REGULATIONS

Title 21
Food and Drugs

Parts 170 to 199

Revised as of April 1, 2013

Containing a codification of documents
of general applicability and future effect

As of April 1, 2013

Published by the Office of the Federal Register
National Archives and Records Administration
as a Special Edition of the Federal Register

U.S. GOVERNMENT OFFICIAL EDITION NOTICE

Legal Status and Use of Seals and Logos

The seal of the National Archives and Records Administration (NARA) authenticates the Code of Federal Regulations (CFR) as the official codification of Federal regulations established under the Federal Register Act. Under the provisions of 44 U.S.C. 1507, the contents of the CFR, a special edition of the Federal Register, shall be judicially noticed. The CFR is prima facie evidence of the original documents published in the Federal Register (44 U.S.C. 1510).

It is prohibited to use NARA's official seal and the stylized Code of Federal Regulations logo on any republication of this material without the express, written permission of the Archivist of the United States or the Archivist's designee. Any person using NARA's official seals and logos in a manner inconsistent with the provisions of 36 CFR part 1200 is subject to the penalties specified in 18 U.S.C. 506, 701, and 1017.

Use of ISBN Prefix

This is the Official U.S. Government edition of this publication and is herein identified to certify its authenticity. Use of the 0–16 ISBN prefix is for U.S. Government Printing Office Official Editions only. The Superintendent of Documents of the U.S. Government Printing Office requests that any reprinted edition clearly be labeled as a copy of the authentic work with a new ISBN.

U.S. GOVERNMENT PRINTING OFFICE

U.S. Superintendent of Documents • Washington, DC 20402–0001

http://bookstore.gpo.gov

Phone: toll-free (866) 512-1800; DC area (202) 512-1800

Table of Contents

Cite this Code: CFR

To cite the regulations in this volume use title, part and section number. Thus, 21 CFR 170.3 *refers to title 21, part 170, section 3.*

Explanation

The Code of Federal Regulations is a codification of the general and permanent rules published in the Federal Register by the Executive departments and agencies of the Federal Government. The Code is divided into 50 titles which represent broad areas subject to Federal regulation. Each title is divided into chapters which usually bear the name of the issuing agency. Each chapter is further subdivided into parts covering specific regulatory areas.

Each volume of the Code is revised at least once each calendar year and issued on a quarterly basis approximately as follows:

Title 1 through Title 16....................as of January 1
Title 17 through Title 27....................as of April 1
Title 28 through Title 41....................as of July 1
Title 42 through Title 50....................as of October 1

The appropriate revision date is printed on the cover of each volume.

LEGAL STATUS

The contents of the Federal Register are required to be judicially noticed (44 U.S.C. 1507). The Code of Federal Regulations is prima facie evidence of the text of the original documents (44 U.S.C. 1510).

HOW TO USE THE CODE OF FEDERAL REGULATIONS

The Code of Federal Regulations is kept up to date by the individual issues of the Federal Register. These two publications must be used together to determine the latest version of any given rule.

To determine whether a Code volume has been amended since its revision date (in this case, April 1, 2013), consult the "List of CFR Sections Affected (LSA)," which is issued monthly, and the "Cumulative List of Parts Affected," which appears in the Reader Aids section of the daily Federal Register. These two lists will identify the Federal Register page number of the latest amendment of any given rule.

EFFECTIVE AND EXPIRATION DATES

Each volume of the Code contains amendments published in the Federal Register since the last revision of that volume of the Code. Source citations for the regulations are referred to by volume number and page number of the Federal Register and date of publication. Publication dates and effective dates are usually not the same and care must be exercised by the user in determining the actual effective date. In instances where the effective date is beyond the cut-off date for the Code a note has been inserted to reflect the future effective date. In those instances where a regulation published in the Federal Register states a date certain for expiration, an appropriate note will be inserted following the text.

OMB CONTROL NUMBERS

The Paperwork Reduction Act of 1980 (Pub. L. 96–511) requires Federal agencies to display an OMB control number with their information collection request.

Many agencies have begun publishing numerous OMB control numbers as amendments to existing regulations in the CFR. These OMB numbers are placed as close as possible to the applicable recordkeeping or reporting requirements.

PAST PROVISIONS OF THE CODE

Provisions of the Code that are no longer in force and effect as of the revision date stated on the cover of each volume are not carried. Code users may find the text of provisions in effect on any given date in the past by using the appropriate List of CFR Sections Affected (LSA). For the convenience of the reader, a "List of CFR Sections Affected" is published at the end of each CFR volume. For changes to the Code prior to the LSA listings at the end of the volume, consult previous annual editions of the LSA. For changes to the Code prior to 2001, consult the List of CFR Sections Affected compilations, published for 1949-1963, 1964-1972, 1973-1985, and 1986-2000.

"[RESERVED]" TERMINOLOGY

The term "[Reserved]" is used as a place holder within the Code of Federal Regulations. An agency may add regulatory information at a "[Reserved]" location at any time. Occasionally "[Reserved]" is used editorially to indicate that a portion of the CFR was left vacant and not accidentally dropped due to a printing or computer error.

INCORPORATION BY REFERENCE

What is incorporation by reference? Incorporation by reference was established by statute and allows Federal agencies to meet the requirement to publish regulations in the Federal Register by referring to materials already published elsewhere. For an incorporation to be valid, the Director of the Federal Register must approve it. The legal effect of incorporation by reference is that the material is treated as if it were published in full in the Federal Register (5 U.S.C. 552(a)). This material, like any other properly issued regulation, has the force of law.

What is a proper incorporation by reference? The Director of the Federal Register will approve an incorporation by reference only when the requirements of 1 CFR part 51 are met. Some of the elements on which approval is based are:

(a) The incorporation will substantially reduce the volume of material published in the Federal Register.

(b) The matter incorporated is in fact available to the extent necessary to afford fairness and uniformity in the administrative process.

(c) The incorporating document is drafted and submitted for publication in accordance with 1 CFR part 51.

What if the material incorporated by reference cannot be found? If you have any problem locating or obtaining a copy of material listed as an approved incorporation by reference, please contact the agency that issued the regulation containing that incorporation. If, after contacting the agency, you find the material is not available, please notify the Director of the Federal Register, National Archives and Records Administration, 8601 Adelphi Road, College Park, MD 20740-6001, or call 202-741-6010.

CFR INDEXES AND TABULAR GUIDES

A subject index to the Code of Federal Regulations is contained in a separate volume, revised annually as of January 1, entitled CFR INDEX AND FINDING AIDS. This volume contains the Parallel Table of Authorities and Rules. A list of CFR titles, chapters, subchapters, and parts and an alphabetical list of agencies publishing in the CFR are also included in this volume.

An index to the text of "Title 3—The President" is carried within that volume.

The Federal Register Index is issued monthly in cumulative form. This index is based on a consolidation of the "Contents" entries in the daily Federal Register.

A List of CFR Sections Affected (LSA) is published monthly, keyed to the revision dates of the 50 CFR titles.

REPUBLICATION OF MATERIAL

There are no restrictions on the republication of material appearing in the Code of Federal Regulations.

INQUIRIES

For a legal interpretation or explanation of any regulation in this volume, contact the issuing agency. The issuing agency's name appears at the top of odd-numbered pages.

For inquiries concerning CFR reference assistance, call 202–741–6000 or write to the Director, Office of the Federal Register, National Archives and Records Administration, 8601 Adelphi Road, College Park, MD 20740-6001 or e-mail *fedreg.info@nara.gov.*

SALES

The Government Printing Office (GPO) processes all sales and distribution of the CFR. For payment by credit card, call toll-free, 866-512-1800, or DC area, 202-512-1800, M-F 8 a.m. to 4 p.m. e.s.t. or fax your order to 202-512-2104, 24 hours a day. For payment by check, write to: US Government Printing Office – New Orders, P.O. Box 979050, St. Louis, MO 63197-9000.

ELECTRONIC SERVICES

The full text of the Code of Federal Regulations, the LSA (List of CFR Sections Affected), The United States Government Manual, the Federal Register, Public Laws, Public Papers of the Presidents of the United States, Compilation of Presidential Documents and the Privacy Act Compilation are available in electronic format via *www.ofr.gov.* For more information, contact the GPO Customer Contact Center, U.S. Government Printing Office. Phone 202-512-1800, or 866-512-1800 (toll-free). E-mail, *ContactCenter@gpo.gov.*

The Office of the Federal Register also offers a free service on the National Archives and Records Administration's (NARA) World Wide Web site for public law numbers, Federal Register finding aids, and related information. Connect to NARA's web site at *www.archives.gov/federal-register.*

The e-CFR is a regularly updated, unofficial editorial compilation of CFR material and Federal Register amendments, produced by the Office of the Federal Register and the Government Printing Office. It is available at *www.ecfr.gov.*

CHARLES A. BARTH,
Director,
Office of the Federal Register.
April 1, 2013.

THIS TITLE

Title 21—FOOD AND DRUGS is composed of nine volumes. The parts in these volumes are arranged in the following order: Parts 1–99, 100–169, 170–199, 200–299, 300–499, 500–599, 600–799, 800–1299 and 1300 to end. The first eight volumes, containing parts 1–1299, comprise Chapter I—Food and Drug Administration, Department of Health and Human Services. The ninth volume, containing part 1300 to end, includes Chapter II—Drug Enforcement Administration, Department of Justice, and Chapter III—Office of National Drug Control Policy. The contents of these volumes represent all current regulations codified under this title of the CFR as of April 1, 2013.

For this volume, Susannah C. Hurley was Chief Editor. The Code of Federal Regulations publication program is under the direction of Michael L. White, assisted by Ann Worley.

Title 21—Food and Drugs

(This book contains parts 170 to 199)

CHAPTER I—FOOD AND DRUG ADMINISTRATION, DEPARTMENT OF HEALTH AND HUMAN SERVICES (CONTINUED)

(Parts 170 to 199)

EDITORIAL NOTE: Nomenclature changes to chapter I appear at 59 FR 14366, Mar. 28, 1994, and 69 FR 18803, Apr. 9, 2004.

SUBCHAPTER B—FOOD FOR HUMAN CONSUMPTION (CONTINUED)

SUBCHAPTER B—FOOD FOR HUMAN CONSUMPTION (CONTINUED)

PART 170—FOOD ADDITIVES

Subpart A—General Provisions

Subpart B—Food Additive Safety

Subpart C—Specific Administrative Rulings and Decisions

Subpart D—Premarket Notifications

AUTHORITY: 21 U.S.C. 321, 341, 342, 346a, 348, 371.

SOURCE: 42 FR 14483, Mar. 15, 1977, unless otherwise noted.

EDITORIAL NOTE: Nomenclature changes to part 170 appear at 66 FR 56035, Nov. 6, 2001 and 69 FR 13717, Mar. 24, 2004.

Subpart A—General Provisions

§ 170.3 Definitions.

For the purposes of this subchapter, the following definitions apply:

(a) *Secretary* means the Secretary of Health and Human Services.

(b) *Department* means the Department of Health and Human Services.

(c) *Commissioner* means the Commissioner of Food and Drugs.

(d) As used in this part, the term *act* means the Federal Food, Drug, and Cosmetic Act approved June 25, 1936, 52 Stat. 1040 *et seq.*, as amended (21 U.S.C. 301–392).

(e)(1) *Food additives* includes all substances not exempted by section 201(s) of the act, the intended use of which results or may reasonably be expected to result, directly or indirectly, either in their becoming a component of food or otherwise affecting the characteristics of food. A material used in the production of containers and packages is subject to the definition if it may reasonably be expected to become a component, or to affect the characteristics, directly or indirectly, of food packed in the container. "Affecting the characteristics of food" does not include such physical effects, as protecting contents of packages, preserving shape, and preventing moisture loss. If there is no migration of a packaging component from the package to the food, it does not become a component of the food and thus is not a food additive. A substance that does not become a component of food, but that is used, for example, in preparing an ingredient of the food to give a different flavor, texture, or other characteristic in the food, may be a food additive.

(2) *Uses of food additives not requiring a listing regulation.* Use of a substance in a food contact article (e.g., food-packaging or food-processing equipment) whereby the substance migrates, or may reasonably be expected to migrate, into food at such levels that the use has been exempted from regulation as a food additive under § 170.39, and food contact substances used in accordance with a notification submitted under section 409(h) of the act that is effective.

(3) *A food contact substance* is any substance that is intended for use as a component of materials used in manufacturing, packing, packaging, transporting, or holding food if such use is not intended to have any technical effect in such food.

(f) *Common use in food* means a substantial history of consumption of a substance for food use by a significant number of consumers.

(g) The word *substance* in the definition of the term ''food additive'' includes a food or food component consisting of one or more ingredients.

(h) *Scientific procedures* include those human, animal, analytical, and other scientific studies, whether published or unpublished, appropriate to establish the safety of a substance.

(i) *Safe* or *safety* means that there is a reasonable certainty in the minds of competent scientists that the substance is not harmful under the intended conditions of use. It is impossible in the present state of scientific knowledge to establish with complete certainty the absolute harmlessness of the use of any substance. Safety may be determined by scientific procedures or by general recognition of safety. In determining safety, the following factors shall be considered:

(1) The probable consumption of the substance and of any substance formed in or on food because of its use.

(2) The cumulative effect of the substance in the diet, taking into account any chemically or pharmacologically related substance or substances in such diet.

(3) Safety factors which, in the opinion of experts qualified by scientific training and experience to evaluate the safety of food and food ingredients, are generally recognized as appropriate.

(j) The term *nonperishable processed food* means any processed food not subject to rapid decay or deterioration that would render it unfit for consumption. Examples are flour, sugar, cereals, packaged cookies, and crackers. Not included are hermetically sealed foods or manufactured dairy products and other processed foods requiring refrigeration.

(k) *General recognition of safety* shall be determined in accordance with § 170.30.

(l) *Prior sanction* means an explicit approval granted with respect to use of a substance in food prior to September 6, 1958, by the Food and Drug Administration or the United States Department of Agriculture pursuant to the Federal Food, Drug, and Cosmetic Act, the Poultry Products Inspection Act, or the Meat Inspection Act.

(m) *Food* includes human food, substances migrating to food from food-contact articles, pet food, and animal feed.

(n) The following general food categories are established to group specific related foods together for the purpose of establishing tolerances or limitations for the use of direct human food ingredients. Individual food products will be included within these categories according to the detailed classifications lists contained in Exhibit 33B of the report of the National Academy of Sciences/National Research Council report, ''A Comprehensive Survey of Industry on the Use of Food Chemicals Generally Recognized as Safe'' (September 1972), which is incorporated by reference. Copies are available from the National Technical Information Service (NTIS), 5285 Port Royal Rd., Springfield, VA 22161, or at the National Archives and Records Administration (NARA). For information on the availability of this material at NARA, call 202–741–6030, or go to: *http://www.archives.gov/federal_register/code_of_federal_regulations/ibr_locations.html.*

(1) Baked goods and baking mixes, including all ready-to-eat and ready-to-bake products, flours, and mixes requiring preparation before serving.

(2) Beverages, alcoholic, including malt beverages, wines, distilled liquors, and cocktail mix.

(3) Beverages and beverage bases, nonalcoholic, including only special or spiced teas, soft drinks, coffee substitutes, and fruit and vegetable flavored gelatin drinks.

(4) Breakfast cereals, including ready-to-eat and instant and regular hot cereals.

(5) Cheeses, including curd and whey cheeses, cream, natural, grating, processed, spread, dip, and miscellaneous cheeses.

(6) Chewing gum, including all forms.

(7) Coffee and tea, including regular, decaffeinated, and instant types.

(8) Condiments and relishes, including plain seasoning sauces and spreads, olives, pickles, and relishes, but not spices or herbs.

(9) Confections and frostings, including candy and flavored frostings, marshmallows, baking chocolate, and brown, lump, rock, maple, powdered, and raw sugars.

(10) Dairy product analogs, including nondairy milk, frozen or liquid creamers, coffee whiteners, toppings, and other nondairy products.

(11) Egg products, including liquid, frozen, or dried eggs, and egg dishes made therefrom, i.e., egg roll, egg foo young, egg salad, and frozen multicourse egg meals, but not fresh eggs.

(12) Fats and oils, including margarine, dressings for salads, butter, salad oils, shortenings and cooking oils.

(13) Fish products, including all prepared main dishes, salads, appetizers, frozen multicourse meals, and spreads containing fish, shellfish, and other aquatic animals, but not fresh fish.

(14) Fresh eggs, including cooked eggs and egg dishes made only from fresh shell eggs.

(15) Fresh fish, including only fresh and frozen fish, shellfish, and other aquatic animals.

(16) Fresh fruits and fruit juices, including only raw fruits, citrus, melons, and berries, and home-prepared "ades" and punches made therefrom.

(17) Fresh meats, including only fresh or home-frozen beef or veal, pork, lamb or mutton and home-prepared fresh meat-containing dishes, salads, appetizers, or sandwich spreads made therefrom.

(18) Fresh poultry, including only fresh or home-frozen poultry and game birds and home-prepared fresh poultry-containing dishes, salads, appetizers, or sandwich spreads made therefrom.

(19) Fresh vegetables, tomatoes, and potatoes, including only fresh and home-prepared vegetables.

(20) Frozen dairy desserts and mixes, including ice cream, ice milks, sherbets, and other frozen dairy desserts and specialties.

(21) Fruit and water ices, including all frozen fruit and water ices.

(22) Gelatins, puddings, and fillings, including flavored gelatin desserts, puddings, custards, parfaits, pie fillings, and gelatin base salads.

(23) Grain products and pastas, including macaroni and noodle products, rice dishes, and frozen multicourse meals, without meat or vegetables.

(24) Gravies and sauces, including all meat sauces and gravies, and tomato, milk, buttery, and specialty sauces.

(25) Hard candy and cough drops, including all hard type candies.

(26) Herbs, seeds, spices, seasonings, blends, extracts, and flavorings, including all natural and artificial spices, blends, and flavors.

(27) Jams and jellies, home-prepared, including only home-prepared jams, jellies, fruit butters, preserves, and sweet spreads.

(28) Jams and jellies, commercial, including only commercially processed jams, jellies, fruit butters, preserves, and sweet spreads.

(29) Meat products, including all meats and meat containing dishes, salads, appetizers, frozen multicourse meat meals, and sandwich ingredients prepared by commercial processing or using commercially processed meats with home preparation.

(30) Milk, whole and skim, including only whole, lowfat, and skim fluid milks.

(31) Milk products, including flavored milks and milk drinks, dry milks, toppings, snack dips, spreads, weight control milk beverages, and other milk origin products.

(32) Nuts and nut products, including whole or shelled tree nuts, peanuts, coconut, and nut and peanut spreads.

(33) Plant protein products, including the National Academy of Sciences/National Research Council "reconstituted vegetable protein" category, and meat, poultry, and fish substitutes, analogs, and extender products made from plant proteins.

(34) Poultry products, including all poultry and poultry-containing dishes, salads, appetizers, frozen multicourse poultry meals, and sandwich ingredients prepared by commercial processing or using commercially processed poultry with home preparation.

(35) Processed fruits and fruit juices, including all commercially processed fruits, citrus, berries, and mixtures; salads, juices and juice punches, concentrates, dilutions, "ades", and drink substitutes made therefrom.

(36) Processed vegetables and vegetable juices, including all commercially processed vegetables, vegetable dishes, frozen multicourse vegetable meals, and vegetable juices and blends.

(37) Snack foods, including chips, pretzels, and other novelty snacks.

(38) Soft candy, including candy bars, chocolates, fudge, mints, and other chewy or nougat candies.

(39) Soups, home-prepared, including meat, fish, poultry, vegetable, and combination home-prepared soups.

(40) Soups and soup mixes, including commercially prepared meat, fish, poultry, vegetable, and combination soups and soup mixes.

(41) Sugar, white, granulated, including only white granulated sugar.

(42) Sugar substitutes, including granulated, liquid, and tablet sugar substitutes.

(43) Sweet sauces, toppings, and syrups, including chocolate, berry, fruit, corn syrup, and maple sweet sauces and toppings.

(o) The following terms describe the physical or technical functional effects for which direct human food ingredients may be added to foods. They are adopted from the National Academy of Sciences/National Research Council national survey of food industries, reported to the Food and Drug Administration under the contract title "A Comprehensive Survey of Industry on the Use of Food Chemicals Generally Recognized as Safe" (September 1972), which is incorporated by reference. Copies are available from the National Technical Information Service (NTIS), 5285 Port Royal Rd., Springfield, VA 22161, or at the National Archives and Records Administration (NARA). For information on the availability of this material at NARA, call 202–741–6030, or go to: *http://www.archives.gov/federal_register/code_of_federal_regulations/ibr_locations.html.*

(1) *Anticaking agents and free-flow agents*: Substances added to finely powdered or crystalline food products to prevent caking, lumping, or agglomeration.

(2) *Antimicrobial agents*: Substances used to preserve food by preventing growth of microorganisms and subsequent spoilage, including fungistats, mold and rope inhibitors, and the effects listed by the National Academy of Sciences/National Research Council under "preservatives."

(3) *Antioxidants*: Substances used to preserve food by retarding deterioration, rancidity, or discoloration due to oxidation.

(4) *Colors and coloring adjuncts*: Substances used to impart, preserve, or enhance the color or shading of a food, including color stabilizers, color fixatives, color-retention agents, etc.

(5) *Curing and pickling agents*: Substances imparting a unique flavor and/or color to a food, usually producing an increase in shelf life stability.

(6) *Dough strengtheners*: Substances used to modify starch and gluten, thereby producing a more stable dough, including the applicable effects listed by the National Academy of Sciences/National Research Council under "dough conditioner."

(7) *Drying agents*: Substances with moisture-absorbing ability, used to maintain an environment of low moisture.

(8) *Emulsifiers and emulsifier salts*: Substances which modify surface tension in the component phase of an emulsion to establish a uniform dispersion or emulsion.

(9) *Enzymes*: Enzymes used to improve food processing and the quality of the finished food.

(10) *Firming agents*: Substances added to precipitate residual pectin, thus strengthening the supporting tissue

and preventing its collapse during processing.

(11) *Flavor enhancers*: Substances added to supplement, enhance, or modify the original taste and/or aroma of a food, without imparting a characteristic taste or aroma of its own.

(12) *Flavoring agents and adjuvants*: Substances added to impart or help impart a taste or aroma in food.

(13) *Flour treating agents*: Substances added to milled flour, at the mill, to improve its color and/or baking qualities, including bleaching and maturing agents.

(14) *Formulation aids*: Substances used to promote or produce a desired physical state or texture in food, including carriers, binders, fillers, plasticizers, film-formers, and tableting aids, etc.

(15) *Fumigants*: Volatile substances used for controlling insects or pests.

(16) *Humectants*: Hygroscopic substances incorporated in food to promote retention of moisture, including moisture-retention agents and anti-dusting agents.

(17) *Leavening agents*: Substances used to produce or stimulate production of carbon dioxide in baked goods to impart a light texture, including yeast, yeast foods, and calcium salts listed by the National Academy of Sciences/National Research Council under "dough conditioners."

(18) *Lubricants and release agents*: Substances added to food contact surfaces to prevent ingredients and finished products from sticking to them.

(19) *Non-nutritive sweeteners*: Substances having less than 2 percent of the caloric value of sucrose per equivalent unit of sweetening capacity.

(20) *Nutrient supplements*: Substances which are necessary for the body's nutritional and metabolic processes.

(21) *Nutritive sweeteners*: Substances having greater than 2 percent of the caloric value of sucrose per equivalent unit of sweetening capacity.

(22) *Oxidizing and reducing agents*: Substances which chemically oxidize or reduce another food ingredient, thereby producing a more stable product, including the applicable effect listed by the National Academy of Sciences/National Research Council under "dough conditioners."

(23) *pH control agents*: Substances added to change or maintain active acidity or basicity, including buffers, acids, alkalies, and neutralizing agents.

(24) *Processing aids*: Substances used as manufacturing aids to enhance the appeal or utility of a food or food component, including clarifying agents, clouding agents, catalysts, flocculents, filter aids, and crystallization inhibitors, etc.

(25) *Propellants, aerating agents, and gases*: Gases used to supply force to expel a product or used to reduce the amount of oxygen in contact with the food in packaging.

(26) *Sequestrants*: Substances which combine with polyvalent metal ions to form a soluble metal complex, to improve the quality and stability of products.

(27) *Solvents and vehicles*: Substances used to extract or dissolve another substance.

(28) *Stabilizers and thickeners*: Substances used to produce viscous solutions or dispersions, to impart body, improve consistency, or stabilize emulsions, including suspending and bodying agents, setting agents, jellying agents, and bulking agents, etc.

(29) *Surface-active agents*: Substances used to modify surface properties of liquid food components for a variety of effects, other than emulsifiers, but including solubilizing agents, dispersants, detergents, wetting agents, rehydration enhancers, whipping agents, foaming agents, and defoaming agents, etc.

(30) *Surface-finishing agents*: Substances used to increase palatability, preserve gloss, and inhibit discoloration of foods, including glazes, polishes, waxes, and protective coatings.

(31) *Synergists*: Substances used to act or react with another food ingredient to produce a total effect different or greater than the sum of the effects produced by the individual ingredients.

(32) *Texturizers*: Substances which affect the appearance or feel of the food.

[42 FR 14483, Mar. 15, 1977, as amended at 47 FR 11835, Mar. 19, 1982; 53 FR 16546, May 10, 1988; 54 FR 24896, June 12, 1989; 60 FR 36595, July 17, 1995; 67 FR 35729, May 21, 2002]

§ 170.6 Opinion letters on food additive status.

(a) Over the years the Food and Drug Administration has given informal written opinions to inquiries as to the safety of articles intended for use as components of, or in contact with, food. Prior to the enactment of the Food Additives Amendment of 1958 (Pub. L. 85–929; Sept. 6, 1958), these opinions were given pursuant to section 402(a)(1) of the Federal Food, Drug, and Cosmetic Act, which reads in part: "A food shall be deemed to be adulterated if it bears or contains any poisonous or deleterious substance which may render it injurious to health".

(b) Since enactment of the Food Additives Amendment, the Food and Drug Administration has advised such inquirers that an article:

(1) Is a food additive within the meaning of section 201(s) of the act; or

(2) Is generally recognized as safe (GRAS); or

(3) Has prior sanction or approval under that amendment; or

(4) Is not a food additive under the conditions of intended use.

(c) In the interest of the public health, such articles which have been considered in the past by the Food and Drug Administration to be safe under the provisions of section 402(a)(1), or to be generally recognized as safe for their intended use, or to have prior sanction or approval, or not to be food additives under the conditions of intended use, must be reexamined in the light of current scientific information and current principles for evaluating the safety of food additives if their use is to be continued.

(d) Because of the time span involved, copies of many of the letters in which the Food and Drug Administration has expressed an informal opinion concerning the status of such articles may no longer be in the file of the Food and Drug Administration. In the absence of information concerning the names and uses made of all the articles referred to in such letters, their safety of use cannot be reexamined. For this reason all food additive status opinions of the kind described in paragraph (c) of this section given by the Food and Drug Administration are hereby revoked.

(e) The prior opinions of the kind described in paragraph (c) of this section will be replaced by qualified and current opinions if the recipient of each such letter forwards a copy of each to the Department of Health and Human Services, Food and Drug Administration, Center for Food Safety and Applied Nutrition, 5100 Paint Branch Pkwy., College Park, MD 20740, along with a copy of his letter of inquiry, on or before July 23, 1970.

(f) This section does not apply to food additive status opinion letters pertaining to articles that were considered by the Food and Drug Administration to be food additives nor to articles included in regulations in parts 170 through 189 of this chapter if the articles are used in accordance with the requirements of such regulations.

[42 FR 14483, Mar. 15, 1977, as amended at 54 FR 24896, June 12, 1989]

§ 170.10 Food additives in standardized foods.

(a) The inclusion of food ingredients in parts 170 through 189 of this chapter does not imply that these ingredients may be used in standardized foods unless they are recognized as optional ingredients in applicable food standards. Where a petition is received for the issuance or amendment of a regulation establishing a definition and standard of identity for a food under section 401 of the Act, which proposes the inclusion of a food additive in such definition and standard of identity, the provisions of the regulations in this part shall apply with respect to the information that must be submitted with respect to the food additive. Since section 409(b)(5) of the Act requires that the Secretary publish notice of a petition for the establishment of a food-additive regulation within 30 days after filing, notice of a petition relating to a definition and standard of identity shall also be published within that time limitation if it includes a request, so designated, for the establishment of a regulation pertaining to a food additive.

(b) If a petition for a definition and standard of identity contains a proposal for a food-additive regulation, and the petitioner fails to designate it as such, the Commissioner, upon determining that the petition includes a proposal for a food-additive regulation, shall so notify the petitioner and shall thereafter proceed in accordance with the regulations in this part.

(c) A regulation will not be issued allowing the use of a food additive in a food for which a definition and standard of identity is established, unless its issuance is in conformity with section 401 of the Act or with the terms of a temporary permit issued under § 130.17 of this chapter. When the contemplated use of such additive complies with the terms of a temporary permit, the food additive regulation will be conditioned on such compliance and will expire with the expiration of the temporary permit.

§ 170.15 Adoption of regulation on initiative of Commissioner.

(a) The Commissioner upon his own initiative may propose the issuance of a regulation prescribing, with respect to any particular use of a food additive, the conditions under which such additive may be safely used. Notice of such proposal shall be published in the FEDERAL REGISTER and shall state the reasons for the proposal.

(b) Action upon a proposal made by the Commissioner shall proceed as provided in part 10 of this chapter.

[42 FR 14486, Mar. 15, 1977, as amended at 42 FR 15673, Mar. 22, 1977]

§ 170.17 Exemption for investigational use and procedure for obtaining authorization to market edible products from experimental animals.

A food additive or food containing a food additive intended for investigational use by qualified experts shall be exempt from the requirements of section 409 of the Act under the following conditions:

(a) If intended for investigational use in vitro or in laboratory research animals, it bears a label which states prominently, in addition to the other information required by the act, the warning:

Caution. Contains a new food additive for investigational use only in laboratory research animals or for tests in vitro. Not for use in humans.

(b) If intended for use in animals other than laboratory research animals and if the edible products of the animals are to be marketed as food, permission for the marketing of the edible products as food has been requested by the sponsor, and authorization has been granted by the Food and Drug Administration in accordance with § 511.1 of this chapter or by the Department of Agriculture in accordance with 9 CFR 309.17, and it bears a label which states prominently, in addition to the other information required by the Act, the warning:

Caution. Contains a new food additive for use only in investigational animals. Not for use in humans.

Edible products of investigational animals are not to be used for food unless authorization has been granted by the U.S. Food and Drug Administration or by the U.S. Department of Agriculture.

(c) If intended for nonclinical laboratory studies in food-producing animals, the study is conducted in compliance with the regulations set forth in part 58 of this chapter.

[42 FR 14483, Mar. 15, 1977, as amended at 43 FR 60021, Dec. 22, 1978]

§ 170.18 Tolerances for related food additives.

(a) Food additives that cause similar or related pharmacological effects will be regarded as a class, and in the absence of evidence to the contrary, as having additive toxic effects and will be considered as related food additives.

(b) Tolerances established for such related food additives may limit the amount of a common component that may be present, or may limit the amount of biological activity (such as cholinesterase inhibition) that may be present or may limit the total amount of related food additives that may be present.

(c) Where food additives from two or more chemicals in the same class are present in or on a food, the tolerance for the total of such additives shall be the same as that for the additive having the lowest numerical tolerance in this class, unless there are available methods that permit quantitative determination of the amount of each food additive present or unless it is shown that a higher tolerance is reasonably required for the combined additives to accomplish the physical or technical effect for which such combined additives are intended and that the higher tolerance will be safe.

(d) Where residues from two or more additives in the same class are present in or on a food and there are available methods that permit quantitative determination of each residue, the quantity of combined residues that are within the tolerance may be determined as follows:

(1) Determine the quantity of each residue present.

(2) Divide the quantity of each residue by the tolerance that would apply if it occurred alone, and multiply by 100 to determine the percentage of the permitted amount of residue present.

(3) Add the percentages so obtained for all residues present.

(4) The sum of the percentage shall not exceed 100 percent.

§ 170.19 Pesticide chemicals in processed foods.

When pesticide chemical residues occur in processed foods due to the use of raw agricultural commodities that bore or contained a pesticide chemical in conformity with an exemption granted or a tolerance prescribed under section 408 of the Act, the processed food will not be regarded as adulterated so long as good manufacturing practice has been followed in removing any residue from the raw agricultural commodity in the processing (such as by peeling or washing) and so long as the concentration of the residue in the processed food when ready to eat is not greater than the tolerance prescribed for the raw agricultural commodity. But when the concentration of residue in the processed food when ready to eat is higher than the tolerance prescribed for the raw agricultural commodity, the processed food is adulterated unless the higher concentration is permitted by a tolerance obtained under section 409 of the Act. For example, if fruit bearing a residue of 7 parts per million of DDT permitted on the raw agricultural commodity is dried and a residue in excess of 7 parts per million of DDT results on the dried fruit, the dehydrated fruit is adulterated unless the higher tolerance for DDT is authorized by the regulations in this part. Food that is itself ready to eat, and which contains a higher residue than allowed for the raw agricultural commodity, may not be legalized by blending or mixing with other foods to reduce the residue in the mixed food below the tolerance prescribed for the raw agricultural commodity.

Subpart B—Food Additive Safety

§ 170.20 General principles for evaluating the safety of food additives.

(a) In reaching a decision on any petition filed under section 409 of the Act, the Commissioner will give full consideration to the specific biological properties of the compound and the adequacy of the methods employed to demonstrate safety for the proposed use, and the Commissioner will be guided by the principles and procedures for establishing the safety of food additives stated in current publications of the National Academy of Sciences-National Research Council. A petition will not be denied, however, by reason of the petitioner's having followed procedures other than those outlined in the publications of the National Academy of Sciences-National Research Council if, from available evidence, the Commissioner finds that the procedures used give results as reliable as, or more reliable than, those reasonably to be expected from the use of the outlined procedures. In reaching a decision, the Commissioner will give due weight to the anticipated levels and patterns of consumption of the additive specified or reasonably inferrable. For the purposes of this section, the principles for evaluating safety of additives set forth in the abovementioned publications will apply to any substance that may properly be classified as a food additive as defined in section 201(s) of the Act.

(b) Upon written request describing the proposed use of an additive and the proposed experiments to determine its safety, the Commissioner will advise a person who wishes to establish the safety of a food additive whether he believes the experiments planned will yield data adequate for an evaluation of the safety of the additive.

§ 170.22 Safety factors to be considered.

In accordance with section 409(c)(5)(C) of the Act, the following safety factors will be applied in determining whether the proposed use of a food additive will be safe: Except where evidence is submitted which justifies use of a different safety factor, a safety factor in applying animal experimentation data to man of 100 to 1, will be used; that is, a food additive for use by man will not be granted a tolerance that will exceed 1/100th of the maximum amount demonstrated to be without harm to experimental animals.

§ 170.30 Eligibility for classification as generally recognized as safe (GRAS).

(a) General recognition of safety may be based only on the views of experts qualified by scientific training and experience to evaluate the safety of substances directly or indirectly added to food. The basis of such views may be either (1) scientific procedures or (2) in the case of a substance used in food prior to January 1, 1958, through experience based on common use in food. General recognition of safety requires common knowledge about the substance throughout the scientific community knowledgeable about the safety of substances directly or indirectly added to food.

(b) General recognition of safety based upon scientific procedures shall require the same quantity and quality of scientific evidence as is required to obtain approval of a food additive regulation for the ingredient. General recognition of safety through scientific procedures shall ordinarily be based upon published studies which may be corroborated by unpublished studies and other data and information.

(c)(1) General recognition of safety through experience based on common use in food prior to January 1, 1958, may be determined without the quantity or quality of scientific procedures required for approval of a food additive regulation. General recognition of safety through experience based on common use in food prior to January 1, 1958, shall be based solely on food use of the substance prior to January 1, 1958, and shall ordinarily be based upon generally available data and information. An ingredient not in common use in food prior to January 1, 1958, may achieve general recognition of safety only through scientific procedures.

(2) A substance used in food prior to January 1, 1958, may be generally recognized as safe through experience based on its common use in food when that use occurred exclusively or primarily outside of the United States if the information about the experience establishes that the use of the substance is safe within the meaning of the act (see § 170.3(i)). Common use in food prior to January 1, 1958, that occurred outside of the United States shall be documented by published or other information and shall be corroborated by information from a second, independent source that confirms the history and circumstances of use of the substance. The information used to document and to corroborate the history and circumstances of use of the substance must be generally available; that is, it must be widely available in the country in which the history of use has occurred and readily available to interested qualified experts in this country. Persons claiming GRAS status for a substance based on its common use in food outside of the United States should obtain FDA concurrence that the use of the substance is GRAS.

(d) The food ingredients listed as GRAS in part 182 of this chapter or affirmed as GRAS in part 184 or § 186.1 of this chapter do not include all substances that are generally recognized as safe for their intended use in food. Because of the large number of substances the intended use of which results or may reasonably be expected to result, directly or indirectly, in their becoming a component or otherwise affecting the characteristics of food, it is impracticable to list all such substances that are GRAS. A food ingredient of natural biological origin that has been widely consumed for its nutrient properties in the United States prior to January 1, 1958, without known detrimental effects, which is subject only to conventional processing as practiced prior to January 1, 1958, and for which no known safety hazard exists, will ordinarily be regarded as GRAS without specific inclusion in part 182, part 184 or § 186.1 of this chapter.

(e) Food ingredients were listed as GRAS in part 182 of this chapter during 1958–1962 without a detailed scientific review of all available data and information relating to their safety. Beginning in 1969, the Food and Drug Administration has undertaken a systematic review of the status of all ingredients used in food on the determination that they are GRAS or subject to a prior sanction. All determinations of GRAS status or food additive status or prior sanction status pursuant to this review shall be handled pursuant to §§ 170.35, 170.38, and 180.1 of this chapter. Affirmation of GRAS status shall be announced in part 184 or § 186.1 of this chapter.

(f) The status of the following food ingredients will be reviewed and affirmed as GRAS or determined to be a food additive or subject to a prior sanction pursuant to § 170.35, § 170.38, or § 180.1 of this chapter:

(1) Any substance of natural biological origin that has been widely consumed for its nutrient properties in the United States prior to January 1, 1958, without known detrimental effect, for which no health hazard is known, and which has been modified by processes first introduced into commercial use after January 1, 1958, which may reasonably be expected significantly to alter the composition of the substance.

(2) Any substance of natural biological origin that has been widely consumed for its nutrient properties in the United States prior to January 1, 1958, without known detrimental effect, for which no health hazard is known, that has had significant alteration of composition by breeding or selection after January 1, 1958, where the change may be reasonably expected to alter the nutritive value or the concentration of toxic constituents.

(3) Distillates, isolates, extracts, and concentration of extracts of GRAS substances.

(4) Reaction products of GRAS substances.

(5) Substances not of a natural biological origin, including those for which evidence is offered that they are identical to a GRAS counterpart of natural biological origin.

(6) Substances of natural biological origin intended for consumption for other than their nutrient properties.

(g) A food ingredient that is not GRAS or subject to a prior sanction requires a food additive regulation promulgated under section 409 of the act before it may be directly or indirectly added to food.

(h) A food ingredient that is listed as GRAS in part 182 of this chapter or affirmed as GRAS in part 184 or § 186.1 of this chapter shall be regarded as GRAS only if, in addition to all the requirements in the applicable regulation, it also meets all of the following requirements:

(1) It complies with any applicable food grade specifications of the Food Chemicals Codex, 2d Ed. (1972), or, if specifically indicated in the GRAS affirmation regulation, the Food Chemicals Codex, 3d Ed. (1981), which are incorporated by reference, except that any substance used as a component of articles that contact food and affirmed as GRAS in § 186.1 of this chapter shall comply with the specifications therein, or in the absence of such specifications, shall be of a purity suitable for its intended use. Copies may be obtained from the National Academy Press, 2101 Constitution Ave. NW., Washington, DC 20418, or at the National Archives and Records Administration (NARA). For information on the availability of this material at NARA, call 202–741–6030, or go to: *http://www.archives.gov/federal_register/code_of_federal_regulations/ibr_locations.html.*

(2) It performs an appropriate function in the food or food-contact article in which it is used.

(3) It is used at a level no higher than necessary to achieve its intended purpose in that food or, if used as a component of a food-contact article, at a level no higher than necessary to achieve its intended purpose in that article.

(i) If a substance is affirmed as GRAS in part 184 or § 186.1 of this chapter with no limitation other than good manufacturing practice, it shall be regarded as GRAS if its conditions of use are not significantly different from those reported in the regulation as the basis on which the GRAS status of the substance was affirmed. If the conditions of use are significantly different, such use of the substance may not be GRAS. In such a case a manufacturer may not rely on the regulation as authorizing the use but must independently establish that the use is GRAS or must use the substance in accordance with a food additive regulation.

(j) If an ingredient is affirmed as GRAS in part 184 or § 186.1 of this chapter with specific limitation(s), it may be used in food only within such limitation(s) (including the category of food(s), the functional use(s) of the ingredient, and the level(s) of use). Any use of such an ingredient not in full compliance with each such established limitation shall require a food additive regulation.

(k) Pursuant to § 170.35, a food ingredient may be affirmed as GRAS in part 184 or § 186.1 of this chapter for a specific use(s) without a general evaluation of use of the ingredient. In addition to the use(s) specified in the regulation, other uses of such an ingredient may also be GRAS. Any affirmation of GRAS status for a specific use(s), without a general evaluation of use of the ingredient, is subject to reconsideration upon such evaluation.

(l) New information may at any time require reconsideration of the GRAS status of a food ingredient. Any change in part 182, part 184, or § 186.1 of this chapter shall be accomplished pursuant to § 170.38.

[42 FR 14483, Mar. 15, 1977, as amended at 49 FR 5610, Feb. 14, 1984; 53 FR 16546, May 10, 1988]

§ 170.35 Affirmation of generally recognized as safe (GRAS) status.

(a) The Commissioner, either on his initiative or on the petition of an interested person, may affirm the GRAS status of substances that directly or indirectly become components of food.

(b)(1) If the Commissioner proposes on his own initiative that a substance is entitled to affirmation as GRAS, he will place all of the data and information on which he relies on public file in the office of the Division of Dockets Management and will publish in the FEDERAL REGISTER a notice giving the name of the substance, its proposed uses, and any limitations proposed for purposes other than safety.

(2) The FEDERAL REGISTER notice will allow a period of 60 days during which any interested person may review the data and information and/or file comments with the Division of Dockets Management. Copies of all comments received shall be made available for examination in the Division of Dockets Management's office.

(3) The Commissioner will evaluate all comments received. If he concludes that there is convincing evidence that the substance is GRAS as described in § 170.30, he will publish a notice in the FEDERAL REGISTER listing the substance as GRAS in part 182, part 184, or part 186 of this chapter, as appropriate.

(4) If, after evaluation of the comments, the Commissioner concludes that there is a lack of convincing evidence that the substance is GRAS and that it should be considered a food additive subject to section 409 of the Act, he shall publish a notice thereof in the FEDERAL REGISTER in accordance with § 170.38.

(c)(1) Persons seeking the affirmation of GRAS status of substances as provided in § 170.30(e), except those subject to the NAS/NRC GRAS list survey (36 FR 20546; October 23, 1971), shall submit a petition for GRAS affirmation pursuant to part 10 of this chapter. Such petition shall contain information to establish that the GRAS criteria as set forth in § 170.30 (b) or (c) have been met, in the following form:

(i) Description of the substance, including:

(*a*) Common or usual name.

(*b*) Chemical name.

(*c*) Chemical Abstract Service (CAS) registry number.

(*d*) Empirical formula.

(*e*) Structural formula.

(*f*) Specifications for food grade material, including arsenic and heavy metals. (Recommendation for any change in the Food Chemicals Codex monograph should be included where applicable.)

(*g*) Quantitative compositions.

(*h*) Manufacturing process (excluding any trade secrets).

(ii) Use of the substance, including:

(*a*) Date when use began.

(*b*) Information and reports or other data on past uses in food.

(*c*) Foods in which used, and levels of use in such foods, and for what purposes.

(iii) Methods for detecting the substance in food, including:

(*a*) References to qualitative and quantitative methods for determining the substance(s) in food, including the type of analytical procedures used.

(*b*) Sensitivity and reproducibility of such method(s).

(iv) Information to establish the safety and functionality of the substance in food. Published scientific literature, evidence that the substance is identical to a GRAS counterpart of natural biological origin, and other data may be submitted to support safety. Any adverse information or consumer complaints shall be included. Complete bibliographic references shall be provided where a copy of the article is not provided.

(v) A statement signed by the person responsible for the petition that to the best of his knowledge it is a representative and balanced submission that includes unfavorable information, as well as favorable information, known to him pertinent to the evaluation of the safety and functionality of the substance.

(vi) If nonclinical laboratory studies are involved, additional information and data submitted in support of filed petitions shall include, with respect to each nonclinical study, either a statement that the study was conducted in compliance with the requirements set forth in part 58 of this chapter, or, if the study was not conducted in compliance with such regulations, a brief statement of the reason for the noncompliance.

(vii) [Reserved]

(viii) A claim for categorical exclusion under §25.30 or §25.32 of this chapter or an environmental assessment under §25.40 of this chapter.

(2) Within 30 days after the date of filing the petition, the Commissioner will place the petition on public file in the office of the Division of Dockets Management and will publish a notice of filing in the FEDERAL REGISTER giving the name of the petitioner and a brief description of the petition including the name of the substance, its proposed use, and any limitations proposed for reasons other than safety. A copy of the notice will be mailed to the petitioner at the time the original is sent to the FEDERAL REGISTER.

(3)(i) If intended uses of the substance include uses in meat, meat food product, or poultry product subject to regulation by the U.S. Department of Agriculture (USDA) under the Poultry Products Inspection Act (PPIA) (21 U.S.C. 451 *et seq.*) or Federal Meat Inspection Act (FMIA) (21 U.S.C. 601 *et seq.*), FDA shall, upon filing of the petition, forward a copy of the petition or relevant portions thereof to the Food Safety and Inspection Service, USDA, for simultaneous review under the PPIA and FMIA.

(ii) FDA will ask USDA to advise whether the proposed meat and poultry uses comply with the FMIA and PPIA or, if not, whether use of the substance would be permitted in products under USDA jurisdiction under specified conditions or restrictions.

(4) The notice of filing in the FEDERAL REGISTER will allow a period of 60 days during which any interested person may review the petition and/or file comments with the Division of Dockets Management. Copies of all comments received shall be made available for examination in the Division of Dockets Management's office.

(5) The Commissioner will evaluate the petition and all available information including all comments received. If the petition and such information provide convincing evidence that the substance is GRAS as described in §170.30 he will publish an order in the FEDERAL REGISTER listing the substance as GRAS in part 182, part 184, or part 186 of this chapter, as appropriate.

(6) If, after evaluation of the petition and all available information, the Commissioner concludes that there is a lack of convincing evidence that the substance is GRAS and that it should be considered a food additive subject to section 409 of the Act, he shall publish a notice thereof in the FEDERAL REGISTER in accordance with §170.38.

(7) The notice of filing in the FEDERAL REGISTER will request submission of proof of any applicable prior sanction for use of the ingredient under

conditions different from those proposed to be determined to be GRAS. The failure of any person to come forward with proof of such an applicable prior sanction in response to the notice of filing will constitute a waiver of the right to assert or rely on such sanction at any later time. The notice of filing will also constitute a proposal to establish a regulation under part 181 of this chapter, incorporating the same provisions, in the event that such a regulation is determined to be appropriate as a result of submission of proof of such an applicable prior sanction in response to the notice of filing.

(Information collection requirements were approved by the Office of Management and Budget under control number 0910–0132)

[42 FR 14488, Mar. 15, 1977, as amended at 50 FR 7492, Feb. 22, 1985; 50 FR 16668, Apr. 26, 1985; 53 FR 16547, May 10, 1988; 62 FR 40599, July 29, 1997; 65 FR 51762, Aug. 25, 2000]

§ 170.38 Determination of food additive status.

(a) The Commissioner may, in accordance with § 170.35(b)(4) or (c)(5), publish a notice in the FEDERAL REGISTER determining that a substance is not GRAS and is a food additive subject to section 409 of the Act.

(b)(1) The Commissioner, on his own initiative or on the petition of any interested person, pursuant to part 10 of this chapter, may issue a notice in the FEDERAL REGISTER proposing to determine that a substance is not GRAS and is a food additive subject to section 409 of the Act. Any petition shall include all relevant data and information of the type described in § 171.130(b). The Commissioner will place all of the data and information on which he relies on public file in the office of the Division of Dockets Management and will include in the FEDERAL REGISTER notice the name of the substance, its known uses, and a summary of the basis for the determination.

(2) The FEDERAL REGISTER notice will allow a period of 60 days during which any interested person may review the data and information and/or file comments with the Division of Dockets Management. Copies of all comments shall be made available for examination in the Division of Dockets Management's office.

(3) The Commissioner will evaluate all comments received. If he concludes that there is a lack of convincing evidence that the substance is GRAS or is otherwise exempt from the definition of a food additive in section 201(s) of the Act, he will publish a notice thereof in the FEDERAL REGISTER. If he concludes that there is convincing evidence that the substance is GRAS, he will publish an order in the FEDERAL REGISTER listing the substance as GRAS in part 182, part 184, or part 186 of this chapter, as appropriate.

(c) A FEDERAL REGISTER notice determining that a substance is a food additive shall provide for the use of the additive in food or food contact surfaces as follows:

(1) It may promulgate a food additive regulation governing use of the additive.

(2) It may promulgate an interim food additive regulation governing use of the additive.

(3) It may require discontinuation of the use of the additive.

(4) It may adopt any combination of the above three approaches for different uses or levels of use of the additive.

(d) If the Commissioner of Food and Drugs is aware of any prior sanction for use of the substance, he will concurrently propose a separate regulation covering such use of the ingredient under part 181 of this chapter. If the Commissioner is unaware of any such applicable prior sanction, the proposed regulation will so state and will require any person who intends to assert or rely on such sanction to submit proof of its existence. Any regulation promulgated pursuant to this section constitutes a determination that excluded uses would result in adulteration of the food in violation of section 402 of the Act, and the failure of any person to come forward with proof of such an applicable prior sanction in response to the proposal will constitute a waiver of the right to assert or rely on such sanction at any later time. The notice will also constitute a proposal to establish a regulation under part 181 of this chapter, incorporating the same provisions, in the event that such a regulation is determined to be appropriate as a result of submission of proof of such an applicable prior sanction in response to the proposal.

[42 FR 14488, Mar. 15, 1977, as amended at 42 FR 15673, Mar. 22, 1977; 54 FR 24896, June 12, 1989]

§ 170.39 Threshold of regulation for substances used in food-contact articles.

(a) A substance used in a food-contact article (e.g., food-packaging or food-processing equipment) that migrates, or that may be expected to migrate, into food will be exempted from regulation as a food additive because it becomes a component of food at levels that are below the threshold of regulation if:

(1) The substance has not been shown to be a carcinogen in humans or animals, and there is no reason, based on the chemical structure of the substance, to suspect that the substance is a carcinogen. The substance must also not contain a carcinogenic impurity or, if it does, must not contain a carcinogenic impurity with a TD_{50} value based on chronic feeding studies reported in the scientific literature or otherwise available to the Food and Drug Administration of less than 6.25 milligrams per kilogram bodyweight per day (The TD_{50}, for the purposes of this section, is the feeding dose that causes cancer in 50 percent of the test animals when corrected for tumors found in control animals. If more than one TD_{50} value has been reported in the scientific literature for a substance, the Food and Drug Administration will use the lowest appropriate TD50 value in its review.);

(2) The substance presents no other health or safety concerns because:

(i) The use in question has been shown to result in or may be expected to result in dietary concentrations at or below 0.5 parts per billion, corresponding to dietary exposure levels at or below 1.5 micrograms/person/day (based on a diet of 1,500 grams of solid food and 1,500 grams of liquid food per person per day); or

(ii) The substance is currently regulated for direct addition into food, and the dietary exposure to the substance resulting from the proposed use is at or below 1 percent of the acceptable daily intake as determined by safety data in the Food and Drug Administration's files or from other appropriate sources;

(3) The substance has no technical effect in or on the food to which it migrates; and

(4) The substance use has no significant adverse impact on the environment.

(b) Notwithstanding paragraph (a) of this section, the Food and Drug Administration reserves the right to decline to grant an exemption in those cases in which available information establishes that the proposed use may pose a public health risk. The reasons for the agency's decision to decline to grant an exemption will be explained in the Food and Drug Administration's response to the requestor.

(c) A request for the Food and Drug Administration to exempt a use of a substance from regulation as a food additive shall include three copies of the following information (If part of the submitted material is in a foreign language, it must be accompanied by an English translation verified to be complete and accurate in accordance with § 10.20(c)(2) of this chapter):

(1) The chemical composition of the substance for which the request is made, including, whenever possible, the name of the chemical in accordance with current Chemical Abstract Service (CAS) nomenclature guidelines and a CAS registry number, if available;

(2) Detailed information on the conditions of use of the substance (e.g., temperature, type of food with which the substance will come into contact, the duration of the contact, and whether the food-contact article will be for repeated or single use applications);

(3) A clear statement as to whether the request for exemption from regulation as a food additive is based on the fact that the use of the substance in the food-contact article results in a dietary concentration at or below 0.5 parts per billion, or on the fact that it involves the use of a regulated direct food additive for which the dietary exposure is at or below 1 percent of the acceptable dietary intake (ADI);

(4) Data that will enable the Food and Drug Administration to estimate

the daily dietary concentration resulting from the proposed use of the substance. These data should be in the form of:

(i) Validated migration data obtained under worst-case (time/temperature) intended use conditions utilizing appropriate food simulating solvents;

(ii) Information on the amount of the substance used in the manufacture of the food-contact article; or

(iii) Information on the residual level of the substance in the food-contact article. For repeat-use articles, an estimate of the amount of food that contacts a specific unit of surface area over the lifetime of the article should also be provided. (In cases where data are provided only in the form of manufacturing use levels or residual levels of the substance present in the food-contact article, the Food and Drug Administration will calculate a worst-case dietary concentration level assuming 100 percent migration.) A detailed description of the analytical method used to quantify the substance should also be submitted along with data used to validate the detection limit.

(iv) In cases where there is no detectable migration into food or food simulants, or when no residual level of a substance is detected in the food-contact article by a suitable analytical method, the Food and Drug Administration will, for the purposes of estimating the dietary concentration, consider the validated detection limit of the method used to analyze for the substance.

(5) The results of an analysis of existing toxicological information on the substance and its impurities. This information on the substance is needed to show whether an animal carcinogen bioassay has been carried out, or whether there is some other basis for suspecting that the substance is a carcinogen or potent toxin. This type of information on the impurities is needed to show whether any of them are carcinogenic, and, if carcinogenic, whether their TD50 values are greater than 6.25 milligrams per kilogram bodyweight per day in accordance with paragraph (a)(1) of this section.

(6) Information on the environmental impact that would result from the proposed use of the substance. The request should contain either a claim for categorical exclusion as specified in § 25.32 of this chapter or an environmental assessment as specified in § 25.40 of this chapter.

(d) Data to be reviewed under this section shall be submitted to the Food and Drug Administration's Office of Premarket Approval (HFS–200), 5100 Paint Branch Pkwy., College Park, MD 20740.

(e) The Food and Drug Administration will inform the requestor by letter whether the specific food-contact application is exempt from regulation as a food additive or not. Although a substance that migrates to food at a level that results in a dietary concentration at or below the threshold of regulation will not be the subject of a regulation published in the FEDERAL REGISTER and will not appear in the Code of Federal Regulations, the Food and Drug Administration will maintain a list of substances exempted from regulation as food additives under this section on display at the Division of Dockets Management. This list will include the name of the company that made the request, the chemical name of the substance, the specific use for which it has received an exemption from regulation as a food additive, and any appropriate limitations on its use. The list will not include any trade names. This list will enable interested persons to see the types of uses of food-contact materials being exempted under the regulation. Interested persons may also obtain a copy of the list of exempted substances by contacting the Food and Drug Administration's Office of Premarket Approval (HFS–200), 5100 Paint Branch Pkwy., College Park, MD 20740. For actions requiring an environmental assessment, the agency's finding of no significant impact and the evidence supporting that finding, contained in the petitioner's environmental assessment, also will be available for public inspection at the Division of Dockets Management in accordance with § 25.51(b)(2) of this chapter. Requests for copies of releasable information contained in submissions requesting exemptions from the food additive regulations will be handled in accordance with the Food and Drug Administration's Freedom of Information Act procedures, as described in part 20 of this chapter. In particular, data and information that fall within the definitions of a trade secret or confidential commercial or financial information are not available for public disclosure in accordance with § 20.61(c) of this chapter.

(f) If the request for an exemption from regulation as a food additive is not granted, the requestor may submit a petition to the Food and Drug Administration for reconsideration of the decision in accordance with the provisions of § 10.33 of this chapter.

(g) If the Food and Drug Administration receives significant new information that raises questions about the dietary concentration or the safety of a substance that the agency has exempted from regulation, the Food and Drug Administration may reevaluate the substance. If the Food and Drug Administration tentatively concludes that the information that is available about the substance no longer supports an exemption for the use of the food-contact material from the food additive regulations, the agency will notify any persons that requested an exemption for the substance of its tentative decision. The requestors will be given an opportunity to show why the use of the substance should not be regulated under the food additive provisions of the act. If the requestors fail to adequately respond to the new evidence, the agency will notify them that further use of the substance in question for the particular use will require a food additive regulation. This notification will be placed on public display at the Division of Dockets Management as part of the file of uses of substances exempted from regulation as food additives. The Food and Drug Administration recognizes that manufacturers other than those that actually made a request for exemption may also be using exempted substances in food-contact articles under conditions of use (e.g., use levels, temperature, type of food contacted, etc.) that are similar to those for which the exemption was issued. Because only requestors will be notified as part of the revocation process described in this section, the Food and Drug Administration plans to notify other manufacturers by means of a notice published in the FEDERAL REGISTER of its decision to revoke an exemption issued for a specific use of a substance in a food contact article.

(h) Guidance documents to assist requestors in the preparation of submissions seeking exemptions from the food additive regulations are available from the Food and Drug Administration's Office of Premarket Approval (HFS–200), 5100 Paint Branch Pkwy., College Park, MD 20740. Interested persons are encouraged to obtain specific guidance from the Food and Drug Administration on the appropriate protocols to be used for obtaining migration data, on the validation of the analytical methods used to quantify migration levels, on the procedures used to relate migration data to dietary exposures, and on any other issue not specifically covered in the Food and Drug Administration's guidance documents.

[60 FR 36595, July 17, 1995, as amended at 62 FR 40599, July 29, 1997; 65 FR 56479, Sept. 19, 2000]

Subpart C—Specific Administrative Rulings and Decisions

§ 170.45 Fluorine-containing compounds.

The Commissioner of Food and Drugs has concluded that it is in the interest of the public health to limit the addition of fluorine compounds to foods (a) to that resulting from the fluoridation of public water supplies, (b) to that resulting from the fluoridation of bottled water within the limitation established in § 165.110(d) of this chapter, and (c) to that authorized by regulations (40 CFR part 180) under section 408 of the Act.

[42 FR 14483, Mar. 15, 1977, as amended at 72 FR 10357 Mar. 8, 2007]

§ 170.50 Glycine (aminoacetic acid) in food for human consumption.

(a) Heretofore, the Food and Drug Administration has expressed the opinion in trade correspondence that glycine is generally recognized as safe for certain technical effects in human food when used in accordance with good manufacturing practice; however:

(1) Reports in scientific literature indicate that adverse effects were found in cases where high levels of glycine were administered in diets of experimental animals.

(2) Current usage information indicates that the daily dietary intake of glycine by humans may be substantially increasing due to changing use patterns in food technology.

Therefore, the Food and Drug Administration no longer regards glycine and its salts as generally recognized as safe for use in human food and all outstanding letters expressing sanction for such use are rescinded.

(b) The Commissioner of Food and Drugs concludes that by May 8, 1971, manufacturers:

(1) Shall reformulate food products for human use to eliminate added glycine and its salts; or

(2) Shall bring such products into compliance with an authorizing food additive regulation. A food additive petition supported by toxicity data is required to show that any proposed level of glycine or its salts added to foods for human consumption will be safe.

(c) The status of glycine as generally recognized as safe for use in animal feed, as prescribed in § 582.5049 of this chapter, remains unchanged because the additive is considered an essential nutrient in certain animal feeds and is safe for such use under conditions of good feeding practice.

§ 170.60 Nitrites and/or nitrates in curing premixes.

(a) Nitrites and/or nitrates are food additives when combined in curing premixes with spices and/or other flavoring or seasoning ingredients that contain or constitute a source of secondary or tertiary amines, including but not limited to essential oils, disodium inosinate, disodium guanylate, hydrolysates of animal or plant origin (such as hydrolyzed vegetable protein), oleoresins of spices, soy products, and spice extractives. Such food additives may be used only after the establishment of an authorizing food additive regulation. A food additive petition submitted pursuant to §§ 171.1 and 171.100 of this chapter, supported by data demonstrating that nitrosamines are not formed in curing premixes containing such food additives, is required to establish safety.

(b) Nitrites and/or nitrates, when packaged separately from flavoring and seasoning in curing premixes, may continue to be used under prior sanctions in the commercial curing of meat and meat products and poultry products and in accordance with the provisions of §§ 172.170 and 172.175 of this chapter that apply to meat curing preparations for the home curing of meat and meat products, including poultry and wild game. To assure safe use of such ingredients the labeling of the premixes shall bear instructions to the user that such separately packaged ingredients are not to be combined until just prior to use. Encapsulating or coating some or all of the ingredients does not constitute separate packaging.

Subpart D—Premarket Notifications

SOURCE: 67 FR 35729, May 21, 2002, unless otherwise noted.

§ 170.100 Submission of a premarket notification for a food contact substance (FCN) to the Food and Drug Administration (FDA).

(a) An FCN is effective for the food contact substance manufactured or prepared by the manufacturer or supplier identified in the FCN submission. If another manufacturer or supplier wishes to market the same food contact substance for the same use, that manufacturer or supplier must also submit an FCN to FDA.

(1) An FCN must contain all of the information described in § 170.101.

(2) An FCN may incorporate by reference any information in FDA's files provided that the manufacturer or supplier is authorized to reference the information. The FCN must include information establishing that the manufacturer or supplier is authorized to reference information in FDA's files.

(3) Any material submitted in or referenced by an FCN that is in a foreign language must be accompanied by an English translation verified to be complete and accurate.

(b) FDA may choose not to accept an FCN for either of the following:

(1) A use of a food contact substance that is the subject of a regulation in parts 173 through 189 of this chapter; or

(2) A use of a food contact substance that is the subject of an exemption under the threshold of regulation process described in § 170.39.

(c) A petition must be submitted under § 171.1 of this chapter to authorize the safe use of a food contact substance in either of the following circumstances, unless FDA agrees to accept an FCN for the proposed use.

(1) The use of the food contact substance increases the cumulative dietary concentration to a certain level. For a substance that is a biocide (e.g., it is intended to exert microbial toxicity), this level is equal to or greater than 200 parts per billion in the daily diet (0.6 milligram (mg)/person/day). For a substance that is not a biocide, this level is equal to or greater than 1 part per million in the daily diet (3 mg/person/day); or

(2) There exists a bioassay on the food contact substance, FDA has not reviewed the bioassay, and the bioassay is not clearly negative for carcinogenic effects.

(d) A manufacturer or supplier for which a notification is effective must keep a current address on file with FDA.

(1) The current address may be either the manufacturer's (or supplier's) address or the address of the manufacturer's (or supplier's) agent.

(2) FDA will deliver correspondence to the manufacturer's or supplier's current address.

§ 170.101 Information in a premarket notification for a food contact substance (FCN).

An FCN must contain the following:

(a) A comprehensive discussion of the basis for the manufacturer's or supplier's determination that the use of the food contact substance is safe. This discussion must:

(1) Discuss all information and data submitted in the notification; and

(2) Address any information and data that may appear to be inconsistent with the determination that the proposed use of the food contact substance is safe.

(b) All data and other information that form the basis of the determination that the food contact substance is safe under the intended conditions of use. Data must include primary biological data and chemical data.

(c) A good laboratory practice statement for each nonclinical laboratory study, as defined under § 58.3(d) of this chapter, that is submitted as part of the FCN, in the form of either:

(1) A signed statement that the study was conducted in compliance with the good laboratory practice regulations under part 58 of this chapter; or

(2) A brief signed statement listing the reason(s) that the study was not conducted in compliance with part 58 of this chapter.

(3) Data from any study conducted after 1978 but not conducted in compliance with part 58 of this chapter must be validated by an independent third party prior to submission to the Food and Drug Administration (FDA), and the report and signed certification of the validating party must be submitted as part of the notification.

(d) Information to address FDA's responsibility under the National Environmental Policy Act, in the form of either:

(1) A claim of categorical exclusion under § 25.30 or § 25.32 of this chapter; or

(2) An environmental assessment complying with § 25.40 of this chapter.

(e) A completed and signed FDA Form No. 3480.

§ 170.102 Confidentiality of information in a premarket notification for a food contact substance (FCN).

(a) During the 120-day period of the Food and Drug Administration (FDA) review of an FCN, FDA will not disclose publicly any information in that FCN.

(b) FDA will not disclose publicly the information in an FCN that is withdrawn prior to the completion of FDA's review.

(c) Once FDA completes its review of an FCN, the agency will make its conclusion about the FCN publicly available. For example, if FDA objects to a notification 90 days after the date of receipt, the agency would make available its objection at that time.

(d) By submitting an FCN to FDA, the manufacturer or supplier waives any claim to confidentiality of the information required to adequately describe the food contact substance and the intended conditions of use that are the subject of that FCN.

(e) The following data and information in an FCN are available for public disclosure, unless extraordinary circumstances are shown, on the 121st day after receipt of the notification by FDA, except that no data or information are available for public disclosure if the FCN is withdrawn under §170.103.

(1) All safety and functionality data and information submitted with or incorporated by reference into the notification. Safety and functionality data include all studies and tests of a food contact substance on animals and humans and all studies and tests on a food contact substance for establishing identity, stability, purity, potency, performance, and usefulness.

(2) A protocol for a test or study, unless it is exempt from disclosure under §20.61 of this chapter.

(3) A list of all ingredients contained in a food contact substance, excluding information that is exempt from disclosure under §20.61 of this chapter. Where applicable, an ingredient list will be identified as incomplete.

(4) An assay method or other analytical method, unless it serves no regulatory or compliance purpose and is exempt from disclosure under §20.61 of this chapter.

(5) All correspondence and written summaries of oral discussions relating to the notification, except information that is exempt for disclosure under §20.61 of this chapter.

(6) All other information not subject to an exemption from disclosure under subpart D of part 20 of this chapter.

§170.103 Withdrawal without prejudice of a premarket notification for a food contact substance (FCN).

A manufacturer or supplier may withdraw an FCN without prejudice to a future submission to the Food and Drug Administration (FDA) if FDA has not completed review of the FCN. For the purpose of this section, FDA's review is completed when FDA has allowed 120 days to pass without objecting to the FCN or FDA has issued an objection letter.

§170.104 Action on a premarket notification for a food contact substance (FCN).

(a) If the Food and Drug Administration (FDA) does not object to an FCN within the 120-day period for FDA review, the FCN becomes effective.

(b) If an FCN is complete when received, the 120-day review period begins on the date FDA receives the FCN.

(1) If any element required under §170.101 is missing from an FCN, then FDA will not accept that FCN and FDA will send an FCN nonacceptance letter to the manufacturer or supplier. If the manufacturer or supplier submits the missing information before FDA sends an FCN nonacceptance letter, the 120-day review period begins on the date of receipt of the missing information.

(2) If FDA accepts an FCN, then FDA will acknowledge in writing its receipt of that FCN.

(c) Objection to an FCN:

(1) If FDA objects to an FCN, then FDA will send an FCN objection letter. The date of the letter will be the date of FDA's objection for purposes of section 409(h)(2)(A) of the act.

(2) If FDA objects to an FCN within the 120-day period for FDA review, the FCN will not become effective.

(3) FDA may object to an FCN if any part of FDA's 120-day review occurs during a period when this program is not funded as required in section 409(h)(5) of the act.

(d) If FDA and a manufacturer or supplier agree that the notifier may submit a food additive petition proposing the approval of the food contact substance for the use in the manufacturer's or supplier's FCN, FDA will consider that FCN to be withdrawn by the manufacturer or supplier on the date the petition is received by FDA.

§170.105 The Food and Drug Administration's (FDA's) determination that a premarket notification for a food contact substance (FCN) is no longer effective.

(a) If data or other information available to FDA, including data not submitted by the manufacturer or supplier, demonstrate that the intended use of the food contact substance is no longer safe, FDA may determine that the authorizing FCN is no longer effective.

(b) If FDA determines that an FCN is no longer effective, FDA will inform the manufacturer or supplier in writing of the basis for that determination. FDA will give the manufacturer or supplier an opportunity to show why the FCN should continue to be effective and will specify the time that the manufacturer or supplier will have to respond.

(c) If the manufacturer or supplier fails to respond adequately to the safety concerns regarding the notified use, FDA will publish a notice of its determination that the FCN is no longer effective. FDA will publish this notice in the FEDERAL REGISTER, stating that a detailed summary of the basis for FDA's determination that the FCN is no longer effective has been placed on public display and that copies are available upon request. The date that the notice publishes in the FEDERAL REGISTER is the date on which the notification is no longer effective.

(d) FDA's determination that an FCN is no longer effective is final agency action subject to judicial review.

§ 170.106 Notification for a food contact substance formulation (NFCSF).

(a) In order for the Food and Drug Administration (FDA) to accept an NFCSF, any food additive that is a component of the formulation must be authorized for its intended use in that NFCSF.

(b) FDA may publish a notice in the FEDERAL REGISTER stating that the agency has insufficient resources to review NFCSFs. From the date that this notice publishes in the FEDERAL REGISTER, FDA will no longer accept NFCSFs.

(c) An NFCSF must contain the following:

(1) A completed and signed FDA Form No. 3479; and

(2) Any additional documentation required to establish that each component of the formulation already may be marketed legally for its intended use.

PART 171—FOOD ADDITIVE PETITIONS

Subpart A—General Provisions

Subpart B—Administrative Actions on Applications

AUTHORITY: 21 U.S.C. 321, 342, 348, 371.

SOURCE: 42 FR 14489, Mar. 15, 1977, unless otherwise noted.

Subpart A—General Provisions

§ 171.1 Petitions.

(a) Petitions to be filed with the Commissioner under the provisions of section 409(b) of the Federal Food, Drug, and Cosmetic Act (the act) shall be submitted in triplicate (quadruplicate, if intended uses include use in meat, meat food product, or poultry product). If any part of the material submitted is in a foreign language, it shall be accompanied by an accurate and complete English translation. The petition shall state petitioner's post office address to which published notices or orders issued or objections filed pursuant to section 409 of the Act may be sent.

(b) Pertinent information may be incorporated in, and will be considered as part of, a petition on the basis of specific reference to such information submitted to and retained in the files of the Food and Drug Administration. However, any reference to unpublished information furnished by a person other than the applicant will not be considered unless use of such information is authorized in a written statement signed by the person who submitted it. Any reference to published information offered in support of a food additive petition should be accompanied by reprints or photostatic copies of such references.

(c) Petitions shall include the following data and be submitted in the following form:

(Date)

Name of petitioner ________________________
Post-office address ________________________
Date ________________________
Name of food additive and proposed use ____

____

Office of Food Additive Safety (HFS–200), Center for Food Safety and Applied Nutrition, Food and Drug Administration, 5100 Paint Branch Pkwy., College Park, MD 20740.

DEAR SIRS:

The undersigned, ________ submits this petition pursuant to section 409(b)(1) of the Federal Food, Drug, and Cosmetic Act with respect to ________

(Name of the food additive and proposed use)

Attached hereto, in triplicate (quadruplicate, if intended uses include use in meat, meat food product, or poultry product), and constituting a part of this petition are the following:

A. The name and all pertinent information concerning the food additive, including chemical identity and composition of the food additive, its physical, chemical, and biological properties, and specifications prescribing the minimum content of the desired component(s) and identifying and limiting the reaction byproducts and other impurities. Where such information is not available, a statement as to the reasons why it is not should be submitted.

When the chemical identity and composition of the food additive is not known, the petition shall contain information in sufficient detail to permit evaluation regarding the method of manufacture and the analytical controls used during the various stages of manufacturing, processing, or packing of the food additive which are relied upon to establish that it is a substance of reproducible composition. Alternative methods and controls and variations in methods and controls within reasonable limits that do not affect the characteristics of the substance or the reliability of the controls may be specified.

If the food additive is a mixture of chemicals, the petition shall supply a list of all substances used in the synthesis, extraction, or other method of preparation, regardless of whether they undergo chemical change in the process. Each substance should be identified by its common English name and complete chemical name, using structural formulas when necessary for specific identification. If any proprietary preparation is used as a component, the proprietary name should be followed by a complete quantitative statement of composition. Reasonable alternatives for any listed substance may be specified.

If the petitioner does not himself perform all the manufacturing, processing, and packing operations for a food additive, the petition shall identify each person who will perform a part of such operations and designate the part.

The petition shall include stability data, and, if the data indicate that it is needed to insure the identity, strength, quality, or purity of the additive, the expiration date that will be employed.

B. The amount of the food additive proposed for use and the purposes for which it is proposed, together with all directions, recommendations, and suggestions regarding the proposed use, as well as specimens of the labeling proposed for the food additive and any labeling that will be required by applicable provisions of the Federal Food, Drug, and Cosmetic Act on the finished food by reason of the use of the food additive. If the additive results or may reasonably be expected to result from the use of packaging material, the petitioner shall show how this may occur and what residues may reasonably be anticipated.

(Typewritten or other draft-labeling copy will be accepted for consideration of the petition, provided a statement is made that final printed labeling identical in content to the draft copy will be submitted as soon as available and prior to the marketing of the food additive.)

(If the food additive is one for which a tolerance limitation is required to assure its safety, the level of use proposed should be no higher than the amount reasonably required to accomplish the intended physical or other technical effect, even though the safety data may support a higher tolerance.)

C. Data establishing that the food additive will have the intended physical or other technical effect or that it may reasonably be expected to become a component, or to affect the characteristics, directly or indirectly, of food and the amount necessary to accomplish this. These data should include information in sufficient detail to permit evaluation with control data.

D. A description of practicable methods to determine the amount of the food additive in the raw, processed, and/or finished food and of any substance formed in or on such food because of its use. The test proposed shall be one that can be used for food-control purposes and that can be applied with consistent results by any properly equipped and trained laboratory personnel.

E. Full reports of investigations made with respect to the safety of the food additive.

(A petition may be regarded as incomplete unless it includes full reports of adequate tests reasonably applicable to show whether or not the food additive will be safe for its intended use. The reports ordinarily should include detailed data derived from appropriate animal and other biological experiments in which the methods used and the results obtained are clearly set forth. The petition shall not omit without explanation any reports of investigations that would bias an evaluation of the safety of the food additive.)

F. Proposed tolerances for the food additive, if tolerances are required in order to insure its safety. A petitioner may include a proposed regulation.

G. If submitting petition to modify an existing regulation issued pursuant to section 409(c)(1)(A) of the Act, full information on each proposed change that is to be made in the original regulation must be submitted. The petition may omit statements made in the original petition concerning which no change is proposed. A supplemental petition must be submitted for any change beyond the variations provided for in the original petition and the regulation issued on the basis of the original petition.

H. The petitioner is required to submit either a claim for categorical exclusion under §25.30 or 25.32 of this chapter or an environmental assessment under §25.40 of this chapter.

Yours very truly,
Petitioner ______________________
By ______________________
(Indicate authority)

(d) The petitioner will be notified of the date on which his petition is filed; and an incomplete petition, or one that has not been submitted in triplicate, will usually be retained but not filed as a petition under section 409 of the Act. The petitioner will be notified in what respects his petition is incomplete.

(e) The petition must be signed by the petitioner or by his attorney or agent, or (if a corporation) by an authorized official.

(f) The data specified under the several lettered headings should be submitted on separate sheets or sets of sheets, suitably identified. If such data have already been submitted with an earlier application, the present petition may incorporate it by specific reference to the earlier. If part of the data have been submitted by the manufacturer of the food additive as a master file, the petitioner may refer to the master file if and to the extent he obtains the manufacturer's written permission to do so. The manufacturer may authorize specific reference to the data without disclosure to the petitioner. Nothing herein shall prevent reference to published data.

(g) A petition shall be retained but shall not be filed if any of the data prescribed by section 409(b) of the Act are lacking or are not set forth so as to be readily understood.

(h)(1) The following data and information in a food additive petition are available for public disclosure, unless extraordinary circumstances are shown, after the notice of filing of the petition is published in the FEDERAL REGISTER or, if the petition is not promptly filed because of deficiencies in it, after the petitioner is informed that it will not be filed because of the deficiencies involved:

(i) All safety and functionality data and information submitted with or incorporated by reference in the petition.

(ii) A protocol for a test or study, unless it is shown to fall within the exemption established for trade secrets and confidential commercial information in §20.61 of this chapter.

(iii) Adverse reaction reports, product experience reports, consumer complaints, and other similar data and information, after deletion of:

(*a*) Names and any information that would identify the person using the product.

(*b*) Names and any information that would identify any third party involved with the report, such as a physician or hospital or other institution.

(iv) A list of all ingredients contained in a food additive, whether or not it is in descending order of predominance. A particular ingredient or group of ingredients shall be deleted from any such list prior to public disclosure if it is shown to fall within the exemption established in §20.61 of this chapter, and a notation shall be made that any such ingredient list is incomplete.

(v) An assay method or other analytical method, unless it serves no regulatory or compliance purpose and is shown to fall within the exemption established in §20.61 of this chapter.

(2) The following data and information in a food additive petition are not available for public disclosure unless they have been previously disclosed to the public as defined in §20.81 of this chapter or they relate to a product or ingredient that has been abandoned

and they no longer represent a trade secret or confidential commercial or financial information as defined in §20.61 of this chapter:

(i) Manufacturing methods or processes, including quality control procedures.

(ii) Production, sales, distribution, and similar data and information, except that any compilation of such data and information aggregated and prepared in a way that does not reveal data or information which is not available for public disclosure under this provision is available for public disclosure.

(iii) Quantitative or semiquantitative formulas.

(3) All correspondence and written summaries of oral discussions relating to a food additive petition are available for public disclosure in accordance with the provisions of part 20 of this chapter when the food additive regulation is published in the FEDERAL REGISTER.

(4) For purposes of this regulation, safety and functionality data include all studies and tests of a food additive on animals and humans and all studies and tests on a food additive for identity, stability, purity, potency, performance, and usefulness.

(i)(1)(i) Within 15 days after receipt, the Food and Drug Administration will notify the petitioner of the acceptance or nonacceptance of a petition, and if not accepted, the reasons therefor. If accepted, the petitioner will be sent a letter stating this and the date of the letter shall become the date of filing for the purposes of section 409(b)(5) of the act. In cases in which the Food and Drug Administration agrees that a premarket notification for a food contact substance (Food Contact Notification (FCN)) submitted under section 409(h) of the act may be converted to a petition, the withdrawal date for the FCN will be deemed the date of receipt for the petition.

(ii) If the petitioner desires, he may supplement a deficient petition after being notified regarding deficiencies. If the supplementary material or explanation of the petition is deemed acceptable, the petitioner shall be notified. The date of such notification becomes the date of filing. If the petitioner does not wish to supplement or explain the petition and requests in writing that it be filed as submitted, the petition shall be filed and the petitioner so notified.

(iii) Notwithstanding paragraph (i)(1)(ii) of this section, the petition shall not be filed if the Food and Drug Administration determines that the use identified in the petition should be the subject of an FCN under section 409(h) of the act rather than a petition.

(2) The Commissioner will publish in the FEDERAL REGISTER within 30 days from the date of filing of such petition, a notice of the filing, the name of the petitioner, and a brief description of the proposal in general terms. In the case of a food additive which becomes a component of food by migration from packaging material, the notice shall include the name of the migratory substance, and where it is different from that of one of the original components, the name of the parent component, the maximum quantity of the migratory substance that is proposed for use in food, and the physical or other technical effect which the migratory substance or its parent component is intended to have in the packaging material. A copy of the notice will be mailed to the petitioner when the original is forwarded to the FEDERAL REGISTER for publication.

(j) The Commissioner may request a full description of the methods used in, and the facilities and controls used for, the production of the food additive, or a sample of the food additive, articles used as components thereof, or of the food in which the additive is proposed to be used, at any time while a petition is under consideration. The Commissioner shall specify in the request for a sample of the food additive, or articles used as components thereof, or of the food in or on which the additive is proposed to be used, a quantity deemed adequate to permit tests of analytical methods to determine quantities of the food additive present in foods for which it is intended to be used or adequate for any study or investigation reasonably required with respect to the safety of the food additive or the physical or technical effect it produces. The date used for computing the 90-day limit for the purposes of section 409(c)(2) of the

Act shall be moved forward 1 day for each day after the mailing date of the request taken by the petitioner to submit the sample. If the information or sample is requested a reasonable time in advance of the 180 days, but is not submitted within such 180 days after filing of the petition, the petition will be considered withdrawn without prejudice.

(k) If nonclinical laboratory studies are involved, petitions filed with the Commissioner under section 409(b) of the act shall include, with respect to each nonclinical study contained in the petition, either a statement that the study has been, or will be, conducted in compliance with the good laboratory practice regulations as set forth in part 58 of this chapter, or, if any such study was not conducted in compliance with such regulations, a brief statement of the reason for the noncompliance.

(l) [Reserved]

(m) If clinical investigations involving human subjects are involved, petitions filed with the Commissioner under section 409(b) of the Act shall include statements regarding each such clinical investigation relied upon in the petition that it either was conducted in compliance with the requirements for institutional review set forth in part 56 of this chapter, or was not subject to such requirements in accordance with § 56.104 or § 56.105, and that it was conducted in compliance with the requirements for informed consent set forth in part 50 of this chapter.

(n)(1) If intended uses of the food additive include uses in meat, meat food product, or poultry product subject to regulation by the U.S. Department of Agriculture (USDA) under the Poultry Products Inspection Act (PPIA) (21 U.S.C. 451 *et seq.*) or the Federal Meat Inspection Act (FMIA) (21 U.S.C. 601 *et seq.*), FDA shall, upon filing of the petition, forward a copy of the petition or relevant portions thereof to the Food Safety and Inspection Service, USDA, for simultaneous review under the PPIA and FMIA.

(2) FDA will ask USDA to advise whether the proposed meat and poultry uses comply with the FMIA and PPIA, or if not, whether use of the substance would be permitted in products under USDA jurisdiction under specified conditions or restrictions.

[42 FR 14489, Mar. 15, 1977, as amended at 42 FR 15674, Mar. 22, 1977; 46 FR 8952, Jan. 27, 1981; 50 FR 7492, Feb. 22, 1985; 50 FR 16668, Apr. 26, 1985; 62 FR 40599, July 29, 1997; 65 FR 51763, Aug. 25, 2000; 67 FR 35731, May 21, 2002; 72 FR 10357, Mar. 8, 2007]

§ 171.6 Amendment of petition.

After a petition has been filed, the petitioner may submit additional information or data in support thereof. In such cases, if the Commissioner determines that the additional information or data amount to a substantive amendment, the petition as amended will be given a new filing date, and the time limitation will begin to run anew. If nonclinical laboratory studies are involved, additional information and data submitted in support of filed petitions shall include, with respect to each nonclinical study, either a statement that the study was conducted in compliance with the requirements set forth in part 58 of this chapter, or, if the study was not conducted in compliance with such regulations, a brief statement of the reason for the noncompliance.

[50 FR 7492, Feb. 22, 1985, as amended at 50 FR 16668, Apr. 26, 1985]

§ 171.7 Withdrawal of petition without prejudice.

(a) In some cases the Commissioner will notify the petitioner that the petition, while technically complete, is inadequate to justify the establishment of a regulation or the regulation requested by petitioner. This may be due to the fact that the data are not sufficiently clear or complete. In such cases, the petitioner may withdraw the petition pending its clarification or the obtaining of additional data. This withdrawal will be without prejudice to a future filing. Upon refiling, the time limitation will begin to run anew from the date of refiling.

(b) At any time before the order provided for in § 171.100(a) has been forwarded to the FEDERAL REGISTER for publication, the petitioner may withdraw the petition without prejudice to a future filing. Upon refiling the time limitation will begin to run anew.

(c) Any petitioner who has a food additive petition pending before the agency and who subsequently submits a premarket notification for a food contact substance (FCN) for a use or uses described in such petition shall be deemed to have withdrawn the petition for such use or uses without prejudice to a future filing on the date the FCN is received by the Food and Drug Administration.

[42 FR 14489, Mar. 15, 1977, as amended at 67 FR 35731, May 21, 2002]

§ 171.8 Threshold of regulation for substances used in food-contact articles.

Substances used in food-contact articles (e.g., food-packaging or food-processing equipment) that migrate or that may be expected to migrate into food at negligible levels may be reviewed under § 170.39 of this chapter. The Food and Drug Administration will exempt substances whose uses it determines meet the criteria in § 170.39 of this chapter from regulation as food additives and, therefore, a food additive petition will not be required for the exempted use.

[60 FR 36596, July 17, 1995]

Subpart B—Administrative Actions on Applications

§ 171.100 Regulation based on petition.

(a) The Commissioner will forward for publication in the FEDERAL REGISTER, within 90 days after filing of the petition (or within 180 days if the time is extended as provided for in section 409(c)(2) of the Act), a regulation prescribing the conditions under which the food additive may be safely used (including, but not limited to, specifications as to the particular food or classes of food in or on which such additive may be used, the maximum quantity that may be used or permitted to remain in or on such food, the manner in which such additive may be added to or used in or on such food, and any directions or other labeling or packaging requirements for such additive deemed necessary by him to assure the safety of such use), and prior to the forwarding of the order to the FEDERAL REGISTER for publication shall notify the petitioner of such order and the reasons for such action; or by order deny the petition, and shall notify the petitioner of such order and of the reasons for such action.

(b) The regulation shall describe the conditions under which the substance may be safely used in any meat product, meat food product, or poultry product subject to the Federal Meat Inspection Act (FMIA) (21 U.S.C. 601 *et seq.*) or the Poultry Products Inspection Act (PPIA) (21 U.S.C. 451 *et seq.*).

(c) If the Commissioner determines that additional time is needed to study and investigate the petition, he shall by written notice to the petitioner extend the 90-day period for not more than 180 days after the filing of the petition.

[42 FR 14489, Mar. 15, 1977, as amended at 65 FR 51763, Aug. 25, 2000]

§ 171.102 Effective date of regulation.

A regulation published in accordance with § 171.100(a) shall become effective upon publication in the FEDERAL REGISTER.

§ 171.110 Procedure for objections and hearings.

Objections and hearings relating to food additive regulations under section 409 (c), (d), or (h) of the Act shall be governed by part 12 of this chapter.

[42 FR 14491, Mar. 15, 1977, as amended at 42 FR 15674, Mar. 22, 1977]

§ 171.130 Procedure for amending and repealing tolerances or exemptions from tolerances.

(a) The Commissioner, on his own initiative or on the petition of any interested person, pursuant to part 10 of this chapter, may propose the issuance of a regulation amending or repealing a regulation pertaining to a food additive or granting or repealing an exception for such additive.

(b) Any such petition shall include an assertion of facts, supported by data, showing that new information exists with respect to the food additive or that new uses have been developed or old uses abandoned, that new data are available as to toxicity of the chemical, or that experience with the existing regulation or exemption may justify its amendment or repeal. New data shall be furnished in the form specified in §§171.1 and 171.100 for submitting petitions.

[42 FR 14491, Mar. 15, 1977, as amended at 42 FR 15674, Mar. 22, 1977]

PART 172—FOOD ADDITIVES PERMITTED FOR DIRECT ADDITION TO FOOD FOR HUMAN CONSUMPTION

Subpart A—General Provisions

Subpart B—Food Preservatives

Subpart C—Coatings, Films and Related Substances

Subpart D—Special Dietary and Nutritional Additives

Subpart E—Anticaking Agents

Subpart F—Flavoring Agents and Related Substances

Subpart G—Gums, Chewing Gum Bases and Related Substances

Subpart H—Other Specific Usage Additives

AUTHORITY: 21 U.S.C. 321, 341, 342, 348, 371, 379e.

SOURCE: 42 FR 14491, Mar. 15, 1977, unless otherwise noted.

EDITORIAL NOTE: Nomenclature changes to part 172 appear at 61 FR 14482, Apr. 2, 1996, 66 FR 56035, Nov. 6, 2001, 66 FR 66742, Dec. 27, 2001, 68 FR 15355, Mar. 31, 2003, 70 FR 40880, July 15, 2005, 70 FR 67651, Nov. 8, 2005, and 70 FR 72074, Dec. 1, 2005.

Subpart A—General Provisions

§ 172.5 General provisions for direct food additives.

(a) Regulations prescribing conditions under which food additive substances may be safely used predicate usage under conditions of good manufacturing practice. For the purposes of this part, good manufacturing practice shall be defined to include the following restrictions.

(1) The quantity of the substance added to food does not exceed the amount reasonably required to accomplish its intended physical, nutritive, or other technical effect in food.

(2) Any substance intended for use in or on food is of appropriate food grade and is prepared and handled as a food ingredient.

(b) The existence of a regulation prescribing safe conditions of use for a food additive shall not be construed to relieve the use of the substance from compliance with any other provision of the Act.

(c) The existence of any regulation prescribing safe conditions of use for a nutrient substance does not constitute a finding that the substance is useful or required as a supplement to the diet of humans.

Subpart B—Food Preservatives

§ 172.105 Anoxomer.

Anoxomer as identified in this section may be safely used in accordance with the following conditions:

(a) Anoxomer is 1,4-benzenediol, 2-(1,1-dimethylethyl)-polymer with diethenylbenzene, 4-(1,1-dimethylethyl)phenol, 4- methoxyphenol, 4,4′-(1-methylethylidene)bis(phenol) and 4-methylphenol (CAS Reg. No. 60837–57–2) prepared by condensation polymerization of divinylbenzene (*m*- and *p*-) with *tert*-butylhydroquinone, *tert*-butylphenol, hydroxyanisole, *p*-cresol and 4,4′-isopropylidenediphenol.

(b) The polymeric antioxidant meets the following specifications:

(1) Polymer, not less than 98.0 percent as determined by an ultraviolet method entitled "Ultraviolet Assay, "1982, which is incorporated by reference. Copies are available from the Center for Food Safety and Applied Nutrition (HFS–200), Food and Drug Administration, 5100 Paint Branch Pkwy., College Park, MD 20740, or at the National Archives and Records Administration (NARA). For information on the availability of this material at NARA, call 202–741–6030, or go to: *http://www.archives.gov/federal_register/code_of_federal_regulations/ibr_locations.html.*

(2) Molecular weight: Total monomers, dimers and trimers below 500 not more than 1 percent as determined by a method entitled "Low Molecular Weight Anoxomer Analysis," 1982, which is incorporated by reference. Copies are available from the Center for Food Safety and Applied Nutrition (HFS–200), Food and Drug Administration, 5100 Paint Branch Pkwy., College Park, MD 20740, or at the National Archives and Records Administration (NARA). For information on the availability of this material at NARA, call 202–741–6030, or go to: *http://www.archives.gov/federal_register/code_of_federal_regulations/ibr_locations.html.*

(3) Phenol content: Not less than 3.2 milliequivalent/gram and not more than 3.8 milliequivalent/gram as determined by a method entitled "Total Phenols," 1982, which is incorporated by reference. Copies are available from the Center for Food Safety and Applied Nutrition (HFS–200), Food and Drug Administration, 5100 Paint Branch Pkwy., College Park, MD 20740, or at the National Archives and Records Administration (NARA). For information on the availability of this material at NARA, call 202–741–6030, or go to: *http://www.archives.gov/federal_register/code_of_federal_regulations/ibr_locations.html.*

(4) Heavy metals as lead (as Pb), not more than 10 parts per million. Arsenic (as As), not more than 3 parts per million. Mercury (as Hg), not more than 1 part per million.

(c) Anoxomer may be safely used as an antioxidant in food at a level of not more than 5,000 parts per million based on fat and oil content of the food.

[48 FR 18798, Apr. 26, 1983, as amended at 54 FR 24896, June 12, 1989]

§ 172.110 BHA.

The food additive BHA (butylated hydroxyanisole) alone or in combination with other antioxidants permitted in food for human consumption in this subpart B may be safely used in or on specified foods, as follows:

(a) The BHA meets the following specification:

Assay (total BHA), 98.5 percent minimum.
Melting point 48 °C minimum.

(b) The BHA is used alone or in combination with BHT, as an antioxidant in foods, as follows:

Food	Limitations (total BHA and BHT) parts per million
Dehydrated potato shreds	50
Active dry yeast	[1] 1,000
Beverages and desserts prepared from dry mixes	[1] 2
Dry breakfast cereals	50
Dry diced glazed fruit	[1] 32
Dry mixes for beverages and desserts	[1] 90
Emulsion stabilizers for shortenings	200

Food	Limitations (total BHA and BHT) parts per million
Potato flakes	50
Potato granules	10
Sweet potato flakes	50

[1] BHA only.

(c) To assure safe use of the additive:

(1) The label of any market package of the additive shall bear, in addition to the other information required by the Act, the name of the additive.

(2) When the additive is marketed in a suitable carrier, in addition to meeting the requirement of paragraph (c)(1) of this section, the label shall declare the percentage of the additive in the mixture.

(3) The label or labeling of dry mixes for beverages and desserts shall bear adequate directions for use to provide that beverages and desserts prepared from the dry mixes contain no more than 2 parts per million BHA.

§ 172.115 BHT.

The food additive BHT (butylated hydroxytoluene), alone or in combination with other antioxidants permitted in this subpart B may be safely used in or on specified foods, as follows:

(a) The BHT meets the following specification: Assay (total BHT) 99 percent minimum.

(b) The BHT is used alone or in combination with BHA, as an antioxidant in foods, as follows:

Food	Limitations (total BHA and BHT) parts per million
Dehydrated potato shreds	50
Dry breakfast cereals	50
Emulsion stabilizers for shortenings	200
Potato flakes	50
Potato granules	10
Sweetpotato flakes	50

(c) To assure safe use of the additive:

(1) The label of any market package of the additive shall bear, in addition to the other information required by the Act, the name of the additive.

(2) When the additive is marketed in a suitable carrier, in addition to meeting the requirement of paragraph (c)(1) of this section, the label shall declare the percentage of the additive in the mixture.

§ 172.120 Calcium disodium EDTA.

The food additive calcium disodium EDTA (calcium disodium ethylenediaminetetraacetate) may be safely used in designated foods for the purposes and in accordance with the conditions prescribed, as follows:

(a) The additive contains a minimum of 99 percent by weight of either the dihydrate $C_{10}H_{12}O_8N_2CaNa_2 \cdot 2H_2O$ or the trihydrate $C_{10}H_{12}O_8N_2CaNa_2 \cdot 3H_2O$, or any mixture of the two.

(b) It is used or intended for use as follows:

(1) Alone, in the following foods at not to exceed the levels prescribed, calculated as the anhydrous compound:

Food	Limitation (parts per million)	Use
Cabbage, pickled	220	Promote color, flavor, and texture retention.
Canned carbonated soft drinks.	33	Promote flavor retention.
Canned white potatoes	110	Promote color retention.
Clams (cooked canned)	340	Promote color retention.
Crabmeat (cooked canned).	275	Retard struvite formation; promote color retention.
Cucumbers pickled	220	Promote color, flavor, and texture retention.
Distilled alcoholic beverages.	25	Promote stability of color, flavor, and/or product clarity.
Dressings, nonstandardized.	75	Preservative.
Dried lima beans (cooked canned).	310	Promote color retention.
Egg product that is hard-cooked and consists, in a cylindrical shape, of egg white with an inner core of egg yolk.	[1] 200	Preservative.
Fermented malt beverages.	25	Antigushing agent.
French dressing	75	Preservative.
Legumes (all cooked canned, other than dried lima beans, pink beans, and red beans).	365	Promote color retention.
Mayonnaise	75	Do.
Mushrooms (cooked canned).	200	Promote color retention.
Oleomargarine	75	Preservative.
Pecan pie filling	100	Promote color retention.
Pink beans (cooked canned).	165	Promote color retention.
Potato salad	100	Preservative.
Processed dry pinto beans.	800	Promote color retention.
Red beans (cooked canned).	165	Promote color retention.

Food	Limitation (parts per million)	Use
Salad dressing	75	Preservative.
Sandwich spread	100	Do.
Sauces	75	Do.
Shrimp (cooked canned).	250	Retard struvite formation; promote color retention.
Spice extractives in soluble carriers.	60	Promote color and flavor retention.
Spreads, artificially colored and lemon-flavored or orange-flavored.	100	Promote color retention.

[1] By weight of egg yolk portion.

(2) With disodium EDTA (disodium ethylenediaminetetraacetate) in the following foods at not to exceed, in combination, the levels prescribed, calculated as anhydrous $C_{10}H_{12}O_8N_2CaNa_2$:

Food	Limitation (parts per million)	Use
Dressings, nonstandardized	75	Preservative.
French dressing	75	Do.
Mayonnaise	75	Do.
Salad dressing	75	Do.
Sandwich spread	100	Do.
Sauces	75	Do.

(c) To assure safe use of the additive:

(1) The label and labeling of the additive container shall bear, in addition to the other information required by the Act, the name of the additive.

(2) The label or labeling of the additive container shall bear adequate use directions to provide a final food product that complies with the limitations provided in paragraph (b) of this section.

(d) In the standardized foods listed in paragraph (b) of this section, the additives are used only in compliance with the applicable standards of identity for such foods.

[42 FR 14491, Mar. 15, 1977, as amended at 48 FR 10815, Mar. 15, 1983; 58 FR 52222, Oct. 7, 1993; 60 FR 33710, June 29, 1995; 65 FR 48379, Aug. 8, 2000]

§ 172.130 Dehydroacetic acid.

The food additive dehydroacetic acid and/or its sodium salt may be safely used in accordance with the following prescribed conditions:

(a) The food additive meets the following specifications:

Dehydroacetic acid: Melting point, 109 °C–111 °C; assay, minimum 98 percent (dry basis).
Sodium salt of dehydroacetic acid: Assay, minimum 98 percent (dry basis).

(b) It is used or intended for use as a preservative for cut or peeled squash, and is so used that no more than 65 parts per million expressed as dehydroacetic acid remains in or on the prepared squash.

(c) The label or labeling of any package of the additive intended for use in food shall bear adequate directions for use to insure compliance with this section.

§ 172.133 Dimethyl dicarbonate.

Dimethyl dicarbonate (CAS Reg. No. 4525–33–1) may be safely used in food in accordance with the following prescribed conditions:

(a) The additive meets the following specifications:

(1) The additive has a purity of not less than 99.8 percent as determined by the following titration method:

PRINCIPLES OF METHOD

Dimethyl dicarbonate (DMDC) is mixed with excess diisobutylamine with which it reacts quantitatively. The excess amine is backtitrated with acid.

APPARATUS

250-milliliter (mL) Beaker
100-mL Graduate cylinder
25-mL Pipette
10-mL Burette (automatic, eg., Metrohm burette)
Stirrer
Device for potentiometric titration
Reference electrode
Glass electrode

REAGENTS

Acetone, analytical-grade
Solution of 1 *N* diisobutylamine in chlorobenzene, distilled
1 *N* Acetic Acid

PROCEDURE

Accurately weigh in about 2 grams of the sample (W) and dissolve in 100 mL acetone. Add accurately 25 mL of the 1 *N* diisobutylamine solution by pipette and allow to stand for 5 minutes. Subsequently, titrate the reaction mixture potentiometrically with 1 *N* hydrochloric acid (consumption=*a* mL) while stirring. For determining the blank consumption, carry out the analysis without a sample (consumption=*b* mL).

CALCULATION

$$\frac{(b-a)\times 13.4}{W} = \%\ \text{DMDC}$$

NOTE: For adding the diisobutylamine solution, always use the same pipette and wait for a further three drops to fall when the flow has stopped.

(2) The additive contains not more than 2,000 ppm (0.2 percent) dimethyl carbonate as determined by a method entitled "Gas Chromatography Method for Dimethyl Carbonate Impurity in Dimethyl Dicarbonate," which is incorporated by reference in accordance with 5 U.S.C. 552(a). Copies are available from the Center for Food Safety and Applied Nutrition (HFS–200), 5100 Paint Branch Pkwy., College Park, MD 20740, or at the National Archives and Records Administration (NARA). For information on the availability of this material at NARA, call 202–741–6030, or go to: *http://www.archives.gov/federal_register/code_of_federal_regulations/ibr_locations.html.*

(b) The additive is used or intended for use as a microbial control agent in the following beverages under normal circumstances of bottling, canning, or other forms of final packaging, where the viable microbial load has been reduced to 500 microorganisms per milliliter or less by current good manufacturing practices such as heat treatment, filtration, or other technologies prior to the use of dimethyl dicarbonate:

(1) In wine, dealcoholized wine, and low alcohol wine in an amount not to exceed 200 parts per million.

(2) In ready-to-drink teas in an amount not to exceed 250 parts per million.

(3) In carbonated or noncarbonated, nonjuice-containing (less than or equal to 1 percent juice), flavored or unflavored beverages containing added electrolytes (5–20 milliequivalents/liter sodium ion (Na+) and 3–7 milliequivalents/liter potassium ion (K+)) in an amount not to exceed 250 parts per million.

(4) In carbonated, dilute beverages containing juice, fruit flavor, or both, with juice content not to exceed 50 percent, in an amount not to exceed 250 parts per million.

(c) To ensure the safe use of the food additive, the label of the package containing the additive shall bear, in addition to other information required by the Federal Food, Drug, and Cosmetic Act:

(1) The name of the additive "dimethyl dicarbonate."

(2) The intended use of the additive.

(3) Adequate directions for use to ensure compliance with this section.

[53 FR 41329, Oct. 21, 1988, as amended at 58 FR 6091, Jan. 26, 1993; 59 FR 5319, Feb. 4, 1994; 61 FR 14245, Apr. 1, 1996; 61 FR 26788, May 29, 1996; 66 FR 13653, Mar. 7, 2001]

§ 172.135 Disodium EDTA.

The food additive disodium EDTA (disodium ethylenediaminetetraacetate) may be safely used in designated foods for the purposes and in accordance with the following prescribed conditions:

(a) The additive contains a minimum of 99 percent disodium ethylenediaminetetraacetate dihydrate ($C_{10}H_{14}O_8N_2Na_2{\cdot}2H_2O$).

(b) It is used or intended for use as follows:

(1) Alone, in the following foods at not to exceed the levels prescribed, calculated as anhydrous calcium disodium EDTA:

Food	Limitation (parts per million)	Use
Aqueous multivitamin preparations.	150	With iron salts as a stabilizer for vitamin B_{12} in liquid multivitamin preparations.
Canned black-eyed peas	145	Promote color retention.
Canned kidney beans	165	Preservative.
Canned strawberry pie filling	500	Promote color retention.
Cooked sausage	36	As a cure accelerator with sodium ascorbate or ascorbic acid.
Dressings, nonstandardized	75	Preservative.
French dressing	75	Do.
Frozen white potatoes including cut potatoes.	100	Promote color retention.
Gefilte fish balls or patties in packing medium.	[1] 50	Inhibit discoloration.
Legumes (all cooked canned, other than black-eyed peas).	165	Promote color retention.
Mayonnaise	75	Preservative.

Food	Limitation (parts per million)	Use
Ready-to-eat cereal products containing dried bananas.	[2] 315	Promote color retention.
Salad dressing	75	Preservative.
Sandwich spread	100	Do.
Sauces	75	Do.

[1] Based on total weight of finished product including packing medium.

[2] In dried banana component of cereal product.

(2) With calcium disodium EDTA (calcium disodium ethylenediaminetetraacetate; calcium disodium (ethylenedinitrilo) tetraacetate), in the following foods at not to exceed, in combination, the levels prescribed, calculated as anhydrous $C_{10}H_{12}O_8N_2CaNa_2$:

Food	Limitation (parts per million)	Use
Dressings, nonstandardized	75	Preservative.
French dressing	75	Do.
Mayonnaise	75	Do.
Salad dressing	75	Do.
Sandwich spread	100	Do.
Sauces	75	Do.

(3) Alone, as a sequestrant in the nonnutritive sweeteners that are listed in § 180.37 of this chapter and that, in addition, are designed for aqueous solution: *Provided*, That the amount of the additive, calculated as anhydrous calcium disodium EDTA, does not exceed 0.1 percent by weight of the dry nonnutritive sweetener.

(c) To assure the safe use of the additive:

(1) The label and labeling of the additive container shall bear, in addition to the other information required by the act, the name of the additive.

(2) The label or labeling of the additive container shall bear adequate use directions to provide a final food product that complies with the limitations provided in paragraph (b) of this section.

(d) In the standardized foods listed in paragraphs (b) (1) and (2) of this section the additives are used only in compliance with the applicable standards of identity for such foods.

[42 FR 14491, Mar. 15, 1977, as amended at 65 FR 48379, Aug. 8, 2000]

§ 172.140 Ethoxyquin.

(a) Ethoxyquin (1,2-dihydro-6-ethoxy-2,2,4-trimethylquinoline) may be safely used as an antioxidant for preservation of color in the production of chili powder, paprika, and ground chili at levels not in excess of 100 parts per million.

(b) In order to provide for the safe use of the additive in feed prepared in accordance with §§ 573.380 and 573.400 of this chapter, tolerances are established for residues of ethoxyquin in or on edible products of animals as follows:

5 parts per million in or on the uncooked fat of meat from animals except poultry.

3 parts per million in or on the uncooked liver and fat of poultry.

0.5 part per million in or on the uncooked muscle meat of animals.

0.5 part per million in poultry eggs.

Zero in milk.

§ 172.145 Heptylparaben.

(a) The food additive heptylparaben is the chemical *n*-heptyl *p*-hydroxybenzoate.

(b) It may be safely used to inhibit microbiological spoilage in accordance with the following prescribed conditions:

(1) In fermented malt beverages in amounts not to exceed 12 parts per million.

(2) In noncarbonated soft drinks and fruit-based beverages in amounts not to exceed 20 parts per million, when standards of identity established under section 401 of the Act (21 U.S.C. 341) do not preclude such use.

§ 172.150 4-Hydroxymethyl-2,6-di-*tert*-butylphenol.

The food additive 4-hydroxymethyl-2,6-di-*tert*-butylphenol may be safely used in food in accordance with the following prescribed conditions:

(a) The additive has a solidification point of 140 °C–141 °C.

(b) The additive is used as an antioxidant alone or in combination with other permitted antioxidants.

(c) The total amount of all antioxidants added to such food shall not exceed 0.02 percent of the oil or fat content of the food, including the essential (volatile) oil content of the food.

§ 172.155 Natamycin (pimaricin).

(a) Natamycin (CAS Reg. No. 7681–93–8), also known as pimaricin, is a polyene macrolide antimycotic substance possessing an empirical formula of $C_{33}H_{47}NO_{13}$ and a molecular weight of 665.7.

(b) The additive shall conform to the following specifications:

Purity: 97 percent ±2 percent on an anhydrous basis.
Arsenic: Not more than 1 part per million.
Heavy metals (as Pb): Not more than 20 parts per million.

(c) The additive may be applied on cheese, as an antimycotic, in amounts not to exceed 20 milligrams per kilogram (20 parts per million) in the finished product as determined by International Dairy Federation (IDF) Standard 140A:1992, ''Cheese and Cheese Rind-Determination of Natamycin Content-Method by Molecular Absorption Spectrometry and by High-Performance Liquid Chromatography,'' which is incorporated by reference. The Director of the Office of the Federal Register approves this incorporation by reference in accordance with 5 U.S.C. 552(a) and 1 CFR part 51. Copies are available from the Division of Product Policy (HFS–206), Center for Food Safety and Applied Nutrition, Food and Drug Administration, 5100 Paint Branch Pkwy., College Park, MD 20740, or may be examined at the Center for Food Safety and Applied Nutrition's Library, 5100 Paint Branch Pkwy., College Park, MD 20740, or at the National Archives and Records Administration (NARA). For information on the availability of this material at NARA, call 202–741–6030, or go to: *http://www.archives.gov/federal_register/code_of_federal_regulations/ibr_locations.html.*

[47 FR 26823, June 22, 1982, as amended at 50 FR 49536, Dec. 3, 1985; 63 FR 66015, Dec. 1, 1998; 66 FR 13847, Mar. 8, 2001]

§ 172.160 Potassium nitrate.

The food additive potassium nitrate may be safely used as a curing agent in the processing of cod roe, in an amount not to exceed 200 parts per million of the finished roe.

§ 172.165 Quaternary ammonium chloride combination.

The food additive, quaternary ammonium chloride combination, may be safely used in food in accordance with the following conditions:

(a) The additive contains the following compounds: *n*-dodecyl dimethyl benzyl ammonium chloride (CAS Reg. No. 139–07–1); *n*-dodecyl dimethyl ethylbenzyl ammonium chloride (CAS Reg. No. 27479–28–3); *n*-hexadecyl dimethyl benzyl ammonium chloride (CAS Reg. No. 122–18–9); *n*-octadecyl dimethyl benzyl ammonium chloride (CAS Reg. No. 122–19–0); *n*-tetradecyl dimethyl benzyl ammonium chloride (CAS Reg. No. 139–08–2); *n*-tetradecyl dimethyl ethylbenzyl ammonium chloride (CAS Reg. No. 27479–29–4).

(b) The additive meets the following specifications: pH (5 percent active solution) 7.0–8.0; total amines, maximum 1 percent as combined free amines and amine hydrochlorides.

(c) The additive is used as an antimicrobial agent, as defined in § 170.3(o)(2) of this chapter, in raw sugar cane juice. It is added prior to clarification when further processing of the sugar cane juice must be delayed.

(d) The additive is applied to the sugar juice in the following quantities, based on the weight of the raw cane:

Component	Parts per million
n-Dodecyl dimethyl benzyl ammonium chloride	0.25–1.0
n-Dodecyl dimethyl ethylbenzyl ammonium chloride	3.4–13.5
n-Hexadecyl dimethyl benzyl ammonium chloride	1.5–6.0
n-Octadecyl dimethyl benzyl ammonium chloride	0.25–1.0
n-Tetradecyl dimethyl benzyl ammonium chloride	3.0–12.0
n-Tetradecyl dimethyl ethylbenzyl ammonium chloride	1.6–6.5

[50 FR 3890, Jan. 29, 1985]

§ 172.167 Silver nitrate and hydrogen peroxide solution.

An aqueous solution containing a mixture of silver nitrate and hydrogen peroxide may be safely used in accordance with the following prescribed conditions:

(a) The additive is used as an antimicrobial agent in bottled water.

(b) Hydrogen peroxide meets the specifications of the "Food Chemicals Codex," 6th ed. (2008), pp. 463 and 464, which is incorporated by reference. The Director of the Federal Register approves this incorporation by reference in accordance with 5 U.S.C. 552(a) and 1 CFR part 51. You may obtain copies from the United States Pharmacopeial Convention, 12601 Twinbrook Pkwy., Rockville, MD 20852 (Internet address *http://www.usp.org*). Copies may be examined at the Center for Food Safety and Applied Nutrition's Library, Food and Drug Administration, 5100 Paint Branch Pkwy., College Park, MD 20740, 301–436–2163, or at the National Archives and Records Administration (NARA). For information on the availability of this material at NARA, call 202–741–6030 or go to: *http://www.archives.gov/federal_register/code_of_federal_regulations/ibr_locations.html.*

(c) The amount of silver added will not exceed 17 micrograms per kilogram in the treated bottled water, and the amount of hydrogen peroxide will not exceed 23 milligrams per kilogram in the treated bottled water. Analyses for silver and hydrogen peroxide shall be conducted on samples of treated bottled water at the site of bottling, using samples of the water intended for treatment for the blank determination.

(d)(1) The amount of silver in the treated bottled water is determined using the method for silver designated in 21 CFR 165.110(b)(4)(iii)(G)(*2*)(*i*).

(2) The amount of hydrogen peroxide in the treated bottled water is determined using a Hydrogen Peroxide Test Kit from the HACH Co., or equivalent. The manual from the Hydrogen Peroxide Test Kit, Model HYP–1, Catalog Number 22917–00, 1991, is incorporated by reference. The Director of the Federal Register approves this incorporation by reference in accordance with 5 U.S.C. 552(a) and 1 CFR part 51. You may obtain copies of the test kit manual from the HACH Co., P.O. Box 389, Loveland CO, 80359 (1–800–227–4224), Model HYP–1, Catalog Number 22917–00. Copies may be examined at the Center for Food Safety and Applied Nutrition's Library, Food and Drug Administration, 5100 Paint Branch Pkwy., College Park, MD 20740, 301–436–2163, or at the National Archives and Records Administration (NARA). For information on the availability of this material at NARA, call 202–741–6030 or go to: *http://www.archives.gov/federal_register/code_of_federal_regulations/ibr_locations.html.*

(e) Substances generally recognized as safe in or on food may be used to stabilize the additive to ensure that the additive will perform its intended technical effect.

(f) The additive may not be added to bottled water that has been filtered or is intended to be filtered through a silver-containing water filter.

(g) Bottled water must meet the quality standards for bottled water in § 165.110(b)(2) through (b)(5) of this chapter, including the limits specified for total silver and nitrate, unless the water bears a label statement of substandard quality, as provided for under § 165.110(c) of this chapter.

[74 FR 11478, Mar. 18, 2009]

§ 172.170 Sodium nitrate.

The food additive sodium nitrate may be safely used in or on specified foods in accordance with the following prescribed conditions:

(a) It is used or intended for use as follows:

(1) As a preservative and color fixative, with or without sodium nitrite, in smoked, cured sablefish, smoked, cured salmon, and smoked, cured shad, so that the level of sodium nitrate does not exceed 500 parts per million and the level of sodium nitrite does not exceed 200 parts per million in the finished product.

(2) As a preservative and color fixative, with or without sodium nitrite, in meat-curing preparations for the home curing of meat and meat products (including poultry and wild game), with directions for use which limit the amount of sodium nitrate to not more than 500 parts per million in the finished meat product and the amount of sodium nitrite to not more than 200 parts per million in the finished meat product.

(b) To assure safe use of the additive, in addition to the other information required by the Act:

(1) The label of the additive or of a mixture containing the additive shall bear:

(i) The name of the additive.

(ii) A statement of the concentration of the additive in any mixture.

(2) If in a retail package intended for household use, the label and labeling of the additive, or of a mixture containing the additive, shall bear adequate directions for use to provide a final food product that complies with the limitations prescribed in paragraph (a) of this section.

(3) If in a retail package intended for household use, the label of the additive or of a mixture containing the additive, shall bear the statement "Keep out of the reach of children".

§172.175 Sodium nitrite.

The food additive sodium nitrite may be safely used in or on specified foods in accordance with the following prescribed conditions:

(a) It is used or intended for use as follows:

(1) As a color fixative in smoked cured tunafish products so that the level of sodium nitrite does not exceed 10 parts per million (0.001 percent) in the finished product.

(2) As a preservative and color fixative, with or without sodium nitrate, in smoked, cured sablefish, smoked, cured salmon, and smoked, cured shad so that the level of sodium nitrite does not exceed 200 parts per million and the level of sodium nitrate does not exceed 500 parts per million in the finished product.

(3) As a preservative and color fixative, with sodium nitrate, in meat-curing preparations for the home curing of meat and meat products (including poultry and wild game), with directions for use which limit the amount of sodium nitrite to not more than 200 parts per million in the finished meat product, and the amount of sodium nitrate to not more than 500 parts per million in the finished meat product.

(b) To assure safe use of the additive, in addition to the other information required by the Act:

(1) The label of the additive or of a mixture containing the additive shall bear:

(i) The name of the additive.

(ii) A statement of the concentration of the additive in any mixture.

(2) If in a retail package intended for household use, the label and labeling of the additive, or of a mixture containing the additive, shall bear adequate directions for use to provide a final food product which complies with the limitations prescribed in paragraph (a) of this section.

(3) If in a retail package intended for household use, the label of the additive, or of a mixture containing the additive, shall bear the statement "Keep out of the reach of children".

§172.177 Sodium nitrite used in processing smoked chub.

The food additive sodium nitrite may be safely used in combination with salt (NaCl) to aid in inhibiting the outgrowth and toxin formation from *Clostridium botulinum* type E in the commercial processing of smoked chub in accordance with the following prescribed conditions:

(a) All fish in smoking establishments shall be clean and wholesome and shall be expeditiously processed, packed, and stored under adequate sanitary conditions in accordance with good manufacturing practice.

(b) The brining procedure is controlled in such a manner that the water phase portion of the edible portion of the finished smoked product has a salt (NaCl) content of not less than 3.5 percent, as measured in the loin muscle, and the sodium nitrite content of the edible portion of the finished smoked product is not less than 100 parts per million and not greater than 200 parts per million, as measured in the loin muscle.

(c) Smoked chub shall be heated by a controlled heat process which provides a monitoring system positioned in as many strategic locations in the smokehouse as necessary to assure a continuous temperature throughout each fish of at least 160 °F for a minimum of 30 minutes.

(d) The finished product shall be cooled to a temperature of 50 °F or below within 3 hours after smoking and further cooled to a temperature of 38 °F or below within 12 hours after smoking. A temperature of 38 °F or below shall be maintained during all subsequent storage and distribution. All shipping containers, retail packages, and shipping records shall indicate with appropriate notice the perishable nature of the product and specify that the product shall be held under refrigeration (38 °F or below) until consumed.

(e) To assure safe use of the additive:

(1) The label and labeling of the additive container shall bear, in addition to the other information required by the Act, the name of the additive.

(2) The label or labeling of the additive container shall bear adequate directions to assure use in compliance with the provisions of this section.

§ 172.180 Stannous chloride.

The food additive stannous chloride may be safely used for color retention in asparagus packed in glass, with lids lined with an inert material, in an amount not to exceed 20 parts per million calculated as tin (Sn).

§ 172.185 TBHQ.

The food additive TBHQ, which is the chemical 2-(1,1-dimethylethyl)-1,4-benzenediol (Chemical Abstracts Service Registry Number 1948–33–0), also known as tertiary butylhydroquinone, may be safely used in food in accordance with the following prescribed conditions:

(a) The food additive has a melting point of 126.5 °C–128.5 °C.

(b) It is used as an antioxidant alone or in combination with BHA and/or BHT.

(c) The total antioxidant content of a food containing the additive will not exceed 0.02 percent of the oil or fat content of the food, including the essential (volatile) oil content of the food.

§ 172.190 THBP.

The food additive THBP (2,4,5-trihydroxybutyrophenone) may be safely used in food in accordance with the following prescribed conditions:

(a) The food additive has a melting point of 149 °C–153 °C.

(b) It is used as an antioxidant alone or in combination with other permitted antioxidants.

(c) The total antioxidant content of a food containing the additive will not exceed 0.02 percent of the oil or fat content of the food, including the essential (volatile) oil content of the food.

Subpart C—Coatings, Films and Related Substances

§ 172.210 Coatings on fresh citrus fruit.

Coatings may be applied to fresh citrus fruit for protection of the fruit in accordance with the following conditions:

(a) The coating is applied in the minimum amount required to accomplish the intended effect.

(b) The coating may be formulated from the following components, each used in the minimum quantity required to accomplish the intended effect:

(1) Substances generally recognized as safe for the purpose or previously sanctioned for the purpose.

(2) One or more of the following:

Component	Limitations
Fatty acids	Complying with § 172.860.
Oleic acid derived from tall oil fatty acids	Complying with § 172.862.
Partially hydrogenated rosin	Catalytically hydrogenated to a maximum refractive index of 1.5012 at 100 °C. Color of WG or paler.
Pentaerythritol ester of maleic anhydride-modified wood rosin.	Acid number of 134–145; drop-softening point of 127 °C–173 °C; saponification number of less than 280; and a color of M or paler.
Do	Acid number of 176–186; drop-softening point of 110 °C–118 °C; saponification number of less than 280; and a color of M or paler.
Polyethylene glycol	Complying with § 172.820. As a defoamer and dispersing adjuvant.
Polyhydric alcohol diesters of oxidatively refined (Gersthofen process) montan wax acids.	Complying with § 178.3770 of this chapter and having a dropping point of 77 to 83 °C (170.6 to 181.4 °F), as determined by ASTM Method D566–76 (Reapproved 1982), "Standard Test Method for Dropping Point of Lubricating Grease," which is incorporated by reference (Copies are available from the American Society for Testing and Materials, 100 Barr Harbor Dr., West Conshohocken, Philadelphia, PA 19428-2959, or at the National Archives and Records Administration (NARA). For information on the availability of this material at NARA, call 202–741–6030, or go to: *http://www.archives.gov/federal_register/code_of_federal_regulations/ibr_locations.html.*) using as a solvent xylene-ethyl alcohol in a 2:1 ratio instead of toluene-ethyl alcohol in a 2:1 ratio.
Sodium lauryl sulfate	Complying with § 172.822. As a film former.

Component	Limitations
Wood rosin	Color of K or paler.

(3) In lieu of the components listed in paragraph (b) (2) and (4) of this section, the following copolymer and one or more of the listed adjuvants.

Component	Limitations
Vinyl chloride-vinylidene chloride copolymer	As an aqueous dispersion containing a minimum of 75 percent water when applied.
Polyethylene glycol	Complying with § 172.820. As a defoamer and dispersing adjuvant.
Polyvinylpyrrolidone	As an adjuvant.
Potassium persulfate	Do.
Propylene glycol alginate	Do.
Sodium decylbenzenesulfonate	Do.

(4) In lieu of the components listed in paragraph (b) (2) and (3) of this section, the following rosin derivative and either or both of the listed adjuvants:

Component	Limitations
Calcium salt of partially dimerized rosin	Having a maximum drop-softening point of 197 °C and a color of H or paler. It is prepared by reaction with not more than 7 parts hydrated lime per 100 parts of partially dimerized rosin. The partially dimerized rosin is rosin that has been dimerized by sulfuric acid catalyst to a drop-softening point of 95 °C to 105 °C and a color of WG or paler.
Petroleum naphtha	As adjuvant. Complying with § 172.250.
Sperm oil	As adjuvant.

[42 FR 14491, Mar. 15, 1977; 49 FR 5747, Feb. 15, 1984, as amended at 51 FR 2693, Jan. 21, 1986; 52 FR 18911, May 20, 1987; 61 FR 14245, Apr. 1, 1996]

§ 172.215 Coumarone-indene resin.

The food additive coumarone-indene resin may be safely used on grapefruit, lemons, limes, oranges, tangelos, and tangerines in accordance with the following prescribed conditions:

(a) The food additive is manufactured by the polymerization of a crude, heavy coal-tar solvent naphtha meeting the following specifications:

(1) It is a mixture of indene, indan (hydrindene), substituted benzenes, and related compounds.

(2) It contains no more than 0.25 percent tar bases.

(3) 95 percent distills in the range 167 °C–184 °C.

(b) The food additive meets the following specifications:

(1) Softening point, ring and ball: 126 °C minimum as determined by ASTM method E28–67 (Reapproved 1982), "Standard Test Method for Softening Point by Ring-and-Ball Apparatus," which is incorporated by reference. Copies may be obtained from the American Society for Testing Materials, 100 Barr Harbor Dr., West Conshohocken, Philadelphia, PA 19428-2959, or may be examined at the National Archives and Records Administration (NARA). For information on the availability of this material at NARA, call 202-741-6030, or go to: *http://www.archives.gov/federal_register/code_of_federal_regulations/ibr_locations.html.*

(2) Refractive index (n^{25}/D) 1.63–1.64.

(c) It is used or intended for use as a protective coating for grapefruit, lemons, limes, oranges, tangelos, and tangerines whereby the maximum amount of the resin remaining on the fruit does not exceed 200 parts per million on a fresh-weight basis.

(d) To assure safe use of the additive:

(1) The label of the market package or any intermediate premix of the additive shall bear, in addition to the other information required by the act:

(i) The name of the additive, coumarone-indene resin.

(ii) A statement of the concentration of the additive therein.

(2) The label or accompanying labeling shall bear adequate directions that, if followed, will result in a finished food not in conflict with the requirements of this section.

[42 FR 14491, Mar. 15, 1977, as amended at 49 FR 10103, Mar. 19, 1984]

§ 172.225 Methyl and ethyl esters of fatty acids produced from edible fats and oils.

Methyl esters and ethyl esters of fatty acids produced from edible fats and oils may be safely used in food, subject to the following prescribed conditions:

(a) The additive consists of a mixture of either methyl or ethyl esters of fatty acids produced from edible fats and oils and meets the following specifications:

(1) Not less than 90 percent methyl or ethyl esters of fatty acids.

(2) Not more than 1.5 percent unsaponifiable matter.

(b) The additive is used or intended for use at the level not to exceed 3 percent by weight in an aqueous emulsion in dehydrating grapes to produce raisins, whereby the residue of the additive on the raisins does not exceed 200 parts per million.

[57 FR 12711, Apr. 13, 1992]

§ 172.230 Microcapsules for flavoring substances.

Microcapsules may be safely used for encapsulating discrete particles of flavoring substances that are generally recognized as safe for their intended use or are regulated under this part, in accordance with the following conditions:

(a) The microcapsules may be formulated from the following components, each used in the minimum quantity required to accomplish the intended effect:

(1) Substances generally recognized as safe for the purpose.

(2) One or more of the following components:

COMPONENT AND LIMITATIONS

Succinylated gelatin—Not to exceed 15 percent by combined weight of the microcapsule and flavoring oil. Succinic acid content of the gelatin is 4.5 to 5.5 percent.

Arabinogalactan—Complying with § 172.610; as adjuvant.

Silicon dioxide—Complying with § 172.480; as adjuvant.

(3) In lieu of the components listed in paragraph (a)(2) of this section, the following components:

COMPONENT AND LIMITATIONS

Glutaraldehyde—As cross-linking agent for insolubilizing a coacervate of gum arabic and gelatin.

n-Octyl alcohol—As a defoamer.

(4) In lieu of the components listed in paragraphs (a)(2) and (3) of this section, the following component:

COMPONENT AND LIMITATIONS

Petroleum wax—Complying with § 172.886. Not to exceed 50 percent by combined weight of the microcapsule and spice-flavoring substance.

(b) The microcapsules produced from the components listed in paragraphs (a) (1), (2), and (3) of this section may be used for encapsulating authorized flavoring oils for use, in accordance with good manufacturing practice, in foods for which standards of identity established under section 401 of the Act do not preclude such use, except that microcapsules formulated from components listed in paragraph (a)(2) of this section may be used only for encapsulating lemon oil, distilled lime oil, orange oil, peppermint oil, and spearmint oil for use in dry mixes for puddings and gelatin desserts.

(c) The microcapsules produced from the components listed in paragraphs (a) (1) and (4) of this section may be used only for encapsulating authorized spice-flavoring substances for use, in accordance with good manufacturing practice, in frozen pizzas which are to be further processed by heat. Such pizzas shall bear labels or labeling including adequate directions for use to ensure heating to temperatures which will melt the wax to release the spice-flavoring substances.

[45 FR 48123, July 18, 1980]

§ 172.235 Morpholine.

Morpholine may be safely used as a component of food, subject to the following restrictions.

(a) It is used as the salt(s) of one or more of the fatty acids meeting the requirements of § 172.860, as a component of protective coatings applied to fresh fruits and vegetables.

(b) It is used at a level not in excess of that reasonably required to produce its intended effect.

§ 172.250 Petroleum naphtha.

Petroleum naphtha may be safely used in food in accordance with the following conditions:

(a) The additive is a mixture of liquid hydrocarbons, essentially paraffinic and naphthenic in nature obtained from petroleum,

(b) The additive is refined to meet the following specifications when subjected to the procedures described in this paragraph.

(1) Boiling-point range: 175 °F–300 °F.

(2) Nonvolatile residue: 0.002 gram per 100 milliliters maximum.

(3) Ultraviolet absorbance limits, as follows:

Wavelength (milli-microns)	Maximum absorbance per centimeter optical pathlength
280–289	0.15
290–299	.13
300–359	.08
360–400	.02

ANALYTICAL SPECIFICATION FOR PETROLEUM NAPHTHA

GENERAL INSTRUCTIONS

All glassware should be scrupulously cleaned to remove all organic matter such as oil, grease, detergent residues, etc. Examine all glassware, including stoppers and stopcocks, under ultraviolet light to detect any residual fluorescent contamination. As a precautionary measure, it is recommended practice to rinse all glassware with purified isooctane immediately before use. No grease is to be used on stopcocks or joints. Great care to avoid contamination of petroleum naphtha samples in handling and to assure absence of any extraneous material arising from inadequate packaging is essential. Because some of the polynuclear hydrocarbons sought in this test are very susceptible to photo-oxidation, the entire procedure is to be carried out under subdued light.

APPARATUS

Separatory funnels. 250-milliliter, and 2,000-milliliter capacity, equipped with tetrafluoroethylene polymer stopcocks.

Erlenmeyer flask. 125-milliliter with 24/40 standard taper neck.

Evaporation flask. 250-milliliter capacity all-glass flask equipped with 24/40 standard taper stopper having inlet and outlet tubes to permit passage of nitrogen across the surface of the container liquid to be evaporated.

Condenser. 24/40 joints, fitted with drying tube, length optional.

Spectrophotometric cells. Fused quartz cells, optical path length in the range of 5,000 centimeters ±0.005 centimeter; also for checking spectrophotometer performance only, optical path length in the range 1,000 centimeter ±0.005 centimeter. With distilled water in the cells, determine any absorbance difference.

Spectrophotometer. Spectral range 250–400 mμ with spectral slit width of 2 mμ or less; under instrument operating conditions for these absorbance measurements, the spectrophotometer shall also meet the following performance requirements:

Absorbance repeatability, ±0.01 at 0.4 absorbance.
Absorbance accuracy,[1] ±0.05 at 0.4 absorbance.
Wavelength repeatability, ±0.2 millimicron.
Wavelength accuracy, ±1.0 millimicron.

Ultraviolet lamp. Long wavelength (3400–3800A°).

REAGENTS

Isooctane (2,2,4-trimethylpentane). Use 180 milliliters in a 250-milliliter Erlenmeyer flask, add 1 milliliter of purified *n*-hexadecane, insert the head assembly, allow nitrogen gas to flow into the inlet tube and connect the outlet tube to a solvent trap and vacuum line in such a way as to prevent any back flow of condensate into the flask. The

[1] As determined by procedure using potassium chromate for reference standard and described in National Bureau of Standards Circular 484, Spectrophotometry, U.S. Department of Commerce, (1949). The accuracy is to be determined by comparison with the standard values at 290, 345, and 400 millimicrons. The procedure is incorporated by reference. Copies of the material incorporated by reference are available from the Center for Food Safety and Applied Nutrition (HFS–200), Food and Drug Administration, 5100 Paint Branch Pkwy., College Park, MD 20740, or available for inspection at the National Archives and Records Administration (NARA). For information on the availability of this material at NARA, call 202–741–6030, or go to: *http://www.archives.gov/federal_register/code_of_federal_regulations/ibr_locations.html.*

contents of the flask are evaporated on a steam bath until 1 milliliter of residue remains. Dissolve the 1 milliliter of hexadecane residue in isooctane and make up to 25 milliliters. Determine the absorbance in a 5-centimeter path length cell compared to isooctane as reference. The absorbance should not exceed 0.01 per centimeter path length between 280–400 mμ. If necessary, isooctane may be purified by passage through a column of activated silica gel (Grade 12, Davidson Chemical Co., Baltimore, Md., or equivalent) or by distillation.

Methyl alcohol, A.C.S. reagent grade. Use 10 milliliters and proceed as with isooctane. The absorbance per centimeter of path length should be 0.00 between 280–400 mμ. Methyl alcohol may be purified by simple distillation or by refluxing in the presence of potassium hydroxide (10 grams/2 liters) and zinc dust (25 grams/2 liters) for 3 hours followed by distillation.

n-Hexadecane, 99 percent olefin-free. Dilute 1.0 milliliter of *n*-hexadecane to 25 milliliters with isooctane and determine the absorbance in a 5-centimeter cell compared to isooctane as reference between 280–400 mμ. The absorbance per centimeter path length shall not exceed 0.00 in this range. Purify, if necessary, by percolation through activated silica gel or by distillation.

Sodium borohydride. 98 percent.

Water. All distilled water must be extracted with isooctane before use. A series of three successive extracts of 1.5 liters of distilled water with 100-milliliter portions of isooctane is satisfactory.

PROCEDURE

Determination of ultraviolet absorbance. Add a 25-milliliter aliquot of the hydrocarbon solvent together with 1 milliliter of hexadecane to the 125-milliliter Erlenmeyer flask. While flushing with nitrogen, evaporate to 1 milliliter on a steam bath. Nitrogen is admitted through a 8±1-milliliter outer-diameter tube, drawn out into a 2±1-centimeter long and 1±0.5-millimeter inner-diameter capillary tip. This is positioned so that the capillary tip extends 4 centimeters into the flask. The nitrogen flow rate is such that the surface of the liquid is barely disturbed. After the volume is reduced to that of the 1 milliliter of hexadecane, the flask is left on the steam bath for 10 more minutes before removing. Add 10 milliliters of purified isooctane to the flask and reevaporate the solution to a 1-milliliter volume in the same manner as described above, except do not heat for an added 10 minutes. Repeat this operation twice more. Let the flask cool.

Add 10 milliliters of methyl alcohol and about 0.3 gram of sodium borohydride. (Minimize exposure of the borohydride to the atmosphere; a measuring dipper may be used.) Immediately fit a water-cooled condenser equipped with a 24/40 joint and with a drying tube into the flask, mix until the sodium borohydride is dissolved, and allow to stand for 30 minutes at room temperature, with intermittent swirling. At the end of this time, disconnect the flask and evaporate the methyl alcohol on the steam bath under nitrogen until sodium borohydride begins to drop out of solution. Remove the flask and let it cool.

Add 6 milliliters of isooctane to the flask and swirl to wash the crystalline slurry. Carefully transfer the isooctane extract to a 250-milliliter separatory funnel. Dissolve the crystals in the flask with about 25 milliliters of distilled water and pour this also into the separatory funnel. Adjust the water volume in the separatory funnel to about 100 milliliters and shake for 1 minute. After separation of the layers, draw off the aqueous layer into a second 250-milliliter separatory funnel. Transfer the hydrocarbon layer in the first funnel to a 25-milliliter volumetric flask.

Carefully wash the Erlenmeyer flask with an additional 6 milliliters of isooctane, swirl, and transfer to the second separatory funnel. Shake the funnel for 1 minute. After separation of the layers, draw off the aqueous layer into the first separatory funnel. Transfer the isooctane in the second funnel to the volumetric flask. Again wash the Erlenmeyer flask with an additional 6 milliliters of isooctane, swirl, and transfer to the first separatory funnel. Shake the funnel for 1 minute. After separation of the layers, draw off the aqueous layer and discard. Transfer the isooctane layer to the volumetric flask and adjust the volume to 25 milliliters of isooctane. Mix the contents well, then transfer to the first separatory funnel and wash twice with 50-milliliter portions of distilled water. Discard the aqueous layers after each wash.

Determine the ultraviolet absorbance of the isooctane extract in 5-centimeter path length cells compared to isooctane as reference between 280–400 mμ. Determine a reagent blank concurrently with the sample, using 25 milliliters of purified isooctane instead of a solvent sample and measuring the ultraviolet absorbance of the blank between 280–400mμ.

The reagent blank absorbance should not exceed 0.04 per centimeter path length between 280–289 mμ; 0.020 between 290–359 mμ; and 0.010 between 360–400 mμ.

Determination of boiling-point range. Use ASTM method D86–82, "Standard Method for Distillation of Petroleum Products," which is incorporated by reference. Copies may be obtained from the American Society for Testing Materials, 100 Barr Harbor Dr., West Conshohocken, Philadelphia, PA 19428-2959, or may be examined at the National Archives and Records Administration (NARA). For information on the availability of this material at NARA, call 202–741–6030, or go to: *http://www.archives.gov/federal_register/*

code_of_federal_regulations/ ibr_locations.html.

Determination of nonvolatile residue. For hydrocarbons boiling below 121 °C, determine the nonvolatile residue by ASTM method D1353–78, "Standard Test Method for Nonvolatile Matter in Volatile Solvents for Use in Paint, Varnish, Lacquer, and Related Products;" for those boiling above 121 °C, use ASTM method D381–80, "Standard Test Method for Existent Gum in Fuels by Jet Evaporation," which methods are incorporated by reference. Copies may be obtained from the American Society for Testing Materials, 100 Barr Harbor Dr., West Conshohocken, Philadelphia, PA 19428-2959, or may be examined at the National Archives and Records Administration (NARA). For information on the availability of this material at NARA, call 202–741–6030, or go to: *http://www.archives.gov/federal_register/ code_of_federal_regulations/ ibr_locations.html.*

(c) Petroleum naphtha containing antioxidants shall meet the specified ultraviolet absorbance limits after correction for any absorbance due to the antioxidants. Petroleum naphtha may contain antioxidants authorized for use in food in an amount not to exceed that reasonably required to accomplish the intended effect or to exceed any prescribed limitations.

(d) Petroleum naphtha is used or intended for use as a solvent in protective coatings on fresh citrus fruit in compliance with § 172.210.

[42 FR 14491, Mar. 15, 1977, as amended at 47 FR 11835, Mar. 19, 1982; 49 FR 10104, Mar. 19, 1984; 54 FR 24896, June 12, 1989]

§ 172.255 Polyacrylamide.

Polyacrylamide containing not more than 0.2 percent of acrylamide monomer may be safely used as a film former in the imprinting of soft-shell gelatin capsules when the amount used is not in excess of the minimum required to produce the intended effect.

§ 172.260 Oxidized polyethylene.

Oxidized polyethylene may be safely used as a component of food, subject to the following restrictions:

(a) Oxidized polyethylene is the basic resin produced by the mild air oxidation of polyethylene. The polyethylene used in the oxidation process conforms to the density, maximum *n*-hexane extractable fraction, and maximum xylene soluble fraction specifications prescribed in item 2.3 of the table in § 177.1520(c) of this chapter. The oxidized polyethylene has a minimum number average molecular weight of 1,200, as determined by high temperature vapor pressure osmometry; contains a maximum of 5 percent by weight of total oxygen; and has an acid value of 9 to 19.

(b) The additive is used or intended for use as a protective coating or component of protective coatings for fresh avocados, bananas, beets, coconuts, eggplant, garlic, grapefruit, lemons, limes, mango, muskmelons, onions, oranges, papaya, peas (in pods), pineapple, plantain, pumpkin, rutabaga, squash (acorn), sweetpotatoes, tangerines, turnips, watermelon, Brazil nuts, chestnuts, filberts, hazelnuts, pecans, and walnuts (all nuts in shells).

(c) The additive is used in accordance with good manufacturing practice and in an amount not to exceed that required to produce the intended effect.

§ 172.270 Sulfated butyl oleate.

Sulfate butyl oleate may be safely used in food, subject to the following prescribed conditions:

(a) The additive is prepared by sulfation, using concentrated sulfuric acid, of a mixture of butyl esters produced by transesterification of an edible vegetable oil using 1-butanol. Following sulfation, the reaction mixture is washed with water and neutralized with aqueous sodium or potassium hydroxide. Prior to sulfation, the butyl oleate reaction mixture meets the following specifications:

(1) Not less than 90 percent butyl oleate.

(2) Not more than 1.5 percent unsaponifiable matter.

(b) The additive is used or intended for use at a level not to exceed 2 percent by weight in an aqueous emulsion in dehydrating grapes to produce raisins, whereby the residue of the additive on the raisins does not exceed 100 parts per million.

[57 FR 12711, Apr. 13, 1992]

§ 172.275 Synthetic paraffin and succinic derivatives.

Synthetic paraffin and succinic derivatives identified in this section may be safely used as a component of food, subject to the following restrictions:

(a) The additive is prepared with 50 percent Fischer-Tropsch process synthetic paraffin, meeting the definition and specifications of § 172.615, and 50 percent of such synthetic paraffin to which is bonded succinic anhydride and succinic acid derivatives of isopropyl alcohol, polyethylene glycol, and polypropylene glycol. It consists of a mixture of the Fischer-Tropsch process paraffin (alkane), alkyl succinic anhydride, alkyl succinic anhydride isopropyl half ester, dialkyl succinic anhydride polyethylene glycol half ester, and dialkyl succinic anhydride polypropylene glycol half ester, where the alkane (alkyl) has a chain length of 30–70 carbon atoms and the polyethylene and polypropylene glycols have molecular weights of 600 and 260, respectively.

(b) The additive meets the following specifications: Molecular weight, 880–930; melting point, 215°–217 °F; acid number, 43–47; and saponification number, 75–78.

(c) It is used or intended for use as a protective coating or component of protective coatings for fresh grapefruit, lemons, limes, muskmelons, oranges, sweetpotatoes, and tangerines.

(d) It is used in an amount not to exceed that required to produce the intended effect.

§ 172.280 Terpene resin.

The food additive terpene resin may be safely used in accordance with the following prescribed conditions:

(a) The food additive is the beta-pinene polymer obtained by polymerizing terpene hydrocarbons derived from wood. It has a softening point of 112 °C–118 °C, as determined by ASTM method E28–67 (Reapproved 1982), "Standard Test Method for Softening Point By Ring-and-Ball Apparatus," which is incorporated by reference. Copies may be obtained from the American Society for Testing Materials, 100 Barr Harbor Dr., West Conshohocken, Philadelphia, PA 19428-2959, or may be examined at the National Archives and Records Administration (NARA). For information on the availability of this material at NARA, call 202–741–6030, or go to: *http://www.archives.gov/federal_register/code_of_federal_regulations/ibr_locations.html.*

(b) It is used or intended for use as follows:

(1) As a moisture barrier on soft gelatin capsules in an amount not to exceed 0.07 percent of the weight of the capsule.

(2) As a moisture barrier on powders of ascorbic acid or its salts in an amount not to exceed 7 percent of the weight of the powder.

[42 FR 14491, Mar. 15, 1977, as amended at 49 FR 10104, Mar. 19, 1984]

Subpart D—Special Dietary and Nutritional Additives

§ 172.310 Aluminum nicotinate.

Aluminum nicotinate may be safely used as a source of niacin in foods for special dietary use. A statement of the concentration of the additive, expressed as niacin, shall appear on the label of the food additive container or on that of any intermediate premix prepared therefrom.

§ 172.315 Nicotinamide-ascorbic acid complex.

Nicotinamide-ascorbic acid complex may be safely used in accordance with the following prescribed conditions:

(a) The additive is the product of the controlled reaction between ascorbic acid and nicotinamide, melting in the range 141 °C to 145 °C.

(b) It is used as a source of ascorbic acid and nicotinamide in multivitamin preparations.

§ 172.320 Amino acids.

The food additive amino acids may be safely used as nutrients added to foods in accordance with the following conditions:

(a) The food additive consists of one or more of the following individual amino acids in the free, hydrated or anhydrous form or as the hydrochloride, sodium or potassium salts:

L-Alanine
L-Arginine
L-Asparagine
L-Aspartic acid
L-Cysteine
L-Cystine
L-Glutamic acid

L-Glutamine
Aminoacetic acid (glycine)
L-Histidine
L-Isoleucine
L-Leucine
L-Lysine
DL-Methionine (not for infant foods)
L-Methionine
L-Phenylalanine
L-Proline
L-Serine
L-Threonine
L-Tryptophan
L-Tyrosine
L-Valine

(b) The food additive meets the following specifications:

(1) As found in "Food Chemicals Codex," National Academy of Sciences/National Research Council (NAS/NRC), 3d Ed. (1981), which is incorporated by reference (Copies may be obtained from the National Academy Press, 2101 Constitution Ave. NW., Washington, DC 20418, or may be examined at the National Archives and Records Administration (NARA). For information on the availability of this material at NARA, call 202–741–6030, or go to: *http://www.archives.gov/federal_register/code_of_federal_regulations/ibr_locations.html*.) for the following:

L-Alanine
L-Arginine
L-Arginine Monohydrochloride
L-Cysteine Monohydrochloride
L-Cystine
Aminoacetic acid (glycine)
L-Leucine
DL-Methionine
L-Methionine
L-Tryptophan
L-Phenylalanine
L-Proline
L-Serine
L-Threonine
Glutamic Acid Hydrochloride
L-Isoleucine
L-Lysine Monohydrochloride
Monopotassium *L*-glutamate
L-Tyrosine
L-Valine

(2) As found in "Specifications and Criteria for Biochemical Compounds," NAS/NRC Publication, 3rd Ed. (1972), which is incorporated by reference (Copies are available from the Center for Food Safety and Applied Nutrition (HFS–200), Food and Drug Administration, 5100 Paint Branch Pkwy., College Park, MD 20740, or available for inspection at the National Archives and Records Administration (NARA). For information on the availability of this material at NARA, call 202–741–6030, or go to: *http://www.archives.gov/federal_register/code_of_federal_regulations/ibr_locations.html*.) for the following:

L-Asparagine
L-Aspartic acid
L-Glutamine
L-Histidine

(c) The additive(s) is used or intended for use to significantly improve the biological quality of the total protein in a food containing naturally occurring primarily-intact protein that is considered a significant dietary protein source, provided that:

(1) A reasonable daily adult intake of the finished food furnishes at least 6.5 grams of naturally occurring primarily intact protein (based upon 10 percent of the daily allowance for the "reference" adult male recommended by the National Academy of Sciences in "Recommended Dietary Allowances," NAS Publication No. 1694, 7th Ed. (1968), which is incorporated by reference. Copies are available from the Center for Food Safety and Applied Nutrition (HFS–200), Food and Drug Administration, 5100 Paint Branch Pkwy., College Park, MD 20740, or available for inspection at the National Archives and Records Administration (NARA). For information on the availability of this material at NARA, call 202–741–6030, or go to: *http://www.archives.gov/federal_register/code_of_federal_regulations/ibr_locations.html*.

(2) The additive(s) results in a protein efficiency ratio (PER) of protein in the finished ready-to-eat food equivalent to casein as determined by the method specified in paragraph (d) of this section.

(3) Each amino acid (or combination of the minimum number necessary to achieve a statistically significant increase) added results in a statistically significant increase in the PER as determined by the method described in paragraph (d) of this section. The minimum amount of the amino acid(s) to achieve the desired effect must be used and the increase in PER over the primarily-intact naturally occurring protein in the food must be substantiated

as a statistically significant difference with at least a probability (P) value of less than 0.05.

(4) The amount of the additive added for nutritive purposes plus the amount naturally present in free and combined (as protein) form does not exceed the following levels of amino acids expressed as percent by weight of the total protein of the finished food:

	Percent by weight of total protein (expressed as free amino acid)
L-Alanine	6.1
L-Arginine	6.6
L-Aspartic acid (including L-asparagine)	7.0
L-Cystine (including L-cysteine)	2.3
L-Glutamic acid (including L-glutamine)	12.4
Aminoacetic acid (glycine)	3.5
L-Histidine	2.4
L-Isoleucine	6.6
L-Leucine	8.8
L-Lysine	6.4
L- and DL-Methionine	3.1
L-Phenylalanine	5.8
L-Proline	4.2
L-Serine	8.4
L-Threonine	5.0
L-Tryptophan	1.6
L-Tyrosine	4.3
L-Valine	7.4

(d) Compliance with the limitations concerning PER under paragraph (c) of this section shall be determined by the method described in sections 43.212–43.216, "Official Methods of Analysis of the Association of Official Analytical Chemists," 13th Ed. (1980), which is incorporated by reference. Copies may be obtained from the AOAC INTERNATIONAL, 481 North Frederick Ave., suite 500, Gaithersburg, MD 20877, or may be examined at the National Archives and Records Administration (NARA). For information on the availability of this material at NARA, call 202–741–6030, or go to: *http://www.archives.gov/federal_register/code_of_federal_regulations/ibr_locations.html.* Each manufacturer or person employing the additive(s) under the provisions of this section shall keep and maintain throughout the period of his use of the additive(s) and for a minimum of 3 years thereafter, records of the tests required by this paragraph and other records required to assure effectiveness and compliance with this regulation and shall make such records available upon request at all reasonable hours by any officer or employee of the Food and Drug Administration, or any other officer or employee acting on behalf of the Secretary of Health and Human Services and shall permit such officer or employee to conduct such inventories of raw and finished materials on hand as he deems necessary and otherwise to check the correctness of such records.

(e) To assure safe use of the additive, the label and labeling of the additive and any premix thereof shall bear, in addition to the other information required by the Act, the following:

(1) The name of the amino acid(s) contained therein including the specific optical and chemical form.

(2) The amounts of each amino acid contained in any mixture.

(3) Adequate directions for use to provide a finished food meeting the limitations prescribed by paragraph (c) of this section.

(f) The food additive amino acids added as nutrients to special dietary foods that are intended for use solely under medical supervision to meet nutritional requirements in specific medical conditions and comply with the requirements of part 105 of this chapter are exempt from the limitations in paragraphs (c) and (d) of this section and may be used in such foods at levels not to exceed good manufacturing practices.

[42 FR 14491, Mar. 15, 1977; 42 FR 56728, Oct. 28, 1977, as amended at 47 FR 11836, Mar. 19, 1982; 49 FR 10104, Mar. 19, 1984; 54 FR 24897, June 12, 1989; 59 FR 14550, Mar. 29, 1994; 61 FR 14480, Apr. 2, 1996]

§ 172.325 Bakers yeast protein.

Bakers yeast protein may be safely used in food in accordance with the following conditions:

(a) Bakers yeast protein is the insoluble proteinaceous material remaining after the mechanical rupture of yeast cells of *Saccharomyces cerevisiae* and removal of whole cell walls by centrifugation and separation of soluble cellular materials.

(b) The additive meets the following specifications on a dry weight basis:

(1) Zinc salts less than 500 parts per million (ppm) as zinc.

(2) Nucleic acid less than 2 percent.

(3) Less than 0.3 ppm arsenic, 0.1 ppm cadmium, 0.4 ppm lead, 0.05 ppm mercury, and 0.3 ppm selenium.

(c) The viable microbial content of the finished ingredient is:

(1) Less than 10,000 organisms/gram by aerobic plate count.

(2) Less than 10 yeasts and molds/gram.

(3) Negative for *Salmonella*, *E. coli*, coagulase positive *Staphylococci*, *Clostridium perfringens*, *Clostridium botulinum*, or any other recognized microbial pathogen or any harmful microbial toxin.

(d) The ingredient is used in food as a nutrient supplement as defined in § 170.3(o)(20) of this chapter.

§ 172.330 Calcium pantothenate, calcium chloride double salt.

The food additive calcium chloride double salt of calcium pantothenate may be safely used in foods for special dietary uses in accordance with good manufacturing practice and under the following prescribed conditions:

(a) The food additive is of the *d* (dextrorotatory) or the *dl* (racemic) form.

(b) To assure safe use of the additive, the label and labeling of the food additive container, or that of any intermediate premixes prepared therefrom, shall bear, in addition to the other information required by the Act, the following:

(1) The name of the additive "calcium chloride double salt of *d*-calcium pantothenate" or "calcium chloride double salt of *dl*-calcium pantothenate", whichever is appropriate.

(2) A statement of the appropriate concentration of the additive, expressed as pantothenic acid.

§ 172.335 D-Pantothenamide.

The food additive D-pantothenamide as a source of pantothenic acid activity, may be safely used in foods for special dietary use in an amount not in excess of that reasonably required to produce its intended effect.

§ 172.340 Fish protein isolate.

(a) The food additive fish protein isolate may be safely used as a food supplement in accordance with the following prescribed conditions:

(1) The additive shall consist principally of dried fish protein prepared from the edible portions of fish after removal of the heads, fins, tails, bones, scales, viscera, and intestinal contents.

(2) The additive shall be derived only from species of bony fish that are generally recognized by qualified scientists as safe for human consumption and that can be processed as prescribed to meet the required specifications.

(3) Only wholesome fresh fish otherwise suitable for human consumption may be used. The fish shall be handled expeditiously under sanitary conditions. These conditions shall be in accordance with recognized good manufacturing practice for fish to be used as human food.

(4) The additive shall be prepared by extraction with hexane and food-grade ethanol to remove fat and moisture. Solvent residues shall be reduced by drying.

(b) The food additive meets the following specifications: (Where methods of determination are specified, they are Association of Official Analytical Chemists Methods, 13th ed., 1980, which are incorporated by reference).[1]

(1) Protein content, as N × 6.25, shall not be less than 90 percent by weight of the final product, as determined by the method described in section 2.057, Improved Kjeldahl Method for Nitrate-Free Samples (20)—Official Final Action.

(2) Moisture content shall not be more than 10 percent by weight of the final product, as determined by the method described in section 24.003, Air Drying (1)—Official First Action.

(3) Fat content shall not be more than 0.5 percent by weight of the final product, as determined by the method described in section 24.005, Crude Fat or Ether Extract—Official Final Action.

(4) Solvent residues in the final product shall not be more than 5 parts per

[1] Copies are available from: AOAC INTERNATIONAL, 481 North Frederick Ave., suite 500, Gaithersburg, MD 20877, or examined at the National Archives and Records Administration (NARA). For information on the availability of this material at NARA, call 202–741–6030, or go to: *http://www.archives.gov/federal_register/code_of_federal_regulations/ibr_locations.html.*

million of hexane and 3.5 percent ethanol by weight.

[46 FR 38072, July 24, 1981, as amended at 47 FR 53344, Nov. 26, 1982; 54 FR 24897, June 12, 1989]

§ 172.345 Folic acid (folacin).

Folic acid (CAS Reg. No. 59–30–3), also known as folacin or folate, may be safely used in food as a nutrient in accordance with the following prescribed conditions:

(a) Folic acid is the chemical *N*-[4-[[(2-amino-1,4-dihydro-4-oxo-6-pteridinyl)methyl]amino]benzoyl]-*L*-glutamic acid.

(b) Folic acid meets the specifications of the "Food Chemicals Codex," 4th ed. (1996), pp. 157–158, which is incorporated by reference in accordance with 5 U.S.C. 552(a) and 1 CFR part 51. Copies are available from the National Academy Press, Box 285, 2101 Constitution Ave. NW., Washington, DC 20055 (Internet address *http://www.nap.edu*), or may be examined at the Center for Food Safety and Applied Nutrition's Library, Food and Drug Administration, 5100 Paint Branch Pkwy., College Park, MD 20740, or at the National Archives and Records Administration (NARA). For information on the availability of this material at NARA, call 202–741–6030, or go to: *http://www.archives.gov/federal_register/code_of_federal_regulations/ibr_locations.html.*

(c) Folic acid may be added to foods subject to a standard of identity established under section 401 of the Federal Food, Drug, and Cosmetic Act (the act) when the standard of identity specifically provides for the addition of folic acid.

(d) Folic acid may be added, at levels not to exceed 400 micrograms (μg) per serving, to breakfast cereals, as defined under §170.3(n)(4) of this chapter, and to corn grits at a level such that each pound of corn grits contains not more than 1.0 milligram of folic acid.

(e) Folic acid may be added to infant formula in accordance with section 412(i)(1) of the act or with regulations issued under section 412(i)(2) of the act which are codified in §107.100 of this chapter.

(f) Folic acid may be added to a medical food, as defined in section 5(b)(3) of the Orphan Drug Act (21 U.S.C. 360ee(b)(3)), at levels not to exceed the amount necessary to meet the distinctive nutritional requirements of the disease or condition for which the food is formulated.

(g) Folic acid may be added to food for special dietary use at levels not to exceed the amount necessary to meet the special dietary needs for which the food is formulated.

(h) Folic acid may be added to foods represented as meal-replacement products, in amounts not to exceed:

(1) Four hundred μg per serving if the food is a meal-replacement that is represented for use once per day; or

(2) Two hundred μg per serving if the food is a meal-replacement that is represented for use more than once per day.

[61 FR 8807, Mar. 5, 1996, as amended at 61 FR 27779, June 3, 1996; 64 FR 1758, Jan. 12, 1999]

§ 172.350 Fumaric acid and salts of fumaric acid.

Fumaric acid and its calcium, ferrous, magnesium, potassium, and sodium salts may be safely used in food in accordance with the following prescribed conditions:

(a) The additives meet the following specifications:

(1) Fumaric acid contains a minimum of 99.5 percent by weight of fumaric acid, calculated on the anhydrous basis.

(2) The calcium, magnesium, potassium, and sodium salts contain a minimum of 99 percent by weight of the respective salt, calculated on the anhydrous basis. Ferrous fumarate contains a minimum of 31.3 percent total iron and not more than 2 percent ferric iron.

(b) With the exception of ferrous fumarate, fumaric acid and the named salts are used singly or in combination in food at a level not in excess of the amount reasonably required to accomplish the intended effect.

(c) Ferrous fumarate is used as a source of iron in foods for special dietary use, when the use is consistent with good nutrition practice.

§ 172.365 Kelp.

Kelp may be safely added to a food as a source of the essential mineral iodine, provided the maximum intake of the food as may be consumed during a period of one day, or as directed for use in the case of a dietary supplement, will not result in daily ingestion of the additive so as to provide a total amount of iodine in excess of 225 micrograms for foods labeled without reference to age or physiological state; and when age or the conditions of pregnancy or lactation are specified, in excess of 45 micrograms for infants, 105 micrograms for children under 4 years of age, 225 micrograms for adults and children 4 or more years of age, and 300 micrograms for pregnant or lactating women. The food additive kelp is the dehydrated, ground product prepared from *Macrocystis pyrifera*, *Laminaria digitata*, *Laminaria saccharina*, and *Laminaria cloustoni*.

§ 172.370 Iron-choline citrate complex.

Iron-choline citrate complex made by reacting approximately equimolecular quantities of ferric hydroxide, choline, and citric acid may be safely used as a source of iron in foods for special dietary use.

§ 172.372 N-Acetyl-L-methionine.

The food additive *N*-acetyl-L-methionine may be safely added to food (except infant foods and foods containing added nitrites/nitrates) as a source of L-methionine for use as a nutrient in accordance with the following conditions:

(a) *N*-Acetyl-L-methionine (Chemical Abstracts Service Registry No. 65–82–7) is the derivative of the amino acid methionine formed by addition of an acetyl group to the *alpha*-amino group of methionine. It may be in the free, hydrated or anhydrous form, or as the sodium or potassium salts.

(b) The additive meets the following specifications:

(1) Purity assay, on a dry basis: Minimum 99 percent.

(2) Residue on ignition: Maximum 0.1 percent.

(3) Specific optical rotation $[alpha]^{20}_{D}$: Between −19° and −23°.

(4) The additive may contain residues of not more than 500 ppm ethyl acetate; 50 ppm ethyl alcohol; 10 ppm methyl alcohol; and 10 ppm acetone, when used as processing solvents.

(c) The additive is used or intended for use as a source of L-methionine to improve significantly the biological quality of the total protein in a food containing naturally occurring primarily intact vegetable protein that is considered a significant dietary protein source, provided that:

(1) A reasonable daily adult intake of the finished food furnishes at least 6.5 grams of naturally occurring primarily intact vegetable protein.

(2) The additive results in a protein efficiency ratio (PER) of protein in the finished ready-to-eat food equivalent to casein as determined by the method specified in paragraph (d) of this section.

(3) The use of the additive results in a statistically significant increase in the PER as determined by the method described in paragraph (d) of this section. The minimum amount of the additive to achieve the desired effect must be used, and the increase in PER over the primarily intact naturally occurring vegetable protein in the food must be substantiated as a statistically significant difference with at least a probability (P) value of less than 0.05.

(4) The amount of the additive added for nutritive purpose shall not exceed the level that will provide a total of 3.1 percent L- and DL-methionine (expressed as the free amino acid) by weight of the total protein of the finished food, including the amount naturally present in free and combined (as protein) form.

(5) The additive shall not be added to infant foods or to foods containing added nitrites/nitrates.

(d) Compliance with the limitations concerning PER under paragraph (c) of the section shall be determined by the method described in sections 43.212–43.216, "Official Methods of Analysis of the Association of Official Analytical Chemists," 13th Ed. (1980), which is incorporated by reference. Copies may be obtained from the AOAC INTERNATIONAL, 481 North Frederick Ave., suite 500, Gaithersburg, MD 20877, or may be examined at the National Archives and Records Administration

(NARA). For information on the availability of this material at NARA, call 202–741–6030, or go to: *http://www.archives.gov/federal_register/code_of_federal_regulations/ibr_locations.html*. Each manufacturer or person employing the additive under the provisions of this section shall keep and maintain throughout the period of use of the additive and for a minimum of 3 years thereafter, records of the tests required by this paragraph and other records required to assure effectiveness and compliance with this regulation. Those records shall be made available upon request at all reasonable hours by any officer or employee acting on behalf of the Secretary of Health and Human Services. Those officers or employees shall be permitted to conduct inventories of raw and finished materials on hand as are deemed necessary to verify the records.

(e) To assure safe use of the additive, the label and labeling of the additive and any premix thereof shall bear, in addition to the other information required by the Act, the following:

(1) The name of the additive contained therein.

(2) The amounts of additive and each amino acid contained in any mixture.

(3) Adequate directions for use to provide a finished food meeting the limitations prescribed by paragraph (c) of this section.

(f) When the food additive is added as a nutrient to special dietary foods that are intended for use solely under medical supervision to meet nutritional requirements in specific medical conditions and these foods comply with the requirements of part 105 of this chapter, the food additive is exempt from the limitations in paragraphs (c)(1) through (4) and (d) of this section and may be used in those foods at levels not to exceed good manufacturing practices.

[43 FR 27784, June 27, 1978, as amended at 46 FR 59968, Dec. 8, 1981; 49 FR 10104, Mar. 19, 1984; 54 FR 24897, June 12, 1989]

§ 172.375 Potassium iodide.

The food additive potassium iodide may be safely used in accordance with the following prescribed conditions:

(a) Potassium iodide may be safely added to a food as a source of the essential mineral iodine, provided the maximum intake of the food as may be consumed during a period of one day, or as directed for use in the case of a dietary supplement, will not result in daily ingestion of the additive so as to provide a total amount of iodine in excess of 225 micrograms for foods labeled without reference to age or physiological state; and when age or the conditions of pregnancy or lactation are specified, in excess of 45 micrograms for infants, 105 micrograms for children under 4 years of age, 225 micrograms for adults and children 4 or more years of age, and 300 micrograms for pregnant or lactating women.

(b) To assure safe use of the additive, in addition to the other information required by the Act, the label of the additive shall bear:

(1) The name of the additive.

(2) A statement of the concentration of the additive in any mixture.

§ 172.379 Vitamin D_2.

Vitamin D_2 may be used safely in foods as a nutrient supplement defined under § 170.3(o)(20) of this chapter in accordance with the following prescribed conditions:

(a) Vitamin D_2, also known as ergocalciferol, is the chemical 9,10-seco(5Z,7E,22E)-5,7,10(19),22-ergostatetraen-3-ol. Vitamin D_2 is produced by ultraviolet irradiation of ergosterol isolated from yeast and is purified by crystallization.

(b) Vitamin D_2 meets the specifications of the *Food Chemicals Codex*, 6th ed. (2008), pp. 1013 and 1014, which is incorporated by reference. The Director of the Federal Register approves this incorporation by reference in accordance with 5 U.S.C 552(a) and 1 CFR part 51. You may obtain a copy from the United States Pharmacopeial Convention, 12601 Twinbrook Pkwy., Rockville, MD 20852 (Internet address: *http://www.usp.org*). You may inspect a copy at the Center for Food Safety and Applied Nutrition's Library, Food and Drug Administration, 5100 Paint Branch Pkwy., College Park, MD 20740, 301–436–1071, or at the National Archives and Records Administration

(NARA). For information on the availability of this material at NARA, call 202–741–6030, or go to: *http://www.archives.gov/federal_register/code_of_federal_regulations/ibr_locations.html.*

(c) The additive may be used as follows:

Category of Food	Maximum Levels in Food (as Served)
Soy beverages	50 International Units (IU)/100 grams (g)
Soy beverage products	89 IU/100 g
Soy-based butter substitute spreads	330 IU/100 g
Soy-based cheese substitutes and soy-based cheese substitute products	270 IU/100 g

[74 FR 11022, Mar. 16, 2009]

§ 172.380 Vitamin D_3;.

Vitamin D_3 may be used safely in foods as a nutrient supplement defined under § 170.3(o)(20) of this chapter in accordance with the following prescribed conditions:

(a) Vitamin D_3, also known as cholecalciferol, is the chemical 9,10-seco(5Z,7E)-5,7,10(19)-cholestatrien-3-ol. Vitamin D_3 occurs in and is isolated from fish liver oils. It also is manufactured by ultraviolet irradiation of 7-dehydrocholesterol produced from cholesterol and is purified by crystallization.

(b) Vitamin D_3 meets the specifications of the *Food Chemicals Codex*, 5th ed. (2004), pp. 498–499, which is incorporated by reference. The Director of the Office of the Federal Register approves this incorporation by reference in accordance with 5 U.S.C. 552(a) and 1 CFR part 51. You may obtain copies from the National Academy Press, 500 Fifth St. NW., Washington, DC 20001 (Internet address *http://www.nap.edu*). Copies may be examined at the Center for Food Safety and Applied Nutrition's Library, Food and Drug Administration, 5100 Paint Branch Pkwy., College Park, MD 20740, or at the National Archives and Records Administration (NARA). For information on the availability of this material at NARA, call 202–741–6030, or go to: *http://www.archives.gov/federal_register/code_of_federal_regulations/ibr_locations.html.*

(c) The additive may be used as follows:

(1) At levels not to exceed 100 International Units (IU) per 240 milliliters (mL) in 100 percent fruit juices (as defined under § 170.3(n)(35) of this chapter) that are fortified with greater than or equal to 33 percent of the reference daily intake (RDI) of calcium per 240 mL, excluding fruit juices that are specially formulated or processed for infants.

(2) At levels not to exceed 100 IU per 240 mL in fruit juice drinks (as defined under § 170.3(n)(35) of this chapter) that are fortified with greater than or equal to 10 percent of the RDI of calcium per 240 mL, excluding fruit juice drinks that are specially formulated or processed for infants.

(3) At levels not to exceed 140 IU per 240 mL (prepared beverage) in soy-protein based meal replacement beverages (powder or liquid) that are represented for special dietary use in reducing or maintaining body weight in accordance with § 105.66 of this chapter.

(4) At levels not to exceed 100 IU per 40 grams in meal replacement bars or other-type bars that are represented for special dietary use in reducing or maintaining body weight in accordance with § 105.66 of this chapter.

(5) At levels not to exceed 81 IU per 30 grams in cheese and cheese products as defined under § 170.3(n)(5) of this chapter, excluding cottage cheese, ricotta cheese, and hard grating cheeses such as Parmesan and Romano as defined in §§ 133.165 and 133.183 of this chapter, and those defined by standard of identity in § 133.148 of this chapter.

[68 FR 9003, Feb. 27, 2003, as amended at 70 FR 36025, June 22, 2005; 70 FR 37257, June 29, 2005; 70 FR 69438, Nov. 16, 2005]

§ 172.381 Vitamin D_2 bakers yeast.

Vitamin D_2 bakers yeast may be used safely in foods as a source of vitamin

D_2 and as a leavening agent in accordance with the following prescribed conditions:

(a) Vitamin D_2 bakers yeast is the substance produced by exposing bakers yeast (*Saccharomyces cerevisiae*) to ultraviolet light, resulting in the photochemical conversion of endogenous ergosterol in bakers yeast to vitamin D_2 (also known as ergocalciferol or (9,10-seco(5Z,7E,22E)-5,7,10(19),22-ergostatetraen-3-ol)).

(b) Vitamin D_2 bakers yeast may be used alone as an active dry yeast concentrate or in combination with conventional bakers yeast.

(c) The additive may be used in yeast-leavened baked goods and baking mixes and yeast-leavened baked snack foods at levels not to exceed 400 International Units of vitamin D_2 per 100 grams in the finished food.

(d) To assure safe use of the additive, the label or labeling of the food additive container shall bear, in addition to the other information required by the Federal Food, Drug, and Cosmetic Act, adequate directions for use to provide a final product that complies with the limitations prescribed in paragraph (c) of this section.

(e) Labels of manufactured food products containing the additive shall bear, in the ingredient statement, the name of the additive, "vitamin D_2 bakers yeast," in the proper order of decreasing predominance in the finished food.

[77 FR 52231, Aug. 29, 2012]

§ 172.385 Whole fish protein concentrate.

The food additive whole fish protein concentrate may be safely used as a food supplement in accordance with the following prescribed conditions:

(a) The additive is derived from whole, wholesome hake and hakelike fish, herring of the genera *Clupea*, menhaden, and anchovy of the species *Engraulis mordax*, handled expeditiously and under sanitary conditions in accordance with good manufacturing practices recognized as proper for fish that are used in other forms for human food.

(b) The additive consists essentially of a dried fish protein processed from the whole fish without removal of heads, fins, tails, viscera, or intestinal contents. It is prepared by solvent extraction of fat and moisture with isopropyl alcohol or with ethylene dichloride followed by isopropyl alcohol, except that the additive derived from herring, menhaden and anchovy is prepared by solvent extraction with isopropyl alcohol alone. Solvent residues are reduced by conventional heat drying and/or microwave radiation and there is a partial removal of bone.

(c) The food additive meets the following specifications:

(1) Protein content (N × 6.25) shall not be less than 75 percent by weight of the final product, as determined by the method described in section 2.057 in "Official Methods of Analysis of the Association of Official Analytical Chemists" (AOAC), 13th Ed. (1980). Protein quality shall not be less than 100, as determined by the method described in sections 43.212–43.216 of the AOAC. The 13th Ed. is incorporated by reference, and copies may be obtained from the AOAC INTERNATIONAL, 481 North Frederick Ave., suite 500, Gaithersburg, MD 20877, or may be examined at the National Archives and Records Administration (NARA). For information on the availability of this material at NARA, call 202–741–6030, or go to: *http://www.archives.gov/federal_register/code_of_federal_regulations/ibr_locations.html.*

(2) Moisture content shall not exceed 10 percent by weight of the final product, as determined by the method described in section 24.003 of the AOAC. See paragraph (c)(1) of this section for availability of the material incorporated by reference.

(3) Fat content shall not exceed 0.5 percent by weight of the final product, as determined by the method described in section 24.005 of the AOAC. See paragraph (c)(1) of the this section for availability of the material incorporated by reference.

(4) The additive may contain residues of isopropyl alcohol and ethylene dichloride not in excess of 250 parts per million and 5 parts per million, respectively, when used as solvents in the extraction process.

(5) Microwave radiation meeting the requirements of § 179.30 of this chapter

may be used to reduce residues of the solvents used in the extraction process.

(6) The additive shall contain not in excess of 100 parts per million fluorides (expressed as F).

(7) The additive shall be free of *Escherichia coli* and pathogenic organisms, including *Salmonella*, and shall have a total bacterial plate count of not more than 10,000 per gram.

(8) The additive shall have no more than a faint characteristic fish odor and taste.

(d) When the additive is used or intended for use in the household as a protein supplement in food for regular consumption by children up to 8 years of age, the amount of the additive from this source shall not exceed 20 grams per day (about one heaping tablespoon).

(e) When the additive is used as a protein supplement in manufactured food, the total fluoride content (expressed as F) of the finished food shall not exceed 8 ppm based on the dry weight of the food product.

(f) To assure safe use of the additive, in addition to the other information required by the Act:

(1) The label of consumer-sized or bulk containers of the additive shall bear the name "whole fish protein concentrate".

(2) The label or labeling of containers of the additive shall bear adequate directions for use to comply with the limitations prescribed by paragraphs (d) and (e) of this section.

(3) Labels of manufactured foods containing the additive shall bear, in the ingredient statement, the name of the additive, "whole fish protein concentrate" in the proper order of decreasing predominance in the finished food.

[42 FR 14491, Mar. 15, 1977, as amended at 49 FR 10104, Mar. 19, 1984; 54 FR 24897, June 12, 1989]

§ 172.395 Xylitol.

Xylitol may be safely used in foods for special dietary uses, provided the amount used is not greater than that required to produce its intended effect.

§ 172.399 Zinc methionine sulfate.

Zinc methionine sulfate, CAS Reg. No. 56329–42–1, may be safely used in accordance with the following prescribed conditions:

(a) The additive is the product of the reaction between equimolar amounts of zinc sulfate and DL-methionine in purified water.

(b) The additive meets the following specifications:

Zinc content—19 to 22 percent.

$C_5H_{11}NO_2S$ "DL-methionine"—46 to 50 percent.

Cadmium—not more than 0.05 part per million.

(c) The additive is used in tablet form as a source of dietary zinc.

[46 FR 58297, Dec. 1, 1981]

Subpart E—Anticaking Agents

§ 172.410 Calcium silicate.

Calcium silicate, including synthetic calcium silicate, may be safely used in food in accordance with the following prescribed conditions:

(a) It is used as an anticaking agent in food in an amount not in excess of that reasonably required to produce its intended effect.

(b) It will not exceed 2 percent by weight of the food, except that it may be present up to 5 percent by weight of baking powder.

§ 172.430 Iron ammonium citrate.

Iron ammonium citrate may be safely used in food in accordance with the following prescribed conditions:

(a) The additive is the chemical green ferric ammonium citrate.

(b) The additive is used, or intended for use as an anticaking agent in salt for human consumption so that the level of iron ammonium citrate does not exceed 25 parts per million (0.0025 percent) in the finished salt.

(c) To assure safe use of the additive the label or labeling of the additive shall bear, in addition to the other information required by the Act:

(1) The name of the additive.

(2) Adequate directions to provide a final product that complies with the limitations prescribed in paragraph (b) of this section.

§ 172.480 Silicon dioxide.

The food additive silicon dioxide may be safely used in food in accordance with the following conditions:

(a) The food additive is manufactured by vapor phase hydrolysis or by other means whereby the particle size is such as to accomplish the intended effect.

(b) It is used as an anticaking agent, subject to the following conditions:

(1) It is used in only those foods in which the additive has been demonstrated to have an anticaking effect.

(2) It is used in an amount not in excess of that reasonably required to produce its intended effect.

(3) [Reserved]

(4) It is used in an amount not to exceed 2 percent by weight of the food.

(c) It is used or intended for use as a stabilizer in the production of beer, and is removed from the beer by filtration prior to final processing.

(d) It is used or intended for use as an adsorbent for *dl-a*-tocopheryl acetate and pantothenyl alcohol in tableted foods for special dietary use, in an amount not greater than that required to accomplish the intended physical or technical effect.

§ 172.490 Yellow prussiate of soda.

(a) The food additive yellow prussiate of soda (sodium ferrocyanide decahydrate; $Na_4Fe(CN)_6 \cdot 10H_2O$ contains a minimum of 99 percent by weight of sodium ferrocyanide decahydrate.

(b) The additive is used or intended for use as an anticaking agent in salt and as an adjuvant in the production of dendritic crystals of salt in an amount needed to produce its intended effect but not in excess of 13 parts per million calculated as anhydrous sodium ferrocyanide.

[42 FR 14491, Mar. 15, 1977, as amended at 58 FR 17098, Apr. 1, 1993]

Subpart F—Flavoring Agents and Related Substances

§ 172.510 Natural flavoring substances and natural substances used in conjunction with flavors.

Natural flavoring substances and natural adjuvants may be safely used in food in accordance with the following conditions.

(a) They are used in the minimum quantity required to produce their intended physical or technical effect and in accordance with all the principles of good manufacturing practice.

(b) In the appropriate forms (plant parts, fluid and solid extracts, concentrates, absolutes, oils, gums, balsams, resins, oleoresins, waxes, and distillates) they consist of one or more of the following, used alone or in combination with flavoring substances and adjuvants generally recognized as safe in food, previously sanctioned for such use, or regulated in any section of this part.

Common name	Scientific name	Limitations
Aloe	*Aloe perryi* Baker, *A. barbadensis* Mill., *A. ferox* Mill., and hybrids of this sp. with *A. africana* Mill. and *A. spicata* Baker.	
Althea root and flowers	*Althea officinalis* L.	
Amyris (West Indian sandalwood)	*Amyris balsamifera* L.	
Angola weed	*Roccella fuciformis* Ach	In alcoholic beverages only
Arnica flowers	*Arnica montana* L., *A. fulgens* Pursh, *A. sororia* Greene, or *A. cordifolia* Hooker.	Do.
Artemisia (wormwood)	*Artemisia* spp	Finished food thujone free [1]
Artichoke leaves	*Cynara scolymus* L	In alcoholic beverages only
Benzoin resin	*Styrax benzoin* Dryander, *S. paralleloneurus* Perkins, *S. tonkinensis* (Pierre) Craib ex Hartwich, or other spp. of the Section *Anthostyrax* of the genus *Styrax*.	
Blackberry bark	*Rubus,* Section *Eubatus.*	
Boldus (boldo) leaves	*Peumus boldus* Mol	Do.
Boronia flowers	*Boronia megastigma* Nees.	
Bryonia root	*Bryonia alba* L., or *B. diocia* Jacq	Do.
Buchu leaves	*Barosma betulina* Bartl. et Wendl., *B. crenulata* (L.) Hook. or *B. serratifolia* Willd.	
Buckbean leaves	*Menyanthes trifoliata* L	Do.
Cajeput	*Melaleuca leucadendron* L. and other *Melaleuca* spp.	

Common name	Scientific name	Limitations
Calumba root	*Jateorhiza palmata* (Lam.) Miers	Do.
Camphor tree	*Cinnamomum camphora* (L.) Nees et Eberm	Safrole free
Cascara sagrada	*Rhamnus purshiana* DC.	
Cassie flowers	*Acacia farnesiana* (L.) Willd.	
Castor oil	*Ricinus communis* L.	
Catechu, black	*Acacia catechu* Willd.	
Cedar, white (aborvitae), leaves and twigs	*Thuja occidentalis* L	Finished food thujone free [1]
Centuary	*Centaurium umbellatum* Gilib	In alcoholic beverages only
Cherry pits	*Prunus avium* L. or *P. cerasus* L	Not to exceed 25 p.p.m. prussic acid
Cherry-laurel leaves	*Prunus laurocerasus* L	Do.
Chestnut leaves	*Castanea dentata* (Marsh.) Borkh.	
Chirata	*Swertia chirata* Buch.-Ham	In alcoholic beverages only
Cinchona, red, bark	*Cinchona succirubra* Pav. or its hybrids	In beverages only; not more than 83 p.p.m. total cinchona alkaloids in finished beverage
Cinchona, yellow, bark	*Cinchona ledgeriana* Moens, *C. calisaya* Wedd., or hybrids of these with other spp. of *Cinchona*..	Do.
Copaiba	South American spp. of *Copaifera* L.	
Cork, oak	*Quercus suber* L., or *Q. occidentalis* F. Gay	In alcoholic beverages only
Costmary	*Chrysanthemum balsamita* L	Do.
Costus root	*Saussurea lappa* Clarke.	
Cubeb	*Piper cubeba* L. f.	
Currant, black, buds and leaves	*Ribes nigrum* L.	
Damiana leaves	*Turnera diffusa* Willd.	
Davana	*Artemisia pallens* Wall.	
Dill, Indian	*Anethum sowa* Roxb. (*Peucedanum graveolens* Benth et Hook., *Anethum graveolens* L.).	
Dittany (fraxinella) roots	*Dictamnus albus* L	Do.
Dittany of Crete	*Origanum dictamnus* L.	
Dragon's blood (dracorubin)	*Daemonorops* spp.	
Elder tree leaves	*Sambucus nigra* L	In alcoholic beverages only; not to exceed 25 p.p.m. prussic acid in the flavor
Elecampane rhizome and roots	*Inula helenium* L	In alcoholic beverages only
Elemi	*Canarium commune* L. or *C. luzonicum* Miq.	
Erigeron	*Erigeron canadensis* L.	
Eucalyptus globulus leaves	*Eucalyptus globulus* Labill.	
Fir ("pine") needles and twigs	*Abies sibirica* Ledeb., *A. alba* Mill., *A. sachalinesis* Masters or *A. mayriana* Miyabe et Kudo.	
Fir, balsam, needles and twigs	*Abies balsamea* (L.) Mill.	
Galanga, greater	*Alpinia galanga* Willd	Do.
Galbanum	*Ferula galbaniflua* Boiss. et Buhse and other *Ferula* spp.	
Gambir (catechu, pale)	*Uncaria gambir* Roxb.	
Genet flowers	*Spartium junceum* L.	
Gentian rhizome and roots	*Gentiana lutea* L.	
Gentian, stemless	*Gentiana acaulis* L	Do.
Germander, chamaedrys	*Teucrium chamaedrys* L	Do.
Germander, golden	*Teucrium polium* L	Do.
Guaiac	*Guaiacum officinale* L., *G. santum* L., *Bulnesia sarmienti* Lor.	
Guarana	*Paullinia cupana* HBK.	
Haw, black, bark	*Viburnum prunifolium* L.	
Hemlock needles and twigs	*Tsuga canadensis* (L.) Carr. or *T. heterophylla* (Raf.) Sarg.	
Hyacinth flowers	*Hyacinthus orientalis* L.	
Iceland moss	*Cetraria islandica* Ach	Do.
Imperatoria	*Peucedanum ostruthium* (L.). Koch (*Imperatoria ostruthium* L.).	
Iva	*Achillea moschata* Jacq	Do.
Labdanum	*Cistus* spp.	
Lemon-verbena	*Lippia citriodora* HBK	Do.
Linaloe wood	*Bursera delpechiana* Poiss. and other *Bursera* spp.	
Linden leaves	*Tillia* spp	Do.
Lovage	*Levisticum officinale* Koch.	
Lungmoss (lungwort)	*Sticta pulmonacea* Ach.	

Common name	Scientific name	Limitations
Maidenhair fern	*Adiantum capillus-veneris* L	Do.
Maple, mountain	*Acer spicatum* Lam.	
Mimosa (black wattle) flowers	*Acacia decurrens* Willd. var. *dealbata*.	
Mullein flowers	*Verbascum phlomoides* L. or *V. thapsiforme* Schrad	Do.
Myrrh	*Commiphora molmol* Engl., *C. abyssinica* (Berg) Engl., or other *Commiphora* spp.	
Myrtle leaves	*Myrtus communis* L	Do.
Oak, English, wood	*Quercus robur* L	Do.
Oak, white, chips	*Quercus alba* L.	
Oak moss	*Evernia prunastri* (L.) Ach., *E. furfuracea* (L.) Mann, and other lichens.	Finished food thujone free [1]
Olibanum	*Boswellia carteri* Birdw. and other *Boswellia* spp.	
Opopanax (bisabolmyrrh)	*Opopanax chironium* Koch (true opopanax) of *Commiphora erythraea* Engl. var. *Llabrescens*.	
Orris root	*Iris germanica* L. (including its variety *florentina* Dykes) and *I. pallida* Lam.	
Pansy	*Viola tricolor* L	In alcoholic beverages only
Passion flower	*Passiflora incarnata* L.	
Patchouly	*Pogostemon cablin* Benth. and *P. heyneanus* Benth.	
Peach leaves	*Prunus persica* (L.) Batsch	In alcoholic beverages only; not to exceed 25 p.p.m. prussic acid in the flavor
Pennyroyal, American	*Hedeoma pulegioides* (L.) Pers.	
Pennyroyal, European	*Mentha pulegium* L.	
Pine, dwarf, needles and twigs	*Pinus mugo* Turra var. *pumilio* (Haenke) Zenari.	
Pine, Scotch, needles and twigs	*Pinus sylvestris* L.	
Pine, white, bark	*Pinus strobus* L	In alcoholic beverages only
Pine, white oil	*Pinus palustris* Mill., and other *Pinus* spp.	
Poplar buds	*Populus balsamifera* L. (*P. tacamahacca* Mill.), *P. candicans* Ait., or *P. nigra* L.	Do.
Quassia	*Picrasma excelsa* (Sw.) Planch, or *Quassia amara* L.	
Quebracho bark	*Aspidosperma quebracho-blanco* Schlecht, or (*Quebrachia lorentzii* (Griseb)).	*Schinopsis lorentzii* (Griseb.) Engl.
Quillaia (soapbark)	*Quillaja saponaria* Mol.	
Red saunders (red sandalwood)	*Pterocarpus san alinus* L	In alcoholic beverages only
Rhatany root	*Krameria triandra* Ruiz et Pav. or *K. argentea* Mart.	
Rhubarb, garden root	*Rheum rhaponticum* L	Do.
Rhubarb root	*Rheum officinale* Baill., *R. palmatum* L., or other spp. (excepting *R. rhaponticum* L.) or hybrids of *Rheum* grown in China.	
Roselle	*Hibiscus sabdariffa* L	Do.
Rosin (colophony)	*Pinus palustris* Mill., and other *Pinus* spp	Do.
St. Johnswort leaves, flowers, and caulis	*Hypericum perforatum* L	Hypericin-free alcohol distillate form only; in alcoholic beverages only
Sandalwood, white (yellow, or East Indian)	*Santalum album* L.	
Sandarac	*Tetraclinis articulata* (Vahl.), Mast	In alcoholic beverages only
Sarsaparilla	*Smilax aristolochiaefolia* Mill., (Mexican sarsaparilla), *S. regelii* Killip et Morton (Honduras sarsaparilla), *S. febrifuga* Kunth (Ecuadorean sarsaparilla), or undetermined *Smilax* spp. (Ecuadorean or Central American sarsaparilla).	
Sassafras leaves	*Sassafras albidum* (Nutt.) Nees	Safrole free
Senna, Alexandria	*Cassia acutifolia* Delile.	
Serpentaria (Virginia snakeroot)	*Aristolochia serpentaria* L	In alcoholic beverages only
Simaruba bark	*Simaruba amara* Aubl	Do.
Snakeroot, Canadian (wild ginger)	*Asarum canadense* L.	
Spruce needles and twigs	*Picea glauca* (Moench) Voss or *P. mariana* (Mill.) BSP.	
Storax (styrax)	*Liquidambar orientalis* Mill. or *L. styraciflua* L.	
Tagetes (marigold)	*Tagetes patula* L., *T. erecta* L., or *T. minuta* L. (*T. glandulifera* Schrank).	As oil only
Tansy	*Tanacetum vulgare* L	In alcoholic beverages only; finished alcoholic beverage thujone free [1]
Thistle, blessed (holy thistle)	*Onicus benedictus* L	In alcoholic beverages only
Thymus capitatus (Spanish "origanum")	*Thymus capitatus* Hoffmg. et Link.	

Common name	Scientific name	Limitations
Tolu	*Myroxylon balsamum* (L.) Harms.	
Turpentine	*Pinus palustris* Mill. and other *Pinus* spp. which yield terpene oils exclusively.	
Valerian rhizome and roots	*Valeriana officinalis* L.	
Veronica	*Veronica officinalis* L	Do.
Vervain, European	*Verbena officinalis* L	Do.
Vetiver	*Vetiveria zizanioides* Stapf	Do.
Violet, Swiss	*Viola calcarata* L.	
Walnut husks (hulls), leaves, and green nuts	*Juglans nigra* L. or *J. regia* L.	
Woodruff, sweet	*Asperula odorata* L	In alcoholic beverages only
Yarrow	*Achillea millefolium* L	In beverages only; finished beverage thujone free [1]
Yerba santa	*Eriodictyon californicum* (Hook, et Arn.) Torr.	
Yucca, Joshua-tree	*Yucca brevifolia* Engelm.	
Yucca, Mohave	*Yucca schidigera* Roezl ex Ortgies (*Y. mohavensis* Sarg.).	

[1] As determined by using the method (or, in other than alcoholic beverages, a suitable adaptation thereof) in section 9.129 of the "Official Methods of Analysis of the Association of Official Analytical Chemists," 13th Ed. (1980), which is incorporated by reference. Copies may be obtained from the AOAC INTERNATIONAL, 481 North Frederick Ave., suite 500, Gaithersburg, MD 20877, or may be examined at the National Archives and Records Administration (NARA). For information on the availability of this material at NARA, call 202–741–6030, or go to: *http://www.archives.gov/federal_register/code_of_federal_regulations/ibr_locations.html.*

[42 FR 14491, Mar. 15, 1977, as amended at 43 FR 14644, Apr. 7, 1978; 49 FR 10104, Mar. 19, 1984; 54 FR 24897, June 12, 1989; 69 FR 24511, May 4, 2004; 72 FR 10357, Mar. 8, 2007]

§ 172.515 Synthetic flavoring substances and adjuvants.

Synthetic flavoring substances and adjuvants may be safely used in food in accordance with the following conditions.

(a) They are used in the minimum quantity required to produce their intended effect, and otherwise in accordance with all the principles of good manufacturing practice.

(b) They consist of one or more of the following, used alone or in combination with flavoring substances and adjuvants generally recognized as safe in food, prior-sanctioned for such use, or regulated by an appropriate section in this part.

Acetal; acetaldehyde diethyl acetal.
Acetaldehyde phenethyl propyl acetal.
Acetanisole; 4′-methoxyacetophenone.
Acetophenone; methyl phenyl ketone.
Allyl anthranilate.
Allyl butyrate.
Allyl cinnamate.
Allyl cyclohexaneacetate.
Allyl cyclohexanebutyrate.
Allyl cyclohexanehexanoate.
Allyl cyclohexaneproprionate.
Allyl cyclohexanevalerate.
Allyl disulfide.
Allyl 2-ethylbutyrate.
Allyl hexanoate; allyl caproate.
Allyl α-ionone; 1-(2,6,6-trimethyl-2-cyclo-hexene-1-yl)-1,6-heptadiene-3-one.
Allyl isothiocyanate; mustard oil.
Allyl isovalerate.
Allyl mercaptan; 2-propene-1-thiol.
Allyl nonanoate.
Allyl octanoate.
Allyl phenoxyacetate.
Allyl phenylacetate.
Allyl propionate.
Allyl sorbate; allyl 2,4-hexadienoate.
Allyl sulfide.
Allyl tiglate; allyl *trans*-2-methyl-2-butenoate.
Allyl 10-undecenoate.
Ammonium isovalerate.
Ammonium sulfide.
Amyl alcohol; pentyl alcohol.
Amyl butyrate.
α-Amylcinnamaldehyde.
α-Amylcinnamaldehyde dimethyl acetal.
α-Amylcinnamyl acetate.
α-Amylcinnamyl alcohol.
α-Amylcinnamyl formate.
α-Amylcinnamyl isovalerate.
Amyl formate.
Amyl heptanoate.
Amyl hexanoate.
Amyl octanoate.
Anisole; methoxybenzene.
Anisyl acetate.
Anisyl alcohol; *p*-methoxybenzyl alcohol.
Anisyl butyrate
Anisyl formate.
Anisyl phenylacetate.
Anisyl propionate.
Beechwood creosote.
Benzaldehyde dimethyl acetal.
Benzaldehyde glyceryl acetal; 2-phenyl-*m*-dioxan-5-ol.

Benzaldehyde propylene glycol acetal; 4-methyl-2-phenyl-*m*-dioxolane.
Benzenethiol; thiophenol.
Benzoin; 2-hydroxy-2-phenylacetophenone.
Benzophenone; diphenylketone.
Benzyl acetate.
Benzyl acetoacetate.
Benzyl alcohol.
Benzyl benzoate.
Benzyl butyl ether.
Benzyl butyrate.
Benzyl cinnamate.
Benzyl 2,3–dimethylcrotonate; benzyl methyl tiglate.
Benzyl disulfide; dibenzyl disulfide.
Benzyl ethyl ether.
Benzyl formate.
3-Benzyl-4-heptanone; benzyl dipropyl ketone.
Benzyl isobutyrate.
Benzyl isovalerate.
Benzyl mercaptan; α-toluenethiol.
Benzyl methoxyethyl acetal; acetaldehyde benzyl β-methoxyethyl acetal.
Benzyl phenylacetate.
Benzyl propionate.
Benzyl salicylate.
Birch tar oil.
Borneol; *d*-camphanol.
Bornyl acetate.
Bornyl formate.
Bornyl isovalerate.
Bornyl valerate.
β-Bourbonene; 1,2,3,3a,3bβ,4,5,6,6aβ,6bα-decahydro-lα-isopropyl-3a$_a$-methyl-6-methylene-cyclobuta [1,2:3,4] dicyclopentene.
2-Butanol.
2-Butanone; methyl ethyl ketone.
Butter acids.
Butter esters.
Butyl acetate.
Butyl acetoacetate.
Butyl alcohol; 1-butanol.
Butyl anthranilate.
Butyl butyrate.
Butyl butyryllactate; lactic acid, butyl ester, butyrate.
α-Butylcinnamaldehyde.
Butyl cinnamate.
Butyl 2-decenoate.
Butyl ethyl malonate.
Butyl formate.
Butyl heptanoate.
Butyl hexanoate.
Butyl *p*-hydroxybenzoate.
Butyl isobutyrate.
Butyl isovalerate.
Butyl lactate.
Butyl laurate.
Butyl levulinate.
Butyl phenylacetate.
Butyl propionate.
Butyl stearate.
Butyl sulfide.
Butyl 10-undecenoate.
Butyl valerate.
Butyraldehyde.
Cadinene.
Camphene; 2,2-dimethyl-3-methylene-norbornane.
d-Camphor.
Carvacrol; 2-*p*-cymenol.
Carvacryl ethyl ether; 2-ethoxy-*p*-cymene.
Carveol; *p*-mentha-6,8-dien-2-ol.
4-Carvomenthenol; 1-*p*-menthen-4-ol; 4-terpinenol.
cis Carvone oxide; 1,6-epoxy-*p*-menth-8-en-2-one.
Carvyl acetate.
Carvyl propionate.
β-Caryophyllene.
Caryophyllene alcohol.
Caryophyllene alcohol acetate.
β-Caryophyllene oxide; 4-12,12-trimethyl-9-methylene-5-oxatricylo [8.2.0.0^{4,6}] dodecane.
Cedarwood oil alcohols.
Cedarwood oil terpenes.
1,4-Cineole.
Cinnamaldehyde ethylene glycol acetal.
Cinnamic acid.
Cinnamyl acetate.
Cinnamyl alcohol; 3-phenyl-2-propen-1-ol.
Cinnamyl benzoate.
Cinnamyl butyrate.
Cinnamyl cinnamate.
Cinnamyl formate.
Cinnamyl isobutyrate.
Cinnamyl isovalerate.
Cinnamyl phenylacetate.
Cinnamyl propionate.
Citral diethyl acetal; 3,7-dimethyl-2,6-octadienal diethyl acetal.
Citral dimethyl acetal; 3,7-dimethyl-2,6-octadienal dimethyl acetal.
Citral propylene glycol acetal.
Citronellal; 3,7-dimethyl-6-octenal; rhodinal.
Citronellol; 3,7-dimethyl-6-octen-1-ol; *d*-citronellol.
Citronelloxyacetaldehyde.
Citronellyl acetate.
Citronellyl butyrate.
Citronellyl formate.
Citronellyl isobutyrate.
Citronellyl phenylacetate.
Citronellyl propionate.
Citronellyl valerate.
p-Cresol.
Cuminaldehyde; cuminal; *p*-isopropyl benzaldehyde.
Cyclohexaneacetic acid.
Cyclohexaneethyl acetate.
Cyclohexyl acetate.
Cyclohexyl anthranilate.
Cyclohexyl butyrate.
Cyclohexyl cinnamate.
Cyclohexyl formate.
Cyclohexyl isovalerate.
Cyclohexyl propionate.
p-Cymene.
γ-Decalactone; 4-hydroxy-decanoic acid, γ-lactone.
γ-Decalactone; 5-hydroxy-decanoic acid, δ-lactone.

Decanal dimethyl acetal.
1-Decanol; decylic alcohol.
2-Decenal.
3-Decen-2-one; heptylidene acetone.
Decyl actate.
Decyl butyrate.
Decyl propionate.
Dibenzyl ether.
4,4-Dibutyl-γ-butyrolactone; 4,4-dibutyl-4-hydroxy-butyric acid, γ-lactone.
Dibutyl sebacate.
Diethyl malate.
Diethyl malonate; ethyl malonate.
Diethyl sebacate.
Diethyl succinate.
Diethyl tartrate.
2,5-Diethyltetrahydrofuran.
Dihydrocarveol; 8-*p*-menthen-2-ol; 6-methyl-3-isopropenylcyclohexanol.
Dihydrocarvone.
Dihydrocarvyl acetate.
m-Dimethoxybenzene.
p-Dimethoxybenzene; dimethyl hydroquinone.
2,4-Dimethylacetophenone.
α,α-Dimethylbenzyl isobutyrate; phenyldimethylcarbinyl isobutyrate.
2,6-Dimethyl-5-heptenal.
2,6-Dimethyl octanal; isodecylaldehyde.
3,7-Dimethyl-1-octanol; tetrahydrogeraniol.
α,α-Dimethylphenethyl acetate; benzylpropyl acetate; benzyldimethylcarbinyl acetate.
α,α-Dimethylphenethyl alcohol; dimethylbenzyl carbinol.
α,α-Dimethylphenethyl butyrate; benzyldimethylcarbinyl butyrate.
α,α-Dimethylphenethyl formate; benzyldimethylcarbinyl formate.
Dimethyl succinate.
1,3-Diphenyl-2-propanone; dibenzyl ketone.
delta-Dodecalactone; 5-hydroxydodecanoic acid, deltalactone.
γ-Dodecalactone; 4-hydroxydodecanoic acid γ-lactone.
2-Dodecenal.
Estragole.
ρ-Ethoxybenzaldehyde.
Ethyl acetoacetate.
Ethyl 2-acetyl-3-phenylpropionate; ethylbenzyl acetoacetate.
Ethyl aconitate, mixed esters.
Ethyl acrylate.
Ethyl ρ-anisate.
Ethyl anthranilate.
Ethyl benzoate.
Ethyl benzoylacetate.
α-Ethylbenzyl butyrate; α-phenylpropyl butyrate.
Ethyl brassylate; tridecanedioic acid cyclic ethylene glycol diester; cyclo 1,13-ethylenedioxytridecan-1,13-dione.
2-Ethylbutyl acetate.
2-Ethylbutyraldehyde.
2-Ethylbutyric acid.
Ethyl cinnamate.
Ethyl crotonate; *trans*-2-butenoic acid ethylester.
Ethyl cyclohexanepropionate.
Ethyl decanoate.
2-Ethylfuran.
Ethyl 2-furanpropionate.
4-Ethylguaiacol; 4-ethyl-2-methoxyphenol.
Ethyl heptanoate.
2-Ethyl-2-heptenal; 2-ethyl-3-butylacrolein.
Ethyl hexanoate.
Ethyl isobutyrate.
Ethyl isovalerate.
Ethyl lactate.
Ethyl laurate.
Ethyl levulinate.
Ethyl maltol; 2-ethyl-3-hydroxy-4H-pyran-4-one.
Ethyl 2-methylbutyrate.
Ethyl myristate.
Ethyl nitrite.
Ethyl nonanoate.
Ethyl 2-nonynoate; ethyl octyne carbonate.
Ethyl octanoate.
Ethyl oleate.
Ethyl phenylacetate.
Ethyl 4-phenylbutyrate.
Ethyl 3-phenylglycidate.
Ethyl 3-phenylpropionate; ethyl hydrocinnamate.
Ethyl propionate.
Ethyl pyruvate.
Ethyl salicylate.
Ethyl sorbate; ethyl 2,4-hexadienoate.
Ethyl tiglate; ethyl *trans*-2-methyl-2-butenoate.
Ethyl undecanoate.
Ethyl 10-undecenoate.
Ethyl valerate.
Eucalyptol; 1,8-epoxy-*p*-menthane; cineole.
Eugenyl acetate.
Eugenyl benzoate.
Eugenyl formate.
Eugenyl methyl ether; 4-allylveratrole; methyl eugenol.
Farnesol; 3,7,11-trimethyl-2,6,10-dodecatrien-1-ol.
d-Fenchone; *d*-1,3,3-trimethyl-2-norbornanone.
Fenchyl alcohol; 1,3,3-trimethyl-2-norbornanol.
Formic acid
(2-Furyl)-2-propanone; furyl acetone.
1-Furyl-2-propanone; furyl acetone.
Fusel oil, refined (mixed amyl alcohols).
Geranyl acetoacetate; *trans*-3,7-dimethyl-2, 6-octadien-1-yl acetoacetate.
Geranyl acetone; 6,10-dimethyl-5,9-undecadien-2-one.
Geranyl benzoate.
Geranyl butyrate.
Geranyl formate.
Geranyl hexanoate
Geranyl isobutyrate.
Geranyl isovalerate.
Geranyl phenylacetate.
Geranyl propionate.
Glucose pentaacetate.

Guaiacol; μ-methoxyphenol.
Guaiacyl acetate; μ-methoxyphenyl acetate.
Guaiacyl phenylacetate.
Guaiene; 1,4-dimethyl-7-isopropenyl-Δ9,10-octahydroazulene.
Guaiol acetate; 1,4-dimethyl-7-(α-hydroxyisopropyl)-δ9,10-octahydroazulene acetate.
γ-Heptalactone; 4-hydroxyheptanoic acid, γ-lactone.
Heptanal; enanthaldehyde.
Heptanal dimethyl acetal.
Heptanal 1,2-glyceryl acetal.
2,3-Heptanedione; acetyl valeryl.
3-Heptanol.
2-Heptanone; methyl amyl ketone.
3-Heptanone; ethyl butyl ketone.
4-Heptanone; dipropyl ketone.
cis-4-Heptenal; *cis*-4-hepten-1-al.
Heptyl acetate.
Heptyl alcohol; enanthic alcohol.
Heptyl butyrate.
Heptyl cinnamate.
Heptyl formate.
Heptyl isobutyrate.
Heptyl octanoate.
1-Hexadecanol; cetyl alcohol.
ω-6-Hexadecenlactone; 16-hydroxy-6-hexadecenoic acid, ω-lactone; ambrettolide.
γ-Hexalactone; 4-hydroxyhexanoic acid, γ-lactone; tonkalide.
Hexanal; caproic aldehyde.
2,3-Hexanedione; acetyl butyryl.
Hexanoic acid; caproic acid.
2-Hexenal.
2-Hexen-1-ol.
3-Hexen-1-ol; leaf alcohol.
2-Hexen-1-yl acetate.
3-Hexenyl isovalerate.
3-Hexenyl 2-methylbutyrate.
3-Hexenyl phenylacetate; *cis*-3-hexenyl phenylacetate.
Hexyl acetate.
2-Hexyl-4-acetoxytetrahydrofuran.
Hexyl alcohol.
Hexyl butyrate.
α-Hexylcinnamaldehyde.
Hexyl formate.
Hexyl hexanoate.
2-Hexylidene cyclopentanone.
Hexyl isovalerate.
Hexyl 2-methylbutyrate.
Hexyl octanoate.
Hexyl phenylacetate; *n*-hexyl phenylacetate.
Hexyl propionate.
Hydroxycitronellal; 3,7-dimethyl-7-hydroxyoctanal.
Hydroxycitronellal diethyl acetal.
Hydroxycitronellal dimethyl acetal.
Hydroxycitronellol; 3,7-dimethyl-1,7-octanediol.
N-(4-Hydroxy-3-methoxybenzyl)-nonanamide; pelargonyl vanillylamide.
5-Hydroxy-4-octanone; butyroin.
4-(*p*-Hydroxyphenyl)-2-butanone; *p*-hydroxybenzyl acetone.
Indole.
α-Ionone; 4-(2,6,6-trimethyl-2-cyclohexen-1-yl)-3-buten-2-one.
β-Ionone; 4-(2,6,6-trimethyl-1-cyclohexen-1-yl)-3-buten-2-one.
α-Irone; 4-(2,5,6,6-tetramethyl-2-cyclohexene-1-yl)-3-buten-2-one; 6-methylionone.
Isoamyl acetate.
Isoamyl acetoacetate.
Isoamyl alcohol; isopentyl alcohol; 3-methyl-1-butanol.
Isoamyl benzoate.
Isoamyl butyrate.
Isoamyl cinnamate.
Isoamyl formate.
Isoamyl 2-furanbutyrate; α-isoamyl furfurylpropionate.
Isoamyl 2-furanpropionate; α-isoamyl furfurylacetate.
Isoamyl hexanoate.
Isoamyl isobutyrate.
Isoamyl isovalerate.
Isoamyl laurate.
Isoamyl-2-methylbutyrate; isopentyl-2-methylbutyrate.
Isoamyl nonanoate.
Isoamyl octanoate.
Isoamyl phenylacetate.
Isoamyl propionate.
Isoamyl pyruvate.
Isoamyl salicylate.
Isoborneol.
Isobornyl acetate.
Isobornyl formate.
Isobornyl isovalerate.
Isobornyl propionate.
Isobutyl acetate.
Isobutyl acetoacetate.
Isobutyl alcohol.
Isobutyl angelate; isobutyl *cis*-2-methyl-2-butenoate.
Isobutyl anthranilate.
Isobutyl benzoate.
Isobutyl butyrate.
Isobutyl cinnamate.
Isobutyl formate.
Isobutyl 2-furanpropionate.
Isobutyl heptanoate.
Isobutyl hexanoate.
Isobutyl isobutyrate.
α-Isobutylphenethyl alcohol; isobutyl benzyl carbinol; 4-methyl-1-phenyl-2-pentanol.
Isobutyl phenylacetate.
Isobutyl propionate.
Isobutyl salicylate.
2-Isobutylthiazole.
Isobutyraldehyde.
Isobutyric acid.
Isoeugenol; 2-methoxy-4-propenylphenol.
Isoeugenyl acetate.
Isoeugenyl benzyl ether; benzyl isoeugenol.
Isoeugenyl ethyl ether; 2-ethoxy-5-propenylanisole; ethyl isoeugenol.
Isoeugenyl formate.
Isoeugenyl methyl ether; 4-propenylveratrole; methyl isoeugenol.
Isoeugenyl phenylacetate.

Isojasmone; mixture of 2-hexylidenecyclopentanone and 2-hexyl-2-cyclopenten-1-one.
α-Isomethylionone; 4-(2,6,6-trimethyl-2-cyclohexen-1-yl)-3-methyl-3-buten-2-one; methyl γ-ionone.
Isopropyl acetate.
ρ-Isopropylacetophenone.
Isopropyl alcohol; isopropanol.
Isopropyl benzoate.
ρ-Isopropylbenzyl alcohol; cuminic alcohol; ρ-cymen-7-ol.
Isopropyl butyrate.
Isopropyl cinnamate.
Isopropyl formate.
Isopropyl hexanoate.
Isopropyl isobutyrate.
Isopropyl isovalerate.
ρ-Isopropylphenylacetaldehyde; ρ-cymen-7-carboxaldehyde.
Isopropyl phenylacetate.
3-(ρ-Isopropylphenyl)-propionaldehyde; ρ-isopropylhydrocinnamaldehyde; cuminyl acetaldehyde.
Isopropyl propionate.
Isopulegol; *p*-menth-8-en-3-ol.
Isopulegone; *p*-menth-8-en-3-one.
Isopulegyl acetate.
Isoquinoline.
Isovaleric acid.
cis-Jasmone; 3-methyl-2-(2-pentenyl)-2-cyclopenten-1-one.
Lauric aldehyde; dodecanal.
Lauryl acetate.
Lauryl alcohol; 1-dodecanol.
Lepidine; 4-methylquinoline.
Levulinic acid.
Linalool oxide; *cis*- and *trans*-2-vinyl-2-methyl-5-(1′-hydroxy-1′-methylethyl) tetrahydrofuran.
Linalyl anthranilate; 3,7-dimethyl-1,6-octadien-3-yl anthranilate.
Linalyl benzoate.
Linalyl butyrate.
Linalyl cinnamate.
Linalyl formate.
Linalyl hexanoate.
Linalyl isobutyrate.
Linalyl isovalerate.
Linalyl octanoate.
Linalyl propionate.
Maltol; 3-hydroxy-2-methyl-4H-pyran-4-one.
Menthadienol; *p*-mentha-1,8(10)-dien-9-ol.
p-Mentha-1,8-dien-7-ol; perillyl alcohol.
Menthadienyl acetate; *p*-mentha-1,8(10)-dien-9-yl acetate.
p-Menth-3-en-1-ol.
1-*p*-Menthen—9-yl acetate; *p*-menth-1-en-9-yl acetate.
Menthol; 2-isopropyl-5-methylcyclohexanol.
Menthone; *p*-menthan-3-one.
Menthyl acetate; *p*-menth-3-yl acetate.
Menthyl isovalerate; *p*-menth-3-yl isovalerate.
o-Methoxybenzaldehyde.
p-Methoxybenzaldehyde; *p*-anisaldehyde.
o-Methoxycinnamaldehyde.
2-Methoxy-4-methylphenol; 4-methylguaiacol; 2-methoxy-*p*-cresol.
4-(*p*-Methoxyphenyl)-2-butanone; anisyl acetone.
1-(4-Methoxyphenyl)-4-methyl-1-penten-3-one; methoxystyryl isopropyl ketone.
1-(*p*-Methoxyphenyl)-1-penten-3-one; α-methylanisylidene acetone; ethone.
1-(*p*-Methoxyphenyl)-2-propanone; anisylmethyl ketone; anisic ketone.
2-Methoxy-4-vinylphenol; *p*-vinylguaiacol.
Methyl acetate.
4′-Methylacetophenone; *p*-methylacetophenone; methyl *p*-tolyl ketone.
2-Methylallyl butyrate; 2-methyl-2-propenlyl butyrate.
Methyl anisate.
o-Methylanisole; *o*-cresyl methyl ether.
p-Methylanisole; *p*-cresyl methyl ether; *p*-methoxytoluene.
Methyl benzoate.
Methylbenzyl acetate, mixed *o*-,*m*-,*p*-.
α-Methylbenzyl acetate; styralyl acetate.
α-Methylbenzyl alcohol; styralyl alcohol.
α-Methylbenzyl butyrate; styralyl butyrate.
α-Methylbenzyl isobutyrate; styralyl isobutyrate.
α-Methylbenzyl formate; styralyl formate.
α-Methylbenzyl propionate; styralyl propionate.
2-Methyl-3-buten-2-ol.
2-Methylbutyl isovalerate.
Methyl *p-tert*-butylphenylacetate.
2-Methylbutyraldehyde; methyl ethyl acetaldehyde.
3-Methylbutyraldehyde; isovaleraldehyde.
Methyl butyrate.
2-Methylbutyric acid.
α-Methylcinnamaldehyde.
p-Methylcinnamaldehyde.
Methyl cinnamate.
2-Methyl-1,3-cyclohexadiene.
Methylcyclopentenolone; 3-methylcyclopentane-1,2-dione.
Methyl disulfide; dimethyl disulfide.
Methyl ester of rosin, partially hydrogenated (as defined in § 172.615); methyl dihydroabietate.
Methyl heptanoate.
2-Methylheptanoic acid.
6-Methyl-3,5-heptadien-2-one.
Methyl-5-hepten-2-ol.
6-Methyl-5-hepten-2-one.
Methyl hexanoate.
Methyl 2-hexanoate.
Methyl *p*-hydroxybenzoate; methylparaben.
Methyl α-ionone; 5-(2,6,6-trimethyl-2-cyclohexen-1-yl)-4-penten-3-one.
Methyl β-ionone; 5-(2,6,6-trimethyl-1-cyclohexen-1-yl)-4-penten-3-one.
Methyl Δ-ionone; 5-(2,6,6-trimethyl-3-cyclohexen-1-yl-)-4-penten-3-one.
Methyl isobutyrate.
2-Methyl-3-(*p*-isopropylphenyl)-propionaldehyde; α-methyl-*p*-isopropylhydrocinnamal- dehyde; cyclamen aldehyde.
Methyl isovalerate.

Methyl laurate.
Methyl mercaptan; methanethiol.
Methyl *o*-methoxybenzoate.
Methyl *N*-methylanthranilate; dimethyl anthranilate.
Methyl 2-methylbutyrate.
Methyl-3-methylthiopropionate.
Methyl 4-methylvalerate.
Methyl myristate.
Methyl β-naphthyl ketone; 2′-acetonaphthone.
Methyl nonanoate.
Methyl 2-nonenoate.
Methyl 2-nonynoate; methyloctyne carbonate.
2-Methyloctanal; methyl hexyl acetaldehyde.
Methyl octanoate.
Methyl 2-octynoate; methyl heptine carbonate.
4-Methyl-2,3-pentanedione; acetyl isobutyryl.
4-Methyl-2-pentanone; methyl isobutyl ketone.
β-Methylphenethyl alcohol; hydratropyl alcohol.
Methyl phenylacetate.
3-Methyl-4-phenyl-3-butene-2-one.
2-Methyl-4-phenyl-2-butyl acetate; dimethylphenylethyl carbinyl acetate.
2-Methyl-4-phenyl-2-butyl isobutyrate; dimethylphenyl ethylcarbinyl isobutyrate.
3-Methyl-2-phenylbutyraldehyde; α-isopropyl phenylacetaldehyde.
Methyl 4-phenylbutyrate.
4-Methyl-1-phenyl-2-pentanone; benzyl isobutyl ketone.
Methyl 3-phenylpropionate; methyl hydrocinnamate.
Methyl propionate.
3-Methyl-5-propyl-2-cyclohexen-1-one.
Methyl sulfide.
3-Methylthiopropionaldehyde; methional.
2-Methyl-3-tolylpropionaldehyde, mixed *o*-, *m*-, *p*-.
2-Methylundecanal; methyl nonyl acetaldehyde.
Methyl 9-undecenoate.
Methyl 2-undecynoate; methyl decyne carbonate.
Methyl valerate.
2-Methylvaleric acid.
Myrcene; 7-methyl-3-methylene-1,6-octadiene.
Myristaldehyde; tetradecanal.
d-Neomenthol; 2-isopropyl-5-methylcyclohexanol.
Nerol; *cis*-3,7-dimethyl-2,6-octadien-1-ol.
Nerolidol; 3,7,11-trimethyl-1,6,10-dodecatrien-3-ol.
Neryl acetate.
Neryl butyrate.
Neryl formate.
Neryl isobutyrate.
Neryl isovalerate.
Neryl propionate.
2,6-Nonadien-1-ol.
γ-Nonalactone; 4-hydroxynonanoic acid, γ-lactone; aldehyde C–18.
Nonanal; pelargonic aldehyde.
1,3-Nonanediol acetate, mixed esters.
Nonanoic acid; pelargonic acid.
2-Nonanone; methylheptyl ketone.
3-Nonanon-1-yl acetate; 1-hydroxy-3-nonanone acetate.
Nonyl acetate.
Nonyl alcohol; 1-nonanol.
Nonyl octanoate.
Nonyl isovalerate.
Nootkatone; 5,6-dimethyl-8-isopropenylbicyclo[4,4,0]-dec-1-en-3-one.
Ocimene; *trans*-β-ocimene; 3,7-dimethyl-1,3,6-octatriene.
γ-Octalactone; 4-hydroxyoctanoic acid, γ-lactone.
Octanal; caprylaldehyde.
Octanal dimethyl acetal.
1-Octanol; octyl alcohol.
2-Octanol.
3-Octanol.
2-Octanone; methyl hexyl ketone.
3-Octanone; ethyl amyl ketone.
3-Octanon-1-ol.
1-Octen-3-ol; amyl vinyl carbinol.
1-Octen-3-yl acetate.
Octyl acetate.
3-Octyl acetate.
Octyl butyrate.
Octyl formate.
Octyl heptanoate.
Octyl isobutyrate.
Octyl isovalerate.
Octyl octanoate.
Octyl phenylacetate.
Octyl propionate.
ω-Pentadecalactone; 15-hydroxypentadecanoic acid, ω-lactone; pentadecanolide; angelica lactone.
2,3-Pentanedione; acetyl propionyl.
2-Pentanone; methyl propyl ketone.
4-Pentenoic acid.
1-Penten-3-ol.
Perillaldehyde; 4-isopropenyl-1-cyclohexene-1-carboxaldehyde;*p*-mentha-1,8-dien-7-al.
Perillyl acetate; *p*-mentha-1,8-dien-7-yl acetate.
α-Phellandrene; ρ-mentha-1,5-diene.
Phenethyl acetate.
Phenethyl alcohol; β-phenylethyl alcohol.
Phenethyl anthranilate.
Phenethyl benzoate.
Phenethyl butyrate.
Phenethyl cinnamate.
Phenethyl formate.
Phenethyl isobutyrate.
Phenethyl isovalerate.
Phenethyl 2-methylbutyrate.
Phenethyl phenylacetate.
Phenethyl propionate.
Phenethyl salicylate.
Phenethyl senecioate; phenethyl 3,3-dimethylacrylate.
Phenethyl tiglate.
Phenoxyacetic acid.

2-Phenoxyethyl isobutyrate.
Phenylacetaldehyde; α-toluic aldehyde.
Phenylacetaldehyde 2,3-butylene glycol acetal.
Phenylacetaldehyde dimethyl acetal.
Phenylacetaldehyde glyceryl acetal.
Phenylacetic acid; α-toluic acid.
4-Phenyl-2-butanol; phenylethyl methyl carbinol.
4-Phenyl-3-buten-2-ol; methyl styryl carbinol.
4-Phenyl-3-buten-2-one.
4-Phenyl-2-butyl acetate; phenylethyl methyl carbinyl acetate.
1-Phenyl-3-methyl-3-pentanol; phenylethyl methyl ethyl carbinol.
1-Phenyl-1-propanol; phenylethyl carbinol.
3-Phenyl-1-propanol; hydrocinnamyl alcohol.
2-Phenylpropionaldehyde; hydratropaldehyde.
3-Phenylpropionaldehyde; hydrocinnamaldehyde.
2-Phenylpropionalde-hyde dimethyl acetal; hydratropic aldehyde dimethyl acetal.
3-Phenylpropionic acid; hydrocinnamic acid.
3-Phenylpropyl acetate.
2-Phenylpropyl butyrate.
3-Phenylpropyl cinnamate.
3-Phenylpropyl formate.
3-Phenylpropyl hexanoate.
2-Phenylpropyl isobutyrate.
3-Phenylpropyl isobutyrate.
3-Phenylpropyl isovalerate.
3-Phenylpropyl propionate.
2-(3-Phenylpropyl)-tetrahydrofuran.
α-Pinene; 2-pinene.
β-Pinene; 2(10)-pinene.
Pine tar oil.
Pinocarveol; 2(10)-pinen-3-ol.
Piperidine.
Piperine.
d-Piperitone; *p*-menth-1-en-3-one.
Piperitenone; *p*-mentha-1,4(8)-dien-3-one.
Piperitenone oxide; 1,2-epoxy-*p*-menth-4-(8)-en-3-one.
Piperonyl acetate; heliotropyl acetate.
Piperonyl isobutyrate.
Polylimonene.
Polysorbate 20; polyoxyethylene (20) sorbitan monolaurate.
Polysorbate 60; polyoxyethylene (20) sorbitan monostereate.
Polysorbate 80; polyoxyethylene (20) sorbitan monooleate.
Potassium acetate.
Propenylguaethol; 6-ethoxy-*m*-anol.
Propionaldehyde.
Propyl acetate.
Propyl alcohol; 1-propanol.
p-Propyl anisole; dihydroanethole.
Propyl benzoate.
Propyl butyrate.
Propyl cinnamate.
Propyl disulfide.
Propyl formate.
Propyl 2-furanacrylate.
Propyl heptanoate.
Propyl hexanoate.
Propyl *p*-hydroxybenzoate; propylparaben.
3-Propylidenephthalide.
Propyl isobutyrate.
Propyl isovalerate.
Propyl mercaptan.
α-Propylphenethyl alcohol.
Propyl phenylacetate.
Propyl propionate.
Pulegone; *p*-menth-4(8)-en-3-one.
Pyridine.
Pyroligneous acid extract.
Pyruvaldehyde.
Pyruvic acid.
Rhodinol; 3,7-dimethyl-7-octen-1-ol; *l*-citronellol.
Rhodinyl acetate.
Rhodinyl butyrate.
Rhodinyl formate.
Rhodinyl isobutyrate.
Rhodinyl isovalerate.
Rhodinyl phenylacetate.
Rhodinyl propionate.
Rum ether; ethyl oxyhydrate.
Salicylaldehyde.
Santalol, α and β.
Santalyl acetate.
Santalyl phenylacetate.
Skatole.
Sorbitan monostearate.
Styrene.
Sucrose octaacetate.
α-Terpinene.
γ-Terpinene.
α-Terpineol; *p*-menth-1-en-8-ol.
β-Terpineol.
Terpinolene; *p*-menth-1,4(8)-diene.
Terpinyl acetate.
Terpinyl anthranilate.
Terpinyl butyrate.
Terpinyl cinnamate.
Terpinyl formate.
Terpinyl isobutyrate.
Terpinyl isovalerate.
Terpinyl propionate.
Tetrahydrofurfuryl acetate.
Tetrahydrofurfuryl alcohol.
Tetrahydrofurfuryl butyrate.
Tetrahydrofurfuryl propionate.
Tetrahydro-pseudo-ionone; 6,10-dimethyl-9-undecen-2-one.
Tetrahydrolinalool; 3,7-dimethyloctan-3-ol.
Tetramethyl ethylcyclohexenone; mixture of 5-ethyl-2,3,4,5-tetramethyl-2-cyclohexen-1-one and 5-ethyl-3,4,5,6-tetramethyl-2-cyclohexen-1-one.
2-Thienyl mercaptan; 2-thienylthiol.
Thymol.
Tolualdehyde glyceryl acetal, mixed *o*, *m*, *p*.
Tolualdehydes, mixed *o*, *m*, *p*.
p-Tolylacetaldehyde.
o-Tolyl acetate; *o*-cresyl acetate.
p-Tolyl acetate; *p*-cresyl acetate.
4-(*p*-Tolyl)-2-butanone; *p*-methylbenzylacetone.
p-Tolyl isobutyrate.
p-Tolyl laurate.

p-Tolyl phenylacetate.
2-(*p*-Tolyl)-propionaldehyde; *p*-methylhydratropic aldehyde.
Tributyl acetylcitrate.
2-Tridecenal.
2,3-Undecadione; acetyl nonyryl.
γ-Undecalactone; 4-hydroxyundecanoic acid γ-lactone; peach aldehyde; aldehyde C–14.
Undecenal.
2-Undecanone; methyl nonyl ketone.
9-Undecenal; undecenoic aldehyde.
10-Undecenal.
Undecen-1-ol; undecylenic alcohol.
10-Undecen-1-yl acetate.
Undecyl alcohol.
Valeraldehyde; pentanal.
Valeric acid; pentanoic acid.
Vanillin acetate; acetyl vanillin.
Veratraldehyde.
Verbenol; 2-pinen-4-ol.
Zingerone; 4-(4-hydroxy-3-methoxyphenyl)-2-butanone.

(c) Δ-Decalactone and Δ-dodecalactone when used separately or in combination in oleomargarine are used at levels not to exceed 10 parts per million and 20 parts per million, respectively, in accordance with § 166.110 of this chapter.

(d) BHA (butylated hydroxyanisole) may be used as an antioxidant in flavoring substances whereby the additive does not exceed 0.5 percent of the essential (volatile) oil content of the flavoring substance.

[42 FR 14491, Mar. 15, 1977, as amended at 42 FR 23148, May 6, 1977; 43 FR 19843, May 9, 1978; 45 FR 22915, Apr. 4, 1980; 47 FR 27810, June 25, 1982; 48 FR 10812, Mar. 15, 1983; 48 FR 51907, Nov. 15, 1983; 49 FR 5747, Feb. 15, 1984; 50 FR 42932, Oct. 23, 1985; 54 FR 7402, Feb. 21, 1989; 61 FR 14245, Apr. 1, 1996; 69 FR 24511, May 4, 2004]

§ 172.520 Cocoa with dioctyl sodium sulfosuccinate for manufacturing.

The food additive "cocoa with dioctyl sodium sulfosuccinate for manufacturing," conforming to § 163.117 of this chapter and § 172.810, is used or intended for use as a flavoring substance in dry beverage mixes whereby the amount of dioctyl sodium sulfosuccinate does not exceed 75 parts per million of the finished beverage. The labeling of the dry beverage mix shall bear adequate directions to assure use in compliance with this section.

§ 172.530 Disodium guanylate.

Disodium guanylate may be safely used as a flavor enhancer in foods, at a level not in excess of that reasonably required to produce the intended effect.

§ 172.535 Disodium inosinate.

The food additive disodium inosinate may be safely used in food in accordance with the following prescribed conditions:

(a) The food additive is the disodium salt of inosinic acid, manufactured and purified so as to contain no more than 150 parts per million of soluble barium in the compound disodium inosinate with seven and one-half molecules of water of crystallization.

(b) The food additive is used as a flavoring adjuvant in food.

§ 172.540 DL-Alanine.

DL-Alanine (a racemic mixture of D- and L-alanine; CAS Reg. No. 302–72–7) may be safely used as a flavor enhancer for sweeteners in pickling mixtures at a level not to exceed 1 percent of the pickling spice that is added to the pickling brine.

[56 FR 6968, Feb. 21, 1991]

§ 172.560 Modified hop extract.

The food additive modified hop extract may be safely used in beer in accordance with the following prescribed conditions:

(a) The food additive is used or intended for use as a flavoring agent in the brewing of beer.

(b) The food additive is manufactured by one of the following processes:

(1) The additive is manufactured from a hexane extract of hops by simultaneous isomerization and selective reduction in an alkaline aqueous medium with sodium borohydride, whereby the additive meets the following specifications:

(i) A solution of the food additive solids is made up in approximately 0.012 *n* alkaline methyl alcohol (6 milliliters of 1 *n* sodium hydroxide diluted to 500 milliliters with methyl alcohol) to show an absorbance at 253 millimicrons of 0.6 to 0.9 per centimeter. (This absorbance is obtained by approximately 0.03 milligram solids permilliliter.) The ultraviolet absorption spectrum of this solution exhibits the following characteristics: An absorption peak at 253 millimicrons; no absorption peak at 325 to 330 millimicrons; the absorbance at 268 millimicrons does not exceed the absorbance at 272 millimicrons.

(ii) The boron content of the food additive does not exceed 310 parts per million (0.0310 percent), calculated as boron.

(2) The additive is manufactured from hops by a sequence of extractions and fractionations, using benzene, light petroleum spirits, and methyl alcohol as solvents, followed by isomerization by potassium carbonate treatment. Residues of solvents in the modified hop extract shall not exceed 1.0 part per million of benzene, 1.0 part per million of light petroleum spirits, and 250 parts per million of methyl alcohol. The light petroleum spirits and benzene solvents shall comply with the specifications in §172.250 except that the boiling point range for light petroleum spirits is 150 °F–300 °F.

(3) The additive is manufactured from hops by a sequence of extractions and fractionations, using methylene chloride, hexane, and methyl alcohol as solvents, followed by isomerization by sodium hydroxide treatment. Residues of the solvents in the modified hop extract shall not exceed 5 parts per million of methylene chloride, 25 parts per million of hexane, and 100 parts per million of methyl alcohol.

(4) The additive is manufactured from hops by a sequence of extractions and fractionations, using benzene, light petroleum spirits, methyl alcohol, *n*-butyl alcohol, and ethyl acetate as solvents, followed by isomerization by potassium carbonate treatment. Residues of solvents in the modified hop extract shall not exceed 1.0 part per million of benzene, 1.0 part per million of light petroleum spirits, 50 parts per million of methyl alcohol, 50 parts per million of *n*-butyl alcohol, and 1 part per million of ethyl acetate. The light petroleum spirits and benzene solvents shall comply with the specifications in §172.250 except that the boiling point range for light petroleum spirits is 150 °F to 300 °F.

(5) The additive is manufactured from hops by an initial extraction and fractionation using one or more of the following solvents: Ethylene dichloride, hexane, isopropyl alcohol, methyl alcohol, methylene chloride, trichloroethylene, and water; followed by isomerization by calcium chloride or magnesium chloride treatment in ethylene dichloride, methylene chloride, or trichloroethylene and a further sequence of extractions and fractionations using one or more of the solvents set forth in this paragraph. Residues of the solvents in the modified hop extract shall not exceed 125 parts per million of hexane; 150 parts per million of ethylene dichloride, methylene chloride, or trichloroethylene; or 250 parts per million of isopropyl alcohol or methyl alcohol.

(6) The additive is manufactured from hops by an initial extraction and fractionation using one or more of the solvents listed in paragraph (b)(5) of this section followed by: Hydrogenation using palladium as a catalyst in methyl alcohol, ethyl alcohol, or isopropyl alcohol acidified with hydrochloric or sulfuric acid; oxidation with peracetic acid; isomerization by calcium chloride or magnesium chloride treatment in ethylene dichloride, methylene chloride, or trichloroethylene (alternatively, the hydrogenation and isomerization steps may be performed in reverse order); and a further sequence of extractions and fractionations using one or more of the solvents listed in paragraph (b)(5) of this section. The additive shall meet the residue limitations as prescribed in paragraph (b)(5) of this section.

(7) The additive is manufactured from hops as set forth in paragraph (b)(6) of this section followed by reduction with sodium borohydride in aqueous alkaline methyl alcohol, and a sequence of extractions and fractionations using one or more of the solvents listed in paragraph (b)(5) of this section. The additive shall meet the residue limitations as prescribed in paragraph (b)(5) of this section, and a boron content level not in excess of 300 parts per million (0.0300 percent), calculated as boron.

(8) The additive is manufactured from hops as a nonisomerizable nonvolatile hop resin by an initial extraction and fractionation using one or more of the solvents listed in paragraph (b)(5) of this section followed by a sequence of aqueous extractions and removal of nonaqueous solvents to less

than 0.5 percent. The additive is added to the wort before or during cooking in the manufacture of beer.

§ 172.575 Quinine.

Quinine, as the hydrochloride salt or sulfate salt, may be safely used in food in accordance with the following conditions:

Uses	Limitations
In carbonated beverages as a flavor.	Not to exceed 83 parts per million, as quinine. Label shall bear a prominent declaration of the presence of quinine either by the use of the word "quinine" in the name of the article or through a separate declaration.

§ 172.580 Safrole-free extract of sassafras.

The food additive safrole-free extract of sassafras may be safely used in accordance with the following prescribed conditions:

(a) The additive is the aqueous extract obtained from the root bark of the plant *Sassafras albidum* (Nuttall) Nees (Fam. Lauraceae).

(b) It is obtained by extracting the bark with dilute alcohol, first concentrating the alcoholic solution by vacuum distillation, then diluting the concentrate with water and discarding the oily fraction.

(c) The purified aqueous extract is safrole-free.

(d) It is used as a flavoring in food.

§ 172.585 Sugar beet extract flavor base.

Sugar beet extract flavor base may be safely used in food in accordance with the provisions of this section.

(a) Sugar beet extract flavor base is the concentrated residue of soluble sugar beet extractives from which sugar and glutamic acid have been recovered, and which has been subjected to ion exchange to minimize the concentration of naturally occurring trace minerals.

(b) It is used as a flavor in food.

§ 172.590 Yeast-malt sprout extract.

Yeast-malt sprout extract, as described in this section, may be safely used in food in accordance with the following prescribed conditions:

(a) The additive is produced by partial hydrolysis of yeast extract (derived from *Saccharomyces cereviseae*, *Saccharomyces fragilis*, or *Candida utilis*) using the sprout portion of malt barley as the source of enzymes. The additive contains a maximum of 6 percent 5′ nucleotides by weight.

(b) The additive may be used as a flavor enhancer in food at a level not in excess of that reasonably required to produce the intended effect.

Subpart G—Gums, Chewing Gum Bases and Related Substances

§ 172.610 Arabinogalactan.

Arabinogalactan may be safely used in food in accordance with the following conditions:

(a) Arabinogalactan is a polysaccharide extracted by water from Western larch wood, having galactose units and arabinose units in the approximate ratio of six to one.

(b) It is used in the following foods in the minimum quantity required to produce its intended effect as an emulsifier, stabilizer, binder, or bodying agent: Essential oils, nonnutritive sweeteners, flavor bases, nonstandardized dressings, and pudding mixes.

§ 172.615 Chewing gum base.

The food additive chewing gum base may be safely used in the manufacture of chewing gum in accordance with the following prescribed conditions:

(a) The food additive consists of one or more of the following substances that meet the specifications and limitations prescribed in this paragraph, used in amounts not to exceed those required to produce the intended physical or other technical effect.

MASTICATORY SUBSTANCES

NATURAL (COAGULATED OR CONCENTRATED LATICES) OF VEGETABLE ORIGIN

Family	Genus and species
Sapotaceae:	
Chicle	Manilkara zapotilla Gilly and Manilkara chicle Gilly.
Chiquibul	Manilkara zapotilla Gilly.

MASTICATORY SUBSTANCES—Continued

NATURAL (COAGULATED OR CONCENTRATED LATICES) OF VEGETABLE ORIGIN

Family	Genus and species
Crown gum	Manilkara zapotilla Gilly and Manilkara chicle Gilly.
Gutta hang kang	Palaquium leiocarpum Boerl. and Palaquium oblongifolium Burck.
Massaranduba balata (and the solvent-free resin extract of Massaranduba balata).	Manilkara huberi (Ducke) Chevalier.
Massaranduba chocolate	Manilkara solimoesensis Gilly.
Nispero	Manilkara zapotilla Gilly and Manilkara chicle Gilly.
Rosidinha (rosadinha)	Micropholis (also known as Sideroxylon) spp.
Venezuelan chicle	Manilkara williamsii Standley and related spp.
Apocynaceae:	
Jelutong	Dyera costulata Hook, F. and Dyera lowii Hook, F.
Leche caspi (sorva)	Couma macrocarpa Barb. Rodr.
Pendare	Couma macrocarpa Barb. Rodr. and Couma utilis (Mart.) Muell. Arg.
Perillo	Couma macrocarpa Barb. Rodr. and Couma utilis (Mart.) Muell. Arg.
Moraceae:	
Leche de vaca	Brosimum utile (H.B.K.) Pittier and Poulsenia spp.; also Lacmellea standleyi (Woodson), Monachino (Apocynaceae).
Niger gutta	Ficus platyphylla Del.
Tunu (tuno)	Castilla fallax Cook.
Euphorbiaceae:	
Chilte	Cnidoscolus (also known as Jatropha) elasticus Lundell and Cnidoscolus tepiquensis (Cost. and Gall.) McVaugh.
Natural rubber (smoked sheet and latex solids).	Hevea brasiliensis.

Synthetic	Specifications
Butadiene-styrene rubber	Basic polymer.
Isobutylene-isoprene copolymer (butyl rubber).	Do.
Paraffin	Synthesized by Fischer-Tropsch process from carbon monoxide and hydrogen which are catalytically converted to a mixture of paraffin hydrocarbon. Lower molecular weight fractions are removed by distillation. The residue is hydrogenated and further treated by percolation through activated charcoal. The product has a congealing point of 93°–99 °C as determined by ASTM method D938–71 (Reapproved 1981), "Standard Test Method for Congealing Point of Petroleum Waxes, Including Petrolatum," a maximum oil content of 0.5 percent as determined by ASTM method D721–56T, "Tentative Method of Test for Oil Content of Petroleum Waxes," and an absorptivity of less than 0.01 at 290 millimicrons in decahydronaphthalene at 88 °C as determined by ASTM method D2008–80, "Standard Test Method for Ultraviolet Absorbance and Absorptivity of Petroleum Products," which are incorporated by reference. Copies may be obtained from the American Society for Testing Materials, 100 Barr Harbor Dr., West Conshohocken, Philadelphia, PA 19428-2959, or may be examined at the National Archives and Records Administration (NARA). For information on the availability of this material at NARA, call 202–741–6030, or go to: *http://www.archives.gov/federal_register/code_of_federal_regulations/ibr_locations.html.*
Petroleum wax	Complying with § 172.886.
Petroleum wax synthetic	Complying with § 172.888.
Polyethylene	Molecular weight 2,000–21,000.
Polyisobutylene	Minimum molecular weight 37,000 (Flory).
Polyvinyl acetate	Molecular weight, minimum 2,000.

PLASTICIZING MATERIALS (SOFTENERS)

Glycerol ester of partially dimerized rosin	Having an acid number of 3–8, a minimum drop-softening point of 109 °C, and a color of M or paler.
Glycerol ester of partially hydrogenated gum or wood rosin.	Having an acid number of 3–10, a minimum drop-softening point of 79 °C, and a color of N or paler.
Glycerol ester of polymerized rosin	Having an acid number of 3–12, a minimum melting-point of 80 °C, and a color of M or paler.
Glycerol ester of gum rosin	Having an acid number of 5–9, a minimum drop-softening point of 88 °C, and a color of N or paler. The ester is purified by steam stripping.
Glycerol ester of tall oil rosin	Having an acid number of 2–12, a softening point (ring and ball) of 80°–88 °C, and a color of N or paler. The ester is purified by steam stripping.
Glycerol ester of wood rosin	Having an acid number of 3–9, a drop-softening point of 88 °C–96 °C, and a color of N or paler. The ester is purified by steam stripping.
Lanolin	

MASTICATORY SUBSTANCES—Continued

NATURAL (COAGULATED OR CONCENTRATED LATICES) OF VEGETABLE ORIGIN

Family	Genus and species
Methyl ester of rosin, partially hydrogenated	Having an acid number of 4–8, a refractive index of 1.5170–1.5205 at 20 °C, and a viscosity of 23–66 poises at 25 °C. The ester is purified by steam stripping.
Pentaerythritol ester of partially hydrogenated gum or wood rosin.	Having an acid number of 7–18, a minimum drop-softening point of 102 °C, and a color of K or paler.
Pentaerythritol ester of gum or wood rosin	Having an acid number of 6–16, a minimum drop-softening point of 109 °C, and a color of M or paler.
Rice bran wax	Complying with § 172.890.
Stearic acid	Complying with § 172.860.
Sodium and potassium stearates	Complying with § 172.863.
TERPENE RESINS	
Synthetic resin	Consisting of polymers of αpinene, βpinene, and/or dipentene; acid value less than 5, saponification number less than 5, and color less than 4 on the Gardner scale as measured in 50 percent mineral spirit solution.
Natural resin	Consisting of polymers of α-pinene; softening point minimum 155 °C, determined by U.S.P. closed-capillary method, United States Pharmacopeia XX (1980) (page 961).
ANTIOXIDANTS	
Butylated hydroxyanisole	Not to exceed antioxidant content of 0.1% when used alone or in any combination.
Butylated hydroxytoluene	Do.
Propyl gallate	Do.
MISCELLANEOUS	
Sodium sulfate	
Sodium sulfide	Reaction-control agent in synthetic polymer production.

(b) In addition to the substances listed in paragraph (a) of this section, chewing gum base may also include substances generally recognized as safe in food.

(c) To assure safe use of the additive, in addition to the other information required by the act, the label and labeling of the food additive shall bear the name of the additive, "chewing gum base." As used in this paragraph, the term "chewing gum base" means the manufactured or partially manufactured nonnutritive masticatory substance comprised of one or more of the ingredients named and so defined in paragraph (a) of this section.

[42 FR 14491, Mar. 15, 1977, as amended at 45 FR 56051, Aug. 22, 1980; 49 FR 5747, Feb. 15, 1984; 49 FR 10105, Mar. 19, 1984; 66 FR 38153, July 23, 2001; 66 FR 53711, Oct. 24, 2001]

§ 172.620 Carrageenan.

The food additive carrageenan may be safely used in food in accordance with the following prescribed conditions:

(a) The food additive is the refined hydrocolloid prepared by aqueous extraction from the following members of the families Gigartinaceae and Solieriaceae of the class Rodophyceae (red seaweed):

Chondrus crispus.
Chondrus ocellatus.
Eucheuma cottonii.
Eucheuma spinosum.
Gigartina acicularis.
Gigartina pistillata.
Gigartina radula.
Gigartina stellata.

(b) The food additive conforms to the following conditions:

(1) It is a sulfated polysaccharide the dominant hexose units of which are galactose and anhydrogalactose.

(2) Range of sulfate content: 20 percent to 40 percent on a dry-weight basis.

(c) The food additive is used or intended for use in the amount necessary for an emulsifier, stabilizer, or thickener in foods, except for those standardized foods that do not provide for such use.

(d) To assure safe use of the additive, the label and labeling of the additive shall bear the name of the additive, carrageenan.

§172.623 Carrageenan with polysorbate 80.

Carrageenan otherwise meeting the definition and specifications of §172.620 (a) and (b) and salts of carrageenan otherwise meeting the definition of §172.626(a) may be safely produced with the use of polysorbate 80 meeting the specifications and requirements of §172.840 (a) and (b) in accordance with the following prescribed conditions:

(a) The polysorbate 80 is used only to facilitate separation of sheeted carrageenan and salts of carrageenan from drying rolls.

(b) The carrageenan and salts of carrageenan contain not more than 5 percent by weight of polysorbate 80, and the final food containing the additives contains polysorbate 80 in an amount not to exceed 500 parts per million.

(c) The carrageenan and salts of carrageenan so produced are used only in producing foods in gel form and only for the purposes defined in §§172.620(c) and 172.626(b), respectively.

(d) The carrageenan and salts of carrageenan so produced are not used in foods for which standards of identity exist unless the standards provide for the use of carrageenan, or salts of carrageenan, combined with polysorbate 80.

(e) The carrageenan and salts of carrageenan produced in accordance with this section, and foods containing the same, in addition to the other requirements of the Act, are labeled to show the presence of polysorbate 80, and the label or labeling of the carrageenan and salts of carrageenan so produced bear adequate directions for use.

§172.626 Salts of carrageenan.

The food additive salts of carrageenan may be safely used in food in accordance with the following prescribed conditions:

(a) The food additive consists of carrageenan, meeting the provisions of §172.620, modified by increasing the concentration of one of the naturally occurring salts (ammonium, calcium, potassium, or sodium) of carrageenan to the level that it is the dominant salt in the additive.

(b) The food additive is used or intended for use in the amount necessary for an emulsifier, stabilizer, or thickener in foods, except for those standardized foods that do not provide for such use.

(c) To assure safe use of the additive, the label and labeling of the additive shall bear the name of the salt of carrageenan that dominates the mixture by reason of the modification, e.g., "sodium carrageenan", "potassium carrageenan", etc.

§172.655 Furcelleran.

The food additive furcelleran may be safely used in food in accordance with the following prescribed conditions:

(a) The food additive is the refined hydrocolloid prepared by aqueous extraction of furcellaria fastigiata of the class Rodophyceae (red seaweed).

(b) The food additive conforms to the following:

(1) It is a sulfated polysaccharide the dominant hexose units of which are galactose and anhydrogalactose.

(2) Range of sulfate content: 8 percent to 19 percent, on a dry-weight basis.

(c) The food additive is used or intended for use in the amount necessary for an emulsifier, stabilizer, or thickener in foods, except for those standardized foods that do not provide for such use.

(d) To assure safe use of the additive, the label and labeling of the additive shall bear the name of the additive, furcelleran.

§172.660 Salts of furcelleran.

The food additive salts of furcelleran may be safely used in food in accordance with the following prescribed conditions:

(a) The food additive consists of furcelleran, meeting the provisions of §172.655, modified by increasing the concentration of one of the naturally occurring salts (ammonium, calcium, potassium, or sodium) of furcelleran to the level that it is the dominant salt in the additive.

(b) The food additive is used or intended for use in the amount necessary for an emulsifier, stabilizer, or thickener in foods, except for those standardized foods that do not provide for such use.

(c) To assure safe use of the additive, the label and labeling of the additive shall bear the name of the salt of furcelleran that dominates the mixture by reason of the modification, e.g., "sodium furcelleran", "potassium furcelleran", etc.

§ 172.665 Gellan gum.

The food additive gellan gum may be safely used in food in accordance with the following prescribed conditions:

(a) The additive is a high molecular weight polysaccharide gum produced from *Pseudomonas elodea* by a pure culture fermentation process and purified by recovery with isopropyl alcohol. It is composed of tetrasaccharide repeat units, each containing one molecule of rhamnose and glucuronic acid, and two molecules of glucose. The glucuronic acid is neutralized to a mixed potassium, sodium, calcium, and magnesium salt. The polysaccharide may contain acyl (glyceryl and acetyl) groups as the O-glycosidically linked esters.

(b) The strain of *P. elodea* is nonpathogenic and nontoxic in man and animals.

(c) The additive is produced by a process that renders it free of viable cells of *P. elodea*.

(d) The additive meets the following specifications:

(1) Positive for gellan gum when subjected to the following identification tests:

(i) A 1-percent solution is made by hydrating 1 gram of gellan gum in 99 milliliters of distilled water. The mixture is stirred for about 2 hours, using a motorized stirrer and a propeller-type stirring blade. A small amount of the above solution is drawn into a wide bore pipet and transferred into a solution of 10-percent calcium chloride. A tough worm-like gel will form instantly.

(ii) To the 1-percent distilled water solution prepared for identification test (i), 0.50 gram of sodium chloride is added. The solution is heated to 80 °C with stirring, held at 80 °C for 1 minute, and allowed to cool to room temperature without stirring. A firm gel will form.

(2) Residual isopropyl alcohol (IPA) not to exceed 0.075 percent as determined by the procedure described in the Xanthan Gum monograph, the "Food Chemicals Codex," 4th ed. (1996), pp. 437–438, which is incorporated by reference in accordance with 5 U.S.C. 552(a) and 1 CFR part 51. Copies are available from the National Academy Press, Box 285, 2101 Constitution Ave. NW., Washington, DC 20055 (Internet address *http://www.nap.edu*), or may be examined at the Center for Food Safety and Applied Nutrition's Library, Food and Drug Administration, 5100 Paint Branch Pkwy., College Park, MD 20740, or at the National Archives and Records Administration (NARA). For information on the availability of this material at NARA, call 202–741–6030, or go to: *http://www.archives.gov/federal_register/code_of_federal_regulations/ibr_locations.html.*

(e) The additive is used or intended for use in accordance with current good manufacturing practice as a stabilizer and thickener as defined in § 170.3(o)(28) of this chapter. The additive may be used in foods where standards of identity established under section 401 of the Federal Food, Drug, and Cosmetic Act do not preclude such use.

(f) To assure safe use of the additive:

(1) The label of its container shall bear, in addition to other information required by the Federal Food, Drug, and Cosmetic Act, the name of the additive and the designation "food grade".

(2) The label or labeling of the food additive container shall bear adequate directions for use.

[55 FR 39614, Sept. 28, 1990, as amended at 57 FR 55445, Nov. 25, 1992; 64 FR 1758, Jan. 12, 1999]

§ 172.695 Xanthan gum.

The food additive xanthan gum may be safely used in food in accordance with the following prescribed conditions:

(a) The additive is a polysaccharide gum derived from *Xanthomonas campestris* by a pure-culture fermentation process and purified by recovery with isopropyl alcohol. It contains D-glucose, D-mannose, and D-glucuronic acid as the dominant hexose units and is manufactured as the sodium, potassium, or calcium salt.

(b) The strain of *Xanthomonas campestris* is nonpathogenic and nontoxic in man or other animals.

(c) The additive is produced by a process that renders it free of viable cells of *Xanthomonas campestris*.

(d) The additive meets the following specifications:

(1) Residual isopropyl alcohol not to exceed 750 parts per million.

(2) An aqueous solution containing 1 percent of the additive and 1 percent of potassium chloride stirred for 2 hours has a minimum viscosity of 600 centipoises at 75 °F, as determined by Brookfield Viscometer, Model LVF (or equivalent), using a No. 3 spindle at 60 r.p.m., and the ratio of viscosities at 75 °F and 150 °F is in the range of 1.02 to 1.45.

(3) Positive for xanthan gum when subjected to the following procedure:

LOCUST BEAN GUM GEL TEST

Blend on a weighing paper or in a weighing pan 1.0 gram of powdered locust bean gum with 1.0 gram of the powdered polysaccharide to be tested. Add the blend slowly (approximately ½ minute) at the point of maximum agitation to a stirred solution of 200 milliliters of distilled water previously heated to 80 °C in a 400-milliliter beaker. Continue mechanical stirring until the mixture is in solution, but stir for a minimum time of 30 minutes. Do not allow the water temperature to drop below 60 °C.

Set the beaker and its contents aside to cool in the absence of agitation. Allow a minimum time of 2 hours for cooling. Examine the cooled beaker contents for a firm rubbery gel formation after the temperature drops below 40 °C.

In the event that a gel is obtained, make up a 1 percent solution of the polysaccharide to be tested in 200 milliliters of distilled water previously heated to 80 °C (omit the locust bean gum). Allow the solution to cool without agitation as before. Formation of a gel on cooling indicates that the sample is a gelling polysaccharide and not xanthan gum.

Record the sample as "positive" for xanthan gum if a firm, rubbery gel forms in the presence of locust bean gum but not in its absence. Record the sample as "negative" for xanthan gum if no gel forms or if a soft or brittle gel forms both with locust bean gum and in a 1 percent solution of the sample (containing no locust bean gum).

(4) Positive for xanthan gum when subjected to the following procedure:

PYRUVIC ACID TEST

Pipet 10 milliliters of an 0.6 percent solution of the polysaccharide in distilled water (60 milligrams of water-soluble gum) into a 50-milliliter flask equipped with a standard taper glass joint. Pipet in 20 milliliters of 1*N* hydrochloric acid. Weigh the flask. Reflux the mixture for 3 hours. Take precautions to avoid loss of vapor during the refluxing. Cool the solution to room temperature. Add distilled water to make up any weight loss from the flask contents.

Pipet 1 milliliter of a 2,4-dinitrophenylhydrazine reagent (0.5 percent in 2*N* hydrochloric acid) into a 30-milliliter separatory funnel followed by a 2-milliliter aliquot (4 milligrams of water-soluble gum) of the polysaccharide hydrolyzate. Mix and allow the reaction mixture to stand at room temperature for 5 minutes. Extract the mixture with 5 milliliters of ethyl acetate. Discard the aqueous layer.

Extract the hydrazone from the ethyl acetate with three 5 milliliter portions of 10 percent sodium carbonate solution. Dilute the combined sodium carbonate extracts to 100 milliliters with additional 10 percent sodium carbonate in a 10-milliliter volumetric flask. Measure the optical density of the sodium carbonate solution at 375 millimicrons.

Compare the results with a curve of the optical density versus concentration of an authentic sample of pyruvic acid that has been run through the procedure starting with the preparation of the hydrazone.

Record the percent by weight of pyruvic acid in the test polysaccharide. Note "positive" for xanthan gum if the sample contains more than 1.5 percent of pyruvic acid and "negative" for xanthan gum if the sample contains less than 1.5 percent of pyruvic acid by weight.

(e) The additive is used or intended for use in accordance with good manufacturing practice as a stabilizer, emulsifier, thickener, suspending agent, bodying agent, or foam enhancer in foods for which standards of identity established under section 401 of the Act do not preclude such use.

(f) To assure safe use of the additive:

(1) The label of its container shall bear, in addition to other information required by the Act, the name of the additive and the designation "food grade".

(2) The label or labeling of the food additive container shall bear adequate directions for use.

Subpart H—Other Specific Usage Additives

§ 172.710 Adjuvants for pesticide use dilutions.

The following surfactants and related adjuvants may be safely added to pesticide use dilutions by a grower or applicant prior to application to the growing crop:

n-Alkyl (C_8-C_{18}) amine acetate, where the alkyl groups (C_8-C_{18}) are derived from coconut oil, as a surfactant in emulsifier blends at levels not in excess of 5 percent by weight of the emulsifier blends that are added to herbicides for application to corn and sorghum.

Di-*n*-alkyl (C_8-C_{18}) dimethyl ammonium chloride, where the alkyl groups (C_8-C_{18}) are derived from coconut oil, as surfactants in emulsifier blends at levels not in excess of 5 percent by weight of emulsifier blends that are added to herbicides for application to corn or sorghum.

Diethanolamide condensate based on a mixture of saturated and unsaturated soybean oil fatty acids (C_{16}-C_{18}) as a surfactant in emulsifier blends that are added to the herbicide atrazine for application to corn.

Diethanolamide condensate based on stripped coconut fatty acids (C_{10} C_{18}) as a surfactant in emulsifier blends that are added to the herbicide atrazine for application to corn.

α-(*p*-Dodecylphenyl)-*omega*-hydroxypoly (oxyethylene) produced by the condensation of 1 mole of dodecylphenol (dodecyl group is a proplyene tetramer isomer) with an average of 4–14 or 30–70 moles of ethylene oxide; if a blend of products is used, the average number of moles of ethylene oxide reacted to produce any product that is a component of the blend shall be in the range of 4–14 or 30–70.

Ethylene dichloride.

Polyglyceryl phthalate ester of coconut oil fatty acids.

α-[*p*-(1,1,3,3-Tetramethylbutyl) phenyl]-*omega*-hydroxypoly(oxyethylene) produced by the condensation of 1 mole of *p*-(1,1,3,3-tetramethylbutyl) phenol with an average of 4–14 or 30–70 moles of ethylene oxide; if a blend of products is used, the average number of moles of ethylene oxide reacted to produce any product that is a component of the blend shall be in the range of 4–14 or 30–70.

α-[*p*-(1,1,3,3-Tetramethylbutyl) phenyl]-*omega*-hydroxypoly(oxyethylene) produced by the condensation of 1 mole of *p*-(1,1,3,3-tetramethylbutyl) phenol with 1 mole of ethylene oxide.

Sodium acrylate and acrylamide copolymer with a minimum average molecular weight of 10,000,000 in which 30 percent of the polymer is comprised of acrylate units and 70 percent acrylamide units, for use as a drift control agent in herbicide formulations applied to crops at a level not to exceed 0.5 ounces of the additive per acre.

§ 172.712 1,3-Butylene glycol.

The food additive 1,3-butylene glycol (CAS Reg. No. 107–88–0) may be safely used in food in accordance with the following prescribed conditions:

(a) It is prepared by the aldol condensation of acetaldehyde followed by catalytic hydrogenation.

(b) The food additive shall conform to the identity and specifications listed in the monograph entitled "1,3-Butylene Glycol" in the Food Chemicals Codex, 4th ed. (1996), p. 52, which is incorporated by reference in accordance with 5 U.S.C. 552(a) and 1 CFR part 51. Copies are available from the Office of Food Additive Safety (HFS–200), Center for Food Safety and Applied Nutrition, 5100 Paint Branch Pkwy., College Park, MD 20740, 240–402–1200, or may be examined at the Center for Food Safety and Applied Nutrition's Library, Food and Drug Administration, 5100 Paint Branch Pkwy., College Park, MD 20740, or at the National Archives and Records Administration (NARA). For information on the availability of this material at NARA, call 202–741–6030, or go to: *http://www.archives.gov/federal_register/code_of_federal_regulations/ibr_locations.html.*

(c) It is used in the manufacture of sausage casings as a formulation aid as defined in § 170.3(o)(14) of this chapter and as a processing aid as defined in § 170.3(o)(24) of this chapter.

[62 FR 26228, May 13, 1997, as amended at 78 FR 14664, Mar. 7, 2013]

§ 172.715 Calcium lignosulfonate.

Calcium lignosulfonate may be safely used in or on food, subject to the provisions of this section.

(a) Calcium lignosulfonate consists of sulfonated lignin, primarily as calcium and sodium salts.

(b) It is used in an amount not to exceed that reasonably required to accomplish the intended physical or technical effect when added as a dispersing agent and stabilizer in pesticides for preharvest or postharvest application to bananas.

§ 172.720 Calcium lactobionate.

The food additive calcium lactobionate may be safely used in food in accordance with the following prescribed conditions:

(a) The food additive is the calcium salt of lactobionic acid (4-(β,D-galactosido)-D-gluconic acid) produced by the oxidation of lactose.

(b) It is used or intended for use as a firming agent in dry pudding mixes at a level not greater than that required to accomplish the intended effect.

§ 172.723 Epoxidized soybean oil.

Epoxidized soybean oil may be safely used in accordance with the following prescribed conditions:

(a) The additive is prepared by reacting soybean oil in toluene with hydrogen peroxide and formic acid.

(b) It meets the following specifications:

(1) Epoxidized soybean oil contains oxirane oxygen, between 7.0 and 8.0 percent, as determined by the American Oil Chemists' Society (A.O.C.S.) method Cd 9–57, "Oxirane Oxygen," reapproved 1989, which is incorporated by reference in accordance with 5 U.S.C 552(a) and 1 CFR part 51. Copies are available from the American Oil Chemists' Society, P. O. Box 3489, Champaign, IL 61826–3489, or may be examined at the Office of Food Additive Safety (HFS–200), Center for Food Safety and Applied Nutrition, Food and Drug Administration, 5100 Paint Branch Pkwy., College Park, MD 20740, 240–402–1200, or at the National Archives and Records Administration (NARA). For information on the availability of this material at NARA, call 202–741–6030, or go to: *http://www.archives.gov/federal_register/code_of_federal_regulations/ibr_locations.html.*

(2) The maximum iodine value is 3.0, as determined by A.O.C.S. method Cd 1–25, "Iodine Value of Fats and Oils Wijs Method," revised 1993, which is incorporated by reference in accordance with 5 U.S.C. 552(a) and 1 CFR part 51. The availability of this incorporation by reference is given in paragraph (b)(1) of this section.

(3) The heavy metals (as Pb) content cannot be more than 10 parts per million, as determined by the "Heavy Metals Test," of the "Food Chemicals Codex," 4th ed. (1996), pp. 760–761, Method II (with a 2-gram sample and 20 microgram of lead ion in the control), which is incorporated by reference in accordance with 5 U.S.C. 552(a) and 1 CFR part 51. Copies are available from the National Academy Press, Box 285, 2101 Constitution Ave. NW., Washington, DC 20055 (Internet address *http://www.nap.edu*), or may be examined at the Center for Food Safety and Applied Nutrition's Library, Food and Drug Administration, 5100 Paint Branch Pkwy., College Park, MD 20740, or at the National Archives and Records Administration (NARA). For information on the availability of this material at NARA, call 202–741–6030, or go to: *http://www.archives.gov/federal_register/code_of_federal_regulations/ibr_locations.html.*

(c) The additive is used as a halogen stabilizer in brominated soybean oil at a level not to exceed 1 percent.

[60 FR 32903, June 26, 1995, as amended at 64 FR 1759, Jan. 12, 1999; 78 FR 14665, Mar. 7, 2013]

§ 172.725 Gibberellic acid and its potassium salt.

The food additives gibberellic acid and its potassium salt may be used in the malting of barley in accordance with the following prescribed conditions:

(a) The additives meet the following specifications:

(1) The gibberellic acid is produced by deep-culture fermentation of a suitable nutrient medium by a strain of Fusarium moniliforme or a selection of this culture.

(2) The gibberellic acid produced is of 80 percent purity or better.

(3) The empirical formula of gibberellic acid is represented by $C_{19}H_{22}O_6$.

(4) Potassium gibberellate is the potassium salt of the specified gibberellic acid.

(5) The potassium gibberellate is of 80 percent purity or better.

(6) The gibberellic acid or potassium gibberellate may be diluted with substances generally recognized as safe in foods or with salts of fatty acids conforming to § 172.863.

(b) They are used or intended for use in the malting of barley under conditions whereby the amount of either or both additives present in the malt is not in excess of 2 parts per million expressed as gibberellic acid, and the treated malt is to be used in the production of fermented malt beverages or distilled spirits only, whereby the finished distilled spirits contain none and the finished malt beverage contains not more than 0.5 part per million of gibberellic acid.

(c) To insure the safe use of the food additives the label of the package shall bear, in addition to the other information required by the Act:

(1) The name of the additive, "gibberellic acid" or "potassium gibberellate", whichever is appropriate.

(2) An accurate statement of the concentration of the additive contained in the package.

(3) Adequate use directions to provide not more than 2 parts per million of gibberellic acid in the finished malt.

(4) Adequate labeling directions to provide that the final malt is properly labeled as described in paragraph (d) of this section.

(d) To insure the safe use of the additive the label of the treated malt shall bear, in addition to the other information required by the Act, the statements:

(1) "Contains not more than 2 parts per million _____", the blank being filled in with the words "gibberellic acid" or "potassium gibberellate", whichever is appropriate; and

(2) "Brewer's malt—To be used in the production of fermented malt beverages only" or "Distiller's malt—To be used in the production of distilled spirits only", whichever is appropriate.

§ 172.730 Potassium bromate.

The food additive potassium bromate may be safely used in the malting of barley under the following prescribed conditions:

(a)(1) It is used or intended for use in the malting of barley under conditions whereby the amount of the additive present in the malt from the treatment does not exceed 75 parts per million of bromate (calculated as Br), and the treated malt is used only in the production of fermented malt beverages or distilled spirits.

(2) The total residue of inorganic bromides in fermented malt beverages, resulting from the use of the treated malt plus additional residues of inorganic bromides that may be present from uses in accordance with other regulations in this chapter promulgated under sections 408 and/or 409 of the act, does not exceed 25 parts per million of bromide (calculated as Br). No tolerance is established for bromide in distilled spirits because there is evidence that inorganic bromides do not pass over in the distillation process.

(b) To assure safe use of the additive, the label or labeling of the food additive shall bear, in addition to the other information required by the Act, the following:

(1) The name of the additive.

(2) Adequate directions for use.

(c) To assure safe use of the additive, the label or labeling of the treated malt shall bear, in addition to other information required by the Act, the statement, "Brewer's Malt—To be used in the production of fermented malt beverages only", or "Distiller's Malt—To be used in the production of distilled spirits only", whichever is the case.

§ 172.735 Glycerol ester of rosin.

Glycerol ester of wood rosin, gum rosin, or tall oil rosin may be safely used in food in accordance with the following prescribed conditions:

(a) It has an acid number of 3 to 9, a drop-softening point of 88 to 96 °C; and a color of N or paler as determined in accordance with Official Naval Stores Standards of the United States. It is purified by countercurrent steam distillation or steam stripping.

(b) It is used to adjust the density of citrus oils used in the preparation of beverages whereby the amount of the additive does not exceed 100 parts per million of the finished beverage.

[42 FR 14491, Mar. 15, 1977, as amended at 70 FR 15758, Mar. 29, 2005; 72 FR 46896, Aug. 22, 2007]

§ 172.736 Glycerides and polyglycides of hydrogenated vegetable oils.

The food additive glycerides and polyglycides of hydrogenated vegetable oils may be safely used in food in accordance with the following prescribed conditions:

(a) The additive is manufactured by heating a mixture of hydrogenated oils of vegetable origin and polyethylene glycol in the presence of an alkaline catalyst followed by neutralization with any acid that is approved or is generally recognized as safe for this use to yield the finished product.

(b) The additive consists of a mixture of mono-, di- and tri-glycerides and polyethylene glycol mono- and diesters of fatty acids (polyglycides) of hydrogenated vegetable oils and meets the following specifications:

(1) Total ester content, greater than 90 percent as determined by a method entitled "Determination of Esterified Glycerides and Polyoxyethylene Glycols," approved November 16, 2001, printed by Gattefosse S.A.S., and incorporated by reference. The Director of the Office of the Federal Register approves this incorporation by reference in accordance with 5 U.S.C. 552(a) and 1 CFR part 51. You may obtain a copy from the Office of Food Additive Safety, 5100 Paint Branch Pkwy., College Park, MD 20740 or you may examine a copy at the Center for Food Safety and Applied Nutrition's Library, Food and Drug Administration, 5100 Paint Branch Pkwy., College Park, MD 20740, or at the National Archives and Records Administration (NARA). For information on the availability of this material at NARA, call 202–741–6030, or go to *http://www.archives.gov/federal_register/code_of_federal_regulations/ibr_locations.html.*

(2) Acid value, not greater than 2, and hydroxyl value, not greater than 56 as determined by the methods entitled "Acid Value," p. 934 and "Hydroxyl Value," p. 936, respectively, in the Food Chemicals Codex, 5th ed., effective January 1, 2004, and incorporated by reference in accordance with 5 U.S.C. 552(a) and 1 CFR part 51. Copies are available from the National Academies Press, 500 Fifth St. NW., Washington, DC 20055 (Internet address *http://www.nap.edu*), or may be examined at the Center for Food Safety and Applied Nutrition's Library, 5100 Paint Branch Pkwy., College Park, MD 20740, or at the National Archives and Records Administration (NARA). For information on the availability of this material at NARA, call 202–741–6030, or go to *http://www.archives.gov/federal_register/code_of_federal_regulations/ibr_locations.html.*

(3) Lead, not greater than 0.1 mg/kg as determined by the American Oil Chemists' Society (A.O.C.S.) method Ca 18c–91, "Determination of Lead by Direct Graphite Furnace Atomic Absorption Spectrophotometry," updated 1995, and incorporated by reference in accordance with 5 U.S.C. 552(a) and 1 CFR part 51. Copies are available from American Oil Chemists' Society, P. O. Box 3489, Champaign, IL 61826–3489, or may be examined in the library at the Center for Food Safety and Applied Nutrition, 5100 Paint Branch Pkwy., College Park, MD 20740, or at the National Archives and Records Administration (NARA). For information on the availability of this material at NARA, call 202–741–6030, or go to *http://www.archives.gov/federal_register/code_of_federal_regulations/ibr_locations.html.*

(4) 1,4-Dioxane, not greater than 10 milligrams per kilogram (mg/kg), and ethylene oxide, not greater than 1 mg/kg, as determined by a gas chromatographic method entitled "Determination of Ethylene Oxide and 1,4-Dioxane by Headspace Gas Chromatography," approved November 5, 1998, printed by Gattefosse S.A.S., and incorporated by reference in accordance with 5 U.S.C. 552(a) and 1 CFR part 51; see paragraph (b)(1) of this section for availability of the incorporation by reference.

(c) The additive is used or intended for use as an excipient in dietary supplement tablets, capsules, and liquid formulations that are intended for ingestion in daily quantities measured in drops or similar small units of measure.

[71 FR 12620, Mar. 13, 2006]

§ 172.755 Stearyl monoglyceridyl citrate.

The food additive stearyl monoglyceridyl citrate may be safely used in food in accordance with the following provisions:

(a) The additive is prepared by controlled chemical reaction of the following:

Reactant	Limitations
Citric acid	
Monoglycerides of fatty acids.	Prepared by the glycerolysis of edible fats and oils or derived from fatty acids conforming with § 172.860.
Stearyl alcohol	Derived from fatty acids conforming with § 172.860, or derived synthetically in conformity with § 172.864.

(b) The additive stearyl monoglyceridyl citrate, produced as described under paragraph (a) of this section, meets the following specifications:

Acid number 40 to 52.
Total citric acid 15 to 18 percent.
Saponification number 215–255.

(c) The additive is used or intended for use as an emulsion stabilizer in or with shortenings containing emulsifiers.

§ 172.765 Succistearin (stearoyl propylene glycol hydrogen succinate).

The food additive succistearin (stearoyl propylene glycol hydrogen succinate) may be safely used in food in accordance with the following prescribed conditions:

(a) The additive is the reaction product of succinic anhydride, fully hydrogenated vegetable oil (predominantly C_{16} or C_{18} fatty acid chain length), and propylene glycol.

(b) The additive meets the following specifications:

Acid number 50–150.
Hydroxyl number 15–50.
Succinated ester content 45–75 percent.

(c) The additive is used or intended for use as an emulsifier in or with shortenings and edible oils intended for use in cakes, cake mixes, fillings, icings, pastries, and toppings, in accordance with good manufacturing practice.

§ 172.770 Ethylene oxide polymer.

The polymer of ethylene oxide may be safely used as a foam stabilizer in fermented malt beverages in accordance with the following conditions.

(a) It is the polymer of ethylene oxide having a minimum viscosity of 1,500 centipoises in a 1 percent aqueous solution at 25 °C.

(b) It is used at a level not to exceed 300 parts per million by weight of the fermented malt beverage.

(c) The label of the additive bears directions for use to insure compliance with paragraph (b) of this section.

§ 172.775 Methacrylic acid-divinylbenzene copolymer.

Methacrylic acid-divinylbenzene copolymer may be safely used in food in accordance with the following prescribed conditions:

(a) The additive is produced by the polymerization of methacrylic acid and divinylbenzene. The divinylbenzene functions as a cross-linking agent and constitutes a minimum of 4 percent of the polymer.

(b) Aqueous extractives from the additive do not exceed 2 percent (dry basis) after 24 hours at 25 °C.

(c) The additive is used as a carrier of vitamin B_{12} in foods for special dietary use.

§ 172.780 Acacia (gum arabic).

The food additive may be safely used in food in accordance with the following prescribed conditions:

(a) Acacia (gum arabic) is the dried gummy exudate from stems and branches of trees of various species of the genus *Acacia*, family Leguminosae.

(b) The ingredient meets the specifications of "Food Chemicals Codex," 5th Ed. (2004), pp. 210 and 211, which is incorporated by reference. The Director of the Office of the Federal Register approves this incorporation by reference in accordance with 5 U.S.C. 552(a) and 1 CFR part 51. You may obtain copies from the National Academies Press, 500 Fifth St. NW., Washington, DC 20001 (Internet address: *http://www.nap.edu*). Copies may be examined at the Center for Food Safety and Applied Nutrition's Library, Food and Drug Administration, 5100 Paint Branch Pkwy., College Park,

MD 20740, or at the National Archives and Records Administration (NARA). For information on the availability of this material at NARA, call 202–741–6030, or go to: *http://www.archives.gov/federal_register/code_of_federa_regulations/ibr_locations.html.*

(c) The ingredient is used as a thickener, emulsifier, or stabilizer in alcoholic beverages at a use level not to exceed 20 percent in the final beverage.

[70 FR 8034, Feb. 17, 2005]

§ 172.785 *Listeria*-specific bacteriophage preparation.

The additive may be safely used as an antimicrobial agent specific for *Listeria monocytogenes* (*L. monocytogenes*) in accordance with the following conditions:

(a) *Identity.* (1) The additive consists of a mixture of equal proportions of six different individually purified lytic-type (lacking lysogenic activity) bacteriophages (phages) specific against *L. monocytogenes.*

(2) Each phage is deposited at, and assigned an identifying code by, a scientifically-recognized culture collection center, and is made available to FDA upon request.

(3) The additive is produced from one or more cell cultures of *L. monocytogenes* in a safe and suitable nutrient medium.

(b) *Specifications.* (1) The additive achieves a positive lytic result ($OD_{600} \leq 0.06$) when tested against any of the following *L. monocytogenes* isolates available from American Type Culture Collection (ATCC): ATCC 35152 (serogroup 1/2a), ATCC 19118 (serogroup 4b), and ATCC 15313 (serogroup 1/2b). The analytical method for determining the potency of the additive entitled "Determination of Potency of LMP–102™," dated October 9, 2003, and printed by Intralytix, Inc., is incorporated by reference. The Director of the Office of the Federal Register approves this incorporation by reference in accordance with 5 U.S.C. 552(a) and 1 CFR part 51. You may obtain a copy from the Office of Food Additive Safety (HFS–200), Center for Food Safety and Applied Nutrition, Food and Drug Administration, 5100 Paint Branch Pkwy., College Park, MD 20740, or you may examine a copy at the Center for Food Safety and Applied Nutrition's Library, 5100 Paint Branch Pkwy., College Park, MD 20740, or at the National Archives and Records Administration (NARA). For information on the availability of this material at NARA, call 202–741–6030, or go to: *http://www.archives.gov/federal_register/code_of_federal_regulations/ibr_locations.html.*

(2) The mean phage titer of each monophage in the additive is 1×10^9 plaque forming units (PFU)/ml. The analytical method for determining phage titer entitled "Method to Determine Lytic Activity/Phage Titer," dated November 6, 2001, and printed by Intralytix, Inc., is incorporated by reference. Copies are available at locations cited in paragraph (b)(1) of this section.

(3) The phages present in the preparation must not contain a functional portion of any of the toxin-encoding sequences described in 40 CFR 725.421(d). No sequences derived from genes encoding bacterial 16S ribosomal RNA are present in the complete genomic sequence of the phages.

(4) *L. monocytogenes* toxin, listeriolysin O (LLO), is not greater than 5 hemolytic units (HU)/ml. The analytical method for determining LLO entitled "Quantitation of Listeriolysin O Levels in LMP–102™," dated September 27, 2004, and printed by Intralytix, Inc., is incorporated by reference. Copies are available at locations cited in paragraph (b)(1) of this section.

(5) The additive is negative for *L. monocytogenes.* The modified version of the U.S. Department of Agriculture's method for determining *L. monocytogenes* entitled "LMP–102™ *Listeria monocytogenes* Sterility Testing," dated May 24, 2004, and printed by Intralytix, Inc., is incorporated by reference. Copies are available at locations cited in paragraph (b)(1) of this section.

(6) The additive is negative for gram-positive and gram-negative bacteria capable of growing in commonly used microbiological media (e.g., Luria-Bertani (LB) medium), including *Escherichia coli, Salmonella* species and coagulase-positive *Staphylococci,* as determined by the "Method to Determine

Microbial Contamination,'' dated July 11, 2003, and printed by Intralytix, Inc., is incorporated by reference. Copies are available at locations cited in paragraph (b)(1) of this section.

(7) Total organic carbon (TOC) is less than or equal to 36 mg/kg. The analytical method for determining TOC entitled ''Determination of Total Organic Carbon by Automated Analyzer,'' dated March 30, 2001, and printed by Intralytix, Inc., is incorporated by reference. Copies are available at locations cited in paragraph (b)(1) of this section.

(c) *Conditions of use.* The additive is used in accordance with current good manufacturing practice to control *L. monocytogenes* by direct application to meat and poultry products that comply with the ready-to-eat definition in 9 CFR 430.1. Current good manufacturing practice is consistent with direct spray application of the additive at a rate of approximately 1 mL of the additive per 500 cm^2 product surface area.

[71 FR 47731, Aug. 18, 2006]

Subpart I—Multipurpose Additives

§ 172.800 Acesulfame potassium.

Acesulfame potassium (CAS Reg. No. 55589–62–3), also known as acesulfame K, may be safely used as a general-purpose sweetener and flavor enhancer in foods generally, except in meat and poultry, in accordance with current good manufacturing practice and in an amount not to exceed that reasonably required to accomplish the intended technical effect in foods for which standards of identity established under section 401 of the Federal Food, Drug, and Cosmetic Act do not preclude such use, under the following conditions:

(a) Acesulfame potassium is the potassium salt of 6-methyl-1,2,3-oxathiazine-4(3*H*)-one-2,2-dioxide.

(b) The additive meets the following specifications:

(1) Purity is not less than 99 percent on a dry basis. The purity shall be determined by a method titled ''Acesulfame Potassium Assay,'' which is incorporated by reference. Copies are available from the Center for Food Safety and Applied Nutrition (HFS–200), Food and Drug Administration, 5100 Paint Branch Pkwy., College Park, MD 20740, or available for inspection at the National Archives and Records Administration (NARA). For information on the availability of this material at NARA, call 202–741–6030, or go to: *http://www.archives.gov/federal_register/code_of_federal_regulations/ibr_locations.html.*

(2) Fluoride content is not more than 30 parts per million, as determined by method III of the Fluoride Limit Test of the Food Chemicals Codex, 3d Ed. (1981), p. 511, which is incorporated by reference. Copies are available from the National Academy Press, 2101 Constitution Ave. NW., Washington, DC 20418, or available for inspection at the National Archives and Records Administration (NARA). For information on the availability of this material at NARA, call 202–741–6030, or go to: *http://www.archives.gov/federal_register/code_of_federal_regulations/ibr_locations.html.*

(c) If the food containing the additive is represented to be for special dietary uses, it shall be labeled in compliance with part 105 of this chapter.

[53 FR 28382, July 28, 1988, as amended at 57 FR 57961, Dec. 8, 1992; 59 FR 61540, 61543, 61545, Dec. 1, 1994; 60 FR 21702, May 3, 1995; 63 FR 36362, July 6, 1998; 68 FR 75413, Dec. 31, 2003]

§ 172.802 Acetone peroxides.

The food additive acetone peroxides may be safely used in flour, and in bread and rolls where standards of identity do not preclude its use, in accordance with the following prescribed conditions:

(a) The additive is a mixture of monomeric and linear dimeric acetone peroxide, with minor proportions of higher polymers, manufactured by reaction of hydrogen peroxide and acetone.

(b) The additive may be mixed with an edible carrier to give a concentration of: (1) 3 grams to 10 grams of hydrogen peroxide equivalent per 100 grams of the additive, plus carrier, for use in flour maturing and bleaching; or (2) approximately 0.75 gram of hydrogen peroxide equivalent per 100 grams of the additive, plus carrier, for use in dough conditioning.

(c) It is used or intended for use: (1) In maturing and bleaching of flour in a quantity not more than sufficient for such effect; and (2) as a dough-conditioning agent in bread and roll production at not to exceed the quantity of hydrogen peroxide equivalent necessary for the artificial maturing effect.

(d) To insure safe use of the additive, the label of the food additive container and any intermediate premix thereof shall bear, in addition to the other information required by the act:

(1) The name of the additive, "acetone peroxides".

(2) The concentration of the additive expressed in hydrogen peroxide equivalents per 100 grams.

(3) Adequate use directions to provide a final product that complies with the limitations prescribed in paragraph (c) of this section.

§ 172.804 Aspartame.

The food additive aspartame may be safely used in food in accordance with good manufacturing practice as a sweetening agent and a flavor enhancer in foods for which standards of identity established under section 401 of the act do not preclude such use under the following conditions:

(a) Aspartame is the chemical 1-methyl *N*-L-α-aspartyl-L-phenylalanine ($C_{14}H_{18}N_2O_5$).

(b) The additive meets the specifications of the "Food Chemicals Codex," 3d Ed. (1981) pp. 28–29 and First Supplement p. 5, which is incorporated by reference in accordance with 5 U.S.C. 552(a). Copies are available from the National Academy Press, 2101 Constitution Ave. NW., Washington, DC 20418, or may be examined at the Center for Food Safety and Applied Nutrition's Library, Food And Drug Administration, 5100 Paint Branch Pkwy., College Park, MD 20740, or at the National Archives and Records Administration (NARA). For information on the availability of this material at NARA, call 202–741–6030, or go to: *http://www.archives.gov/federal_register/code_of_federal_regulations/ibr_locations.html.*

(c)(1) When aspartame is used as a sugar substitute tablet for sweetening hot beverages, including coffee and tea, L-leucine may be used as a lubricant in the manufacture of such tablets at a level not to exceed 3.5 percent of the weight of the tablet.

(2) When aspartame is used in baked goods and baking mixes, the amount of the additive is not to exceed 0.5 percent by weight of ready-to-bake products or of finished formulations prior to baking. Generally recognized as safe (GRAS) ingredients or food additives approved for use in baked goods shall be used in combination with aspartame to ensure its functionality as a sweetener in the final baked product. The level of aspartame used in these products is determined by an analytical method entitled "Analytical Method for the Determination of Aspartame and Diketopiperazine in Baked Goods and Baking Mixes," October 8, 1992, which was developed by the Nutrasweet Co. Copies are available from the Office of Premarket Approval (HFS–200), Center for Food Safety and Applied Nutrition, 5100 Paint Branch Pkwy., College Park, MD 20740, or are available for inspection at the Center for Food Safety and Applied Nutrition's Library, Food and Drug Administration, 5100 Paint Branch Pkwy., College Park, MD 20740, and at the National Archives and Records Administration (NARA). For information on the availability of this material at NARA, call 202–741–6030, or go to: *http://www.archives.gov/federal_register/code_of_federal_regulations/ibr_locations.html.*

(d) To assure safe use of the additive, in addition to the other information required by the Act:

(1) The principal display panel of any intermediate mix of the additive for manufacturing purposes shall bear a statement of the concentration of the additive contained therein;

(2) The label of any food containing the additive shall bear, either on the principal display panel or on the information panel, the following statement:

PHENYLKETONURICS: CONTAINS PHENYLALANINE

The statement shall appear in the labeling prominently and conspicuously as compared to other words, statements, designs or devices and in bold type and on clear contrasting background in order to render it likely to be read and understood by the ordinary individual under customary conditions of purchase and use.

(3) When the additive is used in a sugar substitute for table use, its label shall bear instructions not to use in cooking or baking.

(4) Packages of the dry, free-flowing additive shall prominently display the sweetening equivalence in teaspoons of sugar.

(e) If the food containing the additive purports to be or is represented for special dietary uses, it shall be labeled in compliance with part 105 of this chapter.

[39 FR 27319, July 26, 1974]

EDITORIAL NOTE: For FEDERAL REGISTER citations affecting § 172.804, see the List of CFR Sections Affected, which appears in the Finding Aids section of the printed volume and at *www.fdsys.gov*.

§ 172.806 Azodicarbonamide.

The food additive azodicarbonamide may be safely used in food in accordance with the following prescribed conditions:

(a) It is used or intended for use:

(1) As an aging and bleaching ingredient in cereal flour in an amount not to exceed 2.05 grams per 100 pounds of flour (0.0045 percent; 45 parts per million).

(2) As a dough conditioner in bread baking in a total amount not to exceed 0.0045 percent (45 parts per million) by weight of the flour used, including any quantity of azodicarbonamide added to flour in accordance with paragraph (a)(1) of this section.

(b) To assure safe use of the additive:

(1) The label and labeling of the additive and any intermediate premix prepared therefrom shall bear, in addition to the other information required by the Act, the following:

(i) The name of the additive.

(ii) A statement of the concentration or the strength of the additive in any intermediate premixes.

(2) The label or labeling of the food additive shall also bear adequate directions for use.

§ 172.808 Copolymer condensates of ethylene oxide and propylene oxide.

Copolymer condensates of ethylene oxide and propylene oxide may be safely used in food under the following prescribed conditions:

(a) The additive consists of one of the following:

(1) α-Hydro-*omega*-hydroxy-poly (oxyethylene) poly(oxypropylene)-(55–61 moles)poly(oxyethylene) block copolymer, having a molecular weight range of 9,760–13,200 and a cloud point above 100 °C in 1 percent aqueous solution.

(2) α-Hydro-*omega*-hydroxy-poly (oxyethylene)poly(oxypropylene)-(53–59 moles)poly(oxyethylene)(14–16 moles) block copolymer, having a molecular weight range of 3,500–4,125 and a cloud point of 9 °C–12 °C in 10 percent aqueous solution.

(3) α-Hydro-*omega*-hydroxy-poly(oxyethylene)/poly(oxypropylene) (minimum 15 moles)/poly(oxyethylene) block copolymer, having a minimum average molecular weight of 1900 and a minimum cloud point of 9 °C–12 °C in 10 percent aqueous solution.

(4) α-Hydro-*omega*-hydroxy-poly(oxyethylene) poly (oxypropylene)-(51–57 moles) poly(oxyethylene) block copolymer, having an average molecular weight of 14,000 and a cloud point above 100 °C in 1 percent aqueous solution.

(b) The additive is used or intended for use as follows:

(1) The additive identified in paragraph (a)(1) of this section is used in practice as a solubilizing and stabilizing agent in flavor concentrates (containing authorized flavoring oils) for use in foods for which standards of identity established under section 401 of the Act do not preclude such use, provided that the weight of the additive does not exceed the weight of the flavoring oils in the flavor concentrate.

(2) The additive identified in paragraph (a)(2) of this section is used as a processing aid and wetting agent in combination with dioctyl sodium sulfosuccinate for fumaric acid as prescribed in § 172.810.

(3) The additive identified in paragraph (a)(3) of this section is used:

(i) As a surfactant and defoaming agent, at levels not to exceed 0.05 percent by weight, in scald baths for poultry defeathering, followed by potable water rinse. The temperatures of the scald baths shall be not less than 125 °F.

(ii) As a foam control and rinse adjuvant in hog dehairing machines at a use level of not more than 5 grams per hog.

(4) The additive identified in paragraph (a)(4) of this section is used as a dough conditioner in yeast-leavened bakery products for which standards of identity established under section 401 of the Act do not preclude such use, provided that the amount of the additive dose not exceed 0.5 percent by weight of the flour used.

[42 FR 14491, Mar. 15, 1977, as amended at 46 FR 57476, Nov. 24, 1981]

§ 172.809 Curdlan.

Curdlan may be safely used in accordance with the following conditions:

(a) Curdlan is a high molecular weight polymer of glucose (β-1,3-glucan; CAS Reg. No. 54724–00–4) produced by pure culture fermentation from the nonpathogenic and nontoxicogenic bacterium *Alcaligenes faecalis* var. *myxogenes*.

(b) Curdlan meets the following specifications when it is tested according to the methods described or referenced in the document entitled "Analytical Methods for Specification Tests for Curdlan," by Takeda Chemical Industries, Ltd., 12–10 Nihonbashi, 2–Chome, Chuo-ku, Tokyo, 103, Japan, 1996, which is incorporated by reference in accordance with 5 U.S.C. 552(a) and 1 CFR part 51. Copies are available from the Office of Food Additive Safety (HFS–200), Center for Food Safety and Applied Nutrition, Food and Drug Administration, 5100 Paint Branch Pkwy., College Park, MD 20740, 240–402–1200, or may be examined at the Center for Food Safety and Applied Nutrition's Library, Food and Drug Administration, 5100 Paint Branch Pkwy., College Park, MD 20740, or at the National Archives and Records Administration (NARA). For information on the availability of this material at NARA, call 202–741–6030, or go to: *http://www.archives.gov/federal_register/code_of_federal_regulations/ibr_locations.html.*

(1) Positive for curdlan.

(2) Assay for curdlan (calculated as anhydrous glucose), not less than 80 percent.

(3) pH of 1 percent aqueous suspension, 6.0–7.5.

(4) Lead, not more than 0.5 mg/kg.

(5) Heavy metals (as Pb), not more than 0.002 percent.

(6) Total nitrogen, not more than 0.2 percent.

(7) Loss on drying, not more than 10 percent.

(8) Residue on ignition, not more than 6 percent.

(9) Gel strength of 2 percent aqueous suspension, not less than 600×10^3 dyne per square centimeter.

(10) Aerobic plate count, not more than 10^3 per gram.

(11) Coliform bacteria, not more than 3 per gram.

(c) Curdlan is used or intended for use in accordance with good manufacturing practice as a formulation aid, processing aid, stabilizer and thickener, and texturizer in foods for which standards of identity established under section 401 of the act do not preclude such use.

[61 FR 65941, Dec. 16, 1996, as amended at 78 FR 14665, Mar. 7, 2013]

§ 172.810 Dioctyl sodium sulfosuccinate.

The food additive dioctyl sodium sulfosuccinate, which meets the specifications of the Food Chemicals Codex, 3d Ed. (1981), pp. 102–104, which is incorporated by reference (Copies may be obtained from the National Academy Press, 2101 Constitution Ave. NW., Washington, DC 20418, or may be examined at the National Archives and Records Administration (NARA). For information on the availability of this material at NARA, call 202–741–6030, or go to: *http://www.archives.gov/federal_register/code_of_federal_regulations/ibr_locations.html.*), may be safely used in food in accordance with the following prescribed conditions:

(a) As a wetting agent in the following fumaric acid-acidulated foods: Dry gelatin dessert, dry beverage base, and fruit juice drinks, when standards of identity do not preclude such use. The labeling of the dry gelatin dessert and dry beverage base shall bear adequate directions for use, and the additive shall be used in such an amount that the finished gelatin dessert will contain not in excess of 15 parts per million of the additive and the finished beverage or fruit juice drink will contain not in excess of 10 parts per million of the additive.

(b) As a processing aid in sugar factories in the production of unrefined cane sugar, in an amount not in excess of 0.5 part per million of the additive per percentage point of sucrose in the juice, syrup, or massecuite being processed, and so used that the final molasses will contain no more than 25 parts per million of the additive.

(c) As a solubilizing agent on gums and hydrophilic colloids to be used in food as stabilizing and thickening agents, when standards of identity do not preclude such use. The additive is used in an amount not to exceed 0.5 percent by weight of the gums or hydrophilic colloids.

(d) As an emulsifying agent for cocoa fat in noncarbonated beverages containing cocoa, whereby the amount of the additive does not exceed 25 parts per million of the finished beverage.

(e) As a dispersing agent in "cocoa with dioctyl sodium sulfosuccinate for manufacturing" that conforms to the provisions of § 163.117 of this chapter and the use limitations prescribed in § 172.520, in an amount not to exceed 0.4 percent by weight thereof.

(f) As a processing aid and wetting agent in combination with α-hydro-*omega* -hydroxy - poly(oxyethylene) - poly-(oxypropylene) (53–59 moles) poly(oxyethylene) (14–16 moles) block copolymer, having a molecular weight range of 3,500–4,125 and a cloud point of 9 °C–12 °C in 10 percent aqueous solution, for fumaric acid used in fumaric acid-acidulated dry beverage base and in fumaric acid-acidulated fruit juice drinks, when standards of identity do not preclude such use. The labeling of the dry beverage base shall bear adequate directions for use, and the additives shall be used in such an amount that the finished beverage or fruit juice drink will contain not in excess of a total of 10 parts per million of the dioctyl sodium sulfosuccinate-block copolymer combination.

[42 FR 14491, Mar. 15, 1977, as amended at 49 FR 10105, Mar. 19, 1984]

§ 172.811 Glyceryl tristearate.

The food additive glyceryl tristearate may be safely used in food in accordance with the following prescribed conditions:

(a) The food additive (CAS Reg. No. 555–43–1) is prepared by reacting stearic acid with glycerol in the presence of a suitable catalyst.

(b) The food additive meets the following specifications:

Acid number: Not to exceed 1.0.
Iodine number: Not to exceed 1.0.
Saponification number: 186–192.
Hydroxyl number: Not to exceed 5.0.
Free glycerol content: Not to exceed 0.5 percent.
Unsaponifiable matter: Not to exceed 0.5 percent.
Melting point (Class II): 69 °C–73 °C.

(c) The additive is used or intended for use as follows when standards of identity established under section 401 of the Act do not preclude such use:

Uses	Limitations
1. As a crystallization accelerator in cocoa products, in imitation chocolate, and in compound coatings.	Not to exceed 1 percent of the combined weight of the formulation.
2. As a formulation aid as defined in § 170.3(o)(14) of this chapter, lubricant and release agent as defined in § 170.3(o)(18) of this chapter, and surface-finishing agent as defined in § 170.3(o)(30) of this chapter in food.	Not to exceed 0.5 percent.
3. As a formulation aid as defined in § 170.3(o)(14) of this chapter in confections.	Not to exceed 3.0 percent of the combined weight of the formulation.
4. As a formulation aid as defined in § 170.3(o)(14) of this chapter in fats and oils as defined in § 170.3 (n)(12) of this chapter.	Not to exceed 1.0 percent of the combined weight of the formulation.
5. As a winterization and fractionation aid in fat and oil processing.	Not to exceed 0.5 percent by weight of the processed fat or oil.

(d) To assure safe use of the additive:

(1) In addition to the other information required by the act, the label or labeling of the additive shall bear the name of the additive.

(2) The label of the additive shall bear adequate directions to provide a final product that complies with the limitations prescribed in paragraph (c) of this section.

[53 FR 21632, June 9, 1988, as amended at 59 FR 24924, May 13, 1994]

§ 172.812 Glycine.

The food additive glycine may be safely used for technological purposes in food in accordance with the following prescribed conditions:

(a) The additive complies with the specifications of the "Food Chemicals Codex," 3d Ed. (1981), p. 140, which is incorporated by reference. Copies may be obtained from the National Academy Press, 2101 Constitution Ave. NW., Washington, DC 20418, or may be examined at the National Archives and Records Administration (NARA). For information on the availability of this material at NARA, call 202–741–6030, or go to: *http://www.archives.gov/federal_register/code_of_federal_regulations/ibr_locations.html.*

(b) The additive is used or intended for use as follows:

Uses	Limitations
As a masking agent for the bitter aftertaste of saccharin used in manufactured beverages and beverage bases.	Not to exceed 0.2 percent in the finished beverage.
As a stabilizer in mono- and diglycerides prepared by the glycerolysis of edible fats or oils.	Not to exceed 0.02 percent of the mono- and diglycerides.

(c) To assure safe use of the additive, in addition to the other information required by the Act:

(1) The labeling of the additive shall bear adequate directions for use of the additive in compliance with the provisions of this section.

(2) The labeling of beverage bases containing the additive shall bear adequate directions for use to provide that beverages prepared therefrom shall contain no more than 0.2 percent glycine.

[42 FR 14491, Mar. 15, 1977, as amended at 49 FR 10105, Mar. 19, 1984]

§ 172.814 Hydroxylated lecithin.

The food additive hydroxylated lecithin may be safely used as an emulsifier in foods in accordance with the following conditions:

(a) The additive is obtained by the treatment of lecithin in one of the following ways, under controlled conditions whereby the separated fatty acid fraction of the resultant product has an acetyl value of 30 to 38:

(1) With hydrogen peroxide, benzoyl peroxide, lactic acid, and sodium hydroxide.

(2) With hydrogen peroxide, acetic acid, and sodium hydroxide.

(b) It is used or intended for use, in accordance with good manufacturing practice, as an emulsifier in foods, except for those standardized foods that do not provide for such use.

(c) To assure safe use of the additive, the label of the food additive container shall bear, in addition to the other information required by the Act:

(1) The name of the additive, "hydroxylated lecithin".

(2) Adequate directions for its use.

§ 172.816 Methyl glucoside-coconut oil ester.

Methyl glucoside-coconut oil ester may be safely used in food in accordance with the following conditions:

(a) It is the methyl glucoside-coconut oil ester having the following specifications:

Acid number: 10–20
Hydroxyl number: 200–300
pH (5% aqueous): 4.8–5.0
Saponification number: 178–190

(b) It is used or intended for use as follows:

(1) As an aid in crystallization of sucrose and dextrose at a level not to exceed the minimum quantity required to produce its intended effect.

(2) As a surfactant in molasses at a level not to exceed 320 parts per million in the molasses.

§ 172.818 Oxystearin.

The food additive oxystearin may be safely used in foods, when such use is not precluded by standards of identity in accordance with the following conditions:

(a) The additive is a mixture of the glycerides of partially oxidized stearic and other fatty acids obtained by heating hydrogenated cottonseed or soybean oil under controlled conditions, in the presence of air and a suitable catalyst which is not a food additive as so defined. The resultant product meets the following specifications:

Acid number: Maximum 15.

Iodine number: Maximum 15.
Saponification number: 225–240.
Hydroxyl number: 30–45.
Unsaponifiable material: Maximum 0.8 percent.
Refractive index (butyro): 60±1 at 48 °C.

(b) It is used or intended for use as a crystallization inhibitor in vegetable oils and as a release agent in vegetable oils and vegetable shortenings, whereby the additive does not exceed 0.125 percent of the combined weight of the oil or shortening.

(c) To insure safe use of the additive, the label and labeling of the additive container shall bear, in addition to the other information required by the Act:

(1) The name of the additive.

(2) Adequate directions to provide an oil or shortening that complies with the limitations prescribed in paragraph (b) of this section.

§ 172.820 Polyethylene glycol (mean molecular weight 200–9,500).

Polyethylene glycol identified in this section may be safely used in food in accordance with the following prescribed conditions:

(a) *Identity*. (1) The additive is an addition polymer of ethylene oxide and water with a mean molecular weight of 200 to 9,500.

(2) It contains no more than 0.2 percent total by weight of ethylene and diethylene glycols when tested by the analytical methods prescribed in paragraph (b) of this section.

(b) *Analytical method*. (1) The analytical method prescribed in the National Formulary XV (1980), page 1244, for polyethylene glycol 400 shall be used to determine the total ethylene and diethylene glycol content of polyethylene glycols having mean molecular weights of 450 or higher.

(2) The following analytical method shall be used to determine the total ethylene and diethylene glycol content of polyethylene glycols having mean molecular weights below 450.

ANALYTICAL METHOD

ETHYLENE GLYCOL AND DIETHYLENE GLYCOL CONTENT OF POLYETHYLENE GLYCOLS

The analytical method for determining ethylene glycol and diethylene glycol is as follows:

APPARATUS

Gas chromatograph with hydrogen flame ionization detector (Varian Aerograph 600 D or equivalent). The following conditions shall be employed with the Varian Aerograph 600 D gas chromatograph:

Column temperature: 165 °C.

Inlet temperature: 260 °C.

Carrier gas (nitrogen) flow rate: 70 milliliters per minute.

Hydrogen and air flow to burner: Optimize to give maximum sensitivity.

Sample size: 2 microliters.

Elution time: Ethylene glycol: 2.0 minutes. Diethylene glycol: 6.5 minutes.

Recorder: −0.5 to +1.05 millivolt, full span, 1 second full response time.

Syringe: 10-microliter (Hamilton 710 N or equivalent).

Chromatograph column: 5 feet × ⅛ inch. I.D. stainless steel tube packed with sorbitol (Mathieson-Coleman-Bell 2768 Sorbitol SX850, or equivalent) 12 percent in H_2O by weight on 60–80 mesh nonacid washed diatomaceous earth (Chromosorb W. Johns-Manville, or equivalent).

REAGENTS AND MATERIALS

Carrier gas, nitrogen: Commercial grade in cylinder equipped with reducing regulator to provide 50 p.s.i.g. to the gas chromatograph.

Ethylene glycol: Commercial grade. Purify if necessary, by distillation.

Diethylene glycol: Commercial grade. Purify, if necessary, by distillation.

Glycol standards: Prepare chromatographic standards by dissolving known amounts of ethylene glycol and diethylene glycol in water. Suitable concentrations for standardization range from 1 to 6 milligrams of each component per milliliter (for example 10 milligrams diluted to volume in a 10-milliliter volumetric flask is equivalent to 1 milligram per milliliter).

STANDARDIZATION

Inject a 2-microliter aliquot of the glycol standard into the gas chromatograph employing the conditions described above. Measure the net peak heights for the ethylene glycol and for the diethylene glycol. Record the values as follows:

A=Peak height in millimeters of the ethylene glycol peak.

B=milligrams of ethylene glycol per milliliter of standard solution.

C=Peak height in millimeters of the diethylene glycol peak.

D=Milligrams of diethylene glycol per milliliter of standard solution.

PROCEDURE

Weigh approximately 4 grams of polyethylene glycol sample accurately into a 10-milliliter volumetric flask. Dilute to volume with water. Mix the solution thoroughly and inject a 2-microliter aliquot into the gas chromatograph. Measure the heights, in millimeters, of the ethylene glycol peak and of the diethylene glycol peak and record as E and F, respectively.

Percent ethylene glycol=(E×B)/(A×sample weight in grams)

Percent diethylene glycol=(F×D)/(C×sample weight in grams)

(c) *Uses.* It may be used, except in milk or preparations intended for addition to milk, as follows:

(1) As a coating, binder, plasticizing agent, and/or lubricant in tablets used for food.

(2) As an adjuvant to improve flavor and as a bodying agent in nonnutritive sweeteners identified in §180.37 of this chapter.

(3) As an adjuvant in dispersing vitamin and/or mineral preparations.

(4) As a coating on sodium nitrite to inhibit hygroscopic properties.

(d) *Limitations.* (1) It is used in an amount not greater than that required to produce the intended physical or technical effect.

(2) A tolerance of zero is established for residues of polyethylene glycol in milk.

[42 FR 14491, Mar. 15, 1977, as amended at 49 FR 10105, Mar. 19, 1984]

§ 172.822 Sodium lauryl sulfate.

The food additive sodium lauryl sulfate may be safely used in food in accordance with the following conditions:

(a) The additive meets the following specifications:

(1) It is a mixture of sodium alkyl sulfates consisting chiefly of sodium lauryl sulfate [$CH_2(CH_2)_{10}CH_2OSO_2Na$].

(2) It has a minimum content of 90 percent sodium alkyl sulfates.

(b) It is used or intended for use:

(1) As an emulsifier in or with egg whites whereby the additive does not exceed the following limits:

Egg white solids, 1,000 parts per million.
Frozen egg whites, 125 parts per million.
Liquid egg whites, 125 parts per million.

(2) As a whipping agent at a level not to exceed 0.5 percent by weight of gelatine used in the preparation of marshmallows.

(3) As a surfactant in:

(i) Fumaric acid-acidulated dry beverage base whereby the additive does not exceed 25 parts per million of the finished beverage and such beverage base is not for use in a food for which a standard of identity established under section 401 of the Act precludes such use.

(ii) Fumaric acid-acidulated fruit juice drinks whereby the additive does not exceed 25 parts per million of the finished fruit juice drink and it is not used in a fruit juice drink for which a standard of identity established under section 401 of the Act precludes such use.

(4) As a wetting agent at a level not to exceed 10 parts per million in the partition of high and low melting fractions of crude vegetable oils and animal fats, provided that the partition step is followed by a conventional refining process that includes alkali neutralization and deodorization of the fats and oils.

(c) To insure the safe use of the additive, the label of the food additive container shall bear, in addition to the other information required by the Act:

(1) The name of the additive, sodium lauryl sulfate.

(2) Adequate use directions to provide a final product that complies with the limitations prescribed in paragraph (b) of this section.

[42 FR 14491, Mar. 15, 1977, as amended at 43 FR 18668, May 2, 1978]

§ 172.824 Sodium mono- and dimethyl naphthalene sulfonates.

The food additive sodium mono- and dimethyl naphthalene sulfonates may be safely used in accordance with the following prescribed conditions:

(a) The additive has a molecular weight range of 245–260.

(b) The additive is used or intended for use:

(1) In the crystallization of sodium carbonate in an amount not to exceed 250 parts per million of the sodium carbonate. Such sodium carbonate is used or intended for use in potable water systems to reduce hardness and aid in sedimentation and coagulation by raising the pH for the efficient utilization of other coagulation materials.

(2) As an anticaking agent in sodium nitrite at a level not in excess of 0.1 percent by weight thereof for authorized uses in cured fish and meat.

(c) In addition to the general labeling requirements of the Act:

(1) Sodium carbonate produced in accordance with paragraph (b)(1) of this section shall be labeled to show the presence of the additive and its label or labeling shall bear adequate directions for use.

(2) Sodium nitrite produced in accordance with paragraph (b)(2) of this section shall bear the labeling required by § 172.175 and a statement declaring the presence of sodium mono- and dimethyl naphthalene sulfonates.

[42 FR 14491, Mar. 15, 1977, as amended at 63 FR 7069, Feb. 12, 1998]

§ 172.826 Sodium stearyl fumarate.

Sodium stearyl fumarate may be safely used in food in accordance with the following conditions:

(a) It contains not less than 99 percent sodium stearyl fumarate calculated on the anhydrous basis, and not more than 0.25 percent sodium stearyl maleate.

(b) The additive is used or intended for use:

(1) As a dough conditioner in yeast-leavened bakery products in an amount not to exceed 0.5 percent by weight of the flour used.

(2) As a conditioning agent in dehydrated potatoes in an amount not to exceed 1 percent by weight thereof.

(3) As a stabilizing agent in nonyeast-leavened bakery products in an amount not to exceed 1 percent by weight of the flour used.

(4) As a conditioning agent in processed cereals for cooking in an amount not to exceed 1 percent by weight of the dry cereal, except for foods for which standards of identity preclude such use.

(5) As a conditioning agent in starch-thickened or flour-thickened foods in an amount not to exceed 0.2 percent by weight of the food.

§ 172.828 Acetylated monoglycerides.

The food additive acetylated monoglycerides may be safely used in or on food in accordance with the following prescribed conditions:

(a) The additive is manufactured by:

(1) The interesterification of edible fats with triacetin and in the presence of catalytic agents that are not food additives or are authorized by regulation, followed by a molecular distillation or by steam stripping; or

(2) The direct acetylation of edible monoglycerides with acetic anhydride without the use of catalyst or molecular distillation, and with the removal by vacuum distillation, if necessary, of the acetic acid, acetic anhydride, and triacetin.

(b) The food additive has a Reichert-Meissl value of 75–200 and an acid value of less than 6.

(c) The food additive is used at a level not in excess of the amount reasonably required to produce its intended effect in food, or in food-processing, food-packing, or food-storage equipment.

[42 FR 14491, Mar. 15, 1977, as amended at 50 FR 3508, Jan. 25, 1985]

§ 172.829 Neotame.

(a) Neotame is the chemical *N*-[*N*-(3,3-dimethylbutyl)-L-α-aspartyl]-L-phenylalanine-1-methyl ester (CAS Reg. No. 165450–17–9).

(b) Neotame meets the following specifications when it is tested according to the methods described or referenced in the document entitled "Specifications and Analytical Methods for Neotame" dated April 3, 2001, by the NutraSweet Co., 699 North Wheeling Rd., Mount Prospect, IL 60056. The Director of the Office of the Federal Register has approved the incorporation by reference of this material in accordance with 5 U.S.C. 552(a) and 1 CFR part 51. Copies are available from the Office of Food Additive Safety (HFS–200), Center for Food Safety and Applied Nutrition, 5100 Paint Branch Pkwy., College Park, MD 20740. Copies may be examined at the Center for Food Safety and Applied Nutrition's Library, 5100 Paint Branch Pkwy., rm. 1C–100, College Park, MD 20740, or at the National Archives and Records Administration (NARA). For information on the availability of this material at NARA, call 202–741–6030, or go to: *http://www.archives.gov/federal_register/code_of_federal_regulations/ibr_locations.html.*

(1) Assay for neotame, not less than 97.0 percent and not more than 102.0 percent on a dry basis.

(2) Free dipeptide acid (*N*-[*N*-(3,3-dimethylbutyl)-L-α-aspartyl]-L-phenylalanine), not more than 1.5 percent.

(3) Other related substances, not more than 2.0 percent.

(4) Lead, not more than 2.0 milligrams per kilogram.

(5) Water, not more than 5.0 percent.

(6) Residue on ignition, not more than 0.2 percent

(7) Specific rotation, determined at 20 °C $[\alpha]_D$: −40.0° to 43.4° calculated on a dry basis.

(c) The food additive neotame may be safely used as a sweetening agent and flavor enhancer in foods generally, except in meat and poultry, in accordance with current good manufacturing practice, in an amount not to exceed that reasonably required to accomplish the intended technical effect, in foods for which standards of identity established under section 401 of the Federal Food, Drug, and Cosmetic Act do not preclude such use.

(d) When neotame is used as a sugar substitute tablet, L-leucine may be used as a lubricant in the manufacture of tablets at a level not to exceed 3.5 percent of the weight of the tablet.

(e) If the food containing the additive purports to be or is represented to be for special dietary use, it shall be labeled in compliance with part 105 of this chapter.

[67 FR 45310, July 9, 2002]

§ 172.830 Succinylated monoglycerides.

The food additive succinylated monoglycerides may be safely used in food in accordance with the following prescribed conditions:

(a) The additive is a mixture of semi- and neutral succinic acid esters of mono- and diglycerides produced by the succinylation of a product obtained by the glycerolysis of edible fats and oils, or by the direct esterification of glycerol with edible fat-forming fatty acids.

(b) The additive meets the following specifications:

Succinic acid content: 14.8%–25.6%
Melting point: 50 °C–60 °C.
Acid number: 70–120

(c) The additive is used or intended for use in the following foods:

(1) As an emulsifier in liquid and plastic shortenings at a level not to exceed 3 percent by weight of the shortening.

(2) As a dough conditioner in bread baking, when such use is permitted by an appropriate food standard, at a level not to exceed 0.5 percent by weight of the flour used.

§ 172.831 Sucralose.

(a) Sucralose is the chemical 1,6-dichloro-1,6-dideoxy-β-D-fructofuranosyl-4-chloro-4-deoxy-α-D-galactopyranoside (CAS Reg. No. 56038–13–2).

(b) The additive meets the specifications of the "Food Chemicals Codex," 4th ed. (1996), pp. 398–400, which is incorporated by reference in accordance with 5 U.S.C. 552(a) and 1 CFR part 51. Copies are available from the Office of Food Additive Safety (HFS–200), Center for Food Safety and Applied Nutrition, Food and Drug Administration, 5100 Paint Branch Pkwy., College Park, MD 20740, 240–402–1200, or may be examined at the Center for Food Safety and Applied Nutrition's Library, 5100 Paint Branch Pkwy., College Park, MD 20740, or at the National Archives and Records Administration (NARA). For information on the availability of this material at NARA, call 202–741–6030, or go to: *http://www.archives.gov/federal_register/code_of_federal_regulations/ibr_locations.html.*

(c) The additive may be used as a sweetener in foods generally, in accordance with current good manufacturing practice in an amount not to exceed that reasonably required to accomplish the intended effect.

(d) If the food containing the additive purports to be or is represented to be for special dietary use, it shall be labeled in compliance with part 105 of this chapter.

[63 FR 16433, Apr. 3, 1998, as amended at 64 FR 43909, Aug. 12, 1999; 78 FR 14665, Mar. 7, 2013]

§ 172.832 Monoglyceride citrate.

A food additive that is a mixture of glyceryl monooleate and its citric acid monoester manufactured by the reaction of glyceryl monooleate with citric acid under controlled conditions may be safely used as a synergist and solubilizer for antioxidants in oils and fats, when used in accordance with the conditions prescribed in this section.

(a) The food additive meets the following specifications:

Acid number, 70–100.
Total citric acid (free and combined), 14 percent–17 percent.

(b) It is used, or intended for use, in antioxidant formulations for addition to oils and fats whereby the additive does not exceed 200 parts per million of the combined weight of the oil or fat and the additive.

(c) To assure safe use of the additive:

(1) The container label shall bear, in addition to the other information required by the Act, the name of the additive.

(2) The label or accompanying labeling shall bear adequate directions for the use of the additive which, if followed, will result in a food that complies with the requirements of this section.

§ 172.833 Sucrose acetate isobutyrate (SAIB).

Sucrose acetate isobutyrate may be safely used in foods in accordance with the following prescribed conditions:

(a) Sucrose acetate isobutyrate (CAS Reg. No. 27216–37–1), or SAIB, is the chemical *alpha*-D-glucopyranoside, O-acetyl-tris-O-(2-methyl-1-oxopropyl)-*beta*-D-fructofuranosyl, acetate tris(2-methyl propanoate).

(b) SAIB, a pale, straw-colored liquid, meets the following specifications: (1) Assay: Not less than 98.8 percent and not more than 101.9 percent, based on the following formula:

$$\text{Assay} = ((\text{SV } 0.10586) \div 56.1) \times 100$$

Where SV = Saponification value

(2) Saponification value: 524–540 determined using 1 gram of sample by the "Guide to Specifications for General Notices, General Analytical Techniques, Identification Tests, Test Solutions, and Other Reference Materials," in the "Compendium of Food Additive Specifications, Addendum 4, Food and Agriculture Organization of the United Nations (FAO), Food and Nutrition Paper 5, Revision 2" (1991), pp. 203 and 204, which is incorporated by reference, in accordance with 5 U.S.C. 552(a) and 1 CFR part 51. Copies are available from the Office of Food Additive Safety (HFS–200), Center for Food Safety and Applied Nutrition, Food and Drug Administration, 5100 Paint Branch Pkwy., College Park, MD 20740, 240–402–1200, or may be examined at the Center for Food Safety and Applied Nutrition's Library, 5100 Paint Branch Pkwy., College Park, MD 20740, or at the National Archives and Records Administration (NARA). For information on the availability of this material at NARA, call 202–741–6030, or go to: *http://www.archives.gov/federal_register/code_of_federal_regulations/ibr_locations.html.*

(3) Acid value: Not to exceed 0.20 determined using 50 grams of sample by the "Guide to Specifications for General Notices, General Analytical Techniques, Identification Tests, Test Solutions, and Other Reference Materials," in the "Compendium of Food Additive Specifications, Addendum 4, FAO Food and Nutrition Paper 5, Revision 2," p. 189 (1991), which is incorporated by reference; see paragraph (b)(2) of this section for availability of the incorporation by reference.

(4) Lead: Not to exceed 1.0 milligrams/kilogram determined by the "Atomic Absorption Spectrophotometric Graphite Furnace Method, Method I," in the "Food Chemicals Codex," 4th ed. (1996), pp. 763 and 764, with an attached modification to the sample digestion section in Appendix III.B (July 1996), which is incorporated by reference. Copies are available from the National Academy Press, 2101 Constitution Ave. NW., Box 285, Washington, DC 20055 (Internet *http://www.nap.edu*), or may be examined at the Center for Food Safety and Applied Nutrition's Library, 5100 Paint Branch Pkwy., College Park, MD 20740, or at the National Archives and Records Administration (NARA). For information on the availability of this material at NARA, call 202–741–6030, or go to: *http://www.archives.gov/federal_register/code_of_federal_regulations/ibr_locations.html.*

(5) Triacetin: Not to exceed 0.10 percent determined by gas chromatography as described in the "Guide to Specifications for General Notices,

General Analytical Techniques, Identification Tests, Test Solutions, and Other Reference Materials,'' in the ''Compendium of Food Additive Specifications, Addendum 4, FAO Food and Nutrition Paper 5, Revision 2,'' (1991), pp. 13–26, which is incorporated by reference; see paragraph (b)(2) of this section for availability of the incorporation by reference.

(c) The food additive is used as a stabilizer (as defined in §170.3(o)(28) of this chapter) of emulsions of flavoring oils in nonalcoholic beverages.

(d) The total SAIB content of a beverage containing the additive does not exceed 300 milligrams/kilogram of the finished beverage.

[64 FR 29958, June 4, 1999; 64 FR 43072, Aug. 9, 1999, as amended at 78 FR 14665, Mar. 7, 2013]

§ 172.834 Ethoxylated mono- and diglycerides.

The food additive ethoxylated mono- and diglycerides (polyoxyethylene (20) mono- and diglycerides of fatty acids) (polyglycerate 60) may be safely used in food in accordance with the following prescribed conditions:

(a) The food additive is manufactured by:

(1) Glycerolysis of edible fats primarily composed of stearic, palmitic, and myristic acids; or

(2) Direct esterification of glycerol with a mixture of primarily stearic, palmitic, and myristic acids;

to yield a product with less than 0.3 acid number and less than 0.2 percent water, which is then reacted with ethylene oxide.

(b) The additive meets the following specifications:

Saponification number, 65–75.
Acid number, 0–2.
Hydroxyl number, 65–80.
Oxyethylene content, 60.5–65.0 percent.

(c) The additive is used or intended for use in the following foods when standards of identity established under section 401 of the Act do not preclude such use:

Use	Limitations
1. As an emulsifier in pan-release agents for and as a dough conditioner in yeast-leavened bakery products.	Not to exceed levels required to produce the intended effects, total not to exceed 0.5 percent by weight of the flour used.
2. As an emulsifier in cakes and cake mixes.	Not to exceed 0.5 percent by weight of the dry ingredients.
3. As an emulsifier in whipped vegetable oil toppings and topping mixes.	Not to exceed 0.45 percent by weight of the finished whipped vegetable oil toppings.
4. As an emulsifier in icings and icing mixes.	Not to exceed 0.5 percent by weight of the finished icings.
5. As an emulsifier in frozen desserts.	Not to exceed 0.2 percent by weight of the finished frozen desserts.
6. As an emulsifier in edible vegetable fat-water emulsions intended for use as substitutes for milk or cream in beverage coffee.	Not to exceed 0.4 percent by weight of the finished vegetable fat-water emulsions.

(d) When the name ''polyglycerate 60'' is used in labeling it shall be followed by either ''polyoxyethylene (20) mono-and diglycerides of fatty acids'' or ''ethoxylated mono- and diglycerides'' in parentheses.

[42 FR 14491, Mar. 15, 1977, as amended at 42 FR 37973, July 26, 1977; 50 FR 49536, Dec. 3, 1985]

§ 172.836 Polysorbate 60.

The food additive polysorbate 60 (polyoxyethylene (20) sorbitan monostearate) which is a mixture of polyoxyethylene ethers of mixed partial stearic and palmitic acid esters of sorbitol anhydrides and related compounds, may be safely used in food in accordance with the following prescribed conditions:

(a) The food additive is manufactured by reacting stearic acid (usually containing associated fatty acids, chiefly palmitic) with sorbitol to yield a product with a maximum acid number of 10 and a maximum water content of 0.2 percent, which is then reacted with ethylene oxide.

(b) The food additive meets the following specifications:

Saponification number 45–55.
Acid number 0–2.
Hydroxyl number 81–96.
Oxyethylene content 65 percent–69.5 percent.

(c) It is used or intended for use as follows:

(1) As an emulsifier in whipped edible oil topping with or without one or a combination of the following:

(i) Sorbitan monostearate;

(ii) Polysorbate 65;

(iii) Polysorbate 80;

whereby the maximum amount of the additive or additives used does not exceed 0.4 percent of the weight of the finished whipped edible oil topping; except that a combination of the additive with sorbitan monostearate may be used in excess of 0.4 percent, provided that the amount of the additive does not exceed 0.77 percent and the amount of sorbitan monostearate does not exceed 0.27 percent of the weight of the finished whipped edible oil topping.

(2) As an emulsifier in cakes and cake mixes, with or without one or a combination of the following:

(i) Polysorbate 65.

(ii) Sorbitan monostearate.

When used alone, the maximum amount of polysorbate 60 shall not exceed 0.46 percent of the cake or cake mix, on a dry-weight basis. When used with polysorbate 65 and/or sorbitan monostearate, it shall not exceed 0.46 percent, nor shall the polysorbate 65 exceed 0.32 percent or the sorbitan monostearate exceed 0.61 percent, and no combination of these emulsifiers shall exceed 0.66 percent of the cake or cake mix, all calculated on a dry-weight basis.

(3) As an emulsifier, alone or in combination with sorbitan monostearate, in nonstandardized confectionery coatings and standardized cacao products specified in §§ 163.123, 163.130, 163.135, 163.140, 163.145, and 163.150 of this chapter, as follows:

(i) It is used alone in an amount not to exceed 0.5 percent of the weight of the finished nonstandardized confectionery coating or standardized cacao product.

(ii) It is used with sorbitan monostearate in any combination of up to 0.5 percent of polysorbate 60 and up to 1 percent of sorbitan monostearate: *Provided*, That the total combination does not exceed 1 percent of the weight of the finished nonstandardized confectionery coating or standardized cacao product.

(4) [Reserved]

(5) As an emulsifier in cake icings and cake fillings, with or without one or a combination of the following:

(i) Polysorbate 65.

(ii) Sorbitan monostearate.

When used alone, the maximum amount of polysorbate 60 shall not exceed 0.46 percent of the weight of the cake icings and cake fillings. When used with polysorbate 65 and/or sorbitan monostearate, it shall not exceed 0.46 percent, nor shall the polysorbate 65 exceed 0.32 percent or the sorbitan monostearate exceed 0.7 percent, and no combination of these emulsifiers shall exceed 1 percent of the weight of the cake icing or cake filling.

(6) To impart greater opacity to sugar-type confection coatings whereby the maximum amount of the additive does not exceed 0.2 percent of the weight of the finished sugar coating.

(7) As an emulsifier in nonstandardized dressings whereby the maximum amount of the additive does not exceed 0.3 percent of the weight of the finished dressings.

(8) As an emulsifier, alone or in combination with polysorbate 80, in shortenings and edible oils intended for use in foods as follows, when standards of identity established under section 401 of the act do not preclude such use:

(i) It is used alone in an amount not to exceed 1 percent of the weight of the finished shortening or oil.

(ii) It is used with polysorbate 80 in any combination providing no more than 1 percent of polysorbate 60 and no more than 1 percent of polysorbate 80, provided that the total combination does not exceed 1 percent of the finished shortening or oil.

(iii) The 1-percent limitation specified in paragraph (c)(8) (i) and (ii) of this section may be exceeded in premix concentrates of shortening or edible oil if the labeling complies with the requirements of paragraph (d) of this section.

(9) As an emulsifier in solid-state, edible vegetable fat-water emulsions intended for use as substitutes for milk or cream in beverage coffee, with or without one or a combination of the following:

(i) Polysorbate 65.

(ii) Sorbitan monostearate.

The maximum amount of the additive or additives shall not exceed 0.4 percent by weight of the finished edible vegetable fat-water emulsion.

(10) As a foaming agent in nonalcoholic mixes, to be added to alcoholic beverages in the preparation of mixed alcoholic drinks, at a level not to exceed 4.5 percent by weight of the nonalcoholic mix.

(11) As a dough conditioner in yeast-leavened bakery products in an amount not to exceed 0.5 percent by weight of the flour used.

(12) As an emulsifier, alone or in combination with sorbitan monostearate, in the minimum quantity required to accomplish the intended effect, in formulations of white mineral oil conforming with § 172.878 and/or petroleum wax conforming with § 172.886 for use as protective coatings on raw fruits and vegetables.

(13) As a dispersing agent in artificially sweetened gelatin desserts and in artificially sweetened gelatin dessert mixes, whereby the amount of the additive does not exceed 0.5 percent on a dry-weight basis.

(14) As an emulsifier in chocolate flavored syrups, whereby the maximum amount of the additive does not exceed 0.05 percent in the finished product.

(15) As a surfactant and wetting agent for natural and artificial colors in food as follows:

(i) In powdered soft drink mixes in an amount not to exceed 4.5 percent by weight of the mix.

(ii) In sugar-based gelatin dessert mixes in an amount not to exceed 0.5 percent by weight of the mix.

(iii) In artificially sweetened gelatin dessert mixes in an amount not to exceed 3.6 percent by weight of the mix.

(iv) In sugar-based pudding mixes in an amount not to exceed 0.5 percent by weight of the mix.

(v) In artificially sweetened pudding mixes in an amount not to exceed 0.5 percent by weight of the mix.

(16) As an emulsifier in ice cream, frozen custard, fruit sherbet, and nonstandardized frozen desserts when used alone or in combination with polysorbate 65 and/or polysorbate 80, whereby the maximum amount of the additives, alone or in combination, does not exceed 0.1 percent of the finished frozen dessert.

(d) To assure safe use of the additive, in addition to the other information required by the Act:

(1) The label of the additive and any intermediate premixes shall bear:

(i) The name of the additive.

(ii) A statement of the concentration or strength of the additive in any intermediate premixes.

(2) The label or labeling shall bear adequate directions to provide a final product that complies with the limitations prescribed in paragraph (c) of this section.

[42 FR 14491, Mar. 15, 1977, as amended at 43 FR 2871, Jan. 25, 1978; 45 FR 58836, Sept. 5, 1980; 46 FR 8466, Jan. 27, 1981; 64 FR 57976, Oct. 28, 1999]

§ 172.838 Polysorbate 65.

The food additive polysorbate 65 (polyoxyethylene (20) sorbitan tristearate), which is a mixture of polyoxyethylene ethers of mixed stearic acid esters of sorbitol anhydrides and related compounds, may be safely used in food in accordance with the following prescribed conditions:

(a) The food additive is manufactured by reacting stearic acid (usually containing associated fatty acids, chiefly palmitic) with sorbitol to yield a product with a maximum acid number of 15 and a maximum water content of 0.2 percent, which is then reacted with ethylene oxide.

(b) The food additive meets the following specifications:

Saponification number 88–98.
Acid number 0–2.
Hydroxyl number 44–60.
Oxyethylene content 46 percent–50 percent.

(c) The additive is used, or intended for use, as follows:

(1) As an emulsifier in ice cream, frozen custard, ice milk, fruit sherbet and nonstandardized frozen desserts when used alone or in combination with polysorbate 80, whereby the maximum amount of the additives, alone or in combination, does not exceed 0.1 percent of the finished frozen dessert.

(2) As an emulsifier in cakes and cake mixes, with or without one or a combination of the following:

(i) Sorbitan monostearate.

(ii) Polysorbate 60.

When used alone, the maximum amount of polysorbate 65 shall not exceed 0.32 percent of the cake or cake mix, on a dry-weight basis. When used with sorbitan monostearate and/or polysorbate 60, it shall not exceed 0.32 percent, nor shall the sorbitan monostearate exceed 0.61 percent or the polysorbate 60 exceed 0.46 percent, and no combination of these emulsifiers shall exceed 0.66 percent of the cake or cake mix, all calculated on a dry-weight basis.

(3) As an emulsifier in whipped edible oil topping with or without one or a combination of the following:

(i) Sorbitan monostearate;

(ii) Polysorbate 60;

(iii) Polysorbate 80;

whereby the maximum amount of the additive or additives used does not exceed 0.4 percent of the weight of the finished whipped edible oil topping.

(4) As an emulsifier in solid-state, edible vegetable fat-water emulsions intended for use as substitutes for milk or cream in beverage coffee, with or without one or a combination of the following:

(i) Sorbitan monostearate.

(ii) Polysorbate 60.

The maximum amount of the additive or additives shall not exceed 0.4 percent by weight of the finished edible vegetable fat-water emulsion.

(5) As an emulsifier in cake icings and cake fillings, with or without one or a combination of the following:

(i) Sorbitan monostearate.

(ii) Polysorbate 60.

When used alone, the maximum amount of polysorbate 65 shall not exceed 0.32 percent of the weight of the cake icing or cake filling. When used with sorbitan monostearate and/or polysorbate 60, it shall not exceed 0.32 percent, nor shall the sorbitan monostearate exceed 0.7 percent or the polysorbate 60 exceed 0.46 percent, and no combination of these emulsifiers shall exceed 1 percent of the weight of the cake icing or cake filling.

(d) To assure safe use of the additive, in addition to the other information required by the Act:

(1) The label of the additive and any intermediate premixes shall bear:

(i) The name of the additive.

(ii) A statement of the concentration or strength of the additive in any intermediate premixes.

(2) The label or labeling shall bear adequate directions to provide a final product that complies with the limitations prescribed in paragraph (c) of this section.

[42 FR 14491, Mar. 15, 1977, as amended at 43 FR 2871, Jan. 20, 1978]

§ 172.840 Polysorbate 80.

The food additive polysorbate 80 (polyoxyethylene (20) sorbitan monooleate), which is a mixture of polyoxyethylene ethers of mixed partial oleic acid esters of sorbitol anhydrides and related compounds, may be safely used in food in accordance with the following prescribed conditions:

(a) The food additive is manufactured by reacting oleic acid (usually containing associated fatty acids) with sorbitol to yield a product with a maximum acid number of 7.5 and a maximum water content of 0.5 percent, which is then reacted with ethylene oxide.

(b) The food additive meets the following specifications:

Saponification number 45–55.
Acid number 0–2.
Hydroxyl number 65–80.
Oxyethylene content 65 percent–69.5 percent.

(c) The additive is used or intended for use as follows:

(1) An emulsifier in ice cream, frozen custard, ice milk, fruit sherbet, and nonstandardized frozen desserts, when used alone or in combination with polysorbate 65 whereby the maximum amount of the additives, alone or in combination, does not exceed 0.1 percent of the finished frozen dessert.

(2) In yeast-defoamer formulations whereby the maximum amount of the additive does not exceed 4 percent of the finished yeast defoamer and the maximum amount of the additive in the yeast from such use does not exceed 4 parts per million.

(3) As a solubilizing and dispersing agent in pickles and pickle products, whereby the maximum amount of the additive does not exceed 500 parts per million.

(4) As a solubilizing and dispersing agent in:

(i) Vitamin-mineral preparations containing calcium caseinate in the absence of fat-soluble vitamins, whereby the maximum intake of polysorbate 80 shall not exceed 175 milligrams from the recommended daily dose of the preparations.

(ii) Fat-soluble vitamins in vitamin and vitamin-mineral preparations containing no calcium caseinate, whereby the maximum intake of polysorbate 80 shall not exceed 300 milligrams from the recommended daily dose of the preparations.

(iii) In vitamin-mineral preparations containing both calcium caseinate and fat-soluble vitamins, whereby the maximum intake of polysorbate 80 shall not exceed 475 milligrams from the recommended daily dose of the preparations.

(5) As a surfactant in the production of coarse crystal sodium chloride whereby the maximum amount of the additive in the finished sodium chloride does not exceed 10 parts per million.

(6) In special dietary foods, as an emulsifier for edible fats and oils, with directions for use which provide for the ingestion of not more than 360 milligrams of polysorbate 80 per day.

(7) As a solubilizing and dispersing agent for dill oil in canned spiced green beans, not to exceed 30 parts per million.

(8) As an emulsifier, alone or in combination with polysorbate 60, in shortenings and edible oils intended for use in foods as follows, when standards of identity established under section 401 of the act do not preclude such use:

(i) It is used alone in an amount not to exceed 1 percent of the weight of the finished shortening or oil.

(ii) It is used with polysorbate 60 in any combination providing no more than 1 percent of polysorbate 80 and no more than 1 percent of polysorbate 60, provided that the total combination does not exceed 1 percent of the finished shortening or oil.

(iii) The 1-percent limitation specified in paragraph (c)(8) (i) and (ii) of this section may be exceeded in premix concentrates of shortening or edible oil if the labeling complies with the requirements of paragraph (d) of this section.

(9) As an emulsifier in whipped edible oil topping with or without one or a combination of the following:

(i) Sorbitan monostearate;

(ii) Polysorbate 60;

(iii) Polysorbate 65;

whereby the maximum amount of the additive or additives used does not exceed 0.4 percent of the weight of the finished whipped edible oil topping.

(10) It is used as a wetting agent in scald water for poultry defeathering, followed by potable water rinse. The concentration of the additive in the scald water does not exceed 0.0175 percent.

(11) As a dispersing agent in gelatin desserts and in gelatin dessert mixes, whereby the amount of the additive does not exceed 0.082 percent on a dry-weight basis.

(12) As an adjuvant added to herbicide use and plant-growth regulator use dilutions by a grower or applicator prior to application of such dilutions to the growing crop. Residues resulting from such use are exempt from the requirement of a tolerance. When so used or intended for use, the additive shall be exempt from the requirements of paragraph (d)(1) of this section.

(13) As a defoaming agent in the preparation of the creaming mixture for cottage cheese and lowfat cottage cheese, as identified in §§ 133.128 and 133.131 of this chapter, respectively, whereby the amount of the additive does not exceed .008 percent by weight of the finished products.

(14) As a surfactant and wetting agent for natural and artificial colors for use in barbecue sauce where the level of the additive does not exceed 0.005 percent by weight of the barbecue sauce.

(d) To assure safe use of the additive, in addition to the other information required by the Act:

(1) The label of the additive and any intermediate premixes shall bear:

(i) The name of the additive.

(ii) A statement of the concentration or strength of the additive in any intermediate premixes.

(2) The label or labeling shall bear adequate directions to provide a final product that complies with the limitations prescribed in paragraph (c) of this section.

[42 FR 14491, Mar. 15, 1977, as amended at 43 FR 2871, Jan. 20, 1978; 45 FR 58835, Sept. 5, 1980; 46 FR 8466, Jan. 27, 1981]

§ 172.841 Polydextrose.

Polydextrose as identified in this section may be safely used in food in accordance with the following prescribed conditions:

(a)(1) Polydextrose (CAS Reg. No. 68424–04–4) is a partially metabolizable water-soluble polymer prepared by the condensation of a melt which consists either of approximately 89 percent D-glucose, 10 percent sorbitol, and 1 percent citric acid or of approximately 90 percent D-glucose, 10 percent sorbitol, and 0.1 percent phosphoric acid, on a weight basis.

(2) Polydextrose may be partially neutralized with potassium hydroxide, or partially reduced by transition metal catalytic hydrogenation in aqueous solution.

(b) The additive meets the specifications of the "Food Chemicals Codex," 5th ed. (January 1, 2004), pp. 336–339, and the First Supplement to the 5th Edition of the Food Chemicals Codex (March 1, 2006), p. 37, which are incorporated by reference. The Director of the Office of the Federal Register approves this incorporation by reference in accordance with 5 U.S.C. 552(a) and 1 CFR part 51. You may obtain a copy from The National Academies Press, 500 Fifth St. NW., Washington, DC 20001 (Internet address *http://www.nap.edu*). You may inspect a copy at the Center for Food Safety and Applied Nutrition's Library, Food and Drug Administration, 5100 Paint Branch Pkwy., College Park, MD 20740, or at the National Archives and Records Administration (NARA). For information on the availability of this material at NARA, call 202–741–6030, or go to: *http://www.archives.gov/federal-register/cfr/ibr-locations.html.*

(c) When standards of identity established under section 401 of the act do not preclude such use, polydextrose may be used in accordance with current good manufacturing practices as a bulking agent, formulation aid, humectant, and texturizer in all foods, except meat and poultry, baby food, and infant formula.

(d) If the food containing the additive purports to be or is represented for special dietary uses, it shall be labeled in compliance with part 105 of this chapter.

(e) The label and labeling of food a single serving of which would be expected to exceed 15 grams of the additive shall bear the statement: "Sensitive individuals may experience a laxative effect from excessive consumption of this product".

[46 FR 30081, June 5, 1981, as amended at 59 FR 37421, July 22, 1994; 60 FR 54425, Oct. 24, 1995; 61 FR 14480, Apr. 2, 1996; 62 FR 30985, June 6, 1997; 63 FR 57597, Oct. 28, 1998; 65 FR 64605, Oct. 30, 2000; 65 FR 79719, Dec. 20, 2000; 72 FR 46564, Aug. 21, 2007]

§ 172.842 Sorbitan monostearate.

The food additive sorbitan monostearate, which is a mixture of partial stearic and palmitic acid esters of sorbitol anhydrides, may be safely used in or on food in accordance with the following prescribed conditions:

(a) The food additive is manufactured by reacting stearic acid (usually containing associated fatty acids, chiefly palmitic) with sorbitol to yield essentially a mixture of esters.

(b) The food additive meets the following specifications:

Saponification number, 147–157
Acid number, 5–10
Hydroxyl number, 235–260

(c) It is used or intended for use, alone or in combination with polysorbate 60 as follows:

(1) As an emulsifier in whipped edible oil topping with or without one or a combination of the following:

(i) Polysorbate 60;

(ii) Polysorbate 65;

(iii) Polysorbate 80;

whereby the maximum amount of the additive or additives used does not exceed 0.4 percent of the weight of the finished whipped edible oil topping; except that a combination of the additive with polysorbate 60 may be used in excess of 0.4 percent: *Provided,* That the amount of the additive does not exceed 0.27 percent and the amount of polysorbate 60 does not exceed 0.77 percent of the weight of the finished whipped edible oil topping.

(2) As an emulsifier in cakes and cake mixes, with or without one or a combination of the following:

(i) Polysorbate 65.

(ii) Polysorbate 60.

When used alone, the maximum amount of sorbitan monostearate shall not exceed 0.61 percent of the cake or cake mix, on a dry-weight basis. When used with polysorbate 65 and/or polysorbate 60, it shall not exceed 0.61 percent, nor shall the polysorbate 65 exceed 0.32 percent or the polysorbate 60 exceed 0.46 percent, and no combination of the emulsifiers shall exceed 0.66 percent of the weight of the cake or cake mix, calculated on a dry-weight basis.

(3) As an emulsifier, alone or in combination with polysorbate 60 in nonstandardized confectionery coatings and standardized cacao products specified in §§ 163.123, 163.130, 163.135, 163.140, 163.145, and 163.150 of this chapter, as follows:

(i) It is used alone in an amount not to exceed 1 percent of the weight of the finished nonstandardized confectionery coating or standardized cacao product.

(ii) It is used with polysorbate 60 in any combination of up to 1 percent sorbitan monostearate and up to 0.5 percent polysorbate 60 provided that the total combination does not exceed 1 percent of the weight of the finished nonstandardized confectionery coating or standardized cacao product.

(4) As an emulsifier in cake icings and cake fillings, with or without one or a combination of the following:

(i) Polysorbate 65.

(ii) Polysorbate 60.

When used alone, the maximum amount of sorbitan monostearate shall not exceed 0.7 percent of the weight of the cake icing or cake filling. When used with polysorbate 65 and/or polysorbate 60, it shall not exceed 0.7 percent, nor shall the polysorbate 65 exceed 0.32 percent or the polysorbate 60 exceed 0.46 percent, and no combination of these emulsifiers shall exceed 1 percent of the weight of the cake icing or cake filling.

(5) As an emulsifier in solid-state, edible vegetable fat-water emulsions intended for use as substitutes for milk or cream in beverage coffee, with or without one or a combination of the following:

(i) Polysorbate 60.

(ii) Polysorbate 65.

The maximum amount of the additive or additives shall not exceed 0.4 percent by weight of the finished edible vegetable fat-water emulsion.

(6) It is used alone as a rehydration aid in the production of active dry yeast in an amount not to exceed 1 percent by weight of the dry yeast.

(7) As an emulsifier, alone or in combination with polysorbate 60, in the minimum quantity required to accomplish the intended effect, in formulations of white mineral oil conforming with § 172.878 and/or petroleum wax conforming with § 172.886 for use as protective coatings on raw fruits and vegetables.

(d) To assure safe use of the additive, in addition to the other information required by the Act:

(1) The label of the additive and any intermediate premixes shall bear:

(i) The name of the additive.

(ii) A statement of the concentration or strength of the additive in any intermediate premixes.

(2) The label or labeling shall bear adequate directions to provide a final product that complies with the limitations prescribed in paragraph (c) of this section.

[42 FR 14491, Mar. 15, 1977, as amended at 43 FR 2871, Jan. 20, 1978]

§ 172.844 Calcium stearoyl-2-lactylate.

The food additive calcium stearoyl-2-lactylate may be safely used in or on food in accordance with the following prescribed conditions:

(a) The additive, which is a mixture of calcium salts of stearoyl lactylic acids and minor proportions of other calcium salts of related acids, is manufactured by the reaction of stearic acid and lactic acid and conversion to the calcium salts.

(b) The additive meets the following specifications:

Acid number, 50–86.
Calcium content, 4.2–5.2 percent.
Lactic acid content, 32–38 percent.
Ester number, 125–164.

(c) It is used or intended for use as follows:

(1) As a dough conditioner in yeast-leavened bakery products and prepared mixes for yeast-leavened bakery products in an amount not to exceed 0.5

part for each 100 parts by weight of flour used.

(2) As a whipping agent in:

(i) Liquid and frozen egg white at a level not to exceed 0.05 percent.

(ii) Dried egg white at a level not to exceed 0.5 percent.

(iii) Whipped vegetable oil topping at a level not to exceed 0.3 percent of the weight of the finished whipped vegetable oil topping.

(3) As a conditioning agent in dehydrated potatoes in an amount not to exceed 0.5 percent by weight thereof.

(d) To assure safe use of the additive:

(1) The label and labeling of the food additive and any intermediate premix prepared therefrom shall bear, in addition to the other information required by the act, the following:

(i) The name of the additive.

(ii) A statement of the concentration or strength of the additive in any intermediate premixes.

(2) The label or labeling of the food additive shall also bear adequate directions of use to provide a finished food that complies with the limitations prescribed in paragraph (c) of this section.

§ 172.846 Sodium stearoyl lactylate.

The food additive sodium stearoyl lactylate (CAS Reg. No. 25–383–997) may be safely used in food in accordance with the following prescribed conditions:

(a) The additive, which is a mixture of sodium salts of stearoyl lactylic acids and minor proportions of sodium salts of related acids, is manufactured by the reaction of stearic acid and lactic acid and conversion to the sodium salts.

(b) The additive meets the specifications of the "Food Chemicals Codex," 3d Ed. (1981), pp. 300–301, which is incorporated by reference. Copies may be obtained from the National Academy Press, 2101 Constitution Ave. NW., Washington, DC 20418, or may be examined at the National Archives and Records Administration (NARA). For information on the availability of this material at NARA, call 202–741–6030, or go to: *http://www.archives.gov/federal_register/code_of_federal_regulations/ibr_locations.html.*

(c) It is used or intended for use as follows when standards of identity established under section 401 of the Act do not preclude such use:

(1) As a dough strengthener, emulsifier, or processing aid in baked products, pancakes, and waffles, in an amount not to exceed 0.5 part for each 100 parts by weight of flour used.

(2) As a surface-active agent, emulsifier, or stabilizer in icings, fillings, puddings, and toppings, at a level not to exceed 0.2 percent by weight of the finished food.

(3) As an emulsifier or stabilizer in liquid and solid edible fat-water emulsions intended for use as substitutes for milk or cream in beverage coffee, at a level not to exceed 0.3 percent by weight of the finished edible fat-water emulsion.

(4) As a formulation aid, processing aid, or surface-active agent in dehydrated potatoes, in an amount not to exceed 0.5 percent of the dry weight of the food.

(5) As an emulsifier, stabilizer, or texturizer in snack dips, at a level not to exceed 0.2 percent by weight of the finished product.

(6) As an emulsifier, stabilizer, or texturizer in cheese substitutes and imitations and cheese product substitutes and imitations, at a level not to exceed 0.2 percent by weight of the finished food.

(7) As an emulsifier, stabilizer, or texturizer in sauces or gravies, and the products containing the same, in an amount not to exceed 0.25 percent by weight of the finished food.

(8) In prepared mixes for each of the foods listed in paragraphs (c) (1) through (7) of this section, provided the additive is used only as specified in each of those paragraphs.

(9) As an emulsifier, stabilizer, or texturizer in cream liqueur drinks, at a level not to exceed 0.5 percent by weight of the finished product.

[45 FR 51767, Aug. 5, 1980, as amended at 49 FR 10105, Mar. 19, 1984; 50 FR 49536, Dec. 3, 1985; 51 FR 1495, Jan. 14, 1986; 51 FR 3333, Jan. 27, 1986; 65 FR 60859, Oct. 13, 2000]

§ 172.848 Lactylic esters of fatty acids.

Lactylic esters of fatty acids may be safely used in food in accordance with the following prescribed conditions:

(a) They are prepared from lactic acid and fatty acids meeting the requirements of § 172.860(b) and/or oleic acid derived from tall oil fatty acids meeting the requirements of § 172.862.

(b) They are used as emulsifiers, plasticizers, or surface-active agents in the following foods, when standards of identity do not preclude their use:

Foods	Limitations
Bakery mixes	
Baked products	
Cake icings, fillings, and toppings	
Dehydrated fruits and vegetables	
Dehydrated fruit and vegetable juices.	
Edible vegetable fat-water emulsions.	As substitutes for milk or cream in beverage coffee.
Frozen desserts	
Liquid shortening	For household use.
Pancake mixes	
Precooked instant rice	
Pudding mixes	

(c) They are used in an amount not greater than required to produce the intended physical or technical effect, and they may be used with shortening and edible fats and oils when such are required in the foods identified in paragraph (b) of this section.

§ 172.850 Lactylated fatty acid esters of glycerol and propylene glycol.

The food additive lactylated fatty acid esters of glycerol and propylene glycol may be safely used in food in accordance with the following prescribed conditions:

(a) The additive is a mixture of esters produced by the lactylation of a product obtained by reacting edible fats or oils with propylene glycol.

(b) The additive meets the following specifications: Water insoluble combined lactic acid, 14–18 percent; and acid number, 12 maximum.

(c) It is used in amounts not in excess of that reasonably required to produce the intended physical effect as an emulsifier, plasticizer, or surface-active agent in food.

§ 172.852 Glyceryl-lacto esters of fatty acids.

Glyceryl-lacto esters of fatty acids (the lactic acid esters of mono- and diglycerides) may be safely used in food in accordance with the following prescribed conditions:

(a) They are manufactured from glycerin, lactic acid, and fatty acids conforming with § 172.860 and/or oleic acid derived from tall oil fatty acids conforming with § 172.862 and/or edible fats and oils.

(b) They are used in amounts not in excess of those reasonably required to accomplish their intended physical or technical effect as emulsifiers and plasticizers in food.

§ 172.854 Polyglycerol esters of fatty acids.

Polyglycerol esters of fatty acids, up to and including the decaglycerol esters, may be safely used in food in accordance with the following prescribed conditions:

(a) They are prepared from corn oil, cottonseed oil, lard, palm oil from fruit, peanut oil, safflower oil, sesame oil, soybean oil, and tallow and the fatty acids derived from these substances (hydrogenated and nonhydrogenated) meeting the requirements of § 172.860(b) and/or oleic acid derived from tall oil fatty acids meeting the requirements of § 172.862.

(b) They are used as emulsifiers in food, in amounts not greater than that required to produce the intended physical or technical effect.

(c) Polyglycerol esters of a mixture of stearic, oleic, and coconut fatty acids are used as a cloud inhibitor in vegetable and salad oils when use is not precluded by standards of identity. The fatty acids used in the production of the polyglycerol esters meet the requirements of § 172.860(b), and the polyglycerol esters are used at a level not in excess of the amount required to perform its cloud-inhibiting effect. Oleic acid derived from tall oil fatty acids conforming with § 172.862 may be used as a substitute for or together with the oleic acid permitted by this paragraph.

(d) Polyglycerol esters of butter oil fatty acids are used as emulsifiers in combination with other approved emulsifiers in dry, whipped topping base. The fatty acids used in the production of the polyglycerol esters meet the requirements of § 172.860(b), and the polyglycerol esters are used at a level not in excess of the amount required to perform their emulsifying effect.

§ 172.856 Propylene glycol mono- and diesters of fats and fatty acids.

Propylene glycol mono- and diesters of fats and fatty acids may be safely used in food, subject to the following prescribed conditions:

(a) They are produced from edible fats and/or fatty acids in compliance with § 172.860 and/or oleic acid derived from tall oil fatty acids in compliance with § 172.862.

(b) They are used in food in amounts not in excess of that reasonably required to produce their intended effect.

§ 172.858 Propylene glycol alginate.

The food additive propylene glycol alginate (CAS Reg. No. 9005–37–2) may be used as an emulsifier, flavoring adjuvant, formulation aid, stabilizer, surfactant, or thickener in foods in accordance with the following prescribed conditions:

(a) The additive meets the specifications of the Food Chemicals Codex, 3d Ed. (1981), p. 256, which is incorporated by reference (Copies are available from the National Academy Press, 2101 Constitution Ave. NW., Washington, DC 20418, or available for inspection at the National Archives and Records Administration (NARA). For information on the availability of this material at NARA, call 202–741–6030, or go to: *http://www.archives.gov/federal_register/code_of_federal_regulations/ibr_locations.html.*), and the additional specification that it shall have up to 85 percent of the carboxylic acid groups esterified with the remaining groups either free or neutralized.

(b) The additive is used or intended for use in the following foods as defined in § 170.3(n) of this chapter, when standards of identity established under section 401 of the act do not preclude such use:

(1) As a stabilizer in frozen dairy desserts, in fruit and water ices, and in confections and frostings at a level not to exceed 0.5 percent by weight of the finished product.

(2) As an emulsifier, flavoring adjuvant, stabilizer, or thickener in baked goods at a level not to exceed 0.5 percent by weight of the finished product.

(3) As an emulsifier, stabilizer, or thickener in cheeses at a level not to exceed 0.9 percent by weight of the finished product.

(4) As an emulsifier, stabilizer, or thickener in fats and oils at a level not to exceed 1.1 percent by weight of the finished product.

(5) As an emulsifier, stabilizer, or thickener in gelatins and puddings at a level not to exceed 0.6 percent by weight of the finished product.

(6) As a stabilizer or thickener in gravies and in sweet sauces at a level not to exceed 0.5 percent by weight of the finished product.

(7) As a stabilizer in jams and jellies at a level not to exceed 0.4 percent by weight of the finished product.

(8) As an emulsifier, stabilizer, or thickener in condiments and relishes at a level not to exceed 0.6 percent by weight of the finished product.

(9) As a flavoring adjunct or adjuvant in seasonings and flavors at a level not to exceed 1.7 percent by weight of the finished product.

(10) As an emulsifier, flavoring adjuvant, formulation aid, stabilizer or thickener, or surface active agent in other foods, where applicable, at a level not to exceed 0.3 percent by weight of the finished product.

(c) To ensure safe use of the additive, the label of the food additive container shall bear, in addition to the other information required by the act:

(1) The name of the additive, "propylene glycol alginate" or "propylene glycol ester of alginic acid".

(2) Adequate directions for use.

[47 FR 29950, July 9, 1982]

§ 172.859 Sucrose fatty acid esters.

Sucrose fatty acid esters identified in this section may be safely used in accordance with the following prescribed conditions:

(a) Sucrose fatty acid esters are the mono-, di-, and tri-esters of sucrose with fatty acids and are derived from sucrose and edible tallow or hydrogenated edible tallow or edible vegetable oils. The only solvents which may be used in the preparation of sucrose fatty acid esters are those generally recognized as safe in food or regulated for such use by an appropriate section in this part. Ethyl acetate or methyl ethyl ketone or dimethyl sulfoxide and isobutyl alcohol (2-methyl-1-

propanol) may be used in the preparation of sucrose fatty acid esters.

(b) Sucrose fatty acid esters meet the following specifications:

(1) The total content of mono-, di-, and tri-esters is not less than 80 percent as determined by a method title "Sucrose Fatty Acid Esters, Method of Assay," which is incorporated by reference. Copies are available from the Center for Food Safety and Applied Nutrition (HFS–200), Food and Drug Administration, 5100 Paint Branch Pkwy., College Park, MD 20740, or available for inspection at the National Archives and Records Administration (NARA). For information on the availability of this material at NARA, call 202–741–6030, or go to: *http://www.archives.gov/federal_register/code_of_federal_regulations/ibr_locations.html.*

(2) The free sucrose content is not more than 5 percent as determined by Test S.2 in the method titled "Sucrose Fatty Acid Esters, Method of Assay," which is incorporated by reference. The availability of this incorporation by reference is given in paragraph (b)(1) of this section.

(3) The acid value is not more than 6.

(4) The residue on ignition (sulfated ash) is not more than 2 percent.

(5) The total ethyl acetate content is not more than 350 parts per million as determined by a method titled "Determination of Ethyl Acetate," which is incorporated by reference. Copies are available from the Center for Food Safety and Applied Nutrition (HFS–200), Food and Drug Administration, 5100 Paint Branch Pkwy., College Park, MD 20740, or available for inspection at the National Archives and Records Administration (NARA). For information on the availability of this material at NARA, call 202–741–6030, or go to: *http://www.archives.gov/federal_register/code_of_federal_regulations/ibr_locations.html.*

(6) Arsenic is not more than 3 parts per million.

(7) Total heavy metal content (as Pb) is not more than 50 parts per million.

(8) Lead is not more than 10 parts per million.

(9) The total content of methyl ethyl ketone or of methanol shall not be more than 10 parts per million as determined by a method titled "Methyl Ethyl Ketone Test; Methyl Alcohol Test," which is incorporated by reference. Copies are available from the Center for Food Safety and Applied Nutrition (HFS–200), Food and Drug Administration, 5100 Paint Branch Pkwy., College Park, MD 20740, or available for inspection at the National Archives and Records Administration (NARA). For information on the availability of this material at NARA, call 202–741–6030, or go to: *http://www.archives.gov/federal_register/code_of_federal_regulations/ibr_locations.html.*

(10) The total dimethyl sulfoxide content is not more than 2 parts per million as determined by a method entitled "Determination of Dimethyl Sulfoxide," which is incorporated by reference. Copies are available from the Center for Food Safety and Applied Nutrition (HFS–200), Food and Drug Administration, 5100 Paint Branch Pkwy., College Park, MD 20740, or available for inspection at the National Archives and Records Administration (NARA). For information on the availability of this material at NARA, call 202–741–6030, or go to: *http://www.archives.gov/federal_register/code_of_federal_regulations/ibr_locations.html.*

(11) The total isobuytl alcohol (2-methyl-1-propanol) content is not more than 10 parts per million as determined by a method entitled "Determination of Isobutyl Alcohol," which is incorporated by reference. Copies are available from the Center for Food Safety and Applied Nutrition (HFS–200), Food and Drug Administration, 5100 Paint Branch Pkwy., College Park, MD 20740, or available for inspection at the National Archives and Records Administration (NARA). For information on the availability of this material at NARA, call 202–741–6030, or go to: *http://www.archives.gov/federal_register/code_of_federal_regulations/ibr_locations.html.*

(c) Sucrose fatty acid esters may be used as follows when standards of identity established under section 401 of the Federal Food, Drug, and Cosmetic Act do not preclude such use:

(1) As emulsifiers as defined in § 170.3(o)(8) of this chapter, or as stabilizers as defined in § 170.3(o)(28) of this chapter, in baked goods and baking mixes as defined in § 170.3(n)(1) of this chapter, in chewing gum as defined in § 170.3(n)(6) of this chapter, in coffee and tea beverages with added dairy ingredients and/or dairy product analogues, in confections and frostings as defined in § 170.3(n)(9) of this chapter, in dairy product analogues as defined in § 170.3(n)(10) of this chapter, in frozen dairy desserts and mixes as defined in § 170.3(n)(20) of this chapter, and in whipped milk products.

(2) As texturizers as defined in § 170.3(o)(32) of this chapter in biscuit mixes, in chewing gum as defined in § 170.3(n)(6) of this chapter, in confections and frostings as defined in § 170.3(n)(9) of this chapter, and in surimi-based fabricated seafood products.

(3) As components of protective coatings applied to fresh apples, avocados, bananas, banana plantains, limes, melons (honeydew and cantaloupe), papaya, peaches, pears, pineapples, and plums to retard ripening and spoiling.

(d) Sucrose fatty acid esters are used in accordance with current good manufacturing practice and in an amount not to exceed that reasonably required to accomplish the intended effect.

[47 FR 55475, Dec. 10, 1982, as amended at 48 FR 38226, Aug. 23, 1983; 52 FR 10883, Apr. 6, 1987; 53 FR 22294, 22297, June 15, 1988; 54 FR 24897, June 12, 1989; 60 FR 44756, Aug. 29, 1995]

§ 172.860 Fatty acids.

The food additive fatty acids may be safely used in food and in the manufacture of food components in accordance with the following prescribed conditions:

(a) The food additive consists of one or any mixture of the following straight-chain monobasic carboxylic acids and their associated fatty acids manufactured from fats and oils derived from edible sources: Capric acid, caprylic acid, lauric acid, myristic acid, oleic acid, palmitic acid, and stearic acid.

(b) The food additive meets the following specifications:

(1) Unsaponifiable matter does not exceed 2 percent.

(2) It is free of chick-edema factor:

(i) As evidenced during the bioassay method for determining the chick-edema factor as prescribed in paragraph (c)(2) of this section; or

(ii) As evidenced by the absence of chromatographic peaks with a retention time relative to aldrin (RA) between 10 and 25, using the gas chromatographic-electron capture method prescribed in paragraph (c)(3) of this section. If chromatographic peaks are found with RA values between 10 and 25, the food additive shall meet the requirements of the bioassay method prescribed in paragraph (c)(2) of this section for determining chick-edema factor.

(c) For the purposes of this section:

(1) Unsaponifiable matter shall be determined by the method described in the 13th Ed. (1980) of the "Official Methods of Analysis of the Association of Official Analytical Chemists," which is incorporated by reference. Copies are available from the AOAC INTERNATIONAL, 481 North Frederick Ave., suite 500, Gaithersburg, MD 20877, or available for inspection at the National Archives and Records Administration (NARA). For information on the availability of this material at NARA, call 202–741–6030, or go to: *http://www.archives.gov/federal_register/code_of_federal_regulations/ibr_locations.html.*

(2) Chick-edema factor shall be determined by the bioassay method described in "Official Methods of Analysis of the Association of Official Analytical Chemists," 13th Ed. (1980), sections 28.127–28.130, which is incorporated by reference. Copies may be obtained from the AOAC INTERNATIONAL, 481 North Frederick Ave., suite 500, Gaithersburg, MD 20877, or may be examined at the National Archives and Records Administration (NARA). For information on the availability of this material at NARA, call 202–741–6030, or go to: *http://www.archives.gov/federal_register/code_of_federal_regulations/ibr_locations.html.*

(3) The gas chromatographic-electron capture method for testing fatty acids for chick-edema shall be the method

described in the "Journal of the Association of Official Analytical Chemists," Volume 50 (No. 1), pages 216–218 (1967), or the modified method using a sulfuric acid clean-up procedure, as described in the "Journal of the Association of the Offical Analytical Chemists," Volume 51 (No. 2), pages 489–490 (1968), which are incorporated by reference. See paragraph (c)(2) of this section for availability of these references.

(d) It is used or intended for use as follows:

(1) In foods as a lubricant, binder, and as a defoaming agent in accordance with good manufacturing practice.

(2) As a component in the manufacture of other food-grade additives.

(e) To assure safe use of the additive, the label and labeling of the additive and any premix thereof shall bear, in addition to the other information required by the act, the following:

(1) The common or usual name of the acid or acids contained therein.

(2) The words "food grade," in juxtaposition with and equally as prominent as the name of the acid.

[42 FR 14491, Mar. 15, 1977, as amended at 47 FR 11837, Mar. 19, 1982; 49 FR 10105, Mar. 19, 1984; 54 FR 24897, June 12, 1989]

§ 172.861 Cocoa butter substitute from coconut oil, palm kernel oil, or both oils.

The food additive, cocoa butter substitute from coconut oil, palm kernel oil, or both oils, may be safely used in food in accordance with the following conditions:

(a) Cocoa butter substitute from coconut oil, palm kernel oil (CAS Reg. No. 85665–33–4), or both oils is a mixture of triglycerides. It is manufactured by esterification of glycerol with food-grade fatty acids (complying with § 172.860) derived from edible coconut oil, edible palm kernel oil, or both oils.

(b) The ingredient meets the following specifications:

Acid number: Not to exceed 0.5.
Saponification number: 220 to 260.
Iodine number: Not to exceed 3.
Melting range: 30 to 44 °C.

(c) The ingredient is used or intended for use as follows:

(1) As coating material for sugar, table salt, vitamins, citric acid, succinic acid, and spices; and

(2) In compound coatings, cocoa creams, cocoa-based sweets, toffees, caramel masses, and chewing sweets as defined in § 170.3 (n)(9) and (n)(38) of this chapter, except that the ingredient may not be used in a standardized food unless permitted by the standard of identity.

(d) The ingredient is used in accordance with current good manufacturing practice and in an amount not to exceed that reasonably required to accomplish the intended effect.

[56 FR 66970, Dec. 27, 1991; 57 FR 2814, Jan. 23, 1992]

§ 172.862 Oleic acid derived from tall oil fatty acids.

The food additive oleic acid derived from tall oil fatty acids may be safely used in food and as a component in the manufacture of food-grade additives in accordance with the following prescribed conditions:

(a) The additive consists of purified oleic acid separated from refined tall oil fatty acids.

(b) The additive meets the following specifications:

(1) Specifications for oleic acid prescribed in the "Food Chemicals Codex." 3d Ed. (1981), pp. 207–208, which is incorporated by reference, except that titer (solidification point) shall not exceed 13.5 °C and unsaponifiable matter shall not exceed 0.5 percent. Copies of the material incorporated by reference may be obtained from the National Academy Press, 2101 Constitution Ave. NW., Washington, DC 20418, or may be examined at the National Archives and Records Administration (NARA). For information on the availability of this material at NARA, call 202–741–6030, or go to: *http://www.archives.gov/federal_register/code_of_federal_regulations/ibr_locations.html.*

(2) The resin acid content does not exceed 0.01 as determined by ASTM method D1240–82, "Standard Test Method for Rosin Acids in Fatty Acids," which is incorporated by reference. Copies may be obtained from the American Society for Testing Materials, 100 Barr Harbor Dr., West Conshohocken,

Philadelphia, PA 19428-2959, or may be examined at the National Archives and Records Administration (NARA). For information on the availability of this material at NARA, call 202–741–6030, or go to: *http://www.archives.gov/federal_register/code_of_federal_regulations/ibr_locations.html.*

(3) The requirements for absence of chick-edema factor as prescribed in § 172.860.

(c) It is used or intended for use as follows:

(1) In foods as a lubricant, binder, and defoaming agent in accordance with good manufacturing practice.

(2) As a component in the manufacture of other food-grade additives.

(d) To assure safe use of the additive, the label and labeling of the additive and any premix thereof shall bear, in addition to the other information required by the Act, the following:

(1) The common or usual name of the acid.

(2) The words "food grade" in juxtaposition with and equally as prominent as the name of the acid.

[42 FR 14491, Mar. 15, 1977, as amended at 49 FR 10105, Mar. 19, 1984]

§ 172.863 Salts of fatty acids.

The food additive salts of fatty acids may be safely used in food and in the manufacture of food components in accordance with the following prescribed conditions:

(a) The additive consists of one or any mixture of two or more of the aluminum, calcium, magnesium, potassium, and sodium salts of the fatty acids conforming with § 172.860 and/or oleic acid derived from tall oil fatty acids conforming with § 172.862.

(b) The food additive is used or intended for use as a binder, emulsifier, and anticaking agent in food in accordance with good manufacturing practice.

(c) To assure safe use of the additive, the label and labeling of the additive and any premix thereof shall bear, in addition to the other information required by the Act, the following:

(1) The common or usual name of the fatty acid salt or salts contained therein.

(2) The words "food grade," in juxtaposition with and equally as prominent as the name of the salt.

§ 172.864 Synthetic fatty alcohols.

Synthetic fatty alcohols may be safely used in food and in the synthesis of food components in accordance with the following prescribed conditions:

(a) The food additive consists of any one of the following fatty alcohols:

(1) Hexyl, octyl, decyl, lauryl, myristyl, cetyl, and stearyl; manufactured by fractional distillation of alcohols obtained by a sequence of oxidation and hydrolysis of organo-aluminums generated by the controlled reaction of low molecular weight trialkylaluminum with purified ethylene (minimum 99 percent by volume C_2H_4), and utilizing the hydrocarbon solvent as defined in paragraph (b) of this section, such that:

(i) Hexyl, octyl, decyl, lauryl, and myristyl alcohols contain not less than 99 percent of total alcohols and not less than 96 percent of straight chain alcohols. Any nonalcoholic impurities are primarily paraffins.

(ii) Cetyl and stearyl alcohols contain not less than 98 percent of total alcohols and not less than 94 percent of straight chain alcohols. Any nonalcoholic impurities are primarily paraffins.

(iii) The synthetic fatty alcohols contain no more than 0.1 weight percent of total diols as determined by a method available upon request from the Commissioner of Food and Drugs.

(2) Hexyl, octyl, and decyl; manufactured by fractional distillation of alcohols obtained by a sequence of oxidation, hydrolysis, and catalytic hydrogenation (catalyst consists of copper, chromium, and nickel) of organo-aluminums generated by the controlled reaction of low molecular weight trialkylaluminum with purified ethylene (minimum 99 percent by volume C_2H_4), and utilizing an external coolant such that these alcohols meet the specifications prescribed in paragraph (a)(1)(i) and (iii) of this section.

(3) n-Octyl; manufactured by the hydrodimerization of 1,3-butadiene, followed by catalytic hydrogenation of the resulting dienol, and distillation to

produce *n*-octyl alcohol with a minimum purity of 99 percent. The analytical method for *n*-octyl alcohol entitled "Test Method [Normal-octanol]" dated October 2003, and printed by Kuraray Co., Ltd., is incorporated by reference. The Director of the Office of the Federal Register approves this incorporation by reference in accordance with 5 U.S.C. 552(a) and 1 CFR part 51. You may obtain a copy from the Office of Food Additive Safety, 5100 Paint Branch Pkwy., College Park, MD 20740, or you may examine a copy at the Center for Food Safety and Applied Nutrition's Library, Food and Drug Administration, 5100 Paint Branch Pkwy., College Park, MD 20740, or at the National Archives and Records Administration (NARA). For information on the availability of this material at NARA, call 202–741–6030, or go to *http://www.archives.gov/federal_register/code_of_federal_regulations/ibr_locations.html.*

(b) The hydrocarbon solvent used in the process described in paragraph (a)(1) of this section is a mixture of liquid hydrocarbons essentially paraffinic in nature, derived from petroleum and refined to meet the specifications described in paragraph (b)(1) of this section when subjected to the procedures described in paragraph (b) (2) and (3) of this section.

(1) The hydrocarbon solvent meets the following specifications:

(i) Boiling-point range: 175 °C–275 °C.

(ii) Ultraviolet absorbance limits as follows:

Wavelength (millicrons)	Maximum absorbance per centimeter optical path length
280–289	0.15
290–299	.12
300–359	.05
360–400	.02

(2) Use ASTM method D86–82, "Standard Method for Distillation of Petroleum Products," which is incorporated by reference, to determine boiling point range. Copies of the material incorporated by reference may be obtained from the American Society for Testing Materials, 100 Barr Harbor Dr., West Conshohocken, Philadelphia, PA 19428-2959, or may be examined at the National Archives and Records Administration (NARA). For information on the availability of this material at NARA, call 202–741–6030, or go to: *http://www.archives.gov/federal_register/code_of_federal_regulations/ibr_locations.html.*

(3) The analytical method for determining ultraviolet absorbance limits is as follows:

General Instructions

All glassware should be scrupulously cleaned to remove all organic matter such as oil, grease, detergent residues, etc. Examine all glassware, including stoppers and stopcocks, under ultraviolet light to detect any residual fluorescent contamination. As a precautionary measure, it is recommended practice to rinse all glassware with purified isooctane immediately before use. No grease is to be used on stopcocks or joints. Great care to avoid contamination of hydrocarbon solvent samples in handling and to assure absence of any extraneous material arising from inadequate packaging is essential. Because some of the polynuclear hydrocarbons sought in this test are very susceptible to photo-oxidation, the entire procedure is to be carried out under subdued light.

Apparatus

Chromatographic tube. 450 millimeters in length (packing section), inside diameter 19 millimeters ±1 millimeter, equipped with a wad of clean Pyrex brand filtering wool (Corning Glass Works Catalog No. 3950 or equivalent). The tube shall contain a 250-milliliter reservoir and a 2-millimeter tetrafluoroethylene polymer stopcock at the opposite end. Overall length of the tube is 670 millimeters.

Stainless steel rod. 2 feet in length, 2 to 4 millimeters in diameter.

Vacuum oven. Similar to Labline No. 3610 but modified as follows: A copper tube one-fourth inch in diameter and 13 inches in length is bent to a right angle at the 4-inch point and plugged at the opposite end; eight copper tubes one-eighth inch in diameter and 5 inches in length are silver soldered in drilled holes (one-eighth inch in diameter) to the one-fourth-inch tube, one on each side at the 5-, 7.5-, 10- and 12.5-inch points; the one-eighth-inch copper tubes are bent to conform with the inner periphery of the oven.

Beakers. 250-milliliter and 500-milliliter capacity.

Graduated cylinders. 25-milliliter, 50-milliliter, and 150-milliliter capacity.

Tuberculin syringe. 1-milliliter capacity, with 3-inch, 22-gauge needle.

Volumetric flask. 5-milliliter capacity.

Spectrophotometric cells. Fused quartz ground glass stoppered cells, optical path length in the range of 1.000 centimeter ±0.005 centimeter. With distilled water in the cells, determine any absorbance difference.

Spectrophotometer. Spectral range 250 millimicrons—400 millimicrons with spectral slit width of 2 millimicrons or less: under instrument operating conditions for these absorbance measurements, the spectrophotometer shall also meet the following performance requirements:

Absorbance repeatability, ±0.01 at 0.4 absorbance.

Absorbance accuracy,[1] ±0.05 at 0.4 absorbance.

Wavelength repeatability, ±0.2 millimicron.

Wavelength accuracy, ±1.0 millimicron.

Nitrogen cylinder. Water-pumped or equivalent purity nitrogen in cylinder equipped with regulator and valve to control flow at 5 p.s.i.g.

REAGENTS AND MATERIALS

Organic solvents. All solvents used throughout the procedure shall meet the specifications and tests described in this specification. The isooctane, benzene, hexane, and 1,2-dichloroethane designated in the list following this paragraph shall pass the following test:

To the specified quantity of solvent in a 250-milliliter beaker, add 1 milliliter of purified *n*-hexadecane and evaporate in the vacuum oven under a stream of nitrogen. Discontinue evaporation when not over 1 milliliter of residue remains. (To the residue from benzene add a 5-milliliter portion of purified isooctane, reevaporate, and repeat once to insure complete removal of benzene.)

Dissolve the 1 milliliter of hexadecane residue in isooctane and make to 5 milliliters volume. Determine the absorbance in the 1-centimeter path length cells compared to isooctane as reference. The absorbance of the solution of the solvent residue shall not exceed 0.02 per centimeter path length between 280 and 300 mμ and shall not exceed 0.01 per centimeter path length between 300 and 400 mμ.

Isooctane (2,2,4-trimethylpentane). Use 10 milliliters for the test described in the preceding paragraph. If necessary, isooctane may be purified by passage through a column of activated silica gel (Grade 12, Davison Chemical Co., Baltimore, Md., or equivalent).

Benzene, spectro grade (Burdick and Jackson Laboratories, Inc., Muskegon, Mich., or equivalent). Use 80 milliliters for the test. If necessary, benzene may be purified by distillation or otherwise.

Hexane, spectro grade (Burdick and Jackson Laboratories, Inc., Muskegon, Mich., or equivalent). Use 650 milliliters for the test. If necessary, hexane may be purified by distillation or otherwise.

1,2-Dichloroethane, spectro grade (Matheson, Coleman, and Bell, East Rutherford, N.J., or equivalent). Use 20 milliliters for test. If necessary, 1,2-dichloroethane may be purified by distillation.

Eluting mixtures:

1. *10 percent 1,2-dichloroethane in hexane.* Pipet 100 milliliters of 1,2-dichloroethane into a 1-liter glass-stoppered volumetric flask and adjust to volume with hexane, with mixing.

2. *40 percent benzene in hexane.* Pipet 400 milliliters of benzene into a 1-liter glass-stoppered volumetric flask and adjust to volume with hexane, with mixing.

n-Hexadecane, 99 percent olefin-free. Dilute 1.0 milliliter of *n*-hexadecane to 5 milliliters with isooctane and determine the absorbance in a 1-centimeter cell compared to isooctane as reference between 280 mμ-400mμ. The absorbance per centimeter path length shall not exceed 0.00 in this range. If necessary, *n*-hexadecane may be purified by percolation through activated silica gel or by distillation.

Silica gel, 28–200 mesh (Grade 12, Davison Chemical Co., Baltimore, Md., or equivalent). Activate as follows: Weigh about 900 grams into a 1-gallon bottle, add 100 milliliters of de-ionized water, seal the bottle and shake and roll at intervals for 1 hour. Allow to equilibrate overnight in the sealed bottle. Activate the gel at 150 °C for 16 hours, in a 2-inch × 7-inch × 12-inch porcelain pan loosely covered with aluminum foil, cool in a dessicator, transfer to a bottle and seal.

PROCEDURE

Determination of ultraviolet absorbance. Before proceeding with the analysis of a sample determine the absorbance in a 1-centimeter path cell for the reagent blank by carrying out the procedure without a sample. Record the absorbance in the wavelength range of 280 to 400 millimicrons. Typical reagent blank absorbance in this range should not exceed 0.04 in the 280 to 299 millimicron

[1] As determined by using potassium chromate for reference standard and described in National Bureau of Standards Circular 484, Spectrophotometry, U.S. Department of Commerce, (1949). The accuracy is to be determined by comparison with the standard values at 290, 345, and 400 millimicrons. Circular 484 is incorporated by reference. Copies are available from the Center for Food Safety and Applied Nutrition (HFS–200), Food and Drug Administration, 5100 Paint Branch Pkwy., College Park, MD 20740, or available for inspection at the National Archives and Records Administration (NARA). For information on the availability of this material at NARA, call 202–741–6030, or go to: *http://www.archives.gov/federal_register/code_of_federal_regulations/ibr_locations.html.*

range, 0.02 in the 300 to 359 millimicron range, and 0.01 in the 360 to 400 millimicron range. If the characteristic benzene peaks in the 250 to 260 millimicron region are present, remove the benzene by the procedure described above under "Reagents and Materials," "Organic Solvents," and record absorbance again.

Transfer 50 grams of silica gel to the chromatographic tube for sample analysis. Raise and drop the column on a semisoft, clean surface for about 1 minute to settle the gel. Pour 100 milliliters of hexane into the column with the stopcock open and allow to drain to about one-half inch above the gel. Turn off the stopcock and allow the column to cool for 30 minutes. After cooling, vibrate the column to eliminate air and stir the top 1 to 2 inches with a small diameter stainless steel rod. Take care not to get the gel above the liquid and onto the sides of the column.

Weigh out 40 grams ±0.1 gram of the hydrocarbon solvent sample into a 250-milliliter beaker, add 50 milliliters of hexane, and pour the solution into the column. Rinse the beaker with 50 milliliters of hexane and add this to the column. Allow the hexane sample solution to elute into a 500-milliliter beaker until the solution is about one-half inch above the gel. Rinse the column three times with 50-milliliter portions of hexane. Allow each hexane rinse to separately elute to about one-half inch above the gel. Replace the eluate beaker (discard the hexane eluate) with a 250-milliliter beaker. Add two separate 25-milliliter portions of 10 percent 1,2-dichloroethane and allow each to separately elute as before. Finally, add 150 milliliters of 10 percent 1,2-dichloroethane for a total of 200 milliliters. When the final 10 percent 1,2-dichloroethane fraction is about one-half inch above the top of the gel bed, replace the receiving beaker (discard the 1,2-dichloroethane eluate) with a 250-milliliter beaker containing 1 milliliter of hexadecane. Adjust the elution rate to 2 to 3 milliliters per minute, add two 25-milliliter portions of 40 percent benzene and allow each to separately elute as before to within about one-half inch of the gel bed. Finally, add 150 milliliters of 40 percent benzene for a total of 200 milliliters. Evaporate the benzene in the oven with vacuum and sufficient nitrogen flow to just ripple the top of the benzene solution. When the benzene is removed (as determined by a constant volume of hexadecane) add 5 milliliters of isooctane and evaporate. Repeat once to insure complete removal of benzene. Remove the beaker and cover with aluminum foil (previously rinsed with hexane) until cool.

Quantitatively transfer the hexadecane residue to a 5-milliliter volumetric flask and dilute to volume with isooctane. Determine the absorbance of the solution in 1-centimeter path length cells between 280 and 400 millimicrons using isooctane as a reference. Correct the absorbance values for any absorbance derived from reagents as determined by carrying out the procedure without a sample. If the corrected absorbance does not exceed the limits prescribed in paragraph (b)(1)(ii) of this section, the sample meets the ultraviolet absorbance specifications for hydrocarbon solvent.

(c) Synthetic fatty alcohols may be used as follows:

(1) As substitutes for the corresponding naturally derived fatty alcohols permitted in food by existing regulations in this part or part 173 of this chapter provided that the use is in compliance with any prescribed limitations.

(2) As substitutes for the corresponding naturally derived fatty alcohols used as intermediates in the synthesis of food additives and other substances permitted in food.

[42 FR 14491, Mar. 15, 1977, as amended at 47 FR 11837, Mar. 19, 1982; 49 FR 10105, Mar. 19, 1984; 54 FR 24897, June 12, 1989; 70 FR 72908, Dec. 8, 2005]

§ 172.866 Synthetic glycerin produced by the hydrogenolysis of carbohydrates.

Synthetic glycerin produced by the hydrogenolysis of carbohydrates may be safely used in food, subject to the provisions of this section:

(a) It shall contain not in excess of 0.2 percent by weight of a mixture of butanetriols.

(b) It is used or intended for use in an amount not to exceed that reasonably required to produce its intended effect.

§ 172.867 Olestra.

Olestra, as identified in this section, may be safely used in accordance with the following conditions:

(a) Olestra is a mixture of octa-, hepta-, and hexa-esters of sucrose with fatty acids derived from edible fats and oils or fatty acid sources that are generally recognized as safe or approved for use as food ingredients. The chain lengths of the fatty acids are no less than 12 carbon atoms.

(b) Olestra meets the specifications of the *Food Chemicals Codex*, 4th edition, 1st supplement (1997), pp. 33–35, which is incorporated by reference. The Director of the Office of the Federal Register approves this incorporation by reference in accordance with 5

U.S.C. 552(a) and 1 CFR part 51. You may obtain copies from the National Academy Press, 2101 Constitution Ave. NW., Washington, DC 20418 (Internet address *http://www.nap.edu*). Copies may be examined at the Center for Food Safety and Applied Nutrition's Library, Food and Drug Administration, 5100 Paint Branch Pkwy., College Park, MD 20740, or at the National Archives and Records Administration (NARA). For information on the availability of this material at NARA, call 202–741–6030, or go to: *http://www.archives.gov/federal_register/code_of_federal_regulations/ibr_locations.html.*

(c) Olestra may be used in place of fats and oils in prepackaged ready-to-eat savory (i.e., salty or piquant but not sweet) snacks and prepackaged, unpopped popcorn kernels that are ready-to-heat. In such foods, the additive may be used in place of fats and oils for frying or baking, in dough conditioners, in sprays, in filling ingredients, or in flavors.

(d) To compensate for any interference with absorption of fat soluble vitamins, the following vitamins shall be added to foods containing olestra: 1.9 milligrams alpha-tocopherol equivalents per gram olestra; 51 retinol equivalents per gram olestra (as retinyl acetate or retinyl palmitate); 12 IU vitamin D per gram olestra; and 8 μg vitamin K_1 per gram olestra.

(e)(1) Vitamins A, D, E, and K present in foods as a result of the requirement in paragraph (d) of this section shall be declared in the listing of ingredients. Such vitamins shall not be considered in determining nutrient content for the nutritional label or for any nutrient claims, express or implied.

(i) An asterisk shall follow vitamins A, D, E, and K in the listing of ingredients;

(ii) The asterisk shall appear as a superscript following each vitamin;

(iii) Immediately following the ingredient list an asterisk and statement, "Dietarily insignificant" shall appear prominently and conspicuously as specified in § 101.2(c) of this chapter;

(2) Olestra shall not be considered as a source of fat or calories for purposes of §§ 101.9 and 101.13 of this chapter.

[61 FR 3171, Jan. 30, 1996; 61 FR 11546, Mar. 21, 1996, as amended at 68 FR 46402, Aug. 5, 2003; 69 FR 29432, May 24, 2004]

§ 172.868 Ethyl cellulose.

The food additive ethyl cellulose may be safely used in food in accordance with the following prescribed conditions:

(a) The food additive is a cellulose ether containing ethoxy (OC_2H_5) groups attached by an ether linkage and containing on an anhydrous basis not more than 2.6 ethoxy groups per anhydroglucose unit.

(b) It is used or intended for use as follows:

(1) As a binder and filler in dry vitamin preparations.

(2) As a component of protective coatings for vitamin and mineral tablets.

(3) As a fixative in flavoring compounds.

§ 172.869 Sucrose oligoesters.

Sucrose oligoesters, as identified in this section, may be safely used in accordance with the following conditions:

(a) Sucrose oligoesters consist of mixtures of sucrose fatty acid esters with an average degree of esterification ranging from four to seven. It is produced by interesterification of sucrose with methyl esters of fatty acids derived from edible fats and oils (including hydrogenated fats and oils). The only solvents which may be used in the preparation of sucrose oligoesters are dimethyl sulfoxide, isobutyl alcohol, and those solvents generally recognized as safe in food.

(b) Sucrose oligoesters meet the specifications in the methods listed in the table in this paragraph. The methods cited for determining compliance with each specification are incorporated by reference, in accordance with 5 U.S.C. 552(a) and 1 CFR part 51. Copies of the methods may be examined at the Center for Food Safety and Applied Nutrition's Library, room 1C–100, 5100 Paint Branch Pkwy., College Park, MD 20740, or at the National Archives and Records Administration (NARA). For information on the availability of this material at NARA, call 202–741–6030, or go to: *http://www.archives.gov/federal_register/code_of_federal_regulations/ibr_locations.html*. Copies of the methods are available from the sources listed in the table in this paragraph:

Specification	Limit	Method Cited	Source for Obtaining Method
(1) Sucrose esters	Not less than 90%	"Method for Analyzing the Purity of Sucrose Fatty Acid Esters," issued by Mitsubishi Chemical Corp., June 17, 1998.	Office of Food Additive Safety, Center for Food Safety and Applied Nutrition (HFS–200), Food and Drug Administration, 5100 Paint Branch Pkwy., College Park, MD 20740.
(2) Mono-, di-, and tri-esters ...	Not more than 45%	"Method for Measuring the Ester Distribution of Sucrose Oligoesters," issued by Mitsubishi Chemical Corp., June 17, 1998.	Do.
(3) Tetra-, penta-, hexa-, and hepta-esters.	Not less than 50%	Do.	Do.
(4) Octa-esters	Not more than 40%	Do.	Do.
(5) Free Sucrose	Not more than 0.5%	"Free Sucrose Method," issued by Mitsubishi Chemical Corp., June 17, 1998.	Do.
(6) Acid Value	Not more than 4.0	"Acid Value," Appendix VII, Method I (Commercial Fatty Acids), in the *Food Chemicals Codex,* 4th ed. (1996), p. 820.	National Academy Press, 2101 Constitution Ave. NW, Washington, DC 20418 (Internet: *http://www.nap.edu*).
(7) Residue on Ignition	Not more than 0.7%	"Residue on Ignition, Appendix IIC, Method I, in the *Food Chemicals Codex,* 4th ed. (1996), pp. 751–752, (using a 1-gram sample).	Do.
(8) Residual Methanol	Not more than 10 milligrams/kilogram.	Method listed in the monograph for "Sucrose Fatty Acid Esters" in the First Supplement to the 4th ed. of the *Food Chemicals Codex* (1997), pp. 44–45.	Do.
(9) Residual Dimethyl Sulfoxide.	Not more than 2.0 milligrams/kilogram.	Do.	Do.
(10) Residual Isobutyl Alcohol	Not more than 10 milligrams/kilogram.	Do.	Do.
(11) Lead	Not more than 1.0 milligram/kilogram.	"Atomic Absorption Spectrophotometric Graphite Furnace Method," Method I, in the *Food Chemicals Codex,* 4th ed. (1996), pp. 763–765.	Do.

(c) The additive is used as an emulsifier (as defined in §170.3(o)(8) of this chapter) or stabilizer (as defined in §170.3(o)(28) of this chapter) in chocolate and in butter-substitute spreads, at a level not to exceed 2.0 percent; except that the additive may not be used in a standardized food unless permitted by the standard of identity.

[68 FR 50072, Aug. 20, 2003]

§ 172.870 Hydroxypropyl cellulose.

The food additive hydroxypropyl cellulose may be safely used in food, except standardized foods that do not provide for such use, in accordance with the following prescribed conditions:

(a) The additive consists of one of the following:

(1) A cellulose ether containing propylene glycol groups attached by an ether linkage that contains, on an anhydrous basis, not more than 4.6 hydroxypropyl groups per anhydroglucose unit. The additive has a minimum viscosity of 10 centipoises for a 10 percent by weight aqueous solution at 25 degrees C.

(2) A cellulose ether containing propylene glycol groups attached by an ether linkage having a hydroxypropoxy (OC_3H_6OH) content of 5 to 16 percent weight in weight (w/w) on an anhydrous basis, i.e., 0.1 to 0.4 hydroxypropyl groups per anhydroglucose unit. The common name for this form of the additive is low substituted hydroxypropyl cellulose.

(b) The additive is used or intended for use as follows:

(1) The additive identified in paragraph (a)(1) of this section is used or intended for use as an emulsifier, film former, protective colloid, stabilizer, suspending agent, or thickener in food, in accordance with good manufacturing practice. The additive also may be used as a binder in dietary supplements, in accordance with good manufacturing practice.

(2) The additive identified in paragraph (a)(2) of this section is used or intended for use as a binder and disintegrator in tablets or wafers containing dietary supplements of vitamins and/or minerals. The additive is used in accordance with good manufacturing practice.

[46 FR 50065, Oct. 9, 1981, as amended at 76 FR 41689, July 15, 2011]

§ 172.872 Methyl ethyl cellulose.

The food additive methyl ethyl cellulose may be safely used in food in accordance with the following prescribed conditions.

(a) The additive is a cellulose ether having the general formula $[C_6H_{(10-x-y)}O_5(CH_3)_x(C_2H_5)_y]_n$, where x is the number of methyl groups and y is the number of ethyl groups. The average value of x is 0.3 and the average value of y is 0.7.

(b) The additive meets the following specifications:

(1) The methoxy content shall be not less than 3.5 percent and not more than 6.5 percent, calculated as OCH_3, and the ethoxy content shall be not less than 14.5 percent and not more than 19 percent, calculated as OC_2H_5, both measured on the dry sample.

(2) The viscosity of an aqueous solution, 2.5 grams of the material in 100 milliliters of water, at 20 °C, is 20 to 60 centipoises.

(3) The ash content on a dry basis has a maximum of 0.6 percent.

(c) The food additive is used as an aerating, emulsifying, and foaming agent, in an amount not in excess of that reasonably required to produce its intended effect.

§ 172.874 Hydroxypropyl methylcellulose.

The food additive hydroxypropyl methylcellulose (CAS Reg. No. 9004–65–3) may be safely used in food, except in standardized foods which do not provide for such use if:

(a) The additive complies with the definition and specifications prescribed in the National Formulary, 12th edition.

(b) It is used or intended for use as an emulsifier, film former, protective colloid, stabilizer, suspending agent, or thickener, in accordance with good manufacturing practice.

(c) To insure safe use of the additive, the container of the additive, in addition to being labeled as required by the general provisions of the act, shall be accompanied by labeling which contains adequate directions for use to provide a final product that complies with the limitations prescribed in paragraph (b) of this section.

[42 FR 14491, Mar. 15, 1977, as amended at 47 FR 38273, Aug. 31, 1982]

§ 172.876 Castor oil.

The food additive castor oil may be safely used in accordance with the following conditions:

(a) The additive meets the specifications of the United States Pharmacopeia XX (1980).

(b) The additive is used or intended for use as follows:

Use and Limitations

Hard candy production—As a release agent and antisticking agent, not to exceed 500 parts per million in hard candy.

Vitamin and mineral tablets—As a component of protective coatings.

[42 FR 14491, Mar. 15, 1977, as amended at 49 FR 10105, Mar. 19, 1984]

§ 172.878 White mineral oil.

White mineral oil may be safely used in food in accordance with the following conditions:

(a) White mineral oil is a mixture of liquid hydrocarbons, essentially paraffinic and naphthenic in nature obtained from petroleum. It is refined to meet the following specifications:

(1) It meets the test requirements of the United States Pharmacopeia XX (1980) for readily carbonizable substances (page 532).

(2) It meets the test requirements of U.S.P. XVII for sulfur compounds (page 400).

(3) It meets the specifications prescribed in the "Journal of the Association of Official Analytical Chemists," Volume 45, page 66 (1962), which is incorporated by reference, after correction of the ultraviolet absorbance for any absorbance due to added antioxidants. Copies of the material incorporated by reference are available from the Center for Food Safety and Applied Nutrition (HFS–200), Food and Drug Administration, 5100 Paint Branch Pkwy., College Park, MD 20740, or available for inspection at the National Archives and Records Administration (NARA). For information on the availability of this material at NARA, call 202–741–6030, or go to: *http://www.archives.gov/federal_register/code_of_federal_regulations/ibr_locations.html.*

(b) White mineral oil may contain any antioxidant permitted in food by regulations issued in accordance with section 409 of the Act, in an amount not greater than that required to produce its intended effect.

(c) White mineral oil is used or intended for use as follows:

Use	Limitation (inclusive of all petroleum hydrocarbons that may be used in combination with white mineral oil)
1. As a release agent, binder, and lubricant in or on capsules and tablets containing concentrates of flavoring, spices, condiments, and nutrients intended for addition to food, excluding confectionery.	Not to exceed 0.6% of the capsule or tablet.
2. As a release agent, binder, and lubricant in or on capsules and tablets containing food for special dietary use.	Not to exceed 0.6% of the capsule or tablet.
3. As a float on fermentation fluids in the manufacture of vinegar and wine to prevent or retard access of air, evaporation, and wild yeast contamination during fermentation.	In an amount not to exceed good manufacturing practice.
4. As a defoamer in food	In accordance with § 173.340 of this chapter.
5. In bakery products, as a release agent and lubricant	Not to exceed 0.15% of bakery products.
6. In dehydrated fruits and vegetables, as a release agent	Not to exceed 0.02% of dehydrated fruits and vegetables.
7. In egg white solids, as a release agent	Not to exceed 0.1% of egg white solids.
8. On raw fruits and vegetables, as a protective coating	In an amount not to exceed good manufacturing practice.
9. In frozen meat, as a component of hot-melt coating	Not to exceed 0.095% of meat.
10. As a protective float on brine used in the curing of pickles	In an amount not to exceed good manufacturing practice.
11. In molding starch used in the manufacture of confectionery	Not to exceed 0.3 percent in the molding starch.
12. As a release agent, binder, and lubricant in the manufacture of yeast	Not to exceed 0.15 percent of yeast.
13. As an antidusting agent in sorbic acid for food use	Not to exceed 0.25 percent in the sorbic acid.
14. As release agent and as sealing and polishing agent in the manufacture of confectionery.	Not to exceed 0.2 percent of confectionery.
15. As a dust control agent for wheat, corn, soybean, barley, rice, rye, oats, and sorghum.	Applied at a level of no more than 0.02 percent by weight of grain.
16. As a dust control agent for rice	ISO 100 oil viscosity (100 centistokes (cSt) at 100 °F) applied at a level of no more than 0.08 percent by weight of the rice grain.

[42 FR 14491, Mar. 15, 1977, as amended at 47 FR 8764, Mar. 2, 1982; 47 FR 11838, Mar. 19, 1982; 48 FR 55728, Dec. 15, 1983; 49 FR 10105, Mar. 19, 1984; 54 FR 24897, June 12, 1989; 63 FR 66014, Dec. 1, 1998]

§ 172.880 Petrolatum.

Petrolatum may be safely used in food, subject to the provisions of this section.

(a) Petrolatum complies with the specifications set forth in the United States Pharmacopeia XX (1980) for white petrolatum or in the National Formulary XV (1980) for petrolatum.

(b) Petrolatum meets the following ultraviolet absorbance limits when subjected to the analytical procedure described in § 172.886(b):

Ultraviolet absorbance per centimeter path length:

Millimicrons	Maximum
280–289	0.25
290–299	.20
300–359	.14
360–400	.04

(c) Petrolatum is used or intended for use as follows:

Use	Limitation (inclusive of all petroleum hydrocarbons that may be used in combination with petrolatum)
In bakery products; as release agent and lubricant	With white mineral oil, not to exceed 0.15 percent of bakery product.
In confectionery; as release agent and as sealing and polishing agent	Not to exceed 0.2 percent of confectionery.
In dehydrated fruits and vegetables; as release agent	Not to exceed 0.02 percent of dehydrated fruits and vegetables.
In egg white solids; as release agent	Not to exceed 0.1 percent of egg white solids.
On raw fruits and vegetables; as protective coating	In an amount not to exceed good manufacturing practice.
In beet sugar and yeast; as defoaming agent	As prescribed in § 173.340 of this chapter.

(d) Petrolatum may contain any antioxidant permitted in food by regulations issued in accordance with section 409 of the Act, in an amount not greater than that required to produce its intended effect.

[42 FR 14491, Mar. 15, 1977, as amended at 49 FR 10105, Mar. 19, 1984]

§ 172.882 Synthetic isoparaffinic petroleum hydrocarbons.

Synthetic isoparaffinic petroleum hydrocarbons may be safely used in food, in accordance with the following conditions:

(a) They are produced by synthesis from petroleum gases and consist of a mixture of liquid hydrocarbons meeting the following specifications:

Boiling point 93–260 °C as determined by ASTM method D86–82, "Standard Method for Distillation of Petroleum Products," which is incorporated by reference. Copies may be obtained from the American Society for Testing Materials, 100 Barr Harbor Dr., West Conshohocken, Philadelphia, PA 19428-2959, or may be examined at the National Archives and Records Administration (NARA). For information on the availability of this material at NARA, call 202–741–6030, or go to: *http://www.archives.gov/federal_register/code_of_federal_regulations/ibr_locations.html.*

Ultraviolet absorbance:

260–319 millimicrons—1.5 maximum.

320–329 millimicrons—0.08 maximum.

330–350 millimicrons—0.05 maximum.

Nonvolatile residual: 0.002 gram per 100 milliliters maximum.

Synthetic isoparaffinic petroleum hydrocarbons containing antioxidants shall meet the specified ultraviolet absorbance limits after correction for any absorbance due to the antioxidants. The ultraviolet absorbance shall be determined by the procedure described for application of mineral oil, disregarding the last sentence of the procedure, under "Specifications" on page 66 of the "Journal of the Association of Official Analytical Chemists," Volume 45 (February 1962), which is incorporated by reference. Copies are available from the Center for Food Safety and Applied Nutrition (HFS–200), Food and Drug Administration, 5100 Paint Branch Pkwy., College Park, MD 20740, or available for inspection at the National Archives and Records Administration (NARA). For information on the availability of this material at NARA, call 202–741–6030, or go to: *http://www.archives.gov/federal_register/code_of_federal_regulations/ibr_locations.html.* For hydrocarbons boiling below 250 °F, the nonvolatile residue shall be determined by ASTM method D1353–78, "Standard Test Method for Nonvolatile Matter in Volatile Solvents for Use in Paint, Varnish, Lacquer, and Related Products;" for those boiling above 121 °C, ASTM method D381–80, "Standard Test Method for Existent Gum in Fuels by Jet Evaporation" shall be used. These methods are incorporated by reference. Copies may be obtained from the American Society for Testing Materials, 100 Barr Harbor Dr., West Conshohocken, Philadelphia, PA 19428-2959, or may be examined at the National Archives and Records Administration (NARA). For information on the availability of this material at NARA, call 202–741–6030, or go to: *http://www.archives.gov/federal_register/code_of_federal_regulations/ibr_locations.html.*

(b) Isoparaffinic petroleum hydrocarbons may contain antioxidants authorized for use in food in an amount not to exceed that reasonably required to accomplish the intended technical effect nor to exceed any prescribed limitations.

(c) Synthetic isoparaffinic petroleum hydrocarbons are used or intended for use as follows:

Uses	Limitations
1. In the froth-flotation cleaning of vegetables.	In an amount not to exceed good manufacturing practice.
2. As a component of insecticide formulations for use on processed foods.	Do.
3. As a component of coatings on fruits and vegetables.	Do.
4. As a coating on shell eggs	Do.
5. As a float on fermentation fluids in the manufacture of vinegar and wine and on brine used in curing pickles, to prevent or retard access of air, evaporation, and contamination with wild organisms during fermentation.	Do.

[42 FR 14491, Mar. 15, 1977, as amended at 47 FR 11838, Mar. 19, 1982; 49 FR 10106, Mar. 19, 1984; 54 FR 24897, June 12, 1989]

§ 172.884 Odorless light petroleum hydrocarbons.

Odorless light petroleum hydrocarbons may be safely used in food, in accordance with the following prescribed conditions:

(a) The additive is a mixture of liquid hydrocarbons derived from petroleum or synthesized from petroleum gases. The additive is chiefly paraffinic, isoparaffinic, or naphthenic in nature.

(b) The additive meets the following specifications:

(1) Odor is faint and not kerosenic.

(2) Initial boiling point is 300 °F minimum.

(3) Final boiling point is 650 °F maximum.

(4) Ultraviolet absorbance limits determined by method specified in § 178.3620(b)(1)(ii) of this chapter, as follows:

Wavelength mμ	Maximum absorbance per centimeter optical pathlength
280–289	4.0
290–299	3.3
300–329	2.3
330–360	.8

(c) The additive is used as follows:

Use	Limitations
As a coating on shell eggs	In an amount not to exceed good manufacturing practice.
As a defoamer in processing beet sugar and yeast.	Complying with § 173.340 of this chapter.
As a float on fermentation fluids in the manufacture of vinegar and wine to prevent or retard access of air, evaporation, and wild yeast contamination during fermentation.	In an amount not to exceed good manufacturing practice.
In the froth-flotation cleaning of vegetables.	Do.
As a component of insecticide formulations used in compliance with regulations issued in parts 170 through 189 of this chapter.	Do.

§ 172.886 Petroleum wax.

Petroleum wax may be safely used in or on food, in accordance with the following conditions:

(a) Petroleum wax is a mixture of solid hydrocarbons, paraffinic in nature, derived from petroleum, and refined to meet the specifications prescribed by this section.

(b) Petroleum wax meets the following ultraviolet absorbance limits when subjected to the analytical procedure described in this paragraph.

	Maximum ultraviolet absorbance per centimeter path length
280–289 millimicrons	0.15

	Maximum ultraviolet absorbance per centimeter path length
290–299 millimicrons	0.12
300–359 millimicrons	0.08
360–400 millimicrons	0.02

ANALYTICAL SPECIFICATION FOR PETROLEUM WAX

GENERAL INSTRUCTIONS

Because of the sensitivity of the test, the possibility of errors arising from contamination is great. It is of the greatest importance that all glassware be scrupulously cleaned to remove all organic matter such as oil, grease, detergent residues, etc. Examine all glassware, including stoppers and stopcocks, under ultraviolet light to detect any residual fluorescent contamination. As a precautionary measure it is recommended practice to rinse all glassware with purified isooctane immediately before use. No grease is to be used on stopcocks or joints. Great care to avoid contamination of wax samples in handling and to assure absence of any extraneous material arising from inadequate packaging is essential. Because some of the polynuclear hydrocarbons sought in this test are very susceptible to photo-oxidation, the entire procedure is to be carried out under subdued light.

APPARATUS

Separatory funnels. 250–milliliter, 500–milliliter, 1,000–milliliter, and preferably 2,000–milliliter capacity, equipped with tetrafluoroethylene polymer stopcocks.

Reservoir. 500–milliliter capacity, equipped with a 24/40 standard taper male fitting at the bottom and a suitable ball-joint at the top for connecting to the nitrogen supply. The male fitting should be equipped with glass hooks.

Chromatographic tube. 180 millimeters in length, inside diameter to be 15.7 millimeters ±0.1 millimeter, equipped with a coarse, fritted-glass disc, a tetrafluoroethylene polymer stopcock, and a female 24/40 standard tapered fitting at the opposite end. (Overall length of the column with the female joint is 235 millimeters.) The female fitting should be equipped with glass hooks.

Disc. Tetrafluoroethylene polymer 2–inch diameter disc approximately 3/16–inch thick with a hole bored in the center to closely fit the stem of the chromatographic tube.

Heating jacket. Conical, for 500–milliliter separatory funnel. (Used with variable transformer heat control.)

Suction flask. 250–milliliter or 500–milliliter filter flask.

Condenser. 24/40 joints, fitted with a drying tube, length optional.

Evaporation flask (optional). 250–milliliter or 500–milliliter capacity all-glass flask equipped with standard taper stopper having inlet and outlet tubes to permit passage of nitrogen across the surface of contained liquid to be evaporated.

Vacuum distillation assembly. All glass (for purification of dimethyl sulfoxide); 2–liter distillation flask with heating mantle; Vigreaux vacuum-jacketed condenser (or equivalent) about 45 centimeters in length and distilling head with separable cold finger condenser. Use of tetrafluoroethylene polymer sleeves on the glass joints will prevent freezing. Do not use grease on stopcocks or joints.

Spectrophotometric cells. Fused quartz cells, optical path length in the range of 5.000 centimeters ±0.005 centimeter; also for checking spectrophotometer performance only, optical path length in the range 1.000 centimeter ±0.005 centimeter. With distilled water in the cells, determine any absorbance differences.

Spectrophotometer. Spectral range 250 millimicrons–400 millimicrons with spectral slit width of 2 millimicrons or less, under instrument operating conditions for these absorbance measurements, the spectrophotometer shall also meet the following performance requirements:

Absorbance repeatability, ±0.01 at 0.4 absorbance.

Absorbance accuracy,[1] ±0.05 at 0.4 absorbance.

Wavelength repeatability, ±0.2 millimicron.

Wavelength accuracy, ±1.0 millimicron.

Nitrogen cylinder. Water-pumped or equivalent purity nitrogen in cylinder equipped with regulator and valve to control flow at 5 p.s.i.g.

[1] As determined by using potassium chromate for reference standard and described in National Bureau of Standards Circular 484, Spectrophotometry, U.S. Department of Commerce, (1949). The accuracy is to be determined by comparison with the standard values at 290, 345, and 400 millimicrons. Circular 484 is incorporated by reference. Copies are available from the Center for Food Safety and Applied Nutrition (HFS–200), Food and Drug Administration, 5100 Paint Branch Pkwy., College Park, MD 20740, or available for inspection at the National Archives and Records Administration (NARA). For information on the availability of this material at NARA, call 202–741–6030, or go to: *http://www.archives.gov/federal_register/code_of_federal_regulations/ibr_locations.html.*

REAGENTS AND MATERIALS

Organic solvents. All solvents used throughout the procedure shall meet the specifications and tests described in this specification. The isooctane, benzene, acetone, and methyl alcohol designated in the list following this paragraph shall pass the following test:

To the specified quantity of solvent in a 250–milliliter Erlenmeyer flask, add 1 milliliter of purified *n*-hexadecane and evaporate on the steam bath under a stream of nitrogen (a) loose aluminum foil jacket around the flask will speed evaporation). Discontinue evaporation when not over 1 milliliter of residue remains. (To the residue from benzene add a 10–milliliter portion of purified isooctane, reevaporate, and repeat once to insure complete removal of benzene.)

Alternatively, the evaporation time can be reduced by using the optional evaporation flask. In this case the solvent and *n*-hexadecane are placed in the flask on the steam bath, the tube assembly is inserted, and a stream of nitrogen is fed through the inlet tube while the outlet tube is connected to a solvent trap and vacuum line in such a way as to prevent any flow-back of condensate into the flask.

Dissolve the 1 milliliter of hexadecane residue in isooctane and make to 25 milliliters volume. Determine the absorbance in the 5–centimeter path length cells compared to isooctane as reference. The absorbance of the solution of the solvent residue (except for methyl alcohol) shall not exceed 0.01 per centimeter path length between 280 and 400 mμ. For methyl alcohol this absorbance value shall be 0.00.

Isooctane (2,2,4–trimethylpentane). Use 180 milliliters for the test described in the preceding paragraph. Purify, if necessary, by passage through a column of activated silica gel (Grade 12, Davison Chemical Company, Baltimore, Maryland, or equivalent) about 90 centimeters in length and 5 centimeters to 8 centimeters in diameter.

Benzene, A.C.S. reagent grade. Use 150 milliliters for the test. Purify, if necessary, by distillation or otherwise.

Acetone, A.C.S. reagent grade. Use 200 milliliters for the test. Purify, if necessary, by distillation.

Eluting mixtures:

1. *10 percent benzene in isooctane.* Pipet 50 milliliters of benzene into a 500–milliliter glass-stoppered volumetric flask and adjust to volume with isooctane, with mixing.

2. *20 percent benzene in isooctane.* Pipet 50 milliliters of benzene into a 250–milliliter glass-stoppered volumetric flask, and adjust to volume with isooctane, with mixing.

3. *Acetone-benzene-water mixture.* Add 20 milliliters of water to 380 milliliters of acetone and 200 milliliters of benzene, and mix.

n-Hexadecane, 99 percent olefin-free. Dilute 1.0 milliliter of *n*-hexadecane to 25 milliliters with isooctane and determine the absorbance in a 5–centimeter cell compared to isooctane as reference point between 280 mμ–400 mμ. The absorbance per centimeter path length shall not exceed 0.00 in this range. Purify, if necessary, by percolation through activated silica gel or by distillation.

Methyl alcohol, A.C.S. reagent grade. Use 10.0 milliliters of methyl alcohol. Purify, if necessary, by distillation.

Dimethyl sulfoxide. Pure grade, clear, water-white, m.p. 18° minimum. Dilute 120 milliliters of dimethyl sulfoxide with 240 milliliters of distilled water in a 500–milliliter separatory funnel, mix and allow to cool for 5–10 minutes. Add 40 milliliters of isooctane to the solution and extract by shaking the funnel vigorously for 2 minutes. Draw off the lower aqueous layer into a second 500–milliliter separatory funnel and repeat the extraction with 40 milliliters of isooctane. Draw off and discard the aqueous layer. Wash each of the 40–milliliter extractives three times with 50–milliliter portions of distilled water. Shaking time for each wash is 1 minute. Discard the aqueous layers. Filter the first extractive through anhydrous sodium sulfate prewashed with isooctane (see *Sodium sulfate under* "Reagents and Materials" for preparation of filter), into a 250–milliliter Erlenmeyer flask, or optionally into the evaporating flask. Wash the first separatory funnel with the second 40–milliliter isooctane extractive, and pass through the sodium sulfate into the flask. Then wash the second and first separatory funnels successively with a 10–milliliter portion of isooctane, and pass the solvent through the sodium sulfate into the flask. Add 1 milliliter of *n*-hexadecane and evaporate the isooctane on the steam bath under nitrogen. Discontinue evaporation when not over 1 milliliter of residue remains. To the residue, add a 10–milliliter portion of isooctane and reevaporate to 1 milliliter of hexadecane. Again, add 10 milliliters of isooctane to the residue and evaporate to 1 milliliter of hexadecane to insure complete removal of all volatile materials. Dissolve the 1 milliliter of hexadecane in isooctane and make to 25–milliliter volume. Determine the reference. The absorbance of the solution should not exceed 0.02 per centimeter path length in the 280 mμ–400 mμ range. (NOTE. Difficulty in meeting this absorbance specification may be due to organic impurities in the distilled water. Repetition of the test omitting the dimethyl sulfoxide will disclose their presence. If necessary to meet the specification, purify the water by redistillation, passage through an ion-exchange resin, or otherwise.)

Purify, if necessary, by the following procedure: To 1,500 milliliters of dimethyl sulfoxide in a 2–liter glass-stoppered flask, add

6.0 milliliters of phosphoric acid and 50 grams of Norit A (decolorizing carbon, alkaline) or equivalent. Stopper the flask, and with the use of a magnetic stirrer (tetrafluoroethylene polymer coated bar) stir the solvent for 15 minutes. Filter the dimethyl sulfoxide through four thicknesses of fluted paper (18.5 centimeters, Schleicher & Schuell, No. 597, or equivalent). If the initial filtrate contains carbon fines, refilter through the same filter until a clear filtrate is obtained. Protect the sulfoxide from air and moisture during this operation by covering the solvent in the funnel and collection flask with a layer of isooctane. Transfer the filtrate to a 2–liter separatory funnel and draw off the dimethyl sulfoxide into the 2–liter distillation flask of the vacuum distillation assembly and distill at approximately 3–millimeter Hg pressure or less. Discard the first 200–milliliter fraction of the distillate and replace the distillate collection flask with a clean one. Continue the distillation until approximately 1 liter of the sulfoxide has been collected.

At completion of the distillation, the reagent should be stored in glass-stoppered bottles since it is very hygroscopic and will react with some metal containers in the presence of air.

Phosphoric acid. 85 percent A.C.S. reagent grade.

Sodium borohydride. 98 percent.

Magnesium oxide (Sea Sorb 43, Food Machinery Company, Westvaco Division, distributed by chemical supply firms, or equivalent). Place 100 grams of the magnesium oxide in a large beaker, add 700 milliliters of distilled water to make a thin slurry, and heat on a steam bath for 30 minutes with intermittent stirring. Stir well initially to insure that all the absorbent is completely wetted. Using a Buchner funnel and a filter paper (Schleicher & Schuell No. 597, or equivalent) of suitable diameter, filter with suction. Continue suction until water no longer drips from the funnel. Transfer the absorbent to a glass trough lined with aluminum foil (free from rolling oil). Break up the magnesia with a clean spatula and spread out the absorbent on the aluminum foil in a layer about 1 centimeter to 2 centimeters thick. Dry for 24 hours at 160 °C ±1 °C. Pulverize the magnesia with mortar and pestle. Sieve the pulverized absorbent between 60–180 mesh. Use the magnesia retained on the 180–mesh sieve.

Celite 545. Johns-Manville Company, diatomaceous earth, or equivalent.

Magnesium oxide-Celite 545 mixture (2+ 1) by weight. Place the magnesium oxide (60–180 mesh) and the Celite 545 in 2 to 1 proportions, respectively, by weight in a glass-stoppered flask large enough for adequate mixing. Shake vigorously for 10 minutes. Transfer the mixture to a glass trough lined with aluminum foil (free from rolling oil) and spread it out on a layer about 1 centimeter to 2 centimeters thick. Reheat the mixture at 160 °C ±1 °C for 2 hours, and store in a tightly closed flask.

Sodium sulfate, anhydrous, A.C.S. reagent grade, preferably in granular form. For each bottle of sodium sulfate reagent used, establish as follows the necessary sodium sulfate prewash to provide such filters required in the method: Place approximately 35 grams of anhydrous sodium sulfate in a 30–milliliter coarse, fritted-glass funnel or in a 65–millimeter filter funnel with glass wool plug; wash with successive 15–milliliter portions of the indicated solvent until a 15–milliliter portion of the wash shows 0.00 absorbance per centimeter path length between 280 mμ and 400 mμ when tested as prescribed under "Organic solvents." Usually three portions of wash solvent are sufficient.

Before proceeding with analysis of a sample, determine the absorbance in a 5–centimeter path cell between 250 mμ and 400 mμ for the reagent blank by carrying out the procedure, without a wax sample, at room temperature, recording the spectra after the extraction stage and after the complete procedure as prescribed. The absorbance per centimeter path length following the extraction stage should not exceed 0.040 in the wavelength range from 280 mμ to 400 mμ; the absorbance per centimeter path length following the complete procedure should not exceed 0.070 in the wavelength range from 280 mμ to 299 mμ, inclusive, nor 0.045 in the wavelength range from 300 mμ to 400 mμ. If in either spectrum the characteristic benzene peaks in the 250 mμ–260 mμ region are present, remove the benzene by the procedure under "Organic solvents" and record absorbance again.

Place 300 milliliters of dimethyl sulfoxide in a 1–liter separatory funnel and add 75 milliliters of phosphoric acid. Mix the contents of the funnel and allow to stand for 10 minutes. (The reaction between the sulfoxide and the acid is exothermic. Release pressure after mixing, then keep funnel stoppered.) Add 150 milliliters of isooctane and shake to preequilibrate the solvents. Draw off the individual layers and store in glass-stoppered flasks.

Place a representative 1–kilogram sample of wax, or if this amount is not available, the entire sample, in a beaker of a capacity about three times the volume of the sample and heat with occasional stirring on a steam bath until the wax is completely melted and homogeneous. Weigh four 25–gram ±0.2 gram portions of the melted wax in separate 100–milliliter beakers. Reserve three of the portions for later replicate analyses as necessary. Pour one weighed portion immediately after remelting (on the steam bath) into a 500–milliliter separatory funnel containing 100 milliliters of the preequilibrated sulfoxide-phosphoric acid mixture that has been heated in the heating jacket at a temperature just high enough to keep the wax melted. (NOTE: In preheating the sulfoxide-acid mixture, remove the stopper of the separatory funnel at intervals to release the pressure.)

Promptly complete the transfer of the sample to the funnel in the jacket with portions of the preequilibrated isooctane, warming the beaker, if necessary, and using a total volume of just 50 milliliters of the solvent. If the wax comes out of solution during these operations, let the stoppered funnel remain in the jacket until the wax redissolves. (Remove stopper from the funnel at intervals to release pressure.) When the wax is in solution, remove the funnel from the jacket and shake it vigorously for 2 minutes. Set up three 250–milliliter separatory funnels with each containing 30 milliliters of preequilibrated isooctane. After separation of the liquid phases, allow to cool until the main portion of the wax-isooctane solution begins to show a precipitate. Gently swirl the funnel when precipitation first occurs on the inside surface of the funnel to accelerate this process. Carefully draw off the lower layer, filter it slowly through a thin layer of glass wool fitted loosely in a filter funnel into the first 250–milliliter separatory funnel, and wash in tandem with the 30–milliliter portions of isooctane contained in the 250–milliliter separatory funnels. Shaking time for each wash is 1 minute. Repeat the extraction operation with two additional portions of the sulfoxide-acid mixture, replacing the funnel in the jacket after each extraction to keep the wax in solution and washing each extractive in tandem through the same three portions of isooctane.

Collect the successive extractives (300 milliliters total) in a separatory funnel (preferably 2–liter), containing 480 milliliters of distilled water, mix, and allow to cool for a few minutes after the last extractive has been added. Add 80 milliliters of isooctane to the solution and extract by shaking the funnel vigorously for 2 minutes. Draw off the lower aqueous layer into a second separatory funnel (preferably 2–liter) and repeat the extraction with 80 milliliters of isooctane. Draw off and discard the aqueous layer. Wash each of the 80–milliliter extractives three times with 100–milliliter portions of distilled water. Shaking time for each wash is 1 minute. Discard the aqueous layers. Filter the first extractive through anhydrous sodium sulfate prewashed with isooctane (see *Sodium Sulfate* under "Reagents and Materials" for preparation of filter) into a 250–milliliter Erlenmeyer flask (or optionally into the evaporation flask). Wash the first separatory funnel with the second 80–milliliter isooctane extractive and pass through the sodium sulfate. Then wash the second and first separatory funnels successively with a 20–milliliter portion of isooctane and pass the solvent through the sodium sulfate into the flask. Add 1 milliliter of *n*-hexadecane and evaporate the isooctane on the steam bath under nitrogen. Discontinue evaporation when not over 1 milliliter of residue remains. To the residue, add a 10–milliliter portion of isooctane, reevaporate to 1 milliliter of hexadecane, and repeat this operation once.

Quantitatively transfer the residue with isooctane to a 25–milliliter volumetric flask, make to volume, and mix. Determine the absorbance of the solution in the 5–centimeter path length cells compared to isooctane as reference between 280 mμ–400 mμ (take care to lose none of the solution in filling the sample cell). Correct the absorbance values for any absorbance derived from reagents as determined by carrying out the procedure without a wax sample. If the corrected absorbance does not exceed the limits prescribed in this paragraph (b), the wax meets the ultraviolet absorbance specifications. If the corrected absorbance per centimeter path length exceeds the limits prescribed in this paragraph (b), proceed as follows:

Quantitatively transfer the isooctane solution to a 125–milliliter flask equipped with 24/40 joint and evaporate the isooctane on the steam bath under a stream of nitrogen to a volume of 1 milliliter of hexadecane. Add 10 milliliters of methyl alcohol and approximately 0.3 gram of sodium borohydride. (Minimize exposure of the borohydride to the atmosphere. A measuring dipper may be used.) Immediately fit a water-cooled condenser equipped with a 24/40 joint and with a drying tube into the flask, mix until the borohydride is dissolved, and allow to stand for 30 minutes at room temperature, with intermittent swirling. At the end of this period, disconnect the flask and evaporate the methyl alcohol on the steam bath under nitrogen until the sodium borohydride begins to come out of the solution. Then add 10 milliliters of isooctane and evaporate to a volume of about 2–3 milliliters. Again, add 10 milliliters of isooctane and concentrate to a volume of approximately 5 milliliters. Swirl the flask repeatedly to assure adequate washing of the sodium borohydride residues.

Fit the tetrafluoroethylene polymer disc on the upper part of the stem of the chromatographic tube, then place the tube with the disc on the suction flask and apply the vacuum (approximately 135 millimeters Hg pressure). Weight out 14 grams of the 2:1 magnesium oxide-Celite 545 mixture and pour the adsorbent mixture into the chromatographic tube in approximately 3–centimeter layers. After the addition of each layer, level off the top of the adsorbent with a flat glass rod or metal plunger by pressing down firmly until the adsorbent is well packed. Loosen the topmost few millimeters of each adsorbent layer with the end of a metal rod before the addition of the next layer. Continue packing in this manner until all the 14 grams of the adsorbent is added to the tube. Level off the top of the adsorbent by pressing down firmly with a flat glass rod or metal plunger to make the depth of the adsorbent bed approximately 12.5 centimeters in depth. Turn off the vacuum and remove the suction flask. Fit the 500–milliliter reservoir onto the top of the chromatographic column and prewet the column by passing 100 milliliters of isooctane through the column. Adjust the nitrogen pressure so that the rate of descent of the isooctane coming off of the column is between 2–3 milliliters per minute. Discontinue pressure just before the last of the isooctane reaches the level of the adsorbent. (CAUTION: Do not allow the liquid level to recede below the adsorbent level at any time.) Remove the reservoir and decant the 5–milliliter isooctane concentrate solution onto the column and with slight pressure again allow the liquid level to recede to barely above the adsorbent level. Rapidly complete the transfer similarly with two 5–milliliter portions of isooctane, swirling the flask repeatedly each time to assure adequate washing of the residue. Just before the final 5–milliliter wash reaches the top of the adsorbent, add 100 milliliters of isooctane to the reservoir and continue the percolation at the 2–3 milliliter per minute rate. Just before the last of the isooctane reaches the adsorbent level, add 100 milliliters of 10 percent benzene in isooctane to the reservoir and continue the percolation at the aforementioned rate. Just before the solvent mixture reaches adsorbent level, add 25 milliliters of 20 percent benzene in isooctane to the reservoir and continue the percolation at 2–3 milliliters per minute until all this solvent mixture has been removed from the column. Discard all the elution solvents collected up to this point. Add 300 milliliters of the acetone-benzene-water mixture to the reservoir and percolate through the column to elute the polynuclear compounds. Collect the eluate in a clean 1–liter separatory funnel. Allow the column to drain until most of the solvent mixture is removed. Wash the eluate three times with 300–milliliter portions of distilled water, shaking well for each wash. (The addition of small amounts of sodium chloride facilitates separation.) Discard the aqueous layer after each wash. After the final separation, filter the residual benzene through anhydrous sodium sulfate prewashed with benzene (see *Sodium sulfate* under "Reagents and Materials" for preparation of filter) into a 250–milliliter Erlenmeyer flask (or optionally into the evaporation flask). Wash the separatory funnel with two additional 20–milliliter portions of benzene which are also filtered through the sodium sulfate. Add 1 milliliter of *n*-hexadecane and completely remove the benzene by evaporation under nitrogen, using the special procedure to eliminate benzene as previously described under "Organic Solvents." Quantitatively transfer the residue with isooctane to a 25–milliliter volumetric flask and adjust to volume. Determine the absorbance of the solution in the 5–centimeter path length cells compared to isooctane as reference between 250 mμ–400 mμ. Correct for any absorbance derived from the reagents as determined by carrying out the procedure without a wax sample. If either spectrum shows the characteristic benzene peaks in the 250 mμ–260 mμ region, evaporate the solution to remove benzene by the procedure under "Organic Solvents." Dissolve the residue, transfer quantitatively, and adjust to volume in isooctane in a 25–milliliter volumetric flask. Record the absorbance again. If the corrected absorbance does not exceed the limits prescribed in this paragraph (b), the wax meets the ultraviolet absorbance specifications.

(c) Petroleum wax may contain one or more of the following adjuvants in amounts not greater than that required to produce their intended effect:

(1) Antioxidants permitted in food by regulations issued in accordance with section 409 of the act.

(2) Poly(alkylacrylate) (CAS Reg. No. 27029–57–8), made from long chain (C_{16}-C_{22}) alcohols and acrylic acid, or poly(alkylmethacrylate) (CAS Reg. No. 179529–36–3), made from long chain (C_{18}-C_{22}) methacrylate esters, having:

(i) A number average molecular weight between 40,000 and 100,000;

(ii) A weight average molecular weight (MW_w) to number average molecular weight (MW_n) ratio (MW_w/MW_n) of not less than 3; and

(iii) Unreacted alkylacrylate or alkylmethacrylate monomer content not in excess of 14 percent, as determined by a method entitled "Method for Determining Weight-Average and Number-Average Molecular Weight and for Determining Alkylacrylate Monomer Content of Poly(alkylacrylate) used as Processing Aid in Manufacture of Petroleum Wax," which is incorporated by reference in accordance with 5 U.S.C. 552(a) and 1 CFR part 51. Copies are available from the Office of Food Additive Safety (HFS–200), Center for Food Safety and Applied Nutrition, Food and Drug Administration, 5100 Paint Branch Pkwy., College Park, MD 20740, 240–402–1200, or may be examined at the Center for Food Safety and Applied Nutrition's Library, Food and Drug Administration, 5100 Paint

Branch Pkwy., College Park, MD 20740 or at the National Archives and Records Administration (NARA). For information on the availability of this material at NARA, call 202–741–6030, or go to: *http://www.archives.gov/federal_register/code_of_federal_regulations/ibr_locations.html.* Petroleum wax shall contain not more than 1,050 parts per million of poly(alkylacrylate) or poly(alkylmethacrylate) residues as determined by a method entitled "Method for Determining Residual Level of Poly(alkylacrylate) in Petroleum Wax," which is incorporated by reference. Copies are available from the addresses cited in this paragraph.

(d) Petroleum wax is used or intended for use as follows:

Use	Limitations
In chewing gum base, as a masticatory substance.	In an amount not to exceed good manufacturing practice.
On cheese and raw fruits and vegetables as a protective coating.	Do.
As a defoamer in food	In accordance with § 173.340 of this chapter.
As a component of microcapsules for spice-flavoring substances.	In accordance with § 172.230 of this chapter.

[42 FR 14491, Mar. 15, 1977, as amended at 45 FR 48123, July 18, 1980; 47 FR 11838, Mar. 19, 1982; 50 FR 32561, Aug. 13, 1985; 51 FR 19544, May 30, 1986; 54 FR 24897, June 12, 1989; 64 FR 44122, Aug. 13, 1999; 78 FR 14665, Mar. 7, 2013]

§ 172.888 Synthetic petroleum wax.

Synthetic petroleum wax may be safely used in or on foods in accordance with the following conditions:

(a) Synthetic petroleum wax is a mixture of solid hydrocarbons, paraffinic in nature, prepared by either catalytic polymerization of ethylene or copolymerization of ethylene with linear (C_3 to C_{12}) alpha-olefins, and refined to meet the specifications prescribed in this section.

(b) Synthetic petroleum wax meets the ultraviolet absorbance limits of § 172.886(b) when subjected to the analytical procedure described therein.

(c) Synthetic petroleum wax has a number average molecular weight of not less than 500 nor greater than 1,200 as determined by vapor pressure osmometry.

(d) Synthetic petroleum wax may contain any antioxidant permitted in food by regulations issued in accordance with section 409 of the act, in an amount not greater than that required to produce its intended effect.

(e) Synthetic petroleum wax is used or intended for use as follows:

Use	Limitations
In chewing gum base, as a masticatory substance.	In accordance with § 172.615 in an amount not to exceed good manufacturing practice.
On cheese and raw fruits and vegetables as a protective coating.	In an amount not to exceed good manufacturing practice.
As a defoamer in food	In accordance with § 173.340 of this chapter.

[42 FR 14491, Mar. 15, 1977, as amended at 59 FR 10986, Mar. 9, 1994]

§ 172.890 Rice bran wax.

Rice bran wax may be safely used in food in accordance with the following conditions:

(a) It is the refined wax obtained from rice bran and meets the following specifications:

Melting point 75 °C to 80 °C.
Free fatty acids, maximum 10 percent.
Iodine number, maximum 20.
Saponification number 75 to 120.

(b) It is used or intended for use as follows:

Food	Limitation in food	Use
Candy	50 p.p.m	Coating.
Fresh fruits and fresh vegetables.	do	Do.
Chewing gum	2½ pct	Plasticizing material.

§ 172.892 Food starch-modified.

Food starch-modified as described in this section may be safely used in food. The quantity of any substance employed to effect such modification shall not exceed the amount reasonably required to accomplish the intended physical or technical effect, nor exceed any limitation prescribed. To insure safe use of the food starch-modified, the label of the food additive container shall bear the name of the additive "food starch-modified" in addition to other information required by the Act. Food starch may be modified by treatment prescribed as follows:

(a) Food starch may be acid-modified by treatment with hydrochloric acid or sulfuric acid or both.

(b) Food starch may be bleached by treatment with one or more of the following:

	Limitations
Active oxygen obtained from hydrogen peroxide and/or peracetic acid, not to exceed 0.45 percent of active oxygen.	
Ammonium persulfate, not to exceed 0.075 percent and sulfur dioxide, not to exceed 0.05 percent.	
Chlorine, as calcium hypochlorite, not to exceed 0.036 percent of dry starch.	The finished food starch-modified is limited to use only as a component of batter for commercially processed foods.
Chlorine, as sodium hypochlorite, not to exceed 0.0082 pound of chlorine per pound of dry starch.	
Potassium permanganate, not to exceed 0.2 percent.	Residual manganese (calculated as Mn), not to exceed 50 parts per million in food starch-modified.
Sodium chlorite, not to exceed 0.5 percent.	

(c) Food starch may be oxidized by treatment with chlorine, as sodium hypochlorite, not to exceed 0.055 pound of chlorine per pound of dry starch.

(d) Food starch may be esterified by treatment with one of the following:

	Limitations
Acetic anhydride	Acetyl groups in food starch-modified not to exceed 2.5 percent.
Adipic anhydride, not to exceed 0.12 percent, and acetic anhydride.	Do.
Monosodium orthophosphate	Residual phosphate in food starch-modified not to exceed 0.4 percent calculated as phosphorus.
1–Octenyl succinic anhydride, not to exceed 3 percent.	
1–Octenyl succinic anhydride, not to exceed 2 percent, and aluminum sulfate, not to exceed 2 percent.	
1-Octenyl succinic anhydride, not to exceed 3 percent, followed by treatment with a *beta*-amylase enzyme that is either an approved food additive of is generally recognized as safe.	Limited to use as a stabilizer or emulsifier in beverages and beverage bases as defined in § 170.3(n)(3) of this chapter.
Phosphorus oxychloride, not to exceed 0.1 percent.	
Phosphorus oxychloride, not to exceed 0.1 percent, followed by either acetic anhydride, not to exceed 8 percent, or vinyl acetate, not to exceed 7.5 percent.	Acetyl groups in food starch-modified not to exceed 2.5 percent.
Sodium trimetaphosphate	Residual phosphate in food starch-modified not to exceed 0.04 percent, calculated as phosphorus.
Sodium tripolyphosphate and sodium trimetaphosphate.	Residual phosphate in food starch-modified not to exceed 0.4 percent calculated as phosphorus.
Succinic anhydride, not to exceed 4 percent.	
Vinyl acetate	Acetyl groups in food starch-modified not to exceed 2.5 percent.

(e) Food starch may be etherified by treatment with one of the following:

	Limitations
Acrolein, not to exceed 0.6 percent.	
Epichlorohydrin, not to exceed 0.3 percent.	
Epichlorohydrin, not to exceed 0.1 percent, and propylene oxide, not to exceed 10 percent, added in combination or in any sequence.	Residual propylene chlorohydrin not more than 5 parts per million in food starch-modified.
Epichlorohydrin, not to exceed 0.1 percent, followed by propylene oxide, not to exceed 25 percent.	Do.
Propylene oxide, not to exceed 25 percent.	Do.

(f) Food starch may be esterified and etherified by treatment with one of the following:

	Limitations
Acrolein, not to exceed 0.6 percent and vinyl acetate, not to exceed 7.5 percent.	Acetyl groups in food starch-modified not to exceed 2.5 percent.
Epichlorohydrin, not to exceed 0.3 percent, and acetic anhydride.	Acetyl groups in food starch-modified not to exceed 2.5 percent.
Epichlorohydrin, not to exceed 0.3 percent, and succinic anhydride, not to exceed 4 percent.	
Phosphorus oxychloride, not to exceed 0.1 percent, and propylene oxide, not to exceed 10 percent.	Residual propylene chlorohydrin not more than 5 parts per million in food starch-modified.

(g) Food starch may be modified by treatment with one of the following:

	Limitations
Chlorine, as sodium hypochlorite, not to exceed 0.055 pound of chlorine per pound of dry starch; 0.45 percent of active oxygen obtained from hydrogen peroxide; and propylene oxide, not to exceed 25 percent.	Residual propylene chlorohydrin not more than 5 parts per million in food starch-modified.
Sodium hydroxide, not to exceed 1 percent.	

(h) Food starch may be modified by a combination of the treatments prescribed by paragraphs (a), (b), and/or (i) of this section and any one of the treatments prescribed by paragraph (c), (d), (e), (f), or (g) of this section, subject to any limitations prescribed by the paragraphs named.

(i) Food starch may be modified by treatment with the following enzymes:

Enzyme	Limitations
Alpha-amylase (E.C. 3.2.1.1)	The enzyme must be generally recognized as safe or approved as a food additive for this purpose. The resulting nonsweet nutritive saccharide polymer has a dextrose equivalent of less than 20.
Beta-amylase (E.C. 3.2.1.2).	
Glucoamylase (E.C. 3.2.1.3).	
Isoamylase (E.C. 3.2.1.68).	
Pullulanase (E.C. 3.2.1.41).	

[42 FR 14491, Mar. 15, 1977, as amended at 43 FR 11697, Mar. 21, 1978; 46 FR 32015, June 19, 1981; 57 FR 54700, Nov. 20, 1992; 58 FR 21100, Apr. 19, 1993; 66 FR 17509, Apr. 2, 2001]

§ 172.894 Modified cottonseed products intended for human consumption.

The food additive modified cottonseed products may be used for human consumption in accordance with the following prescribed conditions:

(a) The additive is derived from:

(1) Decorticated, partially defatted, cooked, ground cottonseed kernels; or

(2) Decorticated, ground cottonseed kernels, in a process that utilizes *n*-hexane as an extracting solvent in such a way that no more than 60 parts per million of *n*-hexane residues and less than 1 percent fat by weight remain in the finished product; or

(3) Glandless cottonseed kernels roasted to attain a temperature of not less than 250 °F in the kernel for not less than 5 minutes for use as a snack food, or in baked goods, or in soft candy; or

(4) Raw glandless cottonseed kernels may be used in hard candy where the kernel temperature during cooking will exceed 250 °F for not less than 5 minutes.

(b) The additive is prepared to meet the following specifications:

(1) Free gossypol content not to exceed 450 parts per million.

(2) It contains no added arsenic compound and therefore may not exceed a maximum natural background level of 0.2 part per million total arsenic, calculated as As.

(c) To assure safe use of the additive, the label of the food additive container shall bear, in addition to other information required by the act, the name of the additive as follows:

(1) The additive identified in paragraph (a)(1) of this section as "partially defatted, cooked cottonseed flour".

(2) The additive identified in paragraph (a)(2) of this section as "defatted cottonseed flour".

(3) The additive identified in paragraph (a)(3) of this section as "roasted glandless cottonseed kernels".

(4) The additive identified in paragraph (a)(4) of this section as "raw glandless cottonseed kernels for use in cooked hard candy".

(d) The Food and Drug Administration and the Environmental Protection Agency have determined that glandless cottonseed kernels permitted for use by this section are a distinct commodity from glanded cottonseed.

§ 172.896 Dried yeasts.

Dried yeast (*Saccharomyces cerevisiae* and *Saccharomyces fragilis*) and dried torula yeast (*Candida utilis*) may be safely used in food provided the total folic acid content of the yeast does not exceed 0.04 milligram per gram of yeast (approximately 0.008 milligram of pteroylglutamic acid per gram of yeast).

§ 172.898 Bakers yeast glycan.

Bakers yeast glycan may be safely used in food in accordance with the following conditions:

(a) Bakers yeast glycan is the comminuted, washed, pasteurized, and dried cell walls of the yeast, *Saccharomyces cerevisiae*. It is composed principally of long chain carbohydrates, not less than 85 percent on a dry solids basis. The carbohydrate is composed of glycan and mannan units in approximately a 2:1 ratio.

(b) The additive meets the following specifications on a dry weight basis: Less than 0.4 part per million (ppm) arsenic, 0.13 ppm cadmium, 0.2 ppm lead, 0.05 ppm mercury, 0.09 ppm selenium, and 10 ppm zinc.

(c) The viable microbial content of the finished ingredient is:

(1) Less than 10,000 organisms/gram by aerobic plate count.

(2) Less than 10 yeasts and molds/gram.

(3) Negative for *Salmonella, E. coli*, coagulase positive *Staphylococci, Clostridium perfringens, Clostridium botulinum*, or any other recognized microbial pathogen or any harmful microbial toxin.

(d) The additive is used or intended for use in the following foods when standards of identity established under section 401 of the Act do not preclude such use:

Use	Limitations
(1) In salad dressings as an emulsifier and emulsifier salt as defined in § 170.3(o)(8) of this chapter, stabilizer and thickener as defined in § 170.3(o)(28) of this chapter, or texturizer as defined in § 170.3(o)(32) of this chapter.	Not to exceed a concentration of 5 percent of the finished salad dressing.
(2) In frozen dessert analogs as a stabilizer and thickener as defined in § 170.3(o)(28) of this chapter, or texturizer as defined in § 170.3(o)(32) of this chapter.	In an amount not to exceed good manufacturing practice.
(3) In sour cream analogs as a stabilizer and thickener as defined in § 170.3(o)(28) of this chapter, or texturizer as defined in § 170.3(o)(32) of this chapter.	Do.
(4) In cheese spread analogs as a stabilizer and thickener as defined in § 170.3(o)(28) of this chapter, or texturizer as defined in § 170.3(o)(32) of this chapter.	Do.
(5) In cheese-flavored and sour cream-flavored snack dips as a stabilizer and thickener as defined in § 170.3(o)(28) of this chapter, or texturizer as defined in § 170.3(o)(32) of this chapter.	Do.

(e) The label and labeling of the ingredient shall bear adequate directions to assure that use of the ingredient complies with this regulation.

[42 FR 14491, Mar. 15, 1977, as amended at 45 FR 58836, Sept. 5, 1980]

PART 173—SECONDARY DIRECT FOOD ADDITIVES PERMITTED IN FOOD FOR HUMAN CONSUMPTION

Subpart A—Polymer Substances and Polymer Adjuvants for Food Treatment

Sec.

Subpart B—Enzyme Preparations and Microorganisms

Subpart C—Solvents, Lubricants, Release Agents and Related Substances

Subpart D—Specific Usage Additives

AUTHORITY: 21 U.S.C. 321, 342, 348.

SOURCE: 42 FR 14526, Mar. 15, 1977, unless otherwise noted.

EDITORIAL NOTE: Nomenclature changes to part 173 appear at 61 FR 14482, Apr. 2, 1996, 66 FR 56035, Nov. 6, 2001, and 66 FR 66742, Dec. 27, 2001.

Subpart A—Polymer Substances and Polymer Adjuvants for Food Treatment

§ 173.5 Acrylate-acrylamide resins.

Acrylate-acrylamide resins may be safely used in food under the following prescribed conditions:

(a) The additive consists of one of the following:

(1) Acrylamide-acrylic acid resin (hydrolyzed polyacrylamide) is produced by the polymerization of acrylamide with partial hydrolysis, or by copolymerization of acrylamide and acrylic acid, with the greater part of the polymer being composed of acrylamide units.

(2) Sodium polyacrylate-acrylamide resin is produced by the polymerization and subsequent hydrolysis of acrylonitrile in a sodium silicate-sodium hydroxide aqueous solution, with the greater part of the polymer being composed of acrylate units.

(b) The additive contains not more than 0.05 percent of residual monomer calculated as acrylamide.

(c) The additive is used or intended for use as follows:

(1) The additive identified in paragraph (a) (1) of this section is used as a flocculent in the clarification of beet sugar juice and liquor or cane sugar juice and liquor or corn starch hydrolyzate in an amount not to exceed 5 parts per million by weight of the juice or 10 parts per million by weight of the liquor or the corn starch hydrolyzate.

(2) The additive identified in paragraph (a)(2) of this section is used to control organic and mineral scale in beet sugar juice and liquor or cane sugar juice and liquor in an amount not to exceed 2.5 parts per million by weight of the juice or liquor.

[42 FR 14526, Mar. 15, 1977, as amended at 46 FR 30494, June 9, 1981]

§ 173.10 Modified polyacrylamide resin.

Modified polyacrylamide resin may be safely used in food in accordance with the following prescribed conditions:

(a) The modified polyacrylamide resin is produced by the copolymerization of acrylamide with not more than 5-mole percent β-methacrylyloxyethyltrimethylammonium methyl sulfate.

(b) The modified polyacrylamide resin contains not more than 0.05 percent residual acrylamide.

(c) The modified polyacrylamide resin is used as a flocculent in the clarification of beet or cane sugar juice in an amount not exceeding 5 parts per million by weight of the juice.

(d) To assure safe use of the additive, the label and labeling of the additive shall bear, in addition to the other information required by the act, adequate directions to assure use in compliance with paragraph (c) of this section.

§ 173.20 Ion-exchange membranes.

Ion-exchange membranes may be safely used in the processing of food under the following prescribed conditions:

(a) The ion-exchange membrane is prepared by subjecting a polyethylene base conforming to § 177.1520 of this chapter to polymerization with styrene until the polystyrene phase of the base is not less than 16 percent nor more than 30 percent by weight. The base is then modified by reaction with chloromethyl methyl ether, and by subsequent amination with trimethylamine, dimethylamine, diethylenetriamine, or dimethylethanolamine.

(b) The ion-exchange membrane is manufactured so as to comply with the following extraction limitations when subjected to the described procedure: Separate square-foot samples of membrane weighing approximately 14 grams each are cut into small pieces and refluxed for 4 hours in 150 cubic centimeters of the following solvents: Distilled water, 5 percent acetic acid, and 50 percent alcohol. Extraction from each sample will not exceed 0.4 percent by weight of sample.

(c) The ion-exchange membrane will be used in the production of grapefruit juice to adjust the ratio of citric acid to total solids of the grapefruit juice produced.

§ 173.21 Perfluorinated ion exchange membranes.

Substances identified in paragraph (a) of this section may be safely used as ion exchange membranes intended for use in the treatment of bulk quantities of liquid food under the following prescribed conditions:

(a) *Identity.* The membrane is a copolymer of ethanesulfonyl fluoride, 2-[1-[difluoro-[(trifluoroethenyl)oxy]methyl]-1,2,2,2-tetrafluoroethoxy]-1,1,2,2,-tetrafluoro-, with tetrafluoroethylene that has been subsequently treated to hydrolyze the sulfonyl fluoride group to the sulfonic acid. The Chemical Abstracts Service name of this polymer is ethanesulfonic acid, 2-[1-[difluoro-[(trifluoroethenyl)oxy]methyl]-1,2,2,2-tetrafluoroethoxy]-1,1,2,2,-tetrafluoro-, polymer with tetrafluoroethane (CAS Reg. No. 31175–20–9).

(b) *Optional adjuvant substances.* The basic polymer identified in paragraph (a) of this section may contain optional adjuvant substances required in the production of such basic polymer. These optional adjuvant substances may include substances used in accordance with § 174.5 of this chapter.

(c) *Conditions of use.* (1) Perfluorinated ion exchange membranes described in paragraph (a) of this section may be used in contact with all types of liquid foods at temperatures not exceeding 70° (158 °F).

(2) Maximum thickness of the copolymer membrane is 0.007 inch (0.017 centimeter).

(3) Perfluorinated ion exchange membranes shall be maintained in a sanitary manner in accordance with current good manufacturing practice so as to prevent microbial adulteration of food.

(4) To assure their safe use, perfluorinated ionomer membranes shall be thoroughly cleaned prior to their first use in accordance with current good manufacturing practice.

[59 FR 15623, Apr. 4, 1994]

§ 173.25 Ion-exchange resins.

Ion-exchange resins may be safely used in the treatment of food under the following prescribed conditions:

(a) The ion-exchange resins are prepared in appropriate physical form, and consist of one or more of the following:

(1) Sulfonated copolymer of styrene and divinylbenzene.

(2) Sulfonated anthracite coal meeting the requirements of ASTM method D388–38, Class I, Group 2, "Standard Specifications for Classification of Coal by Rank," which is incorporated by reference. Copies are available from University Microfilms International, 300 N. Zeeb Rd., Ann Arbor, MI 48106, or available for inspection at the National Archives and Records Administration (NARA). For information on the availability of this material at NARA, call 202–741–6030, or go to: *http://www.archives.gov/federal_register/*

code_of_federal_regulations/ ibr_locations.html.

(3) Sulfite-modified cross-linked phenol-formaldehyde, with modification resulting in sulfonic acid groups on side chains.

(4) Methacrylic acid-divinylbenzene copolymer.

(5) Cross-linked polystyrene, first chloromethylated then aminated with trimethylamine, dimethylamine, diethylenetriamine, or dimethylethanolamine.

(6) Diethylenetriamine, triethylenetetramine, or tetraethylenepentamine cross-linked with epichlorohydrin.

(7) Cross-linked phenol-formaldehyde activated with one or both of the following: Triethylene tetramine and tetraethylenepentamine.

(8) Reaction resin of formaldehyde, acetone, and tetraethylenepentamine.

(9) Completely hydrolyzed copolymers of methyl acrylate and divinylbenzene.

(10) Completely hydrolyzed terpolymers of methyl acrylate, divinylbenzene, and acrylonitrile.

(11) Sulfonated terpolymers of styrene, divinylbenzene, and acrylonitrile or methyl acrylate.

(12) Methyl acrylate-divinylbenzene copolymer containing not less than 2 percent by weight of divinylbenzene, aminolyzed with dimethylaminopropylamine.

(13) Methyl acrylate-divinylbenzene copolymer containing not less than 3.5 percent by weight of divinylbenzene, aminolyzed with dimethylaminopropylamine.

(14) Epichlorohydrin cross-linked with ammonia.

(15) Sulfonated tetrapolymer of styrene, divinylbenzene, acrylonitrile, and methyl acrylate derived from a mixture of monomers containing not more than a total of 2 percent by weight of acrylonitrile and methyl acrylate.

(16) Methyl acrylate-divinylbenzene-diethylene glycol divinyl ether terpolymer containing not less than 3.5 percent by weight of divinylbenzene and not more than 0.6 percent by weight of diethylene glycol divinyl ether, aminolyzed with dimethylaminopropylamine.

(17) Styrene-divinylbenzene cross-linked copolymer, first chloromethylated then aminated with dimethylamine and oxidized with hydrogen peroxide whereby the resin contains not more than 15 percent by weight of vinyl *N,N*-dimethylbenzylamine-*N*-oxide and not more than 6.5 percent by weight of nitrogen.

(18) Methyl acrylate-divinylbenzene-diethylene glycol divinyl ether terpolymer containing not less than 7 percent by weight of divinylbenzene and not more than 2.3 percent by weight of diethylene glycol divinyl ether, aminolyzed with dimethylaminopropylamine and quaternized with methyl chloride.

(19) Epichlorohydrin cross-linked with ammonia and then quaternized with methyl chloride to contain not more than 18 percent strong base capacity by weight of total exchange capacity [Chemical Abstracts Service name: Oxirane (chloromethyl)-, polymer with ammonia, reaction product with chloromethane; CAS Reg. No. 68036–99–7].

(20) Regenerated cellulose, cross-linked and alkylated with epichlorohydrin and propylene oxide, then sulfonated whereby the amount of epichlorohydrin plus propylene oxide employed does not exceed 250 percent by weight of the starting quantity of cellulose.

(b) Ion-exchange resins are used in the purification of foods, including potable water, to remove undesirable ions or to replace less desirable ions with one or more of the following: bicarbonate, calcium, carbonate, chloride, hydrogen, hydroxyl, magnesium, potassium, sodium, and sulfate except that: The ion-exchange resin identified in paragraph (a)(12) of this section is used only in accordance with paragraph (b)(1) of this section, the ion-exchange resin identified in paragraph (a)(13) of this section is used only in accordance with paragraph (b)(2) of this section, the resin identified in paragraph (a)(16) of this section is used only in accordance with paragraph (b)(1) or (b)(2) of this section, the ion-exchange resin identified in paragraph (a)(17) of this section is used only in accordance with paragraph (b)(3) of this section, the ion-exchange resin identified in paragraph (a)(18) of this section is used only in accordance with paragraph (b)(4) of this section, and the ion-exchange resin identified in paragraph (a)(20) of this section is used only in accordance with paragraphs (b)(5) and (d) of this section.

(1) The ion-exchange resins identified in paragraphs (a) (12) and (16) of this section are used to treat water for use in the manufacture of distilled alcoholic beverages, subject to the following conditions:

(i) The water is subjected to treatment through a mixed bed consisting of one of the resins identified in paragraph (a) (12) or (16) of this section and one of the strongly acidic cation-exchange resins in the hydrogen form identified in paragraphs (a) (1), (2), and (11) of this section; or

(ii) The water is first subjected to one of the resins identified in paragraph (a) (12) or (16) of this section and is subsequently subjected to treatment through a bed of activated carbon or one of the strongly acidic cation-exchange resins in the hydrogen form identified in paragraphs (a) (1), (2), and (11) of this section.

(iii) The temperature of the water passing through the resin beds identified in paragraphs (b)(1) (i) and (ii) of this section is maintained at 30 °C or less, and the flow rate of the water passing through the beds is not less than 2 gallons per cubic foot per minute.

(iv) The ion-exchange resins identified in paragraph (a) (12) or (16) of this section are exempted from the requirements of paragraph (c)(4) of this section, but the strongly acidic cation-exchange resins referred to in paragraphs (b)(1) (i) and (ii) of this section used in the process meet the requirements of paragraph (c)(4) of this section, except for the exemption described in paragraph (d) of this section.

(2) The ion-exchange resins identified in paragraphs (a) (13) and (16) of this section are used to treat water and aqueous food only of the types identified under Categories I, II, and VI-B in table 1 of §176.170(c) of this chapter: *Provided*, That the temperature of the water or food passing through the resin beds is maintained at 50 °C or less and the flow rate of the water or food passing through the beds is not less than 0.5 gallon per cubic foot per minute.

(i) The ion-exchange resin identified in paragraph (a)(13) of this section is used to treat water and aqueous food only of the types identified under categories I, II, and VI-B in Table 1 of §176.170(c) of this chapter: *Provided*, That the temperature of the water or food passing through the resin bed is maintained at 50 °C or less and the flow rate of the water or food passing through the bed is not less than 0.5 gallon per cubic foot per minute.

(ii) The ion-exchange resin identified in paragraph (a)(16) of this section is used to treat water and aqueous food only of the types identified under categories I, II, and VI-B in Table 1 of §176.170(c) of this chapter, *Provided*, that either:

(A) The temperature of the water or food passing through the resin bed is maintained at 50 °C or less and the flow rate of the water or food passing through the bed is not less than 0.5 gallon per cubic foot per minute; or

(B) Extracts of the resin will be found to contain no more than 1 milligram/kilogram dimethylaminopropylamine in each of the food simulants, distilled water and 10 percent ethanol, when, following washing and pretreatment of the resin in accordance with §173.25(c)(1), the resin is subjected to the following test under conditions simulating the actual temperature and flow rate of use: "The Determination of 3-Dimethylaminopropylamine in Food Simulating Extracts of Ion Exchange Resins," February 4, 1998, which is incorporated by reference in accordance with 5 U.S.C. 552(a) and 1 CFR part 51. Copies are available from the Office of Food Additive Safety (HFS–200), Center for Food Safety and Applied Nutrition, Food and Drug Administration, 5100 Paint Branch Pkwy., College Park, MD 20740, 240–402–1200, or may be examined at the Center for Food Safety and Applied Nutrition's Library, 5100 Paint Branch Pkwy., College Park, MD 20740, or at the National Archives and Records Administration (NARA). For information on the availability of this material at NARA, call 202–741–6030, or go to: *http://www.archives.gov/federal_register/code_of_federal_regulations/ibr_locations.html.*

(3) The ion-exchange resin identified in paragraph (a)(17) of this section is used only for industrial application to treat bulk quantities of aqueous food, including potable water, or for treatment of municipal water supplies, subject to the condition that the temperature of the food or water passing through the resin bed is maintained at 25 °C or less and the flow rate of the food or water passing through the bed is not less than 2 gallons per cubic foot per minute.

(4) The ion-exchange resin identified in paragraph (a)(18) of this section is used to treat aqueous sugar solutions subject to the condition that the temperature of the sugar solution passing through the resin bed is maintained at 82 °C (179.6 °F) or less and the flow rate of the sugar solution passing through the bed is not less than 46.8 liters per cubic meter (0.35 gallon per cubic foot) of resin bed volume per minute.

(5) The ion-exchange resin identified in paragraph (a)(20) of this section is limited to use in aqueous process streams for the isolation and purification of protein concentrates and isolates under the following conditions:

(i) For resins that comply with the requirements in paragraph (d)(2)(i) of this section, the pH range for the resin shall be no less than 3.5 and no more than 9, and the temperatures of water and food passing through the resin bed shall not exceed 25 °C.

(ii) For resins that comply with the requirements in paragraph (d)(2)(ii) of this section, the pH range for the resin shall be no less than 2 and no more than 10, and the temperatures of water and food passing through the resin shall not exceed 50 °C.

(c) To insure safe use of ion-exchange resins, each ion-exchange resin will be:

(1) Subjected to pre-use treatment by the manufacturer and/or the user in accordance with the manufacturer's directions prescribed on the label or labeling accompanying the resins, to guarantee a food-grade purity of ion-exchange resins, in accordance with good manufacturing practice.

(2) Accompanied by label or labeling to include directions for use consistent with the intended functional purpose of the resin.

(3) Used in compliance with the label or labeling required by paragraph (c)(2) of this section.

(4) Found to result in no more than 1 part per million of organic extractives obtained with each of the named solvents, distilled water, 15 percent alcohol, and 5 percent acetic acid when, having been washed and otherwise treated in accordance with the manufacturer's directions for preparing them for use with food, the ion-exchange resin is subjected to the following test: Using a separate ion-exchange column for each solvent, prepare columns using 50 milliliters of the ready to use ion-exchange resin that is to be tested. While maintaining the highest temperature that will be encountered in use pass through these beds at the rate of 350–450 milliliters per hour the three test solvents distilled water, 15 percent (by volume) ethyl alcohol, and 5 percent (by weight) acetic acid. The first liter of effluent from each solvent is discarded, then the next 2 liters are used to determine organic extractives. The 2-liter sample is carefully evaporated to constant weight at 105 °C; this is total extractives. This residue is fired in a muffle furnace at 850 °C to constant weight; this is ash. Total extractives, minus ash equals the organic extractives. If the organic extractives are greater than 1 part per million of the solvent used, a blank should be run on the solvent and a correction should be made by subtracting the total extractives obtained with the blank from the total extractives obtained in the resin test. The solvents used are to be made as follows:

Distilled water (de-ionized water is distilled).

15 percent ethyl alcohol made by mixing 15 volumes of absolute ethyl alcohol A.C.S. reagent grade, with 85 volumes of distilled de-ionized water.

5 percent acetic acid made by mixing 5 parts by weight of A.C.S. reagent grade glacial acetic acid with 95 parts by weight of distilled de-ionized water.

In addition to the organic extractives limitation prescribed in this paragraph, the ion-exchange resin identified in paragraph (a)(17) of this section, when extracted with each of the named solvents, distilled water, 50 percent alcohol, and 5 percent acetic acid, will be found to result in not more than 7 parts per million of nitrogen extractives (calculated as nitrogen) when the resin in the free-base form is subjected to the following test immediately before each use: Using a separate 1-inch diameter glass ion-exchange column for each solvent, prepare each column using 100 milliliters of ready to use ion-exchange resin that is to be tested. With the bottom outlet closed, fill each ion-exchange column with one of the three solvents at a temperature of 25 °C until the solvent level is even with the top of the resin bed. Seal each column at the top and bottom and store in a vertical position at a temperature of 25 °C. After 96 hours, open the top of each column, drain the solvent into a collection vessel, and analyze each drained solvent and a solvent blank for nitrogen by a standard micro-Kjeldahl method.

(d)(1) The ion-exchange resins identified in paragraphs (a)(1), (a)(2), (a)(11), and (a)(15) of this section are exempted from the acetic acid extraction requirement of paragraph (c)(4) of this section.

(2) The ion-exchange resin identified in paragraph (a)(20) of this section shall comply either with:

(i) The extraction requirement in paragraph (c)(4) of this section by using dilute sulfuric acid, pH 3.5 as a substitute for acetic acid; or

(ii) The extraction requirement in paragraph (c)(4) of this section by using reagent grade hydrochloric acid, diluted to pH 2, as a substitute for acetic acid. The resin shall be found to result in no more than 25 parts per million of organic extractives obtained with each of the following solvents: Distilled water; 15 percent alcohol; and hydrochloric acid, pH 2. Blanks should be run for each of the solvents, and corrections should be made by subtracting the total extractives obtained with the blank from the total extractives obtained in the resin test.

(e) Acrylonitrile copolymers identified in this section shall comply with the provisions of §180.22 of this chapter.

[42 FR 14526, Mar. 15, 1977, as amended at 46 FR 40181, Aug. 7, 1981; 46 FR 57033, Nov. 20, 1981; 49 FR 28830, July 17, 1984; 56 FR 16268, Apr. 22, 1991; 62 FR 7679, Feb. 20, 1997; 64 FR 14609, Mar. 26, 1999; 64 FR 56173, Oct. 18, 1999; 78 FR 14665, Mar. 7, 2013]

§ 173.40 Molecular sieve resins.

Molecular sieve resins may be safely used in the processing of food under the following prescribed conditions:

(a) The molecular sieve resins consist of purified dextran having an average molecular weight of 40,000, cross-linked with epichlorohydrin in a ratio of 1 part of dextran to 10 parts of epichlorohydrin, to give a stable three dimensional structure. The resins have a pore size of 2.0 to 3.0 milliliters per gram of dry resin (expressed in terms of water regain), and a particle size of 10 to 300 microns.

(b) The molecular sieve resins are thoroughly washed with potable water prior to their first use in contact with food.

(c) Molecular sieve resins are used as the gel filtration media in the final purification of partially delactosed whey. The gel bed shall be maintained in a sanitary manner in accordance with good manufacturing practice so as to prevent microbial build-up on the bed and adulteration of the product.

§ 173.45 Polymaleic acid and its sodium salt.

Polymaleic acid (CAS Reg. No. 26099–09–2) and its sodium salt (CAS Reg. No. 70247–90–4) may be safely used in food in accordance with the following prescribed conditions:

(a) The additives have a weight-average molecular weight in the range of 540 to 850 and a number-average molecular weight in the range of 520 to 650, calculated as the acid. Molecular weights shall be determined by a method entitled "Determination of Molecular Weight Distribution of Poly(Maleic) Acid," March 17, 1992, produced by Ciba-Geigy, Inc., Seven Skyline Dr., Hawthorne, NY 10532–2188, which is incorporated by reference in accordance with 5 U.S.C. 552(a) and 1 CFR part 51. Copies are available from the Office of Food Additive Safety

(HFS–200), Center for Food Safety and Applied Nutrition, Food and Drug Administration, 5100 Paint Branch Pkwy., College Park, MD 20740, 240–402–1200, or are available for inspection at the Center for Food Safety and Applied Nutrition's Library, 5100 Paint Branch Pkwy., College Park, MD 20740, or at the National Archives and Records Administration (NARA). For information on the availability of this material at NARA, call 202–741–6030, or go to: *http://www.archives.gov/federal_register/code_of_federal_regulations/ibr_locations.html.*

(b) The additives may be used, individually or together, in the processing of beet sugar juice and liquor or of cane sugar juice and liquor to control mineral scale.

(c) The additives are to be used so that the amount of either or both additives does not exceed 4 parts per million (calculated as the acid) by weight of the beet or cane sugar juice or liquor process stream.

[51 FR 5315, Feb. 13, 1986, as amended at 61 FR 386, Jan. 5, 1996; 78 FR 14665, Mar. 7, 2013]

§ 173.50 Polyvinylpolypyrrolidone.

The food additive polyvinylpolypyrrolidone may be safely used in accordance with the following prescribed conditions:

(a) The additive is a homopolymer of purified vinylpyrrolidone catalytically produced under conditions producing polymerization and cross-linking such that an insoluble polymer is produced.

(b) The food additive is so processed that when the finished polymer is refluxed for 3 hours with water, 5 percent acetic acid, and 50 percent alcohol, no more than 50 parts per million of extractables is obtained with each solvent.

(c) It is used or intended for use as a clarifying agent in beverages and vinegar, followed by removal with filtration.

§ 173.55 Polyvinylpyrrolidone.

The food additive polyvinylpyrrolidone may be safely used in accordance with the following prescribed conditions:

(a) The additive is a polymer of purified vinylpyrrolidone catalytically produced, having an average molecular weight of 40,000 and a maximum unsaturation of 1 percent, calculated as the monomer, except that the polyvinylpyrrolidone used in beer is that having an average molecular weight of 360,000 and a maximum unsaturation of 1 percent, calculated as the monomer.

(b) The additive is used or intended for use in foods as follows:

Food	Limitations
Beer	As a clarifying agent, at a residual level not to exceed 10 parts per million.
Flavor concentrates in tablet form	As a tableting adjuvent in an amount not to exceed good manufacturing practice.
Nonnutritive sweeteners in concentrated liquid form.	As a stabilizer, bodying agent, and dispersant, in an amount not to exceed good manufacturing practice.
Nonnutritive sweeteners in tablet form	As a tableting adjuvant in an amount not to exceed good manufacturing practice.
Vitamin and mineral concentrates in liquid form	As a stabilizer, bodying agent, and dispersant, in an amount not to exceed good manufacturing practice.
Vitamin and mineral concentrates in tablet form	As a tableting adjuvant in an amount not to exceed good manufacturing practice.
Vinegar	As a clarifying agent, at a residual level not to exceed 40 parts per million.
Wine	As a clarifying agent, at a residual level not to exceed 60 parts per million.

§ 173.60 Dimethylamine-epichlorohydrin copolymer.

Dimethylamine-epichlorohydrin copolymer (CAS Reg. No. 25988–97–0) may be safely used in food in accordance with the following prescribed conditions:

(a) The food additive is produced by copolymerization of dimethylamine and epichlorohydrin in which not more than 5 mole-percent of dimethylamine may be replaced by an equimolar amount of ethylenediamine, and in which the mole ratio of total amine to epichlorohydrin is approximately 1:1.

(b) The additive meets the following specifications:

(1) The nitrogen content of the copolymer is 9.4 to 10.8 weight percent on a dry basis.

(2) A 50-percent-by-weight aqueous solution of the copolymer has a minimum viscosity of 175 centipoises at 25 °C as determined by LVT-series Brookfield viscometer using a No. 2 spindle at 60 RPM (or by another equivalent method).

(3) The additive contains not more than 1,000 parts per million of 1,3-dichloro-2-propanol and not more than 10 parts per million epichlorohydrin. The epichlorohydrin and 1,3-dichloro-2-propanol content is determined by an analytical method entitled "The Determination of Epichlorohydrin and 1,3-Dichloro-2-Propanol in Dimethylamine-Epichlorohydrin Copolymer," which is incorporated by reference. Copies are available from the Center for Food Safety and Applied Nutrition (HFS–200), Food and Drug Administration, 5100 Paint Branch Pkwy., College Park, MD 20740, or available for inspection at the National Archives and Records Administration (NARA). For information on the availability of this material at NARA, call 202–741–6030, or go to: *http://www.archives.gov/federal_register/code_of_federal_regulations/ibr_locations.html.*

(4) Heavy metals (as Pb), 2 parts per million maximum.

(5) Arsenic (as As), 2 parts per million maximum.

(c) The food additive is used as a decolorizing agent and/or flocculant in the clarification of refinery sugar liquors and juices. It is added only at the defecation/clarification stage of sugar liquor refining at a concentration not to exceed 150 parts per million of copolymer by weight of sugar solids.

(d) To assure safe use of the additive, the label and labeling of the additive shall bear, in addition to other information required by the Act, adequate directions to assure use in compliance with paragraph (c) of this section.

[48 FR 37614, Aug. 19, 1983, as amended at 54 FR 24897, June 12, 1989]

§ 173.65 Divinylbenzene copolymer.

Divinylbenzene copolymer may be used for the removal of organic substances from aqueous foods under the following prescribed conditions:

(a) The copolymer is prepared in appropriate physical form and is derived by the polymerization of a grade of divinylbenzene which comprises at least 79 weight-percent divinylbenzene, 15 to 20 weight-percent ethylvinylbenzene, and no more than 4 weight-percent nonpolymerizable impurities.

(b) In accordance with the manufacturer's directions, the copolymer described in paragraph (a) of this section is subjected to pre-use extraction with a water soluble alcohol until the level of divinylbenzene in the extract is less than 50 parts per billion as determined by a method titled, "The Determination of Divinylbenzene in Alcohol Extracts of Amberlite XAD–4," which is incorporated by reference. Copies of this method are available from the Center for Food Safety and Applied Nutrition (HFS–200), Food and Drug Administration, 5100 Paint Branch Pkwy., College Park, MD 20740, or available for inspection at the National Archives and Records Administration (NARA). For information on the availability of this material at NARA, call 202–741–6030, or go to: *http://www.archives.gov/federal_register/code_of_federal_regulations/ibr_locations.html.* The copolymer is then treated with water according to the manufacturer's recommendation to remove the extraction solvent to guarantee a food-grade purity of the resin at the time of use, in accordance with current good manufacturing practice.

(c) The temperature of the aqueous food stream contacting the polymer is maintained at 79.4 °C (175 °F) or less.

(d) The copolymer may be used in contact with food only of Types I, II, and VI-B (excluding carbonated beverages) described in table 1 of paragraph (c) of § 176.170 of this chapter.

[50 FR 61, Jan. 2, 1985]

§ 173.70 Chloromethylated aminated styrene-divinylbenzene resin.

Chloromethylated aminated styrene-divinylbenzene copolymer (CAS Reg. No. 60177–39–1) may be safely used in food in accordance with the following prescribed conditions:

(a) The additive is an aqueous dispersion of styrene-divinylbenzene copolymers, first chloromethylated then aminated with trimethylamine, having an average particle size of not more than 2.0 microns.

(b) The additive shall contain no more than 3.0 percent nonvolatile, soluble extractives when tested as follows: One hundred grams of the additive is centrifuged at 17,000 r/min for 2 hours. The resulting clear supernatant is removed from the compacted solids and concentrated to approximately 10 grams on a steam bath. The 10-gram sample is again centrifuged at 17,000 r/min for 2 hours to remove any residual insoluble material. The supernatant from the second centrifugation is then removed from any compacted solids and dried to constant residual weight using a steam bath. The percent nonvolatile solubles is obtained by dividing the weight of the dried residue by the weight of the solids in the original resin dispersion.

(c) The additive is used as a decolorizing and clarification agent for treatment of refinery sugar liquors and juices at levels not to exceed 500 parts of additive solids per million parts of sugar solids.

[50 FR 29209, July 18, 1985]

§ 173.73 Sodium polyacrylate.

Sodium polyacrylate (CAS Reg. No. 9003–04–7) may be safely used in food in accordance with the following prescribed conditions:

(a) The additive is produced by the polymerization of acrylic acid and subsequent hydrolysis of the polyacrylic acid with an aqueous sodium hydroxide solution. As determined by a method entitled "Determination of Weight Average and Number Average Molecular Weight of Sodium Polyacrylate," which is incorporated by reference in accordance with 5 U.S.C. 552(a), the additive has—

(1) A weight average molecular weight of 2,000 to 2,300; and

(2) A weight average molecular weight to number average molecular weight ratio of not more than 1.3. Copies of the method are available from the Center for Food Safety and Applied Nutrition (HFS–200), Food and Drug Administration, 5100 Paint Branch Pkwy., College Park, MD 20740, or available for inspection at the National Archives and Records Administration (NARA). For information on the availability of this material at NARA, call 202–741–6030, or go to: *http://www.archives.gov/federal_register/code_of_federal_regulations/ibr_locations.html.*

(b) The additive is used to control mineral scale during the evaporation of beet sugar juice or cane sugar juice in the production of sugar in an amount not to exceed 3.6 parts per million by weight of the raw juice.

[53 FR 39456, Oct. 7, 1988; 53 FR 49823, Dec. 9, 1988]

§ 173.75 Sorbitan monooleate.

Sorbitan monooleate may be safely used in accordance with the following prescribed conditions:

(a) The additive is produced by the esterification of sorbitol with commercial oleic acid.

(b) It meets the following specifications:

(1) Saponification number, 145–160.

(2) Hydroxyl number, 193–210.

(c) The additive is used or intended for use as follows:

(1) As an emulsifier in polymer dispersions that are used in the clarification of cane or beet sugar juice or liquor in an amount not to exceed 7.5 percent by weight in the final polymer dispersion.

(2) The additive is used in an amount not to exceed 0.70 part per million in sugar juice and 1.4 parts per million in sugar liquor.

[51 FR 11720, Apr. 7, 1986]

Subpart B—Enzyme Preparations and Microorganisms

§ 173.110 Amyloglucosidase derived from *Rhizopus niveus.*

Amyloglucosidase enzyme product, consisting of enzyme derived from *Rhizopus niveus*, and diatomaceous silica as a carrier, may be safely used in food in accordance with the following conditions:

(a) *Rhizopus niveus* is classified as follows: Class, Phycomycetes; order,

Mucorales; family, Mucoraceae; genus, *Rhizopus;* species, *niveus.*

(b) The strain of *Rhizopus niveus* is nonpathogenic and nontoxic in man or other animals.

(c) The enzyme is produced by a process which completely removes the organism *Rhizopus niveus* from the amyloglucosidase.

(d) The additive is used or intended for use for degrading gelatinized starch into constituent sugars, in the production of distilled spirits and vinegar.

(e) The additive is used at a level not to exceed 0.1 percent by weight of the gelatinized starch.

§ 173.115 Alpha-acetolactate decarboxylase (α-ALDC) enzyme preparation derived from a recombinant Bacillus subtilis.

The food additive alpha-acetolactate decarboxylase (α-ALDC) enzyme preparation, may be safely used in accordance with the following conditions:

(a) The food additive is the enzyme preparation derived from a modified *Bacillus subtilis* strain that contains the gene coding for α-ALDC from *Bacillus brevis.*

(b)(1) The manufacturer produces the additive from a pure culture fermentation of a strain of *Bacillus subtilis* that is nonpathogenic and nontoxigenic in man or other animals.

(2) The manufacturer may stabilize the enzyme preparation with glutaraldehyde or with other suitable approved food additives or generally recognized as safe substances.

(3) The enzyme preparation must meet the general and additional requirements for enzyme preparations in the *Food Chemicals Codex,* 4th ed., 1996, pp. 133–134, which is incorporated by reference. The Director of the Office of the Federal Register approves this incorporation by reference in accordance with 5 U.S.C. 552(a) and 1 CFR part 51. Copies may be obtained from the National Academy Press, 2101 Constitution Ave. NW., Washington, DC 20055, or may be examined at the Center for Food Safety and Applied Nutrition, 5100 Paint Branch Pkwy., College Park, MD 20740, or at the National Archives and Records Administration (NARA). For information on the availability of this material at NARA, call 202–741–6030, or go to: *http://www.archives.gov/federal_register/code_of_federal_regulations/ibr_locations.html.*

(c) The additive is used in an amount not in excess of the minimum required to produce its intended effect as a processing aid in the production of alcoholic malt beverages and distilled liquors.

[66 FR 27022, May 16, 2001]

§ 173.120 Carbohydrase and cellulase derived from *Aspergillus niger*.

Carbohydrase and cellulase enzyme preparation derived from *Aspergillus niger* may be safely used in food in accordance with the following prescribed conditions:

(a) *Aspergillus niger* is classified as follows: Class, Deuteromycetes; order, Moniliales; family, Moniliaceae; genus, *Aspergillus;* species, *niger.*

(b) The strain of *Aspergillus niger* is nonpathogenic and nontoxic in man or other animals.

(c) The additive is produced by a process that completely removes the organism *Aspergillus niger* from the carbohydrase and cellulase enzyme product.

(d) The additive is used or intended for use as follows:

(1) For removal of visceral mass (bellies) in clam processing.

(2) As an aid in the removal of the shell from the edible tissue in shrimp processing.

(e) The additive is used in an amount not in excess of the minimum required to produce its intended effect.

§ 173.130 Carbohydrase derived from *Rhizopus oryzae*.

Carbohydrase from *Rhizopus oryzae* may be safely used in the production of dextrose from starch in accordance with the following prescribed conditions:

(a) *Rhizopus oryzae* is classified as follows: Class, Phycomycetes; order, Mucorales; family, Mucoraceae; genus, *Rhizopus;* species, *Rhizopus oryzae.*

(b) The strain of *Rhizopus oryzae* is nonpathogenic and nontoxic.

(c) The carbohydrase is produced under controlled conditions to maintain nonpathogenicity and nontoxicity, including the absence of aflatoxin.

(d) The carbohydrase is produced by a process which completely removes the organism *Rhizopus oryzae* from the carbohydrase product.

(e) The carbohydrase is maintained under refrigeration from production to use and is labeled to include the necessity of refrigerated storage.

§ 173.135 Catalase derived from *Micrococcus lysodeikticus.*

Bacterial catalase derived from *Micrococcus lysodeikticus* by a pure culture fermentation process may be safely used in destroying and removing hydrogen peroxide used in the manufacture of cheese, in accordance with the following conditions.

(a) The organism *Micrococcus lysodeikticus* from which the bacterial catalase is to be derived is demonstrated to be nontoxic and nonpathogenic.

(b) The organism *Micrococcus lysodeikticus* is removed from the bacterial catalase prior to use of the bacterial catalase.

(c) The bacterial catalase is used in an amount not in excess of the minimum required to produce its intended effect.

§ 173.140 Esterase-lipase derived from *Mucor miehei.*

Esterase-lipase enzyme, consisting of enzyme derived from *Mucor miehei* var. *Cooney et Emerson* by a pure culture fermentation process, with maltodextrin or sweet whey as a carrier, may be safely used in food in accordance with the following conditions:

(a) *Mucor miehei* var. *Cooney et Emerson* is classified as follows: Class, Phycomycetes; subclass, Zygomycetes; order, Mucorales; family, Mucoraceae; genus, *Mucor;* species, *miehei;* variety *Cooney et Emerson.*

(b) The strain of *Mucor miehei* var. *Cooney et Emerson* is nonpathogenic and nontoxic in man or other animals.

(c) The enzyme is produced by a process which completely removes the organism *Mucor miehei* var. *Cooney et Emerson* from the esterase-lipase.

(d) The enzyme is used as a flavor enhancer as defined in § 170.3(o)(12).

(e) The enzyme is used at levels not to exceed current good manufacturing practice in the following food categories: cheeses as defined in § 170.3(n)(5) of this chapter; fat and oils as defined in § 170.(3)(n)(12) of this chapter; and milk products as defined in § 170.(3)(n)(31) of this chapter. Use of this food ingredient is limited to nonstandarized foods and those foods for which the relevant standards of identity permit such use.

(f) The enzyme is used in the minimum amount required to produce its limited technical effect.

[47 FR 28090, June 29, 1982; 48 FR 2748, Jan. 21, 1983]

§ 173.145 Alpha-Galactosidase derived from *Mortierella vinaceae* var. *raffinoseutilizer.*

The food additive alpha-galactosidase and parent mycelial microorganism *Mortierella vinaceae* var. *raffinoseutilizer* may be safely used in food in accordance with the following conditions:

(a) The food additive is the enzyme alpha-galactosidase and the mycelia of the microorganism *Mortierella vinaceae* var. *raffinoseutilizer* which produces the enzyme.

(b) The nonpathogenic microorganism matches American Type Culture Collection (ATCC) No. 20034,[1] and is classified as follows:

Class: Phycomycetes.
Order: Mucorales.
Family: Mortierellaceae.
Genus: *Mortierella.*
Species: *vinaceae.*
Variety: *raffinoseutilizer.*

(c) The additive is used or intended for use in the production of sugar (sucrose) from sugar beets by addition as mycelial pellets to the molasses to increase the yield of sucrose, followed by removal of the spent mycelial pellets by filtration.

(d) The enzyme removal is such that there are no enzyme or mycelial residues remaining in the finished sucrose.

[42 FR 14526, Mar. 15, 1977, as amended at 54 FR 24897, June 12, 1989]

§ 173.150 Milk-clotting enzymes, microbial.

Milk-clotting enzyme produced by pure-culture fermentation process may

---

[1] Available from: American Type Culture Collection, 12301 Parklawn Drive, Rockville, MD 20852.

be safely used in the production of cheese in accordance with the following prescribed conditions:

(a) Milk-clotting enzyme is derived from one of the following organisms by a pure-culture fermentation process:

(1) *Endothia parasitica* classified as follows: Class, Ascomycetes; order, Sphaeriales; family, Diaporthacesae; genus, *Endothia;* species, *parasitica.*

(2) *Bacillus cereus* classified as follows: Class, Schizomycetes; order, Eubacteriales; family, Bacillaceae; genus, *Bacillus;* species, *cereus* (Frankland and Frankland).

(3) *Mucor pusillus* Lindt classified as follows: Class, Phycomycetes; subclass, Zygomycetes; order, Mucorales; family, Mucoraceae; genus, *Mucor;* species, *pusillus;* variety, *Lindt.*

(4) *Mucor miehei Cooney et Emerson* classified as follows: Class, Phycomycetes; subclass, Zygomycetes; order, Mucorales; family, Mucoraceae; genus, *Mucor;* species, *miehei;* variety, *Cooney et Emerson.*

(5) *Aspergillus oryzae* modified by recombinant deoxyribonucleic (DNA) techniques to contain the gene coding for aspartic proteinase from *Rhizomucor miehei* var. *Cooney et Emerson* as defined in paragraph (a)(4) of this section, and classified as follows: Class, Blastodeuteromycetes (Hyphomycetes); order, Phialidales (Moniliales); genus, *Aspergillus*; species *oryzae.*

(b) The strains of organism identified in paragraph (a) of this section are nonpathogenic and nontoxic in man or other animals.

(c) The additive is produced by a process that completely removes the generating organism from the milk-clotting enzyme product.

(d) The additive is used in an amount not in excess of the minimum required to produce its intended effect in the production of those cheeses for which it is permitted by standards of identity established pursuant to section 401 of the Act.

[42 FR 14526, Mar. 15, 1977; 42 FR 56728, Oct. 28, 1977, as amended at 62 FR 59284, Nov. 3, 1997]

§ 173.160 *Candida guilliermondii.*

The food additive *Candida guilliermondii* may be safely used as the organism for fermentation production of citric acid in accordance with the following conditions:

(a) The food additive is the enzyme system of the viable organism *Candida guilliermondii* and its concomitant metabolites produced during the fermentation process.

(b)(1) The nonpathogenic and nontoxicogenic organism descending from strain, American Type Culture Collection (ATCC) No. 20474,[1] is classified as follows:

Class: Deuteromycetes.
Order: Moniliales.
Family: Cryptococcaceae.
Genus: *Candida.*
Species: *guilliermondii.*
Variety: *guilliermondii.*

(2) The toxonomic characteristics of the reference culture strain ATCC No. 20474 agree in the essentials with the standard description for *Candida guilliermondii* variety *guilliermondii* listed in "The Yeasts—A Toxonomic Study;" 2d Ed. (1970), by Jacomina Lodder, which is incorporated by reference. Copies are available from the Center for Food Safety and Applied Nutrition (HFS–200), Food and Drug Administration, 5100 Paint Branch Pkwy., College Park, MD 20740, or available for inspection at the National Archives and Records Administration (NARA). For information on the availability of this material at NARA, call 202–741–6030, or go to: *http://www.archives.gov/federal_register/code_of_federal_regulations/ibr_locations.html.*

(c)(1) The additive is used or intended for use as a pure culture in the fermentation process for the production of citric acid using an acceptable aqueous carbohydrate substrate.

(2) The organism *Candida quilliermondii* is made nonviable and is completely removed from the citric acid during the recovery and purification process.

(d) The additive is so used that the citric acid produced conforms to the specifications of the "Food Chemicals Codex," 3d Ed. (1981), under "Citric acid," pp. 86–87, which is incorporated

[1] Available from: American Type Culture Collection, 12301 Parklawn Drive, Rockville, MD 20852.

by reference. Copies may be obtained from the National Academy Press, 2101 Constitution Ave. NW., Washington, DC 20418, or may be examined at the National Archives and Records Administration (NARA). For information on the availability of this material at NARA, call 202–741–6030, or go to: *http://www.archives.gov/federal_register/code_of_federal_regulations/ibr_locations.html.*

[42 FR 14526, Mar. 15, 1977, as amended at 47 FR 11838, Mar. 19, 1982; 49 FR 10106, Mar. 19, 1984; 54 FR 24897, June 12, 1989]

§ 173.165 *Candida lipolytica.*

The food additive *Candida lipolytica* may be safely used as the organism for fermentation production of citric acid in accordance with the following conditions:

(a) The food additive is the enzyme system of the organism *Candida lipolytica* and its concimitant metabolites produced during the fermentation process.

(b)(1) The nonpathogenic organism is classified as follows:

Class: Deuteromycetes.
Order: Moniliales.
Family: Cryptococcaceae.
Genus: *Candida.*
Species: *lipolytica.*

(2) The taxonomic characteristics of the culture agree in essential with the standard description for *Candida lipolytica* variety *lipolytica* listed in "The Yeasts—A Toxonomic Study," 2d Ed. (1970), by Jacomina Lodder, which is incorporated by reference. Copies are available from the Center for Food Safety and Applied Nutrition (HFS–200), Food and Drug Administration, 5100 Paint Branch Pkwy., College Park, MD 20740, or available for inspection at the National Archives and Records Administration (NARA). For information on the availability of this material at NARA, call 202–741–6030, or go to: *http://www.archives.gov/federal_register/code_of_federal_regulations/ibr_locations.html.*

(c) The additive is used or intended for use as a pure culture in the fermentation process for the production of citric acid from purified normal alkanes.

(d) The additive is so used that the citric acid produced conforms to the specifications of the "Food Chemicals Codex," 3d Ed. (1981), pp. 86–87, which is incorporated by reference. Copies may be obtained from the National Academy Press, 2101 Constitution Ave. NW., Washington, DC 20418, or may be examined at the National Archives and Records Administration (NARA). For information on the availability of this material at NARA, call 202–741–6030, or go to: *http://www.archives.gov/federal_register/code_of_federal_regulations/ibr_locations.html.* The additive meets the following ultraviolet absorbance limits when subjected to the analytical procedure described in this paragraph:

Ultraviolet absorbance per centimeter path length	Maximum
280 to 289 millimicrons	0.25
290 to 299 millimicrons	0.20
300 to 359 millimicrons	0.13
360 to 400 millimicrons	0.03

ANALYTICAL PROCEDURE FOR CITRIC ACID

GENERAL INSTRUCTIONS

Because of the sensitivity of the test, the possibility of errors arising from contamination is great. It is of the greatest importance that all glassware be scrupulously cleaned to remove all organic matter such as oil, grease, detergent residues, etc. Examine all glassware including stoppers and stopcocks, under ultraviolet light to detect any residual fluorescent contamination. As a precautionary measure it is recommended practice to rinse all glassware with purified isooctane immediately before use. No grease is to be used on stopcocks or joints. Great care to avoid contamination of citric acid samples in handling is essential to assure absence of any extraneous material arising from inadequate packaging. Because some of the polynuclear hydrocarbons sought in this test are very susceptible to photo-oxidation, the entire procedure is to be carried out under subdued light.

APPARATUS

1. Aluminum foil, oil free.
2. Separatory funnels, 500-milliliter capacity, equipped with tetrafluoroethylene polymer stopcocks.
3. Chromatographic tubes: (a) 80-millimeter ID × 900-millimeter length equipped with tetrafluoroethylene polymer stopcock and course fritted disk; (b) 18-millimeter ID × 300-millimeter length equipped with tetrafluoroethylene polymer stopcock.
4. Rotary vacuum evaporator, Buchi or equivalent.

5. Spectrophotometer—Spectral range 250–400 nanometers with spectral slit width of 2 nanometers or less; under instrument operating conditions for these absorbance measurements, the spectrophotometer shall also meet the following performance requirements:

Absorbance repeatability, ±0.01 at 0.4 absorbance.

Wavelength repeatability, ±0.2 nanometer.

Wavelength accuracy, ±1.0 nanometer.

The spectrophotometer is equipped with matched 1 centimeter path length quartz microcuvettes with 0.5-milliliter volume capacity.

6. Vacuum oven, minimum inside dimensions: 200 mm × 200 mm × 300 mm deep.

REAGENTS AND MATERIALS

Organic solvents. All solvents used throughout the procedure shall meet the specifications and tests described in this specification. The methyl alcohol, isooctane, benzene, hexane and 1,2-dichloroethane designated in the list following this paragraph shall pass the following test:

The specified quantity of solvent is added to a 250-milliliter round bottom flask containing 0.5 milliliter of purified *n*-hexadecane and evaporated on the rotary evaporator at 45 °C to constant volume. Six milliliters of purified isooctane are added to this residue and evaporated under the same conditions as above for 5 minutes. Determine the absorbance of the residue compared to purified *n*-hexadecane as reference. The absorbance of the solution of the solvent residue shall not exceed 0.03 per centimeter path length between 280 and 299 nanometers and 0.01 per centimeter path length between 300 and 400 nanometers.

Methyl alcohol, A.C.S. reagent grade. Use 100 milliliters for the test described in the preceding paragraph. If necessary, methyl alcohol may be purified by distillation through a Virgreaux column discarding the first and last ten percent of the distillate or otherwise.

Benzene, spectrograde (Burdick and Jackson Laboratories, Inc., Muskegon, Mich., or equivalent). Use 80 milliliters for the test. If necessary, benzene may be purified by distillation or otherwise.

Isooctane (2,2,4-trimethylpentane). Use 100 milliliters for the test. If necessary, isooctane may be purified by passage through a column of activated silica gel, distillation or otherwise.

Hexane, spectrograde (Burdick and Jackson Laboratories, Inc., Muskegon, Mich., or equivalent). Use 100 milliliters for the test. If necessary, hexane may be purified by distillation or otherwise.

1,2-Dichloroethane, spectrograde (Matheson, Coleman and Bell, East Rutherford, N.J., or equivalent). Use 100 milliliters for the test. If necessary, 1,2-dichloroethane may be purified by distillation or otherwise.

ELUTING MIXTURES

1. *10 percent 1,2-dichloroethane in hexane.* Prepare by mixing the purified solvents in the volume ratio of 1 part of 1,2-dichloroethane to 9 parts of hexane.

2. *40 percent benzene in hexane.* Prepare by mixing the purified solvents in the volume ratio of 4 parts of benzene to 6 parts of hexane.

n-Hexadecane, 99 percent olefin-free. Determine the absorbance compared to isooctane as reference. The absorbance per centimeter path length shall not exceed 0.00 in the range of 280–400 nanometers. If necessary, *n*-hexadecane may be purified by percolation through activated silica gel, distillation or otherwise.

Silica gel, 28–200 mesh (Grade 12, Davison Chemical Co., Baltimore, MD, or equivalent). Activate as follows: Slurry 900 grams of silica gel reagent with 2 liters of purified water in a 3-liter beaker. Cool the mixture and pour into a 80 × 900 chromatographic column with coarse fritted disc. Drain the water, wash with an additional 6 liters of purified water and wash with 3,600 milliliters of purified methyl alcohol at a relatively slow rate. Drain all of the solvents and transfer the silica gel to an aluminum foil-lined drying dish. Place foil over the top of the dish. Activate in a vacuum oven at low vacuum (approximately 750 millimeters Mercury or 27 inches of Mercury below atmospheric pressure) at 173° to 177 °C for at least 20 hours. Cool under vacuum and store in an amber bottle.

Sodium sulfate, anhydrous, A.C.S. reagent grade. This reagent should be washed with purified isooctane. Check the purity of this reagent as described in § 172.886 of this chapter.

Water, purified. All water used must meet the specifications of the following test:

Extract 600 milliliters of water with 50 milliliters of purified isooctane. Add 1 milliliter of purified *n*-hexadecane to the isooctane extract and evaporate the resulting solution to 1 milliliter. The absorbance of this residue shall not exceed 0.02 per centimeter path length between 300–400 nanometers and 0.03 per centimeter path length between 280–299 nanometers. If necessary, water may be purified by distillation, extraction with purified organic solvents, treatment with an absorbent (e.g., activated carbon) followed by filtration of the absorbent or otherwise.

PROCEDURE

Separate portions of 200 milliliters of purified water are taken through the procedure for use as control blanks. Each citric acid sample is processed as follows: Weigh 200 grams of anhydrous citric acid into a 500 milliliter flask and dissolve in 200 milliliters of pure water. Heat the solution to 60 °C and transfer to a 500 milliliter separatory funnel. Rinse the flask with 50 milliliters of isooctane and add the isooctane to the separatory funnel. Gently shake the mixture 90 times (caution: vigorous shaking will cause emulsions) with periodic release of the pressure caused by shaking.

Allow the phases to separate for at least 5 minutes. Draw off the lower aqueous layer into a second 500-milliliter separatory funnel and repeat the extraction with a second aliquot of 50 milliliters of isooctane. After separation of the layers, draw off and discard the water layer. Combine both isooctane extracts in the funnel containing the first extract. Rinse the funnel which contained the second extract with 10 milliliters of isooctane and add this portion to the combined isooctane extract.

A chromatographic column containing 5.5 grams of silica gel and 3 grams of anhydrous sodium sulfate is prepared for each citric acid sample as follows: Fit 18 × 300 column with a small glass wool plug. Rinse the inside of the column with 10 milliliters of purified isooctane. Drain the isooctane from the column. Pour 5.5 grams of activated silica gel into the column. Tap the column approximately 20 times on a semisoft, clean surface to settle the silica gel. Carefully pour 3 grams of anhydrous sodium sulfate onto the top of the silica gel in the column.

Carefully drain the isooctane extract of the citric acid solution into the column in a series of additions while the isooctane is draining from the column at an elution rate of approximately 3 milliliters per minute. Rinse the separatory funnel with 10 milliliters of isooctane after the last portion of the extract has been applied to the column and add this rinse to the column. After all of the extract has been applied to the column and the solvent layer reaches the top of the sulfate bed, rinse the column with 25 milliliters of isooctane followed by 10 milliliters of a 10-percent dichloroethane in hexane solution. For each rinse solution, drain the column until the solvent layer reaches the top of the sodium sulfate bed. Discard the rinse solvents. Place a 250-milliliter round bottom flask containing 0.5 milliliter of purified *n*-hexadecane under the column. Elute the polynuclear aromatic hydrocarbons from the column with 30 milliliters of 40-percent benzene in hexane solution. Drain the eluate until the 40-percent benzene in the hexane solvent reaches the top of the sodium sulfate bed.

Evaporate the 40-percent benzene in hexane eluate on the rotary vacuum evaporator at 45 °C until only the *n*-hexadecane residue of 0.5 milliliter remains. Treat the *n*-hexadecane residue twice with the following wash step: Add 6 milliliters of purified isooctane and remove the solvents by vacuum evaporation at 45 °C to constant volume, i.e., 0.5 milliliter. Cool the *n*-hexadecane residue and transfer the solution to an 0.5-milliliter microcuvette. Determine the absorbance of this solution compared to purified *n*-hexadecane as reference. Correct the absorbance values for any absorbance derived from the control reagent blank. If the corrected absorbance does not exceed the limits prescribed, the samples meet the ultraviolet absorbance specifications.

The reagent blank is prepared by using 200 milliliters of purified water in place of the citric acid solution and carrying the water sample through the procedure. The typical control reagent blank should not exceed 0.03 absorbance per centimeter path length between 280 and 299 nanometers, 0.02 absorbance per centimeter path length between 300 and 359 nanometers, and 0.01 absorbance per centimeter path length between 360 and 400 nanometers.

[42 FR 14491, Mar. 15, 1977, as amended at 47 FR 11838, Mar. 19, 1982; 49 FR 10106, Mar. 19, 1984; 54 FR 24897, June 12, 1989]

§ 173.170 Aminoglycoside 3′-phosphotransferase II.

The food additive aminoglycoside 3′-phosphotransferase II may be safely used in the development of genetically modified cotton, oilseed rape, and tomatoes in accordance with the following prescribed conditions:

(a) The food additive is the enzyme aminoglycoside 3′-phosphotransferase II (CAS Reg. No. 58943–39–8) which catalyzes the phosphorylation of certain aminoglycoside antibiotics, including kanamycin, neomycin, and gentamicin.

(b) Aminoglycoside 3′-phosphotransferase II is encoded by the kan^r gene originally isolated from transposon Tn^5 of the bacterium *Escherichia coli*.

(c) The level of the additive does not exceed the amount reasonably required for selection of plant cells carrying the kan^r gene along with the genetic material of interest.

[59 FR 26711, May 23, 1994]

Subpart C—Solvents, Lubricants, Release Agents and Related Substances

§ 173.210 Acetone.

A tolerance of 30 parts per million is established for acetone in spice oleoresins when present therein as a residue from the extraction of spice.

§ 173.220 1,3-Butylene glycol.

1,3-Butylene glycol (1,3-butanediol) may be safely used in food in accordance with the following prescribed conditions:

(a) The substance meets the following specifications:

(1) 1,3-Butylene glycol content: Not less than 99 percent.

(2) Specific gravity at 20/20 °C: 1.004 to 1.006.

(3) Distillation range: 200°–215 °C.

(b) It is used in the minimum amount required to perform its intended effect.

(c) It is used as a solvent for natural and synthetic flavoring substances except where standards of identity issued under section 401 of the act preclude such use.

§ 173.228 Ethyl acetate.

Ethyl acetate (CAS Reg. No. 141–78–6) may be safely used in food in accordance with the following conditions:

(a) The additive meets the specifications of the Food Chemicals Codex,[1] (Ethyl Acetate; p. 372, 3d Ed., 1981), which are incorporated by reference.

(b) The additive is used in accordance with current good manufacturing practice as a solvent in the decaffeination of coffee and tea.

[47 FR 146, Jan. 5, 1982, as amended at 49 FR 28548, July 13, 1984]

§ 173.230 Ethylene dichloride.

A tolerance of 30 parts per million is established for ethylene dichloride in spice oleoresins when present therein as a residue from the extraction of spice; *Provided, however,* That if residues of other chlorinated solvents are also present the total of all residues of such solvents shall not exceed 30 parts per million.

§ 173.240 Isopropyl alcohol.

Isopropyl alcohol may be present in the following foods under the conditions specified:

(a) In spice oleoresins as a residue from the extraction of spice, at a level not to exceed 50 parts per million.

(b) In lemon oil as a residue in production of the oil, at a level not to exceed 6 parts per million.

(c) In hops extract as a residue from the extraction of hops at a level not to exceed 2.0 percent by weight: *Provided,* That,

(1) The hops extract is added to the wort before or during cooking in the manufacture of beer.

(2) The label of the hops extract specifies the presence of the isopropyl alcohol and provides for the use of the hops extract only as prescribed by paragraph (c)(1) of this section.

§ 173.250 Methyl alcohol residues.

Methyl alcohol may be present in the following foods under the conditions specified:

(a) In spice oleoresins as a residue from the extraction of spice, at a level not to exceed 50 parts per million.

(b) In hops extract as a residue from the extraction of hops, at a level not to exceed 2.2 percent by weight; *Provided,* That:

(1) The hops extract is added to the wort before or during cooking in the manufacture of beer.

(2) The label of the hops extract specifies the presence of methyl alcohol and provides for the use of the hops extract only as prescribed by paragraph (b)(1) of this section.

§ 173.255 Methylene chloride.

Methylene chloride may be present in food under the following conditions:

(a) In spice oleoresins as a residue from the extraction of spice, at a level not to exceed 30 parts per million; *Provided,* That, if residues of other chlorinated solvents are also present, the total of all residues of such solvents shall not exceed 30 parts per million.

(b) In hops extract as a residue from the extraction of hops, at a level not to exceed 2.2 percent, *Provided,* That:

[1] Copies may be obtained from: National Academy Press, 2101 Constitution Ave. NW., Washington, DC 20418 or examined at the National Archives and Records Administration (NARA). For information on the availability of this material at NARA, call 202–741–6030, or go to: *http://www.archives.gov/federal_register/code_of_federal_regulations/ibr_locations.html.*

(1) The hops extract is added to the wort before or during cooking in the manufacture of beer.

(2) The label of the hops extract identifies the presence of the methylene chloride and provides for the use of the hops extract only as prescribed by paragraph (b)(1) of this section.

(c) In coffee as a residue from its use as a solvent in the extraction of caffeine from green coffee beans, at a level not to exceed 10 parts per million (0.001 percent) in decaffeinated roasted coffee and in decaffeinated soluble coffee extract (instant coffee).

§ 173.270 Hexane.

Hexane may be present in the following foods under the conditions specified:

(a) In spice oleoresins as a residue from the extraction of spice, at a level not to exceed 25 parts per million.

(b) In hops extract as a residue from the extraction of hops, at a level not to exceed 2.2 percent by weight; *Provided*, That:

(1) The hops extract is added to the wort before or during cooking in the manufacture of beer.

(2) The label of the hops extract specifies the presence of the hexane and provides for the use of the hops extract only as prescribed by paragraph (b)(1) of this section.

§ 173.275 Hydrogenated sperm oil.

The food additive hydrogenated sperm oil may be safely used in accordance with the following prescribed conditions:

(a) The sperm oil is derived from rendering the fatty tissue of the sperm whale or is prepared by synthesis of fatty acids and fatty alcohols derived from the sperm whale. The sperm oil obtained by rendering is refined. The oil is hydrogenated.

(b) It is used alone or as a component of a release agent or lubricant in bakery pans.

(c) The amount used does not exceed that reasonably required to accomplish the intended lubricating effect.

§ 173.280 Solvent extraction process for citric acid.

A solvent extraction process for recovery of citric acid from conventional *Aspergillus niger* fermentation liquor may be safely used to produce food-grade citric acid in accordance with the following conditions:

(a) The solvent used in the process consists of a mixture of *n*-octyl alcohol meeting the requirements of § 172.864 of this chapter, synthetic isoparaffinic petroleum hydrocarbons meeting the requirements of § 172.882 of this chapter, and tridodecyl amine.

(b) The component substances are used solely as a solvent mixture and in a manner that does not result in formation of products not present in conventionally produced citric acid.

(c) The citric acid so produced meets the specifications of the "Food Chemicals Codex," 3d Ed. (1981), pp. 86–87, which is incorporated by reference (Copies may be obtained from the National Academy Press, 2101 Constitution Ave. NW., Washington, DC 20418, or may be examined at the National Archives and Records Administration (NARA). For information on the availability of this material at NARA, call 202–741–6030, or go to: *http://www.archives.gov/federal_register/code_of_federal_regulations/ibr_locations.html.*), and the polynuclear aromatic hydrocarbon specifications of § 173.165.

(d) Residues of *n*-octyl alcohol and synthetic isoparaffinic petroleum hydrocarbons are removed in accordance with good manufacturing practice. Current good manufacturing practice results in residues not exceeding 16 parts per million (ppm) *n*-octyl alcohol and 0.47 ppm synthetic isoparaffinic petroleum hydrocarbons in citric acid.

(e) Tridodecyl amine may be present as a residue in citric acid at a level not to exceed 100 parts per billion.

[42 FR 14491, Mar. 15, 1977, as amended at 49 FR 10106, Mar. 19, 1984]

§ 173.290 Trichloroethylene.

Tolerances are established for residues of trichloroethylene resulting from its use as a solvent in the manufacture of foods as follows:

Decaffeinated ground coffee	25 parts per million.
Decaffeinated soluble (instant) coffee extract.	10 parts per million.

Spice oleoresins	30 parts per million (provided that if residues of other chlorinated solvents are also present, the total of all residues of such solvents in spice oleoresins shall not exceed 30 parts per million).

Subpart D—Specific Usage Additives

§ 173.300 Chlorine dioxide.

Chlorine dioxide (CAS Reg. No. 10049–04–4) may be safely used in food in accordance with the following prescribed conditions:

(a)(1) The additive is generated by one of the following methods:

(i) Treating an aqueous solution of sodium chlorite with either chlorine gas or a mixture of sodium hypochlorite and hydrochloric acid.

(ii) Treating an aqueous solution of sodium chlorate with hydrogen peroxide in the presence of sulfuric acid.

(iii) Treating an aqueous solution of sodium chlorite by electrolysis.

(2) The generator effluent contains at least 90 percent (by weight) of chlorine dioxide with respect to all chlorine species as determined by Method 4500–ClO_2 E in the "Standard Methods for the Examination of Water and Wastewater," 20th ed., 1998, or an equivalent method. Method 4500–ClO_2 E ("Amperometric Method II") is incorporated by reference in accordance with 5 U.S.C. 552(a) and 1 CFR part 51. You may obtain a copy from the Center for Food Safety and Applied Nutrition (HFS–200), Food and Drug Administration, 5100 Paint Branch Pkwy., College Park, MD 20740, or the American Public Health Association, 800 I St. NW., Washington, DC 20001–3750. You may inspect a copy at the Center for Food Safety and Applied Nutrition's Library, 5100 Paint Branch Pkwy., College Park, MD, or at the National Archives and Records Administration (NARA). For information on the availability of this material at NARA, call 202–741–6030, or go to: *http://www.archives.gov/federal_register/code_of_federal_regulations/ibr_locations.html.*

(b)(1) The additive may be used as an antimicrobial agent in water used in poultry processing in an amount not to exceed 3 parts per million (ppm) residual chlorine dioxide as determined by Method 4500–ClO_2 E, referenced in paragraph (a)(2) of this section, or an equivalent method.

(2) The additive may be used as an antimicrobial agent in water used to wash fruits and vegetables that are not raw agricultural commodities in an amount not to exceed 3 ppm residual chlorine dioxide as determined by Method 4500–ClO_2 E, referenced in paragraph (a)(2) of this section, or an equivalent method. Treatment of the fruits and vegetables with chlorine dioxide shall be followed by a potable water rinse or by blanching, cooking, or canning.

[60 FR 11900, Mar. 3, 1995. Redesignated at 61 FR 14245, Apr. 1, 1996, as amended at 61 FR 14480, Apr. 2, 1996; 63 FR 38747, July 20, 1998; 65 FR 34587, May 31, 2000; 70 FR 7396, Feb. 14, 2005]

§ 173.310 Boiler water additives.

Boiler water additives may be safely used in the preparation of steam that will contact food, under the following conditions:

(a) The amount of additive is not in excess of that required for its functional purpose, and the amount of steam in contact with food does not exceed that required to produce the intended effect in or on the food.

(b) The compounds are prepared from substances identified in paragraphs (c) and (d) of this section, and are subject to the limitations, if any, prescribed:

(c) List of substances:

Substances	Limitations
Acrylamide-sodium acrylate resin	Contains not more than 0.05 percent by weight of acrylamide monomer.

Substances	Limitations
Acrylic acid/2-acrylamido-2-methyl propane sulfonic acid copolymer having a minimum weight average molecular weight of 9,900 and a minimum number average molecular weight of 5,700 as determined by a method entitled "Determination of Weight Average and Number Average Molecular Weight of 60/40 AA/AMPS" (October 23, 1987), which is incorporated by reference in accordance with 5 U.S.C. 552(a). Copies may be obtained from the Center for Food Safety and Applied Nutrition (HFS–200), Food and Drug Administration, 5100 Paint Branch Pkwy., College Park, MD 20740, or may be examined at the National Archives and Records Administration (NARA). For information on the availability of this material at NARA, call 202–741–6030, or go to: *http://www.archives.gov/federal_register/code_of_federal_regulations/ibr_locations.html.*.	Total not to exceed 20 parts per million (active) in boiler feedwater.
Ammonium alginate.	
Cobalt sulfate (as catalyst).	
1-hydroxyethylidene-1,1-diphosphonic acid (CAS Reg. No. 2809–21–4) and its sodium and potassium salts.	
Lignosulfonic acid.	
Monobutyl ethers of polyethylene-polypropylene glycol produced by random condensation of a 1:1 mixture by weight of ethylene oxide and propylene oxide with butanol.	Minimum mol. wt. 1,500.
Poly(acrylic acid-*co*-hypophosphite), sodium salt (CAS Reg. No. 71050–62–9), produced from a 4:1 to a 16:1 mixture by weight of acrylic acid and sodium hypophosphite.	Total not to exceed 1.5 parts per million in boiler feed water. Copolymer contains not more than 0.5 percent by weight of acrylic acid monomer (dry weight basis).
Polyethylene glycol	As defined in § 172.820 of this chapter.
Polymaleic acid [CAS Reg. No. 26099–09–2], and/or its sodium salt. [CAS Reg. No. 30915–61–8 or CAS Reg. No. 70247–90–4].	Total not to exceed 1 part per million in boiler feed water (calculated as the acid).
Polyoxypropylene glycol	Minimum mol. wt. 1,000.
Potassium carbonate.	
Potassium tripolyphosphate.	
Sodium acetate.	
Sodium alginate.	
Sodium aluminate.	
Sodium carbonate.	
Sodium carboxymethylcellulose	Contains not less than 95 percent sodium carboxymethylcellulose on a dry-weight basis, with maximum substitution of 0.9 carboxymethylcellulose groups per anhydroglucose unit, and with a minimum viscosity of 15 centipoises for 2 percent by weight aqueous solution at 25 °C; by the method prescribed in the "Food Chemicals Codex," 4th ed. (1996), pp. 744–745, which is incorporated by reference in accordance with 5 U.S.C. 552(a) and 1 CFR part 51. Copies are available from the National Academy Press, Box 285, 2101 Constitution Ave. NW., Washington, DC 20055 (Internet address *http://www.nap.edu*), or may be examined at the Center for Food Safety and Applied Nutrition's Library, Food and Drug Administration, 5100 Paint Branch Pkwy., College Park, MD 20740, or at the National Archives and Records Administration (NARA). For information on the availability of this material at NARA, call 202–741–6030, or go to: *http://www.archives.gov/federal_register/code_of_federal_regulations/ibr_locations.html.*
Sodium glucoheptonate	Less than 1 part per million cyanide in the sodium glucoheptonate.
Sodium hexametaphosphate.	
Sodium humate.	
Sodium hydroxide.	
Sodium lignosulfonate.	
Sodium metabisulfite.	
Sodium metasilicate.	
Sodium nitrate.	
Sodium phosphate (mono-, di-, tri-).	
Sodium polyacrylate.	
Sodium polymethacrylate.	
Sodium silicate.	
Sodium sulfate.	
Sodium sulfite (neutral or alkaline).	
Sodium tripolyphosphate.	

Substances	Limitations
Sorbitol anhydride esters: a mixture consisting of sorbitan monostearate as defined in § 172.842 of this chapter; polysorbate 60 ((polyoxyethylene (20) sorbitan monostearate)) as defined in § 172.836 of this chapter; and polysorbate 20 ((polyoxyethylene (20) sorbitan monolaurate)), meeting the specifications of the Food Chemicals Codex, 4th ed. (1996), pp. 306–307, which is incorporated by reference in accordance with 5 U.S.C. 552(a) and 1 CFR part 51. Copies are available from the National Academy Press, 2101 Constitution Ave. NW., Box 285, Washington, DC 20055 (Internet *http://www.nap.edu*), or may be examined at the Center for Food Safety and Applied Nutrition's Library, Food and Drug Administration, 5100 Paint Branch Pkwy., College Park, MD 20740, or at the National Archives and Records Administration (NARA). For information on the availability of this material at NARA, call 202–741–6030, or go to: *http://www.archives.gov/federal_register/code_of_federal_regulations/ibr_locations.html.*.	The mixture is used as an anticorrosive agent in steam boiler distribution systems, with each component not to exceed 15 parts per million in the steam.
Tannin (including quebracho extract).	
Tetrasodium EDTA.	
Tetrasodium pyrophosphate.	

(d) Substances used alone or in combination with substances in paragraph (c) of this section:

Substances	Limitations
Cyclohexylamine	Not to exceed 10 parts per million in steam, and excluding use of such steam in contact with milk and milk products.
Diethylaminoethanol	Not to exceed 15 parts per million in steam, and excluding use of such steam in contact with milk and milk products.
Hydrazine	Zero in steam.
Morpholine	Not to exceed 10 parts per million in steam, and excluding use of such steam in contact with milk and milk products.
Octadecylamine	Not to exceed 3 parts per million in steam, and excluding use of such steam in contact with milk and milk products.
Trisodium nitrilotriacetate	Not to exceed 5 parts per million in boiler feedwater; not to be used where steam will be in contact with milk and milk products.

(e) To assure safe use of the additive, in addition to the other information required by the Act, the label or labeling shall bear:

(1) The common or chemical name or names of the additive or additives.

(2) Adequate directions for use to assure compliance with all the provisions of this section.

[42 FR 14526, Mar. 15, 1977, as amended at 45 FR 73922, Nov. 7, 1980; 45 FR 85726, Dec. 30, 1980; 48 FR 7439, Feb. 22, 1983; 49 FR 5748, Feb. 15, 1984; 49 FR 10106, Mar. 19, 1984; 50 FR 49536, Dec. 3, 1985; 53 FR 15199, Apr. 28, 1988; 54 FR 31012, July 26, 1989; 55 FR 12172, Apr. 2, 1990; 61 FR 14245, Apr. 1, 1996; 64 FR 1759, Jan. 12, 1999; 64 FR 29227, June 1, 1999]

§ 173.315 Chemicals used in washing or to assist in the peeling of fruits and vegetables.

Chemicals may be safely used to wash or to assist in the peeling of fruits and vegetables in accordance with the following conditions:

(a) The chemicals consist of one or more of the following:

(1) Substances generally recognized as safe in food or covered by prior sanctions for use in washing fruits and vegetables.

(2) Substances identified in this subparagraph and subject to such limitations as are provided:

Substances	Limitations
A mixture of alkylene oxide adducts of alkyl alcohols and phosphate esters of alkylene oxide adducts of alkyl alcohols consisting of: α-alkyl (C_{12}-C_{18})-*omega*-hydroxy-poly (oxyethylene) (7.5–8.5 moles)/poly (oxypropylene) block copolymer having an average molecular weight of 810; α-alkyl (C_{12}-C_{18})-*omega*-hydroxy-poly (oxyethylene) (3.3–3.7 moles) polymer having an average molecular weight of 380, and subsequently esterified with 1.25 moles phosphoric anhydride; and α-alkyl (C_{10}-C_{12})-*omega*-hydroxypoly (oxyethylene) (11.9–12.9 moles)/poly (oxypropylene) copolymer, having an average molecular weight of 810, and subsequently esterified with 1.25 moles phosphoric anhydride.	May be used at a level not to exceed 0.2 percent in lye-peeling solution to assist in the lye peeling of fruit and vegetables.
Aliphatic acid mixture consisting of valeric, caproic, enanthic, caprylic, and pelargonic acids.	May be used at a level not to exceed 1 percent in lye peeling solution to assist in the lye peeling of fruits and vegetables.
Polyacrylamide	Not to exceed 10 parts per million in wash water. Contains not more than 0.2 percent acrylamide monomer. May be used in the washing of fruits and vegetables.
Potassium bromide	May be used in the washing or to assist in the lye peeling of fruits and vegetables.
Sodium *n*-alkylbenzene-sulfonate (alkyl group predominantly C_{12} and C_{13} and not less than 95 percent C_{10} to C_{16}).	Not to exceed 0.2 percent in wash water. May be used in washing or to assist in the lye peeling of fruits and vegetables.
Sodium dodecylbenzene-sulfonate (alkyl group predominantly C_{12} and not less than 95% C_{10} to C_{16}).	Do.
Sodium 2 ethyl-hexyl sulfate	Do.
Sodium hypochlorite	May be used in the washing or to assist in the lye peeling of fruits and vegetables.
Sodium mono- and dimethyl naphthalene sulfonates (mol. wt. 245–260)	Not to exceed 0.2 percent in wash water. May be used in the washing or to assist in the lye peeling of fruits and vegetables.

(3) Sodium mono- and dimethyl naphthalene sulfonates (mol. wt. 245–260) may be used in the steam/scald vacuum peeling of tomatoes at a level not to exceed 0.2 percent in the condensate or scald water.

(4) Substances identified in this paragraph (a)(4) for use in flume water for washing sugar beets prior to the slicing operation and subject to the limitations as are provided for the level of the substances in the flume water:

Substance	Limitations
α-Alkyl-*omega*-hydroxypoly-(oxyethylene) produced by condensation of 1 mole of C_{11}-C4863$_{15}$ straight chain randomly substituted secondary alcohols with an average of 9 moles of ethylene oxide.	Not to exceed 3 ppm.
Linear undecylbenzenesulfonic acid.	Do.
Dialkanolamide produced by condensing 1 mole of methyl laurate with 1.05 moles of diethanolamine.	Not to exceed 2 ppm.
Triethanolamine	Do.
Ethylene glycol monobutyl ether	Not to exceed 1 ppm.
Oleic acid conforming with § 172.860 of this chapter.	Do.
Tetrapotassium pyrophosphate	Not to exceed 0.3 ppm.
Monoethanolamine	Do.
Ethylene dichloride	Not to exceed 0.2 ppm.
Tetrasodium ethylenediamine-tetraacetate.	Not to exceed 0.1 ppm.

(5) Substances identified in this paragraph (a)(5) for use on fruits and vegetables that are not raw agricultural commodities and subject to the limitations provided:

Substances	Limitations
Hydrogen peroxide	Used in combination with acetic acid to form peroxyacetic acid. Not to exceed 59 ppm in wash water.
1-Hydroxyethylidene-1,1-diphosphonic acid.	May be used only with peroxyacetic acid. Not to exceed 4.8 ppm in wash water.
Peroxyacetic acid	Prepared by reacting acetic acid with hydrogen peroxide. Not to exceed 80 ppm in wash water.

(b) The chemicals are used in amounts not in excess of the minimum required to accomplish their intended effect.

(c) The use of the chemicals listed under paragraphs (a)(1), (a)(2), and (a)(4) is followed by rinsing with potable water to remove, to the extent possible, residues of the chemicals.

(d) To assure safe use of the additive:

(1) The label and labeling of the additive container shall bear, in addition to the other information required by the act, the name of the additive or a statement of its composition.

(2) The label or labeling of the additive container shall bear adequate use directions to assure use in compliance with all provisions of this section.

[42 FR 14526, Mar. 15, 1977, as amended at 42 FR 29856, June 10, 1977; 42 FR 32229, June 24, 1977; 43 FR 54926, Nov. 24, 1978; 61 FR 46376, 46377, Sept. 3, 1996; 63 FR 7069, Feb. 12, 1998; 64 FR 38564, July 19, 1999]

§ 173.320 Chemicals for controlling microorganisms in cane-sugar and beet-sugar mills.

Agents for controlling microorganisms in cane-sugar and beet-sugar mills may be safely used in accordance with the following conditions:

(a) They are used in the control of microorganisms in cane-sugar and/or beet-sugar mills as specified in paragraph (b) of this section.

(b) They are applied to the sugar mill grinding, crusher, and/or diffuser systems in one of the combinations listed in paragraph (b) (1), (2), (3), or (5) of this section or as a single agent listed in paragraph (b) (4) or (6) of this section. Quantities of the individual additives in parts per million are expressed in terms of the weight of the raw cane or raw beets.

(1) Combination for cane-sugar mills:

	Parts per million
Disodium cyanodithioimidocarbonate	2.5
Ethylenediamine	1.0
Potassium *N*-methyldithiocarbamate	3.5

(2) Combination for cane-sugar mills:

	Parts per million
Disodium ethylenebisdithiocarbamate	3.0
Sodium dimethyldithiocarbamate	3.0

(3) Combinations for cane-sugar mills and beet-sugar mills:

	Parts per million
(i) Disodium ethylenebisdithiocarbamate	3.0
Ethylenediamine	2.0
Sodium dimethyldithiocarbamate	3.0
(ii) Disodium cyanodithioimidocarbonate	2.9
Potassium *N*-methyldithiocarbamate	4.1

(4) Single additive for cane-sugar mills and beet-sugar mills.

	Parts per million
2,2-Dibromo-3-nitrilopropionamide (CAS Reg. No. 10222–01–2). *Limitations:* By-product molasses, bagasse, and pulp containing residues of 2,2-dibromo-3-nitrilopropionamide are not authorized for use in animal feed.	Not more than 10.0 and not less than 2.0.

(5) Combination for cane-sugar mills:

	Parts per million
n-Dodecyl dimethyl benzyl ammonium chloride	0.05±0.005
n-Dodecyl dimethyl ethylbenzyl ammonium chloride	0.68±0.068
n-Hexadecyl dimethyl benzyl ammonium chloride	0.30±0.030
n-Octadecyl dimethyl benzyl ammonium chloride	0.05±0.005
n-Tetradecyl dimethyl benzyl ammonium chloride	0.60±0.060
n-Tetradecyl dimethyl ethylbenzyl ammonium chloride	0.32±0.032

Limitations. Byproduct molasses, bagasse, and pulp containing residues of these quaternary ammonium salts are not authorized for use in animal feed.

(6) Single additive for beet-sugar mills:

	Parts per million
Glutaraldehyde (CAS Reg. No. 111–30–8).	Not more than 250.

(c) To assure safe use of the additives, their label and labeling shall conform to that registered with the Environmental Protection Agency.

[42 FR 14526, Mar. 15, 1977, as amended at 47 FR 35756, Aug. 17, 1982; 50 FR 3891, Jan. 29, 1985; 57 FR 8065, Mar. 6, 1992]

§ 173.322 Chemicals used in delinting cottonseed.

Chemicals may be safely used to assist in the delinting of cottonseed in accordance with the following conditions:

(a) The chemicals consist of one or more of the following:

(1) Substances generally recognized as safe for direct addition to food.

(2) Substances identified in this paragraph and subject to such limitations as are provided:

Substances	Limitations
alpha-Alkyl-*omega*-hydroxypoly-(oxyethylene) produced by condensation of a linear primary alcohol containing an average chain length of 10 carbons with poly(oxyethylene) having an average of 5 ethylene oxide units.	May be used at an application rate not to exceed 0.3 percent by weight of cottonseeds to enhance delinting of cottonseeds intended for the production of cottonseed oil. Byproducts including lint, hulls, and meal may be used in animal feed.
An alkanomide produced by condensation of coconut oil fatty acids and diethanolamine, CAS Reg. No. 068603–42–9.	May be used at an application rate not to exceed 0.2 percent by weight of cottonseeds to enhance delinting of cottonseeds intended for the production of cottonseed oil. Byproducts including lint, hulls, and meal may be used in animal feed.

[47 FR 8346, Feb. 26, 1982]

§ 173.325 Acidified sodium chlorite solutions.

Acidified sodium chlorite solutions may be safely used in accordance with the following prescribed conditions:

(a) The additive is produced by mixing an aqueous solution of sodium chlorite (CAS Reg. No. 7758–19–2) with any generally recognized as safe (GRAS) acid.

(b)(1) The additive is used as an antimicrobial agent in poultry processing water in accordance with current industry practice under the following conditions:

(i) As a component of a carcass spray or dip solution prior to immersion of the intact carcass in a prechiller or chiller tank;

(ii) In a prechiller or chiller solution for application to the intact carcass;

(iii) As a component of a spray or dip solution for application to poultry carcass parts;

(iv) In a prechiller or chiller solution for application to poultry carcass parts; or

(v) As a component of a post-chill carcass spray or dip solution when applied to poultry meat, organs, or related parts or trim.

(2) When used in a spray or dip solution, the additive is used at levels that result in sodium chlorite concentrations between 500 and 1,200 parts per million (ppm), in combination with any GRAS acid at a level sufficient to achieve a solution pH of 2.3 to 2.9.

(3) When used in a prechiller or chiller solution, the additive is used at levels that result in sodium chlorite concentrations between 50 and 150 ppm, in combination with any GRAS acid at levels sufficient to achieve a solution pH of 2.8 to 3.2.

(c) The additive is used as an antimicrobial agent in accordance with current industry practice in the processing of red meat, red meat parts, and organs as a component of a spray or in the processing of red meat parts and organs as a component of a dip. Applied as a dip or spray, the additive is used at levels that result in sodium chlorite concentrations between 500 and 1,200 ppm in combination with any GRAS acid at levels sufficient to achieve a solution pH of 2.5 to 2.9.

(d)(1) The additive is used as an antimicrobial agent in water and ice that are used to rinse, wash, thaw, transport, or store seafood in accordance with current industry standards of good manufacturing practice. The additive is produced by mixing an aqueous solution of sodium chlorite with any GRAS acid to achieve a pH in the range of 2.5 to 2.9 and diluting this solution with water to achieve an actual use concentration of 40 to 50 parts per million (ppm) sodium chlorite. Any seafood that is intended to be consumed raw shall be subjected to a potable water rinse prior to consumption.

(2) The additive is used as a single application in processing facilities as an antimicrobial agent to reduce pathogenic bacteria due to cross-contamination during the harvesting, handling, heading, evisceration, butchering, storing, holding, packing, or packaging of finfish and crustaceans; or following the filleting of finfish; in accordance with current industry standards of good manufacturing practice. Applied as a dip or spray, the additive is used at levels that result in a sodium chlorite concentration of 1,200 ppm, in combination with any GRAS acid at levels sufficient to achieve a pH of 2.3 to 2.9. Treated seafood shall be cooked prior to consumption.

(e) The additive is used as an antimicrobial agent on raw agricultural commodities in the preparing, packing, or holding of the food for commercial purposes, consistent with section

201(q)(1)(B)(i) of the act, and not applied for use under section 201(q)(1)(B)(i)(I), (q)(1)(B)(i)(II), or (q)(1)(B)(i)(III) of the act, in accordance with current industry standards of good manufacturing practice. Applied as a dip or a spray, the additive is used at levels that result in chlorite concentrations of 500 to 1200 parts per million (ppm), in combination with any GRAS acid at levels sufficient to achieve a pH of 2.3 to 2.9. Treatment of the raw agricultural commodities with acidified sodium chlorite solutions shall be followed by a potable water rinse, or by blanching, cooking, or canning.

(f) The additive is used as an antimicrobial agent on processed, comminuted or formed meat food products (unless precluded by standards of identity in 9 CFR part 319) prior to packaging of the food for commercial purposes, in accordance with current industry standards of good manufacturing practice. Applied as a dip or spray, the additive is used at levels that result in sodium chlorite concentrations of 500 to 1200 ppm, in combination with any GRAS acid at levels sufficient to achieve a pH of 2.5 to 2.9.

(g) The additive is used as an antimicrobial agent in the water applied to processed fruits and processed root, tuber, bulb, legume, fruiting (i.e., eggplant, groundcherry, pepino, pepper, tomatillo, and tomato), and cucurbit vegetables in accordance with current industry standards of good manufacturing practices, as a component of a spray or dip solution, provided that such application be followed by a potable water rinse and a 24-hour holding period prior to consumption. However, for processed leafy vegetables (i.e., vegetables other than root, tuber, bulb, legume, fruiting, and cucurbit vegetables) and vegetables in the Brassica [Cole] family, application must be by dip treatment only, and must be preceded by a potable water rinse and followed by a potable water rinse and a 24-hour holding period prior to consumption. When used in a spray or dip solution, the additive is used at levels that result in sodium chlorite concentrations between 500 and 1,200 ppm, in combination with any GRAS acid at a level sufficient to achieve a solution pH of 2.3 to 2.9.

(h) The concentration of sodium chlorite is determined by a method entitled "Determination of Sodium Chlorite: 50 ppm to 1500 ppm Concentration," September 13, 1995, developed by Alcide Corp., Redmond, WA, which is incorporated by reference in accordance with 5 U.S.C. 552(a) and 1 CFR part 51. Copies are available from the Office of Food Additive Safety (HFS–200), Center for Food Safety and Applied Nutrition, Food and Drug Administration, 5100 Paint Branch Pkwy., College Park, MD 20740, 240–402–1200, or may be examined at the Center for Food Safety and Applied Nutrition's Library, 5100 Paint Branch Pkwy., College Park, MD 20740 20204–0001, or at the National Archives and Records Administration (NARA). For information on the availability of this material at NARA, call 202–741–6030, or go to: *http://www.archives.gov/federal_register/code_of_federal_regulations/ibr_locations.html.*

[61 FR 17829, Apr. 23, 1996, as amended at 63 FR 11119, Mar. 6, 1998; 64 FR 44123, Aug. 13, 1999; 64 FR 49982, Sept. 15, 1999; 65 FR 1776, Jan. 12, 2000; 65 FR 16312, Mar. 28, 2000; 66 FR 22922, May 7, 2001; 66 FR 31841, June 13, 2001; 67 FR 15720, Apr. 3, 2002; 69 FR 78304, Dec. 30, 2004; 78 FR 14665, Mar. 7, 2013]

§ 173.340 Defoaming agents.

Defoaming agents may be safely used in processing foods, in accordance with the following conditions:

(a) They consist of one or more of the following:

(1) Substances generally recognized by qualified experts as safe in food or covered by prior sanctions for the use prescribed by this section.

(2) Substances listed in this paragraph (a)(2) of this section, subject to any limitations imposed:

Substances	Limitations
Dimethylpolysiloxane (substantially free from hydrolyzable chloride and alkoxy groups; no more than 18 percent loss in weight after heating 4 hours at 200 °C; viscosity 300 to 1,050 centistokes at 25 °C; refractive index 1.400–1.404 at 25 °C).	10 parts per million in food, or at such level in a concentrated food that when prepared as directed on the labels, the food in its ready-for-consumption state will have not more than 10 parts per million except as follows: Zero in milk; 110 parts per million in dry gelatin dessert mixes labeled for use whereby no more than 16 parts per million is present in the ready-to-serve dessert; 250 parts per million in salt labeled for cooking purposes, whereby no more than 10 parts per million is present in the cooked food.
Formaldehyde	As a preservative in defoaming agents containing dimethylpolysiloxane, in an amount not exceeding 1.0 percent of the dimethylpolysiloxane content.
α-Hydro-*omega*-hydroxy-poly (oxyethylene)/poly(oxypropylene) (minimum 15 moles)/poly(oxyethylene) block copolymer (CAS Reg. No. 9003–11–6) as defined in § 172.808(a)(3) of this chapter.	For use as prescribed in § 172.808(b)(3) of this chapter.
Polyacrylic acid, sodium salt	As a stabilizer and thickener in defoaming agents containing dimethylpolysiloxane in an amount reasonably required to accomplish the intended effect.
Polyethylene glycol	As defined in § 172.820 of this chapter.
Polyoxyethylene 40 monostearate	As defined in U.S.P. XVI.
Polysorbate 60	As defined in § 172.836 of this chapter.
Polysorbate 65	As defined in § 172.838 of this chapter.
Propylene glycol alginate	As defined in § 172.858 of this chapter.
Silicon dioxide	As defined in § 172.480 of this chapter.
Sorbitan monostearate	As defined in § 172.842 of this chapter.
White mineral oil: Conforming with § 172.878 of this chapter	As a component of defoaming agents for use in wash water for sliced potatoes at a level not to exceed 0.008 percent of the wash water.

(3) Substances listed in this paragraph (a)(3), provided they are components of defoaming agents limited to use in processing beet sugar and yeast, and subject to any limitations imposed:

Substances	Limitations
Aluminum stearate	As defined in § 172.863 of this chapter.
Butyl stearate.	
BHA	As an antioxidant, not to exceed 0.1 percent by weight of defoamer.
BHT	Do.
Calcium stearate	As defined in § 172.863 of this chapter.
Fatty acids	As defined in § 172.860 of this chapter.
Formaldehyde	As a preservative.
Hydroxylated lecithin	As defined in § 172.814 of this chapter.
Isopropyl alcohol.	
Magnesium stearate	As defined in § 172.863 of this chapter.
Mineral oil: Conforming with § 172.878 of this chapter	Not more than 150 p.p.m. in yeast, measured as hydrocarbons.
Odorless light petroleum hydrocarbons: Conforming with § 172.884 of this chapter.	
Petrolatum: Conforming with § 172.880 of this chapter	
Petroleum wax: Conforming with § 172.886 of this chapter.	
Petroleum wax, synthetic.	
Polyethylene glycol (400)dioleate: Conforming with § 172.820(a)(2) of this chapter and providing the oleic acid used in the production of this substance complies with § 172.860 or § 172.862 of this chapter.	As an emulsifier not to exceed 10 percent by weight of defoamer formulation.
Synthetic isoparaffinic petroleum hydrocarbons: Conforming with § 172.882 of this chapter.	
Oleic acid derived from tall oil fatty acids	Complying with § 172.862 of this chapter.
Oxystearin	As defined in § 172.818 of this chapter.
Polyoxyethylene (600) dioleate.	
Polyoxyethylene (600) monoricinoleate.	
Polypropylene glycol	Molecular weight range, 1,200–3,000.
Polysorbate 80	As defined in § 172.840 of this chapter.
Potassium stearate	As defined in § 172.863 of this chapter.
Propylene glycol mono- and diesters of fats and fatty acids	As defined in § 172.856 of this chapter.
Soybean oil fatty acids, hydroxylated.	
Tallow, hydrogenated, oxidized or sulfated.	
Tallow alcohol, hydrogenated.	

(4) The substances listed in this paragraph (a)(4), provided they are components of defoaming agents limited to use in processing beet sugar only, and subject to the limitations imposed:

Substances	Limitations
n-Butoxypoly(oxyethylene)-poly(oxypropylene)glycol.	Viscosity range, 4,850–5,350 Saybolt Universal Seconds (SUS) at 37.8 °C (100 °F). The viscosity range is determined by the method "Viscosity Determination of *n*-butoxypoly(oxyethylene)-poly(oxypropylene) glycol" dated April 26, 1995, developed by Union Carbide Corp., P.O. Box 670, Bound Brook, NJ 08805, which is incorporated by reference in accordance with 5 U.S.C. 552(a) and 1 CFR part 51. Copies of the material incorporated by reference are available from the Division of Petition Control, Center for Food Safety and Applied Nutrition (HFS–215), Food and Drug Administration, 5100 Paint Branch Pkwy., College Park, MD 20740, and may be examined at the Center for Food Safety and Applied Nutrition's Library, 5100 Paint Branch Pkwy., College Park, MD 20740, or at the National Archives and Records Administration (NARA). For information on the availability of this material at NARA, call 202–741–6030, or go to: *http://www.archives.gov/federal_register/code_of_federal_regulations/ibr_locations.html.*
Monoester of alpha-hydro-omega-hydroxy-poly(oxyethylene) poly(oxypropylene) poly(oxyethylene) (15 mole minimum) blocked copolymer derived from low erucic acid rapeseed oil.	

(b) They are added in an amount not in excess of that reasonably required to inhibit foaming.

[42 FR 14526, Mar. 15, 1977, as amended at 43 FR 2872, Jan. 20, 1978; 46 FR 30493, June 9, 1981; 46 FR 57476, Nov. 24, 1981; 60 FR 54036, Oct. 19, 1995; 61 FR 632, Jan. 9, 1996; 63 FR 29134, May 28, 1998]

§ 173.342 Chlorofluorocarbon 113 and perfluorohexane.

A mixture of 99 percent chlorofluorocarbon 113 (1,1,2-trichloro-1,2,2-trifluoroethane) (CAS Reg. No. 76–13–1, also known as fluorocarbon 113, CFC 113 and FC 113) and 1 percent perfluorohexane (CAS Reg. No. 355–42–0) may be safely used in accordance with the following prescribed conditions:

(a) The additive chlorofluorocarbon 113 has a purity of not less than 99.99 percent.

(b) The additive mixture is intended for use to quickly cool or crust-freeze chickens sealed in intact bags composed of substances regulated in parts 174, 175, 177, 178, and § 179.45 of this chapter and conforming to any limitations or specifications in such regulations.

[55 FR 8913, Mar. 9, 1990]

§ 173.345 Chloropentafluoroethane.

The food additive chloropentafluoroethane may be safely used in food in accordance with the following prescribed conditions:

(a) The food additive has a purity of not less than 99.97 percent, and contains not more than 200 parts per million saturated fluoro compounds and 10 parts per million unsaturated fluoro compounds as impurities.

(b) The additive is used or intended for use alone or with one or more of the following substances: Carbon dioxide, nitrous oxide, propane, and octafluorocyclobutane complying with § 173.360, as an aerating agent for foamed or sprayed food products, with any propellant effect being incidental and no more than is minimally necessary to achieve the aerating function, except that use is not permitted for those standardized foods that do not provide for such use.

(c) To assure safe use of the additive

(1) The label of the food additive container shall bear, in addition to the other information required by the act, the following:

(i) The name of the additive, chloropentafluoroethane.

(ii) The percentage of the additive present in the case of a mixture.

(iii) The designation ''food grade''.

(2) The label or labeling of the food additive container shall bear adequate directions for use.

[42 FR 14526, Mar. 15, 1977, as amended at 43 FR 11317, Mar. 17, 1978; 43 FR 14644, Apr. 7, 1978]

§ 173.350 Combustion product gas.

The food additive combustion product gas may be safely used in the processing and packaging of the foods designated in paragraph (c) of this section for the purpose of removing and displacing oxygen in accordance with the following prescribed conditions:

(a) The food additive is manufactured by the controlled combustion in air of butane, propane, or natural gas. The combustion equipment shall be provided with an absorption-type filter capable of removing possible toxic impurities, through which all gas used in the treatment of food shall pass; and with suitable controls to insure that any combustion products failing to meet the specifications provided in this section will be prevented from reaching the food being treated.

(b) The food additive meets the following specifications:

(1) Carbon monoxide content not to exceed 4.5 percent by volume.

(2) The ultraviolet absorbance in isooctane solution in the range 255 millimicrons to 310 millimicrons not to exceed one-third of the standard reference absorbance when tested as described in paragraph (e) of this section.

(c) It is used or intended for use to displace or remove oxygen in the processing, storage, or packaging of beverage products and other food, except fresh meats.

(d) To assure safe use of the additive in addition to the other information required by the act, the label or labeling of the combustion device shall bear adequate directions for use to provide a combustion product gas that complies with the limitations prescribed in paragraph (b) of this section, including instructions to assure proper filtration.

(e) The food additive is tested for compliance with paragraph (b)(2) by the following empirical method:

Spectrophotometric measurements. All measurements are made in an ultraviolet spectrophotometer in optical cells of 5 centimeters in length, and in the range of 255 millimicrons to 310 millimicrons, under the same instrumental conditions. The standard reference absorbance is the absorbance at 275 millimicrons of a standard reference solution of naphthalene (National Bureau of Standards Material No. 577 or equivalent in purity) containing a concentration of 1.4 milligrams per liter in purified isooctane, measured against isooctane of the same spectral purity in 5-centimeter cells. (This absorbance will be approximately 0.30.)

Solvent. The solvent used is pure grade isooctane having an ultraviolet absorbance not to exceed 0.05 measured against distilled water as a reference. Upon passage of purified inert gas through some isooctane under the identical conditions of the test, a lowering of the absorbance value has been observed. The absorbance of isooctane to be used in this procedure shall not be more than 0.02 lower in the range 255 millimicrons to 310 millimicrons, inclusive, than that of the untreated solvent as measured in a 5-centimeter cell. If necessary to obtain the prescribed purities, the isooctane may be passed through activated silica gel.

Apparatus. To assure reproducible results, the additive is passed into the isooctane solution through a gas-absorption train consisting of the following components and necessary connections:

1. A gas flow meter with a range up to 30 liters per hour provided with a constant differential relay or other device to maintain a constant flow rate independent of the input pressure.

2. An absorption apparatus consisting of an inlet gas dispersion tube inserted to the bottom of a covered cylindrical vessel with a suitable outlet on the vessel for effluent gas. The dimensions and arrangement of tube and vessel are such that the inlet tube introduces the gas at a point not above 5¼ inches below the surface of the solvent through a sintered glass outlet. The dimensions of the vessel are such, and both inlet and vessel are so designed, that the gas can be bubbled through 60 milliliters of isooctane solvent at a rate up to 30 liters per hour without mechanical loss of solvent. The level corresponding to 60 milliliters should be marked on the vessel.

3. A cooling bath containing crushed ice and water to permit immersion of the absorption vessel at least to the solvent level mark.

Caution. The various parts of the absorption train must be connected by gas-tight tubing and joints composed of materials which will neither remove components from nor add components to the gas stream. The gas source is connected in series to the flow-rate device, the flow meter, and the absorption apparatus in that order. Ventilation should be provided for the effluent gases which may contain carbon monoxide.

Sampling procedure. Immerse the gas-absorption apparatus containing 60 milliliters of isooctane in the coolant bath so that the solvent is completely immersed. Cool for at least 15 minutes and then pass 120 liters of the test gas through the absorption train at a rate of 30 liters per hour or less. Maintain the coolant bath at 0 °C throughout. Remove the absorption vessel from the bath, disconnect, and warm to room temperature. Add isooctane to bring the contents of the absorption vessel to 60 milliliters, and mix. Determine the absorbance of the solution in the 5-centimeter cell in the range 255 millimicrons to 310 millimicrons, inclusive, compared to isooctane. The absorbance of the solution of combustion product gas shall not exceed that of the isooctane solvent at any wavelength in the specified range by more than one-third of the standard reference absorbance.

§ 173.355 Dichlorodifluoromethane.

The food additive dichlorodifluoromethane may be safely used in food in accordance with the following prescribed conditions:

(a) The additive has a purity of not less than 99.97 percent.

(b) It is used or intended for use, in accordance with good manufacturing practice, as a direct-contact freezing agent for foods.

(c) To assure safe use of the additive:

(1) The label of its container shall bear, in addition to the other information required by the act, the following:

(i) The name of the additive, dichlorodifluoromethane, with or without the parenthetical name "Food Freezant 12".

(ii) The designation "food grade".

(2) The label or labeling of the food additive container shall bear adequate directions for use.

§ 173.356 Hydrogen peroxide.

Hydrogen peroxide (CAS Reg. No. 7722–84–1) may be safely used to treat food in accordance with the following conditions:

(a) The additive meets the specifications of the *Food Chemicals Codex*, 7th ed. (2010), pp. 496 and 497, which is incorporated by reference. The Director of the Federal Register approves this incorporation by reference in accordance with 5 U.S.C. 552(a) and 1 CFR part 51. You may obtain copies from the United States Pharmacopeial Convention, 12601 Twinbrook Pkwy., Rockville, MD 20852 (Internet address *http://www.usp.org*). Copies may be examined at the Center for Food Safety and Applied Nutrition's Library, Food and Drug Administration, 5100 Paint Branch Pkwy., College Park, MD 20740, 301–436–2163, or at the National Archives and Records Administration (NARA). For information on the availability of this material at NARA, call 202–741–6030, or go to: *http://www.archives.gov/federal_register/code_of_federal_regulations/ibr_locations.html.*

(b) The additive is used as an antimicrobial agent in the production of modified whey (including, but not limited to, whey protein concentrates and whey protein isolates) by ultrafiltration methods, at a level not to exceed 0.001 percent by weight of the whey, providing that residual hydrogen peroxide is removed by appropriate chemical or physical means during the processing of the modified whey.

[76 FR 11330, Mar. 2, 2011]

§ 173.357 Materials used as fixing agents in the immobilization of enzyme preparations.

Fixing agents may be safely used in the immobilization of enzyme preparations in accordance with the following conditions:

(a) The materials consist of one or more of the following:

(1) Substances generally recognized as safe in food.

(2) Substances identified in this subparagraph and subject to such limitations as are provided:

Substances	Limitations
Acrylamide-acrylic acid resin: Complying with § 173.5(a)(1) and (b) of this chapter.	May be used as a fixing material in the immobilization of glucose isomerase enzyme preparations for use in the manufacture of high fructose corn syrup, in accordance with § 184.1372 of this chapter.
Cellulose triacetate	May be used as a fixing material in the immobilization of lactase for use in reducing the lactose content of milk.
Diethylaminoethyl-cellulose	May be used as a fixing material in the immobilization of glucose isomerase enzyme preparations for use in the manufacture of high fructose corn syrup, in accordance with § 184.1372 of this chapter.

Substances	Limitations
Dimethylamine-epichlorohydrin resin: Complying with § 173.60(a) and (b) of this chapter.	May be used as a fixing material in the immobilization of glucose isomerase enzyme preparations for use in the manufacture of high fructose corn syrup, in accordance with § 184.1372 of this chapter.
Glutaraldehyde	Do.
Periodic acid (CAS Reg. No. 10450–60–9)..	May be used as a fixing material in the immobilization of glucoamylase enzyme preparations from *Aspergillus niger* for use in the manufacture of beer.
Polyethylenimine reaction product with 1,2-dichloroethane (CAS Reg. No. 68130–97–2) is the reaction product of homopolymerization of ethylenimine in aqueous hydrochloric acid at 100 °C and of cross-linking with 1,2-dichloroethane. The finished polymer has an average molecular weight of 50,000 to 70,000 as determined by gel permeation chromatography. The analytical method is entitled "Methodology for Molecular Weight Detection of Polyethylenimine," which is incorporated by reference in accordance with 5 U.S.C. 552(a) and 1 CFR part 51. Copies may be obtained from the Division of Petition Control, Center for Food Safety and Applied Nutrition (HFS–200), 5100 Paint Branch Pkwy., College Park, MD 20740, and may be examined at the Center for Food Safety and Applied Nutrition's Library, 5100 Paint Branch Pkwy., College Park, MD 20740, or at the National Archives and Records Administration (NARA). For information on the availability of this material at NARA, call 202–741–6030, or go to: *http://www.archives.gov/federal_register/code_of_federal_regulations/ibr_locations.html*..	May be used as a fixing material in the immobilization of: 1. Glucose isomerase enzyme preparations for use in the manufacture of high fructose corn syrup, in accordance with § 184.1372 of this chapter. 2. Glucoamylase enzyme preparations from *Aspergillus niger* for use in the manufacture of beer. Residual ethylenimine in the finished polyethylenimine polymer will be less than 1 part per million as determined by gas chromatography-mass spectrometry. The residual ethylenimine is determined by an analytical method entitled "Methodology for Ethylenimine Detection in Polyethylenimine," which is incorporated by reference in accordance with 5 U.S.C. 552(a) and 1 CFR part 51. Residual 1,2-dichloroethane in the finished polyethylenimine polymer will be less than 1 part per million as determined by gas chromatography. The residual 1,2-dichloroethane is determined by an analytical method entitled, "Methodology for Ethylenedichloride Detection in Polyethylenimine," which is incorporated by reference in accordance with 5 U.S.C. 552(a) and 1 CFR part 51. Copies may be obtained from the Division of Petition Control, Center for Food Safety and Applied Nutrition (HFS–215), 5100 Paint Branch Pkwy., College Park, MD 20740, or may be examined at the Center for Food Safety and Applied Nutrition's Library, 5100 Paint Branch Pkwy., College Park, MD 20740, or at the National Archives and Records Administration (NARA). For information on the availability of this material at NARA, call 202–741–6030, or go to: *http://www.archives.gov/federal_register/code_of_federal_regulations/ibr_locations.html.*

(b) The fixed enzyme preparation is washed to remove residues of the fixing materials.

[48 FR 5716, Feb. 8, 1983, as amended at 52 FR 39512, Oct. 22, 1987; 55 FR 12172, Apr. 2, 1990; 59 FR 36937, July 20, 1994; 61 FR 4873, Feb. 9, 1996; 61 FR 14245, Apr. 1, 1996; 67 FR 42716, June 25, 2002]

§ 173.360 Octafluorocyclobutane.

The food additive octafluorocyclo-butane may be safely used as a propellant and aerating agent in foamed or sprayed food products in accordance with the following conditions:

(a) The food additive meets the following specifications:

99.99 percent octafluorocyclobutane.

Less than 0.1 part per million fluoroolefins, calculated as perfluoroisobutylene.

(b) The additive is used or intended for use alone or with one or more of the following substances: Carbon dioxide, nitrous oxide, and propane, as a propellant and aerating agent for foamed or sprayed food products, except for those standardized foods that do not provide for such use.

(c) To assure safe use of the additive:

(1) The label of the food additive container shall bear, in addition to the other information required by the act, the following:

(i) The name of the additive, octafluorocyclobutane.

(ii) The percentage of the additive present in the case of a mixture.

(iii) The designation "food grade".

(2) The label or labeling of the food additive container shall bear adequate directions for use.

§ 173.368 Ozone.

Ozone (CAS Reg. No. 10028–15–6) may be safely used in the treatment, storage, and processing of foods, including meat and poultry (unless such use is precluded by standards of identity in 9 CFR part 319), in accordance with the following prescribed conditions:

(a) The additive is an unstable, colorless gas with a pungent, characteristic odor, which occurs freely in nature. It is produced commercially by passing electrical discharges or ionizing radiation through air or oxygen.

(b) The additive is used as an antimicrobial agent as defined in § 170.3(o)(2) of this chapter.

(c) The additive meets the specifications for ozone in the *Food Chemicals Codex*, 4th ed. (1996), p. 277, which is incorporated by reference. The Director of the Office of the Federal Register approves this incorporation by reference in accordance with 5 U.S.C. 552(a) and 1 CFR part 51. Copies are available from the National Academy Press, 2101 Constitution Ave. NW., Washington, DC 20055, or may be examined at the Office of Food Additive Safety (HFS–200), Center for Food Safety and Applied Nutrition, Food and Drug Administration, 5100 Paint Branch Pkwy., College Park, MD 20740, 240–402–1200, and at the National Archives and Records Administration (NARA). For information on the availability of this material at NARA, call 202–741–6030, or go to: *http://www.archives.gov/federal_register/code_of_federal_regulations/ibr_locations.html.*

(d) The additive is used in contact with food, including meat and poultry (unless such use is precluded by standards of identity in 9 CFR part 319 or 9 CFR part 381, subpart P), in the gaseous or aqueous phase in accordance with current industry standards of good manufacturing practice.

(e) When used on raw agricultural commodities, the use is consistent with section 201(q)(1)(B)(i) of the Federal Food, Drug, and Cosmetic Act (the act) and not applied for use under section 201(q)(1)(B)(i)(I), (q)(1)(B)(i)(II), or (q)(1)(B)(i)(III) of the act.

[66 FR 33830, June 26, 2001; 67 FR 271, Jan. 3, 2002, as amended at 78 FR 14665, Mar. 7, 2013]

§ 173.370 Peroxyacids.

Peroxyacids may be safely used in accordance with the following prescribed conditions:

(a) The additive is a mixture of peroxyacetic acid, octanoic acid, acetic acid, hydrogen peroxide, peroxyoctanoic acid, and 1-hydroxyethylidene-1,1-diphosphonic acid.

(b)(1) The additive is used as an antimicrobial agent on meat carcasses, parts, trim, and organs in accordance with current industry practice where the maximum concentration of peroxyacids is 220 parts per million (ppm) as peroxyacetic acid, and the maximum concentration of hydrogen peroxide is 75 ppm.

(2) The additive is used as an antimicrobial agent on poultry carcasses, poultry parts, and organs in accordance with current industry standards of good manufacturing practice (unless precluded by the U.S. Department of Agriculture's standards of identity in 9 CFR part 381, subpart P) where the maximum concentration of peroxyacids is 220 parts per million (ppm) as peroxyacetic acid, the maximum concentration of hydrogen peroxide is 110 ppm, and the maximum concentration of 1-hydroxyethylidene-1,1-diphosphonic acid (HEDP) is 13 ppm.

(c) The concentrations of peroxyacids and hydrogen peroxide in the additive are determined by a method entitled "Hydrogen Peroxide and Peracid (as Peracetic Acid) Content," July 26, 2000, developed by Ecolab, Inc., St. Paul, MN, which is incorporated by reference. The concentration of 1-hydroxyethylidene-1,1-diphosphonic acid is determined by a method entitled "Determination of 1-hydroxyethylidene-1,1-diphosphonic acid (HEDP) Peroxyacid/Peroxide-Containing Solutions," August 21, 2001, developed by Ecolab, Inc., St. Paul, MN, which is incorporated by reference. The Director of the Office of the Federal Register approves these incorporations by reference in accordance with 5 U.S.C. 552(a) and 1 CFR part 51. You may obtain copies of these methods from the Division of Petition Review, Center for Food Safety and Applied Nutrition, Food and Drug Administration, 5100 Paint Branch Pkwy., College Park, MD 20740, or you may examine a copy at the Center for Food Safety and Applied Nutrition's Library, 5100 Paint Branch Pkwy., College Park, MD 20740, or at the National Archives and Records Administration (NARA). For information on the availability of this material at NARA, call 202–741–6030, or go to: *http://www.archives.gov/federal_register/*

code_of_federal_regulations/ ibr_locations.html.

[65 FR 70660, Nov. 27, 2000, as amended at 66 FR 48208, Sept. 19, 2001; 67 FR 61784, Oct. 2, 2002]

§ 173.375 Cetylpyridinium chloride.

Cetylpyridinium chloride (CAS Reg. No. 123–93–5) may be safely used in food in accordance with the following conditions:

(a) The additive meets the specifications of the United States Pharmacopeia (USP)/National Formulary (NF) described in USP 30/NF 25, May 1, 2007, pp. 1700–1701, which is incorporated by reference. The Director of the Office of the Federal Register approves this incorporation by reference in accordance with 5 U.S.C. 552(a) and 1 CFR part 51. You may obtain copies from the United States Pharmacopeial Convention, Inc., 12601 Twinbrook Pkwy., Rockville, MD 20852, or you may examine a copy at the Center for Food Safety and Applied Nutrition's Library, Food and Drug Administration, 5100 Paint Branch Pkwy., College Park, MD 20740, or at the National Archives and Records Administration (NARA). For information on the availability of this material at NARA, call 202–741–6030, or go to: *http://www.archives.gov/federal-register/cfr/ibr-locations.html.*

(b) The additive is used in food as an antimicrobial agent as defined in §170.3(o)(2) of this chapter to treat the surface of raw poultry carcasses. The solution in which the additive is used to treat raw poultry carcasses shall also contain propylene glycol (CAS Reg. No. 57–55–6) complying with §184.1666 of this chapter, at a concentration of 1.5 times that of cetylpyridinium chloride.

(c) The additive is used as follows:

(1) As a fine mist spray of an ambient temperature aqueous solution applied to raw poultry carcasses prior to immersion in a chiller, at a level not to exceed 0.3 gram cetylpyridinium chloride per pound of raw poultry carcass, provided that the additive is used in systems that collect and recycle solution that is not carried out of the system with the treated poultry carcasses; or

(2) As a liquid aqueous solution applied to raw poultry carcasses either prior to or after chilling at an amount not to exceed 5 gallons of solution per carcass, provided that the additive is used in systems that recapture at least 99 percent of the solution that is applied to the poultry carcasses. The concentration of cetylpyridinium chloride in the solution applied to the carcasses shall not exceed 0.8 percent by weight. When application of the additive is not followed by immersion in a chiller, the treatment will be followed by a potable water rinse of the carcass.

[72 FR 67576, Nov. 29, 2007, as amended at 76 FR 59248, Sept. 26, 2011]

§ 173.385 Sodium methyl sulfate.

Sodium methyl sulfate may be present in pectin in accordance with the following conditions.

(a) It is present as the result of methylation of pectin by sulfuric acid and methyl alcohol and subsequent treatment with sodium bicarbonate.

(b) It does not exceed 0.1 percent by weight of the pectin.

§ 173.395 Trifluoromethane sulfonic acid.

Trifluoromethane sulfonic acid has the empirical formula CF_3SO_3H (CAS Reg. No. 1493–13–6). The catalyst (Trifluoromethane sulfonic acid) may safely be used in the production of cocoa butter substitute from palm oil (1-palmitoyl-2-oleoyl-3-stearin) (see §184.1259 of this chapter) in accordance with the following conditions:

(a) The catalyst meets the following specifications:

Appearance, Clear liquid.
Color, Colorless to amber.
Neutralization equivalent, 147–151.
Water, 1 percent maximum.
Fluoride ion, 0.03 percent maximum.
Heavy metals (as Pb), 30 parts per million maximum.
Arsenic (as As), 3 parts per million maximum.

(b) It is used at levels not to exceed 0.2 percent of the reaction mixture to catalyze the directed esterification.

(c) The esterification reaction is quenched with steam and water and the catalyst is removed with the aqueous phase. Final traces of catalyst are removed by washing batches of the product three times with an aqueous solution of 0.5 percent sodium bicarbonate.

(d) No residual catalyst may remain in the product at a detection limit of 0.2 part per million fluoride as determined by the method described in "Official Methods of Analysis of the Association of Official Analytical Chemists," sections 25.049–25.055, 13th Ed. (1980), which is incorporated by reference. Copies may be obtained from the AOAC INTERNATIONAL, 481 North Frederick Ave., suite 500, Gaithersburg, MD 20877, or may be examined at the National Archives and Records Administration (NARA). For information on the availability of this material at NARA, call 202–741–6030, or go to: *http://www.archives.gov/federal_register/code_of_federal_regulations/ibr_locations.html.*

[43 FR 54237, Nov. 11, 1978, as amended at 49 FR 10106, Mar. 19, 1984; 54 FR 24897, June 12, 1989; 70 FR 40880, July 15, 2005; 70 FR 67651, Nov. 8, 2005]

§ 173.400 Dimethyldialkylammonium chloride.

Dimethyldialkylammonium chloride may be safely used in food in accordance with the following prescribed conditions:

(a) The food additive is produced by one of the following methods:

(1) Ammonolysis of natural tallow fatty acids to form amines that are subsequently reacted with methyl chloride to form the quaternary ammonium compounds consisting primarily of dimethyldioctadecylammonium chloride and dimethyldihexadecylammonium chloride. The additive may contain residues of isopropyl alcohol not in excess of 18 percent by weight when used as a processing solvent.

(2) Ammonolysis of natural tallow fatty acids to form amines that are then reacted with 2-ethylhexanal, reduced, methylated, and subsequently reacted with methyl chloride to form the quaternary ammonium compound known as dimethyl(2-ethylhexyl) hydrogenated tallow ammonium chloride and consisting primarily of dimethyl(2-ethylhexyl)octadecylammonium chloride and dimethyl(2-ethylhexyl)hexadecylammonium chloride.

(b) The food additive described in paragraph (a)(1) of this section contains not more than a total of 2 percent by weight of free amine and amine hydrochloride. The food additive described in paragraph (a)(2) of this section contains not more than 3 percent by weight, each, of free amine and amine hydrochloride as determined by A.O.C.S. method Te 3a–64, "Acid Value and Free Amine Value of Fatty Quaternary Ammonium Chlorides," 2d printing including additions and revisions 1990, which is incorporated by reference in accordance with 5 U.S.C. 552(a) and 1 CFR part 51. Copies are available from the Center for Food Safety and Applied Nutrition (HFS–200), Food and Drug Administration, 5100 Paint Branch Pkwy., College Park, MD 20740, and from the American Oil Chemists' Society, P.O. Box 5037, Station A, Champaign, IL 61820, or available for inspection at the National Archives and Records Administration (NARA). For information on the availability of this material at NARA, call 202–741–6030, or go to: *http://www.archives.gov/federal_register/code_of_federal_regulations/ibr_locations.html.*

(c) The food additive is used as a decolorizing agent in the clarification of refinery sugar liquors under the following limitations:

(1) The food additive described in paragraph (a)(1) of this section is added only at the defecation/clarification stage of sugar liquor refining in an amount not to exceed 700 parts per million by weight of sugar solids.

(2) The food additive described in paragraph (a)(2) of this section is used under the following conditions:

(i) The additive is adsorbed onto a support column composed of suitable polymers that are regulated for contact with aqueous food. Excess nonadsorbed additive shall be rinsed away with potable water prior to passage of sugar liquor through the column.

(ii) The residue of the additive in the decolorized sugar liquor prior to crystallization shall not exceed 1 part per million of sugar as determined by a method entitled "Colorimetric Determination of Residual Quaternary Ammonium Compounds (Arquad HTL8) in Sugar and Sugar Solutions," June 13, 1990, which is incorporated by reference in accordance with 5 U.S.C. 552(a) and 1

CFR part 51. Copies are available from the Center for Food Safety and Applied Nutrition (HFS–200), Food and Drug Administration, 5100 Paint Branch Pkwy., College Park, MD 20740, or available for inspection at the National Archives and Records Administration (NARA). For information on the availability of this material at NARA, call 202–741–6030, or go to: *http://www.archives.gov/federal_register/code_of_federal_regulations/ibr_locations.html.*

(d) To assure safe use of the additive, the label and labeling of the additive shall bear, in addition to other information required by the Federal Food, Drug, and Cosmetic Act, adequate directions to assure use in compliance with paragraph (c) of this section.

[56 FR 42686, Aug. 29, 1991]

§ 173.405 Sodium dodecylbenzenesulfonate.

Sodium dodecylbenzenesulfonate (CAS No. 25155–30–0) may be safely used in accordance with the following prescribed conditions:

(a) The additive is an antimicrobial agent used in wash water for fruits and vegetables. The additive may be used at a level not to exceed 111 milligrams per kilogram in the wash water. Fruits and vegetables treated by the additive do not require a potable water rinse.

(b) The additive is limited to use in commissaries, cafeterias, restaurants, retail food establishments, nonprofit food establishments, and other food service operations in which food is prepared for or served directly to the consumer.

(c) To assure safe use of the additive, the label or labeling of the additive container shall bear, in addition to the other information required by the Federal Food, Drug, and Cosmetic Act, adequate directions to assure use in compliance with the provisions of this section.

[77 FR 71697, Dec. 4, 2012]

PART 174—INDIRECT FOOD ADDITIVES: GENERAL

Sec.

AUTHORITY: 21 U.S.C. 321, 342, 348, 371.

§ 174.5 General provisions applicable to indirect food additives.

(a) Regulations prescribing conditions under which food additive substances may be safely used predicate usage under conditions of good manufacturing practice. For the purpose of this part and parts 175, 176, and 177 of this chapter, good manufacturing practice shall be defined to include the following restrictions:

(1) The quantity of any food additive substance that may be added to food as a result of use in articles that contact food shall not exceed, where no limits are specified, that which results from use of the substance in an amount not more than reasonably required to accomplish the intended physical or technical effect in the food-contact article; shall not exceed any prescribed limitations; and shall not be intended to accomplish any physical or technical effect in the food itself, except as such may be permitted by regulations in parts 170 through 189 of this chapter.

(2) Any substance used as a component of articles that contact food shall be of a purity suitable for its intended use.

(b) The existence in the subchapter B of a regulation prescribing safe conditions for the use of a substance as an article or component of articles that contact food shall not be construed to relieve such use of the substance or article from compliance with any other provision of the Federal Food, Drug, and Cosmetic Act. For example, if a regulated food-packaging material were found on appropriate test to impart odor or taste to a specific food product such as to render it unfit within the meaning of section 402(a)(3) of the Act, the regulation would not be construed to relieve such use from compliance with section 402(a)(3).

(c) The existence in this subchapter B of a regulation prescribing safe conditions for the use of a substance as an article or component of articles that contact food shall not be construed as implying that such substance may be safely used as a direct additive in food.

(d) Substances that under conditions of good manufacturing practice may be safely used as components of articles that contact food include the following, subject to any prescribed limitations:

(1) Substances generally recognized as safe in or on food.

(2) Substances generally recognized as safe for their intended use in food packaging.

(3) Substances used in accordance with a prior sanction or approval.

(4) Substances permitted for use by regulations in this part and parts 175, 176, 177, 178 and § 179.45 of this chapter.

(5) Food contact substances used in accordance with an effective premarket notification for a food contact substance (FCN) submitted under section 409(h) of the act.

[42 FR 14534, Mar. 15, 1977, as amended at 67 FR 35731, May 21, 2002]

§ 174.6 Threshold of regulation for substances used in food-contact articles.

Substances used in food-contact articles (e.g., food-packaging or food-processing equipment) that migrate, or that may be expected to migrate, into food at negligible levels may be reviewed under § 170.39 of this chapter. The Food and Drug Administration will exempt substances whose uses it determines meet the criteria in § 170.39 of this chapter from regulation as food additives and, therefore, a food additive petition will not be required for the exempted use.

[60 FR 36596, July 17, 1995]

PART 175—INDIRECT FOOD ADDITIVES: ADHESIVES AND COMPONENTS OF COATINGS

AUTHORITY: 21 U.S.C. 321, 342, 348, 379e.

SOURCE: 42 FR 14534, Mar. 15, 1977, unless otherwise noted.

EDITORIAL NOTE: Nomenclature changes to part 175 appear at 61 FR 14482, Apr. 2, 1996, 66 FR 56035, Nov. 6, 2001, and 70 FR 72074, Dec. 1, 2005.

Subpart A [Reserved]

Subpart B—Substances for Use Only as Components of Adhesives

§ 175.105 Adhesives.

(a) Adhesives may be safely used as components of articles intended for use in packaging, transporting, or holding food in accordance with the following prescribed conditions:

(1) The adhesive is prepared from one or more of the optional substances named in paragraph (c) of this section, subject to any prescribed limitations.

(2) The adhesive is either separated from the food by a functional barrier or used subject to the following additional limitations:

(i) *In dry foods.* The quantity of adhesive that contacts packaged dry food shall not exceed the limits of good manufacturing practice.

(ii) *In fatty and aqueous foods.* (*a*) The quantity of adhesive that contacts packaged fatty and aqueous foods shall not exceed the trace amount at seams and at the edge exposure between packaging laminates that may occur within the limits of good manufacturing practice.

(*b*) Under normal conditions of use the packaging seams or laminates will remain firmly bonded without visible separation.

(b) To assure safe usage of adhesives, the label of the finished adhesive container shall bear the statement "food-packaging adhesive".

(c) Subject to any limitation prescribed in this section and in any other regulation promulgated under section 409 of the Act which prescribes safe conditions of use for substances that may be employed as constituents of adhesives, the optional substances used in the formulation of adhesives may include the following:

(1) Substances generally recognized as safe for use in food or food packaging.

(2) Substances permitted for use in adhesives by prior sanction or approval and employed under the specific conditions of use prescribed by such sanction or approval.

(3) Flavoring substances permitted for use in food by regulations in this part, provided that such flavoring substances are volatilized from the adhesives during the packaging fabrication process.

(4) Color additives approved for use in food.

(5) Substances permitted for use in adhesives by other regulations in this subchapter and substances named in this subparagraph: *Provided, however,* That any substance named in this paragraph and covered by a specific regulation in this subchapter, must meet any specifications in such regulation.

Substances	Limitations
Abietic acid.	
Acetone.	
Acetone-formaldehyde condensate (CAS Reg. No. 25619–09–4).	
Acetone-urea-formaldehyde resin.	
N-Acetyl ethanolamine.	
Acetyl tributyl citrate.	
Acetyl triethyl citrate.	
2-Acrylamido-2-methyl-propanesulfonic acid, homopolymer, sodium salt (CAS Reg. No. 35641–59–9).	
Albumin, blood.	
(2-Alkenyl) succinic anhydrides in which the alkenyl groups are derived from olefins which contain not less than 78 percent C_{30} and higher groups (CAS Reg. No. 70983–55–0).	
4-[2-[2-2-(Alkoxy (C_{12}-C_{15}) ethoxy) ethoxy]ethyl] disodium sulfosuccinate.	
1-Alkyl (C_6-C_{18}) amino-3-amino-propane monoacetate.	
Alkylated (C_4 and/or C_8) phenols.	
Alkyl (C_7-$C1_2$) benzene.	
Alkyl (C_{10}-C_{20}) dimethylbenzyl ammonium chloride.	
n-Alkyl(C_{12}, C_{14}, C_{16}, or C_{18}) dimethyl (ethylbenzyl) ammonium cyclohexylsulfamate.	For use as preservative only.
Alkyl ketene dimers as described in § 176.120 of this chapter.	
Alkyl (C_7-C_{12}) naphthalene.	
alpha Olefin sulfonate [alkyl group is in the range of C_{10}-C_{18} with not less than 50 percent C_{14}-C_{16}], ammonium, calcium, magnesium, potassium, and sodium salts.	
2-[(2-aminoethyl)amino]ethanol (CAS Reg. No. 111–41–1).	
3-Aminopropanediol	For use only in the preparation of polyurethane resins.
Aluminum.	
Aluminum acetate.	
Aluminum di(2-ethylhexoate).	
Aluminum potassium silicate.	
N-β-Aminoethyl-*gamma*-aminopropyl trimethoxysilane.	
3-(Aminomethyl)-3,5,5-trimethylcyclohexylamine.	
Aminomethylpropanol.	
Ammonium benzoate	For use as preservative only.
Ammonium bifluoride	For use only as bonding agent for aluminum foil, stabilizer or preservative. Total fluoride from all sources not to exceed 1 percent by weight of the finished adhesive.
Ammonium borate.	
Ammonium citrate.	
Ammonium persulfate.	
Ammonium polyacrylate.	
Ammonium potassium hydrogen phosphate.	
Ammonium silico-fluoride	For use only as bonding agent for aluminum foil, stabilizer, or preservative. Total fluoride from all sources not to exceed 1 percent by weight of the finished adhesive.

Substances	Limitations
Ammonium sulfamate.	
Ammonium thiocyanate.	
Ammonium thiosulfate.	
Amyl acetate.	
Anhydroenneaheptitol.	
Animal glue as described in § 178.3120 of this chapter.	
2-Anthraquinone sulfonic acid, sodium salt	For use only as polymerization-control agent.
Antimony oxide.	
Asbestos.	
Asphalt, paraffinic and naphthenic.	
Azelaic acid.	
Azo-*bis*-isobutyronitrile.	
Balata rubber.	
Barium acetate.	
Barium peroxide.	
Barium sulfate.	
Bentonite.	
Benzene (benzol).	
1,4-Benzenedicarboxylic acid, bis[2-(1,1-dimethylethyl)-6-[[3-(1,1-dimethylethyl)-2-hydroxy-5-methylphenyl]methyl]-4-methyl-phenyl]ester (CAS Reg. No. 57569–40–1).	For use as a stabilizer.
1,2–Benzisothiazolin–3–one (CAS Registry No. 2634–33–5)	For use as preservative only.
Benzothiazyldisulfide.	
p-Benzoxyphenol	For use as preservative only.
Benzoyl peroxide.	
Benzyl alcohol.	
Benzyl benzoate.	
Benzyl bromoacetate	For use as preservative only.
p-Benzyloxyphenol	Do.
BHA (butylated hydroxyanisole).	
BHT (butylated hydroxytoluene).	
Bicyclo[2.2.1]hept-2-ene-6-methyl acrylate.	
2-Biphenyl diphenyl phosphate.	
Bis(benzoate-*O*)(2-propanolato)aluminum (CAS Reg. No. 105442–85–1)	For use only as a reactant in the preparation of polyester resins.
1,2-Bis(3,5-di-*tert*-butyl-4-hydroxyhydrocinnamoyl)hy-drazine (CAS Reg. No. 32687–78–8).	For use at a level not to exceed 2 percent by weight of the adhesive.
1,3-Bis(2-benzothiazolylmercaptomethyl) urea.	
4,4′-Bis(α,α-dimethylbenzyl)diphenylamine.	
2,6-Bis(1,1-dimethylethyl)-4-(1-methylpropyl)phenol (CAS Reg. No. 17540–75–9).	For use as an antioxidant and/or stabilizer only.
2,6-Bis (1-methylheptadecyl)-*p*-cresol.	
4-[[4, 6-Bis(octylthio)6-Bis(octylthio)6-Bis(octylthio)-*s*-triazin-2-yl]amino]-2,6-di-*tert*-butylphenol (CAS Reg. No. 991–84–4).	
Bis(tri-*n*-butyltin) oxide	For use as preservative only.
Bis(trichloromethyl)sulfone C.A. Registry No. 3064–70–8	Do.
Borax.	
Boric acid.	
2-Bromo-2-nitro-1, 3-propanediol (CAS Reg. No. 52–51–7)	For use only as an antibacterial preservative.
Butanedioic acid, sulfo-1,4-di-(C_9-C_{11} alkyl) ester, ammonium salt (also known as butanedioic acid, sulfo-1,4-diisodecyl ester, ammonium salt [CAS Reg. No. 144093–88–9])..	For use as a surface active agent in adhesives.
1,3-Butanediol.	
1,4-Butanediol.	
1,4-Butanediol modified with adipic acid.	
Butoxy polyethylene polypropylene glycol (molecular weight 900–4,200).	
Butyl acetate.	
Butyl acetyl ricinoleate.	
Butyl alcohol.	
Butylated reaction product of *p*-cresol and dicyclopentadiene	As identified in § 178.2010(b) of this chapter.
Butylated, styrenated cresols identified in § 178.2010(b) of this chapter.	
Butyl benzoate.	
Butyl benzyl phthalate.	
Butyldecyl phthalate	
1,3-Butylene glycoldiglycolic acid copolymer.	
tert-Butyl hydroperoxide.	
4,4′-Butylidenebis(6-*tert*-butyl-*m*-cresol).	
Butyl lactate.	
Butyloctyl phthalate.	
p-*tert*-Butylphenyl salicylate.	
Butyl phthalate butyl glycolate.	
p-*tert*-Butylpyrocatechol	For use only as polymerization-control agent.
Butyl ricinoleate.	
Butyl rubber polymer.	

Substances	Limitations
Butyl stearate.	
Butyl titanate, polymerized.	
Butyraldehyde.	
Calcium ethyl acetoacetate.	
Calcium nitrate.	
Calcium metasilicate.	
Camphor.	
Camphor fatty acid esters.	
Candelilla wax.	
epsilon-Caprolactam-(ethylene-ethyl acrylate) graft polymer.	
Carbon black, channel process.	
Carbon disulfide-1,1′-methylenedipiperidine reaction product.	
Carbon tetrachloride.	
Carboxymethylcellulose.	
Castor oil, polyoxyethylated (4–84 moles ethylene oxide).	
Cellulose acetate butyrate.	
Cellulose acetate propionate.	
Ceresin wax (ozocerite).	
Cetyl alcohol.	
Chloracetamide.	
Chloral hydrate.	
Chlorinated liquid *n*-paraffins with chain lengths of C_{10}-C_{17}, containing 40–70 percent chlorine by weight.	
Chlorinated pyridine mixture with active ingredients consisting of 2,3,5,6-tetrachloro-4-(methylsulfonyl) pyridine, 2,3,5,6-tetrachloro-4-(methylsulfinyl) pyridine and pentachloropyridine.	For use as preservative only.
Chlorinated rubber polymer (natural rubber polymer containing approximately 67 percent chlorine).	
1-(3-Chloroallyl)-3,5,7-triaza-1-azoniaadamantane chloride	For use as preservative only.
Chlorobenzene.	
4-Chloro-3,5-dimethylphenol (*p*-chloro-*m*-xylenol)	For use as preservative only.
4-Chloro-3-methylphenol	Do.
5-Chloro-2-methyl-4-isothiazolin-3-one (CAS Reg. No. 26172–55–4) and 2-methyl-4-isothiazolin-3-one (CAS Reg. No. 2682–20–4) mixture at a ratio of 3 parts to 1 part, manufactured from methyl-3-mercaptopropionate (CAS Reg. No. 2935–90–2). The mixture may contain magnesium nitrate (CAS Reg. No. 10377–60–3) at a concentration equivalent to the isothiazolone active ingredients (weight/weight).	For use only as an antimicrobial agent in polymer latex emulsions.
Chloroform.	
Chloroprene.	
Chromium caseinate.	
Chromium nitrate.	
Chromium potassium sulfate.	
Cobaltous acetate.	
Coconut fatty acid amine salt of tetrachlorophenol	For use as preservative only.
Copal.	
Copper 8-quinolinolate	For use as preservative only.
Coumarone-indene resin.	
Cresyl diphenyl phosphate.	
Cumene hydroperoxide.	
Cyanoguanidine.	
Cyclized rubber as identified in § 176.170(b)(2) of this chapter.	
Cyclohexane.	
1,4-Cyclohexanedimethanoldibenzoate (CAS Reg. No. 35541–81–2).	
Cyclohexanol.	
Cyclohexanone resin.	
Cyclohexanone-formaldehyde condensate.	
N-Cyclohexyl *p*-toluene sulfonamide.	
(η^5-Cyclopentadienyl)-(η^6-isopropylbenzene)iron(II) hexafluorophosphate (CAS Reg. No. 32760–80–8).	For use only as a photoinitiator.
Damar.	
Defoaming agents as described in § 176.210 of this chapter.	
Dehydroacetic acid	
Diacetone alcohol.	
Diacetyl peroxide.	
N,N′-Dialkoyl-4,4′-diaminodiphenylmethane mixtures where; the alkoyl groups are derived from marine fatty acids (C_{12}-C_{24}).	
2,5-Di-*tert*-amylhydroquinone.	
Diamines derived from dimerized vegetable oil acids.	
Diaryl-*p*-phenylenediamine, where the aryl group may be phenyl, tolyl, or xylyl.	
1,2–Dibromo–2,4–dicyanobutane (CAS Registry No. 3569–65–7)	For use as a preservative only.
2,2-Dibromo-3-nitrilopropionamide (CAS Reg. No. 10222–01–2).	For use as a preservative only.

Substances	Limitations
Di(butoxyethyl) phthalate.	
2,5-Di-*tert*-butylhydroquinone.	
Dibutyl maleate.	
2,6-Di-*tert*-butyl-4-methylphenol	For use as preservative only.
Di(C_7, C_9-alkyl)adipate.	
Dibutyl phthalate.	
Dibutyl sebacate.	
Dibutyltin dilaurate for use only as a catalyst for polyurethane resins.	
1,2-Dichloroethylene (mixed isomers).	
Dicumyl peroxide.	
Dicyclohexyl phthalate.	
Diethanolamine.	
Diethanolamine condensed with animal or vegetable fatty acids.	
Diethylamine.	
Diethylene glycol.	
Diethylene glycol adipic acid copolymer.	
Diethylene glycol dibenzoate.	
Diethylene glycol hydrogenated tallowate monoester.	
Diethylene glycol laurate.	
Diethylene glycol monobutyl ether.	
Diethylene glycol monobutyl ether acetate.	
Diethylene glycol monoethyl ether.	
Diethylene glycol monoethyl ether acetate.	
Diethylene glycol monomethyl ether.	
Diethylene glycol monooleate.	
Diethylene glycol monophenyl ether.	
Diethylene glycol copolymer of adipic acid and phthalic anhydride.	
Di(2-ethylhexyl) adipate.	
Di(2-ethylhexyl)hexahydrophthalate.	
Di(2-ethylhexyl)phthalate.	
Diethyl oxalate.	
Diethyl phthalate.	
Dihexyl phthalate.	
Dihydroabietylphthalate.	
Di(2-hydroxy-5-*tert*-butylphenyl) sulfide.	
2,2′-Dihydroxy-5,5′-dichlorodiphenylmethane (dichlorophene).	
4,5-Dihydroxy-2-imidazolidinone.	
4-(Diiodomethylsulfonyl) toluene CA Registry No.: 20018–09–01	For use as an antifungal preservative only.
Diisobutyl adipate.	
Diisobutyl ketone.	
Diisobutylphenoxyethoxyethyl dimethyl benzyl ammonium chloride.	
Diisobutyl phthalate.	
Diisodecyl adipate.	
Diisodecyl phthalate.	
Diisooctyl phthalate.	
Diisopropylbenzene hydroperoxide.	
N,N-Dimethylcyclohexylamine dibutyldithiocarbamate.	
Dimethyl formamide.	
Dimethyl hexynol.	
2,2-Dimethyl-1,3-propanediol dibenzoate.	
Dimethyl octynediol.	
N-(1,1-dimethyl-3-oxobutyl) acrylamide.	
Dimethyl phthalate.	
3,5-Dimethyl-1,3,5,2*H*-tetrahydrothiadiazine-2-thione	For use as preservative only.
Di-β-naphthyl-*p*-phenylenediamine.	
4,6-Dinonyl-*o*-cresol.	
Dinonylphenol.	
Di-*n*-octyldecyl adipate.	
Dioctyldiphenylamine.	
Dioctylphthalate.	
Dioctylsebacate.	
Dioxane.	
Dipentaerythritol pentastearate.	
Dipentamethylene-thiuram-tetrasulfide.	
Dipentene	
Dipentene resins.	
Dipentene-*beta*-pinene-styrene resins.	
Dipentene-styrene resin (CAS Registry No. 64536–06–7).	
Diphenyl-2-ethylhexyl phosphate.	
Diphenyl, hydrogen ated.	
N,N′-Diphenyl-*p*-phenylenediamine.	
Diphenyl phthalate.	
1,3-Diphenyl-2-thiourea.	
Dipropylene glycol.	

Substances	Limitations
Dipropylene glycol dibenzoate.	
Dipropylene glycol monomethyl ether.	
Dipropylene glycol copolymer of adipic acid and phthalic anhydride.	
Disodium cyanodithioimidocarbonate.	
Disodium 4-isodecyl sulfosuccinate (CAS Reg. No. 37294–49–8).	
N,N'-Distearoylethylenediamine.	
Distearyl thiodipropionate.	
3,5-Di-*tert*-butyl-4-hydroxyhydrocinnamic acid triester with 1,3,5-tris(2-hydroxyethyl)-*s*-triazine-2,4,6(1*H*, 3*H*, 5*H*)-trione.	For use as antioxidant only.
4,4'-Dithiodimorpholine.	
n-Dodecylmercaptan.	
tert-Dodecylmercaptan.	
Dodecylphenoxybenzene-disulfonic acid and/or its calcium, magnesium, and sodium salts.	
Elemi gum.	
Epichlorohydrin-4,4'-isopropylidenediphenol resin.	
Epichlorohydrin-4,4'-*sec*-butylidenediphenol resin.	
Epichlorohydrin-4,4'-isopropylidene-di-o-cresol resin.	
Epichlorohydrin-phenolformaldehyde resin.	
Erucamide (erucylamide).	
Ethanolamine.	
Ethoxylated primary linear alcohols of greater than 10 percent ethylene oxide by weight having molecular weights of 390 to 7,000 (CAS Reg. No. 97953–22–5).	
Ethoxypropanol butyl ether.	
Ethyl alcohol (ethanol).	
5-Ethyl-1,3-diglycidyl-5-methylhydantoin (CAS Reg. No. 15336–82–0).	
Ethylene-acrylic acid-carbon monoxide copolymer (CAS Reg. No. 97756–27–9).	
Ethylene-acrylic acid copolymer, partial sodium salt containing no more than 20 percent acrylic acid by weight, and no more than 16 percent of the acrylic acid as the sodium salt (CAS Reg. No. 25750–82–7).	
Ethylenediamine.	
Ethylenediaminetetra-acetic acid, calcium, ferric, potassium, or sodium salts, single or mixed.	
Ethylene dichloride.	
Ethylene glycol.	
Ethylene glycol monobutyl ether.	
Ethylene glycol monobutyl ether acetate.	
Ethylene glycol monoethyl ether.	
Ethylene glycol monoethyl ether acetate.	
Ethylene glycol monoethyl ether ricinoleate.	
Ethylene glycol monomethyl ether.	
Ethylene glycol monophenyl ether.	
Ethylene-carbon monoxide copolymer (CAS Reg. No. 25052–62–4) containing not more than 30 weight percent of the units derived from carbon monoxide.	
Ethylene-maleic anhydride copolymer, ammonium or potassium salt.	
Ethylene-methacrylic acid copolymer partial salts: Ammonium, calcium, magnesium, sodium, and/or zinc.	
Ethylene-methacrylic acid-vinyl acetate copolymer partial salts: Ammonium, calcium, magnesium, sodium, and/or zinc.	
Ethylene-octene-1 copolymers containing not less than 70 weight percent ethylene (CAS Reg. No. 26221–73–8).	
Ethylene-propylene-dicyclopentadiene copolymer rubber.	
Ethylene, propylene, 1,4-hexadiene and 2,5-norbornadiene tetrapolymer.	
Ethylene-vinyl acetate carbon monoxide terpolymer (CAS Registry No. 26337–35–9) containing not more than 15 weight percent of units derived from carbon monoxide.	
2,2'-Ethylidenebis (4,6-di-*tert*-butylphenol) (CAS Reg. No. 35958–30–6).	
Ethyl-*p*-hydroxybenzoate	For use as preservative only.
Ethyl hydroxyethylcellulose.	
Ethyl lactate.	
2,2'-Ethylidenebis(4,6-di-*tert*-butylphenyl)fluorophosphonite (CAS Reg. No. 118337–09–0).	For use as an antioxidant and/or stabilizer only.
Ethyl phthalyl ethyl glycolate.	
Ethyl-*p*-toluene sulfonamide	
Fats and oils derived from animal or vegetable sources, and the hydrogenated, sulfated, or sulfonated forms of such fats and oils.	
Fatty acids derived from animal or vegetable fats and oils; and salts of such acids, single or mixed, as follows:	
Aluminum.	
Ammonium.	
Calcium.	

Substances	Limitations
Magnesium.	
Potassium.	
Sodium.	
Zinc.	
Ferric chloride.	
Fluosilicic acid (hydrofluosilicic acid)	For use only as bonding agent for aluminum foil, stabilizer, or preservative. Total fluoride from all sources not to exceed 1 percent by weight of the finished adhesive.
Formaldehyde.	
Formaldehyde *o*- and *p*-toluene sulfonamide.	
Formamide.	
Fumaratochromium (III) nitrate.	
Furfural.	
Furfuryl alcohol.	
Fumaric acid.	
gamma-Aminopropyltrimethoxysilane (CAS Reg. No. 13822–56–5).	
Glutaraldehyde.	
Glycerides, di- and monoesters.	
Glycerol polyoxypropylene triol, minimum average molecular weight 250 (CAS Reg. No. 25791–96–2).	For use only in the preparation of polyester and polyurethane resins in adhesives.
Glyceryl borate (glycol boriborate resin).	
Glyceryl ester of damar, copal, elemi, and sandarac.	
Glyceryl monobutyl ricinoleate.	
Glyceryl monohydroxy stearate.	
Glyceryl monohydroxy tallowate.	
Glyceryl polyoxypropylene triol (average molecular weight 1,000).	
Glyceryl tribenzoate.	
Glycol diacetate.	
Glyoxal.	
Heptane.	
Hexamethylenetetramine.	
Hexane.	
Hexanetriols.	
Hexylene glycol.	
Hydroabietyl alcohol.	
Hydrocarbon resins (produced by polymerization of mixtures of mono- and di-unsaturated hydrocarbons of the aliphatic, alicyclic, and monobenzenoid type derived both from cracked petroleum and terpene stocks) (CAS Reg. No. 68239–99–6).	
Hydrocarbon resins (produced by the polymerization of styrene and *alpha*-methyl styrene), hydrogenated (CAS Reg. No. 68441–37–2).	
Hydrofluoric acid	For use only as bonding agent for aluminum foil, stabilizer, or preservative. Total fluoride from all sources not to exceed 1 percent by weight of the finished adhesive.
Hydrogen peroxide.	
Hydrogenated dipentene resin (CAS Reg. No. 106168–39–2).	
Hydrogenated dipentene-styrene copolymer resin (CAS Reg. No. 106168–36–9).	
Hydrogenated-*beta*-pinene-*alpha*-pinene-dipentene copolymer resin (CAS Reg. No. 106168–37–0).	
a-Hydro-*omega*-hydroxypoly-(oxytetramethylene)	For use only in the preparation of polyurethane resins.
Hydroquinone.	
Hydroquinone monobenzyl ether.	
Hydroquinone monoethyl ether.	
2(2′-Hydroxy-3′,5′ di-*tert*-amylphenyl) benzotriazole.	
Hydroxyacetic acid.	
7-Hydroxycoumarin.	
Hydroxyethylcellulose.	
2–Hydroxy-1-[4-(2-hydroxyethoxy)phenyl]-2-methyl-1-propanone(CAS Reg. No. 106797–53–9).	For use only as a photoinitiator at a level not to exceed 5 percent by weight of the adhesive.
1-(2-Hydroxyethyl)-1-(4-chlorobutyl)-2 alkyl (C_6-C_{17}) imidazolinium chloride.	
Hydroxyethyldiethylenetriamine.	
β-Hydroxyethyl pyridinium 2-mercaptobenzothiazol.	
Hydroxyethyl starch.	
Hydroxyethylurea	
Hydroxylamine sulfate.	
5-Hydroxymethoxymethyl-1-aza-3,7-dioxabicyclo[3.3.0]octane, 5-hydroxymethyl-1-aza-3,7-dioxabicyclo[3.3.0]octane, and 5-hydroxypoly-[methyleneoxy]methyl-1-aza-3,7-dioxabicyclo[3.3.0] octane mixture.	For use only as an antibacterial preservative.
Hydroxypropyl methylcellulose.	

Substances	Limitations
2-(Hydroxymethyl)-2-methyl-1,3-propanediol tribenzoate.	
2-Imidazolidinone.	
3–Iodo–2–propynyl-N-butyl carbamate (CAS Reg. No. 55406–53–6)	For use only as an antifungal preservative.
Iodoform	For use only as polymerization-control agent.
Isoascorbic acid.	
Isobutyl alcohol (isobutanol).	
Isobutylene-isoprene copolymer.	
Isodecyl benzoate (CAS Reg. No. 131298–44–7).	
Isophorone.	
Isopropanolamine (mono-, di-, tri-).	
Isopropyl acetate.	
Isopropyl alcohol (isopropanol).	
Isopropyl-*m*- and *p*-cresol (thymol derived).	
4,4′-Isopropylidenediphenol.	
4,4′-Isopropylidenediphenol, polybutylated mixture	For use as preservative only.
Isopropyl peroxydicarbonate.	
p-Isopropoxy diphenylamine.	
4,4′-Isopropylidene-bis(*p*-phenyleneoxy)-di-2-propanol.	
Itaconic acid.	
Japan wax.	
Kerosene.	
Lauroyl peroxide.	
Lauroyl sulfate salts:	
Ammonium.	
Magnesium.	
Potassium.	
Sodium.	
Lauryl alcohol.	
Lauryl pyridinium 5-chloro-2-mercaptobenzothiazole.	
Lignin calcium sulfonate.	
Lignin sodium sulfonate.	
Linoleamide (linoleic acid amide).	
Magnesium fluoride	For use only as bonding agent for aluminum foil, stabilizer, or preservative. Total fluoride from all sources not to exceed 1 percent by weight of the finished adhesives.
Magnesium glycerophosphate.	
Maleic acid.	
Maleic anhydride-diisobutylene copolymer, ammonium or sodium salt.	
Manganese acetate.	
Marine oil fatty acid soaps, hydrogenated.	
Melamine.	
Melamine-formaldehyde copolymer.	
2-Mercaptobenzothiazole.	
2-Mercaptobenzothiazole and dimethyl dithiocarbamic acid mixture, sodium salt.	For use as preservative only.
2-Mercaptobenzothiazole, sodium or zinc salt	For use as preservative only.
Methacrylate-chromic chloride complex, ethyl or methyl ester.	
p-Menthane hydroperoxide.	
Methyl acetate.	
Methyl acetyl ricinoleate.	
Methyl alcohol (methanol).	
Methylcellulose.	
Methylene chloride.	
4,4′-Methylenebis(2,6-di-*tert*-butylphenol).	
2,2-Methylenebis (4-ethyl-6-*tert*-butylphenol).	
2,2-Methylenebis (4-methyl-6-nonylphenol).	
2,2-Methylenebis (4-methyl-6-*tert*-butylphenol).	
Methyl ethyl ketone.	
Methyl ethyl ketone-formaldehyde condensate.	
2-Methylhexane.	
1-Methyl-2-hydroxy-4-isopropyl benzene.	
Methyl isobutyl ketone.	
Methyl oleate.	
Methyl oleate-palmitate mixture.	
Methyl phthalyl ethyl glycolate.	
Methyl ricinoleate.	
Methyl salicylate.	
a-Methylstyrene-vinyltoluene copolymer resins (molar ratio 1 *a* methylstyrene to 3 vinyltoluene).	
Methyl tallowate.	
Mineral oil.	
Monochloracetic acid.	
Monooctyldiphenylamine.	

Substances	Limitations
Montan wax.	
Morpholine.	
Myristic acid-chromic chloride complex.	
Myristyl alcohol.	
Naphtha.	
Naphthalene, monosulfonated.	
Naphthalene sulfonic acid-formaldehyde condensate, sodium salt.	
α-Naphthylamine.	
α,α′,α″,α‴-Neopentane tetrayltetrakis [*omega*-hydroxypoly (oxypropylene) (1–2 moles)], average molecular weight 400.	
Nitric acid.	
μ-Nitrobiphenyl.	
Nitrocellulose.	
2-Nitropropane.	
α-(*p*-Nonylphenyl)-*omega*-hydroxypoly (oxyethylene) mixture of dihydrogen phosphate and monohydrogen phosphate esters; the nonyl group is a propylene trimer isomer and the poly (oxyethylene) content averages 6–9 moles or 50 moles.	
α(*p*-Nonylphenyl)-*omega*-hydroxypoly (oxyethylene) produced by the condensation of 1 mole of *p*-nonylphenol (nonyl group is a propylene trimer isomer) with an average of 1–40 moles of ethylene oxide.	
α-(*p*-Nonylphenyl)-*omega*-hydroxypoly (oxyethylene) sulfate, ammonium salt: the nonyl group is a propylene trimer isomer and the poly (oxyethylene) content averages 9 or 30 moles.	
endo-cis-5-Norbornene-2,3-dicarboxylic anhydride.	
α-*cis*-9-Octadecenyl-*omega*-hydroxypoly (oxyethylene); the octadecenyl group is derived from oleyl alcohol and the poly (oxyethylene) content averages 20 moles.	
Octadecyl 3,5-di-*tert*-butyl-4-hydroxyhydrocinnamate.	
Octyl alcohol.	
Octyldecyl phthalate.	
Octylphenol.	
Octylphenoxyethanols.	
Octylphenoxypolyethoxy-polypropoxyethanol (13 moles of ethylene oxide and propylene oxide).	
Odorless light petroleum hydrocarbons.	
Oleamide (oleic acid amide).	
Oleic acid, sulfated.	
2,2′-Oxamidobis[ethyl 3-(3,5-di-*tert*-butyl-4-hydroxyphenyl)propionate] (CAS Reg. No. 70331–94–1).	
Oxazoline.	
α-(oxiranylmethyl)-ω-(oxiranylmethoxy)poly[oxy(methyl-1,2-ethanediyl)], (alternative name: epichlorohydrin-polypropylene glycol) (CAS Reg. No. 26142–30–3).	For use as a reactant in the preparation of epoxy-based resins.
2,2′-[oxybis[(methyl-2,1-ethanediyl)-oxymethylene]]bisoxirane, (alternative name: epichlorohydrin-dipropylene glycol) (CAS Reg. No. 41638–13–5).	For use as a reactant in the preparation of epoxy-based resins.
n-Oxydiethylene-benzothiazole.	
Palmitamide (palmitic acid amide).	
Paraffin (C_{12}-C_{20}) sulfonate.	
Paraformaldehyde.	
Pentachlorophenol.	
Pentaerythritol ester of maleic anhydride.	
Pentaerythritol monostearate	For use as preservative only.
Pentaerythritol tetrabenzoate [CAS Registry No. 4196–86–5].	
Pentaerythritol tetrastearate.	
2,4-Pentanedione.	
Pentasodium diethylenetriaminepentaacetate (CAS Reg. No. 140–01–2).	
Perchloroethylene.	
Petrolatum.	
Petroleum hydrocarbon resin (cyclopentadiene type), hydrogenated.	
Petroleum hydrocarbon resin (produced by the catalytic polymerization and subsequent hydrogenation of styrene, vinyltoluene, and indene types from distillates of cracked petroleum stocks).	
Petroleum hydrocarbon resins (produced by the homo-and copolymerization of dienes and olefins of the aliphatic, alicyclic, and monobenzenoid arylalkene types from distillates of cracked petroleum stocks).	
Phenol	For use as preservative only.
Phenol-coumarone-indene resin.	
Phenolic resins as described in § 175.300(b)(3)(vi).	
Phenothiazine	For use only as polymerization-control agent.
Phenyl-β-naphthylamine (free of β-naphthylamine).	
o-Phenylphenol	For use as preservative only.

Substances	Limitations
o-Phthalic acid.	
Pimaric acid	
Pine oil.	
Piperazine.	
Piperidinium pentamethylenedithiocarbamate.	
Poly(acrylamide-[2-acrylamide-2-methylpropylsulfonate]-dimethylidiallyl ammonium chloride) sodium salt (CAS Reg. No. 72275-68-4).	
Polyamides derived from reaction of one or more of the following acids with one or more of the following amines:	
Acids:	
Azelaic acid.	
Dimerized vegetable oil acids.	
Amines:	
Bis(hexamethylene) triamine and higher homologues.	
Diethylenetriamine.	
Diphenylamine.	
Ethylenediamine.	
Hexamethylenediamine.	
Poly(oxypropylene)diamine (weight average molecular weight 2010) (CAS Reg. No. 9046–10–0).	
Poly(oxypropylene)diamine (weight average molecular weight 440) (CAS Reg. No. 9046–10–0).	
Tetraethylenepentamine.	
Triethylenetetramine.	
Polybutene, hydrogenated.	
Polybutylene glycol (molecular weight 1,000).	
Poly [2(diethylamino) ethyl methacrylate] phosphate.	
Polyester of adipic acid, phthalic acid, and propylene glycol, terminated with butyl alcohol.	
Polyester of diglycolic acid and propylene glycol containing ethylene glycol monobutyl ether as a chain stopper.	
Polyester resins (including alkyd type), as the basic polymer, formed as esters when one or more of the following acids are made to react with one or more of the following alcohols:	
Acids:	
Azelaic acid.	
Dimethyl 1,4-cyclohexanedicarboxylate (CAS Reg. No. 94–60–0).	
Dimethyl-5-sulfoisophthalic acid (CAS Reg. No. 50975–82–1) and/or its sodium salt (CAS Reg. No. 3965–55–7).	
Polybasic and monobasic acids identified in § 175.300(b)(3)(vii)(*a*) and (*b*).	
5-sulfo-1,3-benzenedicarboxylic acid, monosodium salt (CAS Reg. No. 6362–79–4).	
Tetrahydrophthalic acid.	
Alcohols:	
1,4-Cyclohexanedimethanol.	
2,2-Dimethyl-1,3-propanediol.	
1,6-Hexanediol (CAS Reg. No. 629–11–8).	
Polyhydric and monohydric alcohols identified in § 175.300(b)(3)(vii)(*c*) and (*d*).	
Polyethyleneadipate modified with ethanolamine with the molar ratio of the amine to the adipic acid less than 0.1 to 1.	For use only in the preparation of polyurethan resins.
Polyethylene glycol (molecular weight 200–6,000).	
Polyethylene glycol mono-isotridecyl ether sulfate, sodium salt (CAS Reg. No. 150413–26–6).	
Polyethyleneglycol alkyl(C_{10}-C_{12}) ether sulfosuccinate, disodium salt (CAS Reg. No. 68954–91–6).	
Polyethylene, oxidized.	
Polyethylene resins, carboxyl modified, identified in § 177.1600 of this chapter.	
Polyethylenimine.	
Polyethylenimine-epichlorohydrin resins.	
Poly(ethyloxazoline) (CAS Reg. No. 25805-17-8).	
Polyisoprene.	
Polymeric esters of polyhydric alcohols and polycarboxylic acids prepared from glycerin and phthalic anhydride and modified with benzoic acid, castor oil, coconut oil, linseed oil, rosin, soybean oil, styrene, and vinyl toluene.	
Polymers: Homopolymers and copolymers of the following monomers:.	
Acrylamide.	
Acrylic acid.	
Acrylonitrile.	

Substances	Limitations
Allylmethacrylate (CAS Reg. No. 00096–05–09).	
Butadiene.	
Butene.	
N-tert-Butylacrylamide.	
Butyl acrylate.	
1,3-Butylene glycol dimethacrylate.	
Butyl methacrylate.	
Crotonic acid.	
Decyl acrylate.	
Diallyl fumarate.	
Diallyl maleate.	
Diallyl phthalate.	
Dibutyl fumarate.	
Dibutyl itaconate.	
Dibutyl maleate.	
Di(2-ethylhexyl) maleate.	
Dimethyl-α-methylstyrene.	
Dioctyl fumarate.	
Dioctyl maleate.	
Divinylbenzene.	
Ethyl acrylate.	
Ethylene.	
Ethylene cyanohydrin.	
2-Ethylhexyl acrylate.	
Ethyl methacrylate.	
Fatty acids, $C_{10\text{-}13}$-branched, vinyl esters (CAS Reg. No. 184785–38–4).	
Fumaric acid and/or its methyl, ethyl, propyl, butyl, amyl hexyl, heptyl and octyl esters.	
Glycidyl methacrylate.	
1–Hexene (CAS Reg. No. 592–41–6).	
2-Hydroxyethyl acrylate.	
2-Hydroxyethyl methacrylate.	
2-Hydroxypropyl methacrylate.	
Isobutyl acrylate.	
Isobutylene.	
Itaconic acid.	
Maleic acid, diester with 2-hydroxyethanesulfonic acid, sodium salt.	
Maleic anhydride.	
Methacrylic acid.	
Methyl acrylate.	
N,N'-Methylenebisacrylamide.	
Methyl methacrylate.	
N-Methylolacrylamide.	
Methyl styrene.	
-Methyl styrene.	
Monoethyl maleate.	
Monomethyl maleate.	
Mono (2-ethylhexyl) maleate.	
5-Norbornene-2 3-dicarboxylic acid, mono-*n*-butyl ester.	
1-Octene (CAS Reg. No. 111–66–0).	
Propyl acrylate.	
Propylene.	
Styrene.	
Triallyl cyanurate.	
Vinyl acetate.	
Vinyl alcohol (from alcoholysis or hydrolysis of vinyl acetate units).	
Vinyl butyrate.	
Vinyl chloride.	
Vinyl crotonate.	
Vinyl ethyl ether.	
Vinyl hexoate.	
Vinylidene chloride.	
Vinyl methyl ether.	
Vinyl pelargonate.	
Vinyl propionate.	
Vinyl pyrrolidone.	
Vinyl stearate.	
Polyoxyalkylated-phenolic resin (phenolic resin obtained from formaldehyde plus butyl- and/or amylphenols, oxyalkylated with ethylene oxide and/or propylene oxide).	
Poly(oxycaproyl) diols and triols (minimum molecular weight 500).	
Polyoxyethylated (40 moles) tallow alcohol sulfate, sodium salt.	
Polyoxyethylene (20 mol)—anhydrous lanolin adduct.	

Substances	Limitations
Polyoxyethylene (molecular weight 200) dibenzoate.	
Polyoxyethylene (molecular weight 200–600) esters of fatty acids derived from animal or vegetable fats and oils (including tall oil).	
Polyoxyethylene (15 moles) ester of rosin.	
Polyoxyethylene (4–5 moles) ether of phenol.	
Polyoxyethylene (25 moles)—glycerol adduct.	
Polyoxyethylene (40 moles) stearate.	
Polyoxyethylene (5–15 moles) tridecyl alcohol.	
Polyoxypropylene (3 moles) tridecyl alcohol sulfate.	
Polyoxypropylene (20 moles) butyl ether.	
Polyoxypropylene (40 moles) butyl ether.	
Polyoxypropylene (20 moles) oleate butyl ether.	
Polyoxypropylene-polyoxyethylene condensate (minimum molecular weight 1,900).	
Polypropylene glycol (minimum molecular weight 150).	
Polypropylene glycol (3–4 moles) triether with 2-ethyl-2-(hydroxymethyl)-1,3-propane-diol, average molecular weight 730.	
Polypropylene glycol dibenzoate (CAS Reg. No. 72245–46–6)	For use as a plasticizer at levels not to exceed 20 percent by weight of the finished adhesive.
Polypropylene, noncrystalline.	
Polysiloxanes:	
Diethyl polysiloxane.	
Dihydrogen polysiloxane.	
Dimethyl polysiloxane.	
Diphenyl polysiloxane.	
Ethyl hydrogen polysiloxane.	
Ethyl phenyl polysiloxane.	
Methyl ethyl polysiloxane.	
Methyl hydrogen polysiloxane.	
Methyl phenyl polysiloxane.	
Phenyl hydrogen polysiloxane.	
Polysorbate 60.	
Polysorbate 80.	
Polysorbate 20 (polyoxyethylene (20) sorbitan monolaurate).	
Polysorbate 40 (polyoxyethylene (20) sorbitan monopalmitate).	
Poly[styrene-co-disodium maleate-co-α-(*p*-nonyl-phenyl)-*omega*-(*p*-vinyl-benzyl)poly(oxyethylene)] terpolymer.	
Polytetrafluoroethylene..	
Polyurethane resins produced by: (1) reacting diisocyanates with one or more of the polyols or polyesters named in this paragraph, or (2) reacting the chloroformate derivatives of one or more of the polyols or polyesters named in this paragraph with one or more of the polyamines named in this paragraph, or (3) reacting toluene diisocyanate or 4,4′ methylenebis(cyclohexylisocyanate) (CAS Reg. No. 5124–30–1) with: (i) one or more of the polyols or polyesters named in this paragraph and with either *N*-methyldiethanolamine (CAS Reg. No. 105–59–9) and dimethyl sulfate (CAS Reg. No. 77–78–1) or dimethylolpropionic acid (CAS Reg. No. 4767–03–7) and triethylamine (CAS Reg. No. 121–44–8), or (ii) a fumaric acid-modified polypropylene glycol or fumaric acid-modified tripropylene glycol), triethylamine (CAS Reg. No. 107–15–3), and ethylenediamine (CAS Reg. No. 121–44–8), or (4) reacting *meta*-tetramethylxylene diisocyanate (CAS Reg. No. 2778–42–9) with one or more of the polyols and polyesters listed in this paragraph and with dimethylolpropionic acid (CAS Reg. No. 4767–03–7) and triethylamine (CAS Reg. No. 121–44–8), *N*-methyldiethanolamine (CAS Reg. No. 105–59–9), 2–dimethylaminoethanol (CAS Reg. No. 108–01–0), 2–dimethylamino–2–methyl–1–propanol (CAS Reg. No. 7005–47–2), and/or 2–amino–2–methyl–1–propanol (CAS Reg. No. 124–68–5).	
Polyvinyl alcohol modified so as to contain not more than 3 weight percent of comonomer units derived from 1-alkenes having 12 to 20 carbon atoms.	
Polyvinyl butyral.	
Polyvinyl formal.	
Potassium ferricyanide	For use only as polymerization-control agent.
Potassium *N*-methyldithiocarbamate.	
Potassium pentachlorophenate	For use as preservative only.
Potassium permanganate.	
Potassium persulfate.	
Potassium phosphates (mono-, di-, tribasic).	
Potassium tripolyphosphate.	
α, α′, α″-1,2,3-Propanetriyltris [*omega*-(2,3-epoxypropoxy) poly (oxypropylene) (24 moles)].	
β-Propiolactone.	

Substances	Limitations
Propyl alcohol (propanol).	
Propylene carbonate.	
Propylene glycol and *p-p'*-isopropylidenediphenol diether.	
Propylene glycol dibenzoate (CAS Reg. No. 19224–26–1)	For use as a plasticizer at levels not to exceed 20 percent by weight of the finished adhesive.
Propylene glycol esters of coconut fatty acids.	
Propylene glycol monolaurate.	
Propylene glycol monomethyl ether.	
Propylene glycol monostearate.	
α, α', α''-[Propylidynetris (methylene)] tris [*omega*-hydroxypoly (oxypropylene) (1.5 moles minimum)], minimum molecular weight 400.	
Quaternary ammonium chloride (hexadecyl, octadecyl derivative)	For use as preservative only.
Rosin (wood, gum, and tall oil rosin), rosin dimers, decarboxylated rosin (including rosin oil, disproportionated rosin, and these substances as modified by one or more of the following reactants:.	
Alkyl (C_1-C_9) phenolformaldehyde.	
Ammonia.	
Ammonium caseinate-*p*-Cyclohexylphenolformaldehyde.	
Diethylene glycol.	
Dipentaerythritol.	
Ethylene glycol.	
Formaldehyde.	
Fumaric acid.	
Glycerin.	
Hydrogen.	
Isophthalic acid.	
4,4'-Isopropylidenediphenol-epichlorohydrin (epoxy).	
4,4'-Isopropylidenediphenol-formaldehyde.	
Maleic anhydride.	
Methyl alcohol.	
Pentaerythritol.	
Phthalic anhydride.	
Polyethylene glycol.	
Phenol-formaldehyde.	
Phenyl μ-cresol-formaldehyde.	
p-Phenylphenol-formaldehyde.	
Sulfuric acid.	
Triethylene glycol.	
Xylenol-formaldehyde.	
Rosin salts (salts of wood, gum, and tall oil rosin, and the dimers thereof, decarboxylated rosin disproportionated rosin, hydrogenated rosin):	
Aluminum.	
Ammonium.	
Calcium.	
Magnesium.	
Potassium.	
Sodium.	
Zinc.	
Rosin, gasoline-insoluble fraction.	
Rubber hydrochloride polymer.	
Rubber latex, natural.	
Salicylic acid	For use as preservative only.
Sandarac.	
Sebacic acid.	
Shellac.	
Silicon dioxide as defined in § 172.480(a) of this chapter.	
Sodium alkyl (C_2-$C_{13.5}$ aliphatic) benezenesulfonate.	
Sodium aluminum pyrophosphate.	
Sodium aluminum sulfate.	
Sodium bisulfate.	
Sodium calcium silicate.	
Sodium capryl polyphosphate.	
Sodium carboxymethylcellulose.	
Sodium chlorate.	
Sodium chlorite.	
Sodium chromate.	
Sodium decylsulfate.	
Sodium dehydroacetate	For use as preservative only.
Sodium di-(2-ethylhexoate).	
Sodium di-(2-ethylhexyl) pyrophosphate.	
Sodium dihexylsulfosuccinate.	
Sodium dissobutylphenoxydiethoxyethyl sulfonate.	
Sodium diisobutylphenoxymonoethoxyethyl sulfonate.	
Sodium diisopropyl- and triisopropylnaphthalenesulfonate.	

Substances	Limitations
Sodium dimethyldithiocarbamate.	
Sodium dioctylsulfosuccinate.	
Sodium *n*-dodecylpolyethoxy (50 moles) sulfate.	
Sodium ethylene ether of nonylphenol sulfate.	
Sodium 2-ethylhexyl sulfate.	
Sodium fluoride	For use only as bonding agent for aluminum foil, stabilizer, or preservative. Total fluoride for all sources not to exceed 1 percent by weight of the finished adhesive.
Sodium formaldehyde sulfoxylate.	
Sodium formate.	
Sodium heptadecylsulfate.	
Sodium hypochlorite.	
Sodium isododecylphenoxypolyethoxy (40 moles) sulfate.	
Sodium *N*-lauroyl sarcosinate.	
Sodium metaborate.	
Sodium α-naphthalene sulfonate.	
Sodium nitrate.	
Sodium nitrite.	
Sodium oleoyl isopropanolamide sulfosuccinate.	
Sodium pentachlorophenate	For use as preservative only.
Sodium perborate.	
Sodium persulfate.	
Sodium μ-phenylphenate	For use as preservative only.
Sodium polyacrylate.	
Sodium polymethacrylate.	
Sodium polystyrene sulfonate.	
Sodium salicylate	For use as preservative only.
Sodium salt of 1-hydroxy 2(1H)-pyridine thione	Do.
Sodium tetradecylsulfate.	
Sodium thiocyanate.	
Sodium bis-tridecylsulfosuccinate.	
Sodium xylene sulfonate.	
Sorbitan monooleate.	
Sorbitan monostearate.	
Soybean oil, epoxidized.	
Spermaceti wax.	
Sperm oil wax.	
Stannous 2-ethylhexanoate	For use only as a catalyst for polyurethane resins.
Stannous stearate.	
Starch hydrolysates.	
Starch or starch modified by one or more of the treatments described in §§ 172.892 and 178.3520 of this chapter.	
Starch, reacted with a urea-formaldehyde resin.	
Starch, reacted with formaldehyde.	
Stearamide (stearic acid amide).	
Stearic acid.	
Stearic acid-chromic chloride complex.	
Stearyl-cetyl alcohol, technical grade, approximately 65 percent–80 percent stearyl and 20 percent–35 percent cetyl.	
Strontium salicylate.	
Styrenated phenol.	
Styrene block polymers with 1,3-butadiene.	
Styrene-maleic anhydride copolymer, ammonium or potassium salt.	
Styrene-maleic anhydride copolymer (partially methylated) sodium salt.	
Styrene-methacrylic acid copolymer, potassium salt.	
Sucrose acetate isobutyrate.	
Sucrose benzoate.	
Sucrose octaacetate.	
2–sulfoethyl methacrylate (CAS Registry No. 10595–80–9)	For use at levels not to exceed 2 percent by weight of the dry adhesive.
α-Sulfo-omega-(dodecyloxy)poly (oxyethylene), ammonium salt.	
Sulfonated octadecylene (sodium form).	
Sulfosuccinic acid 4-ester with polyethylene glycol dodecyl ether disodium salt (alcohol moiety produced by condensation of 1 mole of *n*-dodecyl alcohol and an average of 5–6 moles of ethylene oxide, Chemical Abstracts Service Registry No. 039354–45–5).	
Sulfosuccinic acid 4-ester with polyethylene glycol nonylphenyl ether, disodium salt (alcohol moiety produced by condensation of 1 mole of nonylphenol and an average of 9–10 moles of ethylene oxide) (CAS Reg. No. 9040–38–4).	
Sulfur.	
Synthetic primary linear aliphatic alcohols whose weight average molecular weight is greater than 400 (CAS Reg. No. 71750–71–5).	

Substances	Limitations
Synthetic wax polymer as described in § 176.170(a)(5) of this chapter.	
Tall oil.	
Tall oil fatty acids, linoleic and oleic.	
Tall oil fatty acid methyl ester.	
Tall oil, methyl ester.	
Tall oil pitch.	
Tall oil soaps.	
Tallow alcohol (hydrogenated).	
Tallow amine, secondary (hexadecyl, octadecyl), of hard tallow.	
Tallow, blown (oxidized).	
Tallow, propylene glycol ester.	
Terpene resins (α-and β-pinene) homopolymers, copolymers, and condensates with phenol, formaldehyde, coumarone, and/or indene.	
Terphenyl.	
Terphenyl, hydrogenated.	
Terpineol.	
Tetraethylene pentamine.	
Tetraethylthiuram disulfide.	
Tetrahydrofuran.	
Tetrahydrofurfuryl alcohol.	
Tetra-isopropyl titanate.	
Tetrakis[methylene (3,5-di-*tert*-butyl-4-hydroxy-hydro-cinnamate)] methane.	
A[*p*-(1,1,3,3-Tetramethylbutyl) phenyl]-*omega*-hydroxypoly-(oxyethylene) produced by the condensation of 1 mole of *p*-(1,1,3,3-tetramethylbutyl) phenol with an average of 1–40 moles of ethylene oxide.	
A-[*p*-(1,1,3,3-Tetramethylbutyl) phenyl]-*omega*-hydroxy-poly(oxyethylene) mixture of dihydrogen phosphate and monohydrogen phosphate esters and their sodium, potassium, and ammonium salts having a poly(oxyethylene) content averaging 6–9 or 40 moles.	
Tetramethyl decanediol.	
Tetramethyl decynediol.	
Tetramethyl decynediol plus 1–30 moles of ethylene oxide.	
Tetramethylthiuram monosulfide.	
Tetrasodium *N*-(1,2-dicarboxyethyl)*N*-octadecylsulfosuccinamate.	
4,4′-Thiobis-6-*tert*-butyl-*m*-cresol.	
Thiodiethylene-bis(3,5-di-*tert*-butyl-4-hydroxyhydrocinnamate).	
2,2′-(2,5-Thiophenediyl) bis[5-*tert*-butylbenzoxazole].	
Thiram.	
Thymol	For use as preservative only.
Titanium dioxide.	
Titanium dioxide-barium sulfate.	
Titanium dioxide-calcium sulfate.	
Titanium dioxide-magnesium silicate.	
Toluene.	
Toluene 2,4-diisocyanate.	
Toluene 2,6-diisocyanate.	
o- and *p*-Toluene ethyl sulfonamide.	
o- and *p*-Toluene sulfonamide.	
p-Toluene sulfonic acid.	
p-(*p*′-Toluene-sulfonylamide)-diphenylamide.	
Triazine-formaldehyde resins as described in § 175.300(b)(3)(xiii).	
Tributoxyethyl phosphate.	
Tributylcitrate.	
Tri-*tert*-butyl-*p*-phenyl phenol	For use as preservative only.
Tributyl phosphate.	
Tributyltin chloride complex of ethylene oxide condensate of dehydroabietylamine.	For use as preservative only.
Tri-*n*-butyltin acetate	For use as preservative only.
Tri-*n*-butyltin neodecanoate	Do.
1,1,1-Trichloroethane.	
1,1,2-Trichloroethane.	
Trichloroethylene.	
Tri-β-chloroethylphosphate.	
Tridecyl alcohol.	
Triethanolamine.	
3-(Triethoxysilyl) propylamine.	
Triethylene glycol.	
Triethylene glycol dibenzoate.	
Triethylene glycol di(2-ethylhexoate).	
Triethylene glycol polyester of benzoic acid and phthalic acid.	
Triethylhexyl phosphate.	
Triethylphosphate.	
2,4,5-Trihydroxy butyrophenone.	

Substances	Limitations
Triisopropanolamine.	
Trimethylol propane.	
2,2,4-Trimethylpentanediol-1,3-diisobutyrate.	
Trimeric aromatic amine resin from diphenylamine and acetone of molecular weight approximately 500.	
Tri(nonylphenyl) phosphite-formaldehyde resins	As identified in § 177.2600(c)(4)(iii) of this chapter. For use only as a stabilizer.
Triphenylphosphate.	
Tripropylene glycol monomethyl ether.	
1,3,5-Tris (3,5-di-*tert*-butyl-4-hydroxy-benzyl)-triazine-2,4,6 (1H,3H,5H)-trione.	
Tris (*p*-tertiary butyl phenyl) phosphate.	
Tris(2-methyl-4-hydroxy-5-*tert*-butyl-phenyl)butane.	
Trisodium *N*-hydroxyethylethylenediaminetriacetate (CAS Reg. No. 139–89–9).	
Turpentine.	
Urea-formaldehyde resins as described in § 175.300(b)(3)(xii).	
Vegetable oil, sulfonated or sulfated, potassium salt.	
Vinyl acetate-maleic anhydride copolymer, sodium salt.	
Waxes, petroleum.	
Wax, petroleum, chlorinated (40% to 70% chlorine).	
Waxes, synthetic paraffin (Fischer-Tropsch process).	
3-(2-Xenolyl)-1,2-epoxypropane.	
Xylene.	
Xylene (or toluene) alkylated with dicyclopentadiene.	
Zein.	
Zinc acetate.	
Zinc ammonium chloride.	
Zinc dibenzyl dithiocarbamate.	
Zinc dibutyldithiocarbamate.	
Zinc diethyldithiocarbamate.	
Zinc di(2-ethylhexoate).	
Zinc formaldehyde sulfoxylate.	
Zinc naphthenate and dehydroabietylamine mixture.	
Zinc nitrate.	
Zinc orthophosphate.	
Zinc resinate.	
Zinc sulfide.	
Zineb (zinc ethylenebis-dithiocarbamate).	
Ziram (zinc dimethyldithiocarbamate).	

[42 FR 14534, Mar. 15, 1977; 42 FR 56728, Oct. 28, 1977]

EDITORIAL NOTE: For FEDERAL REGISTER citations affecting § 175.105, see the List of CFR Sections Affected, which appears in the Finding Aids section of the printed volume and at *www.fdsys.gov*.

§ 175.125 Pressure-sensitive adhesives.

Pressure-sensitive adhesives may be safely used as the food-contact surface of labels and/or tapes applied to food, in accordance with the following prescribed conditions:

(a) Pressure-sensitive adhesives prepared from one or a mixture of two or more of the substances listed in this paragraph may be used as the food-contact surface of labels and/or tapes applied to poultry, dry food, and processed, frozen, dried, or partially dehydrated fruits or vegetables.

(1) Substances generally recognized as safe in food.

(2) Substances used in accordance with a prior sanction or approval.

(3) Color additives listed for use in or on food in parts 73 and 74 of this chapter.

(4) Substances identified in § 172.615 of this chapter other than substances used in accordance with paragraph (a)(2) of this section.

(5) Polyethylene, oxidized; complying with the identity prescribed in § 177.1620(a) of this chapter.

(6) 4-[[4, 6-Bis(octylthio)-*s*-triazin-2-yl]amino]-2,6-di-*tert*-butylphenol (CAS Reg. No. 991–84–4) as an antioxidant/stabilizer at a level not to exceed 1.5 percent by weight of the finished pressure-sensitive adhesive.

(7) 2,2′-(2,5-Thiophenediyl)-bis(5-*tert*-butylbenzoxazole) (CAS Reg. No. 7128–64–5) as an optical brightener at a level

not to exceed 0.05 percent by weight of the finished pressure-sensitive adhesive.

(8) 2-Hydroxy-1-[4-(2-hydroxyethoxy) phenyl]-2-methyl-1-propanone (CAS Reg. No. 106797–53–9) as a photoinitiator at a level not to exceed 5 percent by weight of the pressure-sensitive adhesive.

(9) Butanedioic acid, sulfo-1,4-di-(C_9-C_{11} alkyl) ester, ammonium salt (also known as butanedioic acid sulfo-1, 4-diisodecyl ester, ammonium salt [CAS Reg. No. 144093–88–9]) as a surface active agent at a level not to exceed 3.0 percent by weight of the finished pressure-sensitive adhesive.

(b) Pressure-sensitive adhesives prepared from one or a mixture of two or more of the substances listed in this paragraph may be used as the food-contact surface of labels and/or tapes applied to raw fruit and raw vegetables.

(1) Substances listed in paragraphs (a)(1), (a)(2), (a)(3), (a)(5), (a)(6), (a)(7), (a)(8), and (a)(9) of this section, and those substances prescribed by paragraph (a)(4) of this section that are not identified in paragraph (b)(2) of this section.

(2) Substances identified in this subparagraph and subject to the limitations provided:

BHA.
BHT.
Butadiene-acrylonitrile copolymer.
Butadiene-acrylonitrile-styrene copolymer.
Butadiene-styrene copolymer.
Butyl rubber.
Butylated reaction product of *p*-cresol and dicyclopentadiene produced by reacting *p*-cresol and dicyclopentadiene in an approximate mole ratio of 1.5 to 1.0, respectively, followed by alkylation with isobutylene so that the butyl content of the final product is not less than 18 percent, for use at levels not to exceed 1.0 percent by weight of the adhesive formulation.
Chlorinated natural rubber.
Isobutylene-styrene copolymer.
Petrolatum.
Polybutene-1.
Polybutene, hydrogenated; complying with the identity prescribed under §178.3740(b) of this chapter.
Polyisobutylene.
cis-1,4-Polyisoprene.
Polystyrene.
Propyl gallate.
Rapeseed oil, vulcanized.
Rosins and rosin derivatives as provided in §178.3870 of this chapter.
Rubber hydrochloride.
Rubber (natural latex solids or crepe, smoked or unsmoked).
Terpene resins (α- and β-pinene), homopolymers, copolymers, and condensates with phenol, formaldehyde, coumarone, and/or indene.
Tetrasodium ethylenediaminetetraacetate.
Tri(mixed mono- and dinonylphenyl) phosphite (which may contain not more than 1 percent by weight of triisopropanolamine).

(c) Acrylonitrile copolymers identified in this section shall comply with the provisions of §180.22 of this chapter.

[42 FR 14534, Mar. 15, 1977, as amended at 42 FR 15674, Mar. 22, 1977; 48 FR 15617, Apr. 12, 1983; 63 FR 3464, Jan. 23, 1998; 63 FR 51528, Sept. 28, 1998; 64 FR 48291, Sept. 3, 1999]

Subpart C—Substances for Use as Components of Coatings

§ 175.210 Acrylate ester copolymer coating.

Acrylate ester copolymer coating may safely be used as a food-contact surface of articles intended for packaging and holding food, including heating of prepared food, subject to the provisions of this section:

(a) The acrylate ester copolymer is a fully polymerized copolymer of ethyl acrylate, methyl methacrylate, and methacrylic acid applied in emulsion form to molded virgin fiber and heat-cured to an insoluble resin.

(b) Optional substances used in the preparation of the polymer and in the preparation and application of the emulsion may include substances named in this paragraph, in an amount not to exceed that required to accomplish the desired technical effect and subject to any limitation prescribed: *Provided, however*, That any substance named in this paragraph and covered by a specific regulation in subchapter B of this chapter must meet any specifications in such regulation.

List of substances	Limitations
Aluminum stearate.	
Ammonium lauryl sulfate.	
Borax	Not to exceed the amount required as a preservative in emulsion defoamer.
Disodium hydrogen phosphate	Do.
Formaldehyde.	

List of substances	Limitations
Glyceryl monostearate.	
Methyl cellulose.	
Mineral oil.	
Paraffin wax.	
Potassium hydroxide.	
Potassium persulfate.	
Tallow.	
Tetrasodium pyrophosphate.	
Titanium dioxide.	

(c) The coating in the form in which it contacts food meets the following tests:

(1) An appropriate sample when exposed to distilled water at 212 °F for 30 minutes shall yield total chloroform-soluble extractables not to exceed 0.5 milligram per square inch.

(2) An appropriate sample when exposed to *n*-heptane at 120 °F for 30 minutes shall yield total chloroform-soluble extractables not to exceed 0.5 milligram per square inch.

§ 175.230 Hot-melt strippable food coatings.

Hot-melt strippable food coatings may be safely applied to food, subject to the provisions of this section.

(a) The coatings are applied to and used as removable coatings for food.

(b) The coatings may be prepared, as mixtures, from the following substances:

(1) Substances generally recognized as safe in food.

(2) Substances identified in this subparagraph.

List of substances	Limitations
Acetylated monoglycerides	Complying with 172.828 of this chapter.
Cellulose acetate butyrate.	
Cellulose acetate propionate.	
Mineral oil, white	For use only as a component of hot-melt strippable food coatings applied to frozen meats and complying with § 172.878 of this chapter.

§ 175.250 Paraffin (synthetic).

Synthetic paraffin may be safely used as an impregnant in, coating on, or component of coatings on articles used in producing, manufacturing, packing, processing, preparing, treating, packaging, transporting, or holding food in accordance with the following prescribed conditions:

(a) The additive is synthesized by the Fischer-Tropsch process from carbon monoxide and hydrogen, which are catalytically converted to a mixture of paraffin hydrocarbons. Lower molecular-weight fractions are removed by distillation. The residue is hydrogenated and may be further treated by percolation through activated charcoal. This mixture can be fractionated into its components by a solvent separation method, using synthetic isoparaffinic petroleum hydrocarbons complying with § 178.3530 of this chapter.

(b) Synthetic paraffin shall conform to the following specifications:

(1) *Congealing point.* There is no specification for the congealing point of synthetic paraffin components, except those components that have a congealing point below 50 °C when used in contact with food Types III, IVA, V, VIIA, and IX identified in table 1 of § 176.170(c) of this chapter and under conditions of use E, F, and G described in table 2 of § 176.170(c) of this chapter shall be limited to a concentration not exceeding 15 percent by weight of the finished coating. The congealing point shall be determined by ASTM method D938–71 (Reapproved 1981), "Standard Test Method for Congealing Point of Petroleum Waxes, Including Petrolatum," which is incorporated by reference. Copies may be obtained from the American Society for Testing Materials, 100 Barr Harbor Dr., West Conshohocken, Philadelphia, PA 19428-2959, or may be examined at the National Archives and Records Administration (NARA). For information on the availability of this material at NARA, call 202–741–6030, or go to: *http://www.archives.gov/federal_register/code_of_federal_regulations/ibr_locations.html.*

(2) *Oil content.* The substance has an oil content not exceeding 2.5 percent as determined by ASTM method D721–56T, "Tentative Method of Test for Oil Content of Petroleum Waxes" (Revised 1956), which is incorporated by reference. See paragraph (b)(1) of this section for availability of the incorporation by reference.

(3) *Absorptivity.* The substance has an absorptivity at 290 millimicrons in

decahydronaphthalene at 88 °C not exceeding 0.01 as determined by ASTM method E131–81a, "Standard Definitions of Terms and Symbols Relating to Molecular-Spectroscopy," which is incorporated by reference. See paragraph (b)(1) of this section for availability of the incorporation by reference.

(c) The provisions of this section are not applicable to synthetic paraffin used in food-packaging adhesives complying with § 175.105.

[42 FR 14534, Mar. 15, 1977, as amended at 47 FR 11839, Mar. 19, 1982; 49 FR 10106, Mar. 19, 1984; 51 FR 47010, Dec. 30, 1986; 60 FR 39645, Aug. 3, 1995]

§ 175.260 Partial phosphoric acid esters of polyester resins.

Partial phosphoric acid esters of polyester resins identified in this section and applied on aluminum may be safely used as food-contact coatings, in accordance with the following prescribed conditions:

(a) For the purpose of this section, partial phosphoric acid esters of polyester resins are prepared by the reaction of trimellitic anhydride with 2,2-dimethyl-1,3-propanediol followed by reaction of the resin thus produced with phosphoric acid anhydride to produce a resin having an acid number of 81 to 98 and a phosphorus content of 4.05 to 4.65 percent by weight.

(b) The coating is chemically bonded to the metal and cured at temperatures exceeding 450 °F.

(c) The finished food-contact coating, when extracted with the solvent or solvents characterizing the type of food and under the conditions of time and temperature characterizing the conditions of its intended use, as determined from tables 1 and 2 of § 175.300(d), yields total extractives in each extracting solvent not to exceed 0.3 milligrams per square inch of food-contact surface, as determined by the methods described in § 175.300(e), and the coating yields 2,2-dimethyl-1,3-propanediol in each extracting solvent not to exceed 0.3 micrograms per square inch of food-contact surface. In testing the finished food-contact articles, a separate test sample is to be used for each required extracting solvent.

§ 175.270 Poly(vinyl fluoride) resins.

Poly(vinyl fluoride) resins identified in this section may be safely used as components of food-contact coatings for containers having a capacity of not less than 5 gallons, subject to the provisions of this section.

(a) For the purpose of this section, poly(vinyl fluoride) resins consist of basic resins produced by the polymerization of vinyl fluoride.

(b) The poly(vinyl fluoride) basic resins have an intrinsic viscosity of not less than 0.75 deciliter per gram as determined by ASTM method D1243–79, "Standard Test Method for Dilute Solution Viscosity of Vinyl Chloride Polymers," which is incorporated by reference. Copies may be obtained from the American Society for Testing Materials, 100 Barr Harbor Dr., West Conshohocken, Philadelphia, PA 19428-2959, or may be examined at the National Archives and Records Administration (NARA). For information on the availability of this material at NARA, call 202–741–6030, or go to: *http://www.archives.gov/federal_register/code_of_federal_regulations/ibr_locations.html.*

(1) *Solvent.* *N,N*-Dimethylacetamide, technical grade.

(2) *Solution.* Powdered resin and solvent are heated at 120 °C until the resin is dissolved.

(3) *Temperature.* Flow times of the solvent and solution are determined at 110 °C.

(4) *Viscometer.* Cannon-Ubbelohde size 50 semimicro dilution viscometer (or equivalent).

(5) *Calculation.* The calculation method used is that described in appendix X 1.3 (ASTM method D1243–79, "Standard Test Method for Dilute Solution Viscosity of Vinyl Chloride Polymers," which is incorporated by reference; see paragraph (b) of this section for availability of the incorporation by reference) with the reduced viscosity determined for three concentration levels not greater than 0.5 gram per deciliter and extrapolated to zero concentration for intrinsic viscosity. The following formula is used for determining reduced viscosity:

$$\text{Reduced viscosity in terms of deciliters per gram} = \frac{t - to}{to \times c}$$

where:

t=Solution efflux time.
to=Solvent efflux time.
c=Concentration of solution in terms of grams per deciliter.

[42 FR 14534, Mar. 15, 1977, as amended at 47 FR 11839, Mar. 19, 1982; 49 FR 10107, Mar. 19, 1984]

§ 175.300 Resinous and polymeric coatings.

Resinous and polymeric coatings may be safely used as the food-contact surface of articles intended for use in producing, manufacturing, packing, processing, preparing, treating, packaging, transporting, or holding food, in accordance with the following prescribed conditions:

(a) The coating is applied as a continuous film or enamel over a metal substrate, or the coating is intended for repeated food-contact use and is applied to any suitable substrate as a continuous film or enamel that serves as a functional barrier between the food and the substrate. The coating is characterized by one or more of the following descriptions:

(1) Coatings cured by oxidation.

(2) Coatings cured by polymerization, condensation, and/or cross-linking without oxidation.

(3) Coatings prepared from prepolymerized substances.

(b) The coatings are formulated from optional substances that may include:

(1) Substances generally recognized as safe in food.

(2) Substances the use of which is permitted by regulations in this part or which are permitted by prior sanction or approval and employed under the specific conditions, if any, of the prior sanction or approval.

(3) Any substance employed in the production of resinous and polymeric coatings that is the subject of a regulation in subchapter B of this chapter and conforms with any specification in such regulation. Substances named in this paragraph (b)(3) and further identified as required:

(i) Drying oils, including the triglycerides or fatty acids derived therefrom:

Beechnut.
Candlenut.
Castor (including dehydrated).
Chinawood (tung).
Coconut.
Corn.
Cottonseed.
Fish (refined).
Hempseed.
Linseed.
Oiticica.
Perilla.
Poppyseed.
Pumpkinseed.
Safflower.
Sesame.
Soybean.
Sunflower.
Tall oil.
Walnut.

The oils may be raw, heat-bodied, or blown. They may be refined by filtration, degumming, acid or alkali washing, bleaching, distillation, partial dehydration, partial polymerization, or solvent extraction, or modified by combination with maleic anhydride.

(ii) Reconstituted oils from triglycerides or fatty acids derived from the oils listed in paragraph (b)(3)(i) of this section to form esters with:

Butylene glycol.
Ethylene glycol.
Pentaerythritol.
Polyethylene glycol.
Polypropylene glycol.
Propylene glycol.
Sorbitol.
Trimethylol ethane.
Trimethylol propane.

(iii) Synthetic drying oils, as the basic polymer:

Butadiene and methylstyrene copolymer.
Butadiene and styrene copolymer, blown or unblown.
Maleic anhydride adduct of butadiene styrene.
Polybutadiene.

(iv) Natural fossil resins, as the basic resin:

Copal.
Damar.
Elemi.
Gilsonite.
Glycerol ester of damar, copal, elemi, and sandarac.
Sandarac.
Shellac.
Utah coal resin.

(v) Rosins and rosin derivatives, with or without modification by polymerization, isomerization, incidental decarboxylation, and/or hydrogenation, as follows:

(*a*) Rosins, refined to color grade of K or paler:

Gum rosin.
Tall oil rosin.
Wood rosin.

(*b*) Rosin esters formed by reacting rosin (paragraph (b)(3)(v)(*a*) of this section) with:

4,4′-*sec*-Butylidenediphenol-epichlorohydrin (epoxy).
Diethylene glycol.
Ethylene glycol.
Glycerol.
4,4′-Isopropylidenediphenol-epichlorohydrin (epoxy).
Methyl alcohol.
Pentaerythritol.

(*c*) Rosin esters (paragraph (b)(3)(v)(*b*) of this section) modified by reaction with:

Maleic anhydride.
o-, *m*-, and *p*-substituted phenol-formaldehydes listed in paragraph (b)(3)(vi) of this section.
Phenol-formaldehyde.

(*d*) Rosin salts:

Calcium resinate (limed rosin).
Zinc resinate.

(vi) Phenolic resins as the basic polymer formed by reaction of phenols with formaldehyde:

(*a*) Phenolic resins formed by reaction of formaldehyde with:

Alkylated (methyl, ethyl, propyl, isopropyl, butyl) phenols.
p-*tert*-Amylphenol.
4,4′-*sec*-Butylidenediphenol.
p-*tert*-Butylphenol.
o-, *m*-, and *p*-Cresol.
p-Cyclohexylphenol.
4,4′-Isopropylidenediphenol.
p-Nonylphenol.
p-Octylphenol.
3-Pentadecyl phenol mixture obtained from cashew nut shell liquid.
Phenol.
Phenyl *o*-cresol.
p-Phenylphenol.
Xylenol.

(*b*) Adjunct for phenolic resins: Aluminum butylate.

(vii) Polyester resins (including alkyd-type), as the basic polymers, formed as esters of acids listed in paragraph (b)(3)(vii) (*a*) and (*b*) of this section by reaction with alcohols in paragraph (b)(3)(vii) (*c*) and (*d*) of this section.

(*a*) Polybasic acids:

Adipic.
1,4-cyclohexanedicarboxylic (CAS Reg. No. 1076–97–7).
Dimerized fatty acids derived from oils listed in paragraph (b)(3)(i) of this section.
Fumaric.
Isophthalic.
Maleic.
2,6-Naphthalenedicarboxylic.
2,6-Naphthalenedicarboxylic, dimethyl ester.
Orthophthalic.
Sebacic.
Terephthalic.
Terpene-maleic acid adduct.
Trimellitic.

(*b*) Monobasic acids:

Benzoic acid.
4,4-Bis(4′-hydroxyphenyl)-pentanoic acid.
tert-Butyl benzoic acid.
Fatty acids derived from oils listed in paragraph (b)(3)(i) of this section.
Rosins listed in paragraph (b)(3)(v)(*a*) of this section, for use only as reactants in oil-based or fatty acid-based alkyd resins.

(*c*) Polyhydric alcohols:

Butylene glycol.
Diethylene glycol.
2,2-Dimethyl-1,3-propanediol for use only in forming polyester resins for coatings intended for use in contact with non-alcoholic foods.
Ethylene glycol.
Glycerol.
Mannitol.
α-Methyl glucoside.
Pentaerythritol.
Propylene glycol.
Sorbitol.
Triethylene glycol, for use as a component in polyester resins for coatings not exceeding a coating weight of 4 milligrams per square inch and that are intended for contact under conditions of use D, E, F or G described in table 2 of paragraph (d) of this section with alcoholic beverages containing less than 8 percent alcohol.
Trimethylol ethane.
Trimethylol propane.

(*d*) Monohydric alcohols:

Cetyl alcohol.
Decyl alcohol.
Lauryl alcohol.
Myristyl alcohol.
Octyl alcohol.
Stearyl alcohol.

(*e*) Catalysts:

Dibutyltin oxide (CAS Reg. No. 818–08–6), not to exceed 0.2 percent of the polyester resin.
Hydroxybutyltin oxide (CAS Reg. No. 2273–43–0), not to exceed 0.2 percent of the polyester resin.
Monobutyltin tris(2-ethylhexoate) (CAS Reg. No. 23850–94–4), not to exceed 0.2 percent of the polyester resin.

(viii) Epoxy resins, catalysts, and adjuncts:

(*a*) Epoxy resins, as the basic polymer:

(Alkoxy C_{10}-C_{16})-2,3-epoxypropane, in which the alkyl groups are even numbered and consist of a maximum of 1 percent C_{10} carbon atoms and a minimum of 48 percent C_{12} carbon atoms and a minimum of 18 percent C_{14} carbon atoms, for use only in coatings that are intended for contact with dry bulk foods at room temperature.
4,4′-*sec*-Butylidenediphenol-epichlorohydrin.
4,4′-*sec*-Butylidenediphenol-epichlorohydrin reacted with one or more of the drying oils or fatty acids listed in paragraph (b)(3)(i) of this section.
4,4′-*sec*-Butylidenediphenol-epichlorohydrin chemically treated with one or more of the following substances:
  Allyl ether of mono-, di-, or trimethylol phenol.
  4,4′-*sec*-Butylidenediphenol-formaldehyde.
  4,4′-Isopropylidenediphenol-formaldehyde.
  Melamine-formaldehyde.
  Phenol-formaldehyde.
  Urea-formaldehyde.
Epoxidized polybutadiene.
Glycidyl ethers formed by reacting phenolnovolak resins with epichlorohydrin.
4,4′-Isopropylidenediphenol-epichlorohydrin.
4,4′-Isopropylidenediphenol-epichlorohydrin reacted with one or more of the drying oils or fatty acids listed in paragraph (b)(3)(i) of this section.
4,4′-Isopropylidenediphenol-epichlorohydrin chemically treated with one or more of the following substances:
  Allyl ether of mono-, di-, or trimethylol phenol.
  4,4′-*sec*-Butylidenediphenol-formaldehyde.
  4,4′-Isopropylidenediphenol-formaldehyde.
  Melamine-formaldehyde.
  2,2′-[(1-methylethylidene)bis[4,1-phenyleneoxy[1-(butoxymethyl)-2,1-ethanediyl]oxymethylene]]bisoxirane, CAS Reg. No. 71033–08–4, for use only in coatings intended for contact with bulk dry foods at temperatures below 100 °F.
  Phenol-formaldehyde.
  Urea-formaldehyde.

(*b*) Catalysts and cross-linking agents for epoxy resins:

3-(Aminomethyl)-3,5,5-trimethylcyclohexylamine reacted with phenol and formaldehyde in a ratio of 2.6:1.0:2.0, for use only in coatings intended for repeated use in contact with foods only of the types identified in paragraph (d) of this section, table 1, under Category I and Category VIII, at temperatures not exceeding 88 °C (190 °F).
N-*Beta*-(aminoethyl)-*gamma*-aminopropyltrimethoxysilane (CAS Reg. No. 1760–24–3), for use only in coatings at a level not to exceed 1.3 percent by weight of the resin when such coatings are intended for repeated use in contact with foods only of the types identified in paragraph (d) of this section, table 1, under Types I, II, and III, under conditions of use C, D, E, or F as described in table 2 of paragraph (d) of this section; or when such coatings are intended for repeated use in contact with foods of the types identified in paragraph (d) of this section, table 1, under Types V, VI, VII, and VIII, under conditions of use E or F as described in table 2 of paragraph (d) of this section. Use shall be limited to coatings for tanks of capacity greater than 530,000 gallons.
Benzyl alcohol (CAS Reg. No. 100–51–6), for use only in coatings at a level not to exceed 4 percent by weight of the resin when such coatings are intended for repeated use in contact with foods only of the types identified in paragraph (d) of this section, table 1, under Types I, II, and III, under conditions of use C, D, E, or F as described in table 2 of paragraph (d) of this section; or when such coatings are intended for repeated use in contact with foods of the types identified in paragraph (d) of this section, table 1, under Types V, VI, VII, and VIII, under conditions of use E or F as described in table 2 of paragraph (d) of this section. Use shall be limited to coatings for tanks of capacity greater than 530,000 gallons.
Catalysts and cross-linking agents for epoxy resins:
  3-Aminomethyl-3,5,5-trimethylcyclohexylamine (CAS Reg. No. 2855–0913–092).
Cyanoguanidine.
Dibutyl phthalate, for use only in coatings for containers having a capacity of 1,000 gallons or more when such containers are intended for repeated use in contact with alcoholic beverages containing up to 8 percent of alcohol by volume.
3-Diethylaminopropylamine (CAS Reg. No. 104–78–9), for use in coatings at a level not to exceed 6 percent by weight of the resin when such coatings are intended for repeated use in contact with foods only of the types identified in paragraph (d) of this section, table 1, under Types I, II, and III, under conditions of use C, D, E, or F as described in table 2 of paragraph (d) of this

section; or when such coatings are intended for repeated use in contact with foods of the types identified in paragraph (d) of this section, table 1, under Types V, VI, VII, and VIII, under conditions of use E or F as described in table 2 of paragraph (d) of this section. Use shall be limited to coatings for tanks of capacity greater than 530,000 gallons.

Diethylenetriamine.

Diphenylamine.

Ethylenediamine.

Isophthalyl dihydrazide for use only in coatings subject to the provisions of paragraph (c) (3) or (4) of this section.

4,4′-Methylenedianiline, for use only in coatings for containers having a capacity of 1,000 gallons or more when such containers are intended for repeated use in contact with alcoholic beverages containing up to 8 percent of alcohol by volume.

N-Oleyl-1,3-propanediamine with not more than 10 percent by weight of diethylaminoethanol.

3-Pentadecenyl phenol mixture (obtained from cashew nutshell liquid) reacted with formaldehyde and ethylenediamine in a ratio of 1:2:2 (CAS Reg. No. 68413–28–5).

Polyamine produced when 1 mole of the chlorohydrin diether of polyethylene glycol 400 is made to react under dehydrohalogenating conditions with 2 moles of *N*-octadecyltrimethylenediamine for use only in coatings that are subject to the provisions of paragraph (c) (3) or (4) of this section and that contact food at temperatures not to exceed room temperature.

Polyethylenepolyamine (CAS Reg. No. 68131–73–7), for use only in coatings intended for repeated use in contact with food, at temperatures not to exceed 180 °F (82 °C).

Salicylic acid, for use only in coatings for containers having a capacity of 1,000 gallons or more when such containers are intended for repeated use in contact with alcoholic beverages containing up to 8 percent of alcohol by volume.

Salicylic acid (CAS Reg. No. 69–72–7), for use only in coatings at a level not to exceed 0.35 percent by weight of the resin when such coatings are intended for repeated use in contact with foods only of the types identified in paragraph (d) of this section, table 1, under Types I, II, and III, under conditions of use C, D, E, or F as described in table 2 of paragraph (d) of this section; or when such coatings are intended for repeated use in contact with foods of the types identified in paragraph (d) of this section, table 1, under Types V, VI, VII, and VIII, under conditions of use E or F as described in table 2 of paragraph (d) of this section. Use shall be limited to coatings for tanks of capacity greater than 530,000 gallons.

Stannous 2-ethylhexanoate for use only as a catalyst at a level not to exceed 1 percent by weight of the resin used in coatings that are intended for contact with food under conditions of use D, E, F, and G described in table 2 of paragraph (d) of this section.

Styrene oxide, for use only in coatings for containers having a capacity of 1,000 gallons or more when such containers are intended for repeated use in contact with alcoholic beverages containing up to 8 percent of alcohol by volume.

Tetraethylenepentamine.

Tetraethylenepentamine reacted with equimolar quantities of fatty acids.

Tri(dimethylaminomethyl) phenol and its salts prepared from the fatty acid moieties of the salts listed in paragraph (b)(3)(xxii)(*b*) of this section, for use only in coatings subject to the provisions of paragraph (c) (3) or (4) of this section.

Triethylenetetramine.

Trimellitic anhydride (CAS Reg. No. 552–30–7) for use only as a cross-linking agent at a level not to exceed 15 percent by weight of the resin in contact with food under all conditions of use, except that resins intended for use with foods containing more than 8 percent alcohol must contact such food only under conditions of use D, E, F, and G described in table 2 of paragraph (d) of this section.

Trimellitic anhydride adducts of ethylene glycol and glycerol, prepared by the reaction of 1 mole of trimellitic anhydride with 0.4–0.6 mole of ethylene glycol and 0.04–0.12 mole of glycerol, for use only as a cross-linking agent at a level not to exceed 10 percent by weight of the cured coating, provided that the cured coating only contacts food containing not more than 8 percent alcohol.

Meta-Xylylenediamine (1,3-benzenedimethanamine, CAS Reg. No. 1477–55–0), for use only in coatings at a level not to exceed 3 percent by weight of the resin when such coatings are intended for repeated use in contact with foods only of the types identified in paragraph (d) of this section, table 1, under Types I, II, and III, under conditions of use C, D, E or F as described in table 2 of paragraph (d) of this section; or when such coatings are intended for repeated use in contact with foods of the types identified in paragraph (d) of this section, table 1, under Types V, VI, VII, and VIII, under conditions of use E or F as described in table 2 of paragraph (d) of this section. Use shall be limited to coatings for tanks of capacity greater than 530,000 gallons.

Para-Xylylenediamine (1,4 benzenedimethanamine, CAS Reg. No. 539–48–0), for use only in coatings at a level not to exceed 0.6 percent by weight of the resin when such coatings are intended for repeated use in contact with foods only of the types identified in paragraph (d) of this section, table 1, under Types I, II, III, under conditions of use C, D, E, or F as described in table 2 of paragraph (d) of this section; or when such coatings are intended for repeated use in contact with foods of the types identified in paragraph (d) of this section, table 1, under Types V, VI, VII, and VIII, under conditions of use E and F as described in table 2 of paragraph (d) of this section. Use shall be limited to coatings for tanks of capacity greater than 530,000 gallons.

(*c*) Adjuncts for epoxy resins:

Aluminum butylate.
Benzoic acid, for use as a component in epoxy resins for coatings not exceeding a coating weight of 4 milligrams per square inch and that are intended for contact under conditions of use D, E, F or G described in table 2 of paragraph (d) of this section with alcoholic beverages containing less than 8 percent alcohol.
Polyamides from dimerized vegetable oils and the amine catalysts listed in paragraph (b)(3)(viii)(*b*) of this section, as the basic polymer.
Silane coupled silica, prepared from the reaction of microcrystalline quartz with *N-beta*-(*N*-vinylbenzylamino) ethyl-*gamma*-aminopropyltrimethoxy silane, monohydrogen chloride, for use only in coatings intended for repeated use in contact with foods only of the types identified in paragraph (d) of this section, table 1, under Category I and Category VIII, at temperatures not exceeding 88 °C (190 °F).
Succinic anhydride, for use as a component in epoxy resins for coatings not exceeding a coating weight of 4 milligrams per square inch, and that are intended for contact under conditions of use D, E, F or G described in table 2 of paragraph (d) of this section with alcoholic beverages containing less than 8 percent alcohol.

(ix) Coumarone-indene resin, as the basic polymer.

(x) Petroleum hydrocarbon resin (cyclopentadiene type), as the basic polymer.

(xi) Terpene resins, as the basic polymer, from one or more of the following:

Dipentene.
Hydrogenated dipentene resin (CAS Reg. No. 106168–39–2). For use only with coatings in contact with acidic and aqueous foods.
Hydrogenated-*beta*-pinene-*alpha*-pinene-dipentene copolymer resin (CAS Reg. No. 106168–37–0). For use only with coatings in contact with acidic and aqueous foods.
α-Pinene.
β-Pinene.

(xii) Urea-formaldehyde, resins and their curing catalyst:

(*a*) Urea-formaldehyde resins, as the basic polymer:

Urea-formaldehyde.
Urea-formaldehyde chemically modified with methyl, ethyl, propyl, isopropyl, butyl, or isobutyl alcohol.
Urea-formaldehyde chemically modified with one or more of the amine catalysts listed in paragraph (b)(3)(viii)(*b*) of this section.

(*b*) Curing (cross-linking) catalyst for urea-formaldehyde resins:

Dodecyl benzenesulfonic acid (C.A. Registry No. 27176–87–0).

(xiii) Triazine-formaldehyde resins and their curing catalyst:

(*a*) Triazine-formaldehyde resins, as the basic polymer:

Benzoguanamine-formaldehyde.
Melamine-formaldehyde.
Melamine-formaldehyde chemically modified with one or more of the following amine catalysts:
Amine catalysts listed in paragraph (b)(3)(viii)(*b*) of this section.
Dimethylamine-2-methyl-1-propanol.
Methylpropanolamine.
Triethanolamine.
Melamine-formaldehyde chemically modified with methyl, ethyl, propyl, isopropyl, butyl, or isobutyl alcohol.

(*b*) Curing (cross-linking) catalyst for triazine-formaldehyde resins:

Dodecyl benzenesulfonic acid (C.A. Registry No. 27176–87–0).

(xiv) Modifiers (for oils and alkyds, including polyesters), as the basic polymer:

Butyl methacrylate.
Cyclopentadiene.
Methyl, ethyl, butyl, or octyl esters of acrylic acid.
Methyl methacrylate.
Styrene.
Vinyl toluene.

(xv) Vinyl resinous substance, as the basic polymers:

Polyvinyl acetate.
Polyvinyl alcohol.
Polyvinyl butyral.
Polyvinyl chloride.
Polyvinyl formal.
Polyvinylidene chloride.
Polyvinyl pyrrolidone.
Polyvinyl stearate.
Vinyl chloride-acetate-2,3-epoxypropyl methacrylate copolymers containing not more than 10 weight percent of total polymer units derived from 2,3-epoxypropyl methacrylate and not more than 0.1 weight percent of unreacted 2,3-epoxypropyl methacrylate monomer for use in coatings for containers.

Vinyl chloride-acetate, hydroxyl-modified copolymer.
Vinyl chloride-acetate, hydroxyl-modified copolymer, reacted with trimellitic anhydride.
Vinyl chloride copolymerized with acrylamide and ethylene in such a manner that the finished copolymers have a minimum weight average molecular weight of 30,000 and contain not more than 3.5 weight percent of total polymer units derived from acrylamide; the acrylamide portion may or may not be subsequently partially hydrolyzed.
Vinyl chloride copolymerized with one or more of the following substances:
Acrylonitrile.
Fumaric acid and/or its methyl, ethyl, propyl, butyl, amyl, hexyl, heptyl, or octyl esters.
Maleic acid and/or its methyl, ethyl, propyl, butyl, amyl, hexyl, heptyl, or octyl esters.
5-Norbornene-2,3-dicarboxylic acid, mono-*n*-butyl ester; for use such that the finished vinyl chloride copolymers contain not more than 4 weight percent of total polymer units derived from this comonomer.
Vinyl acetate.
Vinylidene chloride.
Vinyl chloride-vinylidene chloride-2,3-epoxypropyl methacrylate copolymers containing not more than 10 weight percent of total polymer units derived from 2,3-epoxypropyl methacrylate and not more than 0.05 weight percent of unreacted 2,3-epoxypropyl methacrylate monomer based on polymer solids for use only in coatings for containers intended for contact with foods under conditions B, C, D, E, F, G, or H described in table 2 of paragraph (d) of this section.

(xvi) Cellulosics, as the basic polymer:

Carboxymethylcellulose.
Cellulose acetate.
Cellulose acetate-butyrate.
Cellulose acetate-propionate.
Ethylcellulose.
Ethyl hydroxyethylcellulose.
Hydroxyethylcellulose.
Hydroxypropyl methylcellulose.
Methylcellulose.
Nitrocellulose.

(xvii) Styrene polymers, as the basic polymer:

Polystyrene.
α-Methyl styrene polymer.
Styrene copolymerized with one or more of the following:
Acrylonitrile.
α-Methylstyrene.

(xviii) Polyethylene and its copolymers as the basic polymer:

Ethylene-ethyl acrylate copolymer.
Ethylene-isobutyl acrylate copolymers containing no more than 35 weight percent of total polymer units derived from isobutyl acrylate.
Ethylene-vinyl acetate copolymer.
Polyethylene.

(xix) Polypropylene as the basic polymer:

Polypropylene.
Maleic anhydride adduct of polypropylene The polypropylene used in the manufacture of the adduct complies with §177.1520(c), item 1.1; and the adduct has a maximum combined maleic anhydride content of 0.8 percent and a minimum intrinsic viscosity of 0.9, determined at 135 °C on a 0.1 percent solution of the modified polypropylene in decahydronaphthalene as determined by a method titled "Method for Determination of Intrinsic Viscosity of Maleic Anhydride Adduct of Polypropylene," which is incorporated by reference. Copies are available from the Center for Food Safety and Applied Nutrition (HFS–200), Food and Drug Administration, 5100 Paint Branch Pkwy., College Park, MD 20740, or available for inspection at the National Archives and Records Administration (NARA). For information on the availability of this material at NARA, call 202–741–6030, or go to: *http://www.archives.gov/federal_register/code_of_federal_regulations/ibr_locations.html.*

(xx) Acrylics and their copolymers, as the basic polymer:

Acrylamide with ethylacrylate and/or styrene and/or methacrylic acid, subsequently reacted with formaldehyde and butanol.
Acrylic acid and the following esters thereof:
Ethyl.
Methyl.
Butyl acrylate-styrene-methacrylic acid-hydroxyethyl methacrylate copolymers containing no more than 20 weight percent of total polymer units derived from methacrylic acid and containing no more than 7 weight percent of total polymer units derived from hydroxyethyl methacrylate; for use only in coatings that are applied by electrodeposition to metal substrates.
Butyl acrylate-styrene-methacrylic acid-hydroxypropyl methacrylate copolymers containing no more than 20 weight percent of total polymer units derived from methacrylic acid and containing no more than 7 weight percent of total polymer units derived from hydroxypropyl methacrylate; for use only in coatings that are applied by electrodeposition to metal substrates and that are intended for contact, under condition of use D, E, F, or G described in table 2 of paragraph (d) of this section, with food

containing no more than 8 percent of alcohol.

Ethyl acrylate-styrene-methacrylic acid copolymers for use only as modifiers for epoxy resins listed in paragraph (b)(3)(viii)(*a*) of this section.

Ethyl acrylate-methyl methacrylate-styrene-methacrylic acid copolymers for use only as modifiers for epoxy resins listed in paragraph (b)(3)(viii)(*a*) of this section.

2-Ethylhexyl acrylate-ethyl acrylate copolymers prepared by copolymerization of 2-ethylhexyl acrylate and ethyl acrylate in a 7/3 weight ratio and having a number average molecular weight range of 5,800 to 6,500 and a refractive index, n_{D25}° (40 percent in 2,2,4-trimethyl pentane) of 1.4130–1.4190; for use as a modifier for nylon resins complying with § 177.1500 of this chapter and for phenolic and epoxy resins listed in paragraph (b)(3) (vi) and (viii) of this section, respectively, at a level not to exceed 1.5 percent of the coating.

2-Ethylhexyl acrylate-methyl methacrylate-acrylic acid copolymers for use only as modifiers for epoxy resins listed in paragraph (b)(3)(viii) of this section.

Methacrylic acid and the following esters thereof:

Butyl.
Ethyl.
Methyl.

Methacrylic acid or its ethyl and methyl esters copolymerized with one or more of the following:

Acrylic acid.
Ethyl acrylate.
Methyl acrylate.

n-Butyl acrylate-styrene-methacrylic acid-hydroxyethyl methacrylate copolymers containing no more than 2 weight percent of total polymer units derived from methacrylic acid and containing no more than 9.5 weight percent of total polymer units derived from hydroxyethyl methacrylate; for use only in coatings in contact with dry food (food type VIII in table 1 of paragraph (d) of this section). 2-(Dimethylamino) ethanol (C.A.S. Registry No. 108–01–0) may be employed as an optional adjuvant substance limited to no more than 2 weight percent based on polymer solids in the coating emulsion.

Styrene polymers made by the polymerization of any combination of styrene or alpha methyl styrene with acrylic acid, methacrylic acid, 2-ethyl hexyl acrylate, methyl methacrylate, and butyl acrylate. The styrene and alpha methyl styrene, individually, may constitute from 0 to 80 weight percent of the polymer. The other monomers, individually, may be from 0 to 40 weight percent of the polymer. The polymer number average molecular weight (M_n) shall be at least 2,000 (as determined by gel permeation chromatography). The acid number of the polymer shall be less than 250. The monomer content shall be less than 0.5 percent. The polymers are for use only in contact with food of Types IV-A, V, VII in table 1 of paragraph (d) of this section, under use conditions E through G in table 2 of paragraph (d), and with food of Type VIII without use temperature restriction.

(xxi) Elastomers, as the basic polymer:

Butadiene-acrylonitrile copolymer.
Butadiene-acrylonitrile-styrene copolymer.
Butadiene-styrene copolymer.
Butyl rubber.
Chlorinated rubber.
2-Chloro-1,3-butadiene (neoprene).
Natural rubber (natural latex or natural latex solids, smoked or unsmoked).
Polyisobutylene.
Rubber hydrochloride.
Styrene-isobutylene copolymer.

(xxii) Driers made by reaction of a metal from paragraph (b)(3)(xxii)(*a*) of this section with acid, to form the salt listed in paragraph (b)(3)(xxii)(*b*) of this section:

(*a*) Metals:

Aluminum.
Calcium.
Cerium.
Cobalt.
Iron.
Lithium.
Magnesium.
Manganese.
Zinc.
Zirconium.

(*b*) Salts:

Caprate.
Caprylate.
Isodecanoate.
Linoleate.
Naphthenate.
Neodecanoate.
Octoate (2-ethylhexoate).
Oleate.
Palmitate.
Resinate.
Ricinoleate.
Soyate.
Stearate.
Tallate.

(xxiii) Waxes:

Paraffin, Type I.
Paraffin, Type II.
Polyethylene.
Sperm oil.
Spermaceti.

(xxiv) Plasticizers:

Acetyl tributyl citrate.

Acetyl triethyl citrate.
Butyl phthalyl butyl glycolate.
Butyl stearate.
p-tert-Butyl phenyl salicylate.
Dibutyl sebacate.
Diethyl phthalate.
Diisobutyl adipate.
Diisooctyl phthalate.
Epoxidized soybean oil (iodine number maximum 14; oxirane oxygen content 6% minimum), as the basic polymer.
Ethyl phthalyl ethyl glycolate.
2-Ethylhexyl diphenyl phosphate.
di-2-Ethylhexyl phthalate.
Glycerol.
Glyceryl monooleate.
Glyceryl triacetate.
Monoisopropyl citrate.
Propylene glycol.
Sorbitol.
Mono-, di-, and tristearyl citrate.
Triethyl citrate.
Triethylene glycol.
3-(2-Xenolyl)-1,2-epoxypropane.

(xxv) Release agents, as the basic polymer, when applicable:

N,N′-Dioleoylethylenediamine (CAS Reg. No. 110–31–6) for use only in ionomeric resins complying with § 177.1330 of this chapter and in ethylene vinyl acetate copolymers complying with § 177.1350 of this chapter at a level not to exceed 0.0085 milligram per square centimeter (0.055 milligram per square inch) in the finished food-contact article.
N,N′-Distearoyl ethylenediamine.
Linoleic acid amide.
Oleic acid amide.
Palmitic acid amide.
Petrolatum.
Polyethylene wax.
Polyoxyethylene glycol monooleate (mol. wt. of the polyoxyethylene glycol moiety greater than 300).
Polytetrafluoroethylene.
Silicones (not less than 300 centistokes viscosity): Dimethylpolysiloxanes and/or methylphenylpolysiloxanes. The methylphenylpolysiloxanes contain not more than 2.0 percent by weight of cyclosiloxanes having up to and including 4 siloxy units.
Silicones (not less than 100 centistokes viscosity): Dimethylpolysiloxanes and/or methylphenylpolysiloxanes limited to use only on metal substrates. The methylphenylpolysiloxanes contain not more than 2.0 percent by weight of cyclosiloxanes having up to and including 4 siloxy units.

(xxvi) Colorants used in accordance with § 178.3297 of this chapter.

(xxvii) Surface lubricants:

Cottonseed oil and other edible oils.
Dibutyl sebacate.
Dioctyl sebacate.
Glyceryl monostearate.
Lanolin.
Mineral oil, white.
Palm oil.
Paraffin, Type I.
Paraffin, Type II.
Petrolatum.
Stearic acid.

(xxviii) Silicones and their curing catalysts:

(*a*) Silicones as the basic polymer:

Siloxane resins originating from methyl hydrogen polysiloxane, dimethyl polysiloxane, and methylphenyl polysiloxane.
Siloxane resins originating from the platinum-catalyzed reaction product of vinyl-containing dimethylpolysiloxane (CAS Reg. No. 68083–18–1 and CAS Reg. No. 68083–19–2) with methylhydrogen polysiloxane (CAS Reg. No. 63148–57–2) and dimethylmethylhydrogen polysiloxane (CAS Reg. No. 68037–59–2), where the platinum content does not exceed 150 parts per million. The following substances may be used as optional polymerization inhibitors:
3,5-Dimethyl-1-hexyne-3-ol (CAS Reg. No. 107–54–0), at a level not to exceed 0.53 weight-percent;
1-Ethynylcyclohexene (CAS Reg. No. 931–49–7), at a level not to exceed 0.64 weight-percent;
Bis(methoxymethyl)ethyl maleate (CAS Reg. No. 102054–10–4), at a level not to exceed 1.0 weight-percent;
Methylvinyl cyclosiloxane (CAS Reg. No. 68082–23–5); and
Tetramethyltetravinylcyclotetrasiloxane (CAS Reg. No. 2554–06–5).

(*b*) Curing (cross-linking) catalysts for silicones (the maximum amount of tin catalyst used shall be that required to effect optimum cure but shall not exceed 1 part of tin per 100 parts of siloxane resins solids):

Dibutyltin dilaurate.
Stannous oleate.
Tetrabutyl titanate.

(xxix) Surface active agents:

Ethylene oxide adduct of 2,4,7,9-tetramethyl-5-decyn-4,7-diol (CAS Reg. No. 9014–85–1).
Poly[2-(diethylamino) ethyl methacrylate] phosphate (minimum intrinsic viscosity in water at 25 °C is not less than 9.0 deciliters per gram as determined by ASTM method D1243–79, "Standard Test Method for Dilute Solution Viscosity of Vinyl Chloride Polymers," which is incorporated by reference (Copies may be obtained from the American Society for Testing Materials, 100 Barr Harbor Dr., West Conshohocken,

Philadelphia, PA 19428-2959, or may be examined at the National Archives and Records Administration (NARA). For information on the availability of this material at NARA, call 202–741–6030, or go to: *http://www.archives.gov/federal_register/code_of_federal_regulations/ibr_locations.html.*), for use only as a suspending agent in the manufacture of vinyl chloride copolymers and limited to use at levels not to exceed 0.1 percent by weight of the copolymers.

Sodium dioctyl sulfosuccinate.
Sodium dodecylbenzenesulfonate
Sodium lauryl sulfate.
2,4,7,9-Tetramethyl-5-decyn-4,7-diol (C.A.S. Reg. No. 126-86-3), for use only in can coatings which are subsequently dried and cured at temperatures of at least 193 °C (380 °F) for 4 minutes.

(xxx) Antioxidants:

Butylated hydroxyanisole.
Butylated hydroxytoluene.
Gum guaiac.
Dilauryl thiodipropionate.
Nordihydroguaiaretic acid.
Propyl gallate.
Distearyl thiodipropionate.
Thiodipropionic acid.
2,4,5-Trihydroxybutyrophenone.

(xxxi) Can end cements (sealing compounds used for sealing can ends only): In addition to the substances listed in paragraph (b) of this section and those listed in § 177.1210(b)(5) of this chapter, the following may be used:

Butadiene-styrene-divinylbenzene copolymer (CAS Reg. No. 26471–45–4) for use only at levels not to exceed 23.8 percent by weight of the cement solids in can end cements.
Butadiene-styrene-fumaric acid copolymer.
4,4′-Butylidenebis (6-*tert*-butyl-*m*-cresol).
Dibenzamido phenyl disulfide.
Di-β-naphthyl phenylenediamine.
Dipentamethylene thiuram tetrasulfide.
Isobutylene-isoprene-divinylbenzene copolymers for use only at levels not to exceed 15 percent by weight of the dry cement composition.
Naphthalene sulfonic acid-formaldehyde condensate, sodium salt, for use only at levels not to exceed 0.6 percent by weight of the cement solids in can end cements for containers having a capacity of not less than 5 gallons.
Sodium decylbenzene sulfonate.
Sodium nitrite for use only at levels not to exceed 0.3 percent by weight of the cement solids in can end cements for containers having a capacity of not less than 5 gallons.
Sodium pentachlorophenate for use as a preservative at 0.1 percent by weight in can-sealing compounds on containers having a capacity of 5 gallons or more.
Sodium phenylphenate.
Styrene-maleic anhydride resin, partial methyl and butyl (*sec-* or *iso-*) esters, for use only at levels not in excess of 3 percent of the cement solids in can end cement formulations.
Tetrasodium EDTA (tetrasodium ethylenediaminetetraacetate).
Tri (mixed mono- and dinonylphenyl) phosphite.
Zinc dibutyldithiocarbamate.

(xxxii) Side seam cements: In addition to the substances listed in paragraph (b)(3) (i) to (xxx), inclusive, of this section, the following may be used.

p-tert-Butyl perbenzoate as a catalyst for epoxy resin.
epsilon-Caprolactam-(ethylene-ethyl acrylate) graft polymer.
Dicumyl peroxide for use only as polymerization catalyst.
4–(Diiodomethylsulfonyl) toluene (CAS Reg. No. 20018–09–1) for use as a preservative at a level not to exceed 0.3 percent by weight in can-sealing cements.
Diisodecyl phthalate for use only as plasticizer in side seam cements for containers intended for use in contact with food only of the types identified in paragraph (d) of this section, table 1, under Categories I, II, and VI.
4,4′-Bis(*alpha,alpha*-dimethylbenzyl)diphenylamine, CAS Reg. No. 10081–67–1.
Ethyl toluene sulfonamide.
N,N′-Hexamethylenebis(3,5-di-*tert*-butyl-4-hydroxyhydrocinnamide), CAS Reg. No. 23128–74–7.
Polyamides consisting of the following:
  Copolymer of *omega*-laurolactam and *espilon*-caprolactam, CAS Reg. No. 25191–04–2 (Nylon 12/6).
  Homopolymer of *omega*-aminododecanoic acid, CAS Reg. No. 24937–16–4.
  Homopolymer of *omega*-laurolactam, CAS Reg. No. 25038–74–8 (Nylon 12).
Polyamides derived from the following acids and amines:
  Acids:
    Adipic.
    Azelaic.
    Sebacic.
    Vegetable oil acids (with or without dimerization).
  Amines:
    Diethylenetriamine.
    Diphenylamine.
    Ethylenediamine.
    Hexamethylenediamine.
    Tetraethylenepentamine.
    Triethylenetetramine.
Polypropylene glycol CAS Reg. No. 25322–69–4.

Sodium pentachlorophenate for use as a preservative at 0.1 percent by weight in can-sealing compounds on containers having a capacity of 5 gallons or more.

Tetrakis [methylene(3,5-di-*tert*-butyl-4-hydroxyhydrocinnamate)]methane, CAS Reg. No. 6683–19–8.

Toluene sulfonamide formaldehyde resin (basic polymer).

Triethylene glycol methacrylate for use only as polymerization cross-linking agent in side seam cements for containers intended for use in contact with food only of the types identified in paragraph (d) of this section, table 1, under Categories I, II, and VI.

Urea.

(xxxiii) Miscellaneous materials:

Ammonium citrate.

Ammonium potassium phosphate.

Bentonite, modified by reaction with benzyl dimethyl alkyl ammonium chloride, where the alkyl groups are derived from hydrogenated tallow (CAS Reg. No. 71011–24–0). For use only as a rheological agent in coatings intended to contact food under repeated use conditions.

Bentonite, modified by reaction with sodium stearate and benzyl dimethyl alkyl ammonium chloride, where the alkyl groups are derived from hydrogenated tallow (CAS Reg. No. 121888–68–4). For use as a rheological agent only in coatings intended to contact dry food under repeated-use conditions.

Calcium acetate.

Calcium ethyl acetoacetate.

Calcium glycerophosphate.

Calcium, sodium, and potassium oleates.

Calcium, sodium, and potassium ricinoleates.

Calcium, sodium, and potassium stearates.

Castor oil, hydrogenated.

Castor oil, hydrogenated polymer with ethylenediamine, 12-hydroxyoctadecanoic acid and sebacic acid (CAS Reg. No. 68604–06–8). The condensation product formed by the reaction of hydrogenated castor oil with polyamide derived from ethylenediamine, sebacic acid and 12-hydroxystearic acid, for use only in coatings at a level not to exceed 3.2 percent by weight of the resin when such coatings are intended for repeated use in contact with foods only of the types identified in paragraph (d) of this section, table 1, under Types I, II, and III, under conditions of use C, D, E, or F as described in table 2 of paragraph (d) of this section; or when such coatings are intended for repeated use in contact with foods of the types identified in paragraph (d) of this section, table 1, under Types V, VI, VII, and VIII, under conditions of use E or F as described in table 2 of paragraph (d) of this section. Use shall be limited to coatings for tanks of capacity greater than 530,000 gallons.

Castor oil, sulfated, sodium salt (CAS Reg. No. 68187–76–8), for use only in coatings for containers intended for repeated use.

Cetyl alcohol.

5-Chloro-2-methyl-4-isothiazolin-3-one (CAS Reg. No. 26172–55–4) and 2-methyl-4-isothiazolin-3-one (CAS Reg. No. 2682–20–4) mixture, at a ratio of 3 parts to 1 part, respectively, manufactured from methyl-3-mercaptopropionate (CAS Reg. No. 2935–90–2) and optionally containing magnesium nitrate (CAS Reg. No. 10377–60–3) at a concentration equivalent to the isothiazolone active ingredients (weight/weight). For use only as an antimicrobial agent in emulsion-based silicone coatings at a level not to exceed 50 milligrams per kilogram (based on isothiazolone active ingredient) in the coating formulations.

Cyclohexanone-formaldehyde resin produced when 1 mole of cyclohexanone is made to react with 1.65 moles of formaldehyde such that the finished resin has an average molecular weight of 600–610 as determined by ASTM method D2503–82, "Standard Test Method for Molecular Weight (Relative Molecular Mass) of Hydrocarbons by Thermoelectric Measurement of Vapor Pressure," which is incorporated by reference. Copies may be obtained from the American Society for Testing Materials, 100 Barr Harbor Dr., West Conshohocken, Philadelphia, PA 19428-2959, or may be examined at the National Archives and Records Administration (NARA). For information on the availability of this material at NARA, call 202–741–6030, or go to: *http://www.archives.gov/federal_register/code_of_federal_regulations/ibr_locations.html*. For use only in contact with nonalcoholic and nonfatty foods under conditions of use E, F, and G, described in table 2 of paragraph (d) this section.

Decyl alcohol.

1,2-Dibromo-2,4-dicyanobutane (CAS Reg No. 35691–65–7). For use as an antimicrobial agent at levels not to exceed 500 milligrams per kilogram in emulsion-based silicone coatings.

Disodium hydrogen phosphate.

Ethyl acetoacetate.

Hectorite, modified by reaction with a mixture of benzyl methyl dialkyl ammonium chloride and dimethyl dialkyl ammonium chloride, where the alkyl groups are derived from hydrogenated tallow (CAS Reg. No. 121888–67–3). For use as a rheological agent only in coatings intended to contact dry food under repeated-use conditions.

Lauryl alcohol.

Lecithin.

Magnesium, sodium, and potassium citrate.

Magnesium glycerophosphate.

Magnesium stearate.

Mono-, di-, and tricalcium phosphate.
Monodibutylamine pyrophosphate as sequestrant for iron.
Mono-, di-, and trimagnesium phosphate.
Myristyl alcohol.
Octyl alcohol.
Phosphoric acid.
Polybutene, hydrogenated; complying with the identity and limitations prescribed by §178.3740 of this chapter.
Poly(ethylene oxide).
Siloxanes and silicones, dimethyl, 3-hydroxypropyl group-terminated, diesters with poly(2-oxepanone), diacetates (CAS Reg. No. 116810–47–0) at a level not to exceed 0.025 weight percent of the finished coating having no greater than a 0.5 mil thickness for use as a component of polyester, epoxy, and acrylic coatings complying with paragraphs (b)(3)(vii), (viii), and (xx) of this section, respectively.
Silver chloride-coated titanium dioxide for use only as a preservative in latex emulsions at a level not to exceed 2.2 parts per million (based on silver ion concentration) in the dry coating.
Sodium pyrophosphate.
Stannous chloride.
Stannous stearate.
Stannous sulfate.
Stearyl alcohol.
2-Sulfoethyl methacrylate, sodium salt (CAS Reg. No. 1804–87–1). For use only in copolymer coatings on metal under conditions of use E, F, and G described in table 2 of paragraph (d) of this section, and limited to use at a level not to exceed 2.0 percent by weight of the dry copolymer coating.
Tetrasodium pyrophosphate.
Tridecyl alcohol produced from tetrapropylene by the oxo process, for use only as a processing aid in polyvinyl chloride resins.
Trimethylolpropane (CAS Reg. No. 77–99–6). For use as a pigment dispersant at levels not to exceed 0.45 percent by weight of the pigment.
Vinyl acetate-dibutyl maleate copolymers produced when vinyl acetate and dibutyl maleate are copolymerized with or without one of the monomers: Acrylic acid or glycidyl methacrylate. For use only in coatings for metal foil used in contact with foods that are dry solids with the surface containing no free fat or oil. The finished copolymers shall contain at least 50 weight-percent of polymer units derived from vinyl acetate and shall contain no more than 5 weight-percent of total polymer units derived from acrylic acid or glycidyl methacrylate.

(xxxiv) Polyamide resins derived from dimerized vegetable oil acids (containing not more than 20 percent of monomer acids) and ethylenediamine, as the basic resin, for use only in coatings that contact food at temperatures not to exceed room temperature.

(xxxv) Polyamide resins having a maximum acid value of 5 and a maximum amine value of 8.5 derived from dimerized vegetable oil acids (containing not more than 10 percent of monomer acids), ethylenediamine, and 4,4-bis (4-hydroxyphenyl) pentanoic acid (in an amount not to exceed 10 percent by weight of said polyamide resins); as the basic resin, for use only in coatings that contact food at temperatures not to exceed room temperature provided that the concentration of the polyamide resins in the finished food-contact coating does not exceed 5 milligrams per square inch of food-contact surface.

(xxxvi) Methacrylonitrile grafted polybutadiene copolymers containing no more than 41 weight percent of total polymer units derived from methacrylonitrile; for use only in coatings that are intended for contact, under conditions of use D, E, F, or G described in table 2 of paragraph (d) of this section, with food containing no more than 8 percent of alcohol.

(xxxvii) Polymeric resin as a coating component prepared from terephthalic acid, isophthalic acid, succinic anhydride, ethylene glycol, diethylene glycol, and 2,2-dimethyl-1,3-propanediol for use in contact with aqueous foods and alcoholic foods containing not more than 20 percent (by volume) of alcohol under conditions of use D, E, F, and G described in table 2 of §176.170 of this chapter. The resin shall contain no more than 30 weight percent of 2,2-dimethyl-1,3-propanediol.

(c) The coating in the finished form in which it is to contact food, when extracted with the solvent or solvents characterizing the type of food, and under conditions of time and temperature characterizing the conditions of its intended use as determined from tables 1 and 2 of paragraph (d) of this section, shall yield chloroform-soluble extractives, corrected for zinc extractives as zinc oleate, not to exceed the following:

(1) From a coating intended for or employed as a component of a container not to exceed 1 gallon and intended for one-time use, not to exceed

0.5 milligram per square inch nor to exceed that amount as milligrams per square inch that would equal 0.005 percent of the water capacity of the container, in milligrams, divided by the area of the food-contact surface of the container in square inches. From a fabricated container conforming with the description in this paragraph (c)(1), the extractives shall not exceed 0.5 milligram per square inch of food-contact surface nor exceed 50 parts per million of the water capacity of the container as determined by the methods provided in paragraph (e) of this section.

(2) From a coating intended for or employed as a component of a container having a capacity in excess of 1 gallon and intended for one-time use, not to exceed 1.8 milligrams per square inch nor to exceed that amount as milligrams per square inch that would equal 0.005 percent of the water capacity of the container in milligrams, divided by the area of the food-contact surface of the container in square inches.

(3) From a coating intended for or employed as a component of a container for repeated use, not to exceed 18 milligrams per square inch nor to exceed that amount as milligrams per square inch that would equal 0.005 percent of the water capacity of the container in milligrams, divided by the area of the food-contact surface of the container in square inches.

(4) From coating intended for repeated use, and employed other than as a component of a container, not to exceed 18 milligrams per square inch of coated surface.

(d) Tables:

TABLE 1—TYPES OF FOOD

I. Nonacid (pH above 5.0), aqueous products; may contain salt or sugar or both, and including oil-in-water emulsions of low- or high-fat content.
II. Acidic (pH 5.0 or below), aqueous products; may contain salt or sugar or both, and including oil-in-water emulsions of low- or high-fat content.
III. Aqueous, acid or nonacid products containing free oil or fat; may contain salt, and including water-in-oil emulsions of low- or high-fat content.
IV. Dairy products and modifications:
  A. Water-in-oil emulsion, high- or low-fat.
  B. Oil-in-water emulsion, high- or low-fat.
V. Low moisture fats and oils.
VI. Beverages:
  A. Containing alcohol.
  B. Nonalcoholic.
VII. Bakery products.
VIII. Dry solids (no end test required).

TABLE 2—TEST PROCEDURES FOR DETERMINING AMOUNT OF EXTRACTIVES FROM RESINOUS OR POLYMERIC COATINGS, USING SOLVENTS SIMULATING TYPES OF FOODS AND BEVERAGES

Condition of use	Types of food (see Table 1)	Extractant		
		Water (time and temperature)	Heptane[1,2] (time and temperature)	8% alcohol (time and temperature)
A. High temperature heat-sterilized (e.g., over 212 °F).	I, IV–B	250 °F, 2 hr	.	
	III, IV–A, VII	do	150 °F, 2 hr.	
B. Boiling water-sterilized	II	212 °F, 30 min	.	
	III, VII	do	120 °F, 30 min.	
C. Hot filled or pasteurized above 150 °F.	II, IV–B	Fill boiling, cool to 100 °F.	.	
	III, IV–A	do	120 °F, 15 min.	
	V		do.	
D. Hot filled or pasteurized below 150 °F.	II, IV–B, VI–B	150 °F, 2 hr	.	
	III, IV–A	do	100 °F, 30 min.	
	V		do.	
	VI–A			150 °F, 2 hr.
E. Room temperature filled and stored (no thermal treatment in the container).	II, IV–B, VI–B	120 °F, 24 hr	.	
	III, IV–A	do	70 °F, 30 min.	
	V, VII		do.	
	VI–A			120 °F, 24 hr.
F. Refrigerated storage (no thermal treatment in the container).	I, II, III, IV–A, IV–B, VI–B,VII.	70 °F, 48 hr	.	
	VI–A			70 °F, 48 hr.

TABLE 2—TEST PROCEDURES FOR DETERMINING AMOUNT OF EXTRACTIVES FROM RESINOUS OR POLYMERIC COATINGS, USING SOLVENTS SIMULATING TYPES OF FOODS AND BEVERAGES—Continued

Condition of use	Types of food (see Table 1)	Extractant		
		Water (time and temperature)	Heptane[1,2] (time and temperature)	8% alcohol (time and temperature)
G. Frozen storage (no thermal treatment in the container).	I, II, III, IV–B, VII ...	70 °F, 24 hr	.	
H. Frozen storage: Ready-prepared foods intended to be re-heated in container at time of use:				
1. Aqueous or oil in water emulsion of high or low fat.	I, II, IV–B	212 °F, 30 min	.	
2. Aqueous, high or low free oil or fat.	III, IV–A, VII	do	120 °F, 30 min.	

[1] Heptane extractant not to be used on wax-lined containers.
[2] Heptane extractivity results must be divided by a factor of five in arriving at the extractivity for a food product.

(e) *Analytical methods*—(1) *Selection of extractability conditions.* First ascertain the type of food product (table 1, paragraph (d) of this section) that is being packed commercially in the test container and the normal conditions of thermal treatment used in packaging the type of food involved. Using table 2 (paragraph (d) of this section), select the food-simulating solvent or solvents (demineralized distilled water, heptane, and/or 8 percent ethyl alcohol) and the time-temperature exaggerations of the container-use conditions. Aqueous products (Types I, II, IV-B, and VI-B) require only a water-extractability test at the temperature and time conditions shown for the most severe "conditions of use." Aqueous products with free oil or fat, and water-oil emulsions (types III, IV-A, and VII) will require determinations of both water extractability and heptane extractability. Low-moisture fats and oils (type V with no free water) require only the heptane extractability. Alcoholic beverages (type VI-A) require only the 8 percent alcohol extractant. Having selected the appropriate extractant or extractants simulating various types of foods and beverages and the time-temperature exaggerations over normal use, follow the applicable extraction procedure. Adapt the procedure, when necessary, for containers having a capacity of over 1 gallon.

(2) *Selection of coated-container samples.* For consumer-sized containers up to 1 gallon, quadruplicate samples of representative containers (using for each replicate sample the number of containers nearest to an area of 180 square inches) should be selected from the lot to be examined.

(3) *Cleaning procedure preliminary to determining the amount of extractables from coated containers.* Quadruplicate samples of representative containers should be selected from the lot to be examined and must be carefully rinsed to remove extraneous material prior to the actual extraction procedure. Soda fountain pressure-type hot water rinsing equipment, consisting in its simplest form of a ⅛-inch–¼-inch internal diameter metal tube attached to a hot water line and bent so as to direct a stream of water upward, may be used. Be sure hot water has reached a temperature of 190 °F–200 °F before starting to rinse the container. Invert the container over the top of the fountain and direct a strong stream of hot water against the bottom and all sides for 1 minute, drain, and allow to dry.

(4) *Exposure conditions*—(i) *Water (250 °F for 2 hours), simulating high-temperature heat sterilization.* Fill the container within ¼-inch of the top with a measured volume of demineralized distilled water. Cover the container with clean aluminum foil and place the container on a rack in a pressure cooker. Add a small amount of demineralized distilled water to the pressure cooker, but do not allow the water to touch the

bottom of the container. Close the cooker securely and start to heat over a suitable burner. When a steady stream of steam emerges from the vent, close the vent and allow the pressure to rise to 15 pounds per square inch (250 °F) and continue to maintain this pressure for 2 hours. Slowly release the pressure, open the pressure cooker when the pressure reads zero, and composite the water of each replicate immediately in a clean Pyrex flask or beaker. Proceed with the determination of the amount of extractives by the method described in paragraph (e)(5) of this section.

(ii) *Water (212 °F for 30 minutes), simulating boiling water sterilization.* Fill the container within ¼-inch of the top with a measured volume of boiling, demineralized distilled water. Cover the container with clean aluminum foil and place the container on a rack in a pressure cooker in which a small amount of demineralized distilled water is boiling. Do not close the pressure vent, but operate at atmospheric pressure so that there is a continuous escape of a small amount of steam. Continue to heat for 30 minutes, then remove the test container and composite the contents of each replicate immediately in a clean Pyrex flask or beaker. Proceed with the determination of the amount of extractives by the method described in paragraph (e)(5) of this section.

(iii) *Water (from boiling to 100 °F), simulating hot fill or pasteurization above 150 °F.* Fill the container within ¼-inch of the top with a measured volume of boiling, demineralized distilled water. Insert a thermometer in the water and allow the uncovered container to stand in a room at 70 °F–85 °F. When the temperature reads 100 °F, composite the water from each replicate immediately in a clean Pyrex flask or beaker. Proceed with the determination of the amount of extractives by the method described in paragraph (e)(5) of this section.

(iv) *Water (150° for 2 hours), simulating hot fill or pasteurization below 150 °F.* Preheat demineralized distilled water to 150 °F in a clean Pyrex flask. Fill the container within ¼-inch of the top with a measured volume of the 150 °F water and cover with clean aluminum foil. Place the test container in an oven maintained at 150 °F. After 2 hours, remove the test container from the oven and immediately composite the water of each replicate in a clean Pyrex flask or beaker. Proceed with the determination of the amount of extractives by the method described in paragraph (e)(5) of this section.

(v) *Water (120 °F for 24 hours), simulating room temperature filling and storage.* Preheat demineralized distilled water to 120 °F in a clean Pyrex flask. Fill the container within ¼-inch of the top with a measured volume of the 120 °F water and cover with clean aluminum foil. Place the test container in an incubator or oven maintained at 120 °F. After 24 hours, remove the test container from the incubator and immediately composite the water of each replicate in a clean Pyrex flask or beaker. Proceed with the determination of the amount of extractives by the method described in paragraph (e)(5) of this section.

(vi) *Water (70 °F for 48 hours), simulating refrigerated storage.* Bring demineralized distilled water to 70 °F in a clean Pyrex flask. Fill the container within ¼-inch of the top with a measured volume of the 70 °F water, and cover with clean aluminum foil. Place the test container in a suitable room maintained at 70 °F. After 48 hours, immediately composite the water of each replicate in a clean Pyrex flask or beaker. Proceed with the determination of the amount of extractives by the method described in paragraph (e)(5) of this section.

(vii) *Water (70 °F for 24 hours), simulating frozen storage.* Bring demineralized distilled water to 70 °F in a clean Pyrex flask. Fill the container within ¼-inch of the top with a measured volume of the 70 °F water and cover with clean aluminum foil. Place the container in a suitable room maintained at 70 °F. After 24 hours, immediately composite the water of each replicate in a clean Pyrex flask or beaker. Proceed with the determination of the amount of extractives by the method described in paragraph (e)(5) of this section.

(viii) *Water (212 °F for 30 minutes), simulating frozen foods reheated in the container.* Fill the container to within ¼-

inch of the top with a measured volume of boiling, demineralized distilled water. Cover the container with clean aluminum foil and place the container on a rack in a pressure cooker in which a small amount of demineralized distilled water is boiling. Do not close the pressure vent, but operate at atmospheric pressure so that there is a continuous escape of a small amount of steam. Continue to heat for 30 minutes, then remove the test container and composite the contents of each replicate immediately in a clean Pyrex flask or beaker. Proceed with the determination of the amount of extractives by the method described in paragraph (e)(5) of this section.

(ix) *Heptane (150 °F for 2 hours) simulating high-temperature heat sterilization for fatty foods only.* Preheat redistilled reagent-grade heptane (boiling point 208 °F) carefully in a clean Pyrex flask on a water bath or nonsparking hot plate in a well-ventilated hood to 150 °F. At the same time preheat a pressure cooker or equivalent to 150 °F in an incubator. This pressure cooker is to serve only as a container for the heptane-containing test package inside the incubator in order to minimize the danger of explosion. Fill the test container within ¼-inch of the top with a measured volume of the 150 °F heptane and cover with clean aluminum foil. Place the test container in the preheated pressure cooker and then put the assembly into a 150 °F incubator. After 2 hours, remove the pressure cooker from the incubator, open the assembly, and immediately composite the heptane of each replicate in a clean Pyrex flask or beaker. Proceed with the determination of the amount of extractives by the method described in paragraph (e)(5) of this section.

(x) *Heptane (120 °F for 30 minutes), simulating boiling water sterilization of fatty foods only.* Preheat redistilled reagent-grade heptane (boiling point 208 °F) carefully in a clean Pyrex flask on a water bath or nonsparking hot plate in a well-ventilated hood to 120 °F. At the same time, preheat a pressure cooker or equivalent to 120 °F in an incubator. This pressure cooker is to serve only as a vented container for the heptane-containing test package inside the incubator in order to minimize the danger of explosion. Fill the test container within ¼-inch of the top with a measured volume of the 120 °F heptane and cover with clean aluminum foil. Place the test container in the preheated pressure cooker and then put the assembly into a 120 °F incubator. After 30 minutes, remove the pressure cooker from the incubator, open the assembly, and immediately composite the heptane of each replicate in a clean Pyrex flask or beaker. Proceed with the determination of the amount of extractives by the method described in paragraph (e)(5) of this section.

(xi) *Heptane (120 °F for 15 minutes), simulating hot fill or pasteurization above 150 °F for fatty foods only.* Preheat redistilled reagent-grade heptane (boiling point 208 °F) carefully in a clean Pyrex flask on a water bath or nonsparking hot plate in a well-ventilated hood to 120 °F. At the same time, preheat a pressure cooker or equivalent to 120 °F in an incubator. This pressure cooker is to serve only as a container for the heptane-containing test package inside the incubator in order to minimize the danger of explosion. Fill the test container within ¼-inch of the top with a measured volume of the 120 °F heptane and cover with clean aluminum foil. Place the test container in the preheated pressure cooker and then put the assembly into a 120 °F incubator. After 15 minutes, remove the pressure cooker from the incubator, open the assembly, and immediately composite the heptane of each replicate in a clean Pyrex flask or beaker. Proceed with the determination of the amount of extractives by the method described in paragraph (e)(5) of this section.

(xii) *Heptane (100 °F for 30 minutes), simulating hot fill or pasteurization below 150 °F for fatty foods only.* Preheat redistilled reagent-grade heptane (boiling point 208 °F) carefully in a clean Pyrex flask on a water bath or nonsparking hot plate in a well-ventilated hood to 100 °F. At the same time, preheat a pressure cooker or equivalent to 100 °F in an incubator. This pressure cooker is to serve only as a container for the heptane-containing test package inside the incubator in order to minimize the danger of explosion. Fill the test container within ¼-inch of the top with a measured volume of the 100 °F heptane and cover with clean aluminum foil. Place the test container in the preheated pressure cooker and then put the assembly into a 100 °F incubator. After 30 minutes, remove the pressure cooker from the incubator, open the assembly and immediately composite the heptane of each replicate in a clean Pyrex flask or beaker. Proceed with the determination of the amount of extractives by the method described in paragraph (e)(5) of this section.

(xiii) *Heptane (70 °F for 30 minutes), simulating room temperature filling and storage of fatty foods only.* Fill the test container within ¼-inch of the top with a measured volume of the 70 °F heptane and cover with clean aluminum foil. Place the test container in a suitable room maintained at 70 °F. After 30 minutes, composite the heptane of each replicate in a clean Pyrex flask or beaker. Proceed with the determination of the amount of extractives by the method described in paragraph (e)(5) of this section.

(xiv) *Heptane (120 °F for 30 minutes), simulating frozen fatty foods reheated in the container.* Preheat redistilled reagent-grade heptane (boiling point 208 °F) carefully in a clean Pyrex flask on a water bath or hot plate in a well-ventilated hood to 120 °F. At the same time, preheat a pressure cooker to 120 °F in an incubator. This pressure cooker is to serve only as a container for the heptane-containing test package inside the incubator in order to minimize the danger of explosion. Fill the test container within ¼-inch of the top with a measured volume of the 120 °F heptane and cover with clean aluminum foil. Place the test container in the preheated pressure cooker and then put the assembly into a 120 °F incubator. After 30 minutes, remove the pressure cooker from the incubator, open the assembly and immediately composite the heptane from each replicate into a clean Pyrex flask. Proceed with the determination of the amount of extractives by the method described in paragraph (e)(5) of this section.

(xv) *Alcohol—8 percent (150 °F for 2 hours), simulating alcoholic beverages hot filled or pasteurized below 150 °F.* Preheat 8 percent (by volume) ethyl alcohol in demineralized distilled water to 150 °F in a clean Pyrex flask. Fill the test container with within ¼-inch of the top with a measured volume of the 8 percent alcohol. Cover the container with clean aluminum foil and place in an oven maintained at 150 °F. After 2 hours, remove the container from the oven and immediately composite the alcohol from each replicate in a clean Pyrex flask. Proceed with the determination of the amount of extractives by the method described in paragraph (e)(5) of this section.

(xvi) *Alcohol—8 percent (120 °F for 24 hours), simulating alcoholic beverages room-temperature filled and stored.* Preheat 8 percent (by volume) ethyl alcohol in demineralized distilled water to 120 °F in a clean Pyrex flask. Fill the test container within ¼-inch of the top with a measured volume of the 8 percent alcohol, cover the container with clean aluminum foil and place in an oven or incubator maintained at 120 °F. After 24 hours, remove the container from the oven or incubator and immediately composite the alcohol from each replicate into a clean Pyrex flask. Proceed with the determination of the amount of extractives by the method described in paragraph (e)(5) of this section.

(xvii) *Alcohol—8 percent (70 °F for 48 hours), simulating alcoholic beverages in refrigerated storage.* Bring 8 percent (by volume) ethyl alcohol in demineralized distilled water to 70 °F in a clean Pyrex flask. Fill the test container within ¼-inch of the top with a measured volume of the 8 percent alcohol. Cover the container with clean aluminum foil. Place the test container in a suitable room maintained at 70 °F. After 48 hours, immediately composite the alcohol from each replicate into a clean Pyrex flask. Proceed with the determination of the amount of extractives by the method described in paragraph (e)(5) of this section.

NOTE: The tests specified in paragraph (e)(4) (i) through (xvii) of this section are applicable to flexible packages consisting of coated metal contacting food, in which case the closure end is double-folded and clamped with metal spring clips by which the package can be suspended.

(5) *Determination of amount of extractives*—(i) *Total residues.* Evaporate the food-simulating solvents from paragraph (e)(4) (i) to (xvii), inclusive, of

this section to about 100 milliliters in the Pyrex flask and transfer to a clean, tared platinum dish, washing the flask three times with the solvent used in the extraction procedure, and evaporate to a few milliliters on a nonsparking low-temperature hotplate. The last few milliliters should be evaporated in an oven maintained at a temperature of 212 °F. Cool the platinum dish in a desiccator for 30 minutes and weigh the residue to the nearest 0.1 milligram (*e*). Calculate the extractives in milligrams per square inch and in parts per million for the particular size of container being tested and for the specific food-simulating solvent used.

(*a*) *Water and 8-percent alcohol.*

$$\text{Milligrams extractives per square inch} = \frac{e}{s}$$

$$\text{Extractives residue} = \frac{Ex = (e)(a)(1000)}{(c)(s)}$$

(*b*) *Heptane.*

$$\text{Milligrams extractives per square inch} = \frac{e}{(s)(F)}$$

$$\text{Extractives residue} = \frac{Ex = (e)(a)(1000)}{(c)(s)(F)}$$

where:

Ex=Extractives residue in ppm for any container size.
e=Milligrams extractives per sample tested.
a=Total coated area, including closure in square inches.
c=Water capacity of container, in grams.
s=Surface of coated area tested, in square inches.
F=Five, the ratio of the amount of extractives removed from a coated container by heptane under exaggerated time-temperature test conditions compared to the amount extracted by a fat or oil from a container tested under exaggerated conditions of thermal sterilization and use.
e′=Chloroform-soluble extractives residue.
ee′=Zinc corrected chloroform-soluble extractive residue.
e′ or *ee′* is substituted for *e* in the above equations when necessary.

If when calculated by the equations in paragraph (e)(5)(i) (*a*) and (*b*) of this section, the concentration of extractives residue (*Ex*) exceeds 50 parts per million or the extractives in milligrams per square inch exceed the limitations prescribed in paragraph (c) of this section for the particular container size, proceed to paragraph (e)(5)(ii) of this section (method for determining the amount of chloroform-soluble extractives residue).

(ii) *Chloroform-soluble extractives residue.* Add 50 milliliters of chloroform (freshly distilled reagent grade or a grade having an established consistently low blank) to the dried and weighed residue, (*e*), in the platinum dish, obtained in paragraph (e)(5)(i) of this section. Warm carefully, and filter through Whatman No. 41 filter paper in a Pyrex funnel, collecting the filtrate in a clean, tared platinum dish. Repeat the chloroform extraction, washing the filter paper with this second portion of chloroform. Add this filtrate to the original filtrate and evaporate the total down to a few milliliters on a low-temperature hotplate. The last few milliliters should be evaporated in an oven maintained at 212 °F. Cool the platinum dish in a desiccator for 30 minutes and weigh to the nearest 0.1 milligram to get the chloroform-soluble extractives residue (*e′*). This *e′* is substituted for *e* in the equations in paragraph (e)(5)(i) (*a*) and (*b*) of this section. If the concentration of extractives (*Ex*) still exceeds 50 parts per million or the extractives in milligrams per square inch exceed the limitations prescribed in paragraph (c) of this section for the particular container size, proceed as follows to correct for zinc extractives ("C" enamels only): Ash the residue in the platinum dish by heating gently over a Meeker-type burner to destroy organic matter and hold at red heat for about 1 minute. Cool in the air for 3 minutes, and place the platinum dish in the desiccator for 30 minutes and weigh to the nearest 0.1 milligram. Analyze this ash for zinc by standard Association of Official Agricultural Chemists methods or equivalent. Calculate the zinc in the ash as zinc oleate, and subtract from the weight of chloroform-soluble extractives residue (*e′*) to obtain the zinc-corrected chloroform-soluble extractives residue (*ee′*). This *ee′* is substituted for *e* in the formulas in paragraph (e)(5)(i) (*a*) and (*b*) of this section. To comply with the limitations in paragraph (c) of this section, the chloroform-soluble extractives residue (but after correction for the zinc extractives in case of "C" enamels) must not exceed 50 parts per million and must not exceed in milligrams per square inch the limitations for the particular article as prescribed in paragraph (c) of this section.

(f) *Equipment and reagent requirements*—(1) *Equipment*.

Rinsing equipment, soda fountain pressure-type hot water, consisting in simplest form of a ⅛-inch–¼-inch inside diameter metal tube attached to a hot water line delivering 190 °F–200 °F water and bent so as to direct a stream of water upward.

Pressure cooker, 21-quart capacity with pressure gage, safety release, and removable rack, 12.5 inches inside diameter × 11 inches inside height, 20 pounds per square inch safe operating pressure.

Oven, mechanical convection, range to include 120 °F–212 °F explosion-proof, inside dimensions (minimum), 19″ × 19″ × 19″, constant temperature to ±2 °F (water bath may be substituted).

Incubator, inside dimensions (minimum) 19″ × 19″ × 19″ for use at 100 °F±2 °F explosion proof (water bath may be substituted).

Constant-temperature room or chamber 70 °F±2 °F minimum inside dimensions 19″ × 19″ × 19″.

Hot plate, nonsparking (explosion proof), top 12″ × 20″, 2,500 watts, with temperature control.

Platinum dish, 100-milliliter capacity minimum.

All glass, Pyrex or equivalent.

(2) *Reagents*.

Water, all water used in extraction procedure should be freshly demineralized (deionized) distilled water.

Heptane, reagent grade, freshly redistilled before use, using only material boiling at 208 °F.

Alcohol, 8 percent (by volume), prepared from undenatured 95 percent ethyl alcohol diluted with demineralized or distilled water.

Chloroform, reagent grade, freshly redistilled before use, or a grade having an established, consistently low blank.

Filter paper, Whatman No. 41 or equivalent.

(g) In accordance with good manufacturing practice, finished coatings intended for repeated food-contact use shall be thoroughly cleansed prior to their first use in contact with food.

(h) Acrylonitrile copolymers identified in this section shall comply with the provisions of § 180.22 of this chapter.

[42 FR 14534, Mar. 15, 1977]

EDITORIAL NOTE: For FEDERAL REGISTER citations affecting § 175.300, see the List of CFR Sections Affected, which appears in the Finding Aids section of the printed volume and at *www.fdsys.gov*.

§ 175.320 Resinous and polymeric coatings for polyolefin films.

Resinous and polymeric coatings may be safely used as the food-contact surface of articles intended for use in producing, manufacturing, packing, processing, preparing, treating, packaging, transporting, or holding food, in accordance with the following prescribed conditions:

(a) The coating is applied as a continuous film over one or both sides of a base film produced from one or more of the basic olefin polymers complying with § 177.1520 of this chapter. The base polyolefin film may contain optional adjuvant substances permitted for use in polyolefin film by applicable regulations in parts 170 through 189 of this chapter.

(b) The coatings are formulated from optional substances which are:

(1) Substances generally recognized as safe for use in or on food.

(2) Substances the use of which is permitted under applicable regulations in parts 170 through 189 of this chapter, by prior sanctions, or approvals.

(3) Substances identified in this paragraph (b)(3) and subject to such limitations as are provided:

List of substances	Limitations
(i) Resins and polymers:	
Acrylic acid polymer and its ethyl or methyl esters.	
Acrylamide copolymerized with ethyl acrylate and/or styrene and/or methacrylic acid, and the copolymer subsequently reacted with formaldehyde and butanol.	
Butadiene-acrylonitrile copolymer.	
Butadiene-acrylonitrile-styrene terpolymer.	
Butyl rubber.	

List of substances	Limitations
N,N'-Diphenyl-*p*-phenylenediamine	For use only as a polymerization inhibitor in 2-sulfoethyl methacrylate, sodium salt.
2-Ethylhexyl acrylate copolymerized with one or more of the following:	
Acrylonitrile.	
Itaconic acid.	
Methacrylonitrile.	
Methyl acrylate.	
Methyl methacrylate.	
4,4'-Isopropylidenediphenolepichlorohydrin average molecular weight 900.	
Melamine-formaldehyde as the basic polymer or chemically modified with methyl alcohol.	
Methacrylic acid and its ethyl or methyl esters copolymerized with one or more of the following:	
Acrylic acid.	
Ethyl acrylate.	
Methyl acrylate.	
α-Methyl styrene polymer.	
α-Methylstyrene-vinyltoluene copolymer resins (molar ratio 1 α-methylstyrene to 3 vinyltoluene).	For use only in coatings that contact food under conditions of use D, E, F, or G described in table 2 of § 176.170(c) of this chapter, provided that the concentration of α-methylstyrene-vinyltoluene copolymer resins in the finished food-contact coating does not exceed 1.0 milligram per square inch of food-contact surface.
Petroleum alicyclic hydrocarbon resins	As defined in § 176.170 of this chapter. Blended with butyl rubber for use as a component of coatings on polyolefin fabric for bulk packaging of raw fruits and vegetables and used at a level not to exceed 30 percent by weight of the total coating solids.
Polyamide resins (CAS Reg. No. 68139–70–8), as the basic resin, derived from:	For use only in coatings for polypropylene films that contact food at temperatures not to exceed room temperature.
Dimerized vegetable oil or tall oil acids containing not more than 20 percent of monomer acids.	
Azelaic acid (CAS Reg. No. 123–99–9) in an amount not to exceed 3.7 percent by weight of the polyamide resin.	
Ethylenediamine (CAS Reg. No. 107–15–3).	
Piperazine (CAS Reg. No. 110–85–0) in an amount not to exceed 6.4 percent by weight of the polyamide resin.	
Polyamide resins, derived from dimerized vegetable oil acids (containing not more than 20% of monomer acids) and ethylenediamine, as the basic resin.	For use only in coatings for polyolefin films that contact food at temperatures not to exceed room temperature.
Polyamide resins having a maximum acid value of 5 and a maximum amine value of 8.5 derived from dimerized vegetable oil acids (containing not more than 10 percent of monomer acids), ethylenediamine, and 4,4-bis (4-hydroxyphenyl) pentanoic acids (in an amount not to exceed 10 percent by weight of said polyamide resins); as the basic resin.	For use only in coatings that contact food at temperatures not to exceed room temperature provided that the concentration of the polyamide resins in the finished food-contact coating does not exceed 5 milligrams per square inch of food-contact surface.
Polyester resins formed by reaction of one or more of the following polybasic acids and monobasic acids with one or more of the following polyhydric alcohols:	
Polybasic acids:	
Adipic.	
Azelaic	For use in forming polyester resins intended for use in coatings that contact food only of the type identified in § 176.170(c) of this chapter, table 1, under Category VIII, and under conditions of use E, F, or G, described in table 2 of § 176.170(c) of this chapter.
Dimerized fatty acids derived from:	
Animal, marine or vegetable fats and oils.	
Tall oil.	
Fumaric.	
Isophthalic.	
Maleic.	
o-Phthalic.	
Sebacic.	
Terephthalic.	
Trimellitic.	
Monobasic acids:	
Fatty acids derived from:	
Animal, marine, or vegetable fats and oils.	

List of substances	Limitations
Gum rosin	As defined in § 178.3870 of this chapter. For use in forming polyester resins intended for use in coatings that contact food only of the type identified in § 176.170(c) of this chapter, table 1, under Category VIII, and under conditions of use E, F, or G described in table 2 of § 176.170(c) of this chapter.
Polyhydric alcohols:	
1,3-Butylene glycol.	
Diethylene glycol.	
2,2-Dimethyl-1,3-propanediol.	
Dipropylene glycol.	
Ethylene glycol.	
Glycerol.	
Mannitol.	
α-Methyl glucoside.	
Pentaerythritol.	
Propylene glycol.	
Sorbitol.	
Trimethylol ethane.	
Trimethylol propane.	
Polyethylenimine	For use only as a primer subcoat to anchor epoxy surface coatings to the base sheet.
Polystyrene.	
Polyvinyl acetate.	
Polyvinyl chloride	
Siloxanes and silicones: platinum-catalyzed reaction product of vinyl-containing dimethylpolysiloxane (CAS Reg. No. 68083–18–1 and CAS Reg. No. 68083–19–2) with methylhydrogen polysiloxane (CAS Reg. No. 63148–57–2) and dimethylmethylhydrogen polysiloxane (CAS Reg. No. 68037–59–2). The following substances may be used as optional polymerization inhibitors:.	Platinum content not to exceed 150 parts per million.
3,5-Dimethyl-1-hexyne-3-ol (CAS Reg. No. 107–54–0), at a level not to exceed 0.53 weight percent;.	
1-Ethynylcyclohexene (CAS Reg. No. 931–49–7), at a level not to exceed 0.64 weight percent;.	
Bis(methoxymethyl)ethyl maleate (CAS Reg. No. 102054–10–4), at a level not to exceed 1.0 weight percent;.	
Methylvinyl cyclosiloxane (CAS Reg. No. 68082–23–5); and.	
Tetramethyltetravinylcyclotetrasiloxane (CAS Reg. No. 2554–06–5)..	
Siloxanes and silicones; platinum-catalyzed reaction product of vinyl-containing dimethylpolysiloxane (CAS Reg. Nos. 68083–19–2 and 68083–18–1), with methyl hydrogen polysiloxane (CAS Reg. No. 63148–57–2). Dimethyl maleate (CAS Reg. No. 624–48–6) and vinyl acetate (CAS Reg. No. 108–05–4) may be used as optional polymerization inhibitors.	Platinum content not to exceed 100 parts per million. For use only as a surface coating under the following conditions: 1. In coatings for olefin polymers provided the coating contacts food only of the types identified in § 176.170(c) of this chapter, table 1, under Types I, II, VI, and VII-B when used under conditions of use E, F, and G described in table 2 in § 176.170(c) of this chapter. 2. In coatings for olefin polymers provided the coating contacts food only of the types identified in § 176.170(c) of this chapter, table 1, under Types III, IV, V, VII-A, VIII, and IX when used under conditions of use A through H described in table 2 in § 176.170(c) of this chapter.
Siloxanes and silicones; platinum-catalyzed reaction product of vinyl-containing dimethylpolysiloxane (CAS Reg. Nos. 68083–19–2 and 68083–18–1), with methyl hydrogen polysiloxane (CAS Reg. No. 63148–57–2). Dimethyl maleate (CAS Reg. No. 624–48–6), vinyl acetate (CAS Reg. No. 108–05–4), dibutyl maleate (CAS Reg. No. 105–76–0) and diallyl maleate (CAS Reg. No. 999–21–3) may be used as optional polymerization inhibitors. The polymer may also contain C_{16}-C_{18} olefins (CAS Reg. No. 68855–60–7) as a control release agent.	Platinum content not to exceed 100 parts per million. For use only as a release coating for pressure sensitive adhesives.
Styrene copolymerized with one or more of the following:	
Acrylonitrile.	
α-Methyl styrene.	

List of substances	Limitations
Styrene polymers made by the polymerization of any combination of styrene or alpha methyl styrene with acrylic acid, methacrylic acid, 2-ethyl hexyl acrylate, methyl methacrylate, and butyl acrylate. The styrene and alpha methyl styrene, individually, may constitute from 0 to 80 weight percent of the polymer. The other monomers, individually, may be from 0 to 40 weight percent of the polymer. The polymer number average molecular weight (M_n) shall be at least 2,000 (as determined by gel permeation chromatography). The acid number of the polymer shall be less than 250. The monomer content shall be less than 0.5 percent.	For use only in contact with foods of Types IV-A, V, and VII in table 1 of § 176.170(c) of this chapter, under use conditions E through G in table 2 of § 176.170(c), and with foods of Types VIII and IX without use temperature restriction.
Styrene-isobutylene copolymer.	
Terpene resins consisting of polymers of α-pinene, β-pinene, and/or dipentene; acid value less than 5, saponification number less than 5, and color less than 4 on the Gardner scale as measured in 50 percent mineral spirits solution.	
2-Sulfoethyl methacrylate, sodium salt Chemical Abstracts Service No. 1804–87–1].	For use only in copolymer coatings under conditions of use E, F, and G described in table 2 of § 176.170(c) of this chapter and limited to use at a level not to exceed 2.0 percent by weight of the dry copolymer coating.
Vinyl chloride-acetate, hydroxyl-modified copolymer or maleic acid-modified copolymer.	
Vinyl chloride copolymerized with one or more of the following:	
Acrvlonitrile.	
Vinyl acetate.	
Vinylidene chloride.	
Vinylidene chloride copolymerized with one or more of the following:	
Acrylic acid and its methyl, ethyl, propyl, butyl, or octyl esters.	
Acrylonitrile.	
Itaconic acid.	
Methacrylic acid and its methyl, ethyl, propyl, butyl, or octyl esters.	
Methacrylonitrile.	
Vinyl chloride.	
(ii) Plasticizers:	
Acetyl tributyl citrate.	
Acetyl triethyl citrate.	
Butyl phthalyl butyl glycolate.	
Butyl stearate.	
Dibutyl sebacate.	
Diethyl phthalate.	
2-Ethylhexyl diphenyl phosphate.	
Ethyl phthalyl ethyl glycolate.	
Glycerol monooleate	
Glycerol triacetate.	
Triethyl citrate.	
(iii) Adjuvants (release agents, waxes, and dispersants):	
Acetone.	
Amides (unsubstituted) of fatty acids from vegetable or animal oils.	
n-Butyl acetate.	
n-Butyl alcohol.	
Candelilla wax.	
Carnauba wax.	
5-Chloro-2-methyl-4-isothiazolin-3-one (CAS Reg. No. 26172–55–4) and 2-methyl-4-isothiazolin-3-one (CAS Reg. No. 2682–20–4) mixture, at a ratio of 3 parts to 1 part, respectively, manufactured from methyl-3-mercaptopropionate (CAS Reg. No. 2935–90–2) and optionally containing magnesium nitrate (CAS Reg. No. 10377–60–3) at a concentration equivalent to the isothiazolone active ingredients (weight/weight)..	For use only as an antimicrobial agent in emulsion-based silicone coatings at a level not to exceed 50 milligrams per kilogram (based on isothiazolone active ingredient) in the coating formulation.
1,2-Dibromo-2,4-dicyanobutane (CAS Reg. No. 35691–65–7).	For use as an antimicrobial agent at levels not to exceed 500 milligrams per kilogram in emulsion-based silicone coating.
Ethyl acetate.	
Fatty acids from vegetable or animal oils and their aluminum, ammonium, calcium, magnesium, and sodium salts.	
Hexane.	

List of substances	Limitations
Methyl ethyl ketone.	
N,N-Dioleoylethylenediamine (CAS Reg. No. 110–31–6) ...	For use only in ionomeric resins complying with § 177.1330 of this chapter and in ethylene vinyl acetate copolymers complying with § 177.1350 of this chapter at a level not to exceed 0.0085 milligram per square centimeter (0.055 milligram per square inch) in the finished food-contact article.
Petroleum waxes conforming to specifications included in a regulation in subchapter B of this chapter.	
Polyvinyl alcohol, minimum viscosity of 4% aqueous solution at 20 °C of 4 centipoises and percent alcoholysis of 87–100.	For use only as a dispersing agent at levels not to exceed 6% of total coating weight in coatings for pol-yolefin films provided the finished polyolefin films contact food only of the types identified in § 176.170(c) of this chapter, table 1, under Types V, VIII, and IX.
Sodium dioctyl sulfosuccinate.	
Sodium dodecylbenzenesulfonate.	
Sodium lauryl sulfate.	
Sorbitan and sorbitol esters of fatty acids from vegetable or animal oils.	
Spermaceti wax.	
Tetrahydrofuran.	
Toluene.	
(iv) Preservatives:	
Silver chloride-coated titanium dioxide	For use only as a preservative in latex emulsions at a level not to exceed 2.2 parts per million (based on silver ion concentration) in the dry coating.

(c) The coating in the finished form in which it is to contact food, when extracted with the solvent or solvents characterizing the type of food, and under conditions of time and temperature characterizing the conditions of its intended use as determined from tables 1 and 2 of § 176.17(c) of this chapter, shall yield net chloroform-soluble extractives not to exceed 0.5 milligram per square inch of coated surface.

(d) Acrylonitrile copolymers identified in this section shall comply with the provisions of § 180.22 of this chapter.

[42 FR 14534, Mar. 15, 1977, as amended at 43 FR 7206, Feb. 21, 1978; 45 FR 6541, Jan. 29, 1980; 47 FR 22512, May 25, 1982; 49 FR 36497, Sept. 18, 1984; 50 FR 47209, Nov. 15, 1985; 56 FR 49674, Oct. 1, 1991; 61 FR 14246, Apr. 1, 1996; 63 FR 71017, Dec. 23, 1998; 64 FR 2568, Jan. 15, 1999; 65 FR 6892, Feb. 11, 2000; 65 FR 37041, June 13, 2000]

§ 175.350 Vinyl acetate/crotonic acid copolymer.

A copolymer of vinyl acetate and crotonic acid may be safely used as a coating or as a component of a coating which is the food-contact surface of polyolefin films intended for packaging food, subject to the provisions of this section.

(a) The copolymer may contain added optional substances to impart desired properties.

(b) The quantity of any optional substance does not exceed the amount reasonably required to accomplish the intended physical or technical effect nor any limitations further provided.

(c) Any optional substance that is the subject of a regulation in parts 174, 175, 176, 177, 178, and § 179.45 of this chapter conforms with any specifications in such regulation.

(d) Optional substances as provided in paragraph (a) of this section include:

(1) Substances generally recognized as safe in food.

(2) Substances subject to prior sanction or approval for uses with a copolymer of vinyl acetate and crotonic acid and used in accordance with such sanction or approval.

(3) Substances identified in this subparagraph and subject to such limitations as are provided:

List of substances	Limitations
Silica.	
Japan wax.	

(e) Copolymer of vinyl acetate and crotonic acid used as a coating or as a component of a coating conforming with the specifications of paragraph (e)(1) of this section are used as provided in paragraph (e)(2) of this section.

(1) *Specifications.* (i) The chloroform-soluble portion of the water extractives

of the coated film obtained with distilled water at 120 °F for 24 hours does not exceed 0.5 milligram per square inch of coated surface.

(ii) The chloroform-soluble portion of the *n*-heptane extractives of the coated film obtained with *n*-heptane at 70 °F for 30 minutes does not exceed 0.5 milligram per square inch of coated surface.

(2) *Conditions of use.* The copolymer of vinyl acetate and crotonic acid is used as a coating or as a component of a coating for polyolefin films for packaging bakery products and confectionery.

§ 175.360 Vinylidene chloride copolymer coatings for nylon film.

Vinylidene chloride copolymer coatings identified in this section and applied on nylon film may be safely used as food-contact surfaces, in accordance with the following prescribed conditions:

(a) The coating is applied as a continuous film over one or both sides of a base film produced from nylon resins complying with § 177.1500 of this chapter.

(b) The coatings are prepared from vinylidene chloride copolymers produced by copolymerizing vinylidene chloride with one or more of the monomers acrylic acid, acrylonitrile, ethyl acrylate, methacrylic acid, methyl acrylate, methyl methacrylate (CAS Reg. No. 80–62–6; maximum use level 6 weight percent) and 2-sulfoethyl methacrylate (CAS Reg. No. 10595–80–9; maximum use level 1 weight percent). The finished copolymers contain at least 50 weight percent of polymer units derived from vinylidene chloride. The finished coating produced from vinylidene chloride copolymers produced by copolymerizing vinylidene chloride with methyl methacrylate and/or 2-sulfoethyl methacrylate, or with methyl methacrylate and/or 2-sulfoethyl methacrylate together with one or more of the other monomers from this section, is restricted to use at or below room temperature.

(c) Optional adjuvant substances employed in the production of the coatings or added thereto to impart desired properties may include sodium dodecylbenzenesulfonate.

(d) The coating in the finished form in which it is to contact food, when extracted with the solvent or solvents characterizing the type of food, and under conditions of time and temperature characterizing the conditions of its intended use as determined from tables 1 and 2 of § 176.170(c) of this chapter, shall yield net chloroform-soluble extractives not to exceed 0.5 milligram per square inch of coated surface when tested by the methods described in § 176.170(d) of this chapter.

(e) Acrylonitrile copolymers identified in this section shall comply with the provisions of § 180.22 of this chapter.

[42 FR 14534, Mar. 15, 1977, as amended at 43 FR 7206, Feb. 21, 1978; 45 FR 76998, Nov. 21, 1980; 47 FR 54430, Dec. 3, 1982]

§ 175.365 Vinylidene chloride copolymer coatings for polycarbonate film.

Vinylidene chloride copolymer coatings identified in this section and applied on polycarbonate film may be safely used as food-contact surfaces, in accordance with the following prescribed conditions:

(a) The coating is applied as a continuous film over one or both sides of a base film produced from polycarbonate resins complying with § 177.1580 of this chapter.

(b) The coatings are prepared from vinylidene chloride copolymers produced by copolymerizing vinylidene chloride with acrylonitrile, methyl acrylate, and acrylic acid. The finished copolymers contain at least 50 weight-percent of polymer units derived from vinyldene chloride.

(c) Optional adjuvant substances employed in the production of the coatings or added thereto to impart desired properties may include sodium dodecylbenzenesulfonate in addition to substances described in § 174.5(d) of this chapter.

(d) The coating in the finished form in which it is to contact food, when extracted with the solvent or solvents characterizing the type of food, and under the conditions of time and temperature characterizing the conditions of its intended use as determined from tables 1 and 2 of § 176.170(c) of this chapter, shall yield net chloroform-soluble extractives in each extracting solvent not to exceed 0.5 milligram per square inch of coated surface as determined by the methods described in § 176.170(d) of this chapter. In testing the finished food-contact articles, a separate test sample is to be used for each required extracting solvent.

(e) Acrylonitrile copolymers identified in this section shall comply with the provisons of § 180.22 of this chapter.

§ 175.380 Xylene-formaldehyde resins condensed with 4,4′-isopropylidenediphenol-epichlorohydrin epoxy resins.

The resins identified in paragraph (a) of this section may be safely used as a food-contact coating for articles intended for use in contact with food, in accordance with the following prescribed conditions.

(a) The resins are produced by the condensation of xylene-formaldehyde resin and 4,4′-isopropylidenediphenol-epichlorohydrin epoxy resins, to which may have been added certain optional adjuvant substances required in the production of the resins or added to impart desired physical and technical properties. The optional adjuvant substances may include resins produced by the condensation of allyl ether of mono-, di-, or trimethylol phenol and capryl alcohol and also may include substances identified in § 175.300(b)(3), with the exception of paragraph (b)(3)(xxxi) and (xxxii) of that section.

(b) The resins identified in paragraph (a) of this section may be used as a food-contact coating for articles intended for contact at temperatures not to exceed 160 °F with food of Types I, II, VI-A and B, and VIII described in table 1 of § 176.170(c) of this chapter provided that the coating in the finished form in which it is to contact food meets the following extractives limitations when tested by the methods provided in § 175.300(e):

(1) The coating when extracted with distilled water at 180 °F for 24 hours yields total extractives not to exceed 0.05 milligram per square inch of food-contact surface.

(2) The coating when extracted with 8 percent (by volume) ethyl alcohol in distilled water at 160 °F for 4 hours yields total extractives not to exceed 0.05 milligram per square inch of food-contact surface.

(c) The resins identified in paragraph (a) of this section may be used as a food-contact coating for articles intended for contact at temperatures not to exceed room temperature with food of Type VI-C described in table 1 of § 176.170(c) of this chapter provided the coating in the finished form in which it is to contact food meets the following extractives limitations when tested by the methods provided in § 175.300(e):

(1) The coating when extracted with distilled water at 180 °F for 24 hours yields total extractives not to exceed 0.05 milligram per square inch of food-contact surface.

(2) The coating when extracted with 50 percent (by volume) ethyl alcohol in distilled water at 180 °F for 24 hours yields total extractives not to exceed 0.05 milligram per square inch.

§ 175.390 Zinc-silicon dioxide matrix coatings.

Zinc-silicon dioxide matrix coatings may be safely used as the food-contact surface of articles intended for use in producing, manufacturing, packing, processing, preparing, treating, packaging, transporting, or holding food, subject to the provisions of this section;

(a) The coating is applied to a metal surface, cured, and washed with water to remove soluble substances.

(b) The coatings are formulated from optional substances which include:

(1) Substances generally recognized as safe.

(2) Substances for which safe conditions of use have been prescribed in § 175.300.

(3) Substances identified in paragraph (c) of this section, subject to the limitations prescribed.

(c) The optional substances permitted are as follows:

List of substances	Limitations
Ethylene glycol	As a solvent removed by water washing.
Iron oxide.	
Lithium hydroxide	Removed by water washing.
Methyl orange	As an acid-base indicator.
Potassium dichromate	Removed by water washing.
Silica gel.	
Sodium silicate.	
Zinc, as particulate metal.	

(d) The coating in the finished form in which it is to contact food, when extracted with the solvent or solvents characterizing the type of food, and under the conditions of its intended use as shown in table 1 and 2 of §175.300(d) (using 20 percent alcohol as the solvent when the type of food contains approximately 20 percent alcohol) shall yield total extractives not to exceed those prescribed in §175.300(c)(3); lithium extractives not to exceed 0.025 milligram per square inch of surface; and chromium extractives not to exceed 0.05 microgram per square inch of surface.

(e) The coatings are used as food-contact surfaces for bulk reusable containers intended for storing, handling, and transporting food.

PART 176—INDIRECT FOOD ADDITIVES: PAPER AND PAPERBOARD COMPONENTS

Subpart A [Reserved]

Subpart B—Substances for Use Only as Components of Paper and Paperboard

Sec.

AUTHORITY: 21 U.S.C. 321, 342, 346, 348, 379e.

SOURCE: 42 FR 14554, Mar. 15, 1977, unless otherwise noted.

EDITORIAL NOTE: Nomenclature changes to part 176 appear at 61 FR 14482, Apr. 2, 1996, 66 FR 56035, Nov. 6, 2001, and 70 FR 72074, Dec. 1, 2005.

Subpart A [Reserved]

Subpart B—Substances for Use Only as Components of Paper and Paperboard

§ 176.110 Acrylamide-acrylic acid resins.

Acrylamide-acrylic acid resins may be safely used as components of articles intended for use in producing, manufacturing, packing, processing, preparing, treating, packaging, transporting, or holding food, subject to the provisions of this section.

(a) Acrylamide-acrylic acid resins are produced by the polymerization of acrylamide with partial hydrolysis or by the copolymerization of acrylamide and acrylic acid.

(b) The acrylamide-acrylic acid resins contain less than 0.2 percent residual monomer.

(c) The resins are used as adjuvants in the manufacture of paper and paperboard in amounts not to exceed that necessary to accomplish the technical effect and not to exceed 2 percent by weight of the paper or paperboard.

§ 176.120 Alkyl ketene dimers.

Alkyl ketene dimers may be safely used as a component of articles intended for use in producing, manufacturing, packing, processing, preparing, treating, packaging, transporting, or holding food, subject to the provisions of this section.

(a) The alkyl ketene dimers are manufactured by the dehydrohalogenation of the acyl halides derived from the fatty acids of animal or vegetable fats and oils.

(b) The alkyl ketene dimers are used as an adjuvant in the manufacture of paper and paperboard under such conditions that the alkyl ketene dimers and their hydrolysis products dialkyl ketones do not exceed 0.4 percent by weight of the paper or paperboard.

(c) The alkyl ketene dimers may be used in the form of an aqueous emulsion which may contain sodium lignosulfonate as a dispersant.

§ 176.130 Anti-offset substances.

Substances named in paragraphs (b) and (c) of this section may be safely used to prevent the transfer of inks employed in printing and decorating paper and paperboard used for food packaging in accordance with the provisions of this section:

(a) The substances are applied to the nonfood contact, printed side of the paper or paperboard in an amount not greater than that required to accomplish the technical effect nor greater than any specific limitations, where such are provided.

(b) Anti-offset powders are prepared from substances that are generally recognized as safe in food, substances for which prior sanctions or approvals were granted and which are used in accordance with the specific provisions of such sanction or approval, and substances named in paragraph (c) of this section.

(c) The substances permitted are as follows:

Substances	Limitations
Carbon tetrachloride.	
Methyl hydrogen polysiloxanes.	
Industrial starch—modified	Complying with § 178.3520 of this chapter.
Stannous oleate.	
Zinc-2-ethyl hexoate.	

§ 176.150 Chelating agents used in the manufacture of paper and paperboard.

The substances named in paragraph (a) of this section may be safely used in the manufacture of paper and paperboard, in accordance with the conditions prescribed in paragraphs (b) and (c) of this section:

(a) Chelating agents:

List of substances	Limitations
Ammonium fructoheptonate.	
Ammonium glucoheptonate.	
Disodium ethylenediamine tetraacetate.	
Pentasodium salt of diethylenetriamine pentaacetate.	
Sodium fructoheptonate.	
Sodium glucoheptonate.	
Tetrasodium ethylenediamine tetraacetate.	
Trisodium *N*-hydroxyethyl ethylenediamine triacetate.	

(b) Any one or any combination of the substances named is used or intended for use as chelating agents.

(c) The substances are added in an amount not greater than that required to accomplish the intended technical effect nor greater than any specific limitation, where such is provided.

§ 176.160 Chromium (Cr III) complex of *N*-ethyl-*N*-heptadecylfluoro-octane sulfonyl glycine.

The chromium (Cr III) complex of *N*-ethyl - *N* -heptadecylfluoro-octane sulfonyl glycine containing up to 20 percent by weight of the chromium (Cr III) complex of heptadecylfluoro-octane sulfonic acid may be safely used as a component of paper for packaging dry food when used in accordance with the following prescribed conditions.

(a) The food additive is used as a component of paper in an amount not to exceed 0.5 percent by weight of the paper.

(b)(1) The food-contact surface of the paper is overcoated with a polymeric or resinous coating at least ⅓-mil in thickness, that meets the provision of § 176.170; or

(2) The treated paper forms one or more plies of a paper in a multiwall bag and is separated from the food by at least one ply of packaging films or grease-resistant papers which serves as a functional barrier between the food additive and the food. Such packaging films or grease-resistant papers conform with appropriate food additive regulations.

(c) The labeling of the food additive shall contain adequate directions for its use to insure compliance with the requirements of paragraphs (a) and (b) of this section.

§ 176.170 Components of paper and paperboard in contact with aqueous and fatty foods.

Substances identified in this section may be safely used as components of the uncoated or coated food-contact surface of paper and paperboard intended for use in producing, manufacturing, packaging, processing, preparing, treating, packing, transporting, or holding aqueous and fatty foods, subject to the provisions of this section. Components of paper and paperboard in contact with dry food of the type identified under Type VIII of table 1 in paragraph (c) of this section are subject to the provisions of § 176.180.

(a) Substances identified in paragraph (a) (1) through (5) of this section may be used as components of the food-contact surface of paper and paperboard. Paper and paperboard products shall be exempted from compliance with the extractives limitations prescribed in paragraph (c) of this section: *Provided*, That the components of the food-contact surface consist entirely of one or more of the substances identified in this paragraph: *And provided further*, That if the paper or paperboard when extracted under the conditions prescribed in paragraph (c) of this section exceeds the limitations on extractives contained in paragraph (c) of this section, information shall be available from manufacturing records from which it is possible to determine that only substances identified in this paragraph (a) are present in the food-contact surface of such paper or paperboard.

(1) Substances generally recognized as safe in food.

(2) Substances generally recognized as safe for their intended use in paper and paperboard products used in food packaging.

(3) Substances used in accordance with a prior sanction or approval.

(4) Substances that by regulation in parts 170 through 189 of this chapter may be safely used without extractives limitations as components of the uncoated or coated food-contact surface of paper and paperboard in contact with aqueous or fatty food, subject to the provisions of such regulation.

(5) Substances identified in this paragraph, as follows:

List of Substances	Limitations
Acetyl peroxide	For use only as polymerization catalyst.
Acrylamide-methacrylic acid-maleic anhydride copolymers containing not more than 0.2 percent of residual acrylamide monomer and having an average nitrogen content of 14.9 percent such that a 1 percent by weight aqueous solution has a minimum viscosity of 600 centipoises at 75 °F, as determined by LVG-series Brookfield viscometer (or equivalent) using a No. 2 spindle at 30 r.p.m.	For use only as a retention aid employed prior to the sheet-forming operation in the manufacture of paper and paperboard in such an amount that the finished paper and paperboard will contain the additive at a level not in excess of 0.05 percent by weight of dry fibers in the finished paper and paperboard.
Acrylamide-β-methacrylyloxyethyltrimethylammonium methyl sulfate copolymer resins containing not more than 10 molar percent of β-methacrylyloxyethyltrimethylammonium methyl sulfate and containing less than 0.2% of residual acrylamide monomer.	For use only as a retention aid and flocculant employed prior to the sheet-forming operation in the manufacture of paper and paperboard.
Acrylic acid, sodium salt copolymer with polyethyleneglycol allyl ether (CAS Reg. No. 86830–15–1).	For use only in paper mill boilers.
Acrylic acid copolymer with 2-acrylamido-2-methylpropane-sulfonic acid (CAS Reg. No. 40623–75–4) and/or its ammonium/alkali metal mixed salts. The copolymer is produced by poly-merization of acrylic acid and 2-acrylamido-2-methylpropane-sulfonic acid in a weight ratio of 60/40, such that a 28 percent by weight aqueous solution of the polymer has a viscosity of 75–150 centipoises at 25 °C as determined by LV-series Brookfield viscometer (or equivalent) using a No. 2 spindle at 60 r.p.m.	For use only as a scale inhibitor prior to the sheet-forming operation in the manufacture of paper and paperboard and used at a level not to exceed 1.0 kilogram (2.2 pounds) of copolymer per 907 kilograms (1 ton) of dry paper and paperboard fibers.
Acrylonitrile polymer, reaction product with ethylenediamine sulfate having a nitrogen content of 22.5–25.0 percent (Kjeldahl dry basis) and containing no more than 0.075 percent monomer as ethylenediamine. The finished resin in a 24 percent by weight aqueous solution has a viscosity of 1,000–2,000 centipoises at 25 °C as determined by LVT-series Brookfield viscometer using a No. 4 spindle at 50 r.p.m. (or by other equivalent method).	For use only as a size promoter and retention aid at a level not to exceed 0.5 percent by weight of the dry paper and paperboard.
Acrylonitrile polymer with styrene, reaction product with ethylenediamine acetate, having a nitrogen content of 7.4–8.3 percent (Kjeldahl dry basis) and containing no more than 0.25 percent monomer as ethylenediamine.	1. For use only as a sizing material applied after the sheet-forming operation in the manufacture of paper and paperboard in such amount that the paper and paperboard will contain the additive at a level not in excess of 0.25 percent by weight of the dry paper and paperboard. 2. For use only as a sizing material applied prior to the sheet-forming operation in the manufacture of paper and paperboard in such amount that the paper and paperboard will contain the additive at a level not in excess of 1.0 percent by weight of the dry paper and paperboard.

List of Substances	Limitations
1-Alkenyl olefins, containing not less than 72 percent of C_{30} and higher olefins.	For use only under the following conditions: 1. In coatings for paper and paperboard with food of Types I, II, IV-B, and VII-B described in table 1 of paragraph (c) of this section under conditions of use E, F, and G described in table 2 of paragraph (c) of this section. 2. In coatings for paper and paperboard with food of Type VIII described in table I of paragraph (c) of this section under conditions of use A through H described in table 2 of paragraph (c) of this section.
(2-Alkenyl) succinic anhydrides mixture, in which the alkenyl groups are derived from olefins which contain not less than 95 percent of C_{15}-C_{21} groups.	For use only as a sizing agent employed prior to the sheet-forming operation in the manufacture of paper and paperboard and limited to use at a level not to exceed 1 percent by weight of the finished dry paper and paperboard fibers.
Alkyl(C_{12}-C_{20})methacrylatemethacrylic acid copolymers (CAS Reg. No. 27401–06–5).	For use only as stabilizers employed prior to the sheet-forming operation in the manufacture of paper and paperboard.
tert-Alkyl(C_8-C_{16})mercaptans	For use only as polymerization-control agent.
Aluminum acetate.	
2-Amino-2-methyl-1-propanol (CAS Reg. No. 124–68–5)	For use as a dispersant for pigment suspension at a level not to exceed 0.25 percent by weight of pigment. The suspension is used as a component of coatings for paper and paperboard under conditions of use described in paragraph (c) of this section, table 2, conditions of use E through G.
Ammonium bis(*N*-ethyl-2-perfluoroalkylsulfonamido ethyl) phosphates, containing not more than 15% ammonium mono (*N*-ethyl-2-perfluoroalkylsulfonamido ethyl) phosphates, where the alkyl group is more than 95% C_8 and the salts have a fluorine content of 50.2% to 52.8% as determined on a solids basis.	For use only as an oil and water repellant at a level not to exceed 0.17 pound (0.09 pound of fluorine) per 1,000 square feet of treated paper or paperboard of a sheet basis weight of 100 pounds or less per 3,000 square feet of paper or paperboard, and at a level not to exceed 0.5 pound (0.26 pound of fluorine) per 1,000 square feet of treated paper or paperboard having a sheet basis weight greater than 100 lb. per 3,000 square feet as determined by analysis for total fluorine in the treated paper or paperboard without correction for any fluorine that might be present in the untreated paper or paperboard, when such paper or paperboard is used as follows: 1. In contact, under conditions of use C, D, E, F, G, or H described in table 2 of paragraph (c) of this section, with nonalcoholic food. 2. In contact with bakery products of Type VII, VIII, and IX described in table I of paragraph (c) of this section under good manufacturing practices of commercial and institutional baking.
Ammonium persulfate.	
Ammonium thiosulfate.	
Ammonium zirconium carbonate (CAS Reg. No. 32535–84–5) and its tartaric acid adduct.	For use only as an insolubilizer for binders used in coatings for paper and paperboard, and limited to use at a level not to exceed 2.5 percent by weight of coating solids.
Ammonium zirconium citrate (CAS Reg. No. 149564–62–5), ammonium zirconium lactate-citrate (CAS Reg. No. 149564–64–7), ammonium zirconium lactate (CAS Reg. No. 149564–63–6).	For use as insolubilizers with protein binders in coatings for paper and paperboard, at a level not to exceed 1.4 percent by weight of coating solids.
Anionic polyurethane, produced by reacting the preliminary adduct formed from the reaction of glyceryl monostearate and 2,4-toluenediisocyanate with not more than 10 mole percent *N*-methyldiethanolamine and not less than 90 mole percent dimethylolpropionic acid. The final product is a 15 to 20 percent by weight aqueous solution, having a Brookfield viscosity of 25 to 100 centipoises at 24 °C (75 °F).	For use only as a surface sizing agent at a level not to exceed 0.1 percent by weight of dry paper and paperboard.
9,10–Anthraquinone (Chemical Abstracts Service Registry No. 84–65–1) which has a purity of not less than 98 percent.	For use only as a pulping aid in the alkaline pulping of lignocellulosic material at levels not to exceed 0.1 percent by weight of the raw lignocellulosic material.

List of Substances	Limitations
Aromatic petroleum hydrocarbon resin, hydrogenated (CAS Reg. No. 88526–47–0), produced by the catalytic polymerization of aromatic substituted olefins from low boiling distillates of cracked petroleum stocks with a boiling point no greater than 220 °C (428 °F), and the subsequent catalytic reduction of the resulting aromatic petroleum hydrocarbon resin. The resin meets the following specifications: softening point 85 °C (185 °F) minimum, as determined by ASTM Method E 28–67 (Reapproved 1982), "Standard Test Method for Softening Point by Ring-and-Ball Apparatus," and aniline point 70 °C (158 °F) minimum, as determined by ASTM Method D 611–82, "Standard Test Methods for Aniline Point and Mixed Aniline Point of Petroleum Products and Hydrocarbon Solvents," which are incorporated by reference in accordance with 5 U.S.C. 552(a) and 1 CFR part 51. Copies may be obtained from the American Society for Testing and Materials, 100 Barr Harbor Dr., West Conshohocken, Philadelphia, PA 19428-2959, or may be examined at the National Archives and Records Administration (NARA). For information on the availability of this material at NARA, call 202–741–6030, or go to: *http://www.archives.gov/federal_register/code_of_federal_regulations/ibr_locations.html.*.	For use only as modifiers in wax polymer blend coatings for paper and paperboard at a level not to exceed 50 weight-percent of the coating solids under conditions of use E, F, and G identified in table 2 of paragraph (c) of this section.
Azo-bisisobutyronitrile	For use only as polymerization catalyst.
1,2-Benzisothiazolin-3-one (CAS Registry No. 2634–33–5)	For use only as a preservative in paper coating compositions and limited to use at a level not to exceed 0.01 mg/in^2 (0.0016 mg/cm^2) of the finished paper and paperboard.
Benzoyl peroxide	Do.
N,N-Bis(2-hydroxyethyl)alkyl (C_{12}-C_{18})amide	For use only as an adjuvant to control pulp absorbency and pitch content in the manufacture of paper and paperboard prior to the sheet forming operation.
Bis(methoxymethyl)tetrakis-[(octadecyloxy)-methyl]melamine resins having a 5.8–6.5 percent nitrogen content (CAS Reg. No. 68412–27–1).	For use only under the following conditions: 1. As a water repellant employed prior to the sheet-forming operation in the manufacture of paper and paperboard in such amount that the finished paper and paperboard will contain the additive at a level not in excess of 1.6 percent by weight of the finished dry paper and paperboard fibers. 2. The finished paper and paperboard will be used in contact with nonalcoholic foods only. 3. As a water repellant employed after the sheet-forming operation in the manufacture of paper and paperboard in such amount that the finished paper and paperboard will contain the additive at a level not to exceed 1.6 percent by weight of the finished dry paper and paperboard fibers. The finished paper and paperboard will be used only in contact with food of Types I, II, IV-B, VI, VII-B, and VIII described in table 1 of paragraph (c) of this section.
2-Bromo-2-nitro-1,3-propanediol (CAS Reg. No. 52–51–7)	For use only as an antimicrobial/preservative in fillers, pigment slurries, starch sizing solutions, and latex coatings at levels not to exceed 0.01 percent by weight of those components.
Butanedioic acid, sulfo-1,4-di-(C_9-C_{11} alkyl) ester, ammonium salt (also known as butanedioic acid, sulfo-1,4-diisodecyl ester, ammonium salt [CAS Reg. No. 144093–88–9])..	For use as a surface active agent in package coating inks at levels not to exceed 3 percent by weight of the coating ink.
tert-Butyl hydroperoxide	For use only as polymerization catalyst.
tert-Butyl peroxide	Do.
Calcium isostearate	For use only with *n*-decyl alcohol as a stabilizing material for aqueous calcium stearate dispersions intended for use as components of coatings for paper and paperboard.
Carrageenan and salts of carrageenan as described in §§ 172.620 and 172.626 of this chapter.	
Castor oil, hydrogenated.	
Castor oil, sulfated, ammonium, potassium, or sodium salt.	
Cellulose, regenerated.	
Chloracetamide	For use only as polymerization-control agent.
Cobaltous acetate	For use only as polymerization catalyst.
Cumene hydroperoxide	Do.
Cyanoguanidine	For use only: 1. As a modifier for amino resins. 2. As a fluidizing agent in starch and protein coatings for paper and paperboard.
n-Decyl alcohol	For use only with calcium isostearate as a stabilizing material for aqueous calcium stearate dispersions intended for use as components of coatings for paper and paperboard.

List of Substances	Limitations
Dialdehyde guar gum	For use only as a wet-strength agent employed prior to the sheet-forming operation in the manufacture of paper and paperboard and used at a level not to exceed 1% by weight of the finished dry paper and paperboard fibers.
Dialdehyde locust bean gum	Do.
Dialkyl(C_{16}-C_{18})carbamoyl chloride (CAS Reg. No. 41319–54–4) manufactured by the reaction of secondary amines derived from fatty acids of animal or vegetable sources with phosgene.	For use as a sizing agent at a level not to exceed 0.2 percent by weight of the dry fiber.
Diallyldimethyl ammonium chloride polymer with acrylamide and potassium acrylate, produced by copolymerizing either (1) diallyldimethyl ammonium chloride and acrylamide in a weight ratio of 50/50, with 4.4 percent of the acrylamide subsequently hydrolyzed to potassium acrylate or (2) polymerized diallyldimethyl ammonium chloride, acrylamide and potassium acrylate (as acrylic acid) in a weight ratio of 50/47.8/2.2, respectively, so that the finished resin in a 1 percent by weight aqueous solution (active polymer) has a viscosity of more than 22 centipoises at 22 °C (72 °F) as determined by LVF series, Brookfield Viscometer using No. 1 spindle at 60 RPM (or by other equivalent method) (CAS Reg. No. 25136–75–8).	For use only as a retention and/or drainage aid employed prior to the sheet-forming operations in the manufacture of paper and paperboard and limited to use at a level not to exceed 0.05 percent by weight of the finished paper and paperboard.
Diallyldimethylammonium chloride with acrylamide (CAS Reg. No. 26590–05–6). The copolymer is produced by copolymerizing diallyldimethylammonium chloride with acrylamide in a weight ratio of 50–50 so that the finished resin in a 1 percent by weight aqueous solution (active polymer) has a viscosity of more than 22 centipoises at 22 °C (71.6 °F), as determined by LVF-series Brookfield viscometer using a No. 1 spindle at 60 r.p.m. (or by other equivalent method).	For use only as a drainage and/or retention aid employed prior to the sheet-forming operation in the manufacture of paper and paperboard and limited to use at a level not to exceed 0.05 percent by weight of the finished paper and paperboard.
Diallyldiethylammonium chloride polymer with acrylamide, and diallyldimethylammonium chloride, produced by copolymerizing acrylamide, diallyldiethylammonium chloride, and diallyldimethylammonium chloride, respectively, in the following weight ratios and having viscosities determined at 22 °C, by LVF-series Brookfield viscometer using a No. 1 spindle at 60 r.p.m. (or by other equivalent method), as follows:.	
1. Weight ratio: 50–2.5–47.5. The finished resin in a 1 percent by weight aqueous solution has a minimum viscosity of 22 centipoises.	For use only as a retention aid employed prior to the sheet-forming operation in the manufacture of paper and paperboard and limited to use at a level not to exceed 0.05 percent by weight of the finished paper and paperboard.
2. Weight ratio: 25–2.5–72.5. The finished resin in a 0.20 percent by weight aqueous solution has a minimum viscosity of 20 centipoises.	For use only as a drainage and/or retention aid employed prior to the sheet-forming operation in the manufacture of paper and paperboard and limited to use at a level not to exceed 0.075 percent by weight of the finished paper and paperboard.
3. Weight ratio: 80–2.5–17.5. The finished resin in a 0.30 percent by weight aqueous solution has a minimum viscosity of 50 centipoises.	For use only as a drainage and/or retention aid employed prior to the sheet-forming operation in the manufacture of paper and paperboard and limited to use at a level not to exceed 0.075 percent by weight of the finished paper and paperboard.
Diallyldiethylammonium chloride polymer with acrylamide, potassium acrylate, and diallyldimethylammonium chloride. The polymer is produced by copolymerizing either: (1) acrylamide, diallyldiethylammonium chloride, and diallyldimethylammonium chloride in a weight ratio of 50–2.5–47.5, respectively, with 4.4 percent of the acrylamide subsequently hydrolyzed to potassium acrylate, or (2) acrylamide, potassium acrylate (as acrylic acid), diallyldiethylammonium chloride, and diallyldimethylammonium chloride in a weight ratio of 47.8–2.2–2.5–47.5, so that the finished resin in a 1 percent by weight aqueous solution has a minimum viscosity of 22 centipoises at 22 °C, as determined by LVF-series Brookfield viscometer using a No. 1 spindle at 60 r.p.m. (or by other equivalent method).	For use only as a retention aid employed prior to the sheet-forming operation in the manufacture of paper and paperboard and limited to use at a level not to exceed 0.05 percent by weight of the finished paper and paperboard.

List of Substances	Limitations
Diallyldimethylammonium chloride polymer with acrylamide, reaction product with glyoxal, produced by copolymerizing not less than 90 weight percent of acrylamide and not more than 10 weight percent of diallyldimethylammonium chloride, which is then cross-linked with not more than 30 weight percent of glyoxal, such that a 10 percent aqueous solution has a minimum viscosity of 25 centipoises at 25 °C as determined by Brookfield viscometer Model RVF, using a No. 1 spindle at 100 r.p.m.	For use only as a dry and wet strength agent employed prior to the sheet-forming operation in the manufacture of paper and paperboard in such an amount that the finished paper and paperboard will contain the additive at a level not in excess of 2 percent by weight of the dry fibers in the finished paper and paperboard.
2,2-Dibromo-3-nitrilopropionamide (CAS Reg. No.10222–01–2).	For use as a preservative at a level not to exceed 100 parts per million in coating formulations and in component slurries and emulsions, used in the production of paper and paperboard and coatings for paper and paperboard.
2,5-Di-*tert*-butyl hydroquinone	For use only as an antioxidant for fatty based coating adjuvants provided it is used at a level not to exceed 0.005% by weight of coating solids.
Diethanolamine	For use only: 1. As an adjuvant to control pulp absorbency and pitch content in the manufacture of paper and paperboard prior to the sheet-forming operation. 2.In paper mill boilers.
Diethanolamine salts of mono- and bis (1*H*,1*H*,2*H*,2*H*-perfluoroalkyl) phosphates where the alkyl group is even-numbered in the range C_8-C_{18} and the salts have a fluorine content of 52.4% to 54.4% as determined on a solids basis.	For use only as an oil and water repellant at a level not to exceed 0.17 pound (0.09 pound of fluorine) per 1,000 square feet of treated paper or paperboard, as determined by analysis for total fluorine in the treated paper or paperboard without correction for any fluorine which might be present in the untreated paper or paperboard, when such paper or paperboard is used in contact with nonalcoholic foods under the conditions of use described in paragraph (c) of this section, table 2, conditions of use (B) through (H).
Diethyl(2-hydroxyethyl) methylammonium methyl sulfate, acrylate, polymer with acrylamide, chemical abstract service registry No. [26796–75–8] having 90–95 mole pct. acrylamide, a nitrogen content of not more than 19.7 pct. (Kjeldahl, dry basis), and a residual acrylamide monomer content of not more than 0.1 pct. The finished polymer in a 1 pct. by weight aqueous solution has a minimum viscosity of 900 centipoises at 25 °C as determined by LVT-series Brookfield viscometer using a No. 2 spindle at 12 r.p.m. (or by equivalent method).	For use only as a retention aid and drainage aid employed prior to the sheet-forming operation in the manufacture of paper and paperboard at a level not to exceed 0.15 pct. by weight of finished dry paper and paperboard fibers.
Diethylenetriamine	For use only as a modifier for amino resins.
N,N-Diisopropanolamide of tallow fatty acids	For use only as an adjuvant to control pulp absorbency and pitch content in the manufacture of paper and paperboard prior to the sheet-forming operation.
Dimethylamine-epichlorohydrin copolymer in which not more than 5 mole-percent of dimethylamine may be replaced by an equimolar amount of ethylenediamine and in which the ratio of total amine to epichlorohydrin does not exceed 1:1. The nitrogen content of the copolymer shall be 9.4 to 10.8 weight percent on a dry basis and a 10 percent by weight aqueous solution of the final product has a minimum viscosity of 5.0 centipoises at 25 °C, as determined by LVT-series Brookfield viscometer using a No. 1 spindle at 60 r.p.m. (or by other equivalent method).	For use only: 1. As a retention aid employed before the sheet-forming operation in the manufacture of paper and paperboard and limited to use at a level not to exceed 1 percent by weight of the finished paper and paperboard. 2. At the size press at a level not to exceed 0.017 percent by weight of the finished paper and paperboard.
N-[(Dimethylamino)methyl]-acrylamide polymer with acrylamide and styrene having a nitrogen content of not more than 16.9 percent and a residual acrylamide monomer content of not more than 0.2 percent on a dry basis.	For use only as a dry-strength agent employed prior to the sheet-forming operation in the manufacture of paper and paperboard and used at a level not to exceed 1 percent by weight of finished dry paper or paperboard fibers.
N,N'-Dioleoylethylenediamine.	
Diphenylamine	For use only as an antioxidant for fatty based coating adjuvants provided it is used at a level not to exceed 0.005% by weight of coating solids.
Dipropylene glycol.	
Disodium salt of 1,4-dihydro-9,10-dihydroxyanthracene (CAS Reg. No. 73347–80–5).	For use only as a catalyst in the alkaline pulping of lignocellulosic materials at levels not to exceed 0.1 percent by weight of the raw lignocellulosic materials.
N,N'-Distearoylethylenediamine.	

List of Substances	Limitations
n-Dodecylguanidine acetate	For use only as an antimicrobial agent in paper and paperboard under the following conditions: 1. For contact only with nonalcoholic food having a pH above 5 and provided it is used at a level not to exceed 0.4 percent by weight of the paper and paperboard. 2. For use in the outer ply of multiwall paper bags for contact with dry food of Type VIII described in table I of paragraph (c) of this section and provided it is used at a level of 0.8 percent by weight of the paper.
n-Dodecylguanidine hydrochloride	For use only as an antimicrobial agent in paper and paperboard under the following conditions: 1. For contact only with nonalcoholic food having a pH above 5 and provided it is used at a level not to exceed 0.4 percent by weight of the paper and paperboard. 2. For use in the outer ply of multiwall paper bags for contact with dry food of Type VIII described in table I of paragraph (c) of this section and provided it is used at a level of 0.8 percent by weight of the paper.
Fatty acids derived from animal and vegetable fats and oils and salts of such acids, single or mixed, as follows: Aluminum. Ammonium. Calcium. Magnesium. Potassium. Sodium. Zinc.	
Ferric chloride.	
Ferrous ammonium sulfate.	
Fish oil, hydrogenated.	
Fish oil, hydrogenated, potassium salt.	
Furcelleran and salts of furcelleran as described in §§ 172.655 and 172.660 of this chapter.	
Glutaraldehyde (CAS Reg. No. 111–30–8)	For use only as an antimicrobial agent in pigment and filler slurries used in the manufacture of paper and paperboard at levels not to exceed 300 parts per million by weight of the slurry solids.
Glyceryl lactostearate.	
Glyceryl mono-1,2-hydroxystearate.	
Glyceryl monoricinoleate.	
Guar gum modified by treatment with β-diethylamino- ethyl chloride hydrochloride.	For use only as a retention aid and/or drainage aid employed prior to the sheet-forming operation in the manufacture of paper and paperboard.
Guar gum modified by treatment with not more than 25 weight percent of 2,3-epoxypropyltri-methylammonium chloride such that the finished product has a maximum chlorine content of 4.5 percent, a maximum nitrogen content of 3.0 percent, and a minimum viscosity in 1-percent-by-weight aqueous solution of 1,000 centipoises at 77 °F, as determined by RV-series Brookfield viscometer (or equivalent) using a No. 3 spindle at 20 r.p.m.	For use only as a retention aid and/or internal size employed prior to the sheet-forming operation in the manufacture of paper and paperboard, and limited to use at a level: (1) Not to exceed 0.15 percent by weight of the finished dry paper and paperboard fibers intended for use in contact with all types of foods, except (2) not to exceed 0.30 pct. by weight of the finished dried paper and paperboard fibers for use with nonalcoholic and nonfatty food of types identified under Types I, II, IV-B, VI-B, VII-B, and VIII of table I in par. (c) of this section.
N,N,N′,N′,N″,N″-Hexakis (methoxymethyl)-1,3,5-triazine-2,4,6-triamine polymer with stearyl alcohol, α-octadecenyl-omega-hydroxypoly(oxy-1,2-ethanediyl), and alkyl (C20+) alcohols (CAS Reg. No. 130328–24–4).	For use only as a water-repellent applied to the surface of paper and paperboard at levels not to exceed 1 percent by weight of the finished dry paperboard fibers. The finished paper and paperboard will be used in contact with aqueous foods under conditions of use B through G as described in table 2 of paragraph (c) of this section.
Hexamethylenetetramine	For use only as polymerization cross-linking agent for protein, including casein.
Hydroquinone and the monomethyl or monoethyl ethers of hydroquinone.	For use only as an inhibitor for monomers.
Hydroxymethyl-5,5-dimethylhydantoin (CAS Reg. No. 27636–82–4), mixture with 1,3-bis(hydroxymethyl)-5,5-dimethylhydantoin (CAS Reg. No. 6440–58–0).	For use only as a preservative in clay-type fillers at a level not to exceed a combined total of 1,200 milligrams/kilograms hydroxymethyl-5,5-dimethylhydantoin and 1,3-bis(hydroxymethyl)-5,5-dimethylhydantoin in the filler.
Hydroxypropyl guar gum having a minimum viscosity of 5,000 centipoises at 25 °C., as determined by RV-series Brookfield viscometer using a No. 4 spindle at 20 r.p.m. (or other suitable method) and using a test sample prepared by dissolving 5 grams of moisture-free hydroxypropyl guar gum in 495 milliliters of a 70 percent by weight aqueous propylene glycol solution.	For use only as a dry strength and formation aid agent employed prior to the sheet-forming operation in the manufacture of paper and paperboard and used at a level not to exceed 1.5 percent by weight of finished dry paper or paperboard fibers.

List of Substances	Limitations
12-Hydroxystearic acid-polyethylene glycol block copolymers (CAS Reg. No. 70142–34–6) produced by the reaction of polyethylene glycol (minimum molecular weight 200) with 12-hydroxystearic acid.	For use only as a surfactant for dispersions of polyacrylamide retention and drainage aids employed prior to the sheet forming operation in the manufacture of paper and paperboard.
Imidazolium compounds, 2–(C_{17} and C_{17}-unsaturated alkyl)-1–[2–(C_{18} and C_{18}-unsaturated amido)ethyl]-4,5-dihydro-1-methyl, methyl sulfates (CAS Reg. No. 72749–55–4)..	For use only at a level not to exceed 0.5 percent by weight of the dry paper and paperboard.
Isopropyl *m*- and *p*-cresols (thymol derived)	For use only as an antioxidant for fatty based coating adjuvants provided it is used as a level not to exceed 0.005% by weight of coating solids.
Isopropyl peroxydicarbonate	For use only as polymerization catalyst.
Japan wax.	
Lanolin.	
Lauryl peroxide	For use only as polymerization catalyst.
Lauryl sulfate salts:	
Ammonium.	
Magnesium.	
Potassium.	
Sodium.	
Lecithin, hydroxylated.	
Lignin sulfonate and its calcium, potassium, and sodium salts.	
Maleic anhydride, polymer with ethyl acrylate and vinyl acetate, hydrolyzed (CAS Reg. No. 113221–69–5) and/or its ammonium, potassium, and sodium salts.	For use only as a deposit control additive prior to the sheet forming operation to prevent scale buildup in the manufacture of paper and paperboard in contact with food, at a level not to exceed 0.075 percent (as the acid) by weight of the dry paper and paperboard.
Methacrylic acid-acrylic acid copolymer (CAS Reg. No. 25751–21–7).	For use only as a boiler water additive at a level not to exceed 50 parts per million in the boiler water.
N-methyldiallylamine hydrochloride polymer with epichlorohydrin having a nitrogen content of 4.8 to 5.9 percent (Kjeldahl dry basis) such that a 20 percent by weight aqueous solution has a minimum viscosity of 30 centipoises and maximum viscosity of 100 centipoises at 25 °C, as determined by LVF Model Brookfield viscometer using a No. 1 spindle at 60 r.p.m. (or equivalent method).	For use only as a retention aid, flocculating agent, and wet-strength agent employed in the manufacture of paper and paperboard prior to the sheet-forming operation and limited to use at a level not to exceed 1.5 percent by weight of the dry paper and paperboard.
Methyl naphthalene sulfonic acid-formaldehyde condensate, sodium salt.	For use only as an adjuvant to control pulp absorbency and pitch content in the manufacture of paper and paperboard prior to the sheet-forming operation.
N-methyl-*N*-(tall oil acyl) taurine, sodium salt (CAS Reg. No. 61791–41–1).	For use only to control scale formation in the manufacture of paper and paperboard prior to the sheetforming operation at a level not to exceed 0.015 percent by weight of the dry paper and paperboard.
Mineral oil, white.	
Mono-, di-, tri-(1-methyl-1-phenylethyl)-phenol, ethoxylated, sulfated, ammonium salt with an average of 12 to 16 moles of ethylene oxide (CAS Reg. No. 68130–71–2).	For use only as an emulsifier for rosin based sizing at a level not to exceed 0.03 percent by weight of the finished dry paper and paperboard.
Monoglyceride citrate.	
Monoisopropanolamine (CAS Reg. No. 78–96–6)	For use as a dispersant for titanium dioxide suspensions at a level not to exceed 0.68 percent by weight of titanium dioxide. The finished paper and paperboard will be used in contact with all food types under conditions of use E through G described in table 2 of paragraph (c) of this section.
Mustardseed oil, sulfated, ammonium, potassium, or sodium salt.	
Naphthalene sulfonic acid-formaldehyde condensate, sodium salt.	For use only as an adjuvant to control pulp absorbency and pitch content in the manufacture of paper and paperboard prior to the sheet-forming operation.
Nitrocellulose, 10.9–12.2% nitrogen.	
Oleic acid, sulfated, ammonium, potassium, or sodium salt.	
N-Oleoyl-*N'*-stearoylethylenediamine.	
Oxystearin.	
Paraformaldehyde	For use only as setting agent for protein.
Pentanoic acid, 4,4–bis [(*gamma-omega*-perfluoro-C_{8-20}-alkyl)thio] derivatives, compounds with diethanolamine (CAS Reg. No. 71608-61-2).	For use only as an oil and water repellent and used at a level not to exceed 8 pounds per ton of the finished paper or paperboard when such paper or paperboard is used in contact with nonalcoholic foods under conditions of use E through H described in table 2 of paragraph (c) of this section.
Perfluoroalkyl acrylate copolymer (CAS Reg. No. 92265–81–1) containing 35 to 40 weight percent fluorine, produced by the copolymerization of ethanaminium, *N,N,N*-trimethyl-2-[(2-methyl-1-oxo-2-propenyl)-oxy]-, chloride; 2-propenoic acid, 2-methyl-, oxiranylmethyl ester; 2-propenoic acid, 2-ethoxyethyl ester; and 2-propenoic acid, 2[[(heptadecafluoro-octyl)sulfonyl] methyl amino]ethyl ester.	For use only as an oil and water repellent at a level not to exceed 0.5 percent by weight of the finished paper and paperboard in contact with nonalcoholic foods under conditions of use C, D, E, F, G, or H described in table 2 of paragraph (c) of this section.

List of Substances	Limitations
Perfluoroalkyl substituted phosphate ester acids, ammonium salts formed by the reaction of 2,2-bis[(γ,ω-perfluoro$C_{4\text{-}20}$ alkylthio) methyl]-1,3-propanediol, polyphosphoric acid and ammonium hydroxide.	For use only as an oil and water repellant at a level not to exceed 0.44 percent perfluoroalkyl actives by weight of the finished paper and paperboard in contact with non-alcoholic foods under condition of use H as described in table 2 of paragraph (c) of this section; and in contact with food of types III, IV-A, V, VII-A, and IX described in table 1 of paragraph (c) of this section under conditions of use C through G as described in table 2 of paragraph (c) of this section.
Petrolatum	Complying with § 178.3700 of this chapter.
Petroleum asphalt, steam and vacuum refined to meet the following specifications: Softening point 88° C to 93° C, as determined by ASTM method D36–76, "Standard Test Method for Softening Point of Bitumen (Ring-and-Ball Apparatus);" penetration at 25° C not to exceed 0.3 mm, as determined by ASTM method D5–73 (Reapproved 1978), "Standard Test Method for Penetration of Bituminous Materials," which are incorporated by reference (Copies may be obtained from the American Society for Testing Materials, 100 Barr Harbor Dr., West Conshohocken, Philadelphia, PA 19428-2959, or may be examined at the National Archives and Records Administration (NARA). For information on the availability of this material at NARA, call 202–741–6030, or go to: *http://www.archives.gov/federal_register/code_of_federal_regulations/ibr_locations.html.*); and maximum weight loss not to exceed 3% when distilled to 371° C, nor to exceed an additional 1.1% when further distilled between 371° C and thermal decomposition.	For use only as a component of internal sizing of paper and paperboard intended for use in contact only with raw fruits, raw vegetables, and dry food of the type identified under Type VIII of table 1 in paragraph (c) of this section, and provided that the asphalt is used at a level not to exceed 5% by weight of the finished dry paper and paperboard fibers.
Petroleum wax, synthetic	Complying with § 178.3720 of this chapter.
Phenothiazine	For use only as antioxidant in dry rosin size.
Phenyl acid phosphate	For use only as polymerization catalyst in melamine-formaldehyde modified alkyd coatings and limited to use at a level not to exceed 2% by weight of the coating solids.
Phenyl-β-naphthylamine	For use only as antioxidant in dry rosin size and limited to use at a level not to exceed 0.4% by weight of the dry rosin size.
Phosphoric acid esters and polyesters (and their sodium salts) of triethanolamine formed by the reaction of triethanolamine with polyphosphoric acid to produce a mixture of esters having an average nitrogen content of 1.5 percent and an average phosphorus content of 32 percent (as PO_4).	For use as an adjuvant prior to the sheet forming operation to control pitch and scale formation in the manufacture of paper and paperboard intended for use in contact with food only of the types identified in paragraph (c) of this section, table 1, under Types I, IV, V, VII, VIII, and IX, and used at a level not to exceed 0.075 percent by weight of dry paper or paperboard fibers.
Poly[acrylamide-acrylic acid-*N*-(dimethyl-aminomethyl)acrylamide], produced by reacting 2.40 to 3.12 parts by weight of polyacrylamide with 1.55 parts dimethylamine and 1 part formaldehyde, and containing no more than 0.2 percent monomer as acrylamide.	For use only as a drainage aid and retention aid employed prior to the sheet-forming operation in the manufacture of paper and paperboard for use in contact with fatty foods under conditions of use described in paragraph (c) of this section, table 2, conditions of use E, F, and G.
Poly(2-aminoethyl acrylate nitrate-*co*-2-hydroxypropyl acrylate) produced when one mole of hydroxypropyl acrylate and three moles of acrylic acid are reacted with three moles of ethylenimine and three moles of nitric acid, such that a 35 percent by weight aqueous solution has a minimum viscosity of 150 centipoises at 72 °F., as determined by RVF-series Brookfield viscometer (or equivalent) using a No. 2 spindle at 20 r.p.m.	For use only as a retention and drainage aid employed prior to the sheet-forming operation in the manufacture of paper and paperboard at a level not to exceed 0.2 percent by weight of dry paper or paperboard fiber.
Polyacrolein (1 part) -sodium bisulfite (0.7 part) adduct, containing excess bisulfite (ratio of excess bisulfite to adduct not to exceed 1.5 to 1).	For use only as an agent in modifying starches and starch gums used in the production of paper and paperboard and limited to use at a level not to exceed 0.09 mg/in^2 of the finished paper and paperboard.
Poly[acrylamide-acrylic acid-*N*-(dimethylaminomethyl) acrylamide] (C.A. Registry No. 53800–41–2), produced by reacting 9.6–16.4 parts by weight of polyacrylamide with 1.6 parts dimethylamine and 1 part formaldehyde, and containing no more than 0.2% monomer as acrylamide, such that a 20% aqueous solution has a minimum viscosity of 4,000 cP at 25 °C., as determined by Brookfield viscometer model RVT, using a No. 5 spindle at 20 r/min (or equivalent method).	For use only as a drainage aid, retention aid, or dry-strength agent employed prior to the sheet-forming operation in the manufacture of paper and paperboard at a level not to exceed 0.25 percent by weight of finished dry paper and paperboard fibers, when such paper or paperboard is used in contact with fatty foods under conditions of use described in paragraph (c) of this section, table 2, conditions of use E, F, and G.

List of Substances	Limitations
Polyamide-epichlorohydrin modified resin produced by reacting adipic acid with diethylene triamine to produce a basic polyamide which is modified by reaction with formic acid and formaldehyde and further reacted with epichlorohydrin in the presence of ammonium hydroxide to form a water-soluble cationic resin having a nitrogen content of 13–16 percent (Kjeldahl, dry basis) such that a 35 percent by weight aqueous solution has a minimum viscosity of 75 centipoises at 25 °C, as determined by Brookfield viscometer using a No. 1 spindle at 12 r.p.m.	For use only as a retention aid and flocculant employed prior to the sheet-forming operation in the manufacture of paper and paperboard and used at a level not to exceed 0.2 percent dry resin by weight of finished dry paper or paperboard fibers.
Polyamide-epichlorohydrin water-soluble thermosetting resins [CAS Reg. No. 68583–79–9] prepared by reacting adipic acid with diethylenetriamine to form a basic polyamide and further reacting the polyamide with an epichlorohydrin and dimethylamine mixture such that the finished resins have a nitrogen content of 17.0 to 18.0 percent of a dry basis, and that a 30-percent-by-weight aqueous solution has a minimum viscosity of 350 centipoises at 20 °C, as determined by a Brookfield viscometer using a No. 3 spindle at 30 r.p.m. (or equivalent method).	For use only under the following conditions: 1. As a retention aid employed prior to the sheet-forming operation in the manufacture of paper and paperboard and limited to use at a level not to exceed 0.12 percent by weight of dry paper or paperboard. 2. The finished paper or paperboard will be used in contact with food only of the types identified in paragraph (c) of this section, table 1, under types I and IV-B and under conditions of use described in paragraph (c) of this section, table 2, conditions of use F and G.
Polyamide-epichlorohydrin water-soluble thermosetting resin (CAS Reg. No. 96387–48–3) prepared by reacting *N*-methylbis(3-aminopropyl) amine with oxalic acid and urea to form a basic polyamide and further reacting the polyamide with epichlorohydrin.	For use only as a wet strength agent and/or retention aid employed prior to the sheet-forming operation in the manufacture of paper and paperboard and used at a level not to exceed 1.5 percent by weight of dry paper and paperboard fibers.
Polyamide-epichlorohydrin water-soluble thermosetting resins prepared by reacting adipic acid, isophthalic acid, itaconic acid or dimethyl glutarate with diethylenetriamine to form a basic polyamide and further reacting the polyamide with one of the following: Epichlorohydrin. Epichlorohydrin and ammonia mixture. Epichlorohydrin and sodium hydrosulfite mixture.	For use only in the manufacture of paper and paperboard under conditions such that the resins do not exceed 1.5 percent by weight of the paper or paperboard.
Polyamidoamine-ethyleneimine-epichlorohydrin resin prepared by reacting hexanedioic acid, *N*-(2-aminoethyl)-1,2-ethanediamine, (chloromethyl)oxirane, ethyleneimine (aziridine), and polyethylene glycol, partly neutralized with sulfuric acid (CAS Reg. No. 167678–45–7).	For use only as a retention aid employed prior to the sheet-forming operation in the manufacture of paper and paperboard at a level not to exceed 0.12 percent resin by weight of the finished dry paper or paperboard.
Polyamidol-epichlorohydrin modified resin produced by reacting glutaric acid dimethyl ester with diethylene-triamine to produce a basic polyamide which is modified by reaction with formaldehyde and further reacted with epicholorohydrin to form a water soluble cationic resin having a nitrogen content of 10.9–11.9 percent and a chlorine content of 13.8–14.8 percent, on a dry basis, and a minimum viscosity, in 12.5 percent by weight aqueous solution, of 10 centipoises at 25 °C, as determined by a Brookfield Model LVF viscometer using a No. 1 spindle at 60 r.p.m. (or equivalent method).	For use only as a wet strength agent employed prior to the sheet-forming operation in the manufacture of paper and paperboard, and used at a level not to exceed 2.5 percent by weight of dry paper and paperboard fibers when such paper or paperboard is used in contact with food under conditions of use E through G described in table 2 of paragraph (c) of this section.
Polyamine-epichlorohydrin resin produced by the reaction of epichlorohydrin with monomethylamine to form a prepolymer and further reaction of this prepolymer with *N,N,N′,N′*-tetramethylethylenediamine such that the finished resin having a nitrogen content of 11.6 to 14.8 percent and a chlorine content of 20.8 to 26.4 percent and a minimum viscosity, in 25 percent by weight aqueous solution, of 500 centipoises at 25 °C, as determined by LV-series Brookfield viscometer using a No. 2 spindle at 12 r.p.m. (or by other equivalent method).	For use only as a flocculant, drainage aid, formation aid, retention aid, or strength additive employed prior to the sheet-forming operation in the manufacture of paper and paperboard, and used at a level not to exceed 0.12 percent by weight of dry paper and paperboard fibers.
Polyamine-epichlorohydrin resin produced by the reaction of *N,N*-dimethyl-1,3-propanediamine with epichlorohydrin and further reacted with sulfuric acid, Chemical Abstracts Service Registry Number [27029–41–0], such that the finished resin has a maximum nitrogen content of 14.4 percent (dry basis) and a minimum viscosity in 30 percent by weight aqueous solution (pH 4–6) of 50 centipoises at 25 °C, as determined by Brookfield LVT model viscometer, using a No. 1 spindle at 12 r.p.m. (or equivalent method).	For use only as a clarifier in the treatment of influent water to be used in the manufacture of paper and paperboard, and used at a level not to exceed 20 parts per million of the influent water.

List of Substances	Limitations
Polyamine-epichlorohydrin water-soluble thermosetting resin produced by reacting epichlorohydrin with: (i) polyamines comprising at least 95 percent by weight C_4 to C_6 aliphatic diamines and/or their self-condensation products, and/or (ii) prepolymers produced by reacting 1,2-dichloroethane with the polyamines in (i). The finished resin has a nitrogen content of 5.0 to 9.0 percent, a chlorine content of 18.0 to 35.0 percent on a dry basis, and a minimum viscosity, in a 25 percent by weight aqueous solution, of 50 centipoises at 20 °C (68 °F), as determined by Brookfield HAT model viscometer using a No. 1H spindle at 50 r.p.m. (or equivlent method).	For use only as a wetstrength agent and/or retention aid employed prior to the sheet-forming operation in the manufacture of paper and paperboard, and used at a level not to exceed 1 percent by weight of dry paper and paperboard fibers.
Polyamine-epichlorohydrin water-soluble thermosetting resin produced by reacting epichlorohydrin with: (i) polyamines comprising at least 95 percent by weight C_4 to C_6 aliphatic diamines and/or their self-condensation products and/or (ii) hexamethylenediamine, and/or (iii) bis(hexamethylene) triamine and higher homologues, and/or (iv) prepolymers produced by reacting 1,2-dichloroethane with the polyamines in (i) and/or (ii) and/or (iii). The finished resin has a nitrogen content of 5.0 to 9.0 percent, a chlorine content of 18.0 to 35.0 percent on a dry basis, and a minimum viscosity, in a 25 percent by weight aqueous solution, of 50 centipoises at 20 °C (68 °F), as determined by Brookfield HAT model viscometer using a No. 1H spindle at 50 r.p.m. (or equivalent method).	For use only as a wet-strength agent and/or retention aid employed prior to the sheet-forming operation in the manufacture of paper and paperboard, and used at a level not to exceed 1 percent by weight of dry paper and paperboard fibers.
Polyamine-epichlorohydrin water soluble thermosetting resin prepared by reacting hexamethylenediamine with 1,2-dichloroethane to form a prepolymer and further reacting this prepolymer with epichlorohydrin. This resin is then reacted with nitrilotris (methylene-phosphonic acid), pentasodium salt, such that the finished resin has a nitrogen content of 5.0–5.3 percent; a chlorine content of 29.7–31.3 percent; and a phosphorus content of 2.0–2.2 percent, on a dry basis, and a minimum viscosity, in 25 percent by weight aqueous solution, of 50 centipoises at 25 °C., as determined on a Brookfield HAT model viscometer using a No. 1H spindle at 50 r.p.m. (or equivalent method).	For use only as a wet-strength agent and/or retention aid employed prior to the sheet-forming operation in the manufacture of paper and paperboard, and used at a level not to exceed 1 percent by weight of dry paper and paperboard fibers.
Polyamine resin produced by the reaction of 1,2-dichloroethane with bis(hexamethylene)triamine and higher homologues such that the finished resin has a nitrogen content of 13.0–15.0 percent on a dry basis, and a minimum viscosity in 25-percent-by-weight aqueous solution of 75 centipoises at 25 °C., as determined by Brookfield HAT model viscometer using a No. 1 spindle at 50 r.p.m. (or equivalent method).	For use only as a retention aid and/or flocculent employed prior to the sheet-forming operation in the manufacture of paper and paperboard and used at a level not to exceed 0.1 percent by weight of dry paper or paperboard fibers.
Polyaminoamide-epichlorohydrin modified resin produced by reacting adipic acid with diethylenetriamine to produce a polyamide which is modified by reaction with diethylaminopropylamine and further reacted with dichloroethyl ether to form a polyamide intermediate. This polyamide intermediate is then reacted with epichlorohydrin such that the finished resins have a nitrogen content of 10.9–12.4 percent (Kjeldahl, dry basis) and a minimum viscosity in 40 percent-by-weight aqueous solution of 250 centipoises at 22 °C, as determined by a Brookfield Model LVT viscometer using a No. 2 spindle at 30 r.p.m. (or equivalent method).	For use only as a wet-strength agent and/or retention aid employed prior to the sheet-forming operation in the manufacture of paper and paperboard, and used at a level not to exceed 0.5 percent by weight of the finished dry paper and paperboard.
Polybutene, hydrogenated; complying with the identity prescribed under § 178.3740(b) of this chapter.	For use only as provided in §§ 175.300, 178.3740 and 178.3860 of this chapter.
Poly(diallyldimethylammonium chloride) (CAS Reg. No. 26062–79–3) produced by the polymerization of (diallyldimethylammonium chloride) so that the finished resin has a nitrogen content of 8.66±0.4 percent on a dry weight basis and a minimum viscosity in a 40 percent by weight aqueous solution of 1,000 centipoises at 25 °C (77 °F), determined by LVF Model Brookfield Viscometer using a No. 3 spindle at 30 r.p.m. (or equivalent method). The level of residual monomer is not to exceed 1 percent by weight of the polymer (dry basis).	For use only: 1. As a pigment dispersant and/or retention aid prior to the sheet-forming operation in the manufacture of paper and paperboard, and used at a level not to exceed 10 pounds of active polymer per ton of finished paper and paperboard. 2. As a pigment dispersant in coatings at a level not to exceed 3.5 pounds of active polymer per ton of finished paper and paperboard.

List of Substances	Limitations
Poly (diallyldimethylammonium chloride) (CAS Reg. No. 26062–79–3) produced by the polymerization of diallyldimethylammonium chloride so that the finished resin has a nitrogen content of 8.66±0.4 percent on a dry basis and a minimum viscosity in a 15 weight-percent aqueous solution of 10 centipoises at 25 °C (77 °F), as determined by LVF Model Brookfield viscometer using a No. 1 spindle at 60 r/min (or equivalent method). The level of residual monomer is not to exceed 1 weight-percent of the polymer (dry basis).	For use only as a flocculant employed prior to the sheet-forming operation in the manufacture of paper and paperboard, and used at a level not to exceed 10 mg/L (10 parts per million) of influent water.
Poly(1,2-dimethyl-5-vinylpyridinium methyl sulfate) having a nitrogen content of 5.7 to 7.3 percent and a sulfur content of 11.7 to 13.3 percent by weight on a dry basis and having a minimum viscosity in 30-percent-by-weight aqueous solution of 2,000 centipoises at 25 °C., as determined by LV-series Brookfield viscometer (or equivalent) using a No. 4 spindle at 60 r.p.m.	For use only as an adjuvant employed in the manufacture of paper and paperboard prior to the sheet-forming operation.
Polyester resin produced by reacting dimethylolpropionic acid (CAS Registry No. 4767–03–7) as a comonomer, at no more than 30 percent by weight of total polymer solids in reaction with 2,2-dimethyl-1,3-propanediol, phthalic anhydride and isophthalic acid, such that the polyester resin has a viscosity of 200–600 centipoises at 80 °F as determined by a Brookfield RVT viscometer using a number 3 spindle at 50 rpm (or equivalent method).	For use only as a surface-sizing compound applied after the sheet-forming operation in the manufacture of paper and paperboard and limited to use at levels not to exceed 0.1 percent by weight of finished dry paper or paperboard.
Polyethylene, oxidized; complying with the identity prescribed in § 177.1620(a) of this chapter.	For use only as component of coatings that contact food only of the type identified under Type VII-B of table 1 in paragraph (c) of this section, and limited to use at a level not to exceed 50 percent by weight of the coating solids.
Polyethyleneamine mixture produced when 1 mole of ethylene dichloride, 1.05 moles of ammonia, and 2 moles of sodium hydroxide are made to react so that a 10 percent aqueous solution has a minimum viscosity of 40 centipoises at 77 °F, as determined by Brookfield viscometer using a No. 1 spindle at 60 r.p.m.	For use only as a retention aid employed prior to the sheet-forming operation in the manufacture of paper and paperboard.
Polyethylene glycol (200) dilaurate	For use only as an adjuvant employed in the manufacture of paper and paperboard prior to the sheet-forming operation.
Polyethylene glycol (400) dioleate.	
Polyethylene glycol (400) esters of coconut oil fatty acids.	
Polyethylene glycol (600) esters of tall oil fatty acids.	
Polyethylene glycol (400) monolaurate.	
Polyethylene glycol (600) monolaurate.	
Polyethylene glycol (400) monooleate.	
Polyethylene glycol (600) monooleate.	
Polyethylene glycol (400) monostearate.	
Polyethylene glycol (600) monostearate.	
Polyethylene glycol (3,000) monostearate.	
Polyethylenimine, produced by the polymerization of ethylenimine.	For use only as an adjuvant employed prior to sheet formation in paper-making systems operated at a pH of 4.5 or higher, and limited to use at a level not to exceed 5% by weight of finished dry paper or paperboard fibers.
Poly(isobutene)/maleic anhydride adduct, diethanolamine reaction product. The mole ratio of poly(isobutene)/maleic anydride adduct to diethanolamine is 1:1.	For use only as a surfactant for dispersions of polyacrylamide retention and drainage aids employed prior to the sheet formation operation in the manufacture of paper and paperboard.
Polymethacrylic acid, sodium salt, having a viscosity in 30-percent-by-weight aqueous solution of 125–325 centipoises at 25 °C as determined by LV-series Brookfield viscometer (or equivalent) using a No. 2 spindle at 60 r.p.m.	For use only as a coating adjuvant for controlling viscosity when used at a level not to exceed 0.3% by weight of coating solids.
Polymethacrylic acid, sodium salt, having a viscosity in 40-percent-by-weight aqueous solution of 400–700 centipoises at 25 °C, as determined by LV-series Brookfield viscometer (or equivalent) using a No. 2 spindle at 30 r.p.m.	For use only as a coating adjuvant for controlling viscosity when used at a level not to exceed 0.1% by weight of coating solids.

List of Substances	Limitations
Poly[(methylimino)(2-hydroxytrimethylene)hydrochloride] produced by reaction of 1:1 molar ratio of methylamine and epichlorohydrin so that a 31-percent aqueous solution at 25° C has a Stokes viscosity range of 2.5-4.0 as determined by ASTM method D1545–76 (Reapproved; 1981), "Standard Test Method for Viscosity of Transparent Liquids by Bubble Time Method," which is incorporated by reference. Copies may be obtained from the American Society for Testing Materials, 100 Barr Harbor Dr., West Conshohocken, Philadelphia, PA 19428-2959, or may be examined at the National Archives and Records Administration (NARA). For information on the availability of this material at NARA, call 202–741–6030, or go to: *http://www.archives.gov/federal_register/code_of_federal_regulations/ibr_locations.html.*.	For use only as a retention aid employed prior to the sheet-forming operation in such an amount that finished paper and paperboard will contain the additive at a level not in excess of 1 percent by weight of the dry paper and paperboard.
Poly[oxyethylene (dimethyliminio) ethylene (dimethyliminio) ethylene dichloride] produced by reacting equimolar quantities of *N,N,N,N*-tetramethylethylene-diamine and dichlorethyl ether to yield a solution of the solid polymer in distilled water at 25° C with a reduced viscosity of not less than 0.15 deciliter per gram as determined by ASTM method D1243–79, "Standard Test Method for -Dilute Solution Viscosity of Vinyl Chloride Polymers," which is incorporated by reference. Copies may be obtained from the American Society for Testing Materials, 100 Barr Harbor Dr., West Conshohocken, Philadelphia, PA 19428-2959, or may be examined at the National Archives and Records Administration (NARA). For information on the availability of this material at NARA, call 202–741–6030, or go to: *http://www.archives.gov/federal_register/code_of_federal_regulations/ibr_locations.html.*). The following formula is used for determining reduced viscosity:. Reduced viscosity in terms of deciliters per gram=$(t-t_0)/(t-C)$, where: t=Solution efflux time t_o=Water efflux time C=Concentration of solution in terms of grams per deciliter	For use only to improve dry-strength of paper and paperboard and as a retention and drainage aid employed prior to the sheet-forming operation in the manufacture of paper and paperboard and limited to use at a level not to exceed 0.1 percent by weight of the finished dry paper and paperboard fibers.
Polypropylene glycol (minimum molecular weight 1,000).	
Potassium persulfate.	
2-Propenoic acid, telomer with sodium 2-methyl-2-[(1-oxo-2-propenyl)amino]-1-propane sulfonate and sodium phosphinate (CAS Reg. No. 110224–99–2).	For use only as a deposit control additive employed prior to the sheet forming operation in the manufacture of paper and paperboard and at a level not to exceed 0.15 percent by weight of the dry paper and paperboard.
Propylene glycol alginate.	
Protein hydrolysate from animal hides or soybean protein condensed with oleic and/or stearic acid.	
Rapeseed oil, sulfated ammonium, potassium, or sodium salt.	
Ricebran oil, sulfated ammonium, potassium, or sodium salt.	
Rosin and rosin derivatives	As provided in § 178.3870 of this chapter.
Siloxanes (silicones), dimethyl, isopropyl methyl, methyl 1-methyl-C_{9-49}-alkyl (CAS Reg. No. 144635–08–5).	For use only as a component of polyolefin coatings with § 177.1520 of this chapter at a level not to exceed 3 percent by weight. The finished coating will be used only for paper and paperboard that contact food of types VI-A and VI-B of table 1 in paragraph (c) of this section, and under conditions of use C, D, and E, as described in table 2 in paragraph (c) of this section, with a maximum hot fill temperature of 200 °F (94 °C).
Silver chloride-coated titanium dioxide	For use only as a preservative in polymer latex emulsions at a level not to exceed 2.2 parts per million (based on silver ion concentration) in the dry coating.
Sodium carboxymethyl guar gum having a minimum viscosity of 2,700 centipoises at 25 °C after 24 hours as determined by RV-series Brookfield viscometer (or equivalent) using a No. 4 spindle at 20 r.p.m. and using a test sample prepared by dissolving 8 grams of sodium carboxymethyl guar gum in 392 milliliters of 0.2-percent-by-weight aqueous sodium *o*-phenylphenate solution.	For use only as a dry-strength and formation-aid agent employed prior to the sheet-forming operation in the manufacture of paper and paperboard and used at a level not to exceed 1% by weight of finished dry paper or paperboard fibers.
Sodium dioctyl sulfosuccinate.	
Sodium formaldehyde sulfoxylate	For use only as polymerization catalyst.
Sodium hypochlorite.	
Sodium *N*-methyl-*N*-oleyltaurate	For use only as an adjuvant to control pulp absorbency and pitch content in the manufacture of paper and paperboard prior to the sheet-forming operation.

List of Substances	Limitations
Sodium nitrite	For use only: 1. At levels not to exceed 0.2% by weight of lubricants or release agents applied at levels not to exceed 1 lb. per ton of finished paper or paperboard. 2. As an anticorrosion agent at levels not to exceed 0.2% by weight of wax emulsions used as internal sizing in the manufacture of paper and paperboard prior to the sheet-forming operation.
Sodium persulfate.	
Sodium polyacrylate	For use only: 1. As a thickening agent for natural rubber latex coatings, provided it is used at a level not to exceed 2 percent by weight of coating solids. 2. As a pigment dispersant in coatings at a level not to exceed 0.25 percent by weight of pigment.
Sodium poly(isopropenylphosphonate) (CAS Reg. No. 118632–18–1).	For use only in paper mill boilers.
Sodium zinc potassium polyphosphate (CAS Reg. No. 65997–17–3).	For use only as a pigment dispersant in coatings at a level not to exceed 1 percent by weight of pigment.
Sperm oil, sulfated, ammonium, potassium, or sodium salt.	
Stannous oleate.	
Stearyl-2-lactylic acid and its calcium salt.	
Styrene-butadiene copolymers produced by copolymerizing styrene-butadiene with one or more of the monomers: acrylamide, acrylic acid, fumaric acid, 2-hydroxyethyl acrylate, itaconic acid, methacrylic acid, and *N*-methylolacrylamide (CAS Reg. No. 53504–31–7). The finished copolymers shall contain not more than 10 weight percent of total polymer units derived from acrylic acid, fumaric acid, 2-hydroxyethyl acrylate, itaconic acid, and methacrylic acid, and shall contain not more than 3 weight percent of total polymer units derived from *N*-methylolacrylamide, and shall contain not more than 2 weight percent of polymer units derived from acrylamide..	
Styrene-maleic anhydride copolymer, amidated, ammonium sodium salt; having, in a 25 percent by weight aqueous solution at pH 8.8, a minimum viscosity of 600 centipoises at 25 °C as determined by Brookfield model LVT viscometer using a No. 3 spindle at 60 r.p.m. (or equivalent method).	For use only as a surface size at a level not to exceed 1 percent by weight of paper or paperboard substrate.
Styrene-maleic anhydride copolymer, sodium salt (minimum molecular weight 30,000).	For use only: 1. As a coating thickening agent at a level not to exceed 1% by weight of coating solids. 2. As surface size at a level not to exceed 1% by weight of paper or paperboard substrate.
Styrene-methacrylic acid copolymer, potassium salt (minimum molecular weight 30,000).	For use only as a coating thickening agent at a level not to exceed 1% by weight of coating solids.
Synthetic wax polymer prepared by the catalytic polymerization of alpha olefins such that the polymer has a maximum iodine number of 18 and a minimum number average molecular weight of 2,400.	For use only as a component of petroleum wax and/or synthetic petroleum wax complying with § 178.3710 or § 178.3720 of this chapter at levels not to exceed 5 percent by weight of the wax: 1. Under conditions of use F and G described in table 2 of paragraph (c) of this section for all foods. 2. Under conditions of use E described in table 2 of paragraph (c) of this section for food Types I, II, IV-B, VI, VII-B and VIII as described in table 1 of paragraph (c) of this section.
Tallow.	
Tallow alcohol.	
Tallow alcohol, hydrogenated.	
Tallow fatty acid, hydrogenated.	
Tallow hydrogenated.	
Tallow sulfated, ammonium, potassium, or sodium salt.	
Tetraethylenepentamine	For use only as a modifier for amino resins.
1,4,4a,9a-Tetrahydro-9, 10-anthracenedione (CAS Reg. No. 56136–14–2).	For use only as a catalyst in the alkaline pulping of lignocellulosic materials at levels not to exceed 0.1 percent by weight of the raw lignocellulosic materials.
N,N,N′, N′-Tetramethylethylenediamine polymer with bis-(2-chloroethyl) ether, first reacted with not more than 5 percent by weight 1-chloro-2,3-epoxypropane and then reacted with not more than 5 percent by weight poly (acrylic acid) such that a 50 percent by weight aqueous solution of the product has a nitrogen content of 4.7–4.9 percent and viscosity of 350–700 centipoises at 25 °C as determined by LV series Brookfield viscometer using a No. 2 spindle at 60 r.p.m. (or by other equivalent method).	For use only as a flocculent, drainage aid or retention aid employed prior to the sheet forming operation in the manufacture of paper and paperboard and limited to use at a level not to exceed 0.2 percent by weight of the finished dry paper and paperboard fibers.

List of Substances	Limitations
Tetrasodium *N*- (1,2-dicarboxyethyl) - *N* - octadecylsulfo-succinamate.	For use only as an emulsifier in aqueous dispersions of rosin sizes complying with § 178.3870(a)(4) of this chapter and limited to use prior to the sheet-forming operation in the manufacture of paper and paperboard at a level not to exceed 0.02 pct by weight of finished paper and paperboard.
Triethanolamine	For use only to adjust pH during the manufacture of amino resins permitted for use as components of paper and paperboard.
Triethylene glycol adipic acid monoester produced by reacting equimolar quantities of triethylene glycol and adipic acid.	For use only as a curl-control agent at a level not to exceed 2% by weight of coated or uncoated paper and paperboard.
Triethylenetetramine	For use only as a modifier for amino resins.
1,3,5-Triethylhexahydro-1,3,5-triazine (CAS Registry No. 7779–27–3).	For use only as an antimicrobial agent for coating, binder, pigment, filler, sizing, and similar formulations added prior to the heat drying step in the manufacture of paper and paperboard and limited to use at a level between 0.05 and 0.15 percent by weight of the formulation.
Undecafluorocyclohexanemethanol ester mixture of dihydrogen phosphate, compound with 2,2′ iminodiethanol (1:1); hydrogen phosphate, compound with 2,2′-iminodiethanol (1:1); and P,P′-dihydrogen pyrophosphate, compound with 2,2′-iminodiethanol (1:2); where the ester mixture has a fluorine content of 48.3 pct to 53.1 pct as determined on a solids basis.	For use only as an oil repellent at a level not to exceed 0.087 lb (0.046 lb of fluorine) per 1,000 ft^2 of treated paper or paperboard, as determined by analysis for total fluorine in the treated paper or paperboard without correction for any fluorine which might be present in the untreated paper or paperboard, when such paper or paperboard is used in contact with food only of the types identified in paragraph (c) of this section, table 1, under Types IVA, V, VIIA, VIII, and IX, and under the conditions of use B through G described in table 2 of paragraph (c) of this section.
Viscose rayon fibers.	
Wax, petroleum	Complying with § 178.3710 of this chapter.
Xanthan gum, conforming to the identity and specifications prescribed in § 172.695 of this chapter, except that the residual isopropyl alcohol shall not exceed 6,000 parts per million.	For use only at a maximum level of 0.125 percent by weight of finished paper as a suspension aid or stabilizer for aqueous pigment slurries employed in the manufacture of paper and paperboard.
Xylene sulfonic acid-formaldehyde condensate, sodium salt	For use only as an adjuvant to control pulp absorbency and pitch content in the manufacture of paper and paperboard prior to the sheet-forming operation.
Zeolite Na-A (CAS Reg. No. 68989–22–0)	For use as a pigment extender at levels not to exceed 5.4 percent by weight of the finished paper and paperboard.
Zinc formaldehyde sulfoxylate	For use only as polymerization catalyst.
Zinc octoate.	
Zirconium oxide	For use only as a component of waterproof coatings where the zirconium oxide is present at a level not to exceed 1 percent by weight of the dry paper or paperboard fiber and where the zirconium oxide is produced by hydrolysis of zirconium acetate.

(b) Substances identified in paragraphs (b) (1) and (2) of this section may be used as components of the food-contact surface of paper and paperboard, provided that the food-contact surface of the paper or paperboard complies with the extractives limitations prescribed in paragraph (c) of this section.

(1) Substances identified in §175.300(b)(3) of this chapter with the exception of those identified in paragraphs (b)(3) (v), (xv), (xx), (xxvi), (xxxi), and (xxxii) of that section and paragraph (a) of this section.

(2) Substances identified in this paragraph (b)(2) follow:

List of substances	Limitations
Acrylamide copolymerized with ethyl acrylate and/or stryene and/or methacrylic acid, subsequently reacted with formaldehyde and butyl alcohol.	
Acrylamide copolymerized with ethylene and vinyl chloride in such a manner that the finished copolymers have a minimum weight average molecular weight of 30,000 and contain not more than 3.5 weight percent of total polymer units derived from acrylamide, and in such a manner that the acrylamide portion may or may not be subsequently partially hydrolyzed.	For use only as coatings or components of coatings.
2-Acrylamido-2-methyl-propanesulfonic acid, homopolymer, sodium salt (CAS Reg. No. 35641–59–9).	For use only in coatings at a level not to exceed 0.01 mg/in^2
Acrylic and modified acrylic polymers	Complying with § 177.1010 of this chapter.

List of substances	Limitations
Acrylic copolymers produced by copolymerizing 2 or more of the acrylate monomers butyl acrylate, ethyl acrylate, ethyl methacrylate, methyl acrylate, methyl methacrylate, and *n*-propyl methacrylate, or produced by copolymerizing one or more of such acrylate monomers together with one or more of the monomers acrylic acid, acrylonitrile, butadiene, 2-ethyl-hexyl acrylate, fumaric acid, glycidyl methacrylate, *n*-hexyl-methacrylate, itaconic acid, methacrylic acid, styrene, vinyl acetate, vinyl chloride, and vinylidene chloride. The finished copolymers shall contain at least 50 weight percent of polymer units derived from one or more of the monomers butyl acrylate, ethyl acrylate, ethyl methacrylate, methyl acrylate, methyl methacrylate, and *n*-propyl methacrylate; and shall contain not more than 5 weight percent of total polymer units derived from acrylic acid, fumaric acid, glycidyl methacrylate, *n*-hexyl methacrylate, itaconic acid, and methacrylic acid. The provision limiting the finished acrylic copolymers to not more than 5 units derived from acrylic acid, fumaric acid, glycidyl methacrylate, *n*-hexyl methacrylate, itaconic acid, and methacrylic acid is not applicable to finished acrylic copolymers used as coating adjuvants at a level not exceeding 2 weight percent of total coating solids.	
Alkyl mono- and disulfonic acids, sodium salts (produced from *n*-alkanes in the range of C_{10}-C_{18} with not less than 50 percent C_{14}-C_{16})..	For use only: 1. As emulsifiers for vinylidene chloride copolymer coatings and limited to use at levels not to exceed 2 percent by weight of the coating solids. 2. As emulsifiers for vinylidene chloride copolymer or homopolymer coatings at levels not to exceed a total of 2.6 percent by weight of coating solids. The finished polymer contacts food only of types identified in paragraph (c) of this section, table 1, under Types I, II, III, IV, V, VIA, VIB, VII, VIII, and IX and under conditions of use E, F, and G described in table 2 of paragraph (c) of this section.
2-Bromo-4′-hydroxyacetophenone	For use only as a preservative for coating formulations, binders, pigment slurries, and sizing solutions at a level not to exceed 0.006 percent by weight of the coating, solution, slurry or emulsion.
Butanedioic acid, sulfo-1,4-di-(C_9-C_{11} alkyl) ester, ammonium salt (also known as butanedioic acid, sulfo-1,4-diisodecyl ester, ammonium salt [CAS Reg. No. 144093–88–9])..	For use as a surface active agent in package coating inks at levels not to exceed 3 percent by weight of the coating ink.
Butylbenzyl phthalate	Complying with § 178.3740 of this chapter.
Butyl oleate, sulfated, ammonium, potassium, or sodium salt.	
Butyraldehyde.	
Captan (*N*-trichloromethylmercapto-4-cyclohexene-1, 2-dicarboximide).	For use only as a mold- and mildew-proofing agent in coatings intended for use in contact with food only of the types identified in paragraph (c) of this section, table 1, under Type I, II, VI-B, and VIII.
Castor Oil, polyoxyethylated (42 moles ethylene oxide)	For use only as an emulsifier in nitrocellulose coatings for paper and paperboard intended for use in contact with food only of the types identified in paragraph (c) of this section, table 1, under Types IV A, V, VII A, VIII, and IX; and limited to use at a level not to exceed 8 percent by weight of the coating solids.
1-(3-Chloroallyl)-3,5,7-triaza-1- azoniaadamantane chloride (CAS Reg. No. 4080–31–3).	For use only: 1. As a preservative at a level of 0.3 weight percent in latexes used as pigment binders in paper and paperboard intended for use in contact with nonacidic, nonalcoholic food and under the conditions of use described in paragraph (c) of this section, table 2, conditions of use E, F, and G. 2. As a preservative at a level not to exceed 0.07 weight percent in latexes and 0.05 weight percent in pigment slurries used as components of coatings for paper and paperboard intended for use in contact with food.

List of substances	Limitations
5-Chloro-2-methyl-4-isothiazolin-3-one (CAS Reg. No. 26172–55–4) and 2-methyl-4-isothiazolin-3-one (CAS Reg. No. 2682–20–4) mixture at a ratio of 3 parts to 1 part, manufactured from methyl-3-mercaptopropionate (CAS Reg. No. 2935–90–2). The mixture may contain magnesium nitrate (CAS Reg. No. 10377–60–3) at a concentration equivalent to the isothiazolone active ingredients (weight/weight).	For use only: 1. As an antimicrobial agent for polymer latex emulsions in paper coatings at a level not to exceed 50 parts per million (based on isothiazolone active ingredients) in the coating formulation. 2. As an antimicrobial agent for finished coating formulations and for additives used in the manufacture of paper and paperboard including fillers, binders, pigment slurries, and sizing solutions at a level not to exceed 25 parts per million (based on isothiazolone active ingredients) in the coating formulations and additives.
Copper 8-quinolinolate	For use only as preservative for coating formulations.
Cyclized rubber produced when natural pale crepe rubber dissolved in phenol is catalytically cyclized so that the finished cyclized rubber has a melting point of 145 °C to 155 °C as determined by ASTM method E28–67 (Reapproved 1982), "Standard Test Method for Softening Point by Ring-and-Ball Apparatus," which is incorporated by reference (Copies may be obtained from the American Society for Testing Materials, 100 Barr Harbor Dr., West Conshohocken, Philadelphia, PA 19428-2959, or may be examined at the National Archives and Records Administration (NARA). For information on the availability of this material at NARA, call 202–741–6030, or go to: *http://www.archives.gov/federal_register/code_of_federal_regulations/ibr_locations.html.*), and contains no more than 4000 ppm of residual-free phenol as determined by a gas liquid chromatographic procedure titled "Determination of Free Phenol in Cyclized Rubber Resin," which is incorporated by reference. Copies are available from the Center for Food Safety and Applied Nutrition (HFS–200), Food and Drug Administration, 5100 Paint Branch Pkwy., College Park, MD 20740, or available for inspection at the National Archives and Records Administration (NARA). For information on the availability of this material at NARA, call 202–741–6030, or go to: *http://www.archives.gov/federal_register/code_of_federal_regulations/ibr_locations.html.*.	For use only in coatings for paper and paperboard intended for use in contact with food only of the types identified in paragraph (c) of this section, table 1, under Types VIII and IX.
1,2-Dibromo-2,4-dicyanobutane (CAS Reg. No. 35691–65–7)	For use only as a preservative at levels not more than 0.05 weight percent and not less than 0.01 weight percent: in latexes used as pigment binders in coatings; in pigment slurries used in coatings; and/or in coatings themselves. The total level of the preservative in the finished coating shall not exceed 0.04 weight percent of the finished coating solids.
Dibutyl phthalate.	
Dibutyl sebacate.	
Di(C_7,C_9-alkyl) adipate	Complying with § 178.3740 of this chapter.
Dicyclohexyl phthalate.	
Diethylene glycol dibenzoate (CAS Reg. No. 120–55–8)	For use only as a plasticizer for polyvinyl acetate coatings at a level not to exceed 5 percent by weight of the coating solids under conditions described in paragraph (c) of this section, table 2, conditions of use E, F, and G.
Diethylene glycol ester of the adduct of terpene and maleic anhydride.	
Dihydroxy dichlorodiphenyl methane	For use only as preservative for coating formulations.
Dimethylpolysiloxane, 100 centistokes viscosity.	
Dimethylpolysiloxane-beta-phenylethyl methyl polysiloxane copolymer (2:1), 200 to 400 centistokes viscosity.	
N,N'-Diphenyl-*p*-phenylenediamine	For use only as polymerization inhibitor in 2-sulfoethyl methacrylate, sodium salt.
Dipropylene glycol dibenzoate (CAS Reg. No. 27138–31–4)	1. For use only as a plasticizer for polyvinyl acetate coatings at a level not to exceed 5 percent by weight of the coating solids under conditions described in paragraph (c) of this section, table 2, condition of use E. 2. For use only as a plasticizer for polyvinyl acetate coatings at a level not to exceed 10 percent by weight of the coating solids under conditions described in paragraph (c) of this section, table 2, conditions of use F and G.
Disodium *N*-octadecylsulfosuccinamate	For use only as an emulsifier in resin latex coatings and limited to use at a level not to exceed 0.05% by weight of the coating solids.
EDTA (ethylenediaminetetraacetic acid) and its sodium and/or calcium salts.	

List of substances	Limitations
Ethanedial, polymer with tetrahydro-4-hydroxy-5-methyl-2(1H)pyrimidinone, propoxylated (CAS Reg. No. 118299-90-4).	For use only as an insolubilizer for starch-based coatings and limited to use at a level not to exceed 5.0 percent by weight of the coating.
Ethylene-acrylic acid copolymers produced by the copolymerization of ethylene and acrylic acid and/or their partial ammonium salts. The finished copolymer shall contain no more than 25 weight percent of polymer units derived from acrylic acid and no more than 0.35 weight percent of residual monomeric acrylic acid, and have a melt index not to exceed 350 as determined by ASTM method D1238–82, "Standard Test Method for Flow Rates of Thermoplastics by Extrusion Plastometer," which is incorporated by reference. Copies may be obtained from the American Society for Testing Materials, 100 Barr Harbor Dr., West Conshohocken, Philadelphia, PA 19428-2959, or may be examined at the National Archives and Records Administration (NARA). For information on the availability of this material at NARA, call 202–741–6030, or go to: *http://www.archives.gov/federal_register/code_of_federal_regulations/ibr_locations.html.*.	
Formaldehyde	For use only as preservative for coating formulations.
Glyoxal	For use only as an insolubilizing agent in starch- and protein-based coatings that contact nonalcoholic foods, and limited to use at a level not to exceed 6 percent by weight of the starch or protein fraction of the coating solids.
Glyceryl monobutyl ricinoleate.	
Hydroxymethyl derivatives (mixture of mono and poly) of [N-(1, 1-dimethyl-3-oxobutyl) acrylamide] produced by reacting 1 mole of the [N-(1,1-dimethyl-3-oxobutyl) acrylamide] with 3 moles of formaldehyde such that the finished product has a maximum nitrogen content of 6.2 percent and a maximum hydroxyl content of 15 percent by weight on a dry basis.	For use only as a comonomer in polyvinyl acetate latex coatings and limited to use at a level not to exceed 1 percent by weight of dry polymer solids.
Isobutyl oleate, sulfated, ammonium, potassium, or sodium salt.	
Maleic anhydride adduct of butadiene-styrene copolymer.	
α-Methylstyrene-vinyltoluene copolymer resins (molar ratio 1α-methylstyrene to 3 vinyltoluene).	
Modified kaolin clay (CAS Reg. No. 1344–00–9) is produced by the reaction of sodium silicate (CAS Reg. No. 1344–09–8) and kaolinite clay (CAS Reg. No. 1332–58–7) under hydrothermal conditions. The reaction product has a molecular weight between 246 and 365 and consists of 46 to 55 percent silicon dioxide (SiO_2), 28 to 42 percent aluminum oxide ($A1_2O_3$), and 2 to 7 percent of sodium oxide (Na_2O). The reaction product will not consist of more than 70 percent modified kaolin clay.	For use only as a component of coatings in paper and paperboard products at a level not to exceed 9 percent by weight of the coating intended for use in contact with food of Types I through IX described in table 1 of paragraph (c) of this section under conditions of use C through H described in table 2 of paragraph (c) of this section.
Naphthalene sulfonic acid-formaldehyde condensate, sodium salt.	
Oleyl alcohol.	
Oxazolidinylethylmethacrylate (CAS Registry No. 46236–15–1) copolymer with ethyl acrylate and methyl methacrylate, and containing not more than 6 percent by weight of oxazolidinylethylmethacrylate. Maximum nitrogen content shall be 0.5 percent and number average molecular weight of that portion of the copolymer soluble in tetrahydrofuran shall be not less than 50,000.	For use only as a binder for pigment coatings as a binder level not to exceed 4.0 percent by weight of dry paper or paperboard.
Pentaerythritol tetrastearate.	

List of substances	Limitations
Petroleum alicyclic hydrocarbon resins, or the hydrogenated product thereof, meeting the following specifications: Softening point 97 °C minimum, as determined by ASTM method E28–67 (Reapproved 1982), "Standard Test Method for Softening Point by Ring and Ball Apparatus;" aniline point 120 °C minimum, as determined by ASTM method D611–82, "Standard Test Methods for Aniline Point and Mixed Aniline Point of Petroleum Products and Hydrocarbon Solvents," which are incorporated by reference (Copies may be obtained from the American Society for Testing Materials, 100 Barr Harbor Dr., West Conshohocken, Philadelphia, PA 19428-2959, or may be examined at the National Archives and Records Administration (NARA). For information on the availability of this material at NARA, call 202–741–6030, or go to: *http://www.archives.gov/federal_register/code_of_federal_regulations/ibr_locations.html.*). Specific gravity 0.96–0.99 (20 °C/20 °C). Such petroleum hydrocarbon resins are produced by the catalytic polymerization of dienes and olefins from low-boiling distillates of cracked petroleum stocks that contain no material boiling over 200 °C and that meet the ultraviolet absorbance limits prescribed in § 172.880(b) of this chapter when subjected to the analytical procedure described in § 172.886(b) of this chapter, modified as follows: Treat the product as in the first paragraph under "Procedure" in § 172.250(b)(3) of this chapter. Then proceed with § 172.886(b) of this chapter, starting with the paragraph commencing with "Promptly complete transfer of the sample * * *".	For use only as modifiers in waxpolymer blend coatings for corrugated paperboard intended for use in bulk packaging or raw fruits, raw vegetables, iced meat, iced fish, and iced poultry; and limited to use at a level not to exceed 30 weight-percent of the coating solids.
Polyester resin formed by the reaction of the methyl ester of rosin, phthalic anhydride, maleic anhydride and ethylene glycol, such that the polyester resin has an acid number of 4 to 11, a drop-softening point of 70 °C–92 °C., and a color of K or paler.	
Polyester resin produced by reacting the acid groups in montan wax with ethylene glycol.	
Polyethylene, oxidized	Complying with § 177.1620 of this chapter.
Polyethylene reacted with maleic anhydride such that the modified polyethylene has a saponification number not in excess of 6 after Soxhlet extraction for 24 hours with anhydrous ethyl alcohol.	
Polyoxyethylated (40 moles) tallow alcohol sulfate, sodium salt	Not to exceed 300 p.p.m. in finished coated paper or paperboard.
Polyoxypropylene-polyoxyethylene block polymers (minimum molecular weight 6,800).	
Polyvinyl acetate.	
Polyvinyl alcohol (minimum viscosity of 4% aqueous solution at 20 °C. of 4 centipoises).	
Polyvinyl butyral.	
Polyvinyl formal.	
Polyvinylidene chloride.	
Polyvinyl pyrrolidone.	
Polyvinyl stearate.	
Propylene glycol mono- and diesters of fats and fatty acids.	
Siloxanes and silicones; platinum-catalyzed reaction product of vinyl-containing dimethyl polysiloxane (CAS Reg. Nos. 68083–19–2 and 68083–18–1) with methyl hydrogen polysiloxane (CAS Reg. No. 63148–57–2) or dimethyl (methyl hydrogen) polysiloxane (CAS Reg. No. 68037–59–2). Diallyl maleate (CAS Reg No. 999–21–3), dimethyl maleate (CAS Reg. No. 624–48–6), 1-ethynyl-1-cyclohexanol (CAS Reg. No. 78–27–3) and vinyl acetate (CAS Reg. No. 108–05–4) may be used as optional polymerization inhibitors.	For use only as a surface coating. Platinum content not to exceed 200 parts per million. 1. In coatings for paper and paperboard provided the coating contacts food only of the types identified in paragraph (c) of this section, table 1, under Types I, II, VI, and VII-B when used under conditions of use E, F, and G described in table 2 of paragraph (c) of this section. 2. In coatings for paper and paperboard provided the coating contacts food only of the types identified in paragraph (c) of this section, table 1, under Types III, IV, V, VII-A, VIII, and IX when used under conditions of use A through H described in table 2 of paragraph (c) of this section.

List of substances	Limitations
Siloxanes and silicones; platinum-catalyzed reaction product of vinyl-containing dimethylpolysiloxane (CAS Reg. Nos. 68083–19–2 and 68083–18–1), with methyl hydrogen polysiloxane (CAS Reg. No. 63148–57–2). Dimethyl maleate (CAS Reg. No. 624–48–6), vinyl acetate (CAS Reg. No. 108–05–4), dibutyl maleate (CAS Reg. No. 105–76–0) and diallyl maleate (CAS Reg. No. 999–21–3) may be used as optional polymerization inhibitors. The polymer may also contain C_{16}-C_{18} olefins (CAS Reg. No. 68855–60–7) as a control release agent.	Platinum content not to exceed 100 parts per million. For use only as a release coating for pressure sensitive adhesives.
Sodium decylbenzenesulfonate.	
Sodium dihexyl sulfosuccinate.	
Sodium *n*-dodecylpolyethoxy (50 moles) sulfate-sodium isododecylphenoxypolyethoxy (40 moles) sulfate mixtures.	For use only as an emulsifier in coatings that contact food only of the types identified in paragraph (c) of this section, table 1, under Types IV-A, V, VII, VIII, and IX; and limited to use at levels not to exceed 0.75 percent by weight of the coating solids.
Sodium 2-ethylhexyl sulfate.	
Sodium oleoyl isopropanolamide sulfosuccinate.	
Sodium pentachlorophenate	For use only as preservative for coating formulations.
Sodium *o*-phenylphenate	Do.
Sodium vinyl sulfonate polymerized.	
Sodium xylenesulfonate (CAS Reg. No. 1300–72–7)	For use only in paper and paperboard coatings at levels not to exceed 0.01 percent by weight of the finished paper and paperboard.
Styrene copolymers produced by copolymerizing styrene with maleic anhydride and its methyl and butyl (*sec*- or *iso*-) esters. Such copolymers may contain β-nitrostyrene as a polymerization chain terminator.	For use only as a coating or component of coatings and limited to use at a level not to exceed 1% by weight of paper or paperboard substrate.
Styrene polymers made by the polymerization of any combination of styrene or alpha methyl styrene with acrylic acid, methacrylic acid, 2-ethyl hexyl acrylate, methyl methacrylate, and butyl acrylate. The styrene and alpha methyl styrene, individually, may constitute from 0 to 80 weight percent of the polymer. The other monomers, individually, may be from 0 to 40 weight percent of the polymer. The polymer number average molecular weight (M_n) shall be at least 2,000 (as determined by gel permeation chromatography). The acid number of the polymer shall be less than 250. The monomer content shall be less than 0.5 percent.	For use only in contact with foods of Types IV-A, V, and VII in table 1 of paragraph (c) of this section, under use conditions E through G in table 2 of paragraph (c), and with foods of Types VIII and IX without use temperature restriction.
Styrene-acrylic copolymers (CAS Reg. No. 25950–40–7 produced by polymerizing 77 to 83 parts by weight of styrene with 13 to 17 parts of methyl methacrylate, 3 to 4 parts of butyl methacrylate, 0.5 to 2.5 parts of methacrylic acid, and 0.1 to 0.3 part of butyl acrylate such that the finished copolymers have a minimum number average molecular weight greater than 100,000 and a level of residual styrene monomer in the polymer not to exceed 0.1 percent by weight.	For use only as a component of coatings and limited to use at a level not to exceed 20 percent by weight of the coating solids.
Styrene-butadiene copolymers produced by copolymerizing styrene-butadiene with one or more of the monomer: acrylamide, acrylic acid, fumaric acid, 2-hydroxyethyl acrylate, itaconic acid, and methacrylic acid. The finished copolymers shall contain not more than 10 weight percent of total polymer units derived from acrylic acid, fumaric acid, 2-hydroxyethyl acrylate, itaconic acid and methacrylic acid, and shall contain not more than 2 weight percent of polymer units derived from acrylamide.	
Styrene-butadiene copolymers with 2-hydroxyethyl acrylate and acrylic acid containing not more than 15 weight percent acrylic acid and no more than 20 weight percent of a combination of 2-hydroxyethyl acrylate and acrylic acid.	
Styrene-butadiene-vinylidene chloride copolymers containing not more than 40 weight percent of vinylidene chloride in the finished copolymers. The finished copolymers may contain not more than 10 weight percent of total polymer units derived from acrylic acid, fumaric acid, 2-hydroxyethyl acrylate, itaconic acid, and/or methacrylic acid.	For use only as coatings or components of coatings.

List of substances	Limitations
Styrene-dimethylstyrene-α-methylstyrene copolymers produced by polymerizing equimolar ratios of the three comonomers such that the finished copolymers have a minimum average molecular weight of 835 as determined by ASTM method D2503–82, "Standard Test Method for Molecular Weight (Relative Molecular Mass) of Hydrocarbons by Thermoelectric Measurement of Vapor Pressure," which is incorporated by reference. Copies may be obtained from the American Society for Testing Materials, 100 Barr Harbor Dr., West Conshohocken, Philadelphia, PA 19428-2959, or may be examined at the National Archives and Records Administration (NARA). For information on the availability of this material at NARA, call 202–741–6030, or go to: *http://www.archives.gov/federal_register/code_of_federal_regulations/ibr_locations.html.*.	For use only in coatings for paper and paperboard intended for use in contact with nonfatty food and limited to use at a level not to exceed 50% by weight of the coating solids.
Styrene-isobutylene copolymers (weight average molecular weight not less than 6,300).	For use only in coatings for paper and paperboard intended for use in contact under conditions of use D G described in table 2 of paragraph (c) of this section, with food of Types I, II, IV-B, VI-B, VII-B, and VIII described in table 1 of paragraph (c) of this section; and limited to use at a level not to exceed 40 percent by weight of the coating solids.
Styrene-maleic anhydride copolymers	For use only as a coating or component of coatings and limited for use at a level not to exceed 2 percent by weight of paper or paperboard substrate.
Styrene-methacrylic acid copolymers containing no more than 5 weight percent of polymer units derived from methacrylic acid.	
Styrene-vinylidene chloride copolymers containing not more than 40 weight percent of vinylidene chloride in the finished copolymers. The finished copolymers may contain not more than 5 weight percent of total polymer units derived from acrylic acid, fumaric acid, itaconic acid, and/or methacrylic acid.	For use only as coatings or components of coatings.
2-Sulfoethyl methacrylate, sodium salt [Chemical Abstracts Service No. 1804–87–1].	For use only in copolymer coatings under conditions of use E, F, and G described in paragraph (c) of this section, table 2, and limited to use at a level not to exceed 2.0 percent by weight of the dry copolymer coating.
α[*p*-(1,1,3,3-Tetramethylbutyl) phenyl]-*omega*-hydroxypoly (oxyethylene) hydrogen sulfate, sodium salt mixture with α-[*p*-(1,1,3,3-tetramethylbutyl)-phenyl]-*omega*-hydroxypoly (oxyethylene) with both substances having a poly(oxyethylene) content averaging 3 moles.	For use only as a surface-active agent at levels not to exceed 3 percent by weight of vinyl acetate polymer with ethylene and *N*-(hydroxymethyl) acrylamide intended for use in coatings for paper and paperboard intended for use in contact with foods: 1. Of the types identified in paragraph (c) of this section, table 1, under Types I, II, III, IV, VI-B, and VII, and under the conditions of use described in paragraph (c) of this section, table 2, conditions of use E, F, and G. 2. Of the types identified in paragraph (c) of this section, table 1, under Types V, VIII and IX and under the conditions of use described in paragraph (c) of this section, table 2, conditions of use C, D, E, F, and G.
Tetrasodium *N*-(1,2-dicarboxyethyl)-*N*-octadecylsulfo-succinamate.	For use only as an emulsifier in resin latex coatings, and limited to use at a level not to exceed 0.05% by weight of the coating solids.
Toluenesulfonamide-formaldehyde resins.	

List of substances	Limitations
Vinyl acetate copolymers produced by copolymerizing vinyl acetate with one or more of the monomers acrylamide, acrylic acid, acrylonitrile, bicyclo-[2.2.1]*hept*-2-ene-6-methylacrylate, butyl acrylate, crotonic acid, decyl acrylate, diallyl fumarate, diallyl maleate, diallyl phthalate, dibutyl fumarate, dibutyl itaconate, dibutylmaleate, di(2-ethylhexyl) maleate, divinyl benzene, ethyl acrylate, 2-ethyl-hexyl acrylate, fumaric acid, itaconic acid, maleic acid, methacrylic acid, methyl acrylate, methyl methacrylate, mono(2-ethylhexyl) maleate, monoethyl maleate, styrene, vinyl butyrate, vinyl crotonate, vinyl hexoate, vinylidene chloride, vinyl pelargonate, vinyl propionate, vinyl pyrrolidone, vinyl stearate, and vinyl sulfonic acid. The finished copolymers shall contain at least 50 weight percent of polymer units derived from vinyl acetate and shall contain no more than 5 weight percent of total polymer units derived from acrylamide, acrylic acid, crotonic acid, decyl acrylate, dibutyl itaconate, di(2-ethylhexyl) maleate, fumaric acid, itaconic acid, maleic acid, methacrylic acid, mono(2-ethylhexyl) maleate, monoethyl maleate, vinyl butyrate, vinyl hexoate, vinyl pelargonate, vinyl propionate, vinyl stearate, and vinyl sulfonic acid.	
Vinyl acetate polymer with ethylene and *N*-(hydroxymethyl) acrylamide containing not more than 6 weight percent of total polymer units derived from *N*-(hydroxymethyl) acrylamide.	For use only in coatings for paper and paperboard intended for use in contact with foods: 1. Of the types identified in paragraph (c) of this section, table 1, under Types I, II, III, IV, VI B, and VII and under the conditions of use described in paragraph (c) of this section, table 2, conditions of use E, F, and G. 2. Of the types identified in paragraph (c) of this section, table 1, under Types V, VIII, and IX and under the conditions of use described in paragraph (c) of this section, table 2, conditions of use C, D, E, F, and G.
Vinyl chloride copolymers produced by copolymerizing vinyl chloride with one or more of the monomers acrylonitrile; fumaric acid and its methyl, ethyl, propyl, butyl, amyl, hexyl, heptyl, or octyl esters; maleic acid and its methyl, ethyl, propyl, butyl, amyl, hexyl, heptyl, or octyl esters; maleic anhydride; 5-norbornene-2, 3-dicarboxylic acid, mono-*n*-butyl ester; vinyl acetate-and vinylidene chloride. The finished copolymers shall contain at least 50 weight percent of polymer units derived from vinyl chloride: shall contain no more than 5 weight percent of total polymer units derived from fumaric and/or maleic acid and/or their methyl, ethyl, propyl, butyl, amyl, heptyl, or octyl monoesters or from maleic anhydride or from mono-*n*-butyl ester of 5-norbornene-2, 3-dicarboxylic acid (however, in any case the finished copolymers shall contain no more than 4 weight percent of total polymer units derived from mono-*n*-butyl ester of 5-norbornene-2,3-dicarboxylic acid).	
Vinyl chloride-vinyl acetate hydroxyl-modified copolymers.	
Vinyl chloride-vinyl acetate hydroxyl-modified copolymers reacted with trimellitic anhydride.	
Vinylidene chloride copolymers produced by copolymerizing vinylidene chloride with one or more of the monomers acrylamide acrylic acid, acrylonitrile, butyl acrylate, butyl methacrylate ethyl acrylate, ethyl methacrylate, fumaric acid, itaconic acid, methacrylic acid, methyl acrylate, methyl methacrylate, octadecyl methacrylate, propyl acrylate, propyl methacrylate, vinyl chloride and vinyl sulfonic acid. The finished copolymers shall contain at least 50 weight percent of polymer units derived from vinylidene chloride; and shall contain no more than 5 weight percent of total polymer units derived from acrylamide, acrylic acid, fumaric acid, itaconic acid, methacrylic acid, octadecyl methacrylate, and vinyl sulfonic acid.	
Colorants:.	
Aluminum	For use as a colorant only.
Aluminum hydrate	Do.
Aluminum and potassium silicate (mica)	Do.
Aluminum mono-, di-, and tristearate	Do.
Aluminum silicate (China clay)	Do.
Barium sulfate	Do.
Bentonite	Do.
Bentonite, modified with dimethyldioctadecylammonium ion	Do.
Burnt umber	Do.

List of substances	Limitations
Calcium carbonate	Do.
Calcium silicate	Do.
Calcium sulfate	Do.
Carbon black (channel process)	Do.
Cobalt aluminate	Do.
Diatomaceous earth	Do.
Iron oxides	Do.
Magnesium oxide	Do.
Magnesium silicate (talc)	Do.
Phthalocyanine blue (C.I. pigment blue 15, 15:1, 15:2, 15:3, and 15:4; C.I. No. 74160; CAS Reg. No. 147–14–8).	Do.
Raw sienna	Do.
Silica	Do.
Tartrazine lake (certified FD&C Yellow No. 5 only)	Do.
Titanium dioxide	Do.
Titanium dioxide-barium sulfate	Do.
Titanium dioxide-magnesium silicate.	Do.
Zinc carbonate	Do.
Zinc oxide	Do.

(c) The food-contact surface of the paper and paperboard in the finished form in which it is to contact food, when extracted with the solvent or solvents characterizing the type of food, and under conditions of time and temperature characterizing the conditions of its intended use as determined from tables 1 and 2 of this paragraph, shall yield net chloroform-soluble extractives (corrected for wax, petrolatum, mineral oil and zinc extractives as zinc oleate) not to exceed 0.5 milligram per square inch of food-contact surface as determined by the methods described in paragraph (d) of this section.

TABLE 1—TYPES OF RAW AND PROCESSED FOODS

I. Nonacid, aqueous products; may contain salt or sugar or both (pH above 5.0).

II. Acid, aqueous products; may contain salt or sugar or both, and including oil-in-water emulsions of low- or high-fat content.

III. Aqueous, acid or nonacid products containing free oil or fat; may contain salt, and including water-in-oil emulsions of low- or high-fat content.

IV. Dairy products and modifications:
- A. Water-in-oil emulsions, high- or low-fat.
- B. Oil-in-water emulsions, high- or low-fat.

V. Low-moisture fats and oil.

VI. Beverages:
- A. Containing up to 8 percent of alcohol.
- B. Nonalcoholic.
- C. Containing more than 8 percent alcohol.

VII. Bakery products other than those included under Types VIII or IX of this table:
- A. Moist bakery products with surface containing free fat or oil.
- B. Moist bakery products with surface containing no free fat or oil.

VIII. Dry solids with the surface containing no free fat or oil (no end test required).

IX. Dry solids with the surface containing free fat or oil.

TABLE 2—TEST PROCEDURES WITH TIME TEMPERATURE CONDITIONS FOR DETERMINING AMOUNT OF EXTRACTIVES FROM THE FOOD-CONTACT SURFACE OF UNCOATED OR COATED PAPER AND PAPERBOARD, USING SOLVENTS SIMULATING TYPES OF FOODS AND BEVERAGES

Condition of use	Types of food (see table 1)	Food-simulating solvents			
		Water	Heptane [1]	8 percent alcohol	50 percent alcohol
		Time and temperature	Time and temperature	Time and temperature	Time and temperature
A. High temperature heat-sterilized (e.g., over 212 °F).	I, IV-B, VII-B	250 °F, 2 hr	......	......	......
	III, IV-A, VII-A	......do	150 °F, 2 hr	......	......
B. Boiling water sterilized	II, VII-B	212 °F, 30 min.			
	III, VII-A	......do	120 °F, 30 min.	......	......

TABLE 2—TEST PROCEDURES WITH TIME TEMPERATURE CONDITIONS FOR DETERMINING AMOUNT OF EXTRACTIVES FROM THE FOOD-CONTACT SURFACE OF UNCOATED OR COATED PAPER AND PAPERBOARD, USING SOLVENTS SIMULATING TYPES OF FOODS AND BEVERAGES—Continued

Condition of use	Types of food (see table 1)	Food-simulating solvents			
		Water	Heptane [1]	8 percent alcohol	50 percent alcohol
		Time and temperature	Time and temperature	Time and temperature	Time and temperature
C. Hot filled or pasteurized above 150 °F	II, IV-B, VII-B	Fill boiling, cool to 100 °F.			
	III, IV-A, VII-A	......do	120 °F, 15 min.		
	V, IX		......do		
D. Hot filled or pasteurized below 150 °F	II, IV-B, VI-B,				
	VII-B	150 °F, 2 hr			
	III, IV-A, VII-A	......do	100 °F, 30 min.		
	V, IX		......do		
	VI-A			150 °F, 2 hr	
	VI-C				150 °F, 2 hr.
E. Room temperature filled and stored (no thermal treatment in the container).	I, II, IV-B, VI-B, VII-B.	120 °F, 24 hr			
	III, IV-A, VII-A	......do	70 °F, 30 min.		
	V, IX		......do		
	VI-A			120 °F, 24 hr	
	VI-C				120 °F, 24 hr.
F. Refrigerated storage (no thermal treatment in the container).	III, IV-A, VII-A	70 °F, 48 hr	70 °F, 30 min.		
	I, II, IV-B, VI-B, VII-B.	......do			
	VI-A			70 °F, 48 hr	
	VI-C				70 °F, 48 hr.
G. Frozen storage (no thermal treatment in the container).	I, II, IV-B, VII-B	70 °F, 24 hr			
	III, VII-A	......do	70 °F, 30 min.		
H. Frozen or refrigerated storage: Ready-prepared foods intended to be reheated in container at time of use:					
1. Aqueous or oil-in-water emulsion of high- or low-fat.	I, II, IV-B, VII-B	212 °F, 30 min.			
2. Aqueous, high- or low-free oil or fat	III, IV-A, VII-A, IX	......do	120 °F, 30 min.		

[1] Heptane extractability results must be divided by a factor of five in arriving at the extractability for a food product having water-in-oil emulsion or free oil or fat. Heptane food-simulating solvent is not required in the case of wax-polymer blend coatings for corrugated paperboard containers intended for use in bulk packaging of iced meat, iced fish, and iced poultry.

(d) *Analytical methods*—(1) *Selection of extractability conditions*. First ascertain the type of food product (table 1, paragraph (c) of this section) that is being packed commercially in the paper or paperboard and the normal conditions of thermal treatment used in packaging the type of food involved. Using table 2, paragraph (c) of this section, select the food-simulating solvent or solvents and the time-temperature exaggerations of the paper or paperboard use conditions. Having selected the appropriate food-simulating solvent or solvents and the time-temperature exaggeration over normal use, follow the applicable extraction procedure.

(2) *Reagents*—(i) *Water*. All water used in extraction procedures should be freshly demineralized (deionized) distilled water.

(ii) *n-Heptane*. Reagent grade, freshly redistilled before use, using only material boiling at 208 °F.

(iii) *Alcohol*. 8 or 50 percent (by volume), prepared from undenatured 95 percent ethyl alcohol diluted with demineralized (deionized) distilled water.

(iv) *Chloroform*. Reagent grade, freshly redistilled before use, or a grade having an established consistently low blank.

(3) *Selection of test method.* Paper or paperboard ready for use in packaging shall be tested by use of the extraction cell described in "Official Methods of Analysis of the Association of Official Analytical Chemists," 13th Ed. (1980), sections 21.010–21.015, under "Exposing Flexible Barrier Materials for Extraction," which is incorporated by reference (Copies may be obtained from the AOAC INTERNATIONAL, 481 North Frederick Ave., suite 500, Gaithersburg, MD 20877, or may be examined at the National Archives and Records Administration (NARA). For information on the availability of this material at NARA, call 202–741–6030, or go to: *http://www.archives.gov/federal_register/code_of_federal_regulations/ibr_locations.html.*); also described in ASTM method F34–76 (Reapproved 1980), "Standard Test Method for Liquid Extraction of Flexible Barrier Materials," which is incorporated by reference (copies may be obtained from the American Society for Testing Materials, 100 Barr Harbor Dr., West Conshohocken, Philadelphia, PA 19428-2959, or may be examined at the National Archives and Records Administration (NARA). For information on the availability of this material at NARA, call 202–741–6030, or go to: *http://www.archives.gov/federal_register/code_of_federal_regulations/ibr_locations.html.*), except that formed paper and paperboard products may be tested in the container by adapting the in-container methods described in §175.300(e) of this chapter. Formed paper and paperboard products such as containers and lids, that cannot be tested satisfactorily by any of the above methods may be tested in specially designed extraction equipment, usually consisting of clamping devices that fit the closure or container so that the food-contact surface can be tested, or, if flat samples can be cut from the formed paper or paperboard products without destroying the integrity of the food-contact surface, they may be tested by adapting the following "sandwich" method:

(i) *Apparatus.* (*a*) Thermostated (±1.0 °F) water bath, variable between 70 °F and 120 °F water bath cover capable of holding at least one 800-milliliter beaker partially submersed in bath.

(*b*) Analytical balance sensitive to 0.1 milligram with an approximate capacity of 100 grams.

(*c*) Tongs.

(*d*) Hood and hot-plate facilities.

(*e*) Forced draft oven.

For each extraction, the following additional apparatus is necessary:

(*f*) One No. 2 paper clip.

(*g*) One 800-milliliter beaker with watch-glass cover.

(*h*) One 250-milliliter beaker.

(*i*) Five 2½-inch-square aluminum screens (standard aluminum window screening is acceptable).

(*j*) One wire capable of supporting sample stack.

(ii) *Procedure.* (*a*) For each extraction, accurately cut eight 2½-inch-square samples from the formed paper or paperboard product to be tested.

(*b*) Carefully stack the eight 2½-inch-square samples and the five 2½-inch-square aluminum screens in sandwich form such that the food-contact side of each sample is always next to an aluminum screen, as follows: Screen, sample, sample, screen, sample, sample, screen, etc. Clip the sandwich together carefully with a No. 2 paper clip, leaving just enough space at the top to slip a wire through.

(*c*) Place an 800-milliliter beaker containing 100-milliliters of the appropriate food-simulating solvent into the constant temperature bath, cover with a watch glass and condition at the desired temperature.

(*d*) After conditioning, carefully lower the sample sandwich with tongs into the beaker.

(*e*) At the end of the extraction period, using the tongs, carefully lift out the sample sandwich and hang it over the beaker with the wire.

(*f*) After draining, pour the food-simulating solvent solution into a tared 250-milliliter beaker. Rinse the 800-milliliter beaker three times, using a total of not more than 50 milliliters of the required solvent.

(*g*) Determine total nonvolatile extractives in accordance with paragraph (d)(5) of this section.

(4) *Selection of samples.* Quadruplicate samples should be tested, using for each replicate sample the number of

cups, containers, or preformed or converted products nearest to an area of 100 square inches.

(5) *Determination of amount of extractives*—(i) *Total residues.* At the end of the exposure period, remove the test container or test cell from the oven and combine the solvent for each replicate in a clean Pyrex (or equivalent) flask or beaker being sure to rinse the test container or cell with a small quantity of clean solvent. Evaporate the food-simulating solvents to about 100 milliliters in the flask or beaker, and transfer to a clean, tared evaporating dish (platinum or Pyrex), washing the flask three times with small portions of solvent used in the extraction procedure, and evaporate to a few milliliters on a nonsparking, low-temperature hotplate. The last few milliliters should be evaporated in an oven maintained at a temperature of approximately 221 °F. Cool the evaporating dish in a desiccator for 30 minutes and weigh the residue to the nearest 0.1 milligram, (*e*). Calculate the extractives in milligrams per square inch of the container or sheeted paper or paperboard surface.

(*a*) *Water and 8- and 50-percent alcohol.* Milligrams extractives per square inch=(*e*)/(*s*).

(*b*) *Heptane.* Milligrams extractives per square inch=*(e)/(s)(F)*

where:

e=Milligrams extractives per sample tested.
s=Surface area tested, in square inches.
F=Five, the ratio of the amount of extractives removed by heptane under exaggerated time-temperature test conditions compared to the amount extracted by a fat or oil under exaggerated conditions of thermal sterilization and use.
e′=Chloroform-soluble extractives residue.
ee′=Corrected chloroform-soluble extractives residue.
e′ or *ee′* is substituted for *e* in the above equations when necessary.

If when calculated by the equations in paragraph (d)(5)(i) (*a*) and (*b*) of this section, the extractives in milligrams per square inch exceeds the limitations prescribed in paragraph (c) of this section, proceed to paragraph (d)(5)(ii) of this section (method for determining the amount of chloroform-soluble extractives residues).

(ii) *Chloroform-soluble extractives residue.* Add 50 milliliters of chloroform (freshly distilled reagent grade or a grade having an established consistently low blank) to the dried and weighed residue, (*e*), in the evaporating dish obtained in paragraph (d)(5)(i) of this section. Warm carefully, and filter through Whatman No. 41 filter paper (or equivalent) in a Pyrex (or equivalent) funnel, collecting the filtrate in a clean, tared evaporating dish (platinum or Pyrex). Repeat the chloroform extraction, washing the filter paper with this second portion of chloroform. Add this filtrate to the original filtrate and evaporate the total down to a few milliliters on a low-temperature hotplate. The last few milliliters should be evaporated in an oven maintained at approximately 221 °F. Cool the evaporating dish in a desiccator for 30 minutes and weigh to the nearest 0.1 milligram to get the chloroform-soluble extractives residue (′). This ′ is substituted for *e* in the equations in paragraph (d)(5)(i) (*a*) and (*b*) of this section. If the chloroform-soluble extractives in milligrams per square inch still exceeds the limitation prescribed in paragraph (c) of this section, proceed to paragraph (d)(5)(iii) of this section (method for determining corrected chloroform-soluble extractives residue).

(iii) *Corrected chloroform-soluble extractives residue*—(*a*) *Correction for zinc extractives.* Ash the residue in the evaporating dish by heating gently over a Meker-type burner to destroy organic matter and hold at red heat for about 1 minute. Cool in the air for 3 minutes, and place the evaporating dish in the desiccator for 30 minutes and weigh to the nearest 0.1 milligram. Analyze this ash for zinc by standard Association of Official Agricultural Chemists methods or equivalent. Calculate the zinc in the ash as zinc oleate, and subtract from the weight of chloroform-soluble extractives residue (′) to obtain the zinc-corrected chloroform-soluble extractives residue (*e′*). This *e′* is substituted for *e* in the equations in paragraph (d)(5)(i) (*a*) and (*b*) of this section.

(*b*) *Correction for wax, petrolatum, and mineral oil*—(*1*) *Apparatus.* Standard 10 millimeter inside diameter × 60 centimeter chromatographic column (or standard 50-milliliter buret with an inside diameter of 10–11 millimeters) with a stopcock of glass, perfluorocarbon resin, or equivalent material. The column (or buret) may be optionally equipped with an integral coarse, fritted glass disc and the top of the column (or buret) may be optionally fitted with a 100-millimeter solvent reservoir.

(*2*) *Preparation of column.* Place a snug pledget of fine glass wool in the bottom of the column (or buret) if the column (or buret) is not equipped with integral coarse, fritted glass disc. Overlay the glass wool pledget (or fritted glass disc) with a 15–20 millimeter deep layer of fine sand. Measure in a graduated cylinder 15 milliliters of chromatographic grade aluminum oxide (80–200 mesh) that has been tightly settled by tapping the cylinder. Transfer the aluminum oxide to the chromatographic tube, tapping the tube during and after the transfer so as to tightly settle the aluminum oxide. Overlay the layer of aluminum oxide with a 1.0–1.5 centimeter deep layer of anhydrous sodium sulfate and on top of this place an 8–10 millimeter thick plug of fine glass wool. Next carefully add about 25 milliliters of heptane to the column with stopcock open, and allow the heptane to pass through the column until the top level of the liquid just passes into the top glass wool plug in the column, and close stopcock.

(*3*) *Chromatographing of sample extract*—(*i*) *For chloroform residues weighing 0.5 gram or less.* To the dried and weighed chloroform-soluble extract residue in the evaporating dish, obtained in paragraph (d)(5)(ii) of this section, add 20 milliliters of heptane and stir. If necessary, heat carefully to dissolve the residue. Additional heptane not to exceed a total volume of 50 milliliters may be used if necessary to complete dissolving. Cool to room temperature. (If solution becomes cloudy, use the procedure in paragraph (d)(5)(iii)(*b*)(*3*)(*ii*) of this section to obtain an aliquot of heptane solution calculated to contain 0.1–0.5 gram of chloroform-soluble extract residue.) Transfer the clear liquid solution to the column (or buret). Rinse the dish with 10 millimeters of additional heptane and add to column. Allow the liquid to pass through the column into a clean, tared evaporating dish (platinum or Pyrex) at a dropwise rate of about 2 milliliters per minute until the liquid surface reaches the top glass wool plug; then close the stopcock temporarily. Rinse the Pyrex flask which contained the filtrate with an additional 10–15 milliliters of heptane and add to the column. Wash (elute) the column with more heptane collecting about 100 milliliters of total eluate including that already collected in the evaporating dish. Evaporate the combined eluate in the evaporating dish to dryness on a steam bath. Dry the residue for 15 minutes in an oven maintained at a temperature of approximately 221 °F. Cool the evaporating dish in a desiccator for 30 minutes and weigh the residue to the nearest 0.1 milligram. Subtract the weight of the residue from the weight of chloroform-soluble extractives residue (′) to obtain the wax-, petrolatum-, and mineral oil-corrected chloroform-soluble extractives residue (*e*′). This *e*′ is substituted for *e* in the equations in paragraph (d)(5)(i) (*a*) and (*b*) of this section.

(*ii*) For chloroform residues weighing more than 0.5 gram. Redissolve the dried and weighed chloroform-soluble extract residue as described in paragraph (d)(5)(iii)(*b*)(*3*)(*i*) of this section using proportionately larger quantities of heptane. Transfer the heptane solution to an appropriate-sized volumetric flask (i.e., a 250-milliliter flask for about 2.5 grams of residue) and adjust to volume with additional heptane. Pipette out an aliquot (about 50 milliliters) calculated to contain 0.1–0.5 gram of the chloroform-soluble extract residue and analyze chromatographically as described in paragraph (d)(5)(iii)(*b*)(*3*)(*i*) of this section. In this case the weight of the dried residue from the heptane eluate must be multiplied by the dilution factor to obtain the weight of wax, petrolatum, and mineral oil residue to be subtracted from the weight of chloroform-soluble extractives residue (′) to obtain the wax-, petrolatum-, and mineral oil-corrected chloroform-soluble extractives residue (*e*′). This *e*′ is substituted for *e* in the equations in paragraph (d)(5)(i) (*a*) and (*b*) of this section. (Note: In the case of chloroform-soluble extracts which contain high melting waxes (melting point greater than 170 °F), it may be necessary to dilute the heptane solution further so that a 50-milliliter aliquot will contain only 0.1–0.2 gram of the chloroform-soluble extract residue.)

(e) Acrylonitrile copolymers identified in this section shall comply with the provisions of § 180.22 of this chapter, except where the copolymers are restricted to use in contact with food only of the type identified in paragraph (c), table 1 under Category VIII.

[42 FR 14554, Mar. 15, 1977]

EDITORIAL NOTE: For FEDERAL REGISTER citations affecting § 176.170, see the List of CFR Sections Affected, which appears in the Finding Aids section of the printed volume and at *www.fdsys.gov*.

§ 176.180 Components of paper and paperboard in contact with dry food.

The substances listed in this section may be safely used as components of the uncoated or coated food-contact surface of paper and paperboard intended for use in producing, manufacturing, packing, processing, preparing, treating, packaging, transporting, or holding dry food of the type identified in § 176.170(c), table 1, under Type VIII, subject to the provisions of this section.

(a) The substances are used in amounts not to exceed that required to accomplish their intended physical or technical effect, and are so used as to accomplish no effect in food other than that ordinarily accomplished by packaging.

(b) The substances permitted to be used include the following:

(1) Substances that by § 176.170 and other applicable regulations in parts 170 through 189 of this chapter may be safely used as components of the uncoated or coated food-contact surface of paper and paperboard, subject to the provisions of such regulation.

(2) Substances identified in the following list:

List of substances	Limitations
Acrylamide polymer with sodium 2-acrylamido-2-methylpropane-sulfonate (CAS Reg. No. 38193–60–1).	For use at a level not to exceed 0.015 weight percent of dry fiber.
(2-Alkenyl) succinic anhydrides in which the alkenyl groups are derived from olefins which contain not less than 78 percent C_{30} and higher groups (CAS Reg. No. 70983–55–0)..	
4-[2-[2-(2-Alkoxy(C_{12}-C_{15}) ethoxy) ethoxy]ethyl]disodium sulfosuccinate.	For use as a polymerization emulsifier and latex emulsion stabilizer at levels not to exceed 5 percent by weight of total emulsion solids.
Alkyl mono- and disulfonic acids, sodium salts (produced from *n*-alkanes in the range of C_{10}-C_{18} with not less than 50 percent C_{14}-C_{16})..	
Aluminum and calcium salts of FD & C dyes on a substrate of alumina.	Colorant.
Ammonium nitrate..	
Amylose..	
Barium metaborate	For use as preservative in coatings and sizings.
1,2-Benzisothiazolin-3-one (CAS Registry No. 2634–33–5)	For use only as a preservative in paper coating compositions and limited to use at a level not to exceed 0.02 mg/in² (0.0031 mg/cm²) of finished paper and paperboard.
N,N-Bis(hydroxyethyl)lauramide.	
Bis(trichloromethyl) sulfone C.A. Registry No. 3064–70–8	For use only as a preservative in coatings.
Borax	For use as preservative in coatings.
Boric acid	Do.
Butanedioic acid, sulfo-1,4-di-(C_9-C_{11} alkyl) ester, ammonium salt (also known as butanedioic acid, sulfo-1,4-diisodecyl ester, ammonium salt [CAS Reg. No. 144093–88–9])..	For use as a surface active agent in package coating inks at levels not to exceed 3 percent by weight of the coating ink.
sec-Butyl alcohol..	
Butyl benzyl phthalate..	
Candelilla wax..	
Carbon tetrachloride..	
Castor oil, polyoxyethylated (42 moles ethylene oxide)..	
Cationic soy protein hydrolyzed (hydrolyzed soy protein isolate modified by treatment with 3-chloro-2-hydroxypropyl-trimethylammonium chloride).	For use only as a coating adhesive, pigment structuring agent, and fiber retention aid.
Cationic soy protein (soy protein isolate modified by treatment with 3-chloro-2-hydroxypropyltrimethyl-ammonium chloride).	For use only as a coating adhesive, pigment structuring agent, and fiber retention aid.
Chloral hydrate	Polymerization reaction-control agent.
N-Cyclohexyl-*p*-toluene sulfonamide..	
2,5-Di-*tert*-butyl hydroquinone.	

List of substances	Limitations
Diethanolamine..	
Diethylene glycol dibenzoate (CAS Reg. No. 120–55–8)	For use only as a plasticizer in polymeric substances.
Diethylene glycol monobutyl ether..	
Diethylene glycol monoethyl ether..	
Diethylenetriamine..	
N,N-Diisopropanolamide of tallow fatty acids..	
N-[(dimethylamino)methyl]acrylamide polymer with acrylamide and styrene..	
N,N-Dioleoylethylenediamine, *N,N*-dilinoeoyl-ethylenediamine, and N-oleoyl-N-linoleoyl-ethylenediamine mixture produced when tall oil fatty acids are made to react with ethylenediamine such that the finished mixture has a melting point of 212°–228 °F, as determined by ASTM method D127–60, and an acid value of 10 maximum. ASTM Method D127–60 "Standard Method of Test for Melting Point of Petrolatum and Microcrystalline Wax" (Revised 1960) is incorporated by reference. Copies are available from University Microfilms International, 300 N. Zeeb Rd., Ann Arbor, MI 48106, or available for inspection at the National Archives and Records Administration (NARA). For information on the availability of this material at NARA, call 202–741–6030, or go to: *http://www.archives.gov/federal_register/code_of_federal_regulations/ibr_locations.html*..	
Diphenylamine..	
Dipropylene glycol dibenzoate (CAS Reg. No. 27138–31–4)	For use only as plasticizer in polymeric substances.
Disodium *N*-octadecylsulfosuccinamate..	
tert-Dodecyl thioether of polyethylene glycol..	
Erucamide (erucylamide)..	
Ethanedial, polymer with tetrahydro-4-hydroxy-5-methyl-2(1*H*)pyrimidinone, propoxylated..	
Ethylene oxide	Fumigant in sizing.
Ethylene oxide adduct of mono-(2-ethylhexyl) *o*-phosphate..	
Fatty acid (C_{12}-C_{18}) diethanolamide..	
Fish oil fatty acids, hydrogenated, potassium salt..	
Formaldehyde..	
Glyceryl monocaprate..	
Glyceryl tribenzoate (CAS Reg. No. 614–33–5)	For use only as a plasticizer in polymeric coatings.
Glyoxal..	
Glyoxal-urea-formaldehyde condensate (CAS Reg. No. 27013–01–0) formed by reaction in the molar ratio of approximately 47:33:15, respectively. The reaction product has a number average molecular weight of 278±14 as determined by a suitable method.	For use as an insolubilizer for starch in coatings.
Glyoxal-urea polymer (CAS Reg. No. 53037–34–6)	For use as an insolubilizer for starch.
Hexamethylenetetramine	Polymerization crosslinking agent for protein, including casein. As neutralizing agent with myristochromic chloride complex and stearato-chromic chloride complex.
Hexylene glycol (2-methyl-2,4-pentanediol)..	
Hydroabietyl alcohol..	
5-Hydroxymethoxymethyl-1-aza-3,7-dioxabicyclo[3.3.0] octane, 5-hydroxymethyl-1-aza-3,7-dioxabicyclo[3.3.0]octane, and 5-hydroxypoly-[methyleneoxy]methyl-1-aza-3,7-dioxabicyclo[3.3.0] octane mixture.	For use only as an antibacterial preservative.
Imidazolium compounds, 2–(C_{17} and C_{17}-unsaturated alkyl)-1–[2–(C_{18} and C_{18}-unsaturated amido)ethyl]-4,5-dihydro-1-methyl, methyl sulfates (CAS Reg. No. 72749–55–4)..	For use only at levels not to exceed 0.5 percent by weight of the dry paper and paperboard.
Isopropanolamine hydrochloride..	
Isopropyl *m*- and *p*-cresol (thymol derived)..	
Itaconic acid..	
Maleic anhydride-diisobutylene copolymer, ammonium or sodium salt..	
Melamine-formaldehyde modified with:	Basic polymer.
Alcohols (ethyl, butyl, isobutyl, propyl, or isopropyl).	
Diethylenetriamine.	
Imino-bis-butylamine.	
Imino-bis-ethyleneimine.	
Imino-bis-propylamine.	
Polyamines made by reacting ethylenediamine or trimethylenediamine with dichloroethane or dichloropropane.	
Sulfanilic acid.	
Tetraethylenepentamine.	
Triethylenetetramine.	
Methyl alcohol..	
Methyl ethers of mono-, di-, and tripropylene glycol..	

List of substances	Limitations
Methyl naphthalene sulfonic acid-formaldehyde condensate, sodium salt..	
Methylated poly(*N*-1,2-dihydroxyethylene-1,3-imidazolidin-2-one).	For use only only as an in solubilizer for starch.
Modified polyacrylamide resulting from an epichlorohydrin addition to a condensate of formaldehyde-dicyandiamide-diethylene triamine and which product is then reacted with polyacrylamide and urea to produce a resin having a nitrogen content of 5.6 to 6.3 percent and having a minimum viscosity in 56 percent-by-weight aqueous solution of 200 centipoises at 25 °C, as determined by LVT-series Brookfield viscometer using a No. 4 spindle at 60 r.p.m. (or equivalent method).	For use only as a dry strength and pigment retention aid agent employed prior to the sheetforming operation in the manufacture of paper and paperboard and used at a level not to exceed 1 percent by weight of dry fibers.
Mono- and di(2-alkenyl)succinyl esters of polyethylene glycol containing not less than 90 percent of the diester product and in which the alkenyl groups are derived from olefins that contain not less than 95 percent of C_{15}-C_{21} groups.	For use only as an emulsifier.
Monoglyceride citrate..	
Myristo chromic chloride complex..	
Naphthalene sulfonic acid-formaldehyde condensate, sodium salt..	
Nickel..	
β-Nitrostyrene	Basic polymer.
Octadecanoic acid, reaction products with 2-[(2-aminoethyl)amino]ethanol and urea (CAS Reg. No. 68412–14–6), and the acetate salts thereof (CAS Reg. No. 68784–21–4), which may be emulsified with ethoxylated tallow alkyl amines (CAS Reg. No. 61791–26–2).	For use prior to sheet forming at levels not to exceed 12 pounds per ton of paper.
α-*cis*-9-Octadecenyl-*omega*-hydroxypoly (oxyethylene); the octadecenyl group is derived from oleyl alcohol and the poly(oxyethylene) content averages not less than 20 moles..	
α-(*p*-Nonylphenyl)-*omega*-hydroxypoly (oxyethylene) sulfate, ammonium salt; the nonyl group is a propylene trimer isomer and the poly (oxyethylene) content averages 9 or 30 moles..	
Oleic acid reacted with *N*-alkyl-(C_{16}-C_{18}) trimethylenediamine..	
Oxidized soy isolate having 50 to 70 percent of its cystine residues oxidized to cysteic acid.	For use as a binder adhesive component of coatings.
Petroleum alicyclic hydrocarbon resins, or the hydrogenated product thereof, complying with the identity prescribed in § 176.170(b)(2).	For use as modifiers at levels up to 30 weight-percent of the solids content of wax-polymer blend coatings.
Petroleum hydrocarbon resins (produced by the catalytic polymerization and subsequent hydrogenation of styrene, vinyltoluene, and indene types from distillates of cracked petroleum stocks)..	
Petroleum hydrocarbons, light and odorless..	
o-Phthalic acid modified hydrolyzed soy protein isolate..	
Pine oil..	
Poly(2-aminoethyl acrylate nitrate-*co*-2-hydroxypropyl acrylate) complying with the identity described in § 176.170(a)..	
Polyamide-epichloro hydrin modified resins resulting from the reaction of the initial caprolactam-itaconic acid product with diethylenetriamine and then condensing this prepolymer with epichlorohydrin to form a cationic resin having a nitrogen content of 11–15 percent and chlorine level of 20–23 percent on a dry basis..	
Polyamide-ethyleneimine-epichlorohydrin resin is prepared by reacting equimolar amounts of adipic acid and three amines (21 mole percent of 1,2-ethanediamine, 51 mole percent of N-(2-aminoethyl)-1,3-propanediamine, and 28 mole percent of N, N′-1,2-ethanediylbis(1,3-propanediamine)) to form a basic polyamidoamine which is modified by reaction with ethyleneimine (5.5:1.0 ethyleneimine:polyamidoamine). The modified polyamidoamine is reacted with a crosslinking agent made by condensing approximately 34 ethylene glycol units with (chloromethyl)oxirane, followed by pH adjustment with formic acid or sulfuric acid to provide a finished product as a formate (CAS Reg. No. 114133–44–7) or a sulfate (CAS Reg. No. 167678–43–5), having a weight-average molecular weight of 1,300,000 and a number-average molecular weight of 16,000..	

List of substances	Limitations
Polyamide-ethyleneimine-epichlorohydrin resin (CAS Reg. No. 115340–77–7), prepared by reacting equimolar amounts of adipic acid and *N*-(2-aminoethyl)-1,2-ethanediamine to form a basic polyamidoamine which is modified by reaction with ethyleneimine, and further reacted with formic acid and (chloromethyl)oxirane-α-hydro-omega-hydroxypoly(oxy-1,2-ethanediyl)..	
Polybutene, hydrogenated; complying with the identity prescribed under § 178.3740(b) of this chapter..	
Poly [2-(diethylamino) ethyl methacrylate] phosphate..	
Polyethylene glycol (200) dilaurate..	
Polyethylene glycol monoisotridecyl ether sulfate, sodium salt (CAS Reg. No. 150413–26–6).	For use only as a surfactant at levels not to exceed 3 percent in latex formulations used in pigment binders for paper and paperboard.
Polymers: Homopolymers and copolymers of the following monomers:	Basic polymer.
Acrylamide.	
Acrylic acid and its methyl, ethyl, butyl, propyl, or octyl esters.	
Acrylonitrile.	
Butadiene.	
Crotonic acid.	
Cyclol acrylate.	
Decyl acrylate.	
Diallyl fumarate.	
Diallyl maleate.	
Diallyl phthalate.	
Dibutyl fumarate.	
Dibutyl itaconate.	
Dibutyl maleate.	
Di(2-ethylhexyl) maleate.	
Dioctyl fumarate.	
Dioctyl maleate.	
Divinylbenzene.	
Ethylene.	
2-Ethylhexyl acrylate.	
Fumaric acid.	
Glycidyl methacrylate.	
2-Hydroxyethyl acrylate.	
N-(Hydroxymethyl) acrylamide.	
Isobutyl acrylate.	
Isobutylene.	
Isoprene.	
Itaconic acid.	
Maleic anhydride and its methyl or butyl esters.	
Methacrylic acid and its methyl, ethyl, butyl, or propyl esters.	
Methylstyrene.	
Mono(2-ethylhexyl) maleate.	
Monoethyl maleate.	
5-Norbornene-2,3-dicarboxylic acid, mono-*n*-butyl ester.	
Styrene.	
Vinyl acetate.	
Vinyl butyrate.	
Vinyl chloride.	
Vinyl crotonate.	
Vinyl hexoate.	
Vinylidene chloride.	
Vinyl pelargonate.	
Vinyl propionate.	
Vinyl pyrrolidone.	
Vinyl stearate.	
Vinyl sulfonic acid.	
Polymer prepared from urea, ethanedial, formaldehyde, and propionaldehyde (CAS Reg. No. 106569–82–8).	For use only as a starch and protein reactant in paper and paperboard coatings.
Polyoxyethylene (minimum 12 moles) ester of tall oil (30%–40% rosin acids)..	
Polyoxypropylene-polyoxyethylene glycol (minimum molecular weight 1,900)..	
Polyvinyl alcohol..	
Potassium titanate fibers produced by calcining titanium dioxide, potassium chloride, and potassium carbonate, such that the finished crystalline fibers have a nominal diameter of 0.20–0.25 micron, a length-to-diameter ratio of approximately 25:1 or greater, and consist principally of $K_2Ti_4O_9$ and $K_2Ti_6O_{13}$..	

List of substances	Limitations
Sodium diisobutylphenoxy diethoxyethyl sulfonate..	
Sodium diisobutylphenoxy monoethoxy ethylsulfonate..	
Sodium *n*-dodecylpolyethoxy (50 moles) sulfate..	
Sodium isododecylphenoxypolyethoxy (40 moles) sulfate..	
Sodium *N*-methyl-*N*-oleyl taurate..	
Sodium methyl siliconate..	
Sodium nitrite..	
Sodium polyacrylate..	
Sodium bis-tridecylsulfosuccinate..	
Sodium xylene sulfonate..	
Stearato chromic chloride complex..	
Styrene-allyl alcohol copolymers..	
Styrene-methacrylic acid copolymer, potassium salt..	
Tetraethylenepentamine	Polymerization cross-linking agent.
α-[*p*-(1,1,3,3-Tetramethylbutyl)phenyl]-*omega* hydroxypoly(oxyethylene) mixture of dihydrogen phosphate and monohydrogen phosphate esters and their sodium, potassium, and ammonium salts having a poly(oxyethylene) content averaging 6–9 or 40 moles..	
α-[*p*-(1,1,3,3-Tetramethylbutyl)phenyl or *p*-nonylphenyl]-*omega*-hydroxypoly (oxyethylene) where nonyl group is a propylene trimer isomer..	
Tetrasodium *N*-(1,2-dicarboxyethyl)-*N*-octadecyl sulfosuccinamate..	
Toluene..	
Triethanolamine..	
Triethylenetetramine	Polymerization cross-linking agent.
Triethylenetetramine monoacetate, partially stearoylated..	
Urea-formaldehyde chemically modified with:	
Alcohol (methyl, ethyl, butyl, isobutyl, propyl, or isopropyl).	
Aminomethylsulfonic acid.	
Diaminobutane.	
Diaminopropane.	
Diethylenetriamine.	
N,N'-Dioleoylethylenediamine.	
Diphenylamine.	
N,N'-Distearoylethylenediamine.	
Ethylenediamine.	
Guanidine.	
Imino-bis-butylamine.	
Imino-bis-ethylamine.	
Imino-bis-propylamine.	
N-Oleoyl-*N'*-stearoylethylenediamine.	
Polyamines made by reacting ethylenediamine or triethylenediamine with dichloroethane or dichloropropane.	
Tetraethylenepentamine.	
Triethylenetetramine.	
Xylene..	
Xylene sulfonic acid-formaldehyde condensate, sodium salt..	
Zinc stearate..	

[42 FR 14554, Mar. 15, 1977]

EDITORIAL NOTE: For additional FEDERAL REGISTER citations affecting § 176.180, see the List of CFR Sections Affected, which appears in the Finding Aids section of the printed volume and at *www.fdsys.gov*.

§ 176.200 Defoaming agents used in coatings.

The defoaming agents described in this section may be safely used as components of articles intended for use in producing, manufacturing, packing, processing, preparing, treating, packaging, transporting, or holding food, subject to the provisions of this section.

(a) The defoaming agents are prepared as mixtures of substances described in paragraph (d) of this section.

(b) The quantity of any substance employed in the formulation of defoaming agents does not exceed the amount reasonably required to accomplish the intended physical or technical effect in the defoaming agents or any limitation further provided.

(c) Any substance employed in the production of defoaming agents and which is the subject of a regulation in parts 174, 175, 176, 177, 178 and § 179.45 of this chapter conforms with any specification in such regulation.

(d) Substances employed in the formulation of defoaming agents include:

(1) Substances generally recognized as safe in food.

(2) Substances subject to prior sanction or approval for use in defoaming agents and used in accordance with such sanction or approval.

(3) Substances identified in this paragraph (d)(3) and subject to such limitations as are provided:

List of substances	Limitations
n-Butyl alcohol.	
tert-Butyl alcohol.	
Butyl stearate.	
Castor oil, sulfated, ammonium, potassium, or sodium salt.	
Cetyl alcohol.	
Cyclohexane.	
Cyclohexanol.	
Diethylene glycol monolaurate.	
Diethylene glycol monostearate.	
Dimers and trimers of unsaturated C_{18} fatty acids derived from:	For use only at levels not to exceed 0.1% by weight of total coating solids.
Animal and vegetable fats and oils.	
Tall oil.	
Dimethylpolysiloxane.	
α-(Dinonylphenyl)-ω-hydroxy-poly(oxy-1,2-ethanediyl), containing 7 to 24 moles of ethylene oxide per mole of dinonylphenol (CAS Reg. No. 9014–93–1).	For use only in defoaming agents for the production of styrene-butadiene coatings at a level not to exceed 0.05 percent by weight of the finished coating.
Dipropylene glycol.	
Ethyl alcohol.	
Fats and oils derived from animal, marine, or vegetable sources:	
Fatty acids derived from animal, marine, or vegetable fats and oils, and salts of such acids, single or mixed, as follows:	
Aluminum..	
Ammonium..	
Calcium..	
Magnesium..	
Potassium..	
Sodium..	
Zinc..	
Formaldehyde	For use as preservative of defoamer only.
Glyceryl mono-12-hydroxystearate.	
Glyceryl monostearate.	
Hexane.	
Hexylene glycol (2-methyl-2,4-pentanediol).	
Isobutyl alcohol.	
Isopropyl alcohol.	
Kerosene.	
Lecithin hydroxylated.	
Methyl alcohol.	
Methylcellulose.	
Methyl esters of fatty acids derived from animal, marine, or vegetable fats and oils.	
Methyl oleate.	
Methyl palmitate.	
Mineral oil.	
Mustardseed oil, sulfated, ammonium, potassium, or sodium salt.	
Myristyl alcohol.	
Naphtha.	
β-Naphthol	For use as preservative of defoamer only.
Nonylphenol.	
Odorless light petroleum hydrocarbons	As defined in § 178.3650 of this chapter.
Oleic acid, sulfated, ammonium, potassium, or sodium salt.	
Parachlorometacresol	For use as preservative of defoamer only.
Peanut oil, sulfated, ammonium, potassium, or sodium salt.	
Petrolatum.	
Pine oil.	
Polyacrylic acid, sodium salt	As a stabilizer and thickener in defoaming agents containing dimethylpolysiloxane.
Polyethylene.	

List of substances	Limitations
Polyethylene, oxidized.	
Polyethylene glycol (200) dilaurate.	
Polyethylene glycol (400) dioleate.	
Polyethylene glycol (600) dioleate.	
Polyethylene glycol (400) esters of coconut oil fatty acids.	
Polyethylene glycol (400) monooleate.	
Polyethylene glycol (600) monooleate.	
Polyethylene glycol (600) monoricinoleate.	
Polyethylene glycol (400) monostearate.	
Polyoxybutylene-polyoxypropylene-polyoxyethylene glycol (min. mol. wt. 3,700).	
Polyoxyethylated (min. 3 mols) cetyl alcohol.	
Polyoxyethylated (min. 5 mols) oleyl alcohol.	
Polyoxyethylated (min. 1.5 mols) tridecyl alcohol.	
Polyoxyethylene (min. 15 mols) ester of rosin.	
Polyoxyethylene (min. 8 mols) monooleate.	
Polyoxyethylene (40) stearate.	
Polyoxypropylated (min. 20 mols) butyl alcohol.	
Polyoxypropylene glycol (min. mol. wt. 200).	
Polyoxypropylene (min. 20 mols) oleate butyl ether.	
Polyoxypropylene-polyoxyethylene glycol (min. mol. wt. 1,900).	
Polyoxypropylene (min. 40 mols) stearate butyl ether.	
Potassium pentachlorophenate	For use as preservative of defoamer only.
Potassium trichlorophenate	Do.
Propylene glycol monoester of soybean oil fatty acids.	
Propylene glycol monoester of tallow fatty acids.	
Ricebran oil, sulfated, ammonium, potassium, or sodium salt.	
Rosins and rosin derivatives	As provided in § 178.3870 of this chapter.
Silica.	
Sodium 2-mercaptobenzothiazole	For use as preservative of defoamer only.
Sodium pentachlorophenate	Do.
Sodium trichlorophenate	Do.
Sperm oil, sulfated, ammonium, potassium, or sodium salt.	
Stearyl alcohol.	
Tall oil fatty acids.	
Tallow fatty acids, hydrogenated or sulfated.	
Tallow, sulfated, ammonium, potassium, or sodium salt.	
Triethanolamine.	
Triisopropanolamine.	
Waxes, petroleum.	

(e) The defoaming agents are used as follows:

(1) The quantity of defoaming agent or agents used shall not exceed the amount reasonably required to accomplish the intended effect, which is to prevent or control the formation of foam.

(2) The defoaming agents are used in the preparation and application of coatings for paper and paperboard.

[42 FR 14554, Mar. 15, 1977, as amended at 62 FR 39772, July 24, 1997]

§ 176.210 Defoaming agents used in the manufacture of paper and paperboard.

Defoaming agents may be safely used in the manufacture of paper and paperboard intended for use in packaging, transporting, or holding food in accordance with the following prescribed conditions:

(a) The defoaming agents are prepared from one or more of the substances named in paragraph (d) of this section, subject to any prescribed limitations.

(b) The defoaming agents are used to prevent or control the formation of foam during the manufacture of paper and paperboard prior to and during the sheet-forming process.

(c) The quantity of defoaming agent or agents added during the manufacturing process shall not exceed the amount necessary to accomplish the intended technical effect.

(d) Substances permitted to be used in the formulation of defoaming agents include substances subject to prior sanctions or approval for such use and employed subject to the conditions of such sanctions or approvals, substances generally recognized as safe for use in food, substances generally recognized as safe for use in paper and paperboard, and substances listed in this paragraph, subject to the limitations, if any, prescribed.

(1) Fatty triglycerides, and the fatty acids, alcohols, and dimers derived therefrom:

Beef tallow.
Castor oil.
Coconut oil.
Corn oil.
Cottonseed oil.
Fish oil.
Lard oil.
Linseed oil.
Mustardseed oil.
Palm oil.
Peanut oil.
Rapeseed oil.
Ricebran oil.
Soybean oil.
Sperm oil.
Tall oil.

(2) Fatty triglycerides, and marine oils, and the fatty acids and alcohols derived therefrom (paragraph (d)(1) of this section) reacted with one or more of the following, with or without dehydration, to form chemicals of the category indicated in parentheses:

Aluminum hydroxide (soaps).
Ammonia (amides).
Butanol (esters).
Butoxy-polyoxypropylene, molecular weight 1,000–2,500 (esters).
Butylene glycol (esters).
Calcium hydroxide (soaps).
Diethanolamine (amides).
Diethylene glycol (esters).
Ethylene glycol (esters).
Ethylene oxide (esters and ethers).
Glycerin (mono- and diglycerides).
Hydrogen (hydrogenated compounds).
Hydrogen (amines).
Isobutanol (esters).
Isopropanol (esters).
Magnesium hydroxide (soaps).
Methanol (esters).
Morpholine (soaps).
Oxygen (air-blown oils).
Pentaerythritol (esters).
Polyoxyethylene, molecular weights 200, 300, 400, 600, 700, 1,000, 1,540, 1,580, 1,760, 4,600 (esters).
Polyoxypropylene, molecular weight 200–2,000 (esters).
Potassium hydroxide (soaps).
Propanol (esters).
Propylene glycol (esters).
Propylene oxide (esters).
Sodium hydroxide (soaps).
Sorbitol (esters).
Sulfuric acid (sulfated and sulfonated compounds).
Triethanolamine (amides and soaps).
Triisopropanolamine (amides and soaps).
Trimethylolethane (esters).
Zinc hydroxide (soaps).

(3) Miscellaneous:

Alcohols and ketone alcohols mixture (still-bottom product from C_{12}-C_{18} alcohol manufacturing process).
Amyl alcohol.
Butoxy polyethylene polypropylene glycol molecular weight 900–4,200.
Butoxy-polyoxypropylene molecular weight 1,000–2,500.
Butylated hydroxyanisole.
Butylated hydroxytoluene.
Calcium lignin sulfonate.
Capryl alcohol.
p-Chlorometacresol.
Cyclohexanol.
Diacetyltartaric acid ester of tallow monoglyceride.
1,2-Dibromo-2,4-dicyanobutane (CAS Reg. No. 35691–65–7), for use as a preservative at a level not to exceed 0.05 weight-percent of the defoaming agent.
Diethanolamine.
Diethylene triamine.
Di-(2-ethylhexyl) phthalate.
2,6-Dimethyl heptanol-4 (nonyl alcohol).
Dimethylpolysiloxane.
Di-*tert*-butyl hydroquinone.
Dodecylbenzene sulfonic acids.
Ethanol.
2-Ethylhexanol.
Ethylenediamine tetraacetic acid tetrasodium salt.
Formaldehyde.
Heavy oxo-fraction (a still-bottom product of iso-octyl alcohol manufacture, of approximate composition: Octyl alcohol 5 percent nonyl alcohol 10 percent, decyl and higher alcohols 35 percent, esters 45 percent, and soaps 5 percent).
2-Heptadecenyl-4-methyl-4-hydroxymethyl-2-oxazoline.
Hexylene glycol (2-methyl-2-4-pentanediol).
12-Hydroxystearic acid.
Isobutanol.
Isopropanol.
Isopropylamine salt of dodecylbenzene sulfonic acid.
Kerosine.
Lanolin.
Methanol.
Methyl 12-hydroxystearate.
Methyl taurine-oleic acid condensate, molecular weight 486.
a,a′-[Methylenebis[4-(1,1,3,3-tetramethylbutyl)-*o*-phenylene]]*bis*[*omega*-hydroxypoly (oxyethylene)] having 6–7.5 moles of ethylene oxide per hydroxyl group.
Mineral oil.
Mono-, di-, and triisopropanolamine.
Mono- and diisopropanolamine stearate.
Monobutyl ether of ethylene glycol.
Monoethanolamine.

Morpholine.
Myristyl alcohol.
Naphtha.
β-Naphthol.
Nonylphenol.
Odorless light petroleum hydrocarbons.
Oleyl alcohol.
Petrolatum.
o-Phenylphenol.
Pine oil.
Polybutene, hydrogenated; complying with the identity prescribed under § 178.3740(b) of this chapter.
Polyethylene.
Polyethylene, oxidized (air-blown).
Polymer derived from *N*-vinyl pyrrolidone and copolymers derived from the mixed alkyl (C_{12}-C_{15}, C_{16}, C_{18}, C_{20}, and C_{22}) methacrylate esters, butyl methacrylate (CAS Reg. No. 97–88–1), isobutyl methacrylate (CAS Reg. No. 97–86–9) and methyl methacrylate (CAS Reg. No. 80–62–6); the combined polymer contains no more than 5 weight percent of polymer units derived from *N*-vinyl pyrrolidone and is present at a level not to exceed 7 parts per million by weight of the finished dry paper and paperboard fibers.
Polyoxyethylene (4 mols) decyl phosphate.
Polyoxyethylene (4 mols) di(2-ethyl hexanoate).
Polyoxyethylene (15 mols) ester of rosin.
Polyoxyethylene (3–15 mols) tridecyl alcohol.
Polyoxypropylene, molecular weight 200–2,000.
Polyoxypropylene-polyoxethylene condensate, minimum molecular weight 950.
Polyoxypropylene-ethylene oxide condensate of ethylene diamine, molecular weight 1,700–3,800.
Polyvinyl pyrrolidone, molecular weight 40,000.
Potassium distearyl phosphate.
Potassium pentachlorophenate.
Potassium trichlorophenate.
Rosins and rosin derivatives identified in § 175.105(c)(5) of this chapter.
Silica.
Siloxanes and silicones, dimethyl, methylhydrogen, reaction products with polyethylene-polypropylene glycol monoallyl ether (CAS Reg. No. 71965–38–3).
Sodium alkyl (C_9-C_{15}) benzene-sulfonate.
Sodium dioctyl sulfosuccinate.
Sodium distearyl phosphate.
Sodium lauryl sulfate.
Sodium lignin sulfonate.
Sodium 2-mercaptobenzothiazole.
Sodium naphthalenesulfonic acid (3 mols) condensed with formaldehyde (2 mols).
Sodium orthophenylphenate.
Sodium pentachlorophenate.
Sodium petroleum sulfonate, molecular weight 440–450.
Sodium trichlorophenate.
Stearyl alcohol.
α-[*p*-(1,1,3,3-Tetramethylbutyl) phenyl-, *p*-nonylphenyl-, or *p*-dodecylphenyl]-*omega*-hydroxypoly(oxyethylene) produced by the condensation of 1 mole of *p*-alkylphenol (alkyl group is 1,1,3,3-tetramethylbutyl, a propylene trimer isomer, or a propylene tetramer isomer) with an average of 1.5–15 moles of ethylene oxide.
Tetrahydrofurfuryl alcohol.
Tributoxyethyl phosphate.
Tributyl phosphate.
Tridecyl alcohol.
Triethanolamine.
Triethylene glycol di(2-ethyl hexanoate).
Tri-(2-ethylhexyl) phosphate.
Tristearyl phosphate.
Wax, petroleum, Type I and Type II.
Wax, petroleum (oxidized).
Wax (montan).

[42 FR 14554, Mar. 15, 1977, as amended at 47 FR 17986, Apr. 27, 1982; 47 FR 46495, Oct. 19, 1982; 47 FR 56845, Dec. 21, 1982; 54 FR 24897, June 12, 1989; 57 FR 31313, July 15, 1992; 61 FR 14246, Apr. 1, 1996]

§ 176.230 3,5-Dimethyl-1,3,5,2*H*-tetrahydrothiadiazine-2-thione.

3,5-Dimethyl-1,3,5,2*H*-tetrahydrothiadiazine-2-thione may safely be used as a preservative in the manufacture and coating of paper and paperboard intended for use in contact with food in accordance with the following prescribed conditions:

(a) It is used as follows:

(1) In the manufacture of paper and paperboard as a preservative for substances added to the pulp suspension prior to the sheet-forming operation provided that the preservative is volatilized by heat in the drying and finishing of the paper and paperboard.

(2) As a preservative for coatings for paper and paperboard, *Provided*, That the preservative is volatilized by heat in the drying and finishing of the coated paper or paperboard.

(b) The quantity used shall not exceed the least amount reasonably required to accomplish the intended technical effect and shall not be intended to nor, in fact, accomplish any physical or technical effect in the food itself.

(c) The use of a preservative in any substance or article subject to any regulation in parts 174, 175, 176, 177, 178 and § 179.45 of this chapter must comply with any specifications and limitations prescribed by such regulation for the substance or article.

§ 176.250 Poly-1,4,7,10,13-pentaaza-15-hydroxyhexadecane.

Poly-1,4,7,10,13-pentaaza-15-hydroxyhexadecane may be safely used as a retention aid employed prior to the sheet-forming operation in the manufacture of paper and paperboard intended for use in contact with food in an amount not to exceed that necessary to accomplish the intended physical or technical effect and not to exceed 6 pounds per ton of finished paper or paperboard.

§ 176.260 Pulp from reclaimed fiber.

(a) Pulp from reclaimed fiber may be safely used as a component of articles used in producing, manufacturing, packing, processing, preparing, treating, packaging, transporting, or holding food, subject to the provisions of paragraph (b) of this section.

(b) Pulp from reclaimed fiber is prepared from the paper and paperboard products described in paragraphs (b) (1) and (2) of this section, by repulping with water to recover the fiber with the least possible amount of nonfibrous substances.

(1) Industrial waste from the manufacture of paper and paperboard products excluding that which bears or contains any poisonous or deleterious substance which is retained in the recovered pulp and that migrates to the food, except as provided in regulations promulgated under sections 406 and 409 of the Federal Food, Drug, and Cosmetic Act.

(2) Salvage from used paper and paperboard excluding that which (i) bears or contains any poisonous or deleterious substance which is retained in the recovered pulp and that migrates to the food, except as provided in regulations promulgated under sections 406 and 409 of the act or (ii) has been used for shipping or handling any such substance.

§ 176.300 Slimicides.

(a) Slimicides may be safely used in the manufacture of paper and paperboard that contact food, in accordance with the following prescribed conditions:

(1) Slimicides are used as antimicrobial agents to control slime in the manufacture of paper and paperboard.

(2) Subject to any prescribed limitations, slimicides are prepared from one or more of the slime-control substances named in paragraph (c) of this section to which may be added optional adjuvant substances as provided for under paragraph (d) of this section.

(3) Slimicides are added to the process water used in the production of paper or paperboard, and the quantity added shall not exceed the amount necessary to accomplish the intended technical effect.

(b) To insure safe usage, the label or labeling of slimicides shall bear adequate directions for use.

(c) Slime-control substances permitted for use in the preparation of slimicides include substances subject to prior sanction or approval for such use and the following:

List of substances	Limitations
Acrolein.	
Alkenyl (C_{16}-C_{18}) dimethylethyl-ammonium bromide.	
n-Alkyl (C_{12}-C_{18}) dimethyl benzyl ammonium chloride.	
1,2-Benzisothiazolin-3-one	At a level of 0.06 pound per ton of dry weight fiber.
Bis(1,4-bromoacetoxy)-2-butene.	
5,5-Bis(bromoacetoxymethyl) *m*-dioxane.	
2,6-Bis(dimethylaminomethyl) cyclohexanone.	
1,2-Bis(monobromoacetoxy) ethane [CA Reg. No. 3785–34–0]	At a maximum level of 0.10 pound per ton of dry weight fiber.
Bis(trichloromethyl)sulfone.	
4-Bromoacetoxymethyl-*m*-dioxolane.	
2-Bromo-4′-hydroxyacetophenone.	
2-Bromo-2-nitropropane-1,3-diol (CAS Reg. No. 52–51–7)	At a maximum level of 0.6 pound per ton of dry weight fiber.
β-Bromo-β-nitrostyrene	At a maximum level of 1 pound per ton of dry weight fiber.
Chloroethylenebisthiocyanate.	
5-Chloro-2 - methyl - 4 - isothiazolin-3-one calcium chloride and 2-methyl-4-isothiazolin-3-one calcium chloride mixture at a ratio of 3 parts to 1 part.	At a level of 2.5 pounds per ton of dry weight fiber.
Chlorinated levulinic acids.	
Chloromethyl butanethiolsulfonate.	
Cupric nitrate.	

List of substances	Limitations
n-Dialkyl (C_{12}-C_{18}) benzylmethylammonium chloride.	
1,2-Dibromo-2,4-dicyanobutane (CAS Reg. No. 35691–65–7) ..	At a maximum level of 0.005% of dry weight fiber.
2,2-Dibromo-3-nitrilopropionamide	At a maximum level of 0.1 lb/ton of dry weight fiber.
2,3-Dibromopropionaldehyde.	
4,5-dichloro-1, 2-dithiol-3-one (CAS Reg. No. 1192–52–5)	For use only at levels not to exceed 10 milligrams per kilogram in the pulp slurry.
1,3-Dihalo-5,5-dimethylhydantoin (where the dihalo (halogen) may be bromine and/or chlorine) that may contain no more than 20 weight percent 1,3-dihalo-5-ethyl-5-methylhydantoin (where the dihalo (halogen) may be bromine and/or chlorine)..	At a maximum level of 1.0 kilogram (kg) per 1,000 kg of dry weight fiber.
4-(Diiodomethylsulfonyl) toluene (CAS Reg. No. 20018–09–1).	At a maximum level of 0.2 pound per ton (100 grams/1,000 kilograms) of dry weight fiber.
3,5-Dimethyl 1,3,5,2*H*-tetrahydrothiadiazine-2-thione.	
Dipotassium and disodium ethylenebis(dithiocarba-mate).	
Disodium cyanodithioimidocarbonate.	
n-Dodecylguanidine hydrochloride	At a maximum level of 0.20 pound per ton of dry weight fiber.
Glutaraldehyde (CAS Reg. No. 111-30-8).	
2-(*p*-hydroxyphenyl) glyoxylohydroximoyl chloride (CAS Registry No. 34911–46–1).	At a level of 0.02 pound per ton of dry weight fiber.
2-Hydroxypropyl methanethiol sulfonate.	
2-Mercaptobenzothiazole.	
Methylenebisbutanethiolsulfonate.	
Methylenebisthiocyanate.	
2-Nitrobutyl bromoacetate [CA Reg. No. 32815–96–6]	At a maximum level of 0.15 pound per ton of dry weight fiber.
N-[α-(Nitroethyl)benzyl] ethylenediamine.	
Potassium 2-mercaptobenzothiazole.	
Potassium *N*-hydroxymethyl-*N*-methyldithiocarba-mate.	
Potassium *N*-methyldithiocarbamate.	
Potassium pentachlorophenate.	
Potassium trichlorophenate.	
Silver fluoride	Limit of addition to process water not to exceed 0.024 pound, calculated as silver fluoride, per ton of paper produced.
Silver nitrate.	
Sodium dimethyldithiocarbamate.	
Sodium 2-mercaptobenzothiazole.	
Sodium pentachlorophenate.	
Sodium trichlorophenate.	
1,3,6,8-Tetraazatricyclo[6.2.1.13,6] dodecane.	
3,3,4,4-Tetrachlorotetrahydrothiophene-1,1-dioxide.	
Tetrakis(hydroxymethyl)phosphonium sulfate (CAS Reg. No. 55566–30–8).	Maximum use level of 84 mg/kg in the pulp slurry. The additive may also be added to water, which when introduced into the pulp slurry, results in a concentration in the pulp slurry not to exceed 84 mg/kg.
2-(Thiocyanomethylthio) benzothiazole.	
Vinylene bisthiocyanate.	

(d) Adjuvant substances permitted to be used in the preparation of slimicides include substances generally recognized as safe for use in food, substances generally recognized as safe for use in paper and paperboard, substances permitted to be used in paper and paperboard by other regulations in this chapter, and the following:

Acetone.
Butlylene oxide.
Dibutyl phthalate.
Didecyl phthalate.
N,N-Dimethylformamide.
Dodecyl phthalate.
Ethanolamine.
Ethylene glycol.
Ethylenediamine.
N-methyl-2-pyrrolidone (CAS Reg. No. 872–50–4).
a,a′-[Methylenebis[4-(1,1,3,3-tetramethylbutyl)-*o*-phenylene]] *bis*[*omega*-hydroxypoly (oxyethylene)] having 6–7.5 moles of ethylene oxide per hydroxyl group.
Monomethyl ethers of mono-, di-, and tripropylene glycol.
Nonylphenol reaction product with 9 to 12 molecules of ethylene oxide.
Octylphenol reaction product with 25 molecules of propylene oxide and 40 molecules of ethylene oxide.

[42 FR 14554, Mar. 15, 1977, as amended at 42 FR 41854, Aug. 19, 1977; 44 FR 75627, Dec. 21, 1979; 46 FR 36129, July 14, 1981; 49 FR 5748, Feb. 15, 1984; 51 FR 19059, May 27, 1986; 51 FR 43734, Dec. 4, 1986; 54 FR 18103, Apr. 27, 1989; 55 FR 31825, Aug. 6, 1990; 64 FR 46130, Aug. 24, 1999; 64 FR 69900, Dec. 15, 1999; 65 FR 40497, June 30, 2000; 65 FR 70790, Nov. 28, 2000; 69 FR 24512, May 4, 2004]

§ 176.320 Sodium nitrate-urea complex.

Sodium nitrate-urea complex may be safely used as a component of articles intended for use in producing, manufacturing, packing, processing, preparing, treating, packaging, transporting, or holding food, subject to the provisions of this section.

(a) Sodium nitrate-urea complex is a clathrate of approximately two parts urea and one part sodium nitrate.

(b) Sodium nitrate-urea complex conforming to the limitations prescribed in paragraph (b)(1) of this section is used as provided in paragraph (b)(2) of this section.

(1) *Limitations.* (i) It is used as a plasticizer in glassine and greaseproof paper.

(ii) The amount used does not exceed that required to accomplish its intended technical effect or exceed 15 percent by weight of the finished paper.

(2) *Conditions of use.* The glassine and greaseproof papers are used for packaging dry food or as the food-contact surface for dry food.

§ 176.350 Tamarind seed kernel powder.

Tamarind seed kernel powder may be safely used as a component of articles intended for use in producing, manufacturing, packing, processing, preparing, treating, packaging, transporting, or holding food, subject to the provisions of this section.

(a) Tamarind seed kernel powder is the ground kernel of tamarind seed (*Tamarindus indica* L.) after removal of the seed coat.

(b) It is used in the manufacture of paper and paperboard.

PART 177—INDIRECT FOOD ADDITIVES: POLYMERS

Subpart A [Reserved]

Subpart B—Substances for Use as Basic Components of Single and Repeated Use Food Contact Surfaces

Sec.

Subpart C—Substances for Use Only as Components of Articles Intended for Repeated Use

AUTHORITY: 21 U.S.C. 321, 342, 348, 379e.

SOURCE: 42 FR 14572, Mar. 15, 1977, unless otherwise noted.

EDITORIAL NOTE: Nomenclature changes to part 177 appear at 61 FR 14482, Apr. 2, 1996, 66 FR 56035, Nov. 6, 2001, 66 FR 66742, Dec. 27, 2001, 68 FR 15355, Mar. 31, 2003, and 70 FR 72074, Dec. 1, 2005.

Subpart A [Reserved]

Subpart B—Substances for Use as Basic Components of Single and Repeated Use Food Contact Surfaces

§ 177.1010 Acrylic and modified acrylic plastics, semirigid and rigid.

Semirigid and rigid acrylic and modified acrylic plastics may be safely used as articles intended for use in contact with food, in accordance with the following prescribed conditions. The acrylic and modified acrylic polymers or plastics described in this section also may be safely used as components of articles intended for use in contact with food.

(a) The optional substances that may be used in the formulation of the semirigid and rigid acrylic and modified acrylic plastics, or in the formulation of acrylic and modified acrylic components of articles, include substances generally recognized as safe in food, substances used in accordance with a prior sanction or approval, substances permitted for use in such plastics by regulations in parts 170 through 189 of this chapter, and substances identified in this paragraph. At least 50 weight-percent of the polymer content of the acrylic and modified acrylic materials used as finished articles or as components of articles shall consist of polymer units derived from one or more of the acrylic or methacrylic monomers listed in paragraph (a)(1) of this section.

(1) Homopolymers and copolymers of the following monomers:

n-Butyl acrylate.
n-Butyl methacrylate.
Ethyl acrylate.
2-Ethylhexyl acrylate.
Ethyl methacrylate.

Methyl acrylate.
Methyl methacrylate.

(2) Copolymers produced by copolymerizing one or more of the monomers listed in paragraph (a)(1) of this section with one or more of the following monomers:

Acrylonitrile.
Methacrylonitrile.
α-Methylstyrene.
Styrene.
Vinyl chloride.
Vinylidene chloride.

(3) Polymers identified in paragraphs (a)(1) and (2) of this section containing no more than 5 weight-percent of total polymer units derived by copolymerization with one or more of the monomers listed in paragraph (a)(3)(i) and (ii) of this section. Monomers listed in paragraph (a)(3)(ii) of this section are limited to use only in plastic articles intended for repeated use in contact with food.

(i) List of minor monomers:

Acrylamide.
Acrylic acid
1,3-Butylene glycol dimethacrylate.
1,4-Butylene glycol dimethacrylate.
Diethylene glycol dimethacrylate.
Diproplylene glycol dimethacrylate.
Divinylbenzene.
Ethylene glycol dimethacrylate.
Itaconic acid.
Methacrylic acid.
N-Methylolacrylamide.
N-Methylolmethacrylamide.
4-Methyl-1,4-pentanediol dimethacrylate.
Propylene glycol dimethacrylate.
Trivinylbenzene.

(ii) List of minor monomers limited to use only in plastic articles intended for repeated use in contact with food:

Allyl methacrylate [Chemical Abstracts Service Registry No. 96–05–9]
tert-Butyl acrylate.
tert-Butylaminoethyl methacrylate.
sec-Butyl methacrylate.
tert-Butyl methacrylate.
Cyclohexyl methacrylate.
Dimethylaminoethyl methacrylate.
2-Ethylhexyl methacrylate.
Hydroxyethyl methacrylate.
Hydroxyethyl vinyl sulfide.
Hydroxypropyl methacrylate.
Isobornyl methacrylate.
Isobutyl methacrylate.
Isopropyl acrylate.
Isopropyl methacrylate.
Methacrylamide.
Methacrylamidoethylene urea.
Methacryloxyacetamidoethylethylene urea.
Methacryloxyacetic acid.
n-Propyl methacrylate.
3,5,5-Trimethylcyclohexyl methacrylate.

(4) Polymers identified in paragraphs (a)(1), (2), and (3) of this section are mixed together and/or with the following polymers, provided that no chemical reactions, other than addition reactions, occur when they are mixed:

Butadiene-acrylonitrile copolymers.
Butadiene-acrylonitrile-styrene copolymers.
Butadiene-acrylonitrile-styrene-methyl methacrylic copolymers.
Butadiene-styrene copolymers.
Butyl rubber.
Natural rubber.
Polybutadiene.
Poly (3-chloro-1,3-butadiene).
Polyester identified in § 175.300(b)(3)(vii) of this chapter.
Polyvinyl chloride.
Vinyl chloride copolymers complying with § 177.1980.
Vinyl chloride-vinyl acetate copolymers.

(5) Antioxidants and stabilizers identified in § 175.300(b)(3)(xxx) of this chapter and the following:

Di-*tert*-butyl-*p*-cresol.
2-Hydroxy-4-methoxybenzophenone.
2-Hydroxy-4-methoxy-2-carboxybenzophenone.
3-Hydroxyphenyl benzoate.
p-Methoxyphenol.
Methyl salicylate.
Octadecyl 3,5-di-*tert*-butyl-4-hydroxyhydrocinnamate (CAS Reg. No. 2082–79–3): For use only: (1) At levels not exceeding 0.2 percent by weight in semirigid and rigid acrylic and modified acrylic plastics, where the finished articles contact foods containing not more than 15 percent alcohol; and (2) at levels not exceeding 0.01 percent by weight in semirigid and rigid acrylic and modified acrylic plastics intended for repeated food-contact use where the finished article may be used for foods containing more than 15 percent alcohol.
Phenyl salicylate.

(6) Release agents: Fatty acids derived from animal and vegetable fats and oils, and fatty alcohols derived from such acids.

(7) Surface active agent: Sodium dodecylbenzenesulfonate.

(8) Miscellaneous materials:

Di(2-ethylhexyl) phthalate, for use only as a flow promoter at a level not to exceed 3 weight-percent based on the monomers.
Dimethyl phthalate.

Oxalic acid, for use only as a polymerization catalyst aid.
Tetraethylenepentamine, for use only as a catalyst activator at a level not to exceed 0.5 weight-percent based on the monomers.
Toluene.
Xylene.

(b) The semirigid and rigid acrylic and modified acrylic plastics, in the finished form in which they are to contact food, when extracted with the solvent or solvents characterizing the type of food and under the conditions of time and temperature as determined from tables 1 and 2 of § 176.170(c) of this chapter, shall yield extractives not to exceed the following, when tested by the methods prescribed in paragraph (c) of this section. The acrylic and modified acrylic polymers or plastics intended to be used as components of articles also shall yield extractives not to exceed the following limitations when prepared as strips as described in paragraph (c)(2) of this section:

(1) Total nonvolatile extractives not to exceed 0.3 milligram per square inch of surface tested.

(2) Potassium permanganate oxidizable distilled water and 8 and 50 percent alcohol extractives not to exceed an absorbance of 0.15.

(3) Ultraviolet-absorbing distilled water and 8 and 50 percent alcohol extractives not to exceed an absorbance of 0.30.

(4) Ultraviolet-absorbing *n*-heptane extractives not to exceed an absorbance of 0.10.

(c) *Analytical methods*—(1) *Selection of extractability conditions.* These are to be chosen as provided in § 176.170(c) of this chapter.

(2) *Preparation of samples.* Sufficient samples to allow duplicates of all applicable tests shall be cut from the articles or formed from the plastic composition under tests, as strips about 2.5 inches by about 0.85-inch wide by about 0.125-inch thick. The total exposed surface should be 5 square inches ±0.5-square inch. The samples, after preparation, shall be washed with a clean brush under hot tapwater, rinsed under running hot tapwater (140 °F minimum), rinsed with distilled water, and air-dried in a dust-free area or in a desiccator.

(3) *Preparation of solvents.* The water used shall be double-distilled water, prepared in a still using a block tin condenser. The 8 and 50 percent (by volume) alcohol solvents shall be prepared from ethyl alcohol meeting the specifications of the United States Pharmacopeia XX and diluted with double-distilled water that has been prepared in a still using a tin block condenser. The *n*-heptane shall be spectrophotometric grade. Adequate precautions must be taken to keep all solvents dust-free.

(4) *Blank values on solvents.* (i) Duplicate determinations of residual solids shall be run on samples of each solvent that have been exposed to the temperature-time conditions of the extraction test without the plastic sample. Sixty milliliters of exposed solvent is pipetted into a clean, weighed platinum dish, evaporated to 2–5 milliliters on a nonsparking, low-temperature hot plate and dried in 212 °F oven for 30 minutes. The residue for each solvent shall be determined by weight and the average residue weight used as the blank value in the total solids determination set out in paragraph (c)(6) of this section. The residue for an acceptable solvent sample shall not exceed 0.5 milligram per 60 milliliters.

(ii) For acceptability in the ultraviolet absorbers test, a sample of each solvent shall be scanned in an ultraviolet spectrophotometer in 5-centimeter silica spectrophotometric absorption cells. The absorbance of the distilled water when measured versus air in the reference cell shall not exceed 0.03 at any point in the wavelength region of 245 to 310 mμ. The absorbance of the 8 percent alcohol when measured versus distilled water in the reference cell shall not exceed 0.01 at any point in the wavelength region of 245 to 310 mμ. The absorbance of the 50 percent alcohol when measured versus distilled water in the reference cell shall not exceed 0.05 at any point in the wavelength region of 245 to 310 mμ. The absorbance of the heptane when measured versus distilled water in the reference cell shall not exceed 0.15 at 245, 0.09 at 260, 0.04 at 270, and 0.02 at any point in the wavelength region of 280 to 310 mμ.

(iii) Duplicate ultraviolet blank determinations shall be run on samples of each solvent that has been exposed to the temperature-time conditions of the extraction test without the plastic sample. An aliquot of the exposed solvent shall be measured versus the unexposed solvent in the reference cell. The average difference in the absorbances at any wavelength in the region of 245 to 310 mμ shall be used as a blank correction for the ultraviolet absorbers measured at the same wavelength according to paragraph (c)(8)(ii) of this section.

(iv) The acceptability of the solvents for use in the permanganate test shall be determined by preparing duplicate permanganate test blanks according to paragraph (c)(7)(iv) of this section. For this test, the directions referring to the sample extract shall be disregarded. The blanks shall be scanned in 5-centimeter silica spectrophotometric cells in the spectrophotometer versus the appropriate solvent as reference. The absorbance in distilled water in the wavelength region of 544 to 552 mμ should be 1.16 but must not be less than 1.05 nor more than 1.25. The absorbance in the 8 and 50 percent alcohol must not be less than 0.85 nor more than 1.15.

(v) Duplicate permanganate test determinations shall be run on samples of distilled water and 8 and 50 percent alcohol solvents that have been exposed to the temperature-time conditions of the extraction test without the plastic sample. The procedure shall be as described in paragraph (c)(7)(iv) of this section, except that the appropriate exposed solvent shall be substituted where the directions call for sample extract. The average difference in the absorbances in the region of 544 to 552 mμ shall be used as a blank correction for the determination of permanganate oxidizable extractives according to paragraph (c)(7)(iv) of this section.

(5) *Extraction procedure.* For each extraction, place a plastic sample in a clean 25 millimeters × 200 millimeters hard-glass test tube and add solvent equal to 10 milliliters of solvent per square inch of plastic surface. This amount will be between 45 milliliters and 55 milliliters. The solvent must be preequilibrated to the temperature of the extraction test. Close the test tube with a ground-glass stopper and expose to the specified temperature for the specified time. Cool the tube and contents to room temperature if necessary.

(6) *Determination of total nonvolatile extractives.* Remove the plastic strip from the solvent with a pair of clean forceps and wash the strip with 5 milliliters of the appropriate solvent, adding the washings to the contents of the test tube. Pour the contents of the test tube into a clean, weighed platinum dish. Wash the tube with 5 milliliters of the appropriate solvent and add the solvent to the platinum dish. Evaporate the solvent to 2–5 milliliters on a nonsparking, low-temperature hotplate. Complete the evaporation in a 212 °F oven for 30 minutes. Cool the dish in a desiccator for 30 minutes and weigh to the nearest 0.1 milligram. Calculate the total nonvolatile extractives as follows:

$$\text{Milligrams extractives per square inch} = \frac{e-b}{s}$$

$$\text{Extractives in parts per million} = \frac{eb}{s} \times 100$$

where:

e=Total increase in weight of the dish, in milligrams.

b=Blank value of the solvent in milligrams, as determined in paragraph (c)(4)(i) of this section.

s=Total surface of the plastic sample in square inches.

(7) *Determination of potassium permanganate oxidizable extractives.* (i) Pipette 25 milliliters of distilled water into a clean 125-milliliter Erlenmeyer flask that has been rinsed several times with aliquots of distilled water. This is the blank. Prepare a distilled water solution containing 1.0 part per million of *p*-methoxyphenol (melting point 54–56 °C, Eastman grade or equivalent). Pipette 25 milliliters of this *p*-methoxyphenol solution into a rinsed Erlenmeyer flask. Pipette exactly 3.0 milliliters of 154 parts per million aqueous potassium permanganate solution into the *p*-methoxyphenol and exactly 3.0 milliliters into the blank, in that order. Swirl both flasks to mix the contents and then transfer aliquots from each flask into matched 5-centimeter spectrophotometric absorption cells. The cells are placed in the spectrophotometer cell compartment with

the *p*-methoxyphenol solution in the reference beam. Spectrophotometric measurement is conducted as in paragraph (c)(7)(iv) of this section. The absorbance reading in the region 544–552 mμ should be 0.24 but must be not less than 0.12 nor more than 0.36. This test shall be run in duplicate. For the purpose of ascertaining compliance with the limitations in paragraph (b)(2) of this section, the absorbance measurements obtained on the distilled water extracts according to paragraph (c)(7)(iv) of this section shall be multiplied by a correction factor, calculated as follows:

$$\frac{0.24}{\text{Average of duplicate } \rho\text{-methoxyphenol absorbance determinations according to this paragraph (c)(7)(i) of this section}} = \text{Correction factor for water extracts.}$$

(ii) The procedure in paragraph (c)(7)(i) of this section is repeated except that, in this instance, the solvent shall be 8 percent alcohol. The absorbance in the region 544–552 mμ should be 0.26 but must be not less than 0.13 nor more than 0.39. This test shall be run in duplicate. For the purpose of ascertaining compliance with the limitations prescribed in paragraph (b)(2) of this section, the absorbance measurements obtained on the 8 percent alcohol extracts according to paragraph (c)(7)(iv) of this section shall be multiplied by a correction factor, calculated as follows:

$$\frac{0.26}{\text{Average of duplicate } \rho\text{-methoxyphenol absorbance determination according to this paragraph (c)(7)(ii) of this section}} = \text{Correction factor for aqueous 8 percent alcohol extracts.}$$

(iii) The procedure in paragraph (c)(7)(i) of this section is repeated except that, in this instance, the solvent shall be 50 percent alcohol. The absorbance in the region 544–552 mμ should be 0.25 but must be not less than 0.12 nor more than 0.38. This test shall be run in duplicate. For the purpose of ascertaining compliance with the limitations prescribed in paragraph (b)(2) of this section, the absorbance measurements obtained on the 50 percent alcohol extracts according to paragraph (c)(7)(iv) of this section shall be multiplied by a correction factor, calculated as follows:

$$\frac{0.25}{\text{Average of duplicate } \rho\text{-methoxyphenol absorbance determinations according to paragraph (c)(7)(ii) of this section}} = \text{Correction factor for 50 percent aqueous alcohol extracts.}$$

(iv) *Water and 8 and 50 percent alcohol extracts.* Pipette 25 milliliters of the appropriate solvent into a clean, 125-milliliter Erlenmeyer flask that has been rinsed several times with aliquots of the same solvent. This is the blank. Into another similarly rinsed flask, pipette 25 milliliters of the sample extract that has been exposed under the conditions specified in paragraph (c)(5) of this section. Pipette exactly 3.0 milliliters of 154 parts per million aqueous potassium permanganate solution into the sample and exactly 3.0 milliliters into the blank, in that order. Before use, the potassium permanganate solution shall be checked as in paragraph (c)(7)(i) of this section. Both flasks are swirled to mix the contents, and then aliquots from each flask are transferred to matched 5-centimeter spectrophotometric absorption cells. Both cells are placed in the spectrophotometer cell compartment with the sample solution in the reference beam. The spectrophotometer is adjusted for 0 and 100 percent transmittance at 700 mμ. The spectrum is scanned on the absorbance scale from 700 mμ to 500 mμ in such a way that the region 544 mμ to 552 mμ is scanned within 5 minutes to 10 minutes of the time that permanganate was added to the solutions. The height of the absorbance peak shall be measured, corrected for the blank as determined in paragraph (c)(4)(v) of this section, and multiplied by the appropriate correction factor determined according to paragraph (c)(7) (i), (ii), and (iii) of this section. This test shall be run in duplicate and the two results averaged.

(8) *Determination of ultraviolet-absorbing extractives.* (i) A distilled water solution containing 1.0 part per million of *p*-methoxyphenol (melting point 54 °C–56 °C. Eastman grade or equivalent) shall be scanned in the region 360 to 220 mμ in 5-centimeter silica spectrophotometric absorption cells versus a distilled water reference. The absorbance at the wavelength of maximum absorbance (should be about 285 mμ) is about 0.11 but must be not less than 0.08 nor more than 0.14. This test shall be run in duplicate. For the purpose of ascertaining compliance with the limitations prescribed in paragraph (b) (3) and (4) of this section, the absorbance obtained on the extracts according to paragraph (c)(8)(ii) of this section shall be multiplied by a correction factor, calculated as follows:

$$\frac{0.11}{\text{Average of duplicate } p\text{-methoxyphenol absorbance determinations according to this paragraph (c)(8)(i) of this section}} = \text{Correction factor for ultraviolet absorbers test.}$$

(ii) An aliquot of the extract that has been exposed under the conditions specified in paragraph (c)(5) of this section is scanned in the wavelength region 360 to 220 mμ versus the appropriate solvent reference in matched 5-centimeter silica spectrophotometric absorption cells. The height of any absorption peak shall be measured, corrected for the blank as determined in paragraph (c)(4)(iii) of this section, and multiplied by the correction factor determined according to paragraph (c)(8)(i) of this section.

(d) In accordance with current good manufacturing practice, finished semirigid and rigid acrylic and modified acrylic plastics, and articles containing these polymers, intended for repeated use in contact with food shall be thoroughly cleansed prior to their first use in contact with food.

(e) Acrylonitrile copolymers identified in this section shall comply with the provisions of § 180.22 of this chapter.

(f) The acrylic and modified acrylic polymers identified in and complying with this section, when used as components of the food-contact surface of an article that is the subject of a regulation in this part and in parts 174, 175, 176, and 178 of this chapter, shall comply with any specifications and limitations prescribed by such regulation for the article in the finished form in which it is to contact food.

[42 FR 14572, Mar. 15, 1977; 42 FR 56728, Oct. 28, 1977, as amended at 43 FR 54927, Nov. 24, 1978; 45 FR 67320, Oct. 10, 1980; 46 FR 46796, Sept. 22, 1981; 49 FR 10108, Mar. 19, 1984; 49 FR 13139, Apr. 3, 1984; 50 FR 31045, July 24, 1985]

§ 177.1020 Acrylonitrile/butadiene/styrene co-polymer.

Acrylonitrile/butadiene/styrene copolymer identified in this section may be safely used as an article or component of articles intended for use with all foods, except those containing alcohol, under conditions of use E, F, and G described in table 2 of § 176.170(c) of this chapter.

(a) *Identity.* For the purpose of this section, the acrylonitrile/butadiene/styrene copolymer consists of:

(1) Eighty-four to eighty-nine parts by weight of a matrix polymer containing 73 to 78 parts by weight of acrylonitrile and 22 to 27 parts by weight of styrene; and

(2) Eleven to sixteen parts by weight of a grafted rubber consisting of (i) 8 to 13 parts of butadiene/styrene elastomer containing 72 to 77 parts by weight of butadiene and 23 to 28 parts by weight of styrene and (ii) 3 to 8 parts by weight of a graft polymer having the same composition range as the matrix polymer.

(b) *Adjuvants.* The copolymer identified in paragraph (a) of this section may contain adjuvant substances required in its production. Such adjuvants may include substances generally recognized as safe in food, substances used in accordance with prior sanction, substances permitted in this part, and the following:

Substance	Limitations
2-Mercapto- ethanol	The finished copolymer shall contain not more than 100 ppm 2-mercaptoethanol acrylonitrile adduct as determined by a method titled "Analysis of Cycopac Resin for Residual β-(2-Hydroxyethylmercapto) propionitrile," which is incorporated by reference. Copies are available from the Bureau of Foods (HFS–200), Food and Drug Administration, 5100 Paint Branch Pkwy., College Park, MD 20740, or available for inspection at the National Archives and Records Administration (NARA). For information on the availability of this material at NARA, call 202–741–6030, or go to: *http://www.archives.gov/federal_register/code_of_federal_regulations/ibr_locations.html.*

(c) *Specifications.* (1) Nitrogen content of the copolymer is in the range of 16 to 18.5 percent as determined by Micro-Kjeldahl analysis.

(2) Residual acrylonitrile monomer content of the finished copolymer articles is not more than 11 parts per million as determined by a gas chromatographic method titled "Determination of Residual Acrylonitrile and Styrene Monomers-Gas Chromatographic Internal Standard Method," which is incorporated by reference. Copies are available from the Center for Food Safety and Applied Nutrition (HFS–200), Food and Drug Administration, 5100 Paint Branch Pkwy., College Park, MD 20740, or available for inspection at the National Archives and Records Administration (NARA). For information on the availability of this material at NARA, call 202–741–6030, or go to: *http://www.archives.gov/federal_register/code_of_federal_regulations/ibr_locations.html.*

(d) *Extractive limitations.* (1) Total nonvolatile extractives not to exceed 0.0005 milligram per square inch surface area when the finished food contact article is exposed to distilled water, 3 percent acetic acid, or *n*-heptane for 8 days at 120 °F.

(2) The finished food-contact article shall yield not more than 0.0015 milligram per square inch of acrylonitrile monomer when exposed to distilled water and 3 percent acetic acid at 150 °F for 15 days when analyzed by a polarographic method titled "Extracted Acrylonitrile by Differential Pulse Polarography," which is incorporated by reference. Copies are available from the Center for Food Safety and Applied Nutrition (HFS–200), Food and Drug Administration, 5100 Paint Branch Pkwy., College Park, MD 20740, or available for inspection at the National Archives and Records Administration (NARA). For information on the availability of this material at NARA, call 202–741–6030, or go to: *http://www.archives.gov/federal_register/code_of_federal_regulations/ibr_locations.html.*

(e) Acrylonitrile copolymers identified in this section shall comply with the provisions of § 180.22 of this chapter.

(f) Acrylonitrile copolymers identified in this section are not authorized to be used to fabricate beverage containers.

[42 FR 14572, Mar. 15, 1977, as amended at 42 FR 48543, Sept. 23, 1977; 47 FR 11841, Mar. 19, 1982; 54 FR 24897, June 12, 1989]

§ 177.1030 Acrylonitrile/butadiene/styrene/methyl methacrylate copolymer.

Acrylonitrile/butadiene/styrene/methyl methacrylate copolymer identified in this section may be safely used as an article or component of articles intended for use with food identified in table 1 of § 176.170(c) of this chapter as Type I, II, III, IVA, IVB, V, VIB, (except bottles intended to hold carbonated beverages), VIIA, VIIB, VIII and IX, under conditions of use C, D, E, F, and G described in table 2 of § 176.170(c) of this chapter with a high temperature limitation of 190 °F.

(a) *Identity.* For the purpose of this section, acrylonitrile/butadiene/styrene/methyl methacrylate copolymer consists of: (1) 73 to 79 parts by weight of a matrix polymer containing 64 to 69 parts by weight of acrylonitrile, 25 to 30 parts by weight of styrene and 4 to 6 parts by weight of methyl methacrylate; and (2) 21 to 27 parts by weight of a grafted rubber consisting of (i) 16 to 20 parts of butadiene/styrene/elastomer containing 72 to 77 parts by weight of butadiene and 23 to 28 parts by weight of styrene and (ii) 5 to 10 parts by weight of a graft polymer having the same composition range as the matrix polymer.

(b) *Adjuvants.* The copolymer identified in paragraph (a) of this section may contain adjuvant substances required in its production. Such adjuvants may include substances generally recognized as safe in food, substances used in accordance with prior sanction, substances permitted under applicable regulations in this part, and the following:

Substances	Limitations
2–Mercaptoethanol ..	The finished copolymer shall contain not more than 800 ppm 2–mercaptoethanol acrylonitrile adduct as determined by a method titled "Analysis of Cycopac Resin for Residual β–(2–Hydroxyethylmercapto) propionitrile," which is incorporated by reference. Copies are available from the Bureau of Foods (HFS–200), Food and Drug Administration, 5100 Paint Branch Pkwy., College Park, MD 20740, or available for inspection at the National Archives and Records Administration (NARA). For information on the availability of this material at NARA, call 202–741–6030, or go to: *http://www.archives.gov/federal_register/code_of_federal_regulations/ibr_locations.html.*

(c) *Specifications.* (1) Nitrogen content of the copolymer is in the range of 13.0 to 16.0 percent as determined by Micro-Kjeldahl analysis.

(2) Residual acrylonitrile monomer content of the finished copolymer articles is not more than 11 parts per million as determined by a gas chromatographic method titled "Determination of Residual Acrylonitrile and Styrene Monomers-Gas Chromatographic Internal Standard Method," which is incorporated by reference. Copies are available from the Center for Food Safety and Applied Nutrition (HFS–200), Food and Drug Administration, 5100 Paint Branch Pkwy., College Park, MD 20740, or available for inspection at the National Archives and Records Administration (NARA). For information on the availability of this material at NARA, call 202–741–6030, or go to: *http://www.archives.gov/federal_register/code_of_federal_regulations/ibr_locations.html.*

(d) *Extractive limitations.* (1) Total nonvolatile extractives not to exceed 0.0005 milligram per square inch surface area of the food-contact article when exposed to distilled water, 3 percent acetic acid, 50 percent ethanol, and *n*-heptane for 10 days at 120 °F.

(2) The finished food-contact article shall yield not more than 0.0025 milligram per square inch of acrylonitrile monomer when exposed to distilled water, 3 percent acetic acid and *n*-heptane at 190 °F for 2 hours, cooled to

120 °F (80 to 90 minutes) and maintained at 120 °F for 10 days when analyzed by a polarographic method titled "Extracted Acrylonitrile by Differential Pulse Polarography," which is incorporated by reference. Copies are available from the Center for Food Safety and Applied Nutrition (HFS–200), Food and Drug Administration, 5100 Paint Branch Pkwy., College Park, MD 20740, or available for inspection at the National Archives and Records Administration (NARA). For information on the availability of this material at NARA, call 202–741–6030, or go to: *http://www.archives.gov/federal_register/code_of_federal_regulations/ibr_locations.html.*

(e) Acrylonitrile copolymers identified in this section shall comply with the provisions of § 180.22 of this chapter.

(f) Acrylonitrile copolymers identified in this section are not authorized to be used to fabricate beverage containers.

[42 FR 14572, Mar. 15, 1977, as amended at 42 FR 48543, Sept. 23, 1977; 47 FR 11841, Mar. 19, 1982; 54 FR 24898, June 12, 1989]

§ 177.1040 Acrylonitrile/styrene copolymer.

Acrylonitrile/styrene copolymers identified in this section may be safely used as a component of packaging materials subject to the provisions of this section.

(a) *Identity.* For the purposes of this section acrylonitrile/styrene copolymers are basic copolymers meeting the specifications prescribed in paragraph (c) of this section.

(b) *Adjuvants.* (1) The copolymers identified in paragraph (c) of this section may contain adjuvant substances required in their production, with the exception that they shall not contain mercaptans or other substances which form reversible complexes with acrylonitrile monomer. Permissible adjuvants may include substances generally recognized as safe in food, substances used in accordance with prior sanction, substances permitted under applicable regulations in this part, and those authorized in paragraph (b)(2) of this section.

(2) The optional adjuvants for the acrylonitrile/styrene copolymer identified in paragraphs (c) (1) and (3) of this section are as follows:

Substances	Limitation
Condensation polymer of toluene sulfonamide and formaldehyde.	0.15 pct maximum.

(c) *Specifications.*

Acrylonitrile/styrene copolymers	Maximum residual acrylonitrile monomer content of finished article	Nitrogen content of copolymer	Maximum extractable fractions at specified temperatures and times	Conformance with certain specifications
1. Acrylonitrile/styrene copolymer consisting of the copolymer produced by polymerization of 66–72 parts by weight of acrylonitrile and 28–34 parts by weight of styrene; for use with food of Type VI-B identified in table 1 of § 176.170(c) of this chapter under conditions of use C, D, E, F, G described in table 2 of § 176.170(c) of this chapter.	80 ppm[1]	17.4 to 19 pct.	Total nonvolatile extractives not to exceed 0.01 mg/in ^{2} surface area of the food contact article when exposed to distilled water and 3 pct acetic acid for 10 d at 66 °C (150 °F). The extracted copolymer shall not exceed 0.001 mg/in ^{2} surface area of the food contact article when exposed to distilled water and 3 pct acetic acid for 10 d at 66 °C (150 °F)[1].	Minimum number average molecular weight is 30,000.[1]
2. Acrylonitrile/styrene copolymer consisting of the copolymer produced by polymerization of 45–65 parts by weight of acrylonitrile and 35–55 parts by weigth of styrene; for use with food of Types, I, II, III, IV, V, VI (except bottles), VII, VIII, and IX identified in table 1 of § 176.170(c) of this chapter under conditions B (not to exceed 93 °C (200 °F)), C, D, E, F, G described in table 2 of § 176.170(c) of this chapter.	50 ppm[1]	12.2 to 17.2 pct.	Extracted copolymer not to exceed 2.0 ppm in aqueous extract or *n*-heptane extract obtained when 100 g sample of the basic copolymer in the form of particles of a size that will pass through a U.S. Standard Sieve No. 6 and that will be held on a U.S. Standard Sieve No. 10 is extracted with 250 mil of deionized water or reagent grade *n*-heptane at reflux temperature for 2 h.[1]	Minimum 10 pct solution viscosity at 25 °C (77 °F) is 10cP.[1]

Acrylonitrile/styrene copolymers	Maximum residual acrylonitrile monomer content of finished article	Nitrogen content of copolymer	Maximum extractable fractions at specified temperatures and times	Conformance with certain specifications
3. Acrylonitrile/styrene copolymer consisting of the copolymer produced by polymerization of 66–72 parts by weight of acrylonitrile and 28–34 parts by weight of styrene; for use with food of Types VI-A and VI-B identified in table 1 of § 176.170(c) of this chapter under conditions of use C, D, E, F, G described in table 2 of § 176.170(c) of this chapter.	0.10 ppm (calculated on the basis of the weight of the acrylonitrile copolymer resin in the finished articles). [2]	17.4 to 19 pct.	Total nonvolatile extractives not to exceed 0.01 mg/in[2] surface area of the food contact article when exposed to distilled water and 3 pct acetic acid for 10 d at 66 °C (150 °F). The extracted copolymer shall not exceed 0.001 mg/in[2] surface area of the food contact article when exposed to distilled water and 3 pct acetic acid for 10 d at 66 °C (150 °F). [1].	Maximum carbon dioxide permeability at 23 °C (73 °F) for the finished article is 0.04 barrer. [3]

[1] Use methods for determination of residual acrylonitrile monomer content, maximum extractable fraction, number average molecular weight, and solution viscosity, titled: "Determination of Residual Acrylonitrile and Styrene Monomers-Gas Chromatographic Internal Standard Method"; "Infrared Spectrophotometric Determination of Polymer Extracted from Barex 210 Resin Pellets"; "Procedure for the Determination of Molecular Weights of Acrylonitrile/Styrene Copolymers," and "Analytical Method for 10% Solution Viscosity of Tyril," which are incorproated by reference. Copies are available from the Center for Food Safety and Applied Nutrition (HFS–200), 5100 Paint Branch Pkwy., College Park, MD 20740, or may be examined at the National Archives and Records Administration (NARA). For information on the availability of this material at NARA, call 202–741–6030, or go to: *http://www.archives.gov/federal_register/code_of_federal_regulations/ibr_locations.html.*

[2] As determined by the method titled "Headspace Sampling and Gas-Solid Chromatographic Determination of Residual Acrylonitrile in Acrylonitrile Copolyemr Solutions," which is incorporated by reference. Copies are available from the Center for Food Safety and Applied Nutrition (HFS–200), 5100 Paint Branch Pkwy., College Park, MD 20740, or may be examined at the National Archives and Records Administration (NARA). For information on the availability of this material at NARA, call 202–741–6030, or go to: *http://www.archives.gov/federal_register/code_of_federal_regulations/ibr_locations.html.*

[3] As determined on appropriately shaped test samples of the article or acrylonitrile copolymer layer in a multilayer construction by ASTM method D–1434–82, "Standard Method for Determining Gas Permeability Characteristics of Plastic Film and Sheeting," which is incorporated by reference. Copies are available from the Center for Food Safety and Applied Nutrition (HFS–200), 5100 Paint Branch Pkwy., College Park, MD 20740, and the American Society for Testing Materials, 100 Barr Harbor Dr., West Conshohocken, Philadelphia, PA 19428-2959, or may be examined at the National Archives and Records Administration (NARA). For information on the availability of this material at NARA, call 202–741–6030, or go to: *http://www.archives.gov/federal_register/code_of_federal_regulations/ibr_locations.html.*

(d) *Interim listing.* Acrylonitrile copolymers identified in this section shall comply with the provisions of § 180.22 of this chapter.

(e) Acrylonitrile copolymer identified in this section may be used to fabricate beverage containers only if they comply with the specifications of item 3 in paragraph (c) of this section.

[42 FR 14572, Mar. 15, 1977, as amended at 42 FR 48543, Sept. 23, 1977; 47 FR 11841, Mar. 19, 1982; 49 FR 36643, Sept. 19, 1984; 52 FR 33803, Sept. 8, 1987]

§ 177.1050 Acrylonitrile/styrene copolymer modified with butadiene/styrene elastomer.

Acrylonitrile/styrene copolymer modified with butadiene/styrene elastomer identified in this section may be safely used as a component of bottles intended for use with foods identified in table I of § 176.170(c) of this chapter as Type VI-B under conditions for use E, F, or G described in table 2 of § 176.170(c) of this chapter.

(a) *Identity.* For the purpose of this section, acrylonitrile/styrene copolymer modified with butadiene/styrene elastomer consists of a blend of:

(1) 82–88 parts by weight of a matrix copolymer produced by polymerization of 77–82 parts by weight of acrylonitrile and 18–23 parts of styrene; and

(2) 12–18 parts by weight of a grafted rubber consisting of (i) 8–12 parts of butadiene/styrene elastomer containing 77–82 parts by weight of butadiene and 18–23 parts by weight of styrene and (ii) 4–6 parts by weight of a graft copolymer consisting of 70–77 parts by weight of acrylonitrile and 23–30 parts by weight of styrene.

(b) *Adjuvants.* The modified copolymer identified in paragraph (a) of this section may contain adjuvant substances required in its production. Such adjuvants may include substances generally recognized as safe in food, substances used in accordance with prior sanction, substances permitted under applicable regulations in this part, and the following:

Substances	Limitations
n-Dodecylmercaptan	The finished copolymer shall contain not more than 500 parts per million (ppm) dodecylmercaptan as dodecylmercapto-propionitrile as determined by the method titled, "Determination of β-Dodecylmercaptopropionitrile in NR–16 Polymer," which is incorporated by reference. Copies are available from the Center for Food Safety and Applied Nutrition (HFS–200), Food and Drug Administration, 5100 Paint Branch Pkwy., College Park, MD 20740, or available for inspection at the National Archives and Records Administration (NARA). For information on the availability of this material at NARA, call 202–741–6030, or go to: *http://www.archives.gov/federal_register/code_of_federal_regulations/ibr_locations.html.*

(c) *Specifications.* (1) Nitrogen content of the modified copolymer is in the range of 17.7–19.8 percent.

(2) Intrinsic viscosity of the matrix copolymer in butyrolactone is not less than 0.5 deciliter/gram at 35 °C, as determined by the method titled "Molecular Weight of Matrix Copolymer by Solution Viscosity," which is incorporated by reference. Copies are available from the Center for Food Safety and Applied Nutrition (HFS–200), Food and Drug Administration, 5100 Paint Branch Pkwy., College Park, MD 20740, or available for inspection at the National Archives and Records Administration (NARA). For information on the availability of this material at NARA, call 202–741–6030, or go to: *http://www.archives.gov/federal_register/code_of_federal_regulations/ibr_locations.html.*

(3) Residual acrylonitrile monomer content of the modified copolymer articles is not more than 11 ppm as determined by a gas chromatographic method titled "Determination of Residual Acrylonitrile and Styrene Monomers-Gas Chromatographic Internal Standard Method," which is incorporated by reference. Copies are available from the Center for Food Safety and Applied Nutrition (HFS–200), Food and Drug Administration, 5100 Paint Branch Pkwy., College Park, MD 20740, or available for inspection at the National Archives and Records Administration (NARA). For information on the availability of this material at NARA, call 202–741–6030, or go to: *http://www.archives.gov/federal_register/code_of_federal_regulations/ibr_locations.html.*

(d) *Extractives limitations.* The following extractives limitations are determined by an infrared spectrophotometric method titled "Infrared Spectrophotometric Determination of Polymer Extracted from Borex® 210 Resin Pellets," which is incorporated by reference. Copies are available from the Center for Food Safety and Applied Nutrition (HFS–200), Food and Drug Administration, 5100 Paint Branch Pkwy., College Park, MD 20740, or available for inspection at the National Archives and Records Administration (NARA). For information on the availability of this material at NARA, call 202–741–6030, or go to: *http://www.archives.gov/federal_register/code_of_federal_regulations/ibr_locations.html.* Copies are applicable to the modified copolymers in the form of particles of a size that will pass through a U.S. Standard Sieve No. 6 and that will be held on a U.S. Standard Sieve No. 10:

(1) The extracted copolymer shall not exceed 2.0 ppm in aqueous extract obtained when a 100-gram sample of copolymer is extracted with 250 milliliters of freshly distilled water at reflux temperature for 2 hours.

(2) The extracted copolymer shall not exceed 0.5 ppm in *n*-heptane when a 100-gram sample of the basic copol-ymer is extracted with 250 milliliters spectral grade *n*-heptane at reflux temperature for 2 hours.

(e) *Accelerated extraction end test.* The modified copolymer shall yield acrylonitrile monomer not in excess of 0.4 ppm when tested as follows:

(1) The modified copolymer shall be in the form of eight strips ½ inch by 4 inches by .03 inch.

(2) The modified copolymer strips shall be immersed in 225 milliliters of 3 percent acetic acid in a Pyrex glass pressure bottle.

(3) The pyrex glass pressure bottle is then sealed and heated to 150 °F in either a circulating air oven or a thermostat controlled bath for a period of 8 days.

(4) The Pyrex glass pressure bottle is then removed from the oven or bath

and cooled to room temperature. A sample of the extracting solvent is then withdrawn and analyzed for acrylonitrile monomer by a gas chromatographic method titled "Gas-Solid Chromatographic Procedure for Determining Acrylonitrile Monomer in Acrylonitrile-Containing Polymers and Food Simulating Solvents," which is incorporated by reference. Copies, are available from the Center for Food Safety and Applied Nutrition (HFS–200), Food and Drug Administration, 5100 Paint Branch Pkwy., College Park, MD 20740, or available for inspection at the National Archives and Records Administration (NARA). For information on the availability of this material at NARA, call 202–741–6030, or go to: *http://www.archives.gov/federal_register/code_of_federal_regulations/ibr_locations.html.*

(f) Acrylonitrile copolymers identified in this section shall comply with the provisions of § 180.22 of this chapter.

(g) Acrylonitrile copolymers identified in this section are not authorized to be used to fabricate beverage containers.

[42 FR 14572, Mar. 15, 1977, as amended at 42 FR 48544, Sept. 23, 1977; 47 FR 11841, Mar. 19, 1982; 47 FR 16775, Apr. 20, 1982; 54 FR 24898, June 12, 1989]

§ 177.1060 *n*-Alkylglutarimide/acrylic copolymers.

n-Alkylglutarimide/acrylic copolymers identified in this section may be safely used as articles or components of articles intended for use in contact with food subject to provisions of this section and part 174 of this chapter.

(a) *Identity.* For the purpose of this section, *n*-alkylglutarimide/acrylic copolymers are copolymers obtained by reaction of substances permitted by § 177.1010(a) (1), (2), and (3) with the following substance: Monomethylamine (CAS Reg. No. 74–89–5), to form *n*-methylglutarimide/acrylic copolymers.

(b) *Adjuvants.* The copolymers identified in paragraph (a) of this section may contain adjuvant substances required in their production. The optional adjuvant substances required in the production of the basic polymer may include substances permitted for such use by applicable regulations, as set forth in part 174 of this chapter.

(c) *Specifications.* Maximum nitrogen content of the copolymer determined by micro-Kjeldahl analysis, shall not exceed 8 percent.

(d) *Limitations.* (1) The *n*-alkylglutarimide/acrylic copolymers in the finished form in which they shall contact food, when extracted with the solvent or solvents characterizing the type of food and under the conditions of time and temperature described in tables 1 and 2 of § 176.170(c) of this chapter, shall yield extractives not to exceed the limitations of § 177.1010(b) of this chapter, when prepared as strips, as described in § 177.1010(c)(2) of this chapter.

(2) The *n*-alkylglutarimide/acrylic copolymers shall not be used as polymer modifiers in vinyl chloride homo- or copolymers.

(e) *Conditions of use.* The *n*-alkylglutarimide/acrylic copolymers are used as articles or components of articles (other than articles composed of vinyl chloride homo- or copolymers) intended for use in contact with all foods except beverages containing more than 8 percent alcohol under conditions of use D, E, F, and G as described in table 2 of § 176.170(c) of this chapter.

[54 FR 20382, May 11, 1989, as amended at 58 FR 17098, Apr. 1, 1993]

§ 177.1200 Cellophane.

Cellophane may be safely used for packaging food in accordance with the following prescribed conditions:

(a) Cellophane consists of a base sheet made from regenerated cellulose to which have been added certain optional substances of a grade of purity suitable for use in food packaging as constituents of the base sheet or as coatings applied to impart desired technological properties.

(b) Subject to any limitations prescribed in this part, the optional substances used in the base sheet and coating may include:

(1) Substances generally recognized as safe in food.

(2) Substances for which prior approval or sanctions permit their use in cellophane, under conditions specified in such sanctions and substances listed in § 181.22 of this chapter.

(3) Substances that by any regulation promulgated under section 409 of the act may be safely used as components of cellophane.

(4) Substances named in this section and further identified as required.

(c) *List of substances:*

List of substances	Limitations (residue and limits of addition expressed as percent by weight of finished packaging cellophane)
Acrylonitrile-butadiene copolymer resins	As the basic polymer.
Acrylonitrile-butadiene-styrene copolymer resins	Do.
Acrylonitrile-styrene copolymer resins	Do.
Acrylonitrile-vinyl chloride copolymer resins	Do.
N-Acyl sarcosines where the acyl group is lauroyl or stearoyl	For use only as release agents in coatings at levels not to exceed a total of 0.3 percent by weight of the finished packaging cellophane.
Alkyl ketene dimers identified in § 176.120 of this chapter.	
Aluminum hydroxide.	
Aluminum silicate.	
Ammonium persulfate.	
Ammonium sulfate.	
Behenamide.	
Butadiene-styrene copolymer	As the basic polymer.
1,3-Butanediol.	
n-Butyl acetate	0.1 percent.
n-Butyl alcohol	Do.
Calcium ethyl acetoacetate.	
Calcium stearoyl-2-lactylate identified in § 172.844 of this chapter.	Not to exceed 0.5 percent weight of cellophane.
Carboxymethyl hydroxyethylcellulose polymer.	
Castor oil, hydrogenated.	
Castor oil phthalate with adipic acid and fumaric acid-diethylene glycol polyester.	As the basic polymer.
Castor oil phthalate, hydrogenated	Alone or in combination with other phthalates where total phthalates do not exceed 5 percent.
Castor oil, sulfonated, sodium salt.	
Cellulose acetate butyrate.	
Cellulose acetate propionate.	
Cetyl alcohol.	
Clay, natural.	
Coconut oil fatty acid (C_{12}-C_{18}) diethanolamide, coconut oil fatty acid (C_{12}-C_{18}) diethanolamine soap, and diethanolamine mixture having total alkali (calculated as potassium hydroxide) of 16–18% and having an acid number of 25–35.	For use only as an adjuvant employed during the processing of cellulose pulp used in the manufacture of cellophane base sheet.
Copal resin, heat processed	As basic resin.
Damar resin.	
Defoaming agents identified in § 176.200 of this chapter.	
Dialkyl ketones where the alkyl groups are lauryl or stearyl	Not to exceed a total of 0.35 percent.
Dibutylphthalate	Alone or in combination with other phthalates where total phthalates do not exceed 5 percent.
Dicyclohexyl phthalate	Do.
Diethylene glycol ester of the adduct of terpene and maleic anhydride.	
Di(2-ethylhexyl) adipate.	
Di(2-ethylhexyl) phthalate	Alone or in combination with other phthalates where total phthalates do not exceed 5 percent.
Diisobutyl phthalate	Do.
Dimethylcyclohexyl phthalate	Do.
Dimethyldialkyl (C_8-C_{18}) ammonium chloride	0.005 percent for use only as a flocculant for slip agents.
Di-*n*-ocyltin bis (2-ethylhexyl maleate)	For use only as a stabilizer at a level not to exceed 0.55 percent by weight of the coating solids in vinylidene chloride copolymer waterproof coatings prepared from vinylidene chloride copolymers identified in this paragraph, provided that such vinylidene chloride copolymers contain not less than 90 percent by weight of polymer units derived from vinylidene chloride.

List of substances	Limitations (residue and limits of addition expressed as percent by weight of finished packaging cellophane)
N,N′-Dioleoyethylenediamine, N,N′-dilinoleoylethylene-diamine and N-oleoyl-N′linoleoylethylene-diamine mixture produced when tall oil fatty acids are made to react with ethylene-diamine such that the finished mixture has a melting point of 212°–228 °F., as determined by ASTM method D127–60 ("Standard Method of Test for Melting Point of Petrolatum and Microcrystalline Wax" (Revised 1960), which is incorporated by reference; copies are available from University Microfilms International, 300 N. Zeeb Rd., Ann Arbor, MI 48106, or available for inspection at the National Archives and Records Administration (NARA). For information on the availability of this material at NARA, call 202–741–6030, or go to: *http://www.archives.gov/federal_register/code_of_federal_regulations/ibr_locations.html.*), and an acid value of 10 maximum.	0.5 percent.
N,N′-Dioleoylethylenediamine (*N,N′*-ethylenebisoleamide).	
Disodium EDTA.	
Distearic acid ester of di(hydroxyethyl) diethylenetriamine monoacetate.	0.06 percent.
N,N′-Distearoylethylenediamine (*N,N′*-ethylenebis stearamide).	
Epoxidized polybutadiene	For use only as a primer subcoat to anchor surface coatings to the base sheet.
Erucamide.	
Ethyl acetate.	
Ethylene-vinyl acetate copolymers complying with § 177.1350.	
2-Ethylhexyl alcohol	0.1 percent for use only as lubricant.
Fatty acids derived from animal and vegetable fats and oils, and the following salts of such acids, single or mixed: Aluminum, ammonium, calcium, magnesium, potassium, sodium.	
Ferrous ammonium sulfate.	
Fumaric acid.	
Glycerin-maleic anhydride	As the basic polymer.
Glycerol diacetate.	
Glycerol monoacetate.	
Hydroxyethyl cellulose, water-insoluble.	
Hydroxypropyl cellulose identified in § 172.870 of this chapter.	
Isopropyl acetate	Residue limit 0.1 percent
Isopropyl alcohol	Do.
Itaconic acid.	
Lanolin.	
Lauryl alcohol.	
Lauryl sulfate salts: ammonium, magnesium, potassium, sodium.	
Maleic acid	1 percent.
Maleic acid adduct of butadienestyrene copolymer.	
Melamine formaldehyde	As the basic polymer.
Melamine-formaldehyde modified with one or more of the following: Butyl alcohol, diaminopropane, diethylenetriamine, ethyl alcohol, guanidine, imino-bis-butylamine, imino-bis-ethylamine, imino-bis-propylamine, methyl alcohol, polyamines made by reacting ethylenediamine or trimethylenediamine with dichloroethane or dichloropropane, sulfanilic acid, tetraethylenepentamine, triethanolamine, triethylenetetramine.	As the basic polymer, and used as a resin to anchor coatings to substrate.
Methyl ethyl ketone	Residue limit 0.1 percent
Methyl hydrogen siloxane	0.1 percent as the basic polymer.
α-Methylstyrene-vinyltoluene copolymer resins (molar ratio 1α-methylstyrene to 3 vinyltoluene).	
Mineral oil, white.	
Mono- and bis-(octadecyldiethylene oxide) phosphates (CAS Reg. No. 62362–49–6).	For use only as a release agent at a level not to exceed 0.6 percent by weight of coatings for cellophane.
Naphthalenesulfonic acid-formaldehyde condensate, sodium salt.	0.1 percent, for use only as an emulsifier.
Nitrocellulose, 10.9 percent–12.2 percent nitrogen.	
Nylon resins complying with § 177.1500.	
n-Octyl alcohol	For use only as a defoaming agent in the manufacture of cellophane base sheet.
Olefin copolymers complying with § 177.1520.	
Oleic acid reacted with *N*-alkyl trimethylenediamine (alkyl C_{16} to C_{18}).	
Oleic acid, sulfonated, sodium salt.	
Oleyl palmitamide.	

List of substances	Limitations (residue and limits of addition expressed as percent by weight of finished packaging cellophane)
N,N′-Oleoyl-stearylethylenediamine (*N*-(2-stearoyl-aminoethyl)oleamide).	
Paraffin, synthetic, complying with § 175.250 of this chapter.	
Pentaerythritol tetrastearate	0.1 percent.
Polyamide resins derived from dimerized vegetable oil acids (containing not more than 20 percent of monomer acids) and ethylenediamine as the basic resin.	For use only in cellophane coatings that contact food at temperatures not to exceed room temperature.
Polyamide resins having a maximum acid value of 5 and a maximum amine value of 8.5 derived from dimerized vegetable oil acids (containing not more than 10 percent monomer acids), ethylenediamine, and 4,4-bis(4-hydroxyphenyl)pentanoic acid (in an amount not to exceed 10 percent by weight of said polyamide resins).	As the basic resin, for use only in coatings that contact food at temperatures not to exceed room temperature provided that the concentration of the polyamido resins in the finished food-contact coating does not exceed 5 milligrams per square inch of food-contact surface.
Polybutadiene resin (molecular weight range 2,000–10,200; bromine number range 210–320).	For use only as an adjuvant in vinylidene chloride copolymer coatings.
Polycarbonate resins complying with §.177.1580.	
Polyester resin formed by the reaction of the methyl ester of rosin, phthalic anhydride, maleic anhydride, and ethylene glycol, such that the polyester resin has an acid number of 4 to 11, a drop-softening point of 70 °C–92 °C, and a color of K or paler.	
Polyethylene.	
Polyethyleneaminostearamide ethyl sulfate produced when stearic acid is made to react with equal parts of diethylenetriamine and triethylenetetramine and the reaction product is quaternized with diethyl sulfate.	0.1 percent.
Polyethylene glycol (400) monolaurate.	
Polyethylene glycol (600) monolaurate.	
Polyethylene glycol (400) monooleate.	
Polyethylene glycol (600) monooleate.	
Polyethylene glycol (400) monostearate.	
Polyethylene glycol (600) monostearate.	
Polyethylene, oxidized: complying with the identity prescribed in § 177.1620(a).	
Polyethylenimine	As the basic polymer, for use as a resin to anchor coatings to the substrate and for use as an impregnant in the food-contact surface of regenerated cellulose sheet in an amount not to exceed that required to improve heat-sealable bonding between coated and uncoated sides of cellophane.
Polyisobutylene complying with § 177.1420.	
Polyoxypropylene-polyoxyethylene block polymers (molecular weight 1,900–9,000).	For use as an adjuvant employed during the processing of cellulose pulp used in the manufacture of cellophane base sheet.
Polypropylene complying with § 177.1520.	
Polystyrene	As the basic polymer.
Polyvinyl acetate	Do.
Polyvinyl alcohol (minimum viscosity of 4 percent aqueous solution at 20 °C of 4 centipoises).	
Polyvinyl chloride	As the basic polymer.
Polyvinyl stearate	Do.
n-Propyl acetate	Residue limit 0.1 percent.
n-Propyl alcohol	Do.
Rapeseed oil, blown.	
Rosins and rosin derivatives as provided in § 178.3870 of this chapter.	
Rubber, natural (natural latex solids).	
Silica.	
Silicic acid.	
Sodium *m*-bisulfite.	
Sodium dioctyl sulfosuccinate.	
Sodium dodecylbenzenesulfonate.	
Sodium lauroyl sarcosinate	0.35 percent; for use only in vinylidene chloride copolymer coatings.
Sodium oleyl sulfate-sodium cetyl sulfate mixture	For use only as an emulsifier for coatings; limit 0.005 percent where coating is applied to one side only and 0.01 percent where coating is applied to both sides.
Sodium silicate.	
Sodium stearoyl-2-lactylate identified in § 172.846 of this chapter.	Not to exceed 0.5 percent weight of cellophane.
Sodium sulfate.	
Sodium sulfite.	
Spermaceti wax.	
Stannous oleate.	

List of substances	Limitations (residue and limits of addition expressed as percent by weight of finished packaging cellophane)
2-Stearamido-ethyl stearate.	
Stearyl alcohol.	
Styrene-maleic anhydride resins	As the basic polymer.
Terpene resins identified in § 172.615 of this chapter.	
Tetrahydrofuran	Residue limit of 0.1 percent.
Titanium dioxide.	
Toluene	Residue limit of 0.1 percent.
Toluene sulfonamide formaldehyde	0.6 percent as the basic polymer.
Triethylene glycol.	
Triethylene glycol diacetate, prepared from triethylene glycol containing not more than 0.1 percent of diethylene glycol.	
2,2,4-Trimethyl-1,3 pentanediol diisobutyrate	For use only in cellophane coatings and limited to use at a level not to exceed 10 percent by weight of the coating solids except when used as provided in § 178.3740 of this chapter
Urea (carbamide).	
Urea formaldehyde	As the basic polymer.
Urea formaldehyde modified with methanol, ethanol, butanol diethylenetriamine, triethylenetetramine, tetraethylenepentamine, guanidine, sodium sulfite, sulfanilic acid, imino-bis-ethylamine, imino-bis-propylamine, imino-bis-butylamine, diaminopropane, diaminobutane, aminomethylsulfonic acid, polyamines made by reacting ethylenediamine or trimethylenediamine with dichlorethane or dichloropropane.	As the basic polymer, and used as a resin to anchor coatings to the substrate.
Vinyl acetate-vinyl chloride copolymer resins	As the basic polymer.
Vinyl acetate-vinyl chloride-maleic acid copolymer resins	Do.
Vinylidene chloride copolymerized with one or more of the following: Acrylic acid, acrylonitrile, butyl acrylate, butyl methacrylate, ethyl acrylate, 2-ethylhexyl acrylate, 2-ethylhexyl methacrylate, ethyl methacrylate, itaconic acid, methacrylic acid, methyl acrylate, methyl methacrylate, propyl acrylate, propyl methacrylate, vinyl chloride.	Do.
Vinylidene chloride-methacrylate decyloctyl copolymer	Do.
Wax, petroleum, complying with § 178.3710 of this chapter.	

(d) Any optional component listed in this section covered by a specific food additive regulation must meet any specifications in that regulation.

(e) Acrylonitrile copolymers identified in this section shall comply with the provisions of § 180.22 of this chapter.

[42 FR 14572, Mar. 15, 1977, as amended at 47 FR 11842, Mar. 19, 1982; 64 FR 57978, Oct. 28, 1999]

§ 177.1210 Closures with sealing gaskets for food containers.

Closures with sealing gaskets may be safely used on containers intended for use in producing, manufacturing, packing, processing, preparing, treating, packaging, transporting, or holding food in accordance with the following prescribed conditions:

(a) Closures for food containers are manufactured from substances generally recognized as safe for contact with food; substances that are subject to the provisions of prior sanctions; substances authorized by regulations in parts 174, 175, 176, 177, 178 and § 179.45 of this chapter; and closure-sealing gaskets, as further prescribed in this section.

(b) Closure-sealing gaskets and overall discs are formulated from substances identified in § 175.300(b) of this chapter, with the exception of paragraph (b)(3) (v), (xxxi), and (xxxii) of that section, and from other optional substances, including the following:

(1) Substances generally recognized as safe in food.

(2) Substances used in accordance with the provisions of a prior sanction or approval within the meaning of section 201(s) of the act.

(3) Substances that are the subject of regulations in parts 174, 175, 176, 177, 178 and § 179.45 of this chapter and used in accordance with the conditions prescribed.

(4) Substances identified in paragraph (b)(5) of this section, used in amounts not to exceed those required to accomplish the intended physical or technical effect and in conformance

with any limitation provided; and further provided that any substance employed in the production of closure-sealing gasket compositions that is the subject of a regulation in parts 174, 175, 176, 177, 178 and § 179.45 of this chapter conforms with the identity or specifications prescribed.

(5) Substances that may be employed in the manufacture of closure-sealing gaskets include:

TABLE 1

List of substances	Limitations (expressed as percent by weight of closure-sealing gasket composition)
Arachidy-l-behenyl amide (C_{20}-C_{22}fatty acid amides)	5 percent.
Azodicarbonamide	1. 2 percent. 2. 5 percent; for use only in the manufacture of polyethylene complying with item 2.1 in § 177.1520(c) of this chapter.
Balata rubber.	
Benzyl alcohol	1 percent.
Brominated isobutylene-isoprene copolymers, produced when isobutylene-isoprene copolymers complying with § 177.1420(a)(2) are modified by bromination with not more than 2.3 weight-percent of bromine and having a Mooney Viscosity (ML 1+8 (125 °C)) of 27 or higher. The viscosity is determined by the American Society for Testing and Materials (ASTM) method D 1646–81, "Standard Test Method for Rubber—Viscosity and Vulcanization Characteristics (Mooney Viscometer)," which is incorporated by reference in accordance with 5 U.S.C. 522(a) and 1 CFR part 51. Copies are available from the AOAC INTERNATIONAL, 481 North Frederick Ave., Suite 500, Gaithersburg, MD 20877-2504 and the Center for Food Safety and Applied Nutrition (HFS–200), Food and Drug Administration, 5100 Paint Branch Pkwy., College Park, MD 20740, or available for inspection at the National Archives and Records Administration (NARA). For information on the availability of this material at NARA, call 202–741–6030, or go to: *http://www.archives.gov/federal_register/code_of_federal_regulations/ibr_locations.html.*.	
1,3-Butanediol.	
Calcium tin stearate	2 percent.
Calcium zinc stearate	Do.
Carbon, activated	1 percent.
Castor oil, hydrogenated	2 percent.
Chlorinated isobutylene-isoprene copolymers complying with § 177.1420.	
Coco amide (coconut oil fatty acids amides)	2 percent.
Cork (cleaned, granulated).	
Diebenzamide phenyl disulfide	1 percent; for use only in vulcanized natural or synthetic rubber gasket compositions.
Di(C_7, C_9-alkyl) adipate	Complying with § 178.3740 of this chapter; except that, there is no limitation on polymer thickness.
Di-2-ethylhexyl adipate.	
Di-2-ethylhexyl sebacate	2 percent.
Di-2-ethylhexyl terephthalate (CAS Reg. No. 006422–86–2).	For use as a plasticizer at levels not exceeding 75 parts per hundred by weight of permitted vinyl chloride homo- and/or copolymer resins used in contact with food of Types I, II, IV-B, VI-A, VI-B, VI-C (up to 15 percent alcohol by volume), VII-B, and VIII described in § 176.170(c) of this chapter, table 1, and under conditions of use A through H described in § 176. 170 (c) of this chapter, table 2.
Dihexyl ester of sodium sulfosuccinate	1 percent.
Diisodecyl phthalate	No limitation on amount used but for use only in closure-sealing gasket compositions used in contact with non-fatty foods containing no more than 8 percent of alcohol.
Di-β-naphthyl-*p*-phenylenediamine	1 percent.
Dipentamethylenethiurametetrasulfide	0.4 percent; for use only in vulcanized natural or synthetic rubber gasket compositions.
Eicosane (technical grade) (water-white mixture of predominantly straight-chain paraffin hydrocarbons averaging 20 carbon atoms per molecule).	
Epoxidized linseed oil.	
Epoxidized linseed oil modified with trimellitic anhydride.	
Epoxidized safflower oil.	
Epoxidized safflower oil modified with trimellitic anhydride.	
Epoxidized soybean oil modified with trimellitic anhydride.	

TABLE 1—Continued

List of substances	Limitations (expressed as percent by weight of closure-sealing gasket composition)
Erucylamide	5 percent.
Ethylene-propylene copolymer.	
Ethylene-propylene modified copolymer elastomers produced when ethylene and propylene are copolymerized with 5-methylene-2-norbornene and/or 5-ethylidine-2-norbornene. The finished copolymer elastomers so produced shall contain not more than 5 weight-percent of total polymer units derived from 5-methylene-2-norbornene and/or 5-ethylidine-2-norbornene, and shall have a minimum viscosity average molecular weight of 120,000 as determined by the method described in § 177.1520(d)(5), and a minimum Mooney viscosity of 35 as determined by the method described in § 177.1520(d)(6).	
Ethylene-vinyl acetate copolymer.	
Glyceryl mono-12-hydroxystearate (hydrogenated glyceryl ricinoleate).	2 percent.
Gutta-percha.	
Hexamethylenetetramine	1 percent.
Hexylene glycol	0.5 percent.
Isobutylene-isoprene copolymers complying with § 177.1420.	
Maleic anhydride-polyethylene copolymer	5 percent.
Maleic anhydride-styrene copolymer	Do.
2,2′-Methylenebis[6-(1-methylcylcohexyl)-*p*-cresol]	1 percent.
Mixed octylated diphenylamine (CAS Reg. No. 68411–46–1)	0.1 percent in isobutylene-isoprene and chlorinated isobutylene-isoprene copolymers complying with § 177.1420, and brominated isobutylene-isoprene copolymers complying with this section.
Naphthalene sulfonic acid-formaldehyde condensate, sodium salt.	0.2 percent.
Natural rubber (crepe, latex, mechanical dispersions).	
α-*cis*-9-Octadecenyl-*omega*-hydroxypoly (oxyethylene); the octadecenyl group is derived from oleyl alcohol and the poly (oxyethylene) content averages 20 moles.	0.5 percent.
Oleyl alcohol	1 percent.
4,4′-Oxybis (benzene sulfonyl hydrazide)	0.5 percent.
Paraformaldehyde	1 percent.
Polybutadiene.	
Poly-*p*-dinitroso benzene (activator for butyl rubber)	1 percent; for use only in vulcanized natural or synthetic rubber gasket compositions.
Polyethylene glycol 400 esters of fatty acids derived from animal and vegetable fats and oils.	1 percent.
Polyisobutylene complying with § 177.1420.	
Polyoxypropylene-polyoxyethylene condensate, average mol. wt. 2750–3000.	0.05 percent.
Polyurethane resins manufactured from diphenylmethane diisocyanate, 1,4-butanediol, and adipic acid (CAS Reg. No. 26375–23–5)..	For use only: No limitation on amount used, but for use only in closure gasket compositions used in contact with food types VI-A and VI-C (up to 15 percent alcohol) under conditions of use D, E, F, and G, as described in § 176.170(c) of this chapter, tables 1 and 2, respectively.
Potassium benzoate	1 percent.
Potassium perchlorate	Do.
Potassium propionate	2 percent.
Potassium and sodium persulfate	1 percent.
Resorcinol	0.24 percent; for use only as a reactive adjuvant substance employed in the production of gelatin-bonded cord compositions for use in lining crown closures. The gelatin so used shall be technical grade or better.
Rosins and rosin derivatives as defined in § 175.300(b)(3)(v) of this chapter for use only in resinous and polymeric coatings on metal substrates; for all other uses as defined in § 178.3870 of this chapter.	
Sodium cetyl sulfate	1 percent.
Sodium decylbenzenesulfonate	Do.
Sodium decyl sulfate	Do.
Sodium formaldehyde sulfoxylate	0.05 percent.
Sodium lauryl sulfate	1 percent.
Sodium lignin sulfonate	0.2 percent.
Sodium myristyl sulfate (sodium tetradecyl sulfate)	0.6 percent.

TABLE 1—Continued

List of substances	Limitations (expressed as percent by weight of closure-sealing gasket composition)
Sodium nitrite	0.2 percent; for use only in annular ring gaskets applied in aqueous dispersions to closures for containers having a capacity of not less than 5 gallons.
Sodium *o*-phenylphenate	0.05 percent.
Sodium polyacrylate	5 percent.
Sodium and potassium pentachlorophenate	0.05 percent.
Sodium salt of trisopropyl naphthalenesulfonic acid	0.2 percent.
Sodium tridecylsulfate	0.6 percent.
Stearic acid amide	5 percent.
Sulfur	For use only as a vulcanizing agent in vulcanized natural or synthetic rubber gasket compositions at a level not to exceed 4 percent by weight of the elastomer content of the rubber gasket composition.
Tallow, sulfated	1 percent.
Tin-zinc stearate	2 percent.
Tri(mixed mono- and dinonylphenyl) phosphite	1 percent.
Vinyl chloride-vinyl stearate copolymer.	
Zinc dibutyldithiocarbamate	0.8 percent; for use only in vulcanized natural or synthetic rubber gasket compositions.

TABLE 2—MAXIMUM EXTRACTIVES TOLERANCES

[In parts per million]

Type of closure-sealing gasket composition	Chloroform fraction of water extractives	Chloroform fraction of heptane extractives	Chloroform fraction of alcohol extractives
1. Plasticized polymers, including unvulcanized or vulcanized or otherwise cured natural and synthetic rubber formed in place as overall discs or annular rings from a hot melt, solution, plastisol, organisol, mechanical dispersion, or latex	50	500	50
2. Preformed overall discs or annular rings of plasticized polymers, including unvulcanized natural or synthetic rubber	50	250	50
3. Preformed overall discs or annular rings of vulcanized plasticized polymers, including natural or synthetic rubber	50	50	50
4. Preformed overall discs or annular rings of polymeric or resinous-coated paper, paperboard, plastic, or metal foil substrates	50	250	50
5. Closures with sealing gaskets or sealing compositions as described in 1, 2, 3, and 4, and including paper, paperboard, and glassine used for dry foods only	(1)	(1)	(1)

[1] Extractability tests not applicable.

(c) The closure assembly to include the sealing gasket or sealing compound, together with any polymeric or resinous coating, film, foil, natural cork, or glass that forms a part of the food-contact surface of the assembly, when extracted on a suitable glass container with a solvent or solvents characterizing the type of foods, and under conditions of time and temperature characterizing the conditions of its use as determined from tables 3 and 4 shall yield net chloroform-soluble extractives (corrected for zinc as zinc oleate) not to exceed the tolerances specified in table 2, calculated on the basis of the water capacity of the container on which the closure is to be used. Employ the analytical method described in §175.300 of this chapter, adapting the procedural details to make the method applicable to closures; such as, for example, placing the closed glass container on its side to assure contact of the closure's food-contacting surface with the solvent.

TABLE 3—TYPES OF FOOD

I. Nonacid (pH above 5.0), aqueous products; may contain salt or sugar or both, and including oil-in-water emulsions of low- or high-fat content.
II. Acidic (pH 5.0 or below), aqueous products; may contain salt or sugar or both, and including oil-in-water emulsions of low- or high-fat content.
III. Aqueous, acid or nonacid products containing free oil or fat; may contain salt, and including water-in-oil emulsions of low- or high-fat content.
IV. Dairy products and modifications:
  A. Water-in-oil emulsions, high- or low-fat.
  B. Oil-in-water emulsions, high- or low-fat.
V. Low-moisture fats and oils.
VI. Beverages:

A. Containing alcohol.
B. Nonalcoholic.

VII. Bakery products.
VIII. Dry solids (no end-test required).

TABLE 4—TEST PROCEDURES WITH TIME-TEMPERATURE CONDITIONS FOR DETERMINING AMOUNT OF EXTRACTIVES FROM CLOSURE-SEALING GASKETS, USING SOLVENTS SIMULATING TYPES OF FOODS AND BEVERAGES

Conditions of use	Types of food (see Table 3)	Extractant		
		Water (time and temperature)	Heptane[1] (time and temperature)	8% alcohol (time and temperature)
A. High temperature heat-sterilized (e.g., over 212 °F).	I, IV–B	250 °F, 2 hr	.	
	III, IV–A, VII	do	150 °F, 2 hr.	
B. Boiling water-sterilized	II	212 °F, 30 min	.	
	III, VII	do	120 °F, 30 min.	
C. Hot filled or pasteurized above 150 °F.	II, IV–B	Fill boiling, cool to 100 °F.	.	
	III, IV–A	do	120 °F, 15 min.	
	V		do.	
D. Hot filled or pasteurized below 150 °F.	II, IV–B, VI–B	150 °F, 2 hr	.	
	III, IV–A	do	100 °F, 30 min.	
	V		do.	
	VI–A			150 °F, 2 hr.
E. Room temperature filled and stored (no thermal treatment in the container).	II, IV–B, VI–B	120 °F, 24 hr	.	
	III, IV–A	do	70 °F, 30 min.	
	V		do.	
	VI–A			120 °F, 24 hr.
F. Refrigerated storage (no thermal treatment).	I, II, III, IV–A, IV–B, VI–B,VII.	70 °F, 48 hr	70 °F, 30 min.	
	VI–A			70 °F, 48 hr.
G. Frozen storage (no thermal treatment in the container).	I, II, III, IV–B, VII	70 °F, 24 hr	.	

[1]Heptane extractant not applicable to closure-sealing gaskets overcoated with wax.

[42 FR 14572, Mar. 15, 1977; 42 FR 56728, Oct. 28, 1977, as amended at 47 FR 22090, May 21, 1982; 49 FR 5748, Feb. 15, 1984; 55 FR 34555, Aug. 23, 1990; 61 FR 14480, Apr. 2, 1996; 65 FR 26745, May 9, 2000; 65 FR 52908, Aug. 31, 2000; 70 FR 67651, Nov. 8, 2005; 76 FR 59249, Sept. 26, 2011; 78 FR 14665, Mar. 7, 2013]

§ 177.1211 Cross-linked polyacrylate copolymers.

Cross-linked polyacrylate copolymers identified in paragraph (a) of this section may be safely used as articles or components of articles intended for use in contact with food in accordance with the following prescribed conditions:

(a) *Identity*. For the purpose of this section, the cross-linked polyacrylate copolymers consist of:

(1) The grafted copolymer of cross-linked sodium polyacrylate identified as 2-propenoic acid, polymers with *N,N*-di-2-propenyl-2-propen-1-amine and hydrolyzed polyvinyl acetate, sodium salts, graft (CAS Reg. No. 166164–74–5); or

(2) 2-propenoic acid, polymer with 2-ethyl-2-(((1-oxo-2-propenyl)oxy)methyl)-1,3-propanediyl di-2-propenoate and sodium 2-propenoate (CAS Reg. No. 76774–25–9).

(b) *Adjuvants*. The copolymers identified in paragraph (a) of this section may contain optional adjuvant substances required in the production of such copolymers. The optional adjuvant substances may include substances permitted for such use by regulations in parts 170 through 179 of this chapter, substances generally recognized as safe in food, and substances used in accordance with a prior sanction or approval.

(c) *Extractives limitations*. The copolymers identified in paragraph (a) of this section, in the finished form in which they will contact food, must yield low molecular weight (less than 1,000 Daltons) extractives of no more than 0.15 percent by weight of the total polymer when extracted with 0.2 percent by weight of aqueous sodium chloride solution at 20 °C for 24 hours. The low molecular weight extractives shall be determined using size exclusion chromatography or an equivalent method. When conducting the extraction test, the copolymer, with no other absorptive media, shall be confined either in a finished absorbent pad or in any suitable flexible porous article, (such as a "tea bag" or infuser), under an applied pressure of 0.15 pounds per square inch (for example, a 4×6 inch square pad is subjected to a 1.6 kilograms applied mass). The solvent used shall be at least 60 milliliters aqueous sodium chloride solution per gram of copolymer.

(d) *Conditions of use.* The copolymers identified in paragraph (a)(1) of this section are limited to use as a fluid absorbent in food-contact materials used in the packaging of frozen or refrigerated poultry. The copolymers identified in paragraph (a)(2) of this section are limited to use as a fluid absorbent in food-contact materials used in the packaging of frozen or refrigerated meat and poultry.

[64 FR 28098, May 25, 1999, as amended at 65 FR 16817, Mar. 30, 2000]

§177.1240 1,4-Cyclohexylene dimethylene terephthalate and 1,4-cyclohexylene dimethylene isophthalate copolymer.

Copolymer of 1,4-cyclohexylene dimethylene terephthalate and 1,4-cyclohexylene dimethylene isophthalate may be safely used as an article or component of articles used in producing, manufacturing, packing, processing, preparing, treating, packaging, transporting, or holding food, subject to the provisions of this section:

(a) The copolymer is a basic polyester produced by the catalytic condensation of dimethyl terephthalate and dimethyl isophthalate with 1,4-cyclohexanedimethanol, to which may have been added certain optional substances required in its production or added to impart desired physical and technical properties.

(b) The quantity of any optional substance employed in the production of the copolymer does not exceed the amount reasonably required to accomplish the intended physical or technical effect or any limitation further provided.

(c) Any substance employed in the production of the copolymer that is the subject of a regulation in parts 174, 175, 176, 177, 178 and §179.45 of this chapter conforms with any specification in such regulation.

(d) Substances employed in the production of the copolymer include:

(1) Substances generally recognized as safe in food.

(2) Substances subject to prior sanction or approval for use in the copolymer and used in accordance with such sanction or approval.

(3) Substances which by regulation in parts 174, 175, 176, 177, 178 and §179.45 of this chapter may be safely used as components of resinous or polymeric coatings and film used as food-contact surfaces, subject to the provisions of such regulation.

(e) The copolymer conforms with the following specifications:

(1) The copolymer, when extracted with distilled water at reflux temperature for 2 hours, yields total extractives not to exceed 0.05 percent.

(2) The copolymer, when extracted with ethyl acetate at reflux temperature for 2 hours, yields total extractives not to exceed 0.7 percent.

(3) The copolymer, when extracted with *n*-hexane at reflux temperature for 2 hours, yields total extractives not to exceed 0.05 percent.

[42 FR 14572, Mar. 15, 1977; 49 FR 5748, Feb. 15, 1984, as amended at 55 FR 34555, Aug. 23, 1990]

§177.1310 Ethylene-acrylic acid copolymers.

The ethylene-acrylic acid copolymers identified in paragraph (a) of this section may be safely used as components of articles intended for use in contact with food subject to the provisions of this section.

(a) The ethylene-acrylic acid copolymers consist of basic copolymers produced by the copolymerization of ethylene and acrylic acid such that the finished basic copolymers contain no more than:

(1) 10 weight-percent of total polymer units derived from acrylic acid when used in accordance with paragraph (b) of this section; and

(2) 25 weight-percent of total polymer units derived from acrylic acid when used in accordance with paragraph (c) of this section.

(b) The finished food-contact articles made with no more than 10 percent total polymer units derived from acrylic acid, when extracted with the solvent or solvents characterizing the type of food and under the conditions of its intended use as determined from tables 1 and 2 of § 176.170(c) of this chapter, yield net acidified chloroform-soluble extractives not to exceed 0.5 milligram per square inch of food-contact surface when tested by the methods prescribed in § 177.1330(e)(1), (3)(i) through (iv), (4), (5), and (6), except that

(1) The total residue method using 3 percent acetic acid, as prescribed in § 177.1330(e)(6)(i)(*a*), does not apply, and

(2) The net acidified chloroform-soluble extractives from paper and paperboard complying with § 176.170 of this chapter may be corrected for wax, petrolatum, and mineral oil as provided in § 176.170(d)(5)(iii)(*b*) of this chapter.

If the finished food-contact article is itself the subject of a regulation in parts 174, 175, 176, 177, 178, and § 179.45 of this chapter, it shall also comply with any specifications and limitations prescribed for it by that regulation.

(c) The finished food-contact layer made with basic copolymers containing more than 10 weight-percent but no more than 25 weight-percent of total polymer units derived from acrylic acid and with a maximum thickness of 0.0025 inch (2.5 mils) may be used in contact with food types I, II, IVB, VIA, VIB, VIIB, and VIII identified in table 1 of § 176.170(c) of the chapter under conditions of use B through H as described in table 2 of § 176.170(c) of this chapter, and in contact with food types III, IVA, V, VIIA, and IX identified in table 1 of § 176.170(c) of this chapter under conditions of use E through G as described in table 2 of § 176.170(c) of this chapter.

(d) The provisions of this section are not applicable to ethylene-acrylic acid copolymers used in food-packaging adhesives complying with § 175.105 of this chapter.

[42 FR 14572, Mar. 15, 1977, as amended at 51 FR 19060, May 27, 1986; 53 FR 44009, Nov. 1, 1988]

§ 177.1312 Ethylene-carbon monoxide copolymers.

The ethylene-carbon monoxide copolymers identified in paragraph (a) of this section may be safely used as components of articles intended for use in contact with food subject to the provisions of this section.

(a) *Identity.* For the purposes of this section, ethylene-carbon monoxide copolymers (CAS Reg. No. 25052–62–4) consist of the basic polymers produced by the copolymerization of ethylene and carbon monoxide such that the copolymers contain not more than 30 weight-percent of polymer units derived from carbon monoxide.

(b) *Conditions of use.* (1) The polymers may be safely used as components of the food-contact or interior core layer of multilaminate food-contact articles.

(2) The polymers may be safely used as food-contact materials at temperatures not to exceed 121 °C (250 °F).

(c) *Specifications.* (1) Food-contact layers formed from the basic copolymer identified in paragraph (a) of this section shall be limited to a thickness of not more than 0.01 centimeter (0.004 inch).

(2) The copolymers identified in paragraph (a) of this section shall have a melt index not greater than 500 as determined by ASTM method D1238–82, condition E "Standard Test Method for Flow Rates of Thermoplastics by Extrusion Plastometer," which is incorporated by reference in accordance with 5 U.S.C. 552(a) and 1 CFR part 51. Copies may be obtained from the American Society for Testing Materials, 100 Barr Harbor Dr., West Conshohocken, Philadelphia, PA 19428-2959, or may be examined at the Center for Food Safety and Applied Nutrition (HFS–200), Food and Drug Administration, 5100 Paint Branch Pkwy., College Park, MD 20740, or at the National Archives and Records Administration (NARA). For information on the availability of this material at NARA, call 202–741–6030, or go to: *http://www.archives.gov/federal_register/*

code_of_federal_regulations/ ibr_locations.html.

(3) The basic copolymer identified in paragraph (a) of this section, when extracted with the solvent or solvents characterizing the type of food and under the conditions of time and temperature characterizing the conditions of its intended use, as determined from tables 1 and 2 of § 176.170(c) of this chapter, yields net chloroform-soluble extractives in each extracting solvent not to exceed 0.5 milligram per square inch of food-contact surface when tested by methods described in § 176.170(d) of this chapter.

(4) The provisions of this section are not applicable to ethylene-carbon monoxide copolymers complying with § 175.105 of this chapter.

[57 FR 32422, July 22, 1992]

§ 177.1315 Ethylene-1, 4-cyclohexylene dimethylene terephthalate copolymers.

Ethylene-1, 4-cyclohexylene dimethylene terephthalate copolymer may be safely used as articles or components of articles intended for use in contact with food subject to provisions of this section and of part 174 of this chapter.

(a) *Identity.* For the purposes of this section, ethylene-1,4-cyclohexylene dimethylene terephthalate copolymers (1,4-benzene dicarboxylic acid, dimethyl ester, polymerized with 1,4-cyclohexanedimethanol and 1,2-ethanediol) (CAS Reg. No. 25640–14–6) or (1,4-benzenedicarboxylic acid, polymerized with 1,4-cyclohexanedimethanol and 1,2-ethanediol) (CAS Reg. No. 25038–91–9) are basic copolymers meeting the specifications prescribed in paragraph (b) of this section, to which may have been added certain optional substances required in their production or added to impart desired physical or technical properties.

(b) *Specifications:*

Ethylene-1,4-cyclohexylene dimethylene terephthalate copolymers	Inherent viscosity	Maximum extractable fractions of the copolymer in the finished form at specified temperatures and times (expressed in micrograms of the terephthaloyl moletles/square centimeter of food-contact surface)	Test for orientability	Conditions of use
1. *Non-oriented* ethylene-1,4-cyclohexylene dimethylene terephthalate copolymer is the reaction product of dimethyl terephthalate or terephthalic acid with a mixture containing 99 to 66 mole percent of ethylene glycol and 1 to 34 mole percent of 1,4-cyclohexanedimethanol (70 percent *trans* isomer, 30 percent *cls* isomer).	Inherent viscosity of a 0.50 percent solution of the copolymer in phenol-tetrachloroethane (60:40 ratio wt/wt) solvent is not less than 0.669 as determined by using a Wagner viscometer (or equivalent) and calculated from the following equation: Inherent viscosity = (Natural logarithm of (N_r)/(c) where: N_r=Ratio of flow time of the polymer solution to that of the solvent, and c=concentration of the test solution expressed in grams per 100 milliliters.	(1) 0.23 microgram per square centimeter (1.5 micrograms per square inch) of food-contact surface when extracted with water added at 82.2 °C (180 °F) and allowed to cool to 48.9 °C (120 °F) in contact with the food-contact article.	No test required ...	In contact with foods, including foods containing not more than 25 percent (by volume) aqueous alcohol, excluding carbonated beverages and beer. Conditions of hot fill not to exceed 82.2 °C (180 °F), storage at temperatures not in excess of 48.9 °C (120 °F). No thermal treatment in the container.

Ethylene-1,4-cyclohexylene dimethylene terephthalate copolymers	Inherent viscosity	Maximum extractable fractions of the copolymer in the finished form at specified temperatures and times (expressed in micrograms of the terephthaloyl moieties/square centimeter of food-contact surface)	Test for orientability	Conditions of use
	......do	(2) 0.23 microgram per square centimeter (1.5 micrograms per square inch) of food-contact surface when extracted with 3 percent (by volume) aqueous acetic acid added at 82.2 °C (180 °F) and allowed to cool to 48.9 °C (120 °F) in contact with the food-contact article.	......do	Do.
	......do	(3) 0.08 microgram per square centimeter (0.5 microgram per square inch) of food-contact surface when extracted for 2 hours with *n*-heptane at 48.9 °C (120 °F). The heptane extractable results are to be divided by a factor of 5.	......do	Do.
	......do	(4) 0.16 microgram per square centimeter (1.0 microgram per square inch) of food-contact surface when extracted for 24 hours with 25 percent (by volume) aqueous ethanol at 48.9 °C (120 °F).	......do	Do.
2. *Oriented* ethylene-1,4-cyclohexylene dimethylene terephthalate copolymer is the reaction product of dimethyl terephthalate or terephthalic acid with a mixture containing 99 to 85 mole percent ethylene glycol and 1 to 15 mole percent of 1,4-cyclohexane-dimethanol (70 percent *trans* isomer, 30 percent *cis* isomer).	......do	(1) 0.23 microgram per square centimeter (1.5 micrograms per square inch) of food-contact surface of the oriented copolymer when extracted with water added at 87.8 °C (190 °F) and allowed to cool to 48.9 °C (120 °F) in contact with the food-contact article.	When extracted with heptane at 65.6 °C (150 °F) for 2 hours: terephthaloyl moieties do not exceed 0.09 microgram per square centimeter (0.60 microgram per square inch) of food-contact surface.	In contact with nonalcoholic foods including carbonated beverages. Conditions of hot fill not exceeding 87.8 °C (190 °F), storage at temperatures not in excess of 48.9 °C (120 °F). No thermal treatment in the container.
	......do	(2) 0.23 microgram per square centimeter (1.5 micrograms per square inch) of food-contact surface of oriented copolymer when extracted with 3 percent (by volume) aqueous acetic acid added at 87.8 °C (190 °F) and allowed to cool to 48.9 °C (120 °F) in contact with the food-contact article.	......do	Do.
	......do	(3) 0.08 microgram per square centimeter (0.5 microgram per square inch) of food-contact surface of oriented copolymer when extracted for 2 hours with *n*-heptane at 48.9 °C (120 °F). The heptane extractable results are to be divided by a factor of 5.	......do	Do.

Ethylene-1,4-cyclohexylene dimethylene terephthalate copolymers	Inherent viscosity	Maximum extractable fractions of the copolymer in the finished form at specified temperatures and times (expressed in micrograms of the terephthaloyl moieties/square centimeter of food-contact surface)	Test for orientability	Conditions of use
	......do	(4) 0.23 microgram per square centimeter (1.5 micrograms per square inch) of food-contact surface of oriented copolymer when extracted with 20 percent (by volume) aqueous ethanol heated to 65.6 °C (150 °F) for 20 minutes and allowed to cool to 48.9 °C (120 °F) in contact with the food-contact article.	......do	In contact with foods and beverages containing up to 20 percent (by volume) alcohol. Conditions of thermal treatment in the container not exceeding 65.6 °C (150 °F) for 20 minutes. Storage at temperatures not in excess of 48.9 °C (120 °F).
	......do	(5) 0.23 microgram per square centimeter (1.5 micrograms per square inch) of food-contact surface of oriented copolymer when extracted with 50 percent (by volume) aqueous ethanol at 48.9 °C (120 °F) for 24 hours.	......do	In contact with foods and beverages containing up to 50 percent (by volume) alcohol. Conditions of fill and storage not exceeding 48.9 °C (120 °F). No thermal treatment in the container.
3. Ethylene-1,4-cyclohexylene dimethylene terephthalate copolymer is the reaction product of dimethyl terephthalate or terephthalic acid with a mixture containing 99 to 95 mole percent of ethylene glycol and 1 to 5 mole percent of 1,4-cyclohexanedimethanol (70 percent *trans* isomer, 30 percent *cis* isomer).	No test required ...	For each corresponding condition of use, must meet specifications described in § 177.1630(f), (g), (h), or (j).	No test required ...	For each corresponding specification, may be used as a base sheet and base polymer in accordance with conditions of use described in § 177.1630(f), (g), (h), or (j).

(c) *Analytical method for determination of extractability*. The total extracted terephthaloyl moieties can be determined in the extracts, without evaporation of the solvent, by measuring the ultraviolet (UV) absorbance at 240 nanometers. The spectrophotometer (Varian 635–D, or equivalent) is zeroed with a sample of the solvent taken from the same lot used in the extraction tests. The concentration of the total terephthaloyl moieties in water, 3 percent acetic acid, and in 8 percent aqueous alcohol is calculated as bis(2-hydroxyethyl terephthalate) by reference to standards prepared in the appropriate solvent. Concentration of the terephthaloyl moieties in heptane is calculated as cyclic trimer $(C_6H_4CO_2C_2H_4CO_2)_3$, by reference to standards prepared in 95:5 percent (v/v) heptane: tetrahydrofuran.

[45 FR 39252, June 10, 1980, as amended at 47 FR 24288, June 4, 1982; 49 FR 25629, June 22, 1984; 51 FR 22929, June 24, 1986; 60 FR 57926, Nov. 24, 1995]

§ 177.1320 Ethylene-ethyl acrylate copolymers.

Ethylene-ethyl acrylate copolymers may be safely used to produce packaging materials, containers, and equipment intended for use in producing, manufacturing, packing, processing, preparing, treating, packaging, transporting, or holding food, in accordance with the following prescribed conditions:

(a) Ethylene-ethyl acrylate copolymers consist of basic resins produced by the catalytic copolymerization of ethylene and ethyl acrylate, to which may have been added certain optional substances to impart desired technological properties to the resin. Subject to any limitations prescribed in this section, the optional substances may include:

(1) Substances generally recognized as safe in food and food packaging.

(2) Substances the use of which is permitted under applicable regulations in parts 170 through 189 of this chapter, prior sanction, or approvals.

(b) The ethyl acrylate content of the copolymer does not exceed 8 percent by weight unless it is blended with polyethylene or with one or more olefin copolymers complying with § 177.1520 or with a mixture of polyethylene and one or more olefin copolymers, in such proportions that the ethyl acrylate content of the blend does not exceed 8 percent by weight, or unless it is used in a coating complying with § 175.300 or § 176.170 of this chapter, in such proportions that the ethyl acrylate content does not exceed 8 percent by weight of the finished coating.

(c) Ethylene-ethyl acrylate copolymers or the blend shall conform to the specifications prescribed in paragraph (c)(1) of this section and shall meet the ethyl acrylate content limits prescribed in paragraph (b) of this section, and the extractability limits prescribed in paragraph (c)(2) of this section, when tested by the methods prescribed for polyethylene in § 177.1520.

(1) *Specifications*—(i) *Infrared identification.* Ethylene-ethyl acrylate copolymers can be identified by their characteristic infrared spectra.

(ii) *Quantitative determination of ethyl acrylate content.* The ethyl acrylate can be determined by the infrared spectra. Prepare a scan from 10.5 microns to 12.5 microns. Obtain a baseline absorbance at 11.6 microns and divide by the plaque thickness to obtain absorbance per mil. From a previously prepared calibration curve, obtain the amount of ethyl acrylate present.

(iii) *Specific gravity.* Ethylene-ethyl acrylate copolymers have a specific gravity of not less than 0.920 nor more than 0.935, as determined by ASTM method D1505–68 (Reapproved 1979), "Standard Test Method for Density of Plastics by the Density-Gradient Technique," which is incorporated by reference. Copies may be obtained from the American Society for Testing Materials, 100 Barr Harbor Dr., West Conshohocken, Philadelphia, PA 19428-2959, or may be examined at the National Archives and Records Administration (NARA). For information on the availability of this material at NARA, call 202–741–6030, or go to: *http://www.archives.gov/federal_register/code_of_federal_regulations/ibr_locations.html.*

(2) *Limitations.* Ethylene-ethyl acrylate copolymers or the blend may be used in contact with food except as a component of articles used for packaging or holding food during cooking provided they meet the following extractability limits:

(i) Maximum soluble fraction of 11.3 percent in xylene after refluxing and subsequent cooling to 25 °C.

(ii) Maximum extractable fraction of 5.5 percent when extracted with *n*-hexane at 50 °C.

(d) The provisions of paragraphs (b) and (c)(2) of this section are not applicable to ethylene-ethyl acrylate copolymers used in the formulation of adhesives complying with § 175.105 of this chapter.

[42 FR 14572, Mar. 15, 1977, as amended at 49 FR 10108, Mar. 19, 1984]

§ 177.1330 Ionomeric resins.

Ionomeric resins manufactured from either ethylene-methacrylic acid copolymers (and/or their ammonium, calcium, magnesium, potassium, sodium, and/or zinc partial salts), ethylene-methacrylic acid-vinyl acetate copolymers (and/or their ammonium, calcium, magnesium, potassium, sodium, and/or zinc partial salts,), or methacrylic acid polymers with ethylene and isobutyl acrylate (and/or their potassium, sodium and/or zinc partial salts) may be safely used as articles or components of articles intended for use in contact with food, in accordance with the following prescribed conditions:

(a) For the purpose of this section, the ethylene-methacrylic acid copolymers consist of basic copolymers produced by the copolymerization of ethylene and methacrylic acid such that the copolymers contain no more than 20 weight percent of polymer units derived from methacrylic acid, and the ethylene-methacrylic acid-vinyl acetate copolymers consist of basic copolymers produced by the copolymerization of ethylene, methacrylic acid, and vinyl acetate such that the copolymers contain no more than 15 weight percent of polymer units derived from methacrylic acid.

(b) For the purpose of this section, the methacrylic acid copolymers with ethylene and isobutyl acrylate consist of basic copolymers produced by the copolymerization of methacrylic acid, ethylene, and isobutyl acrylate such that the copolymers contain no less than 70 weight percent of polymer units derived from ethylene, no more than 15 weight percent of polymer units derived from methacrylic acid, and no more than 20 weight percent of polymer units derived from isobutyl acrylate. From 20 percent to 70 percent of the carboxylic acid groups may optionally be neutralized to form sodium or zinc salts.

(c) The finished food-contact article described in paragraph (a) of this section, when extracted with the solvent or solvents characterizing the type of food and under the conditions of time and temperature characterizing the conditions of its intended use as determined from tables 1 and 2 of §176.170(c) of this chapter, yields net acidified chloroform-soluble extractives in each extracting solvent not to exceed 0.5 milligram per square inch of food-contact surface when tested by the methods described in paragraph (e)(1) of this section, and if the finished food-contact article is itself the subject of a regulation in parts 174, 175, 176, 177, 178 and §179.45 of this chapter, it shall also comply with any specifications and limitations prescribed for it by that regulation.

NOTE: In testing the finished food-contact article, use a separate test sample for each required extracting solvent.

(d) The finished food-contact article described in paragraph (b) of this section, when extracted according to the methods listed in paragraph (e)(2) of this section and referenced in this paragraph (d), using the solvent or solvents characterizing the type of food as determined from table I of paragraph (f) of this section, shall yield net acidified chloroform-soluble extractives as follows:

(1) *For fatty food use.* (i) For films of 2 mil (0.002 inches) thickness or less, extractives shall not exceed 0.70 milligram/square inch[1] (0.109 milligram/square centimeter) of food-contact surface (*n*-heptane extractions) when extracted by the abbreviated method cited in paragraph (e)(2)(i) of this section.

(ii) For films of greater than 2 mils (0.002 inch) thickness, extractives shall not exceed 0.40 milligram/square inch[1] (0.062 milligram/square centimeter) of food-contact surface (*n*-heptane extractions) when extracted by the abbreviated method cited in paragraph (e)(2)(i) of this section, or

(iii) Alternatively, for films of greater than 2 mils thickness, extractives shall not exceed 0.70 milligram/square inch[1] (0.109 milligram/square centimeter) of food-contact surface (*n*-heptane extractions) when extracted by the equilibrium method cited in paragraph (e)(2)(ii) of this section.

(2) *For aqueous foods.* (i) The net acidified chloroform-soluble extractives shall not exceed 0.02 milligram/square inch[2](0.003 milligram/square centimeter) of food-contact surface (water, acetic acid, or ethanol/water extractions) when extracted by the abbreviated method cited in paragraph (e)(2)(i) of this section.

(ii) Alternatively, the net acidified chloroform-soluble extractives shall not exceed 0.05 milligram/square inch[3] (0.078 mg/square centimeter) of food-contact surface (water, acetic acid, or ethanol/water extractions) when extracted by the equilibrium method cited in paragraph (e)(2)(ii) of this section. If when exposed to *n*-heptane, a particular film splits along die lines, thus permitting exposure of both sides of the film to the extracting solvent,

[1] Average of four separate values, no single value of which differs from the average of those values by more then ±10 percent.

[2] Average of four separate values, no single value of which differs from the average of those values by more than ±50 percent.

[3] See footnote 2 to paragraph (d)(2)(i) of this section.

the results for that film sample are invalid and the test must be repeated for that sample until no splitting by the solvent occurs. If the finished food-contact article is itself the subject of a regulation in parts 174, 175, 176, 177, 178 and § 179.45 of this chapter, it shall also comply with any specifications and limitations prescribed for it by that regulation.

NOTE: In testing the finished food-contact article, use a separate test sample for each required extracting solvent.

(e) *Analytical methods*—(1) *Selection of extractability conditions for ionomeric resins.* First ascertain the type of food (table 1 of § 176.170(c) of this chapter) that is being packed or used in contact with the finished food-contact article described in paragraph (a) of this section, and also ascertain the normal conditions of thermal treatment used in packaging or contacting the type of food involved. Using table 2 of § 176.170 (c) of this chapter, select the food-simulating solvent or solvents and the time-temperature test conditions that correspond to the intended use of the finished food-contact article. Having selected the appropriate food-simulating solvent or solvents and time-temperature exaggeration over normal use, follow the applicable extraction procedure.

(2) *Selection of extractability conditions for ionomeric resins.* Using table I of paragraph (f) of this section ascertain the type of food that is being packed or used in contact with the finished food-contact article described in paragraph (b) of this section, and also ascertain the food-simulating solvent or solvents that correspond to the intended use of the finished food-contact article.

(i) *Abbreviated test.* For intended use involving food contact at or below 120 °F (49 °C), the appropriate food-simulating solvent is to contact the food-contact film for the time and temperatures as follows:

Solvent	Time	Temperature
n-Heptane	[1] 2	120 °F (49 °C).
Water, 3% acetic acid, or 8%/50% ethanol.	[1] 48	120 °F (49 °C).

[1] Hours

(ii) *Equilibrium test.* For intended use involving food contact at or below 120 °F (49 °C), the appropriate food-simulating solvent is to contact the food-contact film at a temperature of 120 °F until equilibrium is demonstrated.

Solvent	Minimum extraction times (hours)
n-Heptane	8, 10, 12
Water, 3% acetic acid, or 8%/50% ethanol	72, 96, 120

The results from a series of extraction times demonstrate equilibrium when the net chloroform-soluble extractives are unchanging within experimental error appropriate to the method as described in paragraphs (d) (1)(i) and (2)(i) of this section. Should equilibrium not be demonstrated over the above time series, extraction times must be extended until three successive unchanging values for extractives are obtained. In the case where intended uses involve temporary food contact above 120 °F, the food-simulating solvent is to be contacted with the food-contact article under conditions of time and temperature that duplicate the actual conditions in the intended use. Subsequently the extraction is to be continued for the time period and under the conditions specified in the above table.

(3) *Reagents*—(i) *Water.* All water used in extraction procedures should be freshly demineralized (deionized) distilled water.

(ii) *n-Heptane.* Reagent grade, freshly redistilled before use, using only material boiling at 208 °F (97.8 °C).

(iii) *Alcohol.* 8 or 50 percent (by volume), prepared from undenatured 95 percent ethyl alcohol diluted with demineralized (deionized), distilled water.

(iv) *Chloroform.* Reagent grade, freshly redistilled before use, or a grade having an established, consistently low blank.

(v) *Acetic acid.* 3 percent (by weight), prepared from glacial acetic acid diluted with demineralized (deionized), distilled water.

(4) *Selection of test method.* The finished food-contact articles shall be tested either by the extraction cell described in the *Journal of the Association of Official Agricultural Chemists*, Vol. 47, No. 1, p. 177–179 (February 1964), also

described in ASTM method F34–76 (Reapproved 1980), "Standard Test Method for Liquid Extraction of Flexible Barrier Materials," which are incorporated by reference, or by adapting the in-container methods described in §175.300(e) of this chapter. Copies of the material incorporated by reference are available from the Center for Food Safety and Applied Nutrition (HFS–200), Food and Drug Administration, 5100 Paint Branch Pkwy., College Park, MD 20740, and the American Society for Testing Materials, 100 Barr Harbor Dr., West Conshohocken, Philadelphia, PA 19428-2959, respectively, or may be examined at the National Archives and Records Administration (NARA). For information on the availability of this material at NARA, call 202–741–6030, or go to: *http://www.archives.gov/federal_register/code_of_federal_regulations/ibr_locations.html.*

(5) *Selection of samples.* Quadruplicate samples should be tested, using for each replicate sample the number of finished articles with a food-contact surface nearest to 100 square inches.

(6) *Determination of amount of extractives*—(i) *Total residues.* At the end of the exposure period, remove the test container or test cell from the oven, if any, and combine the solvent for each replicate in a clean Pyrex (or equivalent) flask or beaker, being sure to rinse the test container or cell with a small quantity of clean solvent. Evaporate the food-simulating solvents to about 100 milliliters in the flask, and transfer to a clean, tared evaporating dish (platinum or Pyrex), washing the flask three times with small portions of solvent used in the extraction procedure, and evaporate to a few milliliters on a nonsparking, low-temperature hotplate. The last few milliliters should be evaporated in an oven maintained at a temperature of 221 °F (105 °C). Cool the evaporating dish in a desiccator for 30 minutes and weigh the residues to the nearest 0.1 milligram, *e*. Calculate the extractives in milligrams per square inch of the container or material surface.

(*a*) *Water, 3 percent acetic acid, and 8 percent and 50 percent alcohol.* Milligrams extractives per square inch=e/s.

(*b*) *Heptane.* Milligrams extractives per square inch=$(e)/(s)(F)$

where:

e=Milligrams extractives per sample tested.

s=Surface area tested, in square inches.

F=Five, the ratio of the amount of extractives removed by heptane under exaggerated time-temperature test conditions compared to the amount extracted by a fat or oil under exaggerated conditions of thermal sterilization and use.

e'=Acidified chloroform-soluble extractives residue. e' is substituted for e in the above equations when necessary (See paragraph (e)(6)(ii) of this section for method to obtain e').

If when calculated by the equations in paragraphs (e)(6)(i) (a) and (b) of this section, the extractives in milligrams per square inch exceed the limitations prescribed in paragraphs (c) or (d) of this section, proceed to paragraph (e)(6)(ii) of this section (method for determining the amount of acidified chloroform-soluble extractives residue).

(ii) *Acidified chloroform-soluble extractives residue.* Add 3 milliliters of 37 percent ACS reagent grade hydrochloric acid and 3 milliliters of distilled water to the evaporating dish containing the dried and weighed residue, *e*, obtained in paragraph (e)(6)(i) of this section. Mix well so every portion of the residue is wetted with the hydrochloric acid solution. Then add 50 milliliters of chloroform. Warm carefully, and filter through Whatman No. 41 filter paper (or equivalent) in a Pyrex (or equivalent) funnel, collecting the filtrate in a clean separatory funnel. Shake for 1 minute, then draw off the chloroform layer into a clean tared evaporating dish (platinum or Pyrex). Repeat the chloroform extraction, washing the dish, the filter paper, and the separatory funnel with this second portion of chloroform. Add this filtrate to the original filtrate and evaporate the total down to a few milliliters on a low-temperature hotplate. The last few milliliters should be evaporated in an oven maintained at 221 °F. Cool the evaporating dish in a desiccator for 30 minutes and weigh to the nearest 0.1 milligram to get the acidified chloroform-soluble extractives residue, e'. This e' is substituted for e in the equations in paragraphs (e)(6)(i) (a) and (b) of this section.

(f) The types of food and appropriate solvents are as follows:

TABLE 1

Types of food	Appropriate solvent
1. Nonacid (pH above 5.0), aqueous products; may contain salt or sugar or both, and including oil-in-water emulsions of low- or high-fat content.	Water, *n*-heptane.
2. Acidic (pH 5.0 or below), aqueous products; may contain salt or sugar or both, and including oil-in-water emulsions of low- or high-fat content.	*n*-heptane, water, 3% acetic acid.
3. Aqueous, acid or nonacid products containing free oil or fat; may contain salt, and including water-in-oil emulsions of low- or high-fat content.	Water, *n*-heptane, 3% acetic acid.
4. Dairy products and modifications:	
Water, *n*-heptane.	
i. Water-in-oil emulsions, high or low fat.	
ii. Oil-in-water emulsions, high or low fat.	
5. Low moisture fats and oils	*n*-heptane.
6. Beverages:	
i. Containing up to 8% alcohol	8% ethanol/water.
ii. Nonalcoholic	3% acetic acid.
iii. Containing more than 8% alcohol.	50% ethanol/water.
7. Bakery products	Water, *n*-heptane.
8. Dry solids (without free fat or oil).	No extraction test required.
9. Dry solids (with free fat or oil)	*n*-heptane.

(g) The provisions of paragraphs (c) and (d) of this section are not applicable to the ionomeric resins that are used in food-packaging adhesives complying with § 175.105 of this chapter.

[45 FR 22916, Apr. 4, 1980, as amended at 49 FR 10108, Mar. 19, 1984; 49 FR 37747, Sept. 26, 1984; 53 FR 44009, Nov. 1, 1988; 54 FR 24898, June 12, 1989]

§ 177.1340 Ethylene-methyl acrylate copolymer resins.

Ethylene-methyl acrylate copolymer resins may be safely used as articles or components of articles intended for use in contact with food, in accordance with the following prescribed conditions:

(a) For the purpose of this section, the ethylene-methyl acrylate copolymer resins consist of basic copolymers produced by the copolymerization of ethylene and methyl acrylate such that the copolymers contain no more than 25 weight percent of polymer units derived from methyl acrylate.

(b) The finished food-contact article, when extracted with the solvent or solvents characterizing the type of food and under the conditions of time and temperature characterizing the conditions of its intended use as determined from tables 1 and 2 of § 176.170(c) of this chapter, yields net chloroform-soluble extractives (corrected for zinc extractives as zinc oleate) in each extracting solvent not to exceed 0.5 milligram per square inch of food-contact surface when tested by the methods described in § 176.170(d) of this chapter. If the finished food-contact article is itself the subject of a regulation in parts 174, 175, 176, 177, 178 and § 179.45 of this chapter, it shall also comply with any specifications and limitations prescribed for it by that regulation.

NOTE: In testing the finished food-contact article, use a separate test sample for each required extracting solvent.

(c) The provisions of this section are not applicable to ethylene-methyl acrylate copolymer resins used in food-packaging adhesives complying with § 175.105 of this chapter.

§ 177.1345 Ethylene/1,3-phenylene oxyethylene isophthalate/terephthalate copolymer.

Ethylene/1, 3-phenylene oxyethylene isophthalate/terephthalate copolymer (CAS Reg. No. 87365–98–8) identified in paragraph (a) of this section may be safely used, subject to the provisions of this section, as the non-food-contact layer of laminate structures subject to the provisions of § 177.1395, and in blends with polyethylene terephthalate polymers complying with § 177.1630.

(a) *Identity*. For the purpose of this section, ethylene/1,3-phenylene oxyethylene isophthalate/terephthalate copolymer consists of the basic copolymer produced by the catalytic polycondensation of isophthalic acid and terephthalic acid with ethylene glycol and 1,3-bis(2-hydroxyethoxy)benzene such that the finished resin contains between 42 and 48 mole-percent of isophthalic moieties, between 2 and 8 mole-percent of terephthalic moieties, and not more than 10 mole-percent of 1,3-bis(2-hydroxyethoxy)benzene moieties.

(b) *Specifications*—(1) *Density*. Ethylene/1,3-phenylene oxyethylene isophthalate/terephthalate copolymer identified in paragraph (a) of this section has a density of 1.33±0.02 grams per cubic centimeter measured by ASTM Method D 1505–85 (Reapproved 1990), "Standard Test Method for Density of Plastics by the Density-Gradient Technique," which is incorporated by reference in accordance with 5 U.S.C. 552(a) and 1 CFR part 51. Copies may be obtained from the American Society for Testing and Materials, 100 Barr Harbor Dr., West Conshohocken, Philadelphia, PA 19428-2959, or may be examined at the Center for Food Safety and Applied Nutrition's Library, Food and Drug Administration, 5100 Paint Branch Pkwy., College Park, MD 20740, and at the National Archives and Records Administration (NARA). For information on the availability of this material at NARA, call 202–741–6030, or go to: *http://www.archives.gov/federal_register/code_of_federal_regulations/ibr_locations.html.*

(2) *Softening point.* Ethylene/1,3–phenylene oxyethylene isophthalate/terephthalate copolymer identified in paragraph (a) of this section has a softening point of 63±5 °C as measured by ASTM Method D 1525–87, "Standard Test Method for VICAT Softening Temperature of Plastics," which is incorporated by reference in accordance with 5 U.S.C. 552(a) and 1 CFR part 51. The availability of this material is provided in paragraph (b)(1) of this section.

(c) *Optional adjuvant substances.* Ethylene/1,3–phenylene oxyethylene isophthalate/terephthalate copolymer, identified in paragraph (a) of this section, may contain optional adjuvant substances required in their production. The optional adjuvants may include substances used in accordance with § 174.5 of this chapter.

(d) *Limitations.* Copolymer blends described above shall not exceed 30 percent by weight of ethylene/1, 3-phenylene oxyethylene isophthalate/terephthalate copolymer. The finished blend may be used in contact with food only under conditions of use C through G, as described in table 2 of § 176.170(c) of this chapter, except that with food identified as Type III, IV-A, V, VII-A, and IX in § 176.170(c), table 1, the copolymer may be used under condition of use C at temperatures not to exceed 160 °F (71 °C).

[57 FR 43399, Sept. 21, 1992, as amended at 59 FR 62318, Dec. 5, 1994; 61 FR 14481, Apr. 2, 1996; 62 FR 34628, June 27, 1997]

§ 177.1350 Ethylene-vinyl acetate copolymers.

Ethylene-vinyl acetate copolymers may be safely used as articles or components of articles intended for use in producing, manufacturing, packing, processing, preparing, treating, packaging, transporting, or holding food in accordance with the following prescribed conditions:

(a)(1) Ethylene-vinyl acetate copolymers consist of basic resins produced by the catalytic copolymerization of ethylene and vinyl acetate to which may have been added certain optional substances to impart desired technological or physical properties to the resin. Subject to any limitations prescribed in this section, the optional substances may include:

(i) Substances generally recognized as safe in food and food packaging.

(ii) Substances the use of which is permitted under applicable regulations in parts 170 through 189 of this chapter, prior sanction, or approvals.

(iii) Substances identified in § 175.300(b)(3) (xxv), (xxvii), (xxx), and (xxxiii) of this chapter, and colorants used in accordance with § 178.3297 of this chapter.

(iv) Erucamide as identified in § 178.3860 of this chapter.

(v) Xanthan gum as identified in § 172.695 for use as a thickening agent at a level not to exceed 1 percent by weight of coating solids in aqueous dispersions of ethylene-vinyl acetate copolymers, where such copolymers are used only as coatings or a component of coatings.

(vi) The copolymer of vinylidene fluoride and hexafluoropropene (CAS Reg. No. 9011–17–0), containing 65 to 71 percent fluorine and having a Mooney Viscosity of at least 28, for use as a processing aid at a level not to exceed 0.2 percent by weight of ethylene-vinyl acetate copolymers.

(2) Maleic anhydride-grafted ethylene-vinyl acetate copolymers (CAS

Reg. No. 28064–24–6) consist of basic resins produced by the catalytic copolymerization of ethylene and vinyl acetate, followed by reaction with maleic anhydride. Such polymers shall contain not more than 11 percent of polymer units derived from vinyl acetate by weight of total polymer prior to reaction with maleic anhydride, and not more than 2 percent of grafted maleic anhydride by weight of the finished polymer. Optional adjuvant substances that may be added to the copolymers include substances generally recognized as safe in food and food packaging, substances the use of which is permitted under applicable regulations in parts 170 through 189 of this chapter, and substances identified in § 175.300(b)(3)(xxv), (xxvii), (xxxiii), and (xxx) of this chapter and colorants for polymers used in accordance with the provisions of § 178.3297 of this chapter.

(b)(1) Ethylene-vinyl acetate copolymers, with or without the optional substances described in paragraph (a) of this section, when extracted with the solvent or solvents characterizing the type of food, and under conditions of time and temperature characterizing the conditions of their intended use as determined from tables 1 and 2 of § 176.170(c) of this chapter, shall yield net chloroform-soluble extractives corrected for zinc as zinc oleate not to exceed 0.5 milligram per square inch of an appropriate sample.

(2) Maleic anhydride grafted ethylene-vinyl acetate copolymers shall have a melt flow index not to exceed 2.1 grams per 10 minutes as determined by ASTM method D 1238–82, "Standard Test Method for Flow Rates of Thermoplastics by Extrusion Plastometer," which is incorporated by reference in accordance with 5 U.S.C. 552(a). Copies may be obtained from the American Society for Testing Materials, 100 Barr Harbor Dr., West Conshohocken, Philadelphia, PA 19428-2959, or at the Office of Food Additive Safety (HFS–200), Center for Food Safety and Applied Nutrition, Food and Drug Administration, 5100 Paint Branch Pkwy., College Park, MD 20740, 240–402–1200, or may be examined at the Center for Food Safety and Applied Nutrition's Library, 5100 Paint Branch Pkwy., College Park, MD 20740, or at the National Archives and Records Administration (NARA). For information on the availability of this material at NARA, call 202–741–6030, or go to: *http://www.archives.gov/federal_register/code_of_federal_regulations/ibr_locations.html.* Compliance of the melt flow index specification shall be determined using conditions and procedures corresponding to those described in the method as Condition E, Procedure A). The copolymers shall be used in blends with other polymers at levels not to exceed 17 percent by weight of total polymer, subject to the limitation that when contacting food of types III, IV-A, V, VI-C, VII-A, and IX, identified in § 176.170(c) of this chapter, Table 1, the polymers shall be used only under conditions of use C, D, E, F, and G, described in § 176.170(c) of this chapter, Table 2.

(c) The provisions of paragraph (b) of this section are not applicable to ethylene-vinyl acetate copolymers used in food-packaging adhesives complying with § 175.105 of this chapter.

(d) Ethylene-vinyl acetate copolymers may be irradiated under the following conditions to produce molecular crosslinking of the polymers to impart desired properties such as increased strength and increased ability to shrink when exposed to heat:

(1) Electron beam source of ionizing radiation at a maximum energy of 3 million electron volts: Maximum absorbed dose not to exceed 150 kiloGray (15 megarads).

(2) The finished food-contact film shall meet the extractives limitations prescribed in paragraph (e)(2) of this section.

(3) The ethylene-vinyl acetate copolymer films may be further irradiated in accordance with the provisions of paragraph (e)(1) of this section: *Provided,* That the total accumulated radiation dose from both electron beam and gamma ray radiation does not exceed 150 kiloGray (15 megarads).

(e) Ethylene-vinyl acetate copolymer films intended for contact with food may be irradiated to control the growth of microorganisms under the following conditions:

(1) Gamma photons emitted from a cobalt–60 sealed source in the dose

range of 5–50 kiloGray (0.5–5.0 megarads).

(2) The irradiated ethylene-vinyl acetate copolymer films, when extracted with reagent grade n-heptane (freshly redistilled before use) according to methods described under § 176.170(d)(3) of this chapter, at 75 °F for 30 minutes shall yield total extractives not to exceed 4.5 percent by weight of the film.

[42 FR 14572, Mar. 15, 1977, as amended at 43 FR 29287, July 7, 1978; 54 FR 35874, Aug. 30, 1989; 55 FR 18595, May 3, 1990; 56 FR 42932, Aug. 30, 1991; 64 FR 47108, Aug. 30, 1999; 78 FR 14665, Mar. 7, 2013]

§ 177.1360 Ethylene-vinyl acetate-vinyl alcohol copolymers.

Ethylene-vinyl acetate-vinyl alcohol copolymers (CAS Reg. No. 26221–27–2) may be safely used as articles or components of articles intended for use in contact with food, in accordance with the following prescribed conditions:

(a) Ethylene-vinyl acetate-vinyl alcohol copolymers are produced by the partial or complete alcoholysis or hydrolysis of those ethylene-vinyl acetate copolymers complying with § 177.1350.

(1) Those copolymers containing a minimum of 55 percent ethylene and a maximum of 30 percent vinyl alcohol units by weight may be used in contact with foods as described in paragraph (b) of this section.

(2) Those copolymers containing a minimum of 55 percent ethylene and a maximum of 15 percent vinyl alcohol units by weight may be used in contact with foods as described in paragraph (c) of this section.

(3) Those copolymers containing 17 to 40 percent ethylene and 60 to 83 percent vinyl alcohol units by weight may be used in contact with foods as described in paragraph (d) of this section.

(b) The finished food-contact article shall not exceed 0.013 centimeter (0.005 inch) thickness and shall contact foods only of the types identified in table 1 of § 176.170(c) of this chapter in Categories I, II, IV-B, VI, VII-B, and VIII under conditions of use D through G described in table 2 of § 176.170(c) of this chapter. Film samples of 0.013 centimeter (0.005) inch thickness representing the finished article shall meet the following extractive limitation when tested by ASTM method F34–76 (Reapproved 1980), "Standard Test Method for Liquid Extraction of Flexible Barrier Materials," which is incorporated by reference. Copies may be obtained from the American Society for Testing Materials, 100 Barr Harbor Dr., West Conshohocken, Philadelphia, PA 19428-2959, or may be examined at the National Archives and Records Administration (NARA). For information on the availability of this material at NARA, call 202–741–6030, or go to: *http://www.archives.gov/federal_register/code_of_federal_regulations/ibr_locations.html.*

(1) The film when extracted with distilled water at 21 °C (70 °F) for 48 hours yields total extractives not to exceed 0.0047 milligram per square centimeter (0.03 milligram per square inch) of food-contact surface.

(2) The film when extracted with 50 percent ethyl alcohol at 21 °C (70 °F) for 48 hours yields total extractives not to exceed 0.0062 milligram per square centimeter (0.04 milligram per square inch) of food-contact surface.

(c) The finished food-contact article shall not exceed 0.0076 centimeter (0.003 inch) thickness and shall contact foods only of the types identified in table 1 of § 176.170(c) of this chapter in Categories III, IV-A, VII-A, and IX under conditions of use F and G described in table 2 of § 176.170(c) of this chapter. Film samples of 0.0076 centimeter (0.003 inch) thickness representing the finished articles shall meet the following extractive limitation when tested by ASTM method F34–76 (Reapproved 1980), "Standard Test Method for Liquid Extraction of Flexible Barrier Materials," which is incorporated by reference. The availability of this incorporation by reference is given in paragraph (b) of this section. The film when extracted with *n*-heptane at 38 °C (100 °F) for 30 minutes yields total extractives not to exceed 0.0078 milligram per square centimeter (0.05 milligram per square inch) of food-contact surface, after correcting the total extractives by dividing by a factor of five.

(d) The finished food-contact article shall not exceed 0.018 centimeter (0.007 inch) thickness and may contact all foods, except those containing more than 8 percent alcohol, under conditions of use B through H described in table 2 of § 176.170(c) of this chapter. Film samples of 0.018 centimeter (0.007 inch) thickness representing the finished articles shall meet the following extractive limitation when tested by ASTM method F34–76 (Reapproved 1980), "Standard Test Methods for Liquid Extraction of Flexible Barrier Materials," which is incorporated by reference. The availability of this incorporation by reference is given in paragraph (b) of this section. The film when extracted with distilled water at 100 °C (212 °F) for 30 minutes yields ethylene-vinyl acetate-vinyl alcohol oligomers not to exceed 0.093 milligram per square centimeter (0.6 milligram per square inch) of food contact surface as determined by a method entitled "Analytical Method of Determining the Amount of EVOH in the Extractives Residue of EVOH Film," dated March 23, 1987, as developed by the Kuraray Co., Ltd., which is incorporated by reference in accordance with 5 U.S.C. 552(a) and 1 CFR part 51. Copies may be obtained from the Office of Food Additive Safety (HFS–200)), Center for Food Safety and Applied Nutrition, Food and Drug Administration, 5100 Paint Branch Pkwy., College Park, MD 20740, 240–402–1200, or may be examined at the Center for Food Safety and Applied Nutrition's Library, 5100 Paint Branch Pkwy., College Park, MD 20740, or at the National Archives and Records Administration (NARA). For information on the availability of this material at NARA, call 202–741–6030, or go to: *http://www.archives.gov/federal_register/code_of_federal_regulations/ibr_locations.html.*

(e) The provisions of this section are not applicable to ethylene-vinyl acetate-vinyl alcohol copolymers used in the food-packaging adhesives complying with § 175.105 of this chapter.

[47 FR 41531, Sept. 21, 1982, as amended at 49 FR 10108, Mar. 19, 1984; 65 FR 17135, Mar. 31, 2000; 78 FR 14665, Mar. 7, 2013]

§ 177.1380 Fluorocarbon resins.

Fluorocarbon resins may be safely used as articles or components of articles intended for use in contact with food, in accordance with the following prescribed conditions:

(a) For the purpose of this section, fluorocarbon resins consist of basic resins produced as follows:

(1) Chlorotrifluoroethylene resins produced by the homopolymerization of chlorotrifluoroethylene.

(2) Chlorotrifluoroethylene-1,1-difluoroethylene copolymer resins produced by copolymerization of chlorotrifluoroethylene and 1,1-difluoroethylene.

(3) Chlorotrifluoroethylene-1,1-difluoroethylene-tetrafluoroethylene co-polymer resins produced by copolymerization of chlorotrifluoroethylene, 1,1-difluoroethylene, and tetrafluoroethylene.

(4) Ethylene-chlorotrifluoroethylene copolymer resins produced by copolymerization of nominally 50 mole percent of ethylene and 50 mole percent of chlorotrifluoroethylene. The copolymer shall have a melting point of 239 to 243 °C and a melt index of less than or equal to 20 as determined by ASTM Method D 3275–89 "Standard Specification for E-CTFE-Fluoroplastic Molding, Extrusion, and Coating Materials," which is incorporated by reference in accordance with 5 U.S.C. 552(a) and 1 CFR part 51. Copies may be obtained from the American Society for Testing and Materials, 1916 Race St., Philadelphia, PA 19013, or may be examined at the National Archives and Records Administration (NARA). For information on the availability of this material at NARA, call 202–741–6030, or go to: *http://www.archives.gov/federal_register/code_of_federal_regulations/ibr_locations.html.*

(b) Fluorocarbon resins that are identified in paragraph (a) of this section and that comply with extractive limitations prescribed in paragraph (c) of this section may be used as articles or components of articles intended for use in contact with food as follows:

(1) Fluorocarbon resins that are identified in paragraphs (a)(1), (a)(2), and (a)(3) of this section and that comply only with the extractive limitations prescribed in paragraphs (c)(1) and (c)(2) of this section may be used when such use is limited to articles or components of articles that are intended for repeated use in contact with food or

that are intended for one-time use in contact with foods only of the types identified in § 176.170(c) of this chapter, table 1, under Types I, II, VI, VII-B, and VIII.

(2) Fluorocarbon resins that are identified in paragraph (a)(4) of this section and that comply with the extractive limitations prescribed in paragraphs (c)(1) and (c)(2) of this section may be used only when such use is limited to articles or components of articles that are intended for repeated use in contact with food.

(3) In accordance with current good manufacturing practice, those food-contact articles intended for repeated use shall be thoroughly cleansed prior to their first use in contact with food.

(c) Extractives limitations are applicable to the basic resins in the form of pellets that have been ground or cut into small particles that will pass through a U.S. Standard Sieve No. 6 and that will be held on a U.S. Standard Sieve No. 10.

(1) A 100-gram sample of the resin pellets, when extracted with 100 milliliters of distilled water at reflux temperature for 8 hours, shall yield total extractives not to exceed 0.003 percent by weight of the resins.

(2) A 100-gram sample of the resin pellets, when extracted with 100 milliliters of 50 percent (by volume) ethyl alcohol in distilled water at reflux temperature for 8 hours, shall yield total extractives not to exceed 0.003 percent by weight of the resins.

(3) A 100-gram sample of the resin pellets, when extracted with 100 milliliters of *n*-heptane at reflux temperature for 8 hours, shall yield total extractives not to exceed 0.01 percent by weight of the resins.

[42 FR 14572, Mar. 15, 1977, as amended at 57 FR 185, Jan. 3, 1992]

§ 177.1390 Laminate structures for use at temperatures of 250 °F and above.

(a) The high-temperature laminates identified in this section may be safely used for food contact at temperatures not exceeding 135 °C (275 °F) unless otherwise specified. These articles are layered constructions that are optionally bonded with adhesives. The interior (food-contact) layer(s) may be separated from the exterior layer(s) by a functional barrier, such as aluminum foil. Upon review of the physical properties of a particular construction, the Food and Drug Administration may consider other layers to serve as functional barriers. This regulation is not intended to limit these constructions as to shape, degree of flexibility, thickness, or number of layers. These layers may be laminated, extruded, co-extruded, or fused.

(b) When containers subject to this regulation undergo heat sterilization to produce shelf-stable foods, certain control measures (in addition to the food additive requirements in paragraphs (c) and (d) of this section) are necessary to ensure proper food sterilization and package integrity. Refer to parts 108, 110, 113, and 114 of this chapter for details.

(c) Subject to the provisions of this paragraph, food-contact articles produced from high-temperature laminates may be safely used to package all food types except those containing more than 8 percent ethyl alcohol.

(1) *Polymeric films/layers*. Films or layers not separated from food by a functional barrier must meet the following requirements:

(i) Films/layers may consist of the following:

(*a*) Polyolefin resins complying with item 2.2 or 3.2 of the table in § 177.1520(c).

(*b*) Polymeric resin blends formulated from a base polymer complying with item 2.2 or 3.2 of the table in § 177.1520(c) blended with no more than 10 percent by weight of a copolymer of ethylene and vinyl acetate complying with § 177.1350.

(*c*) Polymeric resin blends formulated from a base polymer complying with item 2.2 or 3.2 of the table in § 177.1520(c) blended with no more than 38 percent by weight of a homopolymer of isobutylene complying with § 177.1420(a)(1).

(*d*) Polyethylene phthalate resins complying with § 177.1630(e)(4) (i) and (ii).

(*e*) Nylon MXD–6 resins that comply with item 10.3 of the table in § 177.1500(b) of this chapter when extracted with water and heptane under the conditions of time and temperature specified for condition of use A, as set forth in Table 2 of § 176.170(c) of this chapter.

(*f*) Nylon 6/12 resins (CAS Reg. No. 25191–04–2) complying with item 13.3 of the table in § 177.1500(b), for use as nonfood-contact layers of laminated films and in rigid multilaminate constructions with polypropylene outer layers. Laminate structures with authorized food-contact materials yield no more than 0.15 milligrams of *epsilon*-caprolactam and 0.04 milligrams of *omega*-laurolactam per square inch when extracted with 95 percent ethanol at 121 °C (250 °F) for 2 hours.

(*g*) Polymeric resins that comply with an applicable regulation in this chapter which permits food type and time/temperature conditions to which the container will be exposed, including sterilization processing.

(ii) Adjuvants used in these layers must comply with an applicable regulation that permits food type and time/temperature conditions to which the container will be exposed, including sterilization processing.

(2) *Adhesives.* The use of adhesives in these containers is optional. Adhesives may be formulated from the following substances, subject to the prescribed limitations:

(i) Any substance suitable for use in formulating adhesives that complies with an applicable regulation of this chapter which permits food type and time/temperature conditions to which the container will be exposed, including sterilization processing.

(ii) Substances complying with § 175.105 of this chapter may be used in these constructions, provided they are separated from the interior (food-contact) layer(s) by a functional barrier as discussed under paragraph (a) of this section.

(iii) Maleic anhydride adduct of polypropylene complying with § 175.300 of this chapter.

(iv) Polyester-urethane adhesive for use at temperatures not exceeding 121 °C (250 °F) and formulated from the following:

(*a*) Polyester-urethanediol resin prepared by the reaction of a mixture of polybasic acids and polyhydric alcohols listed in § 175.300(b)(3)(vii) of this chapter, 3-isocyanatomethyl-3,5,5-trimethylcyclohexyl isocyanate (CAS Reg. No. 4098–71–9) and optional trimethoxysilane coupling agents containing amino, epoxy, ether, and/or mercapto groups not to exceed 3 percent by weight of the cured adhesive.

(*b*) Urethane cross-linking agent comprising not more than 25 percent by weight of the cured adhesive and formulated from 3-isocyanatomethyl-3,5,5-trimethylcyclohexyl isocyanate (CAS Reg. No. 4098–71–9) adduct of trimethylol propane (Cas Reg. No. 77–99–6) and/or 1,3-bis(isocyanatomethyl) benzene (CAS Reg. No. 25854–16–4) adduct of trimethylol propane.

(v) Polyester-epoxy-urethane adhesives formulated from the following:

(*a*) Polyester resin formed by the reaction of polybasic acids and polyhydric alcohols listed in § 175.300(b)(3)(vii) of this chapter. Azelaic acid may also be used as a polybasic acid.

(*b*) Epoxy resin listed in § 175.300(b)(3)(viii)(*a*) of this chapter and comprising no more than 30 percent by weight of the cured adhesive.

(*c*) Urethane cross-linking agent comprising no more than 14 percent weight of the cured adhesive and formulated from 3-isocyanatomethyl-3,5.5-trimethylcyclohexyl isocyanate cyanurate (CAS Reg. No. 53880–05–0).

(vi) Polyurethane-polyester resin-epoxy adhesives formulated from the following mixture:

(*a*)(*1*) Polyester-polyurethanediol resins prepared by the reaction of a mixture of polybasic acids and polyhydric alcohols listed in § 175.300(b)(3)(vii) of this chapter and 3-isocyanatomethyl-3,5,5-trimethylcyclohexyl isocyanate (CAS Reg. No. 4098–71–9).

(*2*) Polyester resin formed by the reaction of polybasic acids and polyhydric alcohols listed in § 175.300(b)(3)(vii) of this chapter. Additionally, azelaic acid and 1,6-hexanediol may also be used as reactants in lieu of a polyhydric alcohol.

(*3*) Epoxy resin listed in § 175.300(b)(3)(viii)(*a*) of this chapter and comprising not more than 5 percent by weight of the cured adhesive.

(*4*) Optional trimethoxy silane curing agents, containing amino, epoxy, ether, or mercapto groups not in excess of 3 percent of the cured adhesive.

(*b*) Urethane cross-linking agent, comprising not more than 20 percent by weight of the cured adhesive, and formulated from trimethylol propane (CAS Reg. No. 77–99–6) adducts of 3–isocyanatomethyl-3,5,5–trimethylcyclohexyl isocyanate (CAS Reg. No. 4098–71–9) or 1,3-bis(isocyanatomethyl)benzene (CAS Reg. No. 25854–16–4).

(vii) Polyester-polyurethane resin-acid dianhydride adhesives for use at temperatures not to exceed 121 °C (250 °F), in contact only with food Types I, II, VIA, VIB, VIIB, and VIII as described in Table I of § 176.170 of this chapter, and formulated from the following mixture:

(*a*)(*1*) Polyesterpolyurethanediol resins prepared by the reaction of a mixture of polybasic acids and polyhydric alcohols listed in § 175.300(b)(3)(vii) of this chapter and 3-isocyanatomethyl-3,5,5-trimethylcyclohexyl isocyanate (CAS Reg. No. 4098–71–9). Additionally, dimethylol propionic acid and 1,6-hexanediol may be used alone or in combination as reactants in lieu of a polybasic acid and a polyhydric alcohol.

(*2*) Acid dianhydride formulated from 3a,4,5,7a-tetrahydro-7-methyl-5-(tetrahydro-2,5-dioxo-3-furanyl)-1,3-isobenzofurandione (CAS Reg. No. 73003–90–4), comprising not more than one percent of the cured adhesive.

(*b*) Urethane cross-linking agent, comprising not more than twelve percent by weight of the cured adhesive, and formulated from trimethylol propane (CAS Reg. No. 77–99–6) adducts of 3-isocyanatomethyl-3,5,5-trimethylcyclohexyl isocyanate (CAS Reg. No. 4098–71–9) and/or 1,3-bis(isocyanatomethyl)benzene (CAS Reg. No. 363–48–31).

(3) *Test specifications*. These specifications apply only to materials on the food-contact side of a functional barrier, if present. All tests must be performed on containers made under production conditions. Laminated structures submitted to extraction procedures must maintain complete structural integrity (particularly with regard to delamination) throughout the test.

(i) *Nonvolatile extractives*. (*a*) For use at temperatures not to exceed 121 °C (250 °F): The container interior (food-contact side) shall be extracted with deionized distilled water at 121 °C (250 °F) for 2 hours.

(*1*) The chloroform-soluble fraction of the total nonvolatile extractives for containers using adhesives listed in paragraphs (c)(2)(i), (c)(2)(ii), (c)(2)(iii), (c)(2)(iv), and (c)(2)(vii) of this section shall not exceed 0.0016 milligram per square centimeter (0.01 milligram per square inch) as determined by a method entitled "Determination of Non-Volatile Chloroform Soluble Residues in Retort Pouch Water Extracts," which is incorporated by reference. Copies are available from the Center for Food Safety and Applied Nutrition (HFS–200), Food and Drug Administration, 5100 Paint Branch Pkwy., College Park, MD 20740, and may be examined at the Center for Food Safety and Applied Nutrition's Library, 5100 Paint Branch Pkwy.; College Park, MD 20740, or at the National Archives and Records Administration (NARA). For information on the availability of this material at NARA, call 202–741–6030, or go to: *http://www.archives.gov/federal_register/code_of_federal_regulations/ibr_locations.html.*

(*2*) The chloroform-soluble fraction of the total nonvolatile extractives for containers using adhesives listed in paragraph (c)(2)(v) of this section shall not exceed 0.016 milligram per square centimeter (0.10 milligram per square inch) as determined by a method titled "Determination of Non-volatile Chloroform Soluble Residues in Retort Pouch Water Extracts," which is incorporated by reference in paragraph (c)(3)(i)(*a*)(*1*) of this section.

(*b*) For use at temperatures not to exceed 135 °C (275 °F): The container interior (food-contact side) shall be extracted with deionized distilled water at 135 °C (275 °F) for 1 hour.

(*1*) The chloroform-soluble fraction of the total nonvolatile extractives for containers using no adhesive, or adhesives listed in paragraphs (c)(2) (i), (ii), and (iii) of this section shall not exceed 0.0020 milligram per square centimeter

(0.013 milligram per square inch) as determined by a method titled "Determination of Non-volatile Chloroform Soluble Residues in Retort Pouch Water Extracts," which is incorporated by reference. The availability of this incorporation by reference is given in paragraph (c)(3)(i)(*a*)(*1*) of this section.

(*2*) The chloroform-soluble fraction of the total nonvolatile extractives for containers using adhesives listed in paragraph (c)(2)(v) of this section shall not exceed 0.016 milligram per square centimeter (0.10 milligram per square inch) as determined by a method titled "Determination of Non-volatile Chloroform Soluble Residues in Retort Pouch Water Extracts," which is incorporated by reference. The availability of this incorporation by reference is given in paragraph (c)(3)(i)(*a*)(*1*) of this section.

(*3*) The chloroform-soluble fraction of the total nonvolatile extractives for containers using adhesives listed in paragraph (c)(2)(vi) of this section shall not exceed 0.008 milligram per square centimeter (0.05 milligram per square inch) as determined by a method entitled, "Determination of Non-volatile Chloroform Soluble Residues in Retort Pouch Water Extracts," which is incorporated by reference in paragraph (c)(3)(i)(*a*)(*1*) of this section.

(ii) *Volatiles.* Volatile substances employed in the manufacture of high-temperature laminates must be removed to the greatest extent possible in keeping with good manufacturing practice prescribed in § 174.5(a) of this chapter.

(d) Nylon 12/aluminum foil high-temperature laminates: Subject to the provisions of this paragraph, containers constructed of nylon 12 laminated to aluminum foil may be safely used at temperatures no greater than 250 °F (121 °C) in contact with all food types except those containing more than 8 percent alcohol.

(1) The container is constructed of aluminum foil to which nylon 12 film is fused. Prior to fusing the nylon 12, the aluminum foil may be optionally precoated with a coating complying with § 175.300 of this chapter.

(2) Nylon 12 resin complying with § 177.1500 and having an average thickness not to exceed 0.0016 inch (41 microns) may be used as the food-contact surface of the container.

(3) Container test specifications. On exposure to distilled water at 250 °F (121 °C) for 2 hours, extractives from the food-contact side of the nylon 12 multilayered construction shall not exceed 0.05 milligram per square inch (0.0078 milligram per square centimeter) as total nonvolatile extractives.

[45 FR 2843, Jan. 15, 1980, as amended at 47 FR 49639, Nov. 2, 1982; 48 FR 236, Jan. 4, 1983; 48 FR 15242, Apr. 8, 1983; 48 FR 17347, Apr. 22, 1983; 49 FR 7558, Mar. 1, 1984; 52 FR 33575, Sept. 4, 1987; 53 FR 39084, Oct. 5, 1988; 54 FR 24898, June 12, 1989; 61 FR 14481, Apr. 2, 1996; 63 FR 55943, Oct. 20, 1998; 64 FR 4785, Feb. 1, 1999; 64 FR 46272, Aug. 25, 1999; 69 FR 15668, Mar. 26, 2004]

§ 177.1395 Laminate structures for use at temperatures between 120 °F and 250 °F.

(a) The laminates identified in this section may be safely used at the specified temperatures. These articles are layered structures that are optionally bonded with adhesives. In these articles, the food-contact layer does not function as a barrier to migration of components from non-food-contact layers. The layers may be laminated, extruded, coextruded, or fused.

(b) Laminate structures may be manufactured from:

(1) Polymers and adjuvants complying with § 177.1390 of this chapter.

(2) Any polymeric resin listed in these regulations so long as the use of the resin in the structure complies with the conditions of use (food type and time/temperature) specified in the regulation for that resin.

(3) Optional adjuvant substances used in accordance with § 174.5 of this chapter.

(4) The following substances in non-food-contact layers only:

Substances	Limitations
Ethylene/1,3–phenylene oxyethylene isophthalate/terephthalate copolymer (CAS Reg. No. 87365–98–8) complying with § 177.1345.	For use only with polyethylene terephthalate as the food-contact layer, complying with § 177.1630 under conditions of use C through G described in table 2 of § 176.170(c) of this chapter. Laminate structures, when extracted with 8 percent ethanol at 150 °F for 2 hours shall not yield *m*-pheny lenedioxy-O,O′-diethyl isophthalate or cyclic bis(ethylene isophthalate) in excess of 7.8 micrograms/square decimeter (0.5 microgram/square inch) of food-contact surface.
Nylon 6/12 resins complying with § 177.1500(b), item 13.2, of this chapter (CAS Reg. No. 25191–04–2).	For use with nonalcoholic foods at temperatures not to exceed 100 °C (212 °F). Laminate structures with authorized food-contact materials yield no more than 0.15 milligram of *epsilon*-caprolactam and 0.04 milligram of *omega*-laurolactam per square inch when extracted with water at 100 °C (212 °F) for 5 hours.
Nylon 6/66 resins complying with § 177.1500(b), item 4.2 of this chapter (CAS Reg. 24993–04–2).	For use only with: 1. Nonalcoholic foods at temperatures not to exceed 82.2 °C (180 °F). Laminate structures with authorized food-contact materials yield no more than 0.15 milligram of *epsilon*-caprolactam per square inch when extracted with water at 82.2 °C (180 °F) for 5 hours. 2. Nonalcoholic foods at temperatures not to exceed 100 °C (212 °F). Laminate films with authorized food-contact materials yield no more than 0.15 milligram of *epsilon*-caprolactam per square inch when extracted with water at 100 °C (212 °F) for 5 hours.
Nylon 6/69 resins complying with § 177.1500(b), item 14, of this chapter (CAS Reg. No. 51995–62–1).	For use with nonalcoholic foods under conditions of use B, C, D, E, F, G, and H described in table 2 of § 176.170 of this chapter. Laminate structures with authorized food-contact materials may contain nylon 6/69 resins provided that the nitrogen content of aqueous extracts of a representative laminate (obtained at 100 °C (212 °F) for 8 hours) does not exceed 15 micrograms per square centimeter (100 micrograms per square inch).

[52 FR 33575, Sept. 4, 1987, as amended at 53 FR 19772, May 31, 1988; 57 FR 43399, Sept. 21, 1992; 58 FR 32610, June 11, 1993; 62 FR 53957, Oct. 17, 1997]

§ 177.1400 Hydroxyethyl cellulose film, water-insoluble.

Water-insoluble hydroxyethyl cellulose film may be safely used for packaging food in accordance with the following prescribed conditions:

(a) Water-insoluble hydroxyethyl cellulose film consists of a base sheet manufactured by the ethoxylation of cellulose under controlled conditions, to which may be added certain optional substances of a grade of purity suitable for use in food packaging as constituents of the base sheet or as coatings applied to impart desired technological properties.

(b) Subject to any limitations prescribed in parts 170 through 189 of this chapter, the optional substances used in the base sheet and coating may include:

(1) Substances generally recognized as safe in food.

(2) Substances permitted to be used in water-insoluble hydroxyethyl cellulose film by prior sanction or approval and under conditions specified in such sanctions or approval, and substances listed in part 181, subpart B of this chapter.

(3) Substances that by any regulation promulgated under section 409 of the act may be safely used as components of water-insoluble hydroxyethyl cellulose film.

(4) Substances identified in and used in compliance with § 177.1200(c).

(c) Any substance employed in the production of the water-insoluble hydroxyethyl cellulose film described in this section that is the subject of a regulation in parts 174, 175, 176, 177, 178 and § 179.45 of this chapter conforms with any specification in such regulation.

§ 177.1420 Isobutylene polymers.

Isobutylene polymers may be safely used as components of articles intended for use in producing, manufacturing, packing, processing, preparing, treating, packaging, transporting, or holding food, in accordance with the following prescribed conditions:

(a) For the purpose of this section, isobutylene polymers are those produced as follows:

(1) Polyisobutylene produced by the homopolymerization of isobutylene such that the finished polymers have a molecular weight of 750,000 (Flory) or higher.

(2) Isobutylene-isoprene copolymers produced by the copolymerization of isobutylene with not more than 3 molar percent of isoprene such that the finished polymers have a molecular weight of 300,000 (Flory) or higher.

(3) Chlorinated isobutylene-isoprene copolymers produced when isobutylene-isoprene copolymers (molecular weight 300,000 (Flory) or higher) are modified by chlorination with not more than 1.3 weight-percent of chlorine.

(b) The polymers identified in paragraph (a) of this section may contain optional adjuvant substances required in the production of the polymers. The optional adjuvant substances required in the production of the polymers may include substances generally recognized as safe in food, substances used in accordance with a prior sanction or approval, and aluminum chloride.

(c) The provisions of this section are not applicable to polyisobutylene used in food-packaging adhesives complying with § 175.105 of this chapter.

§ 177.1430 Isobutylene-butene copolymers.

Isobutylene-butene copolymers identified in paragraph (a) of this section may be safely used as components of articles intended for use in contact with food, subject to the provisions of this section.

(a) For the purpose of this section, isobutylene-butene copolymers consist of basic copolymers produced by the copolymerization of isobutylene with mixtures of *n*-butenes such that the finished basic copolymers contain not less than 45 weight percent of polymer units derived from isobutylene and meet the specifications prescribed in paragraph (b) of this section when tested by the methods described in paragraph (c) of this section.

(b) *Specifications:*

Isobutylene-butene copolymers	Molecular weight (range)	Viscosity (range)	Maximum bromine value
1. Used as release agents in petroleum wax complying with § 178.3710 of this chapter.	300 to 5,000 ...	40 to 20,000 seconds Saybolt at 200 °F.	40
2. Used as plasticizers in polyethylene or polypropylene complying with § 177.1520, and in polystyrene complying with § 177.1640.	300 to 5,000 ...	40 to 20,000 seconds Saybolt at 200 °F.	40
3. Used as components of nonfood articles complying with §§ 175.300, 176.170, 176.210, 177.2260(d)(2), 177.2800, and 178.3570 (provided that addition to food does not exceed 10 parts per million), or § 176.180 of this chapter.	300 to 5,000 ...	40 to 20,000 seconds Saybolt at 200 °F.	40
4. Used as production aids in the manufacture of expanded (foamed) polystyrene articles complying with § 177.1640 of this chapter.	150 to 5,000 ...	Less than 20,000 seconds Saybolt at 200 °F.	90.
5. Used in release coatings on backings or linings for pressure-sensitive adhesive labels complying with § 175.125 of this chapter.	150 to 5,000 ...	Less than 20,000 seconds Saybolt at 200 °F.	90

(c) The analytical methods for determining whether isobutylene-butene copolymers conform to the specifications in paragraph (b) are as follows:

(1) *Molecular weight.* Molecular weight shall be determined by American Society for Testing and Materials (ASTM) method D2503–82, "Standard Test Method for Molecular Weight

(Relative Molecular Mass) of Hydrocarbons by Thermoelectric Measurement of Vapor Pressure," which is incorporated by reference. Copies may be obtained from the American Society for Testing Materials, 100 Barr Harbor Dr., West Conshohocken, Philadelphia, PA 19428-2959, or may be examined at the National Archives and Records Administration (NARA). For information on the availability of this material at NARA, call 202–741–6030, or go to: *http://www.archives.gov/federal_register/code_of_federal_regulations/ibr_locations.html.*

(2) *Viscosity.* Viscosity shall be determined by ASTM method D445–74, "Test for Kinematic Viscosity of Transparent and Opaque Liquids," which is incorporated by reference. The availability of this incorporation by reference is given in paragraph (c)(1) of this section.

(3) *Maximum bromine value.* Maximum bromine value shall be determined by ASTM method D1492–78, "Standard Test Method for Bromine Index of Aromatic Hydrocarbons by Coulometric Titration," which is incorporated by reference. The availability of this incorporation by reference is given in paragraph (c)(1) of this section.

(d) The provisions of this section are not applicable to isobutylene-butene copolymers used as provided under §175.105 of this chapter.

[52 FR 11641, Apr. 10, 1987, as amended at 63 FR 36175, July 2, 1998]

§ 177.1440 4,4′-Isopropylidenediphenol-epichlorohydrin resins minimum molecular weight 10,000.

4,4′-Isopropylidenediphenol-epichlorohydrin resins having a minimum molecular weight of 10,000 may be safely used as articles or components of articles intended for use in producing, manufacturing, packing, processing, preparing, treating, packaging, transporting, or holding food in accordance with the following prescribed conditions:

(a) 4,4′-Isopropylidenediphenol-epichlorohydrin resins consist of basic resins produced by the condensation of equimolar amounts of 4,4′-isopropylidenediphenol and epichlorohydrin terminated with phenol, to which may have been added certain optional adjuvant substances required in the production of the resins.

(b) The optional adjuvant substances required in the production of the resins may include substances generally recognized as safe in food, substances used in accordance with a prior sanction or approval, and the following:

List of substances	Limitations
Butyl alcohol	Not to exceed 300 p.p.m. as residual solvent in finished resin.
Ethyl alcohol.	
Toluene	Not to exceed 1,000 p.p.m. as residual solvent in finished resin.

(c) 4,4′-Isopropylidenediphenol-epichlorohydrin resins shall meet the following nonvolatile extractives limitations:

(1) Maximum extractable nonvolatile fraction of 2 parts per million when extracted with distilled water at 70 °C for 2 hours, using a volume-to-surface ratio of 2 milliliters per square inch.

(2) Maximum extractable nonvolatile fraction of 3 parts per million when extracted with *n*-heptane at 70 °C for 2 hours, using a volume-to-surface ratio of 2 milliliters per square inch.

(3) Maximum extractable nonvolatile fraction of 6 parts per million when extracted with 10 percent (by volume) ethyl alcohol in distilled water at 70 °C for 2 hours, using a volume-to-surface ratio of 2 milliliters per square inch.

(d) The provisions of this section are not applicable to 4,4′-isopropylidenediphenol-epichlorohydrin resins listed in other sections of subchapter B of this chapter.

§ 177.1460 Melamine-formaldehyde resins in molded articles.

Melamine-formaldehyde resins may be safely used as the food-contact surface of molded articles intended for use in producing, manufacturing, packing, processing, preparing, treating, packaging, transporting, or holding food in accordance with the following prescribed conditions:

(a) For the purpose of this section, melamine-formaldehyde resins are those produced when 1 mole of melamine is made to react with not more than 3 moles of formaldehyde in water solution.

(b) The resins may be mixed with refined woodpulp and the mixture may contain other optional adjuvant substances which may include the following:

List of substances	Limitations
Colorants used in accordance with § 178.3297 of this chapter.	
Dioctyl phthalate	For use as lubricant.
Hexamethylenetetramine	For use only as polymerization reaction control agent.
Phthalic acid anhydride	Do.
Zinc stearate	For use as lubricant.

(c) The molded melamine-formaldehyde articles in the finished form in which they are to contact food, when extracted with the solvent or solvents characterizing the type of food and under the conditions of time and temperature as determined from tables 1 and 2 of § 175.300(d) of this chapter, shall yield net chloroform-soluble extractives not to exceed 0.5 milligram per square inch of food-contact surface.

[42 FR 14572, Mar. 15, 1977, as amended at 56 FR 42933, Aug. 30, 1991]

§ 177.1480 Nitrile rubber modified acrylonitrile-methyl acrylate copolymers.

Nitrile rubber modified acrylonitrile-methyl acrylate copolymers identified in this section may be safely used as components of articles intended for food-contact use under conditions of use D, E, F, or G described in table 2 of § 176.170(c) of this chapter, subject to the provisions of this section.

(a) For the purpose of this section, nitrile rubber modified acrylonitrile-methyl acrylate copolymers consist of basic copolymers produced by the graft copolymerization of 73–77 parts by weight of acrylonitrile and 23–27 parts by weight of methyl acrylate in the presence of 8–10 parts by weight of butadiene-acrylonitrile copolymers containing approximately 70 percent by weight of polymer units derived from butadiene.

(b) The nitrile rubber modified acrylonitrile-methyl acrylate basic copolymers meet the following specifications and extractives limitations:

(1) *Specifications.* (i) Nitrogen content is in the range 16.5–19 percent as determined by Kjeldahl analysis.

(ii) Intrinsic viscosity in acetonitrile at 25 °C is not less than 0.29 deciliter per gram as determined by ASTM method D1243–79, "Standard Test Method for Dilute Solution Viscosity of Vinyl Chloride Polymers," which is incorporated by reference. Copies may be obtained from the American Society for Testing Materials, 100 Barr Harbor Dr., West Conshohocken, Philadelphia, PA 19428-2959, or may be examined at the National Archives and Records Administration (NARA). For information on the availability of this material at NARA, call 202–741–6030, or go to: *http://www.archives.gov/federal_register/code_of_federal_regulations/ibr_locations.html.*

(iii) Residual acrylonitrile monomer content is not more than 11 parts per million as determined by gas chromatography.

(iv) Acetonitrile-soluble fraction after refluxing the base polymer in acetonitrile for 1 hour is not greater than 95 percent by weight of the basic copolymers.

(2) *Extractives limitations.* The following extractive limitations are determined by an infrared spectrophotometric method titled, "Infrared Spectrophotometric Determination of Polymer Extracted from Borex® 210 Resin Pellets," which is incorporated by reference. Copies are available from the Center for Food Safety and Applied Nutrition (HFS–200), Food and Drug Administration, 5100 Paint Branch Pkwy., College Park, MD 20740, or available for inspection at the National Archives and Records Administration (NARA). For information on the availability of this material at NARA, call 202–741–6030, or go to: *http://www.archives.gov/federal_register/code_of_federal_regulations/ibr_locations.html.*Copies are applicable to the basic copolymers in the form of particles of a size that will pass through a U.S. standard sieve No. 6 and that will be held on a U.S. standard sieve No. 10:

(i) Extracted copolymer not to exceed 2.0 parts per million in aqueous extract obtained when a 100-gram sample of the basic copolymers is extracted with 250 milliliters of demineralized (deionized) water at reflux temperature for 2 hours.

(ii) Extracted copolymer not to exceed 0.5 part per million in *n*-heptane extract obtained when a 100-gram sample of the basic copolymers is extracted with 250 milliliters of reagent grade *n*-heptane at reflux temperature for 2 hours.

(c) Acrylonitrile copolymers identified in this section shall comply with the provisions of § 180.22 of this chapter.

(d) Acrylonitrile copolymers identified in this section are not authorized to be used to fabricate beverage containers.

[42 FR 14572, Mar. 15, 1977, as amended at 42 FR 48544, Sept. 23, 1977; 47 FR 11843, Mar. 19, 1982; 47 FR 16775, Apr. 20, 1982; 49 FR 10109, Mar. 19, 1984; 54 FR 24898, June 12, 1989; 61 FR 14481, Apr. 2, 1996]

§ 177.1500 Nylon resins.

The nylon resins listed in paragraph (a) of this section may be safely used to produce articles intended for use in processing, handling, and packaging food, subject to the provisions of this section:

(a) The nylon resins are manufactured as described in this paragraph so as to meet the specifications prescribed in paragraph (b) of this section when tested by the methods described in paragraph (d) of this section.

(1) Nylon 66 resins are manufactured by the condensation of hexamethylenediamine and adipic acid.

(2) Nylon 610 resins are manufactured by the condensation of hexamethylenediamine and sebacic acid.

(3) Nylon 66/610 resins are manufactured by the condensation of equal-weight mixtures of nylon 66 salts and nylon 610 salts.

(4) Nylon 6/66 resins manufactured by the condensation and polymerization of Nylon 66 salts and *epsilon*-caprolactam.

(5) Nylon 11 resins are manufactured by the condensation of 11-aminoundecanoic acid.

(6) Nylon 6 resins are manufactured by the polymerization of *epsilon*-caprolactam.

(7) Nylon 66T resins are manufactured by the condensation of hexamethyl-enediamine, adipic acid, and terephthalic acid such that composition in terms of ingredients is 43.1±0.2 weight percent hexamethylenediamine, 35.3±1.2 weight percent adipic acid, and 21.6±1.2 weight percent terephthalic acid.

(8) Nylon 612 resins are manufactured by the condensation of hexamethylenediamine and dodecanedioic acid.

(9) Nylon 12 resins are manufactured by the condensation of *omega*-laurolactam.

(10)(i) Impact modified Nylon MXD-6 resins (CAS Reg. No. 59655-05-9) manufactured by the condensation of adipic acid, 1,3-benzenedimethanamine, and *alpha*-(3-aminopropyl)-*omega*-(3-aminopropoxy)poly- oxyethylene under such conditions that the *alpha*-(3-aminopropyl)-*omega*-(3-aminopropoxy) polyoxyethylene monomer content does not exceed 7 percent by weight of the finished resin.

(ii) Nylon MXD-6 resins (CAS Reg. No. 25718-70-1) manufactured by the condensation of adipic acid and 1,3-benzenedimethanamine.

(11) Nylon 12T resins are manufactured by the condensation of *omega*-laurolactam (CAS Reg. No. 0947-04-6), isophthalic acid (CAS Reg. No. 0121-91-5), and bis(4-amino-3-methylcyclohexyl)methane (CAS Reg. No. 6864-37-5) such that the composition in terms of ingredients is 34.4±1.5 weight percent *omega*-laurolactam, 26.8±0.4 weight percent isophthalic acid, and 38.8±0.5 weight percent bis(4-amino-3-methylcyclohexyl)-methane.

(12) Nylon 6I/6T resins (CAS Reg. No. 25750-23-6) are manufactured by the condensation of hexamethylenediamine, terephthalic acid, and isophthalic acid such that 65 to 80 percent of the polymer units are derived from hexamethylene isophthalamide.

(13)(i) Nylon 6/12 resins (CAS Reg. No. 25191-04-2) are manufactured by the copolymerization of a 1 to 1 ratio by weight of *epsilon*-caprolactam and *omega*-laurolactam.

(ii) Nylon 6/12 resins (CAS Reg. No. 25191-04-2) are manufactured by the copolymerization of a ratio of at least 80 weight percent of *epsilon*-caprolactam and no more than 20 weight percent of *omega*-laurolactam.

(14) Nylon 6/69 resins (CAS Reg. No. 51995-62-1) are manufactured by the condensation of 49.5+0.5 weight percent *epsilon*-caprolactam, 19.4+0.2 weight

percent hexamethylenediamine and 31.2+0.3 weight percent azelaic acid.

(15) Nylon 46 resins (CAS Reg. No. 50327–77–0) are manufactured by the condensation of 1,4-butanediamine and adipic acid.

(16) Nylon resins PA 6–3–T (CAS Registry No. 26246–77–5) are manufactured by the condensation of 50 mol percent 1,4-benzenedicarboxylic acid, dimethyl ester and 50 mol percent of an equimolar mixture of 2,2,4-trimethyl-1,6-hexanediamine and 2,4,4-trimethyl-1,6-hexanediamine.

(b) *Specifications:*

Nylon resins	Specific gravity	Melting point (degrees Fahrenheit)	Solubility in boiling 4.2*N* HC1	Viscosity No. (mL/g)	Maximum extractable fraction in selected solvents (expressed in percent by weight of resin)			
					Water	95 percent ethyl alcohol	Ethyl acetate	Benzene
1. Nylon 66 resins	1.14±.015	475–495	Dissolves in 1 h.		1.5	1.5	0.2	0.2
2. Nylon 610 resins	1.09±.015	405–425	Insoluble after 1 h.		1.0	2.0	1.0	1.0
3.1 Nylon 66/610 resins	1.10±.015	375–395	Dissolves in 1 h.		1.5	2.0	1.0	1.0
4.1 Nylon 6/66 resins, *epsilon*-caprolactam monomer content not to exceed 0.7 percent by weight.	1.13±.015	440–460	......do		2.0	2.0	1.5	1.5
4.2 Nylon 6/66 resins with combined caprolactam content greater than 60 percent and residual *epsilon*-caprolactam monomer content not to exceed 0.4 percent by weight. For use only as specified in § 177.1395 of this chapter (CAS Reg. No. 24993–04–2).	1.14±.015	380–425	......do		0.8	1.0	0.5	0.5
5.1 Nylon 11 resins for use in articles intended for 1-time use or repeated use in contact with food.	1.04±.015	355–375	Insoluble after 1 h.		.30	.35	.25	.3
5.2 Nylon 11 resins for use only: a. In articles intended for repeated use in contact with food. b. In side-seam cements for articles intended for 1-time use in contact with food and which are in compliance with § 175.300 of this chapter.	1.04±.015	355–375	......do		.35	1.60	.35	.40
6.1 Nylon 6 resins	1.15±.015	392–446	Dissolves in 1 h.		1.0	2.0	1.0	1.0
6.2 Nylon 6 resins for use only in food-contact films having an average thickness not to exceed 0.001 in.	1.15±.015	392–446	......do		1.5	2.0	1.0	1.0
7. Nylon 66T resins for use only in food-contact films having an average thickness not to exceed 0.001 in.	1.16±.015	482–518	Insoluble after 1 h.		1.0	1.0	.25	.25
8. Nylon 612 resins for use only in articles intended for repeated use in contact with food at temperatures not to exceed 212 °F.	1.06±.015	406–420	......do		.50	1.50	.50	.50

Nylon resins	Specific gravity	Melting point (degrees Fahrenheit)	Solubility in boiling 4.2*N* HC1	Viscosity No. (mL/g)	Maximum extractable fraction in selected solvents (expressed in percent by weight of resin)			
					Water	95 percent ethyl alcohol	Ethyl acetate	Benzene
9. Nylon 12 resins for use only:. a. In food-contact films having an average thickness not to exceed 0.0016 inch intended for use in contact with nonalcoholic food under the conditions of use A (sterilization not to exceed 30 minutes at a temperature not to exceed 250 °F), and B through H of table 2 of § 176.170(c) of this chapter, except as provided in § 177.1390(d) b. In coatings intended for repeated use in contact with all food types described in table 1 of § 176.170(c) of this chapter, except those containing more than 8 percent alcohol, under conditions of use B through H described in table 2 of § 176.170(c) of this chapter.	1.01±.015	335–355	......do	....	1.0	2.0	1.50	1.50
10.1 Nylon MXD–6 and impact modified Nylon MXD–6 film having an average thickness not to exceed 40 microns (0.0016 inch) for use in processing, handling, and packaging of food of types V and IX listed in table 1 of § 176.170(c) of this chapter under conditions of use C, D, E, F, G, and H in table 2 of § 176.170(C) of this chapter.	1.21±0.02	437–491	Dissolves in 1h.	....	2.0	2.5	1.0	1.0
10.2 Impact modified Nylon MXD–6 resins for use as polymer use as polymer modifiers in Nylon 6 resin films complying with paragraph (a)(6) of this section, at levels not to exceed 13 percent by weight of films whose average thickness will not exceed 15 microns (0.6 mils). The finished film is used for packaging, transporting, or holding food, excluding beverages containing more than 8 percent alcohol (by volume) at temperatures not to exceed 49 °C (120 °F) (conditions of use E, F, and G in table 2 of § 176.170(c) of this chapter).	1.21±0.02	437–491	do	....	2.0	2.5	1.0	1.0

Nylon resins	Specific gravity	Melting point (degrees Fahrenheit)	Solubility in boiling 4.2*N* HC1	Viscosity No. (mL/g)	Maximum extractable fraction in selected solvents (expressed in percent by weight of resin)			
					Water	95 percent ethyl alcohol	Ethyl acetate	Benzene
10.3 Nylon MXD–6 resins for use only as nonfood-contact layers of: (1) Multilayer films and (2) rigid plastic containers composed of polypropylene food-contact and exterior layers, as defined in § 177.1520(c), item 1.1(a) and 1.1(b), of this chapter. The finished food-contact laminate, in the form in which it contacts food, when extracted with the food simulating solvent or solvents characterizing the conditions of the intended use as determined from Table 2 of § 176.170(c) of this chapter, shall yield not more than 0.5 micrograms of *m*-xylylenediamine-adipic acid cyclic monomer per square inch of food-contact surface, when the food simulating solvent is analyzed by any appropriate, properly validated method.	1.22±0.02	455–470	Dissolves in 1 h.		1.0	1.5	0.2	0.2
11. Nylon 12T resins for use in contact with all types of food except those containing more than 8 percent alcohol.	1.06±0.015	N/A	Insoluble after 1 hour.	....	0.1	....	0.5	0.5
12. Nylon 6I/6T resins for use in contact with all types of food except alcoholic beverages containing more than 8 percent alcohol.	1.207±0.1	N/A	Insoluble after 1 hour.	....	0.2	1.0	0.1	0.1
13.1 Nylon 6/12 resins for use only in food-contact films having an average thickness not to exceed 51 microns (0.002 inch). The finished film is intended to contact all foods except those containing more than 8 percent ethanol under conditions of use B, C, D, E, F, G, and H listed in table 2 of § 176.170(c) of this chapter.	1.06±0.015	260–285	Dissolves in 1 hour.	Greater than 140	2.0	....	1.5	1.5
13.2 Nylon 6/12 resins with residual *epsilon*-caprolactam not to exceed 0.5 percent by weight and residual *omega*-laurolactam not to exceed 0.1 percent by weight. For use only as specified in § 177.1395 of this chapter.	1.10±0.15	380–400	Dissolves in 1 h.	Greater than 160	0.8	1.0	0.5	0.5

Nylon resins	Specific gravity	Melting point (degrees Fahrenheit)	Solubility in boiling 4.2*N* HC1	Viscosity No. (mL/g)	Maximum extractable fraction in selected solvents (expressed in percent by weight of resin)			
					Water	95 percent ethyl alcohol	Ethyl acetate	Benzene
13.3 Nylon 6/12 resins with residual *epsilon*-caprolactam not to exceed 0.8 percent by weight and residual *omega*-laurolactam not to exceed 0.1 percent by weight. For use only as specified in § 177.1390 of this chapter.	1.13 ±0.15	400–420	Dissolves in 1 h.	....	1.0	1.5	0.5	0.5
14. Nylon 6/69 resins for use only as specified in 21 CFR 177.1395 of this chapter.	1.09±0.02	270–277	....	>140 using the method described in § 177.1500(c)(5)(ii) of this chapter.	3.0			
15. Nylon 46 resins for use only in food-contact membrane filters intended for repeated use. The finished membrane filter is intended to contact beverages containing no more than 13 percent alcohol, under conditions of use E, F, and G listed in table 2 of § 176.170(c) of this chapter.	1.18±0.015	551–592	Dissolves in 1 h.	....	0.3	0.2	0.2	0.3
16. Nylon resins PA 6–3–T for repeated-use (excluding bottles) in contact with food of type VIA and VIB described in table 1 of § 176.170(c) of this chapter under conditions of use D through H described in table 2 of § 176.170(c) of this chapter with a hot-fill temperature limitation of 40 °C.	1.12±0.03	NA	Insoluble after 1 h.	> 110	0.007	0.64	0.003	0

(c) *Nylon modifier*—(1) *Identity*. Copolyester-graft-acrylate copolymer is the substance 1,4-benzenedicarboxylic acid, polymer with 1,4-butanediol, (*E*)-2-butenedioic acid, 1,2-ethanediol, ethyl 2-propenoate, hexanedioic acid and 2-propenoic acid, graft (CAS Reg. No. 175419–23–5), and is derived from grafting of 25 weight percent of acrylic polymer with 75 weight percent of copolyester. The copolyester is polymerized terephthalic acid (55 mol%), adipic acid (40 mol%), and fumaric acid (5 mol%) with ethylene glycol (40 mol%) and 1,4-butanediol (60 mol%). The acrylic polymer is made from acrylic acid (70 mol%) and ethyl acrylate (30 mol%).

(2) *Specifications*. The finished copolyester-graft-acrylate copolymer shall meet the following specifications:

(i) Weight average molecular weight 15,000–35,000,

(ii) pH 7.2 to 8.2, and

(iii) Glass transition temperature −15 to −25 °C.

(3) *Conditions of use*. (i) Copolyester-graft acrylate copolymer described in paragraph (c)(1) of this section is intended to improve the adhesive qualities of film. It is limited for use as a modifier of Nylon 6 and Nylon 6 modified with Nylon MXD–6 at a level not to exceed 0.17 weight percent of the additive in the finished film.

(ii) The finished film is used for packaging, transporting, or holding all types of foods under conditions of use B through H, described in table 2 of §176.170(c) of this chapter, except that in the case of Nylon 6 films modified with Nylon MXD–6 (complying with §177.1500, item 10.2), the use complies with the conditions of use specified in table 2.

(iii) *Extractives.* Food contact films described in paragraphs (c)(1) of this section, when extracted with solvent or solvents prescribed for the type of food and under conditions of time and temperature specified for the intended use, shall yield total extractives not to exceed 0.5 milligram per inch squared of food-contact surface when tested by the methods described in §176.170(d) of this chapter.

(iv) *Optional adjuvant substances.* The substances employed in the production of Nylon modifiers listed in paragraph (c)(1) of this section may include:

(A) Substances generally recognized as safe for use in food and food packaging;

(B) Substances subject to prior sanction or approval for use in Nylon resins and used in accordance with such sanctions or approval; and

(C) Optional substances required in the production of the additive identified in this paragraph and other optional substances that may be required to accomplish the intended physical or technical effect.

(d) *Analytical methods*—(1) *Specific gravity.* Specific gravity shall be determined by weighing a 1-gram to 5-gram sample first in air and then in freshly boiled distilled water at 23 °C±2 °C.

(2) *Melting point.* The melting point shall be determined as follows: Use a hot-stage apparatus. The use of crossed nicol prisms with a microscope hot stage and reading of the thermometer when the birefringence disappears increases the accuracy. If the crossed nicol apparatus is not available, use the lowest temperature at which the sample becomes transparent or the sharp edges or corners of the sample become rounded as the melting point. In case of doubt as to the onset of melting, the sample is prodded with a sharp instrument. If it sticks to the heating block, it is considered to have melted. If the melting point is low, dry the sample in an oven at 85 °C for 24 hours in a nitrogen atmosphere then repeat the test.

(3) *Solubility in boiling 4.2N HCl.* The test shall be run on a sample approximately the size of a ⅛-inch cube in at least 25 milliliters of 4.2 normal hydrochloric acid.

(4) *Maximum extractable fraction in selected solvents.* The procedure for determining the maximum extractable fraction of the nylon resins in selected solvents is as follows:

(i) Film should be cut with ordinary scissors into pieces of a convenient size such as ¼-inch squares, for the extraction tests described in this section. The granules of nylon molding powders are in the proper form for the extraction tests. Samples of fabricated articles such as pipe, fittings, and other similar articles must be cut to approximately the size of the molding powder. This can be done conveniently by using a small-scale commercial plastics granulator and cutting the sample through a screen having ¼-inch mesh. Fine particles should be separated from the cut resin by screening through a 20-mesh screen. The material retained on the screen is suitable for the extraction tests.

(ii) The organic solvents must be of American Chemical Society analytical reagent grade; distilled water is used. Approximately 30 grams of the prepared sample is weighed to the nearest milligram. The weighed resin is transferred to a 500-milliliter round-bottom flask equipped with a reflux condenser. Approximately 300-milliliters of solvent is added to the flask and the contents refluxed gently for 8 hours with a heating mantle. The solvent is then filtered off immediately while still hot, using a Buchner funnel approximately 5 inches in diameter, a suction flask, and a hardened filter paper (Whatman No. 50 or equivalent). The paper is wet with the solvent and a slight suction applied just before starting the filtration. The resin is washed twice with approximately 100-milliliter portions of solvent and the combined filtrate and washings are reduced to approximately 25 milliliters by evaporation at reduced pressure (50 millimeters to 100 millimeters of mercury, absolute), heating as necessary. The contents of the flask are transferred to an evaporation dish (which has been held in a vacuum desiccator over anhydrous calcium sulfate until constant weight has been attained) and carefully evaporated to dryness. The weight of the solid residue is determined by difference after holding in a vacuum desiccator over anhydrous calcium sulfate until constant weight has been attained. The percent of solids extracted is calculated by dividing the weight of the solid residue by the weight of the sample and multiplying by 100.

(5) *Viscosity number (VN).* (i) The viscosity number (VN) for Nylon 6/12 resin in a 96 percent sulfuric acid solution (5 milligrams resin per milliliter) shall be determined at 25 °C (77 °F) by method ISO 307–1984(E), "Plastics-Polyamides-Determination of Viscosity Number," which is incorporated by reference. Copies are available from the Center for Food Safety and Applied Nutrition (HFS–200), Food and Drug Administration, 5100 Paint Branch Pkwy., College Park, MD 20740, or available for inspection at the National Archives and Records Administration (NARA). For information on the availability of this material at NARA, call 202–741–6030, or go to: *http://www.archives.gov/federal_register/code_of_federal_regulations/ibr_locations.html.*

(ii) The viscosity number (VN) for Nylon 6/69 and Nylon PA–6–3–T resins in a 99 percent cresol solution (5 milligrams resin per milliliter) shall be determined at 25 °C (77 °F) by method ISO 307–1984(E), "Plastics-Polyamides-Determination of Viscosity Number," which is incorporated by reference. The availability of this incorporation by reference is given in paragraph (d)(5)(i) of this section.

[42 FR 14572, Mar. 15, 1977]

EDITORIAL NOTE: For FEDERAL REGISTER citations affecting §177.1500, see the List of CFR Sections Affected, which appears in the Finding Aids section of the printed volume and at *www.fdsys.gov.*

§ 177.1520 Olefin polymers.

The olefin polymers listed in paragraph (a) of this section may be safely used as articles or components of articles intended for use in contact with food, subject to the provisions of this section.

(a) For the purpose of this section, olefin polymers are basic polymers manufactured as described in this paragraph, so as to meet the specifications prescribed in paragraph (c) of this section, when tested by the methods described in paragraph (d) of this section.

(1)(i) Polypropylene consists of basic polymers manufactured by the catalytic polymerization of propylene.

(ii) Propylene homopolymer consists of basic polymers manufactured by the catalytic polymerization of propylene with a metallocene catalyst.

(2)(i) Polyethylene consists of basic polymers manufactured by the catalytic polymerization of ethylene.

(ii) Fumaric acid-grafted polyethylene (CAS Reg. No. 26877–81–6) consists of basic polymers manufactured by the catalytic polymerization of ethylene followed by reaction with fumaric acid in the absence of free radical initiators. Such polymers shall contain grafted fumaric acid at levels not to exceed 2 percent by weight of the finished polymer.

(3) Olefin basic copolymers consist of basic copolymers manufactured by the catalytic copolymerization of:

(i) Two or more of the 1-alkenes having 2 to 8 carbon atoms. Such olefin basic copolymers contain not less than 96 weight-percent of polymer units derived from ethylene and/or propylene, except that:

(*a*)(*1*) Olefin basic copolymers manufactured by the catalytic copolymerization of ethylene and hexene-1 or ethylene and octene-1 shall contain not less than 90 weight-percent of polymer units derived from ethylene;

(*2*) Olefin basic copolymers manufactured by the catalytic copolymerization of ethylene and hexene-1 shall contain not less than 80 but not more than 90 weight percent of polymer units derived from ethylene.

(*3*) Olefin basic copolymers manufactured by the catalytic copolymerization of ethylene and pentene-1 shall contain not less than 90 weight-percent of polymer units derived from ethylene.

(*4*) Olefin basic copolymers manufactured by the catalytic polymerization of ethylene and octene-1 shall contain not less than 50 weight-percent of polymer units derived from ethylene.

(*b*) Olefin basic copolymers manufactured by the catalytic copolymerization of ethylene and 4-methylpentene-1 shall contain not less than 89 weight-percent of polymer units derived from ethylene;

(*c*)(*1*) Olefin basic copolymers manufactured by the catalytic copolymerization of two or more of the monomers ethylene, propylene, butene-1, 2-methylpropene-1, and 2,4,4-trimethylpentene-1 shall contain not less than 85 weight-percent of polymer units derived from ethylene and/or propylene;

(*2*) Olefin basic copolymers manufactured by the catalytic copolymerization of propylene and butene-1 shall contain greater than 15 but not greater than 35 weight percent of polymer units derived from butene-1 with the remainder being propylene.

(*d*) Olefin basic terpolymers manufactured by the catalytic copolymerization of ethylene, hexene-1, and either propylene or butene-1, shall contain not less than 85 weight percent polymer units derived from ethylene.

(*e*) Olefin basic copolymers manufactured by the catalytic polymerization of ethylene and octene-1, or ethylene, octene-1, and either hexene-1, butene-1, propylene, or 4-methylpentene-1 shall contain not less than 80 weight percent of polymer units derived from ethylene.

(ii) 4-Methylpentene-1 and 1-alkenes having from 6 to 18 carbon atoms. Such olefin basic copolymers shall contain not less than 95 molar percent of polymer units derived from 4-methylpentene-1, except that copolymers manufactured with 1-alkenes having from 12 to 18 carbon atoms shall contain not less than 97 molar percent of polymer units derived from 4-methylpentene-1; or

(iii) Ethylene and propylene that may contain as modifiers not more than 5 weight-percent of total polymer units derived by copolymerization with one or more of the following monomers:

5-Ethylidine-2-norbornene.
5-Methylene-2-norbornene.

(iv) Ethylene and propylene that may contain as a modifier not more than 4.5 weight percent of total polymer units derived by copolymerization with 1,4-hexadiene.

(v) Ethylene and butene-1 copolymers (CAS Reg. No. 25087–34–7) that shall contain not less than 80 weight percent of polymer units derived from ethylene.

(vi) Olefin basic copolymers (CAS Reg. No. 61615–63–2) manufactured by the catalytic copolymerization of ethylene and propylene with 1,4-hexadiene, followed by reaction with fumaric acid in the absence of free radical initiators. Such polymers shall contain not more than 4.5 percent of polymer units deriving from 1,4-hexadiene by weight of total polymer prior to reaction with fumaric acid and not more than 2.2 percent of grafted fumaric acid by weight of the finished polymer.

(vii) Ethylene and 2-norbornene (CAS Reg. No. 26007–43–2) copolymers that shall contain not less than 30 and not more than 70 mole percent of polymer units derived from 2-norbornene.

(4) Poly(methylpentene) consists of basic polymers manufactured by the catalytic polymerization of 4-methylpentene-1.

(5) Polyethylene graft copolymers consist of polyethylene complying with item 2.2 of paragraph (c) of this section which subsequently has 3a,4,7,7a-tetrahydromethyl-4,7-methanoisobenzofuran-1,3-dione grafted onto it at a level not to exceed 1.7 percent by weight of the finished copolymer.

(6) Ethylene-maleic anhydride copolymers (CAS Reg. No. 9006–26–2) containing no more than 2 percent by weight of copolymer units derived from maleic anhydride.

(b) The basic olefin polymers identified in paragraph (a) of this section may contain optional adjuvant substances required in the production of such basic olefin polymers. The optional adjuvant substances required in the production of the basic olefin polymers or finished food-contact articles may include substances permitted for such use by applicable regulations in parts 170 through 189 of this chapter, substances generally recognized as safe in food and food packaging, substances used in accordance with a prior sanction or approval, and the following:

Substance	Limitations
Aromatic petroleum hydrocarbon resin, hydrogenated (CAS Reg. No. 88526–47–0), produced by the catalytic polymerization of aromatic-substituted olefins from distillates of cracked petroleum stocks with a boiling point no greater than 220 °C (428 °F), and the subsequent catalytic hydrogenation of the resulting aromatic petroleum hydrocarbon resin, having a minimum softening point of 110 °C (230 °F), as determined by ASTM Method E 28–67 (Reapproved 1982), "Standard Test Method for Softening Point by Ring-and-Ball Apparatus," and a minimum aniline point of 107 °C (225 °F), as determined by ASTM Method D 611–82, "Standard Test Methods for Aniline Point and Mixed Aniline Point of Petroleum Products and Hydrocarbon Solvents," both of which are incorporated by reference in accordance with 5 U.S.C. 552(a) and 1 CFR part 51. Copies are available from the American Society for Testing and Materials, 100 Barr Harbor Dr., West Conshohocken, Philadelphia, PA 19428-2959, or from the Center for Food Safety and Applied Nutrition (HFS–200), Food and Drug Administration, 5100 Paint Branch Pkwy., College Park, MD 20740, or may be examined at the National Archives and Records Administration (NARA). For information on the availability of this material at NARA, call 202–741–6030, or go to: *http://www.archives.gov/federal_register/code_of_federal_regulations/ibr_locations.html.*.	For use only as an adjuvant at levels not to exceed 25 percent by weight in blends with polypropylene complying with paragraph (c), item 1.1 of this section. The finished polymer may be used in contact with food Types I, II, IV-B, VI-A through VI-C, VII-B, and VIII identified in table 1 of § 176.170(c) of this chapter and under conditions of use B through H described in table 2 of § 176.170(c) of this chapter; and with food Types III, IV-A, V, VII-A, and IX identified in table 1 of § 176.170(c) of this chapter and under conditions of use D through G described in table 2 of § 176.170(c) of this chapter.
Colorants used in accordance with § 178.3297 of this chapter.	
2,5-Dimethyl-2,5-di(*tert*-butylperoxy)hexane (CAS Reg. No. 78–63–7).	For use as an initiator in the production of propylene homopolymer complying with § 177.1520(c), item 1.1 and olefin copolymers complying with § 177.1520(c), items 3.1 and 3.2 and containing not less than 75 weight percent of polymer units derived from propylene, provided that the maximum concentration of *tert*-butyl alcohol in the polymer does not exceed 100 parts per million, as determined by a method titled "Determination of *tert*-Butyl Alcohol in Polypropylene," which is incorporated by reference. Copies are available from the Center for Food Safety and Applied Nutrition (HFS–200), Food and Drug Administration, 5100 Paint Branch Pkwy., College Park, MD 20740, or available for inspection at the National Archives and Records Administration (NARA). For information on the availability of this material at NARA, call 202–741–6030, or go to: *http://www.archives.gov/federal_register/code_of_federal_regulations/ibr_locations.html.*
Methyl methacrylate/butyl acrylate-grafted polypropylene copolymer containing methyl methacrylate/butyl acrylate-grafted polypropylene (CAS Reg. No. 121510–09–6), methyl methacrylate/butyl acrylate copolymer (CAS Reg. No. 25852–37–3), methyl methacrylate homopolymer (CAS Reg. No. 9011–14–7), and polypropylene (CAS Reg. No. 9003–07–0), resulting from the reaction of a mixture of methyl methacrylate and butyl acrylate with polypropylene. The finished product contains no more than 55 percent by weight of polymer units derived from methyl methacrylate and butyl acrylate as determined by a method entitled, "Determination of the Total Acrylic in PP-MMA/BA Polymers," which is incorporated by reference in accordance with 5 U.S.C. 552(a) and 1 CFR part 51. Copies are available from the Office of Premarket Approval, Center for Food Safety and Applied Nutrition (HFS–200), Food and Drug Administration, 5100 Paint Branch Pkwy., College Park, MD 20740, or may be examined at the Center for Food Safety and Applied Nutrition's Library, 5100 Paint Branch Pkwy., College Park, MD 20740, or at the National Archives and Records Administration (NARA). For information on the availability of this material at NARA, call 202–741–6030, or go to: *http://www.archives.gov/federal_register/code_of_federal_regulations/ibr_locations.html.*.	For use only at levels not to exceed 6 percent by weight of olefin polymers complying with paragraph (c) of this section, items 1.1, 3.1a, 3.2a, and 3.2b, where the copolymers complying with items 3.1a, 3.2a, and 3.2b contain not less than 85 weight-percent of polymer units derived from propylene.

Substance	Limitations
Petroleum hydrocarbon resins (cyclopentadiene-type), hydrogenated (CAS Reg. No. 68132–00–3) produced by the thermal polymerization of dicyclopentadiene and cyclodiene codimers (consisting of a mixture of cyclopentadiene, methyl cyclopentadiene, and C_4-C_5 acyclic dienes), followed by hydrogenation and having a ring-and-ball softening point of 119 °C minimum as determined by ASTM Method E 28–67 (Reapproved 1982), "Standard Test Method for Softening Point by Ring-and-Ball Apparatus," and a minimum viscosity of 3,000 centipoise, measured at 160 °C, as determined by ASTM Method D 3236–88, "Standard Test Method for Apparent Viscosity of Hot Melt Adhesives and Coating Materials," both of which are incorporated by reference in accordance with 5 U.S.C. 552(a) and 1 CFR part 51. Copies are available from the American Society for Testing and Materials, 100 Barr Harbor Dr., West Conshohocken, Philadelphia, PA 19428-2959, or from the Center For Food Safety and Applied Nutrition (HFS–200), Food and Drug Administration, 5100 Paint Branch Pkwy., College Park, MD 20740, or may be examined at the National Archives and Records Administration (NARA). For information on the availability of this material at NARA, call 202–741–6030, or go to: *http://www.archives.gov/federal_register/code_of_federal_regulations/ibr_locations.html.*.	For use only as an adjuvant at levels not to exceed 30 percent by weight in blends with: (1) Polypropylene complying with paragraph (c), item 1.1 of this section, or (2) a copolymer of propylene and ethylene containing not less than 94 weight percent propylene and complying with paragraph (c), item 3.2 of this section. The average thickness of the food-contact film is not to exceed 0.1 millimeter (0.004 inch). The finished polymer may be used in contact with (1) Food types I, II, IV-B, VI-A, VI-B, VII-B, and VIII identified in table 1 of § 176.170(c) of this chapter and under conditions of use C through G described in table 2 of § 176.170(c) of this chapter; and (2) food types III, IV-A, V, VI-C, VII-A, and IX identified in table 1 of § 176.170(c) of this chapter and under conditions of use D through G described in table 2 of § 176.170(c) of this chapter.
Polymethylsilsesquioxane (CAS Reg. No. 68554–70–1)	For use only as a surface lubricant or anti-blocking agent in films.
Poly(vinylidene fluoride) homopolymer (CAS Reg. No. 24937–79–9), having a melt viscosity of 6 to 37 kilopoise at a shear rate of 100^{-1} seconds at 232 °C as determined by ASTM Method D 3835–79 (Reapproved 1983), "Standard Test Method for Rheological Properties of Thermoplastics with a Capillary Rheometer" using a capillary of 15:1 L/D, which is incorporated by reference in accordance with 5 U.S.C. 552(a) and 1 CFR part 51. Copies are available from the Center for Food Safety and Applied Nutrition (HFS–200), Food and Drug Administration, 5100 Paint Branch Pkwy., College Park, MD 20740, or may be examined at the National Archives and Records Administration (NARA). For information on the availability of this material at NARA, call 202–741–6030, or go to: *http://www.archives.gov/federal_register/code_of_federal_regulations/ibr_locations.html.*.	For use only as a processing aid in the production of olefin polymers complying with paragraph (c) of this section at levels not to exceed 1.0 percent by weight of the polymer. The finished polymers may be used only under the conditions described in § 176.170(c) of this chapter, table 2, under conditions of use B though H.
Polyoxyethylene-grafted polydimethylsiloxane (CAS Reg. No. 68937–54–2).	For use as an extrusion aid in the production of extruded olefin polymers that comply with § 177.1520(c) at levels not to exceed 0.3 percent by weight of the polymer. The finished polymer is used in contact with foods under conditions of use B through H described in table 2 of § 176.170 of this chapter.
Triisopropanolamine (CAS Reg. No. 122–20–3)	For use as a Zeigler-Natta-type catalyst deactivator and antioxidant in the production of olefin polymers complying with § 177.1520(c), items 2.1, 2.2, and 2.3, and having a minimum density of 0.94 grams per cubic centimeter, and copolymers complying with § 177.1520(c), items 3.1 and 3.2, for use in contact with all foods under the following conditions of use: (a) films with a maximum thickness of 0.102 millimeter (0.004 inch) may be used under conditions A through H defined in table 2 of § 176.170(c) of this chapter; and (b) articles with thickness greater than 0.102 millimeter (0.004 inch) may be used under conditions C through G defined in table 2 of § 176.170(c) of this chapter.
Trimethylpyridine and dimethylpyridine mixture having percent by weight composition as follows: 2,4,6-trimethylpyridine (CAS Reg. No. 108–75–8), not less than 60 percent; 2,3,6-trimethylpyridine (CAS Reg. No. 1462–84–6), not more than 27 percent; 3,5-dimethylpyridine (CAS Reg. No. 591–22–0), not more than 12 percent; and other dimethylpyridines, not more than 6 percent.	For use only as an adjuvant substance in the production of propylene homopolymers complying with items 1.1, 1.2, and 1.3, and propylene copolymers complying with items 3.1, and 3.2 of paragraph (c) of this section provided that the adjuvant is used at a level not to exceed 20 parts per million by weight of the olefin polymers.

Substance	Limitations
Vinylidene fluoride-hexafluoropropene copolymer (CAS Reg. No. 9011–17–0) having a fluorine content of 65 to 71 percent and a Mooney viscosity of at least 28, as determined by a method entitled "Mooney Viscosity," which is incorporated by reference in accordance with 5 U.S.C. 552(a). Copies are available from the Center for Food Safety and Applied Nutrition (HFS–200), Food and Drug Administration, 5100 Paint Branch Pkwy., College Park, MD 20740, or may be examined at the National Archives and Records Administration (NARA). For information on the availability of this material at NARA, call 202–741–6030, or go to: *http://www.archives.gov/federal_register/code_of_federal_regulations/ibr_locations.html.*.	For use only as an extrusion aid in the production of extruded olefin polymers at levels not to exceed 0.2 percent by weight of the polymer. The finished polymers may be used only under the conditions described in § 176.170(c) of this chapter, table 2, under conditions of use B through H.
Vinylidene fluoride-hexafluoropropene copolymer (CAS Reg. No. 9011–17–0), having a vinylidene fluoride content of not less than 87 percent but less than 100 percent by weight and a melt viscosity of 12 to 27 kilopoise at a shear rate of 100^{-1} seconds at 232 °C as determined by ASTM Method D 3835–79 (Reapproved 1983), "Standard Test Method for Rheological Properties of Thermoplastics with a Capillary Rheometer" using a capillary of 15:1 L/D, which is incorporated by reference in accordance with 5 U.S.C. 552(a) and 1 CFR part 51. Copies are available from the Center for Food Safety and Applied Nutrition (HFS–200), Food and Drug Administration, 5100 Paint Branch Pkwy., College Park, MD 20740, or may be examined at the National Archives and Records Administration (NARA). For information on the availability of this material at NARA, call 202–741–6030, or go to: *http://www.archives.gov/federal_register/code_of_federal_regulations/ibr_locations.html.*.	For use only as a processing aid in the production of olefin polymers complying with paragraph (c) of this section at levels not to exceed 1.0 percent by weight of the polymer. The finished polymers may be used only under the conditions described in § 176.170(c) of this chapter, table 2, under conditions of use B though H.

(c) *Specifications:*

Olefin polymers	Density	Melting Point (MP) or softening point (SP) (*Degrees Centigrade*)—	Maximum extractable fraction (expressed as percent by weight of the polymer) in *N*-hexane at specified temperatures	Maximum soluble fraction (expressed as percent by weight of polymer) in xylene at specified temperatures
1.1a. Polypropylene described in paragraph (a)(1)(i) of this section	0.880–0.913	MP: 160°–180 °C	6.4 pct at reflux temperature	9.8 pct at 25 °C
1.1b. Propylene homopolymer described in paragraph (a)(1)(ii) of this section	0.880–0.913–	MP: 150°–180 °C	6.4 pct at reflux temperature	9.8 pct at 25 °C
1.2. Polypropylene, noncrystalline; for use only to plasticize polyethylene described under items 2.1 and 2.2 of this table, provided that such plasticized polymers meet the maximum extractable fraction and maximum soluble fraction specifications prescribed for such basic polyethylene	0.80–0.88			
1.3. Polypropylene, noncrystalline, for use only: To plasticize polypropylene described by item 1.1 of this table, provided that such plasticized polymers meet the maximum extractable fraction and maximum soluble fraction specifications prescribed for such basic polypropylene, and further provided that such plasticized polypropylene contacts food only of the types identified in § 176.170(c) of this chapter, table 1, under Types I, II, IV-B, VI-B, VII-B, and VIII; and for use at levels not to exceed 50 pct by weight of any mixture employed as a food-contact coating provided such coatings contact food only of the types identified in § 176.170(c) of this chapter, table 1, under Types I, II, IV-B, VI-B, VII-B, and VIII	0.80–0.88	SP:115°–138 °C.		
2.1. Polyethylene for use in articles that contact food except for articles used for packing or holding food during cooking	0.85–1.00	....	5.5 pct at 50 °C	11.3 pct at 25 °C

Olefin polymers	Density	Melting Point (MP) or softening point (SP) (*Degrees Centigrade*)—	Maximum extractable fraction (expressed as percent by weight of the polymer) in *N*-hexane at specified temperatures	Maximum soluble fraction (expressed as percent by weight of polymer) in xylene at specified temperatures
2.2. Polyethylene for use in articles used for packing or holding food during cooking	0.85–1.00	....	2.6 pct at 50 °C	Do.
2.3. Polyethylene for use only as component of food-contact coatings at levels up to and including 50 percent by weight of any mixture employed as a food-contact coating	0.85–1.00	....	53 pct at 50 °C	75 pct at 25 °C
2.4. Olefin polymers described in paragraph (a)(2)(ii) of this section, having a melt flow index not to exceed 17 grams/per 10 minutes as determined by the method described in paragraph (d)(7) of this section, for use in blends with other polymers at levels not to exceed 20 percent by weight of total polymer, subject to the limitation that when contacting food of types III, IV-A, V, VI-C, VII-A, and IX identified in § 176.170(c) of this chapter, Table 1, the polymers shall be used only under conditions of use C, D, E, F, and G, described in § 176.170(c) of this chapter, Table 2.				
3.1a. Olefin copolymers described in paragraph (a)(3)(i) of this section for use in articles that contact food except for articles used for packing or holding food during cooking; except olefin copolymers described in paragraph (a)(3)(i)(*a*)(*3*) of this section and listed in item 3.1c of this table and olefin copolymers described in paragraph (a)(3)(i)(*e*) of this section and listed in item 3.1b of this table	0.85–1.00	....	5.5 pct at 50 °C	30 pct at 25 °C
3.1b. Olefin copolymers described in paragraph (a)(3)(i)(*e*) of this section for use in contact with food only under conditions of use D, E, F, G, and H described in § 176.170(c) of this chapter, table 2	0.9–1.00	....	Do	Do.
3.1c. Olefin copolymers described in paragraph (a)(3)(i)(*a*)(*3*) of this section for use in contact with food only under conditions of use B, C, D, E, F, G, and H described in § 176.170(c) of this chapter, table 2; except that such copolymers when used in contact with food of the types identified in § 176.170(c), table 1, under types III, IVA, V, VIIA, and IX, shall be used only under conditions of use D, E, F, and G described in § 176.170(c) of this chapter, table 2	Not less than 0.92			

Olefin polymers	Density	Melting Point (MP) or softening point (SP) (*Degrees Centigrade*)—	Maximum extractable fraction (expressed as percent by weight of the polymer) in *N*-hexane at specified temperatures	Maximum soluble fraction (expressed as percent by weight of polymer) in xylene at specified temperatures
3.2a. Olefin copolymers described in paragraph (a)(3)(i) of this section for use in articles used for packing or holding food during cooking; except olefin copolymers described in paragraph (a)(3)(i)(*c*)(*2*) of this section and listed in item 3.2b of this table; except that olefin copolymers containing 89 to 95 percent ethylene with the remainder being 4-methyl-pentene-1 contacting food Types III, IVA, V, VIIA, and IX identified in § 176.170(c) of this chapter, table 1, shall not exceed 0.051 millimeter (mm) (0.002 inch (in)) in thickness when used under conditions of use A and shall not exceed 0.102 mm (0.004 in) in thickness when used under conditions of use B, C, D, E, and H described in § 176.170(c) of this chapter, table 2. Additionally, olefin copolymers described in (a)(3)(i)(*a*)(*2*) of this section may be used only under conditions of use B, C, D, E, F, G, and H described in § 176.170(c) of this chapter, table 2, in contact with all food types identified in § 176.170(c) of this chapter, table 1	0.85–1.00	....	2.6 pct at 50 °C	Do.
3.2b. Olefin copolymers described in paragraph (a)(3)(i)(*c*)(*2*) of this section have a melt flow index no greater than 10 grams per 10 minutes as determined by the method described in paragraph (d)(7) of this section, and the thickness of the finished polymer contacting food shall not exceed 0.025 mm (0.001 in). Additionally, optional adjuvants permitted for use in olefin copolymers complying with item 3.2a of this table may be used in the production of this copolymer	Do.			
3.2c. Olefin copolymers described in paragraph (a)(3)(i)(*a*)(*4*) of this section have a melt flow index no greater than 50 grams per 10 minutes as determined by the method described in paragraph (d)(7) of this section. Articles manufactured using these polymers may be used with all types of food under conditions of use C through H as described in table 2 of § 176.170(c) of this chapter	0.85–0.92			
3.3a. Olefin copolymers described in paragraph (a)(3)(ii) of this section and manufactured with 1-alkenes having from 6 to 10 carbon atoms				
3.3b. Olefin copolymers described in paragraph (a)(3)(ii) of this section, provided that such olefin polymers have a melt temperature of 220 °C to 250 °C (428 °F to 482 °F) as determined by the method described in paragraph (d)(8) of this section and minimum intrinsic viscosity of 1.0 as determined in paragraph (d)(9) of this section.				

Olefin polymers	Density	Melting Point (MP) or softening point (SP) (*Degrees Centigrade*)—	Maximum extractable fraction (expressed as percent by weight of the polymer) in *N*-hexane at specified temperatures	Maximum soluble fraction (expressed as percent by weight of polymer) in xylene at specified temperatures
3.4. Olefin copolymers, primarily non-crystalline, described in par. (a)(3) (iii) of this section provided that such olefin polymers have a minimum viscosity average molecular weight of 120,000 as determined by the method described in par. (d)(5) of this section and a minimum Mooney viscosity of 35 as determined by the method described in par. (d)(6) of this section, and further provided that such olefin copolymers contact food only of the types identified in § 176.170(c) of this chapter, table 1, under Types I, II, III, IV-B, VI, VII, VIII, and IX	0.85–0.90			
3.5. Olefin copolymers, primarily non-crystalline, described in paragraph (a)(3)(iv) of this section, provided that such olefin polymers have a minimum viscosity average molecular weight of 95,600 as determined by the method described in paragraph (d)(5) of this section, and further provided that such olefin polymers are used only in blends with olefin polymers described under items 1.1, 2.1, and 2.2 of this table at a maximum level of 25 pct by weight, and provided that such olefin copolymers contact food only of the types identified in § 176.170 (c) of this chapter, table 1, under Types I, II, IV-B, VI, VII-B, and VIII at temperatures not exceeding 190 °F	0.85–0.90			
3.6. Olefin copolymers described in paragraph (a)(3)(v) of this section for use in blends with olefin polymer resins have a melt flow index no greater than 5 grams/10 minutes as determined by the method described in paragraph (d)(7) of this section and the thickness of the finished blends shall not exceed 0.1 millimeter (0.004 inch). The ethylene/butene-1 copolymer may be used subject to the following conditions: (1) For use at a level not to exceed 20 weight percent in polypropylene as described under item 1.1 of this table. (2) For use at a level not to exceed 40 weight percent in polyethylene as described under items 2.1 and 2.2 of this table. (3) For use at a level not to exceed 40 weight percent in olefin copolymers as described under items 3.1 and 3.2 of this table	Not less than 0.88			

Olefin polymers	Density	Melting Point (MP) or softening point (SP) (*Degrees Centigrade*)—	Maximum extractable fraction (expressed as percent by weight of the polymer) in *N*-hexane at specified temperatures	Maximum soluble fraction (expressed as percent by weight of polymer) in xylene at specified temperatures
3.7. Ethylene/propylene copolymers, meeting the identity described in paragraph (a)(3)(i) of this section, containing not less than 80 mole-percent of polymer units derived from ethylene and having a minimum viscosity average molecular weight of 95,000 as determined by the method described in paragraph (d)(5) of this section, and a minimum Mooney viscosity of 13 as determined by the method described in paragraph (d)(6) of this section. Ethylene/propylene copolymers described in this item 3.7 are to be used only in blends with other olefin polymers complying with this section, at levels not to exceed 30 percent by weight of the total polymer blend, and in contact with food only of types identified in § 176.170(c) of this chapter, Table 1, under Types I, II, III, IV-B, VI, VII, VIII, and IX. Additionally, optional adjuvants permitted for use in olefin copolymers complying with item 3.4 of this table may be used in the production of this copolymer	Not less than 0.86			
3.8. Olefin polymers described in paragraph (a)(3)(vi) of this section, having a melt flow index not to exceed 9.2 grams per 10 minutes as determined by the method described in paragraph (d)(7) of this section, for use in blends with other polymers at levels not to exceed 8 percent by weight of total polymer, subject to the limitation that when contacting food of types III, IV-A, V, VI-C, VII-A, and IX, identified in § 176.170(c) of this chapter, Table 1, the polymers shall be used only under conditions of use C, D, E, F, and G, described in § 176.170(c) of this chapter, Table 2.				
3.9. Olefin copolymers described in paragraph (a)(3)(vii) of this section may only be used in contact with dry foods, Type VIII, as identified in § 176.170(c) of this chapter, Table 1	Not less than 1.0			
4. Poly(methylpentene)	0.82–0.85	MP: 235°–250 °C	6.6 pct at reflux temperature	7.5 pct at 25 °C
5. Polyethylene copolymer described in paragraph (a)(5) of this section and having a melt index not to exceed 2, for use, either alone or in blends with other olefin polymers, subject to the limitation that when contacting foods of types III, IV-A, V, VI-C, VII-A, VIII, and IX identified in § 176.170(c) of this chapter, table 1, the thickness of the film (in mils) containing the polyethylene graft copolymer times the concentration of the polyethylene graft copolymer shall not exceed a value of 2	Not less than 0.94	....	0.45 pct at 15 °C	1.8 pct at 25 °C
6. Ethylene-maleic anhydride copolymers described in paragraph (a)(6) of this section for use as the adhesive component in multilaminate structures, or as the sealant layer in flexible packaging, in contact with food at temperatures not exceeding 49 °C (120 °F)	0.92 or greater	....	1.36 pct at 50 °C	2.28 pct at 25 °C

(d) The analytical methods for determining whether olefin polymers conform to the specifications prescribed in this section are as follows, and are applicable to the basic polymer in film form not exceeding 4 mils in thickness.

The film to be tested shall be cut into approximately 1-inch squares by any convenient method that avoids contamination by dust, dirt, or grease (NOTE: Do not touch samples with bare fingers—use forceps to hold or transfer samples).

(1) *Density*. Density shall be determined by ASTM method D1505–68 (Reapproved 1979), "Standard Test Method for Density of Plastics by the Density-Gradient Technique," which is incorporated by reference. Copies may be obtained from the American Society for Testing Materials, 100 Barr Harbor Dr., West Conshohocken, Philadelphia, PA 19428-2959, or may be examined at the National Archives and Records Administration (NARA). For information on the availability of this material at NARA, call 202–741–6030, or go to: *http://www.archives.gov/federal_register/code_of_federal_regulations/ibr_locations.html.*

(2) *Melting point or softening point*—(i) *Melting point*. The melting point shall be determined by ASTM method D2117–82, "Standard Test Method for Melting Point of Semicrystalline Polymers by the Hot Stage Microscopy Method," which is incorporated by reference. The availability of this incorporation by reference is given in paragraph (d)(1) of this section.

(ii) *Softening point*. The softening point shall be determined by ASTM method E28–67 (Reapproved 1982), "Standard Test Method for Softening Point by Ring-and-Ball Apparatus," which is incorporated by reference. The availability of this incorporation by reference is given in paragraph (d)(1) of this section.

(3) *Maximum extractable fraction in n-hexane*—(i) *Olefin copolymers described in paragraph (a)(3)(ii) of this section, polypropylene, and poly(methylpentene).* A sample is refluxed in the solvent for 2 hours and filtered at the boiling point. The filtrate is evaporated and the total residue weighed as a measure of the solvent extractable fraction.

(*a*) *Apparatus*. (*1*) Erlenmeyer flasks, 250-milliliter, with ground joint.

(*2*) Condensers, Allihn, 400-millimeter jacket, with ground joint.

(*3*) Funnels, ribbed 75-millimeter diameter, stem cut to 40 millimeters.

(*4*) Funnels, Buchner type, with coarse-porosity fritted disc, 60-millimeter diameter.

(*5*) Bell jar for vacuum filtration into beaker.

(*b*) *Reagent*. *n*-Hexane, commercial grade, specific gravity 0.663–0.667 (20 °C/20 °C), boiling range 66 °C-69 °C, or equivalent.

(*c*) *Procedure*. Weigh 1 gram of sample accurately and place in a 250-milliliter Erlenmeyer flask containing two or three boiling stones. Add 100 milliliters of solvent, attach the flask to the condenser (use no grease), and reflux the mixture for 2 hours. Remove the flask from the heat, disconnect the condenser, and filter rapidly, while still hot, through a small wad of glass wool packed in a short-stem funnel into a tared 150-millimeter beaker. Rinse the flask and filter with two 10-milliliter portions of the hot solvent, and add the rinsings to the filtrate. Evaporate the filtrate on a stream bath with the aid of a stream of nitrogen. Dry the residue in a vacuum oven at 110 °C for 2 hours, cool in a desiccator, and weigh to the nearest 0.0001 gram. Determine the blank on 120 milliliters of solvent evaporated in a tared 150-milliliter beaker. Correct the sample residue for this blank if significant. Calculation:

$$\frac{\text{Grams of residue}}{\text{Grams of sample} \times 100} = \text{Percent extractable with } n\text{-hexane.}$$

(ii) *Olefin copolymers described in paragraph (a)(3)(i) of this section and polyethylene.* A preweighed sample is extracted at 50 °C for 2 hours and filtered. The filtrate is evaporated and the total residue weighed as a measure of the solvent extractable fraction. Alternatively, the sample is reweighed after the extraction period to give a measure of the solvent extractable fraction. The maximum *n*-hexane-extractable fraction may be determined by the methods set forth in paragraphs (d)(3)(ii)(*a*) through (d)(3)(ii)(*i*) of this section.

(*a*) *Extraction apparatus.* Two-liter, straight-walled, Pyrex (or equivalent) resin kettles, fitted with three-hole ground-glass covers are most convenient for this purpose. The cover is fitted with a thermometer, a gas-tight stirrer driven by an air motor or explosion-proof electric motor, and a reflux condenser. The kettle is fitted with an electric heating mantle of appropriate size and shape, which is controlled by a variable-voltage transformer.

(*b*) *Evaporating apparatus.* Rapid evaporation of large volumes of solvent requires special precautions to prevent contamination by dust. This is facilitated by a special "gas" cover consisting of an inverted flat Pyrex crystallizing dish of an appropriate size (190 millimeters × 100 millimeters) to fit a 1-liter beaker. Through the center of the dish are sealed an inlet tube for preheated, oxygen-free nitrogen, and an outlet tube located 1 inch off center. Nitrogen is fed from the supply source through a coil of ¼-inch stainless steel tubing immersed in the same steam bath used to supply heat for solvent evaporation. All connections are made with flexible tetrafluoroethylene tubing.

(*c*) *Reagents*—(*1*) *n-Hexane.* Spectrograde *n*-hexane.

(*2*) *Nitrogen.* High-purity dry nitrogen containing less than 10 parts per million of oxygen.

(*d*) *Procedure.* Transfer 2.5 grams (accurately weighed to nearest 0.001 gram) of the polymer to the resin kettle. Add 1 liter of solvent and clamp top in position. Start water flowing through jacket of the reflux condenser and apply air pressure to the stirring motor to produce vigorous agitation. Turn on heating jacket with transformer set at a predetermined voltage to bring the temperature of the contents to 50 °C within 20–25 minutes. As the thermometer reading approaches 45 °C–47 °C, reduce the voltage to the predetermined setting that will just maintain the temperature at 50 °C. Do not overshoot the prescribed temperature. Should this occur discard the test and start afresh. Exactly 2 hours after the solvent temperature has reached 50 °C, disconnect the heater, remove the resin kettle from the heating jacket, and decant the solvent, while still warm, through a coarse filter paper placed on top of a fritted-glass funnel, collecting the filtrate in a tared, glass-stoppered Erlenmeyer flask of 1-liter capacity. Determine the weight of the filtrate recovered to the nearest gram. Recovery should be at least 90 percent of the original solvent. Losses due to evaporation during heating and filtering have been found not to exceed 10 percent. Transfer about half of the solvent filtrate to a 1-liter beaker placed on an opening in the steam bath and immediately cover with the special "gas" cover, the inlet tube of which has been attached with flexible tetrafluoroethylene tubing to a source of high-purity nitrogen in series with a stainless steel heating coil immersed directly in the body of the steam bath. Maintain a positive flow of warm nitrogen gas throughout the evaporation of the solvent, adding the remainder of the filtrate from the Erlenmeyer flask as the evaporation proceeds. When the volume of the solvent has been reduced to about 50 milliliters, transfer the concentrated liquid to a previously tared weighing dish of suitable size. Wash the beaker twice with 20–30 milliliter portions of warm solvent, adding the washings to the weighing dish while continuing to evaporate the remainder of the solvent under the gas cover with its flow of warm nitrogen directed toward the center of the dish. In the event that an insoluble residue that cannot be removed with warm solvent remains in the beaker, it may be necessary to heat with a small amount of a higher boiling solvent such as benzene or toluene, transferring these washings to the weighing dish before final evaporation to dryness. Transfer the weighing dish with its residue to a vacuum desiccator, and allow it to remain overnight (at least 12 hours), after which the net weight of the dry residue is determined to the nearest 0.0001 gram. Correct the result for any solvent blank equivalent to the nonvolatile matter determined to be contained in the amount of solvents used in the test.

(*e*) *Extraction apparatus for alternate method.* Two-liter extraction vessel, such as a resin kettle or round bottom flask, fitted with an Allihn condenser (size C), a 45/50 male joint with a Teflon sleeve, and a Teflon coated stir bar. Water bath maintained at 49.5 °C ±0.5 °C containing a submersible magnetic stirrer motor with power supply. Other suitable means of maintaining temperature control, such as electric heating mantles, may be used provided that the temperature range can be strictly maintained.

(*f*) *Sample basket (Optional).* A perforated stainless steel cylindrical basket that is approximately 1.5 inches in diameter, 1.6 inches high, and has perforations of 0.125 inches in diameter for 33 holes/in^2, or 40 percent open area. The basket should pass freely through the 45/50 female joint of the extraction flask. A No. 6–32 stainless steel eyebolt is attached to the lid for positioning the basket in the extraction vessel. The positioning rod, approximately 18 inches long and made from 1/16 inch outside diameter 316 stainless steel welding rod or equivalent and hooked at both ends, is used to position the basket in the extraction apparatus.

(*g*) *Vacuum oven.* Capable of maintaining 80 °C ±5 °C and a minimum of 635 millimeters of mercury pressure.

(*h*) *Reagents. n*-Hexane, reagent or spectrograde, aromatic free (less than 1 milligram per liter), minimum 85 percent *n*-hexane. This reagent may be reused until it contains a maximum of 1.5 grams polyolefin extractables or has been used for 12 determinations.

(*i*) *Procedure.* Assemble the extraction vessel, condenser, and magnetic stir bar. Add *n*-hexane (1 liter) to the extraction vessel and clamp the assembly into a water bath set at 49.5 °C ±0.5 °C. Start the water flowing through the jacket of the reflux condenser. Adjust the air flow through the stirring motor to give a smooth and uniform stir rate. Allow the *n*-hexane to preheat for 1 hour to bring the temperature to 49.5 °C±0.5 °C. Temperature is a critical factor in this analysis and it must not vary more than 1 °C. If the temperature exceeds these limits, the test must be discontinued and restarted. Blown, compression molded, or extrusion cast films can be tested. Ideally, the film should be prepared by the same process as will be used with the production resin. Using gloves and metal tweezers to avoid sample contamination, cut about 2.7 grams of the prepared film (4 mils or less in thickness) into about 1-inch squares using clean sharp scissors. Proceed with Option 1 or 2.

Option 1. Using tweezers and noting the number of film pieces, transfer 2.5 grams (accurately weighed to 0.1 milligram) of polymer to the extraction vessel. Extract the film sample for 2 hours. Allow the vessel to cool and filter the contents through a fritted porcelain funnel. Wash the film pieces with fresh *n*-hexane, aspirate to dryness, and transfer, using tweezers, to a beaker. Recount the film pieces to verify that none were lost during the transfer. Place the beaker in the vacuum oven for 2 hours at 80 °C ±5 °C. After 2 hours, remove and place in a desiccator to cool to room temperature (about 1 hour). After cooling, reweigh the film pieces to the nearest 0.1 milligram. Calculate the percent hexane-extractables content from the weight loss of the original sample. Multiply the result by 0.935 and compare with extraction limits in paragraph (c) of this section. Repeat the above procedure for successive samples.

Option 2. Transfer 2.5±0.05 grams of the prepared 1-inch film sections into a tared sample basket and accurately weigh to the nearest 0.1 milligram. Carefully raise the condenser until the hook on the positioning rod is above the neck of the 2-liter extraction vessel. The basket should be totally below the level of *n*-hexane solvent. Extract the sample resin film for 2 hours and then raise the basket above the solvent level to drain momentarily. Remove the basket and rinse the contents by immersing several times in fresh *n*-hexane. Allow the basket to dry between rinsings. Remove the excess solvent by briefly blowing the basket with a stream of nitrogen or dry air. Place the basket in the vacuum oven for 2 hours at 80 °C ±5 °C. After 2 hours, remove and place in a desiccator to cool to room temperature (about 1 hour). After cooling, reweigh the basket to the nearest 0.1 milligram. Calculate the percent hexane extractables content from the weight loss of the original sample. Multiply the result by 0.935 and compare with extraction limits in paragraph (c) of this section. Repeat the above procedure for successive samples. The same solvent charge should remain clear and can be used for at least 12 determinations. Applications of solvent reuse should be confirmed for each resin type before use.

(4) *Maximum soluble fraction in xylene*—(i) *Olefin copolymers described in paragraph (a)(3)(ii) of this section, polypropylene, and poly(methylpen-tene).* A sample is dissolved completely in xylene by heating and stirring in a bottle with little free space. The solution is allowed to cool without stirring, whereupon the insoluble portion precipitates and is filtered off; the total solids content of the filtrate is then determined as a measure of the soluble fraction.

(*a*) *Apparatus.* (*1*) Pyrex (or equivalent) reagent bottle, 125-milliliter, glass-stoppered.

(*2*) Heating mantle of size for 150-milliliter beaker (or suitable aluminum block to fit the 125-milliter bottle described in paragraph (d)(4)(i)(*a*)(*1*) of this section.

(*3*) Magnetic stirrer for use under the heating mantle (combination magnetic stirrer and hotplate may be used if aluminum block is used in place of heating mantle).

(*4*) Variable-voltage transformer, 7.5 amperes.

(*5*) Tetrafluoroethylene-resin-coated stirring bar, 1-inch long.

(*6*) Constant temperature water bath maintained at 25 °C±0.5 °C.

(*7*) *Aluminum* dishes, 18 millimeters × 60 millimeters, disposable.

(*8*) Funnel, Buchner type, with coarse-porosity fritted disc, 30–60 millimeter diameter.

(*b*) *Reagent.* Xylene with antioxidant. Dissolve 0.020 gram of phenyl-β- naphthylamine in 1 liter of industrial grade xylene having specific gravity 0.856–0.867 (20 °C/20 °C) and boiling range 123 °C–160 °C.

(*c*) *Procedure.* Weigh 1 to 2 grams of sample to the nearest 0.001 gram and place in a 125-milliliter Pyrex reagent bottle containing a 1-inch long tetrafluoroethylene-resin-coated stirring bar. Add 100 milliliters of solvent, set the stopper in lightly, and place the bottle in the heating mantle or aluminum block maintained at a temperature of 120 °C, and stir with a magnetic stirrer until the sample is completely dissolved. Remove the bottle from the heat and allow it to cool 1 hour in the air, without stirring. Then place the bottle in a water bath maintained at 25 °C ±0.5 °C, and allow to stand 1 hour without stirring. Next, remove the bottle from the water bath, shake, and pour part of the contents into the coarse-porosity fritted-glass funnel. Apply suction, and draw 30–40 milliliters of filtrate through, adding more slurry to the funnel, and catching the filtrate in a large test tube. (If the slurry is hard to filter, add 10 grams of diatomaceous earth filter aid to the bottle and shake vigorously just prior to the filtration.) Pipet a suitable aliquot (preferably 20 milliliters) of the filtrate into a tared aluminum disposable dish. Place the dish on a steam bath covered with a fresh sheet of aluminum foil and invert a short-stemmed 4-inch funnel over the dish. Pass nitrogen (heated if desired) down through the funnel at a rate sufficient to just ripple the surface of the solvent. When the liquid has evaporated, place the dish in a vacuum oven at 140 °C and less than 50 millimeters mercury pressure for 2 hours. Cool in a desiccator and weigh. (Note: If the residue value seems high, redry in the vacuum oven for one-half hour to ensure complete removal of all xylene solvent.) Calculation:

$$\frac{\text{Grams of residue}}{\text{Grams of sample}} \times \frac{\text{100 milliters}}{\text{volume of aliquot in milliliters}} \times 100 = \text{Percent soluble in xylene}$$

(ii) *Olefin copolymers described in paragraph (a)(3)(i) of this section and polyethylene.* A sample is extracted in xylene at reflux temperature for 2 hours and filtered. The filtrate is evaporated and the total residue weighed as a measure of soluble fraction.

(*a*) *Apparatus*—(*1*) *Extraction apparatus.* Two-liter, straight-walled Pyrex (or equivalent) resin kettles, fitted with ground-glass covers, are most convenient for this purpose. The cover is equipped with a thermometer and an efficient reflux condenser. The kettle is fitted with an electric heating mantle of appropriate size and shape which is controlled by a variable-voltage transformer.

(*2*) *Constant temperature water bath.* It must be large enough to permit immersion of the extraction kettle and set to maintain 25 °C ±0.1 °C.

(*3*) *Evaporating apparatus.* Gas cover consisting of a flat Pyrex crystallizing dish (190 millimeters × 100 millimeters) inverted to fit over a 1-liter beaker with 8-millimeter gas inlet tube sealed through center and an outlet tube 1 inch off center. The beaker with gas cover is inserted in an electric heating mantle equipped with a variable-voltage transformer. The outlet tube is attached to an efficient condenser mounted on a receiving flask for solvent recovery and having an outlet for connection to an aspirator pump. The heating mantle (with the beaker) is mounted on a magnetic stirring device. An infrared heat lamp is mounted vertically 3–4 inches above the gas cover to prevent condensation of the solvent inside the cover. Make all connections with flexible tetrafluoroethylene tubing.

(*b*) *Reagents*—(*1*) *Xylene.* American Chemical Society reagent grade that has been redistilled through a fractionating column to reduce the nonvolatile residue.

(*2*) *Nitrogen.* High-purity dry nitrogen containing less than 10^4 parts per million oxygen.

(*c*) *Procedure.* Transfer 5 grams ±0.001 gram of sample to the resin kettle, add 1,000 milliliters (840 grams) of xylene, and clamp top in position after inserting a piece of glass rod to prevent bumping during reflux. Start water flowing through the jacket of the reflux condenser and apply full voltage (115 volts) to the heating mantle. When the xylene starts to boil, reduce the voltage to a level just sufficient to maintain reflux. After refluxing for at least 2 hours, disconnect the power source to the mantle, remove the kettle, and allow to cool in air until the temperature of the contents drops to 50 °C, after which the kettle may be rapidly cooled to 25 °C–30 °C by immersing in a cold water bath. Transfer the kettle to a constant temperature bath set to maintain 25 °C ±0.1 °C, and allow to equilibrate for a least 1 hour (may be left overnight if convenient). Break up any precipitated polymers that may have formed, and decant the xylene solution successively through a fast filter paper and then through a fritted-glass filter into a tared 1-liter Erlenmeyer flask, collecting only the first 450 milliliters—500 milliliters of filtrate (any attempt to collect more of the xylene solution usually results in clogging the filter and risking losses). Reweigh the Erlenmeyer flask and calculate the weight of the filtrate obtained to the nearest 0.1 gram. Transfer the filtrate, quantitatively, from the Erlenmeyer flask to the 1-liter beaker, insert the beaker in its heating mantle, add a glass-coated magnetic stirring bar, and mount the gas cover in place, connecting the inlet tube to the nitrogen source and the outlet to the condenser of the receiving flask. Start a flow of nitrogen (2 to 3 liters per minute) into the gas cover and connect an aspirator to the receiver using a free-flow rate equivalent to 6–7 liters of air per minute. With the infrared lamp on, adjust the voltage to the heating mantle to give a distillation rate of 12–13 milliliters per minute when the magnetic stirrer is revolving just fast enough to promote good boiling. When the volume of solvent in the beaker has been reduced to 30–50 milliliters, transfer the concentrated extractive to a suitable weighing dish that has been previously tared (dry). Rinse the beaker twice with 10–20 milliliter portions of fresh xylene, adding the rinsings to the weighing dish. Evaporate the remainder of the xylene on an electric hotplate set at low heat under the gas cover with a stream of nitrogen directed toward the center of the dish.

Avoid any charring of the residue. Transfer the weighing dish to a vacuum desiccator at room temperature and allow to remain under reduced pressure for at least 12 hours (overnight), after which determine the net weight of the residue to the nearest 0.0001 gram. Correct the result for nonvolatile solvent blank obtained by evaporating the equivalent amount of xylene under identical conditions. Calculate the weight of residue originally present in the total weight of solvent (840 grams), using the appropriate factor based on the weight of filtrate evaporated.

(5) *Viscosity average molecular weight olefin copolymers described in paragraphs (a)(3) (iii) and (iv) of this section.* The viscosity average molecular weight shall be determined from the kinematic viscosity (using ASTM method D445–74, "Test for Kinematic Viscosity of Transparent and Opaque Liquids" (Revised 1974), which is incorporated by reference; copies are available from American Society for Testing and Materials (ASTM), 100 Barr Harbor Dr., West Conshohocken, Philadelphia, PA 19428-2959, or available for inspection at the National Archives and Records Administration (NARA). For information on the availability of this material at NARA, call 202–741–6030, or go to: *http://www.archives.gov/federal_register/code_of_federal_regulations/ibr_locations.html.*) of solutions of the copolymers in solvents and at temperatures as follows:

(i) Olefin polymers described in paragraph (a)(3)(iii) of this section in decahydronaphthalene at 135 °C.

(ii) Olefin polymers described in paragraph (a)(3)(iv) of this section in tetrachloroethylene at 30 °C.

(6) *Mooney viscosity—olefin copolymers described in paragraph (a)(3)(iii) of this section.* Mooney viscosity is determined by ASTM method D1646–81, "Standard Test Method for Rubber—Viscosity and Vulcanization Characteristics (Mooney Viscometer)," which is incorporated by reference (the availability of this incorporation by reference is given in paragraph (d)(1) of this section), using the large rotor at a temperature of 100 °C, except that a temperature of 127 °C shall be used for those copolymers whose Mooney viscosity cannot be determined at 100 °C. The apparatus containing the sample is warmed for 1 minute, run for 8 minutes, and viscosity measurements are then made.

(7) *Melt flow index.* The melt flow index of olefin polymers described below shall be determined by ASTM method D–1238–82, "Standard Test Method for Flow Rates of Thermoplastics by Extrusion Plastometer," which is incorporated by reference in accordance with 5 U.S.C. 552(a). The availability of this incorporation by reference is given in paragraph (d)(1) of this section. The olefin polymers and test conditions and procedures are as follows:

List of polymers	Conditions/procedures
Olefin copolymers described in paragraph (a)(3)(i)(*c*)(*2*) of this section.	Condition L, procedure A.
Olefin copolymers described in paragraph (a)(3)(v) of this section.	Condition E, procedure A.
Olefin polymers described in paragraph (a)(2)(ii) of this section.	Condition E, procedure A.
Olefin polymers described in paragraph (a)(3)(vi) of this section.	Condition E, procedure A.

(8) *Melting peak temperature.* The melt temperature of the olefin polymers described in paragraph (a)(3)(ii) of this section shall be determined by ASTM method D 3418–82, "Standard Test Method for Transition Temperatures of Polymers by Thermal Analysis," which is incorporated by reference in accordance with 5 U.S.C. 552(a). The availability of this incorporation by reference is given in paragraph (d)(1) of this section.

(9) *Intrinsic viscosity.* The intrinsic viscosity of the olefin polymers described in paragraph (a)(3)(ii) of this section shall be determined by ASTM method D 1601–78, "Standard Test Method for Dilute Solution Viscosity of Ethylene Polymers," which is incorporated by reference in accordance with 5 U.S.C. 552(a). The availability of this incorporation by reference is given in paragraph (d)(1) of this section.

(e) Olefin copolymers described in paragraph (a)(3) (i) of this section and polyethylene, alone or in combination, may be subjected to irradiation bombardment from a source not to exceed 2.3 million volts intensity to cause molecular crosslinking of the polymers to impart desired properties, such as increased strength and increased ability to shrink when exposed to heat.

(f) The olefin polymers identified in and complying with this section, when used as components of the food-contact surface of any article that is the subject of a regulation in parts 174, 175, 176, 177, 178, and § 179.45 of this chapter, shall comply with any specifications and limitations prescribed by such regulation for the article in the finished form in which it is to contact food.

(g) The provisions of this section are not applicable to olefin polymers identified in § 175.105(c) (5) of this chapter and used in food-packaging adhesives complying with § 175.105 of this chapter.

[42 FR 14572, Mar. 15, 1977]

EDITORIAL NOTE: For FEDERAL REGISTER citations affecting § 177.1520, see the List of CFR Sections Affected, which appears in the Finding Aids section of the printed volume and at *www.fdsys.gov*.

§ 177.1550 Perfluorocarbon resins.

Perfluorocarbon resins identified in this section may be safely used as articles or components of articles intended to contact food, subject to the provisions of this section:

(a) *Identity*. For the purpose of this section, perfluorocarbon resins are those produced by: (1) The homopolymerization and/or copolymerization of hexafluoropropylene and tetrafluoroethylene, and (2) the copolymerization of perfluoropropylvinylether and tetrafluoroethylene (CAS Reg. No. 26655–00–5). The resins shall meet the extractives limitations in paragraph (d) of this section.

(b) *Optional components*. The perfluorocarbon resins identified in paragraph (a) of this section as well as articles or coating made from these resins may include the following optional components except that the resin identified in paragraph (a)(2) of this section may not be used with the optional component, lithium polysilicate, mentioned in paragraph (b)(4) of this section.

(1) Substances generally recognized as safe (GRAS) in food or food packaging subject to any limitations cited on their use.

(2) Substances used in accordance with a prior sanction or approval, subject to any limitations cited in the prior sanction or approval.

(3) Substances authorized under applicable regulations in this part and in parts 175 and 178 of this chapter and subject to any limitations prescribed therein.

(4) The following substances, subject to any limitations prescribed:

List of substances	Limitations
Lithium polysilicate containing not more than 20 weight percent silica, not more than 2.1 percent lithium oxide and having a maximum mole ratio of SiO_2/Li_2O of 8.5 to 1.	For use only as a component of repeated-use coatings not exceeding 0.030 millimeter (0.0012 inch) in thickness where the coatings are thermally cured at minimum sintering temperatures of 371 °C (700 °F). Lithium extractives shall not exceed 1.55 milligrams per square decimeter (0.1 milligram per square inch) of coating surface when tested in accordance with paragraph (e)(2) of this section.
Naphthalene sulfonic acid formaldehyde condensate, sodium salt.	For use only: 1. As a component of repeated-use coatings, based on the perfluorocarbon resin identified in paragraph (a)(1) of this section, not to exceed 0.030 millimeter (0.0012 inch) in thickness, and at a level not to exceed 0.4 weight percent of the coating. 2. As a component of repeated-use coatings, based on the perfluorocarbon resin identified in paragraph (a)(2) of this section, not to exceed 0.10 millimeter (0.004 inch) in thickness, and at a level not to exceed 0.4 weight percent of the coating.

(c) *Optional processing*. Poly- tetrafluoroethylene resins may be irradiated by either a cobalt-60 sealed source, at a maximum dose of gamma radiation not to exceed 7.5 megarads, or an electron beam at energy levels not to exceed 2.5 million electron volts with a maximum dosage of 7.5 megarads, to produce lubricant powders having a particle diameter of not more than 20 microns for use only as components of articles intended for repeated use in contact with food.

(d) *Specifications*—(1) *Infrared identification*. Perfluorocarbon resins can be identified by their characteristic infrared spectra.

(2) *Melt-viscosity.* (i) The perfluorocarbon resins identified in paragraph (a)(1) of this section shall have a melt viscosity of not less than 10^4 poises at 380 °C (716 °F) as determined by ASTM method D1238–82, "Standard Test Method for Flow Rates of Thermoplastics by Extrusion Plastometer," which is incorporated by reference. Copies may be obtained from the American Society for Testing Materials, 100 Barr Harbor Dr., West Conshohocken, Philadelphia, PA 19428-2959, or may be examined at the National Archives and Records Administration (NARA). For information on the availability of this material at NARA, call 202–741–6030, or go to: *http://www.archives.gov/federal_register/code_of_federal_regulations/ibr_locations.html.* The melt viscosity of the perfluorocarbon resins identified in paragraph (a)(1) of this section shall not vary more than 50 percent within one-half hour at 380 °C (716 °F).

(ii) Perfluorocarbon resins identified in paragraph (a)(2) of this section shall have a melt viscosity of not less than 10^4 poises at 372 °C (702 °F) as determined by a more detailed method titled "Determination of Melt Viscosity, Molecular Weight Distribution Index and Viscosity Stability," which is incorporated by reference. Copies are available from the Center for Food Safety and Applied Nutrition (HFS–200), Food and Drug Administration, 5100 Paint Branch Pkwy., College Park, MD 20740, or available for inspection at the National Archives and Records Administration (NARA). For information on the availability of this material at NARA, call 202–741–6030, or go to: *http://www.archives.gov/federal_register/code_of_federal_regulations/ibr_locations.html.*

(3) *Thermal instability index.* The thermal instability index of the tetrafluoroethylene homopolymer shall not exceed 50 as determined by ASTM method D1457–56T, "Test for Thermal Instablility index of Tetrafluoroethylene Homopolymer" (Revised 1956), which is incorporated by reference. Copies are available from University Microfilms International, 300 N. Zeeb Rd., Ann Arbor, MI 48106, or available for inspection at the National Archives and Records Administration (NARA). For information on the availability of this material at NARA, call 202–741–6030, or go to: *http://www.archives.gov/federal_register/code_of_federal_regulations/ibr_locations.html.* The requirements of this paragraph do not apply to polytetrafluoroethylene resin lubricant powders described in paragraph (c) of this section.

(e) *Limitations.*[1] (1) Perfluorocarbon-molded articles having a surface area of 6.45 square decimeters (100 square inches) or more and at least 1.27 millimeters (0.05 inch) thick shall be extracted at reflux temperatures for 2 hours separately with distilled water, 50 percent ethanol, *n*-heptane, and ethyl acetate.

(2) Perfluorocarbon resins identified in paragraphs (a)(1) and (2) of this section and intended for use as coatings or components of coatings shall meet extractability limits prescribed in paragraph (e)(3) of this section when the resins in the form of coatings described in paragraphs (e)(2) (i) and (ii) of this section are extracted at reflux temperatures for 2 hours separately with distilled water, 8 percent ethanol, and *n*-heptane:

(i) Perfluorocarbon resin coatings based on resins identified in paragraph (a)(1) of this section shall be applied to both sides of a 0.025-millimeter (0.001 inch) thick aluminum foil to a thickness of 0.025 millimeter (0.001 inch) after thermal curing at 399 °C (750 °F) for 10 minutes. If a primer is used, the total thickness of the primer plus topcoat shall equal 0.025 millimeter (0.001 inch) after heat curing.

(ii) Perfluorocarbon resin coatings based on resins identified in paragraph (a)(2) of this section shall be applied to both sides of a 0.025-millimeter (0.001

[1] A more detailed procedure of extraction conditions is entitled, "Preparation of Extracts," which is incorporated by reference. Copies are available from the Center for Food Safety and Applied Nutrition (HFS–200), Food and Drug Administration, 5100 Paint Branch Pkwy., College Park, MD 20740, or available for inspection at the National Archives and Records Administration (NARA). For information on the availability of this material at NARA, call 202–741–6030, or go to: *http://www.archives.gov/federal_register/code_of_federal_regulations/ibr_locations.html.*

inch) thick aluminum foil to a thickness of 0.10 millimeter (0.004 inch) after thermal curing at 427 °C (800 °F) for 10 minutes. If a primer is used, the total thickness of the primer plus topcoat shall equal 0.10 millimeter (0.004 inch) after heat curing.

(3) The extracted surfaces shall meet the following extractability limits:

(i) Total extractives not to exceed 3.1 milligrams per square decimeter (0.2 milligram per square inch).

(ii) Fluoride extractives calculated as fluorine not to exceed 0.46 milligram per square decimeter (0.03 milligram per square inch).

(f) *Conditions of use.* Perfluorocarbon resins identified in paragraph (a)(2) of this section are limited to use as coatings or components of coatings for articles intended for repeated food-contact use.

[43 FR 44834, Sept. 29, 1978, as amended at 47 FR 11843, Mar. 19, 1982; 47 FR 14699, Apr. 6, 1982; 49 FR 10109, Mar. 19, 1984; 50 FR 1502, Jan. 11, 1985; 54 FR 24898, June 12, 1989; 61 FR 14481, Apr. 2, 1996]

§ 177.1555 Polyarylate resins.

Polyarylate resins (CAS Reg. No. 51706–10–6) may be safely used as articles or components of articles intended for use in contact with food in accordance with the following prescribed conditions:

(a) *Identity.* Polyarylate resins (1, 3-benzenedicarboxylic acid, diphenyl ester, polymer with diphenyl 1,4-benzenedicarboxylate and 4-4′-(1-methylethylidine) bis(phenol)) are formed by melt polycondensation of bisphenol-A with diphenylisophthalate and diphenylterephthalate.

(b) *Specifications.* (1) The finished copolymers shall contain from 70 to 80 weight percent of polymer units derived from diphenylisophthalate and 20 to 30 weight percent of polymer units derived from diphenylterephthalate.

(2) Polyarylate resins shall have a minimum weight average molecular weight of 20,000.

(3) Polyarylate resins may be identified by their characteristic infrared spectra.

(c) *Extractive limitations.* The finished polyarylate resins in sheet form at least 0.5 millimeter (0.020 inch) thick, when extracted with water at 121 °C (250 °F) for 2 hours, shall yield total nonvolatile extractives not to exceed 2.33 micrograms per square centimeter (15 micrograms per square inch) of the exposed resin surface.

(d) *Limitations.* Polyarylate resin articles may be used in contact with all foods except beverages containing more than 8 volume percent ethanol under conditions of use A through H, described in table 2 of § 176.170(c) of this chapter.

[52 FR 35540, Sept. 22, 1987]

§ 177.1556 Polyaryletherketone resins.

The poly(oxy-1,4-phenylenecarbonyl-1,4-phenyleneoxy-1,4-phenylenecarbonyl-1,4-phenylenecarbonyl-1,4-phenylene) resins (CAS Reg. No. 55088–54–5 and CAS Reg. No. 60015–05–6 and commonly referred to as polyaryletherketone resins) identified in paragraph (a) of this section may be safely used as articles or components of articles intended for repeated use in contact with food, subject to the provisions of this section.

(a) *Identity.* Polyaryletherketone resins consist of basic resins produced by reacting 4,4′-diphenoxy benzophenone and terephthaloyl dichloride in such a way that the finished resins have a minimum weight average molecular weight of 20,000 grams per mole, as determined by light scattering measurements in sulfuric acid at room temperature.

(b) *Optional adjuvant substances.* The basic polyaryletherketone resins identified in paragraph (a) of this section may contain optional adjuvant substances required in the production of such basic resins. These adjuvants may include substances used in accordance with § 174.5 of this chapter and the following:

(1) Benzoyl chloride, poly(tetrafluoro ethylene).

(2) [Reserved]

(c) *Extractive limitations.* The finished food-contact article yields net total extractives in each extracting solvent not to exceed 0.052 milligram per square inch (corresponding to 0.008 milligram per square centimeter) of food-contact surface, when extracted at reflux temperature for 2 hours with the following solvents: Distilled water, 50 percent (by volume) ethyl alcohol in distilled water, 3 percent acetic acid (by weight) in distilled water, and *n*-heptane.

(d) In testing the finished food-contact article made of polyaryletherketone resin, use a separate test sample for each required extracting solvent.

[61 FR 42381, Aug. 15, 1996]

§ 177.1560 Polyarylsulfone resins.

Polyarylsulfone resins (CAS Reg. No. 79293–56–4) may be safely used as articles or components of articles intended for use in contact with food, at temperatures up to and including normal baking temperatures, in accordance with the following prescribed conditions:

(a) *Identity*. Polyarylsulfone resins are copolymers containing not more than 25 percent of oxy-*p*-phenylene-oxy-*p*-phenylenesulfonyl-*p*-phenylene polymer units and not less than 75 percent of oxy-*p*-phenylenesulfonyl-*p*-phenylene-oxy-*p*-phenylenesulfonyl-*p*-phenylene polymer units. The copolymers have a minimum reduced viscosity of 0.40 deciliter per gram in 1-methyl-2-pyrrolidinone in accordance with ASTM method D2857–70 (Reapproved 1977), "Standard Test Method for Dilute Solution Viscosity of Polymers," which is incorporated by reference. Copies may be obtained from the American Society for Testing and Materials, 100 Barr Harbor Dr., West Conshohocken, Philadelphia, PA 19428-2959, or may be examined at the National Archives and Records Administration (NARA). For information on the availability of this material at NARA, call 202–741–6030, or go to: *http://www.archives.gov/federal_register/code_of_federal_regulations/ibr_locations.html.*

(b) *Optional adjuvant substances*. The basic polyarylsulfone resins identified in paragraph (a) of this section may contain optional adjuvant substances required in the production of such basic copolymers. These optional adjuvant substances may include substances permitted for such use by regulations in parts 170 through 179 of this chapter, substances generally recognized as safe in food, substances used in accordance with a prior sanction of approval, and substances named in this paragraph and further identified as required:

Substances	Limitations
Sulfolane	Not to exceed 0.15 percent as residual solvent in the finished basic resin.

(c) *Extractive limitations*. The finished polyarylsulfone resin when extracted for 2 hours with the following solvents at the specified temperatures yields total extractives in each extracting solvent not to exceed 0.008 milligram per square centimeter of food-contact surface: distilled water at 121 °C (250 °F), 50 percent (by volume) ethyl alcohol in distilled water at 71.1 °C (160 °F), 3 percent acetic acid in distilled water at 100 °C (212 °F), and *n*-heptane at 65.6 °C (150 °F).

NOTE: In testing the finished polyarylsulfone resin use a separate test sample for each required extracting solvent.

[50 FR 31046, July 24, 1985]

§ 177.1570 Poly-1-butene resins and butene/ethylene copolymers.

The poly-1-butene resins and butene/ethylene copolymers identified in this section may be safely used as articles or components of articles intended for use in contact with food subject to the provisions of this section.

(a) *Identity*. Poly-1-butene resins are produced by the catalytic polymerization of 1-butene liquid monomer. Butene/ethylene copolymers are produced by the catalytic polymerization of 1-butene liquid monomer in the presence of small amounts of ethylene monomer so as to yield no higher than a 6-weight percent concentration of polymer units derived from ethylene in the copolymer.

(b) *Specifications and limitations*. Poly-1-butene resins and butene/ethylene copolymers shall conform to the specifications prescribed in paragraph (b)(1) of this section, and shall meet the extractability limits prescribed in paragraph (b)(2) of this section.

(1) *Specifications*—(i) *Infrared identification*. Poly-1-butene resins and butene/ethylene copolymers can be identified by their characteristic infrared spectra.

(ii) *Viscosity*. Poly-1-butene resins and the butene/ethylene copolymers have an intrinsic viscosity 1.0 to 3.2 as determined by ASTM method D1601–78, "Standard Test Method for Dilute Solution Viscosity of Ethylene Polymers," which is incorporated by reference. Copies may be obtained from the American Society for Testing Materials, 100 Barr Harbor Dr., West Conshohocken, Philadelphia, PA 19428-2959, or may be examined at the National Archives and Records Administration (NARA). For information on the availability of this material at NARA, call 202–741–6030, or go to: *http://www.archives.gov/federal_register/code_of_federal_regulations/ibr_locations.html.*

(iii) *Density.* Poly-1-butene resins have a density of 0.904 to 0.920 gms/cm^3, and butene/ethylene copolymers have a density of 0.890 to 0.916 gms/cm^3 as determined by ASTM method D1505–68 (Reapproved 1979), "Standard Test Method for Density of Plastics by the Density-Gradient Technique," which is incorporated by reference. The availability of this incorporation by reference is given in paragraph (b)(1)(ii) of this section.

(iv) *Melt index.* Poly-1-butene resins have a melt index of 0.1 to 24 and the butene/ethylene copolymers have a melt index of 0.1 to 20 as determined by ASTM method D1238–82, condition E, "Standard Test Method for Flow Rates of Thermoplastics by Extrusion Plastometer," which is incorporated by reference. The availability of this incorporation by reference is given in paragraph (b)(1)(ii) of this section.

(2) *Limitations.* Poly-1-butene resins and butene/ethylene copolymers for use in articles that contact food, and for articles used for packing or holding food during cooking shall yield no more than the following extractables:

(i) Poly-1-butene resins may be used as articles or components of articles intended for use in contact with food, provided that the maximum extractables do not exceed 2.5 percent by weight of the polymer when film or molded samples are tested for 2 hours at 50 °C (122 °F) in *n*-heptane.

(ii) Butene/ethylene copolymers containing no more than 6 percent by weight of polymer units derived from ethylene may be used as articles or components of articles intended for contact with food under conditions of use B, C, D, E, F, G, or H described in table 2 of § 176.170(c) of this chapter, subject to the provisions of this section and provided that the maximum extractables from test films 0.1 to 0.2 millimeter (0.004 to 0.008 inch) in thickness do not exceed 0.80 percent by weight of the polymer when extracted in a soxhlet extractor for 6 hours with refluxing 95 percent ethanol.

(iii) Poly-1-butene resins may be used as articles or components of articles intended for packaging or holding food during cooking, provided that the thickness of such polymers in the form in which they contact food shall not exceed 0.1 millimeter (0.004 inch) and yield maximum extractables of not more than 2.5 percent by weight of the polymer when films are extracted for 2 hours at 50 °C (122 °F) in *n*-heptane.

[42 FR 14572, Mar. 15, 1977, as amended at 49 FR 10109, Mar. 19, 1984; 50 FR 31349, Aug. 2, 1985]

§ 177.1580 Polycarbonate resins.

Polycarbonate resins may be safely used as articles or components of articles intended for use in producing, manufacturing, packing, processing, preparing, treating, packaging, transporting, or holding food, in accordance with the following prescribed conditions:

(a) Polycarbonate resins are polyesters produced by:

(1) The condensation of 4,4′-isopropylidenediphenol and carbonyl chloride to which may have been added certain optional adjuvant substances required in the production of the resins; or by

(2) The reaction of molten 4,4′-isopropylidenediphenol with molten diphenyl carbonate in the presence of the disodium salt of 4,4′-isopropylidenediphenol.

(3) The condensation of 4,4′-isopropylidenediphenol, carbonyl chloride, and 0.5 percent weight maximum of *a*2,*a*6-bis (6-hydroxy-*m*-tolyl) mesitol to which may have been added certain optional adjuvant substances required in the production of branched polycarbonate resins.

(b) The optional adjuvant substances required in the production of resins produced by the methods described in paragraph (a)(1) and (3) of this section may include substances generally recognized as safe in food, substances used in accordance with a prior sanction or approval, and the following:

List of substances	Limitations
p-tert-Butylphenol	
Chloroform	
p-Cumylphenol (CAS Reg. No. 599–64–4).	For use only as a chain terminator at a level not to exceed 5 percent by weight of the resin.
Ethylene dichloride.	
Heptane.	
Methylene chloride.	
Monochlorobenzene	Not to exceed 500 p.p.m. as residual solvent in finished resin.
Pentaerythritol tetrastearate (CAS Reg. No. 115–83–3).	For use only as a mold release agent, at a level not to exceed 0.5 percent by weight of the finished resin.
Phenol (CAS Reg. No. 108–95–2).	
Pyridine.	
Toluene: (CAS Reg. No. 108–88–3).	Not to exceed 800 parts per million as residual solvent in finished resin.
Triethylamine.	

(c) Polycarbonate resins shall conform to the specification prescribed in paragraph (c)(1) of this section and shall meet the extractives limitations prescribed in paragraph (c)(2) of this section.

(1) *Specification*. Polycarbonate resins can be identified by their characteristic infrared spectrum.

(2) *Extractives limitations*. The polycarbonate resins to be tested shall be ground or cut into small particles that will pass through a U.S. standard sieve No. 6 and that will be held on a U.S. standard sieve No. 10.

(i) Polycarbonate resins, when extracted with distilled water at reflux temperature for 6 hours, shall yield total extractives not to exceed 0.15 percent by weight of the resins.

(ii) Polycarbonate resins, when extracted with 50 percent (by volume) ethyl alcohol in distilled water at reflux temperature for 6 hours, shall yield total extractives not to exceed 0.15 percent by weight of the resins.

(iii) Polycarbonate resins, when extracted with *n*-heptane at reflux temperature for 6 hours, shall yield total extractives not to exceed 0.15 percent by weight of the resins.

(d) Polycarbonate resins may be used in accordance with this section except in infant feeding bottles (baby bottles) and spill-proof cups, including their closures and lids, designed to help train babies and toddlers to drink from cups (sippy cups).

[42 FR 14572, Mar. 15, 1977, as amended at 46 FR 23227, Apr. 24, 1981; 49 FR 4372, Feb. 6, 1984; 50 FR 14096, Apr. 10, 1985; 53 FR 29656, Aug. 8, 1988; 59 FR 43731, Aug. 25, 1994; 77 FR 41902, July 17, 2012]

§ 177.1585 Polyestercarbonate resins.

Polyestercarbonate resins may be safely used as articles or components of articles intended for use in producing, manufacturing, packing, processing, preparing, treating, packaging, or holding food, in accordance with the following prescribed conditions:

(a) Polyestercarbonate resins (CAS Reg. No. 71519–80–7) are produced by the condensation of 4,4′-isopropylidenediphenol, carbonyl chloride, terephthaloyl chloride, and isophthaloyl chloride such that the finished resins are composed of 45 to 85 molepercent ester, of which up to 55 mole-percent is the terephthaloyl isomer. The resins are manufactured using a phthaloyl chloride/carbonyl chloride mole ratio of 0.81 to 5.7/1 and isophthaloyl chloride/terephthaloyl chloride mole ratio of 0.81/1 or greater. The resins are also properly identified by CAS Reg. No. 114096–64–9 when produced with the use of greater than 2 but not greater than 5 weight percent *p*-cumylphenol (CAS Reg. No. 599–64–4), as an optional adjuvant substance in accordance with paragraph (b)(2) of this section.

(b) *Optional adjuvants*. The optional adjuvant substances required in the production of resins identified in paragraph (a) of this section may include:

(1) Substances used in accordance with § 174.5 of this chapter.

(2) Substances identified in § 177.1580(b).

(3) Substances regulated in § 178.2010(b) of this chapter for use in polycarbonate resins complying with § 177.1580:

Provided, That the substances are used in accordance with any limitation on concentration, conditions of use, and food types specified in § 178.2010(b) of this chapter.

(c) Polyestercarbonate resins shall conform to the specifications prescribed in paragraph (c)(1) of this section and shall meet the extractive limitations prescribed in paragraph (c)(2) of this section.

(1) *Specifications.* Polyestercarbonate resins identified in paragraph (a) of this section can be identified by their characteristic infrared spectrum. The resins shall comply with either or both of the following specifications:

(i) The solution intrinsic viscosity of the polyestercarbonate resins shall be a minimum of 0.44 deciliter per gram, as determined by a method entitled "Intrinsic Viscosity (IV) of Lexan® Polyestercarbonate Resin by a Single Point Method Using Dichloromethane as the Solvent," developed by the General Electric Co., September 20, 1985, which is incorporated by reference in accordance with 5 U.S.C. 552(a) and 1 CFR part 51. Copies are available from the Office of Premarket Approval, Center for Food Safety and Applied Nutrition (HFS–215), Food and Drug Administration, 5100 Paint Branch Pkwy., College Park, MD 20740, or may be examined at the Center for Food Safety and Applied Nutrition's Library, Food and Drug Administration, 5100 Paint Branch Pkwy., College Park, MD 20740, or at the National Archives and Records Administration (NARA). For information on the availability of this material at NARA, call 202–741–6030, or go to: *http://www.archives.gov/federal_register/code_of_federal_regulations/ibr_locations.html.*

(ii) A minimum weight-average molecular weight of 27,000, as determined by gel permeation chromatography using polystyrene standards.

(2) *Extractives limitations.* The polyestercarbonate resins to be tested shall be ground or cut into small particles that will pass through a U.S. standard sieve No. 6 and that will be held on U.S. standard sieve No. 10.

(i) Polyestercarbonate resins, when extracted with distilled water at reflux temperature for 6 hours, shall yield total nonvolatile extractives not to exceed 0.005 percent by weight of the resins.

(ii) Polyestercarbonate resins, when extracted with 50 percent (by volume) ethyl alcohol in distilled water at reflux temperature for 6 hours, shall yield total nonvolatile extractives not to exceed 0.005 percent by weight of the resins.

(iii) Polyestercarbonate resins, when extracted with *n*-heptane at reflux temperature for 6 hours, shall yield total nonvolatile extractives not to exceed 0.002 percent by weight of the resins.

(3) *Residual methylene chloride levels in polyestercarbonate resins.* Polyestercarbonate resin articles in the finished form shall not contain residual methylene chloride in excess of 5 parts per million as determined by a method titled "Analytical Method for Determination of Residual Methylene Chloride in Polyestercarbonate Resin," developed by the General Electric Co., July 23, 1991, which is incorporated by reference in accordance with 5 U.S.C. 552(a) and 1 CFR part 51. Copies are available from the Center for Food Safety and Applied Nutrition (HFS–200), Food and Drug Administration, 5100 Paint Branch Pkwy., College Park, MD 20740, or may be examined at the National Archives and Records Administration (NARA). For information on the availability of this material at NARA, call 202–741–6030, or go to: *http://www.archives.gov/federal_register/code_of_federal_regulations/ibr_locations.html.*

[57 FR 3940, Feb. 3, 1992, as amended at 64 FR 27178, May 19, 1999]

§ 177.1590 Polyester elastomers.

The polyester elastomers identified in paragraph (a) of this section may be safely used as the food-contact surface of articles intended for use in contact with bulk quantities of dry food of the type identified in § 176.170(c) of this chapter, table 1, under Type VIII, in accordance with the following prescribed conditions:

(a) For the purpose of this section, polyester elastomers are those produced by the ester exchange reaction when one or more of the following phthalates—dimethyl terephthalate, dimethyl orthophthalate, and dimethyl isophthalate—is made to react with alpha-hydroomega-hydroxypoly (oxytetramethylene) and/or 1,4-

butanediol such that the finished elastomer has a number average molecular weight between 20,000 and 30,000.

(b) Optional adjuvant substances employed in the production of the polyester elastomers or added thereto to impart desired technical or physical properties may include the following substances:

List of substances	Limitations
4,4′ - Bis (*alpha, alpha*-dimethyl-benzyl) diphenylamine.	For use only as an antioxidant.
Tetrabutyl titanate	For use only as a catalyst.

(c) An appropriate sample of the finished polyester elastomer in the form in which it contacts food when subjected to ASTM method D968–81, "Standard Test Methods for Abrasion Resistance of Organic Coatings by the Falling Abrasive Tester," which is incorporated by reference (Copies may be obtained from the American Society for Testing Materials, 100 Barr Harbor Dr., West Conshohocken, Philadelphia, PA 19428-2959, or may be examined at the National Archives and Records Administration (NARA). For information on the availability of this material at NARA, call 202–741–6030, or go to: *http://www.archives.gov/federal_register/code_of_federal_regulations/ibr_locations.html.*), using No. 50 emery abrasive in lieu of Ottawa sand, shall exhibit an abrasion coefficient of not less than 100 liters per mil of thickness.

[42 FR 14572, Mar. 15, 1977, as amended at 49 FR 10109, Mar. 19, 1984]

§ 177.1595 Polyetherimide resin.

The polyetherimide resin identified in this section may be safely used as an article or component of an article intended for use in contact with food, subject to the provisions of this section.

(a) *Identity.* For the purpose of this section, the polyetherimide resin is 1,3-isobenzofurandione, 5,5′[(1-methylethylidene)bis(4,1-phenyleneoxy)] bispolymer with 1,3-benzenediamine (CAS Reg. No. 61128–46–9), and is derived from the condensation reaction of *m*-phenylenediamine and bisphenol A-dianhydride.

(b) *Optional adjuvants.* The basic polymer identified in paragraph (a) of this section may contain optional adjuvant substances required in the production of basic resins or finished food-contact articles. The optional adjuvant substances required in the production of the basic polymer may include substances permitted for such use by applicable regulations as set forth in part 174 of this chapter.

(c) *Specifications and extractives limitations*—(1) *Specifications.* Polyetherimide resin identified in paragraph (a) of this section shall have an intrinsic viscosity in chloroform at 25 °C (77 °F) of not less than 0.35 deciliter per gram as determined by a method titled "Intrinsic Viscosity of ULTEM Polyetherimide Using Chloroform as the Solvent," which is incorporated by reference. Copies are available from the Center for Food Safety and Applied Nutrition (HFS–200), Food and Drug Administration, 5100 Paint Branch Pkwy., College Park, MD 20740, or available for inspection at the National Archives and Records Administration (NARA). For information on the availability of this material at NARA, call 202–741–6030, or go to: *http://www.archives.gov/federal_register/code_of_federal_regulations/ibr_locations.html.*

(2) *Extractive limitations.* Extractive limitations are applicable to the basic polyetherimide resin in the form of molded discs of thickness 0.16 centimeter (0.063 inch). The resin discs when extracted with distilled water at 121 °C (250 °F) for 2 hours yield total nonvolatile extractives of not more than 12.3 micrograms per square centimeter.

[50 FR 31351, Aug. 2, 1985; 50 FR 35535, Sept. 3, 1985]

§ 177.1600 Polyethylene resins, carboxyl modified.

Carboxyl-modified polyethylene resins may be safely used as the food-contact surface of articles intended for use in contact with food in accordance with the following prescribed conditions:

(a) For the purpose of this section, carboxyl-modified polyethylene resins consist of basic polymers produced when ethylene-methyl acrylate basic copolymers, containing no more than 25 weight percent of polymer units derived from methyl acrylate, are made to react in an aqueous medium with one or more of the following substances:

Ammonium hydroxide.
Calcium carbonate.
Potassium hydroxide.
Sodium hydroxide.

(b) The finished food-contact article, when extracted with the solvent or solvents characterizing the type of food and under the conditions of time and temperature characterizing the conditions of its intended use as determined from tables 1 and 2 of § 176.170(c) of this chapter, yields total extractives in each extracting solvent not to exceed 0.5 milligram per square inch of food-contact surface as determined by the methods described in § 176.170(d) of this chapter; and if the finished food-contact article is itself the subject of a regulation in parts 174, 175, 176, 177, 178, and § 179.45 of this chapter, it shall also comply with any specifications and limitations prescribed for it by that regulation. In testing the finished food-contact articles, a separate test sample is to be used for each required extracting solvent.

(c) The provisions of paragraph (b) of this section are not applicable to carboxyl-modified polyethylene resins used in food-packaging adhesives complying with § 175.105 of this chapter.

§ 177.1610 Polyethylene, chlorinated.

Chlorinated polyethylene identified in this section may be safely used as articles or components of articles that contact food, except for articles used for packing or holding food during cooking, subject to the provisions of this section.

(a) For the purpose of this section, chlorinated polyethylene consists of basic polymers produced by the direct chlorination of polyethylene conforming to the density, maximum *n*-hexane extractable fraction, and maximum xylene soluble fraction specifications prescribed under item 2.1 of the table in § 177.1520(c). Such chlorinated polyethylene contains a maximum of 60 percent by weight of total chlorine, as determined by ASTM 1method D1303–55 (Reapproved 1979), "Standard Test Method for Total Chlorine in Vinyl Chloride Polymers and Copolymers," which is incorporated by reference (Copies may be obtained from the American Society for Testing Materials, 100 Barr Harbor Dr., West Conshohocken, Philadelphia, PA 19428-2959, or may be examined at the National Archives and Records Administration (NARA). For information on the availability of this material at NARA, call 202–741–6030, or go to: *http://www.archives.gov/federal_register/code_of_federal_regulations/ibr_locations.html.*), and has a 7.0 percent maximum extractable fraction in *n*-hexane at 50 °C, as determined by the method described in § 177.1520(d)(3)(ii).

(b) Chlorinated polyethylene may be used in contact with all types of food, except that when used in contact with fatty food of Types III, IV-A, V, VII-A, and IX described in table 1 of § 176.170(c) of this chapter, chlorinated polyethylene is limited to use only as a modifier admixed at levels not exceeding 15 weight percent in plastic articles prepared from polyvinyl chloride and/or from vinyl chloride copolymers complying with § 177.1980.

[42 FR 14572, Mar. 15, 1977, as amended at 49 FR 10109, Mar. 19, 1984; 59 FR 14550, Mar. 29, 1994]

§ 177.1615 Polyethylene, fluorinated.

Fluorinated polyethylene, identified in paragraph (a) of this section, may be safely used as food-contact articles in accordance with the following prescribed conditions:

(a) Fluorinated polyethylene food-contact articles are produced by modifying the surface of polyethylene articles through action of fluorine gas in combination with gaseous nitrogen as an inert diluent. Such modification affects only the surface of the polymer, leaving the interior unchanged. Fluorinated polyethylene articles are manufactured from basic resins containing not less than 85 weight-percent of polymer units derived from ethylene and identified in § 177.1520 (a)(2) and (3)(i).

(b) Fluorinated polyethylene articles conform to the specifications and use limitations of § 177.1520(c), items 2.1 and 3.1.

(c) The finished food-contact article, when extracted with the solvent or solvents characterizing the type of food and under conditions of time and temperature characterizing the conditions of its intended use as determined from tables 1 and 2 of § 176.170(c) of this chapter, yields fluoride ion not to exceed 5 parts per million calculated on the basis of the volume of food held by the food-contact article.

[48 FR 39057, Aug. 29, 1983]

§ 177.1620 Polyethylene, oxidized.

Oxidized polyethylene identified in paragraph (a) of this section may be safely used as a component of food-contact articles, in accordance with the following prescribed conditions:

(a) Oxidized polyethylene is the basic resin produced by the mild air oxidation of polyethylene conforming to the density, maximum *n*-hexane extractable fraction, and maximum xylene soluble fraction specifications prescribed under item 2.3 of the table in § 177.1520(c). Such oxidized polyethylene has a minimum number average molecular weight of 1,200, as determined by high temperature vapor pressure osmometry, contains a maximum of 5 percent by weight of total oxygen, and has an acid value of 9 to 19.

(b) The finished food-contact article, when extracted with the solvent or solvents characterizing the type of food and under the conditions of time and temperature characterizing the conditions of its intended use as determined from tables 1 and 2 of § 176.170(c) of this chapter, yields net acidified chloroform-soluble extractives not to exceed 0.5 milligram per square inch of food-contact surface when tested by the methods described in § 177.1330(c), except that net acidified chloroform-soluble extractives from paper and paperboard complying with § 176.170 of this chapter may be corrected for wax, petrolatum, and mineral oil as provided in § 176.170(d) (5)(iii)(*b*) of this chapter. If the finished food-contact article is itself the subject of a regulation in parts 174, 175, 176, 177, 178 and § 179.45 of this chapter, it shall also comply with any specifications and limitations prescribed for it by such regulations. (NOTE: In testing the finished food-contact article, use a separate test sample for each extracting solvent.)

(c) The provisions of this section are not applicable to oxidized polyethylene used as provided in §§ 175.105 and 176.210 of this chapter, and § 177.2800. The provisions of paragraph (b) of this section are not applicable to oxidized polyethylene used as provided in §§ 175.125 and 176.170(a)(5) of this chapter and § 177.1200.

§ 177.1630 Polyethylene phthalate polymers.

Polyethylene phthalate polymers identified in this section may be safely used as, or components of plastics (films, articles, or fabric) intended for use in contact with food in accordance with the following prescribed conditions:

(a) Polyethylene phthalate films consist of a base sheet of ethylene terephthalate polymer, ethylene terephthalate-isophthalate copolymer, or ethylene-1,4-cyclohexylene dimethylene terephthalate copolyesters described in § 177.1315(b)(3), to which have been added optional substances, either as constituents of the base sheet or as constituents of coatings applied to the base sheet.

(b) Polyethylene phthalate articles consist of a base polymer of ethylene terephthalate polymer, or ethylene-1,4-cyclohexylene dimethylene terephthalate copolyesters described in § 177.1315(b)(3), to which have been added optional substances, either as constituents of the base polymer or as constituents of coatings applied to the base polymer.

(c)(1) Polyethylene phthalate spunbonded nonwoven fabric consist of continuous filaments of ethylene terephthalate polymer and ethylene terephthalate-isophthalate copolymer to which may have been added optional adjuvant substances required in their preparation and finishing.

(2) The ethylene terephthalate-isophthalate copolymer component of the fabric shall not exceed 25 percent by weight. The filaments may be blended with other fibers regulated for the specific use and the spunbonded fabric may be further bonded by application of heat and/or pressure.

(3) The fabric shall be used only in accordance with paragraph (i) of this section.

(d) The quantity of any optional substance employed in the production of polyethylene phthalate plastics does not exceed the amount reasonably required to accomplish the intended physical or technical effect or any limitations further provided. Any substance employed in the production of polyethylene phthalate plastics that is the subject of a regulation in parts 174, 175, 176, 177, 178 and 179 of this chapter conforms with any specification in such regulation.

(e) Substances employed in the production of polyethylene phthalate plastics include:

(1) Substances generally recognized as safe in food.

(2) Substances subject to prior sanction or approval for use in polyethylene phthalate plastics and used in accordance with such sanction or approval.

(3) Substances which by regulation in parts 174, 175, 176, 177, 178 and § 179.45 of this chapter may be safely used as components of resinous or polymeric food-contact surfaces subject to the provisions of such regulation.

(4) Substances identified in this paragraph (e)(4) subject to the limitations prescribed:

LIST OF SUBSTANCES AND LIMITATIONS

(i) Base sheet:

Ethylene terephthalate copolymers: Prepared by the condensation of dimethyl terephthalate or terephthalic acid with ethylene glycol, modified with one or more of the following: Azelaic acid, dimethyl azelate, dimethyl sebacate, sebacic acid.

Ethylene terephthalate copolymers: Prepared by the condensation of dimethyl terephthalate or terephthalic acid with ethylene glycol, modified with one or more of the following: Azelaic acid, dimethyl azelate, dimethyl sebacate, sebacic acid, pyromellitic dianhydride. The level of pyromellitic dianhydride shall not exceed 0.5 percent by weight of the finished copolymer which may be used under conditions of use E through H as described in table 2 of § 176.170(c) of this chapter.

Ethylene terephthalate-isophthalate copolymers: Prepared by the condensation of dimethyl terephthalate or terephthalic acid and dimethyl isophthalate or isophthalic acid with ethylene glycol. The finished copolymers contain either:

(*a*) 77 to 83 weight percent or

(*b*) At least 97 weight percent of polymer units derived from ethylene terephthalate.

(ii) Base sheet and base polymer:

Ethylene-1,4-cyclohexylene dimethylene terephthalate copolyesters described in § 177.1315(b)(3).

Ethylene terephthalate polymer: Prepared by the condensation of dimethyl terephthalate and ethylene glycol.

Ethylene terephthalate polymer: Prepared by the condensation of terephthalic acid and ethylene glycol.

(iii) Coatings:

Acrylic copolymers (CAS Reg. No. 30394–86–6): Prepared by reaction of ethyl acrylate (CAS Reg. No. 140–88–5), methyl methacrylate (CAS Reg. No. 80–62–6), and methacrylamide (CAS Reg. No. 79–39–0) blended with melamine-formaldehyde resin (CAS Reg. No. 68002–20–0). For use in coatings for polyethylene phthalate films complying with paragraph (a) of this section.—

Ethylene azelate-terephthalate copolymer: The copolymer, dissolved in 1,1,2-trichloroethane and/or methylene chloride, may be used as a heat-activated sealant on polyethylene terephthalate film intended for sealing polyethylene terephthalate pouches that are used as containers of either nonalcoholic beverages or alcoholic beverages containing not more than 15 percent ethyl alcohol. The copolymer has a terephthalate/azelate molecular ratio of 1.25/1.00 and a relative viscosity of not less than 1.5 as determined by a method title "General Procedure of Determining the Relative Viscosity of Resin Polymers," which is incorporated by reference. Copies are available from the Center for Food Safety and Applied Nutrition (HFS–200), Food and Drug Administration, 5100 Paint Branch Pkwy., College Park, MD 20740, or available for inspection, at the National Archives and Records Administration (NARA). For information on the availability of this material at NARA, call 202–741–6030, or go to: *http://www.archives.gov/federal_register/code_of_federal_regulations/ibr_locations.html.* Total residual copolymer solvent (1,1,2-trichloroethane and/or methylene chloride) shall not exceed 0.13 milligram per square inch of film, and food contact of the film shall be limited to not more than 1 square inch per 250 grams of beverage.

2-Ethylhexyl acrylate copolymerized with one or more of the following:

Acrylonitrile.

Methacrylonitrile.

Methyl acrylate.

Methyl methacrylate.

Itaconic acid.

Vinylidene chloride copolymerized with one or more of the following:

Methacrylic acid and its methyl, ethyl, propyl, butyl, or octyl esters.

Acrylic acid and its methyl, ethyl, propyl, butyl, or octyl esters.

Acrylonitrile.
Methacrylonitrile.
Vinyl chloride.
Itaconic acid.

Styrene-maleic anhydride resin, partial 2-butoxyethyl ester, ammonium salt (CAS Reg. No. 68890–80–2). For use only as a coating for polyethylene phthalate films complying with paragraph (a) of this section, at levels not to exceed 0.025 gram per square meter (0.016 milligram per square inch) of the film, in contact with food of types VIII and IX in table 1 of §176.170(c) of this chapter, under use conditions E, F, and G in table 2 of §176.170(c) of this chapter.

(iv) Emulsifiers:

Sodium dodecylbenzenesulfonate: As an adjuvant in the application of coatings to the base sheet or base polymer.

Sodium lauryl sulfate: As an adjuvant in the application of coatings to the base sheet or base polymer.

2-Sulfoethyl methacrylate, sodium salt (CAS Reg. No. 1804–87–1). For use only in copolymer coatings on polyethylene phthalate film under conditions of use E, F, and G described in table 2 of §175.300(d) of this chapter, and limited to use at a level not to exceed 2.0 percent by weight of the dry copolymer coating.

(v) Modifier:

1,4-Benzenedicarboxylic acid, dimethyl ester, polymer with 1,4-butanediol and α-hydro-*omega*-hydroxypoly(oxy-1,4-butanediyl) CAS Reg. No. 9078–71–1) meeting the following specifications:

Melting point: 200° to 215 °C as determined by ASTM method D2117–82, "Standard Test Method for Melting Point of Semicrystalline Polymers by the Hot Stage Microscopy Method," which is incorporated by reference. Copies may be obtained from the American Society for Testing Materials, 100 Barr Harbor Dr., West Conshohocken, Philadelphia, PA 19428-2959, or may be examined at the National Archives and Records Administration (NARA). For information on the availability of this material at NARA, call 202–741–6030, or go to: *http://www.archives.gov/federal_register/code_of_federal_regulations/ibr_locations.html.*

Density: 1.15 to 1.20 as determined by ASTM method D1505–68 (Reapproved 1979), "Standard Test Method for Density of Plastics by the Density-Gradient Technique," which is incorporated by reference. Copies may be obtained from the American Society for Testing Materials, 100 Barr Harbor Dr., West Conshohocken, Philadelphia, PA 19428-2959, or may be examined at the National Archives and Records Administration (NARA). For information on the availability of this material at NARA, call 202–741–6030, or go to: *http://www.archives.gov/federal_register/code_of_federal_regulations/ibr_locations.html.*

The modifier is used at a level not to exceed 5 percent by weight of polyethylene terephthalate film. The average thickness of the finished film shall not exceed 0.016 millimeter (0.0006 inch).

Hexanedioic acid polymer with 1,3-benzenedimethanamine (CAS Reg. No. 25718–70–1) meeting the specifications in §177.1500(b), item 10, when tested by the methods given in §177.1500(c). The modifier is used in polyethylene terephthalate at a level not to exceed 30 percent by weight of the polyethylene terephthalate.

Chloroform-soluble extractives shall not exceed 0.08 milligram/centimeter^2 (0.5 milligram/inch^2) of food-contact surface of the modified polyethylene terephthalate article when exposed to the following solvents at temperatures and times indicated:

(*a*) Distilled water at 49 °C (120 °F) for 24 hours;

(*b*) *n*-Heptane at 49 °C (120 °F) for 24 hours;

(*c*) 8 percent ethyl alcohol at 49 °C (120 °F) for 24 hours.

For use in contact with all types of foods except (*a*) those containing more than 8 percent alcohol, or (*b*) those at temperatures over 49 °C (120 °F).

(f) Polyethylene phthalate plastics conforming with the specifications prescribed in paragraph (f)(1) of this section are used as provided in paragraph (f)(2) of this section:

(1) *Specifications.* (i) The food contact surface, when exposed to distilled water at 250 °F for 2 hours, yields chloroform-soluble extractives not to exceed 0.5 mg/in^2 of food contact surface exposed to the solvent; and

(ii) The food contact surface, when exposed to *n*-heptane at 150 °F for 2 hours, yields chloroform-soluble extractives not to exceed 0.5 mg/in^2 of food contact surface exposed to the solvent.

(2) *Conditions of use.* The plastics are used for packaging, transporting, or holding food, excluding alcoholic beverages, at temperatures not to exceed 250 °F.

(g) Polyethylene phthalate plastics conforming with the specifications prescribed in paragraph (g)(1) of this section are used as provided in paragraph (g)(2) of this section.

(1) *Specifications.* (i) The food contact surface meets the specifications in paragraph (f)(1) of this section; and

(ii) The food contact surface when exposed to 50 percent ethyl alcohol at 120 °F for 24 hours, yields chloroform-soluble extractives not to exceed 0.5 mg/in^2 of food contact surface exposed to the solvent.

(2) *Conditions of use.* The plastics are used for packaging, transporting, or holding alcoholic beverages that do not exceed 50 percent alcohol by volume.

(h) Uncoated polyethylene phthalate plastics consisting of a base sheet or base polymer prepared as prescribed from substances identified in paragraphs (e)(4)(i) and (ii) of this section and conforming with the specifications prescribed in paragraph (h)(1) of this section are used as provided in paragraph (h)(2) of this section:

(1) *Specifications.* (i) The food contact surface, when exposed to distilled water at 250 °F for 2 hours yields chloroform-soluble extractives not to exceed 0.02 milligram/inch^2 of food contact surface exposed to the solvent; and

(ii) The food contact surface, when exposed to *n*-heptane at 150 °F for 2 hours, yields chloroform-soluble extractives not to exceed 0.02 milligram/inch^2 of food contact surface exposed to the solvent.

(2) *Conditions of use.* The plastics are used to contain foods during oven baking or oven cooking at temperatures above 250 °F.

(i) Polyethylene phthalate fabric, identified in paragraph (c) of this section and conforming with the specifications prescribed in paragraph (i)(1) of this section, is used only as provided in paragraph (i)(2) of this section.

(1) *Specifications.* Chloroform-soluble extractives shall not exceed 0.2 milligram/inch^2 of food-contact surface when exposed to the following solvents at temperatures and times indicated:

(i) Distilled water at 212 °F for 2 hours.

(ii) *n*-Heptane at 150 °F for 2 hours.

(iii) 50 percent ethyl alcohol at 120 °F for 24 hours.

(2) *Conditions of use.* The plastics are intended for:

(i) Dry food contact.

(ii) Bulk food (excluding alcoholic beverages) repeated use applications, including filtration, at temperatures not exceeding 212 °F.

(iii) Filtration of bulk alcoholic beverages, not exceeding 50 percent alcohol by volume, at temperatures not exceeding 120 °F.

(j) Polyethylene phthalate plastics, composed of ethylene terephthalate-isophthalate containing a minimum of 98 weight percent of polymer units derived from ethylene terephthalate, or ethylene-1,4-cyclohexylene dimethylene terephthalate copolyesters described in § 177.1315(b)(3), conforming with the specifications prescribed in paragraph (j)(1) of this section, are used as provided in paragraph (j)(2) of this section.

(1) *Specifications.* (i) The food contact surface meets the specifications in paragraph (f)(1) of this section and

(ii)(*a*) *Containers with greater than 500 mL capacity.* The food-contact surface when exposed to 95 percent ethanol at 120 °F for 24 hours should not yield chloroform-soluble extractives in excess of 0.005 mg/in^2.

(*b*) *Containers with less than or equal to 500 mL capacity.* The food contact surface when exposed to 95 percent ethanol at 120 °F for 24 hours should not yield chloroform-soluble extractives in excess of 0.05 mg/in^2.

(2) *Conditions of use.* The plastics are used for packaging, transporting, or holding alcoholic foods that do not exceed 95 percent alcohol by volume.

[42 FR 14572, Mar. 15, 1977, as amended at 42 FR 18611, Apr. 8, 1977; 44 FR 40886, July 13, 1979; 45 FR 6541, Jan. 29, 1980; 47 FR 11844, Mar. 19, 1982; 47 FR 53346, Nov. 26, 1982; 48 FR 30361, July 1, 1983; 49 FR 10110, Mar. 19, 1984; 50 FR 31047, July 24, 1985; 51 FR 3772, Jan. 30, 1986; 52 FR 32917, Sept. 1, 1987; 54 FR 15750, Apr. 19, 1989; 54 FR 24898, June 12, 1989; 60 FR 57927, Nov. 24, 1995; 60 FR 61654, Dec. 1, 1995; 61 FR 46718, Sept. 5, 1996]

§ 177.1632 Poly(phenyleneterephthalamide) resins.

Poly(phenyleneterephthalamide) resins identified in paragraph (a) of this section may be safely used as articles or components of articles intended for repeated contact with food.

(a) *Identity.* For the purpose of this section, the poly(phenyleneterephthalamide) resins (CAS Reg. No.

26125–61–1) are produced by the polymerization of terephthalolyl chloride with *p*-phenylenediamine. The poly(phenyleneterephthalamide) resin fibers and yarns may contain optional adjuvant substances required in their preparation and finishing.

(b) *Optional adjuvant substances.* The poly(phenyleneterephthalamide) resins identified in paragraph (a) of this section may contain the following optional adjuvant substances, subject to any limitation on their use:

(1) Optional adjuvant substances authorized for this use in accordance with § 174.5 of this chapter.

(2) Optional finish components, total weight not to exceed 1 percent by weight of the base polymer, as follows:

List of substances	Limitations
Diundecylphthalate (CAS Reg. No. 3648–20–2).	
Mono- and dipotassium salts of lauryl phosphate (CAS Reg. No. 39322–78–6).	
o-Phenylphenol (CAS Reg. No. 90–43–7).	For use as a fungicide for finish coating materials. Not to exceed 0.01 percent by weight of the base polymer.
Poly(oxyethylene/oxypropylene)monobutylether (CAS Reg. No. 9038–95–3).	
Poly(oxyethylene) mono(nonylphenyl)ether (CAS Reg. No. 9016–45–9).	
Polyvinyl methylether (CAS Reg. No. 9003–09–2).	
Poly(oxyethylene) sorbitol monolaurate tetraoleate (CAS Reg. No. 71243–28–2).	
Poly(oxyethylene) sorbitol hexaoleate (CAS Reg. No. 57171–56–9).	
4,4′-Butylidenebis (6-*tert*-butyl-*m*-cresol) (CAS Reg. No. 85–60–9).	For use only as an oxidation inhibitor for finish coating materials. Not to exceed 0.01 percent by weight of the base polymer.

(c) *Specifications.* (1) Poly(phenyleneterephthalamide) resins in the form of continuous filament yarns or fibers that have been scoured in accordance with paragraph (d)(1) of this section, when refluxed in a 50 percent ethanol/water mixture for 24 hours, yields total extractables not exceeding 0.5 percent by weight of the sample.

(2) Poly(phenyleneterephthalamide) resins in the form of pulp, when refluxed in a 50 percent ethanol/water mixture for 24 hours, yields total extractables not exceeding 0.65 percent by weight of the sample.

(d) *Conditions of use.* (1) Poly(phenyleneterephthalamide) resins in the form of continuous filament yarns and fibers may be used as components of articles intended for repeated use in contact with food at temperatures not to exceed 260 °C (500 °F). All items are scoured prior to use by agitation in a water bath containing 0.5 gram/liter of tetrasodium pyrophosphate and 0.5 percent detergent. The items are agitated at 80 °C (180 °F) for 20 minutes, and then subjected to a cold water rinse.

(2) Poly(phenyleneterephthalamide) resins in the form of pulp may be used as gaskets and packing for food processing equipment at temperatures not to exceed 260 °C (500 °F).

[57 FR 3125, Jan. 28, 1992, as amended at 69 FR 24512, May 4, 2004]

§ 177.1635 Poly(p-methylstyrene) and rubber-modified poly(p-methylstyrene).

Poly(*p*-methylstyrene) and rubber-modified poly(*p*-methylstyrene) identified in this section may be safely used as components of articles intended for use in contact with food, subject to the provisions of this section:

(a) *Identity.* For the purposes of this section, poly(*p*-methylstyrene) and rubber-modified poly(*p*-methylstyrene) are basic polymers, manufactured as described in this paragraph, meeting the specifications prescribed in paragraph (c) of this section.

(1) Poly(*p*-methylstyrene) (CAS Reg. No. 24936–41–2) polymer produced by the polymerization of *p*-methylstyrene.

(2) Rubber-modified poly(*p*-methylstyrene) (CAS Reg. No. 33520–88–6) polymer produced by combining styrene-butadiene copolymer and/or polybutadiene with poly(*p*-methylstyrene), either during or after polymerization of the poly(*p*-methylstyrene), such that the finished polymers contain not less than 75 weight percent of total polymer units derived from *p*-methylstyrene) monomer.

(b) *Optional adjuvants.* The basic polymers identified in paragraph (a) of this section may contain optional adjuvant substances required in the production of such basic polymers. Such optional adjuvant substances may include substances permitted for such use by applicable regulations in this chapter, substances generally recognized as safe in food, substances generally recognized as safe in indirect additives, and substances used in accordance with prior sanction or approval.

(c) *Specifications.* (1) Poly(*p*-methylstyrene) basic polymers identified in paragraph (a)(1) of this section shall contain not more than 1 weight percent of total residual *p*-methystyrene monomer, as determined by a gas chromatographic method titled, "Gas Chromatographic Determination of PMS and PET in PPMS Basic Polymers," which is incorporated by reference. Copies are available from the Center for Food Safety and Applied Nutrition (HFS–200), Food and Drug Administration, 5100 Paint Branch Pkwy., College Park, MD 20740, or available for inspection at the National Archives and Records Administration (NARA). For information on the availability of this material at NARA, call 202–741–6030, or go to: *http://www.archives.gov/federal_register/code_of_federal_regulations/ibr_locations.html.*

(2) Rubber-modified poly(*p*-methylstyrene) basic polymers identified in paragraph (a)(2) of this section shall contain not more than 0.5 weight percent of total residual *p*-methylstyrene monomer, as determined by the method identified in paragraph (c)(1) of this section

(d) *Other specifications and limitations.* The poly(*p*-methylstyrene) and rubber-modified poly(*p*-methylstyrene) identified in and complying with this section, when used as components of the food-contact surface of any article that is the subject of a regulation in parts 175, 176, 177, 178 and § 179.45 of this chapter, shall comply with any specifications and limitations prescribed by such regulation for the article in the finished form in which it is to contact food.

(e) *Conditions of use.* Poly(*p*-methylstyrene) basic polymers and rubber-modified poly(*p*-methylstyrene) basic polymers identified in paragraphs (a)(1) and (a)(2), respectively, of this section shall be used in contact with food only under conditions of use B through H set forth in table 2 of § 176.170(c) of this chapter.

[48 FR 31384, July 8, 1983, as amended at 54 FR 24898, June 12, 1989; 55 FR 52989, Dec. 26, 1990]

§ 177.1637 Poly(oxy-1,2-ethanediyloxycarbonyl-2,6-naphthalenediylcarbonyl) resins.

Poly(oxy-1,2-ethanediyloxycarbonyl-2,6-naphthalenediylcarbonyl) resins identified in paragraph (a) of this section may be safely used as articles or components of articles intended for use in contact with food in accordance with the following conditions:

(a) *Identity.* For the purpose of this section, poly(oxy-1,2-ethanediyloxycarbonyl-2,6-naphthalenediylcarbonyl) resins (CAS Reg. No. 24968–11–4) are polymers formed by catalytic transesterification of 2,6-dimethylnaphthalene dicarboxylate with ethylene glycol followed by catalytic polycondensation.

(b) *Specifications*—(1) *Density.* The density of poly(oxy-1,2-ethanediyloxycarbonyl-2,6-naphthalenediylcarbonyl) resins shall be between 1.33 and 1.40 grams per cubic centimeter.

(2) *Inherent viscosity.* The finished food-contact article shall have a minimum inherent viscosity of 0.55 deciliter per gram in a solution of 0.1 gram of polymer in 100 milliliters of a 25/40/35 (weight/weight/weight) solution of *p*-chlorophenol/tetrachloroethane/phenol. The viscosity is determined by Eastman Chemical Co.'s method ECD-A-AC-G-V-1-5, "Determination of Dilute Solution Viscosity of Polyesters," dated May 31, 1988, which is incorporated by reference in accordance with 5 U.S.C. 552(a) and 1 CFR part 51. Copies are available from the Office of Food Additive Safety (HFS–200), Center for Food Safety and Applied Nutrition, Food and Drug Administration, 5100 Paint Branch Pkwy., College Park, MD 20740, 240–402–1200, or may be examined at the Center for Food Safety and Applied Nutrition's Library, Food and Drug Administration, 5100 Paint Branch Pkwy.,

College Park, MD 20740, or at the National Archives and Records Administration (NARA). For information on the availability of this material at NARA, call 202–741–6030, or go to: *http://www.archives.gov/federal_register/code_of_federal_regulations/ibr_locations.html.*

(c) *Extraction limitations.* A 0.5 millimeter (0.02 inch) thick sheet of resin when extracted with water at 121 °C (250 °F) for 2 hours shall yield total nonvolatile extractives not exceeding 2.0 micrograms per square inch of exposed resin surface.

(d) *Conditions of use.* The finished food contact article shall be:

(1) Used in contact only with food of Types I, II, IVB, VIA, VIB, VIIB, and VIII identified in table 1 of §176.170(c) of this chapter, under conditions of use A through H described in table 2 of §176.170(c) of this chapter; and with food of Types III, IVA, V, VIC, VIIA, and IX identified in table 1 of §176.170(c) of this chapter, under conditions of use C through H described in table 2 of §176.170(c) of this chapter; and

(2) Identified in a manner that will differentiate the article from articles made of other polymeric resins to facilitate collection and sorting.

[61 FR 14965, Apr. 4, 1996, as amended at 78 FR 14666, Mar. 7, 2013]

§177.1640 Polystyrene and rubber-modified polystyrene.

Polystyrene and rubber-modified polystyrene identified in this section may be safely used as components of articles intended for use in contact with food, subject to the provisions of this section.

(a) *Identity.* For the purposes of this section, polystyrene and rubber-modified polystyrene are basic polymers manufactured as described in this paragraph so as to meet the specifications prescribed in paragraph (c) of this section when tested by the method described in paragraph (d) of this section.

(1) Polystyrene consists of basic polymers produced by the polymerization of styrene.

(2) Rubber-modified polystyrene consists of basic polymers produced by combining styrene-butadiene copolymers and/or polybutadiene with polystyrene, either during or after polymerization of the polystyrene, such that the finished basic polymers contain not less than 75 weight percent of total polymer units derived from styrene monomer.

(b) *Optional adjuvants.* The basic polymers identified in paragraph (a) of this section may contain optional adjuvant substances required in the production of such basic polymers. Such optional adjuvant substances may include substances permitted for such use by regulations in parts 170 through 189 of this chapter, substances generally recognized as safe in food, and substances used in accordance with a prior sanction or approval.

(c) *Specifications.* (1) Polystyrene basic polymers identified in paragraph (a)(1) of this section shall contain not more than 1 weight percent of total residual styrene monomer, as determined by the method described in paragraph (d) of this section, except that when used in contact with fatty foods of Types III, IV-A, V, VII-A, and IX described in table 1 of §176.170(c) of this chapter, such polystyrene basic polymers shall contain not more than 0.5 weight percent of total residual styrene monomer.

(2) Rubber-modified polystyrene basic polymers identified in paragraph (a)(2) of this section shall contain not more than 0.5 weight percent of total residual styrene monomer, as determined by the method described in paragraph (d) of this section.

(d) *Analytical method for determination of total residual styrene monomer content*—(1) *Scope.* This method is suitable for the determination of residual styrene monomer in all types of styrene polymers.

(2) *Principle.* The sample is dissolved in methylene chloride. An aliquot of the solution is injected into a gas chromatograph. The amount of styrene monomer present is determined from the area of the resulting peak.

(3) *Apparatus*—(i) *Gas chromatograph.* Beckman GC-2A gas chromatograph with hydrogen flame detector or apparatus of equivalent sensitivity.

(ii) *Chromatograph column.* One-quarter inch outside diameter stainless steel tubing (0.028 inch wall thickness), 4 feet in length, packed with 20 percent polyethylene glycol (20,000 molecular weight) on alkaline treated 60–80 mesh firebrick.

(iii) *Recorder*. Millivolt range of 0–1, chart speed of 30 inches per hour.

(4) *Reagents*. Compressed air, purified; helium gas; hydrogen gas; methylene chloride, redistilled; and styrene monomer, redistilled.

(5) *Operating conditions for the gas chromatograph*. (i) The column is operated at a temperature of 100 °C with a helium flow rate of 82 milliliters per minute.

(ii) The hydrogen burner is operated with 15 pounds per square inch of air pressure and 7 pounds per square inch of hydrogen pressure.

(iii) The attenuation of the hydrogen flame detector is set at 2×10^2.

(6) *Standardization*. (i) Prepare a standard solution by weighing accurately 15 to 20 milligrams of styrene monomer into a 2-ounce bottle containing 25.0 milliliters of methylene chloride. Cap the bottle tightly and shake to thoroughly mix the solution.

(ii) By means of a microliter syringe, inject 1 microliter of the standard solution into the gas chromatograph. Measure the area of the styrene monomer peak which emerges after approximately 12 minutes.

(7) *Procedure*. (i) Transfer 1 gram of sample (accurately weighed to the nearest 0.001 gram to a 2-ounce bottle and add several glass beads. Pipette 25.0 milliliters of methylene chloride into the bottle. Cap the bottle tightly and place on a mechanical shaker. Shake until the polymer is completely dissolved. If any insoluble residue remains, allow the bottle to stand (or centrifuge at a low speed) until a clear supernatant layer appears.

(ii) By means of a microliter syringe, inject 3 microliters of the clear supernatant liquid into the gas chromatograph.

(iii) Measure the area of the resulting styrene monomer peak. Compare the sample peak area with the area produced by the standard styrene monomer solution. Calculation:

Percent residual styrene monomer=Milligrams monomer in standard×peak area of sample/Peak area of monomer standard×sample weight in grams×30

(e) *Other specifications and limitations*. The polystyrene and rubber-modified polystyrene identified in and complying with this section, when used as components of the food-contact surface of any article that is the subject of a regulation in parts 174, 175, 176, 177, 178 and §179.45 of this chapter, shall comply with any specifications and limitations prescribed by such regulation for the article in the finished form in which it is to contact food.

(f) *Nonapplicability*. The provisions of this section are not applicable to polystyrene and rubber-modified polystyrene used in food-packaging adhesives complying with §175.105 of this chapter.

§ 177.1650 Polysulfide polymer-polyepoxy resins.

Polysulfide polymer-polyepoxy resins may be safely used as the food-contact surface of articles intended for packaging, transporting, holding, or otherwise contacting dry food, in accordance with the following prescribed conditions:

(a) Polysulfide polymer-polyepoxy resins are the reaction products of liquid polysulfide polymers and polyfunctional epoxide resins, cured with the aid of tri(dimethylaminomethyl) phenol, to which have been added certain optional substances to impart desired technological properties to the resins. Subject to any limitations prescribed in this section, the optional substances may include:

(1) Substances generally recognized as safe in food and food packaging.

(2) Substances the use of which is permitted under applicable regulations in this part, prior sanctions, or approvals.

(3) Substances named in this subparagraph and further identified as required:

List of substances	Limitations
Bis(2-chloroethyl) formal.	
Bis(dichloropropyl) formal	Cross-linking agent.
Butyl alcohol	Solvent.
Carbon black (channel process).	
Chlorinated paraffins	Cross-linking agent.
Epoxidized linseed oil.	
Epoxidized soybean oil.	
Epoxy resins (as listed in §175.300(b)(3)(viii)(*a*) of this chapter)..	

List of substances	Limitations
Ethylene glycol monobutyl ether	Solvent.
Magnesium chloride.	
Methyl isobutyl ketone	Solvent.
Naphthalene sulfonic acid-formaldehyde condensate, sodium salt.	
Sodium dibutyl naphthalene sulfonate.	Wetting agent.
Sodium hydrosulfide.	
Sodium polysulfide.	
β,β′,γ,γ′-Tetrachloro normal propyl ether.	Cross-linking agent.
Titanium dioxide.	
Toluene	Solvent.
Trichloroethane	Cross-linking agent.
1,2,3-Trichloropropane	Do.
Urea-formaldehyde resins.	
Xylene	Solvent.

(b) The resins are used as the food-contact surface for dry food.

(c) An appropriate sample of the finished resin in the form in which it contacts food, when subjected to ASTM method D968–81, "Standard Test Methods for Abrasion Resistance of Organic Coatings by the Falling Abrasive Tester," which is incorporated by reference (Copies may be obtained from the American Society for Testing Materials, 100 Barr Harbor Dr., West Conshohocken, Philadelphia, PA 19428-2959, or may be examined at the National Archives and Records Administration (NARA). For information on the availability of this material at NARA, call 202–741–6030, or go to: *http://www.archives.gov/federal_register/code_of_federal_regulations/ibr_locations.html.*), using No. 50 Emery abrasive in lieu of Ottawa sand, shall exhibit and abrasion coefficient of not less than 20 liters per mil of film thickness.

[42 FR 14572, Mar. 15, 1977, as amended at 49 FR 10110, Mar. 19, 1984]

§ 177.1655 Polysulfone resins.

Polysulfone resins identified in paragraph (a) of this section may be safely used as articles or components of articles intended for use in contact with food, in accordance with the following prescribed conditions:

(a) For the purpose of this section, polysulfone resins are:

(1) Poly(oxy-*p*-phenylenesulfonyl-*p*-phenyleneoxy-*p*-phenyleneisopropylidene-*p*-phenylene) resins (CAS Reg. No. 25154–01–2) consisting of basic resins produced when the disodium salt of 4,4′-isopropylidenediphenol is made to react with 4,4′-dichlorodiphenyl sulfone in such a way that the finished resins have a minimum number average molecular weight of 15,000, as determined by osmotic pressure in monochlorobenzene; or

(2) 1,1′-Sulfonylbis[4-chlorobenzene] polymer with 4,4′-(1-methylethylidene)bis[phenol] (minimum 92 percent) and 4,4′-sulfonylbis[phenol] (maximum 8 percent) (CAS Reg. No. 88285–91–0) produced when a mixture of 4,4′-isopropylidenediphenol (minimum 92 percent) and 4,4′-sulfonylbis[phenol] (maximum 8 percent) is made to react with 4,4′-dichlorodiphenyl sulfone in such a way that the finished resin has a minimum number average molecular weight of 26,000, as determined by osmotic pressure in dimethylformamide.

(b) The basic polysulfone resins identified in paragraph (a) of this section may contain optional adjuvant substances required in the production of such basic resins. The optional adjuvant substances required in the production of the basic polysulfone resins may include substances described in § 174.5(d) of this chapter and the following:

List of substances	Limitations
Dimethyl sulfoxide	Not to exceed 50 parts per million as residual solvent in finished basic resin in paragraph (a)(1) of this section.
Monochlorobenzene	Not to exceed 500 parts per million as residual solvent in finished basic resin in paragraph (a)(1) of this section.
N-methyl-2-pyrrolidone.	Not to exceed 0.01 percent (100 parts per million) as residual solvent in finished basic resin in paragraph (a)(2) of this section.

(c) Polysulfone resins, when extracted at reflux temperatures for 6 hours with the solvents—distilled water, 50 percent (by volume) ethyl alcohol in distilled water, 3 percent acetic acid in distilled water, and *n*-heptane, yield total extractives in each extracting solvent not to exceed 0.0078 milligram per square centimeter (0.05 milligram per square inch) of resin surface. Note: In testing the finished polysulfone resins, use a separate resin test sample for each required extracting solvent.

(d) Polysulfone resins intended for repeated use in contact with food may be used under conditions of use A through H in table 2 of § 176.170(c) of this chapter. The resins intended for single-service food-contact use may be used only under condition of use H described in table 2 of § 176.170(c) of this chapter.

[51 FR 882, Jan. 9, 1986; 51 FR 4165, Feb. 3, 1986; 61 FR 29475, June 11, 1996]

§ 177.1660 Poly (tetramethylene terephthalate).

Poly(tetramethylene terephthalate) (poly (oxytetramethyleneoxyterephthaloyl)) [Chemical Abstracts Service Registry No. 24968–12–5] identified in this section may be safely used as articles or components of articles intended to contact food, in accordance with the following prescribed conditions:

(a) *Identity*. For the purpose of this section, poly (tetramethylene terephthalate) is the reaction product of dimethyl terephthalate with 1,4-butanediol to which may have been added certain optional substances to impart desired technological properties to the polymer.

(b) *Optional adjuvant substances*. Poly(tetramethylene terephthalate) identified in paragraph (a) of this section may contain optional adjuvant substances. The quantity of any optional adjuvant substance employed in the production of the polymer does not exceed the amount reasonably required to accomplish the intended technical or physical effect. Such adjuvants may include substances generally recognized as safe in food, substances used in accordance with prior sanction, and substances permitted under applicable regulations in this part.

(c) *Specifications*. (1) Inherent viscosity of a 0.50 percent solution of the polymer in phenol/tetrachloroethane (60/40 weight ratio) solvent is not less than 0.6 as determined using a Wagner viscometer (or equivalent) and calculated from the following equation:

$$\text{Inherent viscosity} = \frac{(\text{natural logarithm of } N_r)}{(c)}$$

where:

N_r=Ratio of flow time of the polymer solution to that of the solvent and c=polymer concentration of the test solution in grams per 100 milliliters.

(2) Poly(tetramethylene terephthalate) in the finished form in which it is to contact food shall yield total extractives as follows:

(i) Not to exceed 0.08 milligram per square inch of food contact surface when extracted for 2 hours at 250 °F with distilled water.

(ii) Not to exceed 0.02 milligram per square inch of food contact surface when extracted for 2 hours at 150 °F with *n*-heptane.

(iii) Not to exceed 0.04 milligram per square inch of food contact surface when extracted for 2 hours at 212 °F with 3 percent aqueous acetic acid.

(iv) Not to exceed 0.02 milligram per square inch of food contact surface when extracted for 2 hours at 65.6 °C (150 °F) with 50 percent ethanol.

[42 FR 14572, Mar. 15, 1977, as amended at 50 FR 20748, May 20, 1985; 52 FR 20069, May 29, 1987]

§ 177.1670 Polyvinyl alcohol film.

Polyvinyl alcohol film may be safely used in contact with food of the types identified in § 176.170(c) of this chapter, table 1, under Types V, VIII, and IX, in accordance with the following prescribed conditions:

(a) The polyvinyl alcohol film is produced from polyvinyl alcohol having a minimum viscosity of 4 centipoises when a 4-percent aqueous solution is tested at 20 °C.

(b) The finished food-contact film for use in contact with Food Types V or IX, when extracted with the solvent characterizing the type of food and under the conditions of time and temperature characterizing its intended use as determined from tables 1 and 2 of § 176.170(c) of this chapter, yields total extractives not to exceed 0.078 milligram per square centimeter (0.5 milligram per square inch) of food-contact surface when tested by ASTM method F34–76 (Reapproved 1980), "Standard Test Method for Liquid Extraction of Flexible Barrier Materials," which is incorporated by reference. Copies may be obtained from the American Society for Testing Materials, 100 Barr Harbor Dr., West Conshohocken, Philadelphia, PA 19428-2959, or may be examined at the National Archives and

Records Administration (NARA). For information on the availability of this material at NARA, call 202–741–6030, or go to: *http://www.archives.gov/federal_register/code_of_federal_regulations/ibr_locations.html.*

(c) The finished food-contact film shall not be used as a component of food containers intended for use in contact with water.

[42 FR 14572, Mar. 15, 1977, as amended at 49 FR 10110, Mar. 19, 1984]

§ 177.1680 Polyurethane resins.

The polyurethane resins identified in paragraph (a) of this section may be safely used as the food-contact surface of articles intended for use in contact with bulk quantities of dry food of the type identified in § 176.170(c) of this chapter, table 1, under Type VIII, in accordance with the following prescribed conditions:

(a) For the purpose of this section, polyurethane resins are those produced when one or more of the isocyanates listed in paragraph (a)(1) of this section is made to react with one or more of the substances listed in paragraph (a)(2) of this section:

(1) Isocyanates:

Bis(isocyanatomethyl) benzene (CAS Reg. No. 25854–16–4).
Bis(isocyanatomethyl) cyclohexane (CAS Reg. No. 38661–72–2).
4,4′-Diisocyanato-3,3′-dimethylbiphenyl (bitolylene diisocyanate).
Diphenylmethane diisocyanate.
Hexamethylene diisocyanate.
3-Isocyanatomethyl - 3,5,5 - trimethylcyclohexyl isocyanate.
4,4-Methylenebis(cyclohexyl isocyanate).
Toluene diisocyanate.

(2) List of substances:

Adipic acid.
1,4-Butanediol.
1,3-Butylene glycol.
1,4-Cyclohexane dimethanol (CAS Reg. No. 105–08–8).
2,2-Dimethyl-1,3-propanediol.
Ethylene glycol.
1,6-Hexanediol (CAS Reg. No. 629–11–8).α-Hydro-ω-hydroxypoly(oxy-1,4-butanediyl) (CAS Reg. No. 25190–06–1).
α-Hydro-*omega*-hydroxypoly (oxytetramethylene).
α,α′-(Isopropylidenedi-*p*-phenylene)bis[*omega*-hydroxypoly (oxypropylene)(3–4 moles)], average molecular weight 675.
Maleic anhydride.
Methyl oxirane polymer with oxirane (CAS Reg. No. 9003–11–6).
Methyl oxirane polymer with oxirane, ether with 1,2,3-propanetriol (CAS Reg. No. 9082–00–2).
α,α′α″,α‴-Neopentanetetrayltetrakis [*omega*-hydroxypoly (oxypropylene) (1–2 moles)], average molecular weight 400.
Pentaerythritol-linseed oil alcoholysis product.
Phthalic anhydride.
Polybutylene glycol.
Polyethyleneadipate modified with ethanolamine with the molar ratio of the amine to the adipic acid less than 0.1 to 1.
Poly(oxycarbonylpentamethylene).
Polyoxypropylene ethers of 4.4′-isopropylidenediphenol (containing an average of 2–4 moles of propylene oxide).
Polypropylene glycol.
α,α′,α″-1,2,3-Propanetriyltris [*omega*-hydroxypoly (oxypropylene) (15–18 moles)], average molecular weight 3,000.
Propylene glycol.
α,α′,α″-[Propylidynetris (methylene)] tris [*omega*-hydroxypoly (oxypropylene) (minimum 1.5 moles)], minimum molecular weight 400.
α-[ρ(1,1,3,3-Tetramethylbutyl) - phenyl]-*omega*-hydroxypoly(oxyethylene) (5 moles), average molecular weight 425.
Trimethylol propane.

(b) Optional adjuvant substances employed in the production of the polyurethane resins or added thereto to impart desired technical or physical properties may include the following substances:

List of substances	Limitations
1-[(2-Aminoethyl)amino]2-propanol	As a curing agent.
1-(3-Chloroallyl)-3,5,7-triaza-1-azoniaadamantane chloride	As a preservative.
Colorants used in accordance with § 178.3297 of this chapter..	
Dibutyltin diacetate	As a catalyst.
Dibutyltin dichloride	Do.
Dibutyltin dilaurate	Do.
N,N-Dimethyldodecylamine	Do.
N-Dodecylmorpholine	Do.
a,a′-[Isopropylidenebis[*p*-phenyleneoxy(2-hydroxytrimethylene)]]bis[*omega*-hydroxypoly-(oxyethylene) (136–170 moles)], average molecular weight 15,000.	As a stabilizer.
4,4′-Methylenedianiline	As a curing agent.

List of substances	Limitations
1,1′,1″-Nitrilotri-2-propanol	Do.
2,2′-(*p*-Phenylenedioxy) diethanol	Do.
Polyvinyl isobutyl ether.	
Polyvinyl methyl ether.	
Soyaalkyd resin	Conforming in composition with § 175.300 of this chapter and containing litharge not to exceed that residual from its use as the reaction catalyst and creosol not to exceed that required as an antioxidant.
Tetrakis [methylene–(2,5–di-*tert*-butyl-4-hydroxyhydrocinnamate)]methane (CAS Reg. No. 6683–19–8).	Stabilizer.
N,N,N′N′-Tetrakis (2-hydroxypropyl)ethylenediamine	As a curing agent.
Triethanolamine	Do.
Trimethyleneglycol di (*p*-aminobenzoate) (CAS Reg. No. 57609–64–0).	As a curing agent.

(c) An appropriate sample of the finished resin in the form in which it contacts food, when subjected to ASTM method D968–81, "Standard Test Methods for Abrasion Resistance of Organic Coatings by the Falling Abrasive Tester," which is incorporated by reference (Copies may be obtained from the American Society for Testing Materials, 100 Barr Harbor Dr., West Conshohocken, Philadelphia, PA 19428-2959, or may be examined at the National Archives and Records Administration (NARA). For information on the availability of this material at NARA, call 202–741–6030, or go to: *http://www.archives.gov/federal_register/code_of_federal_regulations/ibr_locations.html.*), using No. 50 Emery abrasive in lieu of Ottawa sand, shall exhibit an abrasion coefficient of not less than 20 liters per mil of film thickness.

[42 FR 14572, Mar. 15, 1977, as amended at 46 FR 57033, Nov. 20, 1981; 49 FR 10110, Mar. 19, 1984; 50 FR 51847, Dec. 20, 1985; 56 FR 15278, Apr. 16, 1991; 56 FR 42933, Aug. 30, 1991]

§ 177.1810 Styrene block polymers.

The styrene block polymers identified in paragraph (a) of this section may be safely used as articles or as components of articles intended for use in contact with food, subject to provisions of this section.

(a) For the purpose of this section, styrene block polymers are basic polymers manufactured as described in this paragraph, so that the finished polymers meet the specifications prescribed in paragraph (b) of this section, when tested by the methods described in paragraph (c) of this section.

(1) Styrene block polymers with 1,3-butadiene are those produced by the catalytic solution polymerization of styrene and 1,3-butadiene.

(2) Styrene block polymers with 2-methyl-1,3-butadiene are those produced by the catalytic solution polymerization of styrene and 2-methyl-1,3-butadiene.

(3) Styrene block polymers with 1,3-butadiene, hydrogenated are those produced by the catalytic solution polymerization of styrene and 1,3-butadiene, and subsequently hydrogenated.

(b) *Specifications:*

Styrene block polymers	Molecular weight (minimum)	Solubility	Glass transition points	Maximum extractable fraction in distilled water at specified temperatures, times, and thicknesses	Maximum extractable fraction in 50 percent ethanol at specified temperatures, times, and thicknesses
1. (i) Styrene block polymers with 1,3-butadiene; for use as articles or as components of articles that contact food of Types I, II, IV-B, VI, VII-B, and VIII identified in table 1 in § 176.170(c) of this chapter under conditions of use D, E, F, and G described in table 2 in § 176.170(c) of this chapter.	29,000	Completely soluble in toluene.	−98 °C (−144 °F) to −71 °C (−96 °F) and 86 °C (187 °F) to 122 °C (252 °F).	0.0039 mg/cm^2 (0.025 mg/in^2) of surface at reflux temperature for 30 min on a 0.19 cm (0.075 in) thick sample.	0.002 mg/cm^2 (0.01 mg/in^2) of surface at 66 °C (150 °F) for 2 hr on a 0.19 cm (0.075 in) thick sample.

Styrene block polymers	Molecular weight (minimum)	Solubility	Glass transition points	Maximum extractable fraction in distilled water at specified temperatures, times, and thicknesses	Maximum extractable fraction in 50 percent ethanol at specified temperatures, times, and thicknesses
(ii) Styrene block polymers with 1,3-butadiene; for use as components of pressure-sensitive adhesives that contact food of Types I, II, IV-B, VI, VII-B, and VIII identified in table 1 in § 176.170(c) of this chapter under conditions of use C, D, E, F and G described in table 2 in § 176.170(c) of this chapter, provided the pressure-sensitive adhesives be applied only to closure tapes for sealing containers having a capacity of not less than 160 cc (5.5 fluid ounces) and that the area of the adhesive exposed to food shall not exceed 4.03 cm^2 (0.625 in^2). The pressure-sensitive adhesive may contain terpene resins as identified in § 175.125(b)(2) of this chapter.	29,000	......do	......do	......do	Do.
2. Styrene block polymers with 2-methyl-1,3-butadiene; for use as articles or as components of articles that contact food of Types I, II, IV-B, VI, VII-B, and VIII identified in table 1 in § 176.170(c) of this chapter.	29,000	......do	−65 °C (−85 °F) to −47 °C (−53 °F) and 86 °C (187 °F) to 122 °C (252 °F).	0.002 mg/cm^2 (0.01 mg/in^2) of surface at reflux temperature for 2 hr on a 0.071 cm (0.028 in) thick sample. (Optionally, maximum net residue soluble in chloroform shall not exceed 0.00020 mg/cm^2 (0.0013 mg/in^2) of surface.).	0.002 mg/cm^2 (0.01 mg/in^2) of surface at 66 °C (150 °F) for 2 hr on a 0.071 cm (0.028 in) thick sample. (Optionally, maximum net residue soluble in chloroform shall not exceed 0.00040 mg/cm^2 (0.0025 mg/in^2) of surface.)
3. (i) Styrene block polymers with 1,3-butadiene, hydrogenated (CAS Reg. No. 66070–58–4): for use as articles or as components of articles that contact food of Types I, II, IV-B, VI, VII-B, and VIII identified in table 1 in § 176.170(c) of this chapter.	16,000	......do	−50 °C (−58 °F) to −30 °C (−22 °F) and 92 °C (198 °F) to 98 °C (208 °F).	0.002 mg/cm^2 (0.01 mg/in^2) of surface at reflux temperature for 2 hr on a 0.071 cm (0.028 in) thick sample.	0.002 mg/cm^2 (0.01 mg/in^2) of surface at 66 °C (150 °F) for 2 hr on a 0.071 cm (0.028 in) thick sample.
(ii) Styrene block polymers with 1,3-butadiene, hydrogenated (CAS Reg. No. 66070–58–4): for use at levels not to exceed 42.4 percent by weight as a component of closures with sealing gaskets that would contact food of Types III, IV-A, V, VII-A, VIII, and IX identified in table 1 in § 176.170(c) of this chapter, and in condition of use D as described under table 2 in § 176.170(c) of this chapter.	16,000	......do	......do	......do	Do.

(c) The analytical methods for determining whether styrene block polymers conform to the specifications prescribed in this section are as follows and are applicable to the finished polymer.

(1) *Molecular weight.* Molecular weight shall be determined by intrinsic viscosity (or other suitable method).

(2) *Glass transition points.* The glass transition points shall be determined by either of the following methods:

(i) ASTM method D2236–70 (''Standard Method of Test for Dynamic Mechanical Properties of Plastics by Means of Torsional Pendulum,'' which is incorporated by reference; copies are available from American Society for Testing and Materials (ASTM), 100

Barr Harbor Dr., West Conshohocken, Philadelphia, PA 19428-2959, or available for inspection at the National Archives and Records Administration (NARA). For information on the availability of this material at NARA, call 202–741–6030, or go to: *http://www.archives.gov/federal_register/code_of_federal_regulations/ibr_locations.html.*) modified by using a forced resonant vibration instead of a fixed vibration and by using frequencies of 25 to 40 cycles per second instead of 0.1 to 10 cycles per second.

(ii) Direct reading viscoelastometric method titled "Direct Reading Viscoelastrometric Method for Determining Glass Transition Points of Styrene Block Polymers" (which is incorporated by reference; copies are available from the Center for Food Safety and Applied Nutrition (HFS–200), Food and Drug Administration, 5100 Paint Branch Pkwy., College Park, MD 20740, or available for inspection at the National Archives and Records Administration (NARA). For information on the availability of this material at NARA, call 202–741–6030, or go to: *http://www.archives.gov/federal_register/code_of_federal_regulations/ibr_locations.html.*), by which the glass transition points are determined in the tensile mode of deformation at a frequency of 35 hertz using a Rheovibron Model DDV-II (or equivalent) Direct Reading Viscoelastometer. Take maxima in the out-of-phase component of the complex modulus as the glass transition points. For block polymers of low styrene content or for simple block polymers, the polymer may be treated with 0.3 part per hundred dicumyl peroxide and cured for 30 minutes at 153 °C to accentuate the upper transition point.

(3) *Maximum extractable fractions in distilled water and 50 percent ethanol and the maximum net residue solubles in chloroform.* The maximum extractable fractions in distilled water and 50 percent ethanol, and the maximum net residue solubles in chloroform, shall be determined in accordance with § 176.170(d)(3) of this chapter using a sandwich form of the finished copolymer of the specified thickness and for the time and temperature specified in paragraph (b) of this section.

(d) The provisions of this section are not applicable to butadiene-styrene copolymers listed in other sections of this subpart.

(e) The provisions of this section are not applicable to styrene block polymers with 1,3-butadiene listed in § 175.105 of this chapter.

[42 FR 14572, Mar. 15, 1977, as amended at 42 FR 43621, Aug. 30, 1977; 47 FR 11844, Mar. 19, 1982; 51 FR 16828, May 7, 1986; 54 FR 24898, June 12, 1989; 58 FR 65546, Dec. 15, 1993]

§ 177.1820 Styrene-maleic anhydride copolymers.

Styrene-maleic anhydride copolymers identified in paragraph (a) of this section may be safely used as articles or components of articles intended for use in contact with food, subject to provisions of this section.

(a) For the purpose of this section, styrene-maleic anhydride copolymers are those produced by the polymerization of styrene and maleic anhydride so that the finished polymers meet the specifications prescribed in paragraph (b) of this section, when tested by the methods described in paragraph (c) of this section.

(b) *Specifications:*

Styrene-maleic copolymers	Molecular weight (minimum number average)	Residual styrene monomer	Residual maleic anhydride monomer	Maximum extractable fraction in distilled water at specified temperatures, times, and particle size	Maximum extractable fraction in *n*-heptane at specified temperatures, times, and particle size
1. Styrene-maleic anhydride copolymers containing not more than 15 pct maleic anhydride units by weight; for use as articles or as components of articles that contact food of Types I, II, III, IV-A, IV-B, V, VI-B (except carbonated beverages), VII-A, VII-B, VIII, and IX identified in table 1 in § 176.170(c) of this chapter under conditions of use B, C, D, E, F, G, and H described in table 2 in § 176.170(c) of this chapter.	70,000	0.3 weight percent.	0.1 weight percent.	0.006 weight percent at reflux temperature for 1 hr utilizing particles of a size that will pass through a U.S. standard sieve No. 10 and will be held on a U.S. standard sieve No. 20.	0.02 weight percent at 73 °F for 2 hr utilizing particles of a size that will pass through a U.S. standard sieve No. 10 and will be held on a U.S. standard sieve No. 20.
2. Styrene-maleic anhydride copolymer modified with butadiene, (CAS Reg. No. 27288–99–9) containing not more than 15 percent maleic anhydride units by weight and not more than 20 percent styrene-butadiene and/or butadiene rubber units by weight; for use (except carbonated beverage bottles) as articles or as components of articles that contact food of Types I, II, III, IV-A, IV-B, V, VI, VII-A, VII-B, VIII, and IX identified in table I in § 176.170(c) of this chapter under conditions of use B, C, D, E, F, G, and H described in table 2 in § 176.170(c) of this chapter.	....	0.3	0.1	0.015 weight percent at reflux temperature for 1 hour utilizing particles of a size that will pass through a U.S. standard sieve No. 10 and will be held on a U.S. standard sieve No. 20.	1.0 weight percent at 23 °C (73 °F) for 2 hours utilizing particles of a size that will pass through a U.S. standard sieve No. 10 and will be held on a U.S. standard sieve No. 20.

(c) The analytical methods for determining conformance with specifications for styrene-maleic anhydride copolymers prescribed in this section are as follows:

(1) *Molecular weight.* Molecular weight shall be determined by membrane osmometry.

(2) *Residual styrene monomer content.* Residual styrene monomer content shall be determined by the method described in § 177.1640(d).

(3) *Residual maleic anhydride monomer content.* Residual maleic anhydride monomer content shall be determined by a gas chromatographic method titled "Determination of Residual Maleic Anhydride in Polymers by Gas Chromatography," which is incorporated by reference. Copies are available from the Center for Food Safety and Applied Nutrition (HFS–200), Food and Drug Administration, 5100 Paint Branch Pkwy., College Park, MD 20740, or available for inspection at the National Archives and Records Administration (NARA). For information on the availability of this material at NARA, call 202–741–6030, or go to: *http://www.archives.gov/federal_register/code_of_federal_regulations/ibr_locations.html.*

(d) The provisions of this section are not applicable to styrene-maleic anhydride copolymers listed in other sections of this subpart.

[42 FR 14572, Mar. 15, 1977, as amended at 47 FR 11844, Mar. 19, 1982; 47 FR 14698, Apr. 6, 1982; 54 FR 24898, June 12, 1989]

§ 177.1830 Styrene-methyl methacrylate copolymers.

Styrene-methyl methacrylate copolymers identified in this section may be safely used as components of plastic articles intended for use in contact with food, subject to the provisions of this section.

(a) For the purpose of this section, styrene-methyl methacrylate copolymers consist of basic copolymers produced by the copolymerization of styrene and methyl methacrylate such that the finished basic copolymers contain more than 50 weight percent of polymer units derived from styrene.

(b) The finished plastic food-contact article, when extracted with the solvent or solvents characterizing the type of food and under the conditions of time and temperature characterizing the conditions of intended use as determined from tables 1 and 2 of § 176.170(c) of this chapter, yields extractives not to exceed the following when tested by the methods prescribed in § 177.1010(c);

(1) Total nonvolatile extractives not to exceed 0.3 milligram per square inch of surface tested.

(2) Potassium permanganate oxidizable distilled water and 8 and 50 percent alcohol extractives not to exceed an absorbance of 0.15.

(3) Ultraviolet-absorbing distilled water and 8 and 50 percent alcohol extractives not to exceed an absorbance of 0.30.

(4) Ultraviolet-absorbing *n*-heptane extractives not to exceed an absorbance of 0.40.

§ 177.1850 Textryls.

Textryls identified in this section may be safely used as articles or components of articles, intended for use in producing, manufacturing, packing, processing, preparing, treating, packaging, transporting or holding food, subject to the provisions of this section.

(a) Textryls are nonwoven sheets prepared from natural or synthetic fibers, bonded with fibryl (Fibryl consists of a polymeric resin in fibrous form commingled with fiber to facilitate sheet formation and subsequently heat cured to fuse the fibryl and effect bonding).

(b) Textryls are prepared from the fibers, fibryls, and adjuvants identified in paragraph (c) of this section, and subject to limitations prescribed in that paragraph, provided that any substance that is the subject of a regulation in parts 174, 175, 176, 177, 178 and § 179.45 of this chapter conforms with any specifications in such regulation for that substance as a component of polymeric resins used as food contact surfaces.

(c) The fibers, fibryls, and adjuvants permitted are as follows:

Substances	Limitations
(1) Fibers prepared from polyethylene terephthalate resins.	Conforming with § 177.1630.
(2) Fibryls prepared from vinyl chloride-vinyl acetate copolymer.	As the basic polymer.
(3) Adjuvant substance, dimethylformamide.	As a solvent in the preparation of fibryl.

(d) Textryls meeting the conditions of test prescribed in paragraph (d)(1) of this section are used as prescribed in paragraph (d)(2) of this section.

(1) *Conditions of test.* Textryls, when extracted with distilled water at reflux temperature for 1 hour, yield total extractives not to exceed 1 percent.

(2) *Uses.* Textryls are used for packaging or holding food at ordinary temperatures and in the brewing of hot beverages.

§ 177.1900 Urea-formaldehyde resins in molded articles.

Urea-formaldehyde resins may be safely used as the food-contact surface of molded articles intended for use in contact with food, in accordance with the following prescribed conditions:

(a) For the purpose of this section, urea-formaldehyde resins are those produced when 1 mole of urea is made to react with not more than 2 moles of formaldehyde in water solution.

(b) The resins may be mixed with refined wood pulp and the mixture may contain other optional adjuvant substances which may include the following:

List of substances	Limitations
Hexamethylenetetramine	For use only as polymerization-control agent.
Tetrachlorophthalic acid anhydride.	Do.
Zinc stearate	For use as lubricant.

(c) The finished food-contact article, when extracted with the solvent or solvents characterizing the type of food and under the conditions of time and temperature characterizing the conditions of its intended use as determined from tables 1 and 2 of § 175.300(d) of this chapter, yields total extractives in each extracting solvent not to exceed 0.5 milligram per square inch of food-contact surface as determined by the methods described in § 175.300(e) of this chapter.

NOTE: In testing the finished food-contact article, use a separate test sample for each required extracting solvent.

§ 177.1950 Vinyl chloride-ethylene copolymers.

The vinyl chloride-ethylene copolymers identified in paragraph (a) of this section may be safely used as components of articles intended for contact with food, under conditions of use D, E, F, or G described in table 2 of § 176.170 (c) of this chapter, subject to the provisions of this section.

(a) For the purpose of this section, vinyl chloride-ethylene copolymers consist of basic copolymers produced by the copolymerization of vinyl chloride and ethylene such that the finished basic copolymers meet the specifications and extractives limitations prescribed in paragraph (c) of this section, when tested by the methods described in paragraph (d) of this section.

(b) The basic vinyl chloride-ethylene copolymers identified in paragraph (a) of this section may contain optional adjuvant substances required in the production of such basic copolymers. The optional adjuvant substances required in the production of the basic vinyl chloride-ethylene copolymers may include substances permitted for such use by regulations in parts 170 through 189 of this chapter, substances generally recognized as safe in food, and substances used in accordance with a prior sanction or approval.

(c) The vinyl chloride-ethylene basic copolymers meet the following specifications and extractives limitations:

(1) *Specifications.* (i) Total chlorine content is in the range of 53 to 56 percent as determined by any suitable analytical procedure of generally accepted applicability.

(ii) Intrinsic viscosity in cyclohexanone at 30 °C is not less than 0.50 deciliter per gram as determined by ASTM method D1243–79, "Standard Test Method for Dilute Solution Viscosity of Vinyl Chloride Polymers," which is incorporated by reference. Copies may be obtained from the American Society for Testing Materials, 100 Barr Harbor Dr., West Conshohocken, Philadelphia, PA 19428-2959, or may be examined at the National Archives and Records Administration (NARA). For information on the availability of this material at NARA, call 202–741–6030, or go to: *http://www.archives.gov/federal_register/code_of_federal_regulations/ibr_locations.html.*

(2) *Extractives limitations.* The following extractives limitations are determined by the methods described in paragraph (d) of this section:

(i) Total extractives do not exceed 0.10 weight-percent when extracted with *n*-heptane at 150 °F for 2 hours.

(ii) Total extractives do not exceed 0.03 weight-percent when extracted with water at 150 °F for 2 hours.

(iii) Total extractives obtained by extracting with water at 150 °F for 2 hours contain no more than 0.5 milligram of vinyl chloride-ethylene copolymer per 100 grams of sample tested as determined from the organic chlorine content. The organic chlorine content is determined as described in paragraph (d)(3) of this section.

(d) Analytical methods: The analytical methods for determining whether vinyl chloride-ethylene basic copolymers conform to the extractives limitations prescribed in paragraph (c) of this section are as follows and are applicable to the basic copolymers in powder form having a particle size such that 100 percent will pass through a U.S. Standard Sieve No. 40 and 80 percent will pass through a U.S. Standard Sieve No. 80:

(1) *Reagents*—(i) *Water.* All water used in these procedures shall be demineralized (deionized), freshly distilled water.

(ii) *n-Heptane.* Reagent grade, freshly distilled *n*-heptane shall be used.

(2) *Determination of total amount of extractives.* All determinations shall be done in duplicate using duplicate blanks. Approximately 400 grams of sample (accurately weighed) shall be placed in a 2-liter Erlenmeyer flask. Add 1,200 milliliters of solvent and cover the flask with aluminum foil. The covered flask and contents are suspended in a thermostated bath and are kept, with continual shaking at 150 °F for 2 hours. The solution is then filtered through a No. 42 Whatman filter paper, and the filtrate is collected in a graduated cylinder. The total amount of filtrate (without washing) is measured and called *A* milliliters. The filtrate is transferred to a Pyrex (or equivalent) beaker and evaporated on a steam bath under a stream of nitrogen

to a small volume (approximately 50–60 milliliters). The concentrated filtrate is then quantitatively transferred to a tared 100-milliliter Pyrex beaker using small, fresh portions of solvent and a rubber policeman to effect the transfer. The concentrated filtrate is evaporated almost to dryness on a hotplate under nitrogen, and is then transferred to a drying oven at 230 °F in the case of the aqueous extract or to a vacuum oven at 150 °F in the case of the heptane extract. In the case of the aqueous extract, the evaporation to constant weight is completed in 15 minutes at 230 °F; and in the case of heptane extract, it is overnight under vacuum at 150 °F. The residue is weighed and corrected for the solvent blank. Calculation:

$$\frac{\text{Grams of corrected residue}}{\text{Grams of sample}} \times \frac{\text{1,200 milliliters}}{\text{Volume of filtrate A in milliliters}} \times 100 = \text{Total extractives expressed as percent by weight of sample.}$$

(3) *Vinyl chloride-ethylene copolymer content of aqueous extract*—(i) *Principle.* The vinyl chloride-ethylene copolymer content of the aqueous extract can be determined by determining the organic chlorine content and calculating the amount of copolymer equivalent to the organic chlorine content.

(ii) *Total organic chlorine content.* A weighed sample of approximately 400 grams is extracted with 1,200 milliliters of water at 150 °F for 2 hours, filtered, and the volume of filtrate is measured (*A* milliliters) as described in paragraph (d)(2) of this section.

(*a*) A slurry of Amberlite IRA–400, or equivalent, is made with distilled water in a 150-milliliter beaker. The slurry is added to a chromatographic column until it is filled to about half its length. This should give a volume of resin of 15–25 milliliters. The liquid must not be allowed to drain below the top of the packed column.

(*b*) The column is regenerated to the basic (OH) form by slowly passing through it (10–15 milliliters per minute) 10 grams of sodium hydroxide dissolved in 200 milliliters of water. The column is washed with distilled water until the effluent is neutral to phenolphthalein. One drop of methyl red indicator is added to the *A* milliliters of filtered aqueous extract and, if on the basic side (yellow), nitric acid is added drop by drop until the solution turns pink.

(*c*) The extract is deionized by passing it through the exchange column at a rate of 10–15 milliliters per minute. The column is washed with 200 milliliters of distilled water. The deionized extract and washings are collected in a 1,500-milliliter beaker. The solution is evaporated carefully on a steam plate to a volume of approximately 50 milliliters and then transferred quantitatively, a little at a time, to a clean 22-milliliter Parr cup, also on the steam plate. The solution is evaporated to dryness. Next 0.25 gram of sucrose and 0.5 gram of benzoic acid are added to the cup. One scoop (approximately 15 grams) of sodium peroxide is then added to the cup. The bomb is assembled and ignition is conducted in the usual fashion.

(*d*) After the bomb has cooled, it is rinsed thoroughly with distilled water and disassembled. The top of the bomb is rinsed into a 250-milliliter beaker with distilled water. The beaker is placed on the steam plate. The bomb cup is placed in the beaker and carefully tipped over to allow the water to leach out the combustion mixture. After the bubbling has stopped, the cup is removed from the beaker and rinsed thoroughly. The solution is cooled to room temperature and cautiously neutralized with concentrated nitric acid by slowly pouring the acid down a stirring rod until the bubbling ceases. The solution is cooled and an equal volume of acetone is added.

(*e*) The solution is titrated with 0.005 *N* silver nitrate using standard potentiometric titration techniques with a silver electrode as indicator and a potassium nitrate modified calomel electrode as a reference electrode. An expanded scale recording titrimeter.

Metrohm Potentiograph 2336 or equivalent, should be used; a complete blank must be run in duplicate.

(iii) *Calculations.*

$$\frac{\text{Milligrams of aqueous extracted}}{\text{copolymer per 100-gram sample}} = \frac{T \times F \times 64.3}{\text{Weight of sample in grams}} \times 100$$

where:

T=Milliliters of silver nitrate (sample minus blank)×normality of silver nitrate.

F=1,200/A (as defined above)

(e) The vinyl chloride-ethylene copolymers identified in and complying with this section, when used as components of the food-contact surface of any article that is the subject of a regulation in parts 174, 175, 176, 177, 178 and §179.45 of this chapter, shall comply with any specifications and limitations prescribed by such regulation for the article in the finished form in which it is to contact food.

(f) The provisions of this section are not applicable to vinyl chloride-ethylene copolymers used as provided in §§175.105 and 176.180 of this chapter.

[42 FR 14572, Mar. 15, 1977, as amended at 49 FR 10110, Mar. 19, 1984]

§ 177.1960 Vinyl chloride-hexene-1 copolymers.

The vinyl chloride-hexene-1 copolymers identified in paragraph (a) of this section or as components of articles intended for use in contact with food, under conditions of use D, E, F, or G described in table 2 of §176.170(c) of this chapter, subject to the provisions of this section.

(a) *Identity.* For the purposes of this section vinyl chloride-hexene-1 copolymers consist of basic copolymers produced by the copolymerization of vinyl chloride and hexene-1 such that the finished copolymers contain not more than 3 mole-percent of polymer units derived from hexene-1 and meet the specifications and extractives limitations prescribed in paragraph (b) of this section. The copolymers may optionally contain hydroxypropyl methylcellulose and trichloroethylene used as a suspending agent and chain transfer agent, respectively, in their production.

(b) *Specifications and limitations.* The vinyl chloride-hexene-1 basic copolymers meet the following specifications and extractives limitations:

(1) *Specifications.* (i) Total chlorine content is 53 to 56 percent as determined by any suitable analytical procedure of generally accepted applicability.

(ii) Inherent viscosity in cyclohexanone at 30 °C is not less than 0.59 deciliters per gram as determined by ASTM method D1243–79, "Standard Test Method for Dilute Solution Viscosity of Vinyl Chloride Polymers," which is incorporated by reference. Copies may be obtained from the American Society for Testing Materials, 100 Barr Harbor Dr., West Conshohocken, Philadelphia, PA 19428-2959, or may be examined at the National Archives and Records Administration (NARA). For information on the availability of this material at NARA, call 202–741–6030, or go to: *http://www.archives.gov/federal_register/code_of_federal_regulations/ibr_locations.html.*

(2) *Extractives limitations.* The following extractives limitations are determined by the methods prescribed in §177.1970(d).

(i) Total extractives do not exceed 0.01 weight percent when extracted with water at 150 °F for 2 hours.

(ii) Total extractives do not exceed 0.30 weight percent when extracted with *n*-heptane at 150 °F for 2 hours.

(c) *Other specifications and limitations.* The vinyl chloride-hexene-1 copolymers identified in and complying with this section, when used as components of the food-contact surface of any article that is subject to a regulation in parts 174, 175, 176, 177, 178 and §179.45 of this chapter, shall comply with any specifications and limitations prescribed by such regulation for the article in the finished form in which it is to contact food.

[42 FR 14572, Mar. 15, 1977, as amended at 49 FR 10110, Mar. 19, 1984]

§ 177.1970 Vinyl chloride-lauryl vinyl ether copolymers.

The vinyl chloride-lauryl vinyl ether copolymers identified in paragraph (a) of this section may be used as an article or as a component of an article intended for use in contact with food subject to the provisions of this section.

(a) *Identity.* For the purposes of this section vinyl chloride-lauryl vinyl ether copolymers consist of basic copolymers produced by the copolymerization of vinyl chloride and lauryl vinyl ether such that the finished copolymers contain not more than 3 weight-percent of polymer units derived from lauryl vinyl ether and meet the specifications and extractives limitations prescribed in paragraph (c) of this section.

(b) *Optional adjuvant substances.* The basic vinyl chloride-lauryl vinyl ether copolymers identified in paragraph (a) of this section may contain optional adjuvant substances required in the production of such basic copolymers. These optional adjuvant substances may include substances permitted for such use by regulations in parts 170 through 189 of this chapter, substances generally recognized as safe in food, and substances used in accordance with a prior sanction or approval.

(c) *Specifications and limitations.* The vinyl chloride-lauryl vinyl ether basic copolymers meet the following specifications and extractives limitations:

(1) *Specifications.* (i) Total chlorine content is 53 to 56 percent as determined by any suitable analytical procedure of generally accepted applicability.

(ii) Inherent viscosity in cylcoHhexanone at 30 °C is not less than 0.60 deciliter per gram as determined by ASTM method D1243–79, "Standard Test Method for Dilute Solution Viscosity of Vinyl Chloride Polymers," which is incorporated by reference. Copies may be obtained from the American Society for Testing Materials, 100 Barr Harbor Dr., West Conshohocken, Philadelphia, PA 19428-2959, or may be examined at the National Archives and Records Administration (NARA). For information on the availability of this material at NARA, call 202–741–6030, or go to: *http://www.archives.gov/federal_register/code_of_federal_regulations/ibr_locations.html.*

(2) *Extractives limitations.* The following extractives limitations are determined by the method described in paragraph (d) of this section:

(i) Total extractives do not exceed 0.03 weight-percent when extracted with water at 150 °F for 2 hours.

(ii) Total extractives do not exceed 0.60 weight-percent when extracted with *n*-heptane at 150 °F for 2 hours.

(d) *Analytical methods.* The analytical methods for determining total extractives are applicable to the basic copolymers in powder form having a particle size such that 100 percent will pass through a U.S. Standard Sieve No. 40 and such that not more than 10 percent will pass through a U.S. Standard Sieve No. 200.

(1) *Reagents*—(i) *Water.* All water used in these procedures shall be demineralized (deionized), freshly distilled water.

(ii) *n-Heptane.* Reagent grade, freshly distilled *n*-heptane shall be used.

(2) *Determination of total amount of extractives.* Place an accurately weighed sample of suitable size in a clean borosilicate flask, and for each gram of sample add 3 milliliters of solvent previously heated to 150 °F. Maintain the temperature of the contents of the flask at 150 °F for 2 hours using a hot plate while also maintaining gentle mechanical agitation. Filter the contents of the flask rapidly through No. 42 Whatman filter paper with the aid of suction. Transfer the filtrate to flat glass dishes that are warmed on a hot plate and evaporate the solvent with the aid of a stream of filtered air. When the volume of the filtrate has been reduced to 10 to 15 milliliters, transfer the filtrate to tared 50-milliliter borosilicate glass beakers and complete evaporation to a constant weight in a 140 °F vacuum oven. Carry out a corresponding blank determination with each solvent. Determine the weight of the residue corrected for the

solvent blank and calculate the result as percent of the initial weight of the resin sample taken for analysis.

(e) *Other specifications and limitations.* The vinyl chloride-lauryl vinyl ether copolymers identified in and complying with this section, when used as components of the food-contact surface of any article that is subject to a regulation in parts 174, 175, 176, 177, 178 and § 179.45 of this chapter, shall comply with any specifications and limitations prescribed by such regulation for the article in the finished form in which it is to contact food.

[42 FR 14572, Mar. 15, 1977, as amended at 49 FR 10110, Mar. 19, 1984]

§ 177.1980 Vinyl chloride-propylene copolymers.

The vinyl chloride-propylene copolymers identified in paragraph (a) of this section may be safely used as components of articles intended for contact with food, subject to the provisions of this section.

(a) For the purpose of this section, vinyl chloride-propylene copolymers consist of basic copolymers produced by the copolymezation of vinyl chloride and propylene such that the finished basic copolymers meet the specifications and extractives limitations prescribed in paragraph (c) of this section, when tested by the methods described in paragraph (d) of this section.

(b) The basic vinyl chloride-propylene copolymers identified in paragraph (a) of this section may contain optional adjuvant substances required in the production of such basic copolymers. The optional adjuvant substances required in the production of the basic vinyl chloride-propylene copolymers may include substances permitted for such use by regulations in parts 170 through 189 of this chapter, substances generally recognized as safe in food, and substances used in accordance with a prior sanction or approval.

(c) The vinyl chloride-propylene basic copolymers meet the following specifications and extractives limitations:

(1) *Specifications.* (i) Total chlorine content is in the range of 53 to 56 percent as determined by any suitable analytical procedure of generally accepted applicability.

(ii) Intrinsic viscosity in cyclohexanone at 30 °C is not less than 0.50 deciliter per gram as determined by ASTM method D1243–79, "Standard Test Method for Dilute Solution Viscosity of Vinyl Chloride Polymers," which is incorporated by reference. Copies may be obtained from the American Society for Testing Materials, 100 Barr Harbor Dr., West Conshohocken, Philadelphia, PA 19428-2959, or may be examined at the National Archives and Records Administration (NARA). For information on the availability of this material at NARA, call 202–741–6030, or go to: *http://www.archives.gov/federal_register/code_of_federal_regulations/ibr_locations.html.*

(2) *Extractives limitations.* The following extractives limitations are determined by the methods described in paragraph (d) of this section:

(i) Total extractives do not exceed 0.10 weight-percent when extracted with *n*-heptane at 150 °F for 2 hours.

(ii) Total extractives do not exceed 0.03 weight-percent when extracted with water at 150 °F for 2 hours.

(iii) Total extractives obtained by extracting with water at 150 °F for 2 hours contain no more than 0.17 milligram of vinyl chloride-propylene copolymer per 100 grams of sample tested as determined from the organic chlorine content. For the purpose of this section, the organic chlorine content is the difference between the total chlorine and ionic chlorine contents determined as described in paragraph (d) of this section.

(d) Analytical methods: The analytical methods for determining whether vinyl chloride-propylene basic copolymers conform to the extractives limitations prescribed in paragraph (c) of this section are as follows and are applicable to the basic copolymers in powder form having a particle size such that 100 percent will pass through a U.S. Standard Sieve No. 40 and 80 percent will pass through a U.S. Standard Sieve No. 80:

(1) *Reagents*—(i) *Water.* All water used in these procedures shall be demineralized (deionized), freshly distilled water.

(ii) *n-Heptane.* Reagent grade, freshly distilled *n*-heptane shall be used.

(2) *Determination of total amount of extractives.* All determinations shall be done in duplicate using duplicate blanks. Approximately 400 grams of sample (accurately weighed) shall be placed in a 2-liter Erlenmeyer flask. Add 1,200 milliliters of solvent and cover the flask with aluminum foil. The covered flask and contents are suspended in a thermostated bath and are kept, with continual shaking, at 150 °F for 2 hours. The solution is then filtered through a No. 42 Whatman filter paper, and the filtrate is collected in a graduated cylinder. The total amount of filtrate (without washing) is measured and called *A* milliliters. The filtrate is transferred to a Pyrex (or equivalent) beaker and evaporated on a steam bath under a stream of nitrogen to a small volume (approximately 50–60 milliliters). The concentrated filtrate is then quantitatively transferred to a tared 100-milliliter Pyrex beaker using small, fresh portions of solvent and a rubber policeman to effect the transfer. The concentrated filtrate is evaporated almost to dryness on a hotplate under nitrogen, and is then transferred to a drying oven at 230 °F in the case of the aqueous extract or to a vacuum oven at 150 °F in the case of the heptane extract. In the case of the aqueous extract the evaporation to constant weight is completed in 15 minutes at 230 °F; and in the case of heptane extract, it is overnight under vacuum at 150 °F. The residue is weighed and corrected for the solvent blank. Calculation:

$$\frac{\text{Grams of corrected residue}}{\text{Grams of sample}} \times \frac{1{,}200 \text{ milliliters}}{\text{Volume of filtrate } A \text{ in milliliters}} \times 100 = \text{Total extractives expressed as percent by weight of sample.}$$

(3) *Vinyl chloride-propylene copolymer content of aqueous extract*—(i) *Principle.* The vinyl chloride-propylene copolymer content of the aqueous extract can be determined by determining the organic chlorine content and calculating the amount of copolymer equivalent to the organic chlorine content. The organic chlorine content is the difference between the total chlorine content and the ionic chlorine content.

(ii) *Total chlorine content.* A weighed sample is extracted with water at 150 °F for 2 hours, filtered, and the volume of filtrate is measured (*A* milliliters) as described in paragraph (d)(2) of this section. Two drops of 50 percent by weight sodium hydroxide solution are added to prevent loss of chloride from ammonium chloride, if present, and the solution is evaporated to approximately 15 milliliters. The concentrated filtrate is quantitatively transferred to a 22-milliliter Parr bomb fusion cup and gently evaporated to dryness. To the contents of the cup are added 3.5 grams of granular sodium peroxide, 0.1 gram of powdered starch, and 0.02 gram potassium nitrate; and the contents are mixed thoroughly. The bomb is assembled, water is added to the recess at the top of the bomb and ignition is conducted in the usual fashion using a Meeker burner. The heating is continued for 1 minute after the water at the top has evaporated. The bomb is quenched in water, rinsed with distilled water, and placed in a 400-milliliter beaker. The bomb cover is rinsed with water, catching the washings in the same 400-milliliter beaker. The bomb is covered with distilled water and a watch glass and heated until the melt has dissolved. The bomb is removed, rinsed, catching the rinsings in the beaker, and the solution is acidified with concentrated nitric acid using methyl purple as an indicator. The beaker is covered with a watch glass, and the contents are boiled gently for 10–15 minutes. After cooling to room temperature the solution is made slightly alkaline with 50 percent by weight sodium hydroxide solution, then acidified with dilute (1:5) nitric acid. Then 1.5 milliliters of 2 *N* nitric acid per 100 milliliters of solution is added and the solution is titrated with 0.005 *N* silver nitrate to the equivalence potential end point using an expanded scale pH meter (Beckman Model 76, or equivalent). A complete blank must be run in duplicate. Calculation:

$$\frac{\text{Grams of sample}}{(B-C)} \times \frac{\text{1,200 milliliters}}{\text{Volume of filtrate } A \text{ in milliliters}} \times 100 = \text{Milliequivalents of total chlorine in aqueous extract of 100 grams of sample}$$

where:

A=volume of filtrate obtained in extraction.
B=milliliters of silver nitrate solution used in sample titration×normality of silver nitrate solution.
C=milliliters of silver nitrate solution used in blank titration×normality of silver nitrate solution.

(iii) *Ionic chlorine content.* A weighed sample is extracted with water at 150 °F for 2 hours, filtered, and the volume of filtrate is measured (*A* milliliters) as in paragraph (d)(2) of this section. Two drops of 50 percent by weight sodium hydroxide solution are added and the solution is evaporated to approximately 150 milliliters. The solution is quantitatively transferred to a 250-milliliter beaker, methyl purple indicator is added, and the solution is neutralized with 0.1 *N* nitric acid. For each 100 milliliters of solution is added 1.5 milliliters of 2 *N* nitric acid. The solution is titrated with 0.005 *N* silver nitrate to the equivalence potential end point, using the expanded scale pH meter described in paragraph (d)(3)(ii) of this section. A complete blank must be run in duplicate. Calculation:

$$\frac{D-E}{\text{Grams of sample}} \times \frac{\text{1,200 milliliters}}{\text{Volume of filtrate } A \text{ in milliliters}} \times 100 = \text{Milliequivalents of ionic chlorine in aqueous extract of 100 grams of sample.}$$

where:

A=volume of filtrate obtained in extraction.
D=milliliters of silver nitrate solution used in sample titration×normality of silver nitrate solution.
E=milliliters of silver nitrate solution used in blank titration×normality of silver nitrate solution.

(iv) *Organic chlorine content and vinyl chloride-propylene copolymer content of aqueous extract.* The organic chlorine content and the vinyl chloride propylene copolymer content of the aqueous extract is calculated as follows:

(*a*) *Organic chlorine content.* Milliequivalents of organic chlorine in aqueous extract of 100 grams of sample equal milliequivalents of total chlorine in aqueous extract of 100 grams of sample (as calculated in paragraph (d)(3)(ii) of this section) minus milliequivalents of ionic chlorine in aqueous extract of 100 grams of sample (as calculated in paragraph (d)(3)(iii) of this section).

(*b*) *Vinyl chloride-propylene copolymer content.* Milligrams of vinyl chloride-propylene copolymer in aqueous extract of 100 grams of sample equal milliequivalents of organic chlorine in aqueous extract of 100 grams of sample (as calculated in paragraph (d)(3)(iv) (*a*) of this section) multiplied by 84.5.

NOTE: The conversion factor, 84.5, is derived from the equivalent weight of chlorine divided by the chlorine content of the heptane extractable fraction.)

(e) The vinyl chloride-propylene copolymers identified in and complying with this section, when used as components of the food-contact surface of any article that is the subject of a regulation in parts 174, 175, 176, 177, 178 and § 179.45 of this chapter, shall comply with any specifications and limitations prescribed by such regulation for the article in the finished form in which it is to contact food.

(f) The provisions of this section are not applicable to vinyl chloride-propylene copolymers used in food-packaging adhesives complying with § 175.105 of this chapter.

[42 FR 14572, Mar. 15, 1977, as amended at 49 FR 10111, Mar. 19, 1984]

§ 177.1990 Vinylidene chloride/methyl acrylate copolymers.

The vinylidene chloride/methyl acrylate copolymers (CAS Reg. No. 25038–72–6) identified in paragraph (a) of this section may be safely used as an article or as a component of an article intended for use in contact with food subject to the provisions of this section.

(a) *Identity.* For the purposes of this section vinylidene chloride/methyl acrylate copolymers consist of basic copolymers produced by the copolymerization of vinylidene chloride and methyl acrylate such that the copolymers contain not more than 15 weight-percent of polymer units derived from methyl acrylate.

(b) *Optional adjuvant substances.* The basic vinylidene chloride/methyl acrylate copolymers identified in paragraph (a) of this section may contain optional adjuvant substances required in the production of such basic copolymers. These optional adjuvant substances may include substances permitted for such use by regulations in parts 170 through 179 of this chapter, substances generally recognized as safe in food, and substances used in accordance with a prior sanction or approval.

(c) *Specifications.* (1) The methyl acrylate content is determined by an infrared spectrophotometric method titled "Determination of Copolymer Ratio in Vinylidene Chloride/Methyl Acrylate Copolymers," which is incorporated by reference. Copies are available from the Center for Food Safety and Applied Nutrition (HFS–200), Food and Drug Administration, 5100 Paint Branch Pkwy., College Park, MD 20740, or available for inspection at the National Archives and Records Administration (NARA). For information on the availability of this material at NARA, call 202–741–6030, or go to: *http://www.archives.gov/federal_register/code_of_federal_regulations/ibr_locations.html.*

(2) The weight average molecular weight of the copolymer is not less than 50,000 when determined by gel permeation chromatography using tetrahydrofuran as the solvent. The gel permeation chromatograph is calibrated with polystyrene standards. The basic gel permeation chromatographic method is described in ANSI/ASTM D3536–76, "Standard Test Method for Molecular Weight Averages and Molecular Weight Distribution of Polystyrene by Liquid Exclusion Chromatography (Gel Permeation Chromatography-GPC)," which is incorporated by reference. Copies are available from University Microfilms International, 300 North Zeeb Rd., Ann Arbor, MI 48106, or available for inspection at the National Archives and Records Administration (NARA). For information on the availability of this material at NARA, call 202–741–6030, or go to: *http://www.archives.gov/federal_register/code_of_federal_regulations/ibr_locations.html.*

(3) Residual vinylidene chloride and residual methyl acrylate in the copolymer in the form in which it will contact food (unsupported film, barrier layer, or as a copolymer for blending) will not exceed 10 parts per million and 5 parts per million, respectively, as determined by either a gas chromatographic method titled "Determination of Residual Vinylidene Chloride and Methyl Acrylate in Vinylidene Chloride/Methyl Acrylate Copolymer Resins and Films," or, alternatively, "Residual Methyl Acrylate and Vinylidene Chloride Monomers in Saran MA/VDC Resins and Pellets by Headspace Gas Chromatography," dated March 3, 1986, which are incorporated by reference in accordance with 5 U.S.C. 552(a). Copies are available from the Center for Food Safety and Applied Nutrition (HFS–200), Food and Drug Administration, 5100 Paint Branch Pkwy., College Park, MD 20740, or available for inspection at the National Archives and Records Administration (NARA). For information on the availability of this material at NARA, call 202–741–6030, or go to: *http://www.archives.gov/federal_register/code_of_federal_regulations/ibr_locations.html.*

(d) *Extractives limitations*. The basic copolymer resin in the form of granules that will pass through a U.S. Standard Sieve No. 45 (350 microns) shall meet the following extractives limitations:

(1) 10-gram samples of the resin, when extracted separately with 100 milliliters of distilled water at 121 °C (250 °F) for 2 hours, and 100 milliliters of *n*-heptane at 66 °C (150 °F) for 2 hours, shall yield total nonvolatile extractives not to exceed 0.5 percent by weight of the resin.

(2) The basic copolymer in the form of film when extracted separately with distilled water at 121 °C (250 °F) for 2 hours shall yield total nonvolatile extractives not to exceed 0.047 milligram per square centimeter (0.3 milligram per square inch).

(e) *Conditions of use*. The copolymers may be safely used as articles or components of articles intended for use in producing, manufacturing, processing, preparing, treating, packaging, transporting, or holding food, including processing of packaged food at temperatures not to exceed 135 °C (275 °F).

(f) *Other specifications and limitations*. The vinylidene chloride-methyl acrylate copolymers identified in and complying with this section, when used as components of the food contact surface of any article that is subject to a regulation in parts 174 through 178 and §179.45 of this chapter, shall comply with any specifications and limitations prescribed by such regulation for the article in the finished form in which it is to contact food.

[48 FR 38605, Aug. 25, 1983; 48 FR 50077, Oct. 31, 1983, as amended at 53 FR 47185, Nov. 22, 1988; 54 FR 24898, June 12, 1989]

§ 177.2000 Vinylidene chloride/methyl acrylate/methyl methacrylate polymers.

The vinylidene chloride/methyl acrylate/methyl methacrylate polymers (CAS Reg. No. 34364–83–5) identified in paragraph (a) of this section may be safely used as articles or as a component of articles intended for use in contact with food subject to the provisions of this section.

(a) *Identity*. For the purpose of this section, vinylidene chloride/methyl acrylate/methyl methacrylate polymers consist of basic polymers produced by the copolymerization of vinylidene chloride/methyl acrylate/methyl methacrylate such that the basic polymers or the finished food-contact articles meet the specifications prescribed in paragraph (d) of this section.

(b) *Optional adjuvant substances*. The basic vinylidene chloride/methyl acrylate/methyl methacrylate polymers identified in paragraph (a) of this section may contain optional adjuvant substances required in the production of such basic polymers. These optional adjuvant substances may include substances permitted for such use by regulations in parts 170 through 179 of this chapter, substances generally recognized as safe in food, and substances used in accordance with a prior sanction of approval.

(c) *Conditions of use*. The polymers may be safely used as articles or as components of articles intended for use in producing, manufacturing, processing, preparing, treating, packaging, transporting, or holding food, including processing of packaged food at temperatures up to 121 °C (250 °F).

(d) *Specifications and limitations*. The vinylidene chloride/methyl acrylate/methyl methacrylate basic polymers and/or finished food-contact articles meet the following specifications and limitations:

(1)(i) The basic vinylidene chloride/methyl acrylate/methyl methacrylate polymers contain not more than 2 weight percent of polymer units derived from methyl acrylate monomer and not more than 6 weight percent of polymer units derived from methyl methacrylate monomer.

(ii) The basic polymers are limited to a thickness of not more than 0.005 centimeter (0.002 inches).

(2) The weight average molecular weight of the basic polymer is not less than 100,000 when determined by gel permeation chromatography using tetrahydrofuran as the solvent. The gel permeation chromatography is calibrated with polystyrene standards. The basic gel permeation chromatographic method is described in ANSI/ASTM D3536–76, which is incorporated by reference. Copies are available from the American Society for Testing Materials, 100 Barr Harbor Dr., West Conshohocken, Philadelphia, PA 19428-

2959, or available for inspection at the National Archives and Records Administration (NARA). For information on the availability of this material at NARA, call 202–741–6030, or go to: *http://www.archives.gov/federal_register/code_of_federal_regulations/ibr_locations.html.*

(3) The basic polymer or food-contact article described in paragraph (a) of this section, when extracted with the solvent or solvents characterizing the type of food and under the conditions of time and temperature characterizing the conditions of its intended use as determined from tables 1 and 2 of §176.170(c) of this chapter, yields net chloroform-soluble extractives in each extracting solvent not to exceed .08 milligram per square centimeter (0.5 milligram per square inch) of food-contact surface when tested by the methods described in §176.170(d). If the finished food-contact article is itself the subject of a regulation in parts 174 through 178 and §179.45 of this chapter, it shall also comply with any specifications and limitations prescribed for it by the regulation.

[49 FR 29578, July 23, 1984]

Subpart C—Substances for Use Only as Components of Articles Intended for Repeated Use

§ 177.2210 Ethylene polymer, chlorosulfonated.

Ethylene polymer, chlorosulfonated as identified in this section may be safely used as an article or component of articles intended for use in contact with food, subject to the provisions of this section.

(a) Ethylene polymer, chlorosulfonated is produced by chlorosulfonation of a carbon tetrachloride solution of polyethylene with chlorine and sulfuryl chloride.

(b) Ethylene polymer, chlorosulfonated shall meet the following specifications:

(1) Chlorine not to exceed 25 percent by weight.

(2) Sulfur not to exceed 1.15 percent by weight.

(3) Molecular weight is in the range of 95,000 to 125,000.

Methods for the specifications in this paragraph (b), titled "Chlorine and Bromine—Coulometric Titration Method by Aminco Chloridometer," "Hypolon® Synthetic Rubber—Determination of Sulfur by Parr Bomb," and ASTM method D2857–70 (Reapproved 1977), "Standard Test Method for Dilute Solution Viscosity of Polymers," are incorporated by reference. Copies of the ASTM method may be obtained from the American Society for Testing Materials, 100 Barr Harbor Dr., West Conshohocken, Philadelphia, PA 19428-2959. Copies of the other two methods are available from the Center for Food Safety and Applied Nutrition (HFS-200), Food and Drug Administration, 5100 Paint Branch Pkwy., College Park, MD 20740. Copies of all three methods may be examined at the National Archives and Records Administration (NARA). For information on the availability of this material at NARA, call 202–741–6030, or go to: *http://www.archives.gov/federal_register/code_of_federal_regulations/ibr_locations.html.*

(c) The additive is used as the article, or a component of articles, intended for use as liners and covers for reservoirs intended for the storage of water for drinking purposes.

(d) Substances permitted by §177.2600 may be employed in the preparation of ethylene polymers, chlorosulfonated, subject to any limitations prescribed therein.

(e) The finished ethylene copolymers, chlorosulfonated shall conform to §177.2600(e) and (g).

[42 FR 14572, Mar. 15, 1977, as amended at 49 FR 10111, Mar. 19, 1984; 54 FR 24898, June 12, 1989]

§ 177.2250 Filters, microporous polymeric.

Microporous polymeric filters identified in paragraph (a) of this section may be safely used, subject to the provisions of this section, to remove particles of insoluble matter in producing, manufacturing, processing, and preparing bulk quantities of liquid food.

(a) Microporous polymeric filters consist of a suitably permeable, continuous, polymeric matrix of polyvinyl chloride, vinyl chloride-propylene, or vinyl chloride-vinyl acetate, in which finely divided silicon dioxide is embedded. Cyclohexanone may be used as a solvent in the production of the filters.

(b) Any substance employed in the production of microporous polymeric filters that is the subject of a regulation in parts 170 through 189 of this chapter must conform with any specification in such regulation.

(c) Cyclohexanone when used as a solvent in the production of the filters shall not exceed 0.35 percent by weight of the microporous polymeric filters.

(d) The microporous polymeric filters may be colored with colorants used in accordance with § 178.3297 of this chapter.

(e) The temperature of food being processed through the microporous polymeric filters shall not exceed 180 °F.

(f) The microporous polymeric filters shall be maintained in a sanitary manner in accordance with good manufacturing practice so as to prevent potential microbial adulteration of the food.

(g) To assure safe use of the microporous polymeric filters, the label or labeling shall include adequate directions for a pre-use treatment, consisting of washing with a minimum of 2 gallons of potable water at a temperature of 180 °F for each square foot of filter, prior to the filter's first use in contact with food.

[42 FR 14572, Mar. 15, 1977, as amended at 56 FR 42933, Aug. 30, 1991]

§ 177.2260 Filters, resin-bonded.

Resin-bonded filters may be safely used in producing, manufacturing, processing, and preparing food, subject to the provisions of this section.

(a) Resin-bonded filters are prepared from natural or synthetic fibers to which have been added substances required in their preparation and finishing, and which are bonded with resins prepared by condensation or polymerization of resin-forming materials, together with adjuvant substances required in their preparation, application, and curing.

(b) The quantity of any substance employed in the production of the resin-bonded filter does not exceed the amount reasonably required to accomplish the intended physical or technical effect or any limitation further provided.

(c) Any substance employed in the production of resin-bonded filters that is the subject of a regulation in parts 174, 175, 176, 177, 178 and § 179.45 of this chapter conforms with any specification in such regulation.

(d) Substances employed in the production of resin-bonded filters include the following, subject to any limitations provided:

LIST OF SUBSTANCES AND LIMITATIONS

(1) *Fibers:*

Cellulose pulp.
Cotton.
Nylon. (From nylon resins complying with the provisions of applicable regulations in subchapter B of this chapter.
Polyethylene terephthalate complying in composition with the provisions of § 177.1630; for use in inline filtration only as provided for in paragraphs (e) and (f) of this section.
Rayon (viscose).

(2) *Substances employed in fiber finishing:*

BHT.
Butyl (or isobutyl) palmitate or stearate.
2,5-Di-*tert*-butyl hydroquinone for use only in lubricant formulations for rayon fiber finishing and at a usage level not to exceed 0.1 percent by weight of the lubricant formulations.
Dimethylpolysiloxane.
4-Ethyl-4-hexadecyl morpholinium ethyl sulfate for use only as a lubricant in the manufacture of polyethylene terephthalate fibers specified in paragraph (d)(1) of this section at a level not to exceed 0.03 percent by weight of the finished fibers.
Fatty acid (C_{10}-C_{18}) diethanolamide condensates.
Fatty acids derived from animal or vegetable fats and oils, and salts of such acids, single or mixed, as follows:
Aluminum.
Ammonium.
Calcium.
Magnesium.
Potassium.
Sodium.
Triethanolamine.
Fatty acid (C_{10}-C_{18}) mono- and diesters of polyoxyethylene glycol (molecular weight 400–3,000).
Methyl esters of fatty acids (C_{10}-C_{18}).
Mineral oil.
Polybutene, hydrogenated; complying with the identity prescribed under § 178.3740 (b) of this chapter.
Polyoxyethylene (4 mols) ethylenediamine monolauramide for use only in lubricant formulations for rayon fiber finishing and

at a usage level not to exceed 10 percent by weight of the lubricant formulations.
Ricebran oil.
Titanium dioxide.

(3) *Resins:*

Acrylic polymers produced by polymerizing ethyl acrylate alone or with one or more of the monomers: Acrylic acid, acrylonitrile, *N*-methylolacrylamide, and styrene. The finished copolymers shall contain at least 70 weight percent of polymer units derived from ethyl acrylate, no more than 2 weight percent of total polymer units derived from acrylic acid, no more than 10 weight percent of total polymer units derived from acrylonitrile, no more than 2 weight percent of total polymer units derived from *N*-methylolacrylamide, and no more than 25 weight percent of total polymer units derived from styrene. For use only as provided in paragraph (m) of this section.
Melamine-formaldehyde.
Melamine-formaldehyde chemically modified with one or more of the amine catalysts identified in §175.300(b)(3)(xiii) of this chapter.
Melamine-formaldehyde chemically modified with methyl alcohol.
Melamine-formaldehyde chemically modified with urea; for use only as provided for in paragraphs (e), (f), (g), (h), and (i) of this section.
Phenol-formaldehyde resins.
Polyvinyl alcohol.
Polyvinyl alcohol with the copolymer of acrylic acid-allyl sucrose.
Polyvinyl alcohol with melamine formaldehyde.
Polyvinyl acetate with melamine formaldehyde.
p-Toluenesulfonamide-formaldehyde chemically modified with one or more of the amine catalysts identified in §175.300 (b)(3)(xiii) of this chapter.

(4) *Adjuvant substances:*

Dimethyl polysiloxane with methylcellulose and sorbic acid (as an antifoaming agent).
Phosphoric acid.

(5) *Colorants:* Colorants used in accordance with §178.3297 of this chapter.

(e) Resin-bonded filters conforming with the specifications of paragraph (e)(1) of this section are used as provided in paragraph (e)(2) of this section:

(1) *Total extractives.* The finished filter, when exposed to distilled water at 100 °F for 2 hours, yields total extractives not to exceed 2.8 percent by weight of the filter.

(2) *Conditions of use.* It is used to filter milk or potable water at operating temperatures not to exceed 100 °F.

(f) Resin-bonded filters conforming with the specifications of paragraph (f)(1) of this section are used as provided in paragraph (e)(2) of this section:

(1) *Total extractives.* The finished filter, when exposed to distilled water at 145 °F for 2 hours, yields total extractives not to exceed 4 percent by weight of the filter.

(2) *Conditions of use.* It is used to filter milk or potable water at operating temperatures not to exceed 145 °F.

(g) Resin-bonded filters conforming with the specifications of paragraph (g)(1) of this section are used as provided in paragraph (g)(2) of this section:

(1) *Total extractives.* The finished filter, when exposed to *n*-hexane at reflux temperature for 2 hours, yields total extractives not to exceed 0.5 percent by weight of the filter.

(2) *Conditions of use.* It is used to filter edible oils.

(h) Resin-bonded filters conforming with the specifications of paragraph (h)(1) of this section are used as provided in paragraph (h)(2) of this section:

(1) *Total extractives.* The finished filter, when exposed to distilled water at 212 °F for 2 hours, yields total extractives not to exceed 4 percent by weight of the filter.

(2) *Conditions of use.* It is used to filter milk, coffee, tea, and potable water at temperatures not to exceed 212 °F.

(i) Resin-bonded filters conforming with the specifications of paragraph (i)(1) of this section are used as provided in paragraph (i)(2) of this section:

(1) *Total extractives.* The finished filter, when exposed to distilled water for 2 hours at a temperature equivalent to, or higher than, the filtration temperature of the aqueous food, yields total extractives not to exceed 4 percent, by weight, of the filter.

(2) *Conditions of use.* It is used in commercial filtration of bulk quantities of nonalcoholic, aqueous foods having a pH above 5.0.

(j) Resin-bonded filters conforming with the specifications of paragraph (j)(1) of this section are used as provided in paragraph (j)(2) of this section:

(1) *Total extractives.* The finished filter, when exposed to 5 percent (by weight) acetic acid for 2 hours at a temperature equivalent to, or higher than, the filtration temperature of the

aqueous food, yields total extractives not to exceed 4 percent, by weight, of the filter.

(2) *Conditions of use.* It is used in commercial filtration of bulk quantities of nonalcoholic, aqueous foods having a pH of 5.0 or below.

(k) Resin-bonded filters conforming with the specifications of paragraph (k)(1) of this section are used as provided in paragraph (k)(2) of this section:

(1) *Total extractives.* The finished filter, when exposed to 8 percent (by volume) ethyl alcohol in distilled water for 2 hours at a temperature equivalent to, or higher than, the filtration temperature of the alcoholic beverage, yields total extractives not to exceed 4 percent, by weight, of the filter.

(2) *Conditions of use.* It is used in commercial filtration of bulk quantities of alcoholic beverages containing not more than 8 percent alcohol.

(l) Resin-bonded filters conforming with the specifications of paragraph (l)(1) of this section are used as provided in paragraph (l)(2) of this section:

(1) *Total extractives.* The finished filter, when exposed to 50 percent (by volume) ethyl alcohol in distilled water for 2 hours at a temperature equivalent to, or higher than, the filtration temperature of the alcoholic beverage, yields total extractives not to exceed 4 percent, by weight, of the filter.

(2) *Conditions of use.* It is used in commercial filtration of bulk quantities of alcoholic beverages containing more than 8 percent alcohol.

(m) Resin-bonded filters fabricated from acrylic polymers as provided in paragraph (d)(3) of this section together with other substances as provided in paragraph (d), (1), (2), and (4) of this section may be used as follows:

(1) The finished filter may be used to filter milk or potable water at operating temperatures not to exceed 100 °F, provided that the finished filter when exposed to distilled water at 100 °F for 2 hours yields total extractives not to exceed 1 percent by weight of the filter.

(2) The finished filter may be used to filter milk or potable water at operating temperatures not to exceed 145 °F, provided that the finished filter when exposed to distilled water at 145 °F for 2 hours yields total extractives not to exceed 1.2 percent by weight of the filter.

(n) Acrylonitrile copolymers identified in this section shall comply with the provisions of § 180.22 of this chapter.

[42 FR 14572, Mar. 15, 1977, as amended at 56 FR 42933, Aug. 30, 1991]

§ 177.2280 4,4′-Isopropylidenediphenol-epichlorohydrin thermosetting epoxy resins.

4,4′-Isopropylidenediphenol-epichlorohydrin thermosetting epoxy resins may be safely used as articles or components of articles intended for repeated use in producing, manufacturing, packing, processing, preparing, treating, packaging, transporting, or holding food, in accordance with the following prescribed conditions:

(a) The basic thermosetting epoxy resin is made by reacting 4,4′-isopropylidenediphenol with epichlorohydrin.

(b) The resin may contain one or more of the following optional substances provided the quantity used does not exceed that reasonably required to accomplish the intended effect:

Allyl glycidyl ether	As curing system additive.
Di- and tri-glycidyl ester mixture resulting from the reaction of epichlorohydrin with mixed dimers and trimers of unsaturated C_{18} monobasic fatty acids derived from animal and vegetable fats and oils.	As modifier at levels not to exceed equal parts by weight of the 4,4′-isopropylidenediphenol-epichlorohydrin basic resin and limited to use in contact with alcoholic beverages containing not more than 8 percent of alcohol.
1,2-Epoxy-3-phenoxypropane	As curing system additive.
Glyoxal	Do.
4,4′-Isopropylidenediphenol	Do.
4,4′-Methylenedianiline	Do.
m-Phenylenediamine	Do.
Tetrahydrophthalic anhydride	Do.

(c) In accordance with good manufacturing practice, finished articles containing the resins shall be thoroughly cleansed prior to their first use in contact with food.

(d) The provisions of this section are not applicable to 4,4′-isopropylidenediphenol-epichlorohydrin resins listed in other sections of parts 174, 175, 176, 177, 178 and 179 of this chapter.

[42 FR 14572, Mar. 15, 1977; 49 FR 5748, Feb. 15, 1984]

§ 177.2355 Mineral reinforced nylon resins.

Mineral reinforced nylon resins identified in paragraph (a) of this section may be safely used as articles or components of articles intended for repeated use in contact with nonacidic food (pH above 5.0) and at use temperatures not exceeding 212 °F. in accordance with the following prescribed conditions:

(a) For the purpose of this section the mineral reinforced nylon resins consist of nylon 66, as identified in and complying with the specifications of §177.1500, reinforced with up to 40 weight percent of calcium silicate and up to 0.5 weight percent 3-(triethoxysilyl) propylamine (Chemical Abstracts Service Registry No. 000919302) based on the weight of the calcium silicate.

(b) The mineral reinforced nylon resins may contain up to 0.2 percent by weight of titanium dioxide as an optional adjuvant substance.

(c) The mineral reinforced nylon resins with or without the optional substance described in paragraph (b) of this section, and in the form of ⅛-inch molded test bars, when extracted with the solvents, i.e., distilled water and 50 percent (by volume) ethyl alcohol in distilled water, at reflux temperature for 24 hours using a volume-to-surface ratio of 2 milliliters of solvent per square inch of surface tested, shall meet the following extractives limitations:

(1) Total extractives not to exceed 5.0 milligrams per square inch of food-contact surface tested for each solvent.

(2) The ash after ignition of the extractives described in paragraph (c)(1) of this section, not to exceed 0.5 milligram per square inch of food-contact surface tested.

(d) In accordance with good manufacturing practice, finished articles containing the mineral reinforced nylon resins shall be thoroughly cleansed prior to their first use in contact with food.

[42 FR 54533, Oct. 7, 1977, as amended at 42 FR 61594, Dec. 6, 1977]

§ 177.2400 Perfluorocarbon cured elastomers.

Perfluorocarbon cured elastomers identified in paragraph (a) of this section may be safely used as articles or components of articles intended for repeated use in contact with nonacid food (pH above 5.0), subject to the provisions of this section.

(a) *Identity.* (1) For the purpose of this section, perfluorocarbon cured elastomers are produced by terpolymerizing tetrafluorethylene (CAS Reg. No. 116–14–3), perfluoromethyl vinyl ether (CAS Reg. No. 1187–93–5), and perfluoro-2-phenoxypropyl vinyl ether (CAS Reg. No. 24520–19–2) and subsequent curing of the terpolymer (CAS Reg. No. 26658–70–8) using the crosslinking agent, phenol, 4,4′-[2,2,2-trifluoro-1-(trifluoromethyl) ethylidene] bis-,dipotassium salt (CAS Reg. No. 25088–69–1) and accelerator, 1,4,7,10,13,16-hexaoxacyclooctadecane (CAS Reg. No. 17455–13–9).

(2) The perfluorocarbon base polymer shall contain no less than 40 weight-percent of polymer units derived from tetrafluoroethylene, no less than 40 weight-percent of polymer units derived from perfluoromethyl vinyl ether and no more than 5 weight-percent polymer units derived from perfluoro-2-phenoxy-propyl vinyl ether.

(3) The composition limitations of the cured elastomer, calculated as parts per 100 parts of terpolymer, are as follows:

Phenol, 4,4′-[2,2,2-trifluoro-1-(trifluoromethyl)-ethylidene] bis-,dipotassium salt—not to exceed 5 parts.

1,4,7,10,13,16-Hexaoxacyclo-octadecane—not to exceed 5 parts.

(b) *Optional adjuvant substances.* The perfluorocarbon cured elastomer identified in paragraph (a) of this section may contain the following optional adjuvant substances, subject to any limitations cited on their use:

(1) Substances generally recognized as safe (GRAS) in food or food packaging.

(2) Substances used in accordance with a prior sanction.

(3) Substances authorized under applicable regulations in this part and in parts 175 and 178 of this chapter and

subject to any limitations prescribed therein.

(4) Substances identified in this paragraph (b)(4) subject to such limitations as are provided:

Substances	Limitations
Carbon black (channel process of furnace combustion process) (CAS Reg. No. 1333–86–4).	Not to exceed 15 parts per 100 parts of the terpolymer.
Magnesium oxide (CAS Reg. No. 1309–48–4).	Not to exceed 5 parts per 100 parts of the terpolymer.

(c) *Specifications*—(1) *Infrared identification*. Perfluorocarbon cured elastomers may be identified by the characteristic infrared spectra of the pyrolysate breakdown product that is obtained by heating and decomposing the elastomer using the method entitled "Qualitative Identification of Kalrez® by Infrared Examination of Pyrolysate." This method is incorporated by reference. Copies of the method are available from the Center for Food Safety and Applied Nutrition (HFS–200), Food and Drug Administration, 5100 Paint Branch Pkwy., College Park, MD 20740, or available for inspection at the National Archives and Records Administration (NARA). For information on the availability of this material at NARA, call 202–741–6030, or go to: *http://www.archives.gov/federal_register/code_of_federal_regulations/ibr_locations.html.*

(2) *Thermogravimetry*. Perfluorocarbon cured elastomers have a major decomposition peak occurring at 490 ° ±15 °C (914 °F). Less than 1.5 percent of the elastomers will volatilize below 400 °C (752 °F) when run under nitrogen at a 10 °C or 18 °F per minute heating rate using a Du Pont Thermal Analyzer Model 1099 with Model 951 TGA unit or the equivalent.

(d) *Extractive limitations*. Articles fabricated from perfluorocarbon cured elastomers having a thickness of at least 1.0 millimeter (0.039 inch) when extracted at reflux temperatures for 2 hours separately with distilled water, 50 percent ethanol, and *n*-heptane, shall meet the following extractability limits:

(1) Total extractives not to exceed 3.1 milligrams per square decimeter (0.2 milligrams per square inch).

(2) Fluoride extractives calculated as fluorine not to exceed 0.47 milligram per square decimeter (0.03 milligram per square inch).

(e) *Conditions of use*. In accordance with current good manufacturing practice, finished food contact articles containing the perfluorocarbon cured elastomers shall be thoroughly cleaned prior to their first use in contact with food.

[49 FR 43050, Oct. 26, 1984]

§ 177.2410 Phenolic resins in molded articles.

Phenolic resins identified in this section may be safely used as the food-contact surface of molded articles intended for repeated use in contact with nonacid food (pH above 5.0), in accordance with the following prescribed conditions:

(a) For the purpose of this section, the phenolic resins are those produced when one or more of the phenols listed in paragraph (a)(1) of this section are made to react with one or more of the aldehydes listed in paragraph (a)(2) of this section, with or without aniline and/or anhydro-formaldehyde aniline (hexahydro-1, 3,5-triphenyl-s-triazine):

(1) *Phenols:*

p-tert-Amylphenol.
p-tert-Butylphenol.
o-, *m*-, and *p*-Cresol.
p-Octylphenol.
Phenol.
o- and *p*-Phenylethylphenol mixture produced when phenol is made to react with styrene in the presence of sulfuric acid catalyst.

(2) *Aldehydes:*

Acetaldehyde.
Formaldehyde.
Paraldehyde.

(b) Optional adjuvant substances employed in the production of the phenolic resins or added thereto to impart desired technical or physical properties include the following:

Asbestos fiber.	
Barium hydroxide	For use as catalyst.
Calcium stearate	For use as lubricant.
Carbon black (channel process).	
Diatomaceous earth.	
Glass fiber.	
Hexamethylenetetramine	For use as curing agent.
Mica.	
Oxalic acid	For use as catalyst.

Zinc stearate	For use as lubricant.

(c) The finished food-contact article, when extracted with distilled water at reflux temperature for 2 hours, using a volume-to-surface ratio of 2 milliliters of distilled water per square inch of surface tested, shall meet the following extractives limitations:

(1) Total extractives not to exceed 0.15 milligram per square inch of food-contact surface.

(2) Extracted phenol not to exceed 0.005 milligram per square inch of food-contact surface.

(3) No extracted aniline when tested by a spectrophotometric method sensitive to 0.006 milligram of aniline per square inch of food-contact surface.

(d) In accordance with good manufacturing practice, finished molded articles containing the phenolic resins shall be thoroughly cleansed prior to their first use in contact with food.

§ 177.2415 Poly(aryletherketone) resins.

Poly(aryletherketone) resins identified in paragraph (a) of this section may be safely used as articles or components of articles intended for repeated use in contact with food subject to the provisions of this section.

(a) *Identity*. For the purposes of this section, poly(aryletherketone) resins are poly(*p*-oxyphenylene *p*-oxyphenylene *p*-carboxyphenylene) resins (CAS Reg. No. 29658–26–2) produced by the polymerization of hydroquinone and 4,4′-difluorobenzophenone, and have a minimum weight-average molecular weight of 12,000, as determined by gel permeation chromatography in comparison with polystyrene standards, and a minimum mid-point glass transition temperature of 142 °C, as determined by differential scanning calorimetry.

(b) *Optional adjuvant substances*. The basic resins identified in paragraph (a) may contain optional adjuvant substances used in their production. These adjuvants may include substances described in §174.5(d) of this chapter and the following:

Substance	Limitations
Diphenyl sulfone	Not to exceed 0.2 percent by weight as a residual solvent in the finished basic resin.

(c) *Extractive limitations*. The finished food contact article, when extracted at reflux temperatures for 2 hours with the following four solvents, yields in each extracting solvent net chloroform soluble extractives not to exceed 0.05 milligrams per square inch of food contact surface: Distilled water, 50 percent (by volume) ethanol in distilled water, 3 percent acetic acid in distilled water, and *n*-heptane. In testing the final food contact article, a separate test sample shall be used for each extracting solvent.

[63 FR 20315, Apr. 24, 1998]

§ 177.2420 Polyester resins, cross-linked.

Cross-linked polyester resins may be safely used as articles or components of articles intended for repeated use in contact with food, in accordance with the following prescribed conditions:

(a) The cross-linked polyester resins are produced by the condensation of one or more of the acids listed in paragraph (a)(1) of this section with one or more of the alcohols or epoxides listed in paragraph (a)(2) of this section, followed by copolymerization with one or more of the cross-linking agents listed in paragraph (a)(3) of this section:

(1) Acids:

Adipic.
Fatty acids, and dimers thereof, from natural sources.
Fumaric.
Isophthalic.
Maleic.
Methacrylic.
Orthophthalic.
Sebacic.
Terephthalic.
Trimellitic.

(2) Polyols and polyepoxides:

Butylene glycol.
Diethylene glycol.
2,2-Dimethyl-1,3-propanediol.
Dipropylene glycol.
Ethylene glycol.
Glycerol.
4,4′-Isopropylidenediphenol-epichlorohydrin.
Mannitol.
a-Methyl glucoside.

Pentaerythritol.
Polyoxypropylene ethers of 4,4′-isopropylidenediphenol (containing an average of 2–7.5 moles of propylene oxide).
Propylene glycol.
Sorbitol.
Trimethylol ethane.
Trimethylol propane.
2,2,4-Trimethyl-1,3-pentanediol.

(3) Cross-linking agents:

Butyl acrylate.
Butyl methacrylate.
Ethyl acrylate.
Ethylhexyl acrylate.
Methyl acrylate.
Methyl methacrylate.
Styrene.
Triglycidyl isocyanurate (CAS Reg. No. 2451–62–9), for use only in coatings contacting bulk quantities of dry food of the type identified in §176.170(c) of this chapter, table 1, under type VIII.
Vinyl toluene.

(b) Optional adjuvant substances employed to facilitate the production of the resins or added thereto to impart desired technical or physical properties include the following, provided that the quantity used does not exceed that reasonably required to accomplish the intended physical or technical effect and does not exceed any limitations prescribed in this section:

List of substances	Limitations (limits of addition expressed as percent by weight of finished resin)
1. Inhibitors:	Total not to exceed 0.08 percent.
Benzoquinone	0.01 percent.
tert-Butyl catechol.	
TBHQ.	
Di-*tert*-butyl hydroquinone.	
Hydroquinone.	
2. Accelerators:	Total not to exceed 1.5 percent.
Benzyl trimethyl ammonium chloride	0.05 percent.
Calcium naphthenate.	
Cobalt naphthenate.	
Copper naphthenate.	
N, N-Diethylaniline	0.4 percent.
N, N-Dimethylaniline	Do.
Ethylene guanidine hydrochloride	0.05 percent.
3. Catalysts:	Total not to exceed 1.5 percent, except that methyl ethyl ketone peroxide may be used as the sole catalyst at levels not to exceed 2 percent.
Azo-bis-isobutyronitrile.	
Benzoyl peroxide.	
tert-Butyl perbenzoate.	
Chlorbenzoyl peroxide.	
Cumene hydroperoxide.	
Dibutyltin oxide (CAS Reg. No. 818–08–6)	For use in the polycondensation reaction at levels not to exceed 0.2 percent of the polyester resin.
Dicumyl peroxide.	
Hydroxybutyltin oxide (CAS Reg. No. 2273–43–0)	For use in the polycondensation reaction at levels not to exceed 0.2 percent of the polyester resin.
Lauroyl peroxide.	
p-Menthane hydroperoxide.	
Methyl ethyl ketone peroxide.	
Monobutyltin tris(2-ethylhexoate) (CAS Reg. No. 23850–94–4).	For use in the polycondensation reaction at levels not to exceed 0.2 percent of the polyester resin.
4. Solvents for inhibitors, accelerators, and catalysts:	
Butyl benzyl phthalate (containing not more than 1.0 percent by weight of dibenzyl phthalate).	
Dibutyl phthalate.	
Diethylene glycol	As a solvent for benzyl trimethyl ammonium chloride or ethylene guanidine hydrochloride only.
Dimethyl phthalate.	
Methyl alcohol.	
Styrene.	
Triphenyl phosphate.	
5. Reinforcements:	
Asbestos.	
Glass fiber.	
Polyester fiber produced by the condensation of one or more of the acids listed in paragraph (a)(1) of this section with one or more of the alcohols listed in paragraph (a)(2) of this section.	
6. Miscellaneous materials:	
Castor oil, hydrogenated.	
α-Methylstyrene.	

List of substances	Limitations (limits of addition expressed as percent by weight of finished resin)
Polyethylene glycol 6000.	
Silicon dioxide.	
Wax, petroleum	Complying with § 178.3710 of this chapter.

(c) The cross-linked polyester resins, with or without the optional substances described in paragraph (b) of this section, and in the finished form in which they are to contact food, when extracted with the solvent or solvents characterizing the type of food and under the conditions of time and temperature characterizing the conditions of their intended use, as determined from tables 1 and 2 of § 176.170(c) of this chapter, shall meet the following extractives limitations:

(1) Net chloroform-soluble extractives not to exceed 0.1 milligram per square inch of food-contact surface tested when the prescribed food-simulating solvent is water or 8 or 50 percent alcohol.

(2) Total nonvolatile extractives not to exceed 0.1 milligram per square inch of food-contact surface tested when the prescribed food-simulating solvent is heptane.

(d) In accordance with good manufacturing practice, finished articles containing the cross-linked polyester resins shall be thoroughly cleansed prior to their first use in contact with food.

[42 FR 14572, Mar. 15, 1977, as amended at 48 FR 37618, Aug. 19, 1983; 54 FR 48858, Nov. 28, 1989]

§ 177.2430 Polyether resins, chlorinated.

Chlorinated polyether resins may be safely used as articles or components of articles intended for repeated use in producing, manufacturing, packing, processing, preparing, treating, packaging, transporting, or holding food, in accordance with the following prescribed conditions:

(a) The chlorinated polyether resins are produced by the catalytic polymerization of 3,3-bis(chloromethyl)-oxetane, and shall contain not more than 2 percent residual monomer.

(b) In accordance with good manufacturing practice, finished articles containing the chlorinated polyether resins shall be thoroughly cleansed prior to their first use in contact with food.

§ 177.2440 Polyethersulfone resins.

Polyethersulfone resins identified in paragraph (a) of this section may be safely used as articles or components of articles intended for repeated use in contact with food in accordance with the following prescribed conditions:

(a) For the purpose of this section, polyethersulfone resins are:

(1) Poly(oxy-*p*-phenylenesulfonyl-*p*-phenylene) resins (CAS Reg. No. 25667–42–9), which have a minimum number average molecular weight of 16,000.

(2) 1,1′-sulfonylbis[4-chlorobenzene] polymer with 4,4′-(1-methylethylidene)bis[phenol] (maximum 8 percent) and 4,4′-sulfonylbis[phenol] (minimum 92 percent) (CAS Reg. No. 88285–91–0), which have a minimum number average molecular weight of 26,000.

(3) In paragraphs (a)(1) and (a)(2) of this section, the minimum number average molecular weight is determined by reduced viscosity in dimethyl formamide in accordance with ASTM method D2857–70 (Reapproved 1977), "Standard Test Method for Dilute Solution Viscosity of Polymers," which is incorporated by reference. Copies may be obtained from the American Society for Testing Materials, 100 Barr Harbor Dr., West Conshohocken, Philadelphia, PA 19428-2959, or may be examined at the Office of Food Additive Safety (HFS–200), Center for Food Safety and Applied Nutrition, Food and Drug Administration, 5100 Paint Branch Pkwy., College Park, MD 20740, 240–402–1200 or at the National Archives and Records Administration (NARA). For information on the availability of this material at NARA, call 202–741–6030, or go to: *http://www.archives.gov/federal_register/code_of_federal_regulations/ibr_locations.html.*

(b) The basic resins identified in paragraphs (a)(1) and (a)(2) of this section may contain optional adjuvant substances described in § 174.5(d) of this chapter and the following:

List of substances	Limitations
Diphenylsulfone	Not to exceed 0.2 percent as residual solvent in the finished basic resin described in paragraph (a)(1) of this section.
Dimethyl sulfoxide	Not to exceed 0.01 percent as residual solvent in the finished basic resin described in paragraph (a)(1) of this section.
N-methyl-2-pyrrolidone	Not to exceed 0.01 percent as residual solvent in the finished basic resin described in paragraph (a)(2) of this section.

(c) The finished food-contact article, when extracted at reflux temperatures for 2 hours with the following four solvents, yields net chloroform-soluble extractives in each extracting solvent not to exceed 0.02 milligram per square inch of food-contact surface: distilled water, 50 percent (by volume) ethyl alcohol in distilled water, 3 percent acetic acid in distilled water, and *n*-heptane. (Note: In testing the finished food-contact article, use a separate test sample for each required extracting solvent.)

(d) In accordance with good manufacturing practice, finished food-contact articles containing the polyethersulfone resins shall be thoroughly cleansed before their first use in contact with food.

[44 FR 34493, June 15, 1979, as amended at 47 FR 38885, Sept. 3, 1982; 49 FR 10111, Mar. 19, 1984; 50 FR 47211, Nov. 15, 1985; 60 FR 48648, Sept. 20, 1995; 78 FR 14666, Mar. 7, 2013]

§ 177.2450 Polyamide-imide resins.

Polyamide-imide resins identified in paragraph (a) of this section may be safely used as components of articles intended for repeated use in contact with food, in accordance with the following prescribed conditions:

(a) *Identity.* (1) For the purpose of this section the polyamide-imide resins are derived from the condensation reaction of substantially equimolar parts of trimellitic anhydride and *p,p'*-diphenylmethane diisocyanate.

(2) The polyamide-imide resins (CAS Reg. No. 31957–38–7) derived from the condensation reaction of equimolar parts of benzoyl chloride-3,4-dicarboxylic anhydride and 4,4'-diphenylmethanediamine.

(b) *Specifications.* (1) Polyamide-imide resins identified in paragraph (a)(1) of this section shall have a nitrogen content of not less than 7.8 weight percent and not more than 8.2 weight percent. Polyamide-imide resins identified in paragraph (a)(2) of this section shall have a nitrogen content of not less than 7.5 weight percent and not more than 7.8 weight percent. Nitrogen content is determined by the Dumas Nitrogen Determination as set forth in the "Official Methods of Analysis of the Association of Official Analytical Chemists," 13th Ed. (1980), sections 7.016–7.020, which is incorporated by reference in accordance with 5 U.S.C. 552(a). Copies may be obtained from the AOAC INTERNATIONAL, 481 North Frederick Ave., suite 500, Gaithersburg, MD 20877, or may be examined at the National Archives and Records Administration (NARA). For information on the availability of this material at NARA, call 202–741–6030, or go to: *http://www.archives.gov/federal_register/code_of_federal_regulations/ibr_locations.html.*

(2) Polyamide-imide resins identified in paragraph (a)(1) of this section shall have a solution viscosity of not less than 1.200. Polyamide-imide resins identified in paragraph (a)(2) of this section shall have a solution viscosity of not less than 1.190. Solution viscosity shall be determined by a method titled "Solution Viscosity" which is incorporated by reference in accordance with 5 U.S.C. 552(a). Copies are available from the Center for Food Safety and Applied Nutrition (HFS–200), Food and Drug Administration, 5100 Paint Branch Pkwy., College Park, MD 20740, or available for inspection at the National Archives and Records Administration (NARA). For information on the availability of this material at NARA, call 202–741–6030, or go to: *http://www.archives.gov/federal_register/code_of_federal_regulations/ibr_locations.html.*

(3) The polyamide-imide resins identified in paragraph (a)(1) of this section are heat cured at 600 °F for 15 minutes when prepared for extraction tests and the residual monomers: *p,p*-diphenylmethane diisocyanate should not be present at greater than 100 parts per million and trimellitic anhydride

should not be present at greater than 500 parts per million. Residual monomers are determined by gas chromatography (the gas chromatography method titled "Amide-Imide Polymer Analysis—Analysis of Monomer Content," is incorporated by reference in accordance with 5 U.S.C. 552(a). Copies are available from the Center for Food Safety and Applied Nutrition (HFS–200), Food and Drug Administration, 5100 Paint Branch Pkwy., College Park, MD 20740, or available for inspection at the National Archives and Records Administration (NARA). For information on the availability of this material at NARA, call 202–741–6030, or go to: *http://www.archives.gov/federal_register/code_of_federal_regulations/ibr_locations.html.*).

(c) Extractive limitations are applicable to the polyamide-imide resins identified in paragraphs (a) (1) and (2) of this section in the form of films of 1 mil uniform thickness after coating and heat curing at 600 °F for 15 minutes on stainless steel plates, each having such resin-coated surface area of 100 square inches. The cured-resin film coatings shall be extracted in accordance with the method described in §176.170(d)(3) of this chapter, using a plurality of spaced, coated stainless steel plates, exposed to the respective food simulating solvents. The resin shall meet the following extractive limitations under the corresponding extraction conditions:

(1) Distilled water at 250 °F for 2 hours: Not to exceed 0.01 milligram per square inch.

(2) Three percent acetic acid at 212 °F for 2 hours: Not to exceed 0.05 milligram per square inch.

(3) Fifty percent ethyl alcohol at 160 °F for 2 hours: Not to exceed 0.03 milligram per square inch.

(4) *n*-Heptane at 150 °F for 2 hours: Not to exceed 0.05 milligram per square inch.

(d) In accordance with good manufacturing practice, those food contact articles, having as components the polyamide-imide resins identified in paragraph (a) of this section and intended for repeated use shall be thoroughly cleansed prior to their first use in contact with food.

[42 FR 14572, Mar. 15, 1977, as amended at 47 FR 11845, Mar. 19, 1982; 49 FR 10111, Mar. 19, 1984; 54 FR 24898, June 12, 1989; 54 FR 43170, Oct. 23, 1989; 61 FR 14481, Apr. 2, 1996; 70 FR 40880, July 15, 2005; 70 FR 67651, Nov. 8, 2005]

§ 177.2460 Poly(2,6-dimethyl-1,4-phenylene) oxide resins.

The poly(2,6-dimethyl-1,4-phenylene) oxide resins identified in paragraph (a) of this section may be used as an article or as a component of an article intended for use in contact with food subject to the provisions of this section.

(a) *Identity.* For the purposes of this section, poly(2,6-dimethyl-1,4-phenylene) oxide resins consist of basic resins produced by the oxidative coupling of 2,6-xylenol such that the finished basic resins meet the specifications and extractives limitations prescribed in paragraph (c) of this section.

(b) *Optional adjuvant substances.* The basic poly(2,6-dimethyl-1,4-phenylene) oxide resins identified in paragraph (a) of this section may contain optional adjuvant substances required in the production of such basic resins. The optional adjuvant substances required in the production of the basic poly(2,6-dimethyl-1,4-phenylene) oxide resins may include substances permitted for such use by regulations in parts 170 through 189 of this chapter, substances generally recognized as safe in food, substances used in accordance with a prior sanction or approval, and the following:

List of substances	Limitations (expressed as percent by weight of finished basic resin)
Diethylamine	Not to exceed 0.16 percent as residual catalyst.
Methyl alcohol	Not to exceed 0.02 percent as residual solvent.
Toluene	Not to exceed 0.2 percent as residual solvent.

(c) *Specifications and extractives limitations.* The poly(2,6-dimethyl-1,4-phenylene) oxide basic resins meet the following:

(1) *Specifications.* Intrinsic viscosity is not less than 0.30 deciliter per gram as determined by ASTM method D1243–79, "Standard Test Method for Dilute Solution Viscosity of Vinyl Chloride Polymers," which is incorporated by

reference, modified as follows. Copies of the incorporation by reference may be obtained from the American Society for Testing Materials, 100 Barr Harbor Dr., West Conshohocken, Philadelphia, PA 19428-2959, or may be examined at the National Archives and Records Administration (NARA). For information on the availability of this material at NARA, call 202–741–6030, or go to: *http://www.archives.gov/federal_register/code_of_federal_regulations/ibr_locations.html.*

(i) *Solvent:* Chloroform, reagent grade containing 0.01 percent *tert*-butylcatechol.

(ii) *Resin sample:* Powdered resin obtained from production prior to molding or extrusion.

(iii) *Viscometer:* Cannno-Ubbelohde series 25 dilution viscometer (or equivalent).

(iv) *Calculation:* The calculation method used is that described in appendix X.1.3 (ASTM method D1243–79, cited and incorporated by reference in paragraph (c)(1) of this section) with the reduced viscosity determined for three concentration levels (0.4, 0.2, and 0.1 gram per deciliter) and extrapolated to zero concentration for intrinisic viscosity. The following formula is used for determining reduced viscosity:

$$\text{Reduced viscosity in terms of deciliters per gram} = \frac{t - t_o}{t_o \times c}$$

where:

t=Solution efflux time.
t_o=Solvent efflux time.
c=Concentration of solution in terms of grams per deciliter.

(2) *Extractives limitations.* Total resin extracted not to exceed 0.02 weight-percent when extracted with *n*-heptane at 160 °F for 2 hours as determined using 200 milliliters of reagent grade *n*-heptane which has been freshly distilled before use and 25 grams of poly (2,-6-dimethyl-1,4-phenylene) oxide resin. The resin as tested is in pellet form having a particle size such that 100 percent of the pellets will pass through a U.S. Standard Sieve No. 6 and 100 percent of the pellets will be held on a U.S. Standard Sieve No. 10.

(d) *Other limitations.* The poly(2,6-dimethyl-1,4-phenylene) oxide resins identified in and complying with this section, when used as components of the food-contact surface of any article that is the subject of a regulation in parts 174, 175, 176, 177, 178 and § 179.45 of this chapter, shall comply with any specifications and limitations prescribed by such regulation for the article in the finished form in which it is to contact food.

(e) *Uses.* The poly(2,6-dimethyl-1,4-phenylene) oxide resins identified in and complying with the limitations in this section may be used as articles or components of articles intended for repeated food-contact use or as articles or components of articles intended for single-service food-contact use only under the conditions described in § 176.170(c) of this chapter, table 2, conditions of use H.

[42 FR 14572, Mar. 15, 1977, as amended at 49 FR 10111, Mar. 19, 1984; 63 FR 8852, Feb. 23, 1998]

§ 177.2465 Polymethylmethacrylate/poly(trimethoxysilylpropyl)methacrylate copolymers.

Polymethylmethacrylate/poly(trimethoxysilylpropyl) methacrylate copolymers (CAS Reg. No. 26936–30–1) may be safely used as components of surface primers used in conjunction with silicone polymers intended for repeated use and complying with § 175.300 of this chapter and § 177.2600, in accordance with the following prescribed conditions.

(a) *Identity.* For the purpose of this section, polymethylmethacrylate/poly(trimethoxysilylpropyl)methacrylate copolymers are produced by the polymerization of methylmethacrylate and trimethoxysilylpropylmethacrylate.

(b) *Conditions of use.* (1) The polymethylmethacrylate/poly(trimethoxysilylpropyl)methacrylate copolymers are used at levels not to exceed 6.0 percent by weight of the primer formulation.

(2) The copolymers may be used in food contact applications with all food types under conditions of use B through H as described in table 2 of § 176.170(c) of this chapter.

[59 FR 5948, Feb. 9, 1994]

§ 177.2470 Polyoxymethylene copolymer.

Polyoxymethylene copolymer identified in this section may be safely used as an article or component of articles intended for food-contact use in accordance with the following prescribed conditions:

(a) *Identity.* For the purpose of this section, polyoxymethylene copolymers are identified as the following: The reaction product of trioxane (cyclic trimer of formaldehyde) and ethylene oxide (CAS Reg. No. 24969–25–3) or the reaction product of trioxane (cyclic trimer of formaldehyde) and a maximum of 5 percent by weight of butanediol formal (CAS Reg. No. 25214 85–1). Both copolymers may have certain optional substances added to impart desired technological properties to the copolymer.

(b) *Optional adjuvant substances.* The polyoxymethylene copolymer identified in paragraph (a) of this section may contain optional adjuvant substances required in its production. The quantity of any optional adjuvant substance employed in the production of the copolymer does not exceed the amount reasonably required to accomplish the intended technical or physical effect. Such adjuvants may include substances generally recognized as safe in food, substances used in accordance with prior sanction, substances permitted under applicable regulations in parts 170 through 189 of this chapter, and the following:

(1) Stabilizers (total amount of stabilizers not to exceed 2.0 percent and amount of any one stabilizer not to exceed 1.0 percent of polymer by weight)

Calcium ricinoleate.
Cyanoguanidine.
Hexamethylene bis(3,5-di-*tert*-butyl-4-hydroxyhydrocinnamate) (CAS Reg. No. 35074–77–2).
Melamine-formaldehyde resin.
2,2′-Methylenebis(4-methyl-6-*tert*-butylphenol).
Nylon 6/66, weight ratio 2/3.
Tetrakis [methylene (3,5-di-*tert*-butyl-4-hydroxyhydrocinnamate)] methane.

(2) Lubricant: N,N′Distearoylethylenediamine.

(c) *Specifications.* (1) Polyoxymethylene copolymer can be identified by its characteristic infrared spectrum.

(2) Minimum number average molecular weight of the copolymer is 15,000 as determined by a method titled "Number Average Molecular Weight," which is incorporated by reference. Copies are available from the Center for Food Safety and Applied Nutrition (HFS–200), Food and Drug Administration, 5100 Paint Branch Pkwy., College Park, MD 20740, or available for inspection at the National Archives and Records Administration (NARA). For information on the availability of this material at NARA, call 202–741–6030, or go to: *http://www.archives.gov/federal_register/code_of_federal_regulations/ibr_locations.html.*

(d) *Extractive limitations.* (1) Polyoxymethylene copolymer in the finished form in which it is to contact food, when extracted with the solvent or solvents characterizing the type of food and under conditions of time and temperature as determined from tables 1 and 2 of § 175.300(d) of this chapter, shall yield net chloroform-soluble extractives not to exceed 0.5 milligram per square inch of food-contact surface.

(2) Polyoxymethylene copolymer with or without the optional substances described in paragraph (b) of this section, when ground or cut into particles that pass through a U.S.A. Standard Sieve No. 6 and that are retained on a U.S.A. Standard Sieve No. 10, shall yield total extractives as follows:

(i) Not to exceed 0.20 percent by weight of the copolymer when extracted for 6 hours with distilled water at reflux temperature.

(ii) Not to exceed 0.15 percent by weight of the copolymer when extracted for 6 hours with n-heptane at reflux temperature.

(e) *Conditions of use.* (1) The polyoxymethylene copolymer is for use as articles or components of articles intended for repeated use.

(2) Use temperature shall not exceed 250 °F.

(3) In accordance with good manufacturing practice, finished articles containing polyoxymethylene copolymer

shall be thoroughly cleansed before their first use in contact with food.

[42 FR 14572, Mar. 15, 1977, as amended at 48 FR 56204, Dec. 20, 1983; 49 FR 5748, Feb. 15, 1984; 50 FR 1842, Jan. 14, 1985; 50 FR 20560, May 17, 1985; 52 FR 4493, Feb. 12, 1987, 54 FR 24898, June 12, 1989]

§ 177.2480 Polyoxymethylene homopolymer.

Polyoxymethylene homopolymer identified in this section may be safely used as articles or components of articles intended for food-contact use in accordance with the following prescribed conditions:

(a) *Identity.* For the purpose of this section, polyoxymethylene homopolymer is polymerized formaldehyde [Chemical Abstracts Service Registry No. 9002–81–7]. Certain optional adjuvant substances, described in paragraph (b) of this section, may be added to impart desired technological properties to the homopolymer.

(b) *Optional adjuvant substances.* The polyoxymethylene homopolymer identified in paragraph (a) of this section may contain optional adjuvant substances in its production. The quantity of any optional adjuvant substance employed in the production of the homopolymer does not exceed the amount reasonably required to accomplish the intended effect. Such adjuvants may include substances generally recognized as safe in food, substances used in accordance with prior sanction, substances permitted under applicable regulations in this part, and the following:

(1) *Stabilizers.* The homopolymer may contain one or more of the following stabilizers. The total amount of stabilizers shall not exceed 1.9 percent of homopolymer by weight, and the quantity of individual stabilizer used shall not exceed the limitations set forth below:

Substances	Limitations
Hexamethylenebis(3,5-di-*tert*-butyl-4-hydroxy-hydrocinnamate) (CAS Reg. No. 35074–77–2).	At a maximum level of 1 percent by weight of homopolymer. The finished articles shall not be used for foods containing more than 8 percent alcohol.
2,2′-Methylenebis(4-methyl-6-*tert*-butylphenol).	At a maximum level of 0.5 percent by weight of homopolymer.
Nylon 66/610/6 terpolymer, respective proportions of nylon polymers by weight are: 3/2/4.	At a maximum level of 1.5 percent by weight of homopolymer.
Nylon 612/6 copolymer (CAS Reg. No. 51733-10-9), weight ratio 6/1.	Do.
Tetrakis[methylene(3,5-di-*tert*-butyl-4-hydroxy-hydrocinnamate)] methane.	At a maximum level of 0.5 percent by weight of homopolymer.

(2) *Lubricant.* *N,N′*-Distearoylethylenediamine.

(3) *Molding assistant.* Polyethylene glycol 6,000.

(c) *Specifications.* (1) Polyoxymethylene homopolymer can be identified by its characteristic infrared spectrum.

(2) Minimum number average molecular weight of the homopolymer is 25,000.

(3) Density of the homopolymer is between 1.39 and 1.44 as determined by ASTM method D1505–68 (Reapproved 1979), "Standard Test Method for Density of Plastics by the Density-Gradient Technique," which is incorporated by reference. Copies may be obtained from the American Society for Testing Materials, 100 Barr Harbor Dr., West Conshohocken, Philadelphia, PA 19428-2959, or may be examined at the National Archives and Records Administration (NARA). For information on the availability of this material at NARA, call 202–741–6030, or go to: *http://www.archives.gov/federal_register/code_of_federal_regulations/ibr_locations.html.*

(4) Melting point is between 172 °C and 184 °C as determined by ASTM method D2133–66, "Specifications for Acetal Resin Injection Molding and Extrusion Materials" (Revised 1966), which is incorporated by reference. Copies are available from American Society for Testing and Materials (ASTM), 100 Barr Harbor Dr., West Conshohocken, Philadelphia, PA 19428-2959, or available for inspection at the National Archives and Records Administration (NARA). For information on the availability of this material at NARA, call 202–741–6030, or go to: *http://www.archives.gov/federal_register/code_of_federal_regulations/ibr_locations.html.*

(d) *Extractive limitations.* (1) Polyoxymethylene homopolymer, in the finished form which is to contact food, when extracted with the solvent or solvents characterizing the type of food and under conditions of time and temperature characterizing the conditions of intended use under paragraphs (c)(3) and (d) of § 175.300 of this chapter and as limited by paragraph (e) of this section, shall yield net chloroform-soluble extractives not to exceed 0.5 milligram per square inch of food-contact surface.

(2) Polyoxymethylene homopolymer, with or without the optional adjuvant substances described in paragraph (b) of this section, when ground or cut into particles that pass through a U.S.A. Standard Sieve No. 6 and that are retained on a U.S.A. Standard Sieve No. 10, shall yield extractives as follows:

(i) Formaldehyde not to exceed 0.0050 percent by weight of homopolymer as determined by a method titled "Formaldehyde Release and Formaldehyde Analysis," which is incorporated by reference. Copies are available from Center for Food Safety and Applied Nutrition (HFS–200) Food and Drug Administration, 5100 Paint Branch Pkwy., College Park, MD 20740, or available for inspection at the National Archives and Records Administration (NARA). For information on the availability of this material at NARA, call 202–741–6030, or go to: *http://www.archives.gov/federal_register/code_of_federal_regulations/ibr_locations.html.*

(ii) Total extractives not to exceed 0.20 percent by weight of homopolymer when extracted for 6 hours with distilled water at reflux temperature and 0.15 percent by weight of homopolymer when extracted for 6 hours with *n*-heptane at reflux temperature.

(e) *Conditions of use.* (1) Polyoxymethylene homopolymer is for use as articles or components of articles intended for repeated use.

(2) Use temperature shall not exceed 250 °F.

(3) In accordance with good manufacturing practice, finished articles containing polyoxymethylene homopolymer shall be thoroughly cleansed prior to first use in contact with food.

[42 FR 14572, Mar. 15, 1977, as amended at 43 FR 44835, Sept. 29, 1978; 47 FR 11846, Mar. 19, 1982; 47 FR 51562, Nov. 16, 1982; 49 FR 10111, Mar. 19, 1984; 54 FR 24898, June 12, 1989]

§ 177.2490 Polyphenylene sulfide resins.

Polyphenylene sulfide resins (poly(1,4-phenylene sulfide) resins) may be safely used as coatings or components of coatings of articles intended for repeated use in contact with food, in accordance with the following prescribed conditions.

(a) Polyphenylene sulfide resins consist of basic resins produced by the reaction of equimolar parts of *p*-dichlorobenzene and sodium sulfide, such that the finished resins meet the following specifications as determined by methods titled "Oxygen Flask Combustion-Gravimetric Method for Determination of Sulfur in Organic Compounds," "Determination of the Inherent Viscosity of Polyphenylene Sulfide," and "Analysis for Dichlorobenzene in Ryton Polyphenylene Sulfide," which are incorporated by reference. Copies are available from the Center for Food Safety and Applied Nutrition (HFS–200), Food and Drug Administration, 5100 Paint Branch Pkwy., College Park, MD 20740, or available for inspection at the National Archives and Records Administration (NARA). For information on the availability of this material at NARA, call 202–741–6030, or go to: *http://www.archives.gov/federal_register/code_of_federal_regulations/ibr_locations.html.*

(1) Sulfur content: 28.2–29.1 percent by weight of finished resin.

(2) Minimum inherent viscosity: 0.13 deciliters per gram.

(3) Maximum residual *p*-dichlorobenzene: 0.8 ppm.

(b) Subject to any limitations prescribed in parts 170 through 189 of this chapter, the following optional substances may be added to the polyphenylene sulfide basic resins in an amount not to exceed that reasonably required to accomplish the intended physical or technical effect.

(1) Substances generally recognized as safe in food.

(2) Substances used in accordance with prior sanction or approval.

(3) Substances the use of which is permitted in coatings under regulations in parts 170 through 189 of this chapter.

(c) The finished coatings are thermally cured at temperatures of 700 °F and above.

(d) Polyphenylene sulfide resin coatings may be used in contact with food at temperatures not to exceed the boiling point of water; provided that the finished cured coating, when extracted at reflux temperatures for 8 hours separately with distilled water, 50 percent ethanol in water, and 3 percent acetic acid, yields total extractives in each extracting solvent not to exceed 0.02 milligram per square inch of surface and when extracted at reflux temperature for 8 hours with heptane yields total extractives not to exceed 0.1 milligram per square inch of surface.

(e) Polyphenylene sulfide resin coatings containing perfluorocarbon resins complying with §177.1550 may be used in contact with food at temperatures up to and including normal baking and frying temperatures; provided that the finished cured coating, when extracted at reflux temperatures for 2 hours separately with distilled water, 50 percent ethanol in water, 3 percent acetic acid and heptane, yields total extractives in each extracting solvent not to exceed 0.2 milligram per square inch of surface and when extracted at reflux temperature for 1 hour with diphenyl ether yields total extractives not to exceed 4.5 milligrams per square inch of surface.

[42 FR 14572, Mar. 15, 1977, as amended at 47 FR 11846, Mar. 19, 1982; 54 FR 24898, June 12, 1989]

§ 177.2500 Polyphenylene sulfone resins.

The polyphenylene sulfone resins (CAS Reg. No. 31833–61–1) identified in paragraph (a) of this section may be safely used as articles or components of articles intended for repeated use in contact with food, subject to the provisions of this section.

(a) *Identity*. For the purpose of this section, polyphenylene sulfone resins consist of basic resin produced by reacting polyphenylene sulfide with peracetic acid such that the finished resins meet the specifications set forth in paragraph (c) of this section. The polyphenylene sulfide used to manufacture polyphenylene sulfone is prepared by the reaction of sodium sulfide and *p*-dichlorobenzene, and has a minimum weight average molecular weight of 5,000 Daltons.

(b) *Optional adjuvant substances*. The basic polyphenylene sulfone resins identified in paragraph (a) of this section may contain optional adjuvant substances required in the production of such basic resins. These optional adjuvant substances may include substances permitted for such use by regulations in parts 170 through 189 of this chapter, substances generally recognized as safe in food, or substances used in accordance with a prior sanction or approval.

(c) *Specifications*. The glass transition temperature of the polymer is 360±5 °C as determined by the use of differential scanning calorimetry.

[65 FR 15058, Mar. 21, 2000]

§ 177.2510 Polyvinylidene fluoride resins.

Polyvinylidene fluoride resins may be safely used as articles or components of articles intended for repeated use in contact with food, in accordance with the following prescribed conditions:

(a) For the purpose of this section, the polyvinylidene fluoride resins consist of basic resins produced by the polymerization of vinylidene fluoride.

(b) The finished food-contact article, when extracted at reflux temperatures for 2 hours with the solvents distilled water, 50 percent (by volume) ethyl alcohol in distilled water, and *n*-heptane, yields total extractives in each extracting solvent not to exceed 0.01 milligram per square inch of food-contact surface tested; and if the finished food-contact article is itself the subject of a regulation in parts 174, 175, 176, 177, 178 and §179.45 of this chapter, it shall also comply with any specifications and limitations prescribed for it by that regulation. (NOTE: In testing the finished food-contact article, use a separate test sample for each required extracting solvent.)

(c) In accordance with good manufacturing practice, finished food-contact articles containing the polyvinylidene fluoride resins shall be thoroughly cleansed prior to their first use in contact with food.

§ 177.2550 Reverse osmosis membranes.

Substances identified in paragraph (a) of this section may be safely used as reverse osmosis membranes intended for use in processing bulk quantities of liquid food to separate permeate from food concentrate or in purifying water for food manufacturing under the following prescribed conditions:

(a) *Identity*. For the purpose of this section, reverse osmosis membranes may consist of either of the following formulations:

(1) A cross-linked high molecular weight polyamide reaction product of 1,3,5-benzenetricarbonyl trichloride with 1,3-benzenediamine (CAS Reg. No. 83044–99–9) or piperazine (CAS Reg. No. 110–85–0). The membrane is on the food-contact surface, and its maximum weight is 62 milligrams per square decimeter (4 milligrams per square inch) as a thin film composite on a suitable support.

(2) A cross-linked polyetheramine (CAS Reg. No. 101747–84–6), identified as the copolymer of epichlorohydrin, 1,2-ethanediamine and 1,2-dichloroethane, whose surface is the reaction product of this copolymer with 2,4-toluenediisocyanate (CAS Reg. No. of the final polymer is 99811–80–0) for use as the food-contact surface of reverse osmosis membranes used in processing liquid food. The composite membrane is on the food-contact surface and its maximum weight is 4.7 milligrams per square decimeter (0.3 milligrams per square inch) as a thin film composite on a suitable support. The maximum weight of the 2,4-toluenediisocyanate component of the thin film composite is 0.47 milligrams per square decimeter (0.03 milligrams per square inch).

(3) For the purpose of this section, the reverse osmosis membrane consists of a polyaramide identified as 2,4-diaminobenzenesulfonic acid, calcium salt (2:1) polymer with 1,3-benzenediamine, 1,3-benzenedicarbonyl dichloride, and 1,4-benzenedicarbonyl dichloride (CAS Reg. No. 39443–76–0). The membrane is the food contact surface and may be applied as a film on a suitable support. Its maximum weight is 512 milligrams per square decimeter (33 milligrams per square inch).

(4) A cross-linked high molecular weight polyamide reaction product of poly(*N*-vinyl-*N*-methylamine) (CAS Reg. No. 31245–56–4), *N,N'*-bis(3-aminopropyl)ethylenediamine (CAS Reg. No. 10563–26–5), 1,3-benzenedicarbonyl dichloride (CAS Reg. No. 99–63–8) and 1,3,5-benzenetricarbonyl trichloride (CAS Reg. No. 4422–95–1). The membrane is the food-contact surface. Its maximum weight is 20 milligrams per square decimeter (1.3 milligrams per square inch) as a thin film composite on a suitable support.

(5) A polyamide reaction product of 1,3,5-benzenetricarbonyl trichloride polymer (CAS Reg. No. 4422–95–1) with piperazine (CAS Reg. No. 110–85–0) and 1,2-diaminoethane (CAS Reg. No. 107–15–3). The membrane is the food-contact layer and may be applied as a film on a suitable support. Its maximum weight is 15 milligrams per square decimeter (1 milligram per square inch).

(b) *Optional adjuvant substances.* The basic polymer identified in paragraph (a) of this section may contain optional adjuvant substances required in the production of such basic polymer. These optional adjuvant substances may include substances permitted for such use by regulations in parts 170 through 186 of this chapter, substances generally recognized as safe in food, and substances used in accordance with a prior sanction or approval.

(c) *Supports.* Suitable supports for reverse osmosis membranes are materials permitted for such use by regulations in parts 170 through 186 of this chapter, substances generally recognized as safe in food, and substances used in accordance with a prior sanction or approval.

(d) *Conditions of use.* (1) Reverse osmosis membranes described in paragraphs (a)(1), (a)(2), (a)(3), and (a)(5) of this section may be used in contact with all types of liquid food at temperatures up to 80 °C (176 °F).

(2) Reverse osmosis membranes described in paragraph (a)(4) of this section may be used in contact with all types of liquid food, except food containing more than 8 percent alcohol, at temperatures up to 80 °C (176 °F).

(3) Reverse osmosis membranes shall be maintained in a sanitary manner in accordance with current good manufacturing practice so as to prevent microbial adulteration of food.

(4) To assure their safe use, reverse osmosis membranes and their supports shall be thoroughly cleaned prior to their first use in accordance with current good manufacturing practice.

[49 FR 49448, Dec. 20, 1984, as amended at 52 FR 29668, Aug. 11, 1987; 53 FR 31835, Aug. 22, 1988; 53 FR 32215, Aug. 24, 1988; 55 FR 8139, Mar. 7, 1990; 59 FR 9925, Mar. 2, 1994]

§ 177.2600 Rubber articles intended for repeated use.

Rubber articles intended for repeated use may be safely used in producing, manufacturing, packing, processing, preparing, treating, packaging, transporting, or holding food, subject to the provisions of this section.

(a) The rubber articles are prepared from natural and/or synthetic polymers and adjuvant substances as described in paragraph (c) of this section.

(b) The quantity of any substance employed in the production of rubber articles intended for repeated use shall not exceed the amount reasonably required to accomplish the intended effect in the rubber article and shall not be intended to accomplish any effect in food.

(c) Substances employed in the preparation of rubber articles include the following, subject to any limitations prescribed:

(1) Substances generally recognized as safe for use in food or food packaging.

(2) Substances used in accordance with the provisions of a prior sanction or approval.

(3) Substances that by regulation in parts 170 through 189 of this chapter may be safely used in rubber articles, subject to the provisions of such regulation.

(4) Substances identified in this paragraph (c)(4), provided that any substance that is the subject of a regulation in parts 174, 175, 176, 177, 178 and § 179.45 of this chapter conforms with any specification in such regulation.

(i) *Elastomers.*

Acrylonitrile-butadiene copolymer.

Brominated isobutylene-isoprene copolymers complying with § 177.1210.

Butadiene-acrylonitrile-ethylene glycol dimethacrylate copolymers containing not more than 5 weight percent of polymer units derived from ethylene glycol dimethacrylate.

Butadiene-acrylonitrile-methacrylic acid copolymer.

Butadiene-styrene-methacrylic acid copolymer.

Chloroprene polymers.

Chlorotrifluoroethylene-vinylidene fluoride copolymer.

Ethylene-propylene copolymer elastomers which may contain not more than 5 weight-percent of total polymer units derived from 5-methylene-2-norbornene and/or 5-ethylidine-2-norbornene.

Ethylene-propylene-dicyclopentadiene copolymer.

Ethylene-propylene-1,4-hexadiene copolymers containing no more than 8 weight percent of total polymer units derived from 1,4-hexadiene.

Hydrogenated butadiene/acrylonitrile copolymers (CAS Reg. No. 88254–10–8) produced when acrylonitrile/butadiene copolymers are modified by hydrogenation of the olefinic unsaturation to leave either: (1) Not more than 10 percent *trans* olefinic unsaturation and no α, β-olefinic unsaturation as determined by a method entitled "Determination of Residual α, β-Olefinic and Trans Olefinic Unsaturation Levels in HNBR," developed October 1, 1991, by Polysar Rubber Corp., 1256 South Vidal St., Sarnia, Ontario, Canada N7T 7MI; or (2) 0.4 percent to 20 percent olefinic unsaturation and Mooney viscosities greater than 45 (ML 1 + 4 @ 100 °C), as determined by ASTM Standard Method D1646–92, "Standard Test Method for Rubber—Viscosity and Vulcanization Characteristics (Mooney Viscometer)," which are both incorporated by reference in accordance with 5 U.S.C. 552(a) and 1 CFR part 51. Copies of these methods may be obtained from the Office of Food Additive Safety (HFS–200), Center for Food Safety and Applied Nutrition, Food and Drug Administration, 5100 Paint Branch Pkwy., College Park, MD 20740, 240–402–1200, or may be examined at the Center for Food Safety and Applied Nutrition's Library, 5100 Paint Branch Pkwy., College Park, MD 20740, or at the National Archives and Records Administration (NARA). For information on the availability of this material at NARA, call 202–741–6030, or go to: *http://www.archives.gov/federal_register/*

code_of_federal_regulations/ibr_locations.html. A copy of ASTM Standard Method D1646–92 may also be obtained from the American Society for Testing and Materials, 100 Barr Harbor Dr., West Conshohocken, PA 19428–2959.

Isobutylene-isoprene copolymer.

Polyamide/polyether block copolymers (CAS Reg. No. 77402–38–1 prepared by reacting a copolymer of *omega*-laurolactam and adipic acid with poly(tetramethylene ether glycol). The polyamide and polyether components are reacted in ratios such that the polyamide component constitutes a minimum of 30 weight-percent of total polymer units. The copolymers may be used in contact with foods of Types I, II, III, IV, V, VI, VII, VIII, and IX identified in table 1 of §176.170(c) of this chapter at temperatures not to exceed 150 °F except that those copolymers prepared with less than 50 weight-percent of polyamide are limited to use in contact with such foods at temperatures not to exceed 100 °F.

Polybutadiene.

Polyester elastomers derived from the reaction of dimethyl terephthalate, 1,4-butanediol, and α-hydro-omega-hydroxypoly (oxytetramethylene). Additionally, trimethyl trimellitate may be used as a reactant. The polyester elastomers may be used only in contact with foods containing not more than 8 percent alcohol and limited to use in contact with food at temperatures not exceeding 150 °F.

Polyisoprene.

Polyurethane resins (CAS Reg. Nos. 37383–28–1 or 9018–04–6) derived from the reaction of diphenylmethane diisocyanate with 1,4-butanediol and polytetramethylene ether glycol.

Polyurethane resins derived from reactions of diphenylmethane diisocyanate with adipic acid and 1,4-butanediol.

Rubber, natural.

Silicone basic polymer as described in ASTM method D1418–81, "Standard Practice for Rubber and Rubber Latices—Nomenclature," which is incorporated by reference. Copies may be obtained from the American Society for Testing Materials, 100 Barr Harbor Dr., West Conshohocken, Philadelphia, PA 19428-2959, or may be examined at the National Archives and Records Administration (NARA). For information on the availability of this material at NARA, call 202–741–6030, or go to: *http://www.archives.gov/federal_register/code_of_federal_regulations/ibr_locations.html.*

Silicone (Si) elastomers containing methyl groups.

Silicone (Psi) elastomers containing methyl and phenyl groups.

Silicone (Vsi) elastomers containing methyl and vinyl groups.

Silicone (Fsi) elastomers containing methyl and fluorine groups.

Silicone (PVsi) elastomers containing phenyl, methyl, and vinyl groups.

Styrene-butadiene copolymer.

Vinylidene fluoride-hexafluoropropylene copolymers (minimum number average molecular weight 70,000 as determined by osmotic pressure in methyl ethyl ketone).

Vinylidene fluoride-hexafluoropropylene-tetrafluoroethylene copolymers (minimum number average molecular weight 100,000 as determined by osmotic pressure in methyl ethyl ketone).

(ii) *Vulcanization materials*—(*a*) *Vulcanizing agents.*

4,4′-Bis(aminocyclohexyl)methane carbamate for use only as cross-linking agent in the vulcanization of vinylidene fluoridehexafluoropropylene copolymer and vinylidene fluoride-hexafluoropropylene-tetrafluoroethylene copolymer elastomers identified under paragraph (c)(4)(i) of this section and limited to use at levels not to exceed 2.4 percent by weight of such copolymers.

Diisopropyl xanthogen polysulfide (a 1:2:1 mixture of O,O-di(1-methylethyl)trithio-bis-thioformate, O,O-di(1-methylethyl)tetrathio-bis-thioformate, and O,O-di(1-methylethyl)pentathio-bis-thioformate) for use as a cross linking agent in the vulcanization of natural rubber, styrene-butadiene copolymer, acrylonitrile-butadiene copolymer, and ethylene-propylene terpolymers identified under paragraph (c)(4)(i) of this section and limited to use at levels not to exceed 2.4 percent by weight of such copolymers.

Hexamethylenediamine carbamate for use only as cross-linking agent in the vulcanization of vinylidene fluoride-hexafluoropropylene copolymer and vinylidene fluoride-hexafluoropropylene-tetrafluoroethylene copolymer elastomers identified under paragraph (c)(4)(i) of this section and limited to use at levels not to exceed 1.5 percent by weight of such copolymers.

Sulfur, ground.

(*b*) *Accelerators (total not to exceed 1.5 percent by weight of rubber product).*

2-Benzothiazyl-*N*,*N*-diethylthiocarbamyl-sulfide.

Benzoyl peroxide.

1,3-Bis(2-benzothiazolylmercaptomethyl) urea.

N-tert-Butyl-2-benzothiazole sulfenamide.

Butyraldehyde-aniline resin (iodine number 670–705).

Carbon disulfide-1,1′-methylenedipiperidine reaction product.

Copper dimethyldithiocarbamate.

N-Cyclohexyl-2-benzothiazole sulfenamide.

Dibenzoyl-*p*-quinone dioxime.
Dibenzylamine.
Diisopropyl xanthogen polysulfide (a 1:2:1 mixture of O,O-di(1-methylethyl)trithio-bis-thioformate, O,O-di(1-methylethyl)tetrathio-bis-thioformate, and O,O-di(1-methylethyl)pentathio-bis-thioformate).
Di(4-methylbenzoyl) peroxide (CAS Reg. No. 895–85–2) for use only as a crosslinking agent in silicone polymers and elastomers identified under paragraph (c)(4)(i) of this section at levels not to exceed 1 percent by weight of such polymers and elastomers where the total of all accelerators does not exceed 1.5 percent by weight of rubber product.
Di-*tert*-butyl peroxide.
Dibutyl xanthogen disulfide.
2,4-Dichlorobenzoyl peroxide.
Dicumyl peroxide.
N,N-Dimethylcyclohexylamine salt of dibutyldithiocarbamic acid.
2,6-Dimethylmorpholine thiobenzothiazol.
Dipentamethylenethiuram hexasulfide (CAS Reg. No. 971–15–3).
Diphenylguanidine.
Diphenylguanidine phthalate.
1,3-Diphenyl-2-thiourea.
2,2′-Dithiobis[benzothiazole].
4,4′-Dithiodimorpholine.
N,N′-Di-*o*-tolylguanidine.
Di-*o*-tolylguanidine salt of pyrocatecholborate.
Ethylenediamine carbamate.
Heptaldehyde-aniline resin (iodine number 430–445).
Hexamethylenetetramine.
2-Mercaptobenzothiazole.
2-Mercaptothiazoline.
N-Oxydiethylene-benzothiazole-2-sulfenamide.
Piperidinium pentamethylenedithiocarbamate.
Potassium pentamethylenedithiocarbamate.
p-Quinone dioxime.
Sodium dibutyldithiocarbamate.
Sodium dimethyldithiocarbamate.
Stannous oleate for use only as an accelerator for silicone elastomers.
Tetrabutylthiuram monosulfide.
Tetraethylthiuram disulfide.
(1,1,4,4-Tetramethyltetramethylene)bis [*tert*-butyl peroxide].
Tetramethylthiuram monosulfide.
Thiram (tetramethylthiuram disulfide).
Triallyl cyanurate.
Triethylenetetramine.
1,3,5-Triethyl-hexahydro-*s*-triazine (triethyltrimethylenetriamine).
Triphenylguanidine.
Zinc butyl xanathate.
Zinc dibenzyl dithiocarbamate.
Zinc dibutyldithiocarbamate.
Zinc diethyldithiocarbamate.
Zinc 2-mercaptobenzothiazole.
Ziram (zinc dimethyldithiocarbamate).

(*c*) *Retarders (total not to exceed 10 percent of weight of rubber product).*

Cyanoguanidine.
Phthalic anhydride.
Salicylic acid.

(*d*) *Activators (total not to exceed 5 percent by weight of rubber product except magnesium oxide may be used at higher levels).*

Diethylamine.
Fatty acid amines, mixed.
Fatty acids.
Magnesium carbonate.
Magnesium oxide, light and heavy.
Oleic acid, dibutylamine salt (dibutylammonium oleate).
Stannous chloride.
Tall oil fatty acids.
Tetrachloro-*p*-benzoquinone.
Triethanolamine.
Zinc salts of fatty acids.

(iii) *Antioxidants and antiozonants (total not to exceed 5 percent by weight of rubber product).*

Aldol-*a*-naphthylamine.
Alkylated (C_4 and/or C_8) phenols.
BHT (butylated hydroxytoluene).
4-[[4,6-bis(octylthio)-*s*-triazin-2-yl]amino]-2,6-di-*tert*-butylphenol (CAS Reg. No. 991–84–4) for use only as a stabilizer at levels not to exceed 0.5 percent by weight of the finished rubber product.
Butylated reaction product of *p*-cresol and dicyclopentadiene as identified in §178.2010(b) of this chapter.
Butylated, styrenated cresols identified in §178.2010(b) of this chapter.
4,4′-Butylidinebis(6-*tert*-butyl-*m*-cresol).
N-Cyclohexyl-*N′*-phenylphenylenediamine.
p,p′-Diaminodiphenylmethane.
2,5-Di-*tert*-amylhydroquinone.
Diaryl-*p*-phenylenediamine, where the aryl group may be phenyl, tolyl, or xylyl.
2,6-Di-*tert*-butyl-*p*-phenylphenol.
1,2-Dihydro-2,2,4-trimethyl-6-dodecylquinoline.
1,2-Dihydro-2,2,4-trimethyl-6-ethoxyquinoline.
1,2-Dihydro-2,2,4-trimethyl-6-phenylquinoline.
4,4′-Dimethoxydiphenylamine.
4,6-Dinonyl-*o*-cresol.
N,N′-Dioctyl-*p*-phenylenediamine.
Diphenylamine-acetone resin.
Diphenylamine-acetone-formaldehyde resin.
N,N′-Diphenylethylenediamine.
N,N′-Disalicylalpropylenediamine.
N,N′-Di-*o*-tolylethylenediamine.
Hydroquinone monobenzyl ether.
Isopropoxydiphenylamine.
N-Isopropyl-*N′*-phenyl-*p*-phenylenediamine.
2,2′-Methylenebis(6-*tert*-butyl-4-ethylphenol).

2,2′-Methylenebis(4-methyl-6-*tert*-butylphenol).
2,2′-Methylenebis(4-methyl-6-nonylphenol).
2,2′-Methylenebis(4-methyl-6-*tert*-octylphenol).
Monooctyl- and dioctyldiphenylamine.
N,N′-Di-β-naphthyl-*p*-phenylenediamine.
Phenyl-*a*-naphthylamine.
Phenyl-β-naphthylamine.
Phenyl-β-naphthylamine-acetone aromatic amine resin (average molecular weight 600; nitrogen content 5.3 percent).
o- and *p*-Phenylphenol.
Polybutylated (mixture) 4,4′-isopropylidenediphenol.
Sodium pentachlorophenate.
Styrenated cresols produced when 2 moles of styrene are made to react with 1 mole of a mixture of phenol and *o*-, *m*-, and *p*-cresols so that the final product has a Brookfield viscosity at 25 °C of 1400 to 1700 centipoises.
Styrenated phenol.
4,4′-Thiobis (6-*tert*-butyl-*m*-cresol).
Toluene-2,4-diamine.
N-o-Tolyl-*N′*-phenyl-*p*-phenylenediamine.
p(p-Tolylsufanilamide) diphenylamine.
Tri(mixed mono- and dinonylphenyl) phosphite.
Tri(nonylphenyl) phosphite-formaldehyde resins produced when 1 mole of tri(nonylphenyl) phosphite is made to react with 1.4 moles of formaldehyde or produced when 1 mole of nonylphenol is made to react with 0.36 mole of formaldehyde and the reaction product is then further reacted with 0.33 mole of phosphorus trichloride. The finished resins have a minimum viscosity of 20,000 centipoises at 25 °C, as determined by LV-series Brookfield viscometer (or equivalent) using a No. 4 spindle at 12 r.p.m., and have an organic phosphorus content of 4.05 to 4.15 percent by weight.

(iv) *Plasticizers (total not to exceed 30 percent by weight of rubber product unless otherwise specified).*

n-Amyl *n*-decyl phthalate.
Butylacetyl ricinoleate.
n-Butyl ester of tall oil fatty acids.
Butyl laurate.
Butyl oleate.
Butyl stearate.
Calcium stearate.
Castor oil.
Coumarone-indene resins.
2,2′-Dibenzamidodiphenyl disulfide.
Dibenzyl adipate.
Dibutoxyethoxyethyl adipate.
Dibutyl phthalate.
Dibutyl sebacate.
Didecyl adipate.
Didecyl phthalate.
Diisodecyl adipate.
Diisodecyl phthalate.
Diisooctyl adipate.
Diisooctyl sebacate.
Dioctyl adipate.
Dioctyl phthalate.
Dioctyl sebacate.
Dipentene resin.
Diphenyl ketone.
Fatty acids.
Fatty acids, hydrogenated.
Isooctyl ester of tall oil fatty acids.
Lanolin.
a-Methylstyrene-vinyltoluene copolymer resins (molar ratio 1 *a*-methylstyrene to 3 vinyltoluene).
Mineral oil; (1) In rubber articles complying with this section, not to exceed 30 percent by weight; (2) Alone or in combination with waxes, petroleum, total not to exceed 45 percent by weight of rubber articles that contain at least 20 percent by weight of ethylene-propylene copolymer elastomer complying with paragraph (c)(4)(i) of this section, in contact with foods of Types I, II, III, IV, VI, VII, VIII, and IX idenified in table 1 of § 176.170(c) of this chapter.
Montan wax.
n-Octyl *n*-decyl adipate.
n-Octyl *n*-decyl phthalate.
Petrolatum.
Petroleum hydrocarbon resin (cyclopentadiene type), hydrogenated.
Petroleum hydrocarbon resin (produced by the homo- and copolymerization of dienes and olefins of the aliphatic, alicyclic, and monobenzenoid arylalkene types from distillates of cracked petroleum stocks).
Petroleum hydrocarbon resin (produced by the catalytic polymerization and subsequent hydrogenation of styrene, vinyltoluene, and indene types from distillates of cracked petroleum stocks).
Petroleum oil, sulfonated.
Phenol-formaldehyde resin.
Pine tar.
Polybutene.
Polystyrene.
Propylene glycol.
n-Propyl ester of tall oil fatty acids.
Rapeseed oil vulcanized with rubber maker's sulfur.
Rosins and rosin derivatives identified in § 175.105(c)(5) of this chapter.
Soybean oil vulcanized with rubber maker's sulfur.
Styrene-acrylonitrile copolymer.
Terpene resins.
Triethylene glycol dicaprate.
Triethylene glycol dicaprylate.
Waxes, petroleum.
Xylene (or toluene) alkylated with dicyclopentadiene.
Zinc 2-benzamidothiophenate.

(v) *Fillers.*

Aluminum hydroxide.
Aluminum silicate.
Asbestos fiber, chrysotile or crocidolite.
Barium sulfate.

Carbon black (channel process or furnace combustion process; total carbon black not to exceed 50 percent by weight of rubber product; furnace combustion black content not to exceed 10 percent by weight of rubber products intended for use in contact with milk or edible oils).
Cork.
Cotton (floc, fibers, fabric).
Mica.
Nylon (floc, fibers, fabric).
Silica.
Titanium dioxide.
Zinc carbonate.
Zinc sulfide.

(vi) *Colorants.* Colorants used in accordance with §178.3297 of this chapter.

(vii) *Lubricants (total not to exceed 2 percent by weight of rubber product).*

Polyethylene.
Sodium stearate.

(viii) *Emulsifiers.*

Fatty acid salts, sodium or potassium.
Naphthalene sulfonic acid-formaldehyde condensate, sodium salt.
Rosins and rosin-derivatives identified in §175.105(c)(5) of this chapter.
Sodium decylbenzenesulfonate
Sodium dodecylbenzenesulfonate
Sodium lauryl sulfate.
Tall oil mixed soap (calcium, potassium, and sodium).

(ix) *Miscellaneous (total not to exceed 5 percent by weight of rubber product).*

Animal glue as described in §178.3120 of this chapter.
Azodicarbonamide as chemical blowing agent.
2-Anthraquinone sulfonic acid sodium salt for use only as polymerization inhibitor in chloroprene polymers and not to exceed 0.03 percent by weight of the chloroprene polymers.
1,2-Benzisothiazolin-3-one (CAS Reg. No. 2634–33–5) for use as a biocide in uncured liquid rubber latex not to exceed 0.02 percent by weight of the latex solids, where the total of all items listed in paragraph (c)(4)(ix) of this section does not exceed 5 percent of the rubber product.
n-Butyllithium for use only as polymerization catalyst for polybutadiene.
4-*tert*-Butyl-*o*-thiocresol as peptizing agent.
tert-Butyl peracetate.
p-*tert*-Butylpyrocatechol.
Dialkyl (C_8–C_{18}) dimethylammonium chloride for use only as a flocculating agent in the manufacture of silica.
Di- and triethanolamine.
Diethyl xanthogen disulfide.
4-(Diiodomethylsulfonyl) toluene, Chemical Abstracts Service Registry No. 20018–09–01, for use as an antifungal preservative at levels not to exceed 0.3 percent by weight of the sealants and caulking materials.
Dodecyl mercaptan isomers, single or mixed.
2-Ethoxyethanol.
Iodoform.
p-Menthane hydroperoxide.
a-(*p*-Nonylphenyl)-*omega*-hydroxypoly (oxyethylene) mixture of dihydrogen phosphate and monohydrogen phosphate esters, barium salt; the nonyl group is a propylene trimer isomer and the poly (oxyethylene) content averages 9 moles; for use only as residual polymerization emulsifier at levels not to exceed 0.7 percent by weight of ethylene-propylene-1,4-hexadiene copolymers identified under paragraph (c)(4)(i) of this section.
4,4′-Oxybis (benzenesulfonhydrazide) as chemical blowing agent.
Phenothiazine.
Potassium persulfate.
Sodium formaldehyde sulfoxylate.
Sodium polysulfide.
Sodium nitrite.
Sodium salt of ethylenediamine tetraacetic acid and glycine.
Sodium sulfide.
Styrene monomer.
Tall oil.
Thioxylenois as peptizing agents.
Tridecyl mercaptan.
Zinc 4-*tert*-butylthiophenate as peptizing agent.

(d) Rubber articles intended for use with dry food are so formulated and cured under conditions of good manufacturing practice as to be suitable for repeated use.

(e) Rubber articles intended for repeated use in contact with aqueous food shall meet the following specifications: The food-contact surface of the rubber article in the finished form in which it is to contact food, when extracted with distilled water at reflux temperature, shall yield total extractives not to exceed 20 milligrams per square inch during the first 7 hours of extraction, nor to exceed 1 milligram per square inch during the succeeding 2 hours of extraction.

(f) Rubber articles intended for repeated use in contact with fatty foods shall meet the following specifications: The food-contact surface of the rubber article in the finished form in which it is to contact food, when extracted with *n*-hexane at reflux temperature, shall yield total extractives not to exceed 175 milligrams per square inch during the first 7 hours of extraction, nor to exceed 4 milligrams per square inch during the succeeding 2 hours of extraction.

(g) In accordance with good manufacturing practice finished rubber articles intended for repeated use in contact with food shall be thoroughly cleansed prior to their first use in contact with food.

(h) The provisions of this section are not applicable to rubber nursing-bottle nipples.

(i) Acrylonitrile copolymers identified in this section shall comply with the provisions of § 180.22 of this chapter.

[42 FR 14572, Mar. 15, 1977]

EDITORIAL NOTE: For FEDERAL REGISTER citations affecting § 177.2600, see the List of CFR Sections Affected, which appears in the Finding Aids section of the printed volume and at *www.fdsys.gov*.

§ 177.2710 Styrene-divinylbenzene resins, cross-linked.

Styrene-divinylbenzene cross-linked copolymer resins may be safely used as articles or components of articles intended for repeated use in producing, manufacturing, packing, processing, preparing, treating, packaging, transporting, or holding food, in accordance with the following prescribed conditions:

(a) The resins are produced by the copolymerization of styrene with divinylbenzene.

(b) The resins meet the extractives limitations prescribed in this paragraph:

(1) The resins to be tested are ground or cut into small particles that will pass through a U.S. standard sieve No. 3 and that will be held on a U.S. standard sieve No. 20.

(2) A 100-gram sample of the resins, when extracted with 100 milliliters of ethyl acetate at reflux temperature for 1 hour, yields total extractives not to exceed 1 percent by weight of the resins.

(c) In accordance with good manufacturing practice, finished articles containing the resins shall be thoroughly cleansed prior to their first use in contact with food.

§ 177.2800 Textiles and textile fibers.

Textiles and textile fibers may safely be used as articles or components of articles intended for use in producing, manufacturing, packing, processing, preparing, treating, packaging, transporting, or holding food, subject to the provisions of this section.

(a) The textiles and textile fibers are prepared from one or more of the fibers identified in paragraph (d) of this section and from certain other adjuvant substances required in the production of the textiles or textile fibers or added to impart desired properties.

(b) The quantity of any adjuvant substance employed in the production of textiles or textile fibers does not exceed the amount reasonably required to accomplish the intended physical or technical effect or any limitation further provided.

(c) Any substance employed in the production of textiles or textile fibers that is the subject of a regulation in parts 174, 175, 176, 177, 178 and § 179.45 of this chapter conforms with any specification in such regulation.

(d) Substances employed in the production of or added to textiles and textile fibers may include:

(1) Substances generally recognized as safe in food.

(2) Substances subject to prior sanction or approval for use in textiles and textile fibers and used in accordance with such sanction or approval.

(3) Substances generally recognized as safe for use in cotton and cotton fabrics used in dry-food packaging.

(4) Substances that by regulation in this part may safely be used in the production of or as a component of textiles or textile fibers and subject to provisions of such regulation.

(5) Substances identified in this paragraph (d)(5), subject to such limitations as are provided:

List of substances	Limitations
(i) Fibers:	
Cotton.	
Polyethylene terephthalate complying in composition with the provisions of § 177.1630(e)(4)(ii).	For use only in the manufacture of items for repeated use.
Rayon.	

List of substances	Limitations
(ii) Adjuvant substances:	
Aluminum stearate.	
Borax	For use as preservative only.
Butyl-acetyl ricinoleate.	
Colorants used in accordance with § 178.3297 of this chapter..	
Di-*tert*-butyl hydroquinone.	
Dimethylpolysiloxane.	
Ethylenediaminetetraacetic acid, sodium salt.	
4-Ethyl-4-hexadecyl morpholinium ethyl sulfate	For use only as a lubricant in the manufacture of polyethylene terephthalate fibers specified in paragraph (d)(5)(i) of this section at a level not to exceed 0.03 percent by weight of the finished fibers.
Eugenol.	
Fats, oils, fatty acids, and fatty alcohols derived from castor, coconut, cottonseed, fish, mustardseed, palm, peanut, rapeseed, ricebran, soybean, sperm, and tall oils and tallow.	
Fats, oils, fatty acids, and fatty alcohols described in the preceding item reacted with one or more of the following substances:	
n-Butyl and isobutyl alcohol.	
Diethylene glycol.	
Diethanolamine.	
Glycerol.	
Hexylene glycol (2-methyl-2,4-pentanediol).	
Hydrogen.	
Isopropyl alcohol.	
Methyl alcohol.	
Oxygen.	
Polyethylene glycol (molecular weight 400–3,000).	
Potassium hydroxide.	
Propylene glycol.	
Sodium hydroxide.	
Sulfuric acid.	
Formaldehyde	For use as preservative only.
Glyceryl mono-12-hydroxystearate.	
2-(9-Heptadecenyl)-1-[2-(10-octadecenamido)ethyl-2-imidazolinium ethyl sulfate.	
Hexylene glycol (2-methyl,-2,4-pentanediol).	
Isobutyl alcohol.	
Isopropyl alcohol.	
Kerosene.	
Methyl ester of sulfated ricebran oil.	
Mineral oil	For use only at a level not to exceed 0.15 percent by weight of finished fibers.
Mono- and diisopropylated *m*- and *p*-cresols (isothymol derivative).	
N-Oleyl, *N'*-acetyl, *N'*-β-hydroxy-ethylenediamine.	
Petrolatum.	
Petroleum sulfonate.	
Pine oil.	
Polybutene, hydrogenated; complying with the identity prescribed under 21 CFR 178.3740(b) of this chapter.	
Polyethylene, oxidized (air blown).	
Polyvinyl acetate.	
Polyvinyl alcohol.	
Potassium soap of a saponified sulfated castor oil.	
Sodium bis(2,6-dimethylheptyl-4) sulfosuccinate.	
Sodium dioctyl sulfosuccinate.	
Sodium dodecyl benzenesulfonate.	
Sodium fluoride	For use as preservative only.
Sodium hydrosulfite.	
Sodium hypochlorite.	
Sodium lauryl sulfate.	
Sodium 2-mercaptobenzothiazole	Do.
Sodium pentachlorophenate	Do.
Styrene-butadiene copolymer.	
Sulfated butyl, isobutyl and propyl oleate.	
Tallow.	
Tallow, sulfonated.	
Titanium dioxide.	
Triethanolamine.	
Ultramarine blue.	
Waxes, petroleum.	
Zinc hydrosulfite.	

(e) Textile and textile fibers are used as articles or components of articles that contact dry food only.

(f) The provisions of this section are not applicable to jute fibers used as prescribed by § 178.3620(d)(2) of this chapter.

[42 FR 14572, Mar. 15, 1977, as amended at 46 FR 37042, July 17, 1981; 49 FR 4372, Feb. 6, 1984; 49 FR 5748, Feb. 15, 1984; 56 FR 42933, Aug. 30, 1991]

§ 177.2910 Ultra-filtration membranes.

Ultra-filtration membranes identified in paragraphs (a)(1), (a)(2), (a)(3), and (a)(4) of this section may be safely used in the processing of food, under the following prescribed conditions;

(a)(1) Ultra-filtration membranes that consist of paper impregnated with cured phenol-formaldehyde resin, which is used as a support and is coated with a vinyl chloride-acrylonitrile copolymer.

(2) Ultra-filtration membranes that consist of a sintered carbon support that is coated with zirconium oxide (CAS Reg. No. 1314–23–4) containing up to 12 percent yttrium oxide (CAS Reg. No. 1314–36–9).

(3) Ultra-filtration membranes that consist of an aluminum oxide support that is coated with zirconium oxide (CAS Reg. No. 1314–23–4) containing up to 5 percent yttrium oxide (CAS Reg. No. 1314–36–9).

(4) Ultrafiltration membranes that consist of a microporous poly(vinylidene fluoride) membrane with a hydrophilic surface modifier consisting of hydroxypropyl acrylate/tetraethylene glycol diacrylate copolymer.

(b) Any substance employed in the production of ultra-filtration membranes that is the subject of a regulation in parts 174, 175, 176, 177, 178 and § 179.45 of this chapter conforms with the specifications of such regulation.

(c) Ultra-filtration membranes are used in the physical separation of dissolved or colloidally suspended varying molecular size components of liquids during the commercial processing of bulk quantities of food.

(d) Ultra-filtration membranes shall be maintained in a sanitary manner in accordance with good manufacturing practice so as to prevent potential microbial adulteration of the food.

(e) Ultrafiltration membranes identified in paragraph (a)(4) may be used to filter aqueous or acidic foods containing up to 13 percent of alcohol at temperatures not to exceed 21 °C (70 °F).

(f) To assure safe use of the ultra-filtration membranes, the label or labeling shall include adequate directions for a pre-use treatment, consisting of conditioning and washing with a minimum of 8 gallons of potable water prior to their first use in contact with food.

(g) Acrylonitrile copolymers identified in this section shall comply with the provisions of § 180.22 of this chapter.

[42 FR 14572, Mar. 15, 1977, as amended at 53 FR 17925, May 19, 1988; 58 FR 48599, Sept. 17, 1993; 60 FR 54426, Oct. 24, 1995]

PART 178—INDIRECT FOOD ADDITIVES: ADJUVANTS, PRODUCTION AIDS, AND SANITIZERS

Subpart A [Reserved]

Subpart B—Substances Utilized To Control the Growth of Microorganisms

Sec.

Subpart C—Antioxidants and Stabilizers

Subpart D—Certain Adjuvants and Production Aids

AUTHORITY: 21 U.S.C. 321, 342, 348, 379e.

SOURCE: 42 FR 14609, Mar. 15, 1977, unless otherwise noted.

EDITORIAL NOTE: Nomenclature changes to part 178 appear at 61 FR 14482, Apr. 2, 1996, 66 FR 56035, Nov. 6, 2001, 66 FR 66742, Dec. 27, 2001, 68 FR 15355, Mar. 31, 2003, and 70 FR 72074, Dec. 1, 2005.

Subpart A [Reserved]

Subpart B—Substances Utilized To Control the Growth of Microorganisms

§ 178.1005 Hydrogen peroxide solution.

Hydrogen peroxide solution identified in this section may be safely used to sterilize polymeric food-contact surfaces identified in paragraph (e)(1) of this section.

(a) *Identity*. For the purpose of this section, hydrogen peroxide solution is an aqueous solution containing not more than 35 percent hydrogen peroxide (CAS Reg. No. 7722–84–1) by weight, meeting the specifications prescribed in paragraph (c) of this section.

(b) *Optional adjuvant substances*. Hydrogen peroxide solution identified in paragraph (a) of this section may contain substances generally recognized as safe in or on food, substances generally recognized for their intended use in food packaging, substances used in accordance with a prior sanction or approval, and substances permitted by applicable regulations in parts 174 through 179 of this chapter.

(c) *Specifications*. Hydrogen peroxide solution shall meet the specifications of the "Food Chemicals Codex," 3d Ed. (1981), pp. 146–147, which is incorporated by reference (Copies may be obtained from the National Academy Press, 2101 Constitution Ave. NW., Washington, DC 20418, or may be examined at the National Archives and Records Administration (NARA). For information on the availability of this material at NARA, call 202–741–6030, or go to: *http://www.archives.gov/federal_register/code_of_federal_regulations/ibr_locations.html*.), and the United States Pharmacopeia XX (1980), except that hydrogen peroxide may exceed the concentration specified therein.

(d) *Limitations*. No use of hydrogen peroxide solution in the sterilization of food packaging material shall be considered to be in compliance if more than 0.5 part per million of hydrogen peroxide can be determined in distilled water packaged under production conditions (assay to be performed immediately after packaging).

(e) *Conditions of use*. (1) Hydrogen peroxide solution identified in and complying with the specifications in this section may be used by itself or in combination with other processes to treat food-contact surfaces to attain commercial sterility at least equivalent to that attainable by thermal processing for metal containers as provided for in part 113 of this chapter. Food-contact surfaces include the following:

Substances	Limitations
Ethylene-acrylic acid copolymers.	Complying with § 177.1310 of this chapter.
Ethylene-carbon monoxide copolymers.	Complying with § 177.1312 of this chapter.
Ethylene-methyl acrylate copolymer resins.	Complying with § 177.1340 of this chapter.
Ethylene-vinyl acetate copolymers.	Complying with § 177.1350 of this chapter.
Ionomeric resins	Complying with § 177.1330 of this chapter.
Isobutylene polymers ...	Complying with § 177.1420 (a)(1) and (a)(2) of this chapter.
Olefin polymers	Complying with § 177.1520 of this chapter.
Polycarbonate resins ...	Complying with § 177.1580 of this chapter.
Polyethylene-terephthalate polymers.	Complying with § 177.1630 of this chapter (excluding polymers described in § 177.1630(c)) of this chapter.
Poly-l-butene resins and butene/ethylene copolymers.	Complying with § 177.1570 of this chapter.
Polystryrene and rubber-modified polystyrene polymers.	Complying with § 177.1640 of this chapter.
Vinylidene chloride/ methyl acrylate copolymers.	Complying with § 177.1990 of this chapter.

(2) The packaging materials identified in paragraph (e)(1) of this section may be used for packaging all commercially sterile foods except that the olefin polymers may be used in articles for packaging foods only of the types identified in § 176.170(c) of this chapter, table 1, under Categories I, II, III, IV-B, V, and VI.

(3) Processed foods packaged in the materials identified in paragraph (e)(1) of this section shall conform with parts 108, 110, 113, and 114 of this chapter as applicable.

[46 FR 2342, Jan. 9, 1981, as amended at 49 FR 10111, Mar. 19, 1984; 49 FR 32345, Aug. 14, 1984; 49 FR 37747, Sept. 26, 1984; 51 FR 45881, Dec. 23, 1986; 52 FR 26146, July 13, 1987; 53 FR 47186, Nov. 22, 1988; 54 FR 5604, Feb. 6, 1989; 54 FR 13167, Mar. 31, 1989; 54 FR 6365 Feb. 9, 1989; 55 FR 47055, Nov. 9, 1990; 57 FR 32423, July 22, 1992]

§ 178.1010 Sanitizing solutions.

Sanitizing solutions may be safely used on food-processing equipment and utensils, and on other food-contact articles as specified in this section, within the following prescribed conditions:

(a) Such sanitizing solutions are used, followed by adequate draining, before contact with food.

(b) The solutions consist of one of the following, to which may be added components generally recognized as safe and components which are permitted by prior sanction or approval.

(1) An aqueous solution containing potassium, sodium, or calcium hypochlorite, with or without the bromides of potassium, sodium, or calcium.

(2) An aqueous solution containing dichloroisocyanuric acid, trichloroisocyanuric acid, or the sodium or potassium salts of these acids, with or without the bromides of potassium, sodium, or calcium.

(3) An aqueous solution containing potassium iodide, sodium *p*-toluenesulfonchloroamide, and sodium lauryl sulfate.

(4) An aqueous solution containing iodine, butoxy monoether of mixed (ethylene-propylene) polyalkylene glycol having a cloudpoint of 90°–100 °C in 0.5 percent aqueous solution and an average molecular weight of 3,300, and ethylene glycol monobutyl ether. Additionally, the aqueous solution may contain diethylene glycol monoethyl ether as an optional ingredient.

(5) An aqueous solution containing elemental iodine, hydriodic acid, *a*-(*p*-nonylphenyl)-*omega*-hydroxypoly-(oxyethylene) (complying with the identity prescribed in § 178.3400(c) and having a maximum average molecular weight of 748) and/or polyoxyethylene-polyoxypropylene block polymers (having a minimum average molecular weight of 1,900). Additionally, the aqueous solution may contain isopropyl alcohol as an optional ingredient.

(6) An aqueous solution containing elemental iodine, sodium iodide, sodium dioctylsulfosuccinate, and polyoxyethylene-polyoxypropylene block polymers (having a minimum average molecular weight of 1,900).

(7) An aqueous solution containing dodecylbenzenesulfonic acid and either isopropyl alcohol or polyoxyethylene-polyoxypropylene block polymers (having a minimum average molecular weight of 2,800). In addition to use on

food-processing equipment and utensils, this solution may be used on glass bottles and other glass containers intended for holding milk.

(8) An aqueous solution containing elemental iodine, butoxy monoether of mixed (ethylene-propylene) polyalkylene glycol having a minimum average molecular weight of 2,400 and α-lauroyl-*omega*-hydroxypoly (oxyethylene) with an average 8–9 moles of ethylene oxide and an average molecular weight of 400. In addition to use on food-processing equipment and utensils, this solution may be used on beverage containers, including milk containers or equipment. Rinse water treated with this solution can be recirculated as a preliminary rinse. It is not to be used as final rinse.

(9) An aqueous solution containing *n*-alkyl (C_{12}-C_{18}) benzyldimethylammonium chloride compounds having average molecular weights of 351 to 380. The alkyl groups consist principally of groups with 12 to 16 carbon atoms and contain not more than 1 percent each of groups with 8 and 10 carbon atoms. Additionally, the aqueous solution may contain either ethyl alcohol or isopropyl alcohol as an optional ingredient.

(10) An aqueous solution containing trichloromelamine and either sodium lauryl sulfate or dodecylbenzenesulfonic acid. In addition to use on food-processing equipment and utensils and other food-contact articles, this solution may be used on beverage containers except milk containers or equipment.

(11) An aqueous solution containing equal amounts of *n*-alkyl (C_{12}-C_{18}) benzyl dimethyl ammonium chloride and *n*-alkyl (C_{12}-C_{18}) dimethyl ethylbenzyl ammonium chloride (having an average molecular weight of 384). In addition to use on food-processing equipment and utensils, this solution may be used on food-contact surfaces in public eating places.

(12) An aqueous solution containing the sodium salt of sulfonated oleic acid, polyoxyethylene-polyoxypropylene block polymers (having an average molecular weight of 2,000 and 27 to 31 moles of polyoxypropylene). In addition to use on food-processing equipment and utensils, this solution may be used on glass bottles and other glass containers intended for holding milk. All equipment, utensils, glass bottles, and other glass containers treated with this sanitizing solution shall have a drainage period of 15 minutes prior to use in contact with food.

(13) An aqueous solution containing elemental iodine and alkyl (C_{12}-C_{15}) monoether of mixed (ethylene-propylene) polyalkylene glycol, having a cloud-point of 70°–77 °C in 1 percent aqueous solution and an average molecular weight of 807.

(14) An aqueous solution containing iodine, butoxy monoether of mixed (ethylene-propylene) polyalkylene glycol, having a cloud-point of 90°–100 °C in 0.5 percent aqueous solution and an average molecular weight of 3,300, and polyoxyethylene-polyoxypropylene block polymers (having a minimum average molecular weight of 2,000).

(15) An aqueous solution containing lithium hypochlorite.

(16) An aqueous solution containing equal amounts of *n*-alkyl (C_{12}-C_{18}) benzyl dimethyl ammonium chloride and *n*-alkyl (C_{12}-C_{14}) dimethyl ethylbenzyl ammonium chloride (having average molecular weights of 377 to 384), with the optional adjuvant substances tetrasodium ethylenediaminetetraacetate and/or *alpha*-(*p*-nonylphenol)-*omega*-hydroxy poly (oxyethylene) having an average poly- (oxyethylene) content of 11 moles. Alpha-hydro-omega-hydroxypoly-(oxyethylene) poly(oxypropoylene) (15 to 18 mole minimum) poly (oxyethylene) block copolymer, having a minimum molecular weight of 1,900 (CAS Registry No. 9003–11–6) may be used in lieu of alpha- (*p*-nonylphenol)-omega-hydroxy-poly(oxyethylene) having an average poly(oxyethylene) content of 11 moles. In addition to use on food-processing equipment and utensils, this solution may be used on food-contact surfaces in public eating places.

(17) An aqueous solution containing di-*n*-alkyl(C_8-C_{10})dimethyl ammonium chlorides having average molecular weights of 332–361 and either ethyl alcohol or isopropyl alcohol. In addition to use on food-processing equipment and utensils, this solution may be used

on food-contact surfaces in public eating places.

(18) An aqueous solution containing *n*-alkyl(C_{12}-C_{18}) benzyldimethylammonium chloride, sodium metaborate, *alpha*-terpineol and *alpha*[*p*-(1,1,3,3-tetramethylbutyl)phenyl] -*omega*-hydroxy-poly (oxyethylene) produced with one mole of the phenol and 4 to 14 moles ethylene oxide.

(19) An aqueous solution containing sodium dichloroisocyanurate and tetrasodium ethylenediaminetetraacetate. In addition to use on food-processing equipment and utensils, this solution may be used on food-contact surfaces in public eating places.

(20) An aqueous solution containing *ortho*-phenylphenol, *ortho*-benzyl-*para*-chlorophenol, para-tertiaryamylphenol, sodium -*alpha*-alkyl(C_{12}-C_{15})-*omega*-hydroxypoly (oxyethylene) sulfate with the poly(oxyethylene) content averaging one mole, potassium salts of coconut oil fatty acids, and isopropyl alcohol or hexylene glycol.

(21) An aqueous solution containing sodium dodecylbenzenesulfonate. In addition to use on food-processing equipment and utensils, this solution may be used on glass bottles and other glass containers intended for holding milk.

(22) An aqueous solution containing (1) di-*n*-alkyl(C_8-C_{10}) dimethylammonium chloride compounds having average molecular weights of 332–361, (2) *n*-alkyl (C_{12}-C_{18}) benzyldimethylammonium chloride compounds having average molecular weights of 351–380 and consisting principally of alkyl groups with 12 to 16 carbon atoms with or without not over 1 percent each of groups with 8 and 10 carbon atoms, and (3) ethyl alcohol. The ratio of compound (1) to compound (2) is 60 to 40.

(23) An aqueous solution containing *n*-alkyl (C_{12}-C_{16}) benzyldimethylammonium chloride and didecyldimethylammonium chloride.

(24) An aqueous solution containing elemental iodine (CAS Reg. No. 7553–56–2), *alpha*-[*p*-(1,1,3,3-tetramethylbutyl)-phenyl]-*omega*-hydroxypoly-(oxyethylene) produced with one mole of the phenol and 4 to 14 moles ethylene oxide, and *alpha*-alkyl(C_{12}-C_{15})-*omega*-hydroxy[poly(oxyethylene) poly(oxypropylene)] (having an average molecular weight of 965).

(25) An aqueous solution containing elemental iodine (CAS Reg. No. 7553–56–2), potassium iodide (CAS Reg. No. 7681–11–0), and isopropanol (CAS Reg. No. 67–63–0). In addition to use on food processing equipment and utensils, this solution may be used on beverage containers, including milk containers and equipment and on food-contact surfaces in public eating places.

(26) [Reserved]

(27) An aqueous solution containing decanoic acid (CAS Reg. No. 334–48–5), octanoic acid (CAS Reg. No. 124–07–2), and sodium 1-octanesulfonate (CAS Reg. No. 5324–84–5). Additionally, the aqueous solution may contain isopropyl alcohol (CAS Reg. No. 67–63–0) as an optional ingredient.

(28) An aqueous solution containing sulfonated 9-octadecenoic acid (CAS Reg. No. 68988–76–1) and sodium xylenesulfonate (CAS Reg. No. 1300–72–7).

(29) An aqueous solution containing dodecyldiphenyloxidedisulfonic acid (CAS Reg. No. 30260–73–2), sulfonated tall oil fatty acid (CAS Reg. No. 68309–27–3), and neo-decanoic acid (CAS Reg. No. 26896–20–8). In addition to use on food-processing equipment and utensils, this solution may be used on glass bottles and other glass containers intended for holding milk.

(30) An aqueous solution containing hydrogen peroxide (CAS Reg. No. 7722–84–1), peracetic acid (CAS Reg. No. 79–21–0), acetic acid (CAS Reg. No. 64–19–7), and 1-hydroxyethylidene-1,1-diphosphonic acid (CAS Reg. No. 2809–21–4).

(31) An aqueous solution containing elemental iodine, *alpha*-alkyl(C_{10}-C_{14})-*omega*-hydroxypoly(oxyethylene)poly-(oxypropylene) of average molecular weight between 768 and 837, and *alpha*-alkyl(C_{12}-C_{18})-*omega*-hydroxypoly(oxyethylene) poly(oxypropylene) of average molecular weight between 950 and 1,120. In addition to use on food-processing equipment and utensils, this solution may be used on food-contact surfaces in public eating places.

(32) An aqueous solution containing (i) di-*n*-alkyl(C_8-C_{10})dimethyl- ammonium chloride compounds having average molecular weights of 332 to 361, (ii) *n*-alkyl(C_{12}-C_{18})benzyldimethyl- ammonium chloride compounds having average molecular weights of 351 to 380 and consisting principally of alkyl groups with 12 to 16 carbon atoms with no more than 1 percent of groups with 8 and 10, (iii) ethyl alcohol, and (iv) *alpha*-(*p*-nonylphenyl)-*omega*-hydroxypoly(oxyethylene) produced by the condensation of 1 mole of *p*-nonylphenol with 9 to 12 moles of ethylene oxide. The ratio of compound (i) to compound (ii) is 3 to 2.

(33) An aqueous solution containing (i) di-*n*-alkyl-(C_8-C_{10})-dimethylammonium chloride compounds having average molecular weights of 332 to 361; (ii) *n*-alkyl(C_{12}-C_{18}) -benzyldimethylammonium chloride compounds having molecular weights of 351 to 380 and consisting principally of alkyl groups with 12 to 16 carbon atoms with no more than 1 percent of the groups with 8 to 10; and (iii) tetrasodium ethylenediamine tetraacetate. Additionally, the aqueous solution contains either *alpha*-(*p*-nonylphenyl)-*omega*-hydroxypoly-(oxyethylene) or *alpha*-alkyl(C_{11}-C_{15})-*omega*-hydroxypoly-(oxyethylene), each produced with 9 to 13 moles of ethylene oxide. The ratio of compound (i) to compound (ii) is 3 to 2.

(34) An aqueous solution of an equilibrium mixture of oxychloro species (predominantly chlorite, chlorate, and chlorine dioxide) generated either (i) by directly metering a concentrated chlorine dioxide solution, prepared just prior to use, into potable water to provide the concentration of available chlorine dioxide stated in paragraph (c)(29) of this section, or (ii) by acidification of an aqueous alkaline solution of oxychloro species (predominantly chlorite and chlorate) followed by dilution with potable water to provide the concentration of available chlorine dioxide described in paragraph (c)(29) of this section.

(35) An aqueous solution containing decanoic acid (CAS Reg. No. 334–48–5), octanoic acid (CAS Reg. No. 124–07–2), lactic acid (CAS Reg. No. 050–21–5), phosphoric acid (CAS Reg. No. 7664–38–2) and a mixture of the sodium salt of naphthalenesulfonic acid (CAS Reg. No. 1321–69–3); the methyl, dimethyl, and trimethyl dervatives of the sodium salt of naphthalenesulfonic acid; and a mixture of the sodium salt of naphthalenesulfonic acid, and the methyl, dimethyl, and trimethyl derivatives of the sodium salt of naphthalenesulfonic acid alkylated at 3 percent by weight with C_6-C_9 linear olefins, as components of a sanitizing solution to be used on food-processing equipment and utensils. The methyl and dimethyl substituted derivatives (described within this paragraph (b)(35)) constitute no less than 70 percent by weight of the mixture of naphthalenesulfonates.

(36) The sanitizing solution contains decanoic acid (CAS Reg. No. 334–48–5); octanoic acid (CAS Reg. No. 124–07–2); lactic acid (CAS Reg. No. 050–21–5); phosphoric acid (CAS Reg. No. 7664–38–2); a mixture of 1-octanesulfonic acid (CAS Reg. No. 3944–72–7), and 1-octanesulfonic-2-sulfinic acid (CAS Reg. No. 113652–56–5) or 1,2-octanedisulfonic acid (CAS Reg. No. 113669–58–2); the condensate of four moles of poly(oxyethylene)poly(oxypropylene) block copolymers with one mole of ethylenediamine (CAS Reg. No. 11111–34–5); and the optional ingredient FD&C Yellow No. 5 (CAS Reg. No. 001934210). In addition to use on food-processing equipment and utensils, this solution may be used on dairy-processing equipment.

(37) The sanitizing solution contains sodium hypochlorite (CAS Reg. No. 7681–52–9), trisodium phosphate (CAS Reg. No. 7601–54–9), sodium lauryl sulfate (CAS Reg. No. 151–21–3), and potassium permanganate (CAS Reg. No. 7722–64–7). Magnesium oxide (CAS Reg. No. 1309–48–4) and potassium bromide (CAS Reg. No. 7758–02–3) may be added as optional ingredients to this sanitizing solution. In addition to use on food-processing equipment and utensils, this solution may be used on food-contact surfaces in public eating places.

(38) An aqueous solution containing hydrogen peroxide (CAS Reg. No. 7722–84–1); peroxyacetic acid (CAS Reg. No. 79–21–0); acetic acid (CAS Reg. No. 64–

19–7); sulfuric acid (CAS Reg. No. 7664–93–9); and 2,6-pyridinedicarboxylic acid (CAS Reg. No. 499–83–2). In addition to use on food-processing equipment and utensils, this solution may be used on dairy-processing equipment.

(39) An aqueous solution containing phosphoric acid (CAS Reg. No. 7664–38–2); octenyl succinic acid (CAS Reg. No. 28805–58–5); *N,N*-dimethyloctanamine (CAS Reg. No. 7378–99–6); and a mixture of *n*-carboxylic acids (C_6-C_{12}, consisting of not less than 56 percent octanoic acid and not less than 40 percent decanoic acid). This solution may be used on food-processing equipment and utensils, including dairy-processing equipment.

(40) An aqueous solution prepared by combining elemental iodine (CAS Reg. No. 7553–56–2); hydriodic acid (CAS Reg. No. 10034–85–2); sodium *N*-cyclohexyl-*N*-palmitoyl taurate (CAS Reg. No. 132–43–4); chloroacetic acid, sodium salt reaction products with 4,5-dihydro-2-undecyl-1*H*-imidazole-1-ethanol and sodium hydroxide (CAS Reg. No. 68608–66–2); dodecylbenzene sulfonic acid (CAS Reg. No. 27176–87–0); phosphoric acid (CAS Reg. No. 7664–38–2); isopropyl alcohol (CAS Reg. No. 67–63–0); and calcium chloride (CAS Reg. No. 10043–52–4). In addition to use on food-processing equipment and utensils, this solution may be used on dairy-processing equipment.

(41) An aqueous solution containing *n*-alkyl(C_{12}-C_{16})benzyldimethylammonium chloride, having average molecular weights ranging from 351 to 380 wherein the alkyl groups contain principally 12 to 16 carbons and not more than 1 percent each of the groups with 8 and 10 carbon atoms; ammonium chloride (CAS Reg. No. 12125–02–9); calcium stearate (CAS Reg. No. 1592–23–0); sodium bicarbonate (CAS Reg. No. 144–55–8); starch or dextrin, or both starch and dextrin (CAS Reg. No. 9004–53–9); and the optional ingredient methylene blue (CAS Reg. No. 61–73–4). In addition to use on food-processing equipment and utensils, this solution may be used on food-contact surfaces in public eating places.

(42) An aqueous solution containing decanoic acid (CAS Reg. No. 334–48–5), nonanoic acid (CAS Reg. No. 112–05–0), phosphoric acid (CAS Reg. No. 7664–38–2), propionic acid (CAS Reg No. 79–09–04), and sodium 1-octanesulfonate (CAS Reg. No. 5324–84–5). Sulfuric acid (CAS Reg. No. 7664–93–9) may be added as an optional ingredient. In addition to use on food-processing equipment and utensils, this solution may be used on dairy-processing equipment.

(43) An aqueous solution of iodine and hypochlorous acid generated by the dilution of an aqueous acidic (21.5 percent nitric acid) solution of iodine monochloride. In addition to use on food-processing equipment and utensils, this solution may be used on dairy-processing equipment.

(44) An aqueous solution of citric acid, disodium ethylenediaminetetraacetate, sodium lauryl sulfate, and monosodium phosphate. In addition to use on food-processing equipment and utensils, this solution may be used on dairy-processing equipment.

(45) An aqueous solution of hydrogen peroxide, acetic acid, peroxyacetic acid, octanoic acid, peroxyoctanoic acid, sodium 1-octanesulfonate, and 1-hydroxyethylidene-1,1-diphosphonic acid. In addition to use on food-processing equipment and utensils, this solution may be used on food-contact surfaces in public eating places, subject to the limitations in paragraph (c)(39) of this section.

(46) An aqueous solution of chlorine dioxide and related oxychloro species generated by acidification of an aqueous solution of sodium chlorite with a solution of sodium gluconate, citric acid, phosphoric acid, and sodium mono- and didodecylphenoxybenzenedisulfonate. In addition to use on food-processing equipment and utensils, this solution may be used on dairy-processing equipment.

(c) The solutions identified in paragraph (b) of this section will not exceed the following concentrations:

(1) Solutions identified in paragraph (b)(1) of this section will provide not more than 200 parts per million of available halogen determined as available chlorine.

(2) Solutions identified in paragraph (b)(2) of this section will provide not more than 100 parts per million of

available halogen determined as available chlorine.

(3) Solution identified in paragraph (b)(3) of this section will provide not more than 25 parts per million of titratable iodine. The solutions will contain the components potassium iodide, sodium *p*-toluenesulfonchloramide and sodium lauryl sulfate at a level not in excess of the minimum required to produce their intended functional effect.

(4) Solutions identified in paragraph (b)(4), (5), (6), (8), (13), and (14) of this section will contain iodine to provide not more than 25 parts per million of titratable iodine. The adjuvants used with the iodine will not be in excess of the minimum amounts required to accomplish the intended technical effect.

(5) Solutions identified in paragraph (b)(7) of this section will provide not more than 400 parts per million dodecylbenzenesulfonic acid and not more than 80 parts per million of polyoxyethylene-polyoxypropylene block polymers (having a minimum average molecular weight of 2,800) or not more than 40 parts per million of isopropyl alcohol.

(6) Solutions identified in paragraph (b)(9) of this section shall provide when ready to use no more than 200 parts per million of the active quaternary compound.

(7) Solutions identified in paragraph (b)(10) of this section shall provide not more than sufficient trichloromelamine to produce 200 parts per million of available chlorine and either sodium lauryl sulfate at a level not in excess of the minimum required to produce its intended functional effect or not more than 400 parts per million of dodecylbenzenesulfonic acid.

(8) Solutions identified in paragraph (b)(11) of this section shall provide, when ready to use, not more than 200 parts per million of active quaternary compound.

(9) The solution identified in paragraph (b)(12) of this section shall provide not more than 200 parts per million of sulfonated oleic acid, sodium salt.

(10) Solutions identified in paragraph (b)(15) of this section will provide not more than 200 parts per million of available chlorine and not more than 30 ppm lithium.

(11) Solutions identified in paragraph (b)(16) of this section shall provide not more than 200 parts per million of active quaternary compound.

(12) Solutions identified in paragraph (b)(17) of this section shall provide, when ready to use, a level of 150 parts per million of the active quaternary compound.

(13) Solutions identified in paragraph (b)(18) of this section shall provide not more than 200 parts per million of active quaternary compound and not more than 66 parts per million of *alpha*[*p*-(1,1,3,3-tetramethylbutyl) phenyl]-*omega*-hydroxypoly (oxyethylene).

(14) Solutions identified in paragraph (b)(19) of this section shall provide, when ready to use, a level of 100 parts per million of available chlorine.

(15) Solutions identified in paragraph (b)(20) of this section are for single use applications only and shall provide, when ready to use, a level of 800 parts per million of total active phenols consisting of 400 parts per million *ortho*-phenylphenol, 320 parts per million *ortho*-benzyl-*para*-chlorophenol and 80 parts per million *para*-tertiaryamylphenol.

(16) Solution identified in paragraph (b)(21) of this section shall provide not more than 430 parts per million and not less than 25 parts per million of sodium dodecylbenzenesulfonate.

(17) Solutions identified in paragraph (b)(22) of this section shall provide, when ready to use, at least 150 parts per million and not more than 400 parts per million of active quaternary compound.

(18) Solutions identified in paragraph (b)(23) of this section shall provide at least 150 parts per million and not more than 200 parts per million of the active quaternary compound.

(19) Solutions identified in paragraphs (b)(24), (b)(25), and (b)(43) of this section shall provide at least 12.5 parts per million and not more than 25 parts per million of titratable iodine. The adjuvants used with the iodine shall not be in excess of the minimum amounts required to accomplish the intended technical effect.

(20)–(21) [Reserved]

(22) Solutions identified in paragraph (b)(27) of this section shall provide, when ready to use, at least 109 parts per million and not more than 218 parts per million of total active fatty acids and at least 156 parts per million and not more than 312 parts per million of the sodium 1-octanesulfonate.

(23) Solutions identified in paragraph (b)(28) of this section shall provide, when ready to use, at least 156 parts per million and not more than 312 parts per million of sulfonated 9-octadecenoic acid, at least 31 parts per million and not more then 62 parts per million of sodium xylenesulfonate.

(24) Solutions identified in paragraph (b)(29) of this section will provide at least 237 parts per million and not more than 474 parts per million dodecyldiphenyloxidedisulfonic acid, at least 33 parts per million and not more than 66 parts per million sulfonated tall oil fatty acid, and at least 87 parts per million and not more than 174 parts per million neo-decanoic acid.

(25) Solutions identified in paragraph (b)(30) of this section shall provide, when ready to use, not less than 550 parts per million and not more than 1,100 parts per million hydrogen peroxide, not less than 100 parts per million and not more than 200 parts per million peracetic acid, not less than 150 parts per million and not more than 300 parts per million acetic acid, and not less than 15 parts per million and not more than 30 parts per million 1-hydroxyethylidene-1,1-diphosphonic acid.

(26) The solution identified in paragraph (b)(31) of this section shall provide, when ready to use, at least 12.5 parts per million and not more than 25 parts per million of titratable iodine. The adjuvants used with the iodine will not be in excess of the minimum amounts required to accomplish the intended technical effect.

(27) Solutions identified in paragraph (b)(32) of this section shall provide, when ready to use, at least 150 parts per million and no more than 400 parts per million of active quarternary compounds in solutions containing no more than 600 parts per million water hardness. The adjuvants used with the quarternary compounds will not exceed the amounts required to accomplish the intended technical effect.

(28) Solutions identified in paragraph (b)(33) of this section shall provide, when ready to use, at least 150 parts per million and not more than 400 parts per million of active quaternary compounds. The adjuvants used with the quaternary compounds shall not exceed the amounts required to accomplish the intended technical effect. Tetrasodium ethylenediamine tetraacetate shall be added at a minimum level of 60 parts per million. Use of these sanitizing solutions shall be limited to conditions of water hardness not in excess of 300 parts per million.

(29) Solutions identified in paragraph (b)(34) of this section should provide, when ready to use, at least 100 parts per million and not more than 200 parts per million available chlorine dioxide as determined by the method titled "Iodometric Method for the Determination of Available Chlorine Dioxide (50–250 ppm available ClO_2)," which is incorporated by reference. Copies are available from the Center for Food Safety and Applied Nutrition (HFS–200), Food and Drug Administration, 5100 Paint Branch Pkwy., College Park, MD 20740, or available for inspection at the National Archives and Records Administration (NARA). For information on the availability of this material at NARA, call 202–741–6030, or go to: *http://www.archives.gov/federal_register/code_of_federal_regulations/ibr_locations.html.*

(30) Solutions identified in paragraph (b)(35) of this section shall provide, when ready for use, at least 117 parts per million and not more than 234 parts per million of total fatty acids and at least 166 parts per million and not more than 332 parts per million of a mixture of naphthalenesulfonates. The adjuvants phosphoric acid and lactic acid, used with decanoic acid, octanoic acid, and sodium naphthalenesulfonate and its alkylated derivatives, will not be in excess of the minimum amounts required to accomplish the intended technical effects.

(31) Solutions identified in paragraph (b)(36) of this section shall provide, when ready for use, at least 29 parts per million and not more than 58 parts per million decanoic acid; at least 88 parts

per million and not more than 176 parts per million of octanoic acid; at least 69 parts per million and not more than 138 parts per million of lactic acid; at least 256 parts per million and not more than 512 parts per million of phosphoric acid; at least 86 parts per million and not more than 172 parts per million of 1-octanesulfonic acid; at least 51 parts per million and not more than 102 parts per million of 1-octanesulfonic-2-sulfinic acid or 1,2-octanedisulfonic acid; and at least 10 parts per million and not more than 20 parts per million of the condensate of four moles of poly(oxyethylene)poly(oxypropylene) block copolymers with one mole of ethylenediamine. The colorant adjuvant FD&C Yellow No. 5 shall not be used in excess of the minimum amount required to accomplish the intended technical effect.

(32)(i) The solution identified in paragraph (b)(37) of this section without potassium bromide shall provide, when ready to use, at least 100 parts per million and not more than 200 parts per million of available halogen determined as available chlorine; at least 2,958 parts per million and not more than 5,916 parts per million of trisodium phosphate; at least 1 part per million and not more than 3 parts per million of sodium lauryl sulfate; and at least 0.3 part per million and not more than 0.7 part per million on potassium permanganate.

(ii) The solution identified in paragraph (b)(37) of this section with potassium bromide shall provide, when ready to use, at least 25 parts per million and not more than 200 parts per million of available halogen determined as available chlorine; at least 15 parts per million and not more than 46 parts per million of potassium bromide; at least 690 parts per million and not more than 2,072 parts per million of trisodium phosphate; at least 0.3 part per million and not more than 1 part per million of sodium lauryl sulfate; and at least 0.1 part per million and not more than 0.3 part per million of potassium permanganate.

(iii) Magnesium oxide when used in paragraph (c)(32) (i) or (ii) of this section shall not be used in excess of the minimum amount required to accomplish its intended technical effect.

(33) Solutions identified in paragraph (b)(38) of this section shall provide when ready for use not less than 300 parts per million and not more than 465 parts per million of hydrogen peroxide; not less than 200 parts per million and not more than 315 parts per million of peroxyacetic acid; not less than 200 parts per million and not more than 340 parts per million of acetic acid; not less than 10 parts per million and not more than 20 parts per million of sulfuric acid; and not less than 0.75 parts per million and not more than 1.2 parts per million of 2,6-pyridinedicarboxylic acid.

(34) Solutions identified in paragraph (b)(39) of this section shall provide when ready for use not less than 460 parts per million and not more than 625 parts per million of phosphoric acid, and all components shall be present in the following proportions: 1 part phosphoric acid to 0.25 octenyl succinic acid to 0.18 part *N,N*-dimethyloctanamine to 0.062 part of a mixture of *n*-carboxylic acids (C_6-C_{12}, consisting of not less than 56 percent octanoic acid and not less than 40 percent decanoic acid).

(35) Solutions identified in paragraph (b)(40) of this section shall provide when ready for use not less than 12.5 parts per million and not more than 25.0 parts per million of titratable iodine; and not less than 2.7 parts per million and not more than 5.5 parts per million of dodecylbenzene sulfonic acid. All components shall be present in the following proportions: 1.0 part dodecylbenzene sulfonic acid to 43 parts sodium *N*-cyclohexyl-*N*-palmitoyl taurate to 7.7 parts chloroacetic acid, sodium salt, reaction products with 4,5-dihydro-2-undecyl-1*H*-imidazole-1-ethanol and sodium hydroxide to 114 parts phosphoric acid to 57 parts isopropyl alcohol to 3.0 parts calcium chloride.

(36) Solutions identified in paragraph (b)(41) of this section shall provide, when ready for use, not less than 150 parts per million and not more than 200 parts per million of *n*-alkyl(C_{12}-C_{16})benzyldimethylammonium chloride; and not more than 0.4 part per million of the colorant methylene blue. Components shall be present in the product used to prepare the solution in the following proportions: 1 part *n*-alkyl(C_{12}-

C_{16})benzyldimethylammonium chloride to 0.24 part ammonium chloride to 0.08 part calcium stearate to 0.60 part sodium bicarbonate to 0.08 part starch or dextrin, or a combination of starch and dextrin.

(37)(i) The solution identified in paragraph (b)(42) of this section not containing sulfuric acid shall provide when ready for use not less than 45 parts per million and not more than 90 parts per million of decanoic acid; and all components shall be present in the following proportions (weight/weight (w/w)): 1 part decanoic acid to 1 part nonanoic acid to 9.5 parts phosphoric acid to 3.3 parts propionic acid to 3.3 parts sodium 1-octanesulfonate.

(ii) The solution identified in paragraph (b)(42) of this section containing sulfuric acid shall provide when ready for use not less than 45 parts per million and not more than 90 parts per million of decanoic acid; and all components shall be present in the following proportions (w/w): 1 part decanoic acid to 1 part nonanoic acid to 2.8 parts phosphoric acid to 3.3 parts propionic acid to 3.3 parts sodium 1-octanesulfonate to 3.2 parts sulfuric acid.

(38) The solution identified in paragraph (b)(44) of this section shall provide, when ready for use, at least 16,450 parts per million and not more than 32,900 parts per million of citric acid; at least 700 parts per million and not more than 1,400 parts per million of disodium ethylenediaminetetraacetate; at least 175 parts per million and not more than 350 parts per million of sodium lauryl sulfate; and at least 175 parts per million and not more than 350 parts per million of monosodium phosphate.

(39)(i) The solution identified in paragraph (b)(45) of this section, when used on food processing equipment and utensils, including dairy and beverage-processing equipment but excluding food-contact surfaces in public eating places and dairy and beverage containers, shall provide when ready for use at least 72 parts per million and not more than 216 parts per million of hydrogen peroxide; at least 46 parts per million and not more than 138 parts per million of peroxyacetic acid; at least 40 parts per million and not more than 122 parts per million of octanoic acid (including peroxyoctanoic acid); at least 281 parts per million and not more than 686 parts per million of acetic acid; at least 7 parts per million and not more than 34 parts per million of 1-hydroxyethylidene-1,1-diphosphonic acid; and at least 36 parts per million and not more than 109 parts per million of sodium 1-octanesulfonate.

(ii) The solution identified in paragraph (b)(45) of this section, when used on food-contact equipment and utensils in warewashing machines, including warewashing machines in public eating places, at temperatures no less than 120 °F (49 °C) shall provide when ready for use at least 30 parts per million and not more than 91 parts per million of hydrogen peroxide; at least 19 parts per million and not more than 58 parts per million of peroxyacetic acid; at least 17 parts per million and not more than 52 parts per million of octanoic acid (including peroxyoctanoic acid); at least 119 parts per million and not more than 290 parts per million of acetic acid; at least 3 parts per million and not more than 14 parts per million of 1-hydroxyethylidene-1,1-diphosphonic acid; and at least 15 parts per million and not more than 46 parts per million of sodium 1-octanesulfonate.

(iii) The solution identified in paragraph (b)(45) of this section, when used on dairy or beverage containers, shall provide when ready for use at least 36 parts per million and not more than 108 parts per million of hydrogen peroxide; at least 23 parts per million and not more than 69 parts per million of peroxyacetic acid; at least 20 parts per million and not more than 61 parts per million of octanoic acid (including peroxyoctanoic acid); at least 140 parts per million and not more than 343 parts per million of acetic acid; at least 3 parts per million and not more than 17 parts per million of 1-hydroxyethylidene-1,1-diphosphonic acid; and at least 18 parts per million and not more than 55 parts per million of sodium 1-octanesulfonate.

(40) The solution identified in paragraph (b)(46) of this section shall provide, when ready for use, at least 100 parts per million and not more than 200 parts per million of chlorine dioxide as determined by the method developed

by Bio-cide International, Inc., entitled, "Iodometric Method for the Determination of Available Chlorine Dioxide (50–250 ppm Available ClO_2)," dated June 11, 1987, which is incorporated by reference in accordance with 5 U.S.C. 552(a) and 1 CFR part 51. Copies of this method are available from the Office of Food Additive Safety (HFS–200), Center for Food Safety and Applied Nutrition, Food and Drug Administration, 5100 Paint Branch Pkwy., College Park, MD 20740, 240–402–1200, and may be examined at the Center for Food Safety and Applied Nutrition's Library, Food and Drug Administration, 5100 Paint Branch Pkwy., College Park, MD 20740, or at the National Archives and Records Administration (NARA). For information on the availability of this material at NARA, call 202–741–6030, or go to: *http://www.archives.gov/federal_register/code_of_federal_regulations/ibr_locations.html*; at least 380 parts per million and not more than 760 parts per million of sodium gluconate; and at least 960 parts per million and not more than 1,920 parts per million of sodium mono- and didodecylphenoxybenzenedisulfonate. Other components listed under paragraph (b)(46) of this section shall be used in the minimum amount necessary to produce the intended effect.

(d) Sanitizing agents for use in accordance with this section will bear labeling meeting the requirements of the Federal Insecticide, Fungicide, and Rodenticide Act.

[42 FR 14609, Mar. 16, 1977]

EDITORIAL NOTE: For FEDERAL REGISTER citations affecting § 178.1010, see the List of CFR Sections Affected, which appears in the Finding Aids section of the printed volume and at *www.fdsys.gov*.

Subpart C—Antioxidants and Stabilizers

§ 178.2010 Antioxidants and/or stabilizers for polymers.

The substances listed in paragraph (b) of this section may be safely used as antioxidants and/or stabilizers in polymers used in the manufacture of articles or components of articles intended for use in producing, manufacturing, packing, processing, preparing, treating, packaging, transporting, or holding food, subject to the provisions of this section:

(a) The quantity used shall not exceed the amount reasonably required to accomplish the intended technical effect.

(b) List of substances:

Substances	Limitations
N-n-Alkyl-*N'*-(carboxymethyl)-*N,N'*-trimethylenediglycine; the alkyl group is even numbered in the range C_{14}–C_{18} and the nitrogen content is in the range 5.4–5.6 weight percent.	For use only: 1. As component of nonfood articles complying with §§ 175.105 and 177.2600 of this chapter. 2. At levels not to exceed 1.35 percent by weight of natural rubber, butadiene-acrylonitrile, butadiene-acrylonitrile-styrene, and butadiene-styrene polymers that are used in contact with nonalcoholic food at temperatures not to exceed room temperature and that are employed in closure-sealing gaskets complying with § 177.1210 of this chapter or in coatings complying with § 175.300, § 176.170, or § 175.320 of this chapter. The average thickness of such coatings and closure-sealing gaskets shall not exceed 0.004 inch.
Alkylthiophenolics:	For use only:
1. Acid-catalyzed condensation reaction products of 4-nonylphenol, formaldehyde, and 1-dodecanethiol (CAS Reg. No. 164907–73–7)..	1. At levels not to exceed 2 percent by weight of adhesives complying with § 175.105 of this chapter, of pressure-sensitive adhesives complying with § 175.125 of this chapter, and of rubber articles complying with § 177.2600 of this chapter.
2. Acid-catalyzed condensation reaction products of branched 4-nonylphenol, formaldehyde, and 1-dodecanethiol (CAS Reg. No. 203742–97–6)..	2. Do.
p-tert-Amylphenolformaldehyde resins produced when one mole of *p-tert*-amylphenol is made to react under acid conditions with one mole of formaldehyde.	For use only at levels not to exceed 2.1 percent by weight of polyamide resins that are: 1. Derived from dimerized vegetable oil acids (containing not more than 20 percent of monomer acids) and ethylenediamine. 2. Used in compliance with regulations in parts 174, 175, 176, 177, 178 and § 179.45 of this chapter.

Substances	Limitations
1,4-Benzenedicarboxylic acid, bis[2-(1,1-dimethylethyl)-6-[[3-(1,1-dimethylethyl)-2-hydroxy-5-methylphenyl]methyl]-4-methylphenyl]ester (CAS Reg. No. 57569–40–1).	For use only at levels not to exceed 0.075 percent by weight of olefin polymers complying with § 177.1520 of this chapter.
2-(2*H*-Benzotriazol-2-yl)-4,6-bis(1-methyl-1-phenylethyl)phenol (CAS Reg. No. 70321–86–7).	For use only: 1. At levels not to exceed 0.5 percent by weight of polyethylene phthalate polymers complying with § 177.1630 of this chapter. 2. At levels not to exceed 3.0 percent by weight of polycarbonate resins complying with § 177.1580 of this chapter.
2-(2*H*-Benzotriazol-2-yl)-4-(1, 1, 3, 3-tetramethylbutyl) phenol (CAS Reg. No. 3147–75–9).	For use only at levels not to exceed 0.5 percent by weight of polycarbonate resins complying with § 177.1580 of this chapter: *Provided,* That the finished resins contact food only under conditions of use E, F, and G described in table 2 of § 176.170(c) of this chapter.
2-[4,6-Bis(2,4-dimethylphenyl)-1,3,5-triazin-2-yl]-5-(octyloxy)phenol (CAS Reg. No. 2725–22–6)..	For use only: 1. At levels not to exceed 0.3 percent by weight of olefin polymers complying with § 177.1520(c) of this chapter in contact with food types I, II, IV-B, VI, VII-B, and VIII described in § 176.170(c) of this chapter, table 1, under conditions of use D through G as described in § 176.170(c), table 2, of this chapter. 2. At levels not to exceed 0.1 percent by weight of polypropylene complying with § 177.1520(c) of this chapter, items 1.1a, 1.2, and 1.3 in contact with food under conditions of use A through H as described in § 176.170(c), table 2, of this chapter. 3. At levels not to exceed 0.04 percent by weight of polyethylene and olefin copolymers complying with § 177.1520(c) of this chapter, items 2.1, 2.2, 2.3, 3.1a, 3.1b, 3.1c, 3.2a, and 3.2b having a minimum density of 0.94 gram per cubic centimeter, in contact with food under conditions of use A through H as described in § 176.170, table 2, of this chapter provided that the finished articles used in contact with fatty food types III, IV-A, V, VII-A, and IX as described in table 1 of § 176.170(c) of this chapter hold a minimum of 2 gallons (7.6 liters) of food. 4. At levels not to exceed 0.4 percent by weight of ethylene copolymers complying with § 177.1520(c) of this chapter, items 3.1a, 3.1b, 3.1c, 3.2a, and 3.2b, having a density of less than 0.94 gram per cubic centimeter, in contact with food under conditions of use B through H, as described in § 176.170(c), table 2, of this chapter provided that the finished articles used in contact with fatty food types III, IV-A, V, VII-A, and IX hold a minimum of 5 gallons (18.9 liters) of food. 5. At levels not to exceed 0.04 percent by weight of polyethylene having a density of less than 0.94 gram per cubic centimeter, and olefin polymers complying with § 177.1520(c) of this chapter, items 2.1, 2.2, 2.3, 3.3a, 3.3b, 3.4, 3.5, 3.6, 4, 5, and 6, in contact with food under conditions of use D through G as described in § 176.170(c) of this chapter, table 2, provided that the finished articles used in contact with fatty food types III, IV-A, V, VII-A, and IX hold a minimum of 5 gallons (18.9 liters) of food.
β, 3(or 4)-Bis(octadecylthio)cyclohexylethane (CAS Reg. No. 37625–75–5); CAS synonym: 1-[(*beta*-(octadecylthio)ethyl]-3(or 4)-(octadecylthio)cyclohexane.	For use only: 1. At levels not to exceed 0.3 percent by weight of all polymers for use in contact with foods of Types I, II, IV-B, VI, VII-B, and VIII under conditions of use B through H as described in tables 1 and 2 of § 176.170(c) of this chapter. 2. At levels not to exceed 0.3 percent by weight of polyolefins complying with § 177.1520 of this chapter, for use in contact with food of types III, IV-A, V, VII-A, and IX under conditions of use C through G as described in tables 1 and 2 of § 176.170(c) of this chapter.
Bis(2,2,6,6-tetramethyl-4-piperidinyl) sebacate (CAS Reg. No. 52829–07–9).	For use only: 1. In adhesives complying with § 175.105 of this chapter. 2. At levels not to exceed 0.1 percent by weight of pressure-sensitive adhesives complying with § 175.125 of this chapter.

Substances	Limitations
Bis(2,4-di-*tert*-butyl-6-methylphenyl) ethyl phosphite (CAS Reg. No. 145650–60–8).	For use only: 1. At levels not to exceed 0.3 percent by weight of olefin polymers complying with § 177.1520(c) of this chapter. The finished polymers may only be used with food of the types identified in § 176.170(c) of this chapter, table 1, under Categories I, II, IV-B, VI-A, VI-B, VII-B, and VIII, and under conditions of use B through H described in table 2 of § 176.170(c) of this chapter. 2. At levels not to exceed 0.1 percent by weight of propylene polymers complying with § 177.1520(c) of this chapter, items 1.1, 1.2, 1.3, 3.2b, 3.4, or 3.5, or 3.1a (where the density of this polymer is at least 0.85 gram per cubic centimeter and less than 0.91 gram per cubic centimeter). The finished polymers may only be used in contact with food of the types identified in § 176.170(c) of this chapter, table 1, under Categories III, IV-A, V, VI-C, VII-A, and IX, and under conditions of use B through H described in table 2 of § 176.170(c) of this chapter. 3. At levels not to exceed 0.1 percent by weight of high-density ethylene polymers complying with § 177.1520(c) of this chapter, items 2.1, 2.2, 2.3, 3.1a, 3.1b, 3.2a, or 3.6 (where the density of each of these polymers is at least 0.94 gram per cubic centimeter), or 5. The finished polymers may only be used in contact with food of the types identified in § 176.170(c) of this chapter, table 1, under Categories III, IV-A, V, VI-C, VII-A, and IX, and under conditions of use C (maximum temperature 70 °C) through G described in table 2 of § 176.170(c) of this chapter. *Provided,* that the finished food contact articles have a volume of at least 18.9 liters (5 gallons). 4. At levels not to exceed 0.01 percent by weight of low-density ethylene polymers complying with § 177.1520(c) of this chapter, items 2.1, 2.2, 2.3, 3.1a, 3.1b, 3.2a, 3.4, 3.5, or 3.6 (where the density of each of these polymers is less than 0.94 gram per cubic centimeter). The finished polymers may only be used in contact with food of the types identified in § 176.170(c) of this chapter, table 1, under Categories III, IV-A, V, VI-C, VII-A, and IX, and under conditions of use B through H described in table 2 of § 176.170(c) of this chapter. *Provided,* that the average thickness of such polymers in the form in which they contact food shall not exceed 0.001 inch.
1,2-Bis(3,5-di-*tert*-butyl-4-hydroxyhydrocinnamoyl)-hydrazine (CAS Reg. No. 32687–78–8).	For use only: 1. As provided in § 175.105 of this chapter. 2. At levels not exceeding 0.1 percent by weight of acrylonitrile-butadiene-styrene copolymers used in accordance with parts 175, 176, 177, and 181 of this chapter. 3. At levels not exceeding 0.1 percent by weight of polyoxymethylene copolymers complying with § 177.2470 of this chapter and of polyoxymethylene homopolymers complying with § 177.2480 of this chapter.
2,6-Bis(1-methylheptadecyl)-*p*-cresol	For use only at levels not exceeding 0.3 percent by weight of olefin polymers complying with § 177.1520(c) of this chapter, items 1.1, 1.2, 1.3, 2.1, 2.2, 2.3, 3.1, 3.2, 3.3, or 4. The average thickness of such polymers in the form in which they contact fatty food or food containing more than 8 percent of alcohol shall not exceed 0.004 inch.
3,9-Bis[2,4-bis(1-methyl-1-phenylethyl)phenoxy]-2,4,8,10-tetraoxa-3,9-diphosphaspiro[5.5]undecane (CAS Reg. No. 154862–43–8), which may contain not more than 2 percent by weight of triisopropanolamine (CAS Reg. No. 122–20–3).	For use only: 1. At levels not to exceed 0.15 percent by weight of all polymers, except as specified below. 2. At levels not to exceed 0.2 percent by weight of polycarbonate resins complying with § 177.1580 of this chapter. 3. At levels not to exceed 0.3 percent by weight of polyetherimide resins complying with § 177.1595 of this chapter.

Substances	Limitations
5,7-Bis(1,1-dimethylethyl)-3-hydroxy-2(3H)-benzofuranone, reaction products with *o*-xylene (CAS Reg. No. 181314–48–7).	For use only: 1. At levels not to exceed 0.1 percent by weight of olefin polymers complying with § 177.1520(c) of this chapter. The finished polymers may only be used in contact with food of the types identified in § 176.170(c) of this chapter, Table 1, under Categories I, II, IV-B, VI-A, VI-B, VII-B, and VIII, and under conditions of use B through H described in Table 2 of § 176.170(c) of this chapter. 2. At levels not to exceed 0.02 percent by weight of: (a) Propylene polymers and copolymers complying with § 177.1520(c) of this chapter, items 1.1, 1.2, 3.1a, 3.2a, 3.2b, 3.4, or 3.5. The finished polymer may only be used in contact with food of types identified in § 176.170(c) of this chapter, Table 1, under Categories III, IV-A, V, VI-C, VII-A, and IX, and under conditions of use B through H described in Table 2 of § 176.170(c) of this chapter; or (b) Ethylene polymers and copolymers complying with § 177.1520(c) of this chapter, items 2.1, 2.2, 2.3, 3.1a, 3.1b, 3.2a, or 3.6 (where the density of each of these polymers is at least 0.94 gram per cubic centimeter), or 5. The finished polymers may only be used in contact with food of the types identified in § 176.170(c) of this chapter, Table 1, under Categories III, IV-A, V, VI-C, VII-A, and IX, and under conditions of use B through H described in Table 2 of § 176.170(c) of this chapter; provided that the finished food-contact articles have a volume of at least 18.9 liters (5 gallons). 3. At levels not to exceed 0.02 percent by weight of ethylene polymers and copolymers complying with § 177.1520(c) of this chapter, items 2.1, 2.2, 2.3, 3.1a, 3.1b, 3.2a, 3.4, 3.5, or 3.6 (where the density of each of these polymers is less than 0.94 gram per cubic centimeter). The finished polymers may only be used in contact with food of the types identified in § 176.170(c) of this chapter, Table 1, under Categories III, IV-A, V, VI-C, VII-A, and IX, and under conditions of use B through H described in Table 2 of § 176.170(c) of this chapter; provided that the average thickness of such polymers in the form in which they contact food shall not exceed 50 micrometers (0.002 inch).
3,9-Bis[2-{3-(3-*tert*-butyl-4-hydroxy-5-methylphenyl)propionyloxy}-1,1-dimethylethyl]-2,4,8,10-tetraoxaspiro[5.5]undecane (CAS Reg. No. 90498–90–1).	For use only: 1. At levels not to exceed 0.2 percent by weight of polypropylene complying with § 177.1520(c), item 1.1 of this chapter. The finished polymer is to be used in contact with food only under conditions of use D through H described in table 2 of § 176.170(c) of this chapter. 2. At levels not to exceed 0.3 percent by weight of polyethylene complying with § 177.1520(c) of this chapter, item 2.1, provided that the polymer has a minimum density of 0.94 grams per cubic centimeter and is used in contact with food only under conditions of use D through G described in table 2 of § 176.170(c) of this chapter. 3. At levels not to exceed 0.3 percent by weight of olefin polymers complying with § 177.1520(c) of this chapter, items 1.1, 3.1, and 3.2, where the copolymers complying with items 3.1 and 3.2 contain not less than 85 weight percent of polymer units derived from propylene. The finished polymer is to be used in contact with food of types I, II, IV-B, VI-A, VI-B, VI-C, VII-B, and VIII under conditions of use A through H described in tables 1 and 2 of § 176.170(c) of this chapter.

Substances	Limitations
4-[[4,6-Bis(octylthio)-*s*-triazin-2-yl]amino]-2,6-di-*tert*-butylphenol (CAS Reg. No. 991–84–4).	For use only: 1. At levels not to exceed 0.5 percent by weight: in styrene block copolymers complying with § 177.1810 of this chapter; in rosins and rosin derivatives complying with § 175.300(b)(3)(v) of this chapter; in can end cement formulations complying with § 175.300(b)(3)(xxxi) of this chapter; in side seam cement formulations complying with § 175.300(b)(3)(xxxii) of this chapter; in petroleum alicyclic hydrocarbon resins and terpene resins complying with § 175.320(b)(3) of this chapter; in rosin and rosin derivatives complying with § 176.170(a)(5) of this chapter; in petroleum alicyclic hydrocarbon resins or their hydrogenated products complying with § 176.170(b)(2) of this chapter; in terpene resins complying with § 175.300(b)(2)(xi) of this chapter, when such terpene resins are used in accordance with § 176.170(b)(1) of this chapter; in resins and polymers complying with § 176.180(b) of this chapter; in closures with sealing gaskets complying with § 177.1210 of this chapter; in petroleum hydrocarbon resin and rosins and rosin derivatives complying with § 178.3800(b) of this chapter; and in reinforced wax complying with § 178.3850 of this chapter. 2. At levels not to exceed 0.2 percent by weight of the finished cellophane complying with § 177.1200 of this chapter. 3. At levels not to exceed 0.1 percent by weight in polystyrene and rubber-modified polystyrene complying with § 177.1640 of this chapter: *Provided,* That the finished polystyrene and rubber-modified polystyrene polymer contact food only under conditions of use B through G described in table 2 of § 176.170(c) of this chapter. 4. In adhesives complying with § 175.105 of this chapter; in pressure-sensitive adhesives complying with § 175.125 of this chapter; and as provided in § 177.2600 of this chapter.
4,4′-Bis(α,α-dimethylbenzyl)diphenylamine (CAS Reg. No. 10081–67–1).	For use at levels not to exceed 0.3 percent by weight of polypropylene complying with § 177.1520(c) of this chapter. The polypropylene articles are limited to use in contact with non-fatty foods only.
Boric acid (CAS Reg. No. 10043–35–3)	For use only at levels not to exceed 0.16 percent by weight of ethylene-vinyl acetate-vinyl alcohol copolymers complying with § 177.1360(a)(3) and (d) of this chapter.
1,3–Butanediol.	
Butylated reaction product of *p*-cresol and dicyclopentadiene produced by reacting *p*-cresol and dicyclopentadiene in an approximate mole ratio of 1.5 to 1, respectively, followed by alkylation with isobutylene so that the butyl content of the final product is not less than 18 percent.	For use only: 1. As components of nonfood articles complying with §§ 175.105 and 177.2600(c)(4)(iii) of this chapter. 2. At levels not to exceed 1.0 percent by weight of acrylonitrile/butadiene/styrene copolymers. The finished copolymers may be used in contact with food of Types I, II, IV-B, VI-A, VI-B, VII-B, and VIII under conditions of use B through H, as described in tables 1 and 2 of § 176.170(c) of this chapter, and with food of Types III, IV-A, V, VI-C, VII-A, and IX under conditions of use C through G as described in tables 1 and 2 of § 176.170(c) of this chapter.

Substances	Limitations
Butylated, styrenated cresols produced when equal moles of isobutylene, styrene, and a metacresol-paracresol mixture having a no more than 3 °C distillation range including 202 °C are made to react so that the final product meets the following specifications: Not less than 95 percent by weight of total alkylated phenols consisting of 13–25 percent by weight of butylated *m*- and *p*-cresols, 26–38 percent by weight of styrenated *m*- and *p*-cresols, 37–49 percent by weight of butylated styrenated *m*- and *p*-cresols, and not more than 10 percent by weight total of alkylated xylenols, alkylated *o*-cresol, alkylated phenol, and alkylated ethylphenol; acidity not more than 0.003 percent; and refractive index at 25 °C of 1.5550–1.5650, as determined by ASTM method D1218–82, "Standard Test Method for Refractive Index and Refractive Dispersion of Hydrocarbon Liquids," which is incorporated by reference. Copies may be obtained from the American Society for Testing Materials, 100 Barr Harbor Dr., West Conshohocken, Philadelphia, PA 19428-2959, or may be examined at the National Archives and Records Administration (NARA). For information on the availability of this material at NARA, call 202–741–6030, or go to: *http://www.archives.gov/federal_register/code_of_federal_regulations/ibr_locations.html.*.	For use only: 1. As provided in §§ 175.105 and 177.2600 of this chapter. 2. At levels not to exceed 0.5 percent by weight of polystyrene, rubber-modified polystyrene, or olefin polymers complying with § 177.1520 (c) of this chapter, items 1.1, 1.2, 1.3, 2.1, 2.2, 2.3, 3.1, 3.2, 3.3, or 4, or complying with other sections in parts 174, 175, 176, 177, 178 and § 179.45 of this chapter, used in articles that contact food only unded the conditions described in § 176.170(c) of this chapter, table 2, under conditions of use C through G.
2-*tert*-Butyl-*a*(3-*tert*-butyl-4-hydroxyphenyl)-*p*-cumenyl bis(*p*-nonylphenyl) phosphite; the nonyl group is a propylene trimer isomer and the phosphorus content is in the range 3.8–4.0 weight percent.	For use only: 1. As components of nonfood articles complying with §§ 175.105 and 177.2600 of this chapter. 2. At levels not to exceed 1.35 percent by weight of natural rubber, butadiene-acrylonitrile, butadiene-acrylonitrile-styrene, and butadiene-styrene polymers that are used in contact with nonalcoholic food at temperatures not to exceed room temperature and that are employed in closure-sealing gaskets complying with § 177.1210 of this chapter or in coatings complying with § 175.300, § 175.320, or § 176.170 of this chapter. The average thickness of such coatings and closure-sealing gaskets shall not exceed 0.004 inch.
2-(3′-*tert*-Butyl-2′-hydroxy-5′-methyl-phenyl)-5-chlorobenzotriazole with a melting point of 137–141 °C.	For use only at levels not to exceed 0.5 percent by weight of olefin polymers complying with § 177.1520(c) of this chapter, provided that the finished polymer contacts foods only of the types identified in Categories I, II, IV-B, VI-A and B, VII-B, and VIII in table 1, § 176.170 of this chapter.
4,4′-Butylidenebis(6-*tert*-butyl-*m*-cresol)	For use only. 1. As provided in §§ 175.105 and 177.2600 of this chapter. 2. At levels not to exceed 0.5 percent by weight of polypropylene complying with § 177.1520 of this chapter and for use at levels not to exceed 0.3 percent by weight of polyethylene complying with § 177.1520 of this chapter, provided that the finished polypropylene and polyethylene contact food only of the types identified in § 176.170(c) of this chapter, table 1, under Categories I, II, VI-B, and VIII.
Butyric acid, 3,3-bis(3-*tert*-butyl-4-hydroxyphenyl)ethylene ester (CAS Reg. No. 32509–66–3).	For use only: 1. At levels not to exceed 0.5 percent by weight of olefin copolymers complying with § 177.1520(c) of this chapter, items 3.1 and 3.2 except that when used in contact with foods described as types III, IV-A, V, VII-A, and IX in table 1 of § 176.170(c) of this chapter, the olefin copolymers may only be used under conditions of use E, F, and G set forth in table 2 of § 176.170(c) of this chapter. 2. At levels not to exceed 0.5 percent by weight of olefin polymers complying with § 177.1520(c) of this chapter, item 1.1, 3.1, or 3.2 (where the copolymers complying with items 3.1 and 3.2 contain not less than 85 weight-percent of polymer units derived from propylene). 3. At levels not to exceed 0.2 percent by weight of olefin polymers complying with § 177.1520(c) of this chapter, items 2.1, 2.2, 3.1, and 3.2.
Calcium benzoate..	

Substances	Limitations
Calcium bis[monoethyl(3,5-di-*tert*-butyl-4-hydroxy-benzyl)phosphonate] (CAS Reg. No. 65140–91–2).	For use only: 1. At levels not to exceed 0.25 percent by weight of polypropylene that complies with § 177.1520(c) of this chapter, items 1.1, 1.2, and 1.3. 2. At levels not to exceed 0.2 percent by weight of polyethylene and olefin copolymers that comply with § 177.1520(c) of this chapter, items 2.1, 2.2, 2.3, 3.1, 3.2, 3.3, 3.4, 3.5, and 3.6. Finished polymers having a density less than 0.94 gram per cubic centimeter shall be used in contact with food only under conditions of use B through H described in table 2 of § 176.170(c) of this chapter. 3. In adhesives complying with § 175.105 of this chapter. 4. At levels not to exceed 0.5 percent by weight of pressure-sensitive adhesives complying with § 175.125 of this chapter. 5. At levels not to exceed 0.5 percent by weight of rosins and rosin derivatives complying with § 175.300(b)(3)(v) of this chapter. 6. At levels not to exceed 0.5 percent by weight of can end cement formulations complying with § 175.300(b)(3)(xxxi) of this chapter. 7. At levels not to exceed 0.5 percent by weight of side seam cement formulations complying with § 175.300(b)(3)(xxxii) of this chapter. 8. At levels not to exceed 0.5 percent by weight of petroleum alicyclic hydrocarbon resins complying with § 175.320(b)(3) of this chapter. 9. At levels not to exceed 0.5 percent by weight of rosin and rosin derivatives complying with § 176.170(a)(5) of this chapter; and petroleum alicyclic hydrocarbon resins, or the hydrogenated product thereof, complying with § 176.170(b)(2) of this chapter. 10. At levels not to exceed 0.5 percent by weight of resins and polymers used as components of paper and paperboard in contact with dry food in compliance with § 176.180 of this chapter. 11. At levels not to exceed 0.5 percent by weight of closures with sealing gaskets complying with § 177.1210 of this chapter. 12. At levels not to exceed 0.5 percent by weight of the finished rubber article complying with § 177.2600 of this chapter. 13. At levels not to exceed 0.5 percent by weight of petroleum hydrocarbon resin and rosins and rosin derivatives complying with § 178.3800(b). 14. At levels not to exceed 0.5 percent by weight of reinforced wax complying with § 178.3850. 15. At levels not to exceed 0.3 percent by weight of polyethylene phthalate polymers, complying with § 177.1630 of this chapter. Provided, that the finished polymers contact food only under conditions of use B through H described in Table 2 of § 176.170(c) of this chapter.
Calcium myristate..	
Calcium ricinoleate	For use only at levels not to exceed 1 percent by weight of polyoxymethylene copolymer as provided in § 177.2470(b)(1) of this chapter.
Calcium stearate..	
Carbethoxymethyl diethyl phosphonate (CAS Reg. No. 867–13–0).	At levels not to exceed 0.07 percent by weight of polyethylene phthalate polymers complying with § 177.1630 of this chapter.
Cerium stereate (CAS Reg. No. 10119–53–6)	For use only at levels not to exceed 0.5 percent by weight in rigid and semirigid vinyl chloride homo– and copolymer articles modified in accordance with § 178.3790(b)(1) of this chapter that contact food under conditions of use B through H described in table 2 of § 176.170(c) of this chapter.
Cupric acetate and lithium iodide	For use at levels not exceeding 0.025 percent cupric acetate and 0.065 percent lithium iodide by weight of nylon 66 resins complying with § 177.1500 of this chapter; the finished resins are used or are intended to be used to contain foods during oven baking or oven cooking at temperatures above 250 °F. The average thickness of such resins in the form in which they contact food shall not exceed 0.0012 inch.
Cuprous iodide	For use at levels not exceeding 0.01 percent cuprous iodide by weight of nylon 66T resins complying with § 177.1500 of this chapter; the finished resins are used or are intended to be used to contain foods during oven baking or oven cooking at temperatures above 250 °F. The average thickness of such resins in the form in which they contact food shall not exceed 0.001 inch.
Cuprous iodide and cuprous bromide	For use at levels not exceeding 0.0025 percent cuprous iodide and 0.0175 percent cuprous bromide by weight of nylon 66 resins complying with § 177.1500 of this chapter; the finished resins are used or are intended to be used to contain foods during oven baking or oven cooking at temperatures above 250 °F. The average thickness of such resins in the form in which they contact food shall not exceed 0.0015 inch.
Cyanoguanidine	For use only at levels not to exceed 1 percent by weight of polyoxymethylene copolymer as provided in § 177.2470(b)(1) of this chapter.

Substances	Limitations
Cyclic neopentanetetrayl bis(octadecyl phosphite) (CAS Reg. No. 3806–34–6); the phosphorus content is in the range of 7.8 to 8.2 weight percent.	For use only at levels not to exceed 0.1 percent by weight of ethylene-vinyl acetate copolymers complying with § 177.1350 of this chapter that contact food under conditions of use E, F, and G described in table 2 of § 176.170(c) of this chapter.
Cyclic neopentanetetrayl bis(octadecyl phosphite) (CAS Reg. No. 3806–34–6) (which may contain not more than 1 percent by weight of triisopropanolamine (CAS Reg. No. 122–20–3)); the phosphorus content is in the range of 7.8 to 8.2 weight percent.	For use only: 1. At levels not to exceed 0.25 percent by weight of olefin polymers complying with § 177.1520(c) of this chapter, items 1.1, 2.1, and 3.1. 2. At levels not to exceed 0.25 percent by weight of olefin polymers complying with § 177.1520(c) of this chapter, item 2.2, that contact food Types I, II, VI-A, VII-B, and VIII described in table 1 of § 176.170(c) of this chapter under conditions of use B (for boil-in-bag applications), C, D, E, F, G, and H described in table 2 of § 176.170(c) of this chapter. 3. At levels not to exceed 0.15 percent by weight of olefin polymers complying with § 177.1520, items 1.1 and 3.2, that contact food Types I, II, VI-A, VII-B, and VIII described in table 1 of § 176.170(c) of this chapter under conditions of use B (for boil-in-bag applications), C, D, E, F, G, and H described in table 2 of § 176.170(c) of this chapter. 4. At levels not to exceed 0.20 percent by weight of polystyrene and/or rubber modified polystyrene complying with § 177.1640 of this chapter that contact food under conditions of use E, F, and G described in table 2 of § 176.170(c) of this chapter.
4,4′-Cyclohexylidenebis(2-cyclohexylphenol)	For use only at levels not to exceed 0.1 percent by weight of olefin polymers complying with § 177.1520(c) of this chapter, items 1.1, 1.2, 1.3, 2.1, 2.2, 2.3, 3.1, 3.2, 3.3, or 4: *Provided,* That the finished polymers contact food only of the types identified in § 176.170(c) of this chapter, table 1, under Categories I, II, IV-B, VI, VII-B, and VIII.
Dicetyl thiodipropionate having a melting point of 59°–62 °C as determined by ASTM method E324–79, "Standard Test Method for Relative Initial and Final Melting Points and the Melting Range of Organic Chemicals," and a saponification value in the range 176–183 as determined by ASTM method D1962–67 (Reapproved 1979), "Standard Test Method for Saponification Value of Drying Oils, Fatty Acids, and Polymerized Fatty Acids," which are incorporated by reference. Copies may be obtained from the American Society for Testing Materials, 100 Barr Harbor Dr., West Conshohocken, Philadelphia, PA 19428-2959, or may be examined at the National Archives and Records Administration (NARA). For information on the availability of this material at NARA, call 202–741–6030, or go to: *http://www.archives.gov/federal_register/code_of_federal_regulations/ibr_locations.html..*	The concentration of this additive and any other permitted antioxidants in the finished food-contact article shall not exceed a total of 0.5 milligram per square inch of food-contact surface.
Didodecyl– 1,4–dihydro–2,6–dimethyl–3,5–pyridinedicarboxylate (CAS Reg. No. 36265–41–5).	For use only at levels not to exceed 0.3 percenmt by weight in rigid polymer articles modified in accordance with § 178.3790 that contact food, under conditions of use E, F, and G described in table 2 of § 176.170 of this chapter.
2,6-Di(α-methyl benzyl)-4-methyl phenol [Chemical Abstracts Service Registry No. 1817–68–1].	For use only at levels not to exceed 0.2 percent by weight of olefin polymers complying with item 3.4 in § 177.1520(c) of this chapter, provided that such olefin polymers are limited to use at a level not to exceed 25 percent by weight in other olefin polymers complying with § 177.1520 of this chapter; and the total amount in such finished olefin polymers not to exceed 0.05 percent by weight, including the level that may be contributed by its presence at 6 percent in the item "butylated, styrenated cresols * * *" listed in this paragraph; and further provided that the finished olefin polymers are intended for contact with foods, except those containing more than 8 percent alcohol.
2,4-Dimethyl-6-(1-methylpentadecyl)phenol (CAS Reg. No. 134701–20–5).	For use only: 1. At levels not to exceed 0.3 percent by weight of acrylonitrile-butadiene-styrene copolymers used in accordance with applicable regulations in parts 175, 176, 177, and 181 of this chapter, under conditions of use C through H as described in table 2 of § 176.170(c) of this chapter. 2. At levels not to exceed 0.033 percent by weight of rigid polyvinyl chloride, under conditions of use A through H as described in table 2 of § 176.170(c) of this chapter.

Substances	Limitations
Dimethyl succinate polymer with 4-hydroxy-2,2,6,6-tetramethyl-1-piperidineethanol (CAS Reg. No. 65447–77–0).	For use only: 1. At levels not to exceed 0.3 percent by weight of olefin polymers complying with § 177.1520 of this chapter and under conditions of use B through H described in table 2 of § 176.170(c) of this chapter. 2. At levels not to exceed 0.3 percent by weight of ethylene-vinyl acetate copolymers complying with § 177.1350 of this chapter and under conditions of use B through H described in table 2 of § 176.170(c) of this chapter.
Dimethyltin/monomethyltin isooctylmercaptoacetates consisting of 5 to 90 percent by weight of monomethyltin tris (isooctylmercaptoacetate) (CAS Reg. No. 54849–38–6) or monomethyltin tris(2-ethylhexylmercaptoacetate) (CAS Reg. No. 57583–34–3) and 10 to 95 percent by weight of dimethyltin bis (isooctylmercaptoacetate) (CAS Reg. No. 26636–01–1) or dimethyltin bis(2–ethylhexylmercaptoacetate) (CAS Reg. No. 57583–35–4), and no more than 0.4 percent by weight of trimethyltin compounds, and having the following specifications: Tin content (as Sn) in the range of 15 to 21 percent and mercaptosulfur content in the range of 11 to 13.5 percent. Other alkyltin compounds are not to exceed 20 ppm.	For use only at levels not to exceed 2 percent by weight: 1. In rigid polyvinyl chloride used in the manufacture of pipes intended for contact with water in food-processing plants, and 2. In rigid polyvinyl chloride and in rigid vinyl chloride copolymers complying with § 177.1950 of this chapter or § 177.1980 of this chapter for use in contact with food of Types I, II, III, IV (except liquid milk), V, VI, VII, VIII, and IX described in table 1 of § 176.170(c) of this chapter under conditions of use C through G described in table 2 of § 176.170(c) of this chapter at temperatures not to exceed 88 °C (190 °F).
Dimyristyl thiodipropionate having a melting point of 48°–52 °C as determined by ASTM method E324–79, "Standard Test Method for Relative Initial and Final Melting Points and the Melting Range of Organic Chemicals," and a saponification equivalent in the range 280–290 as determined by ASTM method D1962–67 (Reapproved 1979), "Standard Test Method for Saponification Value of Drying Oils, Fatty Acids, and Polymerized Fatty Acids," which are incorporated by reference. Copies may be obtained from the American Society for Testing Materials, 1916 Race St., Philadelphia PA 19103, or may be examined at the National Archives and Records Administration (NARA). For information on the availability of this material at NARA, call 202–741–6030, or go to: *http://www.archives.gov/federal_register/code_of_federal_regulations/ibr_locations.html.*.	Finished food-contact articles containing this additive shall meet the extractives limitations prescribed in § 176.170(c) of this chapter.
Di(*n*-octyl)tin bis(2-ethylhexyl maleate) [CAS Reg. No. 10039–33–5] having 12.5 to 15.0 percent by weight of tin (Sn) and having a saponification number of 260 to 280. The additive is made from di(*n*-octyl)tin oxide meeting the specifications of § 178.2650(a)(1).	For use only at levels not to exceed 0.5 percent by weight of acrylonitrile copolymers complying with §§ 177.1020 and 177.1030 of this chapter and used in contact with all food types under conditions of use C through G described in table 2 of § 176.170(c) of this chapter.
N,N'-Diphenylthiourea	For use only: 1. At levels not to exceed 0.5 percent by weight of polyvinyl chloride and/or vinyl chloride copolymers complying with § 177.1980 of this chapter. 2. At levels not to exceed 0.5 percent by weight of vinyl chloride-vinyl acetate copolymers containing not more than 20 molar percent of vinyl acetate.
2-(4,6-Diphenyl-1,3,5-triazin-2-yl)-5-hexyloxy)phenol (CAS Reg. No. 147315–50–2).	For use only 1. At levels not to exceed 0.5 percent by weight of polycarbonate resins complying with § 177.1580 of this chapter. 2. At levels not to exceed 0.5 percent by weight of polyester elastomers complying with § 177.1590 of this chapter. 3. At levels not to exceed 0.5 percent by weight of polyethylene phthalate polymers complying with § 177.1630 of this chapter, in contact with food under conditions of use A through H described in Table 2 of § 176.170(c) of this chapter.

Substances	Limitations
2,6-Di-*tert*-butyl-4-ethylphenol	For use only in contact with nonalcoholic foods: 1. At levels not exceeding 0.04 mg/in ^{2} of food contact surface and not exceeding 0.1 percent by weight in ethylene polymers and copolymers complying with § 177.1520(c) of this chapter, items 2.1, 2.2, 2.3, 3.1, 3.2, and 3.3; § 177.1340; and § 177.1350 of this chapter. The average thickness of such polymers and copolymers in the form in which they contact food shall not exceed 0.0025 in. 2. At levels not exceeding 0.04 mg/in ^{2} of food contact surface in ethylene polymers and copolymers complying with § 177.1520(c) of this chapter, items 2.1, 2.2, 2.3, 3.1, 3.2, and 3.3; § 177.1340; and § 177.1350 of this chapter. The average thickness of such polymers and copolymers in the form in which they contact food shall be greater than 0.0025 in but shall not exceed 0.025 in.
3,5-Di-*tert*-butyl-4-hydroxyhydrocinnamic acid triester with 1,3,5-tris(2-hydroxyethyl)-s-triazine-2,4,6-(1*H*,3*H*,5*H*)-trione (CAS Reg. No. 34137-09-2).	For use only: 1. At levels not to exceed 0.5 percent by weight of polypropylene complying with § 177.1520 of this chapter in articles that contact food not in excess of high temperature heat-sterilized condition of use A described in § 176.170(c) of this chapter, table 2. 2. At levels not to exceed 0.5 percent by weight of polyethylene complying with § 177.1520 of this chapter in articles that contact food not in excess of high temperature heat-sterilized condition of use A described in 176.170(c) of this chapter, table 2. 3. In adhesives complying with § 175.105 of this chapter. 4. At levels not to exceed 0.25 percent by weight of olefin copolymers complying with § 177.1520(c) of this chapter, items 3.1, 3.2, 3.3, 3.4, 3.5, and 4.0. 5. At levels not to exceed 2 percent by weight of polyester elastomers, complying with § 177.1590 of this chapter, in contact with dry food only, and finished rubber articles for repeated use, complying with § 177.2600 of this chapter, in contact with all foods, at temperatures not to exceed 150 °F.
Di-*tert*-butyl-*m*-cresyl phosphonite condensation product with biphenyl (CAS Reg. No. 178358–58–2) produced by the condensation of 4,6-di-*tert*-butyl-*m*-cresol with the Friedel-Crafts addition product (phosphorus trichloride and biphenyl) so that the food additive has a minimum phosphorus content of 5.0 percent.	For use only: 1. At levels not to exceed 0.1 percent by weight of olefin polymers complying with § 177.1520(c) of this chapter, items 1.1, 2.1, 2.2, 3.1(a), 3.1(b), 3.2(a), or 3.2(b).
Di-*tert*-butylphenyl phosphonite condensation product with biphenyl (CAS Reg. No. 119345–01–6) produced by the condensation of 2,4-di-*tert*-butylphenol with the Friedel-Crafts addition product (phosphorus trichloride and biphenyl) so that the food additive has a minimum phosphorus content of 5.4 percent, an acid value not exceeding 10 mg KOH/gm, and a melting range of 85 °C to 110 °C (185 °F to 230 °F).	For use only: 1. At levels not to exceed 0.1 percent by weight of olefin polymers complying with § 177.1520(c) of this chapter, items 1.1, 1.2, 1.3, 3.2b, 3.3a, 3.3b, 3.4, 3.5, and 3.1a (where the density is not less than 0.85 gram per cubic centimeter and not more than 0.91 gram per cubic centimeter); and 2.1, 2.2, 2.3, 3.1a, 3.1b, 3.2a, and 3.6 (where the density is not less than 0.94 gram per cubic centimeter) and 5. 2. At levels not to exceed 0.1 percent by weight of polycarbonate resins complying with § 177.1580 of this chapter. 3. At levels not to exceed 0.2 percent by weight of polystyrene and 0.3 percent by weight of rubber-modified polystyrene complying with § 177.1640 of this chapter. 4. At levels not to exceed 0.15 percent by weight of olefin polymers complying with § 177.1520(c) of this chapter, items 2.1, 2.2, 2.3, 3.1a, 3.1b, 3.2a, 3.4, 3.5, and 3.6 (where the polyethylene component has a density less than 0.94 gram per cubic centimeter). 5. At levels not to exceed 0.1 percent by weight of repeated use rubber articles complying with § 177.2600 of this chapter.

Substances	Limitations
2,4-Di-*tert*-butylphenyl-3,5-di-*tert*-butyl-4-hydroxybenzoate (CAS Reg. No. 4221–80–1).	For use only: 1. At levels not to exceed 0.6 percent by weight of olefin polymers complying with § 177.1520(c) of this chapter, item 1.1: (1) when used in single-use articles that contact food of types I, II, IV-B, VI-A, VI-B, VII-B, and VIII, identified in table 1 of § 176.170(c) of this chapter; and (2) when used in repeated-use articles that contact food of types I, II, III, IV, V, VI, VII, VIII, and IX identified in table 1 of § 176.170(c) of this chapter. The additive is used under conditions of use B through H described in table 2 of § 176.170(c) of this chapter. 2. At levels not to exceed 0.25 percent by weight of olefin polymers having a density of not less than 0.94 gram per cubic centimeter and complying with § 177.1520(c) of this chapter, items 2.1, 2.2, 3.1, and 3.2: (1) when used in single-use articles that contact food of types I, II, IV-B, VI-A, VI-B, VII-B, and VIII, identified in table 1 of § 176.170(c) of this chapter; and (2) when used in repeated-use articles that contact food of types I, II, III, IV, V, VI, VII, VIII, and IX identified in table 1 of § 176.170(c) of this chapter. The additive is used under conditions of use B through H described in table 2 of § 176.170(c) of this chapter.
2,4-Di-*tert*-pentyl-6-[1-(3,5-di-*tert*-pentyl-2-hydroxyphenyl)ethyl]phenyl acrylate (CAS Reg. No. 123968–25–2).	For use only: 1. At levels not to exceed 0.2 percent by weight of polypropylene complying with § 177.1520 of this chapter in contact with food under conditions of use D through G as described in Table 2 of § 176.170(c) of this chapter, except that polypropylene containing the additive at levels not to exceed 0.075 percent by weight may contact food under conditions of use A through H described in Table 2 of § 176.170(c) of this chapter. 2. At levels not to exceed 1.0 percent by weight of of styrene block polymers complying with § 177.1810 of this chapter. The additive is used under conditions of use D through G as described in Table 2 of § 176.170(c) of this chapter. 3. At levels not to exceed 1.0 percent by weight of polystyrene and rubber modified polystyrene complying with § 177.1640 of this chapter in contact with food under conditions of use D through G as described in Table 2 of § 176.170(c) of this chapter.
N,N″–1,2–Ethanediylbis[N–[3–[[4,6-bis[butyl(1,2,2,6,6-pentamethyl-4-piperidinyl)amino]-1,3,5-triazin-2-yl]amino]propyl]-N′,N″-dibutyl-N′,N″-bis(1,2,2,6,6-pentamethyl-4-piperidinyl)-1,3,5-triazine-2,4,6-triamine] (CAS Reg. No. 106990–43–6).	For use only: 1. At levels not to exceed 0.06 percent by weight of olefin polymers complying with § 177.1520(c) of this chapter, items 1.1a, 1.1b, 1.2, or 1.3. The finished polymers may only be used in contact with food of the Types III, IV-A, V, VI-C, VII-A, and IX as described in table 1 of § 176.170(c) of this chapter, and under conditions of use A through H as described in table 2 of § 176.170(c) of this chapter. 2. At levels not to exceed 0.08 percent by weight of olefin polymers complying with § 177.1520(c) of this chapter. The finished polymers may only be used in contact with food of the Types I, II, IV-B, VI-A, VI-B, VII-B, and VIII as described in table 1 of § 176.170(c) of this chapter, and under conditions of use A through H as described in table 2 of § 176.170(c) of this chapter.
Ethylenebis(oxyethylene)-bis-(3-*tert*-butyl-4-hydroxy-5-methylhydrocinnamate) (CAS Reg. No. 36443–68–2).	1. At levels not to exceed 0.3 percent by weight of polystyrene and/or rubber modified polystyrene polymers complying with § 177.1640 of this chapter. 2. At levels not to exceed 0.3 percent by weight of acrylonitrile-butadiene-styrene copolymers used in accordance with applicable regulations in parts 175, 176, 177, and 181 of this chapter. 3. At levels not to exceed 0.75 percent by weight of polyoxymethylene copolymers used in accordance with § 177.2470 of this chapter. The finished articles shall not be used for foods containing more than 15 percent alcohol. 4. At levels not to exceed 0.25 percent by weight of polyoxymethylene homopolymers used in accordance with § 177.2480 of this chapter. The finished articles shall not be used for foods containing more than 15 percent alcohol. 5. At levels not to exceed 0.2 percent by weight of rigid vinyl chloride plastics prepared from vinyl chloride homopolymers and/or vinly chloride copolymers used in accordance with a prior sanction or applicable regulations in parts 175, 176, and 177 of this chapter. The vinyl chloride copolymers shall contain not less than 50 weight percent of total polymer units derived from vinyl chloride. 6. At levels not to exceed 0.1 percent by weight of vinylidene chloride homopolymers and/or vinylidene chloride copolymers used in accordance with a prior sanction or applicable regulations in parts 175, 176, and 177 of this chapter. The vinylidene chloride copolymers shall contain not less than 50 weight percent of total polymer units derived from vinylidene chloride. 7. In adhesives used in accordance with § 175.105 of this chapter.

Substances	Limitations
2,2′-Ethylidenebis(4,6-di-*tert*-butylphenol) (CAS Reg. No. 35958–30–6).	For use only: 1. At levels not to exceed 0.1 percent by weight of olefin polymers complying with § 177.1520(c) of this chapter, item 1.1, 1.2, 1.3, 3.1, or 3.2 (where the polymers complying with items 3.1 and 3.2 contain primarily polymer units derived from propylene). 2. At levels not to exceed 0.05 percent by weight of olefin polymers complying with § 177.1520(c) of this chapter, item 2.1, 2.2, or 2.3. The finished polymers are to be used only under conditions of use B through H described in table 2 of § 176.170(c) of this chapter. 3. At levels not to exceed 0.075 percent by weight of olefin polymers complying with § 177.1520(c) of this chapter, item 2.1, 2.2, or 2.3 (where the density of each of these polymers is not less than 0.94 g/cc) and item 3.1 or 3.2 (where each of these polymers contains primarily polymer units derived from ethylene). 4. At levels not to exceed 0.05 percent by weight of olefin polymers complying with § 177.1520(c) of this chapter, item 3.3, 3.4, 3.5, or 4. 5. At levels not to exceed 0.1 percent by weight of ethylene vinyl acetate copolymers complying with § 177.1350 of this chapter and under conditions of use C through G described in table 2 of § 176.170(c) of this chapter. 6. At levels not to exceed 0.1 percent by weight of rigid or semirigid polyvinyl chloride and under conditions of use B through H described in table 2 of § 176.170(c) of this chapter. 7. At levels not to exceed 0.2 percent by weight of acrylonitrile-butadiene-styrene copolymers containing less than 30 percent by weight of acrylonitrile and under conditions of use D through G described in table 2 of § 176.170(c) of this chapter. 8. At levels not to exceed 0.1 percent by weight of polystyrene complying with § 177.1640 of this chapter and under conditions of use D through G described in table 2 of § 176.170(c) of this chapter. 9. At levels not to exceed 0.2 percent by weight of rubber-modified polystyrene complying with § 177.1640 of this chapter. 10. In adhesives complying with § 175.105 of this chapter.

Substances	Limitations
2,2′-Ethylidenebis(4,6-di-*tert*-butylphenyl)fluorophosphonite (CAS Reg. No. 118337–09–0).	For use only: 1. As provided in § 175.105 of this chapter. 2. In all polymers used in contact with food of types I, II, IV-B, VI-A, VI-B, VII-B, and VIII, under conditions of use B through H described in Tables 1 and 2 of § 176.170(c) of this chapter at levels not to exceed 0.25 percent by weight of polymers. 3. In polypropylene complying with § 177.1520(c) of this chapter, item 1.1, in contact with food of types III, IV-A, V, VII-A, and IX, under: (a) Conditions of use B through H described in Tables 1 and 2 of § 176.170(c) of this chapter at levels not to exceed 0.25 percent by weight of the polymer; or (b) Condition of use A, limited to levels not to exceed 0.1 percent by weight of the polymer; provided that the food-contact surface has an average thickness not exceeding 375 micrometers (0.015 inch). 4. In olefin copolymers complying with § 177.1520(c) of this chapter, items 3.1a or 3.2a, and containing not less than 85 percent by weight of polymer units derived from propylene, in contact with food of types III, IV-A, V, VII-A, and IX, and under: (a) Conditions of use C through G, described in Tables 1 and 2 of § 176.170(c) of this chapter, limited to levels no greater than 0.2 percent by weight of the copolymers; or (b) Conditions of use A, B, and H, limited to levels no greater than 0.1 percent by weight of the olefin copolymers; provided that the food-contact surface has an average thickness not exceeding 375 micrometers (0.015 inch). 5. In olefin polymers complying with § 177.1520(c) of this chapter, items 1.2 or 1.3 in contact with food of types III, IV-A, V, VII-A, and IX, under conditions of use A through H, described in Tables 1 and 2 of § 176.170(c) of this chapter at levels not to exceed 0.1 percent by weight of the polymers; provided that the food-contact surface has an average thickness not exceeding 375 micrometers (0.015 inch). 6. In polyethylene complying with § 177.1520(c) of this chapter, items 2.1 or 2.2, having a density of not less than 0.94, in contact with food of types III, IV-A, V, VII-A, and IX, and under: (a) Conditions of use B through H, described in Tables 1 and 2 of § 176.170(c) of this chapter limited to levels not to exceed 0.2 percent by weight of the polymers; or (b) Condition of use A, described in Tables 1 and 2 of § 176.170(c) of this chapter, limited to levels not to exceed 0.1 percent by weight of the polymer; provided that the food-contact surface has an average thickness not exceeding 125 micrometers (0.005 inch). 7. In olefin copolymers complying with § 177.1520(c) of this chapter, items 3.1a, 3.1b, 3.2a, or 3.2b, containing not less than 85 percent by weight of polymer units derived from ethylene and having a density of not less than 0.94, in contact with food of types III, IV-A, V, VII-A, and IX, and under: (a) Conditions of use C through G, described in Tables 1 and 2 of § 176.170(c) of this chapter limited to levels not to exceed 0.2 percent by weight of the copolymers; or (b) Conditions of use A, B, and H, limited to levels not to exceed 0.1 percent by weight of the copolymers; provided that the food-contact surface has an average thickness not exceeding 125 micrometers (0.005 inch). 8. In olefin polymers complying with § 177.1520(c) of this chapter, items 3.1a, 3.1b, 3.2a, or 3.2b containing not less than 85 percent by weight of polymer units derived from ethylene, in contact with food of types III, IV-A, V, VII-A, and IX, under conditions of use A through H, as described in Tables 1 and 2 of § 176.170(c) of this chapter at levels not to exceed 0.1 percent by weight of the copolymer; provided that the food-contact surface has an average thickness not exceeding 75 micrometers (0.003 inch). 9. In polyethylene phthalate polymers complying with § 177.1630 of this chapter in contact with food of types III, IV-A, V, VI-C, VII-A, and IX, and under: (a) Conditions of use B through H, described in tables 1 and 2 of § 176.170(c) of this chapter, limited to levels not to exceed 0.3 percent by weight of the polymers; or (b) Condition of use A with food of types III, IV-A, V, VII-A, and IX, and limited to levels not to exceed 0.1 percent by weight of the polymers; provided that the film thickness does not exceed 875 micrometers (0.035 inch).
Hexadecyl 3,5-di-*tert*-butyl-4-hydroxybenzoate (CAS Reg. No. 67845–93–6).	For use only at levels not to exceed 0.5 percent by weight of olefin polymers complying with § 177.1520 of this chapter.

Substances	Limitations
Hexamethylenebis (3,5-di-*tert*-butyl-4-hydroxyhydrocinnamate) (CAS Reg. No. 35074-77-2).	For use only: 1. As provided in § 177.2470(b)(1) and § 177.2480(b)(1) of this chapter. 2. In adhesives complying with § 175.105 of this chapter. 3. At levels not to exceed 1 percent by weight in pressure-sensitive adhesives complying with § 175.125 of this chapter. 4. At levels not to exceed 1 percent by weight in can end cement formulations complying with § 175.300(b)(3)(xxxi) of this chapter. 5. At levels not to exceed 1 percent by weight in side seam cement formulations complying with § 175.300(b)(3)(xxxii) of this chapter. 6. At levels not to exceed 1 percent by weight in petroleum alicyclic hydrocarbon resins, polyamide resins, and terpene resins complying with § 175.320 of this chapter. 7. At levels not to exceed 1 percent by weight in rosin and rosin derivatives when used in accordance with § 176.170(a)(5) of this chapter. 8. At levels not to exceed 1 percent by weight in petroleum alicyclic hydrocarbon resins or their hydrogenated products complying with § 176.170(b)(2) of this chapter. 9. At levels not to exceed 1 percent by weight in terpene resins complying with § 175.300(b)(3)(xi) of this chapter, when such terpene resins are used in accordance with § 176.170(b)(1) of this chapter. 10. At levels not to exceed 1 percent by weight in resins and polymers authorized for use in accordance with § 176.180 of this chapter. 11. At levels not to exceed 1 percent by weight in closures with sealing gaskets complying with § 177.1210 of this chapter. 12. At levels not to exceed 1 percent by weight in rubber articles intended for repeated use complying with § 177.2600 of this chapter. 13. At levels not to exceed 1 percent by weight in petroleum hydrocarbon resin and rosins and rosin derivatives used in accordance with § 178.3800 of this chapter. 14. At levels not to exceed 1 percent by weight in reinforced wax complying with § 178.3850 of this chapter.
N,N'-Hexamethylenebis (*3,5-di-tert-butyl-4-hydroxyhydrocinnamamide*) (CAS Reg. No. 23128–74–7).	For use only: 1. At levels not to exceed 1 percent by weight of nylon resins complying with § 177.1500(b) of this chapter, items 1 through 8, that contact food only of the types identified in categories in § 176.170(c) of this chapter, table 1 except VI-A and VI-C. 2. At levels not to exceed 0.75 percent by weight of nylon 12 resins complying with § 177.1500(b) of this chapter, item 9, that contact food only of the types identified in categories in § 176.170(c) of this chapter, table 1, except VI-A and VI-C. 3. At levels not to exceed 0.6 percent by weight of polyester resins complying with § 175.300(b)(3)(vii) of this chapter. 4. At levels not to exceed 0.6 percent by weight of closures with sealing gaskets complying with § 177.1210 of this chapter. 5. At levels not to exceed 0.6 percent by weight of repeated use rubber articles complying with § 177.2600 of this chapter. 6. At levels not to exceed 0.5 percent by weight of polyoxymethylene copolymer complying with § 177.2470 of this chapter. 7. At levels not to exceed 0.5 percent by weight of polyoxymethylene homopolymer complying with § 177.2480 of this chapter.
1,6–Hexanediamine, *N, N'*-bis(2,2,6,6-tetramethyl-4-piperidinyl)-, polymers with morpholine-2,4,6-trichloro-1,3,5-triazine reaction products, methylated (CAS Reg. No. 193098–40–7).	For use only as a stabilizer at levels not to exceed 0.3 percent by weight of olefin polymers complying with § 177.1520(c) of this chapter. The finished polymers are to contact food only under conditions of use C, D, E, F, and G, as described in Table 2 of § 176.170(c) of this chapter. Provided that the finished food-contact articles have a volume of at least 18.9 liters (5 gallons).

Substances	Limitations
1,6-Hexanediamine, *N,N'*-bis(2,2,6,6-tetramethyl-4-piperidinyl)-, polymer with 2,4,6-trichloro-1,3,5-triazine, reaction products with *N*-butyl-1-butanamine and *N*-butyl-2,2,6,6-tetramethyl-4-piperidinamine (CAS Reg. No. 192268–64–7).	For use only: 1. At levels not to exceed 0.5 percent by weight of propylene polymers and copolymers complying with § 177.1520(c) of this chapter, items 1.1, 1.2, 3.1a, 3.2a, 3.2b, 3.4, or 3.5. The finished polymers may contact food only of the types identified in § 176.170(c) of this chapter, table 1, under categories I, II, IV-B, VI-A, VI-B, VII-B, and VIII, and under conditions of use B through H described in table 2 of § 176.170(c) of this chapter. 2. At levels not to exceed 0.3 percent by weight of propylene polymers and copolymers complying with § 177.1520(c) of this chapter, items 1.1, 1.2, 3.1a, 3.2a, 3.2b, 3.4, or 3.5. The finished polymers may contact food only of the types identified in § 176.170(c) of this chapter, table 1, under categories III, IV-A, V, VI-C, VII-A, and IX, and under conditions of use B through H described in table 2 of § 176.170(c) of this chapter. 3. At levels not to exceed 0.5 percent by weight of ethylene polymers and copolymers complying with § 177.1520(c) of this chapter, items 2.1, 2.2, 2.3, 3.1a, 3.1b, 3.2a, or 3.6 (where the density of each of these polymers is at least 0.94 gram per cubic centimeter), or 5. The finished polymers may contact food only of the types identified in § 176.170(c) of this chapter, table 1, under categories I, II, IV-B, VI-A, VI-B, VII-B, and VIII, and under conditions of use B through H described in table 2 of § 176.170(c) of this chapter. 4. At levels not to exceed 0.05 percent by weight of ethylene polymers and copolymers complying with § 177.1520(c) of this chapter, items 2.1, 2.2, 2.3, 3.1a, 3.1b, 3.2a, or 3.6 (where the density of each of these polymers is at least 0.94 gram per cubic centimeter), or 5. The finished polymers may contact food only of the types identified in § 176.170(c) of this chapter, table 1, under categories III, IV-A, V, VI-C, VII-A, and IX, and under conditions of use B through H described in table 2 of § 176.170(c) of this chapter. 5. At levels not to exceed 0.5 percent by weight of ethylene polymers and copolymers complying with § 177.1520(c) of this chapter, items 2.1, 2.2, 2.3, 3.1a, 3.1b, 3.2a, 3.4, 3.5, or 3.6 (where the density of each of these polymers is less than 0.94 gram per cubic centimeter), or 5. The finished polymers may contact food only of the types identified in § 176.170(c) of this chapter, table 1, under categories I, II, IV-B, VI-A, VI-B, VII-B, and VIII, and under conditions of use C through G described in table 2 of § 176.170(c) of this chapter. 6. At levels not to exceed 0.01 percent by weight of ethylene polymers and copolymers complying with § 177.1520(c) of this chapter, items 2.1, 2.2, 2.3, 3.1a, 3.1b, 3.2a, 3.4, 3.5, or 3.6 (where the density of each of these polymers is less than 0.94 gram per cubic centimeter), or 5. The finished polymers may contact food only of the types identified in § 176.170(c) of this chapter, table 1, under categories III, IV-A, V, VI-C, VII-A, and IX, and under conditions of use C through G described in table 2 of § 176.170(c) of this chapter.
2-Hydroxy-4-isooctoxy-benzophenone. Chemical Abstracts (CA) name: Methanone, [2-hydroxy-4-(isooctyloxy) phenyl]phenyl; CA Registry No. 33059–05–1.	For use only at levels not to exceed 0.5 percent by weight of olefin copolymers complying with § 177.1520(c) of this chapter: Items 1.1, 1.2, 1.3, 2.1, 2.2, 2.3, 3.1, 3.2, 3.3 or 4: *Provided,* That the finished polymer contacts food only of the types identified in § 176.170(c) of this chapter, table 1, under Categories I, VII-B and VIII under conditions of use E, F, and G described in table 2 of § 176.170(c) of this chapter.

Substances	Limitations
2(2′-Hydroxy-5′-methylphenyl)benzotriazole meeting the following specification: melting point 126° –132 °C (258.8° –269.6 °F) (CAS Reg. No. 2440–22–4).	For use only: 1. As component of nonfood articles complying with § 177.1010 of this chapter. 2. At levels not to exceed 0.25 percent by weight of rigid polyvinyl chloride and/or rigid vinyl chloride copolymers complying with § 177.1980 of this chapter. 3. In polystyrene that complies with § 177.1640 of this chapter and that is limited to use in contact with dry food of Type VIII described in table 1 of § 176.170(c) of this chapter. 4. At levels not to exceed 0.25 percent by weight of polystyrene and/or rubber-modified polystyrene polymers complying with § 177.1640 of this chapter intended to contact nonalcoholic food: *Provided,* That the finished basic rubber-modified polystyrene polymers in contact with fatty foods shall contain not less than 90 weight percent of total polymer units derived from styrene monomer. 5. At levels not to exceed 0.5 percent by weight of polycarbonate resins complying with § 177.1580 of this chapter. *Provided,* That the finished polycarbonate resins contact food only of Types I, II, III, IV, V, VI-A, VI-B, VII, VIII, and IX identified in table 1 of § 176.170(c) of this chapter and under conditions of use E, F, and G described in table 2 of § 176.170(c) of this chapter. 6. At levels not to exceed 0.5 percent by weight of ethylene-1,4-cyclohexylene dimethylene terephthalate copolymers complying with § 177.1315 of this chapter and of ethylene phthalate polymers complying with § 177.1630 of this chapter and that contact food only under conditions of use D through G described in table 2, § 176.170(c) of this chapter.
2-Hydroxy-4-*n*-octoxy-benzophenone	For use only at levels not to exceed 0.5 percent by weight of olefin polymers complying with § 177.1520(c) of this chapter, items 1.1, 1.2, 1.3, 2.1, 2.2, 2.3, 3.1, 3.2, 3.3, or 4: *Provided,* That the finished polymer contacts food only of the types identified in § 176.170(c) of this chapter, table 1, under Categories I, IV-B, VII-B, and VIII , and under the conditions of use B through H described in table 2 of § 176.170(c) of this chapter.
4,4′-Isopropylidenediphenol alkyl(C_{12}-C_{15}) phosphites; the phosphorus content is in the range of 5.2–5.6 weight percent.	For use only at levels not exceeding 1.0 percent by weight in rigid polyvinyl chloride and/or rigid vinyl chloride copolymers complying with §§ 177.1950, 177.1970 or 177.1980 of this chapter, and used in contact with food, except milk, only under the conditions described in § 176.170(c) of this chapter, table 2, under conditions of use D through G.
Magnesium salicylate	For use only in rigid polyvinyl chloride and/or in rigid vinyl chloride copolymers complying with § 177.1980 of this chapter: *Provided,* That total salicylates (calculated as the acid) do not exceed 0.3 percent by weight of such polymers.
2-Methyl-4,6-bis-[(octylthio)methyl] phenol (CAS Reg. No. 110553–27–0).	For use only: 1. In adhesives complying with § 175.105 of this chapter. 2. At levels not to exceed 0.5 percent by weight of can-end cements and side-seam cements complying with § 175.300(b)(xxxi) and (xxxii) of this chapter. 3. At levels not to exceed 1 percent by weight of pressure sensitive adhesives complying with § 175.125 of this chapter petrolium alicyclic hydrocarbon resins complying with § 176.170 of this chapter, resins and polymers complying with § 176.180 of this chapter, and closures with sealing gaskets complying with § 177.1210 of this chapter. 4. At levels not to exceed 1.7 percent by weight of the finished rubber products complying with § 177.2600 of this chapter. 5. At levels not to exceed 0.1 percent by weight of petroleum alicyclic hydrocarbon resins complying with § 175.320 of this chapter; rubber-modified polystyrene complying with § 177.1640 of this chapter; and petroleum hydrocarbon resins and rosins and rosins and rosin derivatives complying with § 178.3800 of this chapter. 6. At levels not to exceed 0.2 percent by weight of styrene block polymenrs complying with § 177.1810 of this chapter that contact food of Types I, II, IV-B, VI, VII-B, and VIII described in table 1, § 176.170(c) of this chapter, only under conditions of use C through H described in table 2, § 176.170(c) of this chapter.

Substances	Limitations
2,2′-Methylenebis(4,6-di-*tert*-butylphenyl)2-ethylhexyl phosphite (CAS Reg. No. 126050–54–2).	For use only at levels not to exceed 0.25 percent by weight of polypropylene complying with § 177.1520 of this chapter. The finished polymers may only be used in contact with food of the types identified in § 176.170(c) of this chapter, table 1, under Categories I, II, IV-B, VI-B, VII-B, and VIII under conditions of use B through H described in table 2, § 176.170(c) of this chapter, and with food of the types identified in § 176.170(c) of this chapter, table 1, under Categories III, IV-A, V, VI-A, VI-C, VII-A, and IX under conditions of use C through G described in table 2, § 176.170(c) of this chapter.
2,2′-Methylenebis (6-*tert*-butyl-4-ethylphenol)	For use only: 1. In acrylonitrile-butadiene-styrene copolymers at levels not to exceed 0.6 percent by weight of the copolymer. 2. In semirigid and rigid acrylic and modified acrylic plastics complying with § 177.1010 of this chapter at levels not to exceed 0.1 percent by weight of the plastic.
4,4′-Methylenebis (2,6-di-*tert*-butyl-phenol)	For use only: 1. As provided in § 175.105 of this chapter. 2. At levels not to exceed 0.25 percent by weight of petroleum hydrocarbon resins used in compliance with regulations in parts 174, 175, 176, 177, 178 and § 179.45 of this chapter. 3. At levels not to exceed 0.25 percent by weight of terpene resins used in compliance with regulations in parts 174, 175, 176, 177, 178 and § 179.45 of this chapter. 4. At levels not to exceed 0.5 percent by weight of polyethylene complying with § 177.1520 of this chapter: *Provided,* That the polyethylene end product contacts foods only of the types identified in Categories I, II, IV-B, VI, VII-B, and VIII in table 1, § 176.170(c) of this chapter. 5. At levels not to exceed 0.5 percent by weight of polybutadiene used in rubber articles complying with § 177.2600 of this chapter: *Provided,* That the rubber end product contacts foods only of the types identified in Categories I, II, IV-B, VI, VII-B, and VIII in table 1, § 176.170(c) of this chapter.
2,2′-Methylenebis(4-methyl-6-*tert*-butylphenol)	For use only: 1. At levels not to exceed 0.1 percent by weight of olefin polymers complying with sec. 177.1520(c) of this chapter, items 1.1, 1.2, 1.3, 2.1, 2.2, 2.3, 3.1, 3.2, 3.3, or 4 used in articles that contact food of the types identified in sec. 176.170(c) of this chapter, table 1, under Categories I, II, IV-B, VI, VII-B, and VIII. 2. At levels not to exceed 1 percent by weight of polyoxymethylene copolymer as provided in sec. 177.2470(b)(1) of this chapter. 3. At levels not to exceed 0.5 percent by weight of polyoxymethylene homopolymer as provided in § 177.2480(b)(1) of this chapter.
2,2′-Methylenebis(4-methyl-6-*tert*-butylphenol) monoacrylate (CAS Reg. No. 61167–58–6).	For use only: 1. At levels not to exceed 0.5 percent by weight of polystyrene and rubber-modified polystyrene complying with § 177.1640 of this chapter. 2. At levels not to exceed 0.5 percent by weight of styrene block ploymers complying with § 177.1810 of this chapter. 3. At levels not to exceed 1 percent by weight of adhesives complying with § 175.105 of this chapter and pressure sensitive adhesives complying with § 175.125 of this chapter. 4. At levels not to exceed 0.5 percent by weight of acrylonitrile-butadiene-styrene copolymers that comply with § 177.1020 of this chapter when used in articles that contact food only under conditions of use E, F, and G as described in table 2, § 176.170 (c) of this chapter.
2,2′-Methylenebis[6-(1-methylcyclo-hexyl)-*p*-cresol]	For use only: 1. As provided in § 177.1210 of this chapter. 2. At levels not to exceed 0.2 percent by weight of polyethylene complying with § 177.1520 of this chapter: *Provided,* That the finished polyethylene contacts foods only of the type identified in § 176.170(c) of this chapter, table 1, under Categories I, II, VI-B, and VIII. 3. In polyethylene complying with § 177.1520 of this chapter: *Provided,* That the finished polyethylene contacts foods only of the types identified in § 176.170(c) of this chapter, table 1, under Categories III, IV, V, VI-A, VII, and IX, and only at temperatures not to exceed room temperature: *And further provided,* That percentage concentration of the antioxidant in the polyethylene, when multiplied by the thickness in inches of the finished polyethylene, shall not be greater than 0.0005.
2,2′-Methylenebis(4-methyl-6-nonylphenol) and 2,6-bis(2-hydroxy-3-nonyl-5-methyl-benzyl)-*p*-cresol mixtures (varying proportions).	For use only in acrylonitrile-butadiene-styrene copolymers used in contact with nonalcoholic foods.

Substances	Limitations
Methyltin-2-mercaptoethyloleate sulfide, which is defined as one or more of the following:	For use only in rigid poly(vinyl chloride) and rigid vinyl chloride copolymers complying with §§ 177.1950 and 177.1980 of this chapter, respectively, used in the manufacture of pipes and pipe fittings intended for contact with water in food processing plants, at levels not to exceed: 1. 1.0 percent by weight in pipes, and 2. 2.0 percent by weight in pipe fittings.
1. 9-Octadecenoic acid (Z)-, 2-mercaptoethyl ester, reaction products with dichlorodime thylstannane, sodium sulfide, and trichloromethylstannane (CAS Reg. No. 68442–12–6);	
2. Fatty acids, tall oil, 2-mercaptoethyl esters, reaction products with dichlorodimethylstannane, 2-mercaptoethyl decanoate, 2-mercaptoethyl octanoate, sodium sulfide, and trichloromethylstannane (CAS Reg. No. 151436–98–5); or	
3. Fatty acids, tall oil, 2-mercaptoethyl esters, reaction products with dichlorodimethylstannane, sodium sulfide, and trichloromethylstannane (CAS Reg. No. 201687–57–2);and which has the following specifications: Tin content (as Sn) 5 to 21 percent by weight; mercaptosulfur content 5 to 13 percent by weight; acid value no greater than 4.	
Methyltin-2-Mercaptoethyloleate sulfide may also be used with one or more of the following optional substances:	
1.1a 2-Mercaptoethyl oleate (CAS Reg. No. 59118–78–4),	
1.1b 2-Mercaptoethyl tallate (CAS Reg. No. 68440–24–4),	
1.1c 2-Mercaptoethyl octanoate (CAS Reg. No. 57813–59–9),	
1.1d 2-Mercaptoethyl decanoate (CAS Reg. No. 68928–33–6), alone or in combination; not to exceed 40 percent by weight of the stabilizer formulation;	
2.1 2-Mercaptoethanol (CAS Reg. No. 60–24–2): Not to exceed 2 percent by weight of the stabilizer formulation.	
3.1 Mineral oil (CAS Reg. No. 8012–95–1): Not to exceed 40 percent by weight of the stabilizer formulation.	
4.1 Butylated hydroxytoluene (CAS Reg. No. 128–37–0): Not to exceed 5 percent by weight of the stabilizer formulation.	
The total of the optional substances (1.1a through 4.1) shall not exceed 60 percent by weight of the stabilizer formulation.	
Nylon 66/610/6 terpolymer (see § 177.1500 of this chapter for identification)	For use only at levels not to exceed 1.5 percent by weight of polyoxymethylene homopolymer as provided in § 177.2480 (b)(1) of this chapter.
Nylon 612/6 copolymer. (CAS Reg. No. 51733–10–9), weight ratio 6/1.	For use only at levels not to exceed 1.5 percent by weight of polyoxymethylene homopolymer as provided in § 177.2480(b)(1).

Substances	Limitations
Octadecyl 3,5-di-*tert*-butyl-4-hydroxyhydrocinnamate (CAS Reg. No. 2082–79–3).	For use only: 1. At levels not exceeding 0.25 percent by weight of olefin polymers complying with § 177.1520(c) of this chapter, item 1.1, 1.2, 1.3, 2.1, 2.2, 2.3, 3.1, 3.2, 3.3, or 4. 2. As provided in §§ 175.105 and 177.1010(a)(5) of this chapter. 3. At levels not exceeding 0.25 percent by weight of polystyrene and/or rubber-modified polystyrene polymers complying with § 177.1640 of this chapter, except that the finished basic rubber-modified polystyrene polymers in contact with fatty foods shall contain not less than 85 weight percent of total polymer units derived from styrene monomer. 4. At levels not to exceed 0.5 percent by weight of acrylonitrile-butadiene-styrene copolymers used in accordance with prior sanction or regulations in parts 174, 175, 176, 177, 178 and § 179.45 of this chapter. 5. At levels not exceeding 0.25 percent by weight of olefin copolymers complying with § 177.1520(c) of this chapter, items 3.4 and 3.5 as follows: (a) item 3.4, *Provided*, That the finished copolymer contacts foods only of types identified in § 176.170(c) of this chapter, table 1, under Categories I, II, III, IV-B, VI, VII, VIII, and IX; (b) item 3.5, *Provided*, That the finished copolymer contacts non-fatty foods only of types identified in § 176.170(c) of this chapter, table 1, under Categories I, II, IV-B, VI, VII-B, and VIII. 6. At levels not exceeding 0.05 percent by weight of modified semi-rigid and rigid vinyl chloride plastics modified with methacrylate-butadiene-styrene copolymers in accordance with § 178.3790. 7. At levels not exceeding 0.2 percent by weight of rigid polyvinyl chloride. 8. At levels not to exceed 0.3 percent by weight of polycarbonate resins that comply with § 177.1580 and that contact food only under conditions of use E, F, and G described in table 2, § 176.170(c) of this chapter. 9. At levels not exceeding 0.1 percent by weight of ethylene-vinyl acetate copolymers complying with § 177.1350 of this chapter. 10. At levels not to exceed 0.2 percent by weight of nitrile rubber-modified acrylonitrile-methyl acrylate copolymers that comply with § 177.1480 of this chapter when used in articles that contact food only under conditions of use D, E, F, and G described in table 2, § 176.170(c) of this chapter. 11. At levels not exceeding 0.3 percent by weight of styrene block polymers complying with § 177.1810 of this chapter when used in articles that contact food only of the types identified in § 176.170(c) of this chapter, table 1, under Categories I, II, IV-B, VI, VII-B, and VIII, and under conditions of use D, E, F, and G described in table 2 of § 176.170(c) of this chapter. 12. At levels not exceeding 0.2 percent by weight of vinylidene chloride homopolymers and/or vinylidene chloride copolymers complying with applicable regulations in parts 175, 176, 177, 179, and 181 of this chapter. The vinylidene chloride copolymers shall contain not less than 50 weight percent of total polymer units derived from vinylidene chloride. 13. At levels not exceeding 0.025 percent by weight of chlorinated isobutylene-isoprene copolymers complying with § 177.1420(a)(3) of this chapter. 14. At levels not exceeding 0.5 percent by weight of the finished rubber article complying with § 177.2600 of this chapter.

Substances	Limitations
7-Oxa-3,20-diazadispiro-[5.1.11.2]-heneicosan-21-one,2,2,4,4-tetramethyl-,hydrochloride, reaction products with epichlorohydrin, hydrolyzed, polymerized (CAS Reg. No. 202483–55–4).	For use only: 1. At levels not to exceed 0.5 percent by weight of olefin polymers complying with § 177.1520 of this chapter, items 1.1, 3.1, and 3.2, where the copolymers complying with items 3.1 and 3.2 contain not less than 85 weight percent of polymer units derived from propylene; in contact with all types of food described in Table 1 of § 176.170 of this chapter, provided that the finished food-contact article will have a capacity of at least 18.9 liters (5 gallons) when in contact with food of types III, IV-A, V, VII-A, and IX, described in Table 1 of § 176.170 of this chapter. 2. At levels not to exceed 0.5 percent by weight of olefin polymers complying with § 177.1520 of this chapter, items 2.1, 2.2, 3.1, and 3.2, having a density of not less than 0.94 gram/milliliter, where the copolymers complying with items 3.1 and 3.2 contain not less than 85 weight percent of polymer units derived from ethylene; in contact with food only under conditions of use C, D, E, F, and G, described in Table 2 of § 176.170 of this chapter, provided that the finished food-contact article will have a capacity of at least 18.9 liters (5 gallons) when in contact with food of types III, IV-A, V, VII-A, and IX, described in Table 1 of § 176.170 of this chapter. 3. At levels not to exceed 0.3 percent by weight of olefin polymers complying with § 177.1520 of this chapter, items 2.1, 2.2, 3.1, 3.2, 3.3, 3.4, 3.5, 3.6, and 4.0, having a density of less than 0.94 gram/milliliter, in contact with food only under conditions of use D, E, F, and G, described in Table 2 of § 176.170 of this chapter, provided that the finished food-contact article will have a capacity of at least 18.9 liters (5 gallons) except that, films and molded articles containing not more than 0.2 percent by weight of the stabilizer may contact aqueous food of types I, II, IV-B, VI, and VIII, described in Table 1 of § 176.170 of this chapter with no restrictions on the amount of food contacted.
Oxidized bis (hydrogenated tallow alkyl) amines	For use only: 1. At levels not to exceed 0.1 percent by weight of polypropylene polymers complying with § 177.1520(c) of this chapter, item 1.1, 1.2, 1.3, 3.1a (density not less than 0.85 gram per cubic centimeter and less than 0.91 gram per cubic centimeter), 3.2b, 3.4, and 3.5. The finished polymers may be used in contact with food types I, II, IV-B, VII-B and VIII described in table 1 of § 176.170(c) of this chapter, under conditions of use B through H described in table 2 of § 176.170(c) of this chapter and with food types III, IV-A, V, VI, VII-A, and IX described in table 1 of § 176.170(c) of this chapter, under conditions of use D through H described in table 2 of § 176.170(c) of this chapter. 2. At levels not to exceed 0.075 percent by weight of high-density polyethylene polymers complying with § 177.1520(c) of this chapter, item 2.1, 2.2, 2.3, 3.1a, 3.1b, 3.2a, 3.6 (density not less than 0.94 gram per cubic centimeter), and 5. The finished polymers may be used in contact with food types I, II, IV-B, VII-B and VIII described in table 1 of § 176.170(c) of this chapter, under conditions of use B through H described in table 2 of § 176.170(c) of this chapter, and with food types III, IV-A, V, VI, VII-A and IX described in table 1 of § 176.170(c) of this chapter, under conditions of use D through H described in table 2 of § 176.170(c) of this chapter.
2,2′-Oxamidobis[ethyl 3-(3,5-di-*tert*-butyl-4-hydroxyphenyl)propionate] (CAS Reg. No. 70331–94–1).	For use only: 1. At levels not to exceed 0.5 percent by weight of polystyrene and rubber-modified polystyrene complying with § 177.1640 of this chapter. 2. At levels not to exceed 0.5 percent by weight of olefin polymers complying with § 177.1520(c) of this chapter, items 1.1, 1.2, and 1.3. 3. At levels not to exceed 0.5 percent by weight of olefin polymers complying with § 177.1520(c) of this chapter, items 2.1, 2.2, 2.3, 3.1, 3.2, 3.3, 3.4, 3.5, and 4.0 that contact food Types I, II, IV-B, VI, VII-B and VIII described in table 1 of § 176.170(c) of this chapter. 4. At levels not to exceed 0.1 percent by weight of olefin polymers complying with § 177.1520(c) of this chapter, items 2.1, 2.2, 2.3, 3.1, 3.2, 3.3, and 4.0 that contact food Types III, IV-A, V, VII-A, and IX described in table 1 of § 176.170(c) of this chapter; except that olefin copolymers complying with items 3.1 and 3.2 where the majority of polymer units are derived from propylene may contain the additive at levels not to exceed 0.5 percent by weight. 5. At levels not to exceed 0.1 percent by weight of olefin polymers complying with item 3.4 of § 177.1520(c) of this chapter, that contact food Types III, VII-A, and IX described in table 1 of § 176.170(c) of this chapter; except that olefin copolymers complying with item 3.4 where the majority of the polymer units are derived from propylene may contain the additive at levels not to exceed 0.5 percent by weight.

Substances	Limitations
Pentaerythritol and its stearate ester	For use only in rigid polyvinyl chloride and/or in rigid vinyl chloride copolymers complying with § 177.1980 of this chapter: *Provided,* That the total amount of pentaerythritol and/or pentaerythritol stearate (calculated as free pentaerythritol) does not exceed 0.4 percent by weight of such polymers.
N-Phenylbenzenamine reaction products with 2,4,4-trimethylpentenes (CAS Reg. No. 68411–46–1).	For use at levels not to exceed 0.5 percent by weight of pressure-sensitive adhesives complying with § 175.125 of this chapter.
Phosphoric acid triesters with triethylene glycol (CAS Reg. No. 64502–13–2).	At levels not to exceed 0.1 percent by weight of polyethylene phthalate polymers complying with § 177.1630 of this chapter, such that the polymers contact foods only of Type VI-B described in table 1 of § 176.170(c) of this chapter.
Phosphorous acid, cyclic butylethyl propanediol, 2,4,6-tri-*tert*-butylphenyl ester (CAS Reg. No. 161717–32–4), which may contain not more than 1 percent by weight of triisopropanolamine (CAS Reg. No. 122–20–3).	For use only: 1. At levels not to exceed 0.2 percent by weight of olefin polymers complying with § 177.1520(c) of this chapter, items 1.1, 1.2, or 1.3, and items 2.1, 2.2, or 2.3 (where the density of these polymers is not less than 0.94 gram per cubic centimeter), and items 3.1 or 3.2, provided that the finished polymer contacts foods of types I, II, and VI-B as described in table 1 of § 176.170(c) of this chapter only under conditions of use B, C, D, E, F, G, and H as described in table 2 of § 176.170(c) of this chapter. 2. At levels not to exceed 0.1 percent by weight of olefin polymers complying with § 177.1520(c) of this chapter, items 1.1, 1.2, or 1.3, that contact food of types III, IV, V, VI-A, VI-C, VII, VIII, and IX as described in table 1 of § 176.170(c) of this chapter, only under conditions of use C, D, E, F, and G as described in table 2 of § 176.170(c) of this chapter. 3. At levels not to exceed 0.1 percent by weight of olefin copolymers complying with § 177.1520(c) of this chapter, items 3.1a, 3.1b, 3.2a, or 3.2b, having a density less than 0.94 grams per cubic centimeter, in contact with food only of types III, IV, V, VI-A, VI-C, VII, VIII, and IX and under conditions of use B, C, D, E, F, G, and H as described in tables 1 and 2 of § 176.170(c) of this chapter; provided that the food-contact surface does not exceed 0.003 inch (0.076 mm) in thickness. 4. At levels not to exceed 0.1 percent by weight of olefin polymers complying with § 177.1520(c) of this chapter, items 2.1, 2.2, 2.3, 3.1(a), 3.1(b), 3.1(c), 3.2 (a), or 3.2(b), having a density not less than 0.94 grams per cubic centimeter, in contact with foods only of types III, IV, V, VI-A, VI-C, VII, VIII, and IX identified in Table 1 of § 176.170(c) of this chapter, and under conditions of use B through H as described in Table 2 of § 176.170(c) of this chapter; provided that the food-contact surface does not exceed 0.003 inch (0.076 mm) in thickness.
Phosphorous acid, cyclic neopentanetetrayl bis(2,4-di-*tert*-butylphenyl) ester (CAS Reg. No. 26741–53–7) which may contain not more than 1 percent by weight of triisopropanolamine (CAS Reg. No. 122–20–3).	For use only at levels not to exceed 0.10 percent by weight of olefin polymers complying with § 177.1520(c) of this chapter, item 1.1, 1.2, 1.3, 2.1, 2.2, 2.3, 3.1, or 3.2, and limited to use in contact with food only under conditions of use B, C, D, E, F, G, and H described in table 2 of § 176.170(c) of this chapter. Olefin polymers that contain more than 50 weight-percent of polymer units derived from ethylene shall have a density equal to or greater than 0.94 gram per cubic centimeter.
Phosphorous acid, cyclic neopentanetetrayl bis (2,6-di-*tert*-butyl-4-methylphenyl)ester (CAS Reg. No. 80693–00–1).	For use only: 1. At levels not to exceed 0.25 percent by weight of polypropylene homopolymer and copolymers complying with § 177.1520 of this chapter, for use with all food types described in table 1 of § 176.170(c) of this chapter only under conditions of use B through H described in table 2 of § 176.170(c) of this chapter. 2. At levels not to exceed 0.05 percent by weight of polymers complying with § 177.1520(c) of this chapter, item 3.1 or 3.2, and with a maximum thickness of 100 micrometers (0.004 inch) for use with all food types under conditions of use B, C, D, E, F, G, and H described in table 2 of § 176.170(c) of this chapter.

Substances	Limitations
Phosphorous acid, cyclic neopentanetetrayl bis(2,4-di-*tert*-butylphenyl)ester (CAS Reg. No. 26741–53–7).	For use only: 1. At levels not to exceed 0.86 percent by weight in polyvinyl chloride and/or vinyl chloride copolymers that comply with §§ 177.1950, 177.1960, 177.1970, or 177.1980 of this chapter for use with all food types described in table 1 of § 176.170(c) of this chapter, except those containing more than 15 percent alcohol, under conditions of use B, C, D, E, F, G, and H described in table 2 of § 176.170(c) of this chapter. 2. At levels not to exceed 0.25 percent by weight of polycarbonate resins that comply with § 177.1580 of this chapter for use with all food types described in table 1 of § 176.170(c) of this chapter, except those containing more than 15 percent alcohol, under conditions of use B, C, D, E, F, G, and H described in table 2 of § 176.170(c) of this chapter. 3. At levels not to exceed 0.05 percent by weight in olefin polymers complying with § 177.1520(c) of this chapter, item 3.1, that contain more than 50 weight percent of polymer units derived from ethylene and whose density is less than 0.94 gram per cubic centimeter. The average thickness of such polymers intended for use in contact with food types V and VII-A described in table 1 of § 176.170(c) of this chapter shall not exceed 80 micrometers (0.003 inch).
Poly(1,4-cyclohexylenedimethylene-3,3′-thiodipropionate) partially terminated with stearyl alcohol and produced when approximately equal moles of 1,4-cyclohexanedimethanol and 3,3′-thiodipropionic acid are made to react in the presence of stearyl alcohol so that the final product has an average molecular weight in the range of 1,800–2,200, as determined by vapor pressure osmometry, and has a maximum acid value of 2.5.	For use only: 1. In polypropylene complying with § 177.1520(c) of this chapter, item 1.1, and used in contact with nonfatty, nonalcoholic food. 2. At levels not to exceed 0.5 percent by weight of polypropylene complying with § 177.1520(c) of this chapter, item 1.1, and used in contact with fatty, nonalcoholic food. The average thickness of such polymers in the form in which they contact fatty nonalcoholic food shall not exceed 0.005 inch.
Poly[(1,3-dibutyldistannthianediylidene)-1,3-dithio] having the formula $[C_8H_{18}Sn_2S_3]_n$ (where *n* averages 1.5–2) and produced so as to meet the following specifications: Softening point, 130–145 °C; volatile components at 150 °C, less than 1.0 percent; sulphur (sulfide) content in the range 20.5–22.0 percent; tin content in the range 52.0–53.2 percent.	For use only at levels not to exceed 0.2 by percent weight in polyvinyl chloride resin where such resin constitutes not less than 98.7 percent of a finished semirigid or rigid polyvinyl chloride food-contact surface, provided that the finished food-contact article is employed only to package meat, cheese, and food Types I, VIII, and IX as described in table 1 of § 176.170(c) of this chapter. The finished food-contact article containing this stabilizer, when extracted with refined cottonseed oil at 120 °F for 48 hours, using a volume-to-surface ratio of 2 milliliters per square inch of surface tested, shall yield tin (Sn) not to exceed 0.0005 milligram per square inch of food-contact surface.
Poly[(6-morpholino-s-triazine-2,4-diyl)[(2,2,6,6-tetramethyl-4-piperidyl)imino]hexamethylene [(2,2,6,6-tetramethyl-4-piperidyl)imino]] (CAS Reg. No. 82451–48–7).	For use only: 1. At levels not to exceed 0.3 percent by weight of polypropylene complying with § 177.1520(c) of this chapter, items 1.1, 1.2, and 1.3, and of ethylene polymers complying with § 177.1520(c) of this chapter, items 2.1, 2.3, and 3.1, whose specific gravity is not less than 0.94. The finished polymers are to contact food only under conditions of use D, E, F, and G described in table 2 of § 176.170(c) of this chapter. 2. At levels not to exceed 0.3 percent by weight of olefin polymers complying with § 177.1520(c) of this chapter, items 2.1, 2.3, and 3.1, whose specific gravity is less than 0.94, and of olefin polymers complying with items 3.3., 3.4, 3.5, and 4.0. The finished polymers are to contact food in articles having a volume of at least 18.9 liters (5 gallons) only under conditions of use D, E, F, and G described in table 2 of § 176.170(c) of this chapter.
Poly[[6-[(1,1,3,3-tetramethybutyl) amino]-*s*-triazine-2,4-diyl][2,2,6,6-tetramethyl-4-piperidyl)imino]hexamethylene[(2,2,6,6-tetramethyl-4-piperidyl)imino]] (CAS Reg. No. 70624–18–9).	For use only: 1. At levels not to exceed 0.3 percent by weight of polypropylene complying with § 177.1520 of this chapter. 2. At levels not to exceed 0.2 percent by weight of polyethylene complying with § 177.1520 of this chapter, that has a density equal to or greater than 0.94 gram per cubic centimeter. 3. At levels not to exceed 0.3 percent by weight of polyethylene that has a density less than 0.94 gram per cubic centimeter complying with § 177.1520 of this chapter, items 2.1, 2.2, and 2.3, and of olefin polymers and copolymers complying with items 3.1, 3.2, 3.3, 3.4, 3.5, 3.6, and 4. The finished polymers are to contact food only under conditions of use B through H described in table 2 of § 176.170(c) of this chapter, and when contacting fatty foods of Types III, IV-A, V, VII-A, and IX described in table 1 of § 176.170(c) of this chapter, the finished articles are to have a volume of at least 18.9 liters (5 gallons).

Substances	Limitations
Potassium bromide and either cupric acetate or cupric carbonate.	For use at levels not exceeding 0.18 percent potassium bromide and 0.005 percent copper as cupric acetate or cupric carbonate by weight of nylon 66 resins complying with § 177.1500 of this chapter; the finished resins are used or are intended to be used to contain foods during oven baking or oven cooking at temperatures above 250 °F. The average thickness of such resins in the form in which they contact food shall not exceed 0.0015 inch.
1,3-propanediamine, N,N-1,2-ethanediylbis-, polymer with 2,4,6-trichloro-1,3,5-triazine, reaction products with N-butyl-2,2,6,6-tetramethyl-4-piperidinamine (CAS Reg. No. 136504–96–6).	For use only: 1. At levels not to exceed 0.3 percent by weight of polypropylene complying with § 177.1520(c) of this chapter, items 1.1, 1.2, and 1.3. 2. At levels not to exceed 0.2 percent by weight of olefin polymers having a density greater than or equal to 0.94 grams per cubic centimeter and complying with § 177.1520(c) of this chapter, items 2.1, 2.2, 2.3, 3.1, and 3.2. 3. At levels not to exceed 0.3 percent by weight of olefin polymers having a density less than 0.94 grams per cubic centimeter and complying with § 177.1520(c) of this chapter, items 2.1, 2.2, 2.3, 3.1, 3.2, 3.3, 3.4, 3.5, 3.6, and 4.0. The finished polymers are to contact food only under conditions of use B through H described in Table 2 of § 176.170(c) of this chapter, and when used in contact with fatty foods of Types III, IV-A, V, VII-A, and IX as described in Table 1 of § 176.170(c) of this chapter, the finished articles are to have a volume of at least 18.9 liters (5 gallons).
N,N'-1,3-Propanediylbis (3,5-di-*tert*-butyl-4-hydroxyhydrocinnamamide) (CAS Reg. No. 69851–61–2).	For use only at levels not to exceed 0.6 percent by weight of rubber articles for repeated use complying with § 177.2600 of this chapter.
Siloxanes and silicones, methyl hydrogen, reaction products with 2,2,6,6-tetramethyl-4-(2-propenyloxy)piperidine (CAS Reg. No. 182635–99–0).	For use as an ultraviolet (UV) stabilizer only at levels not to exceed 0.33 percent by weight of polypropylene complying with § 177.1520(c) of this chapter, items 1.1a, 1.1b, 1.2, and 1.3, under conditions of use D, E, F, and G, as described in Table 2 of § 176.170 of this chapter.
Stearoylbenzoylmethane (CAS Reg. No. 58446–52–9) consisting of a mixture of β–diketones produced by the condensation of acetophenone and technical methyl stearate..	For use only at levels not to exceed 0.5 percent by weight of vinyl chloride homopolymers modified in accordance with § 178.3790(b)(1). The finished polymers may be used in contact with food containing up to 50 percent alcohol under conditions of use B through H described in table 2 of § 176.170(c) of this chapter.
Styrenated diphenylamine (CAS Reg. No. 68442–68–2).	For use only in adhesives complying with § 175.105 of this chapter and in rubber articles intended for repeated use complying with § 177.2600 of this chapter.
Tetradecanoic acid, lithium salt (CAS Reg. No. 20336–96–3).	For use only at levels not to exceed 0.15 percent by weight of polypropylene and polypropylene copolymers complying with § 177.1520(c) of this chapter, items 1.1a, 1.1b, 3.1a, 3.1b, 3.1c, 3.2a, and 3.2b. The finished polymers may only be used in contact with food of Types I, II, IV-B, VI-B, VII-B, and VIII as described in table 1 of § 176.170(c) of this chapter under conditions of use B through H as described in table 2 of § 176.170(c) of this chapter, and with food of Types III, IV-A, V, VI-A, VI-C, VII-A, and IX described in table 1 of § 176.170(c) of this chapter under conditions of use C through G as described in table 2 of § 176.170(c) of this chapter.
2-[[2,4,8,10-Tetrakis(1,1-dimethylethyl)dibenzo[d,f][1,3,2]-dioxaphosphepin-6-yl]oxy]-*N,N*-bis[2-[[2,4,8,10-tetrakis(1,1-dimethylethyl)dibenzo[d,f][1,3,2]dioxaphosphepin-6-yl]oxy]ethyl]ethanamine (CAS Reg. No. 80410–33–9).	For use only at levels not to exceed 0.075 percent by weight of olefin copolymers complying with § 177.1520(c) of this chapter, items 1.1, 1.2, 1.3, 2.1, 2.2, or 2.3: *Provided,* That the density of the olefin polymers complying with items 2.1, 2.2, or 2.3 is not less than 0.94 gram per cubic centimeter: *And further provided,* That the finished polymers contact food only of Types I, II, IV-B, VI-A, VI-B, VII-B, and VIII described in table 1, of § 176.170(c) of this chapter, under conditions of use B through H described in table 2 of § 176.170(c) of this chapter and food only of Types III, IV-A, V, VI-C, VII-A, and IX described in table 1 of § 176.170(c) of this chapter, under conditions of use C through G described in table 2 of § 176.170(c) of this chapter.

Substances	Limitations
Tetrakis [methylene(3,5- di-*tert*-butyl-4-hydroxyhydro- cinnamate)] methane (CAS Reg. No. 6683–19–8).	For use only: 1. At levels not to exceed 0.5 percent by weight of all polymers used as indirect additives in food packaging, except as specified below. 2. At levels not to exceed 0.1 percent by weight of petroleum wax or synthetic petroleum wax complying with § 176.170(a)(5) of this chapter. 3. At levels not to exceed 1.0 percent by weight of: (a) Pressure sensitive adhesives complying with § 175.125 of this chapter. (b) Can end cement formulations complying with § 175.300(b)(3)(xxxi) of this chapter. (c) Petroleum alicyclic hydrocarbon resins complying with § 175.320(b)(3) of this chapter, § 176.170(b)(2) of this chapter, or their hydrogenated products complying with § 176.170(b)(2) of this chapter. (d) Rosin and rosin derivatives used in accordance with parts 175 through 178 of this chapter. (e) Terpene resins complying with § 175.300(b)(2)(xi) of this chapter when such terpene resins are used in accordance with § 176.170(b) of this chapter. (f) Resins and polymers complying with § 176.180 of this chapter. (g) Closures with sealing gaskets complying with § 177.1210 of this chapter. (h) Polyoxymethylene copolymer as provided in § 177.2470(b)(1) of this chapter. (i) Petroleum hydrocarbon resin complying with § 178.3800. (j) Reinforced wax complying with § 178.3850.
4,4-Thiobis(6-*tert*-butyl-*m*-cresol)	For use only: 1. As provided in §§ 175.105 and 177.2600 of this chapter. 2. At levels not to exceed 0.25 percent by weight of polyethylene complying with § 177.1520 of this chapter: *Provided,* That the specific gravity of the polyethylene is not less than 0.926: *And further provided,* That the finished polyethylene contacts food only of the types identified in § 176.170(c) of this chapter, table 1, under Categories I, II, VI-B, and VIII.
Thiodiethylene bis(3,5-di-*tert*-butyl-4-hydroxyhydrocinnamate) (CAS Reg. No. 41484-35-9).	For use only: 1. In adhesives complying with § 175.105 of this chapter. 2. At levels not to exceed 0.5 percent by weight of pressure-sensitive adhesives complying with § 175.125 of this chapter, petroleum alicyclic hydrocarbon resins complying with § 176.170 of this chapter, resins and polymers complying with § 176.180 of this chapter, closures with sealing gaskets complying with § 177.1210 of this chapter, and finished rubber products complying with § 177.2600 of this chapter.
Thiodipropionic acid.	
1,3,5-Trimethyl-2,4,6-tris(3,5-di-*tert*-butyl-4-hydroxybenzyl) benzene (CAS Reg. No. 1709–70–2).	For use only: 1. At levels not to exceed 0.5 percent by weight of polymers except nylon resins identified in § 177.1500 of this chapter. 2. At levels not to exceed 1 percent by weight of nylon resins identified in § 177.1500 of this chapter.
Tri(mixed mono-and dinonylphenyl) phosphite (which may contain not more than 1 percent by weight of triisopropanolamine)..	
1, 11-(3, 6, 9-Trioxaundecyl) bis-3-(dodecylthio) propionate (CAS Reg. No. 64253–30–1).	For use only as provided in § 175.300(b)(3)(xxxi) of this chapter at 4.0 parts per 100 parts rubber.
1,3,5-Tris(3,5-di-*tert*-butyl-4-hydroxybenzyl)-*s*-triazine-2,4,6(1*H*,3*H*,5*H*)trione (CAS Reg. No. 27676–62–6).	For use only: 1. At levels not to exceed 0.25 percent by weight of polypropylene complying with § 177.1520 of this chapter. 2. In polyethylene complying with § 177.1520 of this chapter: (a) At levels not to exceed 0.1 weight percent. (b) At levels not to exceed 0.5 weight percent in contact with nonfatty food. 3. At levels not to exceed 0.5 percent by weight of ethylene-propylene-5-ethylidine-2-norbornene terpolymers complying with § 177.1520 of this chapter. The maximum thickness of such polymers in the form in which they contact food shall not exceed 0.005 inch. 4. At levels not exceeding 0.1 percent by weight of olefin copolymers complying with § 177.1520(c) of this chapter, items 3.1, 3.2, 3.3, 3.4, or 3.5. 5. At levels not exceeding 0.25 percent by weight of olefin copolymers complying with § 177.1520(c) of this chapter, items 3.1 and 3.2, and also containing not less than 85 weight percent of polymer units derived from propylene. 6. At levels not to exceed 0.2 percent by weight of olefin polymers complying with § 177.1520(c)(4) of this chapter. The finished polymers may be used in contact with food under conditions of use A through H described in table 2 of § 176.170(c) of this chapter.

Substances	Limitations
1,3,5-Tris(3,5-di-*tert*-butyl-4-hydroxyhydrocinnamoyl) hexahydro-*s*-triazine.	For use only in contact with nonfatty foods: 1. At levels not to exceed 0.25 percent by weight of polypropylene complying with § 177.1520 of this chapter. 2. At levels not to exceed 0.1 percent by weight of polyethylene complying with § 177.1520 of this chapter. 3. At levels not to exceed 0.5 percent by weight of ethylene-propylene-5-ethylidine-2-norbornene terpolymers complying with § 177.1520 of this chapter. The maximum thickness of such polymers in the form in which they contact food shall not exceed 0.005 inch.
1,3,5-Tris(4-*tert*-butyl-3-hydroxy-2,6-dimethylbenzyl)-1,3,5-triazine-2,4,6-(1H,3H,5H)-trione. [CAS Reg. No. 40601–76–1].	For use only: 1. At levels not to exceed 0.1 percent by weight of olefin polymers complying with § 177.1520 of this chapter, under conditions of use A through H described in table 2 of § 176.170(c) of this chapter. 2. At levels not to exceed 0.1 percent by weight of polystyrene and rubber-modified polystyrene that comply with § 177.1640 of this chapter, provided that the finished polystyrene and rubber-modified polystyrene contact food only under the conditions described in § 176.170(c) of this chapter, table 2, under conditions of use E through G.

Substances	Limitations
Tris(2,4-di-*tert*-butylphenyl)phosphite. (CAS Reg. No. 31570–04–4).	For use only: 1. At levels not to exceed 0.5 percent by weight of elastomers used in rubber articles complying with § 177.2600 of this chapter. 2. At levels not to exceed 1 percent by weight of nylon resins complying with § 177.1500 of this chapter: *Provided,* That the finished polymer contacts food only under conditions of use E, F, and G described in table 2 of § 176.170(c) of this chapter. 3. At levels not to exceed 0.3 percent by weight of polycarbonate resins complying with § 177.1580 of this chapter. 4. At levels not to exceeds 0.2 percent by weight of polystyrene and rubber-modified polystyrene polymers complying with § 177.1640 of this chapter: *Provided,* that the finished polymer contacts food only under conditions of use B, C, D, E, F, G, and H described in table 2 of § 176.170(c) of this chapter. 5. At levels not to exceed 0.25 percent by weight of olefin polymers complying with § 177.1520(c) of this chapter, item 1.1, 1.2, or 1.3. 6. At levels not to exceed 0.2 percent by weight of olefin polymers complying with § 177.1520(c) of this chapter, items 2.1, 2.2, 2.3, 3.1(a), 3.1(b), 3.1(c), 3.2(a), or 3.2(b). The finished polymers complying with items 2.1, 2.2, or 2.3 having a density less than 0.94 gram per cubic centimeter and a thickness greater than 0.051 millimeter (0.002 inch), either shall have a level of tris(2,4-di-*tert*-butylphenyl)phosphite that shall not exceed 0.062 milligram per square inch of food-contact surface or shall contact all food types identified in Table 1 of § 176.170(c) of this chapter only under conditions of use E, F, and G described in Table 2 of § 176.170(c) of this chapter. 7. At levels not to exceed 0.2 percent by weight of ethylene-vinyl-acetate copolymers complying with § 177.1350 of this chapter, and that are limited to use in contact with food only under conditions of use E, F, and G described in table 2 of § 176.170(c) of this chapter. The average thickness of such polymers in the form in which they contact fatty food shall not exceed 0.1 millimeter (0.004 inch). 8. At levels not to exceed 0.2 percent by weight of olefin polymers complying with § 177.1520(c) of this chapter, item 4. The finished polymers having a thickness greater than 0.051 millimeter (0.002 inch), shall contact food only under conditions of use E, F, and G described in table 2 of § 176.170(c) of this chapter. 9. At levels not to exceed 0.5 percent by weight of acrylic and modified acrylic plastics, semirigid and rigid, complying with § 177.1010 of this chapter. 10. At levels not to exceed 0.1 percent by weight of isobutylene polymers complying with § 177.1420 of this chapter. 11. In adhesives complying with § 175.105 of this chapter. 12. At levels not to exceed 0.5 percent by weight of pressure sensitive adhesives complying with § 175.125 of this chapter. 13. At levels not to exceed 0.5 percent by weight of can end cement formulations complying with § 175.300(b)(3) (xxxi) of this chapter. 14. At levels not to exceed 0.5 percent by weight of side seam cement formulations complying with § 175.300(b)(3) (xxxii) of this chapter. 15. At levels not to exceed 0.5 percent by weight of petroleum alicyclic hydrocarbon resins complying with § 175.320(b)(3) of this chapter. 16. At levels not to exceed 0.5 percent by weight of petroleum alicyclic hydrocarbon resins or their hydrogenated products complying with § 176.170(b) (2) of this chapter. 17. At levels not to exceed 0.5 percent by weight of resins and polymers complying with § 176.180(b) of this chapter. 18. At levels not to exceed 0.5 percent by weight of rosins and rosin derivatives complying with § 176.210(d)(3) of this chapter. 19. At levels not to exceed 0.5 percent by weight of closures with sealing gaskets complying with § 177.1210 of this chapter. 20. At levels not to exceed 0.5 percent by weight of petroleum hydrocarbon resin, and rosins and rosin derivatives complying with § 178.3800(b). 21. At levels not to exceed 0.5 percent by weight of reinforced wax complying with § 178.3850. 22. At levels not to exceed 0.5 percent by weight of olefin copolymers complying with § 177.1520(c) of this chapter, item 3.3. The finished polymers may be used in contact with food under conditions of use A through H described in table 2 of § 176.170(c) of this chapter. 23. At levels not to exceed 0.15 percent by weight of poly-1-butene resins and butene/ethylene copolymers complying with § 177.1570 of this chapter: *Provided,* that the finished polymer contacts food only under conditions of use B through H described in table 2 of § 176.170(c) of this chapter.

Substances	Limitations
Tris(2-methyl-4-hydroxy-5-*tert*-butylphenyl)butane (CAS Reg. No. 1843–03–4).	For use only: 1. At levels not to exceed 0.25 percent by weight of polymers used as provided in § 176.180 of this chapter. 2. At levels not to exceed 0.25 percent by weight of the following polymers when used in articles that contact food of Types I, II, IV-B, VI-B, VII-B, and VIII described in table 1 of § 176.170(c) of this chapter: Olefin polymers complying with § 177.1520(c) of this chapter, items 1.1, 1.2, 1.3, 2.1, 2.2, 2.3, 3.1, 3.2, 3.3, or 4 or complying with other sections in parts 174, 175, 176, 177, 178 and § 179.45 of this chapter; vinyl chloride polymers; and/or vinyl chloride copolymers complying with § 177.1980 of this chapter. 3. At levels not to exceed 0.1 percent by weight of the following polymers when used in articles that contact food of Types III, IV-A, V, VI-A, VI-C, VII-A, and IX described in table 1 of § 176.170(c) of this chapter: Olefin polymers complying with § 177.1520(c) of this chapter, items 1.1, 1.2, 1.3, 2.1, 2.2, 2.3, 3.1, 3.2, 3.3, or 4 or complying with other sections in parts 174, 175, 176, 177, 178 and § 179.45 of this chapter; vinyl chloride polymers; and/or vinyl chloride copolymers complying with § 177.1980 of this chapter. 4. As provided in § 175.105 of this chapter. 5. At levels not to exceed 0.2 percent by weight of polystyrene and/or modified polystyrene polymers identified in § 177.1640 of this chapter. 6. At levels not to exceed 0.25 percent by weight of acrylonitrile-butadiene-styrene copolymers used in contact with nonalcoholic foods. 7. At levels not to exceed 1 percent by weight of closure-sealing gasket compositions complying with § 177.1210(b) of this chapter.
Zinc dibutyldithiocarbamate (CAS Reg. No. 136–23–2).	For use only: 1. At levels not to exceed 0.2 percent by weight of isobutyleneisoprene copolymers complying with § 177.1420 of this chapter: *Provided,* That the finished copolymers contact food only of the types identified in § 176.170(c) of this chapter, table 1, under Types V, VII, VIII, and IX. 2. At levels not to exceed 0.02 percent by weight of polypropylene polymers complying with § 177.1520(c), item 1.1 of this chapter.
Zinc palmitate.	
Zinc salicylate	For use only in rigid polyvinyl chloride and/or in rigid vinyl chloride copolymers complying with § 177.1980 of this chapter: *Provided,* That total salicylates (calculated as the acid) do not exceed 0.3 percent by weight of such polymers.
Zinc stearate.	

[1] Copies are available from the American Society for Testing and Materials, 1916 Race Street, Philadelphia, Pa. 19103.

[42 FR 14609, Mar. 15, 1977]

EDITORIAL NOTE: For FEDERAL REGISTER citations affecting § 178.2010, see the List of CFR Sections Affected, which appears in the Finding Aids section of the printed volume and at *www.fdsys.gov*.

§ 178.2550 4-Hydroxymethyl-2,6-di-*tert*-butylphenol.

4-Hydroxymethyl-2,6-di-*tert*-butylphenol may be safely used as an antioxidant in articles intended for use in contact with food, in accordance with the following prescribed conditions:

(a) The additive has a solidification point of 140°–141 °C.

(b) The concentration of the additive and any other permitted antioxidants in the finished food-contact article does not exceed a total of 0.5 milligram per square inch of food-contact surface.

§ 178.2650 Organotin stabilizers in vinyl chloride plastics.

The organotin chemicals identified in paragraph (a) of this section may be safety used alone or in combination, at levels not to exceed a total of 3 parts per hundred of resin, as stabilizers in vinyl chloride homopolymers and copolymers complying with the provisions of § 177.1950 or § 177.1980 of this chapter and that are identified for use in contact with food of types I, II, III, IV (except liquid milk), V, VI (except malt beverages and carbonated nonalcoholic beverages), VII, VIII, and IX described in table 1 of § 176.170(c) of this chapter, except for the organotin chemical identified in paragraph (a)(3) of this section, which may be used in contact with food of types I through IX at temperatures not exceeding 75 °C (167 °F), and further that the organotin chemicals identified in paragraphs (a) (5) and (6) of this section may be used in contact with food of types I through IX at temperatures not exceeding 66 °C (150 °F), conditions of use D through G described in table 2 of §176.170(c) of this chapter, and further that dodecyltin chemicals identified in paragraph (a)(7) of this section which may be used in contact with food of types I, II, III, IV (except liquid milk), V, VI (except malt beverages and carbonated nonalcoholic beverages), VII, VIII, and IX described in table 1 of §176.170(c) of this chapter at temperatures not exceeding 71 °C (160 °F), in accordance with the following prescribed conditions:

(a) For the purpose of this section, the organotin chemicals are those listed in paragraphs (a) (1), (2), (3), (4), (5), (6), and (7) of this section.

(1) Di(*n*-octyl)tin S,S′-bis(isooctylmercaptoacetate) is an octyltin chemical having 15.1 to 16.4 percent by weight of tin (Sn) and having 8.1 to 8.9 percent by weight of mercapto sulfur. It is made from di(*n*-octyl)tin dichloride or di(*n*-octyl)tin oxide. The isooctyl radical in the mercaptoacetate is derived from oxo process isooctyl alcohol. Di(*n*-octyl)tin dichloride has an organotin composition that is not less than 95 percent by weight of di(*n*-octyl)tin dichloride and not more than 5 percent by weight of tri(*n*-octyl)tin chloride. Di(*n*-octyl)tin oxide has an organotin composition that is not less than 95 percent by weight of di(*n*-octyl)tin oxide and not more than 5 percent by weight of bis[tri(*n*-octyl)tin] oxide, and/or mono *n*-octyltin oxide.

(2) Di(*n*-octyl) tin maleate polymer is an octyltin chemical having the formula $[(C_8H_{17})_2SnC_4H_2O_4]_n$ (where n is between 2 and 4 inclusive), having 25.2 to 26.6 percent by weight of tin (Sn) and having a saponification number of 225 to 255. It is made from di(*n*-octyl)tin dichloride or di(*n*-octyl)tin oxide meeting the specifications prescribed for di(*n*-octyl) tin dichloride or di(*n*-octyl) tin oxide in paragraph (a)(1) of this section.

(3) $C_{10\text{-}16}$-Alkyl mercaptoacetates reaction products with dichlorodioctylstannane and trichlorooctylstannane (CAS Reg. No. 83447–69–2) is an organotin chemical mixture having 10.8 to 11.8 percent by weight of tin (Sn) and having 8.0 to 8.6 percent by weight of mercapto sulfur. It is made from a mixture of di(*n*-octyl)tin dichloride and (*n*-octyl)tin trichloride which has an organotin composition that is not less than 95 percent by weight di(*n*-octyl)tin dichloride/(*n*-octyl)tin trichloride, and not more than 1.5 percent by weight of tri(*n*-octyl)tin chloride. The alkyl radical in the mercaptoacetate is derived from a mixture of saturated *n*-alcohols which has a composition that is not less than 50 percent by weight tetradecyl alcohol, and that is not more than 50 percent by weight total of decyl alcohol and/or dodecyl alcohol, and/or hexadecyl alcohol.

(4) (*n*-Octyl)tin S,S′S″ tris(isooctylmercaptoacetate) is an octyltin chemical having the formula *n*-$C_8H_{17}Sn(SCH_2CO_2C_8H_{17})_3$ (CAS Reg. No. 26401–86–5) having 13.4 to 14.8 percent by weight of tin (Sn) and having 10.9 to 11.9 percent by weight of mercapto sulfur. It is made from (*n*-octyl)tin trichloride. The isooctyl radical in the mercaptoacetate is derived from oxo process isooctyl alcohol. The (*n*-octyl)tin trichloride has an organotin composition that is not less than 95 percent by weight of (*n*-octyl)tin trichloride and not more than 5 percent by weight of tri(*n*-octyl)tin chloride.

(5) Bis(*beta*-carbobutoxyethyl)tin bis(isooctylmercaptoacetate) (CAS Reg. No. 63397–60–4) is an estertin chemical having 14.0 to 15.0 percent by weight of tin (Sn) and having 7.5 to 8.5 percent by weight of mercapto sulfur. It is made from bis(*beta*-carbobutoxyethyl)tin dichloride. The isooctyl radical in the mercaptoacetate is derived from oxo process primary octyl alcohols. The bis(*beta*-carbobutoxyethyl)tin dichloride has an organotin composition that is not less than 95 percent by weight of bis(*beta*-carbobutoxyethyl)tin dichloride and not more than 5 percent by weight of bis(*beta*-carbobutoxyethyltin trichloride. The triestertin chloride content of bis(*beta*-carbobutoxyethyltin)

dichloride shall not exceed 0.02 percent. p

(6) *Beta*-carbobutoxyethyltin tris(isooctylmercaptoacetate) (CAS Reg. No. 63438–80–2) is an estertin chemical having 13.0 to 14.0 percent by weight of tin (Sn) and having 10.5 to 11.5 percent by weight of mercapto sulfur. It is made from *beta*-carbobutoxyethyltin trichloride. The isooctyl radical in the mercaptoacetate is derived from oxo process primary octyl alcohol. The *beta*-carbobutoxyethyltin trichloride has an organotin composition that is not less than 95 percent by weight of *beta*-carbobutoxyethyltin trichloride and not more than 5 percent total of triestertin chloride and diestertin chloride.

(7) The dodecyltin stabilizer is a mixture of 50 to 60 percent by weight of *n*-dodecyltin S,S′,S″-tris(isooctylmercaptoacetate) (CAS Reg. No. 67649–65–4) and 40 to 50 percent by weight of di(*n*-dodecyl)tin S,S′-di(isooctylmercaptoacetate) (CAS Reg. No. 84030–61–5) having 13 to 14 percent by weight of tin (Sn) and having 8 to 9 percent by weight of mercapto sulfur. It is made from a mixture of dodecyltin trichloride and di(dodecyl)tin dichloride which has not more than 0.2 percent by weight of dodecyltin trichloride, not more than 2 percent by weight of dodecylbutyltin dichloride and not more than 3 percent by weight of tri(dodecyl)tin chloride. The isooctyl radical in the mercaptoacetate is derived from oxo process primary octyl alcohols.

(b) The vinyl chloride plastic containers, film or panels in the finished form in which they are to contact food, shall meet the following limitations:

(1) The finished plastics intended for contact with foods of the types listed in this section shall be extracted with the solvent or solvents characterizing those types of foods as determined from table 2 of §176.170(c) of this chapter at the temperature reflecting the conditions of intended use as determined therein. Additionally, extraction tests for acidic foods shall be included and simulated by 3-percent acetic acid at temperatures specified for water in table 2 of §176.170(c) of this chapter. The extraction tests shall cover at least three equilibrium periodic determinations, as follows:

(i) The exposure time for the first determination shall be at least 72 hours for aqueous solvents, and at least 6 hours for heptane.

(ii) Subsequent determinations shall be at a minimum of 24-hour intervals for aqueous solvents, and 2-hour intervals for heptane. These tests shall yield total octylin stabilizers not to exceed 0.5 parts per million as determined by analytical method entitled "Atomic Absorption Spectrometric Determination of Sub-part-per-Million Quantities of Tin in Extracts and Biological Materials with Graphite Furnace," *Analytical Chemistry*, Vol. 49, p. 1090–1093 (1977), which is incorporated by reference. Copies are available from the Center for Food Safety and Applied Nutrition (HFS–200), Food and Drug Administration, 5100 Paint Branch Pkwy., College Park, MD 20740, or available for inspection at the National Archives and Records Administration (NARA). For information on the availability of this material at NARA, call 202–741–6030, or go to: *http://www.archives.gov/federal_register/code_of_federal_regulations/ibr_locations.html.*

(iii) Subsequent determinations for the dodecyltin mixture described in paragraph (a)(7) of this section shall be at a minimum of 24-hour intervals for aqueous solvents and 2-hour intervals for heptane. These tests shall yield di(*n*-octyl)tin S,S′-bis(isooctylmercaptoacetate), or di(*n*-octyl)tin maleate polymer, or (C_{10}-C_{16})-alkylmercaptoacetate reaction products with dichlorodioctylstannane and trichlorooctylstannane, or *n*-octyltin S,S′,S″-tris(isooctylmercaptoacetate), tris(isooctylmercaptoacetate) and di(*n*-dodecyl)tin bis(isooctylmercaptoacetate) or any combination thereof, not to exceed 0.5 parts per million as determined by an analytical method entitled "Atomic Absorption Spectrophotometric Determination of Sub-part-per-Million Quantities of Tin in Extracts and Biological Materials with Graphite Furnace," *Analytical Chemistry*, Vol. 49, pp. 1090–1093 (1977), which is incorporated by reference in accordance with 5 U.S.C.

552(a). The availability of this incorporation by reference is given in paragraph (b)(1)(ii) of this section.

(2) In lieu of the tests prescribed in paragraph (b) (1) of this section, the finished plastics intended for contact with foods only of Types II, V, VI-A (except malt beverages), and VI-C may be end-tested with food-simulating solvents, under conditions of time and temperature, as specified below, whereby such tests shall yield the octyltin residues cited in paragraph (b)(1) of this section not in excess of 0.5 ppm:

	Food-simulating solvent	Time (hours)	Temperature (degrees Fahrenheit)
Type II	Acetic acid, 3 pct	48	135
Type V	Heptane	2	100
Type VI-A	Ethyl alcohol, 8 pct	24	120
Type VI-C	Ethyl alcohol, 50 percent.	24	120

[42 FR 14609, Mar. 15, 1977, as amended at 47 FR 11847, Mar. 19, 1982; 48 FR 7170, Feb. 18, 1983; 48 FR 42972, Sept. 21, 1983; 48 FR 51612, Nov. 10, 1983; 49 FR 8432, Mar. 7, 1984; 50 FR 62, Jan. 2, 1985; 50 FR 3510, Jan. 25, 1985; 50 FR 37998, Sept. 19, 1985; 50 FR 47212, Nov. 15, 1985; 54 FR 24898, June 12, 1989]

Subpart D—Certain Adjuvants and Production Aids

§ 178.3010 Adjuvant substances used in the manufacture of foamed plastics.

The following substances may be safely used as adjuvants in the manufacture of foamed plastics intended for use in contact with food, subject to any prescribed limitations:

List of substances	Limitations
Azodicarbonamide	For use as a blowing agent in polyethylene complying with item 2.1 in § 177.1520(c) of this chapter at a level not to exceed 5 percent by weight of finished foamed polyethylene.
1,1-Difluoroethane (CAS Reg. No. 75–37–6).	For use as a blowing agent in polystyrene.
Isopentane	For use as a blowing agent in polystyrene.
n-Pentane	Do.
1,1,2,2-Tetrachloroethylene.	For use only as a blowing agent adjuvant in polystyrene at a level not to exceed 0.3 percent by weight of finished foamed polystyrene intended for use in contact with food only of the types identified in § 176.170(c) of this chapter, table 1, under Categories I, II, VI, and VIII.
Toluene	For use only as a blowing agent adjuvant in polystyrene at a level not to exceed 0.35 percent by weight of finished foamed polystyrene.

[47 FR 22090, May 21, 1982, as amended at 58 FR 64895, Dec. 10, 1993]

§ 178.3120 Animal glue.

Animal glue may be safely used as a component of articles intended for use in producing, manufacturing, packing, processing, preparing, treating, packaging, transporting, or holding food, subject to the provisions of this section.

(a) Animal glue consists of the proteinaceous extractives obtained from hides, bones, and other collagen-rich substances of animal origin (excluding diseased or rotted animals), to which may be added other optional adjuvant substances required in its production or added to impart desired properties.

(b) The quantity of any substance employed in the production of animal glue does not exceed the amount reasonably required to accomplish the intended physical or technical effect nor any limitation further provided.

(c) Any substance employed in the production of animal glue and which is the subject of a regulation in parts 174, 175, 176, 177, 178 and § 179.45 of this chapter conforms with any specification in such regulation.

(d) Optional adjuvant substances employed in the production of animal glue include:

(1) Substances generally recognized as safe in food.

(2) Substances subject to prior sanction or approval for use in animal glue and used in accordance with such sanction or approval.

(3) Substances identified in this paragraph (d)(3) and subject to such limitations as are provided:

List of substances	Limitations
Alum (double sulfate of aluminum and ammonium, potassium, or sodium).	
4-Chloro-3-methylphenol(*p*-chlorome-tacresol)	For use as preservative only.
Chromium potassium sulfate (chrome alum)	For use only in glue used as a colloidal flocculant added to the pulp suspension prior to the sheet-forming operation in the manufacture of paper and paper board.
3,5-Dimethyl-1,3,5,*H*-tetrahydrothiadia-zine-2-thione	For use as preservative only.
Disodium cyanodithioimidocarbonate	Do.
Defoaming agents	As provided in § 176.210 of this chapter.
Ethanolamine.	
Ethylenediamine.	
Formaldehyde	For use as a preservative only.
Potassium *N*-methyldithiocarbamate	Do.
Potassium pentachlorophenate	Do.
Rosins and rosin derivatives	As provided in § 178.3870.
Sodium chlorate.	
Sodium dodecylbenzenesulfonate.	
Sodium 2-mercaptobenzothiazole	For use as preservative only.
Sodium pentachlorophenate	Do.
Sodium *o*-phenylphenate	Do.
Zinc dimethyldithiocarbamate	Do.
Zinc 2-mercaptobenzothiazole	Do.

(e) The conditions of use are as follows:

(1) The use of animal glue in any substance or article that is the subject of a regulation in this subpart conforms with any specifications or limitations prescribed by such regulation for the finished form of the substance or article.

(2) It is used as an adhesive or component of an adhesive in accordance with the provisions of § 175.105 of this chapter.

(3) It is used as a colloidal flocculant added to the pulp suspension prior to the sheet-forming operation in the manufacture of paper and paperboard.

(4) It is used as a protective colloid in resinous and polymeric emulsion coatings.

§ 178.3125 Anticorrosive agents.

The substances listed in this section may be used as anticorrosive agents in food-contact materials subject to the provisions of this section:

Substances	Limitations
Zinc hydroxy phosphite (CAS Reg. No. 55799–16–1).	For use only as a component of resinous and polymeric food-contact coatings intended for repeated use in contact with dry foods.

[50 FR 21835, May 29, 1985]

§ 178.3130 Antistatic and/or antifogging agents in food-packaging materials.

The substances listed in paragraph (b) of this section may be safely used as antistatic and/or antifogging agents in food-packaging materials, subject to the provisions of this section:

(a) The quantity used shall not exceed the amount reasonably required to accomplish the intended technical effect.

(b) List of substances:

List of substances	Limitations
N-Acyl sarcosines where the acyl group is lauroyl, oleoyl, or derived from the combined fatty acids of coconut oil.	For use only: 1. As antistatic and/or antifogging agent at levels not to exceed a total of 0.15 pct by weight of polyolefin film used for packaging meat, fresh fruits, and fresh vegetables. The average thickness of such polyolefin film shall not exceed 0.003 inch. 2. As antistatic and/or antifogging agent at levels not to exceed a total of 0.15 pct by weight of ethylene-vinyl acetate copolymer film complying with § 177.1350 of this chapter and used for packaging meat, fresh fruits, fresh vegetables, and dry food of Type VIII described in table 1 of § 176.170(c) of this chapter. The average thickness of such ethylene-vinyl acetate copolymer film shall not exceed 0.003 inch when used for packaging meat, fresh fruits, and fresh vegetables.

List of substances	Limitations
Alpha-(Carboxymethyl)-omega-(tetradecyloxy)polyoxyethylene)	For use only as an antistatic and/or antifogging agent at levels not to exceed 0.2 pct by weight in polyolefin film not exceeding 0.001 inch thickness.
Alkyl mono- and disulfonic acids, sodium salts (produced from *n*-alkanes in the range of C_{10}-C_{18} with not less than 50 percent C_{14}-C_{16}).	For use only: 1. As antistatic agents at levels not to exceed 0.1 percent by weight of polyolefin films that comply with § 177.1520 of this chapter: *Provided,* that the finished olefin polymers contact foods of Types I, II, III, IV, V, VIA, VIB, VII, VIII, and IX described in table 1 of § 176.170(c) of this chapter, and under conditions of use E, F, and G described in table 2 of § 176.170(c) of this chapter. 2. As antistatic agents at levels not to exceed 3.0 percent by weight of polystyrene or rubber-modified polystyrene complying with § 177.1640(c) of this chapter under conditions of use B through H described in table 2 of § 176.170(c) of this chapter.
Aluminum Borate (($9Al_2O_3$)·2(B_2O_3), CAS Reg. No. 11121–16–7) produced by reaction between aluminum oxide and/or aluminum hydroxide with boric acid and/or metaboric acid at temperatures in excess of 1000 °C.	For use only: 1. At levels not to exceed 1 percent by weight of polypropylene films complying with § 177.1520(c) of this chapter, item 1.1, of polyethylene films complying with § 177.1520(c) of this chapter, items 2.1 and 2.2 and having a density greater than 0.94 gram per cubic centimeter, and of polyolefin copolymer films complying with § 177.1520(c) of this chapter, items 3.1(a), 3.1(b), 3.2(a), and 3.2(b). The finished polymers may be used in contact with all food types identified in Table 1 of § 176.170(c) of this chapter, under conditions of use A through H as described in Table 2 of § 176.170(c) of this chapter. The thickness of the films shall not exceed 0.005 inch. 2. At levels not to exceed 2 percent by weight of polypropylene films complying with § 177.1520(c) of this chapter, item 1.1, of polyethylene films complying with § 177.1520(c) of this chapter, items 2.1 and 2.2 and having a density greater than 0.94 gram per cubic centimeter, and of polyolefin copolymer films complying with § 177.1520(c) of this chapter, items 3.1(a), 3.1(b), 3.2(a), and 3.2(b). The finished polymers may be used in contact with all food types identified in Table 1 of § 176.170(c) of this chapter under conditions of use B through H as described in Table 2 of § 176.170(c) of this chapter. The thickness of the films shall not exceed 0.005 inch.
N,N-Bis(2-hydroxyethyl)alkyl(C_{12}-C_{18})amine	For use only as an antistatic agent at levels not to exceed 0.1 pct by weight of polyolefin food-contact films.
N,N-bis(2-hydroxyethyl)alkyl (C_{13}-C_{15}) amine (CAS Reg. No. 70955–14–5).	For use only: 1. As an antistatic agent at levels not to exceed 0.2 percent by weight in molded or extruded high-density polyethylene (having a density ≥0.95 g/cm³ and polypropylene containers that contact food only of the types identified in § 176.170(c) of this chapter, Table 1, under types I, VI-B, VII-B, and VIII, under the conditions of use E through G described in Table 2 of § 176.170(c) of this chapter, provided such foods have a pH above 5.0. 2. As an antistatic agent at levels not to exceed 0.1 percent by weight in molded or extruded polypropylene homopolymers and copolymers that contact food only of the types identified in § 176.170(c) of this chapter, Table 1, under Types II, III, IV, V, VII-A, and IX, under the conditions of use C through G described in Table 2 of § 176.170(c) of this chapter.

List of substances	Limitations
N,N-Bis(2-hydroxyethyl) alkylamine, where the alkyl groups (C_{14}–C_{18}) are derived from tallow..	For use only: 1. As an antistatic agent at levels not to exceed 0.15 pct by weight in molded or extruded polyethylene containers that contact food only of the types identified in § 176.170(c) of this chapter, table 1, under Types I, IV-B, VI-B, VII-B, and VIII, under the conditions of use E through G described in table 2 of § 176.170(c) of this chapter provided such foods have a pH above 5.0. 2. As an antistatic agent at levels not to exceed 0.10 mg. per square inch of food-contact surface in vinylidene chloride copolymer coatings complying with § 175.320, § 177.1200, or § 177.1630 of this chapter, provided that such coatings contact food only of the types identified in § 176.170(c) of this chapter, table 1, under Types I, IV, VII, VIII, and IX under the conditions of use E through G described in table 2 of § 176.170(c) of this chapter. The finished copolymers shall contain at least 70 weight pct of polymer units derived from vinylidene chloride; and shall contain not more than 5 weight pct of total polymer units derived from acrylamide, acrylic acid, fumaric acid, itaconic acid, methacrylic acid, octadecyl methacrylate, and vinyl sulfonic acid.
N,N-Bis(2-hydroxyethyl)dodecanamide produced when diethanolamine is made to react with methyl laurate such that the finished product: Has a minimum melting point of 36 °C; has a minimum amide assay of 90 percent; contains no more than 2 percent by weight of free diethanolamine; and contains no more than 0.5 percent by weight of *N,N,* bis(2-hydroxyethyl)piperazine, as determined by paper chromatography method.	For use only: 1. As an antistatic agent at levels not to exceed 0.5 percent by weight of molded or extruded polyethylene containers intended for contact with honey, chocolate syrup, liquid sweeteners, condiments, flavor extracts and liquid flavor concentrates, grated cheese, light and heavy cream, yogurt, and foods of Type VIII as described in table 1 of § 176.170(c) of this chapter. 2. As an antistatic agent at levels not to exceed 0.2 percent by weight in polypropylene films complying with § 177.1520 of this chapter, and used in contact with food of Types I, II, III, IV, V, VI-B, VII, VIII, and IX described in table 1 of § 176.170(c) of this chapter, and under conditions of use B through H described in table 2 of § 176.170(c) of this chapter. The average thickness of such polypropylene film shall not exceed 0.001 inches (30 micrometers).
N,N-Bis(2-hydroxyethyl) dodecanamide produced when diethanolamine is made to react with methyl laurate such that the finished product: Has a minimum melting point of 36 °C; has a minimum amide assay of 90 percent; contains no more than 2 percent by weight of free diethanolamine; and contains no more than 0.5 percent by weight of *N,N'*-bis(2-hydroxyethyl) piperazine, as determined by paper chromatography method.	For use only as an antistatic agent at levels not to exceed 0.5 percent by weight of molded or extruded polyethylene containers intended for contact with honey, chocolate syrup, liquid sweeteners, condiments, flavor extracts and liquid flavor concentrates, grated cheese, light and heavy cream, yogurt, and foods of Type VIII as described in table 1 of § 176.170(c) of this chapter.
N,N-Bis(2-hydroxyethyl) octadecylamine, Chemical Abstracts Service Registry No. 10213–78–2, N-(2-hydroxyethyl)-*N*-octadecylglycine (monosodium salt), Chemical Abstracts Service Registry No. 66810–88–6, and *N,N*-Bis(2-hydroxyethyl)-*N*-(carboxymethyl) octadecanaminum hydroxide (inner salt), Chemical Abstracts Service Registry No. 24170–14–7, as the major components of a mixture prepared by reacting ethylene oxide with octadecylamine and further reacting this product with sodium monochloroacetate and sodium hydroxide, such that the final product has: A nitrogen content of 3.3–3.8 percent; a melting point of 42°–50 °C; and a pH of 10.0–11.5 in a 1 percent by weight aqueous solution.	For use only as an antistatic agent at levels not to exceed 0.45 percent by weight in polypropylene films complying with § 177.1520 of this chapter, and used for packaging food of Types I, II, III, IV, V, VI-B, VII, VIII, and IX described in table 1 of § 176.170(c) of this chapter, and under conditions of use B through H described in table 2 of § 176.170(c). The average thickness of such polypropylene film shall not exceed 0.002 inch.
α-*n*-Dodecanol-*omega*-hydroxypoly (oxyethylene) produced by the condensation of 1 mole of *n*-dodecanol with an average of 9.5 moles of ethylene oxide to form a condensate having a hydroxyl content of 2.7 to 2.9 pct and having a cloud point of 80 °C to 92 °C in 1 pct by weight aqueous solution.	For use only as an antistatic agent at levels not to exceed 0.2 pct by weight in low-density polyethylene film having an average thickness not exceeding 0.005 inch.
Glycerol ester mixtures of ricinoleic acid, containing not more than 50 percent monoricinoleate, 45 pct diricinoleate, 10 pct triricinoleate, and 3.3 pct free glycerine.	As an antifogging agent at levels not exceeding 1.5 pct by weight of permitted plasticized vinyl chloride homo-and/or copolymers.
N-Methacryloyloxyethyl-*N, N*-dimethylammonium-α-*N*-methyl carboxylate chloride sodium salt, octadecyl methacrylate, ethyl methacrylate, cyclohexyl methacrylate, *N*-vinyl-2-pyrrolidone copolymer (CAS Reg. No. 66822–60–4).	For use only as an antistatic agent at levels not to exceed 0.2 percent by weight of polyolefin films that contact foods under the conditions of use B through H described in table 2 of § 176.170(c) of this chapter. The average thickness of such polyolefin film shall not exceed 0.02 centimeter (0.008 inch).

List of substances	Limitations
Octadecanoic acid 2-[2-hydroxyethyl) octadecylamino]ethyl ester (CAS Reg. No. 52497–24–2), (octadecylimino) diethylene distearate (CAS Reg. No. 94945–28–5), and octadecyl bis(hydroxyethyl)amine (CAS Reg. No. 10213–78–2), as the major components of a mixture prepared by reacting ethylene oxide with octadecylamine and further reacting this product with octadecanoic acid, such that the final product has: a maximum acid value of 5 mg KOH/g and total amine value of 86±6 mg KOH/g as determined by a method entitled "Total Amine Value," which is incorporated by reference. Copies of the method are available from the Center for Food Safety and Applied Nutrition (HFS–200), Food and Drug Administration, 5100 Paint Branch Pkwy., College Park, MD 20740, or available for inspection at the National Archives and Records Administration (NARA). For information on the availability of this material at NARA, call 202–741–6030, or go to: *http://www.archives.gov/federal_register/code_of_federal_regulations/ibr_locations.html.*.	For use only as an antistatic agent at levels such that the product of film thickness in microns times the weight percent additive does not exceed 16, in polypropylene films complying with § 177.1520(c)1.1 of this chapter, and used for packaging food (except for food containing more than 8 percent alcohol) under conditions of use B through H described in table 2 of § 176.170(c) of this chapter.

[42 FR 14609, Mar. 15, 1977, as amended at 45 FR 56797, Aug. 26, 1980; 45 FR 85727, Dec. 30, 1980; 46 FR 13688, Feb. 24, 1981; 47 FR 26824, June 22, 1982; 51 FR 28932, Aug. 13, 1986; 56 FR 41457, Aug. 21, 1991; 58 FR 57556, Oct. 26, 1993; 60 FR 54430, Oct. 24, 1995; 60 FR 18351, Apr. 11, 1995; 62 FR 31511, June 10, 1997; 63 FR 38748, July 20, 1998; 64 FR 62585, Nov. 17, 1999; 76 FR 59249, Sept. 26, 2011]

§ 178.3280 Castor oil, hydrogenated.

Hydrogenated castor oil may be safely used in the manufacture of articles or components of articles intended for use in contact with food subject to the provisions of this section.

(a) The quantity used shall not exceed the amount reasonably required to accomplish the intended technical effect.

(b) The additive is used as follows:

Use	Limitations
1. As a lubricant for vinyl chloride polymers used in the manufacture of articles or components of articles authorized for food-contact use.	For use only at levels not to exceed 4 pct by weight of vinyl chloride polymers.
2. As a component of cellophane	Complying with § 177.1200 of this chapter.
3. As a component of resinous and polymeric coatings	Complying with § 175.300 of this chapter.
4. As a component of paper and paperboard in contact with aqueous and fatty food.	Complying with § 176.170 of this chapter.
5. As a component of closures with sealing gaskets for food containers.	Complying with § 177.1210 of this chapter.
6. As a component of cross-linked polyester resins	Complying with § 177.2420 of this chapter.
7. As a component of olefin polymers complying with § 177.1520 of this chapter.	For use only at levels not to exceed 2 percent by weight of the polymer.

[42 FR 14609, Mar. 15, 1977, as amended at 55 FR 8914, Mar. 9, 1990]

§ 178.3290 Chromic chloride complexes.

Myristo chromic chloride complex and stearato chromic chloride complex may be safely used as release agents in the closure area of packaging containers intended for use in producing, manufacturing, packing, processing, preparing, treating, packaging, transporting, or holding food, subject to the provisions of this section:

(a) The quantity used shall not exceed that reasonably required to accomplish the intended technical effect nor exceed 7 micrograms of chromium per square inch of closure area.

(b) The packaging container which has its closure area treated with the release agent shall have a capacity of not less than 120 grams of food per square inch of such treated closure area.

§ 178.3295 Clarifying agents for polymers.

Clarifying agents may be safely used in polymers that are articles or components of articles intended for use in contact with food, subject to the provisions of this section:

Substances	Limitations
Aluminum, hydroxybis[2,4,8,10-tetrakis(1,1-dimethylethyl)-6-hydroxy-12H-dibenzo[d,g][1,3,2]dioxaphosphocin 6-oxidato]-(CAS Reg. No. 151841–65–5).	For use only as a clarifying agent at levels not to exceed 0.25 percent by weight of polypropylene and polypropylene copolymers complying with § 177.1520(c) of this chapter, items 1.1, 3.1, or 3.2. The finished polymers contact food only of types I, II, IV-B, VI-B, VII-B, and VIII as identified in Table 1 of § 176.170(c) of this chapter, under conditions of use B through H described in Table 2 of § 176.170(c) of this chapter or foods only of types III, IV-A, V, VI-A, VI-C, VII-A, and IX as identified in Table 1 of § 176.170(c) of this chapter, under conditions of use C through G described in Table 2 of § 176.170(c) of this chapter.
Bis(*p*-ethylbenzylidene) sorbitol (CAS Reg. No. 79072–96–1) ...	For use only as a clarifying agent at a level not to exceed 0.35 percent by weight of olefin polymers complying with § 177.1520(c) of this chapter, items 1.1a, 1.1b, 3.1a, 3.2a, or 3.2b, where the copolymers complying with items 3.1a, 3.2a, or 3.2b contain not less than 85 weight percent of polymer units derived from propylene.
Di(*p*-tolylidene) sorbitol (CAS Reg. No. 54686–97–4)	For use only as a clarifying agent at a level not to exceed 0.32 percent by weight in propylene homopolymer complying with § 177.1520(c) of this chapter, item 1.1, and in olefin copolymers complying with § 177.1520(c) of this chapter, item 3.1 (containing at least 85 weight percent of polymer units derived from propylene), in contact with all food types under conditions of use C through G described in table 2 of § 176.170(c) of this chapter.
Dibenzylidene sorbitol (CAS Reg. No. 32647–67–9) formed by the condensation of two moles of benzaldehyde with one mole of sorbitol, such that the final product has a minimum content of 95 percent dibenzylidene sorbitol.	For use only as a clarifying agent for olefin polymers complying with § 177.1520(c) 1.1, 3.1, and 3.2 of this chapter under conditions of use C, D, E, F, and G, described in table 2 of § 176.170(c) of this chapter at a level not exceeding 0.25 percent by weight of the polymer.
Dimethyldibenzylidene sorbitol (CAS Reg. No. 135861–56–2)	For use only as a clarifying agent at a level not to exceed 0.4 percent by weight of olefin polymers complying with § 177.1520(c) of this chapter, items 1.1, 3.1, and 3.2, where the copolymers complying with items 3.1 and 3.2 contain not less than 85 weight percent of polymer units derived from polypropylene. The finished polymers shall be used in contact with food under conditions of use A through H described in table 2 of § 176.170(c) of this chapter.
Polyvinylcyclohexane (CAS Reg. No. 25498–06–0)	For use only as a clarfiying agent for polypropylene complying with § 177.1520(c) of this chapter, item 1.1., and in propylene containing copolymers complying with § 177.1520(c) of this chapter, items 3.1 and 3.2, at a level not exceeding 0.1 percent by weight of the polyolefin.
Sodium di(*p-tert*-butylphenyl)phosphate (CAS Reg. No. 10491–31–3).	For use only as a clarifying agent at a level not exceeding 0.35 parts per hundred of the resin in olefin polymers complying with § 177.1520(c) of this chapter, items 1.1, 3.1, or 3.2 (where the copolymers complying with items 3.1 and 3.2 contain not less than 85 weight percent of polymer units derived from propylene).

Substances	Limitations
Sodium 2,2′-methylenebis(4,6-di-*tert*-butylphenyl)phosphate (CAS Reg. No. 85209–91–2).	For use only: 1. As a clarifying agent at a level not exceeding 0.30 percent by weight of olefin polymers complying with § 177.1520(c) of this chapter, items 1.1, 3.1, or 3.2 (where the copolymers complying with items 3.1 and 3.2 contain not less than 85 weight percent of polymer units derived from polypropylene). The finished polymers contact foods only of types I, II, IV-B, VI-B, VII-B, and VIII as identified in table 1 of § 176.170(c) of this chapter and limited to conditions of use B through H, described in table 2 of § 176.170(c), or foods of all types, limited to conditions of use C through H described in table 2 of § 176.170(c). 2. As a clarifying agent at levels not exceeding 0.10 percent by weight of polypropylene complying with § 177.1520(c) of this chapter, items 1.1(a) or 1.1(b) and of olefin polymers complying with § 177.1520(c) of this chapter, items 3.1(a), 3.1(b), 3.1(c), 3.2(a), or 3.2(b) (where the copolymers contain not less than 85 weight percent of the polymer units derived from polypropylene.) The finished polymers shall be used in contact with foods only under conditions of use A through H described in Table 2 of § 176.170(c) of this chapter. 3. As a clarifying agent at a level not exceeding 0.30 percent by weight of olefin polymers complying with § 177.1520(c) of this chapter, item 2.2, where the finished polymer contacts food only of types I, II, IV-B, VI-A, VI-B, and VII-B as identified in Table 1 of § 176.170(c) of this chapter, and limited to conditions of use B through H described in Table 2 of § 176.170(c) of this chapter, or foods of types III, IV-A, V, VI-C, and VII-A as identified in Table 1 of § 176.170(c) of this chapter and limited to conditions of use C through G described in Table 2 of § 176.170(c) of this chapter.

[46 FR 59236, Dec. 4, 1981, as amended at 52 FR 30920, Aug. 18, 1987; 53 FR 30049, Aug. 10, 1988; 54 FR 12432, Mar. 27, 1989; 54 FR 14734, Apr. 12, 1989; 55 FR 52990, Dec. 26, 1990; 56 FR 1085, Jan. 11, 1991; 59 FR 13650, Mar. 23, 1994; 59 FR 25323, May 16, 1994; 61 FR 33847, July 1, 1996; 61 FR 51588, Oct. 3, 1996; 61 FR 65943, Dec. 16, 1996; 63 FR 56789, Oct. 23, 1998; 63 FR 68392, Dec. 11, 1998; 64 FR 26843, May 18, 1999; 65 FR 16316, Mar. 28, 2000]

§ 178.3297 Colorants for polymers.

The substances listed in paragraph (e) of this section may be safely used as colorants in the manufacture of articles or components of articles intended for use in producing, manufacturing, packing, processing, preparing, treating, packaging, transporting, or holding food, subject to the provisions and definitions set forth in this section:

(a) The term *colorant* means a dye, pigment, or other substance that is used to impart color to or to alter the color of a food-contact material, but that does not migrate to food in amounts that will contribute to that food any color apparent to the naked eye. For the purpose of this section, the term "colorant" includes substances such as optical brighteners and fluorescent whiteners, which may not themselves be colored, but whose use is intended to affect the color of a food-contact material.

(b) The colorant must be used in accordance with current good manufacturing practice, including use levels which are not in excess of those reasonably required to accomplish the intended coloring effect.

(c) Colorants in this section must conform to the description and specifications indicated. If a polymer described in this section is itself the subject of a regulation promulgated under section 409 of the Federal Food, Drug, and Cosmetic Act, it shall also comply with any specifications and limitations prescribed by that regulation. Extraction testing guidelines to conduct studies for additional uses of colorants under this section are available from the Food and Drug Administration free of charge from the Food and Drug Administration, Center for Food Safety and Applied Nutrition, 5100 Paint Branch Pkwy., College Park, MD 20740, 240–402–1200

(d) Color additives and their lakes listed for direct use in foods, under the provisions of the color additive regulations in parts 73, 74, 81, and 82 of this chapter, may also be used as colorants for food-contact polymers.

(e) List of substances:

Substances	Limitations
Aluminum.	
Aluminum hydrate.	
Aluminum and potassium silicate (mica).	
Aluminum mono-, di-, and tristearate.	
Aluminum silicate (China clay).	
4-[[5-[[[4-(Aminocarbonyl) phenyl] amino]carbonyl]- 2-methoxyphenyl]azo]-*N*-(5-chloro-2,4-dimethoxyphenyl)-3-hydroxy-2-naphthalene-carboxamide (C.I. Pigment Red 187, CAS Reg. No. 59487–23–9).	For use at levels not to exceed 1 percent by weight of polymers. The finished articles are to contact foods only under conditions of use B through H described in table 2 of § 176.170(c) of this chapter.
N-[4-(Aminocarbonyl)phenyl]-4-[[1-[[(2,3-dihydro-2-oxo-1*H*-benzimidazol-5-yl)amino]carbonyl]-2-oxopropyl]azo]benzamide (C. I. Pigment Yellow 181, CAS Reg. No. 74441–05–7).	For use at levels not to exceed 1 percent by weight of polymers. The finished articles are to contact food only under conditions of use B through H described in table 2 of § 176.170(c) of this chapter.
Anthra(2,1,9-def:(6,5,10-d′e′f)diisoquinoline-1,3,8,10(2H,9H)-tetrone (C.I. Pigment Violet 29; CAS Reg. No. 81–33–4).	For use at levels not to exceed 1% by weight of polymers. The finished articles are to contact food only under conditions of use B through H as described in Table 2 of § 176.170(c) of this chapter.
Barium sulfate.	
Bentonite.	
Bentonite, modified with 3-dimethyldioctadecylammonium ion.	
1,4-Bis[(2,4,6-trimethylphenyl)amino]-9,10-anthracenedione (CAS Reg. No. 116–75–6).	For use at levels not to exceed 0.0004 percent by weight of polyethylene phthalate polymers complying with § 177.1630 of this chapter.
3,6-Bis(4-chlorophenyl)-2,5-dihydro-pyrrolo[3,4-c]pyrrole-1,4-dione (C.I. Pigment Red 254, CAS Reg. No. 84632–65–5).	For use only at levels not to exceed 1 percent by weight of polymers. The finished articles are to contact food only under conditions of use B through H, described in table 2 of § 176.170(c) of this chapter.
4,4′-Bis(4-anilino-6-diethanolamine-α-triazin-2-ylamino)-2,2′-stilbene disulfonic acid, disodium salt.	For use only in the textile fibers specified in § 177.2800 of this chapter.
4,4′-Bis(4-anilino-6-methylethanolamine-α-triazin-2-ylamino)-2,2′-stilbene disulfonic acid, disodium salt.	Do.
Burnt umber.	
Calcium carbonate.	
Calcium silicate.	
Calcium sulfate.	
Carbon black (channel process, prepared by the impingement process from stripped natural gas).	
4-Chloro-2-[[5-hydroxy-3-methyl-1-(3-sulfophenyl)-1H-pyrazol-4-yl]azo]-5-methylbenzenesulfonic acid, calcium salt (1:1); (C.I. Pigment Yellow 191, CAS Reg. No. 129423–54–7).	For use at levels not to exceed 1.0 percent by weight of the finished polymers. The finished articles are to contact food only under conditions of use B through H as described in table 2 of § 176.170(c) of this chapter.
4-Chloro-2-[[5-hydroxy-3-methyl-1-(3-sulfophenyl)-1H-pyrazol-4-yl]azo]-5-methylbenzenesulfonic acid, diammonium salt (1:2): (C.I. Pigment Yellow 191:1, CAS Reg. No. 154946–66–4).	For use at levels not to exceed 0.5 percent by weight of polymers. The finished articles are to contact food under conditions of use A through H described in Table 2 of § 176.170(c) of this chapter.
Chrome antimony titanium buff rutile (C.I. Pigment Brown 24, CAS Reg. No. 68186–90–3).	For use at levels not to exceed 1 percent by weight of polymers. The finished articles are to contact food only under conditions of use B through H as described in Table 2 of § 176.170(c) of this chapter.
Chromium oxide green, Cr_2O_3 (C.I. Pigment Green 17, C.I. No. 77288).	For use only: 1. In polymers used in contact with food at a level not to exceed 5 percent by weight of the polymer, except as specified below. 2. In olefin polymers complying with § 177.1520 of this chapter. 3. In repeat-use rubber articles complying with § 177.2600 of this chapter; total use is not to exceed 10 percent by weight of rubber articles.

Substances	Limitations
Cobalt aluminate	For use only: 1. In resinous and polymeric coatings complying with § 175.300 of this chapter. 2. Melamine-formaldehyde resins in molded articles complying with § 177.1460 of this chapter. 3. Xylene-formaldehyde resins condensed with 4-4′isopropylidenediphenol-epichlorohydrin epoxy resins complying with § 175.380 of this chapter. 4. Ethylene-vinyl acetate copolymers complying with § 177.1350 of this chapter. 5. Urea-formaldehyde resins in molded articles complying with § 177.1900 of this chapter. 6. At levels not to exceed 5 percent by weight of all polymers except those listed under limitations 1 through 5 of this item. The finished articles are to contact food under conditions of use A through H described in table 2 of § 176.170(c) of this chapter.
Copper chromite black spinel (C.I. Pigment Black 28, CAS Reg. No. 68186–91–4).	For use at levels not to exceed 5 percent by weight of polymers. The finished articles are to contact food only under conditions of use A through H as described in table 2 of § 176.170(c) of this chapter.
D&C Red No. 7 and its lakes.	
Diatomaceous earth.	
4,4′-Diamino-[1,1′-bianthracene]-9,9′,10,10′-tetrone (CAS Reg. No. 4051–63–2).	For use at levels not to exceed 1 percent by weight of polymers. The finished articles are to contact food only under conditions of use B through H described in table 2 of § 176.170(c) of this chapter.
2,9-Dichloro-5,12-dihydroquinone[2,3-b]acridine-7,14-dione (C.I. Pigment Red 202, CAS Reg. No. 3089–17–6).	For use at levels not to exceed 1.0 percent by weight of polymers.
4,5-Dichloro-2-((5-hydroxy-3-methyl-1-(3-sulfophenyl)-1H-pyrazol-4- yl)azo)benzenesulfonic acid, calcium salt(1:1), (C.I. Pigment Yellow 183, CAS Reg. No. 65212–77–3).	For use only: 1. At levels not to exceed 1 percent by weight of polypropylene polymers and copolymers complying with § 177.1520(c) of this chapter, items 1.1a, 1.1b, 1.2, 1.3, 3.1a, 3.1b, 3.1c, 3.2a, 3.2b, 3.4, or 3.5. The finished articles are to contact food only under conditions of use E through G, as described in Table 2 of § 176.170(c) of this chapter. 2. At levels not to exceed 1 percent by weight of high density polyethylene polymers and copolymers complying with § 177.1520(c) of this chapter, items 2.1, 2.2, 2.3, 3.1a, 3.1b, 3.1c, 3.2a, 3.2b, 3.6 (density not less than 0.94 grams per cubic centimeter), or 5. The finished articles are to contact food only under conditions of use E through G, as described in Table 2 of § 176.170(c) of this chapter.
5-[(2,3-Dihydro-6-methyl-2-oxo-1*H*-benzimidazol-5-yl)azo]-2,4,6(1*H,* 3*H,* 5*H*)-pyrimidinetrione (CAS Reg. No. 72102–84–2).	For use at levels not to exceed 1 percent by weight of polymers. The finished articles are to contact food only under conditions of use B through H described in table 2 of § 176.170(c) of this chapter.
2,9-Dimethylanthra(2,1,9-def:6,5,10-d′e′f′)diisoquinoline-1,3,8,10(2H,9H)-tetrone (C.I. Pigment Red 179, CAS Reg. No. 5521–31–3).	For use at levels not to exceed 1 percent by weight of polymers. The finished articles are to contact food only under conditions of use B through H as described in Table 2 of § 176.170(c) of this chapter.
3,3′-[(2,5-Dimethyl-1,4-phenylene)bis[imino(1-acetyl-2-oxo-2,1-ethanediyl)azo]]bis[4-chloro-*N*-(5-chloro-2-methylphenyl)-benzamide] (CAS Reg. No. 5280–80–8).	For use at levels not to exceed 1 percent by weight of polymers. The finished articles are to contact food only under conditions of use B through H described in table 2 of § 176.170(c) of this chapter.
3,3′-[(2,5-Dimethyl-1,4-phenylene)bis[imino-carbonyl(2-hydroxy-3,1-naphthalenediyl) azo]] bis(4-methylbenzoic acid), bis(2-chloroethyl) ester (CAS Reg. No. 68259–05–2).	For use at levels not to exceed 1 percent by weight of polymers. The finished articles are to contact food only under conditions of use B through H described in table 2 of § 176.170(c) of this chapter.
2,2′-[1,2-Ethanediylbis(oxy-2,1-phenyleneazo)]bis[N-(2,3-dihydro-2-oxo-1*H*-benzimidazol-5-yl)]-3-oxo-butanamide (C.I. Pigment Yellow 180, CAS Reg. No. 77804–81–0).	For use at levels not to exceed 1.0 percent by weight of polymers. The finished articles are to contact food only under conditions of use B through G described in table 2 of § 176.170(c) of this chapter.
2,2′-(1,2-Ethenediyldi-4,1-phenylene) bis(benzoxazole) (CAS Reg. No. 1533–45–5).	For use as an optical brightener for all polymers at a level not to exceed 0.025 percent by weight of polymer. The finished polymer shall contact foods only of the types identified in table 1 of § 176.170(c) of this chapter, under categories I, II, IV-B, VI-A, VI-B, VII-B, and VIII at temperatures not to exceed 275 °F.

Substances	Limitations
High-purity furnace black (CAS Reg. No. 1333–86–4) containing total polynuclear aromatic hydrocarbons not to exceed 0.5 parts per million, and benzo[a]pyrene not to exceed 5.0 parts per billion, as determined by a method entitled "Determination of PAH Content of Carbon Black," dated July 8, 1994, as developed by the Cabot Corp., which is incorporated by reference in accordance with 5 U.S.C. 552(a) and 1 CFR part 51. Copies may be obtained from the Office of Food Additive Safety (HFS–200), Center for Food Safety and Applied Nutrition, Food and Drug Administration, 5100 Paint Branch Pkwy., College Park, MD 20740, 240–402–1200, or may be examined at the Center for Food Safety and Applied Nutrition's Library, 5100 Paint Branch Pkwy., College Park, MD 20740, or at the National Archives and Records Administration (NARA). For information on the availability of this material at NARA, call 202–741–6030, or go to: *http://www.archives.gov/federal_register/code_of_federal_regulations/ibr_locations.html*..	For use at levels not to exceed 2.5 percent by weight of the polymer.
Iron oxides.	
Kaolin-modified, produced by treating kaolin with a reaction product of isopropyl titanate and oleic acid in which 1 mole of isopropyl titanate is reacted with 1 to 2 moles of oleic acid. The reaction product will not exceed 8 percent of the modified kaolin. The oleic acid used shall meet the requirements specified in § 172.860 of this chapter.	For use only in olefin polymers complying with § 177.1520 of this chapter at levels not to exceed 40 percent by weight of olefin polymer.
Magnesium oxide.	
Magnesium silicate (talc).	
Manganese Violet (manganese ammonium pyrophosphate; CAS Reg. No. 10101–66–3)..	For use at levels not to exceed 2 percent by weight of polymers. The finished articles are to contact food only under conditions of use A through H as described in table 2 of § 176.170(c) of this chapter.
Mixed methylated 4,4′-bis(2-benzoxazolyl)stilbenes with the major portion consisting of 4-(2-benzoxazolyl)-4′-(5-methyl-2-benzoxazolyl)stilbene (CAS Registry No. 5242–49–9) and lesser portions consisting of 4,4′-bis(5-methyl-2-benzoxazolyl)stilbene (CAS Registry No. 2397–00–4) and 4,4′-bis(2-benzoxazolyl)stilbene (CAS Registry No. 1533–45–5).	For use as an optical brightener only at levels not to exceed 0.05 percent by weight of rigid and semirigid polyvinyl chloride and not to exceed 0.03 percent by weight in all other polymers. The finished food-contact articles shall be used only under conditions of use D, E, F, and G described in table 2 of § 176.170(c) of this chapter.
7-(2*H*-Naphtho[1,2-*d*]triazol-2-yl)-3-phenylcoumarin (CAS Reg. No. 3333–62–8) having a melting point of 250 °C to 251 °C and a nitrogen content of 10.7 to 11.2 percent.	For use as an optical brightener only in: 1. Olefin polymers complying with § 177.1520 of this chapter only at levels such that the product of concentration of the optical brightener (expressed in parts per million by weight of the olefin polymer) multiplied by the thickness of the olefin polymer (expressed in thousandths of an inch and limited to no more than 0.400 inch) shall not exceed 500; provided that the level of the brightener shall not exceed 20 parts per million by weight of the olefin polymer, and further that the olefin polymers shall comply with specifications for items 1.1, 2.1, 3.1, 3.3, and 4 of § 177.1520(c) of this chapter. The polymer may be used under the conditions described in § 176.170(c) of this chapter, table 2, under conditions of use E, F, and G. 2. Polyethylene terephthalate specified in § 177.2800(d)(5)(i) of this chapter at a level not to exceed 0.035 percent by weight of the finished fibers.
Nickel antimony titanium yellow rutile (C.I. Pigment Yellow 53, CAS Reg. No. 8007–18–9).	For use at levels not to exceed 1 percent by weight of polymers. The finished articles are to contact food only under conditions of use B through H as described in Table 2 of § 176.170(c) of this chapter.
1,1′-[(6-Phenyl-1,3,5-triazine-2,4-diyl)diimino]bis-9,10-anthracenedione (CAS Reg. No. 4118–16–5).	For use at levels not to exceed 0.25 percent by weight of polyethylene phthalate polymers that comply with § 177.1630 of this chapter. The finished articles are to contact food only under conditions of use E, F, and G described in table 2, § 176.170(c) of this chapter, except, when such articles are used with food types III, IV-A, and V, described in table 1, § 176.170(c) of this chapter, the finished articles are to contact food only under conditions of use D, E, F, and G.
Phthalocyanine blue (C.I. pigment blue 15, 15:1, 15:2, 15:3, and 15:4; C.I. No. 74160; CAS Reg. No. 147–14–8).	
Phthalocyanine green (C.I. pigment green 7, C.I. No. 74260).	
C.I. Pigment red 38 (C.I. No. 21120)	For use only in rubber articles for repeated use complying with § 177.2600 of this chapter; total use is not to exceed 10 percent by weight of rubber article.

Substances	Limitations
Quinacridone red (C.I. Pigment violet 19, C.I. No. 73900).	
Sienna (raw and burnt).	
Silica.	
2,3,4,5-Tetrachloro-6-cyanobenzoic acid, methyl ester reaction products with *p*-phenyllenediamine and sodium methoxide (CAS reg. No. 106276–80–6).	For use only at levels not to exceed 1 percent by weight of polymers. The finished articles are to contact food only under conditins of use B through H, described in table 2, of § 176.170(c) of this chapter.
4,5,6,7-Tetrachloro-2-[2-(4,5,6,7-tetrachloro-2,3-dihydro-1,3-dioxo-1H-inden-2-yl)-8-quinolinyl]-1H-isoindole-1,3(2H)-dione (C. I. Pigment Yellow 138, CAS Reg. No.30125–47–4).	For use only at levels not to exceed 1 percent by weight of polymers. The finished articles are to contact food only under conditions of use C through H, as described in table 2 of § 176.170(c) of this chapter; provided further that the finished articles shall not be filled at temperatures exceeding 158 °F (70 °C).
2,2′-(2,5-Thiophenediyl)-bis(5-*tert*-butylbenzoxazole) (CAS Reg. No. 7128–64–5).	For use as an optical brightener: 1. In all polymers at levels not to exceed 0.015 percent by weight of the polymer. The finished articles are to contact food only under conditions of use A through H described in table 2 of § 176.170(c) of this chapter. 2. In all polymers at levels not to exceed 0.05 percent by weight of the polymer. The finished articles shall contact foods only of the types identified in table 1 of § 176.170(c) of this chapter, under Categories I, II, IV-B, VI-A, VI-B, VI-C, VII-B, and VIII under conditions of use A through H described in table 2 of § 176.170(c) of this chapter. 3. In adhesives complying with § 175.105 of this chapter and in pressure-sensitive adhesives complying with § 175.125 of this chapter.
Titanium dioxide.	
Titanium dioxide-barium sulfate.	
Titanium dioxide-magnesium silicate.	
Ultramarines	As identified in § 73.2725 of this chapter.
Zinc carbonate	For use only: 1. In resinous and polymeric coatings complying with § 175.300 of this chapter. 2. Melamineformaldehyde resins in molded articles complying with § 177.1460 of this chapter. 3. Xylene-formaldehyde resins condensed with 4-4′-isopropylidene diphenol-epichlorohydrin epoxy resins complying with § 175.380 of this chapter. 4. Ethylene-vinyl acetate copolymers complying with § 177.1350 of this chapter. 5. Urea-formaldehyde resins in molded articles complying with § 177.1900 of this chapter.
Zinc chromate	For use only in rubber articles for repeated use complying with § 177.2600 of this chapter; total use is not to exceed 10 percent by weight of rubber article.
Zinc oxide	For use only: 1. In resinous and polymeric coatings complying with § 175.300 of this chapter. 2. Melamine-formaldehyde resins in molded articles complying with § 177.1460 of this chapter. 3. Xylene-formaldehyde resins condensed with 4-4′-isopropylidene-diphenol-epichlorohydrin epoxy resins complying with § 175.380 of this chapter. 4. Ethylene-vinyl acetate copolymers complying with § 177.1350 of this chapter. 5. Urea-formaldehyde resins in molded articles complying with § 177.1900 of this chapter.
Zinc sulfide	For use at levels not to exceed 10 percent by weight.

[48 FR 46775, Oct. 14, 1983]

EDITORIAL NOTE: For FEDERAL REGISTER citations affecting § 178.3297, see the List of CFR Sections Affected, which appears in the Finding Aids section of the printed volume and at *www.fdsys.gov*.

§ 178.3300 Corrosion inhibitors used for steel or tinplate.

Corrosion inhibitors may be safely used for steel or tinplate intended for use in, or to be fabricated as, food containers or food-processing or handling equipment, subject to the provisions of this section.

(a) The corrosion inhibitors are prepared from substances identified in this section and used subject to the limitations prescribed.

(b) The following corrosion inhibitors or adjuvants are used in amounts not to exceed those reasonably required to accomplish the intended physical or technical effect:

(1) Corrosion inhibitors (active ingredients) used in packaging materials for the packaging of steel or tinplate or articles fabricated therefrom:

List of substances	Limitations
Dicyclohexylamine and its salts of fatty acids derived from animal or vegetable oil.	
Dicyclohexylamine nitrite.	
Morpholine and its salts of fatty acids derived from animal or vegetable oils.	

(2) Adjuvants employed in the application and use of corrosion inhibitors:

List of substances	Limitations
Propylene glycol.	

§ 178.3400 Emulsifiers and/or surface-active agents.

The substances listed in paragraph (c) of this section may be safely used as emulsifiers and/or surface-active agents in the manufacture of articles or components of articles intended for use in producing, manufacturing, packing, processing, preparing, treating, packaging, transporting, or holding food, subject to the provisions of this section.

(a) The quantity used shall not exceed the amount reasonably required to accomplish the intended technical effect; and the quantity that may become a component of food as a result of such use shall not be intended to, nor in fact, accomplish any physical or technical effect in the food itself.

(b) The use as an emulsifier and/or surface-active agent in any substance or article that is the subject of a regulation in parts 174, 175, 176, 177, 178 and § 179.45 of this chapter conforms with any specifications and limitations prescribed by such regulation for the finished form of the substance or article.

(c) List of substances:

List of substances	Limitations
α-Alkyl-, α-alkenyl-, and α-alkylaryl-*omega*-hydroxypoly(oxyethylene) mixture consisting of 30 weight pct of α-(2,4,6-triisobutylphenyl)-*omega*-hydroxypoly(oxyethylene) having an average poly(oxyethylene) content of 7 moles and 70 weight pct of a 1:1 weight ratio mixture of α-(*Z*)-9-octadecenyl-*omega*-hydroxypoly(oxyethylene) having an average poly(oxyethylene) content of 18 moles and α-alkyl(C_{16}-C_{18})-*omega*-hydroxypoly(oxyethylene) having an average poly(oxyethylene) content of 18 moles.	For use only at levels not to exceed 0.5 pct by weight of coatings complying with § 175.320 of this chapter and limited to use as an emulsifier for polyhydric alcohol diesters used as provided in § 178.3770(b). The weight of the finished coating shall not exceed 2 milligrams per square inch of food-contact surface.
n-Alkylbenzenesulfonic acid (alkyl group consisting of not less than 95 percent C_{10} to C_{16}) and its ammonium, calcium, magnesium, potassium, and sodium salts.	For use only as emulsifiers and/or surface active agents as components of nonfood articles complying with §§ 175.300, 175.320, 175.365, 175.380, 176.170, 176.180, 177.1010, 177.1200, 177.1210, 177.1630, 177.2600, and 177.2800 of this chapter and § 178.3120.

List of substances	Limitations
Alkyl mono- and disulfonic acids, sodium salts (produced from *n*-alkanes in the range of C_{10}-C_{18} with not less than 50 percent C_{14}-C_{16}).	For use only: 1. As provided in § 176.170 of this chapter. 2. At levels not to exceed 2 percent by weight of polyvinyl chloride and/or vinyl chloride copolymers complying with § 177.1980 of this chapter. 3. As emulsifiers in vinylidene chloride copolymer or homopolymer coatings at levels not to exceed a total of 2.6 percent by weight of coating solids. The finished polymer contacts food only of the Types I, II, III, IV, V, VIA, VIB, VII, VIII, and IX as identified in table 1 of § 176.170(c) of this chapter, and limited to conditions of use E, F, and G described in table 2 of § 176.170 of this chapter. 4. As emulsifiers and/or surface-active agents at levels not to exceed 3.0 percent by weight of polystyrene or rubber-modified polystyrene complying with § 177.1640(c) of this chapter under conditions of use B through H described in table 2 of § 176.170(c) of this chapter.
α-Alkyl-*omega*-hydroxypoly(oxyethylene) produced by condensation of 1 mole of C_{11}-C_{15} straight-chain randomly substitued secondary alcohols with an average of 7–20 moles of ethylene oxide.	
alpha Olefin sulfonate [alkyl group is in the range of C_{10}-C_{18} with not less than 50 percent C_{14}-C_{16}], ammonium, calcium, magnesium, potassium, and sodium salts.	For use only: 1. In acrylonitrile-butadiene copolymers identified in § 177.2600(c)(4)(i) of this chapter. 2. At levels not to exceed 1 percent by weight of acrylic coatings complying with § 175.300(b)(3)(xx) of this chapter and having a maximum thickness of 0.051 millimeter (0.002 inch). The finished polymers contact food only of the Types V, VIII, and IX as identified in table 1 of § 176.170(c) of this chapter. 3. At levels not to exceed 2 percent by weight of vinyl chloride copolymer coatings having a maximum thickness of 0.051 millimeter (0.002 inch) and complying with § 175.300(b)(3)(xv) of this chapter. The finished polymers contact food only of the Types V, VIII, and IX as identified in table 1 of § 176.170(c) of this chapter. 4. As provided in § 175.105 of this chapter.
Alpha-sulfo-*omega*-(dodecyloxy)poly(oxyethylene) ammonium salt (CAS Reg. No. 32612–48–9).	For use only as an emulsifier at levels not to exceed 0.3 percent by weight of styrene-butadiene copolymer coatings for paper and paperboard complying with § 176.170 of this chapter.
Ammonium salt of epoxidized oleic acid, produced from epoxidized oleic acid (predominantly dihydroxystearic and acetoxyhydroxystearic acids) meeting the following specifications: Acid number 160–180, saponification number 210–235, iodine number 2–15, and epoxy groups 0–0.4 percent.	For use only: 1. As a polymerization emulsifier at levels not to exceed 1.5 pct by weight of vinyl chloride polymers used as components of nonfood articles complying with §§ 175.105, 175.300, 176.170, 176.180, and 177.1210 of this chapter. Such vinyl chloride polymers are limited to polyvinyl chloride and/or vinyl chloride copolymers complying with § 177.1980 of this chapter. 2. As a polymerization emulsifier at levels not to exceed 1.5 pct by weight of vinyl chloride-vinyl acetate copolymers used as components of nonfood articles complying with §§ 175.105, 175.300, 176.170, 176.180, and 177.1210 of this chapter.
Butanedioic acid, sulfo-1,4-di-(C_9-C_{11} alkyl) ester, ammonium salt (also known as butanedioic acid, sulfo-1,4-diisodecyl ester, ammonium salt [CAS Reg. No. 144093–88–9])..	For use as a surface active agent as provided in §§ 175.105, 175.125, 176.170, and 176.180 of this chapter.
α-Di-*sec*-butylphenyl-*omega*-hydroxypoly(oxyethylene) produced by the condensation of 1 mole of di-*sec*-butylphenol with an average of 4–14 or 30–50 moles of ethylene oxide; if a blend of products is used, the average number of moles of ethylene oxide reacted to produce any product that is a component of the blend shall be in the range 4–14 or 30–50; *sec*-butyl groups are predominantly (90 percent or more) *o*-, *p*-substituents.	
Disodium 4-isodecyl sulfosuccinate (CAS Reg. No. 37294–49–8).	For use only as an emulsifier at levels not to exceed 5 percent by weight of polymers intended for use in coatings.
α-Dodecyl-*omega*-hydroxpoly (oxyethylene) mixture of dihydrogen phosphate and monohydrogen phosphate esters that have an acid number (to pH 5.2) of 103–111 and that are produced by the esterification of the condensation product of 1 mole of *n*-dodecyl alcohol with 4–4.5 moles of ethylene oxide.	

List of substances	Limitations
α-(*p-Dodecylphenyl*)-*omega*-hydroxypoly (oxyethylene) produced by the condensation of 1 mole of dodecylphenol (dodecyl group is a propylene tetramer isomer) with an average of 4–14 or 30–50 moles of ethylene oxide; if a blend of products is used, the average number of moles of ethylene oxide reacted to produce any product that is a component of the blend shall be in the range 4–14 or 30–50.	
Naphthalene sulfonic acid-formaldehyde condensate, sodium salt (CAS Reg. No. 9084–06–4).	For use only: 1. At levels not to exceed 10 micrograms/in^2 (0.16 mg/dm^2) in vinylidene chloride copolymer or homopolymer coatings applied to films of propylene polymers complying with § 177.1520 of this chapter. 2. At levels not to exceed 14 micrograms/in^2 (0.21 mg/dm^2) in vinylidene chloride copolymer or homopolymer coatings applied to films of polyethylene phthalate polymers complying with § 177.1630 of this chapter.
α-(*p*-nonylphenyl)-*omega*-hydroxypoly (oxyethylene) mixture of dihydrogen phosphate and monohydrogen phosphate esters that have an acid number (to pH 5.2) of 49–59 and that are produced by the esterification of *a*-(*p*-nonylphenyl)-*omega*-hydroxypoly (oxyethylene) complying with the identity prescribed in § 178.3400(c) and having an average poly(oxyethylene) content of 5.5–6.5 moles.	
α-(*p*-Nonylphenyl)-*omega*-hydroxypoly (oxyethylene) mixture of dihydrogen phosphate and monohydrogen phosphate esters that have an acid number (to pH 5.2) of 62–72 and that are produced by the esterification of ′-(*p*-nonylphenyl)*omega*-hydroxypoly (oxyethylene) complying with the identity prescribed in § 178.3400(c) and having an average poly(oxyethylene) content of 9–10 moles.	
α-(*p*-Nonylphenyl)-*omega*-hydroxypoly (oxyethylene) mixture of dihydrogen phosphate and monohydrogen phosphate esters that have an acid number (to pH 5.2) of 98–110 and that are produced by the esterification of α-(*p*-nonylphenyl)-*omega*-hydroxypoly (oxyethylene) complying with the identity prescribed in § 178.3400(c) and having an average poly(oxyethylene) content of 45–55 moles.	
α-(*p*-Nonylphenyl)-*omega*-hydroxypoly (oxyethylene) produced by the condensation of 1 mole of nonylphenol (nonyl group is a propylene trimer isomer) with an average of 4–14 or 30–50 moles of ethylene oxide: if a blend of products is used, the average number of moles of ethylene oxide reacted to produce any product that is a component of the blend shall be in the range 4–14 or 30–50.	
α-(*p*-Nonylphenyl)-*omega*-hydroxypoly (oxyethylene) sulfate, ammonium or sodium salt: the nonyl group is a propylene trimer isomer and the poly (oxyethylene) content average 4 moles.	
Polyethyleneglycol alkyl(C_{10}-C_{12}) ether sulfosuccinate, disodium salt (CAS Reg. No. 68954–91–6).	For use only at levels not to exceed 5 percent by weight of total monomers used in the emulsion polymerization of polyvinyl acetate, acrylic, and vinyl/acrylic polymers intended for use as coatings for paper and paperboard.
Poly[(methylene-*p*-nonylphenoxy) poly(oxypropylene)(4–12 moles) propanol] of minimum molecular weight 3500.	For use in coatings at levels not to exceed 1 mg per square foot of food-contact surface.
Poly(oxypropylene) (45–48 moles) block polymer with poly(oxyethylene). The finished block polymers meet the following specifications: Average molecular weight 11,000–18,000; hydroxyl number 6.2–10.2; cloud point above 100 °C. for 10 pct solution.	For use only as a surface-active agent at levels not to exceed 0.5 percent by weight of polyolefin film or polyolefin coatings. Such polyolefin film and polyolefin coatings shall have an average thickness not to exceed 0.005 inch and shall be limited to use in contact with foods that have a pH above 5.0 and that contain no more than 8 pct of alcohol.
Polysorbate 20 (polyoxyethylene (20) sorbitan monolaurate) meeting the following specifications: Saponification number 40–50, acid number 0–2, hydroxyl number 60–108, oxyethylene content 70–74 pct.	
Polysorbate 40 (polyoxyethylene (20) sorbitan monopalmitate) meeting the following specifications: Saponification number 41–52, oxyethylene content 66–70.5 pct.	
Polysorbate 60 conforming to the identity prescribed in § 172.836 of this chapter.	
Polysorbate 65 conforming to the identity prescribed in § 172.838 of this chapter.	
Polysorbate 80 conforming to the identity prescribed in § 172.840 of this chapter.	

List of substances	Limitations
Polysorbate 85 (polyoxyethylene (20) sorbitan trioleate) meeting the following specifications: Saponification number 80–95, oxyethylene content 46–50 percent.	
Sodium 1,4-dicylcohexyl sulfosuccinate.	
Sodium 1,4-dihexyl sulfosuccinate.	
Sodium 1,4 diisobutyl sulfosuccinate.	
Sodium dioctyl sulfosuccinate.	
Sodium 1,4-dipentyl sulfosuccinate.	
Sodium 1,4-ditridecyl sulfosuccinate.	
Sodium lauryl sulfate.	
Sodium monoalkylphenoxybenzenedisulfonate and sodium dialkylphenoxybenzenedisulfonate mixtures containing not less than 70 pct of the monoalkylated product where the alkyl group is C_8C_{16}.	
Sorbitan monolaurate meeting the following specifications. Saponification number 153–170; and hydroxyl number 330–360.	
Sorbitan monooleate meeting the following specifications: Saponification number 145–160, hydroxyl number 193–210.	
Sorbitan monopalmitate meeting the following specifications: Saponification No. 140–150; and hydroxyl No. 275–305.	
Sorbitan monostearate conforming to the identity prescribed in § 172.842 of this chapter.	
Sorbitan trioleate meeting the following specifications: Saponification No. 170–190; and hydroxyl No. 55–70.	
Sorbitan tristearate meeting the following specifications: Saponification No. 176–188; and hydroxyl No. 66–80.	
Sulfosuccinic acid 4-ester with polyethylene glycol dodecyl ether, disodium salt (CAS Reg. No. 39354–45–5).	For use only at levels not to exceed 5 percent by weight of total monomers used in the emulsion polymerization of polyvinyl acetate, acrylic, and vinyl/acrylic polymers intended for use as coatings for paper and paperboard.
Sulfosuccinic acid 4-ester with polyethylene glycol nonylphenyl ether, disodium salt (alcohol moiety produced by condensation of 1 mole nonylphenol and an average of 9–10 moles of ethylene oxide) (CAS Reg. No. 9040–38–4).	For use only at levels not to exceed 5 percent by weight of the total coating monomers used in the emulsion polymerization of polyvinyl acetate and vinyl-acrylate copolymers intended for use as coatings for paper and paperboard.
α-[*p*-(1,1,3,3-Tetramethylbutyl)phenyl] *omega*-hydroxypoly(oxyethylene) produced by the condensation of 1 mole of *p*-(1,1,3,3-tetramethylbutyl) phenol with an average of 4–14 or 30–40 moles of ethylene oxide; if a blend of products is used, the average number of moles of ethylene oxide reacted to produce any product that is a component of the blend shall be in the range 4–14 or 30–50.	
Tetrasodium *N*-(1,2-dicarboxyethyl)-*N*-octadecyl-sulfosuccinate	For use only as a polymerization emulsifier for resins applied to tea-bag material.
α-Tridecyl-*omega*-hydroxypoly (oxyethylene) mixture of dihydrogen phosphate and monohydrogen phosphate esters that have an acid number (to pH 5.2) of 75–85 and that are produced by the esterification of the condensation product of one mole of "oxo" process tridecyl alcohol with 5.5–6.5 moles of ethylene oxide.	
α-Tridecyl-*omega*-hydroxypoly (oxyethyl-ene) mixture of dihydrogen phosphate and monohydrogen phosphate esters that have an acid number (to pH 5.2) of 58–70 and that are produced by the esterification of the condensation product of one mole of "oxo" process tridecyl alcohol with 9–10 moles of ethylene oxide.	

(d) The provisions of this section are not applicable to emulsifiers and/or surface-active agents listed in §175.105(c)(5) of this chapter and used in food-packaging adhesives complying with §175.105 of this chapter.

[42 FR 14609, Mar. 15, 1977]

EDITORIAL NOTE: For FEDERAL REGISTER citations affecting §178.3400, see the List of CFR Sections Affected, which appears in the Finding Aids section of the printed volume and at *www.fdsys.gov*.

§178.3450 Esters of stearic and palmitic acids.

The ester stearyl palmitate or palmityl stearate or mixtures thereof may be safely used as adjuvants in food-packaging materials when used in accordance with the following prescribed conditions:

(a) They are used or intended for use as plasticizers or lubricants in polystyrene intended for use in contact with food.

(b) They are added to the formulated polymer prior to extrusion.

(c) The quantity used shall not exceed that required to accomplish the intended technical effect.

§ 178.3480 Fatty alcohols, synthetic.

Synthetic fatty alcohols may be safely used as components of articles intended for use in contact with food, and in synthesizing food additives and other substances permitted for use as components of articles intended for use in contact with food in accordance with the following prescribed conditions:

(a) The food additive consists of fatty alcohols meeting the specifications and definition prescribed in § 172.864 of this chapter, except as provided in paragraph (c) of this section.

(b) It is used or intended for use as follows:

(1) As substitutes for the corresponding naturally derived fatty alcohols permitted for use as components of articles intended for use in contact with food by existing regulations in parts 174, 175, 176, 177, 178 and § 179.45 of this chapter: *Provided*, That the use is in compliance with any prescribed limitations.

(2) As substitutes for the corresponding naturally derived fatty alcohols used as intermediates in the synthesis of food additives and other substances permitted for use as components of food-contact articles.

(c) Synthetic fatty alcohols identified in paragraph (c)(1) of this section may contain not more than 0.8 weight percent of total diols as determined by a method titled "Diols in Monohydroxy Alcohol by Miniature Thin Layer Chromatography (MTLC)," which is incorporated by reference. Copies are available from the Center for Food Safety and Applied Nutrition (HFS–200), Food and Drug Administration, 5100 Paint Branch Pkwy., College Park, MD 20740, or available for inspection at the National Archives and Records Administration (NARA). For information on the availability of this material at NARA, call 202–741–6030, or go to: *http://www.archives.gov/federal_register/code_of_federal_regulations/ibr_locations.html.*

(1) *Synthetic fatty alcohols.* (i) Hexyl, octyl, decyl, lauryl, myristyl, cetyl, and stearyl alcohols meeting the specifications and definition prescribed in § 172.864 of this chapter, except that they may contain not more than 0.8 weight percent total diols.

(ii) Lauryl, myristyl, cetyl, and stearyl alcohols manufactured by the process described in § 172.864(a)(2) of this chapter such that lauryl and myristyl alcohols meet the specifications in § 172.864(a)(1)(i) of this chapter, and cetyl and stearyl alcohols meet the specifications in § 172.864(a)(1)(ii) of this chapter.

(2) *Conditions of use.* (i) Synthetic fatty alcohols as substitutes for the corresponding naturally derived fatty alcohols permitted for use in compliance with § 178.3910.

(ii) Synthetic lauryl alcohol as a substitute for the naturally derived lauryl alcohol permitted as an intermediate in the synthesis of sodium lauryl sulfate used in compliance with § 178.3400.

[42 FR 14609, Mar. 15, 1977, as amended at 47 FR 11847, Mar. 19, 1982; 54 FR 24898, June 12, 1989]

§ 178.3500 Glycerin, synthetic.

Synthetic glycerin may be safely used as a component of articles intended for use in packaging materials for food, subject to the provisions of this section:

(a) It is produced by the hydrogenolysis of carbohydrates, and shall contain not in excess of 0.2 percent by weight of a mixture of butanetriols.

(b) It is used in a quantity not to exceed that amount reasonably required to produce its intended physical or technical effect, and in accordance with any limitations prescribed by applicable regulations in parts 174, 175, 176, 177, 178 and 179 of this chapter. It shall not be intended to, nor in fact accomplish, any direct physical or technical effect in the food itself.

§ 178.3505 Glyceryl tri-(12-acetoxystearate).

Glyceryl tri-(12-acetoxystearate) (CAS Reg. No. 139–43–5) may be safely used as a component of articles intended for use in producing, manufacturing, packing, processing, preparing, treating, packaging, transporting, or holding food, subject to the provisions of this section.

(a) The additive is applied to the surface of calcium carbonate at a level not to exceed 1 weight-percent of the total mixture.

(b) The calcium carbonate/glyceryl tri-(12-acetoxystearate) mixture is used as an adjuvant in polymers in contact with nonfatty foods at a level not to exceed 20 weight-percent of the polymer.

[50 FR 1503, Jan. 11, 1985]

§ 178.3520 Industrial starch-modified.

Industrial starch-modified may be safely used as a component of articles intended for use in producing, manufacturing, packing, processing, preparing, treating, packaging, transporting, or holding food, subject to the provisions of this section.

(a) Industrial starch-modified is identified as follows:

(1) A food starch-modified or starch or any combination thereof that has been modified by treatment with one of the reactants hereinafter specified, in an amount reasonably required to achieve the desired functional effect but in no event in excess of any limitation prescribed, with or without subsequent treatment as authorized in § 172.892 of this chapter.

List of reactants	Limitations
Ammonium persulfate, not to exceed 0.3 pct. or in alkaline starch not to exceed 0.6 pct..	
(4-Chlorobutene-2) trimethylammonium chloride, not to exceed 5 pct.	Industrial starch modified by this treatment shall be used only as internal sizing for paper and paperboard intended for food packaging.
β-Diethylaminoethyl chloride hydrochloride, not to exceed 4 pct.	
Dimethylaminoethyl methacrylate, not to exceed 3 pct.	
Dimethylol ethylene urea, not to exceed 0.375 pct	Industrial starch modified by this treatment shall be used only as internal sizing for paper and paperboard intended for food packaging.
2,3-Epoxypropyltrimethylammonium chloride, not to exceed 5 pct.	
Ethylene oxide, not to exceed 3 pct of reacted ethylene oxide in finished product.	
Phosphoric acid, not to exceed 6 pct and urea, not to exceed 20 pct.	Industrial starch modified by this treatment shall be used only as internal sizing for paper and paperboard intended for food packaging and as surface sizing and coating for paper and paperboard that contact food only of Types IV-A, V, VII, VIII, and IX described in table 1 of § 176.170(c) of this chapter.

(2) A starch irradiated under one of the following conditions to produce free radicals for subsequent graft polymerization with the reactants listed in this paragraph (a)(2):

(i) Radiation from a sealed cobalt 60 source, maximum absorbed dose not to exceed 5.0 megarads.

(ii) An electron beam source at a maximum energy of 7 million electron volts of ionizing radiation, maximum absorbed dose not to exceed 5.0 megarads.

List of reactants	Limitations
Acrylamide and [2-(methacryloyloxy) ethyl]trimethylammonium methyl sulfate, such that the finished industrial starch-modified shall contain:	For use only as a retention aid and dry strength agent employed before the sheet-forming operation in the manufacture of paper and paperboard intended to contact food, and used at a level not to exceed 0.25 pct by weight of the finished dry paper and paperboard fibers.
1. Not more than 60 weight percent vinyl copolymer (of which not more than 32 weight percent is [2-(methacryloyloxy)ethyl] trimethylammonium methyl sulfate).	

List of reactants	Limitations
2. Not more than 0.20 pct residual acrylamide. 3. A minimum nitrogen content of 9.0 pct.	

(b) The following adjuvants may be used as surface-active agents in the processing of industrial starch-modified:

Polyethylene glycol (400) dilaurate.
Polyethylene glycol (400) monolaurate.
Polyoxyethylene (4) lauryl ether.

(c) To insure safe use of the industrial starch-modified, the label of the food additive container shall bear the name of the additive "industrial starch-modified," and in the instance of an industrial starch-modified which is limited with respect to conditions of use, the label of the food additive container shall contain a statement of such limited use.

[42 FR 14609, Mar. 15, 1977, as amended at 42 FR 49453, Sept. 27, 1977]

§ 178.3530 Isoparaffinic petroleum hydrocarbons, synthetic.

Isoparaffinic petroleum hydrocarbons, synthetic, may be safely used in the production of nonfood articles intended for use in producing, manufacturing, packing, processing, preparing, treating, packaging, transporting, or holding food, subject to the provisions of this section.

(a) The isoparaffinic petroleum hydrocarbons, produced by synthesis from petroleum gases consist of a mixture of liquid hydrocarbons meeting the following specifications:

Boiling point 63° –260 °C, as determined by ASTM method D86–82, "Standard Method for Distillation of Petroleum Products," which is incorporated by reference. Copies may be obtained from the American Society for Testing Materials, 100 Barr Harbor Dr., West Conshohocken, Philadelphia, PA 19428-2959, or may be examined at the National Archives and Records Administration (NARA). For information on the availability of this material at NARA, call 202–741–6030, or go to: *http://www.archives.gov/federal_register/code_of_federal_regulations/ibr_locations.html.*

Ultraviolet absorbance:
260–319 millimicrons—1.5 maximum.
320–329 millimicrons—0.08 maximum.
330–350 millimicrons—0.05 maximum.

Nonvolatile residue 0.002 gram per 100 milliliters maximum.

Synthetic isoparaffinic petroleum hydrocarbons containing antioxidants shall meet the specified ultraviolet absorbance limits after correction for any absorbance due to the antioxidants. The ultraviolet absorbance shall be determined by the procedure described for application to mineral oil under "Specifications" on page 66 of the "Journal of the Association of Official Agricultural Chemists," Vol. 45 (February 1962), which is incorporated by reference, disregarding the last sentence of that procedure. For hydrocarbons boiling below 121 °C, the nonvolatile residue shall be determined by ASTM method D1353–78, "Standard Test Method for Nonvolatile Matter in Volatile Solvents for Use in Paint, Varnish, Lacquer, and Related Products;" for those boiling above 121 °C, ASTM procedure D381–80, "Standard Test Method for Existent Gum in Fuels by Jet Evaporation," which are incorporated by reference. Copies may be obtained from the American Society for Testing Materials, 100 Barr Harbor Dr., West Conshohocken, Philadelphia, PA 19428-2959, or may be examined at the National Archives and Records Administration (NARA). For information on the availability of this material at NARA, call 202–741–6030, or go to: *http://www.archives.gov/federal_register/code_of_federal_regulations/ibr_locations.html.*

(b) Isoparaffinic petroleum hydrocarbons may contain antioxidants authorized for use in food in an amount not to exceed that reasonably required to accomplish the intended technical effect.

(c) Isoparaffinic petroleum hydrocarbons are used in the production of nonfood articles. The quantity used shall not exceed the amount reasonably required to accomplish the intended technical effect, and the residual remaining in the finished article shall be the minimum amount reasonably attainable.

[42 FR 14609, Mar. 15, 1977, as amended at 47 FR 11847, Mar. 19, 1982; 49 FR 10112, Mar. 19, 1984]

§ 178.3570 Lubricants with incidental food contact.

Lubricants with incidental food contact may be safely used on machinery used for producing, manufacturing, packing, processing, preparing, treating, packaging, transporting, or holding food, subject to the provisions of this section:

(a) The lubricants are prepared from one or more of the following substances:

(1) Substances generally recognized as safe for use in food.

(2) Substances used in accordance with the provisions of a prior sanction or approval.

(3) Substances identified in this paragraph (a)(3).

Substances	Limitations
Aluminum stearoyl benzoyl hydroxide	For use only as a thickening agent in mineral oil lubricants at a level not to exceed 10 pct by weight of the mineral oil.
N,N-Bis(2-ethylhexyl)-*ar*-methyl-1*H*-benzotriazole-1-methanamine (CAS Reg. No. 94270–86–7).	For use as a copper deactivator at a level not to exceed 0.1 percent by weight of the lubricant.
BHA.	
BHT.	
α-Butyl-*omega*-hydroxypoly(oxyethylene) poly(oxypropylene) produced by random condensation of a 1:1 mixture by weight of ethylene oxide and propylene oxide with butanol; minimum molecular weight 1,500; Chemical Abstracts Service Registry No. 9038–95–3.	Addition to food not to exceed 10 parts per million.
α-Butyl-*omega*-hydroxypoly(oxypropylene); minimum molecular weight 1,500; Chemical Abstracts Service Registry No. 9003–13–8.	Do.
Castor oil	Do.
Castor oil, dehydrated	Do.
Castor oil, partially dehydrated	Do.
Dialkyldimethylammonium aluminum silicate (CAS Reg. No. 68953–58–2), which may contain up to 7 percent by weight 1,6-hexanediol (CAS Reg. No. 629–11–8), where the alkyl groups are derived from hydrogenated tallow fatty acids (C_{14}-C_{18}) and where the aluminum silicate is derived from bentonite.	For use only as a gelling agent in mineral oil lubricants at a level not to exceed 15 percent by weight of the mineral oil.
Dimethylpolysiloxane (viscosity greater than 300 centistokes)	Addition to food not to exceed 1 part per million.
Di (*n*-octyl) phosphite (CAS Reg. No. 1809–14–9)	For use only as an extreme pressure-antiwear adjuvant at a level not to exceed 0.5 percent by weight of the lubricant.
Disodium decanedioate (CAS Reg. No. 17265–14–4)	For use only: 1. As a corrosion inhibitor or rust preventative in mineral oil-bentonite lubricants at a level not to exceed 2 percent by weight of the grease. 2. As a corrosion inhibitor or rust preventative only in greases at a level not to exceed 2 percent by weight of the grease.
Disodium EDTA (CAS Reg. No. 139–33–3)	For use only as a chelating agent and sequestrant at a level not to exceed 0.06 percent by weight of lubricant at final use dilution.
Ethoxylated resin phosphate ester mixture consisting of the following compounds: 1. Poly(methylene-*p-tert*-butyl- phenoxy)poly-(oxyethylene) mixture of dihydrogen phosphate and monohydrogen phosphate esters (0 to 40 percent of the mixture). The resin is formed by condensation of 1 mole of *p-tert*-butylphenol with 2 to 4 moles of formaldehyde and subsequent ethoxylation with 4 to 12 moles of ethylene oxide;. 2. Poly(methylene-*p*-nonylphenoxy) poly(oxyethylene) mixture of dihydrogen phosphate and monohydrogen phosphate esters (0 to 40 percent of the mixture). The resin is formed by condensation of 1 mole of *p*-nonylphenol with 2 to 4 moles of formaldehyde and subsequent ethoxylation with 4 to 12 moles of ethylene oxide; and. 3. *n*-Tridecyl alcohol mixture of dihydrogen phosphate and monohydrogen phosphate esters (40 to 80 percent of the mixture; CAS Reg. No. 56831–62–0).	For use only as a surfactant to improve lubricity in lubricating fluids complying with this section at a level not to exceed 5 percent by weight of the lubricating fluid.
Fatty acids derived from animal or vegetable sources, and the hydrogenated forms of such fatty acids.	
2-(8-Heptadecenyl)-4,5-dihydro-1*H*-imidazole-1-ethanol (CAS Reg. No. 95–38–5).	For use at levels not to exceed 0.5 percent by weight of the lubricant.
Hexamethylenebis(3,5-di-*tert*-butyl-4-hydroxyhydrocinnamate) (CAS Reg. No. 35074–77–2).	For use as an antioxidant at levels not to exceed 0.5 percent by weight of the lubricant.

Substances	Limitations
α-Hydro-*omega*-hydroxypoly (oxyethylene) poly(oxypropylene) produced by random condensation of mixtures of ethylene oxide and propylene oxide containing 25 to 75 percent by weight of ethylene oxide; minimum molecular weight 1,500; Chemical Abstracts Service Registry No. 9003–11–6.	Addition to food not to exceed 10 parts per million.
12-Hydroxystearic acid.	
Isopropyl oleate	For use only as an adjuvant (to improve lubricity) in mineral oil lubricants.
Magnesium ricinoleate	For use only as an adjuvant in mineral oil lubricants at a level not to exceed 10 percent by weight of the mineral oil.
Mineral oil	Addition to food not to exceed 10 parts per million.
N-Methyl-*N-(1-oxo-9- octadecenyl)glycine* (CAS Reg. No. 110–25–8).	For use as a corrosion inhibitor at levels not to exceed 0.5 percent by weight of the lubricant.
N-phenylbenzenamine, reaction products with 2,4,4-trimethylpentene (CAS Reg. No. 68411–46–1).	For use only as an antioxidant at levels not to exceed 0.5 percent by weight of the lubricant.
Petrolatum	Complying with § 178.3700. Addition to food not to exceed 10 parts per million.
Phenyl-α-and/or phenyl-β-naphthylamine	For use only, singly or in combination, as antioxidant in mineral oil lubricants at a level not to exceed a total of 1 percent by weight of the mineral oil.
Phosphoric acid, mono- and dihexyl esters, compounds with tetramethylnonylamines and $C_{11\text{-}14}$ alkylamines.	For use only as an adjuvant at levels not to exceed 0.5 percent by weight of the lubricant.
Phosphoric acid, mono- and diisooctyl esters, reacted with *tert*-alkyl and (C_{12}-C_{14}) primary amines (CAS Reg. No. 68187–67–7).	For use only as a corrosion inhibitor or rust preventative inlubricants at a level not to exceed 0.5 percent by weight of the lubricant.
Phosphorothioic acid, *O, O, O*-triphenyl ester, *tert*-butyl derivatives (CAS Reg. No. 192268–65–8).	For use only as an extreme pressure-antiwear adjuvant at a level not to exceed 0.5 percent by weight of the lubricant.
Polyurea, having a nitrogen content of 9–14 percent based on the dry polyurea weight, produced by reacting tolylene diisocyanate with tall oil fatty acid (C_{16} and C_{18}) amine and ethylene diamine in a 2:2:1 molar ratio.	For use only as an adjuvant in mineral oil lubricants at a level not to exceed 10 percent by weight of the mineral oil.
Polybutene (minimum average molecular weight 80,000)	Addition to food not to exceed 10 parts per million.
Polybutene, hydrogenated; complying with the identity prescribed under § 178.3740.	Do.
Polyethylene	Do.
Polyisobutylene (average molecular weight 35,000–140,000 (Flory)).	For use only as a thickening agent in mineral oil lubricants.
Sodium nitrite	For use only as a rust preventive in mineral oil lubricants at a level not to exceed 3 percent by weight of the mineral oil.
Tetrakis[methylene(3,5-di-*tert*-butyl-4-hydroxyhydro-cinnamate)]methane (CAS Reg. No. 6683–19–8).	For use only as an antioxidant in lubricants at a level not to exceed 0.5 percent by weight of the lubricant.
Thiodiethylenebis (3,5-di-*tert*-butyl-4-hydroxyhydrocinnamate) (CAS Reg. No. 41484-35-9).	For use as an antioxidant at levels not to exceed 0.5 percent by weight of the lubricant.
Tri[2(or 4)-$C_{9\text{-}10}$-branched alkylphenyl]phosphorothioate (CAS Reg. No. 126019–82–7).	For use only as an extreme pressure-antiwear adjuvant at levels not to exceed 0.5 percent by weight of the lubricant.
Triphenyl phosphorothionate (CAS Reg. No. 597–82–0)	For use as an adjuvant in lubricants herein listed at a level not to exceed 0.5 percent by weight of the lubricant.
Tris(2,4-di-*tert*-butylphenyl)phosphite (CAS Reg. NO. 31570–04–4).	For use only as a stabilizer at levels not to exceed 0.5 percent by weight of the lubricant.
Thiodiethylenebis(3,5-di-*tert*-butyl-4-hydroxy-hydro- cinnamate) (CAS Reg. No. 41484–35–9).	For use as an antioxidant at levels not to exceed 0.5 percent by weight of the lubricant.
Zinc sulfide	For use at levels not to exceed 10 percent by weight of the lubricant.

(b) The lubricants are used on food-processing equipment as a protective antirust film, as a release agent on gaskets or seals of tank closures, and as a lubricant for machine parts and equipment in locations in which there is exposure of the lubricated part to food. The amount used is the minimum required to accomplish the desired technical effect on the equipment, and the addition to food of any constituent identified in this section does not exceed the limitations prescribed.

(c) Any substance employed in the production of the lubricants described in this section that is the subject of a regulation in parts 174, 175, 176, 177, 178 and § 179.45 of this chapter conforms with any specification in such regulation.

[42 FR 14609, Mar. 15, 1977]

EDITORIAL NOTE: For FEDERAL REGISTER citations affecting § 178.3570, see the List of CFR Sections Affected, which appears in the Finding Aids section of the printed volume and at *www.fdsys.gov*.

§ 178.3600 Methyl glucoside-coconut oil ester.

Methyl glucoside-coconut oil ester identified in § 172.816(a) of this chapter may be safely used as a processing aid (filter aid) in the manufacture of starch, including industrial starch-modified complying with § 178.3520, intended for use as a component of articles that contact food.

§ 178.3610 α-Methylstyrene-vinyltoluene resins, hydrogenated.

Hydrogenated α-methylstyrene-vinyltoluene copolymer resins having a molar ratio of 1 α-methylstyrene to 3 vinyltoluene may be safely used as components of polyolefin film intended for use in contact with food, subject to the following provisions:

(a) Hydrogenated α-methylstyrene-vinyltoluene copolymer resins have a drop-softening point of 125° to 165 °C and a maximum absorptivity of 0.17 liter per gram centimeter at 266 nanometers, as determined by methods titled "Determination of Softening Point (Drop Method)" and "Determination of Unsaturation of Resin 1977," which are incorporated by reference. Copies are available from the Center for Food Safety and Applied Nutrition (HFS–200), Food and Drug Administration, 5100 Paint Branch Pkwy., College Park, MD 20740, or available for inspection at the National Archives and Records Administration (NARA). For information on the availability of this material at NARA, call 202–741–6030, or go to: *http://www.archives.gov/federal_register/code_of_federal_regulations/ibr_locations.html.*

(b) The polyolefin film is produced from olefin polymers complying with § 177.1520 of this chapter, and the average thickness of the film in the form in which it contacts food does not exceed 0.002 inch.

[42 FR 14609, Mar. 15, 1977, as amended at 47 FR 11847, Mar. 19, 1982; 54 FR 24898, June 12, 1989]

§ 178.3620 Mineral oil.

Mineral oil may be safely used as a component of nonfood articles intended for use in contact with food, subject to the provisions of this section:

(a) White mineral oil meeting the specifications prescribed in § 172.878 of this chapter may be used as a component of nonfood articles provided such use complies with any applicable limitations in parts 170 through 189 of this chapter. The use of white mineral oil in or on food itself, including the use of white mineral oil as a protective coating or release agent for food, is subject to the provisions of § 172.878 of this chapter.

(b) Technical white mineral oil identified in paragraph (b)(1) of this section may be used as provided in paragraph (b)(2) of this section.

(1) Technical white mineral oil consists of specially refined distillates of virgin petroleum or of specially refined distillates that are produced synthetically from petroleum gases. Technical white mineral oil meets the following specifications:

(i) Saybolt color 20 minimum as determined by ASTM method D156–82, "Standard Test Method for Saybolt Color of Petroleum Products (Saybolt Chromometer Method)," which is incorporated by reference. Copies may be obtained from the American Society for Testing Materials, 100 Barr Harbor Dr., West Conshohocken, Philadelphia, PA 19428-2959, or may be examined at the National Archives and Records Administration (NARA). For information on the availability of this material at NARA, call 202–741–6030, or go to: *http://www.archives.gov/federal_register/code_of_federal_regulations/ibr_locations.html.*

(ii) Ultraviolet absorbance limits as follows:

Wavelength (mμ)	Maximum absorbance per centimeter optical pathlength
280 to 289	4.0
290 to 299	3.3
300 to 329	2.3
330 to 350	0.8

Technical white mineral oil containing antioxidants shall meet the specified ultraviolet absorbance limits after correction for any absorbance due to the antioxidants. The ultraviolet absorbance shall be determined by the procedure described for application to mineral oil under "Specification" on page 66 of the "Journal of the Association of

Official Agricultural Chemists," Volume 45 (February 1962) (which is incorporated by reference; copies are available from the Center for Food Safety and Applied Nutrition (HFS–200), Food and Drug Administration, 5100 Paint Branch Pkwy., College Park, MD 20740, or available for inspection at the National Archives and Records Administration (NARA). For information on the availability of this material at NARA, call 202–741–6030, or go to: *http://www.archives.gov/federal_register/code_of_federal_regulations/ibr_locations.html.*), disregarding the last two sentences of that procedure and substituting therefor the following: Determine the absorbance of the mineral oil extract in a 10-millimeter cell in the range from 260–350 mμ, inclusive, compared to the solvent control. If the absorbance so measured exceeds 2.0 at any point in range 280–350 mμ, inclusive, dilute the extract and the solvent control, respectively, to twice their volume with dimethyl sulfoxide and remeasure the absorbance. Multiply the remeasured absorbance values by 2 to determine the absorbance of the mineral oil extract per centimeter optical pathlength.

(2) Technical white mineral oil may be used wherever mineral oil is permitted for use as a component of nonfood articles complying with §§175.105, 176.200, 176.210, 177.2260, 177.2600, and 177.2800 of this chapter and §§178.3570 and 178.3910.

(3) Technical white mineral oil may contain any antioxidant permitted in food by regulations issued in accordance with section 409 of the Act, in an amount not greater than that required to produce its intended effect.

(c) Mineral oil identified in paragraph (c)(1) of this section may be used as provided in paragraph (c)(2) of this section.

(1) The mineral oil consists of virgin petroleum distillates refined to meet the following specifications:

(i) Initial boiling point of 450 °F minimum.

(ii) Color 5.5 maximum as determined by ASTM method D1500–82, "Standard Test Method for ASTM Color of Petroleum Products (ASTM Color Scale)," which is incorporated by reference. The availability of this incorporation by reference is given in paragraph (b)(1)(i) of this section.

(iii) Ultraviolet absorbance limits as follows as determined by the analytical method described in paragraph (c)(3) of this section:

Wavelength (mμ)	Maximum absorbance per centimeter optical pathlength
280 to 289	0.7
290 to 299	0.6
300 to 359	0.4
360 to 400	.09

(2) The mineral oil may be used wherever mineral oil is permitted for use as a component of nonfood articles complying with §§175.105 and 176.210 of this chapter and §178.3910 (for use only in rolling of metallic foil and sheet stock), §§176.200, 177.2260, 177.2600, and 177.2800 of this chapter.

(3) The analytical method for determining ultraviolet absorbance limit is as follows:

GENERAL INSTRUCTIONS

Because of the sensitivity of the test, the possibility of errors arising from contamination is great. It is of the greatest importance that all glassware be scrupulously cleaned to remove all organic matter such as oil, grease, detergent residues, etc. Examine all glassware, including stoppers and stopcocks, under ultraviolet light to detect any residual fluorescent contamination. As a precautionary measure it is recommended practice to rinse all glassware with purified isooctane immediately before use. No grease is to be used on stopcocks or joints. Great care to avoid contamination of oil samples in handling and to assure absence of any extraneous material arising from inadequate packaging is essential. Because some of the polynuclear hydrocarbons sought in this test are very susceptible to photo-oxidation, the entire procedure is to be carried out under subdued light.

APPARATUS

Separatory funnels. 250-milliliter, 500-milliliter, 1,000-milliliter, and preferably 2,000-milliliter capacity, equipped with tetrafluoroethylene polymer stopcocks.

Reservoir. 500-milliliter capacity, equipped with a 24/40 standard taper male fitting at the bottom and a suitable ball-joint at the top for connecting to the nitrogen supply. The male fitting should be equipped with glass hooks.

Chromatographic tube. 180 millimeters in length, inside diameter to be 15.7 millimeters ±0.1 millimeter, equipped with a coarse, fritted-glass disc, a tetrafluoroethylene polymer stopcock, and a female 24/40 standard tapered fitting at the opposite end. (Overall length of the column with the female joint is 235 millimeters.) The female fitting should be equipped with glass hooks.

Disc. Tetrafluoroethylene polymer 2-inch diameter disk approximately 3⁄16-inch thick with a hole bored in the center to closely fit the stem of the chromatographic tube.

Suction flask. 250-milliliter or 500-milliliter filter flask.

Condenser. 24/40 joints, fitted with a drying tube, length optional.

Evaporation flask (optional). 250-milliliter or 500-milliliter capacity all-glass flask equipped with standard taper stopper having inlet and outlet tubes to permit passage of nitrogen across the surface of contained liquid to be evaporated.

Spectrophotometric cells. Fused quartz cells, optical path length in the range of 5,000 centimeter ±0.005 centimeter; also for checking spectrophotometer performance only, optical path length in the range 1,000 centimeter ±0.005 centimeter. With distilled water in the cells, determine any absorbance differences.

Spectrophotometer. Spectral range 250 millimicrons—400 millimicrons with spectral slit width of 2 millimicrons or less; under instrument operating conditions for these absorbance measurements, the spectrophotometer shall also meet the following performance requirements:

Absorbance repeatability, ±0.01 at 0.4 absorbance.

Absorbance accuracy[1] ±0.05 at 0.4 absorbance.

Wavelength accuracy, ±1.0 millimicron.

Nitrogen cylinder. Water-pumped or equivalent purity nitrogen in cylinder equipped with regulator and valve to control flow at 5 p.s.i.g.

REAGENTS AND MATERIALS

Organic solvents. All solvents used throughout the procedure shall meet the specifications and tests described in this specification. The isooctane, benzene, acetone, and methyl alcohol designated in the list following this paragraph shall pass the following test:

To the specified quantity of solvent in a 250-milliliter Erlenmeyer flask, add 1 milliliter of purified *n*-hexadecane and evaporate on the steam bath under a stream of nitrogen (a loose aluminum foil jacket around the flask will speed evaporation). Discontinue evaporation when not over 1 milliliter of residue remains. (To the residue from benzene add a 10-milliliter portion of purified isooctane, reevaporate, and repeat once to insure complete removal of benzene.)

Alternatively, the evaporation time can be reduced by using the optional evaporation flask. In this case the solvent and *n*-hexadecane are placed in the flask on the steam bath, the tube assembly is inserted, and a stream of nitrogen is fed through the inlet tube while the outlet tube is connected to a solvent trap and vacuum line in such a way as to prevent any flow-back of condensate into the flask.

Dissolve the 1 milliliter of hexadecane residue in isooctane and make to 25 milliliters volume. Determine the absorbance in the 5-centimeter path length cells compared to isooctane as reference. The absorbance of the solution of the solvent residue (except for methyl alcohol) shall not exceed 0.01 per centimeter path length between 280 and 400 mμ. For methyl alcohol this absorbance value shall be 0.00.

Isooctane (2,2,4-trimethylpentane). Use 180 milliliters for the test described in the preceding paragraph. Purify, if necessary, by passage through a column of activated silica gel (Grade 12, Davison Chemical Company, Baltimore, Maryland, or equivalent) about 90 centimeters in length and 5 centimeters to 8 centimeters in diameter.

Benzene, A.C.S. reagent grade. Use 150 milliliters for the test. Purify, if necessary, by distillation or otherwise.

Acetone, A.C.S. reagent grade. Use 200 milliliters for the test. Purify, if necessary, by distillation.

Eluting mixtures:

1. *10 percent benzene in isooctane.* Pipet 50 milliliters of benzene into a 250-milliliter glass-stoppered volumetric flask and adjust to volume with isooctane, with mixing.

2. *20 percent benzene in isooctane.* Pipet 50 milliliters of benzene into a 250-milliliter glass-stoppered volumetric flask and adjust to volume with isooctane, with mixing.

3. *Acetone-benzene-water mixture.* Add 20 milliliters of water to 380 milliliters of acetone and 200 milliliters of benzene, and mix.

[1] As determined by procedure using potassium chromate for reference standard and described in National Bureau of Standards Circular 484, Spectrophotometry, U.S. Department of Commerce (1949). The accuracy is to be determined by comparison with the standard values at 290, 345, and 400 millimicrons. Circular 484 is incorporated by reference. Copies are available from the Center for Food Safety and Applied Nutrition (HFS–200), Food and Drug Administration, 5100 Paint Branch Pkwy., College Park, MD 20740, or available for inspection at the National Archives and Records Administration (NARA). For information on the availability of this material at NARA, call 202–741–6030, or go to: *http://www.archives.gov/federal_register/code_of_federal_regulations/ibr_locations.html.*

n-Hexadecane, 99-percent olefin-free. Dilute 1.0 milliliter of *n*-hexadecane to 25 milliliters with isooctane and determine the absorbance in a 5-centimeter cell compared to isooctane as reference point between 280 mμ–400 mμ. The absorbance per centimeter path length shall not exceed 0.00 in this range. Purify, if necessary, by percolation through activated silica gel or by distillation.

Methyl alcohol, A.C.S. reagent grade. Use 10.0 milliliters of methyl alcohol. Purify, if necessary, by distillation.

Dimethyl sulfoxide. Spectrophotometric grade (Crown Zellerbach Corporation, Camas, Washington, or equivalent). Absorbance (1-centimeter cell, distilled water reference, sample completely saturated with nitrogen).

Wavelength	Absorbance (maximum)
261.5	1.00
270	.20
275	.09
280	.06
300	.015

There shall be no irregularities in the absorbance curve within these wavelengths.

Phosphoric acid. 85 percent A.C.S. reagent grade.

Sodium borohydride. 98 percent.

Magnesium oxide (Sea Sorb 43, Food Machinery Company, Westvaco Division, distributed by chemical supply firms, or equivalent). Place 100 grams of the magnesium oxide in a large beaker, add 700 milliliters of distilled water to make a thin slurry, and heat on a steam bath for 30 minutes with intermittent stirring. Stir well initially to insure that all the adsorbent is completely wetted. Using a Buchner funnel and a filter paper (Schleicher & Schuell No. 597, or equivalent) of suitable diameter, filter with suction. Continue suction until water no longer drips from the funnel. Transfer the adsorbent to a glass trough lined with aluminum foil (free from rolling oil). Break up the magnesia with a clean spatula and spread out the adsorbent on the aluminum foil in a layer about 1 centimeter to 2 centimeters thick. Dry for 24 hours at 160 °C ±1 °C. Pulverize the magnesia with mortar and pestle. Sieve the pulverized adsorbent between 60–180 mesh. Use the magnesia retained on the 180-mesh sieve.

Celite 545. Johns Mansville Company, diatomaceous earth, or equivalent.

Magnesium oxide-Celite 545 mixture (2+1) by weight. Place the magnesium oxide (60–180 mesh) and the Celite 545 in 2 to 1 proportions, respectively, by weight in a glass-stoppered flask large enough for adequate mixing. Shake vigorously for 10 minutes. Transfer the mixture to a glass trough lined with aluminum foil (free from rolling oil) and spread it out on a layer about 1 centimeter to 2 centimeters thick. Reheat the mixture at 160 °C ±1 °C for 2 hours, and store in a tightly closed flask.

Sodium sulfate, anhydrous, A.C.S. reagent grade, preferably in granular form. For each bottle of sodium sulfate reagent used, establish as follows the necessary sodium sulfate prewash to provide such filters required in the method: Place approximately 35 grams of anhydrous sodium sulfate in a 30-milliliter course, fritted-glass funnel or in a 65-millimeter filter funnel with glass wool plug; wash with successive 15-milliliter portions of the indicated solvent until a 15-milliliter portion of the wash shows 0.00 absorbance per centimeter path length between 280 mμ and 400 mμ when tested as prescribed under "Organic solvents." Usually three portions of wash solvent are sufficient.

Before proceeding with analysis of a sample, determine the absorbance in a 5-centimeter path cell between 250 millimicrons and 400 millimicrons for the reagent blank by carrying out the procedure, without an oil sample, recording the spectra after the extraction stage and after the complete procedure as prescribed. The absorbance per centimeter pathlength following the extraction stage should not exceed 0.02 in the wavelength range from 280 mμ to 400 mμ; the absorbance per centimeter pathlength following the complete procedure should not exceed 0.02 in the wavelength range from 280 mμ to 400 mμ. If in either spectrum the characteristic benzene peaks in the 250 mμ–260 mμ region are present, remove the benzene by the procedure under "Organic solvents" and record absorbance again.

Place 300 milliliters of dimethyl sulfoxide in a 1-liter separatory funnel and add 75 milliliters of phosphoric acid. Mix the contents of the funnel and allow to stand for 10 minutes. (The reaction between the sulfoxide and the acid is exothermic. Release pressure after mixing, then keep funnel stoppered.) Add 150 milliliters of isooctane and shake to pre-equilibrate the solvents. Draw off the individual layers and store in glass-stoppered flasks.

Weigh a 20-gram sample of the oil and transfer to a 500-milliliter separatory funnel containing 100 milliliters of pre-equilibrated sulfoxide-phosphoric acid mixture. Complete the transfer of the sample with small portions of preequilibrated isooctane to give a total volume of the oil and solvent of 75 milliliters. Shake the funnel vigorously for 2 minutes. Set up three 250-milliliter separatory funnels with each containing 30 milliliters of pre-equilibrated isooctane. After separation of liquid phases, carefully draw off lower layer into the first 250-milliliter separatory funnel and wash in tandem with the 30-milliliter portions of isooctane contained in the 250-milliliter separatory funnels. Shaking time for each wash is 1 minute. Repeat the extraction operation with two additional portions of the sulfoxide-acid mixture and wash each extractive in tandem through the same three portions of isooctane.

Collect the successive extractives (300 milliliters total) in a separatory funnel (preferably 2-liter) containing 480 milliliters of distilled water; mix, and allow to cool for a few minutes after the last extractive has been added. Add 80 milliliters of isooctane to the solution and extract by shaking the funnel vigorously for 2 minutes. Draw off the lower aqueous layer into a second separatory funnel (preferably 2-liter) and repeat the extraction with 80 milliliters of isooctane. Draw off and discard the aqueous layer. Wash each of the 80-milliliter extractives three times with 100-milliliter portions of distilled water. Shaking time for each wash is 1 minute. Discard the aqueous layers. Filter the first extractive through anhydrous sodium sulfate prewashed with isooctane (see Sodium sulfate under "Reagents and Materials" for preparation of filter) into a 250-milliliter Erlenmeyer flask (or optionally into the evaporation flask). Wash the first separatory funnel with the second 80-milliliter isooctane extractive and pass through the sodium sulfate. Then wash the second and first separatory funnels successively with a 20-milliliter portion of isooctane and pass the solvent through the sodium sulfate into the flask. Add 1 milliliter of *n*-hexadecane and evaporate the isooctane on the steam bath under nitrogen. Discontinue evaporation when not over 1 milliliter of residue remains. To the residue, add a 10-milliliter portion of isooctane, reevaporate to 1 milliliter of hexadecane, and repeat this operation once.

Quantitatively transfer the residue with isooctane to a 200-milliliter volumetric flask, make to volume, and mix. Determine the absorbance of the solution in the 1-centimeter pathlength cells compared to isooctane as reference between 280 mμ–400 mμ (take care to lose none of the solution in filling the sample cell). Correct the absorbance values for any absorbance derived from reagents as determined by carrying out the procedure without an oil sample. If the corrected absorbance does not exceed the limits prescribed in this paragraph, the oil meets the ultraviolet absorbance specifications. If the corrected absorbance per centimeter pathlength exceeds the limits prescribed in this paragraph, proceed as follows: Quantitatively transfer the isooctane solution to a 125-milliliter flask equipped with 24/40 joint, and evaporate the isooctane on the steam bath under a stream of nitrogen to a volume of 1 milliliter of hexadecane. Add 10 milliliters of methyl alcohol and approximately 0.3 gram of sodium borohydride. (Minimize exposure of the borohydride to the atmosphere. A measuring dipper may be used.) Immediately fit a water-cooled condenser equipped with a 24/40 joint and with a drying tube into the flask, mix until the borohydride is dissolved, and allow to stand for 30 minutes at room temperature, with intermittent swirling. At the end of this period, disconnect the flask and evaporate the methyl alcohol on the steam bath under nitrogen until the sodium borohydride begins to come out of the solution. Then add 10 milliliters of isooctane and evaporate to a volume of about 2–3 milliliters. Again, add 10 milliliters of isooctane and concentrate to a volume of approximately 5 milliliters. Swirl the flask repeatedly to assure adequate washing of the sodium borohydride residues.

Fit the tetrafluoroethylene polymer disc on the upper part of the stem of the chromatographic tube, then place the tube with the disc on the suction flask and apply the vacuum (approximately 135 millimeters Hg pressure). Weigh out 14 grams of the 2:1 magnesium oxide-Celite 545 mixture and pour the adsorbent mixture into the chromatographic tube in approximately 3-centimeter layers. After the addition of each layer, level off the top of the adsorbent with a flat glass rod or metal plunger by pressing down firmly until the adsorbent is well packed. Loosen the topmost few millimeters of each adsorbent layer with the end of a metal rod before the addition of the next layer. Continue packing in this manner until all the 14 grams of the adsorbent is added to the tube. Level off the top of the adsorbent by pressing down firmly with a flat glass rod or metal plunger to make the depth of the adsorbent bed approximately 12.5 centimeters in depth. Turn off the vacuum and remove the suction flask. Fit the 500-milliliter reservoir onto the top of the chromatographic column and prewet the column by passing 100 milliliters of isooctane through the column. Adjust the nitrogen pressure so that the rate of descent of the isooctane coming off the column is between 2–3 milliliters per minute. Discontinue pressure just before the last of the isooctane reaches the level of the adsorbent. (Caution: Do not allow the liquid level to recede below the adsorbent level at any time.) Remove the reservoir and decant the 5-milliliter isooctane concentrate solution onto the column and with slight pressure again allow the liquid level to recede to barely above the adsorbent level. Rapidly complete the transfer similarly with two 5-milliliter portions of isooctane, swirling the flask repeatedly each time to assure adequate washing of the residue. Just before the final 5-milliliter wash reaches the top of the adsorbent, add 100 milliliters of isooctane to the reservoir and continue the percolation at the 2–3 milliliters per minute rate. Just before the last of the isooctane reaches the adsorbent level, add

100 milliliters of 10 percent benzene in isooctane to the reservoir and continue the percolation at the aforementioned rate. Just before the solvent mixture reaches adsorbent level, add 25 milliliters of 20 percent benzene in isooctane to the reservoir and continue the percolation at 2–3 milliliters per minute until all this solvent mixture has been removed from the column. Discard all the elution solvents collected up to this point. Add 300 milliliters of the acetone-benzene-water mixture to the reservoir and percolate through the column to eluate the polynuclear compounds. Collect the eluate in a clean 1-liter separatory funnel. Allow the column to drain until most of the solvent mixture is removed. Wash the eluate three times with 300-milliliter portions of distilled water, shaking well for each wash. (The addition of small amounts of sodium chloride facilitates separation.) Discard the aqueous layer after each wash. After the final separation, filter the residual benzene through anhydrous sodium sulfate pre-washed with benzene (see Sodium sulfate under "Reagents and Materials" for preparation of filter) into a 250-milliliter Erlenmeyer flask (or optionally into the evaporation flask). Wash the separatory funnel with two additional 20-milliliter portions of benzene which are also filtered through the sodium sulfate. Add 1 milliliter of *n*-hexadecane and completely remove the benzene by evaporation under nitrogen, using the special procedure to eliminate benzene as previously described under "Organic solvents." Quantitatively transfer the residue with isooctane to a 200-milliliter volumetric flask and adjust to volume. Determine the absorbance of the solution in the 1-centimeter pathlength cells compared to isooctane as reference between 250 mμ–400 mμ. Correct for any absorbance derived from the reagents as determined by carrying out the procedure without an oil sample. If either spectrum shows the characteristic benzene peaks in the 250 mμ–260 mμ region, evaporate the solution to remove benzene by the procedure under "Organic solvents." Dissolve the residue, transfer quantitatively, and adjust to volume in isooctane in a 200-milliliter volumetric flask. Record the absorbance again. If the corrected absorbance does not exceed the limits proposed in this paragraph, the oil meets the proposed ultraviolet absorbance specifications.

(d) Mineral oil identified in paragraph (d)(1) of this section may be used as provided in paragraph (d)(2) of this section.

(1) The mineral oil consists of virgin petroleum distillates refined to meet the following specifications:

(i) Distillation endpoint at 760 millimeters pressure not to exceed 371 °C, with a maximum residue not to exceed 2 percent, as determined by ASTM method D86–82, "Standard Method for Distillation of Petroleum Products," which is incorporated by reference. The availability of this incorporation by reference is given in paragraph (b)(1)(i) of this section.

(ii) Ultraviolet absorbance limits as follows as determined by the method described in paragraph (d)(3) of this section.

Wavelength (mμ)	Maximum absorbance per centimeter optical pathlength
280 to 299	2.3
300 to 319	1.2
320 to 359	.8
360 to 400	.3

(iii) Pyrene content not to exceed a maximum of 25 parts per million as determined by the method described in paragraph (d)(3) of this section.

(2) The mineral oil may be used only in the processing of jute fiber employed in the production of textile bags intended for use in contact with the following types of food: Dry grains and dry seeds (for example, beans, peas, rice, and lentils); whole root crop vegetables of the types identified in 40 CFR 180.34(f); unshelled and shelled nuts (including peanuts); and dry animal feed. The finished processed jute fiber shall contain no more than 6 percent by weight of residual mineral oil.

(3) The analytical method for determining ultraviolet absorbance limits and pyrene content is as follows:

I. *Apparatus*. A. Assorted beakers, separatory funnels fitted with tetrafluoroethylene polymer stopcocks, and graduated cylinders.

B. Volumetric flasks, 200-milliliter.

C. A chromatographic column made from nominal 1.3 centimeters outside diameter × 75 centimeters glass tubing tapered at one end and joined to a 2-millimeter-bore tetrafluoroethylene polymer stopcock. The opposite end is flanged and joined to a female 24/40 standard taper fitting. This provides for accommodating the 500-milliliter reservoir described in item I.E below.

D. A chromatographic column made from nominal 1.7 centimeters outside diameter × 115 centimeters glass tubing tapered at one end and joined to a 2-millimeter-bore tetrafluoroethylene polymer stopcock. The opposite end is flanged and joined to a 2.5 centimeters outside diameter × 9.0 centimeters glass tube having a female 24/40 standard taper fitting. This provides for accommodating the 500-milliliter reservoir described in item I. E below.

E. A 500-milliliter reservoir having a 24/40 standard taper male fitting at bottom and a suitable ball joint at the top for connecting to the nitrogen supply. The female fitting of the chromatographic columns described in items I. C and D above and the male fitting of the reservoir described in this item E should both be equipped with glass hooks.

(NOTE: Rubber stoppers are not to be used. Stopcock grease is not to be used on ground-glass joints in this method.)

F. A spectrophotometer equipped to automatically record absorbance of liquid samples in 1-centimeter pathlength cells in the spectral region of 280–400 mμ with a spectral slit width of 2 mμ or less. At an absorbance level of about 0.4, absorbance measurements shall be repeatable within ±0.01 and accurate within ±0.05. Wavelength measurements shall be repeatable with ±0.2 mμ and accurate within ±1.0 mμ. Instrument operating conditions are selected to realize this performance under dynamic (automatic) recording operations. Accuracy of absorbance measurements are determined at 290, 345, and 400 mμ, using potassium chromate as the reference standard. (National Bureau of Standards Circular 484, Spectrophotometry, U.S. Department of Commerce, 1949.)

G. Two fused quartz cells having pathlengths of 1.00±0.005 centimeter or better.

II. *Purity of reagents and materials.* Reagent-grade chemicals shall be used in all tests. It is further specified that each chemical shall be tested for purity in accordance with the instruction given under "Reagents and Materials" in III below. In addition, a blank run by the procedure shall be made on each purified lot of reagents and materials. Unless otherwise indicated, references to water shall be understood to mean distilled water.

III. *Reagents and materials*— A. *Organic solvents.* All solvents used throughout the procedure shall meet the specifications and tests described in this section III. The isooctane, benzene, cyclohexane, nitromethane, and *n*-hexadecane designated shall pass the following test: To the specified quantity of solvent in a 150-milliliter beaker, add 1 milliliter of purified *n*-hexadecane and evaporate on the steam bath under a stream of nitrogen. Discontinue evaporation when not over 1 milliliter of residue remains (to the residue from benzene and nitromethane add a 10-milliliter portion of purified isooctane, re-evaporate, and repeat once to insure complete removal of solvent). Dissolve the 1 milliliter of *n*-hexadecane residue in isooctane and make to 10-milliliter volume. Determine the absorbance in 1.0-centimeter pathlength cells compared to water as reference. The absorbance of the solution of solvent residue shall not exceed 0.05 between 280 and 400 mμ.

1. *Isooctane (2,2,4-trimethylpentane).* Use 240 milliliters for the above test. Purify, if necessary, by passage through a column of activated silica gel.

2. *Benzene.* Use 200 milliliters for the above test. Purify, if necessary, by distillation or otherwise.

3. *Cyclohexane.* Use 70 milliliters for the above test. Purify, if necessary, by distillation, silica gel percolation, or otherwise.

4. *Nitromethane.* Use 125 milliliters for the above test. Purify, if necessary, by distillation or otherwise.

5. *n-Hexadecane.* Determine the absorbance on this solvent directly. Purify, if necessary, by silica gel percolation or otherwise.

B. *Other materials*—1. *Pyrene standard reference.* Pyrene, reagent grade, melting point range 150–152 °C. (Organic Chemical 3627, Eastman Kodak Co., Rochester, N.Y., or equivalent). The standard reference absorbance is the absorbance at 334 millimicrons of a standard reference solution of pyrene containing a concentration of 1.0 milligram per liter in purified isooctane measured against isooctane of the same spectral purity in 1.0-centimeter cells. (This absorbance will be approximately 0.28.)

2. *Chrysene solution.* Prepare a solution at a concentration of 5.0 milligrams per liter by dissolving 5.0 milligrams of chrysene in purified isooctane in a 1-liter volumetric flask. Adjust to volume with isooctane.

3. *Nitrogen gas.* Water pumped or equivalent purity, cylinder with regulator, and valve control flow at 5 p.s.i.

4. *Silica gel.* 100–200 mesh (Davison Chemical, Baltimore, Md., Grade 923, or equivalent), purified and activated by the following procedure: Place about 1 kilogram of silica gel in a large column and wash with contaminant-free benzene until a 200-milliliter sample of the benzene coming off the column will pass the ultraviolet absorption test for benzene. This test is performed as stipulated under "Organic solvents" in A under III above. When the silica gel has been sufficiently cleaned, activate the gel before use by placing the 1-kilogram batch in a shallow container in a layer no greater than 1 inch in depth and heating in an oven (Caution! Explosion Hazard) at 130 °C. for 16 hours, and store in a vacuum desiccator. Reheating about once a week is necessary if the silica gel is repeatedly removed from the desiccator.

5. *Aluminum oxide (Aluminum Co. of America, Grade F-20, or equivalent grade).* 80–200 mesh, purified and activated by the following procedure: Place about 1 kilogram of aluminum

oxide in a large column and wash with contaminant-free benzene until a 200-milliliter sample of the benzene coming off the column will pass the ultraviolet absorption test for benzene. This test is performed as stipulated under "Organic solvents" in A under III above. (Caution! Remove Benzene From Adsorbent Under Vacuum To Minimize Explosion Hazard in Subsequent Heating!) When the aluminum oxide has been sufficiently cleaned and freed of solvent, activate it before use by placing the 1-kilogram batch in a shallow container in a layer no greater than 1 inch in depth. Heat in an oven at 130 °C for 16 hours. Upon removal from heat, store at atmospheric pressure over 80 percent (by weight) sulfuric acid in a desiccator for at least 36 hours before use. This gives aluminum oxide with between 6 to 9.5 percent volatiles. This is determined by heating a weighed sample of the prepared aluminum oxide at 2,000 °F for 2 hours and then quickly reweighing. To insure the proper adsorptive properties of the aluminum oxide, perform the following test:

a. Weigh 50 grams ±1 gram of the activated aluminum oxide and pack into the chromatographic column (1.3 centimeters × 75 centimeters) described under "Apparatus" in C under I above. Use glass wool at the column exit to prevent the aluminum oxide from passing through the column.

b. Place a 250-milliliter graduated cylinder under the column to measure the amount of eluate coming from the column.

c. Prewet the aluminum oxide by passing 40 milliliters of isooctane through the column. Adjust the nitrogen pressure so that the rate of descent of the isooctane coming off the column is between 1.5 to 2.5 milliliters per minute.

d. Just prior to the last of the isooctane reaching the top of the aluminum oxide bed, add 10 milliliters of the isooctane solution containing 5.0 milligrams of chrysene per liter.

e. Continue percolation until the isooctane is just above the aluminum oxide. Then add 200 milliliters of a mixture of benzene and isooctane (33⅓ percent benzene and 66⅔ percent isooctane by volume) to the reservoir and continue percolation.

f. Continue percolation, collecting the eluates (40 milliliters of the prewet solution, 10 milliliters of the sample solution, and 200 milliliters of the gradient solution) in the 250-milliliter graduated cylinder until the level of the gradient solution is just above the aluminum oxide. Add 200 milliliters of the eluting solution of benzene and isooctane (90 percent benzene and 10 percent isooctane by volume) to the column and continue collecting until a total of 250 milliliters of solution has been obtained. This may be discarded. Now begin to collect the final eluate.

g. Place a 100-milliliter graduated cylinder under the column and continue the percolation until a 100-milliliter eluate has been obtained.

h. Measure the amount of chrysene in this 100-milliliter fraction by ultraviolet analysis. If the aluminum oxide is satisfactory, more than 80 percent of the original amount of chrysene should be found in this fraction. (NOTE: If the amount of chrysene recovered is less than 80 percent, the original batch of aluminum oxide should be sieved between 100–160 mesh. Activation and testing of this sieved batch should indicate a satisfactory aluminum oxide for use.)

IV. *Sampling.* Precautions must be taken to insure that an uncontaminated sample of the mineral oil is obtained since ultraviolet absorption is very sensitive to small amounts of extraneous material contaminating the sample through careless handling.

V. *Procedure.* A. *Blank.* Before proceeding with the analysis of a sample, determine the absorbance of the solvent residues by carrying out the procedure without a sample.

B. *Sample.* 1. Weigh out 20.0 grams ±0.1 gram of the mineral oil into a beaker and transfer to a 250-milliliter separatory funnel fitted with a tetrafluoroethylene polymer stopcock, using enough cyclohexane (25 milliliters) to give a final total volume of 50 milliliters (mineral oil plus cyclohexane).

2. Add 25 milliliters of nitromethane saturated with cyclohexane and shake by hand vigorously for 3 minutes. Recover the lower nitromethane layer in a 150-milliliter beaker containing 1 milliliter of *n*-hexadecane and evaporate on the steam bath under nitrogen. Repeat the extraction four more times, recovering each extract in the 150-milliliter beaker. Exercise care not to fill the beaker to such a capacity that solvent losses may occur. Evaporate the combined nitromethane extracts to 1 milliliter of *n*-hexadecane residue containing the nitromethane-soluble mineral oil extractives. (NOTE: Complete removal of the nitromethane is essential. This can be assured by two successive additions of 5 milliliters of isooctane and reevaporation.)

3. Remove the beaker from the steam bath and allow to cool.

4. Weigh 50 grams ±1 gram of activated aluminum oxide and pack into the chromatographic column (1.3 centimeters × 75 centimeters) described under "Apparatus" in C under I above. (NOTE: A small plug of glass wool is placed at the column exit to prevent the aluminum oxide from passing through the column. After adding aluminum oxide, tap the column lightly to remove air voids. All percolations using aluminum oxide are performed under nitrogen pressure. The 500-milliliter reservoir described under "Apparatus" in E under I above is to be used to hold the elution solvents.)

5. Prewet the column by adding 40 milliliters of isooctane to the column. Adjust nitrogen pressure so that rate of descent of the

isooctane coming off the column is 2.0 to 3.0 milliliters per minute. Be careful to maintain the level of solvent in the reservoir to prevent air from entering the aluminum oxide bed. New or additional solvent is added just before the last portion of the previous solvent enters the bed. To minimize possible photo-oxidation effects, the following procedures (steps 6 through 18) shall be carried out in subdued light.

6. Before the last of the isooctane reaches the top of the aluminum oxide bed, release the nitrogen pressure and turn off the stopcock on the column. Transfer the *n*-hexadecane residue from the 150-milliliter beaker from procedure step 3 above onto the column, using several washes of isooctane (total volume of washes should be no greater than 10–15 milliliters).

7. Open the stopcock and continue percolation until the isooctane is about 1 centimeter above the top of the aluminum oxide bed. Add 200 milliliters of isooctane to the reservoir, and continue the percolation at the specified rate.

8. Just before the isooctane surface reaches the top of the aluminum oxide bed, add 200 milliliters of a mixture of benzene and isooctane (33⅓ percent benzene and 66⅔ percent isooctane by volume) to the reservoir, and continue the percolation.

9. Just before the surface of this mixture reaches the top of the aluminum oxide bed, release the nitrogen pressure, turn off the stopcock, and discard all the elution solvents collected up to this point.

10. Add to the reservoir 300 milliliters of a mixture of benzene and isooctane (90 percent benzene and 10 percent isooctane by volume), place a 25-milliliter graduated cylinder under the column, continue the percolation until 20 milliliters of eluate has been collected, and then discard the eluate.

11. At this point, place a clean 250-milliliter Erlenmeyer flask under the column. Continue the percolation and collect all the remaining eluate.

(NOTE: Allow the column to drain completely. An increase in the nitrogen pressure may be necessary as the last of the solvent comes off the column.)

12. Place 1 milliliter of *n*-hexadecane into a 150-milliliter beaker. Place this onto a steam bath under a nitrogen stream and transfer in small portions the eluate from step 11 above. Wash out the Erlenmeyer flask with small amounts of benzene and transfer to the evaporation beaker. Evaporate until only 1 milliliter of hexadecane residue remains. (NOTE: Complete removal of the benzene is essential. This can be assured by two successive additions of 5 milliliters of isooctane and reevaporation.)

13. Remove the beaker from the steam bath and cool.

14. Place a sample of 113.5 grams activated 100- 200-mesh silica gel in a 500-milliliter glass-stoppered Erlenmeyer flask. Add to the silica gel 46.2 grams (41 milliliters) of nitromethane. Stopper and shake the flask vigorously until no lumps of silica gel are observed and then shake occasionally during a period of 1 hour. The resultant nitromethane-treated silica gel is 29 weight-percent nitro-methane and 71 weight-percent silica gel.

15. Place a small plug of glass wool in the tapered end of the 1.7 centimeters outside diameter × 115 centimeters column, described under "Apparatus" in D of I above, adjacent to the stopcock to prevent silica gel from passing through the stopcock. Pack the nitromethane-treated silica gel into the column, tapping lightly. The resultant silica gel bed should be about 95 centimeters in depth. Place into a flask 170 milliliters of isooctane saturated with nitromethane.

16. Place a 100-milliliter graduated cylinder under the column and transfer the residue from the beaker in procedure step 13 above with several washes of the 170 milliliters of isooctane, saturated with nitromethane, onto the top of the column. (Total volume of washes should be no greater than 10 to 15 milliliters.) Permit isooctane solution to enter the silica gel bed until the liquid level is at the top bed level. Place the remaining amount of the 170 milliliters of isooctane, saturated with nitromethane, in the reservoir above the bed for percolation through the silica gel. Apply nitrogen pressure to the top of the column, adjusting the pressure so that the isooctane is collected at the rate of 2.5 to 3.5 milliliters per minute, and percolate isooctane through the bed until a quantity of 75.0 milliliters of eluate is collected. Discard the 75 milliliters of eluate. Turn off the stopcock and add 250 milliliters of benzene to the reservoir above the bed. Use a 400-milliliter beaker to collect the remaining eluate.

17. Open the stopcock, renew the pressure, and percolate the remaining isooctane and benzene through the column eluting the remaining aromatics. Transfer the eluate in small portions from the 400 milliliter beaker to a 150-milliliter beaker containing 1 milliliter of *n*-hexadecane and evaporate on the steam bath under nitrogen. Rinse the 400-milliliter beaker well with small portions of isooctane to obtain a complete transfer.

(NOTE: Complete removal of the nitromethane and benzene is essential. This can be assured by successive additions of 5 milliliters of isooctane and reevaporation.)

18. Transfer the residue with several washes of isooctane into a 200-milliliter volumetric flask. Add isooctane to mark.

19. Record the spectrum of the sample solution in a 1-centimeter cell compared to isooctane from 270 to 400 mμ. After making necessary corrections in the spectrum for cell differences and for the blank absorbance, record the maximum absorbance in each of

the wavelength intervals (mμ), 280–299, 300–319, 320–359, 360–400.

a. If the spectrum then shows no discernible peak corresponding to the absorbance maximum of the pyrene reference standard solution at 334 mμ, the maximum absorbances in the respective wavelength intervals recorded shall not exceed those prescribed in paragraph (d)(1)(ii) of this section.

b. If such a peak is evident in the spectrum of the sample solution, and the spectrum as a whole is not incompatible with that of a pyrene contaminant yielding such a peak of the observed absorbance, calculate the concentration of pyrene that would yield this peak (334 m) by the base-line technique described in ASTM method E169–63 (Reapproved 1981), "Standard Recommended Practices for General Techniques of Ultraviolet Quantitative Analysis," which is incorporated by reference. The availability of this incorporation by reference is given in paragraph (b)(1)(i) of this section. Correct each of the maximum absorbances in the respective specified wavelength intervals by subtracting the absorbance due to pyrene, determined as follows:

$$\text{Absorbance due to pyrene} = \frac{Cp \times Sa}{Sp}$$

where:

Cp=Calculated concentration of pyrene in sample solution;

Sp=Concentration of pyrene reference standard solution in same units of concentration;

Sa=Absorbance of pyrene reference standard solution at wavelength of maximum absorbance of sample solution in the respective specified wavelength intervals.

Also calculate the pyrene content of the oil sample in parts per million as follows:

$$\begin{array}{c}\text{Pyrene content}\\ \text{(p.p.m.)}\end{array} = \frac{(200/1000)\times C}{20/1000} = 10C$$

where:

C=Calculated concentration of pyrene in milligrams per liter of sample solution.

c. The pyrene content so determined shall not exceed 25 p.p.m. The maximum absorbances corrected for pyrene content as described in this step 19 for each of the specified wavelength intervals shall not exceed the limits prescribed in paragraph (d)(1)(ii) of this section.

d. If the spectrum as a whole of the sample solution is in any respect clearly incompatible with the presence of pyrene as the source of the peak at 334 mμ, then the maximum absorbances in the respective wavelength intervals without correction for any assumed pyrene content shall not exceed the limits prescribed in paragraph (d)(1)(ii) of this section.

[42 FR 14609, Mar. 15, 1977, as amended at 47 FR 11847, Mar. 19, 1982; 49 FR 10112, Mar. 19, 1984; 54 FR 24898, June 12, 1989]

§ 178.3650 Odorless light petroleum hydrocarbons.

Odorless light petroleum hydrocarbons may be safely used, as a component of nonfood articles intended for use in contact with food, in accordance with the following prescribed conditions:

(a) The additive is a mixture of liquid hydrocarbons derived from petroleum or synthesized from petroleum gases. The additive is chiefly paraffinic, isoparaffinic, or naphthenic in nature.

(b) The additive meets the following specifications:

(1) Odor is faint and not kerosenic.

(2) Initial boiling point is 300 °F minimum.

(3) Final boiling point is 650 °F maximum.

(4) Ultraviolet absorbance limits determined by method specified in § 178.3620(b)(1)(ii), as follows:

Wavelength (Mμ)	Maximum absorbance per centimeter optical pathlength
280 to 289	4.0
290 to 299	3.3
300 to 329	2.3
330 to 360	.8

(c) The additive is used as follows:

Use	Limitations
As a plasticizer and absorber oil in the manufacture of polyolefin articles authorized for food contact use.	In an amount not to exceed that required to produce intended effect, consistent with good manufacturing practice.
As a lubricant of fibers of textiles authorized for food contact use.	At a use level not to exceed 0.15 percent by weight of finished fibers.
As a component of adhesives	Complying with § 175.105 of this chapter.
As a defoamer in the manufacture of paper and paperboard	Complying with § 176.210 of this chapter.
As a defoamer in coatings	Complying with § 176.200 of this chapter.

§ 178.3690 Pentaerythritol adipate-stearate.

Pentaerythritol adipate-stearate identified in paragraph (a) of this section may be safely used as a lubricant in the fabrication of rigid and semirigid polyvinyl chloride and/or vinyl chloride-propylene copolymers complying with § 177.1980 of this chapter used as articles or components of articles that contact food, excluding food with alcohol content greater than 8 percent under conditions of use of E, F, and G described in table 2 in § 175.300(d) of this chapter, subject to the provisions of this section.

(a) *Identity*. For the purpose of this section, pentaerythritol adipate-stearate is an ester of pentaerythritol with adipic acid and stearic acid and its associated fatty acids (chiefly palmitic), with adipic acid comprising 14 percent and stearic acid and its associated acids (chiefly palmitic) comprising 71 percent of the organic moieties.

(b) *Specifications*. Pentaerythritol adipate-stearate has the following specifications:

(1) Melting point (dropping) of 55–58 °C as determined by ASTM method D566–76 (Reapproved 1982), "Standard Test Method for Dropping Point of Lubricating Grease," which is incorporated by reference. Copies may be obtained from the American Society for Testing Materials, 100 Barr Harbor Dr., West Conshohocken, Philadelphia, PA 19428-2959, or may be examined at the National Archives and Records Administration (NARA). For information on the availability of this material at NARA, call 202–741–6030, or go to: *http://www.archives.gov/federal_register/code_of_federal_regulations/ibr_locations.html.*

(2) Acid value not to exceed 15 as determined by ASTM method D1386–78, "Standard Test Method for Saponification Number (Empirical) of Synthetic and Natural Waxes" (Revised 1978), which is incorporated by reference. Copies are available from American Society for Testing and Materials (ASTM), 100 Barr Harbor Dr., West Conshohocken, Philadelphia, PA 19428-2959, or available for inspection at the National Archives and Records Administration (NARA). For information on the availability of this material at NARA, call 202–741–6030, or go to: *http://www.archives.gov/federal_register/code_of_federal_regulations/ibr_locations.html.*

(3) Saponification number of 270–280 as determined by ASTM method D1387–78, "Standard Test Method for Acid Number (Empirical) of Synthetic and Natural Waxes" (Revised 1978), which is incorporated by reference. Copies are available from American Society for Testing and Materials (ASTM), 100 Barr Harbor Dr., West Conshohocken, Philadelphia, PA 19428-2959, or available for inspection at the National Archives and Records Administration (NARA). For information on the availability of this material at NARA, call 202–741–6030, or go to: *http://www.archives.gov/federal_register/code_of_federal_regulations/ibr_locations.html.*

(4) Iodine number not to exceed 2 as determined by Iodine Absorption Number, Hanus Method, of the "Official Methods of Analysis of the Association of Official Analytical Chemists," sections 28.018–28.019, 13th Ed. (1980), which is incorporated by reference. Copies may be obtained from the AOAC INTERNATIONAL, 481 North Frederick Ave., suite 500, Gaithersburg, MD 20877, or may be examined at the National Archives and Records Administration (NARA). For information on the availability of this material at NARA, call 202–741–6030, or go to: *http://www.archives.gov/federal_register/code_of_federal_regulations/ibr_locations.html.*

(c) The total amount of ester (calculated as free pentaerythritol) shall not exceed 0.4 percent by weight of the polyvinyl chloride and/or the vinyl chloride-propylene copolymers complying with § 177.1980.

[45 FR 1018, Jan. 4, 1980, as amended at 47 FR 11848, Mar. 19, 1982; 49 FR 10112, Mar. 19, 1984; 54 FR 24898, June 12, 1989; 57 FR 18082, Apr. 29, 1992; 70 FR 40880, July 15, 2005; 70 FR 67651, Nov. 8, 2005]

§ 178.3700 Petrolatum.

Petrolatum may be safety used as a component of nonfood articles in contact with food, in accordance with the following conditions:

(a) Petrolatum complies with the specifications set forth in the United

States Pharmacopeia XX (1980) for white petrolatum or in the National Formulary XV (1980) for yellow petrolatum.

(b) Petrolatum meets the following ultraviolet absorbance limits when subjected to the analytical procedure described in § 172.886(b) of this chapter:

Ultraviolet absorbance per centimeter pathlength:

Millimicrons	Maximum
280 to 289	0.25
290 to 299	.20
300 to 359	.14
360 to 400	.04

(c) It is used or intended for use as a protective coating of the surfaces of metal or wood tanks used in fermentation process, in an amount not in excess of that required to produce its intended effect.

(d) Petrolatum as defined by this section may be used for the functions described and within the limitations prescribed by specific regulations in parts 175, 176, 177, and 178 of this chapter which prescribe uses of petrolatum. For the purpose of cross-reference, such specific regulations include: §§ 175.105, 175.125, 175.300, 176.170, 176.200, 176.210, 177.2600, 177.2800, and 178.3570 of this chapter.

(e) Petrolatum may contain any antioxidant permitted in food by regulations issued pursuant to section 409 of the act, in an amount not greater than that required to produce its intended effect.

[42 FR 14609, Mar. 15, 1977, as amended at 49 FR 10113, Mar. 19, 1984; 55 FR 12172, Apr. 2, 1990]

§ 178.3710 Petroleum wax.

Petroleum wax may be safely used as a component of nonfood articles in contact with food, in accordance with the following conditions:

(a) Petroleum wax is a mixture of solid hydrocarbons, paraffinic in nature, derived from petroleum, and refined to meet the specifications prescribed in this section.

(b) The petroleum wax meets the following ultraviolet absorbance limits when subjected to the analytical procedure described in § 172.886(b) of this chapter.

Ultraviolet absorbance per centimeter pathlength:

Millimicrons	Maximum
280 to 289	0.15
290 to 299	.12
300 to 359	.08
360 to 400	.02

(c) Petroleum wax may contain any antioxidant permitted in food by regulations issued in accordance with section 409 of the act, in an amount not greater than that required to produce its intended effect.

(d) Petroleum wax may contain a total of not more than 1 weight percent of residues of the following polymers when such residues result from use of the polymers as processing aids (filter aids) in the production of the petroleum wax: Homopolymers and/or copolymers derived from one or more of the mixed *n*-alkyl (C_{12}, C_{14}, C_{16}, and C_{18}) methacrylate esters where the C_{12} and C_{14} alkyl groups are derived from coconut oil and the C_{16} and C_{18} groups are derived from tallow.

(e) Petroleum wax may contain 2-hydroxy-4-*n*-octoxybenzophenone as a stabilizer at a level not to exceed 0.01 weight percent of the petroleum wax.

(f) Petroleum wax may contain poly(alkylacrylate) (CAS Reg. No. 27029–57–8), as described in § 172.886(c)(2) of this chapter, as a processing aid in the manufacture of petroleum wax.

[42 FR 14609, Mar. 15, 1977, as amended at 51 FR 19545, May 30, 1986]

§ 178.3720 Petroleum wax, synthetic.

Synthetic petroleum wax may be safely used in applications and under the same conditions where naturally derived petroleum wax is permitted in subchapter B of this chapter as a component of articles intended to contact food, provided that the synthetic petroleum wax meets the definition and specifications prescribed in § 172.888 of this chapter.

§ 178.3725 Pigment dispersants.

Subject to the provisions of this regulation, the substances listed in this section may be safely used as pigment dispersants in food-contact materials.

Substances	Limitations
Dimethylolpropionic acid (CAS Reg. No. 4767–03–7)	For use only at levels not to exceed 0.45 percent by weight of the pigment. The pigmented articles may contact all foods under conditions of use A through H as described in Table 2 of § 176.170(c) of this chapter.
Phosphorylated tall oil fatty acids (CAS Reg. No. 68604–99–9), prepared by the reaction of dimethyl hydrogen phosphite with tall oil fatty acids.	For use only at levels not to exceed 1.0 percent by weight of the pigment. The pigmented polymeric films may contact all food under conditions of use D, E, F, and G described in table 2 of § 176.170(c) of this chapter.
Propanoic acid, 3-hydroxy-2-(hydroxymethyl)-2-methyl-, compd. with 1,1′,1″-nitrilotris [2-propanol] (1:1) (CAS Reg. No. 221281–21–6).	For use only at levels not to exceed 0.45 percent by weight of the pigment. The pigmented articles may contact all food under conditions of use A through H as described in Table 2 of § 176.170(c) of this chapter.
Siloxanes and silicones; cetylmethyl, dimethyl, methyl 11-methoxy-11-oxoundecyl (CAS Reg. No. 155419–59–3).	For use only at levels not to exceed 0.5 percent by weight of the pigment. The pigmented polymers may contact all foods under conditions of use C, D, E, F, and G described in Table 2 of § 176.170(c) of this chapter.
Trimethylolethane (CAS Reg. No. 77–85–0)	For use only at levels not to exceed 0.45 percent by weight of inorganic pigment. The pigmented articles may contact all food under conditions of use A through H described in Table 2 of § 176.170(c) of this chapter.

[61 FR 43157, Aug. 21, 1996, as amended at 63 FR 35799, July 1, 1998; 64 FR 48292, Sept. 3, 1999; 64 FR 72273, Dec. 27, 1999; 65 FR 52909, Aug. 31, 2000]

§ 178.3730 Piperonyl butoxide and pyrethrins as components of bags.

Piperonyl butoxide in combination with pyrethrins may be safely used for insect control on bags that are intended for use in contact with dried feed in compliance with §§ 561.310 and 561.340 of this chapter, or that are intended for use in contact with dried food in compliance with §§ 193.60 and 193.390 of this chapter.

§ 178.3740 Plasticizers in polymeric substances.

Subject to the provisions of this regulation, the substances listed in paragraph (b) of this section may be safely used as plasticizers in polymeric substances used in the manufacture of articles or components of articles intended for use in producing, manufacturing, packing, processing, preparing, treating, packaging, transporting, or holding food.

(a) The quantity used shall not exceed the amount reasonably required to accomplish the intended technical effect.

(b) List of substances:

Substances	Limitations
Butylbenzyl phthalate	For use only: 1. As provided in §§ 175.105 and 176.180 of this chapter. 2. In polymeric substances used in food-contact articles complying with § 175.300, § 175.320, or § 176.170 of this chapter: *Provided,* That the butyl benzyl phthalate contains not more than 1 percent by weight of dibenzyl phthalate. 3. In polymeric substances used in other permitted food-contact articles: *Provided,* That the butyl benzyl phthalate contains not more than 1 percent by weight of dibenzyl phthalate; and *Provided further,* That the finished food-contact article, when extracted with the solvent or solvents characterizing the type of food and under the conditions of time and temperature characterizing the conditions of its intended use as determined from tables 1 and 2 of § 175.300(d) of this chapter, shall yield net chloroform-soluble extractives not to exceed 0.5 mg. per square inch, as determined by the methods prescribed in § 175.300(e) of this chapter.
1,3-Butylene glycoladipic acid polyester (1,700–2,200 molecular weight) terminated with a 16 percent by weight mixture of myristic, palmitic, and stearic acids.	For use at levels not exceeding 33 percent by weight of polyvinyl chloride homopolymers used in contact with food (except foods that contain more than 8 percent of alcohol) at temperatures not to exceed room temperature. The average thickness of such homopolymers in the form in which they contact food shall not exceed 0.004 inch.

Substances	Limitations
Di(C_7, C_9-alkyl) adipate, in which the C_7, C_9-alkyl groups are derived from linear alpha olefins by the oxo process.	For use only under the conditions listed below, and excluding use as a component of resinous and polymeric coatings described in § 175.300 of this chapter. 1. At levels not to exceed 24 percent by weight of permitted vinyl chloride homo- and/or copolymers used in contact with nonfatty foods. The average thickness of such polymers in the form in which they contact food shall not exceed 0.005 inch. 2. At levels not to exceed 24 pct by weight of permitted vinyl chloride homo- and/or copolymers used in contact, under conditions of use F and G described in table 2 of § 176.170(c) of this chapter, with fatty foods having a fat and oil content not exceeding a total of 40 pct by weight. The average thickness of such polymers in the form in which they contact food shall not exceed 0.005 inch. 3. At levels not exceeding 35 pct by weight of permitted vinyl chloride homo- and/or copolymers used in contact with nonfatty foods. The average thickness of such polymer in the form in which they contact food shall not exceed 0.002 inch. 4. At levels not exceeding 35 pct by weight of permitted vinyl chloride homo- and/or copolymers used in contact, under conditions of use F and G described in table 2 of § 176.170(c) of this chapter with fatty foods having a fat and oil content not exceeding a total of 40 pct by weight. The average thickness of such polymers in the form in which they contact food shall not exceed 0.002 inch.
Di-*n*-alkyl adipate made from C_6 C_8-C_{10} (predominately C_8 and C_{10}) or C_8-C_{10} synthetic fatty alcohols complying with § 172.864 of this chapter.	For use only: 1. At levels not exceeding 24 pct by weight of permitted vinyl chloride homo- and/or copolymers used in contact with nonfatty foods. The average thickness of such polymers in the form in which they contact food shall not exceed 0.005 inch. 2. At levels not exceeding 24 pct by weight of permitted vinyl chloride homo- and/or copolymers used in contact, under conditions of use F and G described in table 2 of § 176.170(c) of this chapter, with fatty foods having a fat and oil content not exceeding a total of 40 pct by weight. The average thickness of such polymers in the form in which they contact food shall not exceed 0.005 inch. 3. At levels not exceeding 35 pct by weight of permitted vinyl chloride homo- and/or copolymers used in contact with nonfatty foods. The average thickness of such polymers in the form in which they contact food shall not exceed 0.002 inch. 4. At levels not exceeding 35 pct by weight of permitted vinyl chloride homo- and/or copolymers used in contact, under conditions of use F and G described in table 2 of § 176.170(c) of this chapter, with fatty foods having a fat and oil content not exceeding a total of 40 pct by weight. The average thickness of such polymers in which they contact food shall not exceed 0.002 inch.
Dicyclohexyl phthalate	For use only: 1. As provided in §§ 175.105, 176.170, 176.180, and 177.1200 of this chapter. 2. Alone or in combination with other phthalates, in plastic film or sheet prepared from polyvinyl acetate, polyvinyl chloride, and/or vinyl chloride copolymers complying with § 177.1980 of this chapter. Such plastic film or sheet shall be used in contact with food at temperatures not to exceed room temperature and shall contain no more than 10 pct by weight of total phthalates, calculated as phthalic acid.
Di(2-ethylhexyl) adipate	

Substances	Limitations
Diisononyl adipate	For use only: 1. At levels not exceeding 24 pct by weight of permitted vinyl chloride homo- and/or copolymers used in contact with nonfatty, nonalcoholic foods. The average thickness of such polymers in the form in which they contact food shall not exceed 0.005 inch. 2. At levels not exceeding 24 pct by weight of permitted vinyl chloride homo- and/or copolymers used in contact under conditions of use F and G described in table 2 of § 176.170(c) of this chapter with fatty, non-alcoholic foods having a fat and oil content not exceeding a total of 30 pct by weight. The average thickness of such polymers in the form in which they contact food shall not exceed 0.005 inch. 3. At levels not exceeding 35 pct by weight of permitted vinyl chloride homo- and/or copolymers used in contact with nonfatty, nonalcoholic foods. The average thickness of such polymers in the form in which they contact food shall not exceed 0.002 inch. 4. At levels not exceeding 35 pct by weight of permitted vinyl chloride homo- and/or copolymers used in contact, under conditions of use F and G described in table 2 of § 176.170(c) of this chapter with fatty, non-alcoholic foods having a fat and oil content not exceeding a total of 40 pct by weight. The average thickness of such polymers in the form in which they contact food shall not exceed 0.002 inch.
Diisononyl phthalate	For use only at levels not exceeding 43 pct by weight of permitted vinyl chloride homo- and/or copolymers used in contact with food only of the types identified in § 176.170(c) of this chapter, table 1, under Categories I, II, IV-B, and VIII, at temperatures not exceeding room temperature. The average thickness of such polymers in the form in which they contact food shall not exceed 0.005 inch.
Di(2-ethylhexyl) azelate	For use only: 1. At levels not exceeding 24 pct by weight of permitted vinyl chloride homo- and/or copolymers used in contact with nonfatty, nonalcoholic food. The average thickness of such polymers in the form in which they contact food shall not exceed 0.003 inch. 2. At levels not exceeding 24 pct by weight of permitted vinyl chloride homo- and/or copolymers used in contact, under conditions of use F and G described in table 2 of § 176.170(c) of this chapter, with fatty, non-alcoholic food having a fat and oil content not exceeding a total of 30 percent by weight. The average thickness of such polymers in the form in which they contact food shall not exceed 0.003 inch.
Di-*n*-hexylazelate	For use only: 1. In polymeric substances used in contact with nonfatty food. 2. In polymeric substances used in contact with fatty food and limited to use at levels not exceeding 15 pct by weight of such polymeric substance except as provided under limitation 3. 3. At levels greater than 15 but not exceeding 24 pct by weight of permitted vinyl chloride homo- and/or copolymers used in contact, under conditions of use F or G described in table 2 of § 176.170(c) of this chapter, with fatty food having a fat and oil content not exceeding a total of 30 pct by weight. The average thickness of such polymers in the form in which they contact food shall not exceed 0.003 inch.
Dihexyl phthalate	For use only: 1. As provided in § 175.105 of this chapter. 2. In articles that contact food only of the types identified in § 176.170(c) of this chapter, table 1, under Categories I, II, IV-B, VI-B, and VIII.
Diphenyl phthalate	For use only: 1. As provided in § 175.105 of this chapter. 2. Alone or in combination with other phthalates, in plastic film or sheet prepared from polyvinyl acetate, polyvinyl chloride, and/or vinyl chloride copolymers complying with § 177.1980 of this chapter. Such plastic film or sheet shall be used in contact with food at temperatures not to exceed room temperature and shall contain no more than 10 pct by weight of total phthalates, calculated as phthalic acid.
Epoxidized butyl esters of linseed oil fatty acids	Iodine number, maximum 5; oxirane oxygen, minimum 7.8 pct.
Epoxidized linseed oil	Iodine number, maximum 5; oxirane oxygen, minimum 9-pct.
Mineral oil, white.	

Substances	Limitations
Polybutene, hydrogenated (minimum viscosity at 99 °F, 39 Saybolt Universal seconds, as determined by ASTM methods D445–82 ("Standard Test Method for Kinematic Viscosity of Transparent and Opaque Liquids (and the Calculation of Dynamic Viscosity)") and D2161–82 ("Standard Method for Conversion of Kinematic Viscosity to Saybolt Universal Viscosity or to Saybolt Furol Viscosity"), and bromine number of 3 or less, as determined by ASTM method D1492–78 ("Standard Test Method for Bromine Index of Aromatic Hydrocarbons by Coulometric Titration"), which are incorporated by reference. Copies may be obtained from the American Society for Testing Materials, 100 Barr Harbor Dr., West Conshohocken, Philadelphia, PA 19428-2959, or may be examined at the National Archives and Records Administration (NARA). For information on the availability of this material at NARA, call 202–741–6030, or go to: *http://www.archives.gov/federal_register/code_of_federal_regulations/ibr_locations.html..*	For use only: 1. In polymeric substances used in contact with non-fatty food. 2. In polyethylene complying with § 177.1520 of this chapter and used in contact with fatty food, provided that the hydrogenated polybutene is added in an amount not to exceed 0.5 pct by weight of the polyethylene, and further provided that such plasticized polyethylene shall not be used as a component of articles intended for packing or holding food during cooking. 3. In polystyrene complying with § 177.1640 of this chapter and used in contact with fatty food, provided that the hydrogenated polybutene is added in an amount not to exceed 5 pct by weight of the polystyrene, and further provided that such plasticized polystyrene shall not be used as a component of articles intended for packing or holding food during cooking.
Polyisobutylene (mol weight 300–5,000)	For use in polyethylene complying with § 177.1520 of this chapter, provided that the polyisobutylene is added in an amount not exceeding 0.5 pct by weight of the polyethylene, and further provided that such plasticized polyethylene shall not be used as a component of articles intended for packing or holding food during cooking.
Polyisobutylene complying with § 177.1420 of this chapter.	
Polypropylene glycol (CAS registry No. 25322–69–4) (minimum mean molecular weight 1,200).	For use only in polystyrene plastics, identified in § 177.1640(a)(1), in an amount not to exceed 6 pct by weight of the finished food-contact article.
Propylene glycol azelate (average mol. weight 3,000).	For use only at levels not exceeding 41 pct by weight of permitted polyvinyl chloride coatings. Such coatings shall be used only as bulk food contact surfaces of articles intended for repeated use, complying with § 177.2600 of this chapter.
Triethylene glycol	Diethylene glycol content not to exceed 0.1 pct.
2,2,4-Trimethyl-1,3-pentanediol diisobutyrate	For use only in cellulosic plastics in an amount not to exceed 15 pct by weight of the finished food-contact article, provided that the finished plastic article contacts food only of the types identified in § 176.170(c) of this chapter, table 1, under Categories I, II, VI-B, VII-B, and VIII.

(c) The use of the plasticizers in any polymeric substance or article subject to any regulation in parts 174, 175, 176, 177, 178 and 179 of this chapter must comply with any specifications and limitations prescribed by such regulation for the finished form of the substance or article.

[42 FR 14609, Mar. 15, 1977, as amended at 42 FR 44223, Sept. 2, 1977; 45 FR 56052, Aug. 22, 1980; 48 FR 5748, Feb. 15, 1984; 49 FR 10113, Mar. 19, 1984; 51 FR 47011, Dec. 30, 1986]

§ 178.3750 Polyethylene glycol (mean molecular weight 200–9,500).

Polyethylene glycol identified in this section may be safely used as a component of articles intended for use in contact with food, in accordance with the following prescribed conditions:

(a) The additive is an addition polymer of ethylene oxide and water with a mean molecular weight of 200 to 9,500.

(b) It contains no more than 0.2 percent total by weight of ethylene and diethylene glycols if its mean molecular weight is 350 or higher and no more than 0.5 percent total by weight of ethylene and diethylene glycols if its mean molecular weight is below 350, when tested by the analytical methods prescribed in § 172.820(b) of this chapter.

(c) The provisions of paragraph (b) of this section are not applicable to polyethylene glycols used in food-packaging adhesives complying with § 175.105 of this chapter.

§ 178.3760 Polyethylene glycol (400) monolaurate.

Polyethylene glycol (400) monolaurate containing not more than 0.1 percent by weight of ethylene and/or diethylene glycol may be used at a level not to exceed 0.3 percent by weight of twine as a finish on twine to be used for tying meat provided the twine fibers are produced from nylon resins complying with § 177.1500 of this chapter.

§ 178.3770 Polyhydric alcohol esters of oxidatively refined (Gersthofen process) montan wax acids.

Polyhydric alcohol esters of oxidatively refined (Gersthofen process) montan wax acids identified in this section may be safely used as components of articles intended for use in contact with food in accordance with the following prescribed conditions:

(a) The polyhydric alcohol esters identified in this paragraph may be used as lubricants in the fabrication of vinyl chloride plastic food-contact articles prepared from polyvinyl chloride and/or from vinyl chloride copolymers complying with § 177.1980 of this chapter. Such esters meet the following specifications and are produced by partial esterification of oxidatively refined (Gersthofen process) montan wax acids by either ethylene glycol or 1,3-butanediol with or without neutralization of unreacted carboxylic groups with calcium hydroxide:

(1) Dropping point 76°–105 °C, as determined by ASTM method D566–76 (Reapproved 1982), "Standard Test Method for Dropping Point of Lubricating Grease," which is incorporated by reference. Copies may be obtained from the American Society for Testing Materials, 100 Barr Harbor Dr., West Conshohocken, Philadelphia, PA 19428-2959, or may be examined at the National Archives and Records Administration (NARA). For information on the availability of this material at NARA, call 202–741–6030, or go to: *http://www.archives.gov/federal_register/code_of_federal_regulations/ibr_locations.html.*

(2) Acid value 10–20, as determined by ASTM method D1386–78 ("Standard Test Method for Acid Number (Empirical) of Synthetic and Natural Waxes" (Revised 1978), which is incorporated by reference; copies are available from American Society for Testing and Materials (ASTM), 100 Barr Harbor Dr., West Conshohocken, Philadelphia, PA 19428-2959, or available for inspection at the National Archives and Records Administration (NARA). For information on the availability of this material at NARA, call 202–741–6030, or go to: *http://www.archives.gov/federal_register/code_of_federal_regulations/ibr_locations.html.*) using as solvent xylene-ethyl alcohol in a 2:1 ratio instead of toluene-ethyl alcohol in a 2:1 ratio.

(3) Saponification value 100–160, as determined by ASTM method D1387–78 ("Standard Test Method for Saponification Number (Empirical) of Synthetic and Natural Waxes" (Revised 1978), which is incorporated by reference; copies are available from American Society for Testing and Materials (ASTM), 100 Barr Harbor Dr., West Conshohocken, Philadelphia, PA 19428-2959, or available for inspection at the National Archives and Records Administration (NARA). For information on the availability of this material at NARA, call 202–741–6030, or go to: *http://www.archives.gov/federal_register/code_of_federal_regulations/ibr_locations.html.*) using xylene-ethyl alcohol in a 2:1 ratio instead of ethyl alcohol in preparation of potassium hydroxide solution.

(4) Ultraviolet absorbance limits as follows, as determined by the analytical method described in this subparagraph:

Ultraviolet absorbance per centimeter pathlength.

Millimicrons	Maximum
280 to 289	0.07
290 to 299	.06
300 to 359	.04
360 to 400	.01

ANALYTICAL METHOD

GENERAL INSTRUCTIONS

Because of the sensitivity of the test, the possibility of errors arising from contamination is great. It is of the greatest importance that all glassware be scrupulously cleaned to remove all organic matter such as oil, grease, detergent residues, etc. Examine all glassware, including stoppers and stopcocks, under ultraviolet light to detect any residual fluorescent contamination. As a precautionary measure it is recommended practice to rinse all glassware with purified isooctane immediately before use. No grease is to be used on stopcocks or joints. Great care to avoid contamination of wax samples in handling and to assure absence of any extraneous material arising from inadequate packaging is essential. Because some of the polynuclear hydrocarbons sought in this test are very susceptible to photo-oxidation, the entire procedure is to be carried out under subdued light.

APPARATUS

Separatory funnels. 250-milliliter, 500-milliliter, 1,000-milliliter, and preferably 2,000-milliliter capacity, equipped with tetrafluoroethylene polymer stopcocks.

Reservoir. 1,000-milliliter capacity, equipped with a 24/40 standard taper male fitting at the bottom and a suitable balljoint at the top.

Chromatographic tube. 1,200 millimeters in length, inside diameter to be 16.5 millimeters ±0.5 millimeter, equipped with a coarse, fritted-glass disc, a tetrafluoroethylene polymer stopcock, and a female 24/40 standard tapered fitting at the opposite end. (Overall length of the column with the female joint is 1,255 millimeters.) The female fitting should be equipped with glass hooks.

Disc. Tetrafluoroethylene polymer 2-inch diameter disc approximately 3/16-inch thick with a hole bored in the center to closely fit the stem of the chromatographic tube.

Heating jackets. Conical, for 500-milliliter and 1,000-milliliter separatory funnels. (Used with variable transformer heat control.)

Suction flask. 250-milliliter or 500-milliliter filter flask.

Condenser. 24/40 joints, fitted with a drying tube, length optional.

Evaporation flasks (optional). A 250-milliliter or 500-milliliter capacity and a 1-liter capacity all-glass flask equipped with standard taper stopper having inlet and outlet tubes to permit passage of nitrogen across the surface of contained liquid to be evaporated.

Vacuum distillation assembly. All glass (for purification of dimethyl sulfoxide) 2-liter distillation flask with heating mantle; Vigreaux vacuum-jacketed condenser (or equivalent) about 45 centimeters in length and distilling head with separable cold finger condenser. Use of tetrafluoroethylene polymer sleeves on the glass joints will prevent freezing. Do not use grease on stopcocks or joints.

Oil bath. Capable of heating to 90 °C.

Spectrophotometric cells. Fused quartz cells, optical pathlength in the range 1.000 centimeter ±0.005 centimeter. With distilled water in the cells, determine any absorbance differences.

Spectrophotometer. Spectral range 250 millimicrons-400 millimicrons with spectral slit width of 0.2 millimicron or less; under instrument operating conditions for these absorbance measurements. The spectrophotometer shall also meet the following performance requirements:

Absorbance repeatability, ±0.01 at 0.4 absorbance.

Absorbance accuracy,[1] ±0.05 at 0.4 absorbance.

Wavelength repeatability, ±0.2 millimicron.

Wavelength accuracy, ±1.0 millimicron.

Recording time, 50 seconds.

Time constant, 0.6 second.

Sensitivity, 30.

Ordinate scale, 90–100 percent transmission through scale.

Abscissa scale, 8X.

Nitrogen cylinder. Water-pumped or equivalent purity nitrogen in cylinder equipped with regulator and valve to control flow at 5 p.s.i.g.

REAGENTS AND MATERIALS

Organic solvents. All solvents used throughout the procedure shall meet the specifications and tests described in this specification. The isooctane and benzene designated in the list following this paragraph shall pass the following test:

To be specified quantity of solvent in a 250-milliliter Erlenmeyer flask, add 1 milliliter of purified *n*-hexadecane and evaporate on the steam bath under a stream of nitrogen (a loose aluminum foil jacket around the flask will speed evaporation). Discontinue evaporation when not over 1 milliliter of residue remains. (To the residue from benzene add a 10-milliliter portion of purified isooctane, reevaporate, and repeat once to insure complete removal of benzene.)

Alternatively, the evaporation time can be reduced by using the optional evaporation flask. In this case the solvent and *n*-hexadecane are placed in the flask on the steam bath, the tube assembly is inserted, and a stream of nitrogen is fed through the inlet tube while the outlet tube is connected to a solvent trap and vacuum line in such a way as to prevent any flow-back of condensate into the flask.

---

[1] As determined by procedure using potassium chromate for reference standard and described in National Bureau of Standards Circular 484, Spectrometry, U.S. Department of Commerce (1949). The accuracy is to be determined by comparison with the standard values at 290, 345, and 400 millimicrons. Circular 484 is incorporated by reference. Copies are available from the Center for Food Safety and Applied Nutrition (HFS-200), Food and Drug Administration, 5100 Paint Branch Pkwy., College Park, MD 20740, or available for inspection at the National Archives and Records Administration (NARA). For information on the availability of this material at NARA, call 202-741-6030, or go to: *http://www.archives.gov/federal_register/code_of_federal_regulations/ibr_locations.html.*

Dissolve the 1 milliliter of hexadecane residue in isooctane and make up to 25 milliliters volume. Determine the absorbance in the 1-centimeter pathlength cells compared to isooctane as reference. The absorbance of the solution of the solvent residue (except for methyl alcohol) shall not exceed 0.01 per centimeter pathlength between 280 mμ and 400 mμ.

Isooctane (2,2,4-trimethylpentane). Use 180 milliliters for the test described in the preceding paragraph. Purify, if necessary, by passage through a column of activated silica gel (Grade 12, Davison Chemical Co., Baltimore, Md., or equivalent) about 90 centimeters in length and 5 centimeters to 8 centimeters in diameter.

Benzene, A.C.S. reagent grade. Use 150 milliliters for the test. Purify, if necessary, by distillation or otherwise.

n-Hexadecane, 99 percent olefin-free. Dilute 1.0 milliliter of *n*-hexadecane to 25 milliliters with isooctane and determine the absorbance in a 1-centimeter cell compared to isooctane as reference point between 280 mμ-400 mμ. The absorbance per centimeter pathlength shall not exceed 0.00 in this range. If necessary, purify by filtering through a column containing 100 grams of aluminum oxide (use same grade as described below) in the lower half and 100 grams of activated silica gel in the upper half keeping the column at 150 °C., for a period of 15 hours or overnight. The first 100 milliliters of eluate are used. Purification can also be accomplished by distillation.

Dimethyl sulfoxide. Pure grade, clear, water-white, m.p. 18° minimum. Dilute 120 milliliters of dimethyl sulfoxide with 240 milliliters of distilled water in a 500-milliliter separatory funnel, mix and allow to cool for 5–10 minutes. Add 40 milliliters of isooctane to the solution and extract by shaking the funnel vigorously for 2 minutes. Draw off the lower aqueous layer into a second 500-milliliter separatory funnel and repeat the extraction with 40 milliliters of isooctane. Draw off and discard the aqueous layer. Wash each of the 40-milliliter extractives three times with 50-milliliter portions of distilled water. Shaking time for each wash is 1 minute. Discard the aqueous layers. Filter the first extractive through anhydrous sodium sulfate prewashed with isooctane (see *Sodium sulfate* under "Reagents and materials" for preparation of filter), into a 250-milliliter Erlenmeyer flask, or optionally into the evaporating flask. Wash the first separatory funnel with the second 40-milliliter isooctane extractive, and pass through the sodium sulfate into the flask. Then wash the second and first separatory funnels successively with a 10-milliliter portion of isooctane, and pass the solvent through the sodium sulfate into the flask. Add 1 milliliter of *n*-hexadecane and evaporate the isooctane on the steam bath under nitrogen. Discontinue evaporation when not over 1 milliliter of residue remains. To the residue, add a 10-milliliter portion of isooctane and reevaporate to 1 milliliter of hexadecane. Again, add 10 milliliters of isooctane to the residue and evaporate to 1 milliliter of hexadecane to insure complete removal of all volatile materials. Dissolve the 1 milliliter of hexadecane in isooctane and make to 25-milliliter volume. Determine the absorbance in 1-centimeter pathlength cells compared to isooctane as reference. The absorbance of the solution should not exceed 0.02 per centimeter pathlength in the 280 mμ-400 mμ range. (NOTE: Difficulty in meeting this absorbance specification may be due to organic impurities in the distilled water. Repetition of the test omitting the dimethyl sulfoxide will disclose their presence. If necessary to meet the specification, purify the water by redistillation, passage through an ion-exchange resin, or otherwise.)

Purify, if necessary, by the following procedure: To 1,500 milliliters of dimethyl sulfoxide in a 2-liter glass-stoppered flask, add 6.0 milliliters of phosphoric acid and 50 grams of Norit A (decolorizing carbon, alkaline) or equivalent. Stopper the flask, and with the use of a magnetic stirrer (tetrafluoroethylene polymer coated bar) stir the solvent for 15 minutes. Filter the dimethyl sulfoxide through four thicknesses of fluted paper (18.5 centimeters, Schleicher & Schuell, No. 597, or equivalent). If the initial filtrate contains carbon fines, refilter through the same filter until a clear filtrate is obtained. Protect the sulfoxide from air and moisture during this operation by covering the solvent in the funnel and collection flask with a layer of isooctane. Transfer the filtrate to a 2-liter separatory funnel and draw off the dimethyl sulfoxide into the 2-liter distillation flask of the vacuum distillation assembly and distill at approximately 3-millimeter Hg pressure or less. Discard the first 200-milliliter fraction of the distillate and replace the distillate collection flask with a clean one. Continue the distillation until approximately 1 liter of the sulfoxide has been collected.

At completion of the distillation, the reagent should be stored in glass-stoppered bottles since it is very hygroscopic and will react with some metal containers in the presence of air.

Phosphoric acid. 85 percent A.C.S. reagent grade.

Aluminum oxide (80–200 mesh Woelm neutral activity grade 1 [Brockmann], Alupharm Chemicals, New Orleans, La., or equivalent). Pipette 1 milliliter of distilled water into a dry 250-milliliter Erlenmeyer flask equipped with a ground-glass stopper. Stopper the flask and rotate it in such a manner as to completely wet out the inside surfaces. When this has been done add 180 grams of the aluminum oxide and shake until no lumps or wet spots remain. Allow to stand at room temperature for a period of 2 hours. At the end of this time the water should be evenly distributed throughout the aluminum oxide powder, and it should have the same free flowing properties as the original material (flow velocity with water 0.2 milliliter per minute). At this point the aluminum oxide has an activity of 1 as expressed in Brockmann degrees, and the amount of added water is 0.5 percent by volume. This product is used in toto and as is, without further screening.

Sodium sulfate, anhydrous, A.C.S. reagent grade, preferably in granular form. For each bottle of sodium sulfate reagent used, establish as follows the necessary sodium sulfate prewash to provide such filters required in the method: Place approximately 35 grams of anhydrous sodium sulfate in a 30-milliliter coarse, fritted-glass funnel or in a 65-millimeter filter funnel with glass wool plug; wash with successive 15-milliliter portions of the indicated solvent until a 15-milliliter portion of the wash shows 0.00 absorbance per centimeter pathlength between 280 mμ and 400 mμ when tested as prescribed under "Organic solvents." Usually three portions of wash solvent are sufficient.

PROCEDURE

Before proceeding with analysis of a sample, determine the absorbance in a 1-centimeter path cell between 250 mμ and 400 mμ for the reagent blank by carrying out the procedure, without a wax sample, at room temperature, recording the spectrum after the complete procedure as prescribed. The absorbance per centimeter pathlength following the complete procedure should not exceed 0.04 in the wavelength range from 280 mμ to 299 mμ, inclusive, nor 0.02 in the wavelength range from 300 mμ to 400 mμ. If in either spectrum the characteristic benzene peaks in the 250 mμ-260 mμ region are present, remove the benzene by the procedure under "Organic solvents" and record absorbance again. Place 300 milliliters of dimethyl sulfoxide in a 1-liter separatory funnel and add 75 milliliters of phosphoric acid. Mix the contents of the funnel and allow to stand for 10 minutes. (The reaction between the sulfoxide and the acid is exothermic. Release pressure after mixing, then keep funnel stoppered.) Add 150 milliliters of isooctane and shake to preequilibrate the solvents. Draw off the individual layers and store in glass-stoppered flasks.

In a 1-liter separatory funnel place a representative 25-gram sample of wax, add 50 milliliters of isooctane, heat gently, stir until the wax is in solution; add 100 milliliters of preequilibrated sulfoxide-phosphoric acid mixture and shake, making sure it remains in solution. If the wax comes out of solution during these operations, let the stoppered funnel remain in the jacket until the wax redissolves. (Remove stopper from the funnel at intervals to release pressure.) When the wax is in solution, remove the funnel from the jacket and shake it vigorously for 2 minutes. Set up three 250-milliliter separatory funnels with each containing 30 milliliters of preequilibrated isooctane. After separation of the liquid phases, allow to cool until the main portion of the wax-isooctane solution begins to show a precipitate. Gently swirl the funnel when precipitation first occurs on the inside surface of the funnel to accelerate this process. Carefully draw off the lower layer, filter it slowly through a thin layer of glass wool fitted loosely in a filter funnel into the first 250-milliliter separatory funnel, and wash in tandem with the 30-milliliter portions of isooctane contained in the 250-milliliter separatory funnels. Shaking time for each wash is 1 minute. Repeat the extraction operation with two additional portions of the sulfoxide-acid mixture, replacing the funnel in the jacket after each extraction to keep the wax in solution and washing each extractive in tandem through the same three portions of isooctane.

Collect the successive extractives (300 milliliters total) in a separatory funnel (preferably 2-liter), containing 480 milliliters of distilled water, mix, and allow to cool for a few minutes after the last extractive has been added. Add 80 milliliters of isooctane to the solution and extract by shaking the funnel vigorously for 2 minutes. Draw off the lower aqueous layer into a second separatory funnel (preferably 2-liter) and repeat the extraction with 80 milliliters of isooctane. Draw off and discard the aqueous layer. Wash each of the 80-milliliter extractives three times with 100-milliliter portions of distilled water. Shaking time for each wash is 1 minute. Discard the aqueous layers. Filter the first extractive through anhydrous sodium sulfate prewashed with isooctane (see *Sodium sulfate* under "Reagents and Materials" for preparation of filter) into a 250-milliliter Erlenmeyer flask (or optionally into the evaporation flask). Wash the first separatory funnel with the second 80-milliliter isooctane extractive and pass through the sodium sulfate. Then wash the second and first separatory funnels successively with a 20-milliliter portion of isooctane and pass the solvent through the sodium sulfate into the flask. Add 1 milliliter of *n*-hexadecane and evaporate the isooctane using an aspirator vacuum under nitrogen and in an oil bath temperature of approximately 90 °C. Discontinue evaporation when not over 1 milliliter of residue remains. To the residue, add a 10-milliliter portion of isooctane, reevaporate to 1 milliliter of hexadecane, and repeat this operation once.

Reserve the residue for column chromatography on the aluminum oxide. Fit the tetrafluoroethylene polymer disc on the upper part of the stem of the chromatographic tube, then place the tube with the disc on the suction flask and apply the vacuum (approximately 135 millimeters Hg pressure). Weigh out 180 grams of the aluminum oxide and pour the adsorbent mixture into the chromatographic tube in approximately 30-centimeter layers. After the addition of each layer, level off the top of the adsorbent with a flat glass rod or metal plunger by pressing down firmly until the adsorbent is well packed. Loosen the topmost few millimeters of each adsorbent layer with the end of a metal rod before the addition of the next layer. Continue packing in this manner until all the 180 grams of the adsorbent is added to the tube. Level off the top of the adsorbent by pressing down firmly with a flat glass rod or metal plunger to make the depth of the adsorbent bed approximately 80 centimeters in depth. Turn off the vacuum and remove the suction flask. Dissolve the hexadecane residue in 10 milliliters of warm benzene and decant the solution onto the column and allow the liquid level to recede to barely above the adsorbent level. Rapidly complete the transfer similarly with two 10-milliliter portions of benzene swirling the flask repeatedly each time to assure adequate washing of the residue. Fix the 1,000-milliliter reservoir onto the top of the chromatographic column. Just before the final 10-milliliter wash reaches the top of the adsorbent, add 670 milliliters of benzene to the reservoir and continue the percolation at the 2–3 milliliter per minute rate until a total of 670 milliliters of benzene has been utilized. Collect the eluate in a clean 1-liter Erlenmeyer flask (or optionally into a 1-liter evaporation flask). Allow the column to drain until most of the solvent mixture is removed. Add 1 milliliter of *n*-hexadecane and completely remove the benzene by evaporation under nitrogen, using the special procedure to eliminate benzene as previously described under "Organic Solvents." Quantitatively transfer the residue with isooctane to a 25-milliliter volumetric flask and adjust to volume. Determine the absorbance of the solution in the 1-centimeter pathlength cells compared to isooctane as reference between 250 mμ-400 mμ. Correct for any absorbance derived from the reagents as determined by carrying out the procedure without a wax sample. If either spectrum shows the characteristic benzene peaks in the 250 mμ-260 mμ region, evaporate the solution to remove benzene by the procedure under "Organic Solvents." Dissolve the residue, transfer quantitatively, and adjust to volume in isooctane in a 25-milliliter volumetric flask. Record the absorbance again. If the corrected absorbance does not exceed the limits prescribed in paragraph (a) of this section, the wax meets the ultraviolet absorbance specifications.

(b) The polyhydric alcohol esters identified in this paragraph may be used as release agents in resinous and polymeric coatings for polyolefin films complying with §175.320 of this chapter. Such esters meet the following specifications and are produced by partial esterification of oxidatively refined (Gersthofen process) montan wax acids with equimolar proportions of ethylene glycol and 1,3-butanediol:

(1) Dropping point 77°–82 °C, as determined by ASTM method D566–76 (Reapproved 1982), "Standard Test Method for Dropping Point of Lubricating Grease," which is incorporated by reference. The availability of this incorporation by reference is given in paragraph (a)(1) of this section.

(2) Acid value 25–35, as determined by ASTM method D1386–78 ("Standard Test Method for Acid Number (Empirical) of Synthetic and Natural Waxes" (Revised 1978), which is incorporated by reference; copies are available from American Society for Testing and Materials (ASTM), 100 Barr Harbor Dr., West Conshohocken, Philadelphia, PA 19428-2959, or available for inspection at the National Archives and Records Administration (NARA). For information on the availability of this material at NARA, call 202–741–6030, or go to: *http://www.archives.gov/federal_register/code_of_federal_regulations/ibr_locations.html.*) using as solvent xylene-ethyl alcohol in a 2:1 ratio instead of toluene-ethyl alcohol in a 1:2 ratio.

(3) Saponification value 135–150, as determined by ASTM method D1387–78 ("Standard Test Method for Saponification Number (Empirical) of Synthetic and Natural Waxes" (Revised 1978), which is incorporated by reference; copies are available from American Society for Testing and Materials (ASTM), 100 Barr Harbor Dr., West Conshohocken, Philadelphia, PA 19428-2959, or available for inspection at the National Archives and Records Administration (NARA). For information on the availability of this material at NARA, call 202–741–6030, or go to: *http://www.archives.gov/federal_register/code_of_federal_regulations/ibr_locations.html.*) using xylene-ethyl alcohol in a 2:1 ratio instead of ethyl alcohol in preparation of potassium hydroxide solution.

(4) Ultraviolet absorbance limits specified in paragraph (a)(4) of this section, as determined by the analytical method described therein.

(c) The polyhydric alcohol esters of oxidatively refined (Gersthofen process) montan wax acids, identified in paragraph (a) or (b) of this section, may also be used as a component of an aqueous dispersion of vinylidene chloride copolymers, subject to the conditions described in paragraphs (c) (1) and (2) of this section.

(1) The aqueous dispersion of the additive contains not more that 18 percent polyhydric alcohol esters of oxidatively refined (Gersthofen process) montan wax acids, not more than 2 percent poly(oxyethylene) (minimum 20 moles of ethylene oxide) oleyl ether (CAS Reg. No. 9004–98–2), and not more than 1 percent poly(oxyethylene) (minimum 3 moles ethylene oxide) cetyl alcohols (CAS Reg. No. 9004–95–9).

(2) The aqueous dispersion described in paragraph (c)(1) of this section is used as an additive to aqueous dispersions of vinylidene chloride copolymers, regulated in §§ 175.300, 175.320, 175.360, 176.170, 176,180, and 177.1630 of this chapter, at levels not to exceed 1.5 percent (solids basis) in the finished coating.

(d) The polyhydric alcohol esters identified in this paragraph may be used as lubricants in the fabrication of vinyl chloride plastic food contact articles prepared from vinyl chloride polymers. Such esters meet the following specifications and are produced by partial esterification of oxidatively refined (Gersthofen process) montan wax acids with glycerol followed by neutralization:

(1) Dropping point 79 to 85 °C, as determined by the American Society for Testing and Materials (ASTM), Method D–566–76 (Reapproved 1982), "Standard Test Method for Dropping Point of Lubricating Grease," which is incorporated by reference in accordance with 5 U.S.C. 552(a). The availability of this incorporation by reference is given in paragraph (a)(1) of this section.

(2) Acid value 20–30, as determined by ASTM Method D–1386–78 "Standard Test Method for Acid Number (Empirical) of Synthetic and Natural Waxes" (Revised 1978) (which is incorporated by reference in accordance with 5 U.S.C. 552(a); the availability of this incorporation by reference is given in paragraph (a)(2) of this section), using as a solvent xylene-ethyl alcohol in a 2:1 ratio instead of toluene-ethyl alcohol in a 2:1 ratio.

(3) Saponification value 130–160, as determined by ASTM Method D–1387–78 "Standard Test Method for Saponification Number (Empirical) of Synthetic and Natural Waxes" (Revised 1978), (which is incorporated by reference in accordance with 5 U.S.C. 552(a); the availability of this incorporation by reference is given in paragraph (a)(3) of this section), using xylene-ethyl alcohol in a 2:1 ratio instead of ethyl alcohol in the preparation of potassium hydroxide solution.

(4) Ultraviolet absorbance limits specified in paragraph (a)(4) of this section, as determined by the analytical method described therein.

[42 FR 14609, Mar. 15, 1977, as amended at 47 FR 11848, Mar. 19, 1982; 49 FR 10113, Mar. 19, 1984; 51 FR 33895, Sept. 24, 1986; 54 FR 24898, June 12, 1989; 55 FR 28020, July 9, 1990; 58 FR 17512, Apr. 5, 1993; 69 FR 24512, May 4, 2004]

§ 178.3780 Polyhydric alcohol esters of long chain monobasic acids.

Polyhydric alcohol esters of long chain monobasic acids identified in this section may be safely used as lubricants in the fabrication of polyvinyl chloride and/or polyvinyl chloride copolymer articles complying with § 177.1980 of this chapter that contact food of Types I, II, IV-B, VI-B, VII-B, and VIII identified in table 1 in § 176.170(c) of this chapter under conditions of use E, F, and G described in table 2 in § 176.170(c) of this chapter, subject to the provisions of this section.

(a) *Identity*. For the purpose of this section, polyhydric alcohol esters of long chain monobasic acids consist of polyhydric alcohol esters having number average molecular weights in the range of 1,050 to 1,700. The esters are produced by the reaction of either ethylene glycol or glycerol with long chain monobasic acids containing from 9 to 49 carbon atoms obtained by the ozonization of long chain *alpha*-olefins, the unreacted carboxylic acids in the formation of the glycerol esters being neutralized with calcium hydroxide to produce a composition having up to 2 percent by weight calcium. The *alpha*-olefins, obtained from the polymerization of ethylene, have 20 to 50 carbon atoms and contain a minimum of 75 percent by weight straight chain *alpha*-olefins and not more than 25 percent vinylidene compounds.

(b) *Specifications.* The polyhydric alcohol esters have the following specifications:

(1) Melting point of 60–80 °C for the ethylene glycol ester and 90–105 °C for the glycerol ester as determined by the Fisher Johns method as described in "Semimicro Qualitative Organic Analysis—The Systematic Identification of Organic Compounds," by Cheronis and Entrikin, 2d Ed., Interscience Publishers, NY, which is incorporated by reference. Copies are available from the Center for Food Safety and Applied Nutrition (HFS–200), Food and Drug Administration, 5100 Paint Branch Pkwy., College Park, MD 20740, or available for inspection at the National Archives and Records Administration (NARA). For information on the availability of this material at NARA, call 202–741–6030, or go to: *http://www.archives.gov/federal_register/code_of_federal_regulations/ibr_locations.html.*

(2) Acid value 15–25 for each ester as determined by the A.O.C.S. method Trla-64T "Titer Test," which is incorporated by reference. Copies are available from American Association of Oil Chemists, 36 East Wacker Drive, Chicago, IL 60601, or available for inspection at the National Archives and Records Administration (NARA). For information on the availability of this material at NARA, call 202–741–6030, or go to: *http://www.archives.gov/federal_register/code_of_federal_regulations/ibr_locations.html.* The method is modified to use as the acid solvent a 1:1 volume mixture of anhydrous isopropyl alcohol and toluene. The solution is titrated with 0.1*N* methanolic sodium hydroxide.

(3) Saponification value 120–160 for the ethylene glycol ester and 90–130 for the glycerol ester as determined the A.O.C.S. method Trla-64T "Saponification Value," which is incorporated by reference. Copies are available from American Association of Oil Chemists, 36 East Wacker Drive, Chicago, IL 60601, or available for inspection at the National Archives and Records Administration (NARA). For information on the availability of this material at NARA, call 202–741–6030, or go to: *http://www.archives.gov/federal_register/code_of_federal_regulations/ibr_locations.html.*

(4) Ultraviolet absorbance as specified in §178.3770(a)(4) of this chapter when tested by the analytical method described therein.

[42 FR 14609, Mar. 15, 1977, as amended at 47 FR 11849, Mar. 19, 1982; 54 FR 24899, June 12, 1989; 61 FR 14481, Apr. 2, 1996]

§ 178.3790 Polymer modifiers in semirigid and rigid vinyl chloride plastics.

The polymers identified in paragraph (a) of this section may be safely admixed, alone or in mixture with other permitted polymers, as modifiers in semirigid and rigid vinyl chloride plastic food-contact articles prepared from vinyl chloride homopolymers and/or from vinyl chloride copolymers complying with §177.1950, §177.1970, and/or §177.1980 of this chapter, in accordance with the following prescribed conditions:

(a) For the purpose of this section, the polymer modifiers are identified as follows:

(1) Acrylic polymers identified in this subparagraph provided that such polymers contain at least 50 weight-percent of polymer units derived from one or more of the monomers listed in paragraph (a)(1)(i) of this section.

(i) Homopolymers and copolymers of the following monomers:

n-Butyl acrylate.
n-Butyl methacrylate.
Ethyl acrylate.
Methyl methacrylate.

(ii) Copolymers produced by copolymerizing one or more of the monomers listed in paragraph (a)(1)(i) of this section with one or more of the following monomers:

Acrylonitrile.
Butadiene.
a-Methylstyrene.
Styrene.
Vinylidene chloride.

(iii) Polymers identified in paragraphs (a)(1) (i) and (ii) of this section containing no more than 5 weight-percent of total polymer units derived by copolymerization with one or more of the following monomers:

Acrylic acid.
1,3-Butylene glycol dimethacrylate.
Divinylbenzene.
Methacrylic acid.

(iv) Mixtures of polymers identified in paragraph (a)(1) (i), (ii), and (iii) of this section; provided that no chemical reactions, other than addition reactions, occur when they are mixed.

(2) Polymers identified in paragraph (a)(1) of this section combined during their polymerization with butadiene-styrene copolymers; provided that no chemical reactions, other than addition reactions, occur when they are combined. Such combined polymers may contain 50 weight-percent or more of total polymer units derived from the butadiene-styrene copolymers.

(b) The polymer content of the finished plastic food-contact article consists of:

(1) Not less than 80 weight-percent of polymer units derived from the vinyl chloride polymers identified in the introduction to this section and not more than 5 weight-percent of polymer units derived from polymers identified in paragraph (a)(1) of this section and may optionally contain up to 15 weight-percent of polymer units derived from butadiene-styrene copolymers; or

(2) Not less than 50 weight-percent of polymer units derived from the vinyl chloride polymers identified in the introduction to this section, not more than 50 weight-percent of polymer units derived from homopolymers and/or copolymers of ethyl acrylate and methyl methacrylate, and not more than 30 weight-percent of polymer units derived from copolymers of methyl methacrylate, α-methylstyrene and acrylonitrile and may optionally contain up to 15 weight-percent of polymer units derived from butadiene-styrene copolymers.

(c) No chemical reactions, other than addition reactions, occur among the vinyl chloride polymers and the modifying polymers present in the polymer mixture used in the manufacture of the finished plastic food-contact article.

(d) The finished plastic food-contact article, when extracted with the solvent or solvents characterizing the type of food and under the conditions of time and temperature characterizing the conditions of its intended use as determined from tables 1 and 2 of § 176.170(c) of this chapter, yields extractives not to exceed the limits prescribed in § 177.1010 (b) (1), (2), (3), and (4) of this chapter when tested by the methods prescribed in § 177.1010 (c) of this chapter.

(e) Acrylonitrile copolymers identified in this section shall comply with the provisions of § 180.22 of this chapter.

§ 178.3800 Preservatives for wood.

Preservatives may be safely used on wooden articles that are used or intended for use in packaging, transporting, or holding raw agricultural products subject to the provisions of this section:

(a) The preservatives are prepared from substances identified in paragraph (b) of this section and applied in amounts not to exceed those necessary to accomplish the technical effect of protecting the wood from decay, mildew, and water absorption.

(b) The substances permitted are as follows:

List of substances	Limitations
Copper-8-quinolinolate.	
Mineral spirits.	
Paraffin wax	Used singly or in combination so as to constitute not less than 50% of the solids.
Petroleum hydrocarbon resin, produced by the homo- and copolymerization of dienes and olefins of the aliphatic, alicyclic, and monobenzenoid arylalkene type from distillates of cracked petroleum stocks.	Do.
Pentachlorophenol and its sodium salt	Not to exceed 50 p.p.m. in the treated wood, calculated as pentachlorophenol.

List of substances	Limitations
Rosins and rosin derivatives	As provided in § 178.3870.
Zinc salt of sulfonated petroleum.	

§ 178.3850 Reinforced wax.

Reinforced wax may be safely used as an article or component of articles intended for use in producing, manufacturing, packing, processing, transporting, or holding food subject to the provisions of this section.

(a) Reinforced wax consists of petroleum wax to which have been added certain optional substances required in its production, or added to impart desired physical or technical properties.

(b) The quantity of any optional adjuvant substance employed in the production of or added to reinforced wax does not exceed the amount reasonably required to accomplish the intended physical or technical effect or any limitation provided in this section.

(c) Any substance employed in the production of reinforced wax, including any optional substance, that is the subject of a regulation in parts 174, 175, 176, 177, 178 and § 179.45 of this chapter, conforms with any specification in such regulation.

(d) The substances and optional adjuvant substances employed in the production of or added to reinforced wax include:

(1) Substances generally recognized as safe in food.

(2) Substances subject to prior sanction for use in reinforced wax and used in accordance with such sanction or approval.

(3) Substances identified in this subparagraph and subject to any limitations provided therein:

List of substances	Limitations
Copolymer of isobutylene modified with isoprene.	
Petroleum wax, Type I and Type II.	
Polyethylene.	
Rosins and rosin derivatives as provided in § 178.3870.	
Synthetic wax polymer as described in § 176.170(a)(5) of this chapter.	Not to exceed 5 percent by weight of the petroleum wax.

(e) Reinforced wax conforming with the specifications in this paragraph is used as provided in paragraph (e)(2) of this section.

(1) The chloroform-soluble portion of the water extract obtained by exposing reinforced wax to demineralized water at 70 °F for 48 hours shall not exceed 0.5 milligram per square inch of food-contact surface.

(2) It is used as a packaging material or component of packaging materials for cheese and cheese products.

[42 FR 14609, Mar. 15, 1977, as amended at 47 FR 1288, Jan. 12, 1982]

§ 178.3860 Release agents.

Substances listed in paragraph (b) of this section may be safely used as release agents in petroleum wax complying with § 178.3710 and in polymeric resins that contact food, subject to the provisions of this section.

(a) The quantity used shall not exceed the amount reasonably required to accomplish the intended technical effect or any limitations prescribed in this section.

(b) Release agents:

List of substances	Limitations
Erucamide (erucylamide).	
Formaldehyde, polymer with 1-naphthalenol (CAS Reg. No. 25359–91–5).	For use only as an antiscaling or release agent, applied on the internal parts of reactors employed in the production of polyvinyl chloride and acrylic copolymers, provided that the residual levels of the additive in the ploymer do not exceed 4 parts per million.
N,N-Dioleoylethylenediamine	For use only in polyvinyl chloride films in amounts such that the concentration of the substance in these films in the form in which the films contact food shall not exceed 0.055 milligram of the substance per square inch of film.
Oleyl palmitamide.	
Polybutene, hydrogenated; complying with the identity prescribed under § 178.3740(b).	For use only subject to the limitations prescribed for hydrogenated polybutene under § 178.3740(b).

List of substances	Limitations
Poly(vinyl acetate/vinyl *N*-octadecylcarbamate) (CAS Reg. No. 70892–21–6) produced by the reaction between stoichiometrically equivalent amounts of octadecyl isocyanate and vinyl alcohol/vinyl acetate copolymer; minimum average molecular weight is 500,000.	For use only in application to the backing of pressuresensitive adhesive tapes at levels not to exceed 0.2 milligram per square centimeter (1.29 milligrams per square inch) of backing.
Rice bran wax	For use only in plastics intended for contact with dry foods identified as Type VIII in table 1 of § 176.170(c) of this chapter, at levels not in excess of 1.0 percent by weight of the polymer.
Saturated fatty acid amides manufactured from fatty acids derived from animal, marine, or vegetable fats and oils.	
Stearyl erucamide.	

[42 FR 14609, Mar. 15, 1977, as amended at 44 FR 69649, Dec. 4, 1979; 46 FR 51902, Oct. 23, 1981; 61 FR 25396, May 21, 1996; 61 FR 42381, Aug. 15, 1996]

§ 178.3870 Rosins and rosin derivatives.

The rosins and rosin derivatives identified in paragraph (a) of this section may safely be used in the manufacture of articles or components of articles intended for use in producing, manufacturing, packing, processing, preparing, treating, packaging, transporting, or holding food, subject to the provisions of this section.

(a) The rosins and rosin derivatives are identified as follows:

(1) Rosins:

(i) Gum rosin, refined to color grade of K or paler.

(ii) Wood rosin, refined to color grade of K or paler.

(iii) Tall oil rosin, refined to color grade of K or paler.

(iv) Dark tall oil rosin, a fraction resulting from the refining of tall oil rosin produced by multicolumnar distillation of crude tall oil to effect removal of fatty acids and pitch components and having a saponification number of from 110–135 and 32 percent–44 percent rosin acids.

(v) Dark wood rosin, all or part of the residue after the volatile terpene oils are distilled from the oleoresin extracted from pine wood.

(2) Modified rosins manufactured from rosins identified in paragraph (a)(1) of this section:

(i) Partially hydrogenated rosin, catalytically hydrogenated to a maximum refractive index of 1.5012 at 100 °C, and a color of WG or paler.

(ii) Fully hydrogenated rosin, catalytically hydrogenated to a maximum dehydroabietic acid content of 2 percent, a minimum drop-softening point of 79 °C, and a color of X or paler.

(iii) Partially dimerized rosin, dimerized by sulfuric acid catalyst to a drop-softening point of 95°–105 °C and a color of WG or paler.

(iv) Fully dimerized rosin, dimerized by sulfuric acid catalyst, and from which sufficient nondimerized rosin has been removed by distillation to achieve a minimum drop-softening point of 143 °C, and a color of H or paler.

(v) Disproportionated rosin, catalytically disproportionated to a minimum dehydroabietic acid content of 35 percent, a maximum abietic acid content of 1 percent, a maximum content of substituted phenanthrenes (as retene) of 0.25 percent, and a color of WG or paler.

(3) Rosin esters manufactured from rosins and modified rosins identified in paragraphs (a)(1) and (2) of this section:

(i) Glycerol ester of wood rosin purified by steam stripping to have an acid number of 3 to 9, a drop-softening point of 88°–96 °C, and a color of N or paler.

(ii) Glycerol ester of partially hydrogenated wood rosin, having an acid number of 3 to 10, a drop-softening point of 79°–88 °C, and a color of N or paler.

(iii) Glycerol ester of partially dimerized rosin, having an acid number of 3 to 8, a drop-softening point of 109°–119 °C, and a color of M or paler.

(iv) Glycerol ester of fully dimerized rosin, having an acid number of 5 to 16, a drop-softening point of 165°–175 °C, and a color of H or paler.

(v) Glycerol ester of maleic anhydride-modified wood rosin, having an acid number of 30 to 40, a drop-softening point of 138°–146 °C, a color of M or paler, and a saponification number less than 280.

(vi) Methyl ester of rosin, partially hydrogenated, purified by steam stripping to have an acid number of 4 to 8, a refractive index of 1.5170 to 1.5205 at 20 °C, and a viscosity of 23 to 66 poises at 25 °C.

(vii) Pentaerythritol ester of wood rosin, having an acid number of 6 to 16, a drop-softening point of 109°–116 °C, and a color of M or paler.

(viii) Pentaerythritol ester of partially hydrogenated wood rosin, having an acid number of 7 to 18, a drop-softening point of 102°–110 °C, and a color of K or paler.

(ix) Pentaerythritol ester of maleic anhydride-modified wood rosin, having an acid number of 8 to 16, a drop-softening point of 154°–162 °C, a color of M or paler, and having a saponification number less than 280.

(x) Pentaerythritol ester of maleic anhydride-modified wood rosin, having an acid number of 9 to 16, a drop-softening point of 130°–140 °C, a color of N or paler, and having a saponification number less than 280.

(xi) Pentaerythritol ester of maleic anhydride-modified wood rosin, having an acid number of 134 to 145, a drop-softening point of 127°–137 °C, a color of M or paler, and having a saponification number less than 280.

(xii) Pentaerythritol ester of maleic anhydride-modified wood rosin, having an acid number of 30 to 40, a drop-softening point of 131°–137 °C, a color of N or paler, and having a saponification number less than 280.

(xiii) Pentaerythritol ester of maleic anhydride-modified wood rosin, further modified by reaction with 4,4′-isopropyl-idenediphenol-formaldehyde condensate, having an acid number of 10 to 22, a drop-softening point of 162°–172 °C, a color of K or paler, a saponification number less than 280, and a maximum ultraviolet absorbance of 0.14 at 296 mμ (using a 1-centimeter cell and 200 milligrams of the rosin ester per liter of solvent consisting of ethyl alcohol made alkaline by addition of 0.1 percent of potassium hydroxide).

(xiv) Mixed methyl and pentaerythritol ester of maleic anhydride-modified wood rosin, having an acid number of 73 to 83, a drop-softening point of 113°–123 °C, a color of M or paler, and a saponification number less than 280.

(xv) Triethylene glycol ester of partially hydrogenated wood rosin, having an acid number of 2 to 10, a color of K or paler, and a viscosity of 350 to 425 seconds Saybolt at 100 °C.

(xvi) Glycerol ester of maleic anhydride-modified wood rosin, having an acid number of 17 to 23, a drop-softening point of 136°–140 °C, a color of M or paler, and a saponification number less than 280. For use only in cellophane complying with §177.1200 of this chapter.

(xvii) Citric acid-modified glycerol ester of rosin, having an acid number less than 20, a drop-softening point of 105°–115 °C, and a color of K or paler. For use only as a blending agent in coatings for cellophane complying with §177.1200 of this chapter.

(xviii) Glycerol ester of tall oil rosin, purified by steam stripping to have an acid number of 5–12, a softening point of 80°–88 °C, and a color of N or paler.

(xix) Glycerol ester of maleic anhydride-modified tall oil rosin, having an acid number of 30 to 40, a drop-softening point of 141°–146 °C, a color of N or paler, and a saponification number less than 280.

(xx) Glycerol ester of disproportionated tall oil rosin, having an acid number of 5 to 10, a drop-softening point of 84°–93 °C, a color of WG or paler, and a saponification number less than 180.

(4) Rosin salts and sizes—Ammonium, calcium, potassium, sodium, or zinc salts of rosin manufactured by the partial or complete saponification of any one of the rosins or modified rosins identified in paragraph (a)(1) and (2) of this section, or blends thereof, and with or without modification by reaction with one or more of the following:

(i) Formaldehyde.

(ii) Fumaric acid.

(iii) Maleic anhydride.

(iv) Saligenin.

(b) The quantity used shall not exceed the amount reasonably required to accomplish the intended technical effect.

(c) The use in any substance or article that is the subject of a regulation in parts 174, 175, 176, 177, 178 and §179.45 of this chapter shall conform with any specifications and limitations prescribed by such regulation for the finished form of the substance or article.

(d) The provisions of this section are not applicable to rosins and rosin derivatives identified in §175.300(b)(3)(v) of this chapter and used in resinous and polymeric coatings complying with §175.300 of this chapter.

(e) The provisions of this section are not applicable to rosins and rosin derivatives identified in §175.105(c)(5) of this chapter and used in defoaming agents complying with §176.210 of this chapter, food-packaging adhesives complying with §175.105 of this chapter, and rubber articles complying with §177.2600 of this chapter.

(f) The analytical methods for determining whether rosins and rosin derivatives conform to the specifications prescribed in paragraph (a) of this section are as follows:

(1) Color: Color shall be as determined by ASTM method D509–70 (Reapproved 1981), "Standard Methods of Sampling and Grading Rosin," which is incorporated by reference. Copies may be obtained from the American Society for Testing Materials, 100 Barr Harbor Dr., West Conshohocken, Philadelphia, PA 19428-2959, or may be examined at the National Archives and Records Administration (NARA). For information on the availability of this material at NARA, call 202–741–6030, or go to: *http://www.archives.gov/federal_register/code_of_federal_regulations/ibr_locations.html.*

(2) Refractive index: Refractive index shall be as determined by ASTM method D1747–62 (Reapproved 1978), "Standard Test Method for Refractive Index of Viscous Materials," which is incorporated by reference. The availability of this incorporation by reference is given in paragraph (f)(1) of this section.

(3) Acid number: Acid number shall be as determined by ASTM method D465–82, "Standard Test Methods for Acid Number of Rosin," which is incorporated by reference. The availability of this incorporation by reference is given in paragraph (f)(1) of this section.

(4) Viscosity: Viscosity in poises shall be as determined by ASTM method D1824–66 (Reapproved 1980), "Standard Test Method for Apparent Viscosity of Plastisols and Organosols at Low Shear Rates by Brookfield Viscometer," and in Saybolt seconds by ASTM method D88–81, "Standard Test Method for Saybolt Viscosity," which are incorporated by reference. The availability of this incorporation by reference is given in paragraph (f)(1) of this section.

(5) Softening point: Softening point shall be as determined by ASTM method E28–67, "Standard Test Method for Softening Point by Ring and Ball Apparatus" (Reapproved 1977), which is incorporated by reference. Copies are available from American Society for Testing and Materials (ASTM), 100 Barr Harbor Dr., West Conshohocken, Philadelphia, PA 19428-2959, or available for inspection at the National Archives and Records Administration (NARA). For information on the availability of this material at NARA, call 202–741–6030, or go to: *http://www.archives.gov/federal_register/code_of_federal_regulations/ibr_locations.html.*

(6) Analytical methods for determining drop-softening point, saponification number, and any other specifications not listed under paragraphs (f)(1) through (5) of this section, titled: (i) "Determination of Abeitic Acid and Dehydroabietic Acid in Rosins"; (ii) "Determination of Softening Point of Solid Resins"; (iii) "Determination of Saponification Number of Rosin Esters," and (iv) "Determination of Phenolic Modification of Rosin Derivatives," which are incorporated by reference. Copies are available from the Center for Food Safety and Applied Nutrition (HFS–200), Food and Drug Administration, 5100 Paint Branch Pkwy., College Park, MD 20740, or available for inspection at the National Archives and Records Administration (NARA). For information on the availability of this material at NARA, call 202–741–6030, or go to: *http://www.archives.gov/federal_register/*

code_of_federal_regulations/ ibr_locations.html.

[42 FR 14609, Mar. 15, 1977, as amended at 47 FR 11849, Mar. 19, 1982; 49 FR 10113, Mar. 19, 1984; 54 FR 24899, June 12, 1989]

§ 178.3900 Sodium pentachlorophenate.

Sodium pentachlorophenate may be safely used as a preservative for ammonium alginate employed as a processing aid in the manufacture of polyvinyl chloride emulsion polymers intended for use as articles or components of articles that contact food at temperatures not to exceed room temperature. The quantity of sodium pentachlorophenate used shall not exceed 0.5 percent by weight of ammonium alginate solids.

§ 178.3910 Surface lubricants used in the manufacture of metallic articles.

The substances listed in this section may be safely used in surface lubricants employed in the manufacture of metallic articles that contact food, subject to the provisions of this section.

(a) The following substances may be used in surface lubricants used in the rolling of metallic foil or sheet stock provided that total residual lubricant remaining on the metallic article in the form in which it contacts food does not exceed 0.015 milligram per square inch of metallic food-contact surface:

(1) Substances identified in paragraphs (b)(1) and (2) of this section.

(2) Substances identified in this paragraph.

List of substances	Limitations
α-Butyl-Ω--hydroxypoly (oxyethylene)-poly (oxypropylene) (CAS Reg. No. 9038–95–3) produced by random condensation of a 1:1 mixture by weight of ethylene oxide and propylene oxide with butanol and having a minimum molecular weight of 1,000.	
α–Butyl–Ω–hydroxypoly(oxypropylene) (CAS Reg. No. 9003-13–8) having a minimum molecular weight of 1000.	
α–Lauroyl–Ω–hydroxpoly(oxyethylene) (CAS Reg. No. 9004–81–3) having a minimum molecular weight of 200.	
Acetate esters derived from synthetic straight chain alcohols (complying with § 172.864 of this chapter) that have even numbers of carbon atoms in the range C_8-C_{18}.	
alpha-Alkyl–*omega*-hydroxypoly(oxyethylene) produced by the condensation of 1 mole of C_{12}-C_{15} straight chain primary alcohols with an average of 3 moles of ethylene oxide (CAS Reg. No. 68002–97–1).	
Benzotriazole (CAS Reg. No. 95–14–7).	
Bis(hydrogenated tallow alkyl)amine (CAS Reg. No. 61789–79–5).	Not to be used in combination with sodium nitrite.
Bis(hydrogenated tallow alkyl)aminoethanol (CAS Reg. No. 116438–56–3).	
N,N-Bis(2-hydroxyethyl)butylamine (CAS Reg. No. 102–79–4).	
Tert-Butyl alcohol.	
Di(2-ethylhexyl)phthalate.	
Diethyl phthalate.	
Diethylene glycol monobutylether (CAS Reg. No. 112–34–5).	
Dimers, trimers, and/or their partial methyl esters; such dimers and trimers are of unsaturated C_{18} fatty acids derived from animal and vegetable fats and oils and/or tall oil, and such partial methyl esters meet the following specifications: Saponification value 180–200, acid value 70–130, and maximum iodine value 120.	For use only at a level not to exceed 10 percent by weight of finished lubricant formulation.
Di-*n*-octyl sebacate.	
Ethylenediaminetetraacetic acid, sodium salts.	
Isopropyl alcohol.	
Isopropyl laurate (CAS Reg. No. 10233–13–3)	For use at a level not to exceed 10 percent by weight of the finished lubricant formulation.
Isopropyl oleate.	
Isotridecyl alcohol, ethoxylated (CAS Reg. No. 9043–30–5).	
Methyl esters of coconut oil fatty acids.	
Methyl esters of fatty acids (C_{16}-C_{18}) derived from animal and vegetable fats and oils.	
Polybutene, hydrogenated: complying with the identity prescribed under § 178.3740(b).	
Polyethylene glycol (400) monostearate.	
Polyisobutylene (minimum molecular weight 300).	

List of substances	Limitations
Polyoxyethylated (5 moles) tallow amine (CAS Reg. No. 61791–26–2).	
Polyvinyl alcohol.	
Sodium nitrite	For use only as a rust inhibitor in lubricant formulations provided the total residual sodium nitrite on the metallic article in the form in which it contacts food does not exceed 0.007 milligram per square inch of metallic food-contact surface.
Sodium petroleum sulfonate, MW 440–450 (CAS Reg. No. 68608–26–4) derived from naphthenic oil having a Saybolt viscosity range of 500–600 Saybolt Universal Seconds (SUS at 37–8 °C (100 °F) as determined by ASTM method D88–81, "Standard Test Method for Saybolt Viscosity," which is incorporated by reference. Copies are available from the American Society for Testing Materials, 1961 Race St., Philadelphia, PA 19103, or available for inspection at the National Archives and Records Administration (NARA). For information on the availability of this material at NARA, call 202-741-6030, or go to: *http://www.archives.gov/federal_register/code_of_federal_regulations/ibr_locations.html*..	
Synthetic alcohol mixture of straight-and branched-chain alcohols that have even numbers of carbon atoms in the range C_4C_{18} and that are prepared from ethylene, aluminum, and hydrogen such that the finished synthetic alcohol mixture contains not less than 75 pct of straight-chain primary alcohols and contains not less than 85 pct total C_{10} and C_{12} alcohols.	
Synthetic primary alcohol mixture of straight- and branched-chain alcohols that contain at least 99 pct primary alcohols consisting of the following: not less than 70 pct normal alcohols; not less than 96.5 pct C_{12}-C_{15} alcohols; and not more than 2.5 pct alpha, omega C_{13}-C_{16} diols. The alcohols are prepared from linear olefins from a purified kerosene fraction, carbon monoxide and hydrogen using a modified oxo process, such that the finished primary alcohol mixture meets the following specifications: Molecular weight, 207±4; hydroxyl number, 266–276.	For use at a level not to exceed 8 pct by weight of the finished lubricant formulation.
Synthetic primary alcohol mixture of straight- and branched-chain alcohols that contain at least 99 pct primary alcohols consisting of the following: not less than 70 percent normal alcohols; not less than 93 pct C_{12}-C_{13} alcohols; not more than 5 pct C_{14}-C_{15} alcohols; and not more than 2.5 pct alpha, omega, C_{13}-C_{16} diols. The alcohols are prepared from linear olefins from a purified kerosene fraction, carbon monoxide and hydrogen using a modified oxo process, such that the finished primary alcohol mixture meets the following specifications: Molecular weight 194±5; hydroxyl number, 283–296.	For use only at a level not to exceed 8 pct by weight of the finished lubricant formulation.
Tallow, sulfonated.	
Triethanolamine.	

(3) Mineral oil conforming to the identity prescribed in §178.3620(c).

(4) Light petroleum hydrocarbons identified in paragraph (a)(4) (i) of this section: *Provided*, That the total residual lubricant on the metallic article in the form in which it contacts food meets the ultraviolet absorbance limits prescribed in paragraph (a) (4) (ii) of this section as determined by the analytical method described in paragraph (a) (4) (iii) of this section.

(i) Light petroleum hydrocarbons are derived by distillation from virgin petroleum stocks or are synthesized from petroleum gases. They are chiefly paraffinic, isoparaffinic, napthenic, or aromatic in nature, and meet the following specifications:

(*a*) Initial boiling point is 24 °C minimum and final boiling point is 288 °C maximum, as determined by ASTM method D86–82, "Standard Method for Distillation of Petroleum Products," which is incorporated by reference. Copies may be obtained from the American Society for Testing Materials, 100 Barr Harbor Dr., West Conshohocken, Philadelphia, PA 19428-2959, or may be examined at the National Archives and Records Administration (NARA). For information on the availability of this material at NARA, call 202–741–6030, or go to: *http://www.archives.gov/federal_register/code_of_federal_regulations/ibr_locations.html.*

(*b*) Nonvolatile residue is 0.005 gram per 100 milliliters, maximum, as determined by ASTM method D381–80, "Standard Test Method for Existent Gum in Fuels by Jet Evaporation," when the final boiling point is 121 °C or above and by ASTM method D1353–78, "Standard Test Method for Nonvolatile Matter in Volatile Solvents for Use in Paint, Varnish, Lacquer, and Related Products," when the final boiling point is below 121 °C. These ASTM methods are incorporated by reference. The availability of these incorporations by reference is given in paragraph (a)(4)(i)(*a*) of this section.

(*c*) Saybolt color 20 minimum as determined by ASTM method D156–82, "Standard Test Method for Saybolt Color of Petroleum Products (Saybolt Chromometer Method)," which is incorporated by reference. The availability of this incorporation by reference is given in paragraph (a)(4)(i)(*a*) of this section.

(*d*) Aromatic component content shall not exceed 32 percent.

(*e*) Conforms with ultraviolet absorbance limits prescribed in § 178.3620(c) as determined by the analytical method described therein.

(ii) Ultraviolet absorbance limits on residual lubricants are as follows:

Wavelength (mμ)	Maximum absorbance per 5 centimeters optical pathlength
280–289	0.7
290–299	.6
300–359	.4
360–400	.09

(iii) The analytical method for determining ultraviolet absorbance limits on residual lubricants is as follows:

GENERAL INSTRUCTIONS

Because of the sensitivity of the test, the possibility of errors arising from contamination is great. It is of the greatest importance that all glassware be scrupulously cleaned to remove all organic matter such as oil, grease, detergent, residues, etc. Examine all glassware including stoppers and stopcocks, under ultraviolet light to detect any residual fluorescent contamination. As a precautionary measure it is recommended practice to rinse all glassware with purified isooctane immediately before use. No grease is to be used on stopcocks or joints. Great care to avoid contamination of oil samples in handling and to assure absence of any extraneous material arising from inadequate packaging is essential. Because some of the polynuclear hydrocarbons sought in this test are very susceptible to photo-oxidation, the entire procedure is to be carried out under subdued light.

APPARATUS

Separatory funnels. 250-milliliter, 500-milliliter, 1,000-milliliter, and preferably 2,000-milliliter capacity, equipped with tetrafluoroethylene polymer stopcocks.

Evaporation flask (optional). 250-milliliter or 500-milliliter capacity all-glass flask equipped with standard-taper stopper having inlet and outlet tubes to permit passage of nitrogen across the surface of contained liquid to be evaporated.

Spectrophotometric cells. Fused quartz cells, optical path length in the range of 5,000 centimeters ±0.005 centimeter; also for checking spectrophotometer performance only, optical path length in the range 1.000 centimeter ±0.005 centimeter. With distilled water in the cells, determine any absorbance differences.

Spectrophotometer. Special range 250 millicrons-400 millimicrons with spectral slit width of 2 millimicrons or less; under instrument operating conditions for these absorbance measurements, the spectrophotometer shall also meet the following performance requirements:

Absorbance repeatability, ±0.01 at 0.4 absorbance.

Absorbance accuracy,[1] ±0.05 at 0.4 absorbance.

Wavelength repeatability, ±0.2 millimicron.

Wavelength accuracy, ±1.0 millimicron.

---

[1] As determined by procedure using potassium chromate for reference standard and described in National Bureau of Standards Circular 484, Spectrometry, U.S. Department of Commerce (1949), which is incorporated by reference. Copies are available from the Center for Food Safety and Applied Nutrition (HFS–200), Food and Drug Administration, 5100 Paint Branch Pkwy., College Park, MD 20740, or available for inspection at the National Archives and Records Administration (NARA). For information on the availability of this material at NARA, call 202–741–6030, or go to: *http://www.archives.gov/federal_register/code_of_federal_regulations/ibr_locations.html.* The accuracy is to be determined by comparison with the standard values at 210, 345, and 400 millimicrons.

Soxhlet apparatus. 60-millimeter diameter body tubes fitted with condenser and 500-milliliter round-bottom boiling flask. A supply of paper thimbles to fit is required.

Nitrogen cylinder. Water-pumped or equivalent purity nitrogen in cylinder equipped with regulator and valve to control flow at 5 p.s.i.g.

REAGENTS AND MATERIALS

Organic solvents. All solvents used throughout the procedure shall meet the specifications and tests described in this specification. The isooctane (2,2,4-trimethylpentane) shall pass the following test:

Place 180 milliliters of solvent in a 250-milliliter Erlenmeyer flask, add 1 milliliter of purified *n*-hexadecane and evaporate on the steam bath under a stream of nitrogen (a loose aluminum foil jacket around the flask will speed evaporation). Discontinue evaporation when not over 1 milliliter of residue remains.

Alternatively, the evaporation time can be reduced by using the optional evaporation flask. In this case the solvent and *n*-hexadecane are placed in the flask on the steam bath, the tube assembly is inserted, and a stream of nitrogen is fed through the inlet tube while the outlet tube is connected to a solvent trap and vacuum line in such a way as to prevent any flow-back of condensate into the flask.

Dissolve the 1 milliliter of hexadecane residue in isooctane and make to 25 milliliters volume. Determine the absorbance in the 5-centimeter path length cells compared to isooctane as reference. The absorbance of the solution of the solvent residue shall not exceed 0.01 per centimeter path length between 280 and 400 mμ. Purify, if necessary, by passage through a column of activated silica gel (Grade 12, Davison Chemical Co., Baltimore, Maryland, or equivalent) about 90 centimeters in length and 5 centimeters to 8 centimeters in diameter.

n-Hexadecane, 99-percent olefin-free. Dilute 1.0 milliliter of *n*-hexadecane to 25 milliliters with isooctane and determine the absorbance in a 5-centimeter cell compared to isooctane as reference point between 280 mμ-400 mμ. The absorbance per centimeter path length shall not exceed 0.00 in this range. Purify, if necessary, by percolation through activated silica gel or by distillation.

Dimethyl sulfoxide. Spectrophotometric grade (Crown Zellerbach Corp., Camas, Washington, or equivalent). Absorbance (1-centimeter cell, distilled water reference, sample completely saturated with nitrogen).

Wavelength	Absorbance (maximum)
261.5	1.00
270	.20
275	.09
280	.06
300	.015

There shall be no irregularities in the absorbance curve within these wavelengths.

Phosphoric acid. 85 percent A.C.S. reagent grade.

Sodium sulfate, anhydrous, A.C.S. reagent grade, preferably in granular form. For each bottle of sodium sulfate reagent used, establish as follows the necessary sodium sulfate prewash to provide such filters required in the method: Place approximately 35 grams of anhydrous sodium sulfate in a 30-milliliter coarse, fritted-glass funnel or in a 65-milliliter filter funnel with glass wool plug; wash with successive 15-milliliter portions of the indicated solvent until a 15-milliliter portion of the wash shows 0.00 absorbance per centimeter path length between 280 mμ and 400 mμ when tested as prescribed under "Organic solvents." Usually three portions of wash solvent are sufficient.

Before proceeding with analysis of a sample, determine the absorbance in a 5-centimeter path cell between 250 millimicrons and 400 millimicrons for the reagent blank by carrying out the procedure, without a metal sample. The absorbance per centimeter path length should not exceed 0.02 in the wavelength range from 280 mμ to 400 mμ.

Place 300 milliliters of dimethyl sulfoxide in a 1-liter separatory funnel and add 75 milliliters of phosphoric acid. Mix the contents of the funnel and allow to stand for 10 minutes. (The reaction between the sulfoxide and the acid is exothermic. Release pressure after mixing, then keep funnel stoppered.) Add 150 milliliters of isooctane and shake to pre-equilibrate the solvents. Draw off the individual layers and store in glass-stoppered flasks.

PROCEDURE

Sample. Select metal foil or sheet stock for the test which has not been previously contaminated by careless handling or exposure to atmospheric dust and fumes. A commercial coil in the form supplied for spindle mounting in a packaging line or wrapping machine is most suitable. Strip off the outside turn of metal and discard. Carefully avoid contamination or damage from handling the metal (wear gloves). Remove a 16–18-foot length from the coil and place it on a flat surface protected by a length of new kraft paper. Cut four 15-foot strips from the sample, each 3 inches wide (avoid tearing the edges of the strips). Using a piece of suitable glass rod, roll the strips of metal into loose coils and insert each into a Soxhlet thimble. Each turn of coil should be visibly separated from the adjacent turn.

Extraction. Fill each of the four Soxhlet tubes with purified isooctane (see under heading "Reagents and Materials," above) until siphon action occurs and then refill the tube body. Supply heat to the boiling flask and allow extraction to continue for at least 8 hours or until repeated weighings of the dried and cooled coil show no further weight loss.

Combine the isooctane extracts from the four Soxhlet units in a suitable beaker, rinsing each tube and flask into the beaker with fresh purified solvent. Evaporate the solvent under an atmosphere of inert gas (nitrogen) to residual volume of 50–60 milliliters and transfer this solution to a 500-milliliter separatory funnel containing 100 milliliters of pre-equilibrated sulfoxide-phosphoric acid mixture. Complete the transfer of the sample with small portions of pre-equilibrated isooctane to give a total volume of the residue and solvent of 75 milliliters. Shake the funnel vigorously for 2 minutes. Set up three 250-milliliter separatory funnels with each containing 30 milliliters of pre-equilibrated isooctane. After separation of liquid phases, carefully draw off lower layer into the first 250-milliliter separatory funnel and wash in tandem with the 30-milliliter portion of isooctane contained in the 250-milliliter separatory funnels. Shaking time for each wash is 1 minute. Repeat the extraction operation with two additional portions of the sulfoxide-acid mixture and wash each extractive in tandem through the same three portions of isooctane.

Collect the successive extractives (300 milliliters total) in a separatory funnel (preferably 2-liter) containing 480 milliliters of distilled water; mix, and allow to cool for a few minutes after the last extractive has been added. Add 80 milliliters of isooctane to the solution and extract by shaking the funnel vigorously for 2 minutes. Draw off the lower aqueous layer into a second separatory funnel (preferably 2-liter) and repeat the extraction with 80 milliliter of isooctane. Draw off and discard the aqueous layer. Wash each of the 80 milliliter extractives three times with 100-milliliter portions distilled water. Shaking time for each wash is 1 minute. Discard the aqueous layers. Filter the first extractive through anhydrous sodium sulfate pre-washed with isooctane (see sodium sulfate under "Reagents and Materials" for preparation of filter) into a 250-milliliter Erlenmeyer flask (or optionally into the evaporation flask). Wash the first separatory funnel with the second 80-milliliter isooctane extractive and pass through the sodium sulfate. Then wash the second and first separatory funnels successively with a 20-milliliter portion of isooctane and pass the solvent through the sodium sulfate into the flask. Add 1 milliliter of *n*-hexadecane and evaporate the isooctane on the steam bath under nitrogen. Discontinue evaporation when not over 1 milliliter of residue remains. To the residue, add a 10-milliliter portion of isooctane, reevaporate to 1 milliliter of hexadecane, and repeat this operation once.

Quantitatively transfer the residue with isooctane to a 25-milliliter volumetric flask, make to volume, and mix. Determine the absorbance of the solution in 5-centimeter pathlength cells compared to isooctane as reference between 280mμ–400mμ (take care to lose none of the solution in filling the sample cell). Correct the absorbance values for any absorbance derived from reagents as determined by carrying out the procedure without a metal sample. If the corrected absorbance does not exceed the limits prescribed in this paragraph, the residue meets the ultraviolet absorbance specifications.

(b) The following substances may be used in surface lubricants used to facilitate the drawing, stamping, or forming of metallic articles from rolled foil or sheet stock by further processing provided that the total residual lubricant remaining on the metallic article in the form in which it contacts food does not exceed 0.2 milligram per square inch of food-contact surface:

(1) Antioxidants used in compliance with regulations in parts 170 through 189 of this chapter.

(2) Substances identified in this subparagraph.

List of substances	Limitations
Acetyl tributyl citrate.	
Acetyl triethyl citrate.	
Butyl stearate.	
Castor oil.	
Dibutyl sebacate.	
Di(2-ethylhexyl) azelate.	
Di(2-ethylhexyl) sebacate.	
Diisodecyl phthalate.	
Dimethylpolysiloxane	Conforming to the identity prescribed in § 181.28 of this chapter.
Dipropylene glycol.	
Epoxidized soybean oil	Conforming to the identity prescribed in § 181.27 of this chapter.

List of substances	Limitations
Fatty acids derived from animal and vegetable fats and oils, and salts of such acids, single or mixed, as follows:	
Aluminum	
Magnesium	
Potassium	
Sodium	
Zinc	
Fatty alcohols, straight-chain with even number carbon atoms (C_{10} or greater).	
Isobutyl stearate.	
Lanolin.	
Linoleic acid amide.	
Mineral oil	Conforming to the identity prescribed in § 178.3620 (a) or (b).
Mono-, di-, and tristearyl citrate.	
Oleic acid amide.	
Palmitic acid amide.	
Petrolatum	Conforming to the identity prescribed in § 178.3700.
Phosphoric acid, mono- and dihexyl esters, compounds with tetramethylnonylamines and C_{11-14}-alkylamines (CAS Reg. No. 80939–62–4).	For use only at levels not to exceed 0.5 percent by weight of the finished surface lubricant formulation.
Polyethylene glycol (molecular weight 300 or greater)	Mono- and diethylene glycol content not to exceed a total of 0.2 pct.
Stannous stearate.	
Stearic acid amide.	
Stearyl stearate.	
Tetrakis[methylene (3,5-di-*tert*-butyl-4-hydroxyhydrocinnamate)] methane (CAS Registry No. 6683–19–8).	For use at a level not to exceed 0.5 percent by weight of the finished surface lubricant formulation.
Triethylene glycol	Diethylene glycol content not to exceed 0.1 pct.
Wax, petroleum	Complying with § 178.3710.

(c) The substances identified in paragraph (a)(2) of this section may be used in surface lubricants used to facilitate the drawing, stamping, and forming of metallic articles from rolled foil and sheet stock provided that total residual lubricant remaining on the metallic article in the form in which it contacts food does not exceed 0.015 milligram per square inch of food-contact surface.

(d) Subject to any prescribed limitations, the quantity of surface lubricant used in the manufacture of metallic articles shall not exceed the least amount reasonably required to accomplish the intended technical effect and shall not be intended to nor, in fact, accomplish any technical effect in the food itself.

(e) The use of the surface lubricants in the manufacture of any article that is the subject of a regulation in parts 174, 175, 176, 177, 178 and § 179.45 of this chapter must comply with any specifications prescribed by such regulation for the finished form of the article.

(f) Any substance that is listed in this section and the subject of a regulation in parts 174, 175, 176, 177, 178 and § 179.45 of this chapter shall comply with any applicable specifications prescribed by such regulation.

[42 FR 14609, Mar. 15, 1977, as amended at 48 FR 238, Jan. 4, 1983; 49 FR 10113, Mar. 19, 1984; 49 FR 29579, July 23, 1984; 50 FR 36874, Sept. 10, 1985; 52 FR 10223, Mar. 31, 1987; 54 FR 6124, Feb. 8, 1989; 54 FR 24899, June 12, 1989; 56 FR 55456, Oct. 28, 1991; 57 FR 23953, June 5, 1992; 58 FR 17513, Apr. 5, 1993; 64 FR 47110, Aug. 30, 1999; 69 FR 24512, May 4, 2004]

§ 178.3930 Terpene resins.

The terpene resins identified in paragraph (a) of this section may be safely used as components of polypropylene film intended for use in contact with food, and the terpene resins identified in paragraph (b) of this section may be safely used as components of polyolefin film intended for use in contact with food;

(a) Terpene resins consisting of the hydrogenated polymers of terpene hydrocarbons obtainable from sulfate turpentine and meeting the following specifications: Drop-softening point of 118°–138 °C; iodine value less than 20.

(b) Terpene resins consisting of polymers of beta-pinene and meeting the following specifications: Acid value less than 1; saponification number less than 1; color less than 4 on the Gardner scale as measured in 50 percent mineral spirits solution.

§ 178.3940 Tetraethylene glycol di-(2-ethylhexoate).

Tetraethylene glycol di-(2-ethylhexoate) containing not more than 22 parts per million ethylene and/or diethylene glycols may be used at a level not to exceed 0.7 percent by weight of twine as a finish on twine to be used for tying meat provided the twine fibers are produced from nylon resins complying with § 177.1500 of this chapter.

§ 178.3950 Tetrahydrofuran.

Tetrahydrofuran may be safely used in the fabrication of articles intended for packaging, transporting, or storing foods, subject to the provisions of this section.

(a) It is used as a solvent in the casting of film from a solution of polymeric resins of vinyl chloride, vinyl acetate, or vinylidene chloride that have been polymerized singly or copolymerized with one another in any combination, or it may be used as a solvent in the casting of film prepared from vinyl chloride copolymers complying with § 177.1980 of this chapter.

(b) The residual amount of tetrahydrofuran in the film does not exceed 1.5 percent by weight of film.

PART 179—IRRADIATION IN THE PRODUCTION, PROCESSING AND HANDLING OF FOOD

Subpart A [Reserved]

Subpart B—Radiation and Radiation Sources

Sec.

Subpart C—Packaging Materials for Irradiated Foods

AUTHORITY: 21 U.S.C. 321, 342, 343, 348, 373, 374.

SOURCE: 42 FR 14635, Mar. 15, 1977, unless otherwise noted.

EDITORIAL NOTE: Nomenclature changes to part 179 appear at 70 FR 72074, Dec. 1, 2005.

Subpart A [Reserved]

Subpart B—Radiation and Radiation Sources

§ 179.21 Sources of radiation used for inspection of food, for inspection of packaged food, and for controlling food processing.

Sources of radiation for the purposes of inspection of foods, for inspection of packaged food, and for controlling food processing may be safely used under the following conditions:

(a) The radiation source is one of the following:

(1) X-ray tubes producing X-radiation from operation of the tube source at a voltage of 500 kilovolt peak or lower.

(2) Sealed units producing radiations at energy levels of not more than 2.2 million electron volts from one of the following isotopes: Americium-241, cesium-137, cobalt-60, iodine-125, krypton-85, radium-226, and strontium-90.

(3) Sealed units producing neutron radiation from the isotope Californium-252 (CAS Reg. No. 13981–17–4) to measure moisture in food.

(4) Machine sources producing X-radiation at energies no greater than 10 million electron volts (MeV).

(5) Monoenergetic neutron sources producing neutrons at energies not less than 1 MeV but no greater than 14 MeV.

(b) To assure safe use of these radiation sources:

(1) The label of the sources shall bear, in addition to the other information required by the Act:

(i) Appropriate and accurate information identifying the source of radiation.

(ii) The maximum energy of radiation emitted by X-ray tube sources.

(iii) The maximum energy of X-radiation emitted by machine source.

(iv) The minimum and maximum energy of radiation emitted by neutron source.

(2) The label or accompanying labeling shall bear:

(i) Adequate directions for installation and use.

(ii) A statement that no food shall be exposed to radiation sources listed in paragraph (a) (1) and (2) of this section so as to receive an absorbed dose in excess of 10 grays.

(iii) A statement that no food shall be exposed to a radiation source listed in paragraph (a)(3) of this section so as to receive an absorbed dose in excess of 2 milligrays.

(iv) A statement that no food shall be exposed to a radiation source listed in paragraph (a)(4) of this section so as to receive a dose in excess of 0.5 gray (Gy).

(v) A statement that no food shall be exposed to a radiation source listed in paragraph (a)(5) of this section so as to receive a dose in excess of 0.01 gray (Gy).

[42 FR 14635, Mar. 15, 1977, as amended at 48 FR 46022, Oct. 11, 1983; 61 FR 14246, Apr. 1, 1996; 64 FR 69191, Dec. 10, 1999; 66 FR 18539, Apr. 10, 2001; 69 FR 76404, Dec. 21, 2004]

§ 179.25 General provisions for food irradiation.

For the purposes of § 179.26, current good manufacturing practice is defined to include the following restrictions:

(a) Any firm that treats foods with ionizing radiation shall comply with the requirements of part 110 of this chapter and other applicable regulations.

(b) Food treated with ionizing radiation shall receive the minimum radiation dose reasonably required to accomplish its intended technical effect and not more than the maximum dose specified by the applicable regulation for that use.

(c) Packaging materials subjected to irradiation incidental to the radiation treatment and processing of prepackaged food shall be in compliance with § 179.45, shall be the subject of an exemption for such use under § 170.39 of this chapter, or shall be the subject of an effective premarket notification for a food contact substance for such use submitted under § 170.100 of this chapter.

(d) Radiation treatment of food shall conform to a scheduled process. A scheduled process for food irradiation is a written procedure that ensures that the radiation dose range selected by the food irradiation processor is adequate under commercial processing conditions (including atmosphere and temperature) for the radiation to achieve its intended effect on a specific product and in a specific facility. A food irradiation processor shall operate with a scheduled process established by qualified persons having expert knowledge in radiation processing requirements of food and specific for that food and for that irradiation processor's treatment facility.

(e) A food irradiation processor shall maintain records as specified in this section for a period of time that exceeds the shelf life of the irradiated food product by 1 year, up to a maximum of 3 years, whichever period is shorter, and shall make these records available for inspection and copy by authorized employees of the Food and Drug Administration. Such records shall include the food treated, lot identification, scheduled process, evidence of compliance with the scheduled process, ionizing energy source, source calibration, dosimetry, dose distribution in the product, and the date of irradiation.

[51 FR 13399, Apr. 18, 1986, as amended at 67 FR 9585, Mar. 4, 2002; 67 FR 35731, May 21, 2002]

§ 179.26 Ionizing radiation for the treatment of food.

Ionizing radiation for treatment of foods may be safely used under the following conditions:

(a) *Energy sources.* Ionizing radiation is limited to:

(1) Gamma rays from sealed units of the radionuclides cobalt-60 or cesium-137.

(2) Electrons generated from machine sources at energies not to exceed 10 million electron volts.

(3) X rays generated from machine sources at energies not to exceed 5 million electron volts (MeV), except as

permitted by paragraph (a)(4) of this section.

(4) X rays generated from machine sources using tantalum or gold as the target material and using energies not to exceed 7.5 (MeV).

(b) *Limitations.*

Use	Limitations
1. For control of *Trichinella spiralis* in pork carcasses or fresh, non-heat-processed cuts of pork carcasses.	Minimum dose 0.3 kiloGray (kGy) (30 kilorad (krad)); maximum dose not to exceed 1 kGy (100 krad).
2. For growth and maturation inhibition of fresh foods.	Not to exceed 1 kGy (100 krad).
3. For disinfestation of arthropod pests in food.	Do.
4. For microbial disinfection of dry or dehydrated enzyme preparations (including immobilized enzymes).	Not to exceed 10 kGy (1 megarad (Mrad)).
5. For microbial disinfection of the following dry or dehydrated aromatic vegetable substances when used as ingredients in small amounts solely for flavoring or aroma: culinary herbs, seeds, spices, vegetable seasonings that are used to impart flavor but that are not either represented as, or appear to be, a vegetable that is eaten for its own sake, and blends of these aromatic vegetable substances. Turmeric and paprika may also be irradiated when they are to be used as color additives. The blends may contain sodium chloride and minor amounts of dry food ingredients ordinarily used in such blends.	Not to exceed 30 kGy (3 Mrad).
6. For control of food-borne pathogens in fresh (refrigerated or unrefrigerated) or frozen, uncooked poultry products that are: (1) Whole carcasses or disjointed portions (or other parts) of such carcasses that are "ready-to-cook poultry" within the meaning of 9 CFR 381.l(b) (with or without nonfluid seasoning; includes, e.g., ground poultry), or (2) mechanically separated poultry product (a finely comminuted ingredient produced by the mechanical deboning of poultry carcasses or parts of carcasses).	Not to exceed 4.5 kGy for non-frozen products; not to exceed 7.0 kGy for frozen products.
7. For the sterilization of frozen, packaged meats used solely in the National Aeronautics and Space Administration space flight programs.	Minimum dose 44 kGy (4.4 Mrad). Packaging materials used need not comply with § 179.25(c) provided that their use is otherwise permitted by applicable regulations in parts 174 through 186 of this chapter.
8. For control of foodborne pathogens in, and extension of the shelf-life of, refrigerated or frozen, uncooked products that are meat within the meaning of 9 CFR 301.2(rr), meat byproducts within the meaning of 9 CFR 301.2(tt), or meat food products within the meaning of 9 CFR 301.2(uu), with or without nonfluid seasoning, that are otherwise composed solely of intact or ground meat, meat byproducts, or both meat and meat byproducts.	Not to exceed 4.5 kGy maximum for refrigerated products; not to exceed 7.0 kGy maximum for frozen products.
9. For control of *Salmonella* in fresh shell eggs..	Not to exceed 3.0 kGy.
10. For control of microbial pathogens on seeds for sprouting..	Not to exceed 8.0 kGy.
11. For the control of Vibrio bacteria and other foodborne microorganisms in or on fresh or frozen molluscan shellfish..	Not to exceed 5.5 kGy.
12. For control of food-borne pathogens and extension of shelf-life in fresh iceberg lettuce and fresh spinach..	Not to exceed 4.0 kGy.
13. For control of foodborne pathogens, and extension of shelf-life, in unrefrigerated (as well as refrigerated) uncooked meat, meat byproducts, and certain meat food products.	Not to exceed 4.5 kGy.

(c) *Labeling.* (1) The label and labeling of retail packages of foods irradiated in conformance with paragraph (b) of this section shall bear the following logo along with either the statement

"Treated with radiation" or the statement "Treated by irradiation" in addition to information required by other regulations. The logo shall be placed prominently and conspicuously in conjunction with the required statement. The radiation disclosure statement is not required to be more prominent than the declaration of ingredients required under § 101.4 of this chapter. As used in this provision, the term "radiation disclosure statement" means the written statement that discloses that a food has been intentionally subject to irradiation.

(2) For irradiated foods not in package form, the required logo and phrase "Treated with radiation" or "Treated by irradiation" shall be displayed to the purchaser with either (i) the labeling of the bulk container plainly in view or (ii) a counter sign, card, or other appropriate device bearing the information that the product has been treated with radiation. As an alternative, each item of food may be individually labeled. In either case, the information must be prominently and conspicuously displayed to purchasers. The labeling requirement applies only to a food that has been irradiated, not to a food that merely contains an irradiated ingredient but that has not itself been irradiated.

(3) For a food, any portion of which is irradiated in conformance with paragraph (b) of this section, the label and labeling and invoices or bills of lading shall bear either the statement "Treated with radiation—do not irradiate again" or the statement "Treated by irradiation—do not irradiate again" when shipped to a food manufacturer or processor for further processing, labeling, or packing.

[51 FR 13399, Apr. 18, 1986, as amended at 53 FR 12757, Apr. 18, 1988; 53 FR 53209, Dec. 30, 1988; 54 FR 32335, Aug. 7, 1989; 55 FR 14415, Apr. 18, 1990; 55 FR 18544, May 2, 1990; 60 FR 12670, Mar. 8, 1995; 62 FR 64121, Dec. 3, 1997; 63 FR 43876, Aug. 17, 1998; 65 FR 45282, July 21, 2000; 65 FR 64607, Oct. 30, 2000; 69 FR 76846, Dec. 23, 2004; 70 FR 48072, Aug. 16, 2005; 73 FR 49603, Aug. 22, 2008; 77 FR 71316, 71321, Nov. 30, 2012]

§ 179.30 Radiofrequency radiation for the heating of food, including microwave frequencies.

Radiofrequency radiation, including microwave frequencies, may be safely used for heating food under the following conditions:

(a) The radiation source consists of electronic equipment producing radio waves with specific frequencies for this purpose authorized by the Federal Communications Commission.

(b) The radiation is used or intended for use in the production of heat in food wherever heat is necessary and effective in the treatment or processing of food.

§ 179.39 Ultraviolet radiation for the processing and treatment of food.

Ultraviolet radiation for the processing and treatment of food may be safely used under the following conditions:

(a) The radiation sources consist of low pressure mercury lamps emitting

90 percent of the emission at a wavelength of 253.7 nanometers (2,537 Angstroms).

(b) The ultraviolet radiation is used or intended for use as follows:

Irradiated food	Limitations	Use
Food and food products	Without ozone production: high fat-content food irradiated in vacuum or in an inert atmosphere; intensity of radiation, 1 W (of 2,537 A. radiation) per 5 to 10 ft.^{2}.	Surface microorganism control.
Potable water	Without ozone production; coefficient of absorption, 0.19 per cm or less; flow rate, 100 gal/h per watt of 2,537 A. radiation; water depth, 1 cm or less; lamp-operating temperature, 36 to 46 °C..	Sterilization of water used in food production.
Juice products	Turbulent flow through tubes with a minimum Reynolds number of 2,200..	Reduction of human pathogens and other microorganisms.

[42 FR 14635, Mar. 15, 1977, as amended at 65 FR 71057, Nov. 29, 2000]

§ 179.41 Pulsed light for the treatment of food.

Pulsed light may be safely used for treatment of foods under the following conditions:

(a) The radiation sources consist of xenon flashlamps designed to emit broadband radiation consisting of wavelengths covering the range of 200 to 1,100 nanometers (nm), and operated so that the pulse duration is no longer than 2 milliseconds (msec);

(b) The treatment is used for surface microorganism control;

(c) Foods treated with pulsed light shall receive the minimum treatment reasonably required to accomplish the intended technical effect; and

(d) The total cumulative treatment shall not exceed 12.0 Joules/square centimeter (J/cm^2.)

[61 FR 42383, Aug. 15, 1996]

§ 179.43 Carbon dioxide laser for etching food.

Carbon dioxide laser light may be safely used for etching information on the surface of food under the following conditions:

(a) The radiation source consists of a carbon dioxide laser designed to emit pulsed infrared radiation with a wavelength of 10.6 micrometers such that the maximum energy output of the laser does not exceed 9.8×10^{-3} joules per square centimeter (J/cm^2);

(b) The carbon dioxide laser shall be used only for etching information on the skin of fresh, intact citrus fruit, providing the fruit has been adequately washed and waxed prior to laser etching, and the etched area is immediately rewaxed after treatment; and

(c) The maximum total energy to which the etched citrus fruit is exposed from the use of the carbon dioxide laser shall not exceed 1.5×10^{-3} J, and the maximum total etched surface area of the citrus fruit shall not exceed 0.122 cm^2.

[77 FR 34215, June 11, 2012]

Subpart C—Packaging Materials for Irradiated Foods

§ 179.45 Packaging materials for use during the irradiation of prepackaged foods.

The packaging materials identified in this section may be safely subjected to irradiation incidental to the radiation treatment and processing of prepackaged foods, subject to the provisions of this section and to the requirement that no induced radioactivity is detectable in the packaging material itself:

(a) The radiation of the food itself shall comply with regulations in this part.

(b) The following packaging materials may be subjected to a dose of radiation, not to exceed 10 kilograys, unless otherwise indicated, incidental to the use of gamma, electron beam, or X-radiation in the radiation treatment of prepackaged foods:

(1) Nitrocellulose-coated or vinylidene chloride copolymer-coated cellophane complying with § 177.1200 of this chapter.

(2) Glassine paper complying with §176.170 of this chapter.

(3) Wax-coated paperboard complying with §176.170 of this chapter.

(4) Polyolefin film prepared from one or more of the basic olefin polymers complying with §177.1520 of this chapter. The finished film may contain:

(i) Adjuvant substances used in compliance with §§178.3740 and 181.22 through 181.30 of this chapter, sodium citrate, sodium lauryl sulfate, polyvinyl chloride, and materials as listed in paragraph (d)(2)(i) of this section.

(ii) Coatings comprising a vinylidene chloride copolymer containing a minimum of 85 percent vinylidene chloride with one or more of the following comonomers: Acrylic acid, acrylonitrile, itaconic acid, methyl acrylate, and methyl methacrylate.

(5) Kraft paper prepared from unbleached sulfate pulp to which rosin, complying with §178.3870 of this chapter, and alum may be added. The kraft paper is used only as a container for flour and is irradiated with a dose not exceeding 500 grays.

(6) Polyethylene terephthalate film prepared from the basic polymer as described in §177.1630(e)(4)(i) and (ii) of this chapter. The finished film may contain:

(i) Adjuvant substances used in compliance with §§178.3740 and 181.22 through 181.30 of this chapter, sodium citrate, sodium lauryl sulfate, polyvinyl chloride, and materials as listed in paragraph (d)(2)(i) of this section.

(ii) Coatings comprising a vinylidene chloride copolymer containing a minimum of 85 percent vinylidene chloride with one or more of the following comonomers: Acrylic acid, acrylonitrile, itaconic acid, methyl acrylate, and methyl methacrylate.

(iii) Coatings consisting of polyethylene conforming to §177.1520 of this chapter.

(7) Polystyrene film prepared from styrene basic polymer. The finished film may contain adjuvant substances used in compliance with §§178.3740 and 181.22 through 181.30 of this chapter.

(8) Rubber hydrochloride film prepared from rubber hydrochloride basic polymer having a chlorine content of 30–32 weight percent and having a maximum extractable fraction of 2 weight percent when extracted with *n*-hexane at reflux temperature for 2 hours. The finished film may contain adjuvant substances used in compliance with §§178.3740 and 181.22 through 181.30 of this chapter.

(9) Vinylidene chloride-vinyl chloride copolymer film prepared from vinylidene chloride-vinyl chloride basic copolymers containing not less than 70 weight percent of vinylidene chloride and having a viscosity of 0.50–1.50 centipoises as determined by ASTM method D729–81, "Standard Specification for Vinylidene Chloride Molding Compounds," which is incorporated by reference. Copies may be obtained from the American Society for Testing Materials, 100 Barr Harbor Dr., West Conshohocken, Philadelphia, PA 19428-2959, or may be examined at the National Archives and Records Administration (NARA). For information on the availability of this material at NARA, call 202–741–6030, or go to: *http://www.archives.gov/federal_register/code_of_federal_regulations/ibr_locations.html.* The finished film may contain adjuvant substances used in compliance with §§178.3740 and 181.22 through 181.30 of this chapter.

(10) Nylon 11 conforming to §177.1500 of this chapter.

(c) Ethylene-vinyl acetate copolymers complying with §177.1350 of this chapter. The ethylene-vinyl acetate packaging materials may be subjected to a dose of radiation, not to exceed 30 kilogray (3 megarads), incidental to the use of gamma, electron beam, or X-radiation in the radiation treatment of packaged foods.

(d) The following packaging materials may be subjected to a dose of radiation, not to exceed 60 kilograys incidental to the use of gamma, electron beam, or X-radiation in the radiation processing of prepackaged foods:

(1) Vegetable parchments, consisting of a cellulose material made from waterleaf paper (unsized) treated with concentrated sulfuric acid, neutralized, and thoroughly washed with distilled water.

(2) Films prepared from basic polymers and with or without adjuvants, as follows:

(i) Polyethylene film prepared from the basic polymer as described in

§177.1520(a) of this chapter. The finished film may contain one or more of the following added substances:

Substances	Limitations
Amides of erucic, linoleic, oleic, palmitic, and stearic acid	Not to exceed 1 pct by weight of the polymer.
BHA as described in §172.110 of this chapter	Do.
BHT as described in §172.115 of this chapter	Do.
Calcium and sodium propionates	Do.
Petroleum wax as described in §178.3710 of this chapter	Do.
Polypropylene, noncrystalline, as described in §177.1520(c) of this chapter.	Not to exceed 2 pct by weight of the polymer.
Stearates of aluminum, calcium, magnesium, potassium, and sodium as described in §172.863(a) of this chapter.	Not to exceed 1 pct by weight of the polymer.
Triethylene glycol as described in §178.3740(b) of this chapter	Do.
Mineral oil as described in §178.3620 (a) or (b) of this chapter	Do.

(ii) Polyethylene terephthalate film prepared from the basic polymer as described in §177.1630(e)(4)(ii) of this chapter. The finished film may contain one or more of the added substances listed in paragraph (d)(2)(i) of this section.

(iii) Nylon 6 films prepared from the nylon 6 basic polymer as described in §177.1500(a)(6) of this chapter and meeting the specifications of item 6.1 of the table in §177.1500(b) of this chapter. The finished film may contain one or more of the added substances listed in paragraph (d)(2)(i) of this section.

(iv) Vinyl chloride-vinyl acetate copolymer film prepared from the basic copolymer containing 88.5 to 90.0 weight percent of vinyl chloride with 10.0 to 11.5 weight percent of vinyl acetate and having a maximum volatility of not over 3.0 percent (1 hour at 105 °C) and viscosity not less than 0.30 determined by ASTM method D1243–79, "Standard Test Method for Dilute Solution Viscosity of Vinyl Chloride Polymers," Method A, which is incorporated by reference. The availability of this incorporation by reference is given in paragraph (b)(9) of this section. The finished film may contain one or more of the added substances listed in paragraph (d)(2)(i) of this section.

(e) Acrylonitrile copolymers identified in this section shall comply with the provisions of §180.22 of this chapter.

[42 FR 14635, Mar. 15, 1977, as amended at 49 FR 10113, Mar. 19, 1984; 54 FR 7405, Feb. 21, 1989; 54 FR 24899, June 12, 1989; 59 FR 14551, Mar. 29, 1994; 61 FR 14246, Apr. 1, 1996; 66 FR 10575, Feb. 16, 2001]

PART 180—FOOD ADDITIVES PERMITTED IN FOOD OR IN CONTACT WITH FOOD ON AN INTERIM BASIS PENDING ADDITIONAL STUDY

Subpart A—General Provisions

Subpart B—Specific Requirements for Certain Food Additives

AUTHORITY: 21 U.S.C. 321, 342, 343, 348, 371; 42 U.S.C. 241.

EDITORIAL NOTE: Nomenclature changes to part 180 appear at 61 FR 14482, Apr. 2, 1996, and 66 FR 56035, Nov. 6, 2001.

Subpart A—General Provisions

§180.1 General.

(a) Substances having a history of use in food for human consumption or in food contact surfaces may at any time have their safety or functionality brought into question by new information that in itself is not conclusive. An interim food additive regulation for the use of any such substance may be promulgated in this subpart when new information raises a substantial question about the safety or functionality of the substance but there is a reasonable certainty that the substance is not harmful and that no harm to the public health will result from the continued use of the substance for a limited period of time while the question raised is being resolved by further study.

(b) No interim food additive regulation may be promulgated if the new information is conclusive with respect to the question raised or if there is a reasonable likelihood that the substance is harmful or that continued use of the substance will result in harm to the public health.

(c) The Commissioner, on his own initiative or on the petition of any interested person, pursuant to part 10 of this chapter, may propose an interim food additive regulation. A final order promulgating an interim food additive regulation shall provide that continued use of the substance in food is subject to each of the following conditions:

(1) Use of the substance in food or food contact surfaces must comply with whatever limitations the Commissioner deems to be appropriate under the circumstances.

(2) Within 60 days following the effective date of the regulation, an interested person shall satisfy the Commissioner in writing that studies adequate and appropriate to resolve the questions raised about the substance have been undertaken, or the Food and Drug Administration may undertake the studies. The Commissioner may extend this 60-day period if necessary to review and act on proposed protocols. If no such commitment is made, or adequate and appropriate studies are not undertaken, an order shall immediately be published in the FEDERAL REGISTER revoking the interim food additive regulation effective upon publication.

(3) A progress report shall be filed on the studies every January 1 and July 1 until completion. If the progress report is inadequate or if the Commissioner concludes that the studies are not being pursued promptly and diligently or if interim results indicate a reasonable likelihood that a health hazard exists, an order will promptly be published in the FEDERAL REGISTER revoking the interim food additive regulation effective upon publication.

(4) If nonclinical laboratory studies are involved, studies filed with the Commissioner shall include, with respect to each study, either a statement that the study has been or will be conducted in compliance with the good laboratory practice regulations as set forth in part 58 of this chapter, or, if any such study was not conducted in compliance with such regulations, a brief statement of the reason for the noncompliance.

(5) [Reserved]

(6) If clinical investigations involving human subjects are involved, such investigations filed with the Commissioner shall include, with respect to each investigation, a statement that the investigation either was conducted in compliance with the requirements for institutional review set forth in part 56 of this chapter, or was not subject to such requirements in accordance with §§ 56.104 or 56.105, and that it has been or will be conducted in compliance with the requirements for informed consent set forth in part 50 of this chapter.

(d) Promptly upon completion of the studies undertaken on the substance, the Commissioner will review all available data, will terminate the interim food additive regulation, and will either issue a food additive regulation or will require elimination of the substance from the food supply.

(e) The Commissioner may consult with advisory committees, professional organizations, or other experts in the field, in evaluating:

(1) Whether an interim food additive regulation is justified,

(2) The type of studies necessary and appropriate to resolve questions raised about a substance,

(3) Whether interim results indicate the reasonable likelihood that a health hazard exists, or

(4) Whether the data available at the conclusion of those studies justify a food additive regulation.

(f) Where appropriate, an emergency action level may be issued for a substance subject to paragraph (a) of this section that is not an approved food additive, pending the issuance of a final interim food additive regulation. Such an action level shall be issued pursuant to sections 306 and 402(a) of the act to identify, based upon available data, a safe level of use for the substance.

Such an action level shall be issued in a notice published in the FEDERAL REGISTER and shall be followed as soon as practicable by a proposed interim food additive regulation. Where the available data do not permit establishing an action level for the safe use of a substance, use of the substance may be prohibited. The identification of a prohibited substance may be made in part 189 of this chapter when appropriate.

[42 FR 14636, Mar. 15, 1977, as amended at 42 FR 15674, Mar. 22, 1977; 42 FR 52821, Sept. 30, 1977; 46 FR 8952, Jan. 27, 1981; 46 FR 14340, Feb. 27, 1981; 50 FR 7492, Feb. 22, 1985; 54 FR 39634, Sept. 27, 1989]

Subpart B—Specific Requirements for Certain Food Additives

§ 180.22 Acrylonitrile copolymers.

Acrylonitrile copolymers may be safely used on an interim basis as articles or components of articles intended for use in contact with food, in accordance with the following prescribed conditions:

(a) Limitations for acrylonitrile monomer extraction for finished food-contact articles, determined by a method of analysis titled "Gas-Solid Chromatographic Procedure for Determining Acrylonitrile Monomer in Acrylonitrile-Containing Polymers and Food Simulating Solvents," which is incorporated by reference. Copies are available from the Center for Food Safety and Applied Nutrition (HFS–200), Food and Drug Administration, 5100 Paint Branch Pkwy., College Park, MD 20740, or available for inspection at the National Archives and Records Administration (NARA). For information on the availability of this material at NARA, call 202–741–6030, or go to: *http://www.archives.gov/federal_register/code_of_federal_regulations/ibr_locations.html.*

(1) In the case of single-use articles having a volume to surface ratio of 10 milliliters or more per square inch of food contact surface—0.003 milligram/square inch when extracted to equilibrium at 120 °F with food-simulating solvents appropriate to the intended conditions of use.

(2) In the case of single-use articles having a volume to surface ratio of less than 10 milliliters per square inch of food contact surface—0.3 part per million calculated on the basis of the volume of the container when extracted to equilibrium at 120 °F with food-simulating solvents appropriate to the intended conditions of use.

(3) In the case of repeated-use articles—0.003 milligram/square inch when extracted at a time equivalent to initial batch usage utilizing food-simulating solvents and temperatures appropriate to the intended conditions of use.

The food-simulating solvents shall include, where applicable, distilled water, 8 percent or 50 percent ethanol, 3 percent acetic acid, and either *n*-heptane or an appropriate oil or fat.

(b) Where necessary, current regulations permitting the use of acrylonitrile copolymers shall be revised to specify limitations on acrylonitrile/mercaptan complexes utilized in the production of acrylonitrile copolymers. Such copolymers, if they contain reversible acrylonitrile/mercaptan complexes and are used in other than repeated-use conditions, shall be tested to determine the identity of the complex and the level of the complex present in the food-contact article. Such testing shall include determination of the rate of decomposition of the complex at temperatures of 100 °F, 160 °F, and 212 °F using 3 percent acetic acid as the hydrolic agent. Acrylonitrile monomer levels, acrylonitrile/mercaptan complex levels, acrylonitrile oligomer levels, descriptions of the analytical methods used to determine the complex and the acrylonitrile migration, and validation studies of these analytical methods shall be submitted by June 9, 1977, to the Center for Food Safety and Applied Nutrition (HFS–200), Food and Drug Administration, 5100 Paint Branch Pkwy., College Park, MD 20740, unless an extension is granted by the Food and Drug Administration for good cause shown. Analytical methods for the determination of acrylonitrile complexes with *n*-dodecyl-mercaptan, n-octyl mercaptan, and 2-mercaptoethanol, titled "Determination of β-Dodecylmercaptopropionitrile in NR–16R Aqueous Extracts" and "Measurement of β-(2-Hdroxyethylmercapto) Propionitrile in Heptane Food-Simulating Solvent," are incorporated by reference. Copies are available from the Center for Food Safety and Applied Nutrition (HFS–200), Food and Drug Administration, 5100 Paint Branch Pkwy., College Park, MD 20740, or available for inspection at the National Archives and Records Administration (NARA). For information on the availability of this material at NARA, call 202–741–6030, or go to: *http://www.archives.gov/federal_register/code_of_federal_regulations/ibr_locations.html.*

(c) The following data shall be provided for finished food-contact articles intended for repeated use:

(1) Qualitative and quantitative migration values at a time equivalent to initial batch usage, utilizing solvents and temperatures appropriate to the intended conditions of use.

(2) Qualitative and quantitative migration values at the time of equilibrium extractions, utilizing solvents and temperatures appropriate to the intended conditions of use.

(3) Data on the volume and/or weight of food handled during the initial batch time period(s), during the equilibrium test period, and over the estimated life of the food-contact surface.

(d) Where acrylonitrile copolymers represent only a minor component of a polymer system, calculations based on 100 percent migration of the acrylonitrile component may be submitted in lieu of the requirements of paragraphs (a), (b), and (c) of this section in support of the continued safe use of acrylonitrile copolymers.

(e) On or before September 13, 1976, any interested person shall satisfy the Commissioner of Food and Drugs that toxicological feeding studies adequate and appropriate to establish safe conditions for the use of acrylonitrile copolymers have been, or soon will be, undertaken. Toxicity studies of acrylonitrile monomer shall include: (1) Lifetime feeding studies with a mammalian species, preferably with animals exposed in utero to the chemical, (2) studies of multigeneration reproduction with oral administration of the test material, (3) assessment of teratogenic and mutagenic potentials, (4) subchronic oral administration in a nonrodent mammal, (5) tests to determine any synergistic toxic effects between acrylonitrile monomer and cyanide ion, and (6) a literature search on the effects of chronic ingestion of hydrogen cyanide. Data on levels of acrylamide extractable from acrylonitrile copolymers shall also be submitted. Protocols of testing should be submitted for review to the Center for Food Safety and Applied Nutrition (HFS–200), Food and Drug Administration, 5100 Paint Branch Pkwy., College Park, MD 20740.

(f) Acrylonitrile copolymers may be used in contact with food only if authorized in parts 174 through 179 or § 181.32 of this chapter, except that other uses of acrylonitrile copolymers in use prior to June 14, 1976, may continue under the following conditions:

(1) On or before August 13, 1976, each use of acrylonitrile copolymers in a manner not authorized by § 181.32 of this chapter or parts 174 through 179 of this chapter shall be the subject of a notice to the Center for Food Safety and Applied Nutrition (HFS–200), Food and Drug Administration, 5100 Paint Branch Pkwy., College Park, MD 20740. Such notice shall be accompanied by a statement of the basis, including any articles and correspondence, on which the user in good faith believed the use to be prior-sanctioned. The Commissioner of Food and Drugs shall, by notice in the FEDERAL REGISTER, identify any use of acrylonitrile copolymers not in accordance with this paragraph. Those uses are thereafter unapproved food additives and consequently unlawful.

(2) Any use of acrylonitrile copolymers subject to paragraph (f)(1) of this section shall be the subject of a petition submitted on or before December 13, 1976, in accordance with § 171.1 of this chapter, unless an extension of time is granted by the Food and Drug Administration for good cause shown. Any application for extension shall be by petition submitted in accordance with the requirements of part 10 of this chapter. If a petition is denied, in whole or in part, those uses subject to the denial are thereafter unapproved food additives and consequently unlawful.

(3) Any use of acrylonitrile copolymers subject to paragraph (f)(1) of this section shall meet the acrylonitrile

monomer extraction limitation set forth in paragraph (a) of this section and shall be subject to the requirements of paragraph (b) of this section.

(g) In addition to the requirements of this section, the use of acrylonitrile copolymers shall comply with all applicable requirements in other regulations in this part.

[42 FR 14636, Mar. 15, 1977, as amended at 47 FR 11850, Mar. 19, 1982; 54 FR 24899, June 12, 1989; 61 FR 14246, Apr. 1, 1996]

§ 180.25 Mannitol.

(a) Mannitol is the chemical 1,2,3,4,5,6,-hexanehexol ($C_6H_{14}O_6$) a hexahydric alcohol, differing from sorbitol principally by having a different optical rotation. Mannitol is produced by one of the following processes:

(1) The electrolytic reduction or transition metal catalytic hydrogenation of sugar solutions containing glucose or fructose.

(2) The fermentation of sugars or sugar alcohols such as glucose, sucrose, fructose, or sorbitol using the yeast *Zygosaccharomyces rouxii.*

(3) A pure culture fermentation of sugars such as fructose, glucose, or maltose using the nonpathogenic, nontoxicogenic bacterium *Lactobacillus intermedius (fermentum).*

(b) The ingredient meets the specifications of the "Food Chemicals Codex," 3d Ed. (1981), pp. 188–190, which is incorporated by reference. Copies may be obtained from the National Academy Press, 2101 Constitution Ave. NW., Washington, DC 20418, or may be examined at the National Archives and Records Administration (NARA). For information on the availability of this material at NARA, call 202–741–6030, or go to: *http://www.archives.gov/federal_register/code_of_federal_regulations/ibr_locations.html.*

(c) The ingredient is used as an anticaking agent and free-flow agent as defined in §170.3(o)(1) of this chapter, formulation aid as defined in §170.3(o)(14) of this chapter, firming agent as defined in §170.3(o)(10) of this chapter, flavoring agent and adjuvant as defined in §170.3(o)(12) of this chapter, lubricant and release agent as defined in §170.3(o)(18) of this chapter, nutritive sweetener as defined in §170.3(o)(21) of this chapter, processing aid as defined in §170.3(o)(24) of this chapter, stabilizer and thickener as defined in §170.3(o)(28) of this chapter, surface-finishing agent as defined in §170.3(o)(30) of this chapter, and texturizer as defined in §170.3(o)(32) of this chapter.

(d) The ingredient is used in food at levels not to exceed 98 percent in pressed mints and 5 percent in all other hard candy and cough drops as defined in §170.3(n)(25) of this chapter, 31 percent in chewing gum as defined in §170.3(n)(6) of this chapter, 40 percent in soft candy as defined in §170.3(n)(38) of this chapter, 8 percent in confections and frostings as defined in §170.3(n)(9) of this chapter, 15 percent in nonstandardized jams and jellies, commercial, as defined in §170.3(n)(28) of this chapter, and at levels less than 2.5 percent in all other foods.

(e) The label and labeling of food whose reasonably foreseeable consumption may result in a daily ingestion of 20 grams of mannitol shall bear the statement "Excess consumption may have a laxative effect".

(f) In accordance with §180.1, adequate and appropriate feeding studies have been undertaken for this substance. Continued uses of this ingredient are contingent upon timely and adequate progress reports of such tests, and no indication of increased risk to public health during the test period.

(g) Prior sanctions for this ingredient different from the uses established in this regulation do not exist or have been waived.

[42 FR 14636, Mar. 15, 1977, as amended at 49 FR 5610, Feb. 14, 1984; 61 FR 7991, Mar. 1, 1996; 69 FR 65542, Nov. 15, 2004]

§ 180.30 Brominated vegetable oil.

The food additive brominated vegetable oil may be safely used in accordance with the following prescribed conditions:

(a) The additive complies with specifications prescribed in the "Food Chemicals Codex," 3d Ed. (1981), pp. 40–41, which is incorporated by reference, except that free fatty acids (as oleic) shall not exceed 2.5 percent and iodine value shall not exceed 16. Copies of the material incorporated by reference may be obtained from the National Academy Press, 2101 Constitution Ave.

NW., Washington, DC 20418, or may be examined at the National Archives and Records Administration (NARA). For information on the availability of this material at NARA, call 202–741–6030, or go to: *http://www.archives.gov/federal_register/code_of_federal_regulations/ibr_locations.html.*

(b) The additive is used on an interim basis as a stabilizer for flavoring oils used in fruit-flavored beverages, for which any applicable standards of identity do not preclude such use, in an amount not to exceed 15 parts per million in the finished beverage, pending the outcome of additional toxicological studies on which periodic reports at 6-month intervals are to be furnished and final results submitted to the Food and Drug Administration promptly after completion of the studies.

[42 FR 14636, Mar. 15, 1977, as amended at 49 FR 5610, Feb. 14, 1984]

§ 180.37 Saccharin, ammonium saccharin, calcium saccharin, and sodium saccharin.

The food additives saccharin, ammonium saccharin, calcium saccharin, and sodium saccharin may be safely used as sweetening agents in food in accordance with the following conditions, if the substitution for nutritive sweeteners is for a valid special dietary purpose and is in accord with current special dietary food regulations and policies or if the use or intended use is for an authorized technological purpose other than calorie reduction:

(a) Saccharin is the chemical, 1,2-benzisothiazolin-3-one - 1,1 - dioxide ($C_7H_5NO_3S$). The named salts of saccharin are produced by the additional neutralization of saccharin with the proper base to yield the desired salt.

(b) The food additives meet the specifications of the "Food Chemicals Codex," 3d Ed. (1981), pp. 22, 62, 266–267, 297–299, which is incorporated by reference. Copies may be obtained from the National Academy Press, 2101 Constitution Ave. NW., Washington, DC 20418, or may be examined at the National Archives and Records Administration (NARA). For information on the availability of this material at NARA, call 202–741–6030, or go to: *http://www.archives.gov/federal_register/code_of_federal_regulations/ibr_locations.html.*

(c) Authority for such use shall expire when the Commissioner receives the final reports on the ongoing studies in Canada and publishes an order on the safety of saccharin and its salts based on those reports and other available data.

(d) The additives are used or intended for use as a sweetening agent only in special dietary foods, as follows:

(1) In beverages, fruit juice drinks, and bases or mixes when prepared for consumption in accordance with directions, in amounts not to exceed 12 milligrams of the additive, calculated as saccharin, per fluid ounce.

(2) As a sugar substitute for cooking or table use, in amounts not to exceed 20 milligrams of the additive, calculated as saccharin, for each expressed teaspoonful of sugar sweetening equivalency.

(3) In processed foods, in amounts not to exceed 30 milligrams of the additive, calculated as saccharin, per serving of designated size.

(e) The additives are used or intended for use only for the following technological purposes:

(1) To reduce bulk and enhance flavors in chewable vitamin tablets, chewable mineral tablets, or combinations thereof.

(2) To retain flavor and physical properties of chewing gum.

(3) To enhance flavor of flavor chips used in nonstandardized bakery products.

(f) To assure safe use of the additives, in addition to the other information required by the Act:

(1) The label of the additive and any intermediate mixes of the additive for manufacturing purposes shall bear:

(i) The name of the additive.

(ii) A statement of the concentration of the additive, expressed as saccharin, in any intermediate mix.

(iii) Adequate directions for use to provide a final food product that complies with the limitations prescribed in paragraphs (d) and (e) of this section.

(2) The label of any finished food product containing the additive shall bear:

(i) The name of the additive.

(ii) The amount of the additive, calculated as saccharin, as follows:

(*a*) For beverages, in milligrams per fluid ounce;

(*b*) For cooking or table use products, in milligrams per dispensing unit;

(*c*) For processed foods, in terms of the weight or size of a serving which shall be that quantity of the food containing 30 milligrams or less of the additive.

(iii) When the additive is used for calorie reduction, such other labeling as is required by part 105 of this chapter.

[42 FR 14636, Mar. 15, 1977, as amended at 49 FR 5610, Feb. 14, 1984; 72 FR 10357, Mar. 8, 2007]

PART 181—PRIOR-SANCTIONED FOOD INGREDIENTS

Subpart A—General Provisions

Subpart B—Specific Prior-Sanctioned Food Ingredients

AUTHORITY: 21 U.S.C. 321, 342, 348, 371.

SOURCE: 42 FR 14638, Mar. 15, 1977, unless otherwise noted.

EDITORIAL NOTE: Nomenclature changes to part 181 appear at 61 FR 14482, Apr. 2, 1996, and 66 FR 56035, Nov. 6, 2001.

Subpart A—General Provisions

§ 181.1 General.

(a) An ingredient whose use in food or food packaging is subject to a prior sanction or approval within the meaning of section 201(s)(4) of the Act is exempt from classification as a food additive. The Commissioner will publish in this part all known prior sanctions. Any interested person may submit to the Commissioner a request for publication of a prior sanction, supported by evidence to show that it falls within section 201(s)(4) of the Act.

(b) Based upon scientific data or information that shows that use of a prior-sanctioned food ingredient may be injurious to health, and thus in violation of section 402 of the Act, the Commissioner will establish or amend an applicable prior sanction regulation to impose whatever limitations or conditions are necessary for the safe use of the ingredient, or to prohibit use of the ingredient.

(c) Where appropriate, an emergency action level may be issued for a prior-sanctioned substance, pending the issuance of a final regulation in accordance with paragraph (b) of this section. Such an action level shall be issued pursuant to section 402(a) of the Act to identify, based upon available data, conditions of use of the substance that may be injurious to health. Such an action level shall be issued in a notice published in the FEDERAL REGISTER and shall be followed as soon as practicable by a proposed regulation in accordance with paragraph (b) of this section. Where the available data demonstrate that the substance may be injurious at any level, use of the substance may be prohibited. The identification of a prohibited substance may be made in part 189 of this chapter when appropriate.

[42 FR 14638, Mar. 15, 1977, as amended at 42 FR 52821, Sept. 30, 1977; 54 FR 39635, Sept. 27, 1989]

§ 181.5 Prior sanctions.

(a) A prior sanction shall exist only for a specific use(s) of a substance in food, i.e., the level(s), condition(s), product(s), etc., for which there was explicit approval by the Food and Drug Administration or the United States Department of Agriculture prior to September 6, 1958.

(b) The existence of a prior sanction exempts the sanctioned use(s) from the food additive provisions of the Act but not from the other adulteration or the misbranding provisions of the Act.

(c) All known prior sanctions shall be the subject of a regulation published in this part. Any such regulation is subject to amendment to impose whatever limitation(s) or condition(s) may be necessary for the safe use of the ingredient, or revocation to prohibit use of the ingredient, in order to prevent the adulteration of food in violation of section 402 of the Act.

(d) In proposing, after a general evaluation of use of an ingredient, regulations affirming the GRAS status of substances added directly to human food in part 184 of this chapter or substances in food-contact surfaces in part 186 of this chapter, or establishing a food additive regulation for substances added directly to human food in parts 172 and 173 of this chapter or food additives in food-contact surfaces in parts 174, 175, 176, 177, 178 and §179.45 of this chapter, the Commissioner shall, if he is aware of any prior sanction for use of the ingredient under conditions different from those proposed in the regulation, concurrently propose a separate regulation covering such use of the ingredient under this part. If the Commissioner is unaware of any such applicable prior sanction, the proposed regulation will so state and will require any person who intends to assert or rely on such sanction to submit proof of its existence. Any food additive or GRAS regulation promulgated after a general evaluation of use of an ingredient constitutes a determination that excluded uses would result in adulteration of the food in violation of section 402 of the Act, and the failure of any person to come forward with proof of such an applicable prior sanction in response to a proposal will constitute a waiver of the right to assert or rely on such sanction at any later time. The notice will also constitute a proposal to establish a regulation under this part, incorporating the same provisions, in the event that such a regulation is determined to be appropriate as a result of submission of proof of such an applicable prior sanction in response to the proposal.

Subpart B—Specific Prior-Sanctioned Food Ingredients

§ 181.22 Certain substances employed in the manufacture of food-packaging materials.

Prior to the enactment of the food additives amendment to the Federal Food, Drug, and Cosmetic Act, sanctions were granted for the usage of the substances listed in §§181.23, 181.24, 181.25, 181.26, 181.27, 181.28, 181.29, and 181.30 in the manufacture of packaging materials. So used, these substances are not considered "food additives" within the meaning of section 201(s) of the Act, provided that they are of good commercial grade, are suitable for association with food, and are used in accordance with good manufacturing practice. For the purpose of this subpart, good manufacturing practice for food-packaging materials includes the restriction that the quantity of any of these substances which becomes a component of food as a result of use in food-packaging materials shall not be intended to accomplish any physical or technical effect in the food itself, shall be reduced to the least amount reasonably possible, and shall not exceed any limit specified in this subpart.

[42 FR 56728, Oct. 28, 1977]

§ 181.23 Antimycotics.

Substances classified as antimycotics, when migrating from food-packaging material shall include:

Calcium propionate.
Methylparaben (methyl *p*-hydroxybenzoate).
Propylparaben (propyl *p*-hydroxybenzoate).
Sodium benzoate.
Sodium propionate.
Sorbic acid.

[42 FR 14638, Mar. 15, 1977; 42 FR 56728, Oct. 28, 1977]

§ 181.24 Antioxidants.

Substances classified as antioxidants, when migrating from food-packaging material (limit of addition to food, 0.005 percent) shall include:

Butylated hydroxyanisole.
Butylated hydroxytoluene.
Dilauryl thiodipropionate.
Distearyl thiodipropionate.
Gum guaiac.
Nordihydroguairetic acid.
Propyl gallate.

Thiodipropionic acid.
2,4,5-Trihydroxy butyrophenone.

[42 FR 14638, Mar. 15, 1977; 42 FR 56728, Oct. 28, 1977]

§ 181.25 Driers.

Substances classified as driers, when migrating from food-packaging material shall include:

Cobalt caprylate.
Cobalt linoleate.
Cobalt naphthenate.
Cobalt tallate.
Iron caprylate.
Iron linoleate.
Iron naphthenate.
Iron tallate.
Manganese caprylate.
Manganese linoleate.
Manganese naphthenate.
Manganese tallate.

[42 FR 14638, Mar. 15, 1977; 42 FR 56728, Oct. 28, 1977]

§ 181.26 Drying oils as components of finished resins.

Substances classified as drying oils, when migrating from food-packaging material (as components of finished resins) shall include:

Chinawood oil (tung oil).
Dehydrated castor oil.
Linseed oil.
Tall oil.

[42 FR 14638, Mar. 15, 1977; 42 FR 56728, Oct. 28, 1977]

§ 181.27 Plasticizers.

Substances classified as plasticizers, when migrating from food-packaging material shall include:

Acetyl tributyl citrate.
Acetyl triethyl citrate.
p-tert-Butylphenyl salicylate.
Butyl stearate.
Butylphthalyl butyl glycolate.
Dibutyl sebacate.
Di-(2-ethylhexyl) phthalate (for foods of high water content only).
Diethyl phthalate.
Diisobutyl adipate.
Diisooctyl phthalate (for foods of high water content only).
Diphenyl-2-ethylhexyl phosphate.
Epoxidized soybean oil (iodine number maximum 6; and oxirane oxygen, minimum, 6.0 percent).
Ethylphthalyl ethyl glycolate.
Glycerol monooleate.
Monoisopropyl citrate.
Mono, di-, and tristearyl citrate.
Triacetin (glycerol triacetate).
Triethyl citrate.
3-(2-Xenolyl)-1,2-epoxypropane.

[42 FR 14638, Mar. 15, 1977; 42 FR 56728, Oct. 28, 1977, as amended at 50 FR 49536, Dec. 3, 1985]

§ 181.28 Release agents.

Substances classified as release agents, when migrating from food-packaging material shall include:

Dimethylpolysiloxane (substantially free from hydrolyzable chloride and alkoxy groups, no more than 18 percent loss in weight after heating 4 hours at 200 °C.; viscosity 300 centisokes, 600 centisokes at 25 °C, specific gravity 0.96 to 0.97 at 25 °C, refractive index 1.400 to 1.404 at 25 °C).
Linoleamide (linoleic acid amide).
Oleamide (oleic acid amide).
Palmitamide (palmitic acid amide).
Stearamide (stearic acid amide).

[42 FR 14638, Mar. 15, 1977; 42 FR 56728, Oct. 28, 1977]

§ 181.29 Stabilizers.

Substances classified as stabilizers, when migrating from food-packaging material shall include:

Aluminum mono-, di-, and tristearate.
Ammonium citrate.
Ammonium potassium hydrogen phosphate.
Calcium glycerophosphate.
Calcium phosphate.
Calcium hydrogen phosphate.
Calcium oleate.
Calcium acetate.
Calcium carbonate.
Calcium ricinoleate.
Calcium stearate.
Disodium hydrogen phosphate.
Magnesium glycerophosphate.
Magnesium stearate.
Magnesium phosphate.
Magnesium hydrogen phosphate.
Mono-, di-, and trisodium citrate.
Mono-, di-, and tripotassium citrate.
Potassium oleate.
Potassium stearate.
Sodium pyrophosphate.
Sodium stearate.
Sodium tetrapyrophosphate.
Stannous stearate (not to exceed 50 parts per million tin as a migrant in finished food).
Zinc orthophosphate (not to exceed 50 parts per million zinc as a migrant in finished food).
Zinc resinate (not to exceed 50 parts per million zinc as a migrant in finished food).

[42 FR 14638, Mar. 15, 1977; 42 FR 56728, Oct. 28, 1977]

§ 181.30 Substances used in the manufacture of paper and paperboard products used in food packaging.

Substances used in the manufacture of paper and paperboard products used in food packaging shall include:

Aliphatic polyoxyethylene ethers.*
1-Alkyl (C_6-C_{18})3-amino-3-aminopropane monoacetate.*
Borax or boric acid for use in adhesives, sizes, and coatings.*
Butadiene-styrene copolymer.
Chromium complex of perfluoro-octane sulfonyl glycine for use on paper and paperboard which is waxed.*
Disodium cyanodithioimidocarbamate with ethylene diamine and potassium *N*-methyl dithiocarbamate and/or sodium 2-mercaptobenzothiazole (slimicides).*
Ethyl acrylate and methyl methacrylate copolymers of itaconic acid or methacrylic acid for use only on paper and paperboard which is waxed.*
Hexamethylene tetramine as a setting agent for protein, including casein.*
1-(2-Hydroxyethyl)-1-(4-chlorobutyl)-2-alkyl (C_6-C_{17}) imidazolinium chloride.*
Itaconic acid (polymerized).
Melamine formaldehyde polymer.
Methyl acrylate (polymerized).
Methyl ethers of mono-, di-, and tripropylene glycol.*
Myristo chromic chloride complex.
Nitrocellulose.
Polyethylene glycol 400.
Polyvinyl acetate.
Potassium pentachlorophenate as a slime control agent.*
Potassium trichlorophenate as a slime control agent.*
Resins from high and low viscosity polyvinyl alcohol for fatty foods only.
Rubber hydrochloride.
Sodium pentachlorophenate as a slime control agent.*
Sodium-trichlorophenate as a slime control agent.*
Stearato-chromic chloride complex.
Titanium dioxide.*
Urea formaldehyde polymer.
Vinylidine chlorides (polymerized).

§ 181.32 Acrylonitrile copolymers and resins.

(a) Acrylonitrile copolymers and resins listed in this section, containing less than 30 percent acrylonitrile and complying with the requirements of paragraph (b) of this section, may be safely used as follows:

(1) *Films.* (i) Acrylonitrile/butadiene/styrene copolymers—no restrictions.

(ii) Acrylonitrile/butadiene copolymers—no restrictions.

(iii) Acrylonitrile/butadiene copolymer blended with vinyl chloride-vinyl acetate (optional at level up to 5 percent by weight of the vinyl chloride resin) resin—for use only in contact with oleomargarine.

(iv) Acrylonitrile/styrene copolymer—no restrictions.

(2) *Coatings.* (i) Acrylonitrile/butadiene copolymer blended with polyvinyl chloride resins—for use only on paper and paperboard in contact with meats and lard.

(ii) Polyvinyl chloride resin blended with either acrylonitrile/butadiene copolymer or acrylonitrile/butadiene styrene copolymer mixed with neoprene, for use as components of conveyor belts to be used with fresh fruits, vegetables, and fish.

(iii) Acrylonitrile/butadiene/styrene copolymer—no restrictions.

(iv) Acrylonitrile/styrene copolymer—no restrictions.

(3) *Rigid and semirigid containers.* (i) Acrylonitrile/butadiene/styrene copolymer—for use only as piping for handling food products and for repeated-use articles intended to contact food.

(ii) Acrylonitrile/styrene resin—no restrictions.

(iii) Acrylonitrile/butadiene copolymer blended with polyvinyl chloride resin—for use only as extruded pipe.

(b) Limitations for acrylonitrile monomer extraction for finished food-contact articles, determined by using the method of analysis titled "Gas-Solid Chromatographic Procedure for Determining Acrylonitrile Monomer in Acrylonitrile-Containing Polymers and Food-Simulating Solvents," which is incorporated by reference. Copies are available from the Center for Food Safety and Applied Nutrition (HFS–200), Food and Drug Administration, 5100 Paint Branch Pkwy., College Park, MD 20740, or available for inspection at the National Archives and Records Administration (NARA). For information on the availability of this material at NARA, call 202–741–6030, or go to: *http://www.archives.gov/federal_register/*

*Under the conditions of normal use, these substances would not reasonably be expected to migrate to food, based on available scientific information and data.

code_of_federal_regulations/ibr_locations.html.

(1) In the case of single-use articles having a volume to surface ratio of 10 milliliters or more per square inch of food-contact surface—0.003 milligram/square inch when extracted to equilibrium at 120 °F with food-simulating solvents appropriate to the intended conditions of use.

(2) In the case of single-use articles having a volume to surface ratio of less than 10 milliliters per square inch of food-contact surface—0.3 part per million calculated on the basis of the volume of the container when extracted to equilibrium at 120 °F with food-simulating solvents appropriate to the intended conditions of use.

(3) In the case of repeated-use articles—0.003 milligram/square inch when extracted at a time equivalent to initial batch usage utilizing food-simulating solvents and temperatures appropriate to the intended conditions of use.

The food-simulating solvents shall include, where applicable, distilled water, 8 percent or 50 percent ethanol, 3 percent acetic acid, and either *n*-heptane or an appropriate oil or fat.

(c) Acrylonitrile monomer may present a hazard to health when ingested. Accordingly, any food-contact article containing acrylonitrile copolymers or resins that yield acrylonitrile monomer in excess of that amount provided for in paragraph (b) of this section shall be deemed to be adulterated in violation of section 402 of the Act.

[42 FR 14638, Mar. 15, 1977, as amended at 47 FR 11850, Mar. 19, 1982; 54 FR 24899, June 12, 1989]

§ 181.33 Sodium nitrate and potassium nitrate.

Sodium nitrate and potassium nitrate are subject to prior sanctions issued by the U.S. Department of Agriculture for use as sources of nitrite, with or without sodium or potassium nitrite, in the production of cured red meat products and cured poultry products.

[48 FR 1705, Jan. 14, 1983]

§ 181.34 Sodium nitrite and potassium nitrite.

Sodium nitrite and potassium nitrite are subject to prior sanctions issued by the U.S. Department of Agriculture for use as color fixatives and preservative agents, with or without sodium or potassium nitrate, in the curing of red meat and poultry products.

[48 FR 1705, Jan. 14, 1983]

PART 182—SUBSTANCES GENERALLY RECOGNIZED AS SAFE

Subpart A—General Provisions

Subpart B—Multiple Purpose GRAS Food Substances

Subpart C—Anticaking Agents

182.2122 Aluminum calcium silicate.
182.2227 Calcium silicate.
182.2437 Magnesium silicate.
182.2727 Sodium aluminosilicate.
182.2729 Sodium calcium aluminosilicate, hydrated.
182.2906 Tricalcium silicate.

Subpart D—Chemical Preservatives

182.3013 Ascorbic acid.
182.3041 Erythorbic acid.
182.3089 Sorbic acid.
182.3109 Thiodipropionic acid.
182.3149 Ascorbyl palmitate.
182.3169 Butylated hydroxyanisole.
182.3173 Butylated hydroxytoluene.
182.3189 Calcium ascorbate.
182.3225 Calcium sorbate.
182.3280 Dilauryl thiodipropionate.
182.3616 Potassium bisulfite.
182.3637 Potassium metabisulfite.
182.3640 Potassium sorbate.
182.3731 Sodium ascorbate.
182.3739 Sodium bisulfite.
182.3766 Sodium metabisulfite.
182.3795 Sodium sorbate.
182.3798 Sodium sulfite.
182.3862 Sulfur dioxide.
182.3890 Tocopherols.

Subpart E—Emulsifying Agents [Reserved]

Subpart F—Dietary Supplements [Reserved]

Subpart G—Sequestrants

182.6085 Sodium acid phosphate.
182.6197 Calcium diacetate.
182.6203 Calcium hexametaphosphate.
182.6215 Monobasic calcium phosphate.
182.6285 Dipotassium phosphate.
182.6290 Disodium phosphate.
182.6757 Sodium gluconate.
182.6760 Sodium hexametaphosphate.
182.6769 Sodium metaphosphate.
182.6778 Sodium phosphate.
182.6787 Sodium pyrophosphate.
182.6789 Tetra sodium pyrophosphate.
182.6810 Sodium tripolyphosphate.

Subpart H—Stabilizers

182.7255 Chondrus extract.

Subpart I—Nutrients

182.8013 Ascorbic acid.
182.8159 Biotin.
182.8217 Calcium phosphate.
182.8223 Calcium pyrophosphate.
182.8250 Choline bitartrate.
182.8252 Choline chloride.
182.8778 Sodium phosphate.
182.8890 Tocopherols.
182.8892 α-Tocopherol acetate.
182.8985 Zinc chloride.
182.8938 Zinc gluconate.
182.8991 Zinc oxide.
182.8994 Zinc stearate.
182.8997 Zinc sulfate.

AUTHORITY: 21 U.S.C. 321, 342, 348, 371.

SOURCE: 42 FR 14640, Mar. 15, 1977, unless otherwise noted.

Subpart A—General Provisions

§ 182.1 Substances that are generally recognized as safe.

(a) It is impracticable to list all substances that are generally recognized as safe for their intended use. However, by way of illustration, the Commissioner regards such common food ingredients as salt, pepper, vinegar, baking powder, and monosodium glutamate as safe for their intended use. This part includes additional substances that, when used for the purposes indicated, in accordance with good manufacturing practice, are regarded by the Commissioner as generaly recognized as safe for such uses.

(b) For the purposes of this section, good manufacturing practice shall be defined to include the following restrictions:

(1) The quantity of a substance added to food does not exceed the amount reasonably required to accomplish its intended physical, nutritional, or other technical effect in food; and

(2) The quantity of a substance that becomes a component of food as a result of its use in the manufacturing, processing, or packaging of food, and which is not intended to accomplish any physical or other technical effect in the food itself, shall be reduced to the extent reasonably possible.

(3) The substance is of appropriate food grade and is prepared and handled as a food ingredient. Upon request the Commissioner will offer an opinion, based on specifications and intended use, as to whether or not a particular grade or lot of the substance is of suitable purity for use in food and would generally be regarded as safe for the purpose intended, by experts qualified to evaluate its safety.

(c) The inclusion of substances in the list of nutrients does not constitute a finding on the part of the Department that the substance is useful as a supplement to the diet for humans.

(d) Substances that are generally recognized as safe for their intended use within the meaning of section 409 of the act are listed in this part. When the status of a substance has been reevaluated, it will be deleted from this part, and will be issued as a new regulation under the appropriate part, e.g., "affirmed as GRAS" under part 184 or 186 of this chapter; "food additive regulation" under parts 170 through 180 of this chapter; "interim food additive regulation" under part 180 of this chapter; or "prohibited from use in food" under part 189 of this chapter.

[42 FR 14640, Mar. 15, 1977, as amended at 53 FR 44875, Nov. 7, 1988]

§ 182.10 Spices and other natural seasonings and flavorings.

Spices and other natural seasonings and flavorings that are generally recognized as safe for their intended use, within the meaning of section 409 of the Act, are as follows:

Common name	Botanical name of plant source
Alfalfa herb and seed	Medicago sativa L.
Allspice	Pimenta officinalis Lindl.
Ambrette seed	Hibiscus abelmoschus L.
Angelica	Angelica archangelica L. or other spp. of Angelica.
Angelica root	Do.
Angelica seed	Do.
Angostura (cusparia bark)	Galipea officinalis Hancock.
Anise	Pimpinella anisum L.
Anise, star	Illicium verum Hook. f.
Balm (lemon balm)	Melissa officinalis L.
Basil, bush	Ocimum minimum L.
Basil, sweet	Ocimum basilicum L.
Bay	Laurus nobilis L.
Calendula	Calendula officinalis L.
Camomile (chamomile), English or Roman	Anthemis nobilis L.
Camomile (chamomile), German or Hungarian	Matricaria chamomilla L.
Capers	Capparis spinosa L.
Capsicum	Capsicum frutescens L. or Capsicum annuum L.
Caraway	Carum carvi L.
Caraway, black (black cumin)	Nigella sativa L.
Cardamom (cardamon)	Elettaria cardamomum Maton.
Cassia, Chinese	Cinnamomum cassia Blume.
Cassia, Padang or Batavia	Cinnamomum burmanni Blume.
Cassia, Saigon	Cinnamomum loureirii Nees.
Cayenne pepper	Capsicum frutescens L. or Capsicum annuum L.
Celery seed	Apium graveolens L.
Chervil	Anthriscus cerefolium (L.) Hoffm.
Chives	Allium schoenoprasum L.
Cinnamon, Ceylon	Cinnamomum zeylanicum Nees.
Cinnamon, Chinese	Cinnamomum cassia Blume.
Cinnamon, Saigon	Cinnamomum loureirii Nees.
Clary (clary sage)	Salvia sclarea L.
Clover	Trifolium spp.
Coriander	Coriandrum sativum L.
Cumin (cummin)	Cuminum cyminum L.
Cumin, black (black caraway)	Nigella sativa L.
Elder flowers	Sambucus canadensis L.
Fennel, common	Foeniculum vulgare Mill.
Fennel, sweet (finocchio, Florence fennel)	Foeniculum vulgare Mill. var. duice (DC.) Alex.
Fenugreek	Trigonella foenum-graecum L.
Galanga (galangal)	Alpinia officinarum Hance.
Geranium	Pelargonium spp.
Ginger	Zingiber officinale Rosc.
Grains of paradise	Amomum melegueta Rosc.
Horehound (hoarhound)	Marrubium vulgare L.
Horseradish	Armoracia lapathifolia Gilib.
Hyssop	Hyssopus officinalis L.
Lavender	Lavandula officinalis Chaix.
Linden flowers	Tilia spp.
Mace	Myristica fragrans Houtt.
Marigold, pot	Calendula officinalis L.
Marjoram, pot	Majorana onites (L.) Benth.
Marjoram, sweet	Majorana hortensis Moench.
Mustard, black or brown	Brassica nigra (L.) Koch.
Mustard, brown	Brassica juncea (L.) Coss.

Common name	Botanical name of plant source
Mustard, white or yellow	Brassica hirta Moench.
Nutmeg	Myristica fragrans Houtt.
Oregano (oreganum, Mexican oregano, Mexican sage, origan).	Lippia spp.
Paprika	Capsicum annuum L.
Parsley	Petroselinum crispum (Mill.) Mansf.
Pepper, black	Piper nigrum L.
Pepper, cayenne	Capsicum frutescens L. or Capsicum annuum L.
Pepper, red	Do.
Pepper, white	Piper nigrum L.
Peppermint	Mentha piperita L.
Poppy seed	Papayer somniferum L.
Pot marigold	Calendula officinalis L.
Pot marjoram	Majorana onites (L.) Benth.
Rosemary	Rosmarinus officinalis L.
Saffron	Crocus sativus L.
Sage	Salvia officinalis L.
Sage, Greek	Salvia triloba L.
Savory, summer	Satureia hortensis L. (Satureja).
Savory, winter	Satureia montana L. (Satureja).
Sesame	Sesamum indicum L.
Spearmint	Mentha spicata L.
Star anise	Illicium verum Hook. f.
Tarragon	Artemisia dracunculus L.
Thyme	Thymus vulgaris L.
Thyme, wild or creeping	Thymus serpyllum L.
Turmeric	Curcuma longa L.
Vanilla	Vanilla planifolia Andr. or Vanilla tahitensis J. W. Moore.
Zedoary	Curcuma zedoaria Rosc.

[42 FR 14640, Mar. 15, 1977, as amended at 43 FR 3705, Jan. 27, 1978; 44 FR 3963, Jan. 19, 1979; 50 FR 21044, May 22, 1985; 61 FR 14246, Apr. 1, 1996]

§ 182.20 Essential oils, oleoresins (solvent-free), and natural extractives (including distillates).

Essential oils, oleoresins (solvent-free), and natural extractives (including distillates) that are generally recognized as safe for their intended use, within the meaning of section 409 of the Act, are as follows:

Common name	Botanical name of plant source
Alfalfa	Medicago sativa L.
Allspice	Pimenta officinalis Lindl.
Almond, bitter (free from prussic acid)	Prunus amygdalus Batsch, Prunus armeniaca L., or Prunus persica (L.) Batsch.
Ambrette (seed)	Hibiscus moschatus Moench.
Angelica root	Angelica archangelica L.
Angelica seed	Do.
Angelica stem	Do.
Angostura (cusparia bark)	Galipea officinalis Hancock.
Anise	Pimpinella anisum L.
Asafetida	Ferula assa-foetida L. and related spp. of Ferula.
Balm (lemon balm)	Melissa officinalis L.
Balsam of Peru	Myroxylon pereirae Klotzsch.
Basil	Ocimum basilicum L.
Bay leaves	Laurus nobilis L.
Bay (myrcia oil)	Pimenta racemosa (Mill.) J. W. Moore.
Bergamot (bergamot orange)	Citrus aurantium L. subsp. bergamia Wright et Arn.
Bitter almond (free from prussic acid)	Prunus amygdalus Batsch, Prunus armeniaca L., or Prunus persica (L.) Batsch.
Bois de rose	Aniba rosaeodora Ducke.
Cacao	Theobroma cacao L.
Camomile (chamomile) flowers, Hungarian	Matricaria chamomilla L.
Camomile (chamomile) flowers, Roman or English	Anthemis nobilis L.
Cananga	Cananga odorata Hook. f. and Thoms.
Capsicum	Capsicum frutescens L. and Capsicum annuum L.
Caraway	Carum carvi L.
Cardamom seed (cardamon)	Elettaria cardamomum Maton.
Carob bean	Ceratonia siliqua L.
Carrot	Daucus carota L.

Common name	Botanical name of plant source
Cascarilla bark	Croton eluteria Benn.
Cassia bark, Chinese	Cinnamomum cassia Blume.
Cassia bark, Padang or Batavia	Cinnamomum burmanni Blume.
Cassia bark, Saigon	Cinnamomum loureirii Nees.
Celery seed	Apium graveolens L.
Cherry, wild, bark	Prunus serotina Ehrh.
Chervil	Anthriscus cerefolium (L.) Hoffm.
Chicory	Cichorium intybus L.
Cinnamon bark, Ceylon	Cinnamomum zeylanicum Nees.
Cinnamon bark, Chinese	Cinnamomum cassia Blume.
Cinnamon bark, Saigon	Cinnamomum loureirii Nees.
Cinnamon leaf, Ceylon	Cinnamomum zeylanicum Nees.
Cinnamon leaf, Chinese	Cinnamomum cassia Blume.
Cinnamon leaf, Saigon	Cinnamomum loureirii Nees.
Citronella	Cymbopogon nardus Rendle.
Citrus peels	Citrus spp.
Clary (clary sage)	Salvia sclarea L.
Clover	Trifolium spp.
Coca (decocainized)	Erythroxylum coca Lam. and other spp. of Erythroxylum.
Coffee	Coffea spp.
Cola nut	Cola acuminata Schott and Endl., and other spp. of Cola.
Coriander	Coriandrum sativum L.
Cumin (cummin)	Cuminum cyminum L.
Curacao orange peel (orange, bitter peel)	Citrus aurantium L.
Cusparia bark	Galipea officinalis Hancock.
Dandelion	Taraxacum officinale Weber and T. laevigatum DC.
Dandelion root	Do.
Dog grass (quackgrass, triticum)	Agropyron repens (L.) Beauv.
Elder flowers	Sambucus canadensis L. and S. nigra I.
Estragole (esdragol, esdragon, tarragon)	Artemisia dracunculus L.
Estragon (tarragon)	Do.
Fennel, sweet	Foeniculum vulgare Mill.
Fenugreek	Trigonella foenum-graecum L.
Galanga (galangal)	Alpinia officinarum Hance.
Geranium	Pelargonium spp.
Geranium, East Indian	Cymbopogon martini Stapf.
Geranium, rose	Pelargonium graveolens L'Her.
Ginger	Zingiber officinale Rosc.
Grapefruit	Citrus paradisi Macf.
Guava	Psidium spp.
Hickory bark	Carya spp.
Horehound (hoarhound)	Marrubium vulgare L.
Hops	Humulus lupulus L.
Horsemint	Monarda punctata L.
Hyssop	Hyssopus officinalis L.
Immortelle	Helichrysum augustifolium DC.
Jasmine	Jasminum officinale L. and other spp. of Jasminum.
Juniper (berries)	Juniperus communis L.
Kola nut	Cola acuminata Schott and Endl., and other spp. of Cola.
Laurel berries	Laurus nobilis L.
Laurel leaves	Laurus spp.
Lavender	Lavandula officinalis Chaix.
Lavender, spike	Lavandula latifolia Vill.
Lavandin	Hybrids between Lavandula officinalis Chaix and Lavandula latifolin Vill.
Lemon	Citrus limon (L.) Burm. f.
Lemon balm (see balm).	
Lemon grass	Cymbopogon citratus DC. and Cymbopogon lexuosus Stapf.
Lemon peel	Citrus limon (L.) Burm. f.
Lime	Citrus aurantifolia Swingle.
Linden flowers	Tilia spp.
Locust bean	Ceratonia siliqua L,
Lupulin	Humulus lupulus L.
Mace	Myristica fragrans Houtt.
Mandarin	Citrus reticulata Blanco.
Marjoram, sweet	Majorana hortensis Moench.
Maté	Ilex paraguariensis St. Hil.
Melissa (see balm).	
Menthol	Mentha spp.
Menthyl acetate	Do.
Molasses (extract)	Saccarum officinarum L.
Mustard	Brassica spp.
Naringin	Citrus paradisi Macf.
Neroli, bigarade	Citrus aurantium L.
Nutmeg	Myristica fragrans Houtt.

Common name	Botanical name of plant source
Onion	Allium cepa L.
Orange, bitter, flowers	Citrus aurantium L.
Orange, bitter, peel	Do.
Orange leaf	Citrus sinensis (L.) Osbeck.
Orange, sweet	Do.
Orange, sweet, flowers	Do.
Orange, sweet, peel	Do.
Origanum	Origanum spp.
Palmarosa	Cymbopogon martini Stapf.
Paprika	Capsicum annuum L.
Parsley	Petroselinum crispum (Mill.) Mansf.
Pepper, black	Piper nigrum L.
Pepper, white	Do.
Peppermint	Mentha piperita L.
Peruvian balsam	Myroxylon pereirae Klotzsch.
Petitgrain	Citrus aurantium L.
Petitgrain lemon	Citrus limon (L.) Burm. f.
Petitgrain mandarin or tangerine	Citrus reticulata Blanco.
Pimenta	Pimenta officinalis Lindl.
Pimenta leaf	Pimenta officinalis Lindl.
Pipsissewa leaves	Chimaphila umbellata Nutt.
Pomegranate	Punica granatum L.
Prickly ash bark	Xanthoxylum (or Zanthoxylum) Americanum Mill. or Xanthoxylum clava-herculis L.
Rose absolute	Rosa alba L., Rosa centifolia L., Rosa damascena Mill., Rosa gallica L., and vars. of these spp.
Rose (otto of roses, attar of roses)	Do.
Rose buds	Do.
Rose flowers	Do.
Rose fruit (hips)	Do.
Rose geranium	Pelargonium graveolens L'Her.
Rose leaves	Rosa spp.
Rosemary	Rosmarinus officinalis L.
Saffron	Crocus sativus L.
Sage	Salvia officinalis L.
Sage, Greek	Salvia triloba L.
Sage, Spanish	Salvia lavandulaefolia Vahl.
St. John's bread	Ceratonia siliqua L.
Savory, summer	Satureia hortensis L.
Savory, winter	Satureia montana L.
Schinus molle	Schinus molle L.
Sloe berries (blackthorn berries)	Prunus spinosa L.
Spearmint	Mentha spicata L.
Spike lavender	Lavandula latifolia Vill.
Tamarind	Tamarindus indica L.
Tangerine	Citrus reticulata Blanco.
Tarragon	Artemisia dracunculus L.
Tea	Thea sinensis L.
Thyme	Thymus vulgaris L. and Thymus zygis var. gracilis Boiss.
Thyme, white	Do.
Thyme, wild or creeping	Thymus serpyllum L.
Triticum (see dog grass).	
Tuberose	Polianthes tuberosa L.
Turmeric	Curcuma longa L.
Vanilla	Vanilla planifolia Andr. or Vanilla tahitensis J. W. Moore.
Violet flowers	Viola odorata L.
Violet leaves	Do.
Violet leaves absolute	Do.
Wild cherry bark	Prunus serotina Ehrh.
Ylang-ylang	Cananga odorata Hook. f. and Thoms.
Zedoary bark	Curcuma zedoaria Rosc.

[42 FR 14640, Mar. 15, 1977, as amended at 44 FR 3963, Jan. 19, 1979; 47 FR 29953, July 9, 1982; 48 FR 51613, Nov. 10, 1983; 50 FR 21043 and 21044, May 22, 1985]

§ 182.40 Natural extractives (solvent-free) used in conjunction with spices, seasonings, and flavorings.

Natural extractives (solvent-free) used in conjunction with spices, seasonings, and flavorings that are generally recognized as safe for their intended use, within the meaning of section 409 of the Act, are as follows:

Common name	Botanical name of plant source
Apricot kernel (persic oil)	Prunus armeniaca L.
Peach kernel (persic oil)	Prunus persica Sieb. et Zucc.
Peanut stearine	Arachis hypogaea L.
Persic oil (see apricot kernel and peach kernel).	
Quince seed	Cydonia oblonga Miller.

[42 FR 14640, Mar. 15, 1977, as amended at 47 FR 47375, Oct. 26, 1982]

§ 182.50 Certain other spices, seasonings, essential oils, oleoresins, and natural extracts.

Certain other spices, seasonings, essential oils, oleoresins, and natural extracts that are generally recognized as safe for their intended use, within the meaning of section 409 of the Act, are as follows:

Common name	Derivation
Ambergris	Physeter macrocephalus L.
Castoreum	Castor fiber L. and C. canadensis Kuhl.
Civet (zibeth, zibet, zibetum)	Civet cats, Viverra civetta Schreber and Viverra zibetha Schreber.
Cognac oil, white and green	Ethyl oenanthate, so-called.
Musk (Tonquin musk)	Musk deer, Moschus moschiferus L.

§ 182.60 Synthetic flavoring substances and adjuvants.

Synthetic flavoring substances and adjuvants that are generally recognized as safe for their intended use, within the meaning of section 409 of the Act, are as follows:

Acetaldehyde (ethanal).
Acetoin (acetyl methylcarbinol).
Anethole (parapropenyl anisole).
Benzaldehyde (benzoic aldehyde).
N-Butyric acid (butanoic acid).
d- or *l*-Carvone (carvol).
Cinnamaldehyde (cinnamic aldehyde).
Citral (2,6-dimethyloctadien-2,6-*al*-8, geranial, neral).
Decanal (*N*-decylaldehyde, capraldehyde, capric aldehyde, caprinaldehyde, aldehyde C-10).
Ethyl acetate.
Ethyl butyrate.
3-Methyl-3-phenyl glycidic acid ethyl ester (ethyl-methyl-phenyl-glycidate, so-called strawberry aldehyde, C-16 aldehyde).
Ethyl vanillin.
Geraniol (3,7-dimethyl-2,6 and 3,6-octadien-1-*ol*).
Geranyl acetate (geraniol acetate).
Limonene (*d*-, *l*-, and *dl*-).
Linalool (linalol, 3,7-dimethyl-1,6-octadien-3-*ol*).
Linalyl acetate (bergamol).
Methyl anthranilate (methyl-2-aminobenzoate).
Piperonal (3,4-methylenedioxy-benzaldehyde, heliotropin).
Vanillin.

[42 FR 14640, Mar. 15, 1977, as amended at 43 FR 47724, Oct. 17, 1978; 44 FR 3963, Jan. 19, 1979; 44 FR 20656, Apr. 6, 1979; 48 FR 51907, Nov. 15, 1983; 54 FR 7402, Feb. 21, 1989]

§ 182.70 Substances migrating from cotton and cotton fabrics used in dry food packaging.

Substances migrating to food from cotton and cotton fabrics used in dry food packaging that are generally recognized as safe for their intended use, within the meaning of section 409 of the Act, are as follows:

Beef tallow.
Carboxymethylcellulose.
Coconut oil, refined.
Cornstarch.
Gelatin.
Lard.
Lard oil.
Oleic acid.
Peanut oil.
Potato starch.
Sodium acetate.
Sodium chloride.

Sodium silicate.
Sodium tripolyphosphate.
Soybean oil (hydrogenated).
Talc.
Tallow (hydrogenated).
Tallow flakes.
Tapioca starch.
Tetrasodium pyrophosphate.
Wheat starch.
Zinc chloride.

[42 FR 14640, Mar. 15, 1977, as amended at 43 FR 11698, Mar. 21, 1978; 44 FR 28323, May 15, 1979; 45 FR 6085, Jan. 25, 1980; 47 FR 27807, 27814, June 25, 1982; 48 FR 51150, Nov. 7, 1983; 48 FR 51616, Nov. 10, 1983; 48 FR 51909, Nov. 15, 1983; 48 FR 52441, 52443, 52445, 52446, Nov. 18, 1983; 51 FR 16830, May 7, 1986; 51 FR 27171, July 30, 1986; 60 FR 62208, Dec. 5, 1995]

§ 182.90 Substances migrating to food from paper and paperboard products.

Substances migrating to food from paper and paperboard products used in food packaging that are generally recognized as safe for their intended use, within the meaning of section 409 of the Act, are as follows:

Alum (double sulfate of aluminum and ammonium potassium, or sodium).
Aluminum hydroxide.
Aluminum oleate.
Aluminum palmitate.
Casein.
Cellulose acetate.
Cornstarch.
Diatomaceous earth filler.
Ethyl cellulose.
Ethyl vanillin.
Glycerin.
Oleic acid.
Potassium sorbate.
Silicon dioxides.
Sodium aluminate.
Sodium chloride.
Sodium hexametaphosphate.
Sodium hydrosulfite.
Sodium phosphoaluminate.
Sodium silicate.
Sodium sorbate.
Sodium tripolyphosphate.
Sorbitol.
Soy protein, isolated.
Starch, acid modified.
Starch, pregelatinized.
Starch, unmodified.
Talc.
Vanillin.
Zinc hydrosulfite.
Zinc sulfate.

[42 FR 14640, Mar. 15, 1977]

EDITORIAL NOTE: For additional FEDERAL REGISTER citations affecting § 182.90, see the List of CFR Sections Affected, which appears in the Finding Aids section of the printed volume and at *www.fdsys.gov*.

§ 182.99 Adjuvants for pesticide chemicals.

Adjuvants, identified and used in accordance with 40 CFR 180.910 and 40 CFR 180.920, which are added to pesticide use dilutions by a grower or applicator prior to application to the raw agricultural commodity, are exempt from the requirement of tolerances under section 409 of the Federal Food, Drug, and Cosmetic Act (21 U.S.C. 348).

[76 FR 59249, Sept. 26, 2011]

Subpart B—Multiple Purpose GRAS Food Substances

§ 182.1045 Glutamic acid.

(a) *Product*. Glutamic acid.

(b) [Reserved]

(c) *Limitations, restrictions, or explanation*. This substance is generally recognized as safe when used as a salt substitute in accordance with good manufacturing practice.

§ 182.1047 Glutamic acid hydrochloride.

(a) *Product*. Glutamic acid hydrochloride.

(b) [Reserved]

(c) *Limitations, restrictions, or explanation*. This substance is generally recognized as safe when used as a salt substitute in accordance with good manufacturing practice.

§ 182.1057 Hydrochloric acid.

(a) *Product*. Hydrochloric acid.

(b) [Reserved]

(c) *Limitations, restrictions, or explanation*. This substance is generally recognized as safe when used as a buffer and neutralizing agent in accordance with good manufacturing practice.

§ 182.1073 Phosphoric acid.

(a) *Product*. Phosphoric acid.

(b) *Conditions of use*. This substance is generally recognized as safe when used in accordance with good manufacturing practice.

§ 182.1087 Sodium acid pyrophosphate.

(a) *Product*. Sodium acid pyrophosphate.

(b) *Conditions of use.* This substance is generally recognized as safe when used in accordance with good manufacturing practice.

§ 182.1125 Aluminum sulfate.

(a) *Product.* Aluminum sulfate.

(b) *Conditions of use.* This substance is generally recognized as safe when used in accordance with good manufacturing practice.

§ 182.1127 Aluminum ammonium sulfate.

(a) *Product.* Aluminum ammonium sulfate.

(b) *Conditions of use.* This substance is generally recognized as safe when used in accordance with good manufacturing practice.

§ 182.1129 Aluminum potassium sulfate.

(a) *Product.* Aluminum potassium sulfate.

(b) *Conditions of use.* This substance is generally recognized as safe when used in accordance with good manufacturing practice.

§ 182.1131 Aluminum sodium sulfate.

(a) *Product.* Aluminum sodium sulfate.

(b) *Conditions of use.* This substance is generally recognized as safe when used in accordance with good manufacturing practice.

§ 182.1180 Caffeine.

(a) *Product.* Caffeine.

(b) *Tolerance.* 0.02 percent.

(c) *Limitations, restrictions, or explanation.* This substance is generally recognized as safe when used in cola-type beverages in accordance with good manufacturing practice.

§ 182.1217 Calcium phosphate.

(a) *Product.* Calcium phosphate (mono-, di-, and tribasic).

(b) *Conditions of use.* This substance is generally recognized as safe when used in accordance with good manufacturing practice.

§ 182.1235 Caramel.

(a) *Product.* Caramel.

(b) *Conditions of use.* This substance is generally recognized as safe when used in accordance with good manufacturing practice.

§ 182.1320 Glycerin.

(a) *Product.* Glycerin.

(b) *Conditions of use.* This substance is generally recognized as safe when used in accordance with good manufacturing practice.

§ 182.1480 Methylcellulose.

(a) *Product.* U.S.P. methylcellulose, except that the methoxy content shall not be less than 27.5 percent and not more than 31.5 percent on a dry-weight basis.

(b) *Conditions of use.* This substance is generally recognized as safe when used in accordance with good manufacturing practice.

§ 182.1500 Monoammonium glutamate.

(a) *Product.* Monoammonium glutamate.

(b) *Conditions of use.* This substance is generally recognized as safe when used in accordance with good manufacturing practice.

§ 182.1516 Monopotassium glutamate.

(a) *Product.* Monopotassium glutamate.

(b) *Conditions of use.* This substance is generally recognized as safe when used in accordance with good manufacturing practice.

§ 182.1711 Silica aerogel.

(a) *Product.* Silica aerogel as a finely powdered microcellular silica foam having a minimum silica content of 89.5 percent.

(b) [Reserved]

(c) *Limitations, restrictions, or explanation.* This substance is generally recognized as safe when used as a component of an anti-foaming agent in accordance with good manufacturing practice.

§ 182.1745 Sodium carboxymethylcellulose.

(a) *Product.* Sodium carboxymethylcellulose is the sodium salt of carboxymethylcellulose not less than 99.5 percent on a dry-weight basis, with maximum substitution of 0.95 carboxymethyl groups per anhydroglucose unit, and with a minimum viscosity of 25 centipoises for 2 percent by weight aqueous solution at 25 °C.

(b) *Conditions of use.* This substance is generally recognized as safe when used in accordance with good manufacturing practice.

§ 182.1748 Sodium caseinate.

(a) *Product.* Sodium caseinate.

(b) *Conditions of use.* This substance is generally recognized as safe when used in accordance with good manufacturing practice.

§ 182.1778 Sodium phosphate.

(a) *Product.* Sodium phosphate (mono-, di-, and tribasic).

(b) *Conditions of use.* This substance is generally recognized as safe when used in accordance with good manufacturing practice.

§ 182.1781 Sodium aluminum phosphate.

(a) *Product.* Sodium aluminum phosphate.

(b) *Conditions of use.* This substance is generally recognized as safe when used in accordance with good manufacturing practice.

§ 182.1810 Sodium tripolyphosphate.

(a) *Product.* Sodium tripolyphosphate.

(b) *Conditions of use.* This substance is generally recognized as safe when used in accordance with good manufacturing practice.

Subpart C—Anticaking Agents

§ 182.2122 Aluminum calcium silicate.

(a) *Product.* Aluminum calcium silicate.

(b) *Tolerance.* 2 percent.

(c) *Limitations, restrictions, or explanation.* This substance is generally recognized as safe when used in table salt in accordance with good manufacturing practice.

§ 182.2227 Calcium silicate.

(a) *Product.* Calcium silicate.

(b) *Tolerance.* 2 percent and 5 percent.

(c) *Limitations, restrictions, or explanation.* This substance is generally recognized as safe when used at levels not exceeding 2 percent in table salt and 5 percent in baking powder in accordance with good manufacturing practice.

§ 182.2437 Magnesium silicate.

(a) *Product.* Magnesium silicate.

(b) *Tolerance.* 2 percent.

(c) *Limitations, restrictions, or explanation.* This substance is generally recognized as safe when used in table salt in accordance with good manufacturing practice.

§ 182.2727 Sodium aluminosilicate.

(a) *Product.* Sodium aluminosilicate (sodium silicoaluminate).

(b) *Tolerance.* This substance is generally recognized as safe for use at a level not exceeding 2 percent in accordance with good manufacturing practice.

§ 182.2729 Sodium calcium aluminosilicate, hydrated.

(a) *Product.* Hydrated sodium calcium aluminosilicate (sodium calcium silicoaluminate).

(b) *Tolerance.* This substance is generally recognized as safe for use at a level not exceeding 2 percent in accordance with good manufacturing practice.

§ 182.2906 Tricalcium silicate.

(a) *Product.* Tricalcium silicate.

(b) *Tolerance.* 2 percent.

(c) *Limitations, restrictions, or explanation.* This substance is generally recognized as safe when used in table salt in accordance with good manufacturing practice.

Subpart D—Chemical Preservatives

§ 182.3013 Ascorbic acid.

(a) *Product.* Ascorbic acid.

(b) *Conditions of use.* This substance is generally recognized as safe when used in accordance with good manufacturing practice.

§ 182.3041 Erythorbic acid.

(a) *Product.* Erythorbic acid.

(b) *Conditions of use.* This substance is generally recognized as safe when used in accordance with good manufacturing practice.

§ 182.3089 Sorbic acid.

(a) *Product.* Sorbic acid.

(b) *Conditions of use.* This substance is generally recognized as safe when used in accordance with good manufacturing practice.

§ 182.3109 Thiodipropionic acid.

(a) *Product.* Thiodipropionic acid.

(b) *Tolerance.* This substance is generally recognized as safe for use in food when the total content of antioxidants is not over 0.02 percent of fat or oil content, including essential (volatile) oil content of the food, provided the substance is used in accordance with good manufacturing practice.

§ 182.3149 Ascorbyl palmitate.

(a) *Product.* Ascorbyl palmitate.

(b) *Conditions of use.* This substance is generally recognized as safe when used in accordance with good manufacturing practice.

§ 182.3169 Butylated hydroxyanisole.

(a) *Product.* Butylated hydroxyanisole.

(b) *Tolerance.* This substance is generally recognized as safe for use in food when the total content of antioxidants is not over 0.02 percent of fat or oil content, including essential (volatile) oil content of food, provided the substance is used in accordance with good manufacturing practice.

§ 182.3173 Butylated hydroxytoluene.

(a) *Product.* Butylated hydroxytoluene.

(b) *Tolerance.* This substance is generally recognized as safe for use in food when the total content of antioxidants is not over 0.02 percent of fat or oil content, including essential (volatile) oil content of food, provided the substance is used in accordance with good manufacturing practice.

§ 182.3189 Calcium ascorbate.

(a) *Product.* Calcium ascorbate.

(b) *Conditions of use.* This substance is generally recognized as safe when used in accordance with good manufacturing practice.

§ 182.3225 Calcium sorbate.

(a) *Product.* Calcium sorbate.

(b) *Conditions of use.* This substance is generally recognized as safe when used in accordance with good manufacturing practice.

§ 182.3280 Dilauryl thiodipropionate.

(a) *Product.* Dilauryl thiodipropionate.

(b) *Tolerance.* This substance is generally recognized as safe for use in food when the total content of antioxidants is not over 0.02 percent of fat or oil content, including essential (volatile) oil content of the food, provided the substance is used in accordance with good manufacturing practice.

§ 182.3616 Potassium bisulfite.

(a) *Product.* Potassium bisulfite.

(b) [Reserved]

(c) *Limitations, restrictions, or explanation.* This substance is generally recognized as safe when used in accordance with good manufacturing practice, except that it is not used in meats; in food recognized as a source of vitamin B_1; on fruits and vegetables intended to be served raw to consumers or sold raw to consumers, or to be presented to consumers as fresh.

[42 FR 14640, Mar. 15, 1977, as amended at 51 FR 25025, July 9, 1986; 55 FR 9832, Mar. 15, 1990; 59 FR 65939, Dec. 22, 1994]

§ 182.3637 Potassium metabisulfite.

(a) *Product.* Potassium metabisulfite.

(b) [Reserved]

(c) *Limitations, restrictions, or explanation.* This substance is generally recognized as safe when used in accordance with good manufacturing practice, except that it is not used in meats; in food recognized as a source of vitamin B_1; on fruits and vegetables intended to be served raw to consumers or sold raw to consumers, or to be presented to consumers as fresh.

[42 FR 14640, Mar. 15, 1977, as amended at 51 FR 25025, July 9, 1986; 55 FR 9832, Mar. 15, 1990; 59 FR 65939, Dec. 22, 1994]

§ 182.3640 Potassium sorbate.

(a) *Product.* Potassium sorbate.

(b) *Conditions of use.* This substance is generally recognized as safe when used in accordance with good manufacturing practice.

§ 182.3731 Sodium ascorbate.

(a) *Product.* Sodium ascorbate.

(b) *Conditions of use.* This substance is generally recognized as safe when used in accordance with good manufacturing practice.

§ 182.3739 Sodium bisulfite.

(a) *Product.* Sodium bisulfite.

(b) [Reserved]

(c) *Limitations, restrictions, or explanation.* This substance is generally recognized as safe when used in accordance with good manufacturing practice, except that it is not used in meats; in food recognized as a source of vitamin B_1; on fruits or vegetables intended to be served raw to consumers or sold raw to consumers, or to be presented to the consumer as fresh.

[42 FR 14640, Mar. 15, 1977, as amended at 51 FR 25025, July 9, 1986; 55 FR 9832, Mar. 15, 1990; 59 FR 65939, Dec. 22, 1994]

§ 182.3766 Sodium metabisulfite.

(a) *Product.* Sodium metabisulfite.

(b) [Reserved]

(c) *Limitations, restrictions, or explanation.* This substance is generally recognized as safe when used in accordance with good manufacturing practice, except that it is not used in meats; in food recognized as a source of vitamin B_1; on fruits or vegetables intended to be served raw to consumers or sold raw to consumers, or to be presented to consumers as fresh.

[42 FR 14640, Mar. 15, 1977, as amended at 51 FR 25025, July 9, 1986; 55 FR 9833, Mar. 15, 1990; 59 FR 65939, Dec. 22, 1994]

§ 182.3795 Sodium sorbate.

(a) *Product.* Sodium sorbate.

(b) *Conditions of use.* This substance is generally recognized as safe when used in accordance with good manufacturing practice.

§ 182.3798 Sodium sulfite.

(a) *Product.* Sodium sulfite.

(b) [Reserved]

(c) *Limitations, restrictions, or explanation.* This substance is generally recognized as safe when used in accordance with good manufacturing practice, except that it is not used in meats; in food recognized as a source of vitamin B_1; on fruits or vegetables intended to be served raw to consumers or sold raw to consumers, or to be presented to consumers as fresh.

[42 FR 14640, Mar. 15, 1977, as amended at 51 FR 25026, July 9, 1986; 55 FR 9833, Mar. 15, 1990; 59 FR 65939, Dec. 22, 1994]

§ 182.3862 Sulfur dioxide.

(a) *Product.* Sulfur dioxide.

(b) [Reserved]

(c) *Limitations, restrictions, or explanation.* This substance is generally recognized as safe when used in accordance with good manufacturing practice, except that it is not used in meats; in food recognized as a source of vitamin B_1; on fruits or vegetables intended to be served raw to consumers or sold raw to consumers, or to be presented to consumers as fresh.

[42 FR 14640, Mar. 15, 1977, as amended at 51 FR 25026, July 9, 1986; 55 FR 9833, Mar. 15, 1990; 59 FR 65939, Dec. 22, 1994]

§ 182.3890 Tocopherols.

(a) *Product.* Tocopherols.

(b) *Conditions of use.* This substance is generally recognized as safe when used in accordance with good manufacturing practice.

Subpart E—Emulsifying Agents [Reserved]

Subpart F—Dietary Supplements [Reserved]

Subpart G—Sequestrants [1]

§ 182.6085 Sodium acid phosphate.

(a) *Product.* Sodium acid phosphate.

(b) *Conditions of use.* This substance is generally recognized as safe when used in accordance with good manufacturing practice.

§ 182.6197 Calcium diacetate.

(a) *Product.* Calcium diacetate.

(b) *Conditions of use.* This substance is generally recognized as safe when used in accordance with good manufacturing practice.

[1] For the purpose of this subpart, no attempt has been made to designate those sequestrants that may also function as chemical preservatives.

§ 182.6203 Calcium hexametaphosphate.

(a) *Product.* Calcium hexametaphosphate.

(b) *Conditions of use.* This substance is generally recognized as safe when used in accordance with good manufacturing practice.

§ 182.6215 Monobasic calcium phosphate.

(a) *Product.* Monobasic calcium phosphate.

(b) *Conditions of use.* This substance is generally recognized as safe when used in accordance with good manufacturing practice.

§ 182.6285 Dipotassium phosphate.

(a) *Product.* Dipotassium phosphate.

(b) *Conditions of use.* This substance is generally recognized as safe when used in accordance with good manufacturing practice.

§ 182.6290 Disodium phosphate.

(a) *Product.* Disodium phosphate.

(b) *Conditions of use.* This substance is generally recognized as safe when used in accordance with good manufacturing practice.

§ 182.6757 Sodium gluconate.

(a) *Product.* Sodium gluconate.

(b) *Conditions of use.* This substance is generally recognized as safe when used in accordance with good manufacturing practice.

§ 182.6760 Sodium hexametaphosphate.

(a) *Product.* Sodium hexametaphosphate.

(b) *Conditions of use.* This substance is generally recognized as safe when used in accordance with good manufacturing practice.

§ 182.6769 Sodium metaphosphate.

(a) *Product.* Sodium metaphosphate.

(b) *Conditions of use.* This substance is generally recognized as safe when used in accordance with good manufacturing practice.

§ 182.6778 Sodium phosphate.

(a) *Product.* Sodium phosphate (mono-, di-, and tribasic).

(b) *Conditions of use.* This substance is generally recognized as safe when used in accordance with good manufacturing practice.

§ 182.6787 Sodium pyrophosphate.

(a) *Product.* Sodium pyrophosphate.

(b) *Conditions of use.* This substance is generally recognized as safe when used in accordance with good manufacturing practice.

§ 182.6789 Tetra sodium pyrophosphate.

(a) *Product.* Tetra sodium pyrophosphate.

(b) *Conditions of use.* This substance is generally recognized as safe when used in accordance with good manufacturing practice.

§ 182.6810 Sodium tripolyphosphate.

(a) *Product.* Sodium tripolyphosphate.

(b) *Conditions of use.* This substance is generally recognized as safe when used in accordance with good manufacturing practice.

Subpart H—Stabilizers

§ 182.7255 Chondrus extract.

(a) *Product.* Chondrus extract (carrageenin).

(b) *Conditions of use.* This substance is generally recognized as safe when used in accordance with good manufacturing practice.

Subpart I—Nutrients

SOURCE: 45 FR 58838, Sept. 5, 1980, unless otherwise noted.

§ 182.8013 Ascorbic acid.

(a) *Product.* Ascorbic acid.

(b) *Conditions of use.* This substance is generally recognized as safe when used in accordance with good manufacturing practice.

§ 182.8159 Biotin.

(a) *Product.* Biotin.

(b) *Conditions of use.* This substance is generally recognized as safe when used in accordance with good manufacturing practice.

§ 182.8217 Calcium phosphate.

(a) *Product.* Calcium phosphate (mono-, di-, and tribasic).

(b) *Conditions of use.* This substance is generally recognized as safe when used in accordance with good manufacturing practice.

§ 182.8223 Calcium pyrophosphate.

(a) *Product.* Calcium pyrophosphate.

(b) *Conditions of use.* This substance is generally recognized as safe when used in accordance with good manufacturing practice.

§ 182.8250 Choline bitartrate.

(a) *Product.* Choline bitartrate.

(b) *Conditions of use.* This substance is generally recognized as safe when used in accordance with good manufacturing practice.

§ 182.8252 Choline chloride.

(a) *Product.* Choline chloride.

(b) *Conditions of use.* This substance is generally recognized as safe when used in accordance with good manufacturing practice.

§ 182.8778 Sodium phosphate.

(a) *Product.* Sodium phosphate (mono-, di-, and tribasic).

(b) *Conditions of use.* This substance is generally recognized as safe when used in accordance with good manufacturing practice.

§ 182.8890 Tocopherols.

(a) *Product.* Tocopherols.

(b) *Conditions of use.* This substance is generally recognized as safe when used in accordance with good manufacturing practice.

§ 182.8892 α-Tocopherol acetate.

(a) *Product.* α-Tocopherol acetate.

(b) *Conditions of use.* This substance is generally recognized as safe when used in accordance with good manufacturing practice.

§ 182.8985 Zinc chloride.

(a) *Product.* Zinc chloride.

(b) *Conditions of use.* This substance is generally recognized as safe when used in accordance with good manufacturing practice.

§ 182.8988 Zinc gluconate.

(a) *Product.* Zinc gluconate.

(b) *Conditions of use.* This substance is generally recognized as safe when used in accordance with good manufacturing practice.

§ 182.8991 Zinc oxide.

(a) *Product.* Zinc oxide.

(b) *Conditions of use.* This substance is generally recognized as safe when used in accordance with good manufacturing practice.

§ 182.8994 Zinc stearate.

(a) *Product.* Zinc stearate prepared from stearic acid free from chickedema factor.

(b) *Conditions of use.* This substance is generally recognized as safe when used in accordance with good manufacturing practice.

§ 182.8997 Zinc sulfate.

(a) *Product.* Zinc sulfate.

(b) *Conditions of use.* This substance is generally recognized as safe when used in accordance with good manufacturing practice.

PART 184—DIRECT FOOD SUBSTANCES AFFIRMED AS GENERALLY RECOGNIZED AS SAFE

Subpart A—General Provisions

Sec.

Subpart B—Listing of Specific Substances Affirmed as GRAS

AUTHORITY: 21 U.S.C. 321, 342, 348, 371.

SOURCE: 42 FR 14653, Mar 15, 1977, unless otherwise noted.

EDITORIAL NOTE: Nomenclature changes to part 184 appear at 66 FR 56035, Nov. 6, 2001, 66 FR 66742, Dec. 27, 2001, 68 FR 15355, Mar. 31, 2003, 69 FR 13717, Mar. 24, 2004, 70 FR 40880, July 15, 2005, and 70 FR 67651, Nov. 8, 2005.

Subpart A—General Provisions

§ 184.1 Substances added directly to human food affirmed as generally recognized as safe (GRAS).

(a) The direct human food ingredients listed in this part have been reviewed by the Food and Drug Administration and determined to be generally recognized as safe (GRAS) for the purposes and under the conditions prescribed. The regulations in this part shall sufficiently describe each ingredient to identify the characteristics of the ingredient that has been affirmed as GRAS and to differentiate it from other possible versions of the ingredient that have not been affirmed as GRAS. Ingredients affirmed as GRAS in this part are also GRAS as indirect human food ingredients, subject to any limitations prescribed in parts 174, 175, 176, 177, 178 or § 179.45 of this chapter or in part 186 of this chapter. The purity specifications in this part do not apply when the ingredient is used in indirect applications. However, when used in indirect applications, the ingredient must be of a purity suitable for its intended use in accordance with § 170.30(h)(1) of this chapter.

(b) Any ingredient affirmed as GRAS in this part shall be used in accordance with current good manufacturing practice. For the purpose of this part, current good manufacturing practice includes the requirements that a direct human food ingredient be of appropriate food grade; that it be prepared and handled as a food ingredient; and that the quantity of the ingredient added to food does not exceed the amount reasonably required to accomplish the intended physical, nutritional, or other technical effect in food.

(1) If the ingredient is affirmed as GRAS with no limitations on its conditions of use other than current good manufacturing practice, it shall be regarded as GRAS if its conditions of use are consistent with the requirements of paragraph (b), (c), and (d) of this section. When the Food and Drug Administration (FDA) determines that it is appropriate, the agency will describe one or more current good manufacturing practice conditions of use in the regulation that affirms the GRAS status of the ingredient. For example, when the safety of an ingredient has been evaluated on the basis of limited conditions of use, the agency will describe in the regulation that affirms the GRAS status of the ingredient, one or more of these limited conditions of use, which may include the category of food(s), the technical effect(s) or functional use(s) of the ingredient, and the level(s) of use. If the ingredient is used under conditions that are significantly different from those described in the regulation, that use of the ingredient may not be GRAS. In such a case, a manufacturer may not rely on the regulation as authorizing that use but shall independently establish that that use is GRAS or shall use the ingredient in accordance with a food additive regulation. Persons seeking FDA approval of an independent determination that a use of an ingredient is GRAS may submit a GRAS petition in accordance with § 170.35 of this chapter.

(2) If the ingredient is affirmed as GRAS with specific limitation(s), it shall be used in food only within such limitation(s), including the category of food(s), the functional use(s) of the ingredient, and the level(s) of use. Any use of such an ingredient not in full compliance with each such established limitation shall require a food additive regulation.

(3) If the ingredient is affirmed as GRAS for a specific use, without a general evaluation of use of the ingredient, other uses may also be GRAS.

(c) The listing of a food ingredient in this part does not authorize the use of such substance in a manner that may lead to deception of the consumer or to any other violation of the Federal Food, Drug, and Cosmetic Act (the Act).

(d) The listing of more than one ingredient to produce the same technological effect does not authorize use of a combination of two or more ingredients to accomplish the same technological effect in any one food at a combined level greater than the highest level permitted for one of the ingredients.

(e) If the Commissioner of Food and Drugs is aware of any prior sanction for use of an ingredient under conditions different from those proposed to be affirmed as GRAS, he will concurrently propose a separate regulation covering such use of the ingredient under part 181 of this chapter. If the Commissioner is unaware of any such applicable prior sanction, the proposed regulation will so state and will require any person who intends to assert or rely on such sanction to submit proof of its existence. Any regulation promulgated pursuant to this section constitutes a determination that excluded uses would result in adulteration of the food in violation of section 402 of the Act, and the failure of any person to come forward with proof of such an applicable prior sanction in response to the proposal will constitute a waiver of the right to assert or rely on such sanction at any later time. The notice will also constitute a proposal to establish a regulation under part 181 of this chapter, incorporating the same provisions, in the event that such a regulation is determined to be appropriate as a result of submission of proof of such an applicable prior sanction in response to the proposal.

(f) The label and labeling of the ingredient and any intermediate mix of the ingredient for use in finished food shall bear, in addition to the other labeling required by the Act:

(1) The name of the ingredient, except where exempted from such labeling in part 101 of this chapter.

(2) A statement of concentration of the ingredient in any intermediate mix; or other information to permit a food processor independently to determine that use of the ingredients will be in accordance with any limitations and good manufacturing practice gudelines prescribed.

(3) Adequate directions for use to provide a final food product that complies with any limitations prescribed for the ingredient(s).

[42 FR 14653, Mar. 15, 1977, as amended at 42 FR 55205, Oct. 14, 1977; 48 FR 48457, 48459, Oct. 19, 1983; 62 FR 15110, Mar. 31, 1997]

Subpart B—Listing of Specific Substances Affirmed as GRAS

§ 184.1005 Acetic acid.

(a) Acetic acid ($C_2H_4O_2$, CAS Reg. No. 64–19–7) is known as ethanoic acid. It occurs naturally in plant and animal tissues. It is produced by fermentation of carbohydrates or by organic synthesis. The principal synthetic methods currently employed are oxidation of acetaldehyde derived from ethylene, liquid phase oxidation of butane, and reaction of carbon monoxide with methanol derived from natural gas.

(b) The ingredient meets the specifications of the Food Chemicals Codex, 3d Ed. (1981), p. 8, which is incorporated by reference. Copies are available from the National Academy Press, 2101 Constitution Ave. NW., Washington, DC 20418, or available for inspection at the National Archives and Records Administration (NARA). For information on the availability of this material at NARA, call 202–741–6030, or go to: *http://www.archives.gov/federal_register/code_of_federal_regulations/ibr_locations.html.*

(c) The ingredient is used as a curing and pickling agent as defined in § 170.3(o)(5) of this chapter; flavor enhancer as defined in § 170.3(o)(11) of this chapter; flavoring agent and adjuvant as defined in § 170.3(o)(12) of this chapter; pH control agent as defined in § 170.3(o)(23) of this chapter; as a solvent and vehicle as defined in § 170.3(o)(27) of this chapter; and as a boiler water additive complying with § 173.310 of this chapter.

(d) The ingredient is used in food at levels not to exceed current good manufacturing practice in accordance with § 184.1(b)(1). Current good manufacturing practice results in a maximum level as served, of 0.25 percent for baked goods as defined in § 170.3(n)(1) of this chapter; 0.8 percent for cheeses as defined in § 170.3(n)(5) of this chapter and dairy product analogs as defined in § 170.3(n)(10) of this chapter; 0.5 percent for chewing gum as defined in § 170.3(n)(6) of this chapter; 9.0 percent for condiments and relishes as defined in § 170.3(n)(8) of this chapter; 0.5 percent for fats and oils as defined in § 170.3(n)(12) of this chapter; 3.0 percent for gravies and sauces as defined in § 170.3(n)(24) of this chapter; 0.6 percent for meat products as defined in § 170.3(n)(29) of this chapter; and 0.15 percent or less for all other food categories. The ingredient may also be used in boiler water additives at levels not to exceed current good manufacturing practice.

(e) Prior sanctions for this ingredient different from the uses established in this section do not exist or have been waived.

[47 FR 27814, June 25, 1982]

§ 184.1007 Aconitic acid.

(a) Aconitic acid (1,2,3-propenetricarboxylic acid ($C_6H_6O_6$), CAS Reg. No. 000499–12–7) occurs in the leaves and tubers of *Aconitum napellus* L. and other *Ranunculaceae*. Transaconitic acid can be isolated during sugarcane processing, by precipitation as the calcium salt from cane sugar or molasses. It may be synthesized by sulfuric acid dehydration of citric acid, but not by the methanesulfonic acid method.

(b) The ingredient meets the following specifications:

(1) *Assay.* Not less than 98.0 percent of $C_3H_3(COOH)_3$, using the "Food Chemicals Codex," 4th ed. (1996), pp. 102–103, test for citric acid, which is incorporated by reference in accordance with 5 U.S.C. 552(a) and 1 CFR part 51, and a molecular weight of 174.11. Copies of the material incorporated by reference are available from the National Academy Press, Box 285, 2101 Constitution Ave. NW., Washington, DC 20055 (Internet address *http://www.nap.edu*), or may be examined at the Center for Food Safety and Applied Nutrition's

Library, Food and Drug Administration, 5100 Paint Branch Pkwy., College Park, MD 20740, or at the National Archives and Records Administration (NARA). For information on the availability of this material at NARA, call 202–741–6030, or go to: *http://www.archives.gov/federal_register/code_of_federal_regulations/ibr_locations.html.*

(2) *Melting point.* Not less than 195 °C and the determination results in decomposition of aconitic acid.

(3) *Heavy metals (as Pb).* Not more than 10 parts per million.

(4) *Arsenic (as As).* Not more than 3 parts per million.

(5) *Oxalate.* Passes test.

(6) *Readily carbonizable substances.* Passes the test for citric acid of the "Food Chemicals Codex," 4th ed. (1996), pp. 102–103, which is incorporated by reference in accordance with 5 U.S.C. 552(a) and 1 CFR part 51. The availability of this incorporation by reference is given in paragraph (b)(1) of this section.

(7) *Residue on ignition.* Not more than 0.1 percent as determined by the "Food Chemicals Codex," 4th ed. (1996), pp. 102–103, test for citric acid, which is incorporated by reference in accordance with 5 U.S.C. 552(a) and 1 CFR part 51. The availability of this incorporation by reference is given in paragraph (b)(1) of this section.

(c) The ingredient is used as a flavoring substance and adjuvant as defined in §170.3(o)(12) of this chapter.

(d) The ingredient is used in food, in accordance with §184.1(b)(1), at levels not to exceed good manufacturing practice. Current good manufacturing practice results in a maximum level, as served, of 0.003 percent for baked goods as defined in §170.3(n)(1) of this chapter, 0.002 percent for alcoholic beverages as defined in §170.3(n)(2) of this chapter, 0.0015 percent for frozen dairy products as defined in §170.3(n)(20) of this chapter, 0.0035 percent for soft candy as defined in §170.3(n)(38) of this chapter, and 0.0005 percent or less for all other food categories.

(e) Prior sanctions for this ingredient different from the uses established in this section do not exist or have been waived.

[43 FR 47724, Oct. 17, 1978, as amended at 49 FR 5610, Feb. 14, 1984; 64 FR 1759, Jan. 12, 1999]

§ 184.1009 Adipic acid.

(a) Adipic acid ($C_6H_{10}O_4$, CAS Reg. No. 00124–04–9) is also known as 1,4-butanedicarboxylic acid or hexanedioic acid. It is prepared by nitric acid oxidation of cyclohexanol or cyclohexanone or a mixture of the two.

(b) The ingredient meets the specifications of the Food Chemicals Codex, 3d Ed. (1981), p. 11, which is incorporated by reference (Copies are available from the National Academy Press, 2101 Constitution Ave., NW., Washington, DC 20418, or available for inspection at the National Archives and Records Administration (NARA). For information on the availability of this material at NARA, call 202–741–6030, or go to: *http://www.archives.gov/federal_register/code_of_federal_regulations/ibr_locations.html.*), and the following additional specifications:

(1) The adipic acid is converted to its corresponding amide. The amide is purified by recrystallization from water or aqueous ethanol. The melting range of the amide is 219° to 220 °C.

(2) The adipic acid is converted to its corresponding *bis-p-p*-bromophenacyl ester. The ester is purified by recrystallization from ethanol. The melting range of the ester is 153° to 154 °C.

(c) The ingredient is used as a flavoring agent as defined in §170.3(o)(12) of this chapter; leavening agent as defined in §170.3(o)(17) of this chapter; and pH control agent as defined in §170.3(o)(23) of this chapter.

(d) The ingredient is used in foods at levels not to exceed current good manufacturing practice in accordance with §184.1(b)(1). Current good manufacturing practice results in maximum levels, as served, of 0.05 percent for baked goods as defined in §170.3(n)(1) of this chapter; 0.005 percent for nonalcoholic beverages as defined in §170.3(n)(3) of this chapter; 5.0 percent for condiments and relishes as defined in §170.3(n)(8) of this chapter; 0.45 percent for dairy product analogs as defined in §170.3(n)(10) of this chapter; 0.3

percent for fats and oil as defined in § 170.3(n)(12) of this chapter; 0.0004 percent for frozen dairy desserts as defined in § 170.3(n)(20) of this chapter; 0.55 percent for gelatin and puddings as defined in § 170.3(n)(22) of this chapter; 0.1 percent for gravies as defined in § 170.3(n)(24) of this chapter; 0.3 percent for meat products as defined in § 170.3(n)(29) of this chapter; 1.3 percent for snack foods as defined in § 170.3(n)(37) of this chapter; and 0.02 percent or less for all other food categories.

(e) Prior sanctions for adipic acid different from the uses established in this section do not exist or have been waived.

[47 FR 27810, June 25, 1982]

§ 184.1011 Alginic acid.

(a) Alginic acid is a colloidal, hydrophilic polysaccharide obtained from certain brown algae by alkaline extraction.

(b) The ingredient meets the specifications of the Food Chemicals Codex, 3d Ed. (1981), p. 13, which is incorporated by reference. Copies are available from the National Academy Press, 2101 Constitution Ave. NW., Washington, DC 20418, or available for inspection at the National Archives and Records Administration (NARA). For information on the availability of this material at NARA, call 202–741–6030, or go to: *http://www.archives.gov/federal_register/code_of_federal_regulations/ibr_locations.html.*

(c) In accordance with § 184.1(b)(2), the ingredient is used in food only within the following specific limitations:

Category of food	Maximum level of use in food (as served)	Functional use
Soup and soup mixes, § 170.3(n) (40) of this chapter.	Not to exceed current good manufacturing practice.	Emulsifier, emulsifier salt, § 170.3(o)(8) of this chapter; formulation aid, § 170.3(o)(14) of this chapter; stabilizer, thickener, § 170.3(o)(28) of this chapter.

(d) Prior sanctions for this ingredient different from the use established in this section do not exist or have been waived.

[47 FR 47375, Oct. 26, 1982]

§ 184.1012 α-Amylase enzyme preparation from Bacillus stearothermophilus.

(a) α-Amylase enzyme preparation is obtained from the culture filtrate that results from a pure culture fermentation of a nonpathogenic and nontoxicogenic strain of *Bacillus stearothermophilus*. Its characterizing enzyme activity is α-amylase (1,4 α-D glucan glucanohydrolase (E.C. 3.2.1.1)).

(b) The ingredient meets the general and additional requirements for enzyme preparations in the "Food Chemicals Codex," 3d ed. (1981), pp. 107–110, which is incorporated by reference in accordance with 5 U.S.C. 552(a) and 1 CFR part 51. Copies are available from the National Academy Press, 2101 Constitution Ave. NW., Washington, DC 20418, or may be examined at the Office Food Additive Safety (HFS–200), Center for Food Safety and Applied Nutrition, Food and Drug Administration, 5100 Paint Branch Pkwy., College Park, MD 20740, 240–402–1200, or at the National Archives and Records Administration (NARA). For information on the availability of this material at NARA, call 202–741–6030, or go to: *http://www.archives.gov/federal_register/code_of_federal_regulations/ibr_locations.html.*

(c) In accordance with § 184.1(b)(1), the ingredient is used in food with no limitation other than current good manufacturing practices. The affirmation of this ingredient as GRAS as a direct human food ingredient is based upon the following current good manufacturing practice conditions of use:

(1) The ingredient is used as an enzyme, as defined in § 170.3(o)(9) of this chapter, in the hydrolysis of edible starch to produce maltodextrins and nutritive carbohydrate sweeteners.

(2) The ingredient is used at levels not to exceed current good manufacturing practices.

[60 FR 55789, Nov. 3, 1995, as amended at 78 FR 14666, Mar. 7, 2013]

§ 184.1021 Benzoic acid.

(a) Benzoic acid is the chemical benzenecarboxylic acid ($C_7H_6O_2$), occurring in nature in free and combined forms. Among the foods in which benzoic acid occurs naturally are cranberries, prunes, plums, cinnamon, ripe cloves, and most berries. Benzoic acid is manufactured by treating molten phthalic anhydride with steam in the presence of a zinc oxide catalyst, by the hydrolysis of benzotrichloride, or by the oxidation of toluene with nitric acid or sodium bichromate or with air in the presence of a transition metal salt catalyst.

(b) The ingredient meets the specifications of the "Food Chemicals Codex," 3d Ed. (1981), p. 35, which is incorporated by reference. Copies may be obtained from the National Academy Press, 2101 Constitution Ave. NW., Washington, DC 20418, or may be examined at the National Archives and Records Administration (NARA). For information on the availability of this material at NARA, call 202–741–6030, or go to: *http://www.archives.gov/federal_register/code_of_federal_regulations/ibr_locations.html.*

(c) The ingredient is used as an antimicrobial agent as defined in §170.3(o)(2) of this chapter, and as a flavoring agent and adjuvant as defined in §170.3(o)(12) of this chapter.

(d) The ingredient is used in food at levels not to exceed good manufacturing practice. Current usage results in a maximum level of 0.1 percent in food. (The Food and Drug Administration has not determined whether significantly different conditions of use would be GRAS).

(e) Prior sanctions for this ingredient different from those uses established in this section, or different from that set forth in part 181 of this chapter, do not exist or have been waived.

[42 FR 14653, Mar. 15, 1977, as amended at 49 FR 5610, Feb. 14, 1984]

§ 184.1024 Bromelain.

(a) Bromelain (CAS Reg. No. 9001–00–7) is an enzyme preparation derived from the pineapples *Ananas comosus* and *A. bracteatus* L. It is a white to light tan amorphous powder. Its characterizing enzyme activity is that of a peptide hydrolase (EC 3.4.22.32).

(b) The ingredient meets the general requirements and additional requirements for enzyme preparations in the Food Chemicals Codex, 3d ed. (1981), p. 110, which is incorporated by reference in accordance with 5 U.S.C. 552(a) and 1 CFR part 51. Copies are available from the National Academy Press, 2101 Constitution Ave. NW., Washington, DC, or may be examined at Office of Food Additive Safety (HFS–200), Center for Food Safety and Applied Nutrition, Food and Drug Administration, 5100 Paint Branch Pkwy., College Park, MD 20740, 240–402–1200, and at the National Archives and Records Administration (NARA). For information on the availability of this material at NARA, call 202–741–6030, or go to: *http://www.archives.gov/federal_register/code_of_federal_regulations/ibr_locations.html.*

(c) In accordance with §184.1(b)(1), the ingredient is used in food with no limitation other than current good manufacturing practice. The affirmation of this ingredient as GRAS as a direct food ingredient is based upon the following current good manufacturing practice conditions of use:

(1) The ingredient is used as an enzyme as defined in §170.3(o)(9) of this chapter to hydrolyze proteins or polypeptides.

(2) The ingredient is used in food at levels not to exceed current good manufacturing practice.

[60 FR 32910, June 26, 1995, as amended at 78 FR 14666, Mar. 7, 2013]

§ 184.1025 Caprylic acid.

(a) Caprylic acid [$CH_3(CH_2)_6COOH$, CAS Reg. No. 124–07–2] is the chemical name for octanoic acid. It is considered to be a short or medium chain fatty acid. It occurs normally in various foods and is commercially prepared by oxidation of *n*-octanol or by fermentation and fractional distillation of the volatile fatty acids present in coconut oil.

(b) The ingredient meets the specifications of the "Food Chemicals Codex," 3d Ed. (1981), p. 207, which is incorporated by reference. Copies may be obtained from the National Academy Press, 2101 Constitution Ave. NW.,

Washington, DC 20418, or may be examined at the National Archives and Records Administration (NARA). For information on the availability of this material at NARA, call 202–741–6030, or go to: *http://www.archives.gov/federal_register/code_of_federal_regulations/ibr_locations.html.*

(c) The ingredient is used as a flavoring agent and adjuvant as defined in §170.3(o)(12) of this chapter.

(d) The ingredient is used in foods in accordance with §184.1(b)(1), at levels not to exceed good manufacturing practice. Current good manufacturing practices result in maximum levels, as served, of: 0.013 percent for baked goods as defined in §170.3(n)(1) of this chapter; 0.04 percent for cheeses as defined in §170.3(n)(5) of this chapter; 0.005 percent for fats and oils as defined in §170.3(n)(12) of this chapter, for frozen dairy desserts as defined in §170.3(n)(20) of this chapter, for gelatins and puddings as defined in §170.3(n)(22) of this chapter, for meat products as defined in §170.3(n)(29) of this chapter, and for soft candy as defined in §170.3(n)(38) of this chapter; 0.016 percent for snack foods as defined in §170.3(n)(37) of this chapter; and 0.001 percent or less for all other food categories.

(e) Prior sanctions for this ingredient different from the uses established in this section do not exist or have been waived.

[43 FR 19843, May 9, 1978, as amended at 49 FR 5611, Feb. 14, 1984]

§ 184.1027 Mixed carbohydrase and protease enzyme product.

(a) Mixed carbohydrase and protease enzyme product is an enzyme preparation that includes carbohydrase and protease activity. It is obtained from the culture filtrate resulting from a pure culture fermentation of a nonpathogenic strain of *B. licheniformis*.

(b) The ingredient meets the specifications of the Food Chemicals Codex, 3d Ed. (1981), p. 107, which is incorporated by reference. Copies are available from the National Academy Press, 2101 Constitution Ave. NW., Washington, DC 20418, or available for inspection at the National Archives and Records Administration (NARA). For information on the availability of this material at NARA, call 202–741–6030, or go to: *http://www.archives.gov/federal_register/code_of_federal_regulations/ibr_locations.html.*

(c) In accordance with §184.1(b)(1), the ingredient is used in food with no limitation other than current good manufacturing practice. The affirmation of this ingredient as generally recognized as safe as a direct human food ingredient is based upon the following current good manufacturing practice conditions of use:

(1) The ingredient is used as an enzyme, as defined in §170.3(o)(9) of this chapter, to hydrolyze proteins or carbohydrates.

(2) The ingredient is used in the following foods at levels not to exceed current good manufacturing practice: alcoholic beverages, as defined in §170.3(n)(2) of this chapter, candy, nutritive sweeteners, and protein hydrolyzates.

[48 FR 240, Jan. 4, 1983]

§ 184.1033 Citric acid.

(a) Citric acid ($C_6H_8O_7$, CAS Reg. No. 77–92–9) is the compound 2-hydroxy-1,2,3-propanetricarboxylic acid. It is a naturally occurring constituent of plant and animal tissues. It occurs as colorless crystals or a white powder and may be anhydrous or contain one mole of water per mole of citric acid. Citric acid may be produced by recovery from sources such as lemon or pineapple juice; by mycological fermentation using *Candida spp.*, described in §§173.160 and 173.165 of this chapter; and by the solvent extraction process described in §173.280 of this chapter for the recovery of citric acid from *Aspergillus niger* fermentation liquor.

(b) The ingredient meets the specifications of the Food Chemicals Codex, 3d ed. (1981), pp. 86–87, and its third supplement (March 1992), pp. 107–108, which are incorporated by reference in accordance with 5 U.S.C. 552(a) and 1 CFR part 51. Copies are available from the National Academy Press, 2101 Constitution Ave. NW., Washington, DC 20418, and the Center for Food Safety and Applied Nutrition (HFS–200), 5100 Paint Branch Pkwy., College Park, MD 20740, or may be examined at the National Archives and Records Administration

(NARA). For information on the availability of this material at NARA, call 202–741–6030, or go to: *http://www.archives.gov/federal_register/code_of_federal_regulations/ibr_locations.html.*

(c) In accordance with §184.1(b)(1), the ingredient is used in food with no limitations other than current good manufacturing practice.

(d) Prior sanctions for this ingredient different from the uses established in this section do not exist or have been waived.

[59 FR 63895, Dec. 12, 1994]

§ 184.1034 Catalase (bovine liver).

(a) Catalase (bovine liver) (CAS Reg. No. 81457–95–6) is an enzyme preparation obtained from extracts of bovine liver. It is a partially purified liquid or powder. Its characterizing enzyme activity is catalase (EC 1.11.1.6).

(b) The ingredient meets the general requirements and additional requirements for enzyme preparations in the Food Chemicals Codex, 3d ed. (1981), p. 110, which is incorporated by reference in accordance with 5 U.S.C. 552(a) and 1 CFR part 51. Copies are available from the National Academy Press, 2101 Constitution Ave., NW., Washington, DC 20418, or may be examined at the Office of Food Additive Safety (HFS–200), Center for Food Safety and Applied Nutrition, Food and Drug Administration, 5100 Paint Branch Pkwy., College Park, MD 20740, 240–402–1200, and at the National Archives and Records Administration (NARA). For information on the availability of this material at NARA, call 202–741–6030, or go to: *http://www.archives.gov/federal_register/code_of_federal_regulations/ibr_locations.html.*

(c) In accordance with §184.1(b)(1), the ingredient is used in food with no limitation other than current good manufacturing practice. The affirmation of this ingredient as GRAS as a direct food ingredient is based upon the following current good manufacturing practice conditions of use:

(1) The ingredient is used as an enzyme as defined in §170.3(o)(9) of this chapter to decompose hydrogen peroxide.

(2) The ingredient is used in food at levels not to exceed current good manufacturing practice.

[60 FR 32910, June 26, 1995, as amended at 69 FR 24512, May 4, 2004; 78 FR 14666, Mar. 7, 2013]

§ 184.1061 Lactic acid.

(a) Lactic acid ($C_3H_6O_3$, CAS Reg. Nos.: DL mixture, 598–82–3; L-isomer, 79–33–4; D-isomer, 10326–41–7), the chemical 2-hydroxypropanoic acid, occurs naturally in several foods. It is produced commercially either by fermentation of carbohydrates such as glucose, sucrose, or lactose, or by a procedure involving formation of lactonitrile from acetaldehyde and hydrogen cyanide and subsequent hydrolysis to lactic acid.

(b) The ingredient meets the specifications of the Food Chemicals Codex, 3d Ed. (1981), p. 159, which is incorporated by reference. Copies are available from the National Academy Press, 2101 Constitution Avenue, NW., Washington, DC 20418, or available for inspection at the National Archives and Records Administration (NARA). For information on the availability of this material at NARA, call 202–741–6030, or go to: *http://www.archives.gov/federal_register/code_of_federal_regulations/ibr_locations.html.*

(c) In accordance with §184.1(b)(1), the ingredient is used in food with no limitation other than current good manufacturing practice. The affirmation of this ingredient as generally recognized as safe (GRAS) as a direct human food ingredient is based upon the following current good manufacturing practice conditions of use:

(1) The ingredient is used as an antimicrobial agent as defined in §170.3(o)(2) of this chapter; a curing and pickling agent as defined in §170.3(o)(5) of this chapter; a flavor enhancer as defined in §170.3(o)(11) of this chapter; a flavoring agent and adjuvant as defined in §170.3(o)(12) of this chapter; a pH control agent as defined in §170.3(o)(23) of this chapter; and a solvent and vehicle as defined in §170.3(o)(27) of this chapter.

(2) The ingredient is used in food, except in infant foods and infant formulas, at levels not to exceed current good manufacturing practice.

(d) Prior sanctions for this ingredient different from the uses established in this section do not exist or have been waived.

[49 FR 35367, Sept. 7, 1984]

§ 184.1063 Enzyme-modified lecithin.

(a) Enzyme-modified lecithin is prepared by treating lecithin with either phospholipase A_2 (EC 3.1.1.4) or pancreatin.

(b) The ingredient meets the specifications in paragraphs (b)(1) through (b)(8) of this section. Unless otherwise noted, compliance with the specifications listed below is determined according to the methods set forth for lecithin in the Food Chemicals Codex, 4th ed. (1996), pp. 220–221, which are incorporated by reference in accordance with 5 U.S.C. 552(a) and 1 CFR part 51. Copies are available from the National Academy Press, 2101 Constitution Ave. NW., Washington DC 20418, or may be examined at the Center for Food Safety and Applied Nutrition's Library, 5100 Paint Branch Pkwy., College Park, MD 20740, or at the National Archives and Records Administration (NARA). For information on the availability of this material at NARA, call 202–741–6030, or go to: *http://www.archives.gov/federal_register/code_of_federal_regulations/ibr_locations.html.*

(1) Acetone-insoluble matter (phosphatides), not less than 50.0 percent.

(2) Acid value, not more than 40.

(3) Lead, not more than 1.0 part per million, as determined by atomic absorption spectroscopy.

(4) Heavy metals (as Pb), not more than 20 parts per million.

(5) Hexane-insoluble matter, not more than 0.3 percent.

(6) Peroxide value, not more than 20.

(7) Water, not more than 4.0 percent.

(8) Lysolecithin, 50 to 80 mole percent of total phosphatides as determined by "Determination of Lysolecithin Content of Enzyme-Modified Lecithin: Method I," dated 1985, which is incorporated by reference in accordance with 5 U.S.C. 552(a) and 1 CFR part 51. Copies are available from the Office of Food Additive Safety (HFS–200), Center for Food Safety and Applied Nutrition, Food and Drug Administration, 5100 Paint Branch Pkwy., College Park, MD 20740, 240–402–1200, or may be examined at the Center for Food Safety and Applied Nutrition's Library, 5100 Paint Branch Pkwy., College Park, MD 20740, or at the National Archives and Records Administration (NARA). For information on the availability of this material at NARA, call 202–741–6030, or go to: *http://www.archives.gov/federal_register/code_of_federal_regulations/ibr_locations.html.*

(c) In accordance with § 184.1(b)(1), the ingredient is used in food with no limitation other than current good manufacturing practice. The affirmation of this ingredient as generally recognized as safe as a direct human food ingredient is based upon the following current good manufacturing practice conditions of use:

(1) The ingredient is used as an emulsifier as defined in § 170.3(o)(8) of this chapter.

(2) The ingredient is used at levels not to exceed current good manufacturing practice.

[61 FR 45889, Aug. 30, 1996, as amended at 78 FR 14666, Mar. 7, 2013]

§ 184.1065 Linoleic acid.

(a) Linoleic acid ((Z, Z)–9, 12-octadecadienoic acid ($C_{17}H_{31}COOH$) (CAS Reg. No. 60–33–3)), a straight chain unsaturated fatty acid with a molecular weight of 280.5, is a colorless oil at room temperature. Linoleic acid may be prepared from edible fats and oils by various methods including hydrolysis and saponification, the Twitchell method, low pressure splitting with catalyst, continuous high pressure counter current splitting, and medium pressure autoclave splitting with catalyst.

(b) The ingredient must be of a purity suitable for its intended use. The ingredient must also meet the specifications in § 172.860(b) of this chapter.

(c) In accordance with § 184.1(b)(1), the ingredient is used in food with no limitation other than current good manufacturing practice. The affirmation of this ingredient as generally recognized as safe (GRAS) as a direct human food ingredient is based upon the following current good manufacturing practice conditions of use:

(1) The ingredient is used as a flavoring agent and adjuvant as defined in §170.3(o)(12) of this chapter and as a nutrient supplement as defined in §170.3(o)(20) of this chapter.

(2) The ingredient is used in foods at levels not to exceed current good manufacturing practice. The ingredient may be used in infant formula in accordance with section 412(g) of the Federal Food, Drug, and Cosmetic Act (the act) or with regulations promulgated under section 412(a)(2) of the act.

(d) Prior sanctions for this ingredient different from the uses established in this section do not exist or have been waived.

[49 FR 48534, Dec. 13, 1984, as amended at 73 FR 8606, Feb. 14, 2008]

§ 184.1069 Malic acid.

(a) Malic acid ($C_4H_6O_5$, CAS Reg. No. of L-form 97–67–6, CAS Reg. No. of DL-form 617–48–1) is the common name for 1-hydroxy-1, 2-ethanedicarboxylic acid. L (+) malic acid, referred to as L-malic acid, occurs naturally in various foods. Racemic DL-malic acid does not occur naturally. It is made commercially by hydration of fumaric acid or maleic acid.

(b) The ingredient meets the specifications of the "Food Chemicals Codex," 3d Ed. (1981), pp. 183–184, which is incorporated by reference. Copies may be obtained from the National Academy Press, 2101 Constitution Ave. NW., Washington, DC 20418, or may be examined at the National Archives and Records Administration (NARA). For information on the availability of this material at NARA, call 202–741–6030, or go to: *http://www.archives.gov/federal_register/code_of_federal_regulations/ibr_locations.html.*

(c) The ingredients are used as a flavor enhancer as defined in §170.3(o)(11) of this chapter, flavoring agent and adjuvant as defined in §170.3(o)(12) of this chapter, and pH control agent as defined in §170.3(o)(23) of this chapter.

(d) The ingredients are used in food, except baby food, at levels not to exceed good manufacturing practice in accordance with §184.1(b)(1). Current good manufacturing practice results in a maximum level, as served, of 3.4 percent for nonalcoholic beverages as defined in §170.3(n)(3) of this chapter; 3.0 percent for chewing gum as defined in §170.3(n)(6) of this chapter; 0.8 percent for gelatins, puddings, and fillings as defined in §170.3(n)(22) of this chapter; 6.9 percent for hard candy as defined in §170.3(n)(25) of this chapter; 2.6 percent for jams and jellies as defined in §170.3(n)(28) of this chapter; 3.5 percent for processed fruits and fruit juices as defined in §170.3(n)(35) of this chapter; 3.0 percent for soft candy as defined in §170.3(n)(38) of this chapter; and 0.7 percent for all other food categories.

(e) Prior sanctions for malic acid different from the uses established in this section do not exist or have been waived.

[44 FR 20656, Apr. 6, 1979, as amended at 49 FR 5611, Feb. 14, 1984]

§ 184.1077 Potassium acid tartrate.

(a) Potassium acid tartrate ($C_4H_5KO_6$, CAS Reg. No. 868–14–4) is the potassium acid salt of L-(+)-tartaric acid and is also called potassium bitartrate or cream of tartar. It occurs as colorless or slightly opaque crystals or as a white, crystalline powder. It has a pleasant, acid taste. It is obtained as a byproduct of wine manufacture.

(b) The ingredient meets the specifications of the Food Chemicals Codex, 3d Ed. (1981), P. 238, which is incorporated by reference. Copies are available from the National Academy Press, 2101 Constitution Ave. NW., Washington, DC 20418, or available for inspection at the National Archives and Records Administration (NARA). For information on the availability of this material at NARA, call 202–741–6030, or go to: *http://www.archives.gov/federal_register/code_of_federal_regulations/ibr_locations.html.*

(c) In accordance with §184.1(b)(1), the ingredient is used in food with no limitation other than current good manufacturing practice. The affirmation of this ingredient as generally recognized as safe (GRAS) as a direct

human food ingredient is based upon the following current good manufacturing practice conditions of use:

(1) The ingredient is used as an anticaking agent as defined in § 170.3(o)(1) of this chapter; an antimicrobial agent as defined in § 170.3(o)(2) of this chapter; a formulation aid as defined in § 170.3(o)(14) of this chapter; a humectant as defined in § 170.3(o)(16) of this chapter; a leavening agent as defined in § 170.3(o)(17) of this chapter; A pH control agent as defined in § 170.3(o)(23) of this chapter; a processing aid as defined in § 170.3(o)(24) of this chapter; a stabilizer and thickener as defined in § 170.3(o)(28) of this chapter; and a surface-active agent as defined in § 170.3(o)(29) of this chapter.

(2) The ingredient is used in the following foods at levels not to exceed current good manufacturing practice: baked goods as defined in § 170.3(n)(1) of this chapter; confections and frostings as defined in § 170.3(n)(9) of this chapter; gelatins and puddings as defined in § 170.3(n)(22) of this chapter; hard candy as defined in § 170.3(n)(25) of this chapter; jams and jellies as defined in § 170.3(n)(28) of this chapter; and soft candy as defined in § 170.3(n)(38) of this chapter.

(d) Prior sanctions for this ingredient different from the uses established in this section do not exist or have been waived.

[48 FR 52446, Nov. 18, 1983]

§ 184.1081 Propionic acid.

(a) Propionic acid ($C_3H_6O_2$, CAS Reg. No. 79–09–4) is an oily liquid having a slightly pungent, rancid odor. It is manufactured by chemical synthesis or by bacterial fermentation.

(b) The ingredient meets the specifications of the Food Chemicals Codex, 3d Ed. (1981), p. 254, which is incorporated by reference. Copies are available from the National Academy Press, 2101 Constitution Ave. NW., Washington, DC 20418, or available for inspection at the National Archives and Records Administration (NARA). For information on the availability of this material at NARA, call 202–741–6030, or go to: *http://www.archives.gov/federal_register/code_of_federal_regulations/ibr_locations.html.*

(c) In accordance with § 184.1(b)(1), the ingredient is used in food with no limitation other than current good manufacturing practice. The affirmation of this ingredient as generally recognized as safe (GRAS) as a direct human food ingredient is based upon the following current good manufacturing practice conditions of use:

(1) The ingredient is used as an antimicrobial agent as defined in § 170.3(o)(2) of this chapter and a flavoring agent as defined in § 170.3(o)(12) of this chapter.

(2) The ingredient is used in foods at levels not to exceed current good manufacturing practice.

(d) Prior sanctions for this ingredient different from the uses established in this section do not exist or have been waived.

[49 FR 13141, Apr. 3, 1984]

§ 184.1090 Stearic acid.

(a) Stearic acid ($C_{18}H_{36}O_2$, CAS Reg. No. 57–11–4) is a white to yellowish white solid. It occurs naturally as a glyceride in tallow and other animal or vegetable fats and oils and is a principal constituent of most commercially hydrogenated fats. It is produced commercially from hydrolyzed tallow derived from edible sources or from hydrolyzed, completely hydrogenated vegetable oil derived from edible sources.

(b) The ingredient meets the specifications of the Food Chemicals Codex, 3d Ed. (1981), p. 313, which is incorporated by reference, and the requirements of § 172.860(b)(2) of this chapter. Copies of the Food Chemicals Codex are available from the National Academy Press, 2101 Constitution Ave. NW., Washington, DC 20418, or available for inspection at the National Archives and Records Administration (NARA). For information on the availability of this material at NARA, call 202–741–6030, or go to: *http://www.archives.gov/federal_register/code_of_federal_regulations/ibr_locations.html.*

(c) In accordance with § 184.1(b)(1), the ingredient is used in food with no limitation other than current good manufacturing practice. The affirmation of this ingredient as generally recognized as safe (GRAS) as a direct

human food ingredient is based upon the following current good manufacturing practice conditions of use:

(1) The ingredient is used as a flavoring agent and adjuvant as defined in § 170.3(o)(12) of this chapter.

(2) The ingredient is used in foods at levels not to exceed current good manufacturing practice.

(d) Prior sanctions for this ingredient different from the uses established in this section do not exist or have been waived.

[48 FR 52445, Nov. 18, 1983, as amended at 50 FR 49536, Dec. 3, 1985; 69 FR 24512, May 4, 2004]

§ 184.1091 Succinic acid.

(a) Succinic acid ($C_4H_6O_4$, CAS Reg. No. 110–15–6), also referred to as amber acid and ethylenesuccinic acid, is the chemical 1,4-butanedioic acid. It is commercially prepared by hydrogenation of maleic or fumaric acid. It can also be produced by aqueous alkali or acid hydrolysis of succinonitrile.

(b) The ingredient meets the specifications of the "Food Chemicals Codex," 3d Ed. (1981), pp. 314–315, which is incorporated by reference. Copies may be obtained from the National Academy Press, 2101 Constitution Ave. NW., Washington, DC 20418, or may be examined at the National Archives and Records Administration (NARA). For information on the availability of this material at NARA, call 202–741–6030, or go to: *http://www.archives.gov/federal_register/code_of_federal_regulations/ibr_locations.html.*

(c) The ingredient is used as a flavor enhancer as defined in § 170.3(o)(11) of this chapter and pH control agent as defined in § 170.3(o)(23) of this chapter.

(d) The ingredient is used in food at levels not to exceed good manufacturing practice in accordance with § 184.1(b)(1). Current good manufacturing practice results in a maximum level, as served, of 0.084 percent in condiments and relishes as defined in § 170.3(n)(8) of this chapter and 0.0061 percent in meat products as defined in § 170.3(n)(29) of this chapter.

(e) Prior sanctions for this ingredient different from the uses established in this section do not exist or have been waived.

[44 FR 20657, Apr. 6, 1979, as amended at 49 FR 5611, Feb. 14, 1984]

§ 184.1095 Sulfuric acid.

(a) Sulfuric acid (H_2SO_4, CAS Reg. No. 7664–93–9), also known as oil of vitriol, is a clear, colorless, oily liquid. It is prepared by reacting sulfur dioxide (SO_2) with oxygen and mixing the resultant sulfur trioxide (SO_3) with water, or by reacting nitric oxide (NO) with sulfur dioxide and water.

(b) The ingredient meets the specifications of the "Food Chemicals Codex," 3d Ed. (1981), pp. 317–318, which is incorporated by reference. Copies may be obtained from the National Academy Press, 2101 Constitution Ave. NW., Washington, DC 20418, or may be examined at the National Archives and Records Administration (NARA). For information on the availability of this material at NARA, call 202–741–6030, or go to: *http://www.archives.gov/federal_register/code_of_federal_regulations/ibr_locations.html.*

(c) The ingredient is used as a pH control agent as defined in § 170.3(o)(23) of this chapter and processing aid as defined in § 170.3(o)(24) of this chapter.

(d) The ingredient is used in food at levels not to exceed good manufacturing practice in accordance with § 184.1(b)(1). Current good manufacturing practice results in a maximum level, as served, of 0.014 percent for alcoholic beverages as defined in § 170.3(n)(2) of this chapter and 0.0003 percent for cheeses as defined in § 170.3(n)(5) of this chapter.

(e) Prior sanctions for this ingredient different from the uses established in this section do not exist or have been waived.

[45 FR 6085, Jan. 25, 1980, as amended at 49 FR 5611, Feb. 14, 1984]

§ 184.1097 Tannic acid.

(a) Tannic acid (CAS Reg. No. 1401–55–4), or hydrolyzable gallotannin, is a complex polyphenolic organic structure that yields gallic acid and either glucose or quinic acid as hydrolysis products. It is a yellowish-white to light brown substance in the form of an amorphous, bulky powder, glistening scales, or spongy masses. It is also ordorless, or has a faint characteristic odor, and has an astringent taste. Tannic acid is obtained by solvent extraction of nutgalls or excrescences that form on the young twigs of *Quercus infectoria Oliver* and related species of *Quercus*. Tannic acid is also obtained by solvent extraction of the seed pods of Tara (*Caesalpinia spinosa*) or the nutgalls of various sumac species, including *Rhus semialata, R. coriaria, R. galabra*, and *R. typhia*.

(b) The ingredient meets the specifications of the Food Chemicals Codex, 3d Ed. (1981), p. 319, which is incorporated by reference. Copies are available from the National Academy Press, 2101 Constitution Ave. NW., Washington, DC 20418, or available for inspection at the National Archives and Records Administration (NARA). For information on the availability of this material at NARA, call 202–741–6030, or go to: *http://www.archives.gov/federal_register/code_of_federal_regulations/ibr_locations.html.*

(c)(1) In accordance with § 184.1(b)(2), the ingredient is used in food only within the following specific limitations:

Category of food	Maximum level of use in food (as served) (percent)	Functional use
Baked goods and baking mixes, § 170.3(n)(1) of this chapter.	0.01	Flavoring agent and adjuvant, § 170.3(o)(12) of this chapter.
Alcoholic beverages, § 170.3(n)(2) of this chapter	0.015	Flavor enhancer, § 170.3(o)(11) of this chapter; flavoring agent and adjuvant, § 170.3(o)(12) of this chapter; processing aid, § 170.3(o)(24) of this chapter.
Nonalcoholic beverages and beverage bases, § 170.3(n)(3) of this chapter and for gelatins, puddings, and fillings, § 170.3(n)(22) of this chapter.	0.005	Flavoring agent and adjuvant, § 170.3(o)(12) of this chapter; pH control agent, § 170.3(o)(23) of this chapter.
Frozen dairy desserts and mixes, § 170.3(n)(20) of this chapter and for soft candy, § 170.3(n)(38) of this chapter.	0.04	Flavoring agent and adjuvant, § 170.3(o)(12) of this chapter.
Hard candy and cough drops, § 170.3(n)(25) of this chapter.	0.013	Do.
Meat products, § 170.3(n)(29) of this chapter	0.001	Do.

(2) Tannic acid may be used in rendered animal fat in accordance with 9 CFR 318.7.

(d) Prior sanctions for this ingredient different from the uses established in this section do not exist or have been waived.

[50 FR 21043, May 22, 1985]

§ 184.1099 Tartaric acid.

(a) Food grade tartaric acid ($C_4H_6O_6$, CAS Reg. No. 87–69–4) has the L configuration. The L form of tartaric acid is dextrorotatory in solution and is also known as L–(+)–tartaric acid. Tartaric acid occurs as colorless or translucent crystals or as a white, crystalline powder. It is odorless and has an acid taste. It is obtained as a byproduct of wine manufacture.

(b) The ingredient meets the specifications of the Food Chemicals Codex, 3d Ed. (1981), P. 320, which is incorporated by reference. Copies are available from the National Academy Press, 2101 Constitution Ave. NW., Washington, DC 20418, or available for inspection at the National Archives and Records Administration (NARA). For information on the availability of this material at NARA, call 202–741–6030, or go to: *http://www.archives.gov/federal_register/code_of_federal_regulations/ibr_locations.html.*

(c) In accordance with § 184.1(b)(1), the ingredient is used in food with no limitation other than current good manufacturing practice. The affirmation of this ingredient as generally recognized as safe (GRAS) as a direct human food ingredient is based upon the following current good manufacturing practice conditions of use:

(1) The ingredient is used as a firming agent as defined in § 170.3(o)(10) of this chapter; a flavor enhancer as defined in § 170.3(o)(11) of this chapter; a flavoring agent as defined in § 170.3(o)(12) of this chapter; a humectant as defined in § 170.3(o)(16) of this chapter; and a pH control agent as defined in § 170.3(o)(23) of this chapter.

(2) The ingredient is used in foods at levels not to exceed current good manufacturing practice.

(d) Prior sanctions for this ingredient different from the uses established in this section do not exist or have been waived.

[48 FR 52447, Nov. 18, 1983, as amended at 50 FR 49536, Dec. 3, 1985]

§ 184.1101 Diacetyl tartaric acid esters of mono- and diglycerides.

(a) Diacetyl tartaric acid esters of mono- and diglycerides, also know as DATEM, are composed of mixed esters of glycerin in which one or more of the hydroxyl groups of glycerin has been esterified by diacetyl tartaric acid and by fatty acids. The ingredient is prepared by the reaction of diacetyl tartaric anhydride with mono- and diglycerides that are derived from edible sources.

(b) The ingredient meets the specifications of the Food Chemicals Codex, 3d. Ed. (1981), pp. 98–99, which is incorporated by reference in accordance with 5 U.S.C. 552(a). Copies are available from the National Academy Press, 2101 Constitution Avenue NW., Washington, DC 20418, or available for inspection at the National Archives and Records Administration (NARA). For information on the availability of this material at NARA, call 202–741–6030, or go to: *http://www.archives.gov/federal_register/code_of_federal_regulations/ibr_locations.html.*

(c) In accordance with § 184.1(b)(1), the ingredient is used in food with no limitation other than current good manufacturing practice. The affirmation of this ingredient as generally recognized as safe (GRAS) as a direct human food ingredient is based upon the following current good manufacturing practice conditions of use:

(1) The ingredient is used in food as an emulsifier and emulsifier salt as defined in § 170.3(o)(8) of this chapter and a flavoring agent and adjuvant as defined in § 170.3(o)(12) of this chapter.

(2) The ingredient is used in the following foods at levels not to exceed current good manufacturing practice: baked goods and baking mixes as defined in § 170.3(n)(1) of this chapter; nonalcoholic beverages as defined in § 170.3(n)(3) of this chapter; confections and frostings as defined in § 170.3(n)(9) of this chapter; dairy product analogs as defined in § 170.3(n)(10) of this chapter; and fats and oils as defined in § 170.3(n)(12) of this chapter.

(d) Prior sanctions for this ingredient different from the uses established in this section do not exist or have been waived.

(e) *Labeling:* The acronym "DATEM" may be used on food labeling as the alternate common or usual name for the ingredient diacetyl tartaric acid esters of mono- and diglycerides.

[54 FR 7403, Feb. 21, 1989, as amended at 54 FR 13168, Mar. 31, 1989; 54 FR 18382, Apr. 28, 1989; 60 FR 15872, Mar. 28, 1995]

§ 184.1115 Agar-agar.

(a) Agar-agar (CAS Reg. No. PM 9002–18–0) is a dried, hydrophyllic, colloidal polysaccharide extracted from one of a number of related species of red algae (class *Rhodophyceae*).

(b) The ingredient meets the specifications of the "Food Chemicals Codex," 3d Ed. (1981), p. 11, which is incorporated by reference. Copies may be obtained from the National Academy Press, 2101 Constitution Ave. NW., Washington, DC 20418, or may be examined at the National Archives and Records Administration (NARA). For information on the availability of this material at NARA, call 202–741–6030, or go to: *http://www.archives.gov/federal_register/code_of_federal_regulations/ibr_locations.html.*

(c) The ingredient is used in food in accordance with § 184.1(b)(2) under the following conditions:

MAXIMUM USAGE LEVELS PERMITTED

Foods (as served)	Percent	Functions
Baked goods and baking mixes, § 170.3(n)(1) of this chapter	0.8	Drying agent, § 170.3(o)(7) of this chapter; flavoring agent, § 170.3(o)(12) of this chapter; stabilizer, thickener, § 170.3(o)(28) of this chapter.
Confections and frostings, § 170.3(n)(9) of this chapter	2.0	Flavoring agent, § 170.3(o)(12) of this chapter; stabilizer, thickener, § 170.3(o)(28) of this chapter; surface finisher, § 170.3(o)(30) of this chapter.
Soft candy, § 170.3(n)(38) of this chapter	1.2	Stabilizer and thickener, § 170.3(o)(28) of this chapter.
All other food categories	.25	Flavoring agent, § 170.3(o)(12) of this chapter; formulation aid, § 170.3(o)(14) of this chapter; humectant, § 170.3(o)(16) of this chapter; stabilizer, thickener, § 170.3(o)(28) of this chapter.

(d) Prior sanctions for this ingredient different from the uses established in this section do not exist or have been waived.

[44 FR 19391, Apr. 3, 1979, as amended at 49 FR 5611, Feb. 14, 1984]

§ 184.1120 Brown algae.

(a) Brown algae are seaweeds of the species *Analipus japonicus, Eisenia bicyclis, Hizikia fusiforme, Kjellmaniella gyrata, Laminaria angustata, Laminaria claustonia, Laminaria digitata, Laminaria japonica, Laminaria longicruris, Laminaria longissima, Laminaria ochotensis, Laminaria saccharina, Macrocystis pyrifera, Petalonia fascia, Scytosiphon lomentaria* and *Undaria pinnatifida*. They are harvested principally in coastal waters of the northern Atlantic and Pacific oceans. The material is dried and ground or chopped for use in food.

(b) The ingredient meets the specifications for kelp in the Food Chemicals Codex, 3d Ed. (1981), p. 157, which is incorporated by reference. Copies are available from the National Academy Press, 2101 Constitution Ave. NW., Washington, DC 20418, or available for inspection at the National Archives and Records Administration (NARA). For information on the availability of this material at NARA, call 202–741–6030, or go to: *http://www.archives.gov/federal_register/code_of_federal_regulations/ibr_locations.html.*

(c) In accordance with § 184.1(b)(2), the ingredient is used in food only within the following specific limitations:

Category of food	Maximum level of use in food (as served)	Functional use
Spices, seasonings, and flavorings, § 170.3(n) (26) of this chapter.	Not to exceed current good manufacturing practice.	Flavor enhancer, § 170.3(o)(11) of this chapter; flavor adjuvant, § 170.3(o)(12) of this chapter.

(d) Prior sanctions for this ingredient different from the use established in this section do not exist or have been waived.

[47 FR 47376, Oct. 26, 1982]

§ 184.1121 Red algae.

(a) Red algae are seaweeds of the species *Gloiopeltis furcata, Porphyra crispata, Porphyra deutata, Porphyra perforata, Porphyra suborbiculata, Porphyra tenera* and *Rhodymenia palmata. Porphyra* and *Rhodymenia* are harvested principally along the coasts of Japan, Korea, China, Taiwan, and the East and West coasts of the United States. *Gloiopeltis* is harvested principally in southern Pacific coastal waters. The material is dried and ground or chopped for use in food.

(b) The ingredient meets the specifications for kelp in the Food Chemicals Codex, 3d Ed. (1981), p. 157, which is incorporated by reference, except that the loss on drying is not more than 20 percent and the maximum allowable level for iodine is 0.05 percent. Copies are available from the National Academy Press, 2101 Constitution Ave. NW., Washington, DC 20418, or available for inspection at the National Archives and Records Administration (NARA). For information on the availability of this material at NARA, call 202–741–6030, or go to: *http://www.archives.gov/federal_register/*

code_of_federal_regulations/ ibr_locations.html.

(c) In accordance with § 184.1(b)(2), the ingredient is used in food only within the following specific limitations:

Category of food	Maximum level of use in food (as served)	Functional use
Spices, seasonings, and flavorings, § 170.3(n) (26) of this chapter.	Not to exceed current good manufacturing practice.	Flavor enhancer, § 170.3(o)(11) of this chapter; flavor adjuvant, § 170.3(o)(12) of this chapter.

(d) Prior sanctions for this ingredient different from the use established in this section do not exist or have been waived.

[47 FR 47376, Oct. 26, 1982]

§ 184.1133 Ammonium alginate.

(a) Ammonium alginate (CAS Reg. No. 9005–34–9) is the ammonium salt of alginic acid, a natural polyuronide constituent of certain brown algae. Ammonium alginate is prepared by the neutralization of purified alginic acid with appropriate pH control agents.

(b) The ingredient meets the specifications of the Food Chemicals Codex, 3d Ed. (1981), p. 18, which is incorporated by reference. Copies are available from the National Academy Press, 2101 Constitution Ave. NW., Washington, DC 20418, or available for inspection at the National Archives and Records Administration (NARA). For information on the availability of this material at NARA, call 202–741–6030, or go to: *http://www.archives.gov/ federal_register/ code_of_federal_regulations/ ibr_locations.html.*

(c) In accordance with § 184.1(b)(2), the ingredient is used in food only within the following specific limitations:

Category of food	Maximum level of use in food (as served) (percent)	Functional use
Confections, frostings, § 170.3(n)(9) of this chapter.	0.4	Stabilizer, thickener, § 170.3(o)(28) of this chapter.
Fats and oils, § 170.3(n)(12) of this chapter.	0.5	Do.
Gelatins, puddings, § 170.3(n)(22) of this chapter.	0.5	Do.
Gravies and sauces, § 170.3(n)(24) of this chapter.	0.4	Do.
Jams and jellies, § 170.3(n)(28) of this chapter.	0.4	Do.
Sweet sauces, § 170.3(n)(43) of this chapter.	0.5	Do.
All other food categories.	0.1	Humectant, § 170.3(o)(16) of this chapter; stabilizer, thickener, § 170.3(o)(28) of this chapter.

(d) Prior sanctions for ammonium alginate different from the uses established in this section do not exist or have been waived.

[47 FR 29950, July 9, 1982]

§ 184.1135 Ammonium bicarbonate.

(a) Ammonium bicarbonate (NH_4HCO_3, CAS Reg. No. 1066–33–7) is prepared by reacting gaseous carbon dioxide with aqueous ammonia. Crystals of ammonium bicarbonate are precipitated from solution and subsequently washed and dried.

(b) The ingredient meets the specifications of the Food Chemicals Codex, 3d Ed. (1981), p. 19, which is incorporated by reference. Copies are available from the National Academy Press, 2101 Constitution Ave. NW., Washington, DC 20418, or available for inspection at the National Archives and Records Administration (NARA). For information on the availability of this material at NARA, call 202–741–6030, or go to: *http://www.archives.gov/ federal_register/ code_of_federal_regulations/ ibr_locations.html.*

(c) In accordance with § 184.1(b)(1), the ingredient is used in food with no limitation other than current good manufacturing practice. The affirmation of this ingredient as generally recognized as safe (GRAS) as a direct human food ingredient is based upon the following current good manufacturing practice conditions of use:

(1) The ingredient is used as a dough strengthener as defined in §170.3(o)(6) of this chapter; a leavening agent as defined in §170.3(o)(17) of this chapter; a pH control agent as defined in §170.3(o)(23) of this chapter; and a texturizer as defined in §170.3(o)(32) of this chapter.

(2) The ingredient is used in food at levels not to exceed current good manufacturing practice.

(d) Prior sanctions for this ingredient different from the uses established in this section do not exist or have been waived.

[48 FR 52439, Nov. 18, 1983]

§184.1137 Ammonium carbonate.

(a) Ammonium carbonate ($(NH_4)_2CO_3$, CAS Reg. No. 8000–73–5) is a mixture of ammonium bicarbonate (NH_4HCO_3) and ammonium carbamate (NH_2COONH_4). It is prepared by the sublimation of a mixture of ammonium sulfate and calcium carbonate and occurs as a white powder or a hard, white or translucent mass.

(b) The ingredient meets the specifications of the Food Chemicals Codex, 3d Ed. (1981), p. 19, which is incorporated by reference. Copies are available from the National Academy Press, 2101 Constitution Ave. NW., Washington, DC 20418, or available for inspection at the National Archives and Records Administration (NARA). For information on the availability of this material at NARA, call 202–741–6030, or go to: *http://www.archives.gov/federal_register/code_of_federal_regulations/ibr_locations.html.*

(c) In accordance with §184.1(b)(1), the ingredient is used in food with no limitation other than current good manufacturing practice. The affirmation of this ingredient as generally recognized as safe (GRAS) as a direct human food ingredient is based upon the following current good manufacturing practice conditions of use:

(1) The ingredient is used as a leavening agent as defined in §170.3(o)(17) of this chapter and a pH control agent as defined in §170.3(o)(23) of this chapter.

(2) The ingredient is used in food at levels not to exceed current good manufacturing practice.

(d) Prior sanctions for this ingredient different from the uses established in this section do not exist or have been waived.

[48 FR 52439, Nov. 18, 1983]

§184.1138 Ammonium chloride.

(a) Ammonium chloride (NH_4Cl, CAS Reg. No. 12125–02–9) is produced by the reaction of sodium chloride and an ammonium salt in solution. The less soluble sodium salt separates out at elevated temperatures, and ammonium chloride is recovered from the filtrate on cooling. Alternatively, hydrogen chloride formed by the burning of hydrogen in chlorine is dissolved in water and then reacted with gaseous ammonia. Ammonium chloride is crystallized from the solution.

(b) The ingredient meets the specifications of the Food Chemicals Codex, 3d Ed. (1981), p. 20, which is incorporated by reference. Copies are available from the National Academy Press, 2101 Constitution Ave, NW., Washington, DC 20418, or available for inspection at the National Archives and Records Administration (NARA). For information on the availability of this material at NARA, call 202–741–6030, or go to: *http://www.archives.gov/federal_register/code_of_federal_regulations/ibr_locations.html.*

(c) In accordance with §184.1(b)(1), the ingredient is used in food with no limitation other than current good manufacturing practice. The affirmation of this ingredient as generally recognized as safe (GRAS) as a direct human food ingredient is based upon the following current good manufacturing practice conditions of use:

(1) The ingredient is used as a dough strengthener as defined in §170.3(o)(6) of this chapter; a flavor enhancer as defined in §170.3(o)(11) of this chapter; a leavening agent as defined in §170.3(o)(17) of this chapter; and a processing aid as defined in §107.3(o)(24) of this chapter.

(2) The ingredient is used in food at levels not to exceed current good manufacturing practice.

(d) Prior sanctions for this ingredient different from the uses established in

this section do not exist or have been waived.

[48 FR 52439, Nov. 18, 1983]

§ 184.1139 Ammonium hydroxide.

(a) Ammonium hydroxide (NH_4OH, CAS Reg. No. 1336–21–6) is produced by passing ammonia gas into water.

(b) The ingredient meets the specifications of the Food Chemicals Codex, 3d Ed. (1981), p. 20, which is incorporated by reference. Copies are available from the National Academy Press, 2101 Constitution Ave. NW., Washington, DC 20418, or available for inspection at the National Archives and Records Administration (NARA). For information on the availability of this material at NARA, call 202–741–6030, or go to: *http://www.archives.gov/federal_register/code_of_federal_regulations/ibr_locations.html.*

(c) In accordance with § 184.1(b)(1), the ingredient is used in food with no limitation other than current good manufacturing practice. The affirmation of this ingredient as generally recognized as safe (GRAS) as a direct human food ingredient is based upon the following current good manufacturing practice conditions of use:

(1) The ingredient is used as a leavening agent as defined in § 170.3(o)(17) of this chapter; a pH control agent as defined in § 170.3(o)(23) of this chapter; a surface-finishing agent as defined in § 170.3(o)(30) of this chapter; and as a boiler water additive complying with § 173.310 of this chapter.

(2) The ingredient is used in food at levels not to exceed current good manufacturing practice. The ingredient may also be used as a boiler water additive at levels not to exceed current good manufacturing practice.

(d) Prior sanctions for this ingredient different from the uses established in this section do not exist or have been waived.

[48 FR 52440, Nov. 18, 1983, as amended at 59 FR 14551, Mar. 29, 1994]

§ 184.1140 Ammonium citrate, dibasic.

(a) Ammonium citrate, dibasic ($(NH_4)_2HC_6H_5O_7$, CAS Reg. No. 3012–65–5) is the diammonium salt of citric acid. It is prepared by partially neutralizing citric acid with ammonia.

(b) The ingredient must be of a purity suitable for its intended use.

(c) In accordance with § 184.1(b)(1), the ingredient is used in food with no limitation other than current good manufacturing practice. The affirmation of this ingredient as generally recognized as safe (GRAS) as a direct human food ingredient is based upon the following current good manufacturing practice conditions of use:

(1) The ingredient is used as a flavor enhancer as defined in § 170.3(o)(11) of this chapter and as a pH control agent as defined in § 170.3(o)(23) of this chapter.

(2) The ingredient is used in nonalcoholic beverages as defined in § 170.3(n)(3) of this chapter and in cheeses as defined in § 170.3(n)(5) of this chapter at levels not to exceed current good manufacturing practice.

(d) Prior sanctions for this ingredient different from the uses established in this section, or different from those set forth in part 181 of this chapter, do not exist or have been waived.

[59 FR 63896, Dec. 12, 1994, as amended at 73 FR 8606, Feb. 14, 2008]

§ 184.1141a Ammonium phosphate, monobasic.

(a) Ammonium phosphate, monobasic ($NH_4H_2PO_4$, CAS Reg. No. 7722–76–1) is manufactured by reacting ammonia with phosphoric acid at a pH below 5.8.

(b) The ingredient meets the specifications of the Food Chemicals Codex, 3d Ed. (1981), p. 21, which is incorporated by reference. Copies are available from the National Academy Press, 2101 Constitution Ave. NW., Washington, DC 20418, or available for inspection at the National Archives and Records Administration (NARA). For information on the availability of this material at NARA, call 202–741–6030, or go to: *http://www.archives.gov/federal_register/code_of_federal_regulations/ibr_locations.html.*

(c) In accordance with § 184.1(b)(1), the ingredient is used in food with no limitation other than current good manufacturing practice. The affirmation of this ingredient as generally recognized as safe (GRAS) as a direct

human food ingredient is based upon the following current good manufacturing practice conditions of use:

(1) The ingredient is used as a dough strengthener as defined in §170.3(o)(6) of this chapter and a pH control agent as defined in §170.3(o)(23) of this chapter.

(2) The ingredient is used in food at levels not to exceed current good manufacturing practice.

(d) Prior sanctions for this ingredient different from the uses established in this section do not exist or have been waived.

[48 FR 52440, Nov. 18, 1983]

§ 184.1141b Ammonium phosphate, dibasic.

(a) Ammonium phosphate, dibasic ($(NH_4)_2HPO_4$, CAS Reg. No. 7783–28–0) is manufactured by reacting ammonia with phosphoric acid at a pH above 5.8.

(b) The ingredient meets the specifications of the Food Chemicals Codex, 3d Ed. (1981), p. 21, which is incorporated by reference. Copies are available from the National Academy Press, 2101 Constitution Ave. NW., Washington, DC 20418, or available for inspection at the National Archives and Records Administration (NARA). For information on the availability of this material at NARA, call 202–741–6030, or go to: *http://www.archives.gov/federal_register/code_of_federal_regulations/ibr_locations.html.*

(c) In accordance with §184.1(b)(1), the ingredient is used in food with no limitation other than current good manufacturing practice. The affirmation of this ingredient as generally recognized as safe (GRAS) as a direct human food ingredient is based upon the following current good manufacturing practice conditions of use:

(1) The ingredient is used as a dough strengthener as defined in §170.3(o)(6) of this chapter; a firming agent as defined in §170.3(o)(10) of this chapter; a leavening agent as defined in §170.3(o)(17) of this chapter; a pH control agent as defined in §170.3(o)(23) of this chapter; and a processing aid as defined in §170.3(o)(24) of this chapter.

(2) The ingredient is used in food at levels not to exceed current good manufacturing practice.

(d) Prior sanctions for this ingredient different from the uses established in this section do not exist or have been waived.

[48 FR 52440, Nov. 18, 1983]

§ 184.1143 Ammonium sulfate.

(a) Ammonium sulfate ($(NH_4)_2SO_4$, CAS Reg. No. 7783–20–2) occurs naturally and consists of colorless or white, odorless crystals or granules. It is prepared by the neutralization of sulfuric acid with ammonium hydroxide.

(b) The ingredient meets the specifications of the "Food Chemicals Codex," 3d Ed. (1981), pp. 22–23, which is incorporated by reference. Copies may be obtained from the National Academy Press, 2101 Constitution Ave. NW., Washington, DC 20418, or may be examined at the National Archives and Records Administration (NARA). For information on the availability of this material at NARA, call 202–741–6030, or go to: *http://www.archives.gov/federal_register/code_of_federal_regulations/ibr_locations.html.*

(c) The ingredient is used as a dough strengthener as defined in §170.3(o)(6) of this chapter, firming agent as defined in §170.3(o)(10) of this chapter, and processing aid as defined in §170.3(o)(24) of this chapter.

(d) The ingredient is used in food at levels not to exceed good manufacturing practice in accordance with §184.1(b)(1). Current good manufacturing practice results in a maximum level, as served, of 0.15 percent for baked goods as defined in §170.3(n)(1) of this chapter and 0.1 percent for gelatins and puddings as defined in §170.1(n)(22) of this chapter.

(e) Prior sanctions for this ingredient different from the uses established in this section do not exist or have been waived.

[45 FR 6086, Jan. 25, 1980; 45 FR 16469, Mar. 14, 1980, as amended at 49 FR 5611, Feb. 14, 1984]

§ 184.1148 Bacterially-derived carbohydrase enzyme preparation.

(a) Bacterially-derived carbohydrase enzyme preparation is obtained from the culture filtrate resulting from a pure culture fermentation of a nonpathogenic and nontoxigenic strain of

Bacillus subtilis or *B. amyloliquefaciens*. The preparation is characterized by the presence of the enzymes α-amylase (EC 3.2.1.1) and β-glucanase (EC 3.2.1.6), which catalyze the hydrolysis of *O*-glycosyl bonds in carbohydrates.

(b) The ingredient meets the general requirements and additional requirements in the monograph on enzyme preparations in the Food Chemicals Codex, 4th ed. (1996), pp. 128–135, which is incorporated by reference in accordance with 5 U.S.C. 552(a) and 1 CFR part 51. Copies are available from the National Academy Press, 2101 Constitution Ave. NW., Washington, DC 20418, or may be examined at the Center for Food Safety and Applied Nutrition's Library, 5100 Paint Branch Pkwy., College Park, MD 20740, or at the National Archives and Records Administration (NARA). For information on the availability of this material at NARA, call 202–741–6030, or go to: *http://www.archives.gov/federal_register/code_of_federal_regulations/ibr_locations.html.* In addition, antibiotic activity is absent in the enzyme preparation when determined by an appropriate validated method such as the method "Determination of antibiotic activity" in the Compendium of Food Additive Specifications, vol. 2, Joint FAO/WHO Expert Committee on Food Additives (JECFA), Food and Agriculture Organization of the United Nations, Rome, 1992. Copies are available from Bernan Associates, 4611–F Assembly Dr., Lanham, MD 20706, or from The United Nations Bookshop, General Assembly Bldg., rm. 32, New York, NY 10017, or by inquiries sent to *http://www.fao.org.* Copies may be examined at the Center for Food Safety and Applied Nutrition's Library, 5100 Paint Branch Pkwy., College Park, MD 20740.

(c) In accordance with § 184.1(b)(1), the ingredient is used in food with no limitation other than current good manufacturing practice. The affirmation of this ingredient as GRAS as a direct food ingredient is based upon the following current good manufacturing practice conditions of use:

(1) The ingredient is used as an enzyme as defined in § 170.3(o)(9) of this chapter to hydrolyze polysaccharides (e.g., starch).

(2) The ingredient is used in food at levels not to exceed current good manufacturing practice.

[64 FR 19894, Apr. 23, 1999]

§ 184.1150 Bacterially-derived protease enzyme preparation.

(a) Bacterially-derived protease enzyme preparation is obtained from the culture filtrate resulting from a pure culture fermentation of a nonpathogenic and nontoxigenic strain of *Bacillus subtilis* or *B. amyloliquefaciens*. The preparation is characterized by the presence of the enzymes subtilisin (EC 3.4.21.62) and neutral proteinase (EC 3.4.24.28), which catalyze the hydrolysis of peptide bonds in proteins.

(b) The ingredient meets the general requirements and additional requirements in the monograph on enzyme preparations in the Food Chemicals Codex, 4th ed. (1996), pp. 128–135, which is incorporated by reference in accordance with 5 U.S.C. 552(a) and 1 CFR part 51. Copies are available from the National Academy Press, 2101 Constitution Ave. NW., Washington, DC 20418, or may be examined at the Center for Food Safety and Applied Nutrition's Library, 5100 Paint Branch Pkwy., College Park, MD 20740, or at the National Archives and Records Administration (NARA). For information on the availability of this material at NARA, call 202–741–6030, or go to: *http://www.archives.gov/federal_register/code_of_federal_regulations/ibr_locations.html.* In addition, antibiotic activity is absent in the enzyme preparation when determined by an appropriate validated method such as the method "Determination of antibiotic activity" in the Compendium of Food Additive Specifications, vol. 2, Joint FAO/WHO Expert Committee on Food Additives (JECFA), Food and Agriculture Organization of the United Nations, Rome, 1992. Copies are available from Bernan Associates, 4611–F Assembly Dr., Lanham, MD 20706, or from The United Nations Bookshop, General Assembly Bldg., rm. 32, New York, NY 10017, or by inquiries sent to *http://www.fao.org.* Copies may be examined at the Center for Food Safety and Applied Nutrition's Library, 5100 Paint Branch Pkwy., College Park, MD 20740.

(c) In accordance with §184.1(b)(1), the ingredient is used in food with no limitation other than current good manufacturing practice. The affirmation of this ingredient as GRAS as a direct food ingredient is based upon the following current good manufacturing practice conditions of use:

(1) The ingredient is used as an enzyme as defined in §170.3(o)(9) of this chapter to hydrolyze proteins or polypeptides.

(2) The ingredient is used in food at levels not to exceed current good manufacturing practice.

[64 FR 19895, Apr. 23, 1999]

§ 184.1155 Bentonite.

(a) Bentonite ($Al_2O_34SiO_2nH_2O$, CAS Reg. No. 1302–78–9) is principally a colloidal hydrated aluminum silicate. Bentonite contains varying quantities of iron, alkalies, and alkaline earths in the commercial products. Depending on the cations present, natural deposits of bentonite range in color from white to gray, yellow, green, or blue. Bentonite's fine particles provide large total surface area and, hence, pronounced adsorptive capability.

(b) The ingredient must be of a purity suitable for its intended use.

(c) In accordance with §184.1(b)(1), the ingredient is used in food with no limitation other than current good manufacturing practice. The affirmation of this ingredient as generally recognized as safe (GRAS) as a direct human food ingredient is based upon the following current good manufacturing practice conditions of use:

(1) The ingredient is used as a processing aid as defined in §170.3(o)(24) of this chapter.

(2) The ingredient is used in food at levels not to exceed current good manufacturing practice. Current good manufacturing practice results in no significant residue in foods.

(d) Prior sanctions for this ingredient different from the uses established in this section do not exist or have been waived.

[47 FR 43367, Oct. 1, 1982, as amended at 73 FR 8606, Feb. 14, 2008; 76 FR 59249, Sept. 26, 2011]

§ 184.1157 Benzoyl peroxide.

(a) Benzoyl peroxide ($(C_6H_5CO)_2O_2$, CAS Reg. No. 94–36–0) is a colorless, rhombic crystalline solid. It is prepared by reaction of benzoyl chloride, sodium hydroxide, and hydrogen peroxide.

(b) The ingredient meets the specifications of the Food Chemicals Codex, 3d Ed. (1981), p. 35, which is incorporated by reference. Copies are available from the National Academy Press, 2101 Constitution Ave. NW., Washington, DC 20418, or available for inspection at the National Archives and Records Administration (NARA). For information on the availability of this material at NARA, call 202–741–6030, or go to: *http://www.archives.gov/federal_register/code_of_federal_regulations/ibr_locations.html.*

(c) In accordance with §184.1(b)(1), the ingredient is used in food with no limitation other than current good manufacturing practice. The affirmation of this ingredient as generally recognized as safe (GRAS) as a direct human food ingredient is based upon the following current good manufacturing practice conditions of use:

(1) The ingredient is used as a bleaching agent in food.

(2) The ingredient is used in the following foods at levels not to exceed current good manufacturing practice: flour; milk used for production of Asiago fresh and Asiago soft cheese (§133.102), Asiago medium cheese (§133.103), Asiago old cheese (§133.104), Blue cheese (§133.106), Caciocavallo siciliano chesse (§133.111), Gorgonzola cheese (§133.141), Parmesan and reggiano cheese (§133.165), Provolone cheese (§133.181), Romano cheese (§133.183), and Swiss and emmentaler cheese (§133.195) in part 133 of this chapter; and annatto-colored whey, such that the final bleached product conforms to the descriptions and specifications for whey, concentrated whey, or dried whey in §184.1979(a) (1), (2), or (3), respectively.

(d) Prior sanctions for this ingredient different from the uses established in this section do not exist or have been waived.

[51 FR 27173, July 30, 1986]

§ 184.1165 n-Butane and iso-butane.

(a) n-Butane and iso-butane (empirical formula C_4H_{10}, CAS Reg. Nos. 106–97–8 and 75–28–5, respectively) are colorless, flammable gases at normal temperatures and pressures. They are easily liquefied under pressure at room temperature and are stored and shipped in the liquid state. The butanes are obtained from natural gas by fractionation following absorption in oil, adsorption to surface-active agents, or refrigeration.

(b) The ingredients must be of a purity suitable for their intended use.

(c) In accordance with § 184.1(b)(1), these ingredients are used in food with no limitations other than current good manufacturing practice. The affirmation of these ingredients as generally recognized as safe (GRAS) as direct human food ingredients is based upon the following current good manufacturing practice conditions of use:

(1) The ingredients are used as propellants, aerating agents, and gases as defined in § 170.3(o)(25) of this chapter.

(2) The ingredients are used in food at levels not to exceed current good manufacturing practice.

(d) Prior sanctions for these ingredients different from the uses established in this section do not exist or have been waived.

[48 FR 57270, Dec. 29, 1983, as amended at 73 FR 8607, Feb. 14, 2008; 76 FR 59249, Sept. 26, 2011]

§ 184.1185 Calcium acetate.

(a) Calcium acetate (Ca $(C_2H_3O_2)_2$, CAS Reg. No. 62–54–4), also known as acetate of lime or vinegar salts, is the calcium salt of acetic acid. It may be produced by the calcium hydroxide neutralization of acetic acid.

(b) The ingredient meets the specifications of the Food Chemicals Codex, 3d Ed. (1981), p. 44, which is incorporated by reference. Copies are available from the National Academy Press, 2101 Constitution Ave. NW., Washington, DC 20418, or available for inspection at the National Archives and Records Administration (NARA). For information on the availability of this material at NARA, call 202–741–6030, or go to: *http://www.archives.gov/federal_register/code_of_federal_regulations/ibr_locations.html.*

(c) The ingredient is used as a firming agent as defined in § 170.3(o)(10) of this chapter; pH control agent as defined in § 170.3(o)(23) of this chapter; processing aid as defined in § 170.3(o)(24) of this chapter; sequestrant as defined in § 170.3(o)(26) of this chapter; stabilizer and thickener as defined in § 170.3(o)(28) of this chapter; and texturizer as defined in § 170.3(o)(32) of this chapter.

(d) The ingredient is used in food at levels not to exceed current good manufacturing practices in accordance with § 184.1(b)(1). Current good manufacturing practices result in a maximum level, as served, of 0.2 percent for baked goods as defined in § 170.3(n)(1) of this chapter; 0.02 percent for cheese as defined in § 170.3(n)(5) of this chapter; 0.2 percent for gelatins, puddings, and fillings as defined in § 170.3(n)(22) of this chapter; 0.15 percent for sweet sauces, toppings, and syrups as defined in § 170.3(n)(43) of this chapter; and 0.0001 percent for all other food categories.

(e) Prior sanctions for this ingredient different from the uses established in this section or in part 181 of this chapter do not exist or have been waived.

[47 FR 27807, June 25, 1982]

§ 184.1187 Calcium alginate.

(a) Calcium alginate (CAS Reg. No. 9005–35–0) is the calcium salt of alginic acid, a natural polyuronide constituent of certain brown algae. Calcium alginate is prepared by the neutralization of purified alginic acid with appropriate pH control agents, or from sodium alginate by metathesis with appropriate calcium salts.

(b) The ingredient meets the specifications of the Food Chemicals Codex, 3d Ed. (1981), p. 45, which is incorporated by reference. Copies are available from the National Academy Press, 2101 Constitution Ave. NW., Washington, DC 20418, or available for inspection at the National Archives and Records Administration (NARA). For information on the availability of this material at NARA, call 202–741–6030, or go to: *http://www.archives.gov/federal_register/*

code_of_federal_regulations/ ibr_locations.html.

(c) In accordance with §184.1(b)(2), the ingredient is used in food only within the following specific limitations:

Category of food	Maximum level of use in food (as served) (percent)	Functional use
Baked goods, §170.3(n)(1) of this chapter.	0.002	Stabilizer, thickener, §170.3(o)(28) of this chapter.
Alcoholic beverages, §170.3(n)(2) of this chapter.	0.4	Do.
Confections and frostings, §170.3(n)(9) of this chapter.	0.4	Do.
Egg products, §170.3(n)(11) of this chapter.	0.6	Do.
Fats and oils, §170.3(n)(12) of this chapter.	0.5	Do.
Gelatins, puddings, §170.3(n)(22) of this chapter.	0.25	Do.
Gravies and sauces, §170.3(n)(24) of this chapter.	0.4	Do.
Jams and jellies, §170.3(n)(28) of this chapter.	0.5	Do.
Sweet sauces, §170.3(n)(43) of this chapter.	0.5	Do.
All other food categories.	0.3	Do.

(d) Prior sanctions for calcium alginate different from the uses established in this section do not exist or have been waived.

[47 FR 29951, July 9, 1982]

§ 184.1191 Calcium carbonate.

(a) Calcium carbonate ($CaCO_3$, CAS Reg. No. 471–34–1) is prepared by three common methods of manufacture:

(1) As a byproduct in the "Lime soda process";

(2) By precipitation of calcium carbonate from calcium hydroxide in the "Carbonation process"; or

(3) By precipitation of calcium carbonate from calcium chloride in the "Calcium chloride process".

(b) The ingredient meets the specifications of the Food Chemicals Codex, 3d Ed. (1981), p. 46, which is incorporated by reference. Copies are available from the National Academy Press, 2101 Constitution Ave. NW., Washington, DC 20418, or available for inspection at the National Archives and Records Administration (NARA). For information on the availability of this material at NARA, call 202–741–6030, or go to: *http://www.archives.gov/ federal_register/ code_of_federal_regulations/ ibr_locations.html.*

(c) In accordance with §184.1(b)(1), the ingredient is used in food with no limitation other than current good manufacturing practice.

(d) Prior sanctions for this ingredient different from the uses established in this section, or different from that set forth in part 181 of this chapter, do not exist or have been waived.

[48 FR 52441, Nov. 18, 1983]

§ 184.1193 Calcium chloride.

(a) Calcium chloride ($CaCl_2 \cdot 2H_2O$, CAS Reg. No. 10035–04–8) or anhydrous calcium chloride ($CaCl_2$, CAS Reg. No. 10043–52–4) may be commercially obtained as a byproduct in the ammonia-soda (Solvay) process and as a joint product from natural salt brines, or it may be prepared by substitution reactions with other calcium and chloride salts.

(b) The ingredient meets the specifications of the Food Chemicals Codex, 3d Ed. (1981), p. 47, which is incorporated by reference. Copies are available from the National Academy Press, 2101 Constitution Ave. NW., Washington, DC 20418, or available for inspection at the National Archives and Records Administration (NARA). For information on the availability of this material at NARA, call 202–741–6030, or go to: *http://www.archives.gov/ federal_register/ code_of_federal_regulations/ ibr_locations.html.*

(c) The ingredient is used as an anticaking agent as defined in §170.3(o)(1) of this chapter; antimicrobial agent as defined in §170.3(o)(2) of this chapter; curing or pickling agent as defined in §170.3(o)(5) of this chapter; firming agent as defined in §170.3(o)(10) of this chapter; flavor enhancer as defined in §170.3(o)(11) of this chapter; humectant as defined in §170.3(o)(16) of this chapter; nutrient supplement as defined in

§ 170.3(o)(20) of this chapter; pH control agent as defined in § 170.3(o)(23) of this chapter; processing aid as defined in § 170.3(o)(24) of this chapter; stabilizer and thickener as defined in § 170.3(o)(28) of this chapter; surface-active agent as defined in § 170.3(o)(29) of this chapter; synergist as defined in § 170.3(o)(31) of this chapter; and texturizer as defined in § 170.3(o)(32) of this chapter.

(d) The ingredient is used in foods at levels not to exceed current good manufacturing practices in accordance with § 184.1(b)(1). Current good manufacturing practices result in a maximum level, as served, of 0.3 percent for baked goods as defined in § 170.3(n)(1) of this chapter and for dairy product analogs as defined in § 170.3(n)(10) of this chapter; 0.22 percent for nonalcoholic beverages and beverage bases as defined in § 170.3(n)(3) of this chapter; 0.2 percent for cheese as defined in § 170.3(n)(5) of this chapter and for processed fruit and fruit juices as defined in § 170.3(n)(35) of this chapter; 0.32 percent for coffee and tea as defined in § 170.3(n)(7) of this chapter; 0.4 percent for condiments and relishes as defined in § 170.3(n)(8) of this chapter; 0.2 percent for gravies and sauces as defined in § 170.3(n)(24) of this chapter; 0.1 percent for commercial jams and jellies as defined in § 170.3(n)(28) of this chapter; 0.25 percent for meat products as defined in § 170.3(n)(29) of this chapter; 2.0 percent for plant protein products as defined in § 170.3(n)(33) of this chapter; 0.4 percent for processed vegetables and vegetable juices as defined in § 170.3(n)(36) of this chapter; and 0.05 percent for all other food categories.

(e) Prior sanctions for this ingredient different from the uses established in this section do not exist or have been waived.

[47 FR 27808, June 25, 1982, as amended at 61 FR 14247, Apr. 1, 1996]

§ 184.1195 Calcium citrate.

(a) Calcium citrate ($Ca_3(C_6H_5O_7)_2{\cdot}4H_2O$, CAS Reg. No. 813–0994–095) is the calcium salt of citric acid. It is prepared by neutralizing citric acid with calcium hydroxide or calcium carbonate. It occurs as a fine white, odorless powder and usually contains four moles of water per mole of calcium citrate.

(b) The ingredient meets the specifications of the Food Chemicals Codex, 3d ed. (1981), pp. 49 and 50, which is incorporated by reference in accordance with 5 U.S.C. 552(a) and 1 CFR part 51. Copies are available from the National Academy Press, 2101 Constitution Ave. NW., Washington, DC 20418, and the Center for Food Safety and Applied Nutrition (HFS–200), 5100 Paint Branch Pkwy., College Park, MD 20740, or may be examined at the National Archives and Records Administration (NARA). For information on the availability of this material at NARA, call 202–741–6030, or go to: *http://www.archives.gov/federal_register/code_of_federal_regulations/ibr_locations.html.*

(c) In accordance with § 184.1(b)(1), the ingredient is used in food with no limitation other than current good manufacturing practice. Calcium citrate may also be used in infant formula in accordance with section 412(g) of the Federal Food, Drug, and Cosmetic Act (the act) or with regulations promulgated under section 412(a)(2) of the act.

(d) Prior sanctions for this ingredient different from the uses established in this section do not exist or have been waived.

[59 FR 63896, Dec. 12, 1994]

§ 184.1199 Calcium gluconate.

(a) Calcium gluconate ($[CH_2OH(CHOH)_4COO]_2Ca$, CAS Reg. No. 299–28–5) is the calcium salt of gluconic acid which may be produced by neutralization of gluconic acid with lime or calcium carbonate.

(b) The ingredient meets the specifications of the Food Chemicals Codex, 3d Ed. (1981), p. 51, which is incorporated by reference. Copies are available from the National Academy Press, 2101 Constitution Ave. NW., Washington, DC 20418, or available for inspection at the National Archives and Records Administration (NARA). For information on the availability of this material at NARA, call 202–741–6030, or go to: *http://www.archives.gov/federal_register/code_of_federal_regulations/ibr_locations.html.*

(c) The ingredient is used as a firming agent as defined in § 170.3(o)(10) of this chapter; formulation aid as defined in §170.3(o)(14) of this chapter; sequestrant as defined in §170.3(o)(26) of this chapter; stabilizer or thickener as defined in §170.3(o)(28) of this chapter; and texturizer as defined in §170.3(o)(32) of this chapter.

(d) The ingredient is used in foods at levels not to exceed current good manufacturing practices in accordance with §184.1(b)(1). Current good manufacturing practices result in a maximum level, as served, of 1.75 percent for baked goods as defined in §170.3(n)(1) of this chapter; 0.4 percent for dairy product analogs as defined in §170.3(n)(10) of this chapter; 4.5 percent for gelatins and puddings as defined in §170.3(n)(22) of this chapter; and 0.01 percent for sugar substitutes as defined in §170.3(n)(42) of this chapter.

(e) Prior sanctions for this ingredient different from the uses established in this section do not exist or have been waived.

[47 FR 27808, June 25, 1982]

§ 184.1201 Calcium glycerophosphate.

(a) Calcium glycerophosphate ($C_3H_7CaO_6P$, CAS Reg. No. 27214–00–2) is a fine, white, odorless, almost tasteless, slightly hygroscopic powder. It is prepared by neutralizing glycerophosphoric acid with calcium hydroxide or calcium carbonate. The commercial product is a mixture of calcium β-, and *D*-, and *L*-α-glycerophosphate.

(b) The ingredient meets the specifications of the "Food Chemicals Codex," 3d Ed. (1981), pp. 51–52, which is incorporated by reference in accordance with 5 U.S.C. 552(a) and 1 CFR part 51. Copies may be obtained from the National Academy Press, 2101 Constitution Ave. NW., Washington, DC 20418, or may be examined at the National Archives and Records Administration (NARA). For information on the availability of this material at NARA, call 202–741–6030, or go to: *http://www.archives.gov/federal_register/code_of_federal_regulations/ibr_locations.html.*

(c) In accordance with §184.1(b)(1), the ingredient is used in food with no limitation other than current good manufacturing practice. The affirmation of this ingredient as generally recognized as safe (GRAS) as a direct human food ingredient is based upon the following current good manufacturing practice conditions of use:

(1) The ingredient is used as a nutrient supplement as defined in §170.3(o)(20) of this chapter.

(2) The ingredient is used in gelatins, puddings, and fillings as defined in §170.3(n)(22) of this chapter.

(d) Prior sanctions for this ingredient different from the uses established in this section or different from that as set forth in part 181 of this chapter, do not exist or have been waived.

[57 FR 10813, Mar. 31, 1992]

§ 184.1205 Calcium hydroxide.

(a) Calcium hydroxide ($Ca(OH)_2$, CAS Reg. No. 1305–62–0) is also known as slaked lime or calcium hydrate. It is produced by the hydration of lime.

(b) The ingredient meets the specifications of the Food Chemicals Codex, 3d Ed. (1981), p. 52, which is incorporated by reference. Copies are available from the National Academy Press, 2101 Constitution Ave. NW., Washington, DC 20418, or available for inspection at the National Archives and Records Administration (NARA). For information on the availability of this material at NARA, call 202–741–6030, or go to: *http://www.archives.gov/federal_register/code_of_federal_regulations/ibr_locations.html.*

(c) In accordance with §184.1(b)(1), the ingredient is used in food with no limitation other than current good manufacturing practice.

(d) Prior sanctions for this ingredient different from the uses established in this section do not exist or have been waived.

[49 FR 26714, June 29, 1984]

§ 184.1206 Calcium iodate.

(a) Calcium iodate [$Ca(IO_3)_2 \cdot H_2O$, CAS Reg. No. 7789–80–2], also referred to as lautarite, does not occur naturally but can be prepared by passing chlorine into a hot solution of lime ($CaCO_3$) in which iodine has been dissolved.

(b) The ingredient meets the specifications of the "Food Chemicals Codex," 3d Ed. (1981), p. 53, which is incorporated by reference. Copies may be obtained from the National Academy Press, 2101 Constitution Ave. NW.,

Washington, DC 20418, or may be examined at the National Archives and Records Administration (NARA). For information on the availability of this material at NARA, call 202–741–6030, or go to: *http://www.archives.gov/federal_register/code_of_federal_regulations/ibr_locations.html.*

(c) The ingredient is used as a dough strengthener as defined in § 170.3(o)(6) of this chapter.

(d) The ingredient is used in the manufacture of bread in accordance with § 184.1(b)(2) of this chapter in an amount not to exceed 0.0075 percent based on the weight of the flour.

(e) Prior sanctions for this ingredient different from the uses established in this section do not exist or have been waived.

[43 FR 11699, Mar. 21, 1978, as amended at 49 FR 5611, Feb. 14, 1984]

§ 184.1207 Calcium lactate.

(a) Calcium lactate ($C_6H_{10}CaO_6.xH_2O$, where x is any integer up to 5, CAS Reg. No. 814–80–2) is prepared commercially by the neutralization of lactic acid with calcium carbonate or calcium hydroxide.

(b) The ingredient meets the specifications of the Food Chemicals Codex, 3d Ed. (1981), p. 53, which is incorporated by reference. Copies are available from the National Academy Press, 2101 Constitution Avenue NW., Washington, DC 20418, or available for inspection at the National Archives and Records Administration (NARA). For information on the availability of this material at NARA, call 202–741–6030, or go to: *http://www.archives.gov/federal_register/code_of_federal_regulations/ibr_locations.html.*

(c) In accordance with § 184.1(b)(1), the ingredient is used in food with no limitation other than current good manufacturing practice. The affirmation of this ingredient as generally recognized as safe (GRAS) as a direct human food ingredient is based upon the following current good manufacturing practice conditions of use:

(1) The ingredient is used as a firming agent as defined in § 170.3(o)(10) of this chapter; a flavor enhancer as defined in § 170.3(o)(11) of this chapter; a flavoring agent or adjuvant as defined in § 170.3(o)(12) of this chapter; a leavening agent as defined in § 170.3(o)(17) of this chapter; a nutrient supplement as defined in § 170.3(o)(20) of this chapter; and a stabilizer and thickener as defined in § 170.3(o)(28) of this chapter.

(2) The ingredient is used in food, except in infant foods and infant formulas, at levels not to exceed current good manufacturing practice.

(d) Prior sanctions for this ingredient different from the uses established in this section do not exist or have been waived.

[49 FR 35367, Sept. 7, 1984]

§ 184.1210 Calcium oxide.

(a) Calcium oxide (CaO, CAS Reg. No. 1305–78–8) is also known as lime, quick lime, burnt lime, or calx. It is produced from calcium carbonate, limestone, or oyster shells by calcination at temperatures of 1,700–2,450 °F.

(b) The ingredient meets the specifications of the Food Chemicals Codex, 3d Ed. (1981), p. 55, which is incorporated by reference. Copies are available from the National Academy Press, 2101 Constitution Ave. NW., Washington, DC 20418, or available for inspection at the National Archives and Records Administration (NARA). For information on the availability of this material at NARA, call 202–741–6030, or go to: *http://www.archives.gov/federal_register/code_of_federal_regulations/ibr_locations.html.*

(c) In accordance with § 184.1(b)(1), the ingredient is used in food with no limitation other than current good manufacturing practice.

(d) Prior sanctions for this ingredient different from the uses established in this section do not exist or have been waived.

[49 FR 26714, June 29, 1984]

§ 184.1212 Calcium pantothenate.

(a) Calcium pantothenate ($(C_9H_{16}NO_5)_2Ca$, CAS Reg. No. of the *D*-isomer, 137–08–6) is a salt of pantothenic acid, one of the vitamins of the B complex. Only the *D*-isomer of pantothenic acid has vitamin activity, although both the *D*-isomer and the *DL*-

racemic mixture of calcium pantothenate are used in food. Commercial calcium pantothenate is prepared synthetically from isobutyraldehyde and formaldehyde via 1,1-dimethyl-2-hydroxy-propionaldehyde and pantolactone.

(b) Calcium pantothenate meets the specifications of the Food Chemicals Codex, 3d Ed. (1981), p. 56, which is incorporated by reference. Copies are available from the National Academy Press, 2101 Constitution Ave. NW., Washington, DC 20418, or available for inspection at the National Archives and Records Administration (NARA). For information on the availability of this material at NARA, call 202–741–6030, or go to: *http://www.archives.gov/federal_register/code_of_federal_regulations/ibr_locations.html.*

(c) In accordance with §184.1(b)(1), the ingredient is used in food with no limitation other than current good manufacturing practice. The affirmation of this ingredient as generally recognized as safe (GRAS) as a direct human food ingredient is based upon the following current good manufacturing practice conditions of use:

(1) The ingredient is used as a nutrient supplement as defined in §170.3(o)(20) of this chapter.

(2) The ingredient is used in foods at levels not to exceed current good manufacturing practice. Calcium pantothenate may be used in infant formula in accordance with section 412(g) of the Federal Food, Drug, and Cosmetic Act (the act) or with regulations promulgated under section 412(a)(2) of the Act.

(d) Prior sanctions for this ingredient different from the uses established in this section do not exist or have been waived.

[48 FR 51908, Nov. 15, 1983]

§ 184.1221 Calcium propionate.

(a) Calcium propionate ($C_6H_{10}CaO_4$, CAS Reg. No. 4075–81–4) is the calcium salt of propionic acid. It occurs as white crystals or a crystalline solid, possessing not more than a faint odor of propionic acid. It is prepared by neutralizing propionic acid with calcium hydroxide.

(b) The ingredient meets the specifications of the Food Chemicals Codex, 3d Ed. (1981), p. 60, which is incorporated by reference. Copies are available from the National Academy Press, 2101 Constitution Ave. NW., Washington, DC 20418, or available for inspection at the National Archives and Records Administration (NARA). For information on the availability of this material at NARA, call 202–741–6030, or go to: *http://www.archives.gov/federal_register/code_of_federal_regulations/ibr_locations.html.*

(c) In accordance with §184.1(b)(1), the ingredient is used in food with no limitation other than current good manufacturing practice. The affirmation of this ingredient as generally recognized as safe (GRAS) as a direct human food ingredient is based upon the following current good manufacturing practice conditions of use:

(1) The ingredient is used as an antimicrobial agent as defined in §170.3(o)(2) of this chapter.

(2) The ingredient is used in the following foods at levels not to exceed current good manufacturing practice: baked goods as defined in §170.3(n)(1) of this chapter; cheeses as defined in §170.3(n)(5) of this chapter; confections and frostings as defined in §170.3(n)(9) of this chapter; gelatins, puddings, and fillings as defined in §170.3(n)(22) of this chapter; and jams and jellies as defined in §170.3(n)(28) of this chapter.

(d) Prior sanctions for this ingredient different from the uses established in this section do not exist or have been waived.

[49 FR 13141, Apr. 3, 1984]

§ 184.1229 Calcium stearate.

(a) Calcium stearate ($Ca(C_{17}H_{35}COO)_2$, CAS Reg. No. 1529–23–0) is the calcium salt of stearic acid derived from edible sources. It is prepared as a white precipitate by mixing calcium chloride and sodium stearate in aqueous solution.

(b) The ingredient meets the specifications of the Food Chemicals Codex, 3d Ed. (1981), p. 64, which is incorporated by reference, and the requirements of §172.860(b)(2) of this chapter. Copies of the Food Chemicals Codex are available from the National Academy Press, 2101 Constitution Ave. NW., Washington, DC 20418, or available for inspection at the National Archives and Records Administration (NARA). For information on the availability of this material at NARA, call 202–741–6030, or go to: *http://www.archives.gov/federal_register/code_of_federal_regulations/ibr_locations.html.*

(c) In accordance with § 184.1(b)(1), the ingredient is used in food with no limitation other than current good manufacturing practice. The affirmation of this ingredient as generally recognized as safe (GRAS) as a direct human food ingredient is based upon the following current good manufacturing practice conditions of use:

(1) The ingredient is used as a flavoring agent and adjuvant as defined in § 170.3(o)(12) of this chapter; a lubricant and release agent as defined in § 170.3(o)(18) of this chapter; and a stabilizer and thickener as defined in § 170.3(o)(28) of this chapter.

(2) The ingredient is used in foods at levels not to exceed current good manufacturing practice.

(d) Prior sanctions for this ingredient different from the uses established in this section do not exist or have been waived.

[48 FR 52445, Nov. 18, 1983]

§ 184.1230 Calcium sulfate.

(a) Calcium sulfate ($CaSO_4$, CAS Reg. No. 7778–18–9 or $CaSO_4 \cdot 2H_2O$, CAS Reg. No. 10101–41–4), also known as plaster of Paris, anhydrite, and gypsum, occurs naturally and exists as a fine, white to slightly yellow-white odorless powder. The anhydrous form is prepared by complete dehydration of gypsum, below 300 °C, in an electric oven.

(b) The ingredient meets the specifications of the "Food Chemicals Codex," 3d Ed. (1981), p. 66, which is incorporated by reference. Copies may be obtained from the National Academy Press, 2101 Constitution Ave. NW., Washington, DC 20418, or may be examined at the National Archives and Records Administration (NARA). For information on the availability of this material at NARA, call 202–741–6030, or go to: *http://www.archives.gov/federal_register/code_of_federal_regulations/ibr_locations.html.*

(c) The ingredient is used as an anticaking agent as defined in § 170.3(o)(1) of this chapter, color and coloring adjunct as defined in § 170.3(o)(4) of this chapter, dough strengthener as defined in § 170.3(o)(6) of this chapter, drying agent as defined in § 170.3(o)(7) of this chapter, firming agent as defined in § 170.3(o)(10) of this chapter, flour treating agent as defined in § 170.3(o)(13) of this chapter, formulation aid as defined in § 170.3(o)(14) of this chapter, leavening agent as defined in § 170.3(o)(17) of this chapter, nutrient supplement as defined in § 170.3(o)(20) of this chapter, pH control agent as defined in § 170.3(o)(23) of this chapter, processing aid as defined in § 170.3(o)(24) of this chapter, stabilizer and thickener as defined in § 170.3(o)(28) of this chapter, synergist as defined in § 170.3(o)(31) of this chapter, and texturizer as defined in § 170.3(o)(32) of this chapter.

(d) The ingredient is used in food at levels not to exceed good manufacturing practice in accordance with § 184.1(b)(1). Current good manufacturing practice results in a maximum level, as served, of 1.3 percent for baked goods as defined in § 170.3(n)(1) of this chapter, 3.0 percent for confections and frostings as defined in § 170.3(n)(9) of this chapter, 0.5 percent for frozen dairy desserts and mixes as defined in § 170.3(n)(20) of this chapter, 0.4 percent for gelatins and puddings as defined in § 170.3(n)(22) of this chapter, 0.5 percent for grain products and pastas as defined in § 170.3(n)(23) of this chapter, 0.35 percent for processed vegetables as defined in § 170.3(n)(36) of this chapter, and 0.07 percent or less for all other food categories.

(e) Prior sanctions for this ingredient different from the uses established in this section do not exist or have been waived.

[45 FR 6086, Jan. 25, 1980; 45 FR 26319, Apr. 18, 1980, as amended at 49 FR 5611, Feb. 14, 1984]

§ 184.1240 Carbon dioxide.

(a) Carbon dioxide (empirical formula CO_2, CAS Reg. No. 124–38–9) occurs as a colorless, odorless, noncombustible gas at normal temperatures and pressures. The solid form, dry ice, sublimes under atmospheric pressure at a temperature of −78.5 °C. Carbon dioxide is prepared as a byproduct of the manufacture of lime during the "burning" of limestone, from the combustion of carbonaceous material, from fermentation processes, and from gases found in certain natural springs and wells.

(b) The ingredient must be of a purity suitable for its intended use.

(c) In accordance with § 184.1(b)(1), the ingredient is used in food with no limitations other than current good manufacturing practice. The affirmation of this ingredient as generally recognized as safe (GRAS) as a direct human food ingredient is based upon the following current good manufacturing practice conditions of use:

(1) The ingredient is used as a leavening agent as defined in § 170.3(o)(17) of this chapter; a processing aid as defined in § 170.3(o)(24) of this chapter; and a propellant, aerating agent, and gas as defined in § 170.3(o)(25) of this chapter.

(2) The ingredient is used in food at levels not to exceed current good manufacturing practice.

(d) Prior sanctions for this ingredient different from the uses established in this section do not exist or have been waived.

[48 FR 57270, Dec. 29, 1983, as amended at 73 FR 8607, Feb. 14, 2008]

§ 184.1245 Beta-carotene.

(a) *Beta*-carotene (CAS Reg. No. 7235–40–7) has the molecular formula $C_{40}H_{56}$. It is synthesized by saponification of vitamin A acetate. The resulting alcohol is either reacted to form vitamin A Wittig reagent or oxidized to vitamin A aldehyde. Vitamin A Wittig reagent and vitamin A aldehyde are reacted together to form *beta*-carotene.

(b) The ingredient meets the specifications of the Food Chemicals Codex, 3d Ed. (1981), p. 73, which is incorporated by reference. Copies are available from the National Academy Press, 2101 Constitution Ave. NW., Washingtion, DC 20418, or available for inspection at the National Archives and Records Administration (NARA). For information on the availability of this material at NARA, call 202–741–6030, or go to: *http://www.archives.gov/federal_register/code_of_federal_regulations/ibr_locations.html.*

(c) In accordance with § 184.1(b)(1), the ingredient is used in food with no limitation other than current good manufacturing practice. The affirmation of this ingredient as generally recognized as safe (GRAS) as a direct human food ingredient is based upon the following current good manufacturing practice conditions of use:

(1) The ingredient is used as a nutrient supplement as defined in § 170.3(o)(20) of this chapter.

(2) The ingredient is used in the following foods at levels not to exceed current good manufacturing practice: dairy product analogs as defined in § 170.3(n)(10) of this chapter; fats and oils as defined in § 170.3(n)(12) of this chapter; and processed fruits and fruit juices as defined in § 170.3(n)(35) of this chapter. *Beta*-carotene may be used in infant formula as a source of vitamin A in accordance with section 412(g) of the Federal Food, Drug, and Cosmetic Act or with regulations promulgated under section 412(g) of the act.

(d) Prior sanctions for this ingredient different from the uses established in this section do not exist or have been waived.

[52 FR 25211, July 6, 1987]

§ 184.1250 Cellulase enzyme preparation derived from Trichoderma longibrachiatum.

(a) Cellulase enzyme preparation is derived from a nonpathogenic, nontoxicogenic strain of *Trichoderma longibrachiatum* (formerly *T. reesei*). The enzyme, cellulase, catalyzes the endohydrolysis of 1,4-beta-glycosidic linkages in cellulose. It is obtained from the culture filtrate resulting from a pure culture fermentation process.

(b) The ingredient meets the general and additional requirements for enzyme preparations in the monograph specifications on enzyme preparations in the "Food Chemicals Codex," 4th ed. (1996), pp. 129 to 134, which is incorporated by reference in accordance with 5 U.S.C. 552(a) and 1 CFR part 51. Copies are available from the National Academy Press, 2101 Constitution Ave. NW., Box 285, Washington, DC 20055 (Internet *http://www.nap.edu*), or may be examined at the Center for Food

Safety and Applied Nutrition's Library, 5100 Paint Branch Pkwy., College Park, MD 20740, or at the National Archives and Records Administration (NARA). For information on the availability of this material at NARA, call 202–741–6030, or go to: *http://www.archives.gov/federal_register/code_of_federal_regulations/ibr_locations.html.*

(c) In accordance with §184.1(b)(1), the ingredient is used in food with no limitation other than current good manufacturing practice. The affirmation of this ingredient as generally recognized as safe (GRAS) as a direct human food ingredient is based upon the following current good manufacturing practice conditions of use:

(1) The ingredient is used in food as an enzyme as defined in §170.3(o)(9) of this chapter for the breakdown of cellulose.

(2) The ingredient is used in food at levels not to exceed current good manufacturing practice.

[64 FR 28361, May 26, 1999]

§ 184.1257 Clove and its derivatives.

(a) Cloves are the dried unopened flower buds and calyx tubes, harvested before the flowers have opened, of the clove tree *Eugenia caryophyllata* Thunberg, native to tropical Asia. Their derivatives include essential oils (cloves, CAS Reg. No. 8000–34–8; buds; leaves, CAS Reg. No. 8015–97–2; stems, CAS Reg. No. 8015–98–3; and eugenol, CAS Reg. No. 97–53–0), oleoresins, and natural extractives obtained from clove buds, leaves, and stems.

(b) Clove bud oil, clove leaf oil, clove stem oil, and eugenol meet the specifications of the "Food Chemicals Codex," 4th ed. (1996), pp. 104–105, which is incorporated by reference in accordance with 5 U.S.C. 552(a) and 1 CFR part 51. Copies are available from the National Academy Press, Box 285, 2101 Constitution Ave. NW., Washington, DC 20055 (Internet address *http://www.nap.edu*), or may be examined at the Center for Food Safety and Applied Nutrition's Library, Food and Drug Administration, 5100 Paint Branch Pkwy., College Park, MD 20740, or at the National Archives and Records Administration (NARA). For information on the availability of this material at NARA, call 202–741–6030, or go to: *http://www.archives.gov/federal_register/code_of_federal_regulations/ibr_locations.html.* As determined by analytical methods in the "Food Chemicals Codex," clove oleoresin or other natural extractives (other than clove oils) meet the "Food Chemicals Codex" specifications for clove (clove bud) oil and the following modifications:

(1) The assay for phenols, as eugenol, by the "Food Chemicals Codex" test, 4th ed. (pp. 104–105), or the volatile oils content by the "Food Chemicals Codex" test, 4th ed. (pp. 104–105) should conform to the representation of the vendor;

(2) Optical rotation of the volatile oil between −2° and 0°;

(3) Refractive index of the volatile oil between 1.527 and 1.538 at 20 °C;

(4) Specific gravity of the volatile oil between 1.036 and 1.060; and

(5) Residual solvent free, except those solvents that are GRAS or within tolerance levels as specified in part 173, subpart C, of this chapter.

(c) Clove and its derivatives are used as flavoring agents and adjuvants as defined in §170.3(0)(12) of this chapter.

(d) The ingredients are used in food at levels not to exceed good manufacturing practice in accordance with §184.1(b)(1).

(e) Prior sanctions for these ingredients different from the uses established in this section do not exist or have been waived.

[44 FR 3964, Jan. 19, 1979, as amended at 47 FR 11852, Mar. 19, 1982; 49 FR 5611, Feb. 14, 1984; 64 FR 1759, Jan. 12, 1999]

§ 184.1259 Cocoa butter substitute.

(a) The common or usual name for the triglyceride 1-palmitoyl-2-oleoyl-3-stearin is "cocoa butter substitute primarily from palm oil." The common or usual name for the triglyceride 1-3-distearoyl-2-olein is "cocoa butter substitute primarily from high-oleic safflower or sunflower oil."

(1) The ingredient 1-palmitoyl-2-oleoyl-3-stearin is manufactured by:

(i) Directed esterification of fully saturated 1,3-diglycerides (derived from palm oil) with the anhydride of food-grade oleic acid in the presence of the catalyst trifluoromethane sulfonic acid (§ 173.395 of this chapter), or

(ii) By interesterification of partially saturated 1,2,3-triglycerides (derived from palm oil) with ethyl stearate in the presence of a suitable lipase enzyme preparation that is either generally recognized as safe (GRAS) or has food additive approval for such use.

(2) The ingredient 1-3-distearoyl-2-olein is manufactured by interesterification of partially unsaturated 1,2,3-triglycerides (derived from high-oleic safflower or sunflower oil) with ethyl stearate or stearic acid in the presence of a suitable lipase enzyme preparation that is either GRAS or has food additive approval for such use.

(b) The ingredient meets the following specifications:

(1) Over 90 percent triglycerides, not more than 7 percent diglycerides, not more than 1 percent monoglycerides, and not more than 1 percent free fatty acids.

(2) Total glycerides—98 percent minimum.

(3) Heavy metals (as lead), not more than 10 milligrams per kilogram, as determined by the Heavy Metals Test of the "Food Chemicals Codex," 4th ed. (1996), pp. 760–761, which is incorporated by reference in accordance with 5 U.S.C. 552(a) and 1 CFR part 51. Copies are available from the National Academy Press, Box 285, 2101 Constitution Ave. NW., Washington, DC 20055 (Internet address *http://www.nap.edu*), or may be examined at the Center for Food Safety and Applied Nutrition's Library, Food and Drug Administration, 5100 Paint Branch Pkwy., College Park, MD 20740, or at the National Archives and Records Administration (NARA). For information on the availability of this material at NARA, call 202–741–6030, or go to: *http://www.archives.gov/federal_register/code_of_federal_regulations/ibr_locations.html.*

(4) Color—clear, bright, and free from suspended matter.

(5) Odor and taste—free from foreign and rancid odor and taste.

(6) Residual catalyst ("Official Methods of Analysis of the Association of Official Analytical Chemists," 13th Ed. (1980), sections 25.049–25.055, which is incorporated by reference), residual fluorine; limit of detection 0.2 part per million F; multiply fluoride result by 2.63 to convert to residual catalyst. Copies of the material incorporated by reference may be obtained from the AOAC INTERNATIONAL, 481 North Frederick Ave., suite 500, Gaithersburg, MD 20877, or may be examined at the National Archives and Records Administration (NARA). For information on the availability of this material at NARA, call 202–741–6030, or go to: *http://www.archives.gov/federal_register/code_of_federal_regulations/ibr_locations.html.* The ingredient shall be washed three times in batches with 0.5 percent sodium bicarbonate to remove catalyst residuals in accordance with good manufacturing practice.

(7) Residual methanol—5 parts per million maximum.

(8) Residual fatty acid ethyl esters—not more than 20 parts per million as determined by a "Modification of Japan Institute of Oils and Fats: Analysis Method of Residual Ethyl Esters of Fatty Acids" issued by the Fuji Oil Co., which is incorporated by reference. Copies are available from the Office of Food Additive Safety (HFS–200), Center for Food Safety and Applied Nutrition, Food and Drug Administration, 5100 Paint Branch Pkwy., College Park, MD 20740, 240–402–1200, or available for inspection at the National Archives and Records Administration (NARA). For information on the availability of this material at NARA, call 202–741–6030, or go to: *http://www.archives.gov/federal_register/code_of_federal_regulations/ibr_locations.html.*

(9) Hexane—not more than 5 parts per million as determined by the method of Dupuy et al., "Rapid Quantitative Determination of Residual Hexane in Oils by Direct Gas Chromatography," published in the "Journal of the American Oil Chemists' Society," Vol. 52, p. 118–120, 1975, which is incorporated by reference. Copies are available from the Division of Food and Color Additives, Center for Food Safety and Applied Nutrition (HFS–200), Food and Drug Administration, 5100 Paint Branch Pkwy., College Park, MD 20740, or available for inspection at the National Archives and Records Administration (NARA).

For information on the availability of this material at NARA, call 202–741–6030, or go to: *http://www.archives.gov/federal_register/code_of_federal_regulations/ibr_locations.html.*

(c) In accordance with § 184.1(b)(1), the ingredient is used in the following food categories at levels not to exceed current good manufacturing practice: Confections and frostings as defined in § 170.3(n)(9) of this chapter; coatings of soft candy as defined in § 170.3(n)(38) of this chapter; and sweet sauces and toppings as defined in § 170.3(n)(43) of this chapter; except that the ingredient may not be used in a standardized food unless permitted by the standard of identity.

(d) The ingredient is used in food in accordance with § 184.1(b)(1) at levels not to exceed good manufacturing practice.

[43 FR 54239, Nov. 11, 1978, as amended at 47 FR 11852, Mar. 19, 1982; 49 FR 5611, Feb. 14, 1984; 49 FR 22799, June 1, 1984; 52 FR 47920, Dec. 17, 1987; 52 FR 48905, Dec. 28, 1987; 61 FR 36290, July 10, 1996; 64 FR 1760, Jan. 12, 1999; 78 FR 14666, Mar. 7, 2013]

§ 184.1260 Copper gluconate.

(a) Copper gluconate (cupric gluconate $(CH_2OH(CHOH)_4COO)_2Cu$, CAS Reg. No. 527–09–3) is a substance that occurs as light blue to bluish-green, odorless crystals, or as a fine, light blue powder. It is prepared by the reaction of gluconic acid solutions with cupric oxide or basic cupric carbonate.

(b) The ingredient meets the specifications of the Food Chemicals Codex, 3d Ed. (1981), p. 90, which is incorporated by reference. Copies are available from the National Academy Press, 2101 Constitution Ave. NW., Washington, DC. 20418, or available for inspection at the National Archives and Records Administration (NARA). For information on the availability of this material at NARA, call 202–741–6030, or go to: *http://www.archives.gov/federal_register/code_of_federal_regulations/ibr_locations.html.*

(c) In accordance with § 184.1(b)(1), the ingredient is used in food with no limitation other than current good manufacturing practice. The affirmation of this ingredient as generally recognized as safe (GRAS) as a direct human food ingredient is based upon the following current good manufacturing practice conditions of use:

(1) The ingredient is used as a nutrient supplement as defined in § 170.3(o)(20) of this chapter and as a synergist as defined in § 170.3(o)(31) of this chapter.

(2) The ingredient is used in food at levels not to exceed current good manufacturing practice. Copper gluconate may be used in infant formula in accordance with section 412(g) of the Federal Food, Drug, and Cosmetic Act (the Act) or with regulations promulgated under section 412(a)(2) of the Act.

(d) Prior sanctions for this ingredient different from the uses established in this section do not exist or have been waived.

[49 FR 24119, June 12, 1984]

§ 184.1261 Copper sulfate.

(a) Copper sulfate (cupric sulfate, $CuSO_4 \cdot 5\ H_2O$, CAS Reg. No. 7758–99–8) usually is used in the pentahydrate form. This form occurs as large, deep blue or ultramarine, triclinic crystals; as blue granules, or as a light blue powder. The ingredient is prepared by the reaction of sulfuric acid with cupric oxide or with copper metal.

(b) The ingredient must be of a purity suitable for its intended use.

(c) In accordance with § 184.1(b)(1), the ingredient is used in food with no limitation other than current good manufacturing practice. The affirmation of this ingredient as generally recognized as safe (GRAS) as a direct human food ingredient is based upon the following current good manufacturing practice conditions of use:

(1) The ingredient is used as a nutrient supplement as defined in § 170.3(o)(20) of this chapter and as a processing aid as defined in § 170.3(o)(24) of this chapter.

(2) The ingredient is used in food at levels not to exceed current good manufacturing practice. Copper sulfate may be used in infant formula in accordance with section 412(g) of the Federal Food, Drug, and Cosmetic Act (the Act) or with regulations promulgated under section 412(a)(2) of the Act.

(d) Prior sanctions for this ingredient different from the uses established in

this section do not exist or have been waived.

[49 FR 24119, June 12, 1984, as amended at 73 FR 8607, Feb. 14, 2008; 76 FR 59249, Sept. 26, 2011]

§ 184.1262 Corn silk and corn silk extract.

(a) Corn silk is the fresh styles and stigmas of *Zea mays* L. collected when the corn is in milk. The filaments are extracted with dilute ethanol to produce corn silk extract. The extract may be concentrated at a temperature not exceeding 60 °C.

(b) The ingredient must be of a purity suitable for its intended use.

(c) In accordance with § 184.1(b)(2), the ingredients are used in food only within the following specific limitations:

Category of food	Maximum level of use in food (as served) [1]	Functional use
Baked goods and baking mixes, § 170.3(n)(1) of this chapter.	30	Flavoring agent, § 170.3(o)(12) of this chapter.
Nonalcoholic beverages, § 170.3(n)(3) of this chapter.	20	Do.
Frozen dairy desserts, § 170.3(n)(20) of this chapter.	10	Do.
Soft candy, § 170.3(n)(38) of this chapter.	20	Do.
All other food categories.	4	Do.

[1] Parts per million.

(d) Prior sanctions for this ingredient different from the uses established in this section do not exist or have been waived.

[47 FR 29953, July 9, 1982, as amended at 73 FR 8607, Feb. 14, 2008]

§ 184.1265 Cuprous iodide.

(a) Cuprous iodide (copper (I) iodide, CuI, CAS Reg. No. 7681–65–4) is a pure white crystalline powder. It is prepared by the reaction of copper sulfate with potassium iodide under slightly acidic conditions.

(b) The ingredient must be of a purity suitable for its intended use.

(c) In accordance with § 184.1(b)(2), the ingredient is used in food only within the following specific limitations:

Category of food	Maximum treatment level in food	Functional use
Table salt.	0.01 percent	Source of dietary iodine.

(d) Prior sanctions for this ingredient different from the uses established in this section do not exist or have been waived.

[49 FR 24119, June 12, 1984, as amended at 73 FR 8607, Feb. 14, 2008]

§ 184.1271 L-Cysteine.

(a) L-Cysteine is the chemical L-2-amino-3-mercaptopropanoic acid ($C_3H_7O_2NS$).

(b) The ingredient meets the appropriate part of the specification set forth in the "Food Chemicals Codex," 3d Ed. (1981), pp. 92–93, which is incorporated by reference. Copies may be obtained from the National Academy Press, 2101 Constitution Ave. NW., Washington, DC 20418, or may be examined at the National Archives and Records Administration (NARA). For information on the availability of this material at NARA, call 202–741–6030, or go to: *http://www.archives.gov/federal_register/code_of_federal_regulations/ibr_locations.html.*

(c) The ingredient is used to supply up to 0.009 part of total L-cysteine per 100 parts of flour in dough as a dough strengthener as defined in § 170.3(o)(6) of this chapter in yeast-leavened baked goods and baking mixes as defined in § 170.3(n)(1) of this chapter.

(d) This regulation is issued prior to a general evaluation of use of this ingredient in order to affirm as GRAS the specific use named.

[42 FR 14653, Mar. 15, 1977, as amended at 49 FR 5612, Feb. 14, 1984]

§ 184.1272 L-Cysteine monohydrochloride.

(a) L-Cysteine monohydrochloride is the chemical L-2-amino-3-mercaptopropanoic acid monohydrochloride monohydrate ($C_3H_7O_2NS\ HCl\ H_2O$).

(b) The ingredient meets the specifications of the "Food Chemicals

Codex,'' 3d Ed. (1981), pp. 92–93, which is incorporated by reference. Copies may be obtained from the National Academy Press, 2101 Constitution Ave. NW., Washington, DC 20418, or may be examined at the National Archives and Records Administration (NARA). For information on the availability of this material at NARA, call 202–741–6030, or go to: *http://www.archives.gov/federal_register/code_of_federal_regulations/ibr_locations.html.*

(c) The ingredient is used to supply up to 0.009 part of total L-cysteine per 100 parts of flour in dough as a dough strengthener as defined in §170.3(o)(6) of this chapter in yeast-leavened baked goods and baking mixes as defined in §170.3(n)(1) of this chapter.

(d) This regulation is issued prior to a general evaluation of use of this ingredient in order to affirm as GRAS the specific use named.

[42 FR 14653, Mar. 15, 1977, as amended at 49 FR 5612, Feb. 14, 1984]

§ 184.1277 Dextrin.

(a) Dextrin ($(C_6H_{10}O_5)_n \cdot H_2O$, CAS Reg. No. 9004–53–9) is an incompletely hydrolyzed starch. It is prepared by dry heating corn, waxy maize, waxy milo, potato, arrowroot, wheat, rice, tapioca, or sago starches, or by dry heating the starches after: (1) Treatment with safe and suitable alkalis, acids, or pH control agents and (2) drying the acid or alkali treated starch.

(b) The ingredient meets the specification of the Food Chemicals Codex, 3d Ed. (1981), p. 96, which is incorporated by reference. Copies are available from the National Academy Press, 2101 Constitution Ave. NW., Washington, DC 20418, or available for inspection at the National Archives and Records Administration (NARA). For information on the availability of this material at NARA, call 202–741–6030, or go to: *http://www.archives.gov/federal_register/code_of_federal_regulations/ibr_locations.html.*

(c) In accordance with §184.1(b)(1), the ingredient is used in food with no limitation other than current good manufacturing practice. The affirmation of this ingredient as generally recognized as safe (GRAS) as a direct human food ingredient is based upon the following current good manufacturing practice conditions of use:

(1) The ingredient is used as a formulation aid as defined in §170.3(o)(14) of this chapter; as a processing aid as defined in §170.3(o)(24) of this chapter; as a stabilizer and thickener as defined in §170.3(o)(28) of this chapter; and as a surface-finishing agent as defined in §170.3(o)(30) of this chapter.

(2) The ingredient is used in food at levels not to exceed current good manufacturing practice.

(d) Prior sanctions for this ingredient different from the uses established in this section do not exist or have been waived.

[48 FR 51909, Nov. 15, 1983]

§ 184.1278 Diacetyl.

(a) Diacetyl ($C_4H_6O_2$, CAS Reg. No. 431–03–8) is a clear yellow to yellowish green liquid with a strong pungent odor. It is also known as 2,3-butanedione and is chemically synthesized from methyl ethyl ketone. It is miscible in water, glycerin, alcohol, and ether, and in very dilute water solution, it has a typical buttery odor and flavor.

(b) The ingredient meets the specifications of the Food Chemicals Codex, 3d Ed. (1981), p. 368, which is incorporated by reference. Copies are available from the National Academy Press, 2101 Constitution Ave. NW., Washington, DC 20418, or available for inspection at the National Archives and Records Administration (NARA). For information on the availability of this material at NARA, call 202–741–6030, or go to: *http://www.archives.gov/federal_register/code_of_federal_regulations/ibr_locations.html.*

(c) In accordance with §184.1(b)(1), the ingredient is used in food with no limitation other than current good manufacturing practice. The affirmation of this ingredient as generally recognized as safe (GRAS) as a direct human food ingredient is based upon the following current good manufacturing practice conditions of use:

(1) The ingredient is used as a flavoring agent and adjuvant as defined in §170.3(o)(12) of this chapter.

(2) The ingredient is used in food at levels not to exceed current good manufacturing practice.

(d) Prior sanctions for this ingredient different from the uses established in this section do not exist or have been waived.

[48 FR 51907, Nov. 15, 1983]

§ 184.1282 Dill and its derivatives.

(a) Dill (American or European) is the herb and seeds from *Anethum graveolens* L., and dill (Indian) is the herb and seeds from *Anethum sowa*, D.C. Its derivatives include essential oils, oleoresins, and natural extractives obtained from these sources of dill.

(b) Dill oils meet the description and specifications of the "Food Chemicals Codex," 4th ed. (1996), pp. 122–123, which is incorporated by reference in accordance with 5 U.S.C. 552(a) and 1 CFR part 51. Copies are available from the National Academy Press, Box 285, 2101 Constitution Ave. NW., Washington, DC 20055 (Internet address *http://www.nap.edu*), or may be examined at the Center for Food Safety and Applied Nutrition's Library, Food and Drug Administration, 5100 Paint Branch Pkwy., College Park, MD 20740, or at the National Archives and Records Administration (NARA). For information on the availability of this material at NARA, call 202–741–6030, or go to: *http://www.archives.gov/federal_register/code_of_federal_regulations/ibr_locations.html.*

(c) Dill and its derivatives are used as flavoring agents and adjuvants as defined in § 170.3(o)(12) of this chapter.

(d) The ingredients are used in food at levels not to exceed good manufacturing practice.

(e) [Reserved]

(f) Prior sanctions for these ingredients different from the uses established in this section do not exist or have been waived.

[42 FR 14653, Mar. 15, 1977, as amended at 42 FR 55205, Oct. 14, 1977; 49 FR 5612, Feb. 14, 1984; 64 FR 1760, Jan. 12, 1999]

§ 184.1287 Enzyme-modified fats.

(a) Enzyme-modified refined beef fat, enzyme-modified butterfat, and enzyme-modified steam-rendered chicken fat are prepared from refined beef fat; butterfat or milkfat; and steam-rendered chicken fat, respectively, with enzymes that are generally recognized as safe (GRAS). Enzyme-modified milk powder may be prepared with GRAS enzymes from reconstituted milk powder, whole milk, condensed or concentrated whole milk, evaporated milk, or milk powder. The lipolysis is maintained at a temperature that is optimal for the action of the enzyme until appropriate acid development is attained. The enzymes are then inactivated. The resulting product is concentrated or dried.

(b) The ingredients must be of a purity suitable for their intended use.

(c) In accordance with § 184.1(b)(1), the ingredients are used in food with no limitation other than current good manufacturing practice. The affirmation of these ingredients as generally recognized as safe (GRAS) as direct human food ingredients is based upon the following current good manufacturing practice conditions of use:

(1) The ingredients are used as flavoring agents and adjuvants as defined in § 170.3(o)(12) of this chapter.

(2) The ingredients are used in food at levels not to exceed current good manufacturing practice.

(d) Prior sanctions for these ingredients different from the uses established in this section do not exist or have been waived.

[52 FR 25976, July 10, 1987, as amended at 73 FR 8607, Feb. 14, 2008]

§ 184.1293 Ethyl alcohol.

(a) Ethyl alcohol (ethanol) is the chemical C_2H_5OH.

(b) The ingredient meets the specifications of the "Food Chemicals Codex," 4th ed. (1996), p. 136, which is incorporated by reference in accordance with 5 U.S.C. 552(a) and 1 CFR part 51. Copies are available from the National Academy Press, Box 285, 2101 Constitution Ave. NW., Washington, DC 20055 (Internet address *http://www.nap.edu*), or may be examined at the Center for Food Safety and Applied Nutrition's Library, Food and Drug Administration, 5100 Paint Branch Pkwy., College Park, MD 20740, or at the National Archives and Records Administration (NARA). For information on the availability of this material at

NARA, call 202–741–6030, or go to: *http://www.archives.gov/federal_register/code_of_federal_regulations/ibr_locations.html.*

(c) The ingredient is used as an antimicrobial agent as defined in §170.3(o)(2) of this chapter on pizza crusts prior to final baking at levels not to exceed 2.0 percent by product weight.

(d) This regulation is issued prior to general evaluation of use of this ingredient in order to affirm as GRAS the specific use named.

[42 FR 14653, Mar. 15, 1977, as amended at 49 FR 5612, Feb. 14, 1984; 64 FR 1760, Jan. 12, 1999]

§184.1295 Ethyl formate.

(a) Ethyl formate ($C_3H_6O_2$, CAS Reg. No. 109–94–4) is also referred to as ethyl methanoate. It is an ester of formic acid and is prepared by esterification of formic acid with ethyl alcohol or by distillation of ethyl acetate and formic acid in the presence of concentrated sulfuric acid. Ethyl formate occurs naturally in some plant oils, fruits, and juices but does not occur naturally in the animal kingdom.

(b) The ingredient meets the specifications of the "Food Chemicals Codex," 3d Ed. (1981), p. 376, which is incorporated by reference. Copies may be obtained from the National Academy Press, 2101 Constitution Ave. NW., Washington, DC 20418, or may be examined at the National Archives and Records Administration (NARA). For information on the availability of this material at NARA, call 202–741–6030, or go to: *http://www.archives.gov/federal_register/code_of_federal_regulations/ibr_locations.html.*

(c) The ingredient is used as a flavoring agent and adjuvant as defined in §170.3(o)(12) of this chapter.

(d) The ingredient is used in food at levels not to exceed good manufacturing practice in accordance with §184.1(b)(1). Current good manufacturing practice results in a maximum level, as served, of 0.05 percent in baked goods as defined in §170.3(n)(1) of this chapter; 0.04 percent in chewing gum as defined in §170.3(n)(6), hard candy as defined in §170.3(n)(25), and soft candy as defined in §170.3(n)(38) of this chapter; 0.02 percent in frozen dairy desserts as defined in §170.3(n)(20) of this chapter; 0.03 percent in gelatins, puddings, and fillings as defined in §170.3(n)(22) of this chapter; and 0.01 percent in all other food categories.

(e) Prior sanctions for ethyl formate different from the uses established in this section do not exist or have been waived.

[45 FR 22915, Apr. 4, 1980, as amended at 49 FR 5612, Feb. 14, 1984]

§184.1296 Ferric ammonium citrate.

(a) Ferric ammonium citrate (iron (III) ammonium citrate) is prepared by the reaction of ferric hydroxide with citric acid, followed by treatment with ammonium hydroxide, evaporating, and drying. The resulting product occurs in two forms depending on the stoichiometry of the initial reactants.

(1) Ferric ammonium citrate (iron (III) ammonium citrate, CAS Reg. No. 1332–98–5) is a complex salt of undetermined structure composed of 16.5 to 18.5 percent iron, approximately 9 percent ammonia, and 65 percent citric acid and occurs as reddish brown or garnet red scales or granules or as a brownish-yellowish powder.

(2) Ferric ammonium citrate (iron (III) ammonium citrate, CAS Reg. No. 1333–00–2) is a complex salt of undetermined structure composed of 14.5 to 16 percent iron, approximately 7.5 percent ammonia, and 75 percent citric acid and occurs as thin transparent green scales, as granules, as a powder, or as transparent green crystals.

(b) The ingredients meet the specifications of the Food Chemicals Codex, 3d Ed. (1981), pp. 116–117 (Ferric ammonium citrate, brown) and p. 117 (Ferric ammonium citrate, green), which is incorporated by reference. Copies are available from the National Academy Press, 2101 Constitution Ave. NW., Washington, DC 20418, or available for inspection at the National Archives and Records Administration (NARA). For information on the availability of this material at NARA, call 202–741–6030, or go to: *http://www.archives.gov/federal_register/code_of_federal_regulations/ibr_locations.html.*

(c) In accordance with § 184.1(b)(1), the ingredients are used in food as nutrient supplements as defined in § 170.3(o)(20) of this chapter, with no limitation other than current good manufacturing practice. The ingredients may also be used in infant formula in accordance with section 412(g) of the Federal Food, Drug, and Cosmetic Act (the act) (21 U.S.C. 350a(g)) or with regulations promulgated under section 412(a)(2) of the act (21 U.S.C. 350a(a)(2)).

(d) Prior sanctions for these ingredients different from the uses established in this section do not exist or have been waived.

[53 FR 16864, May 12, 1988]

§ 184.1297 Ferric chloride.

(a) Ferric chloride (iron (III) chloride, $FeC1_3$, CAS Reg. No. 7705–08–0) may be prepared from iron and chlorine or from ferric oxide and hydrogen chloride. The pure material occurs as hydroscopic, hexagonal, dark crystals. Ferric chloride hexahydrate (iron (III) chloride hexahydrate, $FeC1_3$. $6H_20$, CAS Reg. No. 10025–77–1) is readily formed when ferric chloride is exposed to moisture.

(b) The ingredient must be of a purity suitable for its intended use.

(c) In accordance with § 184.1(b)(1) the ingredient is used in food as a flavoring agent as defined in § 170.3(o)(12) of this chapter, with no limitation other than current good manufacturing practice.

(d) Prior sanctions for this ingredient different from the uses established in this section do not exist or have been waived.

[53 FR 16864, May 12, 1988, as amended at 73 FR 8607, Feb. 14, 2008]

§ 184.1298 Ferric citrate.

(a) Ferric citrate (iron (III) citrate, $C_6H_5FeO_7$, CAS Reg. No. 2338–05–8) is prepared from reaction of citric acid with ferric hydroxide. It is a compound of indefinite ratio of citric acid and iron.

(b) The ingredient must be of a purity suitable for its intended use.

(c) In accordance with § 184.1(b)(1), the ingredient is used in food as a nutrient supplement as defined in § 170.3(o)(20) of this chapter, with no limitation other than current good manufacturing practice. The ingredient may also be used in infant formula in accordance with section 412(g) of the Federal Food, Drug, and Cosmetic Act (the act) (21 U.S.C. 350a(g)) or with regulations promulgated under section 412(a)(2) of the act (21 U.S.C. 350a(a)(2)).

(d) Prior sanctions for this ingredient different from the uses established in this section do not exist or have been waived.

[53 FR 16865, May 12, 1988, as amended at 73 FR 8607, Feb. 14, 2008]

§ 184.1301 Ferric phosphate.

(a) Ferric phosphate (ferric orthophosphate, iron (III) phosphate, $FePO_4{\cdot}xH_2O$, CAS Reg. No. 10045–86–0) is an odorless, yellowish-white to buff-colored powder and contains from one to four molecules of water of hydration. It is prepared by reaction of sodium phosphate with ferric chloride or ferric citrate.

(b) The ingredient meets the specifications of the Food Chemicals Codex, 3d Ed. (1981), pp. 118–120, which is incorporated by reference. Copies are available from the National Academy Press, 2101 Constitution Ave. NW., Washington, DC 20418, or available for inspection at the National Archives and Records Administration (NARA). For information on the availability of this material at NARA, call 202–741–6030, or go to: *http://www.archives.gov/federal_register/code_of_federal_regulations/ibr_locations.html.*

(c) In accordance with § 184.1(b)(1), the ingredient is used in food as nutrient supplement as defined in § 170.3(o)(20) of this chapter, with no limitation other than current good manufacturing practice. The ingredient may also be used in infant formula in accordance with section 412(g) of the Federal Food, Drug, and Cosmetic Act (the act) (21 U.S.C. 350a(g)) or with regulations promulgated under section 412(a)(2) of the act (21 U.S.C. 350a(a)(2)).

(d) Prior sanctions for this ingredient different from the uses established in this section do not exist or have been waived.

[53 FR 16865, May 12, 1988]

§ 184.1304 Ferric pyrophosphate.

(a) Ferric pyrophosphate (iron (III) pyrophosphate, $Fe_4(P_{207})_3 \cdot xH_2O$, CAS Reg. No. 10058–44–3) is a tan or yellowish white colorless powder. It is prepared by reacting sodium pyrophosphate with ferric citrate.

(b) The ingredient meets the specifications of the Food Chemicals Codex, 3d Ed. (1981), p. 120, which is incorporated by reference. Copies are available from the National Academy Press, 2101 Constitution Ave. NW., Washington, DC 20418, or available for inspection at the National Archives and Records Administration (NARA). For information on the availability of this material at NARA, call 202–741–6030, or go to: *http://www.archives.gov/federal_register/code_of_federal_regulations/ibr_locations.html.*

(c) In accordance with § 184.1(b)(1), the ingredient is used in food as a nutrient supplement as defined in § 170.3(o)(20) of this chapter, with no limitation other than current good manufacturing practice. The ingredient may also be used in infant formula in accordance with section 412(g) of the Federal Food, Drug, and Cosmetic Act (the act) (21 U.S.C. 350a(g)) or with regulations promulgated under section 412(a)(2) of the act (21 U.S.C. 350a(a)(2)).

(d) Prior sanctions for this ingredient different from the uses established in this section do not exist or have been waived.

[53 FR 16865, May 12, 1988; 53 FR 20939, June 7, 1988]

§ 184.1307 Ferric sulfate.

(a) Ferric sulfate (iron (III) sulfate, $Fe_2(SO_4)_3$ CAS Reg. No. 10028–22–5) is a yellow substance that may be prepared by oxidizing iron (II) sulfate or by treating ferric oxide or ferric hydroxide with sulfuric acid.

(b) The ingredient must be of a purity suitable for its intended use.

(c) In accordance with § 184.1(b)(1), the ingredient is used in food as a flavoring agent as defined in § 170.3(o)(12) of this chapter, with no limitation other than current good manufacturing practice.

(d) Prior sanctions for this ingredient different from the uses established in this section do not exist or have been waived.

[53 FR 16865, May 12, 1988, as amended at 73 FR 8607, Feb. 14, 2008]

§ 184.1307a Ferrous ascorbate.

(a) Ferrous ascorbate (CAS Reg. No. 24808–52–4) is a reaction product of ferrous hydroxide and ascorbic acid. It is a blue-violet product containing 16 percent iron.

(b) The ingredient must be of a purity suitable for its intended use.

(c) In accordance with § 184.1(b)(1), the ingredient is used in food as a nutrient supplement as defined in § 170.3(o)(20) of this chapter, with no limitation other than current good manufacturing practice. The ingredient may also be used in infant formula in accordance with section 412(g) of the Federal Food, Drug, and Cosmetic Act (the act) (21 U.S.C. 350a(g)) or with regulations promulgated under section 412(a)(2) of the act (21 U.S.C. 350a(a)(2)).

(d) Prior sanctions for this ingredient different from the uses established in this section do not exist or have been waived.

[53 FR 16865, May 12, 1988, as amended at 69 FR 24512, May 4, 2004; 73 FR 8607, Feb. 14, 2008]

§ 184.1307b Ferrous carbonate.

(a) Ferrous carbonate (iron (II) carbonate, $FeCO_3$, CAS Reg. No. 563–71–3) is an odorless, white solid prepared by treating solutions of iron (II) salts with alkali carbonate salts.

(b) The ingredient must be of a purity suitable for its intended use.

(c) In accordance with § 184.1(b)(1), the ingredient is used in food as a nutrient supplement as defined in § 170.3(o)(20) of this chapter, with no limitation other than current good manufacturing practice. The ingredient may also be used in infant formula in accordance with section 412(g) of the Federal Foods, Drug, and Cosmetic Act (the act) (21 U.S.C. 350a(g)) or with regulations promulgated under section 412(a)(2) of the act (21 U.S.C. 350a(a)(2)).

(d) Prior sanctions for this ingredient different from the uses established in this section do not exist or have been waived.

[53 FR 16865, May 12, 1988, as amended at 73 FR 8607, Feb. 14, 2008]

§ 184.1307c Ferrous citrate.

(a) Ferrous citrate (iron (II) citrate, ($C_6H_6FeO_7$), CAS Reg. No. 23383–11–1) is a slightly colored powder or white crystals. It is prepared from the reaction of sodium citrate with ferrous sulfate or by direct action of citric acid on iron filings.

(b) The ingredient must be of a purity suitable for its intended use.

(c) In accordance with § 184.1(b)(1) the ingredient is used in food as a nutrient supplement as defined in § 170.3(o)(20) of this chapter, with no limitation other than current good manufacturing practice. The ingredient may also be used in infant formula in accordance with section 412(g) of the Federal Food, Drug, and Cosmetic Act (the act) (21 U.S.C. 350a(g)) or with regulations promulgated under section 412(a)(2) of the act (21 U.S.C. 350a(a)(2)).

(d) Prior sanctions for this ingredient different from the uses established in this section do not exist or have been waived.

[53 FR 16866, May 12, 1988, as amended at 73 FR 8607, Feb. 14, 2008]

§ 184.1307d Ferrous fumarate.

(a) Ferrous fumarate (iron (II) fumarate, ($C_4H_2FeO_4$), CAS Reg. No. 141–01–5) is an odorless, reddish-orange to reddish-brown powder. It may contain soft lumps that produce a yellow streak when crushed. It is prepared by admixing hot solutions of ferrous sulfate and sodium fumarate.

(b) The ingredient meets the specifications of the Food Chemicals Codex, 3d Ed. (1981), pp. 120–122, which is incorporated by reference. Copies are available from the National Academy Press, 2101 Constitution Ave NW., Washington, DC 20418, or available for inspection at the National Archives and Records Administration (NARA). For information on the availability of this material at NARA, call 202–741–6030, or go to: *http://www.archives.gov/federal_register/code_of_federal_regulations/ibr_locations.html.*

(c) In accordance with § 184.1(b)(1) the ingredient is used in food as a nutrient supplement as defined in § 170.3(o)(20) of this chapter, with no limitation other than current good manufacturing practice. The ingredient may also be used in infant formula in accordance with section 412(g) of the Federal Food, Drug, and Cosmetic Act (the act) (21 U.S.C. 350a(g)), or with regulations promulgated under section 412(a)(2) of the act (21 U.S.C. 350a(a)(2)).

(d) Prior sanctions for this ingredient different from the uses established in this section do not exist or have been waived.

[53 FR 16866, May 12, 1988]

§ 184.1308 Ferrous gluconate.

(a) Ferrous gluconate (iron (II) gluconate dihydrate, $C_{12}H_{22}FeO_{14} \cdot 2H_2O$, CAS Reg. No. 6047-12-7) is a fine yellowish-gray or pale greenish-yellow powder or granules. It is prepared by reacting hot solutions of barium or calcium gluconate with ferrous sulfate or by heating freshly prepared ferrous carbonate with gluconic acid in aqueous solution.

(b) The ingredient meets the specifications of the Food Chemcials Codex, 3d Ed. (1981), pp. 122–123, which is incorporated by reference. Copies are available from the National Academy Press, 2101 Constitution Avenue NW., Washington, DC 20418, or available for inspection at the National Archives and Records Administration (NARA). For information on the availability of this material at NARA, call 202–741–6030, or go to: *http://www.archives.gov/federal_register/code_of_federal_regulations/ibr_locations.html.*

(c) In accordance with § 184.1(b)(1), the ingredient is used in food as a nutrient supplement as defined in § 170.3(o)(20) of this chapter, with no limitation other than current good manufacturing practice. The ingredient may also be used in infant formula in accordance with section 412(g) of the Federal Food, Drug, and Cosmetic Act (the act) (21 U.S.C. 350a(g)) or with regulations promulgated under section 412(a)(2) of the act (21 U.S.C. 350a(a)(2)).

(d) Prior sanctions for this ingredient different from the uses established in this section do not exist or have been waived.

[53 FR 16866, May 12, 1988; 53 FR 20939, June 7, 1988]

§ 184.1311 Ferrous lactate.

(a) Ferrous lactate (iron (II) lactate, $C_6H_{10}FeO_6$, CAS Reg. No. 5905–52–2) in the trihydrate form is a greenish-white powder or crystalline mass. It is prepared by reacting calcium lactate or sodium lactate with ferrous sulfate, direct reaction of lactic acid with iron filings, reaction of ferrous chloride with sodium lactate, or reaction of ferrous sulfate with ammonium lactate.

(b) The ingredient meets the specifications of the Food Chemicals Codex, 4th ed. (1996), pp. 154 to 155, which is incorporated by reference in accordance with 5 U.S.C. 552(a) and 1 CFR part 51. Copies are available from the National Academy Press, 2101 Constitution Ave. NW., Washington, DC 20418, or may be examined at the Center for Food Safety and Applied Nutrition's library, 5100 Paint Branch Pkwy., College Park, MD 20740, or at the National Archives and Records Administration (NARA). For information on the availability of this material at NARA, call 202–741–6030, or go to: *http://www.archives.gov/federal_register/code_of_federal_regulations/ibr_locations.html.*

(c) In accordance with § 184.1(b)(1), the ingredient is used in food as a nutrient supplement as defined in § 170.3(o)(20) of this chapter and as a color fixative for ripe olives, with no other limitation other than current good manufacturing practice. The ingredient may also be used in infant formula in accordance with section 412(g) of the Federal Food, Drug, and Cosmetic Act (the act) (21 U.S.C. 350a(g)) or with regulations promulgated under section 412(a)(2) of the act (21 U.S.C. 350a(a)(2)).

(d) Prior sanctions for this ingredient different from the uses established in this section do not exist or have been waived.

[53 FR 16866, May 12, 1988, as amended at 61 FR 40319, Aug. 2, 1996]

§ 184.1315 Ferrous sulfate.

(a) Ferrous sulfate heptahydrate (iron (II) sulfate heptahydrate, $FeSO_4 \cdot 7H_2O$, CAS Reg. No. 7782–63–0) is prepared by the action of sulfuric acid on iron. It occurs as pale, bluish-green crystals or granules. Progressive heating of ferrous sulfate heptahydrate produces ferrous sulfate (dried). Ferrous sulfate (dried) consists primarily of ferrous sulfate monohydrate (CAS Reg. No. 17375–41–6) with varying amounts of ferrous sulfate tetrahydrate (CAS Reg. No. 20908–72–9) and occurs as a grayish-white to buff-colored powder.

(b) The ingredients meet the specifications of the Food Chemicals Codex, 3d Ed. (1981), p. 123 (Ferrous sulfate heptahydrate) and p. 124 (ferrous sulfate, dried), which is incorporated by reference. Copies are available from the National Academy Press, 2101 Constitution Ave., NW., Washington, DC 20418, or available for inspection at the National Archives and Records Administration (NARA). For information on the availability of this material at NARA, call 202–741–6030, or go to: *http://www.archives.gov/federal_register/code_of_federal_regulations/ibr_locations.html.*

(c) In accordance with § 184.1(b)(1), the ingredients are used in food as nutrient supplements as defined in § 170.3(o)(20) of this chapter and as a processing aid as defined in § 170.3(o)(24) of this chapter, with no limitation other than current good manufacturing practice. The ingredients may also be used in infant formula in accordance with section 412(g) of the Federal Food, Drug, and Cosmetic Act (the act) (21 U.S.C. 350a(g)) or with regulations promulgated under section 412(a)(2) of the act (21 U.S.C. 350a(a)(2)).

(d) Prior sanctions for these ingredients different from the uses established in this section do not exist or have been waived.

[53 FR 16866, May 12, 1988]

§ 184.1316 Ficin.

(a) Ficin (CAS Reg. No. 9001–33–6) is an enzyme preparation obtained from the latex of species of the genus *Ficus*, which include a variety of tropical fig trees. It is a white to off-white powder. Its characterizing enzyme activity is that of a peptide hydrolase (EC 3.4.22.3).

(b) The ingredient meets the general requirements and additional requirements for enzyme preparations in the Food Chemicals Codex, 3d ed. (1981), p. 110, which is incorporated by reference in accordance with 5 U.S.C. 552(a) and 1 CFR part 51. Copies are available from the National Academy Press, 2101 Constitution Ave., NW., Washington, DC 20418, or may be examined at the Office of Food Additive Safety (HFS–200), Center for Food Safety and Applied Nutrition, Food and Drug Administration, 5100 Paint Branch Pkwy., College Park, MD 20740, 240–402–1200, and at the National Archives and Records Administration (NARA). For information on the availability of this material at NARA, call 202–741–6030, or go to: *http://www.archives.gov/federal_register/code_of_federal_regulations/ibr_locations.html.*

(c) In accordance with §184.1(b)(1), the ingredient is used in food with no limitation other than current good manufacturing practice. The affirmation of this ingredient as GRAS as a direct food ingredient is based upon the following current good manufacturing practice conditions of use:

(1) The ingredient is used as an enzyme as defined in §170.3(o)(9) of this chapter to hydrolyze proteins or polypeptides.

(2) The ingredient is used in food at levels not to exceed current good manufacturing practice.

[60 FR 32910, June 26, 1995, as amended at 78 FR 14666, Mar. 7, 2013]

§ 184.1317 Garlic and its derivatives.

(a) Garlic is the fresh or dehydrated bulb or cloves obtained from *Allium sativum*, a genus of the lily family. Its derivatives include essential oils, oleoresins, and natural extractives obtained from garlic.

(b) Garlic oil meets the specifications of the "Food Chemicals Codex," 3d Ed. (1981), p. 132, which is incorporated by reference. Copies may be obtained from the National Academy Press, 2101 Constitution Ave. NW., Washington, DC 20418, or may be examined at the National Archives and Records Administration (NARA). For information on the availability of this material at NARA, call 202–741–6030, or go to: *http://www.archives.gov/federal_register/code_of_federal_regulations/ibr_locations.html.*

(c) Garlic and its derivatives are used as flavoring agents and adjuvants as defined in §170.3(o)(12) of this chapter.

(d) The ingredients are used in food at levels not to exceed good manufacturing practice.

(e) [Reserved]

(f) Prior sanctions for this ingredient different from the uses established in this section do not exist or have been waived.

[42 FR 14653, Mar. 15, 1977, as amended at 42 FR 55205, Oct. 14, 1977; 49 FR 5612, Feb. 14, 1984]

§ 184.1318 Glucono delta-lactone.

(a) Glucono delta-lactone ($C_6H_{10}O_6$, CAS Reg. No. 90–80–2), also called *D*-gluconic acid delta-lactone or *D*-glucono-1,5-lactone, is the cyclic 1,5-intramolecular ester of *D*-gluconic acid. It is prepared by direct crystallization from the aqueous solution of gluconic acid. Gluconic acid may be produced by the oxidation of *D*-glucose with bromine water, by the oxidation of *D*-glucose by microorganisms that are nonpathogenic and nontoxicogenic to man or other animals, or by the oxidation of *D*-glucose with enzymes derived from these microorganisms.

(b) The ingredient meets the specifications of the Food Chemicals Codex, 3d Ed. (1981), p. 134, which is incorporated by reference. Copies are available from the National Academy Press, 2101 Constitution Ave. NW., Washington, DC 20418, or available for inspection at the National Archives and Records Administration (NARA). For information on the availability of this material at NARA, call 202–741–6030, or go to: *http://www.archives.gov/federal_register/code_of_federal_regulations/ibr_locations.html.*

(c) In accordance with §184.1(b)(1), the ingredient is used in food with no limitation other than current good manufacturing practice. The affirmation of this ingredient as generally recognized as safe (GRAS) as a direct human food ingredient is based upon the following current good manufacturing practice conditions of use:

(1) The ingredient is used as a curing and pickling agent as defined in §170.3(o)(5) of this chapter, leavening agent as defined in §170.3(o)(17) of this chapter; pH control agent as defined in §170.3(o)(23) of this chapter; and sequestrant as defined in §170.3(o)(26) of this chapter.

(2) The ingredient is used at levels not to exceed current good manufacturing practice.

(d) Prior sanctions for this ingredient different from the uses established in this section do not exist or have been waived.

[51 FR 33896, Sept. 24, 1986]

§ 184.1321 Corn gluten.

(a) Corn gluten (CAS Reg. No. 66071–96–3), also known as corn gluten meal, is the principal protein component of corn endosperm. It consists mainly of zein and glutelin. Corn gluten is a byproduct of the wet milling of corn for starch. The gluten fraction is washed to remove residual water soluble proteins. Corn gluten is also produced as a byproduct during the conversion of the starch in whole or various fractions of dry milled corn to corn syrups.

(b) The ingredient must be of a purity suitable for its intended use.

(c) In accordance with §184.1(b)(1), the ingredient is used in food with no limitation other than current good manufacturing practice. The affirmation of this ingredient as generally recognized as safe (GRAS) as a direct human food ingredient is based upon the following current good manufacturing practice conditions of use:

(1) The ingredient is used as a nutrient supplement as defined in §170.3(o)(20) of this chapter and a texturizer as defined in §170.3(o)(32) of this chapter.

(2) The ingredient is used in food at levels not to exceed current good manufacturing practice.

(d) Prior sanctions for this ingredient different from the uses established in this section do not exist or have been waived.

[50 FR 8998, Mar. 6, 1985, as amended at 73 FR 8607, Feb. 14, 2008]

§ 184.1322 Wheat gluten.

(a) Wheat gluten (CAS Reg. No. 8002–80–0) is the principal protein component of wheat and consists mainly of gliadin and glutenin. Wheat gluten is obtained by hydrating wheat flour and mechanically working the sticky mass to separate the wheat gluten from the starch and other flour components. Vital gluten is dried gluten that has retained its elastic properties.

(b) The ingredient must be of a purity suitable for its intended use.

(c) In accordance with §184.1(b)(1), the ingredient is used in food with no limitation other than current good manufacturing practice. The affirmation of this ingredient as generally recognized as safe (GRAS) as a direct human food ingredient is based upon the following current good manufacturing practice conditions of use:

(1) The ingredient is used as a dough strengthener as defined in §170.3(o)(6) of this chapter; a formulation aid as defined in §170.3(o)(14) of this chapter; a nutrient supplement as defined in §170.3(o)(20) of this chapter; a processing aid as defined in §170.3(o)(24) of this chapter; a stabilizer and thickener as defined in §170.3(o)(28) of this chapter; a surface-finishing agent as defined in §170.3(o)(30) of this chapter; and a texturizing agent as defined in §170.3(o)(32) of this chapter.

(2) The ingredient is used in food at levels not to exceed current good manufacturing practice.

(d) Prior sanctions for this ingredient different from the uses established in this section do not exist or have been waived.

[50 FR 8998, Mar. 6, 1985, as amended at 73 FR 8607, Feb. 14, 2008]

§ 184.1323 Glyceryl monooleate.

(a) Glyceryl monooleate is prepared by esterification of commerical oleic acid that is derived either from edible sources or from tall oil fatty acids meeting the requirements of §172.862 of this chapter. It contains glyceryl monooleate ($C_{21}H_{40}O_4$, CAS Reg. No. 25496–72–4) and glyceryl esters of fatty acids present in commercial oleic acid.

(b) The ingredient must be of a purity suitable for its intended use.

(c) In accordance with §184.1(b)(1), the ingredient is used in food with no limitation other than current good manufacturing practice. The affirmation of this ingredient as generally recognized as safe (GRAS) as a direct human food ingredient is based upon the following current good manufacturing practice conditions of use:

(1) The ingredient is used as a flavoring agent and adjuvant as defined in §170.3(o)(12) of this chapter and as a solvent and vehicle as defined in §170.3(o)(27) of this chapter.

(2) The ingredient is used in the following foods at levels not to exceed current good manufacturing practice: baked goods and baking mixes as defined in §170.3(n)(1) of this chapter; nonalcoholic beverages and beverage bases as defined in §170.3(n)(3) of this chapter; chewing gum as defined in §170.3(n)(6) of this chapter; and meat products as defined in §170.3(n)(29) of this chapter.

(d) Prior sanctions for this ingredient different from the use established in this section do not exist or have been waived.

[54 FR 7403 Feb. 21, 1989, as amended at 73 FR 8607, Feb. 14, 2008]

§184.1324 Glyceryl monostearate.

(a) Glyceryl monostearate, also known as monostearin, is a mixture of variable proportions of glyceryl monostearate ($C_{21}H_{42}O_4$, CAS Reg. No. 31566–31–1), glyceryl monopalmitate ($C_{19}H_{38}O_4$, CAS Reg. No. 26657–96–5) and glyceryl esters of fatty acids present in commercial stearic acid. Glyceryl monostearate is prepared by glycerolysis of certain fats or oils that are derived from edible sources or by esterification, with glycerin, of stearic acid that is derived from edible sources.

(b) The ingredient must be of a purity suitable for its intended use.

(c) In accordance with §184.1(b)(1), the ingredient is used in food with no limitation other than current good manufacturing practice.

(d) Prior sanctions for this ingredient different from the uses established in this section do not not exist or have been waived.

[54 FR 7403 Feb. 21, 1989, as amended at 73 FR 8607, Feb. 14, 2008]

§184.1328 Glyceryl behenate.

(a) Glyceryl behenate is a mixture of glyceryl esters of behenic acid made from glycerin and behenic acid (a saturated C_{22} fatty acid). The mixture contains predominately glyceryl dibehenate.

(b) The ingredient meets the following specifications:

(1) 10 to 20 percent monoglyceride, 47 to 59 percent diglyceride, 26 to 38 percent triglyceride, and not more than 2.5 percent free fatty acids.

(2) *Behenic acid.* Between 80 and 90 percent of the total fatty acid content.

(3) *Acid value.* Not more than 4.

(4) *Saponification value.* Between 145 and 165.

(5) *Iodine number.* Not more than 3.

(6) *Heavy metals (as Pb).* Not more than 10 parts per million.

(c) In accordance with §184.1(b)(1) of this chapter, the ingredient is used in food with no limitation other than current good manufacturing practice. The affirmation of this ingredient is generally recognized as safe (GRAS) as a direct human food ingredient is based upon the following current good manufacturing practice conditions of use:

(1) The ingredient is used as a formulation aid, as defined in §170.3(o)(14) of this chapter.

(2) The ingredient is used in excipient formulations for use in tablets at levels not to exceed good manufacturing practice.

[52 FR 42430, Nov. 5, 1987]

§184.1329 Glyceryl palmitostearate.

(a) Glyceryl palmitostearate is a mixture of mono-, di-, and triglyceryl esters of palmitic and stearic acids made from glycerin, palmitic acid, and stearic acid.

(b) The ingredient meets the following specifications:

(1) The substance is a mixture of mono-, di-, and triglycerides of palmitic acid and stearic acid.

(2) Heavy metals (as lead): Not more than 10 parts per million.

(c) In accordance with § 184.1(b)(1), the ingredient is used in food with no limitation other than current good manufacturing practice. The affirmation of this ingredient as generally recognized as safe (GRAS) as a direct human food ingredient is based upon the following current good manufacturing practice conditions of use:

(1) The ingredient is used as a formulation aid, as defined in § 170.3(o)(14) of this chapter.

(2) The ingredient is used in excipient formulations for use in tablets at levels not to exceed good manufacturing practice.

[60 FR 63621, Dec. 12, 1995]

§ 184.1330 Acacia (gum arabic).

(a) Acacia (gum arabic) is the dried gummy exudate from stems and branches of trees of various species of the genus *Acacia*, family Leguminosae.

(b) The ingredient meets the specifications of the "Food Chemicals Codex," 3d Ed. (1981), p. 7, which is incorporated by reference. Copies may be obtained from the National Academy Press, 2101 Constitution Ave. NW., Washington, DC 20418, or may be examined at the National Archives and Records Administration (NARA). For information on the availability of this material at NARA, call 202–741–6030, or go to: *http://www.archives.gov/federal_register/code_of_federal_regulations/ibr_locations.html.*

(c) The ingredient is used in food under the following conditions:

MAXIMUM USAGE LEVELS PERMITTED

Food (as served)	Percent	Function
Beverages and beverage bases, § 170.3(n)(3) of this chapter	2.0	Emulsifier and emulsifier salt, § 170.3(o)(8) of this chapter; flavoring agent and adjuvant, § 170.3(o)(12) of this chapter; formulation aid, § 170.3(o)(14) of this chapter; stabilizer and thickener, § 170.3(o)(28) of this chapter.
Chewing gum, § 170.3(n)(6) of this chapter	5.6	Flavoring agent and adjuvant, § 170.3(o)(12) of this chapter; formulation aid, § 170.3(o)(14) of this chapter; humectant, § 170.3(o)(16) of this chapter; surface-finishing agent, § 170.3(o)(30) of this chapter.
Confections and frostings, § 170.3(n)(9) of this chapter	12.4	Formulation aid, § 170.3(o)(14) of this chapter; stabilizer and thickener, § 170.3(o)(28) of this chapter; surface-finishing agent, § 170.3(o)(30) of this chapter.
Dairy product analogs, § 170.3(n)(10) of this chapter	1.3	Formulation aid, § 170.3(o)(14) of this chapter; stabilizer and thickener, § 170.3(o)(28) of this chapter.
Fats and oils, § 170.3(n)(12) of this chapter	1.5	Formulation aid, § 170.3(o)(14) of this chapter; stabilizer and thickener, § 170.3(o)(28) of this chapter.
Gelatins, puddings, and fillings, § 170.3(n)(22) of this chapter	2.5	Emulsifier and emulsifier salt, § 170.3(o)(8) of this chapter; formulation aid, § 170.3(o)(14) of this chapter.; stabilizer and thickener, § 170.3(o)(28) of this chapter.
Hard candy and cough drops, § 170.3(n)(25) of this chapter	46.5	Flavoring agent and adjuvant, § 170.3(o)(12) of this chapter; formulation aid, § 170.3(o)(14) of this chapter.
Nuts and nut products, § 170.3(n)(32) of this chapter	8.3	Formulation aid, § 170.3(o)(14) of this chapter; surface-finishing agent, § 170.3(o)(30) of this chapter.
Quiescently frozen confection products	6.0	Formulation aid, § 170.3(o)(14) of this chapter; stabilizer and thickener, § 170.3(o)(28) of this chapter.
Snack foods, § 170.3(n)(37) of this chapter	4.0	Emulsifier and emulsifier salt, § 170.3(o)(8) of this chapter; formulation aid, § 170.3(o)(14) of this chapter.
Soft candy, § 170.3(n)(38) of this chapter	85.0	Emulsifier and emulsifier salt, § 170.3(o)(8) of this chapter; firming agent, § 170.3(o)(10) of this chapter; flavoring agent and adjuvant, § 170.3(o)(12) of this chapter; formulation aid, § 170.3(o)(14) of this chapter, humectant, § 170.3(o)(16) of this chapter; stabilizer and thickener, § 170.3(o)(28) of this chapter; surface-finishing agent, § 170.3(o)(30) of this chapter.

MAXIMUM USAGE LEVELS PERMITTED—Continued

Food (as served)	Percent	Function
All other food categories	1.0	Emulsifier and emulsifier salt, § 170.3(o)(8) of this chapter; flavoring agent and adjuvant, § 170.3(o)(12) of this chapter; formulation aid, § 170.3(o)(14) of this chapter; processing aid, § 170.3(o)(24) of this chapter; stabilizer and thickener, § 170.3(o)(28) of this chapter; surface-finishing agent, § 170.3(o)(30) of this chapter; texturizer, § 170.3(o)(32) of this chapter.

(d) [Reserved]

(e) Prior sanctions for this ingredient different from the uses established in this section do not exist or have been waived.

[42 FR 14653, Mar. 15, 1977, as amended at 42 FR 55205, Oct. 14, 1977; 49 FR 5612, Feb. 14, 1983; 53 FR 5766, Feb. 26, 1988]

§ 184.1333 Gum ghatti.

(a) Gum ghatti (Indian gum) is an exudate from wounds in the bark of *Anogeissus latifolia*, a large tree found in the dry deciduous forests of India and Ceylon.

(b) The ingredient complies with the following specifications:

(1) *Viscosity of a 1-percent solution.* Not less than the minimum or within the range claimed by the vendor.

(2) *Limits of impurities*—(i) *Arsenic (as AL).* Not more than 3 parts per million (0.0003 percent);

(ii) *Ash (acid-insoluble).* Not more than 1.75 percent;

(iii) *Ash (total).* Not more than 6.0 percent;

(iv) *Heavy metals (as Pb).* Not more than 40 parts per million (0.004 percent); and

(v) *Lead.* Not more than 10 parts per million (0.001 percent).

(3) *Loss on drying.* Not more than 14 percent dried at 105 °C for 5 hours.

(4) *Identification test.* Add 0.2 ml of diluted lead acetate as outlined in "Official Methods of Analysis of the Association of Official Analytical Chemists," 13th Ed. (1980), section 31.178(b), p. 529, under "Dilute Basic Lead Acetate Standard Solution," which is incorporated by reference (Copies are available from the AOAC INTERNATIONAL, 481 North Frederick Ave., suite 500, Gaithersburg, MD 20877, or may be examined at the National Archives and Records Administration (NARA). For information on the availability of this material at NARA, call 202–741–6030, or go to: *http://www.archives.gov/federal_register/code_of_federal_regulations/ibr_locations.html.*), to 5 ml of a cold 1-in-100 aqueous solution of the gum. An immediate, voluminous, opaque precipitate indicates acacia. A small precipitate or clear solution which produces an opaque flocculent precipitate upon the addition of 1 ml of 3 *N* ammonimum hydroxide indicates gum ghatti.

(c) The ingredient is used in food under the following conditions:

MAXIMUM USAGE LEVELS PERMITTED

Food (as served)	Percent	Function
Beverages and beverage bases, nonalcoholic, § 170.3(n)(3) of this chapter.	0.2	Emulsifier and emulsifier salt, § 170.3(o)(8) of this chapter.
All other food categories	.1	Emulsifier and emulsifier salt, § 170.3(o)(8) of this chapter.

(d) Prior sanctions for this ingredient different from the uses established in this section do not exist or have been waived.

[42 FR 14653, Mar. 15, 1977, as amended at 49 FR 5612, Feb. 14, 1984]

§ 184.1339 Guar gum.

(a) Guar gum is the natural substance obtained from the maceration of the seed of the guar plant, *Cyamopsis tetragonoloba* (Linne) Taub., or *Cyamopsis psoraloides* (Lam.) D.C.

(b) The ingredient meets the specifications of the "Food Chemicals Codex," 3d Ed. (1981), p. 141, which is incorporated by reference. Copies may be obtained from the National Academy Press, 2101 Constitution Ave. NW., Washington, DC 20418, or may be examined at the National Archives and Records Administration (NARA). For information on the availability of this material at NARA, call 202-741-6030, or go to: *http://www.archives.gov/federal_register/code_of_federal_regulations/ibr_locations.html.*

(c) The ingredient is used in food under the following conditions:

MAXIMUM USAGE LEVELS PERMITTED

Food (as served)	Percent	Function
Baked goods and baking mixes, § 170.3(n)(1) of this chapter	0.35	Emulsifier and emulsifier salts, § 170.3(o)(8) of this chapter; formulation aid, § 170.3(o)(14) of this chapter; stabilizer and thickener; § 170.3(o)(28) of this chapter.
Breakfast cereals, § 170.3(n)(4) of this chapter	1.2	Formulation aid, § 170.3(o)(14) of this chapter; stabilizer and thickener, § 170.3(o)(28) of this chapter.
Cheese, § 170.3(n)(5) of this chapter	.8	Do.
Dairy products analogs, § 170.3(n)(10) of this chapter	1.0	Firming agent, § 170.3(o)(10) of this chapter; formulation aid, § 170.3(o)(14) of this chapter; stabilizer and thickener, § 170.3(o)(28) of this chapter.
Fats and oils, § 170.3(n)(12) of this chapter	2.0	Do.
Gravies and sauces, § 170.3(n)(24) of this chapter	1.2	Formulation aid, § 170.3(o)(14) of this chapter; stabilizer and thickener, § 170.3(o)(28) of this chapter.
Jams and jellies, commercial, § 170.3(n)(28) of this chapter	1.0	Do.
Milk products, § 170.3(n)(31) of this chapter	.6	Do.
Processed vegetables and vegetable juices, § 170.3(n)(36) of this chapter.	2.0	Formulation aid, § 170.3(o)(14) of this chapter; stabilizer and thickener, § 170.3(o)(28) of this chapter.
Soups and soup mixes, § 170.3(n)(40) of this chapter	.8	Do.
Sweet sauces, toppings and syrups, § 170.3(n)(43) of this chapter.	1.0	Do.
All other food categories	.5	Emulsifier and emulsifier salts, § 170.3(o)(8) of this chapter; firming agent, § 170.3(o)(10) of this chapter; formulation aid, § 170.3(o)(14) of this chapter; stabilizer and thickener, § 170.3(o)(28) of this chapter.

(d) [Reserved]

(e) Prior sanctions for this ingredient different from the uses established in this section do not exist or have been waived.

[42 FR 14653, Mar. 15, 1977, as amended at 42 FR 55205, Oct. 14, 1977; 49 FR 5612, Feb. 14, 1984]

§ 184.1343 Locust (carob) bean gum.

(a) Locust (carob) bean gum is primarily the macerated endosperm of the seed of the locust (carob) bean tree, *Ceratonia siliqua* (Linne), a leguminous evergreen tree, with lesser quantities of seed coat and germ.

(b) The ingredient meets the specifications of the "Food Chemicals Codex," 3d Ed. (1981), pp. 174–175, which is incorporated by reference. Copies may be obtained from the National Academy Press, 2101 Constitution Ave. NW., Washington, DC 20418, or may be examined at the National Archives and Records Administration (NARA). For information on the availability of this material at NARA, call 202-741-6030, or go to: *http://www.archives.gov/federal_register/code_of_federal_regulations/ibr_locations.html.*

(c) The ingredient is used at levels not to exceed the following maximum levels:

MAXIMUM USAGE LEVELS PERMITTED

Food (as served)	Percent	Function
Baked goods and baking mixes, § 170.3(n)(1) of this chapter.	0.15	Stabilizer and thickener, § 170.3(o)(28) of this chapter.

MAXIMUM USAGE LEVELS PERMITTED—Continued

Food (as served)	Percent	Function
Beverages and beverage bases, nonalcoholic, § 170.3(n)(3) of this chapter.	.25	Do.
Cheeses, § 170.3(n)(5) of this chapter	.8	Do.
Gelatins, puddings, and fillings, § 170.3(n)(22) of this chapter.	.75	Do.
Jams and jellies, commercial, § 170.3(n)(28) of this chapter.	.75	Do.
All other food categories	.5	Do.

(d) [Reserved]

(e) Prior sanctions for this ingredient different from the uses established in this regulation do not exist or have been waived.

[42 FR 14653, Mar. 15, 1977, as amended at 42 FR 55205, Oct. 14, 1977; 49 FR 5612, Feb. 14, 1984]

§ 184.1349 Karaya gum (sterculia gum).

(a) Karaya gum (sterculia gum) is the dried gummy exudate from the trunk of trees of various species of the genus *Sterculia*.

(b) The ingredient meets the specifications of the "Food Chemicals Codex," 3d Ed. (1981), p. 157, which is incorporated by reference. Copies may be obtained from the National Academy Press, 2101 Constitution Ave. NW., Washington, DC 20418, or may be examined at the National Archives and Records Administration (NARA). For information on the availability of this material at NARA, call 202–741–6030, or go to: *http://www.archives.gov/federal_register/code_of_federal_regulations/ibr_locations.html.*

(c) The ingredient is used in food under the following conditions:

MAXIMUM USAGE LEVELS PERMITTED

Food (as served)	Percent	Function
Frozen dairy desserts and mixes, § 170.3(n)(20) of this chapter.	0.3	Formulation aid, § 170.3(o)(14) of this chapter; stabilizer and thickener, § 170.3(o)(28) of this chapter.
Milk products, § 170.3(n)(31) of this chapter	.02	Stabilizer and thickener, § 170.3(o)(28) of this chapter.
Soft candy, § 170.3(n)(38) of this chapter	.9	Emulsifier and emulsifier salt, § 170.3(o)(8) of this chapter; stabilizer and thickener, § 170.3(o)(28) of this chapter.
All other food categories	.002	Formulation aid, § 170.3(o)(14) of this chapter; stabilizer and thickener, § 170.3(o)(28) of this chapter.

(d) [Reserved]

(e) Prior sanctions for this ingredient different from the uses established in this section do not exist or have been waived.

[42 FR 14653, Mar. 15, 1977, as amended at 42 FR 55205, Oct. 14, 1977; 49 FR 5612, Feb. 14, 1984]

§ 184.1351 Gum tragacanth.

(a) Gum tragacanth is the exudate from one of several species of *Astragalus gummifier* Labillardiere, a shrub that grows wild in mountainous regions of the Middle East.

(b) The ingredient meets the specifications of the "Food Chemicals Codex," 3d Ed. (1981), p. 337, which is incorporated by reference. Copies may be obtained from the National Academy Press, 2101 Constitution Ave. NW., Washington, DC 20418, or may be examined at the National Archives and Records Administration (NARA). For information on the availability of this material at NARA, call 202–741–6030, or go to: *http://www.archives.gov/federal_register/code_of_federal_regulations/ibr_locations.html.*

(c) The ingredient is used in food under the following conditions:

MAXIMUM USAGE LEVELS PERMITTED

Food (as served)	Percent	Function
Baked goods and baking mixes, § 170.3(n)(1) of this chapter.	0.2	Emulsifier and emulsifier salt, § 170.3(o)(8) of this chapter; formulation aid, § 170.3(o)(14) of this chapter; stabilizer and thickener, § 170.3(o)(28) of this chapter.
Condiments and relishes, § 170.3(n)(8) of this chapter.	.7	Do.
Fats and oils, § 170.3(n)(12) of this chapter	1.3	Do.
Gravies and sauces, § 170.3(n)(24) of this chapter	.8	Do.
Meat products, § 170.3(n)(29) of this chapter	.2	Formulation aid, § 170.3(o)(14) of this chapter; stabilizer and thickener, § 170.3(o)(28) of this chapter.
Processed fruits and fruit juices, § 170.3(n)(35) of this chapter.	.2	Emulsifier and emulsifier salt, § 170.3(o)(8) of this chapter; formulation aid, § 170.3(o)(14) of this chapter; stabilizer and thickener, § 170.3(o)(28) of this chapter.
All other food categories	.1	Do.

(d) [Reserved]

(e) Prior sanctions for this ingredient different from the uses established in this section do not exist or have been waived.

[42 FR 14653, Mar. 15, 1977, as amended at 42 FR 55205, Oct. 14, 1977; 49 FR 5612, Feb. 14, 1984]

§ 184.1355 Helium.

(a) Helium (empirical formula He, CAS Reg. No. 7440–59–7) is a colorless, odorless, flavorless, nonflammable, inert gas. It is lighter than air and is produced by the liquefaction and purification of natural gas.

(b) The ingredient must be of a purity suitable for its intended use.

(c) In accordance with § 184.1(b)(1), the ingredient is used in food with no limitations other than current good manufacturing practice. The affirmation of this ingredient as generally recognized as safe (GRAS) as a direct human food ingredient is based upon the following current good manufacturing practice conditions of use:

(1) The ingredient is used as a processing aid as defined in § 170.3(o)(24) of this chapter.

(2) The ingredient is used in food at levels not to exceed current good manufacturing practice.

(d) Prior sanctions for this ingredient different from the uses established in this section do not exist or have been waived.

[48 FR 57270, Dec. 29, 1983, as amended at 73 FR 8607, Feb. 14, 2008]

§ 184.1366 Hydrogen peroxide.

(a) Hydrogen peroxide (H_2O_2, CAS Reg. No. 7722–84–1) is also referred to as hydrogen dioxide. It is made by the electrolytic oxidation of sulfuric acid or a sulfate to persulfuric acid or a persulfuric acid salt with subsequent hydrolysis and distillation of the hydrogen peroxide formed; by decomposition of barium peroxide with sulfuric or phosphoric acid; by hydrogen reduction of 2-ethylanthraquinone, followed by oxidation with air, to regenerate the quinone and produce hydrogen peroxide; or by electrical discharge through a mixture of hydrogen, oxygen, and water vapor.

(b) The ingredient meets the specifications of the Food Chemicals Codex, 3d ed. (1981), pp. 146–147,[1] which is incorporated by reference.

(c) In accordance with § 184.1(b)(2), the ingredient is used to treat food only within the following specific limitations:

[1] Copies may be obtained from the National Academy of Sciences, 2101 Constitution Ave. NW, Washington, DC 20037, or examined at the National Archives and Records Administration (NARA). For information on the availability of this material at NARA, call 202–741–6030, or go to: *http://www.archives.gov/federal_register/code_of_federal_regulations/ibr_locations.html.*

Food	Maximum treatment level in food (percent)	Functional use
Milk, intended for use during the cheesemaking process as permitted in the appropriate standards of identity for cheese and related cheese products under part 133 of this chapter.	0.05	Antimicrobial agent as defined in § 170.3 (o)(2) of this chapter
Whey, during the preparation of modified whey by electrodialysis methods.	0.04	do.
Dried eggs, dried egg whites, and dried egg yolks as in §§ 160.105, 160.145, and 160.185 of this chapter.	Amount sufficient for the purpose.	Oxidizing and reducing agent as defined in § 170.3 (o)(22) of this chapter
Tripe	do	Bleaching agent.
Beef feet	Amount sufficient for the purpose. (Hydrogen peroxide may be in the form of a compound salt, sodium carbonate peroxide).	Bleaching agent.
Herring	Amount sufficient for the purpose.	do.
Wine	do	Oxidizing and reducing agent as defined in § 170.3 (o)(22) of this chapter.
Starch	0.15	Antimicrobial agent as defined in § 170.3 (o)(2) of this chapter, to produce thermophile-free starch; Remove sulfur dioxide from starch slurry following steeping and grinding operations of corn refining.
Instant tea	Amount sufficient for the purpose.	Bleaching agent.
Corn syrup	0.15	Reduce sulfur dioxide levels in the finished corn syrup.
Colored (annatto) cheese whey	0.05	Bleaching agent.
Wine vinegar	Amount sufficient for the purpose.	Remove sulfur dioxide from wine prior to fermentation to produce vinegar.
Emulsifiers containing fatty acid esters	1.25	Bleaching agent.

(d) Residual hydrogen peroxide is removed by appropriate physical and chemical means during the processing of food where it has been used according to paragraph (c) of this section.

(e) Prior sanctions for this ingredient different from the uses established in this section do not exist or have been waived.

[46 FR 44439, Sept. 4, 1981, as amended at 51 FR 27172, July 30, 1986]

§ 184.1370 Inositol.

(a) Inositol, or myo-inositol ($C_6H_{12}O_6$, CAS Reg. No. 87–89–8), is *cis*-1,2,3,5-*trans*-4,6-cyclohexanehexol. It occurs naturally and is prepared from an aqueous (0.2 percent sulfur dioxide) extract of corn kernels by precipitation and hydrolysis of crude phytate.

(b) The ingredient meets the specifications of the Food Chemicals Codex, 3d Ed. (1981), p. 150, which is incorporated by reference. Copies are available from the National Academy Press, 2101 Constitution Ave. NW., Washington, DC 20418, or available for inspection at the National Archives and Records Administration (NARA). For information on the availability of this material at NARA, call 202–741–6030, or go to: *http://www.archives.gov/federal_register/code_of_federal_regulations/ibr_locations.html.*

(c) In accordance with § 184.1(b)(1), the ingredient is used in food with no limitations other than current good manufacturing practice. The affirmation of this ingredient as generally recognized as safe (GRAS) as a direct human food ingredient is based upon the following current good manufacturing practice conditions of use:

(1) The ingredient is used as a nutrient supplement as defined in § 170.3(o)(20) of this chapter.

(2) The ingredient is used in special dietary foods as defined in part 105 of this chapter at levels not to exceed current good manufacturing practice. It may also be used in infant formula in accordance with section 412(g) of the Act, or with regulations promulgated under section 412(a)(2) of the Act.

(d) Prior sanctions for this ingredient different from the uses established by this section do not exist or have been waived.

[47 FR 38278, Aug. 31, 1982]

§ 184.1372 Insoluble glucose isomerase enzyme preparations.

(a) Insoluble glucose isomerase enzyme preparations are used in the production of high fructose corn syrup described in § 184.1866. They are derived from recognized species of precisely classified nonpathogenic and nontoxicogenic microorganisms, including *Streptomyces rubiginosus*, *Actinoplanes missouriensis*, *Streptomyces olivaceus*, *Streptomyces olivochromogenes*, and *Bacillus coagulans*, that have been grown in a pure culture fermentation that produces no antibiotics. They are fixed (rendered insoluble) for batch production with GRAS ingredients or may be fixed for further immobilization with either GRAS ingredients or materials approved under § 173.357 of this chapter.

(b) The ingredient meets the general and additional requirements for enzyme preparations in the Food Chemicals Codex, 3d Ed. (1981), p. 107, which is incorporated by reference. Copies are available from the National Academy Press, 2101 Constitution Ave. NW., Washington, DC 20418, or available for inspection at the National Archives and Records Administration (NARA). For information on the availability of this material at NARA, call 202–741–6030, or go to: *http://www.archives.gov/federal_register/code_of_federal_regulations/ibr_locations.html.*

(c) In accordance with § 184.1(b)(1), the ingredient is used in food with no limitation other than current good manufacturing practice. The affirmation of this ingredient as generally recognized as safe (GRAS) as a direct human food ingredient is based upon the following current good manufacturing practice conditions of use:

(1) The ingredient is used as an enzyme, as defined in § 170.3(o)(9) of this chapter, to convert glucose to fructose.

(2) The ingredient is used in high fructose corn syrup, at levels not to exceed current good manufacturing practice.

[48 FR 5720, Feb. 8, 1983, as amended at 61 FR 43450, Aug. 23, 1996]

§ 184.1375 Iron, elemental.

(a) Iron, elemental (CAS Reg. No. 7439–89–6) is metallic iron obtained by any of the following processes: reduced iron, electrolytic iron, and carbonyl iron.

(1) Reduced iron is prepared by reacting ground ferric oxide with hydrogen or carbon monoxide at an elevated temperature. The process results in a grayish-black powder, all of which should pass through a 100-mesh sieve. It is lusterless or has not more than a slight luster. When viewed under a microscope, it appears as an amorphous powder free from particles having a crystalline structure. It is stable in dry air.

(2) Electrolytic iron is prepared by electrodeposition. It is an amorphous, lusterless, grayish-black powder. It is stable in dry air.

(3) Carbonyl iron is prepared by the decomposition of iron pentacarbonyl. It occurs as a dark gray powder. When viewed under a microscope, it appears as spheres built up with concentric shells. It is stable in dry air.

(b) Iron, elemental (carbonyl, electrolytic, or reduced) meets the specifications of the Food Chemicals Codex, 3d Ed. (1981) (iron, carbonyl, p. 151; iron, electrolytic, pp. 151–152; iron, reduced; pp. 152–153), which is incorporated by reference. Copies are available from the National Academy Press, 2101 Constitution Ave. NW., Washington, DC 20418, or available for inspection at the National Archives and Records Administration (NARA). For information on the availability of this material at NARA, call 202–741–6030, or go to: *http://www.archives.gov/federal_register/code_of_federal_regulations/ibr_locations.html.*

(c) In accordance with § 184.1(b)(1), the ingredient is used in food as a nutrient supplement as defined in § 170.3(o)(20) of this chapter, with no limitation other than current good manufacturing practice. The ingredient may also be used in accordance with section 412(g) of the Federal Food,

Drug, and Cosmetic Act (the act) (21 U.S.C. 350a(g)) or with regulations promulgated under section 412(a)(2) of the act (21 U.S.C. 350a(2)).

(d) Prior sanctions for this ingredient different from the uses established in this section do not exist or have been waived.

[53 FR 16867, May 12, 1988]

§ 184.1386 Isopropyl citrate.

(a) Isopropyl citrate is a mixture of the mono-, di-, and triisopropyl esters of citric acid. It is prepared by esterifying citric acid with isopropanol.

(b) The ingredient must be of a purity suitable for its intended use.

(c) In accordance with § 184.1(b)(1), the ingredient is used in food with no limitation other than current good manufacturing practice. The affirmation of this ingredient as generally recognized as safe (GRAS) as a direct human food ingredient is based upon the following current good manufacturing practice conditions of use:

(1) The ingredient is used as an antioxidant as defined in § 170.3(o)(3) of this chapter; a sequestrant as defined in § 170.3(o)(26) of this chapter; and a solvent and vehicle as defined in § 170.3(o)(27) of this chapter.

(2) The ingredient is used in margarine in accordance with § 166.110 of this chapter; in nonalcoholic beverages as defined in § 170.3(n)(3) of this chapter; and in fats and oils as defined in § 170.3(n)(12) of this chapter at levels not to exceed current good manufacturing practice.

(d) Prior sanctions for this ingredient different from the uses established in this section, or different from those set forth in part 181 of this chapter, do not exist or have been waived.

[59 FR 63896, Dec. 12, 1994, as amended at 73 FR 8607, Feb. 14, 2008]

§ 184.1387 Lactase enzyme preparation from Candida pseudotropicalis.

(a) This enzyme preparation is derived from the nonpathogenic, nontoxicogenic yeast *C. pseudotropicalis*. It contains the enzyme lactase (β-D-galactoside galactohydrolase, EC 3.2.1.23), which converts lactose to glucose and galactose. It is prepared from yeast that has been grown by a pure culture fermentation process.

(b) The ingredient meets the general requirements and additional requirements for enzyme preparations in the Food Chemicals Codex, 3d ed. (1981), pp. 107–110, which are incorporated by reference in accordance with 5 U.S.C. 552(a) and 1 CFR part 51. Copies are available from the National Academy Press, 2101 Constitution Ave. NW., Washington, DC 20418, or may be examined at the Center for Food Safety and Applied Nutrition's Library, 5100 Paint Branch Pkwy., College Park, MD 20740, or at the National Archives and Records Administration (NARA). For information on the availability of this material at NARA, call 202–741–6030, or go to: *http://www.archives.gov/federal_register/code_of_federal_regulations/ibr_locations.html.*

(c) In accordance with § 184.1(b)(1), the ingredient is used in food with no limitations other than current good manufacturing practice. The affirmation of this ingredient as generally recognized as safe as a direct human food ingredient is based upon the following current good manufacturing practice conditions of use:

(1) The ingredient is used as an enzyme, as defined in § 170.3(o)(9) of this chapter, to convert lactose to glucose and galactose.

(2) The ingredient is used in food at levels not to exceed current good manufacturing practice. Current good manufacturing practice is limited to use of this ingredient to reduce the lactose content in milk and milk-derived food products where food standards do not preclude such use.

[61 FR 7704, Feb. 29, 1996]

§ 184.1388 Lactase enzyme preparation from Kluyveromyces lactis.

(a) This enzyme preparation is derived from the nonpathogenic, nontoxicogenic yeast *Kluyveromyces lactis* (previously named *Saccharomyces lactis*). It contains the enzyme B-galactoside galactohydrase (CAS Reg. No. CBS 683), which converts lactose to glucose and galactose. It is prepared from yeast that has been grown in a pure culture fermentation and by using materials that are generally recognized as safe or are food additives that have been approved for this use by the Food and Drug Administration.

(b) The ingredient meets the general and additional requirements for enzyme preparations in the Food Chemicals Codex, 3d Ed. (1981), p. 107–110, which is incorporated by reference. Copies are available from the National Academy Press, 2101 Constitution Ave. NW., Washington, DC 20418, or available for inspection at the National Archives and Records Administration (NARA). For information on the availability of this material at NARA, call 202–741–6030, or go to: *http://www.archives.gov/federal_register/code_of_federal_regulations/ibr_locations.html.*

(c) In accordance with §184.1(b)(1), the ingredient is used in food with no limitation other than current good manufacturing practice. The affirmation of this ingredient as generally recognized as safe as a direct human food ingredient is based upon the following current good manufacturing practice conditions of use:

(1) The ingredient is used as an enzyme as defined in §170.3(o)(9) of this chapter to convert lactose to glucose and galactose.

(2) The ingredient is used in food at levels not to exceed current good manufacturing practice. Current good manufacturing practice is to use this ingredient in milk to produce lactase-treated milk, which contains less lactose than regular milk, or lactose-reduced milk, which contains at least 70 percent less lactose than regular milk.

[49 FR 47387, Dec. 4, 1984]

§ 184.1400 Lecithin.

(a) Commercial lecithin is a naturally occurring mixture of the phosphatides of choline, ethanolamine, and inositol, with smaller amounts of othe lipids. It is isolated as a gum following hydration of solvent-extracted soy, safflower, or corn oils. Lecithin is bleached, if desired, by hydrogen peroxide and benzoyl peroxide and dried by heating.

(b) The ingredient meets the specifications of the Food Chemicals Codex, 3d Ed. (1981), pp. 166–167, which is incorporated by reference. Copies are available from the National Academy Press, 2101 Constitution Ave. NW., Washington, DC 20418, or available for inspection at the National Archives and Records Administration (NARA). For information on the availability of this material at NARA, call 202–741–6030, or go to: *http://www.archives.gov/federal_register/code_of_federal_regulations/ibr_locations.html.*

(c) In accordance with §184.1(b)(1), the ingredient is used in food with no limitation other than current good manufacturing practice.

(d) Prior sanctions for this ingredient different from the uses established in this section do not exist or have been waived.

[48 FR 51150, Nov. 7, 1983]

§ 184.1408 Licorice and licorice derivatives.

(a)(1) Licorice (glycyrrhiza) root is the dried and ground rhizome and root portions of *Glycyrrhiza glabra* or other species of *Glycyrrhiza.* Licorice extract is that portion of the licorice root that is, after maceration, extracted by boiling water. The extract can be further purified by filtration and by treatment with acids and ethyl alcohol. Licorice extract is sold as a liquid, paste (“block”), or spray-dried powder.

(2) Ammoniated glycyrrhizin is prepared from the water extract of licorice root by acid precipitation followed by neutralization with dilute ammonia. Monoammonium glycyrrhizinate ($C_{42}H_{61}O_{16}NH_{4}5H_{2}O$, CAS Reg. No. 1407–03–0) is prepared from ammoniated glycyrrhizin by solvent extraction and separation techniques.

(b) The ingredients shall meet the following specifications when analyzed:

(1) *Assay.* The glycyrrhizin content of each flavoring ingredient shall be determined by the method in the Official Methods of Analysis of the Association of Official Analytical Chemists, 13th Ed., §§19.136–19.140, which is incorporated by reference, or by methods 19.CO1 through 19.CO4 in the *Journal of the Association of Official Analytical Chemists,* 65:471–472 (1982), which are also incorporated by reference. Copies of all of these methods are available from the AOAC INTERNATIONAL, 481

North Frederick Ave., suite 500, Gaithersburg, MD 20877, or available for inspection at the National Archives and Records Administration (NARA). For information on the availability of this material at NARA, call 202–741–6030, or go to: *http://www.archives.gov/federal_register/code_of_federal_regulations/ibr_locations.html.*

(2) *Ash.* Not more than 9.5 percent for licorice, 2.5 percent for ammoniated glycyrrhizin, and 0.5 percent for monoammonium glycyrrhizinate on an anhydrous basis as determined by the method in the Food Chemicals Codex, 3d Ed. (1981), p. 466, which is incorporated by reference. Copies are available from the National Academy Press, 2101 Constitution Ave. NW., Washington, DC 20418, or available for inspection at the National Archives and Records Administration (NARA). For information on the availability of this material at NARA, call 202–741–6030, or go to: *http://www.archives.gov/federal_register/code_of_federal_regulations/ibr_locations.html.*

(3) *Acid unsoluble ash.* Not more than 2.5 percent for licorice on an anhydrous basis as determined by the method in the Food Chemicals Codex, 3d Ed. (1981), p. 466, which is incorporated by reference.

(4) *Heavy metals (as Pb).* Not more than 40 parts per million as determined by method II in the Food Chemicals Codex, 3d Ed. (1981), p. 512, which is incorporated by reference.

(5) *Arsenic (As).* Not more than 3 parts per million as determined by the method in the Food Chemicals Codex. 3d Ed. (1981), p. 464, which is incorporated by reference.

(c) In accordance with §184.1(b)(2), these ingredients are used in food only within the following specific limitations:

Category of food	Maximum level in food (percent glycyrrhizin content of food) (as served)	Functional use
Baked foods, §170.3(n)(1) of this chapter	0.05	Flavor enhancer, §170.3(o)(11) of this chapter; flavoring agent, §170.3(o)(12) of this chapter.
Alcoholic beverages, §170.3(n)(2) of this chapter	0.1	Flavor enhancer, §170.3(o)(11) of this chapter; flavoring agent, §170.3(o)(12) of this chapter; surface-active agent, §170.3(o)(29) of this chapter.
Nonalcoholic beverages, §170.3(n)(3) of this chapter	0.15	Do.
Chewing gum, §170.3(n)(6) of this chapter	1.1	Flavor enhancer, §170.3(o)(11) of this chapter; flavoring agent, §170.3(n)(12) of this chapter.
Hard candy, §170.3(n)(25) of this chapter	16.0	Do.
Herbs and seasonings, §170.3(n)(26) of this chapter	0.15	Do.
Plant protein products, §170.3(n)(33) of this chapter	0.15	Do.
Soft candy, §170.3(n)(38) of this chapter	3.1	Do.
Vitamin or mineral dietary supplements	0.5	Do.
All other foods except sugar substitutes, §170.3(n)(42) of this chapter. The ingredient is not permitted to be used as a nonnutritive sweetener in sugar substitutes.	0.1	Do.

(d) Prior sanctions for this ingredient different from the uses established in this section do not exist or have been waived.

[50 FR 21044, May 22, 1985, as amended at 54 FR 24899, June 12, 1989]

§184.1409 Ground limestone.

(a) Ground limestone consists essentially (not less than 94 percent) of calcium carbonate ($CaCO_3$) and is prepared by the crushing, grinding, and classifying of naturally occurring limestone.

(b) The ingredient meets the specifications of the Food Chemicals Codex, 3d Ed. (1981), p. 173, which is incorporated by reference. Copies are available from the National Academy Press, 2101 Constitution Ave. NW., Washington, DC 20418, or available for inspection at the National Archives and Records Administration (NARA). For information on the availability of this material at NARA, call 202–741–6030, or go to: *http://www.archives.gov/federal_register/code_of_federal_regulations/ibr_locations.html.*

(c) In accordance with § 184.1(b)(1), the ingredient is used in food with no limitation other than current good manufacturing practice.

(d) Prior sanctions for this ingredient different from the uses established in this section do not exist or have been waived.

[48 FR 52442, Nov. 18, 1983]

§ 184.1415 Animal lipase.

(a) Animal lipase (CAS Reg. No. 9001–62–1) is an enzyme preparation obtained from edible forestomach tissue of calves, kids, or lambs, or from animal pancreatic tissue. The enzyme preparation may be produced as a tissue preparation or as an aqueous extract. Its characterizing enzyme activity is that of a triacylglycerol hydrolase (EC 3.1.1.3).

(b) The ingredient meets the general requirements and additional requirements for enzyme preparations in the Food Chemicals Codex, 3d ed. (1981), p. 110, which is incorporated by reference in accordance with 5 U.S.C. 552(a) and 1 CFR part 51. Copies are available from the National Academy Press, 2101 Constitution Ave., NW., Washington, DC 20418, or may be examined at the Office of Food Additive Safety (HFS–200), Center for Food Safety and Applied Nutrition, Food and Drug Administration, 5100 Paint Branch Pkwy., College Park, MD 20740, 240–402–1200, and at the National Archives and Records Administration (NARA). For information on the availability of this material at NARA, call 202–741–6030, or go to: *http://www.archives.gov/federal_register/code_of_federal_regulations/ibr_locations.html.*

(c) In accordance with § 184.1(b)(1), the ingredient is used in food with no limitation other than current good manufacturing practice. The affirmation of this ingredient as GRAS as a direct food ingredient is based upon the following current good manufacturing practice conditions of use:

(1) The ingredient is used as an enzyme as defined in § 170.3(o)(9) of this chapter to hydrolyze fatty acid glycerides.

(2) The ingredient is used in food at levels not to exceed current good manufacturing practice.

[60 FR 32911, June 26, 1995, as amended at 78 FR 14666, Mar. 7, 2013]

§ 184.1420 Lipase enzyme preparation derived from Rhizopus niveus.

(a) Lipase enzyme preparation contains lipase enzyme (CAS Reg. No. 9001–62–1), which is obtained from the culture filtrate resulting from a pure culture fermentation of a nonpathogenic and nontoxigenic strain of *Rhizopus niveus*. The enzyme preparation also contains diatomaceous earth as a carrier. The characterizing activity of the enzyme, which catalyzes the interesterification of fats and oils at the 1- and 3-positions of triglycerides, is triacylglycerol lipase (EC 3.1.1.3).

(b) The ingredient meets the general requirements and additional requirements for enzyme preparations in the monograph on Enzyme Preparations in the "Food Chemicals Codex," 4th ed. (1996), pp. 133 and 134, which is incorporated by reference in accordance with 5 U.S.C. 552(a) and 1 CFR part 51. Copies are available from the National Academy Press, 2101 Constitution Ave. NW., Washington, DC 20418, or may be examined at the Center for Food Safety and Applied Nutrition's Library, 5100 Paint Branch Pkwy., College Park, MD 20740, or at the National Archives and Records Administration (NARA). For information on the availability of this material at NARA, call 202–741–6030, or go to: *http://www.archives.gov/federal_register/code_of_federal_regulations/ibr_locations.html.*

(c) In accordance with § 184.1(b)(1), the ingredient is used in food with no limitation other than current good manufacturing practice. The affirmation of this ingredient as generally recognized as safe as a direct human food ingredient is based upon the following current good manufacturing practice conditions of use:

(1) The ingredient is used as an enzyme as defined in § 170.3(o)(9) of this chapter for the interesterification of fats and oils.

(2) The ingredient is used in food at levels not to exceed current good manufacturing practice.

[63 FR 24419, May 4, 1998]

§ 184.1425 Magnesium carbonate.

(a) Magnesium carbonate (molecular formula approximately $(MgCO_3)_4 \cdot Mg(OH)_2 \cdot 5H_2O$, CAS Reg. No. 39409–82–0) is also known as magnesium carbonate hydroxide. It is a white powder formed either by adding an alkaline carbonate (such as sodium carbonate) to a solution of magnesium sulfate or by carbonation of a slurry of magnesium hydroxide followed by boiling of the resulting magnesium carbonate.

(b) The ingredient meets the specifications of the Food Chemicals Codex, 3d Ed. (1981), p. 177, which is incorporated by reference. Copies are available from the National Academy Press, 2101 Constitution Ave. NW., Washington, DC 20418, or available for inspection at the National Archives and Records Administration (NARA). For information on the availability of this material at NARA, call 202–741–6030, or go to: *http://www.archives.gov/federal_register/code_of_federal_regulations/ibr_locations.html.*

(c) In accordance with §184.1(b)(1), the ingredient is used in food with no limitation other than current good manufacturing practice. The affirmation of this ingredient as generally recognized as safe (GRAS) as a direct human food ingredient is based upon the following current good manufacturing practice conditions of use:

(1) The ingredient is used as an anticaking and free-flow agent as defined in §170.3(o)(1) of this chapter; a flour treating agent as defined in §170.3(o)(13) of this chapter; a lubricant and release agent as defined in §170.3(o)(18) of this chapter; a nutrient supplement as defined in §170.3(o)(20) of this chapter; a pH control agent as defined in §170.3(o)(23) of this chapter; a processing aid as defined in §170.3(o)(24) of this chapter; and a synergist as defined in §170.3(o)(31) of this chapter.

(2) The ingredient is used in foods at levels not to exceed current good manufacturing practice.

(d) Prior sanctions for this ingredient different from the uses established in this section do not exist or have been waived.

[50 FR 13558, Apr. 5, 1985; 50 FR 16080, Apr. 24, 1985]

§ 184.1426 Magnesium chloride.

(a) Magnesium chloride ($MgCl_2 \cdot 6H_2O$, CAS Reg. No. 7786–30–3) is a colorless, deliquescent, crystalline material that occurs naturally as the mineral bischofite. It is prepared by dissolving magnesium oxide, hydroxide, or carbonate in aqueous hydrochloric acid solution and crystallizing out magnesium chloride hexahydrate.

(b) The ingredient meets the specifications of the Food Chemicals Codex, 3d Ed. (1981), p. 177, which is incorporated by reference. Copies are available from the National Academy Press, 2101 Constitution Ave. NW., Washington, DC 20418, or available for inspection at the National Archives and Records Administration (NARA). For information on the availability of this material at NARA, call 202–741–6030, or go to: *http://www.archives.gov/federal_register/code_of_federal_regulations/ibr_locations.html.*

(c) In accordance with §184.1(b)(1), the ingredient is used in food with no limitation other than current good manufacturing practice. The affirmation of this ingredient as generally recognized as safe (GRAS) as a direct human food ingredient is based upon the following current good manufacturing practice conditions of use:

(1) The ingredient is used as a flavoring agent and adjuvant as defined in §170.3(o)(12) of this chapter and a nutrient supplement as defined in §170.3(o)(20) of this chapter.

(2) The ingredient is used in foods at levels not to exceed current good manufacturing practice. The ingredient also may be used in infant formula in accordance with section 412(g) of the Federal Food, Drug, and Cosmetic Act (the act) or with regulations promulgated under section 412(a)(2) of the act.

(d) Prior sanctions for this ingredient different from the uses established in this section do not exist or have been waived.

[50 FR 13559, Apr. 5, 1985; 50 FR 16080, Apr. 24, 1985]

§ 184.1428 Magnesium hydroxide.

(a) Magnesium hydroxide ($Mg(OH)_2$, CAS Reg. No. 1309–42–8) occurs naturally as the colorless, crystalline mineral brucite. It is prepared as a white precipitate by the addition of sodium hydroxide to a water soluble magnesium salt or by hydration of reactive grades of magnesium oxide.

(b) The ingredient meets the specifications of the Food Chemicals Codex, 3d Ed. (1981), p. 178, which is incorporated by reference. Copies are available from the National Academy Press, 2101 Constitution Ave. NW., Washington, DC 20418, or available for inspection at the National Archives and Records Administration (NARA). For information on the availability of this material at NARA, call 202–741–6030, or go to: *http://www.archives.gov/federal_register/code_of_federal_regulations/ibr_locations.html.*

(c) In accordance with § 184.1(b)(1), the ingredient is used in food with no limitation other than current good manufacturing practice. The affirmation of this ingredient as generally recognized as safe (GRAS) as a direct human food ingredient is based upon the following current good manufacturing practice conditions of use:

(1) The ingredient is used as a nutrient supplement as defined in § 170.3(o)(20) of this chapter; a pH control agent as defined in § 170.3(o)(23) of this chapter; and a processing aid as defined in § 170.3(o)(24) of this chapter.

(2) The ingredient is used in foods at levels not to exceed current good manufacturing practice.

(d) Prior sanctions for this ingredient different from the uses established in this section do not exist or have been waived.

[50 FR 13559, Apr. 5, 1985, as amended at 64 FR 405, Jan. 5, 1999]

§ 184.1431 Magnesium oxide.

(a) Magnesium oxide (MgO, CAS Reg. No. 1309–48–4) occurs naturally as the colorless, crystalline mineral periclase. It is produced either as a bulky white powder (light) or a relatively dense white powder (heavy) by heating magnesium hydroxide or carbonate. Heating these magnesium salts under moderate conditions (400° to 900 °C for a few hours) produces light magnesium oxide. Heating the salts under more rigorous conditions (1200 °C for 12 hours) produces heavy magnesium oxide. Light magnesium oxide is converted to heavy magnesium oxide by sustained heating at high temperatures.

(b) The ingredient meets the specifications of the Food Chemicals Codex, 3d Ed. (1981), p. 178, which is incorporated by reference. Copies are available from the National Academy Press, 2101 Constitution Ave. NW., Washington, DC 20418, or available for inspection at the National Archives and Records Administration (NARA). For information on the availability of this material at NARA, call 202–741–6030, or go to: *http://www.archives.gov/federal_register/code_of_federal_regulations/ibr_locations.html.*

(c) In accordance with § 184.1(b)(1), the ingredient is used in food with no limitation other than current good manufacturing practice. The affirmation of this ingredient as generally recognized as safe (GRAS) as a direct human food ingredient is based upon the following current good manufacturing practice conditions of use:

(1) The ingredient is used as an anticaking and free-flow agent as defined in § 170.3(o)(1) of this chapter; a firming agent as defined in § 170.3(o)(10) of this chapter; a lubricant and release agent as defined in § 170.3(o)(18) of this chapter; a nutrient supplement as defined in § 170.3(o)(20) of this chapter; and a pH control agent as defined in § 170.3(o)(23) of this chapter.

(2) The ingredient is used in foods at levels not be exceed current good manufacturing practice. The ingredient also may be used in infant formula in accordance with section 412(g) of the Federal Food, Drug, and Cosmetic Act (the act) or with regulations promulgated under section 412(a)(2) of the act.

(d) Prior sanctions for this ingredient different from the uses established in this section do not exist or have been waived.

[50 FR 13559, Apr. 5, 1985]

§ 184.1434 Magnesium phosphate.

(a) Magnesium phosphate includes both magnesium phosphate, dibasic, and magnesium phosphate, tribasic. Magnesium phosphate, dibasic ($MgHPO_4 \cdot 3H_2O$, CAS Reg. No. 7782–0975–094) occurs naturally as the white, crystalline mineral newberyite. It is prepared commercially as a precipitate formed by treating a solution of magnesium sulfate with disodium phosphate under controlled conditions. Magnesium phosphate, tribasic ($Mg_3(PO_4)2 \cdot xH_2O$, CAS Reg. No. 7757–87–1) may contain 4, 5, or 8 molecules of water of hydration. It is produced as a precipitate from a solution of magnesite with phosphoric acid.

(b) Magnesium phosphate, dibasic, meets the specifications of the Food Chemicals Codex, 3d Ed. (1981), p. 179, which is incorporated by reference. Magnesium phosphate, tribasic, meets the specifications of the Food Chemicals Codex, 3d Ed. (1981), p. 180, which is incorporated by reference. Copies are available from the National Academy Press, 2101 Constitution Ave. NW., Washington, DC 20418, or available for inspection at the National Archives and Records Administration (NARA). For information on the availability of this material at NARA, call 202–741–6030, or go to: *http://www.archives.gov/federal_register/code_of_federal_regulations/ibr_locations.html.*

(c) In accordance with § 184.1(b)(1), the ingredient is used in food with no limitation other than current good manufacturing practice. The affirmation of this ingredient as generally recognized as safe (GRAS) as a direct human food ingredient is based upon the following current good manufacturing practice conditions of use:

(1) The ingredient is used as a nutrient supplement as defined in § 170.3(o)(20) of this chapter and a pH control agent as defined in § 170.3(o)(23) of this chapter.

(2) The ingredient is used in foods at levels not to exceed current good manufacturing practice. The ingredient also may be used in infant formula in accordance with section 412(g) of the Federal Food, Drug, and Cosmetic Act (the act) or with regulations promulgated under section 412(a)(2) of the Act.

(d) Prior sanctions for this ingredient different from the uses established in this section do not exist or have been waived.

[50 FR 13560, Apr. 5, 1985, as amended at 69 FR 24512, May 4, 2004]

§ 184.1440 Magnesium stearate.

(a) Magnesium stearate ($Mg(C_{17}H_{34}COO)_2$, CAS Reg. No. 557–04–0) is the magnesium salt of stearic acid. It is produced as a white precipitate by the addition of an aqueous solution of magnesium chloride to an aqueous solution of sodium stearate derived from stearic acid that is obtained from edible sources and that conforms to the requirements of § 172.860(b)(2) of this chapter.

(b) The ingredient meets the specifications of the Food Chemicals Codex, 3d Ed. (1981), p. 182, which is incorporated by reference. Copies are available from the National Academy Press, 2101 Constitution Ave. NW., Washington, DC 20418, or available for inspection at the National Archives and Records Administration (NARA). For information on the availability of this material at NARA, call 202–741–6030, or go to: *http://www.archives.gov/federal_register/code_of_federal_regulations/ibr_locations.html.*

(c) In accordance with § 184.1(b)(1), the ingredient is used in food with no limitation other than current good manufacturing practice. The affirmation of this ingredient as generally recognized as safe (GRAS) as a direct human food ingredient is based upon the following current good manufacturing practice conditions of use:

(1) The ingredient is used as a lubricant and release agent as defined in § 170.3(o)(18) of this chapter; a nutrient supplement as defined in § 170.3(o)(20) of this chapter; and a processing aid as defined in § 170.3(o)(24) of this chapter.

(2) The ingredient is used in foods at levels not to exceed current good manufacturing practice.

(d) Prior sanctions for this ingredient different from the uses established in this section do not exist or have been waived.

[50 FR 13560, Apr. 5, 1985]

§ 184.1443 Magnesium sulfate.

(a) Magnesium sulfate ($MgSO_4 \cdot 7H_2O$, CAS Reg. No. 10034–99–8) occurs naturally as the mineral epsomite. It is prepared by neutralization of magnesium oxide, hydroxide, or carbonate with sulfuric acid and evaporating the solution to crystallization.

(b) The ingredient meets the specifications of the Food Chemicals Codex, 3d Ed. (1981), p. 183, which is incorporated by reference. Copies are available from the National Academy Press, 2101 Constitution Ave. NW., Washington, DC 20418, or available for inspection at the National Archives and Records Administration (NARA). For information on the availability of this material at NARA, call 202–741–6030, or go to: *http://www.archives.gov/federal_register/code_of_federal_regulations/ibr_locations.html.*

(c) In accordance with § 184.1(b)(1), the ingredient is used in food with no limitation other than current good manufacturing practice. The affirmation of this ingredient as generally recognized as safe (GRAS) as a direct human food ingredient is based upon the following current good manufacturing practice conditions of use:

(1) The ingredient is used as a flavor enhancer as defined in § 170.3(o)(11) of this chapter; a nutrient supplement as defined in § 170.3(o)(20) of this chapter; and a processing aid as defined in § 170.3(o)(24) of this chapter.

(2) The ingredient is used in foods at levels not to exceed current good manufacturing practice.

(d) Prior sanctions for this ingredient different from the uses established in this section do not exist or have been waived.

[50 FR 13560, Apr. 5, 1985]

§ 184.1443a Malt.

(a) Malt is an enzyme preparation obtained from barley which has been softened by a series of steeping operations and germinated under controlled conditions. It is a brown, sweet, and viscous liquid or a white to tan powder. Its characterizing enzyme activities are α-amylase (EC 3.2.1.1.) and β-amylase (EC 3.2.1.2).

(b) The ingredient meets the general requirements and additional requirements for enzyme preparations in the Food Chemicals Codex, 3d ed. (1981), p. 110, which is incorporated by reference in accordance with 5 U.S.C. 552(a) and 1 CFR part 51. Copies are available from the National Academy Press, 2101 Constitution Ave., NW., Washington, DC 20418, or may be examined at the Office of Premarket Approval (HFS–200), Food and Drug Administration, 5100 Paint Branch Pkwy., College Park, MD 20740, and at the National Archives and Records Administration (NARA). For information on the availability of this material at NARA, call 202–741–6030, or go to: *http://www.archives.gov/federal_register/code_of_federal_regulations/ibr_locations.html.*

(c) In accordance with § 184.1(b)(1), the ingredient is used in food with no limitation other than current good manufacturing practice. The affirmation of this ingredient as GRAS as a direct food ingredient is based upon the following current good manufacturing practice conditions of use:

(1) The ingredient is used as an enzyme as defined in § 170.3(o)(9) of this chapter to hydrolyze starch or starch-derived polysaccharides.

(2) The ingredient is used in food at levels not to exceed current good manufacturing practice.

[60 FR 32911, June 26, 1995]

§ 184.1444 Maltodextrin.

(a) Maltodextrin ($(C_6H_{10}O_5)_n$, CAS Reg. No. 9050–36–6) is a nonsweet nutritive saccharide polymer that consists of D-glucose units linked primarily by α-1-4 bonds and that has a dextrose equivalent (D.E.) of less than 20. It is prepared as a white powder or concentrated solution by partial hydrolysis of corn starch, potato starch, or rice starch with safe and suitable acids and enzymes.

(b)(1) Maltodextrin derived from corn starch must be of a purity suitable for its intended use.

(2) Maltodextrin derived from potato starch meets the specifications of the Food Chemicals Codex, 3d ed., 3d supp. (1992), p. 125, which are incorporated by reference in accordance with 5 U.S.C. 552(a) and 1 CFR part 51. Copies are

available from the National Academy Press, 2101 Constitution Ave., NW., Washington, DC 20418, or at the Division of Petition Control (HFS–217), Center for Food Safety and Applied Nutrition, Food and Drug Administration, 5100 Paint Branch Pkwy., College Park, MD 20740, or may be examined at the National Archives and Records Administration (NARA). For information on the availability of this material at NARA, call 202–741–6030, or go to: *http://www.archives.gov/federal_register/code_of_federal_regulations/ibr_locations.html.*.

(3) Maltodextrin derived from rice starch meets the specifications of the Food Chemicals Codex, 4th ed. (1996), pp. 239 and 240, which is incorporated by reference in accordance with 5 U.S.C. 552(a) and 1 CFR part 51. Copies are available from the National Academy Press, 2101 Constitution Ave. NW., Washington, DC 20418, or may be examined at the Center for Food Safety and Applied Nutrition's Library, 5100 Paint Branch Pkwy., College Park, MD 20740, or at the National Archives and Records Administration (NARA). For information on the availability of this material at NARA, call 202–741–6030, or go to: *http://www.archives.gov/federal_register/code_of_federal_regulations/ibr_locations.html.*

(c) In accordance with § 184.1(b)(1), the ingredient is used in food with no limitation other than current good manufacturing practice.

(d) Prior sanctions for this ingredient different from the uses established in this section do not exist or have been waived.

[48 FR 51911, Nov. 15, 1983; as amended at 60 FR 48893, Sept. 21, 1995; 63 FR 14611, Mar. 26, 1998]

§ 184.1445 Malt syrup (malt extract).

(a) Malt is the product of barley (*Hordeum vulgare* L.) germinated under controlled conditions. Malt syrup and malt extract are interchangeable terms for a viscous concentrate of water extract of germinated barley grain, with or without added safe preservative. Malt syrup is usually a brown, sweet, and viscous liquid containing varying amounts of amylolytic enzymes and plant constituents. Barley is first softened after cleaning by steeping operations and then allowed to germinate under controlled conditions. The germinated grain then undergoes processing, such as drying, grinding, extracting, filtering, and evaporating, to produce malt syrup (malt extract) with 75 to 80 percent solids or dried malt syrup with higher solids content.

(b) The ingredient must be of a purity suitable for its intended use.

(c) In accordance with § 184.1(b)(1), the ingredient is used in food with no limitation other than current good manufacturing practice. The affirmation of this ingredient as generally recognized as safe (GRAS) as a direct human food ingredient is based upon the following current good manufacturing practice conditions of use:

(1) The ingredient is used as a flavoring agent and adjuvant as defined in § 170.3(o)(12) of this chapter.

(2) The ingredient is used in food at levels not to exceed current good manufacturing practice.

(d) Prior sanctions for this ingredient different from the uses established in this section do not exist or have been waived.

[48 FR 51613, Nov. 10, 1983, as amended at 73 FR 8607, Feb. 14, 2008]

§ 184.1446 Manganese chloride.

(a) Manganese chloride ($MnCl_2$, CAS Reg. No. 7773–01–5) is a pink, translucent, crystalline product. It is also known as manganese dichloride. It is prepared by dissolving manganous oxide, pyrolusite ore (MnO_2), or reduced manganese ore in hydrochloric acid. The resulting solution is neutralized to precipitate heavy metals, filtered, concentrated, and crystallized.

(b) The ingredient meets the specifications of the Food Chemicals Codex, 3d Ed. (1981), p. 186, which is incorporated by reference. Copies are available from the National Academy Press, 2101 Constitution Ave. NW., Washington, DC 20418, or available for inspection at the National Archives and Records Administration (NARA). For information on the availability of this material at NARA, call 202–741–6030, or go to: *http://www.archives.gov/federal_register/code_of_federal_regulations/ibr_locations.html.*

(c) In accordance with § 184.1(b)(1), the ingredient is used in food with no limitation other than current good manufacturing practice. The affirmation of this ingredient as generally recognized as safe (GRAS) as a direct human food ingredient is based upon the following current good manufacturing practice conditions of use:

(1) The ingredient is used as a nutrient supplement as defined in § 170.3(o)(20) of this chapter.

(2) The ingredient may be used in infant formulas in accordance with section 412(g) of the Federal Food, Drug, and Cosmetic Act (the act) or with regulations promulgated under section 412(a)(2) of the act.

(d) Prior sanctions for this ingredient different from the uses established in this section do not exist or have been waived.

[50 FR 19165, May 7, 1985, as amended at 76 FR 59250, Sept. 26, 2011]

§ 184.1449 Manganese citrate.

(a) Manganese citrate ($Mn_3(C_6H_5O_7)_2$, CAS Reg. No. 10024–66–5) is a pale orange or pinkish white powder. It is obtained by precipitating manganese carbonate from manganese sulfate and sodium carbonate solutions. The filtered and washed precipitate is digested first with sufficient citric acid solution to form manganous citrate and then with sodium citrate to complete the reaction.

(b) The ingredient must be of a purity suitable for its intended use.

(c) In accordance with § 184.1(b)(1), the ingredient is used in food with no limitation other than current good manufacturing practice. The affirmation of this ingredient as generally recognized as safe (GRAS) as a direct human food ingredient is based upon the following current good manufacturing practice conditions of use:

(1) The ingredient is used as a nutrient supplement as defined in § 170.3(o)(20) of this chapter.

(2) The ingredient is used in the following foods at levels not to exceed current good manufacturing practice: baked goods as defined in § 170.3(n)(1) of this chapter; nonalcoholic beverages as defined in § 170.3(n)(3) of this chapter; dairy product analogs as defined in § 170.3(n)(10) of this chapter; fish products as defined in § 170.3(n)(13) of this chapter; meat products as defined in § 170.3(n)(29) of this chapter; milk products as defined in § 170.3(n)(31) of this chapter; and poultry products as defined in § 170.3(n)(34) of this chapter. The ingredient may be used in infant formulas in accordance with section 412(g) of the Federal Food, Drug, and Cosmetic Act (the act) or with regulations promulgated under section 412(a)(2) of the act.

(d) Prior sanctions for this ingredient different from the uses established in this section do not exist or have been waived.

[50 FR 19166, May 7, 1985, as amended at 73 FR 8607, Feb. 14, 2008; 76 FR 59250, Sept. 26, 2011]

§ 184.1452 Manganese gluconate.

(a) Manganese gluconate ($C_{12}H_{22}MnO_{14}\cdot 2H_2O$, CAS Reg. No. 648–0953–0998) is a slightly pink colored powder. It is obtained by reacting manganese carbonate with gluconic acid in aqueous medium and then crystallizing the product.

(b) The ingredient meets the specifications of the Food Chemicals Codex, 3d Ed. (1981), p. 186, which is incorporated by reference. Copies are available from the National Academy Press, 2101 Constitution Ave. NW., Washington, DC 20418, or available for inspection at the National Archives and Records Administration (NARA). For information on the availability of this material at NARA, call 202–741–6030, or go to: *http://www.archives.gov/federal_register/code_of_federal_regulations/ibr_locations.html.*

(c) In accordance with § 184.1(b)(1), the ingredient is used in food with no limitation other than current good manufacturing practice. The affirmation of this ingredient as generally recognized as safe (GRAS) as a direct human food ingredient is based upon the following current good manufacturing practice conditions of use:

(1) The ingredient is used as a nutrient supplement as defined in § 170.3(o)(20) of this chapter.

(2) The ingredient is used in the following foods at levels not to exceed current good manufacturing practice: baked goods as defined in § 170.3(n)(1) of

this chapter; nonalcoholic beverages as defined in §170.3(n)(3) of this chapter; dairy product analogs as defined in §170.3(n)(10) of this chapter; fish products as defined in §170.3(n)(13) of this chapter; meat products as defined in §170.3(n)(29) of this chapter; milk products as defined in §170.3(n)(31) of this chapter; and poultry products as defined in §170.3(n)(34) of this chapter. The ingredient may be used in infant formulas in accordance with section 412(g) of the Federal Food, Drug, and Cosmetic Act (the act) or with regulations promulgated under section 412(a)(2) of the act.

(d) Prior sanctions for this ingredient different from the uses established in this section do not exist or have been waived.

[50 FR 19166, May 7, 1985]

§184.1461 Manganese sulfate.

(a) Manganese sulfate ($MnSO_4 \cdot H_2O$, CAS Reg. No. 7785–0987–097) is a pale pink, granular, odorless powder. It is obtained by reacting manganese compounds with sulfuric acid. It is also obtained as a byproduct in the manufacture of hydroquinone. Other manufacturing processes include the action of sulfur dioxide on a slurry of manganese dioxide in sulfuric acid, and the roasting of pyrolusite (MnO_2) ore with solid ferrous sulfate and coal, followed by leaching and crystallization.

(b) The ingredient meets the specifications of the Food Chemicals Codex, 3d Ed. (1981), p. 188, which is incorporated by reference. Copies are available from the National Academy Press, 2101 Constitution Ave. NW., Washington, DC 20418, or available for inspection at the National Archives and Records Administration (NARA). For information on the availability of this material at NARA, call 202–741–6030, or go to: *http://www.archives.gov/federal_register/code_of_federal_regulations/ibr_locations.html.*

(c) In accordance with §184.1(b)(1), the ingredient is used in food with no limitation other than current good manufacturing practice. The affirmation of this ingredient as generally recognized as safe (GRAS) as a direct human food ingredient is based upon the following current good manufacturing practice conditions of use:

(1) The ingredient is used as a nutrient supplement as defined in §170.3(o)(20) of this chapter.

(2) The ingredient is used in the following foods at levels not to exceed current good manufacturing practice: baked goods as defined in §170.3(n)(1) of this chapter; nonalcoholic beverages as defined in §170.3(n)(3) of this chapter; dairy product analogs as defined in §170.3(n)(10) of this chapter; fish products as defined in §170.3(n(13) of this chapter; meat products as defined in §170.3(n)(29) of this chapter; milk products as defined in §170.3(n)(31) of this chapter; and poultry products as defined in §170.3(n)(34) of this chapter.

The ingredient may be used in infant formulas in accordance with section 412(g) of the Federal Food, Drug, and Cosmetic Act (the act) or with regulations promulgated under section 412(a)(2) of the act.

(d) Prior sanctions for this ingredient different from the uses established in this section do not exist or have been waived.

[50 FR 19166, May 7, 1985]

§184.1472 Menhaden oil.

(a) *Menhaden oil.* (1) Menhaden oil is prepared from fish of the genus *Brevoortia,* commonly known as menhaden, by cooking and pressing. The resulting crude oil is then refined using the following steps: Storage (winterization), degumming (optional), neutralization, bleaching, and deodorization. Winterization may separate the oil and produce a solid fraction.

(2) Menhaden oil meets the following specifications:

(i) *Color and state.* Yellow liquid to white solid.

(ii) *Odor.* Odorless to slightly fishy.

(iii) *Saponification value.* Between 180 and 200 as determined by the American Oil Chemists' Society Official Method Cd 3–25—"Saponification Value" (reapproved 1989), which is incorporated by reference in accordance with 5 U.S.C. 552(a) and 1 CFR part 51. Copies of this publication are available from the Office of Food Additive Safety,

Center for Food Safety and Applied Nutrition (HFS-200), Food and Drug Administration, 5100 Paint Branch Pkwy., College Park, MD 20740, or available for inspection at the Center for Food Safety and Applied Nutrition's Library, Food and Drug Administration, 5100 Paint Branch Pkwy., College Park, MD 20740, or at the National Archives and Records Administration (NARA). For information on the availability of this material at NARA, call 202–741–6030, or go to: *http://www.archives.gov/federal_register/code_of_federal_regulations/ibr_locations.html.*

(iv) *Iodine number.* Not less than 120 as determined by the American Oil Chemists' Society Recommended Practice Cd 1d–92—"Iodine Value of Fats and Oils, Cyclohexane—Acetic Acid Method," which is incorporated by reference in accordance with 5 U.S.C. 552(a) and 1 CFR part 51. The availability of this incorporation by reference is given in paragraph (a)(2)(iii) of this section.

(v) *Unsaponifiable matter.* Not more than 1.5 percent as determined by the American Oil Chemists' Society Official Method Ca 6b–53—"Unsaponifiable Matter" (reapproved 1989), which is incorporated by reference in accordance with 5 U.S.C. 552(a) and 1 CFR part 51. The availability of this incorporation by reference is given in paragraph (a)(2)(iii) of this section.

(vi) *Free fatty acids.* Not more than 0.1 percent as determined by the American Oil Chemists' Society Official Method Ca 5a–40—"Free Fatty Acids" (reapproved 1989), which is incorporated by reference in accordance with 5 U.S.C. 552(a) and 1 CFR part 51. The availability of this incorporation by reference is given in paragraph (a)(2)(iii) of this section.

(vii) *Peroxide value.* Not more than 5 milliequivalents per kilogram of oil as determined by the American Oil Chemists' Society Official Method Cd 8–53—"Peroxide Value, Acetic Acid—Chloroform Method" (updated 1992) or Recommended Practice Cd 8b–90—"Peroxide Value, Acetic Acid—Isooctane Method" (updated 1992), which are incorporated by reference in accordance with 5 U.S.C. 552(a) and 1 CFR part 51. The availability of this incorporation by reference is given in paragraph (a)(2)(iii) of this section.

(viii) *Lead.* Not more than 0.1 part per million as determined by the American Oil Chemists' Society Official Method Ca 18c–91—"Determination of Lead by Direct Graphite Furnace Atomic Absorption Spectrometry" (revised 1992), which is incorporated by reference in accordance with 5 U.S.C. 552(a) and 1 CFR part 51. The availability of this incorporation by reference is given in paragraph (a)(2)(iii) of this section.

(ix) *Mercury.* Not more than 0.5 part per million as determined by the method entitled "Biomedical Test Materials Program: Analytical Methods for the Quality Assurance of Fish Oil," published in the "NOAA Technical Memorandum NMFS-SEFC-211," F. M. Van Dolah and S. B. Galloway, editors, National Marine Fisheries Service, U. S. Department of Commerce, pages 71–88, November, 1988, which is incorporated by reference in accordance with 5 U.S.C. 552(a) and 1 CFR part 51. The availability of this incorporation by reference is given in paragraph (a)(2)(iii) of this section.

(3) In accordance with § 184.1(b)(2), the ingredient may be used in food only within the following specific limitations to ensure that total intake of eicosapentaenoic acid or docosahexaenoic acid does not exceed 3.0 grams/person/day:

Category of food	Maximum level of use in food (as served)
Baked goods, baking mixes, § 170.3(n)(1) of this chapter.	5.0 percent
Cereals, § 170.3(n)(4) of this chapter	4.0 percent
Cheese products, § 170.3(n)(5) of this chapter.	5.0 percent
Chewing gum, § 170.3(n)(6) of this chapter	3.0 percent
Condiments, § 170.3(n)(8) of this chapter	5.0 percent
Confections, frostings, § 170.3(n)(9) of this chapter.	5.0 percent
Dairy product analogs, § 170.3(n)(10) of this chapter.	5.0 percent
Egg products, § 170.3(n)(11) of this chapter	5.0 percent
Fats, oils, § 170.3(n)(12) of this chapter, but not in infant formula.	12.0 percent
Fish products, § 170.3(n)(13) of this chapter	5.0 percent
Frozen dairy desserts, § 170.3(n)(20) of this chapter.	5.0 percent
Gelatins, puddings, § 170.3(n)(22) of this chapter.	1.0 percent
Gravies, sauces, § 170.3(n)(24) of this chapter.	5.0 percent
Hard candy, § 170.3(n)(25) of this chapter	10.0 percent
Jams, jellies, § 170.3(n)(28) of this chapter	7.0 percent

Category of food	Maximum level of use in food (as served)
Meat products, § 170.3(n)(29) of this chapter	5.0 percent
Milk products, § 170.3(n)(31) of this chapter	5.0 percent
Nonalcoholic beverages, § 170.3(n)(3) of this chapter.	0.5 percent
Nut products, § 170.3(n)(32) of this chapter ..	5.0 percent
Pastas, § 170.3(n)(23) of this chapter	2.0 percent
Plant protein products, § 170.3(n)(33) of this chapter.	5.0 percent
Poultry products, § 170.3(n)(34) of this chapter.	3.0 percent
Processed fruit juices, § 170.3(n)(35) of this chapter.	1.0 percent
Processed vegetable juices, § 170.3(n)(36) of this chapter.	1.0 percent
Snack foods, § 170.3(n)(37) of this chapter ..	5.0 percent
Soft candy, § 170.3(n)(38) of this chapter	4.0 percent
Soup mixes, § 170.3(n)(40) of this chapter ...	3.0 percent
Sugar substitutes, § 170.3(n)(42) of this chapter.	10.0 percent
Sweet sauces, toppings, syrups, § 170.3(n)(43) of this chapter.	5.0 percent
White granulated sugar, § 170.3(n)(41) of this chapter.	4.0 percent

(4) To ensure safe use of the substance, menhaden oil shall not be used in combination with any other added oil that is a significant source of eicosapentaenoic acid or docosahexaenoic acid.

(b) *Hydrogenated and partially hydrogenated menhaden oils.* (1) Partially hydrogenated and hydrogenated menhaden oils are prepared by feeding hydrogen gas under pressure to a converter containing crude menhaden oil and a nickel catalyst. The reaction is begun at 150 to 160 °C and after 1 hour the temperature is raised to 180 °C until the desired degree of hydrogenation is reached. Hydrogenated menhaden oil is fully hydrogenated.

(2) Partially hydrogenated and hydrogenated menhaden oils meet the following specifications:

(i) *Color.* Opaque white solid.

(ii) *Odor.* Odorless.

(iii) *Saponification value.* Between 180 and 200.

(iv) *Iodine number.* Not more than 119 for partially hydrogenated menhaden oil and not more than 10 for fully hydrogenated menhaden oil.

(v) *Unsaponifiable matter.* Not more than 1.5 percent.—

(vi) *Free fatty acids.* Not more than 0.1 percent.

(vii) *Peroxide value.* Not more than 5 milliequivalents per kilogram of oil.

(viii) *Nickel.* Not more than 0.5 part per million.

(ix) *Mercury.* Not more than 0.5 part per million.

(x) *Arsenic (as As).* Not more than 0.1 part per million.

(xi) *Lead.* Not more than 0.1 part per million.

(3) Partially hydrogenated and hydrogenated menhaden oils are used as edible fats or oils, as defined in § 170.3(n)(12) of this chapter, in food at levels not to exceed current good manufacturing practice.

(4) If the fat or oil is fully hydrogenated, the name to be used on the label of a product containing it shall include the term "hydrogenated," or if it is partially hydrogenated, the name shall include the term "partially hydrogenated," in accordance with § 101.4(b)(14) of this chapter.

[62 FR 30756, June 5, 1997, as amended at 70 FR 14531, Mar. 23, 2005]

§ 184.1490 Methylparaben.

(a) Methylparaben is the chemical methyl *p*-hydroxybenzoate. It is produced by the methanol esterification of *p*-hydroxybenzoic acid in the presence of sulfuric acid, with subsequent distillation.

(b) The ingredient meets the specifications of the "Food Chemicals Codex," 3d Ed. (1981), p. 199, which is incorporated by reference. Copies may be obtained from the National Academy Press, 2101 Constitution Ave. NW., Washington, DC 20418, or may be examined at the National Archives and Records Administration (NARA). For information on the availability of this material at NARA, call 202–741–6030, or go to: *http://www.archives.gov/federal_register/code_of_federal_regulations/ibr_locations.html.*

(c) The ingredient is used as an antimicrobial agent as defined in § 170.3(o)(2) of this chapter.

(d) The ingredient is used in food at levels not to exceed good manufacturing practices. Current good manufacturing practice results in a maximum level of 0.1 percent in food.

(e) Prior sanctions for this ingredient different from the uses established in this regulation do not exist or have been waived.

[42 FR 14653, Mar. 15, 1977, as amended at 49 FR 5612, Feb. 14, 1984]

§ 184.1498 Microparticulated protein product.

(a) Microparticulated protein product is prepared from egg whites or milk protein or a combination of egg whites and milk protein. These protein sources may be used alone or in combination with other safe and suitable ingredients to form the microparticulated product. The mixture of ingredients is high-shear heat processed to achieve a smooth and creamy texture similar to that of fat. Safe and suitable ingredients used in the preparation of the microparticulated protein product must be used in compliance with the limitations of the appropriate regulations in parts 172, 182, and 184 of this chapter.

(b) The ingredient is used in food in accordance with § 184.1(b)(2) at levels not to exceed current good manufacturing practice. The affirmation of the use of this ingredient as generally recognized as safe (GRAS) as a direct human food ingredient is based upon the following conditions of use:

(1) The ingredient is used in food as a thickener as defined in § 170.3(o)(28) of this chapter or as a texturizer as defined in § 170.3(o)(32) of this chapter.

(2) The ingredient is used in frozen dessert-type products except that the ingredient may not be used to replace the milk fat required in standardized frozen desserts.

(3) The name of the ingredient used in the ingredient statement on both bulk and packaged food must include the source of the protein (e.g., "microparticulated egg white protein"), followed by a parenthetical listing of each of the ingredients in the microparticulated protein product, in descending order of predominance. Microparticulated protein product must be used in accordance with this requirement or its addition to food will be considered by FDA to constitute the use of an unapproved food additive (see § 184.1(b)(2)).

[55 FR 6391, Feb. 23, 1990]

§ 184.1505 Mono- and diglycerides.

(a) Mono- and diglycerides consist of a mixture of glyceryl mono- and diesters, and minor amounts of triesters, that are prepared from fats or oils or fat-forming acids that are derived from edible sources. The most prevalent fatty acids include lauric, linoleic, myristic, oleic, palmitic, and stearic. Mono- and diglycerides are manufactured by the reaction of glycerin with fatty acids or the reaction of glycerin with triglycerides in the presence of an alkaline catalyst. The products are further purified to obtain a mixture of glycerides, free fatty acids, and free glycerin that contains at least 90 percent-by-weight glycerides.

(b) The ingredient meets the specifications of the Food Chemicals Codex, 3d Ed. (1981), p. 201, which is incorporated by reference in accordance with 5 U.S.C. 552(a). Copies are available from the National Academy Press, 2101 Constitution Ave. NW., Washington, DC 20418, or available for inspection at the National Archives and Records Administration (NARA). For information on the availability of this material at NARA, call 202–741–6030, or go to: *http://www.archives.gov/federal_register/code_of_federal_regulations/ibr_locations.html.*

(c) In accordance with § 184.1(b)(1), the ingredient is used in food with no limitation other than current good manufacturing practice. The affirmation of this ingredient as generally recognized as safe (GRAS) as a direct human food ingredient is based upon the following current good manufacturing practice conditions of use:

(1) The ingredient is used in food as a dough strengthener as defined in § 170.3(o)(6) of this chapter; an emulsifier and emulsifier salt as defined in § 170.3(o)(8) of this chapter; a flavoring agent and adjuvant as defined in § 170.3(o)(12) of this chapter; a formulation aid as defined in § 170.3(o)(14) of this chapter; a lubricant and release agent as defined in § 170.3(o)(18) of this chapter; a solvent and vehicle as defined in § 170.3(o)(27) of this chapter; a stabilizer and thickener as defined in § 170.3(o)(28) of this chapter; a surface-active agent as defined in § 170.3(o)(29) of this chapter; a surface-finishing

agent as defined in § 170.3(o)(30) of this chapter; and a texturizer as defined in § 170.3(o)(32) of this chapter.

(2) The ingredient is used in food at levels not to exceed current good manufacturing practice.

(d) Prior sanctions for this ingredient different from the uses established in this section do not exist or have been waived.

[54 FR 7403, Feb. 21, 1989, as amended at 57 FR 10616, Mar..27, 1992]

§ 184.1521 Monosodium phosphate derivatives of mono- and diglycerides.

(a) Monosodium phophate derivatives of mono- and diglycerides are composed of glyceride derivatives formed by reacting mono- and diglycerides that are derived from edible sources with phosphorus pentoxide (tetraphosphorus decoxide) followed by neutralization with sodium carbonate.

(b) The ingredient must be of a purity suitable for its intended use.

(c) In accordance with § 184.1(b)(1), the ingredient is used in food with no limitation other than current good manufacturing practice. The affirmation of this ingredient as generally recognized as safe (GRAS) as a direct human food ingredient is based upon the following current good manufacturing practice conditions of use:

(1) The ingredient is used in food as an emulsifier and emulsifier salt as defined in § 170.3(o)(8) of this chapter, a lubricant and release agent as defined in § 170.3(o)(18) of this chapter, and as a surface-active agent as defined in § 170.3(o)(29) of this chapter.

(2) The ingredient is used in the following foods at levels not to exceed current good manufacturing practice: dairy product analogs as defined in § 170.3(n)(10) of this chapter and soft candy as defined in § 170.3(n)(38) of this chapter.

(d) Prior sanctions for this ingredient different from the uses established in this section do not exist or have been waived.

[54 FR 7404, Feb. 21, 1989, as amended at 73 FR 8607, Feb. 14, 2008]

§ 184.1530 Niacin.

(a) Niacin ($C_6H_5NO_2$, CAS Reg. No. 59–67–6) is the chemical 3-pyridinecarboxylic acid (nicotinic acid). It is a non-hygroscopic, stable, white, crystalline solid that sublimes without decomposition at about 230 °C. It is soluble in water and alcohol. It is insoluble in ether.

(b) The ingredient meets the specifications of the "Food Chemicals Codex," 4th ed. (1996), p. 264, which is incorporated by reference in accordance with 5 U.S.C. 552(a) and 1 CFR part 51. Copies are available from the National Academy Press, Box 285, 2101 Constitution Ave. NW., Washington, DC 20055 (Internet address *http://www.nap.edu*), or may be examined at the Center for Food Safety and Applied Nutrition's Library, Food and Drug Administration, 5100 Paint Branch Pkwy., College Park, MD 20740, or at the National Archives and Records Administration (NARA). For information on the availability of this material at NARA, call 202–741–6030, or go to: *http://www.archives.gov/federal_register/code_of_federal_regulations/ibr_locations.html.*

(c) In accordance with § 184.1(b)(1), the ingredient is used in food with no limitation other than current good manufacturing practice. The affirmation of this ingredient as generally recognized as safe (GRAS) as direct human food ingredient is based upon the following current good manufacturing practice conditions of use:

(1) The ingredient is used as a nutrient supplement as defined in § 170.3(o)(20) of this chapter.

(2) The ingredient is used in foods at levels not to exceed current good manufacturing practice. The ingredient may also be used in infant formula in accordance with section 412(g) of the Federal Food, Drug, and Cosmetic Act (the Act) or with regulations promulgated under section 412(a)(2) of the Act.

(d) Prior sanctions for this ingredient different from the uses established in this section do not exist or have been waived.

[48 FR 52033, Nov. 16, 1983; 48 FR 54336, Dec. 2, 1983, as amended at 64 FR 1760, Jan. 12, 1999]

§ 184.1535 Niacinamide.

(a) Niacinamide ($C_6H_6N_2O$, CAS Reg. No. 98–92–0) is the chemical 3-

pyridinecarboxylic acid amide (nicotinamide). It is a white crystalline powder that is soluble in water, alcohol, ether, and glycerol. It melts between 128° and 131 °C.

(b) The ingredient meets the specifications of the Food Chemicals Codex, 3d Ed. (1981), p. 205, which is incorporated by reference. Copies are available from the National Academy Press, 2101 Constitution Ave. NW., Washington, DC 20418, or available for inspection at the National Archives and Records Administration (NARA). For information on the availability of this material at NARA, call 202–741–6030, or go to: *http://www.archives.gov/federal_register/code_of_federal_regulations/ibr_locations.html.*

(c) In accordance with § 184.1(b)(1), the ingredient is used in food with no limitation other than current good manufacturing practice. The affirmation of this ingredient as generally recognized as safe (GRAS) as a direct human food ingredient is based upon the following current good manufacturing practice conditions of use:

(1) The ingredient is used as a nutrient supplement as defined in § 170.3(o)(20) of this chapter.

(2) The ingredient is used in foods at levels not to exceed current good manufacturing practice. The ingredient may also be used in infant formula in accordance with section 412(g) of the Federal Food, Drug, and Cosmetic Act (the act) or with regulations promulgated under section 412(a)(2) of the Act.

(d) Prior sanctions for this ingredient different from the uses established in this section do not exist or have been waived.

[48 FR 52033, Nov. 16, 1983; 48 FR 54336, Dec. 2, 1983]

§ 184.1537 Nickel.

(a) Elemental nickel (CAS Reg. No. 7440–02–0) is obtained from nickel ore by transforming it to nickel sulfide (Ni_3S_2). The sulfide is roasted in air to give nickel oxide (NiO). The oxide is then reduced with carbon to give elemental nickel.

(b) The ingredient must be of a purity suitable for its intended use.

(c) In accordance with § 184.1(b)(1), the ingredient is used in food with no limitation other than current good manufacturing practice. The affirmation of this ingredient as generally recognized as safe (GRAS) as a direct human food ingredient is based upon the following current good manufacturing practice conditions of use:

(1) The ingredient is used as a catalyst as defined in § 170.3(o)(24) of this chapter.

(2) The ingredient is used in the hydrogenation of fats and oils as defined in § 170.3(n)(12) of this chapter at levels not to exceed current good manufacturing practice. Current good manufacturing practice includes the removal of nickel from fats and oils following hydrogenation.

(d) Prior sanctions for this ingredient different from the uses established in this section do not exist or have been waived.

[48 FR 51618, Nov. 10, 1983, as amended at 73 FR 8607, Feb. 14, 2008]

§ 184.1538 Nisin preparation.

(a) Nisin preparation is derived from pure culture fermentations of certain strains of Streptococcus lactis Lancefield Group N. Nisin preparation contains nisin (CAS Reg. No. 1414–45–5), a group of related peptides with antibiotic activity.

(b) The ingredient is a concentrate or dry material that meets the specifications that follow when it is tested as described in "Specifications for Identity and Purity of Some Antibiotics," World Health Organization, FAO Nutrition Meeting Report Series, No. 45A, 1969, which is incorporated by reference. Copies are available from the Division of Dockets Management (HFA–305), Food and Drug Administration, 5630 Fishers Lane, rm. 1061, Rockville, MD 20852, or available for inspection at the National Archives and Records Administration (NARA). For information on the availability of this material at NARA, call 202–741–6030, or go to: *http://www.archives.gov/federal_register/code_of_federal_regulations/ibr_locations.html.*

(1) Nisin content, not less than 900 international units per milligram.

(2) Arsenic, not more than 1 part per million.

(3) Lead, not more than 2 parts per million.

(4) Zinc, not more than 25 parts per million.

(5) Copper, zinc plus copper not more than 50 parts per million.

(6) Total plate count, not more than 10 per gram.

(7) *Escherichia coli*, absent in 10 grams.

(8) *Salmonella*, absent in 10 grams.

(9) Coagulase positive staphylococci, absent in 10 grams.

(c) The ingredient is used as an antimicrobial agent as defined in § 170.3(o)(2) of this chapter to inhibit the outgrowth of *Clostridium botulinum* spores and toxin formation in pasteurized cheese spreads and pasteurized process cheese spreads listed in § 133.175; pasteurized cheese spread with fruits, vegetables, or meats as defined in § 133.176; pasteurized process cheese spread as defined in § 133.179; pasteurized process cheese spread with fruits, vegetables, or meats as defined in § 133.180 of this chapter.

(d) The ingredient is used at levels not to exceed good manufacturing practice in accordance with § 184.1(b)(1) of this chapter. The current good manufacturing practice level is the quantity of the ingredient that delivers a maximum of 250 parts per million of nisin in the finished product as determined by the British Standards Institution Methods, "Methods for the Estimation and Differentiation of Nisin in Processed Cheese," BS 4020 (1974), which is incorporated by reference. Copies are available from the Division of Dockets Management (HFA–305), Food and Drug Administration, rm. 1–23, 12420 Parklawn Dr., Rockville, MD 20857, or available for inspection at the National Archives and Records Administration (NARA). For information on the availability of this material at NARA, call 202–741–6030, or go to: *http://www.archives.gov/federal_register/code_of_federal_regulations/ibr_locations.html.*

[53 FR 11250, Apr. 6, 1988, as amended at 59 FR 14364, Mar. 28, 1994; 68 FR 24879, May 9, 2003]

§ 184.1540 Nitrogen.

(a) Nitrogen (empirical formula N_2, CAS Reg. No. 7727–37–9) is a colorless, odorless, flavorless gas that is produced commercially by the fractionation of liquid air.

(b) The ingredient must be of a purity suitable for its intended use.

(c) In accordance with § 184.1(b)(1), the ingredient is used in food with no limitations other than current good manufacturing practice. The affirmation of this ingredient as generally recognized as safe (GRAS) as a direct human food ingredient is based upon the following current good manufacturing practice conditions of use:

(1) The ingredient is used as a propellant, aerating agent, and gas as defined in § 170.3(o)(25) of this chapter.

(2) The ingredient is used in food at levels not to exceed current good manufacturing practice.

(d) Prior sanctions for this ingredient different from the uses established in this section do not exist or have been waived.

[48 FR 57270, Dec. 29, 1983, as amended at 73 FR 8607, Feb. 14, 2008]

§ 184.1545 Nitrous oxide.

(a) Nitrous oxide (empirical formula N_2O, CAS Reg. No. 10024–97–2) is also known as dinitrogen monoxide or laughing gas. It is a colorless gas, about 50 percent heavier than air, with a slightly sweet smell. It does not burn but will support combustion. Nitrous oxide is manufactured by the thermal decomposition of ammonium nitrate. Higher oxides of nitrogen are removed by passing the dry gas through a series of scrubbing towers.

(b) The ingredient must be of a purity suitable for its intended use.

(c) In accordance with § 184.1(b)(1), the ingredient is used in food with no limitations other than current good manufacturing practice. The affirmation of this ingredient as generally recognized as safe (GRAS) as a direct human food ingredient is based upon the following current good manufacturing practice conditions of use:

(1) The ingredient is used as a propellant, aerating agent, and gas as defined in § 170.3(o)(25) of this chapter.

(2) The ingredient is used in dairy product analogs as defined in § 170.3(n)(10) of this chapter at levels not to exceed current good manufacturing practice.

(d) Prior sanctions for this ingredient different from the uses established in this section do not exist or have been waived.

[48 FR 57270, Dec. 29, 1983, as amended at 73 FR 8607, Feb. 14, 2008]

§ 184.1553 Peptones.

(a) Peptones are a variable mixture of polypeptides, oligopeptides, and amino acids that are produced by partial hydrolysis of casein, animal tissue, soy protein isolate, gelatin, defatted fatty tissue, egg albumin, or lactalbumin (whey protein). Peptones are produced from these proteins using proteolytic enzymes that either are considered to be generally recognized as safe (GRAS) or are regulated as food additives. Peptones are also produced by denaturing any of the proteins listed in this paragraph with safe and suitable acids or heat.

(b) The ingredients must be of a purity suitable for their intended use.

(c) In accordance with § 184.1(b)(1), these ingredients are used in food with no limitation other than current good manufacturing practice. The affirmation of these ingredients as GRAS as direct human food ingredients is based upon the following current good manufacturing practice conditions of use:

(1) These ingredients are used as nutrient supplements as defined in § 170.3(o)(20) of this chapter; as processing aids as defined in § 170.3(o)(24) of this chapter; and as surface-active agents as defined in § 170.3(o)(29) of this chapter.

(2) These ingredients are used in food at levels not to exceed current good manufacturing practice.

(d) Prior sanctions for these ingredients different from the uses established in this section do not exist or have been waived.

[49 FR 25430, June 21, 1984, as amended at 50 FR 49536, Dec. 3, 1985; 73 FR 8607, Feb. 14, 2008]

§ 184.1555 Rapeseed oil.

(a) *Fully hydrogenated rapeseed oil.* (1) Fully hydrogenated rapeseed oil is a mixture of triglycerides in which the fatty acid composition is a mixture of saturated fatty acids. The fatty acids are present in the same porportions which result from the full hydrogenation of fatty acids occurring in natural rapeseed oil. The rapeseed oil is obtained from the *napus* and *campestris* varieties of *Brassica* of the family Cruciferae. It is prepared by fully hydrogenating refined and bleached rapeseed oil at 310–375 °F, using a catalyst such as nickel, until the iodine number is 4 or less.

(2) The ingredient meets the following specifications: Acid value not more than 6, arsenic not more than 3 parts per million, free glycerin not more than 7 percent, heavy metals (as Pb) not more than 10 parts per million, iodine number not more than 4, residue on ignition not more than 0.5 percent.

(3) The ingredient is used as a stabilizer and thickener as defined in § 170.3(o)(28) of this chapter in peanut butter. The use level of the ingredient is limited by good manufacturing practice (GMP) to the minimum amount required to produce the intended effect. Current good manufacturing practices result in a maximum level of 2 percent in peanut butter.

(b) *Superglycerinated fully hydrogenated rapeseed oil.* (1) Superglycerinated fully hydrogenated rapeseed oil is a mixture of mono- and diglycerides with triglycerides as a minor component. The fatty acid composition is a mixture of saturated fatty acids present in the same proportions as those resulting from the full hydrogenation of fatty acids in natural rapeseed oil. It is made by adding excess glycerol to the fully hydrogenated rapeseed oil and heating, in the presence of a sodium hydroxide catalyst, to 330 °F under partial vacuum and steam sparging agitation.

(2) The ingredient meets the specifications of the "Food Chemicals Codex," 3d Ed. (1981), p. 201, relating to mono- and diglycerides, which is incorporated by reference. Copies may be obtained from the National Academy Press, 2101 Constitution Ave. NW., Washington, DC 20418, or may be examined at the National Archives and Records Administration (NARA). For information on the availability of this material at NARA, call 202–741–6030, or go to: *http://www.archives.gov/federal_register/code_of_federal_regulations/*

ibr_locations.html. An additional specification requires the iodine number to be 4 or less.

(3) The ingredient is used as an emulsifier as defined in §170.3(o)(8) of this chapter in shortenings for cake mixes. The use level of the ingredient is limited by good manufacturing practice (GMP) to the minimum amount required to produce the intended effect. Current good manufacturing practices result in a maximum level, as served, of 4 percent of the shortening or 0.5 percent of the total weight of the cake mix.

(c) *Low erucic acid rapeseed oil.* (1) Low erucic acid rapeseed oil, also known as canola oil, is the fully refined, bleached, and deodorized edible oil obtained from certain varieties of *Brassica Napus* or *B. Campestris* of the family *Cruciferae.* The plant varieties are those producing oil-bearing seeds with a low erucic acid content. Chemically, low erucic acid rapeseed oil is a mixture of triglycerides, composed of both saturated and unsaturated fatty acids, with an erucic acid content of no more than 2 percent of the component fatty acids.

(2) Low erucic acid rapeseed oil as defined in paragraph (c)(1) of this section may be partially hydrogenated to reduce the proportion of unsaturated fatty acids. When the partially hydrogenated low erucic acid rapeseed oil is used, it shall be referred to as partially hydrogenated low erucic acid rapeseed oil.

(3) In addition to limiting the content of erucic acid to a level not exceeding 2 percent of the component fatty acids, low erucic acid rapeseed oil and partially hydrogenated low erucic acid rapeseed oil must be of a purity suitable for their intended use.

(4) Low erucic acid rapeseed oil and partially hydrogenated low erucic acid rapeseed oil are used as edible fats and oils in food, except in infant formula, at levels not to exceed current good manufacturing practice.

[42 FR 48336, Sept. 23, 1977, as amended at 49 FR 5613, Feb. 14, 1984; 50 FR 3755, Jan. 28, 1985; 53 FR 52682, Dec. 29, 1988; 73 FR 8608, Feb. 14, 2008]

§ 184.1560 Ox bile extract.

(a) Ox bile extract (CAS Reg. No. 8008–63–7), also known as purified oxgall or sodium choleate, is a yellowish green, soft solid, with a partly sweet, partly bitter, disagreeable taste. It is the purified portion of the bile of an ox obtained by evaporating the alcohol extract of concentrated bile.

(b) Food-grade ox bile extract shall meet the specifications of the U.S. Pharmacopeia (USP), XIV, 1950, p. 410.[1]

(c) The ingredient is used as a surfactant as defined in §170.3 (o)(29) of this chapter.

(d) The ingredient is used in food in accordance with §184.1(b)(1) at levels not to exceed good manufacturing practice. Current good manufacturing practice results in a maximum level, as served, of 0.002 percent for cheese as defined in §170.3(n)(5) of this chapter.

(e) Prior sanctions for this ingredient different from the uses established in this section do not exist or have been waived.

[43 FR 36064, Aug. 15, 1978. Redesignated and amended at 50 FR 49537, Dec. 3, 1985]

§ 184.1563 Ozone.

(a) Ozone (O_3, CAS Reg. No. 10028–15–6) is an unstable blue gas with a pungent, characteristic odor, which occurs freely in nature, It is produced commercially by passing electrical discharges or ionizing radiation through air or oxygen.

(b) The ingredient must be of a purity suitable for its intended use in accordance with §170.30(h)(1) of this chapter.

(c) In accordance with §184.1(b)(2), the ingredient is used to treat food only within the following specific limitations:

[1] Copies may be obtained from: U.S. Pharmacopeial Convention, Inc., 12601 Twinbrook Parkway, Rockville, MD 20852.

Category of food	Maximum treatment level in food	Functional use
Bottled water that prior to ozonation meets the microbiological, physical, chemical, and radiological quality standards of § 165.110 (b)(2) through (b)(5) of this chapter.	Not to exceed current good manufacturing practice. Current good manufacturing practice results in a maximum residual level at the time of bottling of 0.4 milligram of ozone per liter of bottled water.	Antimicrobial agent, § 170.3 (o)(2) of this chapter.

[47 FR 50210, Nov. 5, 1982, as amended at 60 FR 57130, Nov. 13, 1995]

§ 184.1583 Pancreatin.

(a) Pancreatin (CAS Reg. No. 8049–47–6) is an enzyme preparation obtained from porcine or bovine pancreatic tissue. It is a white to tan powder. Its characterizing enzyme activity that of a peptide hydrolase (EC 3.4.21.36).

(b) The ingredient meets the general requirements and additional requirements in the Food Chemicals Codex, 3d ed. (1981), p. 110, which is incorporated by reference in accordance with 5 U.S.C. 552(a) and 1 CFR part 51. Copies are available from the National Academy Press, 2101 Constitution Ave. NW., Washington, DC 20418, or may be examined at the Office of Food Additive Safety (HFS–200), Center for Food Safety and Applied Nutrition, Food and Drug Administration, 5100 Paint Branch Pkwy., College Park, MD 20740, 240–402–1200, and at the National Archives and Records Administration (NARA). For information on the availability of this material at NARA, call 202–741–6030, or go to: *http://www.archives.gov/federal_register/code_of_federal_regulations/ibr_locations.html.*

(c) In accordance with § 184.1(b)(1), the ingredient is used in food with no limitation other than current good manufacturing practice. The affirmation of this ingredient as GRAS as a direct food ingredient is based upon the following current good manufacturing practice conditions of use:

(1) The ingredient is used as an enzyme as defined in § 170.3(o)(9) of this chapter to hydrolyze proteins or polypeptides.

(2) The ingredient is used in food at levels not to exceed current good manufacturing practice.

[60 FR 32911, June 26, 1995, as amended at 78 FR 14666, Mar. 7, 2013]

§ 184.1585 Papain.

(a) Papain (CAS Reg. No. 9001–73–4) is a proteolytic enzyme derived from *Carica papaya* L. Crude latex containing the enzyme is collected from slashed unripe papaya. The food-grade product is obtained by repeated filtration of the crude latex or an aqueous solution of latex or by precipitation from an aqueous solution of latex. The resulting enzyme preparation may be used in a liquid or dry form.

(b) The ingredient meets the specifications of the Food Chemicals Codex, 3d Ed. (1981), pp. 107–110, which is incorporated by reference. Copies are available from the National Academy Press, 2101 Constitution Ave. NW., Washington, DC 20418, or available for inspection at the National Archives and Records Administration (NARA). For information on the availability of this material at NARA, call 202–741–6030, or go to: *http://www.archives.gov/federal_register/code_of_federal_regulations/ibr_locations.html.*

(c) In accordance with § 184.1(b)(1), the ingredient is used in food with no limitation other than currect good manufacturing practice. The affirmation of this ingredient as generally recognized as safe (GRAS) as a direct human food ingredient is based upon the following current good manufacturing conditions of use:

(1) The ingredient is used as an enzyme as defined in § 170.3(o)(9) of this chapter; processing aid as defined in § 170.3(o)(24) of this chapter; and texturizer as defined in § 170.3(o)(32) of this chapter.

(2) The ingredient is used in food at levels not to exceed current good manufacturing practice.

(d) Prior sanctions for this ingredient different from the uses established in this section do not exist or have been waived.

[48 FR 48806, Oct. 21, 1983]

§ 184.1588 Pectins.

(a) The pectins (CAS Reg. No. 9000–69–5) are a group of complex, high molecular weight polysaccharides found in plants and composed chiefly of partially methylated polygalacturonic acid units. Portions of the carboxly group occur as methyl esters, and the remaining carboxyl groups exist in the form of the free acid or as its ammonium, potassium, or sodium (CAS Reg. No. 9000–59–8) salts, and in some types as the acid amide. Thus, the pectins regulated in this section are the high-ester pectins, low-ester pectins, amidated pectins, pectinic acids, and pectinates. Pectin is produced commercially by extracting citrus peel, apple pomace, or beet pulp with hot dilute acid (pH 1.0 to 3.5, 70° to 90 °C). The extract is filtered, and pectin is then precipitated from the clear extract with ethanol or isopropanol, or as the copper or aluminum salt. The acid extract is sometimes spray- or roller-dried, or it is concentrated to be sold as liquid pectin.

(b) The ingredients meet the specifications of the Food Chemical Codex, 3d Ed. (1981), p. 215, which is incorporated by reference. Copies are available from the National Academy Press, 2101 Constitution Ave. NW., Washington, DC 20418, or available for inspection at the National Archives and Records Administration (NARA). For information on the availability of this material at NARA, call 202–741–6030, or go to: *http://www.archives.gov/federal_register/code_of_federal_regulations/ibr_locations.html.*

(c) In accordance with § 184.1(b)(1), the ingredients are used in food with no limitation other than current good manufacturing practice. The affirmation of these ingredients as generally recognized as safe (GRAS) as direct human food ingredients is based upon the following current good manufacturing practice conditions of use:

(1) The ingredients are used as emulsifiers as defined in § 170.3(o)(8) of this chapter and as stabilizers and thickeners as defined in § 170.3(o)(28) of this chapter.

(2) The ingredients are used in food at levels not to exceed current good manufacturing practice.

(d) Prior sanctions for these ingredients different from the uses established in this section do not exist or have been waived.

[48 FR 51149, Nov. 7, 1983]

§ 184.1595 Pepsin.

(a) Pepsin (CAS Reg. No. 9001–75–6) is an enzyme preparation obtained from the glandular layer of hog stomach. It is a white to light tan powder, amber paste, or clear amber to brown liquid. Its characterizing enzyme activity is that of a peptide hydrolase (EC 3.4.23.1).

(b) The ingredient meets the general requirements and additional requirements for enzyme preparations in the Food Chemicals Codex, 3d ed. (1981), p. 110, which is incorporated by reference in accordance with 5 U.S.C. 552(a) and 1 CFR part 51. Copies are available from the National Academy Press, 2101 Constitution Ave. NW., Washington, DC 20418, or may be examined at the Office of Food Additive Safety (HFS–200), Center for Food Safety and Applied Nutrition, Food and Drug Administration, 5100 Paint Branch Pkwy., College Park, MD 20740, 240–402–1200, and at the National Archives and Records Administration (NARA). For information on the availability of this material at NARA, call 202–741–6030, or go to: *http://www.archives.gov/federal_register/code_of_federal_regulations/ibr_locations.html.*

(c) In accordance with § 184.1(b)(1), the ingredient is used in food with no limitation other than current good manufacturing practice. The affirmation of this ingredient as GRAS as a direct food ingredient is based upon the following current good manufacturing practice conditions of use:

(1) The ingredient is used as an enzyme as defined in § 170.3(o)(9) of this chapter to hydrolyze proteins or polypeptides.

(2) The ingredient is used in food at levels not to exceed current good manufacturing practice.

[60 FR 32911, June 26, 1995, as amended at 78 FR 14667, Mar. 7, 2013]

§ 184.1610 Potassium alginate.

(a) Potassium alginate (CAS Reg. No. 9005–36–1) is the potassium salt of alginic acid, a natural polyuronide constituent of certain brown algae. Potassium alginate is prepared by the neutralization of purified alginic acid with appropriate pH control agents.

(b) The ingredient meets the specifications of the Food Chemicals Codex, 3d Ed. (1981), p. 239, which is incorporated by reference. Copies are available from the National Academy Press, 2101 Constitution Ave. NW., Washington, DC 20418, or available for inspection at the National Archives and Records Administration (NARA). For information on the availability of this material at NARA, call 202–741–6030, or go to: *http://www.archives.gov/federal_register/code_of_federal_regulations/ibr_locations.html.*

(c) In accordance with § 184.1(b)(2), the ingredient is used in food only within the following specific limitations:

Category of food	Maximum level of use in food (as served) (percent)	Functional use
Confections and frostings, § 170.3(n)(9) of this chapter.	0.1	Stabilizer, thickener, § 170.3(o)(28) of this chapter
Gelatins and puddings, § 170.3(n)(22) of this chapter.	0.7	Do.
Processed fruits and fruit juices, § 170.3(n)(35) of this chapter.	0.25	Do.
All other food categories.	0.01	Do.

(d) Prior sanctions for potassium alginate different from the uses established in this section do not exist or have been waived.

[47 FR 29951, July 9, 1982]

§ 184.1613 Potassium bicarbonate.

(a) Potassium bicarbonate ($KHCO_3$, CAS Reg. No. 298–14–6) is made by the following processes:

(1) By treating a solution of potassium hydroxide with carbon dioxide;

(2) By treating a solution of potassium carbonate with carbon dioxide.

(b) The ingredient meets the specifications of the Food Chemicals Codex, 3d Ed. (1981), p. 239, which is incorporated by reference. Copies are available from the National Academy Press, 2101 Constitution Ave. NW., Washington, DC 20418, or available for inspection at the National Archives and Records Administration (NARA). For information on the availability of this material at NARA, call 202–741–6030, or go to: *http://www.archives.gov/federal_register/code_of_federal_regulations/ibr_locations.html.*

(c) In accordance with § 184.1(b)(1), the ingredient is used in food with no limitation other than current good manufacturing practice. The affirmation of this ingredient as generally recognized as safe (GRAS) as a direct human food ingredient is based upon the following current good manufacturing practice conditions of use:

(1) The ingredient is used as a formulation aid as defined in § 170.3(o)(14) of this chapter; nutrient supplemlent as defined in § 170.3(o)(20) of this chapter; pH control agent as defined in § 170.3(o)(23) of this chapter; and processing aid as defined in § 170.3(o)(24) of this chapter.

(2) The ingredient is used in food at levels not to exceed current good manufacturing practice.

(d) Prior sanctions for this ingredient different from the uses established in this section do not exist or have been waived.

[48 FR 52442, Nov. 18, 1983]

§ 184.1619 Potassium carbonate.

(a) Potassium carbonate (K_2CO_3, CAS Reg. No. 584–08–7) is produced by the following methods of manufacture:

(1) By electrolysis of potassium chloride followed by exposing the resultant potassium to carbon dioxide;

(2) By treating a solution of potassium hydroxide with excess carbon dioxide to produce potassium carbonate;

(3) By treating a solution of potassium hydroxide with carbon dioxide to produce potassium bicarbonate, which is then heated to yield potassium carbonate.

(b) The ingredient meets the specifications of the Food Chemicals Codex,

3d Ed. (1981), p. 240, which is incorporated by reference. Copies are available from the National Academy Press, 2101 Constitution Ave. NW., Washington, D.C. 20418, or available for inspection at the National Archives and Records Administration (NARA). For information on the availability of this material at NARA, call 202–741–6030, or go to: *http://www.archives.gov/federal_register/code_of_federal_regulations/ibr_locations.html.*

(c) In accordance with §184.1(b)(1), the ingredient is used in food with no limitation other than current good manufacturing practice. the affirmation of this ingredient as generally recognized as safe (GRAS) as a direct human food ingredient is based upon the following current good manufacturing practice conditions of use:

(1) The ingredient is used in food as a flavoring agent and adjuvant as defined in §170.3(o)(12) of this chapter; nutrient supplement as defined in §170.3(o)(20) of this chapter; pH control agent as defined in §170.3(o)(23) of this chapter; and processing aid as defined in §170.3(o)(24) of this chapter.

(2) The ingredient is used in food at levels not to exceed current good manufacturing practice.

(d) Prior sanctions for this ingredient different from the uses established in this section do not exist or have been waived.

[48 FR 52442, Nov. 18, 1983]

§ 184.1622 Potassium chloride.

(a) Potassium chloride (KCl, CAS Reg. No. 7447–40–7) is a white, odorless solid prepared from source minerals by fractional crystallization or flotation. It is soluble in water and glycerol and has a saline taste at low concentration levels.

(b) The ingredient meets the specifications of the Food Chemicals Codex, 3d Ed. (1981), p. 241, which is incorporated by reference. Copies are available from the National Academy Press, 2101 Constitution Ave. NW., Washington, DC 20418, or available for inspection at the National Archives and Records Administration (NARA). For information on the availability of this material at NARA, call 202–741–6030, or go to: *http://www.archives.gov/federal_register/code_of_federal_regulations/ibr_locations.html.*

(c) In accordance with §184.1(b)(1), the ingredient is used in food with no limitation other than current good manufacturing practice. The affirmation of this ingredient as generally recognized as safe (GRAS) as a direct human food ingredient is based upon the following current good manufacturing practice conditions of use:

(1) The ingredient is used as a flavor enhancer as defined in §170.3(o)(11) of this chapter; as a flavoring agent as defined in §170.3(o)(12) of this chapter; as a nutrient supplement as defined in §170.3(o)(20) of this chapter; as a pH control agent as defined in §170.3(o)(23) of this chapter; and as a stabilizer or thickener as defined in §170.3(o)(28) of this chapter.

(2) The ingredient is used in food at levels not to exceed current good manufacturing practice. Potassium chloride may be used in infant formula in accordance with section 412(g) of the Federal Food, Drug, and Cosmetic Act (the Act) or with regulations promulgated under section 412(a)(2) of the Act.

(d) Prior sanctions for this ingredient different from the uses established in this section do not exist or have been waived.

[48 FR 51614, Nov. 10, 1983]

§ 184.1625 Potassium citrate.

(a) Potassium citrate ($C_6H_5K_3O_7 \cdot H_2O$, CAS Reg. No. 006100–0905–096) is the potassium salt of citric acid. It is prepared by neutralizing citric acid with potassium hydroxide or potassium carbonate. It occurs as transparent crystals or a white granular powder, is odorless and deliquescent, and contains one mole of water per mole of potassium citrate.

(b) The ingredient meets the specifications of the Food Chemicals Codex, 3d ed. (1981), p. 242, which is incorporated by reference in accordance with 5 U.S.C. 552(a) and 1 CFR part 51. Copies are available from the National Academy Press, 2101 Constitution Ave. NW., Washington, DC 20418, and the Center for Food Safety and Applied Nutrition (HFS–200), 5100 Paint Branch Pkwy., College Park, MD 20740, or may be examined at the National Archives and Records Administration (NARA). For information on the availability of this material at NARA, call 202–741–6030, or go to: *http://www.archives.gov/federal_register/code_of_federal_regulations/ibr_locations.html.*

(c) In accordance with § 184.1(b)(1), the ingredient is used in food with no limitation other than current good manufacturing practice.

(d) Prior sanctions for this ingredient different from the uses established in this section, or different from those set forth in part 181 of this chapter, do not exist or have been waived.

[59 FR 63896, Dec. 12, 1994]

§ 184.1631 Potassium hydroxide.

(a) Potassium hydroxide (KOH, CAS Reg. No. 1310–58–3) is also known as caustic potash, potash lye, and potassa. The empirical formula is KOH. It is a white, highly deliquescent caustic solid, which is marketed in several forms, including pellets, flakes, sticks, lumps, and powders. Potassium hydroxide is obtained commercially from the electrolysis of potassium chloride solution in the presence of a porous diaphragm.

(b) The ingredient meets the specifications of the Food Chemicals Codex, 3d Ed. (1981), which is incorporated by reference. Copies are available from the National Academy Press, 2101 Constitution Ave. NW., Washington, DC 20418, or available from inspection at the National Archives and Records Administration (NARA). For information on the availability of this material at NARA, call 202–741–6030, or go to: *http://www.archives.gov/federal_register/code_of_federal_regulations/ibr_locations.html.*

(c) In accordance with § 184.1(b)(1), the ingredient is used in food with no limitation other than current good manufacturing practice. The affirmation of this ingredient as generally recognized as safe (GRAS) as a direct human food ingredient is based upon the following current good manufacturing practice conditions of use:

(1) The ingredient is used as a formulation aid as defined in § 170.3(o)(14) of this chapter; a pH control agent as defined in § 170.3(o)(23) of the chapter; a processing aid as defined in § 170.3(o)(24) of this chapter; and a stabilizer and thickener as defined in § 170.3(o)(28) of this chapter.

(2) The ingredient is used in food at levels not to exceed current good manufacturing practice.

(d) Prior sanctions for this ingredient different from the uses established in this section do not exist or have been waived.

[48 FR 52444, Nov. 18, 1983]

§ 184.1634 Potassium iodide.

(a) Potassium iodide (KI, CAS Reg. No. 7681–11–0) is the potassium salt of hydriodic acid. It occurs naturally in sea water and in salt deposits, but can be prepared by reacting hydriodic acid (HI) with potassium bicarbonate ($KHCO_3$).

(b) The ingredient meets the specifications of the "Food Chemicals Codex," 3d Ed. (1981), pp. 246–247, which is incorporated by reference. Copies may be obtained from the National Academy Press, 2101 Constitution Ave. NW., Washington, DC 20418, or may be examined at the National Archives and Records Administration (NARA). For information on the availability of this material at NARA, call 202–741–6030, or go to: *http://www.archives.gov/federal_register/code_of_federal_regulations/ibr_locations.html.*

(c) The ingredient is used as a nutrient supplement as defined in § 170.3(o)(20) of this chapter.

(d) The ingredient is used in table salt in accordance with § 184.1(b)(2) of this chapter as a source of dietary iodine at a maximum level of 0.01 percent.

(e) Prior sanctions for this ingredient different from the uses established in this section do not exist or have been waived.

[43 FR 11699, Mar. 21, 1978, as amended at 49 FR 5613, Feb. 14, 1984; 61 FR 14247, Apr. 1, 1996]

§ 184.1635 Potassium iodate.

(a) Potassium iodate (KIO_3, CAS Reg. No. 7758–05–6) does not occur naturally but can be prepared by reacting iodine with potassium hydroxide.

(b) The ingredient meets the specifications of the "Food Chemicals

Codex,'' 3d Ed. (1981), pp. 245–246, which is incorporated by reference. Copies may be obtained from the National Academy Press, 2101 Constitution Ave. NW., Washington, DC 20418, or may be examined at the National Archives and Records Administration (NARA). For information on the availability of this material at NARA, call 202–741–6030, or go to: *http://www.archives.gov/federal_register/code_of_federal_regulations/ibr_locations.html.*

(c) The ingredient is used as a dough strengthener as defined in §170.3(o)(6) of this chapter.

(d) The ingredient is used in the manufacture of bread in accordance with §184.1(b)(2) of this chapter in an amount not to exceed 0.0075 percent based on the weight of the flour.

(e) Prior sanctions for this ingredient different from the uses established in this section do not exist or have been waived.

[43 FR 11699, Mar. 21, 1978, as amended at 49 FR 5613, Feb. 14, 1984]

§ 184.1639 Potassium lactate.

(a) Potassium lactate ($C_3H_5O_3K$, CAS Reg. No. 996–31–6) is the potassium salt of lactic acid. It is a hydroscopic, white, odorless solid and is prepared commercially by the neutralization of lactic acid with potassium hydroxide.

(b) The ingredient must be of a purity suitable for its intended use.

(c) In accordance with §184.1(b)(1), the ingredient is used in food with no limitation other than current good manufacturing practice. This regulation does not authorize its use in infant foods and infant formulas. The affirmation of this ingredient as generally recognized as safe (GRAS) as a direct human food ingredient is based upon the following current good manufacturing practice conditions of use:

(1) The ingredient is used as a flavor enhancer as defined in §170.3(o)(11) of this chapter; a flavoring agent or adjuvant as defined in §170.3(o)(12) of this chapter; a humectant as defined in §170.3(o)(16) of this chapter; and a pH control agent as defined in §170.3(o)(23) of this chapter.

(2) The ingredient is used in food at levels not to exceed current good manufacturing practice.

(d) Prior sanctions for this ingredient different from the uses established in this section do not exist or have been waived.

[52 FR 10886, Apr. 6, 1987, as amended at 73 FR 8608, Feb. 14, 2008]

§ 184.1643 Potassium sulfate.

(a) Potassium sulfate (K_2SO_4, CAS Reg. No. 7778–80–5) occurs naturally and consists of colorless or white crystals or crystalline powder having a bitter, saline taste. It is prepared by the neutralization of sulfuric acid with potassium hydroxide or potassium carbonate.

(b) The ingredient meets the specifications of the "Food Chemicals Codex,'' 3d Ed. (1981), p. 252, which is incorporated by reference. Copies may be obtained from the National Academy Press, 2101 Constitution Ave. NW., Washington, DC 20418, or may be examined at the National Archives and Records Administration (NARA). For information on the availability of this material at NARA, call 202–741–6030, or go to: *http://www.archives.gov/federal_register/code_of_federal_regulations/ibr_locations.html.*

(c) The ingredient is used as a flavoring agent and adjuvant as defined in §170.3(o)(12) of this chapter.

(d) The ingredient is used in food at levels not to exceed good manufacturing practice in accordance with §184.1(b)(1). Current good manufacturing practice results in a maximum level, as served, of 0.015 percent for nonalcoholic beverages as defined in §170.3(n)(3) of this chapter.

(e) Prior sanctions for this ingredient different from the uses established in this section do not exist or have been waived.

[45 FR 6086, Jan. 25, 1980, as amended at 49 FR 5613, Feb. 14, 1984]

§ 184.1655 Propane.

(a) Propane (empirical formula C_3H_8, CAS Reg. No. 74–98–6) is also known as dimethylmethane or propyl hydrid. It is a colorless, odorless, flammable gas at normal temperatures and pressures. It is easily liquefied under pressure at room temperature and is stored and shipped in the liquid state. Propane is obtained from natural gas by fractionation following absorption in oil, adsorption to surface-active agents, or refrigeration.

(b) The ingredient must be of a purity suitable for its intended use.

(c) In accordance with § 184.1(b)(1), the ingredient is used in food with no limitations other than current good manufacturing practice. The affirmation of this ingredient as generally recognized as safe (GRAS) as a direct human food ingredient is based upon the following current good manufacturing practice conditions of use:

(1) The ingredient is used as a propellant, aerating agent, and gas as defined in § 170.3(o)(25) of this chapter.

(2) The ingredient is used in food at levels not to exceed current good manufacturing practice.

(d) Prior sanctions for this ingredient different from the uses established in this section do not exist or have been waived.

[48 FR 57271, Dec. 29, 1983, as amended at 73 FR 8608, Feb. 14, 2008]

§ 184.1660 Propyl gallate.

(a) Propyl gallate is the *n*-propylester of 3,4,5-trihydroxybenzoic acid ($C_{10}H_{12}O_5$). Natural occurrence of propyl gallate has not been reported. It is commercially prepared by esterification of gallic acid with propyl alcohol followed by distillation to remove excess alcohol.

(b) The ingredient meets the specifications of the "Food Chemicals Codex," 3d Ed. (1981), pp. 257–258, which is incorporated by reference. Copies may be obtained from the National Academy Press, 2101 Constitution Ave. NW., Washington, DC 20418, or may be examined at the National Archives and Records Administration (NARA). For information on the availability of this material at NARA, call 202–741–6030, or go to: *http://www.archives.gov/federal_register/code_of_federal_regulations/ibr_locations.html.*

(c) The ingredient is used as an antioxidant as defined in § 170.3(o)(3) of this chapter.

(d) The ingredient is used in food at levels not to exceed good manufacturing practice in accordance with § 184.1(b)(1). Good manufacturing practice results in a maximum total content of antioxidants of 0.02 percent of the fat or oil content, including the essential (volatile) oil content, of the food.

(e) Prior sanctions for this ingredient different from the uses established in this section, or different from that stated in part 181 of this chapter, do not exist or have been waived.

[42 FR 14653, Mar. 15, 1977, as amended at 44 FR 52826, Sept. 11, 1979; 49 FR 5613, Feb. 14, 1984]

§ 184.1666 Propylene glycol.

(a) Propylene glycol ($C_3H_8O_2$, CAS Reg. No. 57–55–6) is known as 1,2-propanediol. It does not occur in nature. Propylene glycol is manufactured by treating propylene with chlorinated water to form the chlorohydrin which is converted to the glycol by treatment with sodium carbonate solution. It is also prepared by heating glyercol with sodium hydroxide.

(b) The ingredient meets the specifications of the Food Chemicals Codex, 3d Ed. (1981), p. 255, which is incorporated by reference. Copies may be obtained from the National Academy Press, 2101 Constitution Ave. NW., Washington, DC 20418. It is also available for inspection at the National Archives and Records Administration (NARA). For information on the availability of this material at NARA, call 202–741–6030, or go to: *http://www.archives.gov/federal_register/code_of_federal_regulations/ibr_locations.html.*

(c) The ingredient is used as an anticaking agent as defined in § 170.3(o)(1) of this chapter; antioxidant as defined in § 170.3(o)(3) of this chapter; dough strengthener as defined in § 170.3(o)(6) of this chapter; emulsifier as defined in § 170.3(o)(8) of this chapter; flavor agent as defined in § 170.3(o)(12) of this chapter; formulation aid as defined in § 170.3(o)(14) of this chapter; humectant as defined in § 170.3(o)(16) of this chapter; processing aid as defined in § 170.3(o)(24) of this chapter; solvent and vehicle as defined in § 170.3(o)(27) of this chapter; stabilizer and thickener as defined in § 170.3(o)(28) of this chapter; surface-active agent as defined in § 170.3(o)(29) of this chapter; and texturizer as defined in § 170.3(o)(32) of this chapter.

(d) The ingredient is used in foods at levels not to exceed current good manufacturing practice in accordance with § 184.1(b)(1). Current good manufacturing practice results in maximum levels, as served, of 5 percent for alcoholic beverages, as defined in § 170.3(n)(2) of this chapter; 24 percent for confections and frostings as defined in § 170.3(n)(9) of this chapter; 2.5 percent for frozen dairy products as defined in § 170.3(n)(20) of this chapter; 97 percent for seasonings and flavorings as defined in § 170.3(n)(26) of this chapter; 5 percent for nuts and nut products as defined in § 170.3(n)(32) of this chapter; and 2.0 percent for all other food categories.

(e) Prior sanctions for this ingredient different from the uses established in this section do not exist or have been waived.

[47 FR 27812, June 25, 1982]

§ 184.1670 Propylparaben.

(a) Propylparaben is the chemical propyl *p*-hydroxybenzoate. It is produced by the *n*-propanol esterification of *p*-hydroxybenzoic acid in the presence of sulfuric acid, with subsequent distillation.

(b) The ingredient meets the specifications of the "Food Chemicals Codex," 3d Ed. (1981), p. 258, which is incorporated by reference. Copies may be obtained from the National Academy Press, 2101 Constitution Ave. NW., Washington, DC 20418, or may be examined at the National Archives and Records Administration (NARA). For information on the availability of this material at NARA, call 202–741–6030, or go to: *http://www.archives.gov/federal_register/code_of_federal_regulations/ibr_locations.html.*

(c) The ingredient is used as an antimicrobial agent as defined in § 170.3(o)(2) of this chapter.

(d) The ingredient is used in food at levels not to exceed good manufacturing practices. Current good manufacturing practice results in a maximum level of 0.1 percent in food.

(e) Prior sanctions for this ingredient different from the uses established in this regulation do not exist or have been waived.

[42 FR 14653, Mar. 15, 1977, as amended at 49 FR 5613, Feb. 14, 1984]

§ 184.1676 Pyridoxine hydrochloride.

(a) Pyridoxine hydrochloride ($C_8H_{11}NO_3 \cdot HCl$, CAS Reg. No. 58–56–0) is the chemical 3-hydroxy-4,5-dihydroxymethy-2-methylpyridine hydrochloride that is prepared by chemical synthesis.

(b) The ingredient meets the specifications of the Food Chemicals Codex, 3d Ed. (1981), p. 260, which is incorporated by reference. Copies are available from the National Academy Press, 2101 Constitution Ave. NW., Washington, DC 20418, or available for inspection at the National Archives and Records Administration (NARA). For information on the availability of this material at NARA, call 202–741–6030, or go to: *http://www.archives.gov/federal_register/code_of_federal_regulations/ibr_locations.html.*

(c) In accordance with § 184.1(b)(1), the ingredient is used in food with no limitation other than current good manufacturing practice. The affirmation of this ingredient as generally recognized as safe (GRAS) as a direct human food ingredient is based upon the following current good manufacturing practice conditions of use:

(1) The ingredient is used as a nutrient supplement as defined in § 170.3(o)(20) of this chapter.

(2) The ingredient is used in the following foods at levels not to exceed current good manufacturing practice: baked goods as defined in § 170.3(n)(1) of this chapter; nonalcoholic beverages and beverage bases as defined in § 170.3(n)(3) of this chapter; breakfast cereals as defined in § 170.3(n)(4) of this chapter; dairy product analogs as defined in § 170.3(n)(10) of this chapter; meat products as defined in § 170.3(n)(29) of this chapter; milk products as defined in § 170.3(n)(31) of this chapter; plant protein products as defined in § 170.3(n)(33) of this chapter; and snack foods as defined in § 170.3(n)(37) of this chapter. Pyridoxine hydrochloride may be used in infant formula in accordance with section 412(g) of the Federal Food, Drug, and

Cosmetic Act (the Act) or with regulations promulgated under section 412(a)(2) of the Act.

(d) Prior sanctions for this ingredient different from the uses established in this section do not exist or have been waived.

[48 FR 51615, Nov. 10, 1983]

§ 184.1685 Rennet (animal-derived) and chymosin preparation (fermentation-derived).

(a)(1) Rennet and bovine rennet are commercial extracts containing the active enzyme rennin (CAS Reg. No. 9001–98–3), also known as chymosin (International Union of Biochemistry Enzyme Commission (E.C.) 3.4.23.4). Rennet is the aqueous extract prepared from cleaned, frozen, salted, or dried fourth stomachs (abomasa) of calves, kids, or lambs. Bovine rennet is the product from adults of the animals listed above. Both products are called rennet and are clear amber to dark brown liquid preparations or white to tan powders.

(2) Chymosin preparation is a clear solution containing the active enzyme chymosin (E.C. 3.4.23.4). It is derived, via fermentation, from a nonpathogenic and nontoxigenic strain of *Escherichia coli* K–12 containing the prochymosin gene. The prochymosin is isolated as an insoluble aggregate that is acid-treated to destroy residual cellular material and, after solubilization, is acid-treated to form chymosin. It must be processed with materials that are generally recognized as safe, or are food additives that have been approved by the Food and Drug Administration for this use.

(3) Chymosin preparation is a clear solution containing the active enzyme chymosin (E.C. 3.4.23.4). It is derived, via fermentation, from a nonpathogenic and nontoxigenic strain of *Kluyveromyces marxianus* variety *lactis*, containing the prochymosin gene. The prochymosin is secreted by cells into fermentation broth and converted to chymosin by acid treatment. All materials used in the processing and formulating of chymosin must be either generally recognized as safe (GRAS), or be food additives that have been approved by the Food and Drug Administration for this use.

(4) Chymosin preparation is a clear solution containing the active enzyme chymosin (E.C. 3.4.23.4). It is derived, via fermentation, from a nonpathogenic and nontoxigenic strain of *Aspergillus niger* van Tieghem variety *awamori* (Nakazawa) Al-Musallam (synonym *A. awamori* Nakazawa) containing the prochymosin gene. Chymosin is recovered from the fermentation broth after acid treatment. All materials used in the processing and formulating of chymosin preparation must be either generally recognized as safe (GRAS) or be food additives that have been approved by the Food and Drug Administration for this use.

(b) Rennet and chymosin preparation meet the general and additional requirements for enzyme preparations of the "Food Chemicals Codex," 3d Ed. (1981), pp. 107–110, which is incorporated by reference in accordance with 5 U.S.C. 552(a). Copies are available from the National Academy Press, 2101 Constitution Avenue NW., Washington, DC 20418, or are available for inspection at the National Archives and Records Administration (NARA). For information on the availability of this material at NARA, call 202–741–6030, or go to: *http://www.archives.gov/federal_register/code_of_federal_regulations/ibr_locations.html.*

(c) In accordance with § 184.1(b)(1), the ingredient is used in food with no limitation other than current good manufacturing practice. The affirmation of this ingredient as generally recognized as safe as a direct human food ingredient is based upon the following current good manufacturing practice conditions of use:

(1) The ingredient is used as an enzyme as defined in § 170.3(o)(9) of this chapter; a processing aid as defined in § 170.3(o)(24) of this chapter; and a stabilizer and thickener as defined in § 170.3(o)(28) of this chapter.

(2) The ingredient is used in the following foods at levels not to exceed current good manufacturing practice: In cheeses as defined in § 170.3(n)(5) of this chapter; frozen dairy desserts and mixes as defined in § 170.3(n)(20) of this chapter; gelatins, puddings, and fillings

as defined in § 170.3(n)(22) of this chapter; and milk products as defined in § 170.3(n)(31) of this chapter.

(d) Prior sanctions for this ingredient different from the uses established in this section do not exist or have been waived.

[55 FR 10935, Mar. 23, 1990, as amended at 57 FR 6479, Feb. 25, 1992; 58 FR 27202, May 7, 1993]

§ 184.1695 Riboflavin.

(a) Riboflavin ($C_{17}H_{20}N_4O_6$, CAS Reg. No. 83–88–5) occurs as yellow to orange-yellow needles that are crystallized from 2*N* acetic acid, alcohol, water, or pyridine. It may be prepared by chemical synthesis, biosynthetically by the organism *Eremothecium ashbyii*, or isolated from natural sources.

(b) The ingredient meets the specifications of the Food Chemicals Codex, 3d Ed. (1981), p. 262, which is incorporated by reference. Copies are available from the National Academy Press, 2101 Constitution Ave. NW., Washington, DC 20418, or available for inspection at the National Archives and Records Administration (NARA). For information on the availability of this material at NARA, call 202–741–6030, or go to: *http://www.archives.gov/federal_register/code_of_federal_regulations/ibr_locations.html.*

(c) In accordance with § 184.1(b)(1), the ingredient is used in food with no limitation other than current good manufacturing practice. The affirmation of this ingredient as generally recognized as safe (GRAS) as a direct human food ingredient is based upon the following current good manufacturing practice conditions of use:

(1) The ingredient is used as a nutrient supplement as defined in § 170.3(o)(20) of this chapter.

(2) The ingredient is used in foods at levels not to exceed current good manufacturing practice. The ingredient may also be used in infant formula in accordance with section 412(g) of the Federal Food, Drug, and Cosmetic Act (the Act) or with regulations promulgated under section 412(a)(2) of the Act.

(d) Prior sanctions for this ingredient different from the uses established in this section do not exist or have been waived.

[48 FR 51148, Nov. 7, 1983]

§ 184.1697 Riboflavin–5′-phosphate (sodium).

(a) Riboflavin-5′-phosphate (sodium) ($C_{17}H_{20}N_4O_9PNa \cdot 2H_2O$, CAS Reg. No 130–40–5) occurs as the dihydrate in yellow to orange-yellow crystals. It is prepared by phosphorylation of riboflavin with chlorophosphoric acid, pyrophosphoric acid, metaphosphoric acid, or pyrocatechol cyclic phosphate.

(b) The ingredient meets the specifications of the Food Chemicals Codex, 3d Ed. (1981), p. 263, which is incorporated by reference. Copies are available from the National Academy Press, 2101 Constitution Ave. NW., Washington DC 20418, or available for inspection at the National Archives and Records Administration (NARA). For information on the availability of this material at NARA, call 202–741–6030, or go to: *http://www.archives.gov/federal_register/code_of_federal_regulations/ibr_locations.html.*

(c) In accordance with § 184.1(b)(1), the ingredient is used in food with no limitation other than current good manufacturing practice. The affirmation of this ingredient as generally recognized as safe (GRAS) as a direct human food ingredient is based upon the following current good manufacturing practice conditions of use:

(1) The ingredient is used as a nutrient supplement as defined in § 170.3(o)(20) of this chapter.

(2) The ingredient is used in milk products, as defined in § 170.3(n)(31) of this chapter, at levels not to exceed current good manufacturing practice. The ingredient may also be used in infant formulas in accordance with section 412(g) of the Federal Food, Drug, and Cosmetic Act (the Act) or with regulations promulgated under section 412(a)(2) of the Act.

(d) Prior sanctions for this ingredient different from the uses established in this section do not exist or have been waived.

[48 FR 51148, Nov. 7, 1983]

§ 184.1698 Rue.

(a) Rue is the perennial herb of several species of *Ruta* (*Ruta montana* L., *Ruta graveolens* L., *Ruta bracteosa* L., and *Ruta calepensis* L.). The leaves, buds, and stems from the top of the plant are gathered, dried, and then crushed in preparation for use, or left whole.

(b) The ingredient is used in all categories of food in accordance with § 184.1(b)(2) of this chapter at concentrations not to exceed 2 parts per million.

(c) Prior sanctions for this ingredient different from the uses established in this section do not exist or have been waived.

[43 FR 3705, Jan. 27, 1978]

§ 184.1699 Oil of rue.

(a) Oil of rue is the natural substance obtained by steam distillation of the fresh blossoming plants of rue, the perennial herb of several species of *Ruta*—*Ruta montana* L., *Ruta graveolens* L., *Ruta bracteosa* L., and *Ruta calepensis* L.

(b) Oil of rue meets the specifications of the "Food Chemicals Codex," 4th ed. (1996), pp. 342–343, which is incorporated by reference in accordance with 5 U.S.C. 552(a) and 1 CFR part 51. Copies are available from the National Academy Press, Box 285, 2101 Constitution Ave. NW., Washington, DC 20055 (Internet address *http://www.nap.edu*), or may be examined at the Center for Food Safety and Applied Nutrition's Library, Food and Drug Administration, 5100 Paint Branch Pkwy., College Park, MD 20740, or at the National Archives and Records Administration (NARA). For information on the availability of this material at NARA, call 202–741–6030, or go to: *http://www.archives.gov/federal_register/code_of_federal_regulations/ibr_locations.html.*

(c) The ingredient is used in food under the following conditions:

MAXIMUM USAGE LEVELS PERMITTED

Food (as served)	Parts per million	Function
Baked goods and baking mixes, § 170.3(n)(1), of this chapter.	10	Flavoring agent and adjuvant, § 170.3(o)(12) of this chapter.
Frozen dairy desserts and mixes, § 170.3 (n)(20) of this chapter.	10	Do.
Soft candy, § 170.3(n)(38) of this chapter	10	Do.
All other food categories	4	Do.

(d) Prior sanctions for this ingredient different from the uses established in this section do not exist or have been waived.

[42 FR 14653, Mar. 15, 1977, as amended at 49 FR 5613, Feb. 14, 1984; 64 FR 1760, Jan. 12, 1999]

§ 184.1702 Sheanut oil.

(a) Sheanut oil is produced from sheanuts derived from the Shea tree *Butyrospermum parkii* and is composed principally of triglycerides containing an oleic acid moiety at the 2-position and saturated fatty acids, usually stearic or palmitic acids, at the 1- and 3-positions.

(b) The ingredient meets the following specifications when tested using any appropriate validated methodology:

(1) Saponification value of 185 to 195,

(2) Iodine value of 28 to 43,

(3) Unsaponifiable matter not to exceed 1.5 percent,

(4) Free fatty acids not more than 0.1 percent as oleic acid,

(5) Peroxide value not more than 10 milliequivalents/equivalent (meq/eq),

(6) Lead not more than 0.1 part per million (ppm),

(7) Copper not more than 0.1 ppm.

(c) In accordance with § 184.1(b)(3), the ingredient is used in the following food categories at levels not to exceed current good manufacturing practice, except that the ingredient may not be used in a standardized food unless permitted by the standard of identity: Confections and frostings as defined in § 170.3(n)(9) of this chapter, coatings of soft candy as defined in § 170.3(n)(38) of this chapter, and sweet sauces and toppings as defined in §170.3(n)(43) of this chapter.

[63 FR 28895, May 27, 1998]

§ 184.1721 Sodium acetate.

(a) Sodium acetate ($C_2H_3O_2Na$, CAS Reg. No. 127–09–3 or $C_2H_3O_2Na{\cdot}3H_2O$, CAS Reg. No. 6131–90–4) is the sodium salt of acetic acid and occurs naturally in plant and animal tissues. Sodium acetate may occur in either the anhydrous or trihydrated form. It is produced synthetically by the neutralization of acetic acid with sodium carbonate or by treating calcium acetate with sodium sulfate and sodium bicarbonate.

(b) The ingredient meets the specifications of the Food Chemicals Codex, 3d Ed. (1981), pp. 272, 273 which is incorporated by reference. Copies are available from the National Academy Press, 2101 Constitution Ave. NW., Washington, DC 20418, or available for inspection at the National Archives and Records Administration (NARA). For information on the availability of this material at NARA, call 202–741–6030, or go to: *http://www.archives.gov/federal_register/code_of_federal_regulations/ibr_locations.html.*

(c) The ingredient is used as a flavoring agent and adjuvant as defined in §170.3(o)(12) of this chapter; and as a pH control agent as defined in §170.3(o)(23) of this chapter.

(d) The ingredient is used in food at levels not to exceed current good manufacturing practice in accordance with 184.1(b)(1). Current good manufacturing practice results in a maximum level, as served, of 0.007 percent for breakfast cereals as defined in §170.3(n)(4) of this chapter; 0.5 percent for fats and oils as defined in §170.3(n)(12) of this chapter; 0.6 percent for grain products and pastas as defined in §170.3(n)(23) of this chapter and snack foods as defined in §170.3(n)(37) of this chapter; 0.15 percent for hard candy as defined in §170.3(n)(25) of this chapter; 0.12 percent for jams and jellies as defined in §170.3(n)(28) of this chapter and meat products as defined in §170.3(n)(29) of this chapter; 0.2 percent for soft candy as defined in §170.3(n)(38) of this chapter; 0.05 percent for soups and soup mixes as defined in §170.3(n)(40) of this chapter and sweet sauces as defined in §170.3(n)(43) of this chapter.

(e) Prior sanctions for this ingredient different from the uses established in this section do not exist or have been waived.

[47 FR 27815, June 25, 1982]

§ 184.1724 Sodium alginate.

(a) Sodium alginate (CAS Reg. No. 9005–38–3) is the sodium salt of alginic acid, a natural polyuronide constituent of certain brown algae. Sodium alginate is prepared by the neutralization of purified alginic acid with appropriate pH control agents.

(b) The ingredient meets the specifications of the Food Chemicals Codex, 3d Ed. (1981), p. 274, which is incorporated by reference. Copies are available from the National Academy Press, 2101 Constitution Ave. NW., Washington, DC 20418, or available for inspection at the National Archives and Records Administration (NARA). For information on the availability of this material at NARA, call 202–741–6030, or go to: *http://www.archives.gov/federal_register/code_of_federal_regulations/ibr_locations.html.*

(c) In accordance with §184.1(b)(2), the ingredient is used in food only within the following specific limitations:

Category of food	Maximum level of use in food (as served) (percent)	Functional use
Condiments and relishes, §170.3(n)(8) of this chapter, except pimento ribbon for stuffed olives.	1.0	Texturizer, §170.3(o)(32) of this chapter, formulation aid §170.3(o)(14) of this chapter, stabilizer, thickener, §170.3(o)(28) of this chapter.
Pimento ribbon for stuffed olives	6.0	Do.
Confections and frostings, §170.3(n)(9) of this chapter	0.3	Stabilizer, thickener, §170.3(o)(28) of this chapter.

Category of food	Maximum level of use in food (as served) (percent)	Functional use
Gelatins and puddings, § 170.3(n)(22) of this chapter	4.0	Firming agent, § 170.3(o)(10) of this chapter; flavor adjuvant, § 170.3(o)(12) of this chapter; stabilizer, thickener, § 170.3(o)(28) of this chapter.
Hard candy, § 170.3(n)(25) of this chapter	10.0	Stabilizer, thickener, § 170.3(o)(28) of this chapter.
Processed fruits and fruit juices, § 170.3(n)(35) of this chapter.	2.0	Formulation aid, § 170.3(o)(14) of this chapter; texturizer, § 170.3(o)(32) of this chapter.
All other food categories	1.0	Emulsifier, § 170.3(o)(8) of this chapter; firming agent, § 170.3(o)(10) of this chapter; flavor enhancer, § 170.3(o)(11) of this chapter; flavor adjuvant, § 170.3(o)(12) of this chapter; processing aid, § 170.3(o)(24) of this chapter; stabilizer and thickener, § 170.3(o)(28) of this chapter; surface active agent, § 170.3(o)(29) of this chapter.

(d) Prior sanctions for sodium alginate different from the uses established in this section do not exist or have been waived.

[47 FR 29951, July 9, 1982, as amended at 48 FR 52448, Nov. 18, 1983]

§ 184.1733 Sodium benzoate.

(a) Sodium benzoate is the chemical benzoate of soda ($C_7H_5NaO_2$), produced by the neutralization of benzoic acid with sodium bicarbonate, sodium carbonate, or sodium hydroxide. The salt is not found to occur naturally.

(b) The ingredient meets the specifications of the "Food Chemicals Codex," 3d Ed. (1981), p. 278, which is incorporated by reference. Copies may be obtained from the National Academy Press, 2101 Constitution Ave. NW., Washington, DC 20418, or may be examined at the National Archives and Records Administration (NARA). For information on the availability of this material at NARA, call 202–741–6030, or go to: *http://www.archives.gov/federal_register/code_of_federal_regulations/ibr_locations.html.*

(c) The ingredient is used as an antimicrobial agent as defined in §170.3(o)(2) of this chapter, and as a flavoring agent and adjuvant as defined in §170.3(o)(12) of this chapter.

(d) The ingredient is used in food at levels not to exceed good manufacturing practice. Current usage results in a maximum level of 0.1 percent in food. (The Food and Drug Administration has not determined whether significally different conditions of use would be GRAS.)

(e) Prior sanctions for this ingredient different from the uses established in this section, or different from that set forth in part 181 of this chapter, do not exist or have been waived.

[42 FR 14653, Mar. 15, 1977, as amended at 49 FR 5613, Feb. 14, 1984]

§ 184.1736 Sodium bicarbonate.

(a) Sodium bicarbonate ($NaHCO_3$, CAS Reg. No. 144–55–8) is prepared by treating a sodium carbonate or a sodium carbonate and sodium bicarbonate solution with carbon dioxide. As carbon dioxide is absorbed, a suspension of sodium bicarbonate forms. The slurry is filtered, forming a cake which is washed and dried.

(b) The ingredient meets the specifications of the Food Chemicals Codex, 3d Ed. (1981), p. 278, which is incorporated by reference. Copies are available from the National Academy Press, 2101 Constitution Ave. NW., Washington, DC 20418, or available for inspection at the National Archives and Records Administration (NARA). For information on the availability of this material at NARA, call 202–741–6030, or go to: *http://www.archives.gov/federal_register/code_of_federal_regulations/ibr_locations.html.*

(c) In accordance with §184.1(b)(1), the ingredient is used in food with no limitation other than current good manufacturing practice.

(d) Prior sanctions for this ingredient different from the uses established in

this section do not exist or have been waived.

[48 FR 52442, Nov. 18, 1983]

§ 184.1742 Sodium carbonate.

(a) Sodium carbonate (Na_2CO_3, CAS Reg. No. 497–19–8) is produced (1) from purified trona ore that has been calcined to soda ash; (2) from trona ore calcined to impure soda ash and then purified; or (3) synthesized from limestone by the Solvay process.

(b) The ingredient meets the specifications of the Food Chemicals Codex, 3d Ed. (1981), p. 280, which is incorporated by reference. Copies are available from the National Academy Press, 2101 Constitution Ave. NW., Washington, DC 20418, or available for inspection at the National Archives and Records Administration (NARA). For information on the availability of this material at NARA, call 202–741–6030, or go to: *http://www.archives.gov/federal_register/code_of_federal_regulations/ibr_locations.html.*

(c) In accordance with § 184.1(b)(1), the ingredient is used in food with no limitation other than current good manufacturing practice. The affirmation of this ingredient as generally recognized as safe (GRAS) as a direct human food ingredient is based upon the following current good manufacturing practice conditions of use:

(1) The ingredient is used in food as an antioxidant as defined in § 170.3(o)(3) of this chapter; curing and pickling agent as defined in § 170.3(o)(5) of this chapter; flavoring agent and adjuvant as defined in § 170.3(o)(12) of this chapter; pH control agent as defined in § 170.3(o)(23) of this chapter; and processing aid as defined in § 170.3(o)(24) of this chapter.

(2) The ingredient is used in food at levels not to exceed current good manufacturing practice.

(d) Prior sanctions for this ingredient different from the uses established in this section do not exist or have been waived.

[48 FR 52442, Nov. 18, 1983, as amended at 50 FR 49536, Dec. 3, 1985]

§ 184.1751 Sodium citrate.

(a) Sodium citrate ($C_6H_5Na_3O_7{\cdot}2H_2O$, CAS Reg. No. 68–0904–092) is the sodium salt of citric acid. It is prepared by neutralizing citric acid with sodium hydroxide or sodium carbonate. The product occurs as colorless crystals or a white crystalline powder. It may be prepared in an anhydrous state or may contain two moles of water per mole of sodium citrate.

(b) The ingredient meets the specifications of the Food Chemicals Codex, 3d ed. (1981), pp. 283–284, which is incorporated by reference in accordance with 5 U.S.C. 552(a) and 1 CFR part 51. Copies are available from the National Academy Press, 2101 Constitution Ave. NW., Washington, DC 20418, and the Center for Food Safety and Applied Nutrition (HFS–200), 5100 Paint Branch Pkwy., College Park, MD 20740, or may be examined at the National Archives and Records Administration (NARA). For information on the availability of this material at NARA, call 202–741–6030, or go to: *http://www.archives.gov/federal_register/code_of_federal_regulations/ibr_locations.html.*

(c) In accordance with § 184.1(b)(1), the ingredient is used in food with no limitation other than current good manufacturing practice.

(d) Prior sanctions for this ingredient different from the uses established in this section, or different from those set forth in part 181 of this chapter, do not exist or have been waived.

[59 FR 63896, Dec. 12, 1994]

§ 184.1754 Sodium diacetate.

(a) Sodium diacetate ($C_4H_7O_4Na{\cdot}xH_2O$, CAS Reg. No. 126–96–5) is a molecular compound of acetic acid, sodium acetate, and water of hydration. The technical grade is prepared synthetically by reacting sodium carbonate with acetic acid. Special grades are produced by reacting anhydrous sodium acetate and acetic acid.

(b) The ingredient meets the specifications of the Food Chemicals Codex, 3d Ed. (1981), p. 284, which is incorporated by reference. Copies are available from the National Academy Press,

2101 Constitution Ave. NW., Washington, DC 20418, or available for inspection at the National Archives and Records Administration (NARA). For information on the availability of this material at NARA, call 202–741–6030, or go to: *http://www.archives.gov/federal_register/code_of_federal_regulations/ibr_locations.html.*

(c) The ingredient is used as an antimicrobial agent as defined in §170.3(o)(2) of this chapter; flavoring agent and adjuvant as defined in §170.3(o)(12) of this chapter; and pH control agent as defined in §170.3(o)(23) of this chapter.

(d) The ingredient is used in food at levels not to exceed current good manufacturing practice in accordance with §184.1(b)(1). Current good manufacturing practice results in a maximum level, as served, 0.4 percent for baked goods as defined in §170.3(n)(1) of this chapter; 0.1 percent for fats and oils as defined in §170.3(n)(12) of this chapter, meat products as defined in §170.3(n)(29) of this chapter and soft candy as defined in §170.3(n)(38) of this chapter; 0.25 percent for gravies and sauces as defined in §170.3(n)(24) of this chapter; and 0.05 percent for snack foods as defined in §170.3(n)(37) of this chapter and soups and soup mixes as defined in §170.3(n)(40) of this chapter.

(e) Prior sanctions for this ingredient different from the uses established in this section do not exist or have been waived.

[47 FR 27815, June 25, 1982]

§ 184.1763 Sodium hydroxide.

(a) Sodium hydroxide (NaOH, CAS Reg. No. 1310–73–2) is also known as sodium hydrate, soda lye, caustic soda, white caustic, and lye. The empirical formula is NaOH. Sodium hydroxide is prepared commercially by the electrolysis of sodium chloride solution and also by reacting calcium hydroxide with sodium carbonate.

(b) The ingredient meets the specifications of the Food Chemicals Codex, 3d Ed. (1981), which is incorporated by reference. Copies are available from the National Academy Press, 2101 Constitution Ave. NW., Washington, DC 20418, or available for inspection at the National Archives and Records Administration (NARA). For information on the availability of this material at NARA, call 202–741–6030, or go to: *http://www.archives.gov/federal_register/code_of_federal_regulations/ibr_locations.html.*

(c) In accordance with §184.1(b)(1), the ingredient is used in food with no limitation other than current good manufacturing practice. The affirmation of this ingredient as generally recognized as safe (GRAS) as a direct human food ingredient is based upon the following current good manufacturing practice conditions of use:

(1) The ingredient is used as a pH control agent as defined in §170.3(o)(23) of this chapter and as a processing aid as defined in §170.3(o)(24) of this chapter.

(2) The ingredient is used in foods at levels not to exceed current good manufacturing practice.

(d) Prior sanctions for this ingredient different from the uses established in this section do not exist or have been waived.

[48 FR 52444, Nov. 18, 1983]

§ 184.1764 Sodium hypophosphite.

(a) Sodium hypophosphite (NaH_2PO_2, CAS Reg. No. 7681–53–0) is a white, odorless, deliquescent granular powder with a saline taste. It is also prepared as colorless, pearly crystalline plates. It is soluble in water, alcohol, and glycerol. It is prepared by neutralization of hypophosphorous acid or by direct aqueous alkaline hydrolysis of white phosphorus.

(b) The ingredient must be of a purity suitable for its intended use.

(c) In accordance with §184.1(b)(1), the ingredient is used in food with no limitations other than current good manufacturing practice. The affirmation of this ingredient as generally recognized as safe (GRAS) as a direct human food ingredient is based upon the following current good manufacturing practice conditions of use:

(1) The ingredient is used as an emulsifier or stabilizer, as defined in §§170.3(o)(8) and 170.3(o)(28) of this chapter.

(2) The ingredient is used in cod-liver oil emulsions at levels not to exceed current good manufacturing practice.

(d) Prior sanctions for this ingredient different from the use established in this section do not exist or have been waived.

[47 FR 38277, Aug. 31, 1982, as amended at 73 FR 8608, Feb. 14, 2008]

§ 184.1768 Sodium lactate.

(a) Sodium lactate ($C_3H_5O_3N_a$, CAS Reg. No. 72–17–3) is the sodium salt of lactic acid. It is prepared commercially by the neutralization of lactic acid with sodium hydroxide.

(b) The ingredient must be of a purity suitable for its intended use.

(c) In accordance with § 184.1(b)(1), the ingredient is used in food with no limitation other than current good manufacturing practice. This regulation does not authorize its use in infant foods and infant formulas. The affirmation of this ingredient as generally recognized as safe (GRAS) as a direct human food ingredient is based upon the following current good manufacturing practice conditions of use:

(1) The ingredient is used as an emulsifier as defined in § 170.3(o)(8) of this chapter; a flavor enhancer as defined in § 170.3(o)(11) of this chapter; a flavoring agent or adjuvant as defined in § 170.3(o)(12) of this chapter; a humectant as defined in § 170.3(o)(16) of this chapter; and a pH control agent as defined in § 170.3(o)(23) of this chapter.

(2) The ingredient is used in food at levels not to exceed current good manufacturing practice.

(d) Prior sanctions for this ingredient different from the uses established in this section do not exist or have been waived.

[52 FR 10886, Apr. 6, 1987, as amended at 73 FR 8608, Feb. 14, 2008]

§ 184.1769a Sodium metasilicate.

(a) Sodium metasilicate (CAS Reg. No. 6834–92–0) is a strongly alkaline white powder. It does not occur naturally but rather is synthesized by melting sand with sodium carbonate at 1400 °C. The commercially available forms of sodium metasilicate are the anhydrous form (Na_2SiO_3), the pentahydrate ($Na_2SiO_3 \cdot 5H_2O$), and the nonahydrate ($Na_2SiO_3 \cdot 9H_2O$).

(b) The ingredient must be of a purity suitable for its intended use.

(c) In accordance with § 184.1(b)(1), the ingredient is used in food with no limitation other than current good manufacturing practice. The affirmation of this ingredient as generally recognized as safe (GRAS) as a direct human food ingredient is based upon the following current good manufacturing practice conditions of use:

(1) The ingredient is used as a processing aid as defined in § 170.3(o)(24) of this chapter.

(2) The ingredient is used to treat the following foods at levels not to exceed current good manufacturing practice: for use in washing and lye peeling of fruits, vegetables, and nuts when used in accordance with § 173.315 of this chapter; for use as a denuding agent in tripe; for use as a hog scald agent in removing hair; and for use as a corrosion preventative in canned and bottled water when used in accordance with § 165.110 of this chapter.

(d) Prior sanctions for this ingredient different from the uses established in this section do not exist or have been waived.

[50 FR 38781, Sept. 25, 1985; 50 FR 42011, Oct. 17, 1985, as amended at 72 FR 10357, Mar. 8, 2007; 73 FR 8608, Feb. 14, 2008]

§ 184.1784 Sodium propionate.

(a) Sodium propionate ($C_3H_5NaO_2$, CAS Reg. No. 137–40–6) is the sodium salt of propionic acid. It occurs as colorless, transparent crystals or a granular crystalline powder. It is odorless, or has a faint acetic-butyric acid odor, and is deliquescent. It is prepared by neutralizing propionic acid with sodium hydroxide.

(b) The ingredients meets the specifications of the Food Chemicals Codex, 3d Ed. (1981), p. 296, which is incorporated by reference. Copies are available from the National Academy Press, 2101 Constitution Ave. NW., Washington DC 20418, or available for inspection at the National Archives and Records Administration (NARA). For information on the availability of this material at NARA, call 202–741–6030, or go to: *http://www.archives.gov/federal_register/code_of_federal_regulations/ibr_locations.html.*

(c) In accordance with § 184.1(b)(1), the ingredient is used in food with no limitation other than current good manufacturing practice. The affirmation of this ingredient as generally recognized as safe (GRAS) as a direct human food ingredient is based upon the following current good manufacturing practice conditions of use:

(1) The ingredient is used as an antimicrobial agent as defined in § 170.3(o)(2) of this chapter and a flavoring agent as defined in § 170.3(o)(12) of this chapter.

(2) The ingredient is used in the following foods at levels not to exceed current good manufacturing practice: baked goods as defined in § 170.3(n)(1) of this chapter; nonalcoholic beverages as defined in § 170.3(n)(3) of this chapter; cheeses as defined in § 170.3(n)(5) of this chapter; confections and frostings as defined in § 170.3(n)(9) of this chapter; gelatins, puddings, and fillings as defined in § 170.3(n)(22) of this chapter; jams and jellies as defined in § 170.3(n)(28) of this chapter; meat products as defined in § 170.3(n)(29) of this chapter; and soft candy as defined in § 170.3(n)(38) of this chapter.

(d) Prior sanctions for this ingredient different from the uses established in this section do not exist or have been waived.

[49 FR 13142, Apr. 3, 1984]

§ 184.1792 Sodium sesquicarbonate.

(a) Sodium sesquicarbonate ($Na_2CO_3 \cdot NaHCO_3 \cdot 2H_2O$, CAS Reg. No. 533–96–0) is prepared by: (1) Partial carbonation of soda ash solution followed by crystallization, centrifugation, and drying; (2) double refining of trona ore, a naturally occurring impure sodium sesquicarbonate.

(b) The ingredient meets the specifications of the Food Chemicals Codex, 3d Ed. (1981), p. 299, which is incorporated by reference. Copies are available from the National Academy Press, 2101 Constitution Ave. NW., Washington, DC 20418, or available for inspection at the National Archives and Records Administration (NARA). For information on the availability of this material at NARA, call 202–741–6030, or go to: *http://www.archives.gov/federal_register/code_of_federal_regulations/ibr_locations.html.*

(c) In accordance with § 184.1(b)(1), the ingredient is used in food with no limitation other than current good manufacturing practice. The affirmation of this ingredient as generally recognized as safe (GRAS) as a direct human food ingredient is based upon the following current good manufacturing practice conditions of use:

(1) The ingredient is used as a pH control agent as defined in § 170.3(o)(23) of this chapter.

(2) The ingredient is used in cream at levels not to exceed current good manufacturing practice. Current good manufacturing practice utilizes a level of the ingredient sufficient to control lactic acid prior to pasteurization and churning of cream into butter.

(d) Prior sanctions for this ingredient different from the uses established in this section do not exist or have been waived.

[48 FR 52443, Nov. 18, 1983]

§ 184.1801 Sodium tartrate.

(a) Sodium tartrate ($C_4H_4Na_2O_6 \cdot 2H_2O$, CAS Reg. No. 868–18–8) is the disodium salt of L-(+)-tartaric acid. It occurs as transparent, colorless, and odorless crystals. It is obtained as a byproduct of wine manufacture.

(b) The ingredient meets the specifications of the Food Chemicals Codex, 3d Ed. (1981), p. 303, which is incorporated by reference. Copies are available from the National Academy Press, 2101 Constitution Ave. NW., Washington, DC 20418, or available for inspection at the National Archives and Records Administration (NARA). For information on the availability of this material at NARA, call 202–741–6030, or go to: *http://www.archives.gov/federal_register/code_of_federal_regulations/ibr_locations.html.*

(c) In accordance with § 184.1(b)(1), the ingredient is used in food with no limitation other than current good manufacturing practice. The affirmation of this ingredient as generally recognized as safe (GRAS) as a direct human food ingredient is based upon the following current good manufacturing practice conditions of use:

(1) The ingredient is used as an emulsifier as defined in § 170.3(o)(8) of this

chapter and as a pH control agent as defined in § 170.3(o)(23) of this chapter.

(2) The ingredient is used in the following foods at levels not to exceed current good manufacturing practice: cheeses as defined in§ 170.3(n)(5) of this chapter; fats and oils as defined in § 170.3(n)(12) of this chapter; and jams and jellies as defined in § 170.3(n)(28) of this chapter.

(d) Prior sanctions for this ingredient different from the uses established in this section do not exist or have been waived.

[48 FR 52447, Nov. 18, 1983]

§ 184.1804 Sodium potassium tartrate.

(a) Sodium potassium tartrate ($C_4H_4KNaO_6 \cdot 4H_2O$, CAS Reg. No. 304–59–6) is the sodium potassium salt of L-(+)-tartaric acid and is also called the Rochelle salt. It occurs as colorless crystals or as a white, crystalline powder and has a cooling saline taste. It is obtained as a byproduct of wine manufacture.

(b) The ingredient meets the specifications of the Food Chemicals Codex, 3d Ed. (1981), p. 296, which is incorporated by reference. Copies are available from the National Academy Press, 2101 Constitution Ave. NW., Washington, DC 20418, or available for inspection at the National Archives and Records Administration (NARA). For information on the availability of this material at NARA, call 202–741–6030, or go to: *http://www.archives.gov/federal_register/code_of_federal_regulations/ibr_locations.html.*

(c) In accordance with § 184.1(b)(1), the ingredient is used in food with no limitation other than current good manufacturing practice. The affirmation of this ingredient as generally recognized as safe (GRAS) as a direct human food ingredient is based upon the following current good manufacturing practice conditions of use:

(1) The ingredient is used as an emulsifier as defined in § 170.3(o)(8) of this chapter and as a pH control agent as defined in § 170.3(o)(23) of this chapter.

(2) The ingredient is used in the following foods at levels not to exceed current good manufacturing practice: cheeses as defined in § 170.3(n)(5) of this chapter and jams and jellies as defined in § 170.3(n)(28) of this chapter.

(d) Prior sanctions for this ingredient different from the uses established in this section do not exist or have been waived.

[48 FR 52447, Nov. 18, 1983]

§ 184.1807 Sodium thiosulfate.

(a) Sodium thiosulfate ($Na_2S_2O_3 \cdot 5H_2O$, CAS Reg. No. 010102–0917–097) is also known as sodium hyposulfite. It is prepared synthetically by the reaction of sulfides and sulfur dioxide (SO_2), the reaction of sulfur and sulfite, or the oxidation of metal sulfides and hydrosulfides.

(b) The ingredient meets the specifications of the "Food Chemicals Codex," 3d Ed. (1981), p. 304, which is incorporated by reference. Copies may be obtained from the National Academy Press, 2101 Constitution Ave. NW., Washington, DC 20418, or may be examined at the National Archives and Records Administration (NARA). For information on the availability of this material at NARA, call 202–741–6030, or go to: *http://www.archives.gov/federal_register/code_of_federal_regulations/ibr_locations.html.*

(c) The ingredient is used as a formulation aid as defined in § 170.3(o)(14) of this chapter and reducing agent as defined in § 170.3(o)(22) of this chapter.

(d) The ingredient is used in alcoholic beverages and table salt in accordance with § 184.1(b)(1) at levels not to exceed good manufacturing practice. Current good manufacturing practice results in a maximum level, as served, of 0.00005 percent for alcoholic beverages as defined in § 170.3(n)(2) of this chapter and 0.1 percent for table salt as defined in § 170.3(n)(26) of this chapter.

(e) Prior sanctions for this ingredient different from the uses established in this section do not exist or have been waived.

[43 FR 22938, May 30, 1978, as amended at 49 FR 5613, Feb. 4, 1984]

§ 184.1835 Sorbitol.

(a) Sorbitol is the chemical 1,2,3,4,5,6-hexanehexol ($C_6H_{14}O_6$), a hexahydric alcohol, differing from mannitol principally by having a different optical rotation. Sorbitol is produced by the electrolytic reduction, or the transition metal catalytic hydrogenation of sugar solutions containing glucose or fructose.

(b) The ingredient meets the specifications of the "Food Chemicals Codex," 3d Ed. (1981), p. 308, which is incorporated by reference. Copies may be obtained from the National Academy Press, 2101 Constitution Ave. NW., Washington, DC 20418, or may be examined at the National Archives and Records Administration (NARA). For information on the availability of this material at NARA, call 202–741–6030, or go to: *http://www.archives.gov/federal_register/code_of_federal_regulations/ibr_locations.html.*

(c) The ingredient is used as an anticaking agent and free-flow agent as defined in §170.3(o)(1) of this chapter, curing and pickling agent as defined in §170.3(o)(5) of this chapter, drying agent as defined in §170.3(o)(7) of this chapter, emulsifier and emulsifier salt as defined in §170.3(o)(8) of this chapter, firming agent as defined in §170.3(o)(10) of this chapter, flavoring agent and adjuvant as defined in §170.3(o)(12) of this chapter, formulation aid as defined in §170.3(o)(14) of this chapter, humectant as defined in §170.3(o)(16) of this chapter, lubricant and release agent as defined in §170.3(o)(18) of this chapter, nutritive sweetener as defined in §170.3(o)(21) of this chapter, sequestrant as defined in §170.3(o)(26) of this chapter, stabilizer and thickener as defined in §170.3(o)(28) of this chapter, surface-finishing agent as defined in §170.3(o)(30) of this chapter, and texturizer as defined in §170.3(o)(32) of this chapter.

(d) The ingredient is used in food at levels not to exceed good manufacturing practices. Current good manufacturing practice in the use of sorbitol results in a maximum level of 99 percent in hard candy and cough drops as defined in §170.3(n)(25) of this chapter, 75 percent in chewing gum as defined in §170.3(n)(6) of this chapter, 98 percent in soft candy as defined in §170.3(n)(38) of this chapter, 30 percent in nonstandardized jams and jellies, commercial, as defined in §170.3(n)(28) of this chapter, 30 percent in baked goods and baking mixes as defined in §170.3(n)(1) of this chapter, 17 percent in frozen dairy desserts and mixes as defined in §170.3(n)(20) of this chapter, and 12 percent in all other foods.

(e) The label and labeling of food whose reasonably foreseeable consumption may result in a daily ingestion of 50 grams of sorbitol shall bear the statement: "Excess consumption may have a laxative effect."

(f) Prior sanctions for this ingredient different from the uses established in this regulation do not exist or have been waived.

[42 FR 14653, Mar. 15, 1977, as amended at 49 FR 5613, Feb. 14, 1984]

§ 184.1845 Stannous chloride (anhydrous and dihydrated).

(a) Stannous chloride is anhydrous or contains two molecules of water of hydration. Anhydrous stannous chloride ($SnCl_2$, CAS Reg. No. 7772–99–8) is the chloride salt of metallic tin. It is prepared by reacting molten tin with either chlorine or gaseous tin tetrachloride. Dihydrated stannous chloride ($SnCl_2 \cdot 2H_2O$, CAS Reg. No. 10025–69–1) is the chloride salt of metallic tin that contains two molecules of water. It is prepared from granulated tin suspended in water and hydrochloric acid or chlorine.

(b) Both forms of the ingredient meet the specifications of the Food Chemicals Codex, 3d Ed. (1981), p. 312, which is incorporated by reference. Copies are available from the National Academy Press, 2101 Constitution Ave. NW., Washington, DC 20418, or available for inspection at the National Archives and Records Administration (NARA). For information on the availability of this material at NARA, call 202–741–6030, or go to: *http://www.archives.gov/federal_register/code_of_federal_regulations/ibr_locations.html.*

(c) The ingredient is used as an antioxidant as defined in §170.3(o)(3) of this chapter.

(d) The ingredient is used in food at levels not to exceed current good manufacturing practice in accordance with §184.(b)(1). Current good manufacturing practice results in a maximum level, as served, of 0.0015 percent or less; calculated as tin, for all food categories.

(e) Prior sanctions for this ingredient different from those uses established in this section do not exist or have been waived.

[47 FR 27816, June 25, 1982, as amended at 76 FR 59250, Sept. 26, 2011]

§ 184.1848 Starter distillate.

(a) Starter distillate (butter starter distillate) is a steam distillate of the culture of any or all of the following species of bacteria grown on a medium consisting of skim milk usually fortified with about 0.1 percent citric acid: *Streptococcus lactis, S. cremoris, S. lactis subsp. diacetylactis, Leuconostoc citrovorum*, and *L. dextranicum*. The ingredient contains more than 98 percent water, and the remainder is a mixture of butterlike flavor compounds. Diacetyl is the major flavor component, constituting as much as 80 to 90 percent of the mixture of organic flavor compounds. Besides diacetyl, starter distillate contains minor amounts of acetaldehyde, ethyl formate, ethyl acetate, acetone, ethyl alcohol, 2-butanone, acetic acid, and acetoin.

(b) The ingredient must be of a purity suitable for its intended use.

(c) In accordance with §184.1(b)(1), the ingredient is used in food with no limitation other than current good manufacturing practice. The affirmation of this ingredient as generally recognized as safe (GRAS) as a direct human food ingredient is based upon the following current good manufacturing practice conditions of use:

(1) The ingredient is used as a flavoring agent and adjuvant as defined in §170.3(o)(12) of this chapter.

(2) The ingredient is used in food at levels not to exceed current good manufacturing practice.

(d) Prior sanctions for this ingredient different from the uses established in this section do not exist or have been waived.

[48 FR 51907, Nov. 15, 1983, as amended at 73 FR 8608, Feb. 14, 2008]

§ 184.1851 Stearyl citrate.

(a) Stearyl citrate is a mixture of the mono-, di-, and tristearyl esters of citric acid. It is prepared by esterifying citric acid with stearyl alcohol.

(b) The ingredient must be of a purity suitable for its intended use.

(c) In accordance with §184.1(b)(1), the ingredient is used in food with no limitation other than current good manufacturing practice. The affirmation of this ingredient as generally recognized as safe (GRAS) as a direct human food ingredient is based upon the following current good manufacturing practice conditions of use:

(1) The ingredient is used as an antioxidant as defined in §170.3(o)(3) of this chapter; an emulsifier and emulsifier salt as defined in §170.3(o)(8) of this chapter; a sequestrant as defined in §170.3(o)(26) of this chapter; and a surface-active agent as defined in §170.3(o)(29) of this chapter.

(2) The ingredient is used in margarine in accordance with §166.110 of this chapter; in nonalcoholic beverages as defined in §170.3(n)(3) of this chapter; and in fats and oils as defined in §170.3(n)(12) of this chapter at levels not to exceed current good manufacturing practice.

(d) Prior sanctions for this ingredient different from the uses established in this section, or different from those set forth in part 181 of this chapter, do not exist or have been waived.

[59 FR 63897, Dec. 12, 1994, as amended at 73 FR 8608, Feb. 14, 2008]

§ 184.1854 Sucrose.

(a) Sucrose ($C_{12}H_{22}O_{11}$, CAS Reg. No. 57–50–11–1) sugar, cane sugar, or beet sugar is the chemical β-D-fructofuranosyl-α-D-glucopyranoside. Sucrose is obtained by crystallization from sugar cane or sugar beet juice that has been extracted by pressing or diffusion, then clarified and evaporated.

(b) The ingredient must be of a purity suitable for its intended use.

(c) In accordance with §184.1(b)(1), the ingredient is used in food with no limitation other than current good manufacturing practice.

(d) Prior sanctions for this ingredient different from the uses established in

this section do not exist or have been waived.

[53 FR 44876, Nov. 7, 1988; 54 FR 228, Jan. 4, 1989, as amended at 73 FR 8608, Feb. 14, 2008]

§ 184.1857 Corn sugar.

(a) Corn sugar ($C_6H_{12}O_6$, CAS Reg. No. 50–99–7), commonly called D-glucose or dextrose, is the chemical α-D-glucopyranose. It occurs as the anhydrous or the monohydrate form and is produced by the complete hydrolysis of corn starch with safe and suitable acids or enzymes, followed by refinement and crystallization from the resulting hydrolysate.

(b) The ingredient meets the specifications of the Food Chemicals Codex, 3d Ed. (1981), pp. 97–98 under the heading "Dextrose," which is incorporated by reference in accordance with 5 U.S.C. 552(a) and 1 CFR part 1. Copies are available from the National Academy Press, 2101 Constitution Ave., NW., Washington, DC 20418, or available for inspection at the National Archives and Records Administration (NARA). For information on the availability of this material at NARA, call 202–741–6030, or go to: *http://www.archives.gov/federal_register/code_of_federal_regulations/ibr_locations.html.*

(c) In accordance with § 184.1(b)(1), the ingredient is used in food with no limitation other than current good manufacturing practice.

(d) Prior sanctions for this ingredient different from the uses established in this section do not exist or have been waived.

[53 FR 44876, Nov. 7, 1988]

§ 184.1859 Invert sugar.

(a) Invert sugar (CAS Reg. No. 8013–17–0) is an aqueous solution of inverted or partly inverted, refined or partly refined sucrose, the solids of which contain not more than 0.3 percent by weight of ash. The solution is colorless, odorless, and flavorless, except for sweetness. It is produced by the hydrolysis or partial hydrolysis of sucrose with safe and suitable acids or enzymes.

(b) The ingredient must be of a purity suitable for its intended use.

(c) In accordance with § 184.1(b)(1), the ingredient is used in food with no limitation other than current good manufacturing practice.

(d) Prior sanctions for this ingredient different from the uses established in this section do not exist or have been waived.

[53 FR 44876, Nov. 7, 1988; 54 FR 228, Jan. 4, 1989, as amended at 73 FR 8608, Feb. 14, 2008]

§ 184.1865 Corn syrup.

(a) Corn syrup, commonly called "glucose sirup" or "glucose syrup," is obtained by partial hydrolysis of corn starch with safe and suitable acids or enzymes. It may also occur in the dehydrated form (dried glucose sirup). Depending on the degree of hydrolysis, corn syrup may contain, in addition to glucose, maltose and higher saccharides.

(b) The ingredient meets the specifications as defined and determined in § 168.120(b) or § 168.121(a) of this chapter, as appropriate.

(c) In accordance with § 184.1(b)(1), the ingredient is used in food with no limitation other than current good manufacturing practice.

(d) Prior sanctions for this ingredient different from the uses established in this section do not exist or have been waived.

[53 FR 44876, Nov. 7, 1988, as amended at 73 FR 8608, Feb. 14, 2008]

§ 184.1866 High fructose corn syrup.

(a) High fructose corn syrup, a sweet, nutritive saccharide mixture containing either approximately 42 or 55 percent fructose, is prepared as a clear aqueous solution from high dextrose-equivalent corn starch hydrolysate by partial enzymatic conversion of glucose (dextrose) to fructose using an insoluble glucose isomerase enzyme preparation described in § 184.1372. The product containing more than 50 percent fructose (dry weight) is prepared through concentration of the fructose portion of the mixture containing less than 50 percent fructose.

(b) The ingredient shall conform to the identity and specifications listed in the monograph entitled "High-Fructose Corn Syrup" in the Food Chemicals Codex, 4th ed. (1996), pp. 191–192, which is incorporated by reference in accordance with 5 U.S.C. 552(a) and 1 CFR part 51. Copies are available from the Office of Food Additive Safety (HFS–200), Center for Food Safety and Applied Nutrition, Food and Drug Administration, 5100 Paint Branch Pkwy., College Park, MD 20740, 240–402–1200, or may be examined at the Center for Food Safety and Applied Nutrition's Library, 5100 Paint Branch Pkwy., College Park, MD 20740, or at the National Archives and Records Administration (NARA). For information on the availability of this material at NARA, call 202–741–6030, or go to: *http://www.archives.gov/federal_register/code_of_federal_regulations/ibr_locations.html.*

(c) In accordance with §184.1(b)(1), the ingredient is used in food with no limitation other than current good manufacturing practice.

[61 FR 43450, Aug. 23, 1996, as amended at 78 FR 14667, Mar. 7, 2013]

§ 184.1875 Thiamine hydrochloride.

(a) Thiamine hydrochloride ($C_{12}H_{17}ClN_4OS{\cdot}HCl$, CAS Reg. No. 67–03–8) is the chloride-hydrochloride salt of thiamine. It occurs as hygroscopic white crystals or a white crystalline powder. The usual method of preparing this substance is by linking the preformed thiazole and pyrimidine ring systems.

(b) The ingredient meets the specifications of the Food Chemicals Codex, 3d Ed. (1981), p. 324, which is incorporated by reference. Copies are available from the National Academy Press, 2101 Constitution Ave. NW., Washington, DC 20418, or available for inspection at the National Archives and Records Administration (NARA). For information on the availability of this material at NARA, call 202–741–6030, or go to: *http://www.archives.gov/federal_register/code_of_federal_regulations/ibr_locations.html.*

(c) In accordance with §184.1(b)(1), the ingredient is used in food with no limitation other than current good manufacturing practice. The affirmation of this ingredient as generally recognized as safe (GRAS) as a direct human food ingredient is based upon the following current good manufacturing practice conditions of use:

(1) The ingredient is used as a flavoring agent and adjuvant as defined in §170.3(o)(12) of this chapter or as a nutrient supplement as defined in §170.3(o)(20) of this chapter.

(2) The ingredient is used in food at levels not to exceed current good manufacturing practice. Thiamine hydrochloride may be used in infant formula in accordance with section 412(g) of the Federal Food, Drug, and Cosmetic Act (the Act) or with regulations promulgated under section 412(a)(2) of the Act.

(d) Prior sanctions for this ingredient different from the uses established in this section do not exist or have been waived.

[48 FR 55124, Dec. 9, 1983]

§ 184.1878 Thiamine mononitrate.

(a) Thiamine mononitrate ($C_{12}H_{17}N_5O_4S$, CAS Reg. No. 532–43–4) is the mononitrate salt of thiamine. It occurs as white crystals or a white crystalline powder and is prepared from thiamine hydrochloride by dissolving the hydrochloride salt in alkaline solution followed by precipitation of the nitrate half-salt with a stoichiometric amount of nitric acid.

(b) The ingredient meets the specifications of the Food Chemicals Codex, 3d Ed. (1981), p. 325, which is incorporated by reference. Copies are available from the National Academy Press, 2101 Constitution Ave. NW., Washington, DC 20418, or available for inspection at the National Archives and Records Administration (NARA). For information on the availability of this material at NARA, call 202–741–6030, or go to: *http://www.archives.gov/federal_register/code_of_federal_regulations/ibr_locations.html.*

(c) In accordance with §184.1(b)(1), the ingredient is used in food with no limitation other than current good manufacturing practice. The affirmation of this ingredient as generally recognized as safe (GRAS) as a direct human food ingredient is based upon the following current good manufacturing practice conditions of use:

(1) The ingredient is used as a nutrient supplement as defined in §170.3(o)(20) of this chapter.

(2) The ingredient is used in food at levels not to exceed current good manufacturing practice. Thiamine mononitrate may be used in infant formula in accordance with section 412(g) of the Federal Food, Drug, and Cosmetic Act (the Act) or with regulations promulgated under section 412(a)(2) of the Act.

(d) Prior sanctions for this ingredient different from the uses established in this section do not exist or have been waived.

[48 FR 55124, Dec. 9, 1983]

§ 184.1890 α-Tocopherols.

(a) The α-tocopherols that are the subject of this GRAS affirmation regulation are limited to the following:

(1) *d*-α-Tocopherol (CAS Reg. No. 59–02–9) is the chemical [2R,4′R,8prime;R]-2,5,7,8-tetramethyl-2-(4′,8′,12′-trimethyltridecyl)-6-chromanol. It occurs commercially as a concentrate and is a red, nearly odorless, viscous oil. It is obtained by vacuum steam distillation of edible vegetable oil products.

(2) *dl*-α-Tocopherol (CAS Reg. No. 10191–41–0) is a mixture of stereoisomers of 2,5,7,8-tetramethyl-2-(4′,8′,12′-trimethyl-tridecyl)-6-chromanol. It is chemically synthesized by condensing racemic isophytol with trimethyl hydroquinone. It is a pale yellow viscous oil at room temperature.

(b) The ingredients meet the specifications of the Food Chemicals Codex, 3d Ed. (1981), pp. 330–331, which is incorporated by reference. Copies are available from the National Academy Press, 2101 Constitution Ave. NW., Washington, DC 20418, or available for inspection at the National Archives and Records Administration (NARA). For information on the availability of this material at NARA, call 202–741–6030, or go to: *http://www.archives.gov/federal_register/code_of_federal_regulations/ibr_locations.html.*

(c) In accordance with § 184.1(b)(3), the affirmation of the ingredients as generally recognized as safe is limited to the following conditions of use while the agency concludes the general evaluation of all food uses of tocopherols:

(1) The ingredients are used as inhibitors of nitrosamine formation.

(2) The ingredients are used in pump-cured bacon at levels not to exceed current good manufacturing practice.

[49 FR 13348, Apr. 4, 1984]

§ 184.1901 Triacetin.

(a) Triacetin ($C_8 H_{14}O_6$, CAS Reg. No. 102–76–1), also known as 1,2,3,-propanetriol triacetate or glyceryl triacetate, is the triester of glycerin and acetic acid. Triacetin can be prepared by heating glycerin with acetic anhydride alone or in the presence of finely divided potassium hydrogen sulfate. It can also be prepared by the reaction of oxygen with a liquid-phase mixture of allyl acetate and acetic acid using a bromide salt as a catalyst.

(b) The ingredient meets the specifications of the Food Chemicals Codex, 3d Ed. (1981), pp. 337–338, as revised by the First Supplement to the 3d Ed., which is incorporated by reference in accordance with 5 U.S.C. 552(a). Copies are available from the National Academy Press, 2102 Constitution Ave., NW., Washington, DC 20418, or available for inspection at the National Archives and Records Administration (NARA). For information on the availability of this material at NARA, call 202–741–6030, or go to: *http://www.archives.gov/federal_register/code_of_federal_regulations/ibr_locations.html.*

(c) In accordance with § 184.1(b)(1), the ingredient is used in food with no limitation other than current good manufacturing practice. The affirmation of this ingredient as generally recognized as safe (GRAS) as a direct human food ingredient is based upon the following current good manufacturing practice conditions of use:

(1) The ingredient is used in food as a flavoring agent and adjuvant as defined in § 170.3(o)(12) of this chapter; a formulation aid as defined in § 170.3(o)(14) of this chapter; and humectant as defined in § 170.3(o)(16) of this chapter; and a solvent and vehicle as defined in § 170.3(o)(27) of this chapter.

(2) The ingredient is used in the following foods at levels not to exceed current good manufacturing practice: baked goods and baking mixes as defined in § 170.3(n)(1) of this chapter, alcoholic beverages as defined in

§ 170.3(n)(2) of this chapter; nonalcoholic beverages and beverage bases as defined in § 170.3(n)(3) of this chapter; chewing gum as defined in § 170.3(n)(6) of this chapter; confections and frostings as defined in § 170.3(n)(9) of this chapter; frozen dairy dessert and mixes as defined in § 170.3(n)(20) of this chapter; gelatins, puddings, and fillngs as defined in § 170.3(n)(22) of this chapter; hard candy as defined in § 170.3(n)(25) of this chapter; and soft candy as defined in § 170.3(n)(38) of this chapter.

(d) Prior sanctions for this ingredient different from the uses established in this section do not exist or have been waived.

[54 FR 7404, Feb. 21, 1989]

§ 184.1903 Tributyrin.

(a) Tributyrin ($C_{15}H_{26}O_6$, CAS Reg. No. 60–01–5), also known as butyrin or glyceryl tributyrate, is the triester of glycerin and butyric acid. It is prepared by esterification of glycerin with excess butyric acid.

(b) The ingredient meets the specification of the Food Chemicals Codex, 3d Ed. (1981), p. 416, which is incorporated by reference in accordance with 5 U.S.C. 552(a). Copies are available from the National Academy Press, 2101 Constitution Ave. NW., Washington, DC 20418, or available for inspection at the National Archives and Records Administration (NARA). For information on the availability of this material at NARA, call 202–741–6030, or go to: *http://www.archives.gov/federal_register/code_of_federal_regulations/ibr_locations.html.*

(c) In accordance with § 184.1(b)(1), the ingredient is used in food with no limitation other than current good manufacturing practice. The affirmation of this ingredient as generaly recognized as safe (GRAS) as a direct human food ingredient is based upon the following current good manufacturing practice conditions of use:

(1) The ingredient is used in food as a flavoring agent and adjuvant as defined in § 170.3(o)(12) of this chapter.

(2) The ingredient is used in the following foods at levels not to exceed current good manufacturing practice; baked goods as defined in § 170.3(n)(1) of this chapter; alcoholic beverages as defined in § 170.3(n)(2) of this chapter; nonalcoholic beverages as defined in § 170.3(n)(3) of this chapter; fats and oils as defined in § 170.3(n)(12) of this chapter; frozen dairy desserts and mixes as defined in § 170.3(n)(20) of this chapter; gelatins, puddings and fillngs as defined in § 170.3(n)(22) of this chapter; and soft candy as defined in § 170.3(n)(38) of this chapter.

(d) Prior sanctions for this ingredient different from the uses established in this section do not exist or have been waived.

[54 FR 7404, Feb. 21, 1989; 54 FR 10482, Mar. 13, 1989]

§ 184.1911 Triethyl citrate.

(a) Triethyl citrate ($C_{12}H_{20}O_7$, CAS Reg. No. 77–93–0) is the triethyl ester of citric acid. It is prepared by esterifying citric acid with ethyl alcohol and occurs as an odorless, practically colorless, oily liquid.

(b) The ingredient meets the specifications of the Food Chemicals Codex, 3d ed. (1981), p. 339, which is incorporated by reference in accordance with 5 U.S.C. 552(a) and 1 CFR part 51. Copies are available from the National Academy Press, 2101 Constitution Ave. NW., Washington, DC 20418, and the Center for Food Safety and Applied Nutrition (HFS–200), 5100 Paint Branch Pkwy., College Park, MD 20740, or may be examined at the National Archives and Records Administration (NARA). For information on the availability of this material at NARA, call 202–741–6030, or go to: *http://www.archives.gov/federal_register/code_of_federal_regulations/ibr_locations.html.*

(c) In accordance with § 184.1(b)(1), the ingredient is used in food with no limitation other than current good manufacturing practice. The affirmation of this ingredient as generally recognized as safe (GRAS) as a direct human food ingredient is based upon the following current good manufacturing practice conditions of use:

(1) The ingredient is used as a flavoring agent as defined in § 170.3(o)(12) of this chapter; a solvent and vehicle as defined in § 170.3(o)(27) of this chapter; and a surface-active agent as defined in § 170.3(o)(29) of this chapter.

(2) The ingredient is used in foods at levels not to exceed current good manufacturing practice.

(d) Prior sanctions for this ingredient different from the uses established in this section, or different from those set forth in part 181 of this chapter, do not exist or have been waived.

[59 FR 63897, Dec. 12, 1994]

§ 184.1914 Trypsin.

(a) Trypsin (CAS Reg. No. 9002–07–7) is an enzyme preparation obtained from purified extracts of porcine or bovine pancreas. It is a white to tan amorphous powder. Its characterizing enzyme activity is that of a peptide hydrolase (EC 3.4.21.4).

(b) The ingredient meets the general requirements and additional requirements for enzyme preparations in the Food Chemicals Codex, 3d ed. (1981), p. 110, which is incorporated by reference in accordance with 5 U.S.C. 552(a) and 1 CFR part 51. Copies are available from the National Academy Press, 2101 Constitution Ave. NW., Washington, DC 20418, or may be examined at the Office of Food Additive Safety (HFS–200), Center for Food Safety and Applied Nutrition, Food and Drug Administration, 5100 Paint Branch Pkwy., College Park, MD 20740, 240–402–1200, and at the National Archives and Records Administration (NARA). For information on the availability of this material at NARA, call 202–741–6030, or go to: *http://www.archives.gov/federal_register/code_of_federal_regulations/ibr_locations.html.*

(c) In accordance with §184.1(b)(1), the ingredient is used in food with no limitation other than current good manufacturing practice. The affirmation of this ingredient as GRAS as a direct food ingredient is based upon the following current good manufacturing practice conditions of use:

(1) The ingredient is used as an enzyme as defined in §170.3(o)(9) of this chapter to hydrolyze proteins or polypeptides.

(2) The ingredient is used in food at levels not to exceed current good manufacturing practice.

[60 FR 32911, June 26, 1995, as amended at 78 FR 14667, Mar. 7, 2013]

§ 184.1923 Urea.

(a) Urea ($CO(NH_2)_2$, CAS Reg. No. 57–13–6) is the diamide of carbonic acid and is also known as carbamide. It is a white, odorless solid and is commonly produced from CO_2 by ammonolysis or from cyanamide by hydrolysis.

(b) The ingredient must be of a purity suitable for its intended use.

(c) In accordance with §184.1(b)(1), the ingredient is used in food with no limitation other than current good manufacturing practice. The affirmation of this ingredient as generally recognized as safe as a direct human food ingredient is based upon the following current good manufacturing practice conditions of use:

(1) The ingredient is used as a formulation aid as defined in §170.3(o)(14) of this chapter and as a fermentation aid.

(2) The ingredient is used in yeast-raised bakery products; in alcoholic beverages as defined in §170.3(n)(2) of this chapter; and in gelatin products.

(d) Prior sanctions for this ingredient different from the uses established in this section do not exist or have been waived.

[48 FR 51616, Nov. 10, 1983, as amended at 49 FR 19816, May 10, 1984; 73 FR 8608, Feb. 14, 2008]

§ 184.1924 Urease enzyme preparation from Lactobacillus fermentum.

(a) This enzyme preparation is derived from the nonpathogenic, nontoxicogenic bacterium *Lactobacillus fermentum*. It contains the enzyme urease (CAS Reg. No. 9002–13–5), which facilitates the hydrolysis of urea to ammonia and carbon dioxide. It is produced by a pure culture fermentation process and by using materials that are generally recognized as safe (GRAS) or are food additives that have been approved for this use by the Food and Drug Administration (FDA).

(b) The ingredient meets the general and additional requirements for enzyme preparations in the "Food Chemicals Codex," 3d ed. (1981), pp. 107–110, which is incorporated by reference in accordance with 5 U.S.C. 552(a) and 1 CFR part 51. Copies are available from the National Academy Press, 2101 Constitution Ave. NW., Washington, DC 20418, or available for inspection at the

National Archives and Records Administration (NARA). For information on the availability of this material at NARA, call 202–741–6030, or go to: *http://www.archives.gov/federal_register/code_of_federal_regulations/ibr_locations.html.*

(c) In accordance with § 184.1(b)(1), the ingredient is used in food with no limitation other than current good manufacturing practice. The affirmation of this ingredient as GRAS as a direct human food ingredient is based upon the following current good manufacturing practice conditions of use:

(1) The ingredient is used in wine, as defined in 27 CFR 2.5 and 4.10, as an enzyme as defined in § 170.3(o)(9) of this chapter to convert urea to ammonia and carbon dioxide.

(2) The ingredient is used in food at levels not to exceed current good manufacturing practice. Current good manufacturing practice is limited to use of this ingredient in wine to inhibit formation of ethyl carbamate.

[57 FR 60473, Dec. 21, 1992]

§ 184.1930 Vitamin A.

(a)(1) Vitamin A (retinol; CAS Reg. No. 68–26–8) is the alcohol 9,13-dimethyl-7-(1,1,5-trimethyl-6-cyclohexen-5-yl)-7,9,11,13-nonatetraen-15-ol. It may be nearly odorless or have a mild fishy odor. Vitamin A is extracted from fish liver oils or produced by total synthesis from β-ionone and a propargyl halide.

(2) Vitamin A acetate (retinyl acetate; CAS Reg. No. 127–47–9) is the acetate ester of retinol. It is prepared by esterifying retinol with acetic acid.

(3) Vitamin A palmitate (retinyl palmitate; CAS Reg. No. 79–81–2) is the palmitate ester of retinol. It is prepared by esterifying retinol with palmitic acid.

(b) The ingredient meets the specifications for vitamin A in the Food Chemicals Codex, 3d Ed. (1981), p. 342, which is incorporated by reference. Copies are available from the National Academy Press, 2101 Constitution Ave. NW., Washington, DC 20418, or available for inspection at the National Archives and Records Administration (NARA). For information on the availability of this material at NARA, call 202–741–6030, or go to: *http://www.archives.gov/federal_register/code_of_federal_regulations/ibr_locations.html.*

(c) In accordance with § 184.1(b)(1), the ingredient is used in food with no limitation other than current good manufacturing practice. The affirmation of this ingredient as generally recognized as safe (GRAS) as a direct human food ingredient is based upon the following current good manufacturing practice conditions of use:

(1) The ingredient is used in food as a nutrient supplement as defined in § 170.3(o)(20) of this chapter.

(2) The ingredient is used in foods at levels not to exceed current good manufacturing practice. Vitamin A may be used in infant formula in accordance with section 412(g) of the Federal Food, Drug, and Cosmetic Act (the act) or with regulations promulgated under section 412(a)(2) of the Act.

(d) Prior sanctions for this ingredient different from the uses established in this section do not exist or have been waived.

[48 FR 51610, Nov. 10, 1983]

§ 184.1945 Vitamin B_{12}..

(a) Vitamin B_{12}, also known as cyanocobalamin ($C_{63}H_{88}CoN_{14}O_{14}P$, CAS Reg. No. 68–0919–099), is produced commercially from cultures of *Streptomyces griseus.*

(b) The ingredient meets the specifications of the Food Chemicals Codex, 3d Ed. (1981), p. 343, which is incorporated by reference. Copies are available from the National Academy Press, 2101 Constitution Ave. NW., Washington, DC 20418, or available for inspection at the National Archives and Records Administration (NARA). For information on the availability of this material at NARA, call 202–741–6030, or go to: *http://www.archives.gov/federal_register/code_of_federal_regulations/ibr_locations.html.*

(c) In accordance with § 184.1(b)(1), the ingredient is used in food with no limitation other than current good manufacturing practice. The affirmation of this ingredient as generally recognized as safe (GRAS) as a direct human food ingredient is based upon the following current good manufacturing practice conditions of use:

(1) The ingredient is used as a nutrient supplement as defined in §170.3(o)(20) of this chapter.

(2) The ingredient is used in food at levels not to exceed current good manufacturing practice. Vitamin B_{12} also may be used in infant formula in accordance with section 412(g) of the Federal Food, Drug, and Cosmetic Act (the act) or with regulations promulgated under section 412(a)(2) of the act.

(d) Prior sanctions for this ingredient different from the uses established in this section do not exist or have been waived.

[50 FR 6341, Feb. 15, 1985]

§ 184.1950 Vitamin D.

(a) Vitamin D is added to food as the following food ingredients:

(1) Crystalline vitamin D_2 ($C_{28}H_{44}O$, CAS Reg. No. 50–14–6), also known as ergocalciferol, is the chemical 9,10-seco(5Z,7E,22E)-5,7,10(19),22-ergostatetraen-3-ol. The ingredient is produced by ultraviolet irradiation of ergosterol isolated from yeast and related fungi and is purified by crystallization.

(2) Crystalline vitamin D_3 ($C_{27}H_{44}O$, CAS Reg. No. 67–97–0), also known as cholecalciferol, is the chemical 9,10-seco(5Z,7E,)-5,7,10(19)-cholestatrien-3-ol. Vitamin D_3 occurs in, and is isolated from, fish liver oils. It is also manufactured by ultraviolet irradiation of 7-dehydrocholesterol produced from cholesterol. It is purified by crystallization. Vitamin D_3 is the vitamin D form that is produced endogenously in humans through sunlight activation of 7-dehydrocholesterol in the skin.

(3) Vitamin D_2 resin and vitamin D_3 resin are the concentrated forms of irradiated ergosterol (D_2) and irradiated 7-dehydrocholesterol (D_3) that are separated from the reacting materials in paragraphs (a) (1) and (2) of this section. The resulting products are sold as food sources of vitamin D without further purification.

(b) Vitamin D_2 and vitamin D_3 as crystals meet the specifications of the Food Chemicals Codex, 3d Ed. (1981), pp. 344 and 345, which is incorporated by reference. Copies are available from the National Academy Press, 2101 Constitution Ave. NW., Washington, DC 20418, or available for inspection at the National Archives and Records Administration (NARA). For information on the availability of this material at NARA, call 202–741–6030, or go to: *http://www.archives.gov/federal_register/code_of_federal_regulations/ibr_locations.html.* Vitamin D_2 resin and vitamin D_3 resin must be of a purity suitable for their intended use.

(c)(1) In accordance with §184.1(b)(2), the ingredients are used in food as the sole source of added vitamin D only within the following specific limitations:

Category of food	Maximum levels in food (as served)	Functional use
Breakfast cereals, § 170.3(n)(4) of this chapter.	350 (IU/100 grams).	Nutrient supplement, § 170.3(o)(20) of this chapter.
Grain products and pastas, § 170.3(n)(23) of this chapter.	90(IU/100 grams)	Do.
Milk, § 170.3(n)(30) of this chapter.	42 (IU/100 grams)	Do.
Milk products, § 170.3(n)(31) of this chapter.	89 (IU/100 grams)	Do.

(2) Vitamin D may be used in infant formula in accordance with section 412(g) of the Federal Food, Drug, and Cosmetic Act (the act) or with regulations promulgated under section 412(a)(2) of the act.

(3) Vitamin D may be used in margarine in accordance with §166.110 of this chapter.

(d) Prior sanctions for these ingredients different from the uses established in this section do not exist or have been waived.

[50 FR 30152, July 24, 1985, as amended at 73 FR 8608, Feb. 14, 2008]

§ 184.1973 Beeswax (yellow and white).

(a) Beeswax (CAS Reg. No. 8012–89–3) is a secretory product of honey bees used as a structural material in honeycombs. Beeswax is prepared from honeycombs after removal of the honey by draining or centrifuging. The combs are melted in hot water or steam or with solar heat, and strained. The wax is refined by melting in hot water to which sulfuric acid or alkali may be added to extract impurities. The resulting wax is referred to as yellow beeswax. White beeswax is produced by bleaching the constituent pigments of yellow beeswax with peroxides, or preferably it is bleached by sun light.

(b) The ingredient meets the specifications of the "Food Chemicals Codex," 3d Ed. (1981), pp. 34–35, which is incorporated by reference. Copies may be obtained from the National Academy Press, 2101 Constitution Ave. NW., Washington, DC 20418, or may be examined at the National Archives and Records Administration (NARA). For information on the availability of this material at NARA, call 202–741–6030, or go to: *http://www.archives.gov/federal_register/code_of_federal_regulations/ibr_locations.html.*

(c) The ingredient is used as a flavoring agent and adjuvant as defined in §170.3(o)(12) of this chapter, as a lubricant as defined in §170.3(o)(18) of this chapter, and as a surface-finishing agent as defined in §170.3(o)(30) of this chapter.

(d) The ingredient is used in food, in accordance with §184.1(b)(1) of this chapter, at levels not to exceed good manufacturing practice. Current good manufacturing practice results in a maximum level, as served, of: 0.065 percent for chewing gum as defined in §170.3(n)(6) of this chapter; 0.005 percent for confections and frostings as defined in §170.3(n)(9) of this chapter; 0.04 percent for hard candy as defined in §170.3(n)(25) of this chapter; 0.1 percent for soft candy as defined in §170.3(n)(38) of this chapter; and 0.002 percent or less for all other food categories.

[43 FR 14644, Apr. 7, 1978, as amended at 49 FR 5613, Feb. 14, 1984; 50 FR 49536, Dec. 3, 1985]

§ 184.1976 Candelilla wax.

(a) Candelilla wax (CAS Reg. No. 8006–44–8) is obtained from the candelilla plant. It is a hard, yellowish-brown, opaque-to-translucent wax. Candelilla wax is prepared by immersing the plants in boiling water containing sulfuric acid and skimming off the wax that rises to the surface. It is composed of about 50 percent hydrocarbons with smaller amounts of esters and free acids.

(b) The ingredient meets the specifications of the Food Chemicals Codex, 3d Ed. (1981), p. 67, which is incorporated by reference. Copies are available from the National Academy Press, 2101 Constitution Ave. NW., Washington, DC 20418, or available for inspection at the National Archives and Records Administration (NARA). For information on the availability of this material at NARA, call 202–741–6030, or go to: *http://www.archives.gov/federal_register/code_of_federal_regulations/ibr_locations.html.*

(c) In accordance with §184.1(b)(1), the ingredient is used in food with no limitation other than current good manufacturing practice. The affirmation of this ingredient as generally recognized as safe (GRAS) as a direct human food ingredient is based upon the following current good manufacturing practice conditions of use:

(1) The ingredient is used as a lubricant as defined in §170.3(o)(18) of this chapter and as a surface-finishing agent as defined in §170.3(o)(30) of this chapter.

(2) The ingredient is used in the following foods at levels not to exceed current good manufacturing practice: in chewing gum as defined in §170.3(n)(6) of this chapter and in hard candy as defined in §170.3(n)(25) of this chapter.

(d) Prior sanctions for this ingredient different from the uses established in this section do not exist or have been waived.

[48 FR 51617, Nov. 10, 1983]

§ 184.1978 Carnauba wax.

(a) Carnauba wax (CAS Reg. No. 008–015–869) is obtained from the leaves and buds of the Brazilian wax palm *Copernicia cerifera* Martius. The wax is hard, brittle, sparingly soluble in cold organic solvents and insoluble in water. It is marketed in five grades designated No. 1 through No. 5. Grades No. 4 and No. 5 represent the bulk of the commercial trade volume. These commercial grades consist chiefly of C_{24} to C_{32} normal saturated monofunctional fatty acids and normal saturated monofunctional primary alcohols.

(b) The ingredient meets the specifications of the Food Chemicals Codex,

3d Ed. (1981), p. 73, which is incorporated by reference. Copies are available from the National Academy Press, 2101 Constitution Ave. NW., Washington, DC 20418, or available for inspection at the National Archives and Records Administration (NARA). For information on the availability of this material at NARA, call 202–741–6030, or go to: *http://www.archives.gov/federal_register/code_of_federal_regulations/ibr_locations.html.*

(c) In accordance with § 184.1(b)(1), the ingredient is used in food with no limitation other than current good manufacturing practice. The affirmation of this ingredient as generally recognized as safe (GRAS) as a direct human food ingredient is based upon the following current good manufacturing practice conditions of use:

(1) The ingredient is used as an anticaking agent as defined § 170.3(o)(1) of this chapter; as a formulation aid as defined in § 170.3(o)(14) of this chapter; as a lubricant and release agent as defined in § 170.3(o)(18) of this chapter; and as a surface-finishing agent as defined in § 170.3(o)(30) of this chapter.

(2) The ingredient is used in the following foods at levels not to exceed current good manufacturing practice: baked goods and baking mixes as defined in § 170.3(n)(1) of this chapter; chewing gun as defined in § 170.3(n)(6) of this chapter; confections and frostings as defined in § 170.3(n)(9) of this chapter; fresh fruits and fruit juices as defined in § 170.3(n)(16) of this chapter; gravies and sauces as defined in § 170.3(n)(24) of this chapter; processed fruits and fruit juices as defined in § 170.3(n)(35) of this chapter; and soft candy as defined in § 170.3(n)(38) of this chapter.

(d) Prior sanctions for this ingredient different from the uses established in this section do not exist or have been waived.

[48 FR 51147, Nov. 7, 1983]

§ 184.1979 Whey.

(a)(1) *Whey.* Whey is the liquid substance obtained by separating the coagulum from milk, cream, or skim milk in cheesemaking. Whey obtained from a procedure, in which a significant amount of lactose is converted to lactic acid, or from the curd formation by direct acidification of milk, is known as acid whey. Whey obtained from a procedure in which there is insignificant conversion of lactose to lactic acid is known as sweet whey. Sweet whey has a maximum titratable acidity of not more than 0.16 percent, calculated as lactic acid, and an alkalinity of ash of not more than 225 milliliters of 0.1*N* hydrochloric acid per 100 grams. The acidity of whey, sweet or acid, may be adjusted by the addition of safe and suitable pH-adjusting ingredients.

(2) *Concentrated whey.* Concentrated whey is the liquid substance obtained by the partial removal of water from whey, while leaving all other constituents in the same relative proportions as in whey.

(3) *Dry or dried whey.* Dry or dried whey is the dry substance obtained by the removal of water from whey, while leaving all other constituents in the same relative proportions as in whey.

(b) The ingredients meet the following specifications:

(1) The analysis of whey, concentrated whey, and dry (dried) whey, on a dry product basis, based on analytical methods in the referenced sections of "Official Methods of Analysis of the Association of Official Analytical Chemists," 13th ed. (1980), which is incorporated by reference in accordance with 5 U.S.C. 552(a) and 1 CFR part 51, is given in paragraphs (b)(1)(i) through (b)(1)(vii) of this section. Copies may be obtained from the AOAC INTERNATIONAL, 481 North Frederick Ave., suite 500, Gaithersburg, MD 20877, or may be examined at the Center for Food Safety and Applied Nutrition's Library, Food and Drug Administration, 5100 Paint Branch Pkwy., College Park, MD 20740, or at the National Archives and Records Administration (NARA). For information on the availability of this material at NARA, call 202–741–6030, or go to: *http://www.archives.gov/federal_register/code_of_federal_regulations/ibr_locations.html.*

(i) Protein content, 10 to 15 percent—as determined by the methods prescribed in section 16.036 (liquid sample), entitled "Total Nitrogen—Official Final Action" under the heading

"Total Solids," or in section 16.193 (dry sample), entitled "Kjeldahl Method" under the heading "Protein—Official Final Action."

(ii) Fat content, 0.2 to 2.0 percent—as determined by the methods prescribed in section 16.059 (liquid sample), "Reese-Gottlieb Method [Reference Method] (11)—Official Final Action" under the heading "Fat," or in section 16.199 (dry sample), entitled "Fat in Dried Milk (45)—Official Final Action."

(iii) Ash content, 7 to 14 percent—as determined by the methods prescribed in section 16.035 (liquid sample), entitled "Ash (5)—Official Final Action" under the heading "Total Solids," or in section 16.196 (dry sample), entitled "Ash—Official Final Action" under the heading "Dried Milk, Nonfat Dry Milk, and Malted Milk."

(iv) Lactose content, 61 to 75 percent—as determined by the methods prescribed in section 16.057 (liquid sample), entitled "Gravimetric Method—Official Final Action" under the heading "Lactose," or in section 31.061 (dry sample), entitled "Lane-Eynon General Volumetric Method" under the heading "Lactose—Chemical Methods—Official Final Action."

(v) Moisture content, 1 to 8 percent—as determined by the methods prescribed in section 16.192, entitled "Moisture (41)—Official Final Action" under the heading "Dried Milk, Nonfat Dry Milk, and Malted Milk."

(vi) Solids content, variable—as determined by the methods prescribed in section 16.032, entitled "Method I—Official Final Action" under the heading "Total Solids."

(vii) Titratable Acidity, variable—as determined by the methods prescribed in section 16.023, entitled "Acidity (2)—Official Final Action" under the heading "Milk," or by an equivalent potentiometric method.

(2) Limits of impurities are: Heavy metals (as lead). Not more than 10 parts per million (0.001 percent) as determined by the method described in the "Food Chemicals Codex," 4th ed. (1996), pp. 760–761, which is incorporated by reference in accordance with 5 U.S.C. 552(a) and 1 CFR part 51. Copies are available from the National Academy Press, Box 285, 2101 Constitution Ave. NW., Washington, DC 20055 (Internet address *http://www.nap.edu*), or may be examined at the Center for Food Safety and Applied Nutrition's Library, Food and Drug Administration, 5100 Paint Branch Pkwy., College Park, MD 20740, or at the National Archives and Records Administration (NARA). For information on the availability of this material at NARA, call 202–741–6030, or go to: *http://www.archives.gov/federal_register/code_of_federal_regulations/ibr_locations.html.*

(3) The whey must be derived from milk that has been pasteurized, or the whey and modified whey product must be subjected to pasteurization techniques or its equivalent before use in food.

(c) Whey, concentrated whey, and dry (dried) whey may be used in food in accordance with good manufacturing practice as indicated in §184.1(b)(1).

(d) The label on the whey form sold to food manufacturers shall read as follows:

(1) For whey: "(Sweet or acid) whey" or "whey (___% titratable acidity).

(2) For concentrated whey: "Concentrated (sweet or acid) whey, ___% solids" or "Concentrated whey (___% titratable acidity), ___% solids".

(3) For dry (dried) whey: "Dry (dried) (sweet or acid) whey" or "dry (dried) whey, (___% titratable acidity)".

(e) Whey, concentrated whey, or dry (dried) whey in a finished food product shall be listed as "whey."

[46 FR 44439, Sept. 4, 1981; 47 FR 7410, Feb. 19, 1982, as amended at 54 FR 24899, June 12, 1989; 64 FR 1760, Jan. 12, 1999]

§ 184.1979a Reduced lactose whey.

(a) Reduced lactose whey is the substance obtained by the removal of lactose from whey. The lactose content of the finished dry product shall not exceed 60 percent. Removal of the lactose is accomplished by physical separation techniques such as precipitation, filtration, or dialysis. As with whey, reduced lactose whey can be used as a fluid, concentrate, or a dry product form. The acidity of reduced lactose whey may be adjusted by the addition of safe and suitable pH-adjusting ingredients.

(b) The reduced lactose whey meets the following specifications:

(1) The analysis of reduced lactose whey, on a dry product basis, based on analytical methods in the referenced sections of "Official Methods of Analysis of the Association of Official Analytical Chemists," 13th ed. (1980), which is incorporated by reference in accordance with 5 U.S.C. 552(a) and 1 CFR part 51, is given in paragraphs (b)(1)(i) through (b)(1)(vii) of this section. Copies may be obtained from the AOAC INTERNATIONAL, 481 North Frederick Ave., suite 500, Gaithersburg, MD 20877, or may be examined at the Center for Food Safety and Applied Nutrition's Library, Food and Drug Administration, 5100 Paint Branch Pkwy., College Park, MD 20740, or at the National Archives and Records Administration (NARA). For information on the availability of this material at NARA, call 202–741–6030, or go to: *http://www.archives.gov/federal_register/code_of_federal_regulations/ibr_locations.html.*

(i) Protein content, 16 to 24 percent—as determined by the methods prescribed in section 16.036 (liquid sample), entitled "Total Nitrogen—Official Final Action" under the heading "Total Solids," or in section 16.193 (dry sample), entitled "Kjeldahl Method" under the heading "Protein—Official Final Action."

(ii) Fat content, 1 to 4 percent—as determined by the methods prescribed in section 16.059 (liquid sample), "Reese-Gottlieb Method [Reference Method] (11)—Official Final Action" under the heading "Fat," or in section 16.199 (dry sample), entitled "Fat in Dried Milk (45)—Official Final Action."

(iii) Ash content, 11 to 27 percent—as determined by the methods prescribed in section 16.035 (liquid sample), entitled "Ash (5)—Official Final Action" under the heading "Total Solids," or in section 16.196 (dry sample), entitled "Ash—Official Final Action" under the heading "Dried Milk, Nonfat Dry Milk, and Malted Milk."

(iv) Lactose content, not more than 60 percent—as determined by the methods prescribed in section 16.057 (liquid sample), entitled "Gravimetric Method—Official Final Action" under the heading "Lactose," or in section 31.061 (dry sample), entitled "Lane-Eynon General Volumetric Method" under the heading "Lactose—Chemical Methods—Official Final Action."

(v) Moisture content, 1 to 6 percent—as determined by the method prescribed in section 16.192, entitled "Moisture (41)—Official Final Action" under the heading "Dried Milk, Nonfat Dry Milk, and Malted Milk."

(vi) Solids content, variable—as determined by the methods prescribed in section 16.032, entitled "Method I—Official Final Action" under the heading "Total Solids."

(vii) Titratable Acidity, variable—as determined by the methods prescribed in section 16.023, entitled "Acidity (2)—Official Final Action" under the heading "Milk," or by an equivalent potentiometric method.

(2) Limits of impurities are: Heavy metals (as lead). Not more than 10 parts per million (0.001 percent), as determined by the method described in the "Food Chemicals Codex," 4th ed. (1996), pp. 760–761, which is incorporated by reference in accordance with 5 U.S.C. 552(a) and 1 CFR part 51. Copies are available from the National Academy Press, Box 285, 2101 Constitution Ave. NW., Washington, DC 20055 (Internet address *http://www.nap.edu*), or may be examined at the Center for Food Safety and Applied Nutrition's Library, Food and Drug Administration, 5100 Paint Branch Pkwy., College Park, MD 20740, or at the National Archives and Records Administration (NARA). For information on the availability of this material at NARA, call 202–741–6030, or go to: *http://www.archives.gov/federal_register/code_of_federal_regulations/ibr_locations.html.*

(3) The reduced lactose whey shall be derived from milk that has been pasteurized, or the reduced lactose whey shall be subjected to pasteurization techniques or its equivalent before use in food.

(c) Reduced lactose whey may be used in food in accordance with good manufacturing practice as indicated in §184.1(b)(1).

(d) The percent of lactose present on a dry product basis, i.e., "reduced lactose whey (___% lactose)," shall be declared on the label of the package sold to food manufacturers. The percent of lactose may be declared in 5-percent increments, expressed as a multiple of 5, not greater than the actual percentage of lactose in the product, or as an actual percentage provided that an analysis of the product on which the actual percentage is based is supplied to the food manufacturer.

(e) The presence of reduced lactose whey in a finished food product shall be listed as "reduced lactose whey."

[46 FR 44440, Sept. 4, 1981, as amended at 54 FR 24899, June 12, 1989; 64 FR 1760, Jan. 12, 1999]

§ 184.1979b Reduced minerals whey.

(a) Reduced minerals whey is the substance obtained by the removal of a portion of the minerals from whey. The dry product shall not contain more than 7 percent ash. Reduced minerals whey is produced by physical separation techniques such as precipitation, filtration, or dialysis. As with whey, reduced minerals whey can be used as a fluid, concentrate, or a dry product form. The acidity of reduced minerals whey may be adjusted by the additional of safe and suitable pH-adjusting ingredients.

(b) The reduced minerals whey meets the following specifications:

(1) The analysis of reduced minerals whey, on a dry product basis, based on analytical methods in the referenced sections of "Official Methods of Analysis of the Association of Official Analytical Chemists," 13th ed. (1980), which is incorporated by reference in accordance with 5 U.S.C. 552(a) and 1 CFR part 51, is given in paragraphs (b)(1)(i) through (b)(1)(vii) of this section. Copies may be obtained from the AOAC INTERNATIONAL, 481 North Frederick Ave., suite 500, Gaithersburg, MD 20877, or may be examined at the Center for Food Safety and Applied Nutrition's Library, Food and Drug Administration, 5100 Paint Branch Pkwy., College Park, MD 20740, or at the National Archives and Records Administration (NARA). For information on the availability of this material at NARA, call 202–741–6030, or go to: *http://www.archives.gov/federal_register/code_of_federal_regulations/ibr_locations.html.*

(i) Protein content, 10 to 24 percent—as determined by the methods prescribed in section 16.036 (liquid sample), entitled "Total Nitrogen—Official Final Action" under the heading "Total Solids," or in section 16.193 (dry sample), entitled "Kjeldahl Method" under the heading "Protein—Official Final Action."

(ii) Fat content, 1 to 4 percent—as determined by the methods prescribed in section 16.059 (liquid sample), "Reese-Gottlieb Method [Reference Method] (11)—Official Final Action" under the heading "Fat," or in section 16.199 (dry sample), entitled "Fat in Dried Milk (45)—Official Final Action."

(iii) Ash content, maximum 7 percent—as determined by the methods prescribed in section 16.035 (liquid sample), entitled "Ash (5)—Official Final Action" under the heading "Total Solids," or in section 16.196 (dry sample), entitled "Ash—Official Final Action" under the heading "Dried Milk, Nonfat Dry Milk, and Malted Milk."

(iv) Lactose content, maximum 85 percent—as determined by the methods prescribed in section 16.057 (liquid sample), entitled "Gravimetric Method—Official Final Action" under the heading "Lactose," or in section 31.061 (dry sample), entitled "Lane-Eynon General Volumetric Method" under the heading "Lactose—Chemical Methods—Official Final Action."

(v) Moisture content, 1 to 6 percent—as determined by the methods prescribed in section 16.192, entitled "Moisture (41)—Official Final Action" under the heading "Dried Milk, Nonfat Dry Milk, and Malted Milk."

(vi) Solids content, variable—as determined by the methods prescribed in section 16.032, entitled "Method I—Official Final Action" under the heading "Total Solid."

(vii) Titratable Acidity, variable—as determined by the methods prescribed in section 16.023, entitled "Acidity (2)—Official Final Action" under the heading "Milk," or by an equivalent potentiometric method.

(2) Limits of impurities are: Heavy metals (as lead). Not more than 10 parts per million (0.001 percent), as determined by the method described in the "Food Chemicals Codex," 4th ed. (1996), pp. 760–761, which is incorporated by reference in accordance with 5 U.S.C. 552(a) and 1 CFR part 51. Copies

are available from the National Academy Press, Box 285, 2101 Constitution Ave. NW., Washington, DC 20055 (Internet address *http://www.nap.edu*), or may be examined at the Center for Food Safety and Applied Nutrition's Library, Food and Drug Administration, 5100 Paint Branch Pkwy., College Park, MD 20740, or at the National Archives and Records Administration (NARA). For information on the availability of this material at NARA, call 202–741–6030, or go to: *http://www.archives.gov/federal_register/code_of_federal_regulations/ibr_locations.html.*

(3) The reduced minerals whey shall be derived from milk that has been pasteurized, or the reduced minerals whey shall be subjected to pasteurization techniques or its equivalent before use in food.

(c) The reduced minerals whey may be used in food in accordance with good manufacturing practice as indicated in § 184.1(b)(1).

(d) The percent of minerals present on a dry product basis, i.e., "reduced minerals whey (___% minerals)," shall be declared on the label of the package sold to food manufacturers. The percent of minerals may be declared in 2-percent increments expressed as a multiple of 2, not greater than the actual percentage of minerals in the product, or as an actual percentage provided that an analysis of the product on which the actual percentage is based is supplied to the food manufacturer.

(e) The presence of reduced minerals whey in a finished food product shall be listed as "reduced minerals whey".

[46 FR 44441, Sept. 4, 1981, as amended at 54 FR 24899, June 12, 1989; 64 FR 1761, Jan. 12, 1999]

§ 184.1979c Whey protein concentrate.

(a) Whey protein concentrate is the substance obtained by the removal of sufficient nonprotein constituents from whey so that the finished dry product contains not less than 25 percent protein. Whey protein concentrate is produced by physical separation techniques such as precipitation, filtration, or dialysis. As with whey, whey protein concentrate can be used as a fluid, concentrate, or dry product form. The acidity of whey protein concentrate may be adjusted by the addition of safe and suitable pH-adjusting ingredients.

(b) The whey protein concentrate meets the following specifications:

(1) The analysis of whey protein concentrate, on a dry product basis, based on analytical methods in the referenced sections of "Official Methods of Analysis of the Association of Official Analytical Chemists," 13th ed. (1980), which is incorporated by reference in accordance with 5 U.S.C. 552(a) and 1 CFR part 51, is given in paragraphs (b)(1)(i) through (b)(1)(vii) of this section. Copies may be obtained from the AOAC INTERNATIONAL, 481 North Frederick Ave., suite 500, Gaithersburg, MD 20877, or may be examined at the Center for Food Safety and Applied Nutrition's Library, Food and Drug Administration, 5100 Paint Branch Pkwy., College Park, MD 20740, or at the National Archives and Records Administration (NARA). For information on the availability of this material at NARA, call 202–741–6030, or go to: *http://www.archives.gov/federal_register/code_of_federal_regulations/ibr_locations.html.*

(i) Protein content, minimum 25 percent—as determined by the methods prescribed in section 16.036 (liquid sample), entitled "Total Nitrogen—Officials Final Action" under the heading "Total Solids," or in section 16.193 (dry sample), entitled "Kjeldahl Method" under the heading "Protein—Official Final Action."

(ii) Fat content, 1 to 10 percent—as determined by the methods prescribed in section 16.059 (liquid sample), "Reese-Gottlieb Method [Reference Method] (11)—Official Final Action" under the heading "Fat," or in section 16.199 (dry sample), entitled "Fat in Dried Milk (45)—Official Final Action."

(iii) Ash content, 2 to 15 percent—as determined by the methods prescribed in section 16.035 (liquid sample), entitled "Ash (5)—Official Final Action" under the heading "Total Solids," or in section 16.196 (dry sample), entitled "Ash—Official Final Action" under the heading "Dried Milk, Nonfat Dry Milk, and Malted Milk."

(iv) Lactose content, maximum 60 percent—as determined by the methods prescribed in section 16.057 (liquid sample), entitled "Gravimetric Method—Official Final Action" under the heading "Lactose," or in section 31.061 (dry sample), entitled "Lane-Eynon General Volumetric Method" under the heading "Lactose—Chemical Methods—Official Final Action."

(v) Moisture content, 1 to 6 percent—as determined by the methods prescribed in section 16.192, entitled "Moisture (41)—Official Final Action" under the heading "Dried Milk, Nonfat Dry Milk, and Malted Milk."

(vi) Solids content, variable—as determined by the methods prescribed in section 16.032, entitled "Method I—Official Final Action" under the heading "Total Solids."

(vii) Titratable Acidity, variable—as determined by the methods prescribed in section 16.023, entitled "Acidity (2)—Official Final Action" under the heading "Milk," or by an equivalent potentiometric method.

(2) Limits of impurities are: Heavy metals (as lead). Not more than 10 parts per million (0.001 percent), as determined by the method described in the "Food Chemicals Codex," 4th ed. (1996), pp. 760–761, which is incorporated by reference in accordance with 5 U.S.C. 552(a) and 1 CFR part 51. Copies are available from the National Academy Press, Box 285, 2101 Constitution Ave. NW., Washington, DC 20055 (Internet address *http://www.nap.edu*), or may be examined at the Center for Food Safety and Applied Nutrition's Library, Food and Drug Administration, 5100 Paint Branch Pkwy., College Park, MD 20740, or at the National Archives and Records Administration (NARA). For information on the availability of this material at NARA, call 202-741-6030, or go to: *http://www.archives.gov/federal_register/code_of_federal_regulations/ibr_locations.html.*

(3) The whey protein concentrate shall be derived from milk that has been pasteurized, or the whey protein concentrate shall be subjected to pasteurization techniques or its equivalent before use in food.

(c) The whey protein concentrate may be used in food in accordance with good manufacturing practice as indicated in § 184.1(b)(1).

(d) The percent of protein present on a dry product basis, i.e., "whey protein concentrate (___% protein)," shall be declared on the label of the package sold to food manufacturers. The percent of protein may be declared in 5-percent increments, expressed as a multiple of 5, not greater than the actual percentage of protein in the product, or as an actual percentage provided that an analysis of the product on which the actual percentage is based is supplied to the food manufacturer.

(e) The presence of whey protein concentrate in a finished food product shall be listed as "whey protein concentrate".

[46 FR 44441, Sept. 4, 1981, as amended at 54 FR 24899, June 12, 1989; 64 FR 1761, Jan. 12, 1999]

§ 184.1983 Bakers yeast extract.

(a) Bakers yeast extract is the food ingredient resulting from concentration of the solubles of mechanically ruptured cells of a selected strain of yeast, *Saccharomyces cerevisiae*. It may be concentrated or dried.

(b) The ingredient meets the following specifications on a dry weight basis: Less than 0.4 part per million (ppm) arsenic, 0.13 ppm cadmium, 0.2 ppm lead, 0.05 ppm mercury, 0.09 ppm selenium, and 10 ppm zinc.

(c) The viable microbial content of the finished ingredient as a concentrate or dry material is:

(1) Less than 10,000 organisms/gram by aerobic plate count.

(2) Less than 10 yeasts and molds/gram.

(3) Negative for *Salmonella*, *E. coli*, coagulase positive *Staphylococci*, *Clostridium perfringens*, *Clostridium botulinum*, or any other recognized microbial pathogen or any harmful microbial toxin.

(d) The ingredient is used as a flavoring agent and adjuvant as defined in § 170.3(o)(12) of this chapter at a level not to exceed 5 percent in food.

(e) This regulation is issued prior to general evaluation of use of this ingredient in order to affirm as GRAS the specific use named.

§ 184.1984 Zein.

(a) Zein (CAS Reg. No. 9010–66–6) is one of the components of corn gluten. It is produced commercially by extraction from corn gluten with alkaline aqueous isopropyl alcohol containing sodium hydroxide. The extract is then cooled, which causes the zein to precipitate.

(b) The ingredient must be of a purity suitable for its intended use.

(c) In accordance with § 184.1(b)(1), the ingredient is used in food with no limitation other than current good manufacturing practice. The affirmation of this ingredient as generally recognized as safe (GRAS) as a direct human food ingredient is based upon the following current good manufacturing practice conditions of use:

(1) The ingredient is used as a surface-finishing agent as defined in § 170.3(o)(30) of this chapter.

(2) The ingredient is used in food at levels not to exceed current good manufacturing practice.

(d) Prior sanctions for this ingredient different from the uses established in this section do not exist or have been waived.

[50 FR 8999, Mar. 6, 1985, as amended at 73 FR 8608, Feb. 14, 2008]

§ 184.1985 Aminopeptidase enzyme preparation derived from lactococcus lactis.

(a) Aminopeptidase enzyme preparation is derived from the nonpathogenic and nontoxicogenic bacterium *Lactococcus lactis* (previously named *Streptococcus lactis*). The preparation contains the enzyme aminopeptidase (CAS Reg. No. 9031–94–1; EC 3.4.11.1) and other peptidases that hydrolyze milk proteins. The preparation is produced by pure culture fermentation.

(b) The ingredient meets the specifications for enzyme preparations in the Food Chemicals Codex, 3d ed. (1981), pp. 107–110, which are incorporated by reference in accordance with 5 U.S.C. 552(a) and 1 CFR part 51. Copies are available from the National Academy Press, 2101 Constitution Ave. NW., Washington, DC 20418, or may be examined at the Office of Food Additive Safety (HFS–200), Center for Food Safety and Applied Nutrition, Food and Drug Administration, 5100 Paint Branch Pkwy., College Park, MD 20740, 240–402–1200, or at the National Archives and Records Administration (NARA). For information on the availability of this material at NARA, call 202–741–6030, or go to: *http://www.archives.gov/federal_register/code_of_federal_regulations/ibr_locations.html.*

(c) In accordance with § 184.1(b)(1), the ingredient is used in food with no limitations other than current good manufacturing practice. The affirmation of this ingredient as generally recognized as safe as a direct human food ingredient is based upon the following current good manufacturing practice conditions of use:

(1) The ingredient is used as an enzyme, as defined in § 170.3(o)(9) of this chapter, as an optional ingredient for flavor development in the manufacture of cheddar cheese, in accordance with § 133.113 of this chapter, and in the preparation of protein hydrolysates.

(2) The ingredient is used at levels not to exceed current good manufacturing practice.

[60 FR 54193, Oct. 20, 1995, as amended at 78 FR 14667, Mar. 7, 2013]

PART 186—INDIRECT FOOD SUBSTANCES AFFIRMED AS GENERALLY RECOGNIZED AS SAFE

Subpart A—General Provisions

Subpart B—Listing of Specific Substances Affirmed as GRAS

AUTHORITY: 21 U.S.C. 321, 342, 348, 371.

SOURCE: 42 FR 14658, Mar. 15, 1977, unless otherwise noted.

Subpart A—General Provisions

§ 186.1 Substances added indirectly to human food affirmed as generally recognized as safe (GRAS).

(a) The indirect human food ingredients listed in this part have been reviewed by the Food and Drug Administration and determined to be generally recognized as safe (GRAS) for the purposes and under the conditions prescribed, providing they comply with the purity specifications listed in this part or, in the absence of purity specifications, are of a purity suitable for their intended use in accordance with § 170.30(h)(1) of this chapter. Certain ingredients in this part may also be used in food-contact surfaces in accordance with parts 174, 175, 176, 177, 178 or § 179.45 of this chapter. Ingredients affirmed as GRAS for direct use in part 184 of this chapter are also GRAS as indirect human food ingredients in accordance with § 184.1(a) of this chapter.

(b) The regulations in this part do not authorize direct addition of any food ingredient to a food. They authorize only the use of these ingredients as indirect ingredients of food, through migration from their immediate wrapper, container, or other food-contact surface. Any ingredient affirmed as GRAS in this part shall be used in accordance with current good manufacturing practice. For the purpose of this part, current good manufacturing practice includes the requirements that an indirect human food ingredient be of a purity suitable for its intended use, and that it be used at a level no higher than reasonably required to achieve its intended technical effect in the food-contact article.

(1) If the ingredient is affirmed as GRAS with no limitations on its conditions of use other than current good manufacturing practice, it shall be regarded as GRAS if its conditions of use are consistent with the requirements of paragraphs (b), (c), and (d) of this section. When the Food and Drug Administration (FDA) determines that it is appropriate, the agency will describe one or more current good manufacturing practice conditions of use in the regulation that affirms the GRAS status of the indirect ingredient. For example, when the safety of an ingredient has been evaluated on the basis of limited conditions of use, the agency will describe in the regulation that affirms the GRAS status of the indirect ingredient, one or more of these limited conditions of use, which may include the category of food-contact surface(s), technical effect(s) or functional use(s) of the indirect ingredient, and the level(s) of use. If the ingredient is used under conditions that are significantly different from those described in the regulation, such use of a substance may not be GRAS. In such a case, a manufacturer may not rely on the regulation as authorizing that use but shall independently establish that the use is GRAS or shall use the ingredient in accordance with a food additive regulation. Persons seeking FDA approval of an independent determination that a use of an ingredient is GRAS may submit a GRAS petition in accordance with § 170.35 of this chapter.

(2) If the ingredient is affirmed as GRAS with specific limitation(s), it shall be used in food-contact surfaces only within such limitation(s), including the category of food-contact surface(s), the functional use(s) of the ingredient, and the level(s) of use. Any use of such an ingredient not in full compliance with each such established limitation shall require a food additive regulation.

(3) If the ingredient is affirmed as GRAS for a specific use, prior to general evaluation of use of the ingredient, other uses may also be GRAS.

(c) The listing of a food ingredient in this part does not authorize the use of such substance for the purpose of adding the ingredient to the food through extraction from the food-contact surface.

(d) The listing of a food ingredient in this part does not authorize the use of such substance in a manner that may lead to deception to the consumer or to any other violation of the Federal Food, Drug, and Cosmetic Act (the Act).

(e) If the Commissioner of Food and Drugs is aware of any prior sanction for use of an ingredient under conditions different from those proposed to be affirmed as GRAS, he will concurrently propose a separate regulation covering such use of the ingredient under part 181 of this chapter. If the Commissioner is unaware of any such applicable prior sanction, the proposed regulation will so state and will require any person who intends to assert or rely on such sanction to submit proof of its existence. Any regulation promulgated pursuant to this section constitutes a determination that excluded uses would result in adulteration of the food in violation of section 402 of the Act, and the failure of any person to come forward with proof of such an applicable prior sanction in response to the proposal will constitute a waiver of the right to assert or rely on such sanction at any later time. The notice will also constitute a proposal to establish a regulation under part 181 of this chapter, incorporating the same provisions, in the event that such a regulation is determined to be appropriate as a result of submission of proof of such an applicable prior sanction in response to the proposal.

[42 FR 14658, Mar. 15, 1977, as amended at 48 FR 48457, 48459, Oct. 19, 1983]

Subpart B—Listing of Specific Substances Affirmed as GRAS

§ 186.1093 Sulfamic acid.

(a) Sulfamic acid (H_3NO_3S, CAS Reg. No. 5329–14–6) is a white crystalline solid manufactured from urea, sulfur trioxide, and sulfuric acid. It is soluble and highly ionized in water.

(b) In accordance with § 186.1(b)(1), the ingredient is used as an indirect food ingredient with no limitations other than current good manufacturing practice. The affirmation of this ingredient as generally recognized as safe (GRAS) as an indirect human food ingredient is based upon the current good manufacturing practice of using this ingredient in the manufacture of paper and paperboard that contact food.

(c) Prior sanctions for this ingredient different from the uses established in this section do not exist or have been waived.

[47 FR 29954, July 9, 1982]

§ 186.1256 Clay (kaolin).

(a) Clay (kaolin) $Al_2O_{3.2SiO2.nH2}O$, Cas Reg. No. 1332–58–7) consists of hydrated aluminum silicate. The commercial products of clay (kaolin) contain varying quantities of alkalies and alkaline earths. Clay (kaolin) is a white to yellowish or grayish fine powder. There are at least three different minerals, kaolinite, dickite, and nacrite, classified as kaolin. Kaolinite or china clay is whiter, less contaminated with extraneous minerals, and less plastic in water.

(b) In accordance with § 186.1(b)(1), the ingredient is used as an indirect human food ingredient with no limitation other than current good manufacturing practice. The affirmation of this ingredient as generally recognized as safe (GRAS) as an indirect human food ingredient is based upon the following current good manufacturing practice conditions of use:

(1) The ingredient is used in the manufacture of paper and paperboard that contact food.

(2) The ingredient is used at levels not to exceed current good manufacturing practice.

(c) Prior sanctions for this ingredient different from the uses established in this regulation do not exist or have been waived.

[47 FR 43367, Oct. 1, 1982]

§ 186.1275 Dextrans.

(a) Dextrans (CAS Reg. No. 9004–54–0) are high molecular weight polysaccharides produced by bacterial fermentation of sucrose. Commercially available dextrans are synthesized from sucrose by *Leuconostoc mesenteroides* strain NRRL B–512(F). Partial depolymerization and purification of the fermented mixture shall produce a product that is free of viable microorganisms.

(b) The ingredient is used or intended for use as a constituent of food-contact surfaces.

(c) The ingredient is used at levels not to exceed good manufacturing practice.

(d) Prior sanctions for this ingredient different from the uses established in

this section do not exist or have been waived.

[43 FR 29288, July 7, 1978, as amended at 48 FR 48457, Oct. 19, 1983]

§ 186.1300 Ferric oxide.

(a) Ferric oxide (iron (III) oxide, Fe_2O_3, CAS Reg. No. 1309–37–1) occurs naturally as the mineral hematite. It may be prepared synthetically by heating brown iron hydroxide oxide. The product is red-brown to black trigonal crystals.

(b) In accordance with § 186.1(b)(1), the ingredient is used as an indirect human food ingredient with no limitation other than current good manufacturing practice. The affirmation of this ingredient as generally recognized as safe (GRAS) as an indirect human food ingredient is based upon the following current good manufacturing practice conditions of use:

(1) The ingredient is used as a constituent of paper and paperboard used for food packaging.

(2) The ingredient is used at levels not to exceed current good manufacturing practice.

(c) Prior sanctions for this ingredient different from the uses established in this section do not exist or have been waived.

[53 FR 16867, May 12, 1988; 53 FR 20939, June 7, 1988]

§ 186.1316 Formic acid.

(a) Formic acid (CH_2O_2, CAS Reg. No. 64–18–6) is also referred to as methanoic acid or hydrogen carboxylic acid. It occurs naturally in some insects and is contained in the free acid state in a number of plants. Formic acid is prepared by the reaction of sodium formate with sulfuric acid and is isolated by distillation.

(b) Formic acid is used as a constituent of paper and paperboard used for food packaging.

(c) The ingredient is used at levels not to exceed good manufacturing practice in accordance with § 186.1(b)(1).

(d) Prior sanctions for formic acid different from the uses established in this section do not exist or have been waived.

[45 FR 22915, Apr. 4, 1980]

§ 186.1374 Iron oxides.

(a) Iron oxides (oxides of iron, CAS Reg. No. 1332–37–2) are undefined mixtures of iron (II) oxide (CAS Reg. No. 1345–25–1, black cubic crystals) and iron (III) oxide (CAS Reg. No. 1309–37–1, red-brown to black trigonal crystals).

(b) In accordance with § 186.1(b)(1), the ingredient is used as an indirect human food ingredient with no limitation other than current good manufacturing practice. The affirmation of this ingredient as generally recognized as safe (GRAS) as an indirect human food ingredient is based upon the following current good manufacturing practice conditions of use:

(1) The ingredient is used as a constituent of paper and paperboard used for food packaging.

(2) The ingredient is used at levels not to exceed current good manufacturing practice.

(c) Prior sanctions for this ingredient different from the uses established in this section do not exist or have been waived.

[53 FR 16867, May 12, 1988; 53 FR 20939, June 7, 1988, as amended at 69 FR 24512, May 4, 2004]

§ 186.1551 Hydrogenated fish oil.

(a) Hydrogenated fish oil (CAS Reg. No. 91078–95–4) is a class of oils produced by partial hydrogenation of oils expressed from fish, primarily menhaden, and secondarily herring or tuna. Hydrogenation of fish oils uses catalysts composed of either elemental nickel, elemental copper, or a mixture of these elements. The crude hydrogenated fish oil is further processed by alkali refining, bleaching, and deodorization by steam stripping.

(b) Hydrogenation of fish oils results in a final product with a melting point greater than 32 °C as determined by Section Cc 1–25, Official and Tentative Methods of the American Oil Chemists' Society method (reapproved 1973) or equivalent. The product has an approximate fatty acid composition of 30 to 45 percent saturated fatty acids, 40 to 55 percent monoenoic fatty acids, 7 to 15 percent dienoic fatty acids, 3 to 10 percent trienoic fatty acids, and less than 2 percent tetraenoic or higher polyenoic fatty acids. The approximate percentages of total fatty acids by carbon chain length are 15 to 30 percent each of C_{16}, C_{18}, C_{20}, C_{22}, less than 10 percent C_{14} or lower carbon chain length, and less than 1 percent C_{24} or higher carbon chain length fatty acids.

(c) The ingredient is used as a constituent of cotton and cotton fabrics used for dry food packaging.

(d) The ingredient is used at levels not to exceed good manufacturing practice in accordance with § 186.1(b)(1).

(e) Prior sanctions for this ingredient different from the use established in this section do not exist or have been waived.

[44 FR 28323, May 15, 1979, as amended at 49 FR 5614, Feb. 14, 1984; 58 FR 17099, Apr. 1, 1993]

§ 186.1555 Japan wax.

(a) Japan wax (CAS Reg. No. 8001–39–6), also known as Japan tallow or sumac wax, is a pale yellow vegetable tallow, containing glycerides of the C_{19}-C_{23} dibasic acids and a high content of tripalmitin. It is prepared from the mesocarp by hot pressing of immature fruits of the oriental sumac, *Rhus succedanea* (Japan, Taiwan, and Indo-China), *R. vernicifera* (Japan), and *R. trichocarpa* (China, Indo-China, India, and Japan). Japan wax is soluble in hot alcohol, benzene, and naphtha, and insoluble in water and in cold alcohol.

(b) In accordance with paragraph (b)(1) of this section, the ingredient is used as an indirect human food ingredient with no limitation other than current good manufacturing practice. The affirmation of this ingredient as generally recognized as safe (GRAS) as an indirect human food ingredient is based on the following current good manufacturing practice conditions of use:

(1) The ingredient is used as a constituent of cotton and cotton fabrics used for dry food packaging.

(2) The ingredient is used at levels not to exceed current good manufacturing practice.

(c) Prior sanctions for this ingredient different from the uses established in this section do not exist or have been waived.

[60 FR 62208, Dec. 5, 1995]

§ 186.1557 Tall oil.

(a) Tall oil (CAS Reg. No. 8002–26–4) is essentially the sap of the pine tree. It is obtained commercially from the waste liquors of pinewood pulp mills and consists mainly of tall oil resin acids and tall oil fatty acids.

(b) In accordance with § 186.1(b)(1), the ingredient is used as an indirect human food ingredient with no limitation other than current good manufacturing practice. The affirmation of this ingredient as generally recognized as safe (GRAS) as an indirect human food ingredient is based on the following current good manufacturing practice conditions of use:

(1) The ingredient is used as a constituent of cotton and cotton fabrics used for dry food packaging.

(2) The ingredient is used at levels not to exceed current good manufacturing practice.

(c) Prior sanctions for this ingredient different from the uses established in this section, or from those listed in part 181 of this chapter, do not exist or have been waived.

[51 FR 16830, May 7, 1986]

§ 186.1673 Pulp.

(a) Pulp is the soft, spongy pith inside the stem of a plant such as wood, straw, sugarcane, or other natural plant sources.

(b) The ingredient is used or intended for use as a constituent of food packaging containers.

(c) The ingredient is used in paper and paperboard made by conventional paper-making processes at levels not to exceed good manufacturing practice.

(d) Prior sanctions for this ingredient different from the uses established in this section do not exist or have been waived.

§ 186.1750 Sodium chlorite.

(a) Sodium chlorite ($NaClO_2$, CAS Reg. No. 7758–19–2) exists as slightly hygroscopic white crystals or flakes. It is manufactured by passing chlorine dioxide into a solution of sodium hydroxide and hydrogen peroxide.

(b) the ingredient is used at levels from 125 to 250 parts per million as a slimicide in the manufacture of paper and paperboard that contact food.

[45 FR 16470, Mar. 14, 1980]

§ 186.1756 Sodium formate.

(a) Sodium formate ($CHNaO_2$, CAS Reg. No. 141–53–7) is the sodium salt of formic acid. It is produced by the reaction of carbon monoxide with sodium hydroxide.

(b) The ingredient is used as a constituent of paper and paperboard used for food packaging.

(c) The ingredient is used at levels not to exceed good manufacturing practice in accordance with § 186.1(b)(1).

(d) Prior sanctions for sodium formate different from the uses established in this section do not exist or have been waived.

[45 FR 22915, Apr. 4, 1980]

§ 186.1770 Sodium oleate.

(a) Sodium oleate ($C_{18}H_{33}O_2Na$, CAS Reg. No. 143–19–1) is the sodium salt of oleic acid (*cis*-9-octadecenoic acid). It exists as a white to yellowish powder with a slight tallow-like odor. Commercially, sodium oleate is made by mixing and heating flaked sodium hydroxide and oleic acid.

(b) In accordance with § 186.1(b)(1), the ingredient is used as a constituent of paper and paperboard for food packaging and as a component of lubricants with incidental food contact in accordance with § 178.3570 of this chapter, with no limitation other than current good manufacturing practice.

(c) Prior sanctions for this ingredient different from the uses established in this section do not exist or have been waived.

[51 FR 39372, Oct. 28, 1986]

§ 186.1771 Sodium palmitate.

(a) Sodium palmitate ($C_{16}H_{31}O_2Na$, CAS Reg. No. 408–35–5) is the sodium salt of palmitic acid (hexadecanoic acid). It exists as a white to yellow powder. Commercially, sodium palmitate is made by mixing and heating flaked sodium hydroxide and palmitic acid.

(b) In accordance with § 186.1(b)(1), the ingredient is used as a constituent of paper and paperboard for food packaging with no limitation other than current good manufacturing practice.

(c) Prior sanctions for this ingredient different from the uses established in this section do not exist or have been waived.

[51 FR 39372, Oct. 28, 1986]

§ 186.1797 Sodium sulfate.

(a) Sodium sulfate (Na_2SO_4, CAS Reg. No. 7757–82–6), also known as Glauber's salt, occurs naturally and exists as colorless crystals or as a fine, white crystalline powder. It is prepared by the neutralization of sulfuric acid with sodium hydroxide.

(b) The ingredient is used as a constituent of paper and paperboard used for food packaging, and cotton and cotton fabric used for dry food packaging.

(c) The ingredient is used at levels not to exceed good manufacturing practice in accordance with § 186.1(b)(1).

(d) Prior sanctions for this ingredient different from the uses established in this section do not exist or have been waived.

[45 FR 6086, Jan. 25, 1980]

§ 186.1839 Sorbose.

(a) Sorbose (L-sorbose, sorbinose) ($C_6H_{12}O_6$, CAS Reg. No. 87–79–6) is an orthorhombic, bisphenoidal crystalline ketohexose. It was originally identifed in the juice of mature berries from the mountain ash (*Sorbus aucuparia*) where it occurs as the result of microbial oxidation of sorbitol. It also occurs naturally in other plants. Sorbose can be synthesized by the catalytic hydrogenation of glucose to D-sorbitol. The resulting sorbitol can be oxidized by *Acetobacter xylinum* or by *Acetobacter suboxydans*.

(b) The ingredient is used or intended for indirect food use as a constituent of cotton, cotton fabrics, paper, and paperboard in contact with dry food.

(c) The ingredient migrates to food at levels not to exceed good manufacturing practice.

(d) Prior sanctions for this ingredient different from the uses established in this section do not exist or have been waived.

[43 FR 11698, Mar. 21, 1978, as amended at 48 FR 48457, Oct. 19, 1983]

PART 189—SUBSTANCES PROHIBITED FROM USE IN HUMAN FOOD

AUTHORITY: 21 U.S.C. 321, 342, 348, 371, 381.

SOURCE: 42 FR 14659, Mar. 15, 1977, unless otherwise noted.

EDITORIAL NOTE: Nomenclature changes to part 189 appear at 61 FR 14482, Apr. 2, 1996, 66 FR 56035, Nov. 6, 2001, 70 FR 40880, July 15, 2005, and 70 FR 67651, Nov. 8, 2005.

Subpart A—General Provisions

§ 189.1 Substances prohibited from use in human food.

(a) The food ingredients listed in this section have been prohibited from use in human food by the Food and Drug Administration because of a determination that they present a potential risk to the public health or have not been shown by adequate scientific data to be safe for use in human food. Use of any of these substances in violation of this section causes the food involved to be adulterated in violation of the act.

(b) This section includes only a partial list of substances prohibited from use in human food, for easy reference purposes, and is not a complete list of substances that may not lawfully be used in human food. No substance may be used in human food unless it meets all applicable requirements of the act.

(c) The Commissioner of Food and Drugs, either on his own initiative or on behalf of any interested person who has submitted a petition, may publish a proposal to establish, amend, or repeal a regulation under this section on the basis of new scientific evaluation or information. Any such petition shall include an adequate scientific basis to support the petition, pursuant to part 10 of this chapter, and will be published for comment if it contains reasonable grounds.

[42 FR 14659, Mar. 15, 1977, as amended at 54 FR 24899, June 12, 1989]

Subpart B—Prohibited Cattle Materials

§ 189.5 Prohibited cattle materials.

(a) *Definitions*. The definitions and interpretations of terms contained in section 201 of the Federal Food, Drug, and Cosmetic Act (the act) apply to such terms when used in this part. The following definitions also apply:

(1) Prohibited cattle materials means specified risk materials, small intestine of all cattle except as provided in paragraph (b)(2) of this section, material from nonambulatory disabled cattle, material from cattle not inspected and passed, or mechanically separated (MS) (Beef). Prohibited cattle materials do not include the following:

(i) Tallow that contains no more than 0.15 percent insoluble impurities, tallow derivatives, hides and hide-derived products, and milk and milk products, and

(ii) Cattle materials inspected and passed from a country designated under paragraph (e) of this section.

(2) *Inspected and passed* means that the product has been inspected and

passed for human consumption by the appropriate regulatory authority, and at the time it was inspected and passed, it was found to be not adulterated.

(3) *Mechanically Separated (MS)(Beef)* means a meat food product that is finely comminuted, resulting from the mechanical separation and removal of most of the bone from attached skeletal muscle of cattle carcasses and parts of carcasses that meets the specifications contained in 9 CFR 319.5, the regulation that prescribes the standard of identity for MS (Species).

(4) *Nonambulatory disabled cattle* means cattle that cannot rise from a recumbent position or that cannot walk, including, but not limited to, those with broken appendages, severed tendons or ligaments, nerve paralysis, fractured vertebral column, or metabolic conditions.

(5) *Specified risk material* means the brain, skull, eyes, trigeminal ganglia, spinal cord, vertebral column (excluding the vertebrae of the tail, the transverse processes of the thoracic and lumbar vertebrae, and the wings of the sacrum), and dorsal root ganglia of cattle 30 months and older and the tonsils and distal ileum of the small intestine of all cattle.

(6) *Tallow* means the rendered fat of cattle obtained by pressing or by applying any other extraction process to tissues derived directly from discrete adipose tissue masses or to other carcass parts and tissues. Tallow must be produced from tissues that are not prohibited cattle materials or must contain not more than 0.15 percent insoluble impurities as determined by the method entitled "Insoluble Impurities" (AOCS Official Method Ca 3a-46), American Oil Chemists' Society (AOCS), 5th Edition, 1997, incorporated by reference in accordance with 5 U.S.C. 552(a) and 1 CFR part 51, or another method equivalent in accuracy, precision, and sensitivity to AOCS Official Method Ca 3a-46. You may obtain copies of the method from AOCS (*http://www.aocs.org*) 2211 W. Bradley Ave. Champaign, IL 61821. Copies may be examined at the Center for Food Safety and Applied Nutrition's Library, 5100 Paint Branch Pkwy., College Park, MD 20740, or at the National Archives and Records Administration (NARA). For information on the availability of this material at NARA, call 202–741–6030, or go to *http://www.archives.gov/federal_register/code_of_federal_regulations/ibr_locations.html.*

(7) *Tallow derivative* means any chemical obtained through initial hydrolysis, saponification, or trans-esterification of tallow; chemical conversion of material obtained by hydrolysis, saponification, or trans-esterification may be applied to obtain the desired product.

(b) *Requirements.* (1) No human food shall be manufactured from, processed with, or otherwise contain, prohibited cattle materials.

(2) The small intestine is not considered prohibited cattle material if the distal ileum is removed by a procedure that removes at least 80 inches of the uncoiled and trimmed small intestine, as measured from the caeco-colic junction and progressing proximally towards the jejunum, or by a procedure that the establishment can demonstrate is equally effective in ensuring complete removal of the distal ileum.

(c) *Records.* (1) Manufacturers and processors of a human food that is manufactured from, processed with, or otherwise contains, material from cattle must establish and maintain records sufficient to demonstrate that the food is not manufactured from, processed with, or does not otherwise contain, prohibited cattle materials.

(2) Records must be retained for 2 years after the date they were created.

(3) Records must be retained at the manufacturing or processing establishment or at a reasonably accessible location.

(4) The maintenance of electronic records is acceptable. Electronic records are considered to be reasonably accessible if they are accessible from an onsite location.

(5) Records required by this section and existing records relevant to compliance with this section must be available to FDA for inspection and copying.

(6) When filing entry with U.S. Customs and Border Protection, the importer of record of a human food manufactured from, processed with, or otherwise containing, cattle material must affirm that the food was manufactured from, processed with, or otherwise contains, cattle material and must affirm that the food was manufactured in accordance with this section. If a human food is manufactured from, processed with, or otherwise contains, cattle material, then the importer of record must, if requested, provide within 5 days records sufficient to demonstrate that the food is not manufactured from, processed with, or does not otherwise contain, prohibited cattle material.

(7) Records established or maintained to satisfy the requirements of this subpart that meet the definition of electronic records in §11.3(b)(6) of this chapter are exempt from the requirements of part 11 of this chapter. Records that satisfy the requirements of this subpart but that are also required under other applicable statutory provisions or regulations remain subject to part 11 of this chapter.

(d) *Adulteration.* (1) Failure of a manufacturer or processor to operate in compliance with the requirements of paragraphs (b) or (c) of this section renders human food adulterated under section 402(a)(4) of the act.

(2) Human food manufactured from, processed with, or otherwise containing, prohibited cattle materials is unfit for human food and deemed adulterated under section 402(a)(3) of the act.

(3) *Food additive status.* Prohibited cattle materials for use in human food are food additives subject to section 409 of the act, except when used as dietary ingredients in dietary supplements. The use or intended use of any prohibited cattle material in human food causes the material and the food to be adulterated under section 402(a)(2)(C) of the act if the prohibited cattle material is a food additive, unless it is the subject of a food additive regulation or of an investigational exemption for a food additive under §170.17 of this chapter.

(e) *Process for designating countries.* A country seeking designation must send a written request to the Director, Office of the Center Director, Center for Food Safety and Applied Nutrition, Food and Drug Administration, at the address designated in 21 CFR 5.1100. The request shall include information about a country's bovine spongiform encephalopathy (BSE) case history, risk factors, measures to prevent the introduction and transmission of BSE, and any other information relevant to determining whether specified risk materials, the small intestine of cattle except as provided in paragraph (b)(2) of this section, material from nonambulatory disabled cattle, or MS (Beef) from cattle from the country should be considered prohibited cattle materials. FDA shall respond in writing to any such request and may impose conditions in granting any such request. A country designation granted by FDA under this paragraph will be subject to future review by FDA, and may be revoked if FDA determines that it is no longer appropriate.

[70 FR 53068, Sept. 7, 2005, as amended at 71 FR 59668, Oct. 11, 2006; 73 FR 20793, Apr. 17, 2008]

Subpart C—Substances Generally Prohibited From Direct Addition or Use as Human Food

SOURCE: 42 FR 14659, Mar. 15, 1977, unless otherwise noted. Redesignated at 69 FR 42273, July 14, 2004.

§ 189.110 Calamus and its derivatives.

(a) Calamus is the dried rhizome of *Acorus calamus* L. It has been used as a flavoring compound, especially as the oil or extract.

(b) Food containing any added calamus, oil of calamus, or extract of calamus is deemed to be adulterated in violation of the act based upon an order published in the FEDERAL REGISTER of May 9, 1968 (33 FR 6967).

(c) The analytical method used for detecting oil of calamus (β-asarone) is in the "Journal of the Association of Official Analytical Chemists," Volume 56, (Number 5), pages 1281 to 1283, September 1973, which is incorporated by reference. Copies are available from the AOAC INTERNATIONAL, 481 North Frederick Ave., suite 500, Gaithersburg,

MD 20877, also from the Office of Food Additive Safety (HFS–200), Center for Food Safety and Applied Nutrition, Food and Drug Administration, 5100 Paint Branch Pkwy., College Park, MD 20740, 240–402–1200, or available for inspection at the National Archives and Records Administration (NARA). For information on the availability of this material at NARA, call 202–741–6030, or go to: *http://www.archives.gov/federal_register/code_of_federal_regulations/ibr_locations.html.*

[42 FR 14659, Mar. 15, 1977, as amended at 47 FR 11855, Mar. 19, 1982; 54 FR 24899, June 12, 1989; 78 FR 14667, Mar. 7, 2013]

§ 189.113 Cinnamyl anthranilate.

(a) The food additive cinnamyl anthranilate ($C_{16}H_{15}NO_2$, CAS Reg. No. 87–29–6) is the ester of cinnamyl alcohol and anthranilic acid. Cinnamyl anthranilate is a synthetic chemical that has not been identified in natural products at levels detectable by available methodology. It has been used as a flavoring agent in food.

(b) Food containing any added cinnamyl anthranilate is deemed to be adulterated in violation of the act based upon an order published in the FEDERAL REGISTER of October 23, 1985.

[50 FR 42932, Oct. 23, 1985]

§ 189.120 Cobaltous salts and its derivatives.

(a) Cobaltous salts are the chemicals, $CoC_4H_6O_4$, $CoCl_2$, and $CoSO_4$.They have been used in fermented malt beverages as a foam stabilizer and to prevent "gushing."

(b) Food containing any added cobaltous salts is deemed to be adulterated in violation of the act based upon an order published in the FEDERAL REGISTER of August 12, 1966 (31 FR 8788).

§ 189.130 Coumarin.

(a) Coumarin is the chemical 1,2-benzopyrone, $C_9H_6O_2$. It is found in tonka beans and extract of tonka beans, among other natural sources, and is also synthesized. It has been used as a flavoring compound.

(b) Food containing any added coumarin as such or as a constituent of tonka beans or tonka extract is deemed to be adulterated under the act, based upon an order published in the FEDERAL REGISTER of March 5, 1954 (19 FR 1239).

(c) The analytical methods used for detecting coumarin in food are in sections 19.016–19.024 of the "Official Methods of Analysis of the Association of Official Analytical Chemists," 13th Ed. (1980), which is incorporated by reference. Copies may be obtained from the AOAC INTERNATIONAL, 481 North Frederick Ave., suite 500, Gaithersburg, MD 20877, or may be examined at the National Archives and Records Administration (NARA). For information on the availability of this material at NARA, call 202–741–6030, or go to: *http://www.archives.gov/federal_register/code_of_federal_regulations/ibr_locations.html.*

[42 FR 14659, Mar. 15, 1977, as amended at 49 FR 10114, Mar. 19, 1984; 54 FR 24899, June 12, 1989]

§ 189.135 Cyclamate and its derivatives.

(a) Calcium, sodium, magnesium and potassium salts of cyclohexane sulfamic acid, $(C_6H_{12}NO_3S)_2Ca$, $(C_6H_{12}NO_3S)Na$, $(C_6H_{12}NO_3S)_2Mg$, and $(C_6H_{12}NO_3S)K$. Cyclamates are synthetic chemicals having a sweet taste 30 to 40 times that of sucrose, are not found in natural products at levels detectable by the official methodology, and have been used as artificial sweeteners.

(b) Food containing any added or detectable level of cyclamate is deemed to be adulterated in violation of the act based upon an order published in the FEDERAL REGISTER of October 21, 1969 (34 FR 17063).

(c) The analytical methods used for detecting cyclamate in food are in sections 20.162–20.172 of the "Official Methods of Analysis of the Association of Official Analytical Chemists," 13th Ed. (1980), which is incorporated by reference. Copies may be obtained from the AOAC INTERNATIONAL, 481 North Frederick Ave., suite 500, Gaithersburg, MD 20877, or may be examined at the National Archives and Records Administration (NARA). For information on the availability of this material at NARA, call 202–741–6030, or go to: *http://www.archives.gov/federal_register/*

code__of__federal__regulations/ ibr__locations.html.

[42 FR 14659, Mar. 15, 1977, as amended at 49 FR 10114, Mar. 19, 1984; 54 FR 24899, June 12, 1989]

§ 189.140 Diethylpyrocarbonate (DEPC).

(a) Diethylpyrocarbonate is the chemical pyrocarbonic acid diethyl ester, $C_6H_{10}O_5$. It is a synthetic chemical not found in natural products at levels detectable by available methodology and has been used as a ferment inhibitor in alcoholic and nonalcoholic beverages.

(b) Food containing any added or detectable level of DEPC is deemed to be adulterated in violation of the act based upon an order published in the FEDERAL REGISTER of August 2, 1972 (37 FR 15426).

§ 189.145 Dulcin.

(a) Dulcin is the chemical 4-ethoxyphenylurea, $C_9H_{12}N_2O_2$. It is a synthetic chemical having a sweet taste about 250 times that of sucrose, is not found in natural products at levels detectable by the official methodology, and has been proposed for use as an artificial sweetener.

(b) Food containing any added or detectable level of dulcin is deemed to be adulterated in violation of the act, based upon an order published in the FEDERAL REGISTER of January 19, 1950 (15 FR 321).

(c) The analytical methods used for detecting dulcin in food are in sections 20.173–20.176 of the "Official Methods of Analysis of the Association of Official Analytical Chemists," 13th Ed. (1980), which is incorporated by reference. Copies may be obtained from the AOAC INTERNATIONAL, 481 North Frederick Ave., suite 500, Gaithersburg, MD 20877, or may be examined at the National Archives and Records Administration (NARA). For information on the availability of this material at NARA, call 202–741–6030, or go to: *http://www.archives.gov/federal__register/code__of__federal__regulations/ibr__locations.html.*

[42 FR 14659, Mar. 15, 1977, as amended at 49 FR 10114, Mar. 19, 1984; 54 FR 24899, June 12, 1989]

§ 189.155 Monochloroacetic acid.

(a) Monochloroacetic acid is the chemical chloroacetic acid, $C_2H_3ClO_2$. It is a synthetic chemical not found in natural products, and has been proposed as a preservative in alcoholic and nonalcoholic beverages. Monochloroacetic acid is permitted in food package adhesives with an accepted migration level up to 10 parts per billion (ppb) under § 175.105 of this chapter. The official methods do not detect monochloroacetic acid at the 10 ppb level.

(b) Food containing any added or detectable level of monochloroacetic acid is deemed to be adulterated in violation of the act based upon trade correspondence dated December 29, 1941 (TC–377).

(c) The analytical methods used for detecting monochloroacetic acid in food are in sections 20.067–20.072 of the "Official Methods of Analysis of the Association of Official Analytical Chemists," 13th Ed. (1980), which is incorporated by reference. Copies may be obtained from the AOAC INTERNATIONAL, 481 North Frederick Ave., suite 500, Gaithersburg, MD 20877, or may be examined at the National Archives and Records Administration (NARA). For information on the availability of this material at NARA, call 202–741–6030, or go to: *http://www.archives.gov/federal__register/code__of__federal__regulations/ibr__locations.html.*

[42 FR 14659, Mar. 15, 1977, as amended at 49 FR 10114, Mar. 19, 1984; 54 FR 24899, June 12, 1989]

§ 189.165 Nordihydroguaiaretic acid (NDGA).

(a) Nordihydroguaiaretic acid is the chemical 4,4′-(2,3-dimethyltetramethylene) dipyrocatechol, $C_{18}H_{22}O_4$. It occurs naturally in the resinous exudates of certain plants. The commercial product, which is synthesized, has been used as an antioxidant in foods.

(b) Food containing any added NDGA is deemed to be adulterated in violation of the act based upon an order published in the FEDERAL REGISTER of April 11, 1968 (33 FR 5619).

(c) The analytical method used for detecting NDGA in food is in section

20.008(b) of the "Official Methods of Analysis of the AOAC INTERNATIONAL," 13th Ed. (1980), which is incorporated by reference. Copies may be obtained from the AOAC INTERNATIONAL, 481 North Frederick Ave., suite 500, Gaithersburg, MD 20877, or may be examined at the National Archives and Records Administration (NARA). For information on the availability of this material at NARA, call 202–741–6030, or go to: *http://www.archives.gov/federal_register/code_of_federal_regulations/ibr_locations.html.*

[42 FR 14659, Mar. 15, 1977, as amended at 49 FR 10114, Mar. 19, 1984; 54 FR 24900, June 12, 1989]

§ 189.175 P–4000.

(a) P–4000 is the chemical 5-nitro-2-n-propoxyaniline, $C_9H_{12}N_2O_3$. It is a synthetic chemical having a sweet taste about 4000 times that of sucrose, is not found in natural products at levels detectable by the official methodology, and has been proposed for use as an artificial sweetener.

(b) Food containing any added or detectable level of P–4000 is deemed to be adulterated in violation of the act based upon an order published in the FEDERAL REGISTER of January 19, 1950 (15 FR 321).

(c) The analytical methods used for detecting P–4000 in food are in sections 20.177–20.181 of the "Official Methods of Analysis of the Association of Official Analytical Chemists," 13th Ed. (1980), which is incorporated by reference. Copies may be obtained from the AOAC INTERNATIONAL, 481 North Frederick Ave., suite 500, Gaithersburg, MD 20877, or may be examined at the National Archives and Records Administration (NARA). For information on the availability of this material at NARA, call 202–741–6030, or go to: *http://www.archives.gov/federal_register/code_of_federal_regulations/ibr_locations.html.*

[42 FR 14659, Mar. 15, 1977, as amended at 49 FR 10114, Mar. 19, 1984; 54 FR 24900, June 12, 1989]

§ 189.180 Safrole.

(a) Safrole is the chemical 4-allyl-1,2-methylenedioxy-benzene, $C_{10}H_{10}O_2$. It is a natural constituent of the sassafras plant. Oil of sassafras is about 80 percent safrole. Isosafrole and dihydrosafrole are derivatives of safrole, and have been used as flavoring compounds.

(b) Food containing any added safrole, oil of sassafras, isosafrole, or dihydrosafrole, as such, or food containing any safrole, oil of sassafras, isosafrole, or dihydrosafrole, e.g., sassafras bark, which is intended solely or primarily as a vehicle for imparting such substances to another food, e.g., sassafras tea, is deemed to be adulterated in violation of the act based upon an order published in the FEDERAL REGISTER of December 3, 1960 (25 FR 12412).

(c) The analytical method used for detecting safrole, isosafrole and dihydrosafrole is in the "Journal of the Association of Official Analytical Chemists," Volume 54 (Number 4), pages 900 to 902, July 1971, which is incorporated by reference. Copies are available from the Office of Food Additive Safety (HFS–200), Center for Food Safety and Applied Nutrition, Food and Drug Administration, 5100 Paint Branch Pkwy., College Park, MD 20740, 240–402–1200, or available for inspection at the National Archives and Records Administration (NARA). For information on the availability of this material at NARA, call 202–741–6030, or go to: *http://www.archives.gov/federal_register/code_of_federal_regulations/ibr_locations.html.*

[42 FR 14659, Mar. 15, 1977, as amended at 42 FR 56729, Oct. 28, 1977; 47 FR 11855, Mar. 19, 1982; 54 FR 24900, June 12, 1989; 78 FR 14667, Mar. 7, 2013]

§ 189.190 Thiourea.

(a) Thiourea is the chemical thiocarbamide, CH_4N_2S. It is a synthetic chemical, is not found in natural products at levels detectable by the official methodology, and has been proposed as an antimycotic for use in dipping citrus.

(b) Food containing any added or detectable level of thiourea is deemed to be adulterated under the act.

(c) The analytical methods used for detecting thiourea are in sections 20.115–20.126 of the "Official Methods of Analysis of the Association of Official

Analytical Chemists,'' 13th Ed. (1980), which is incorporated by reference. Copies may be obtained from the AOAC INTERNATIONAL, 481 North Frederick Ave., suite 500, Gaithersburg, MD 20877, or may be examined at the National Archives and Records Administration (NARA). For information on the availability of this material at NARA, call 202–741–6030, or go to: *http://www.archives.gov/federal_register/code_of_federal_regulations/ibr_locations.html.*

[42 FR 14659, Mar. 15, 1977, as amended at 49 FR 10114, Mar. 19, 1984; 54 FR 24900, June 12, 1989]

§ 189.191 Chlorofluorocarbon propellants.

The use of chlorofluorocarbons in human food as propellants in self-pressurized containers is prohibited as provided by § 2.125 of this chapter.

[43 FR 11317, Mar. 17, 1978]

Subpart D—Substances Prohibited From Indirect Addition to Human Food Through Food-Contact Surfaces

SOURCE: 42 FR 14659, Mar. 15, 1977, unless otherwise noted. Redesignated at 69 FR 42273, July 14, 2004.

§ 189.220 Flectol H.

(a) Flectol H is the chemical 1,2-dihydro-2,2,4-trimethylquinoline, polymerized, $C_{12}H_{15}N$. It is a synthetic chemical not found in natural products, and has been used as a component of food packaging adhesives.

(b) Food containing any added or detectable level of this substance is deemed to be adulterated in violation of the act based upon an order published in the FEDERAL REGISTER of April 7, 1967 (32 FR 5675).

[42 FR 14659, Mar. 15, 1977, as amended at 58 FR 17099, Apr. 1, 1993]

§ 189.240 Lead solders.

(a) Lead solders are alloys of metals that include lead and are used in the construction of metal food cans.

(b) Food packaged in any container that makes use of lead in can solder is deemed to be adulterated in violation of the Federal Food, Drug, and Cosmetic Act, based upon an order published in the FEDERAL REGISTER of June 27, 1995.

[60 FR 33109, June 27, 1995]

§ 189.250 Mercaptoimidazoline and 2-mercaptoimidazoline.

(a) Mercaptoimidazoline and 2-mercaptoimidazoline both have the molecular formula $C_3H_6N_2S$. They are synthetic chemicals not found in natural products and have been used in the production of rubber articles that may come into contact with food.

(b) Food containing any added or detectable levels of these substances is deemed to be adulterated in violation of the act based upon an order published in the FEDERAL REGISTER of November 30, 1973 (38 FR 33072).

§ 189.280 4,4′-Methylenebis (2-chloroanaline).

(a) 4,4′-Methylenebis (2-chloroanaline) has the molecular formula, $C_{13}H_{12}Cl_2N_2$. It is a synthetic chemical not found in natural products and has been used as a polyurethane curing agent and as a component of food packaging adhesives and polyurethane resins.

(b) Food containing any added or detectable level of this substance is deemed to be adulterated in violation of the act based upon an order published in the FEDERAL REGISTER of December 2, 1969 (34 FR 19073).

§ 189.300 Hydrogenated 4,4′-isopropylidene-diphenolphosphite ester resins.

(a) Hydrogenated 4,4′-isopropylidene-diphenolphosphite ester resins are the condensation product of 1 mole of triphenyl phosphite and 1.5 moles of hydrogenated 4,4′-isopropylidene-diphenol such that the finished resins have a molecular weight in the range of 2,400 to 3,000. They are synthetic chemicals not found in natural products and have been used as antioxidants and as stabilizers in vinyl chloride polymer resins when such polymer resins are used in the manufacture of rigid vinyl chloride polymer bottles.

(b) Food containing any added or detectable levels of these substances is deemed to be adulterated and in violation of the Federal Food, Drug, and Cosmetic Act, based upon an order published in the FEDERAL REGISTER of September 9, 1987 (52 FR 33929).

[54 FR 7188, Feb. 17, 1989]

§ 189.301 Tin-coated lead foil capsules for wine bottles.

(a) Tin-coated lead foil is composed of a lead foil coated on one or both sides with a thin layer of tin. Tin-coated lead foil has been used as a capsule (i.e., as a covering applied over the cork and neck areas) on wine bottles to prevent insect infestation, as a barrier to oxygen, and for decorative purposes. Information received by the Food and Drug Administration establishes that the use of such a capsule on wine bottles may reasonably be expected to result in lead becoming a component of the wine.

(b) The capping of any bottles of wine after February 8, 1996, with a tin-coated lead foil capsule renders the wine adulterated and in violation of section 402(a)(2)(C) of the Federal Food, Drug, and Cosmetic Act because lead from the capsule, which is an unsafe food additive within the meaning of section 409 of the act, may reasonably be expected to become a component of the wine.

[61 FR 4820, Feb. 8, 1996]

PART 190—DIETARY SUPPLEMENTS

Subpart A [Reserved]

Subpart B—New Dietary Ingredient Notification

AUTHORITY: Secs. 201(ff), 301, 402, 413, 701 of the Federal Food, Drug, and Cosmetic Act (21 U.S.C. 321(ff), 331, 342, 350b, 371).

SOURCE: 62 FR 49891, Sept. 23, 1997, unless otherwise noted.

EDITORIAL NOTE: Nomenclature changes to part 190 appear at 66 FR 56035, Nov. 6, 2001.

Subpart A [Reserved]

Subpart B—New Dietary Ingredient Notification

§ 190.6 Requirement for premarket notification.

(a) At least 75 days before introducing or delivering for introduction into interstate commerce a dietary supplement that contains a new dietary ingredient that has not been present in the food supply as an article used for food in a form in which the food has not been chemically altered, the manufacturer or distributor of that supplement, or of the new dietary ingredient, shall submit to the Office of Nutritional Products, Labeling and Dietary Supplements (HFS–820), Center for Food Safety and Applied Nutrition, Food and Drug Administration, 5100 Paint Branch Pkwy., College Park, MD 20740, information including any citation to published articles that is the basis on which the manufacturer or distributor has concluded that a dietary supplement containing such dietary ingredient will reasonably be expected to be safe. An original and two copies of this notification shall be submitted.

(b) The notification required by paragraph (a) of this section shall include:

(1) The name and complete address of the manufacturer or distributor of the dietary supplement that contains a new dietary ingredient, or of the new dietary ingredient;

(2) The name of the new dietary ingredient that is the subject of the premarket notification, including the Latin binomial name (including the author) of any herb or other botanical;

(3) A description of the dietary supplement or dietary supplements that contain the new dietary ingredient including:

(i) The level of the new dietary ingredient in the dietary supplement; and

(ii) The conditions of use recommended or suggested in the labeling of the dietary supplement, or if no conditions of use are recommended or suggested in the labeling of the dietary supplement, the ordinary conditions of use of the supplement;

(4) The history of use or other evidence of safety establishing that the dietary ingredient, when used under

the conditions recommended or suggested in the labeling of the dietary supplement, will reasonably be expected to be safe, including any citation to published articles or other evidence that is the basis on which the distributor or manufacturer of the dietary supplement that contains the new dietary ingredient has concluded that the new dietary supplement will reasonably be expected to be safe. Any reference to published information offered in support of the notification shall be accompanied by reprints or photostatic copies of such references. If any part of the material submitted is in a foreign language, it shall be accompanied by an accurate and complete English translation; and

(5) The signature of the person designated by the manufacturer or distributor of the dietary supplement that contains a new dietary ingredient.

(c) FDA will acknowledge its receipt of a notification made under section 413 of the Federal Food, Drug, and Cosmetic Act (the act) and will notify the submitter of the date of receipt of such a notification. The date that the agency receives the notification submitted under paragraph (a) of this section is the filing date for the notification. For 75 days after the filing date, the manufacturer or distributor of a dietary supplement that contains a new dietary ingredient shall not introduce, or deliver for introduction, into interstate commerce the dietary supplement that contains the new dietary ingredient.

(d) If the manufacturer or distributor of a dietary supplement that contains a new dietary ingredient, or of the new dietary ingredient, provides additional information in support of the new dietary ingredient notification, the agency will review all submissions pertaining to that notification, including responses made to inquiries from the agency, to determine whether they are substantive and whether they require that the 75-day period be reset. If the agency determines that the new submission is a substantive amendment, FDA will assign a new filing date. FDA will acknowledge receipt of the additional information and, when applicable, notify the manufacturer of the new filing date, which is the date of receipt by FDA of the information that constitutes the substantive amendment.

(e) FDA will not disclose the existence of, or the information contained in, the new dietary ingredient notification for 90 days after the filing date of the notification. After the 90th day, all information in the notification will be placed on public display, except for any information that is trade secret or otherwise confidential commercial information.

(f) Failure of the agency to respond to a notification does not constitute a finding by the agency that the new dietary ingredient or the dietary supplement that contains the new dietary ingredient is safe or is not adulterated under section 402 of the act.

[62 FR 49891, Sept. 23, 1997, as amended at 66 FR 17359, Mar. 30, 2001]

PARTS 191–199 [RESERVED]

FINDING AIDS

A list of CFR titles, subtitles, chapters, subchapters and parts and an alphabetical list of agencies publishing in the CFR are included in the CFR Index and Finding Aids volume to the Code of Federal Regulations which is published separately and revised annually.

Table of CFR Titles and Chapters

(Revised as of April 1, 2013)

Title 1—General Provisions

Title 2—Grants and Agreements

Title 2—Grants and Agreements—Continued

Chap.	
Chapter XXVII	Small Business Administration (Parts 2700—2799)
Chapter XXVIII	Department of Justice (Parts 2800—2899)
Chapter XXX	Department of Homeland Security (Parts 3000—3099)
Chapter XXXI	Institute of Museum and Library Services (Parts 3100—3199)
Chapter XXXII	National Endowment for the Arts (Parts 3200—3299)
Chapter XXXIII	National Endowment for the Humanities (Parts 3300—3399)
Chapter XXXIV	Department of Education (Parts 3400—3499)
Chapter XXXV	Export-Import Bank of the United States (Parts 3500—3599)
Chapter XXXVII	Peace Corps (Parts 3700—3799)
Chapter LVIII	Election Assistance Commission (Parts 5800—5899)

Title 3—The President

Chapter I	Executive Office of the President (Parts 100—199)

Title 4—Accounts

Chapter I	Government Accountability Office (Parts 1—199)
Chapter II	Recovery Accountability and Transparency Board (Parts 200—299)

Title 5—Administrative Personnel

Chapter I	Office of Personnel Management (Parts 1—1199)
Chapter II	Merit Systems Protection Board (Parts 1200—1299)
Chapter III	Office of Management and Budget (Parts 1300—1399)
Chapter V	The International Organizations Employees Loyalty Board (Parts 1500—1599)
Chapter VI	Federal Retirement Thrift Investment Board (Parts 1600—1699)
Chapter VIII	Office of Special Counsel (Parts 1800—1899)
Chapter IX	Appalachian Regional Commission (Parts 1900—1999)
Chapter XI	Armed Forces Retirement Home (Parts 2100—2199)
Chapter XIV	Federal Labor Relations Authority, General Counsel of the Federal Labor Relations Authority and Federal Service Impasses Panel (Parts 2400—2499)
Chapter XV	Office of Administration, Executive Office of the President (Parts 2500—2599)
Chapter XVI	Office of Government Ethics (Parts 2600—2699)
Chapter XXI	Department of the Treasury (Parts 3100—3199)
Chapter XXII	Federal Deposit Insurance Corporation (Parts 3200—3299)

Chap.	
Chapter XXIII	Department of Energy (Parts 3300—3399)
Chapter XXIV	Federal Energy Regulatory Commission (Parts 3400—3499)
Chapter XXV	Department of the Interior (Parts 3500—3599)
Chapter XXVI	Department of Defense (Parts 3600— 3699)
Chapter XXVIII	Department of Justice (Parts 3800—3899)
Chapter XXIX	Federal Communications Commission (Parts 3900—3999)
Chapter XXX	Farm Credit System Insurance Corporation (Parts 4000—4099)
Chapter XXXI	Farm Credit Administration (Parts 4100—4199)
Chapter XXXIII	Overseas Private Investment Corporation (Parts 4300—4399)
Chapter XXXIV	Securities and Exchange Commission (Parts 4400—4499)
Chapter XXXV	Office of Personnel Management (Parts 4500—4599)
Chapter XXXVII	Federal Election Commission (Parts 4700—4799)
Chapter XL	Interstate Commerce Commission (Parts 5000—5099)
Chapter XLI	Commodity Futures Trading Commission (Parts 5100—5199)
Chapter XLII	Department of Labor (Parts 5200—5299)
Chapter XLIII	National Science Foundation (Parts 5300—5399)
Chapter XLV	Department of Health and Human Services (Parts 5500—5599)
Chapter XLVI	Postal Rate Commission (Parts 5600—5699)
Chapter XLVII	Federal Trade Commission (Parts 5700—5799)
Chapter XLVIII	Nuclear Regulatory Commission (Parts 5800—5899)
Chapter XLIX	Federal Labor Relations Authority (Parts 5900—5999)
Chapter L	Department of Transportation (Parts 6000—6099)
Chapter LII	Export-Import Bank of the United States (Parts 6200—6299)
Chapter LIII	Department of Education (Parts 6300—6399)
Chapter LIV	Environmental Protection Agency (Parts 6400—6499)
Chapter LV	National Endowment for the Arts (Parts 6500—6599)
Chapter LVI	National Endowment for the Humanities (Parts 6600—6699)
Chapter LVII	General Services Administration (Parts 6700—6799)
Chapter LVIII	Board of Governors of the Federal Reserve System (Parts 6800—6899)
Chapter LIX	National Aeronautics and Space Administration (Parts 6900—6999)
Chapter LX	United States Postal Service (Parts 7000—7099)
Chapter LXI	National Labor Relations Board (Parts 7100—7199)
Chapter LXII	Equal Employment Opportunity Commission (Parts 7200—7299)
Chapter LXIII	Inter-American Foundation (Parts 7300—7399)
Chapter LXIV	Merit Systems Protection Board (Parts 7400—7499)
Chapter LXV	Department of Housing and Urban Development (Parts 7500—7599)

Title 5—Administrative Personnel—Continued

Chap.	
Chapter LXVI	National Archives and Records Administration (Parts 7600—7699)
Chapter LXVII	Institute of Museum and Library Services (Parts 7700—7799)
Chapter LXVIII	Commission on Civil Rights (Parts 7800—7899)
Chapter LXIX	Tennessee Valley Authority (Parts 7900—7999)
Chapter LXX	Court Services and Offender Supervision Agency for the District of Columbia (Parts 8000—8099)
Chapter LXXI	Consumer Product Safety Commission (Parts 8100—8199)
Chapter LXXIII	Department of Agriculture (Parts 8300—8399)
Chapter LXXIV	Federal Mine Safety and Health Review Commission (Parts 8400—8499)
Chapter LXXVI	Federal Retirement Thrift Investment Board (Parts 8600—8699)
Chapter LXXVII	Office of Management and Budget (Parts 8700—8799)
Chapter LXXX	Federal Housing Finance Agency (Parts 9000—9099)
Chapter LXXXII	Special Inspector General for Iraq Reconstruction (Parts 9200—9299)
Chapter LXXXIII	Special Inspector General for Afghanistan Reconstruction (Parts 9300—9399)
Chapter LXXXIV	Bureau of Consumer Financial Protection (Parts 9400—9499)
Chapter XCVII	Department of Homeland Security Human Resources Management System (Department of Homeland Security—Office of Personnel Management) (Parts 9700—9799)
Chapter XCVII	Council of the Inspectors General on Integrity and Efficiency (Parts 9800—9899)

Title 6—Domestic Security

Chapter I	Department of Homeland Security, Office of the Secretary (Parts 1—99)

Title 7—Agriculture

	SUBTITLE A—OFFICE OF THE SECRETARY OF AGRICULTURE (PARTS 0—26)
	SUBTITLE B—REGULATIONS OF THE DEPARTMENT OF AGRICULTURE
Chapter I	Agricultural Marketing Service (Standards, Inspections, Marketing Practices), Department of Agriculture (Parts 27—209)
Chapter II	Food and Nutrition Service, Department of Agriculture (Parts 210—299)
Chapter III	Animal and Plant Health Inspection Service, Department of Agriculture (Parts 300—399)
Chapter IV	Federal Crop Insurance Corporation, Department of Agriculture (Parts 400—499)

Title 7—Agriculture—Continued

Chap.

Chapter XXXVI	National Agricultural Statistics Service, Department of Agriculture (Parts 3600—3699)
Chapter XXXVII	Economic Research Service, Department of Agriculture (Parts 3700—3799)
Chapter XXXVIII	World Agricultural Outlook Board, Department of Agriculture (Parts 3800—3899)
Chapter XLI	[Reserved]
Chapter XLII	Rural Business-Cooperative Service and Rural Utilities Service, Department of Agriculture (Parts 4200—4299)

Title 8—Aliens and Nationality

Chapter I	Department of Homeland Security (Immigration and Naturalization) (Parts 1—499)
Chapter V	Executive Office for Immigration Review, Department of Justice (Parts 1000—1399)

Title 9—Animals and Animal Products

Chapter I	Animal and Plant Health Inspection Service, Department of Agriculture (Parts 1—199)
Chapter II	Grain Inspection, Packers and Stockyards Administration (Packers and Stockyards Programs), Department of Agriculture (Parts 200—299)
Chapter III	Food Safety and Inspection Service, Department of Agriculture (Parts 300—599)

Title 10—Energy

Chapter I	Nuclear Regulatory Commission (Parts 0—199)
Chapter II	Department of Energy (Parts 200—699)
Chapter III	Department of Energy (Parts 700—999)
Chapter X	Department of Energy (General Provisions) (Parts 1000—1099)
Chapter XIII	Nuclear Waste Technical Review Board (Parts 1300—1399)
Chapter XVII	Defense Nuclear Facilities Safety Board (Parts 1700—1799)
Chapter XVIII	Northeast Interstate Low-Level Radioactive Waste Commission (Parts 1800—1899)

Title 11—Federal Elections

Chapter I	Federal Election Commission (Parts 1—9099)
Chapter II	Election Assistance Commission (Parts 9400—9499)

Title 12—Banks and Banking

Chapter I	Comptroller of the Currency, Department of the Treasury (Parts 1—199)
Chapter II	Federal Reserve System (Parts 200—299)
Chapter III	Federal Deposit Insurance Corporation (Parts 300—399)

Title 12—Banks and Banking—Continued

Chap.	
Chapter IV	Export-Import Bank of the United States (Parts 400—499)
Chapter V	Office of Thrift Supervision, Department of the Treasury (Parts 500—599)
Chapter VI	Farm Credit Administration (Parts 600—699)
Chapter VII	National Credit Union Administration (Parts 700—799)
Chapter VIII	Federal Financing Bank (Parts 800—899)
Chapter IX	Federal Housing Finance Board (Parts 900—999)
Chapter X	Bureau of Consumer Financial Protection (Parts 1000—1099)
Chapter XI	Federal Financial Institutions Examination Council (Parts 1100—1199)
Chapter XII	Federal Housing Finance Agency (Parts 1200—1299)
Chapter XIII	Financial Stability Oversight Council (Parts 1300—1399)
Chapter XIV	Farm Credit System Insurance Corporation (Parts 1400—1499)
Chapter XV	Department of the Treasury (Parts 1500—1599)
Chapter XVI	Office of Financial Research (Parts 1600—1699)
Chapter XVII	Office of Federal Housing Enterprise Oversight, Department of Housing and Urban Development (Parts 1700—1799)
Chapter XVIII	Community Development Financial Institutions Fund, Department of the Treasury (Parts 1800—1899)

Title 13—Business Credit and Assistance

Chapter I	Small Business Administration (Parts 1—199)
Chapter III	Economic Development Administration, Department of Commerce (Parts 300—399)
Chapter IV	Emergency Steel Guarantee Loan Board (Parts 400—499)
Chapter V	Emergency Oil and Gas Guaranteed Loan Board (Parts 500—599)

Title 14—Aeronautics and Space

Chapter I	Federal Aviation Administration, Department of Transportation (Parts 1—199)
Chapter II	Office of the Secretary, Department of Transportation (Aviation Proceedings) (Parts 200—399)
Chapter III	Commercial Space Transportation, Federal Aviation Administration, Department of Transportation (Parts 400—1199)
Chapter V	National Aeronautics and Space Administration (Parts 1200—1299)
Chapter VI	Air Transportation System Stabilization (Parts 1300—1399)

Title 15—Commerce and Foreign Trade

	SUBTITLE A—OFFICE OF THE SECRETARY OF COMMERCE (PARTS 0—29)
	SUBTITLE B—REGULATIONS RELATING TO COMMERCE AND FOREIGN TRADE
Chapter I	Bureau of the Census, Department of Commerce (Parts 30—199)

Title 16—Commercial Practices

Title 17—Commodity and Securities Exchanges

Title 18—Conservation of Power and Water Resources

Title 19—Customs Duties

Title 19—Customs Duties—Continued

Chap.	
Chapter II	United States International Trade Commission (Parts 200—299)
Chapter III	International Trade Administration, Department of Commerce (Parts 300—399)
Chapter IV	U.S. Immigration and Customs Enforcement, Department of Homeland Security (Parts 400—599)

Title 20—Employees' Benefits

Chapter I	Office of Workers' Compensation Programs, Department of Labor (Parts 1—199)
Chapter II	Railroad Retirement Board (Parts 200—399)
Chapter III	Social Security Administration (Parts 400—499)
Chapter IV	Employees' Compensation Appeals Board, Department of Labor (Parts 500—599)
Chapter V	Employment and Training Administration, Department of Labor (Parts 600—699)
Chapter VI	Office of Workers' Compensation Programs, Department of Labor (Parts 700—799)
Chapter VII	Benefits Review Board, Department of Labor (Parts 800—899)
Chapter VIII	Joint Board for the Enrollment of Actuaries (Parts 900—999)
Chapter IX	Office of the Assistant Secretary for Veterans' Employment and Training Service, Department of Labor (Parts 1000—1099)

Title 21—Food and Drugs

Chapter I	Food and Drug Administration, Department of Health and Human Services (Parts 1—1299)
Chapter II	Drug Enforcement Administration, Department of Justice (Parts 1300—1399)
Chapter III	Office of National Drug Control Policy (Parts 1400—1499)

Title 22—Foreign Relations

Chapter I	Department of State (Parts 1—199)
Chapter II	Agency for International Development (Parts 200—299)
Chapter III	Peace Corps (Parts 300—399)
Chapter IV	International Joint Commission, United States and Canada (Parts 400—499)
Chapter V	Broadcasting Board of Governors (Parts 500—599)
Chapter VII	Overseas Private Investment Corporation (Parts 700—799)
Chapter IX	Foreign Service Grievance Board (Parts 900—999)
Chapter X	Inter-American Foundation (Parts 1000—1099)
Chapter XI	International Boundary and Water Commission, United States and Mexico, United States Section (Parts 1100—1199)
Chapter XII	United States International Development Cooperation Agency (Parts 1200—1299)
Chapter XIII	Millennium Challenge Corporation (Parts 1300—1399)

Title 22—Foreign Relations—Continued

Chap.	
Chapter XIV	Foreign Service Labor Relations Board; Federal Labor Relations Authority; General Counsel of the Federal Labor Relations Authority; and the Foreign Service Impasse Disputes Panel (Parts 1400—1499)
Chapter XV	African Development Foundation (Parts 1500—1599)
Chapter XVI	Japan-United States Friendship Commission (Parts 1600—1699)
Chapter XVII	United States Institute of Peace (Parts 1700—1799)

Title 23—Highways

Chapter I	Federal Highway Administration, Department of Transportation (Parts 1—999)
Chapter II	National Highway Traffic Safety Administration and Federal Highway Administration, Department of Transportation (Parts 1200—1299)
Chapter III	National Highway Traffic Safety Administration, Department of Transportation (Parts 1300—1399)

Title 24—Housing and Urban Development

	SUBTITLE A—OFFICE OF THE SECRETARY, DEPARTMENT OF HOUSING AND URBAN DEVELOPMENT (PARTS 0—99)
	SUBTITLE B—REGULATIONS RELATING TO HOUSING AND URBAN DEVELOPMENT
Chapter I	Office of Assistant Secretary for Equal Opportunity, Department of Housing and Urban Development (Parts 100—199)
Chapter II	Office of Assistant Secretary for Housing-Federal Housing Commissioner, Department of Housing and Urban Development (Parts 200—299)
Chapter III	Government National Mortgage Association, Department of Housing and Urban Development (Parts 300—399)
Chapter IV	Office of Housing and Office of Multifamily Housing Assistance Restructuring, Department of Housing and Urban Development (Parts 400—499)
Chapter V	Office of Assistant Secretary for Community Planning and Development, Department of Housing and Urban Development (Parts 500—599)
Chapter VI	Office of Assistant Secretary for Community Planning and Development, Department of Housing and Urban Development (Parts 600—699) [Reserved]
Chapter VII	Office of the Secretary, Department of Housing and Urban Development (Housing Assistance Programs and Public and Indian Housing Programs) (Parts 700—799)
Chapter VIII	Office of the Assistant Secretary for Housing—Federal Housing Commissioner, Department of Housing and Urban Development (Section 8 Housing Assistance Programs, Section 202 Direct Loan Program, Section 202 Supportive Housing for the Elderly Program and Section 811 Supportive Housing for Persons With Disabilities Program) (Parts 800—899)
Chapter IX	Office of Assistant Secretary for Public and Indian Housing, Department of Housing and Urban Development (Parts 900—1699)

Title 25—Indians

Title 26—Internal Revenue

Title 27—Alcohol, Tobacco Products and Firearms

Title 28—Judicial Administration

Title 28—Judicial Administration—Continued

Chap.	
Chapter VI	Offices of Independent Counsel, Department of Justice (Parts 600—699)
Chapter VII	Office of Independent Counsel (Parts 700—799)
Chapter VIII	Court Services and Offender Supervision Agency for the District of Columbia (Parts 800—899)
Chapter IX	National Crime Prevention and Privacy Compact Council (Parts 900—999)
Chapter XI	Department of Justice and Department of State (Parts 1100—1199)

Title 29—Labor

	SUBTITLE A—OFFICE OF THE SECRETARY OF LABOR (PARTS 0—99)
	SUBTITLE B—REGULATIONS RELATING TO LABOR
Chapter I	National Labor Relations Board (Parts 100—199)
Chapter II	Office of Labor-Management Standards, Department of Labor (Parts 200—299)
Chapter III	National Railroad Adjustment Board (Parts 300—399)
Chapter IV	Office of Labor-Management Standards, Department of Labor (Parts 400—499)
Chapter V	Wage and Hour Division, Department of Labor (Parts 500—899)
Chapter IX	Construction Industry Collective Bargaining Commission (Parts 900—999)
Chapter X	National Mediation Board (Parts 1200—1299)
Chapter XII	Federal Mediation and Conciliation Service (Parts 1400—1499)
Chapter XIV	Equal Employment Opportunity Commission (Parts 1600—1699)
Chapter XVII	Occupational Safety and Health Administration, Department of Labor (Parts 1900—1999)
Chapter XX	Occupational Safety and Health Review Commission (Parts 2200—2499)
Chapter XXV	Employee Benefits Security Administration, Department of Labor (Parts 2500—2599)
Chapter XXVII	Federal Mine Safety and Health Review Commission (Parts 2700—2799)
Chapter XL	Pension Benefit Guaranty Corporation (Parts 4000—4999)

Title 30—Mineral Resources

Chapter I	Mine Safety and Health Administration, Department of Labor (Parts 1—199)
Chapter II	Bureau of Safety and Environmental Enforcement, Department of the Interior (Parts 200—299)
Chapter IV	Geological Survey, Department of the Interior (Parts 400—499)
Chapter V	Bureau of Ocean Energy Management, Department of the Interior (Parts 500—599)
Chapter VII	Office of Surface Mining Reclamation and Enforcement, Department of the Interior (Parts 700—999)
Chapter XII	Office of Natural Resources Revenue, Department of the Interior (Parts 1200—1299)

Title 31—Money and Finance: Treasury

Chap.	
	SUBTITLE A—OFFICE OF THE SECRETARY OF THE TREASURY (PARTS 0—50)
	SUBTITLE B—REGULATIONS RELATING TO MONEY AND FINANCE
Chapter I	Monetary Offices, Department of the Treasury (Parts 51—199)
Chapter II	Fiscal Service, Department of the Treasury (Parts 200—399)
Chapter IV	Secret Service, Department of the Treasury (Parts 400—499)
Chapter V	Office of Foreign Assets Control, Department of the Treasury (Parts 500—599)
Chapter VI	Bureau of Engraving and Printing, Department of the Treasury (Parts 600—699)
Chapter VII	Federal Law Enforcement Training Center, Department of the Treasury (Parts 700—799)
Chapter VIII	Office of International Investment, Department of the Treasury (Parts 800—899)
Chapter IX	Federal Claims Collection Standards (Department of the Treasury—Department of Justice) (Parts 900—999)
Chapter X	Financial Crimes Enforcement Network, Department of the Treasury (Parts 1000—1099)

Title 32—National Defense

	SUBTITLE A—DEPARTMENT OF DEFENSE
Chapter I	Office of the Secretary of Defense (Parts 1—399)
Chapter V	Department of the Army (Parts 400—699)
Chapter VI	Department of the Navy (Parts 700—799)
Chapter VII	Department of the Air Force (Parts 800—1099)
	SUBTITLE B—OTHER REGULATIONS RELATING TO NATIONAL DEFENSE
Chapter XII	Defense Logistics Agency (Parts 1200—1299)
Chapter XVI	Selective Service System (Parts 1600—1699)
Chapter XVII	Office of the Director of National Intelligence (Parts 1700—1799)
Chapter XVIII	National Counterintelligence Center (Parts 1800—1899)
Chapter XIX	Central Intelligence Agency (Parts 1900—1999)
Chapter XX	Information Security Oversight Office, National Archives and Records Administration (Parts 2000—2099)
Chapter XXI	National Security Council (Parts 2100—2199)
Chapter XXIV	Office of Science and Technology Policy (Parts 2400—2499)
Chapter XXVII	Office for Micronesian Status Negotiations (Parts 2700—2799)
Chapter XXVIII	Office of the Vice President of the United States (Parts 2800—2899)

Title 33—Navigation and Navigable Waters

Chapter I	Coast Guard, Department of Homeland Security (Parts 1—199)
Chapter II	Corps of Engineers, Department of the Army (Parts 200—399)

Title 33—Navigation and Navigable Waters—Continued

Chap.

Chapter IV	Saint Lawrence Seaway Development Corporation, Department of Transportation (Parts 400—499)

Title 34—Education

	SUBTITLE A—OFFICE OF THE SECRETARY, DEPARTMENT OF EDUCATION (PARTS 1—99)
	SUBTITLE B—REGULATIONS OF THE OFFICES OF THE DEPARTMENT OF EDUCATION
Chapter I	Office for Civil Rights, Department of Education (Parts 100—199)
Chapter II	Office of Elementary and Secondary Education, Department of Education (Parts 200—299)
Chapter III	Office of Special Education and Rehabilitative Services, Department of Education (Parts 300—399)
Chapter IV	Office of Vocational and Adult Education, Department of Education (Parts 400—499)
Chapter V	Office of Bilingual Education and Minority Languages Affairs, Department of Education (Parts 500—599)
Chapter VI	Office of Postsecondary Education, Department of Education (Parts 600—699)
Chapter VII	Office of Educational Research and Improvement, Department of Education (799—799) [Reserved]
Chapter XI	National Institute for Literacy (Parts 1100—1199)
	SUBTITLE C—REGULATIONS RELATING TO EDUCATION
Chapter XII	National Council on Disability (Parts 1200—1299)

Title 35 [Reserved]

Title 36—Parks, Forests, and Public Property

Chapter I	National Park Service, Department of the Interior (Parts 1—199)
Chapter II	Forest Service, Department of Agriculture (Parts 200—299)
Chapter III	Corps of Engineers, Department of the Army (Parts 300—399)
Chapter IV	American Battle Monuments Commission (Parts 400—499)
Chapter V	Smithsonian Institution (Parts 500—599)
Chapter VI	[Reserved]
Chapter VII	Library of Congress (Parts 700—799)
Chapter VIII	Advisory Council on Historic Preservation (Parts 800—899)
Chapter IX	Pennsylvania Avenue Development Corporation (Parts 900—999)
Chapter X	Presidio Trust (Parts 1000—1099)
Chapter XI	Architectural and Transportation Barriers Compliance Board (Parts 1100—1199)
Chapter XII	National Archives and Records Administration (Parts 1200—1299)
Chapter XV	Oklahoma City National Memorial Trust (Parts 1500—1599)
Chapter XVI	Morris K. Udall Scholarship and Excellence in National Environmental Policy Foundation (Parts 1600—1699)

Title 37—Patents, Trademarks, and Copyrights

Chap.	
Chapter I	United States Patent and Trademark Office, Department of Commerce (Parts 1—199)
Chapter II	Copyright Office, Library of Congress (Parts 200—299)
Chapter III	Copyright Royalty Board, Library of Congress (Parts 300—399)
Chapter IV	Assistant Secretary for Technology Policy, Department of Commerce (Parts 400—599)

Title 38—Pensions, Bonuses, and Veterans' Relief

Chapter I	Department of Veterans Affairs (Parts 0—199)
Chapter II	Armed Forces Retirement Home (Parts 200—299)

Title 39—Postal Service

Chapter I	United States Postal Service (Parts 1—999)
Chapter III	Postal Regulatory Commission (Parts 3000—3099)

Title 40—Protection of Environment

Chapter I	Environmental Protection Agency (Parts 1—1099)
Chapter IV	Environmental Protection Agency and Department of Justice (Parts 1400—1499)
Chapter V	Council on Environmental Quality (Parts 1500—1599)
Chapter VI	Chemical Safety and Hazard Investigation Board (Parts 1600—1699)
Chapter VII	Environmental Protection Agency and Department of Defense; Uniform National Discharge Standards for Vessels of the Armed Forces (Parts 1700—1799)

Title 41—Public Contracts and Property Management

	SUBTITLE A—FEDERAL PROCUREMENT REGULATIONS SYSTEM [NOTE]
	SUBTITLE B—OTHER PROVISIONS RELATING TO PUBLIC CONTRACTS
Chapter 50	Public Contracts, Department of Labor (Parts 50–1—50–999)
Chapter 51	Committee for Purchase From People Who Are Blind or Severely Disabled (Parts 51–1—51–99)
Chapter 60	Office of Federal Contract Compliance Programs, Equal Employment Opportunity, Department of Labor (Parts 60–1—60–999)
Chapter 61	Office of the Assistant Secretary for Veterans' Employment and Training Service, Department of Labor (Parts 61–1—61–999)
Chapters 62—100	[Reserved]
	SUBTITLE C—FEDERAL PROPERTY MANAGEMENT REGULATIONS SYSTEM
Chapter 101	Federal Property Management Regulations (Parts 101–1—101–99)
Chapter 102	Federal Management Regulation (Parts 102–1—102–299)
Chapters 103	104 [Reserved]

Title 41—Public Contracts and Property Management—Continued

Chap.	
Chapter 105	General Services Administration (Parts 105–1—105–999)
Chapter 109	Department of Energy Property Management Regulations (Parts 109–1—109–99)
Chapter 114	Department of the Interior (Parts 114–1—114–99)
Chapter 115	Environmental Protection Agency (Parts 115–1—115–99)
Chapter 128	Department of Justice (Parts 128–1—128–99)
Chapters 129—200	[Reserved]
	SUBTITLE D—OTHER PROVISIONS RELATING TO PROPERTY MANAGEMENT [RESERVED]
	SUBTITLE E—FEDERAL INFORMATION RESOURCES MANAGEMENT REGULATIONS SYSTEM [RESERVED]
	SUBTITLE F—FEDERAL TRAVEL REGULATION SYSTEM
Chapter 300	General (Parts 300–1—300–99)
Chapter 301	Temporary Duty (TDY) Travel Allowances (Parts 301–1—301–99)
Chapter 302	Relocation Allowances (Parts 302–1—302–99)
Chapter 303	Payment of Expenses Connected with the Death of Certain Employees (Part 303–1—303–99)
Chapter 304	Payment of Travel Expenses from a Non-Federal Source (Parts 304–1—304–99)

Title 42—Public Health

Chapter I	Public Health Service, Department of Health and Human Services (Parts 1—199)
Chapter IV	Centers for Medicare & Medicaid Services, Department of Health and Human Services (Parts 400—599)
Chapter V	Office of Inspector General-Health Care, Department of Health and Human Services (Parts 1000—1999)

Title 43—Public Lands: Interior

	SUBTITLE A—OFFICE OF THE SECRETARY OF THE INTERIOR (PARTS 1—199)
	SUBTITLE B—REGULATIONS RELATING TO PUBLIC LANDS
Chapter I	Bureau of Reclamation, Department of the Interior (Parts 400—999)
Chapter II	Bureau of Land Management, Department of the Interior (Parts 1000—9999)
Chapter III	Utah Reclamation Mitigation and Conservation Commission (Parts 10000—10099)

Title 44—Emergency Management and Assistance

Chapter I	Federal Emergency Management Agency, Department of Homeland Security (Parts 0—399)
Chapter IV	Department of Commerce and Department of Transportation (Parts 400—499)

Title 45—Public Welfare

Chap.	
	SUBTITLE A—DEPARTMENT OF HEALTH AND HUMAN SERVICES (PARTS 1—199)158 I18[RESERVED]
	SUBTITLE B—REGULATIONS RELATING TO PUBLIC WELFARE
Chapter II	Office of Family Assistance (Assistance Programs), Administration for Children and Families, Department of Health and Human Services (Parts 200—299)
Chapter III	Office of Child Support Enforcement (Child Support Enforcement Program), Administration for Children and Families, Department of Health and Human Services (Parts 300—399)
Chapter IV	Office of Refugee Resettlement, Administration for Children and Families, Department of Health and Human Services (Parts 400—499)
Chapter V	Foreign Claims Settlement Commission of the United States, Department of Justice (Parts 500—599)
Chapter VI	National Science Foundation (Parts 600—699)
Chapter VII	Commission on Civil Rights (Parts 700—799)
Chapter VIII	Office of Personnel Management (Parts 800—899)
Chapter X	Office of Community Services, Administration for Children and Families, Department of Health and Human Services (Parts 1000—1099)
Chapter XI	National Foundation on the Arts and the Humanities (Parts 1100—1199)
Chapter XII	Corporation for National and Community Service (Parts 1200—1299)
Chapter XIII	Office of Human Development Services, Department of Health and Human Services (Parts 1300—1399)
Chapter XVI	Legal Services Corporation (Parts 1600—1699)
Chapter XVII	National Commission on Libraries and Information Science (Parts 1700—1799)
Chapter XVIII	Harry S. Truman Scholarship Foundation (Parts 1800—1899)
Chapter XXI	Commission on Fine Arts (Parts 2100—2199)
Chapter XXIII	Arctic Research Commission (Part 2301)
Chapter XXIV	James Madison Memorial Fellowship Foundation (Parts 2400—2499)
Chapter XXV	Corporation for National and Community Service (Parts 2500—2599)

Title 46—Shipping

Chapter I	Coast Guard, Department of Homeland Security (Parts 1—199)
Chapter II	Maritime Administration, Department of Transportation (Parts 200—399)
Chapter III	Coast Guard (Great Lakes Pilotage), Department of Homeland Security (Parts 400—499)
Chapter IV	Federal Maritime Commission (Parts 500—599)

Title 47—Telecommunication

Title 48—Federal Acquisition Regulations System

Title 49—Transportation

Title 50—Wildlife and Fisheries

Alphabetical List of Agencies Appearing in the CFR

(Revised as of April 1, 2013)

Agency	CFR Title, Subtitle or Chapter
Administrative Committee of the Federal Register	1, I
Administrative Conference of the United States	1, III
Advisory Council on Historic Preservation	36, VIII
Advocacy and Outreach, Office of	7, XXV
Afghanistan Reconstruction, Special Inspector General for	22, LXXXIII
African Development Foundation	22, XV
Federal Acquisition Regulation	48, 57
Agency for International Development	2, VII; 22, II
Federal Acquisition Regulation	48, 7
Agricultural Marketing Service	7, I, IX, X, XI
Agricultural Research Service	7, V
Agriculture Department	2, IV; 5, LXXIII
Advocacy and Outreach, Office of	7, XXV
Agricultural Marketing Service	7, I, IX, X, XI
Agricultural Research Service	7, V
Animal and Plant Health Inspection Service	7, III; 9, I
Chief Financial Officer, Office of	7, XXX
Commodity Credit Corporation	7, XIV
Economic Research Service	7, XXXVII
Energy Policy and New Uses, Office of	2, IX; 7, XXIX
Environmental Quality, Office of	7, XXXI
Farm Service Agency	7, VII, XVIII
Federal Acquisition Regulation	48, 4
Federal Crop Insurance Corporation	7, IV
Food and Nutrition Service	7, II
Food Safety and Inspection Service	9, III
Foreign Agricultural Service	7, XV
Forest Service	36, II
Grain Inspection, Packers and Stockyards Administration	7, VIII; 9, II
Information Resources Management, Office of	7, XXVII
Inspector General, Office of	7, XXVI
National Agricultural Library	7, XLI
National Agricultural Statistics Service	7, XXXVI
National Institute of Food and Agriculture	7, XXXIV
Natural Resources Conservation Service	7, VI
Operations, Office of	7, XXVIII
Procurement and Property Management, Office of	7, XXXII
Rural Business-Cooperative Service	7, XVIII, XLII, L
Rural Development Administration	7, XLII
Rural Housing Service	7, XVIII, XXXV, L
Rural Telephone Bank	7, XVI
Rural Utilities Service	7, XVII, XVIII, XLII, L
Secretary of Agriculture, Office of	7, Subtitle A
Transportation, Office of	7, XXXIII
World Agricultural Outlook Board	7, XXXVIII
Air Force Department	32, VII
Federal Acquisition Regulation Supplement	48, 53
Air Transportation Stabilization Board	14, VI
Alcohol and Tobacco Tax and Trade Bureau	27, I
Alcohol, Tobacco, Firearms, and Explosives, Bureau of	27, II
AMTRAK	49, VII
American Battle Monuments Commission	36, IV
American Indians, Office of the Special Trustee	25, VII

Agency	CFR Title, Subtitle or Chapter
Animal and Plant Health Inspection Service	7, III; 9, I
Appalachian Regional Commission	5, IX
Architectural and Transportation Barriers Compliance Board	36, XI
Arctic Research Commission	45, XXIII
Armed Forces Retirement Home	5, XI
Army Department	32, V
Engineers, Corps of	33, II; 36, III
Federal Acquisition Regulation	48, 51
Bilingual Education and Minority Languages Affairs, Office of	34, V
Blind or Severely Disabled, Committee for Purchase from People Who Are	41, 51
Broadcasting Board of Governors	22, V
Federal Acquisition Regulation	48, 19
Bureau of Ocean Energy Management, Regulation, and Enforcement	30, II
Census Bureau	15, I
Centers for Medicare & Medicaid Services	42, IV
Central Intelligence Agency	32, XIX
Chemical Safety and Hazardous Investigation Board	40, VI
Chief Financial Officer, Office of	7, XXX
Child Support Enforcement, Office of	45, III
Children and Families, Administration for	45, II, III, IV, X
Civil Rights, Commission on	5, LXVIII; 45, VII
Civil Rights, Office for	34, I
Council of the Inspectors General on Integrity and Efficiency	5, XCVIII
Court Services and Offender Supervision Agency for the District of Columbia	5, LXX
Coast Guard	33, I; 46, I; 49, IV
Coast Guard (Great Lakes Pilotage)	46, III
Commerce Department	2, XIII; 44, IV; 50, VI
Census Bureau	15, I
Economic Analysis, Bureau of	15, VIII
Economic Development Administration	13, III
Emergency Management and Assistance	44, IV
Federal Acquisition Regulation	48, 13
Foreign-Trade Zones Board	15, IV
Industry and Security, Bureau of	15, VII
International Trade Administration	15, III; 19, III
National Institute of Standards and Technology	15, II
National Marine Fisheries Service	50, II, IV
National Oceanic and Atmospheric Administration	15, IX; 50, II, III, IV, VI
National Telecommunications and Information Administration	15, XXIII; 47, III, IV
National Weather Service	15, IX
Patent and Trademark Office, United States	37, I
Productivity, Technology and Innovation, Assistant Secretary for	37, IV
Secretary of Commerce, Office of	15, Subtitle A
Technology Administration	15, XI
Technology Policy, Assistant Secretary for	37, IV
Commercial Space Transportation	14, III
Commodity Credit Corporation	7, XIV
Commodity Futures Trading Commission	5, XLI; 17, I
Community Planning and Development, Office of Assistant Secretary for	24, V, VI
Community Services, Office of	45, X
Comptroller of the Currency	12, I
Construction Industry Collective Bargaining Commission	29, IX
Consumer Financial Protection Bureau	5, LXXXIV; 12, X
Consumer Product Safety Commission	5, LXXI; 16, II
Copyright Office	37, II
Copyright Royalty Board	37, III
Corporation for National and Community Service	2, XXII; 45, XII, XXV
Cost Accounting Standards Board	48, 99
Council on Environmental Quality	40, V
Court Services and Offender Supervision Agency for the District of Columbia	5, LXX; 28, VIII

Agency	CFR Title, Subtitle or Chapter
Customs and Border Protection	19, I
Defense Contract Audit Agency	32, I
Defense Department	2, XI; 5, XXVI; 32, Subtitle A; 40, VII
Advanced Research Projects Agency	32, I
Air Force Department	32, VII
Army Department	32, V; 33, II; 36, III, 48, 51
Defense Acquisition Regulations System	48, 2
Defense Intelligence Agency	32, I
Defense Logistics Agency	32, I, XII; 48, 54
Engineers, Corps of	33, II; 36, III
National Imagery and Mapping Agency	32, I
Navy Department	32, VI; 48, 52
Secretary of Defense, Office of	2, XI; 32, I
Defense Contract Audit Agency	32, I
Defense Intelligence Agency	32, I
Defense Logistics Agency	32, XII; 48, 54
Defense Nuclear Facilities Safety Board	10, XVII
Delaware River Basin Commission	18, III
District of Columbia, Court Services and Offender Supervision Agency for the	5, LXX; 28, VIII
Drug Enforcement Administration	21, II
East-West Foreign Trade Board	15, XIII
Economic Analysis, Bureau of	15, VIII
Economic Development Administration	13, III
Economic Research Service	7, XXXVII
Education, Department of	2, XXXIV; 5, LIII
Bilingual Education and Minority Languages Affairs, Office of	34, V
Civil Rights, Office for	34, I
Educational Research and Improvement, Office of	34, VII
Elementary and Secondary Education, Office of	34, II
Federal Acquisition Regulation	48, 34
Postsecondary Education, Office of	34, VI
Secretary of Education, Office of	34, Subtitle A
Special Education and Rehabilitative Services, Office of	34, III
Vocational and Adult Education, Office of	34, IV
Educational Research and Improvement, Office of	34, VII
Election Assistance Commission	2, LVIII; 11, II
Elementary and Secondary Education, Office of	34, II
Emergency Oil and Gas Guaranteed Loan Board	13, V
Emergency Steel Guarantee Loan Board	13, IV
Employee Benefits Security Administration	29, XXV
Employees' Compensation Appeals Board	20, IV
Employees Loyalty Board	5, V
Employment and Training Administration	20, V
Employment Standards Administration	20, VI
Endangered Species Committee	50, IV
Energy, Department of	2, IX; 5, XXIII; 10, II, III, X
Federal Acquisition Regulation	48, 9
Federal Energy Regulatory Commission	5, XXIV; 18, I
Property Management Regulations	41, 109
Energy, Office of	7, XXIX
Engineers, Corps of	33, II; 36, III
Engraving and Printing, Bureau of	31, VI
Environmental Protection Agency	2, XV; 5, LIV; 40, I, IV, VII
Federal Acquisition Regulation	48, 15
Property Management Regulations	41, 115
Environmental Quality, Office of	7, XXXI
Equal Employment Opportunity Commission	5, LXII; 29, XIV
Equal Opportunity, Office of Assistant Secretary for	24, I
Executive Office of the President	3, I
Administration, Office of	5, XV
Environmental Quality, Council on	40, V

Agency	CFR Title, Subtitle or Chapter
Independent Counsel, Office of	28, VII
Indian Affairs, Bureau of	25, I, V
Indian Affairs, Office of the Assistant Secretary	25, VI
Indian Arts and Crafts Board	25, II
Indian Health Service	25, V
Industry and Security, Bureau of	15, VII
Information Resources Management, Office of	7, XXVII
Information Security Oversight Office, National Archives and Records Administration	32, XX
Inspector General	
Agriculture Department	7, XXVI
Health and Human Services Department	42, V
Housing and Urban Development Department	24, XII, XV
Institute of Peace, United States	22, XVII
Inter-American Foundation	5, LXIII; 22, X
Interior Department	2, XIV
American Indians, Office of the Special Trustee	25, VII
Bureau of Ocean Energy Management, Regulation, and Enforcement	30, II
Endangered Species Committee	50, IV
Federal Acquisition Regulation	48, 14
Federal Property Management Regulations System	41, 114
Fish and Wildlife Service, United States	50, I, IV
Geological Survey	30, IV
Indian Affairs, Bureau of	25, I, V
Indian Affairs, Office of the Assistant Secretary	25, VI
Indian Arts and Crafts Board	25, II
Land Management, Bureau of	43, II
National Indian Gaming Commission	25, III
National Park Service	36, I
Natural Resource Revenue, Office of	30, XII
Ocean Energy Management, Bureau of	30, V
Reclamation, Bureau of	43, I
Secretary of the Interior, Office of	2, XIV; 43, Subtitle A
Surface Mining Reclamation and Enforcement, Office of	30, VII
Internal Revenue Service	26, I
International Boundary and Water Commission, United States and Mexico, United States Section	22, XI
International Development, United States Agency for	22, II
Federal Acquisition Regulation	48, 7
International Development Cooperation Agency, United States	22, XII
International Joint Commission, United States and Canada	22, IV
International Organizations Employees Loyalty Board	5, V
International Trade Administration	15, III; 19, III
International Trade Commission, United States	19, II
Interstate Commerce Commission	5, XL
Investment Security, Office of	31, VIII
Iraq Reconstruction, Special Inspector General for	5, LXXXVII
James Madison Memorial Fellowship Foundation	45, XXIV
Japan–United States Friendship Commission	22, XVI
Joint Board for the Enrollment of Actuaries	20, VIII
Justice Department	2, XXVIII; 5, XXVIII; 28, I, XI; 40, IV
Alcohol, Tobacco, Firearms, and Explosives, Bureau of	27, II
Drug Enforcement Administration	21, II
Federal Acquisition Regulation	48, 28
Federal Claims Collection Standards	31, IX
Federal Prison Industries, Inc.	28, III
Foreign Claims Settlement Commission of the United States	45, V
Immigration Review, Executive Office for	8, V
Offices of Independent Counsel	28, VI
Prisons, Bureau of	28, V
Property Management Regulations	41, 128
Labor Department	5, XLII
Employee Benefits Security Administration	29, XXV

Agency	CFR Title, Subtitle or Chapter
Employees' Compensation Appeals Board	20, IV
Employment and Training Administration	20, V
Employment Standards Administration	20, VI
Federal Acquisition Regulation	48, 29
Federal Contract Compliance Programs, Office of	41, 60
Federal Procurement Regulations System	41, 50
Labor-Management Standards, Office of	29, II, IV
Mine Safety and Health Administration	30, I
Occupational Safety and Health Administration	29, XVII
Office of Workers' Compensation Programs	20, VII
Public Contracts	41, 50
Secretary of Labor, Office of	29, Subtitle A
Veterans' Employment and Training Service, Office of the Assistant Secretary for	41, 61; 20, IX
Wage and Hour Division	29, V
Workers' Compensation Programs, Office of	20, I
Labor-Management Standards, Office of	29, II, IV
Land Management, Bureau of	43, II
Legal Services Corporation	45, XVI
Library of Congress	36, VII
Copyright Office	37, II
Copyright Royalty Board	37, III
Local Television Loan Guarantee Board	7, XX
Management and Budget, Office of	5, III, LXXVII; 14, VI; 48, 99
Marine Mammal Commission	50, V
Maritime Administration	46, II
Merit Systems Protection Board	5, II, LXIV
Micronesian Status Negotiations, Office for	32, XXVII
Millennium Challenge Corporation	22, XIII
Mine Safety and Health Administration	30, I
Minority Business Development Agency	15, XIV
Miscellaneous Agencies	1, IV
Monetary Offices	31, I
Morris K. Udall Scholarship and Excellence in National Environmental Policy Foundation	36, XVI
Museum and Library Services, Institute of	2, XXXI
National Aeronautics and Space Administration	2, XVIII; 5, LIX; 14, V
Federal Acquisition Regulation	48, 18
National Agricultural Library	7, XLI
National Agricultural Statistics Service	7, XXXVI
National and Community Service, Corporation for	2, XXII; 45, XII, XXV
National Archives and Records Administration	2, XXVI; 5, LXVI; 36, XII
Information Security Oversight Office	32, XX
National Capital Planning Commission	1, IV
National Commission for Employment Policy	1, IV
National Commission on Libraries and Information Science	45, XVII
National Council on Disability	34, XII
National Counterintelligence Center	32, XVIII
National Credit Union Administration	12, VII
National Crime Prevention and Privacy Compact Council	28, IX
National Drug Control Policy, Office of	21, III
National Endowment for the Arts	2, XXXII
National Endowment for the Humanities	2, XXXIII
National Foundation on the Arts and the Humanities	45, XI
National Highway Traffic Safety Administration	23, II, III; 47, VI; 49, V
National Imagery and Mapping Agency	32, I
National Indian Gaming Commission	25, III
National Institute for Literacy	34, XI
National Institute of Food and Agriculture	7, XXXIV
National Institute of Standards and Technology	15, II
National Intelligence, Office of Director of	32, XVII
National Labor Relations Board	5, LXI; 29, I
National Marine Fisheries Service	50, II, IV
National Mediation Board	29, X
National Oceanic and Atmospheric Administration	15, IX; 50, II, III, IV, VI

Agency	CFR Title, Subtitle or Chapter
National Park Service	36, I
National Railroad Adjustment Board	29, III
National Railroad Passenger Corporation (AMTRAK)	49, VII
National Science Foundation	2, XXV; 5, XLIII; 45, VI
Federal Acquisition Regulation	48, 25
National Security Council	32, XXI
National Security Council and Office of Science and Technology Policy	47, II
National Telecommunications and Information Administration	15, XXIII; 47, III, IV
National Transportation Safety Board	49, VIII
Natural Resources Conservation Service	7, VI
Natural Resource Revenue, Office of	30, XII
Navajo and Hopi Indian Relocation, Office of	25, IV
Navy Department	32, VI
Federal Acquisition Regulation	48, 52
Neighborhood Reinvestment Corporation	24, XXV
Northeast Interstate Low-Level Radioactive Waste Commission	10, XVIII
Nuclear Regulatory Commission	2, XX; 5, XLVIII; 10, I
Federal Acquisition Regulation	48, 20
Occupational Safety and Health Administration	29, XVII
Occupational Safety and Health Review Commission	29, XX
Ocean Energy Management, Bureau of	30, V
Offices of Independent Counsel	28, VI
Office of Workers' Compensation Programs	20, VII
Oklahoma City National Memorial Trust	36, XV
Operations Office	7, XXVIII
Overseas Private Investment Corporation	5, XXXIII; 22, VII
Patent and Trademark Office, United States	37, I
Payment From a Non-Federal Source for Travel Expenses	41, 304
Payment of Expenses Connected With the Death of Certain Employees	41, 303
Peace Corps	2, XXXVII; 22, III
Pennsylvania Avenue Development Corporation	36, IX
Pension Benefit Guaranty Corporation	29, XL
Personnel Management, Office of	5, I, XXXV; 45, VIII
Human Resources Management and Labor Relations Systems, Department of Homeland Security	5, XCVII
Federal Acquisition Regulation	48, 17
Federal Employees Group Life Insurance Federal Acquisition Regulation	48, 21
Federal Employees Health Benefits Acquisition Regulation	48, 16
Pipeline and Hazardous Materials Safety Administration	49, I
Postal Regulatory Commission	5, XLVI; 39, III
Postal Service, United States	5, LX; 39, I
Postsecondary Education, Office of	34, VI
President's Commission on White House Fellowships	1, IV
Presidential Documents	3
Presidio Trust	36, X
Prisons, Bureau of	28, V
Procurement and Property Management, Office of	7, XXXII
Productivity, Technology and Innovation, Assistant Secretary	37, IV
Public Contracts, Department of Labor	41, 50
Public and Indian Housing, Office of Assistant Secretary for	24, IX
Public Health Service	42, I
Railroad Retirement Board	20, II
Reclamation, Bureau of	43, I
Recovery Accountability and Transparency Board	4, II
Refugee Resettlement, Office of	45, IV
Relocation Allowances	41, 302
Research and Innovative Technology Administration	49, XI
Rural Business-Cooperative Service	7, XVIII, XLII, L
Rural Development Administration	7, XLII
Rural Housing Service	7, XVIII, XXXV, L
Rural Telephone Bank	7, XVI

Agency	CFR Title, Subtitle or Chapter
Rural Utilities Service	7, XVII, XVIII, XLII, L
Saint Lawrence Seaway Development Corporation	33, IV
Science and Technology Policy, Office of	32, XXIV
Science and Technology Policy, Office of, and National Security Council	47, II
Secret Service	31, IV
Securities and Exchange Commission	5, XXXIV; 17, II
Selective Service System	32, XVI
Small Business Administration	2, XXVII; 13, I
Smithsonian Institution	36, V
Social Security Administration	2, XXIII; 20, III; 48, 23
Soldiers' and Airmen's Home, United States	5, XI
Special Counsel, Office of	5, VIII
Special Education and Rehabilitative Services, Office of	34, III
State Department	2, VI; 22, I; 28, XI
Federal Acquisition Regulation	48, 6
Surface Mining Reclamation and Enforcement, Office of	30, VII
Surface Transportation Board	49, X
Susquehanna River Basin Commission	18, VIII
Technology Administration	15, XI
Technology Policy, Assistant Secretary for	37, IV
Tennessee Valley Authority	5, LXIX; 18, XIII
Thrift Supervision Office, Department of the Treasury	12, V
Trade Representative, United States, Office of	15, XX
Transportation, Department of	2, XII; 5, L
Commercial Space Transportation	14, III
Contract Appeals, Board of	48, 63
Emergency Management and Assistance	44, IV
Federal Acquisition Regulation	48, 12
Federal Aviation Administration	14, I
Federal Highway Administration	23, I, II
Federal Motor Carrier Safety Administration	49, III
Federal Railroad Administration	49, II
Federal Transit Administration	49, VI
Maritime Administration	46, II
National Highway Traffic Safety Administration	23, II, III; 47, IV; 49, V
Pipeline and Hazardous Materials Safety Administration	49, I
Saint Lawrence Seaway Development Corporation	33, IV
Secretary of Transportation, Office of	14, II; 49, Subtitle A
Surface Transportation Board	49, X
Transportation Statistics Bureau	49, XI
Transportation, Office of	7, XXXIII
Transportation Security Administration	49, XII
Transportation Statistics Bureau	49, XI
Travel Allowances, Temporary Duty (TDY)	41, 301
Treasury Department	5, XXI; 12, XV; 17, IV; 31, IX
Alcohol and Tobacco Tax and Trade Bureau	27, I
Community Development Financial Institutions Fund	12, XVIII
Comptroller of the Currency	12, I
Customs and Border Protection	19, I
Engraving and Printing, Bureau of	31, VI
Federal Acquisition Regulation	48, 10
Federal Claims Collection Standards	31, IX
Federal Law Enforcement Training Center	31, VII
Financial Crimes Enforcement Network	31, X
Fiscal Service	31, II
Foreign Assets Control, Office of	31, V
Internal Revenue Service	26, I
Investment Security, Office of	31, VIII
Monetary Offices	31, I
Secret Service	31, IV
Secretary of the Treasury, Office of	31, Subtitle A
Thrift Supervision, Office of	12, V
Truman, Harry S. Scholarship Foundation	45, XVIII
United States and Canada, International Joint Commission	22, IV
United States and Mexico, International Boundary and Water Commission, United States Section	22, XI

List of CFR Sections Affected

All changes in this volume of the Code of Federal Regulations (CFR) that were made by documents published in the FEDERAL REGISTER since January 1, 2008 are enumerated in the following list. Entries indicate the nature of the changes effected. Page numbers refer to FEDERAL REGISTER pages. The user should consult the entries for chapters, parts and subparts as well as sections for revisions.

For changes to this volume of the CFR prior to this listing, consult the annual edition of the monthly List of CFR Sections Affected (LSA). The LSA is available at *www.fdsys.gov*. For changes to this volume of the CFR prior to 2001, see the ''List of CFR Sections Affected, 1949–1963, 1964–1972, 1973–1985, and 1986–2000'' published in 11 separate volumes. The ''List of CFR Sections Affected 1986–2000'' is available at *www.fdsys.gov*.

2008

21 CFR

73 FR Page

Chapter I

179.26 (b) table amended 49603
184.1065 (b) revised 8606
184.1140 (b) revised 8606
184.1155 (b) revised 8606
184.1165 (b) revised 8607
184.1240 (b) revised 8607
184.1261 (b) revised 8607
184.1262 (b) revised 8607
184.1265 (b) revised 8607
184.1287 (b) revised 8607
184.1297 (b) revised 8607
184.1298 (b) revised 8607
184.1307 (b) revised 8607
184.1307a (b) revised 8607
184.1307b (b) revised 8607
184.1307c (b) revised 8607
184.1321 (b) revised 8607
184.1322 (b) revised 8607
184.1323 (b) revised 8607
184.1324 (b) revised 8607
184.1355 (b) revised 8607
184.1386 (b) revised 8607
184.1445 (b) revised 8607
184.1449 (b) revised 8607
184.1521 (b) revised 8607
184.1537 (b) revised 8607
184.1540 (b) revised 8607
184.1545 (b) revised 8607
184.1553 (b) revised 8607
184.1555 (c)(3) revised 8608
184.1639 (b) revised 8608
184.1655 (b) revised 8608

21 CFR—Continued

73 FR Page

Chapter I—Continued

184.1764 (b) revised 8608
184.1768 (b) revised 8608
184.1769a (b) revised 8608
184.1848 (b) revised 8608
184.1851 (b) revised 8608
184.1854 (b) revised 8608
184.1859 (b) revised 8608
184.1865 (b) revised 8608
184.1923 (b) revised 8608
184.1950 (b) revised 8608
184.1984 (b) revised 8608
189.5 (a)(1) revised; (e) added; interim 20793

2009

21 CFR

74 FR Page

Chapter I

172.167 Added 11478
172.379 Added 11022

2010

(No regulations published)

2011

21 CFR

76 FR Page

Chapter I

172.785 Regulation at 71 FR 47731 eff. date confirmed 16285
172.870 (a)(1) and (b)(1) revised 41689

21 CFR—Continued

76 FR Page

Chapter I—Continued

173.356 Added 11330
173.375 Introductory text revised 59248
175.105 (c)(5) table amended 59248
175.300 (d) Table 2 revised 59248
177.1210 (c) Table 4 revised 59249
177.2600 (c)(4)(ix) amended 59249
178.3130 (b) table amended 59249
179 Response to objections 20509
179.26 Regulation at 70 FR 48072 confirmed 15841
182.99 Revised 59249
184.1155 (a) amended 59250
184.1165 (a) amended 59250
184.1261 (a) amended 59250
184.1446 (a) amended 59250
184.1449 (a) amended 59250
184.1845 (a) amended 59250

2012

21 CFR

77 FR Page

Chapter I

172.381 Added 52231
173.405 Added 71697
177.1580 (d) added 41902
179 Policy statement 27586
179.26 (b) table amended 71316, 71321
179.43 Added 34215

2013

(Regulations published from January 1, 2013, through April 1, 2013)

21 CFR

78 FR Page

Chapter I

172.712 (b) amended 14664
172.723 (b)(1) amended 14665
172.809 (b) amended 14665

21 CFR—Continued

78 FR Page

Chapter I—Continued

172.831 (b) amended 14665
172.833 (b)(2) amended 14665
172.886 (c)(2)(iii) amended 14665
173.25 (b)(2)(ii)(B) amended 14665
173.45 (a) amended 14665
173.325 (h) amended 14665
173.368 (c) amended 114665
176.180 (b)(2) table amended 14665
177.1210 (b)(5) Table 1 amended 14665
177.1350 (b)(2) amended 14665
177.1360 (d) amended 14665
177.1500 (b) Table 1 amended 14666
177.1637 (b)(2) amended 14666
177.2440 (a)(3) amended 14666
177.2600 (c)(4)(i) amended 14666
178.1010 (c)(40) amended 14666
178.3297 (c) and (e) amended 14666
184.1012 (b) amended 14666
184.1024 (b) amended 14666
184.1034 (b) amended 14666
184.1063 (b)(8) amended 14666
184.1259 (b)(8) amended 14666
184.1316 (b) amended 14666
184.1415 (b) amended 14666
184.1583 (b) amended 14666
184.1595 (b) amended 14667
184.1866 (b) amended 14667
184.1914 (b) amended 14667
184.1985 (b) amended 14667
189.5 Regulations at 69 FR 42273 and 70 FR 53068 comment period reopened 14012
189.110 (c) amended 14667
189.110—189.191 (Subpart B) Regulation at 69 FR 42273 comment period reopened 14012
189.180 (c) amended 14667
189.220—189.301 (Subpart C) Regulation at 69 FR 42273 comment period reopened 14012

○